D1560964

The Ohio
NATURE ALMANAC

The Ohio NATURE ALMANAC

AN ENCYCLOPEDIA OF INDISPENSABLE INFORMATION ABOUT THE NATURAL BUCKEYE UNIVERSE

Edited by STEPHEN OSTRANDER

Orange Frazer Press

Wilmington, Ohio

ISBN: 1-882203-53-4
Copyright 2001 by *Orange Frazer Press, Inc.*
All rights reserved

Ordering information: Additional copies of *The Ohio Nature Almanac* may be ordered directly from:

CUSTOMER SERVICE DEPARTMENT
Orange Frazer Press, Inc.
Box 214
37$^1/_2$ West Main Street
Wilmington, Ohio 45177

Telephone 1.800.852.9332
for price and shipping information

The Ohio Nature Almanac is a registered trademark of *Orange Frazer Press, Inc.*

The information in this edition was compiled from the most current data available. Any errors, inaccuracies, or omissions are strictly unintentional.

Cover:
Photo of Sunrise, Shawnee State Forest, Scioto County by Ian Adams

Library of Congress Cataloging-in-Publication Data

The Ohio nature almanac : an encyclopedia of indispensable information about the natural buckeye universe / edited by Stephen Ostrander.
       p.cm.
     ISBN 1-882203-53-4 (alk.paper)
      1. Natural history--Ohio--Guidebooks. 2. Recreation areas--Ohio--Guidebooks. 3. Ohio--Guidebooks. I. Ostrander, Stephen.

     QH105.03 035 2000
     508.771--dc21

                                                        00-058861

dedication

To all naturalists who have been captivated by Ohio, from Audubon, Braun, and Cooperrider... to Weber, Williams, and everyone between. Like me, they have realized that Ohio's land and wildlife is as worthy as any mountain in Montana, any coast along California, and any desert in Arizona.

writer and editor
STEPHEN OSTRANDER

editorial assistance
JEAN P. KELLY

illustrations
DIANE MANNING

design and production
ANN DRURY-THOMPSON

Sailing on Turkey Foot Lake, now part of Portage Lakes State Park.

preface

Book writers are supposed to scribble a prophetic preamble to the main text. Some words of wisdom for the reader, for posterity, for the literati. Although such statements appear at the front of the book, they are always written last, with the advantage of hindsight. I'm supposed to tell you what you are going to get out of this book, and how to experience it, the way a loose-tongued chef might divulge a secret recipe. So here goes. Fundamentally, this book is about places that people of all comfort levels can go for outdoor fun. Think of it, too, as a field guide to Ohio's natural history, and as a source of pleasurable reading. As some day I hope to tramp through Yellowstone National Park, you may long to see Dysart Woods or Sheldon's Marsh. Until we fulfill our wishes we can vicariously enjoy them via books and magazines. Catch my drift?

However, as wonderful, informative, and entertaining as these stories are, the memories, instruction and joy you personally harvest from Ohio's natural world will be more nourishing. All the humans who have contributed to this volume engage you to explore, appreciate, protect and expand Ohio's natural world. I don't know what the natural world thinks of all this.

Besides being informative and entertaining, I hope this book is about:

• Freedom, attainable by crossing into a state of grace with the natural world, your ancestor;

• Wondering, a happy consequence of freedom that grabs, enriches, and opens you, and stays until you surrender it; and

• Wandering, the occasions and places for wondering and freedom.

acknowledgements

Several moons ago I was commissioned by my family to hunt and gather wallpaper for the bathroom. Tomes of samplers at the interior decorator's salon fascinated me for hours. I was like the kid in the candy store, who, unable to choose, blows his dough on every confection. So, I went home with 20 rolls of my favorite patterns. My idea being to paste a strip from each roll on the barren bathroom walls. One was a maritime scene reminding me of Melville and Masefield (for the tub). Another featured Southwestern designs and petroglyphs with bright yellows and reds, recalling trips to pueblos, rainbow canyons, and deserts. Others had Rubenesque women, tropical flowers, beach prints, gaudy jungle birds, Venetian sunsets, grape vines, Bert and Ernie, Scottish tartans, Spanish castles, etc. For laughs, I bought a prepasted mural of dogs playing poker (deeply discounted, of course). As I left the store, female patrons were chuckling with their hands covering their mouths, so I figured my selections met their approval. My bathroom would be a gallery of curiosity, I proclaimed to myself, a colosseum for my quirky creativity.

I proudly showed my picks to the femmes who occupy my abode, the spouse and daughter who bring clarity, order, and reason to my lopsided world. With sweeping gestures and crescendos, I revealed my decorative plan. One gasped, the other shrieked. Daughter recovered the fumbled rolls and dashed out the door before I could say Martha Stewart; spouse pickpocketed the receipt and muttered something about my tortured taste being kin to the columns of clutter in my office. Off they rushed to return my trophies. My days of interior designing over.

Four stores and seven days later my wife and daughter unloaded cartons of home decorating accoutrements, which, I was told, will coordinate the bathroom in question with the basement and everything between. Expansive ideas were explained, crude sketches and floor plans unfurled like military maps, and nitty-gritty lists of instructions were issued. They assured me their "sublime decorating concept" would "assemble a confident unspoken message" (their phrases), and connect the bow of their imagination to the stern of my Lazy Boy. Their fairy tale canvas would forever inter my nightmarish-cheesy-flea-market color scheme beneath a layer of vinyl wallcovering. I must trust their judgment, they said. I said that I would, knowing I would have to anyway. It was mid-July. I was told to finish the "sublime decorating concept" by hunting season, or else it would be open season on me. Sounded generous, but realistically I wouldn't be finished before Mother's Day. You cannot rush great art.

Writing this book was similar to the wallpaper adventure. After an Everest effort spanning two years, I amassed a mountain of memories—the manuscript—cramped on several computer diskettes. With my engine wheezing and firing on its last cylinder, I parked on the summit to enjoy the view. It was coasting from here, so I thought. Trouble is, I had forgotten my compass and map, and snow, leaves, and rain had erased my tracks. Nor, as I discovered, was I a master geologist-juggler who could align manuscript chapters in decipherable layers.

JEAN KELLY and ANN DRURY-THOMPSON were helicoptered in to rescue the book (not me). They resuscitated it, flavored it, nurtured it, gave it structure, made it readable and suitable for bookbinding, and for bookshelves. Me? I'm edging off the summit, relying on instinct to reach base camp, then heading to Margaritaville.

special considerations

There are many others to thank, notably contributors, SCOTT RUSSELL SANDERS, JOHN FLEISCHMAN, DAVID BEACH, JANE WARE, DAMAINE VONADA, JAMES BAUMANN who contributed to the book, and MARCY HAWLEY, JOHN BASKIN, AND TAMMY MCKAY at *Orange Frazer Press.*

Also, JEAN BACKS, *Ohio Division of Parks and Recreation,*

WILLIAM SCHULTZ, *Ohio Division of Forestry,*

BILL KUEHNLE, *Ohio Division of Geological Survey,*

JANET BUTLER, *Ohio River Islands National Wildlife Refuge,*

GUY DENNY, NANCY STRAYER, and YETTY ALLEY, *Ohio Division of Natural Areas and Preserves,*

JOHN WISSE and CHIP GROSS, *Ohio Division of Wildlife,*

JAMES M. LYNCH, KAREN KENTOSH and JESSICA WINZLER, *Office of Marketing Services, Ohio Department of Natural Resources,*

DEBORAH GANGLOFF, *American Forestry Association,*

LYNDA ANDREWS AND STAFF, *Wayne National Forest,*

LARRY HENRY, *Highland Nature Sanctuary,*

NANCY KING SMITH, *The Nature Center at Shaker Lakes,*

JIM SPRAGUE, *Buckeye Trail Association (and North Country National Scenic Trail),*

PAUL DANIEL, *American Discovery Trail,*

TERRY BERRIGAN, *Ohio Chapter of the Rails-to-Trail Conservancy,*

M. JANE CHRISTYSON, *Cleveland Metroparks,*

GARY KASTER, *AEP ReCreation Land,*

GARY WINSON and ANNA SCHAFER-NOLAN, *Cuyahoga Valley National Recreation Area,*

ART WEBER, *Toledo Metroparks,*

JAMIE MOONEY, *Miami Valley Regional Bicycle Council,* and

SCOTT MCKEEVER, *Muskingum Water Conservancy District,*

JASON TOCKMAN, *Buckeye Forest Council.*

Before the dam—Copacaw, the falls in Cuyahoga Falls in 1913.

Table of Contents

On balance, humans are a blink in Ohio's geological Deep Time.

humans have a hard time comprehending the deep past. Science's modern creation story remains obscure to most of us. Nevertheless, we put our faith in their observations and judgment in the same way our ancestors trusted their learned and anointed sovereigns.

Ohio's Lenni Lenape (Delaware Indians) devised a creation story that told them how they came to Earth, who they were, how they got here, and how they were connected to all creations. In a broader sense it explained their unique role and special place in a vast, unknown cosmos. The story made sense of life. It served them well and provided comfort, as would the creation stories of later arriving Europeans and Africans.

The Lenni Lenape say the people on Earth descended from the sky-people, who lived happy and content in a land above the sky illuminated by the Tree of Light. In his sleep the chief of the sky-people dreamed that he would die unless the Tree of Light was uprooted. The next day, the brothers of the chief took down the tree, which fell through a hole in the ground when it crashed. A man and his pregnant wife stood beside the hole and watched light rising from the falling tree. A tender life-giving wind rose through the hole.

The man told the woman, "You shall create a new world down there. You shall be the mother of all generations on the Earth." With that he pushed her through the hole and she fell toward the light, and a big blue sea. Birds lifted her before she struck the sea, and they placed her gently on the back of a turtle. The turtle was chosen because he could live on land, swim with fish, and lay eggs like birds. Waterfowl and fish piled mud on the turtle's back. Soon the woman had land that yielded grass, and trees, and water for survival. The turtle said he had orders from "above" to support the woman and her offspring forever.

In time, the woman gave birth to a daughter, who upon reaching maturity entered the sea to fertilize her womb. That union produced twins. The Good Twin came from the womb. The Bad Twin spilled from his mother's armpit and promptly killed her. The Good Twin, known as Sapling, became the Creator (also known as the Great Spirit, or Manitou) who made the sun, moon, plants, animals, and people. He gave a heart and soul to everything he created. The Bad Twin concealed animals in a cave and distorted the world.

Today, scientists have replaced shamans and priests as the tellers of creation stories. Their tale is written in stone, and begins 4.5 billion years ago when an explosion called The Big Bang launched shrapnel into the Universe. One of those hot specks became Earth. Eventually the Earth's outer skin cooled and became enwrapped in a vaporous layer—the atmosphere—that regulated the sphere's temperature and produced the basic ingredients for life. Earth's heart, a blast furnace deep in its core, pushed and circulated molten rivers that cracked the cool surface — lithosphere—into plates.

Imagine two box turtle shells cupped together to form a globe. The scales on the shells represent the Earth's plates. If you hold this make-believe globe long enough you will sense the plates slowly creep, collide, and rearrange themselves. The sphere feels alive. The Lenni Lenape's turtle, it turns out, was not far removed from science.

Scientists call the time period that began 500 million years ago (four billion summers after the turtle was born) the Paleozoic Era, the dawn of the Ordovician Period. The land we know as Ohio was located south of the Equator atop a lithospheric plate named Laurentia. Back then, the landmass was flat, depressed, and submerged by a warm, calm, shallow sea packed with creatures that crawled, swam, squirmed, squirted, floated, and burrowed. Think of a vast tropical lagoon. The remains of these marine buggers accumulated on the sea floor, and

solidified into the fossil-rich limestone characteristic of western and south-western Ohio. Fact is, for much of its geological history, Ohio has been under water and hip-deep in muck.

Over deep time, many millions of years, Laurentia was shoved, jostled, lifted, and spanked. By the middle of the Pennsylvanian Period, 300 million years ago, Ohio sat on the Equator, and Laurentia had fused with other plates to form a pole-to-pole supercontinent called Pangaea. Lush vegetation— giant ferns, conifers, towering rushes and reeds—then covered most of Ohio. This primeval swamp forest died, decayed, and compressed into the coal fields of Eastern and Southeastern Ohio.

Ohio started edging northward as the Mesozoic Era began 245 million years ago. Then something strange occured. Ohio stopped making rock. A band of sedimentary rock (found along the Ohio River between Belmont and Meigs counties) formed during the Permian Period, 285-245 million years ago, but nothing else accumulated until the recent Ice Age. This 245-million-year "gap" in the creation story remains a mystery, though scientists suspect that whatever may have been deposited during the Mesozoic and Cenozoic eras may also have been washed away. Whatever the explanation, the glaciers that later fertilized two-thirds of Ohio with topsoil started with a clean slate.

About 200 million years ago (Mesozoic Era, Triassic Period) Pangaea started to break apart. Churning convection currents under the Earth's skin spread the plates. North America, Asia, Africa, South America went their own way. Ohio reached its current location 50 million years ago, allowing a margin of error of five degrees latitude or longitude and several million years.

This creation story's final chapter, the Ice Age, is easier to picture because its vestiges survive in the polar caps and tallest mountain ranges. Its lingering affect arrives in winter's chill, snow, ice, and floods.

The Big Chill started about a million years ago when the Earth's climate cooled and ice caps grew from polar regions. Four continental-sized glaciers, all named after American states, swept over Canada and across

The Ice Age cometh; a glacial calling card left on Kelleys Island.

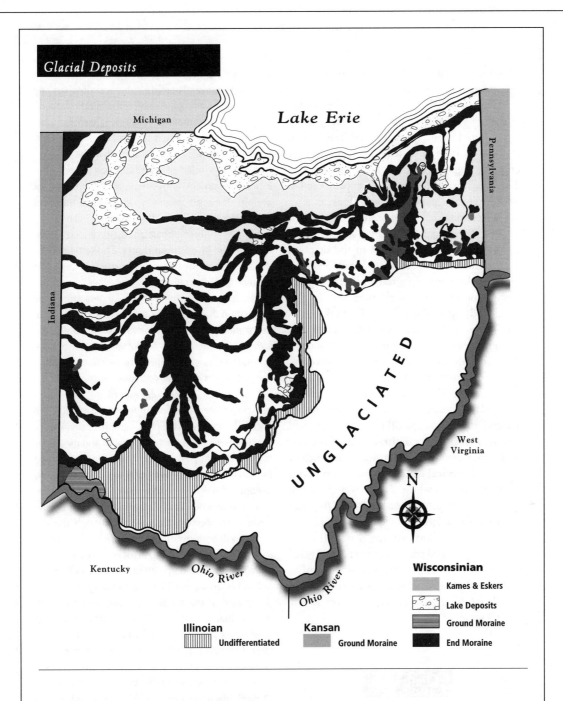

Glacial Deposits

Lake Erie

Michigan

Pennsylvania

Indiana

UNGLACIATED

West
Virginia

N

Kentucky

Ohio River

Ohio River

Wisconsinian
- Kames & Eskers
- Lake Deposits
- Ground Moraine
- End Moraine

Illinoian
- Undifferentiated

Kansan
- Ground Moraine

the Northern United States (and across Europe and Asia). The first ice wave, the Nebraskan, was followed by the Kansan, Illinoian, and Wisconsinan, the latter having the greatest impact on Ohio.

The Wisconsinan started its southbound journey about 40,000 years ago and took six millennia to reach Ohio. Creeping at speeds averaging 160-220 feet a year, it took 12,000 years to spread over the northwestern two-thirds of Ohio, and nearly as long to leave. At a location now forming the Ohio and Ontario border, the ice was

a mile thick and so heavy that it depressed the Earth's surface to make a basin for melting water. Today, the filled basin is called Lake Erie. From that brow the glacier tapered to heights of 50-200 feet at its edge.

Snow and ice piling up in the rear pushed the sheets toward warmer climes. Glaciers, in other words, did not build as they advanced. They did not grow like a rolling snowball. In geological time, they moved in nervous fits and starts, stalling awhile here, bulldozing there. Their paths were determined by forces from the rear, topography, and climate.

Glaciers changed vegetation. Plants that flourished in wet, cold climates replaced those that required warmer and drier habitats. When the Wisconsinan retreated, the vegetation of temperate regions returned. However, pockets of Ice Age flora still exist in places protected as nature preserves, parks, and wildlife areas.

Wisconsinan left its signature on the land as it retreated. Where it parked for a long time, meltwater deposited sediment at its edge in the shape of elongated mounds called moraines. Astute observers can track the route of its retreat by tracing the position of these terminal moraines. It also abandoned "calves," or icebergs that broke off its face. These blocks of ice eventually melted into lakes and ponds—the Wisconsinan's trail of tears. Ohio probably had hundreds of glacial lakes once, resembling Northern Minnesota.

Elsewhere, the Wisconsinan scrubbed and massaged Ohio's terrain, cut new rivers and streams, changed the course of other waterways, and deposited thick layers and mounds of till that became the soil and foundation of one of the richest and most bountiful temperate forests on Earth. Nomadic humans whose ancestors migrated to North America from Asia wandered into Ohio after the Wisconsinan left the stage 12,000 years ago.

The descendants of the first Ohioans departed about 200 years ago after the arrival of humans whose ancestors came from a different continental plate. The latter human horde still scratches this surface, the crusty dome of the Great Turtle. ⌒

—SO

Landscape

Formations

Ohio has been fortunate in that within its boundaries the physical environment has generally been advantageous for human settlement. Ohio's position within the westerly wind belt is such that it experiences considerable variety in weather conditions.

Nearby Lake Erie, by its retention of heat or cold, affects temperatures and length of growing seasons in adjacent shore areas. Ohio's location and topography are such that the region is open to the indraft of warm and humid air; this accounts partially for the state's adequate rainfall for middle-latitude crops and its sometimes tropical summers. Conversely, in winter Ohio is affected by blasts of cold Arctic air and occasional heavy snowfalls.

The low relief of the plains has placed little hindrance on the movement and settlement of people. Railroad, highway, and canal transport have experienced few landform barriers. Even Ohio's moderately hilly southeastern section has been easily traversed by transport routes. The settlement of this area before the rest of the state was in large part the direct result of favorable water access. These hill lands, however, proved to be far less suited for cultivation than the plains topography of the rest of the state. As settlement advanced in Ohio, the various qualities of the landscape throughout the state offered a series of different environments which evoked in part different settlement responses.

Ohio lacks spectacular mountains, but it does possess a wide variety of landscapes. Basically, the state falls into two of the physiographic provinces of North America: the Central Lowland and the Appalachian Plateaus Provinces. The Central Lowland Province, which is of low relief and low elevation, occupies roughly the northwestern half of the state. Here the bedrock is of Paleozoic age, principally Ordovician through Devonian, although the extreme northwestern corner of the state is underlain by rocks of Mississippian age. All rocks are sedimentary, with limestone predominating. Rock strata lie more or less horizontally, with the general regional slope downward to the north, northeast, and east. The Appalachian Plateaus Province extends throughout most of the southeastern half of Ohio. Bedrock is of later Paleozoic age, uplifted but more or less uncontorted and sloping generally down to the east. Shales and sandstones predominate over limestones. Of particular importance to Ohio's economic development are the coal measures associated with the Pennsylvanian-age rocks. The northern portion of the plateaus, because of glaciation, rather resembles the Central Lowland, but the southern portion is much more rugged. The contrast between northwestern and southeastern Ohio is essentially the difference between a youthful plain only slightly scarred by streams and a mature hill country deeply dissected by a well-developed network of rivers tributary to the Ohio River. The river itself is bordered by a flat floodplain along much of its length.

Precious Ice

In parts of Ohio, the hopeful

still pan for gold, which is

possibly present in any

glaciated county. Best bets for

an Ohio gold rush are in sites

along glacial boundaries,

locations where diamonds may

also be found in stream gravels.

According to the Division of

Geological Survey, Ohio

diamonds have a "peculiar

greasy appearance."

What the Glaciers Left Behind

The material left by glacial ice sheets consists of clay, sand, gravel, and boulders in various types of deposits of different modes of origin. Rock debris carried along by a glacier was deposited either directly by the ice or by meltwater from the glacier. Material reaching the ice front was carried off by streams of meltwater to form outwash deposits. These deposits normally consist of sand and gravel. Sand and gravel in forms called kames and eskers were deposited by water on and under the surface of the glacier itself and are recognized by characteristic shapes and composition. The distinctive characteristic of glacial debris by water is that it was sorted by the water that carried it off. The larger boulder-size particles were left behind, while the smaller clay-size particles were carried far away, leaving the intermediate gravel-and-sand-size materials along the stream courses.

Boulder-to-clay-size material deposited directly from the ice was not sorted. Some of the debris was deposited as ridges parallel to the edge of the glacier itself, forming a terminal or end moraine, which marks the position of the retreating ice when it paused for a period of time, possibly a few hundred years. When the ice sheet melted, much of the ground-up rock material still held in the ice was deposited on the surface as ground moraine. The term glacial drift is commonly used to refer to any material deposited at or behind the terminal edge of a glacier. Because the ice that invaded Ohio came from Canada, it carried in many rock types not found in Ohio. Boulders of these foreign rock types are called erratics. Rock collecting in areas covered with glacial drift or in glacial outwash deposits may yield granite, gneiss, trace quantities of gold, and very rarely, diamonds. The bulk of rocks found in glacial deposits, however, will be those types native to Ohio.

Many glacial lakes were formed during the time ice covered Ohio. Lake deposits are primarily very fine-grained clay-and-silt-size sediments. The most extensive area of lake deposits is in northern Ohio bordering Lake Erie. These deposits represent early stages in the development of Lake Erie as it is presently known.

Certain deposits left behind by the ice are of economic importance, particularly sand and gravel, clay, and peat. Sand and gravel, which has been sorted by meltwater, is generally found as kames or eskers or as outwash deposits along major drainageways. Sand and gravel is vital to Ohio's construction industry and deposits are abundant within the state.

Glacial clay is used in cement for common clay products. The minor quantities of peat produced in the state are used mainly for mulch and soil conditioning.

Source: Reprinted with the permission of the Ohio Department of Natural Resources from "Glacial Map of Ohio"

*The clothes maketh the land; well-dressed rock hounds
contemplate the state's geologic destiny.*

Perhaps the single most important factor in the development of the land surface of Ohio has been continental glaciation. Extensive sheets of ice covered Ohio during several widely spaced intervals of glaciation; the latest one, the Wisconsinan, had the greatest effect on Ohio's present landscape. As Alfred Wright noted in 1957 concerning the wide distribution of glacial features in Ohio, "There are many visible landscape features indicating glacial action: glacial scouring is visible in many quarries but with a spectacular example on Kelleys Island; the moraines which festoon much of the state, particularly between Columbus and Hamilton; the beds of former glacial lakes common in northern Ohio; outwash plains such as the one upon which Wright Field (now Wright-Patterson Air Force Base in Dayton) is located; and the millions of boulders which are fragments of rocks not found in the state. Most common, of course, is the glacial drift, which has renewed the base for soils-making materials."

In the early part of the 20th century, high-quality topographic maps were available for the first time, and regional landform analysis, or physiography, was a vibrant and controversial area of scientific research. The big names in geology and geography were physiographers. For more than 50 years, William Morris Davis' familiar, though dated, concept of continuous erosional cycles, which pass through stages of youth, maturity, and old age, served as the unifying concept for the science. Physiographic maps led researchers to regions of similar geology and geologic history. Ohio, for example, was divided into regions that are so familiar they have appeared on the fourth-grade proficiency tests. They include the Lake Plains, Till Plains, Glaciated Appalachian Plateaus, and Unglaciated Appalachian Plateaus. However, as geologic research became more process oriented, physiography faded, and the last update of the Ohio physiographic map appeared during the Great Depression.

Physiographic maps are "in" again; the Ohio, Indiana, and Pennsylvania geological surveys have each recently produced new physiographic or terrain maps. This time it is ecologists and land managers who want the maps for community and habitat studies. More detailed physiographic maps are a key component in developing large-area ecoregions maps, which government agencies plan to use in natural resource management and research. Unique physiographic regions are also unique ecoregions, but the former are much easier to map. In fact, the physiographic divisions of Ohio should seem natural to the observant traveler.

Even early travelers across the Ohio territory could easily identify unique areas such as the Great Black Swamp, Darby Plains, and Oak Openings. As settlement progressed, people noted broad regions where soils were more productive or less productive and where landslides or floods seemed more troublesome than elsewhere. The "new" physiographic regions map of Ohio puts boundaries on such regions and gives rhyme and reason to some puzzling geographic and ecological observations.

A Few of the Regions

Ohio's 33 physiographic regions are an interplay between glacial geology, bedrock geology, topography, soils, and geologic history. For example, if you overlay Ohio's glacial map on the physiographic map, the origin and boundaries of some, but not all, regions become more obvious. For example, the Great Black Swamp occupied region 7, the Maumee Lake Plains. This infamous swamp was a tangle of trees and shrubs in ankle-deep water interspersed with well-drained oak-covered hillocks. These hillocks--Ice Age beach ridges, dunes, bars, and deltas of ancestral Lake Erie--are concentrated in region 7.2, the Maumee Sand Plains. The low, wet areas were clay flats of the deepest part of the lake basin and remain today as region 7.1, the Paulding Clay Basin, which has the distinction of being Ohio's flattest area; for dozens of square miles the difference in elevation between the highest swell and lowest swale is less than five feet.

Glacial geology offers insight in Ohio's highest region as well, the Bellefontaine Upland (region 3.3) in west-central Ohio. The high point of Ohio, Campbell Hill (1,549 feet above sea level), by rights should be a crag of bedrock that resisted the onslaught of glaciers. Instead, the glaciers piled more than 300 feet of debris over a mere bump of bedrock. More end moraines drape this area than any other.

Escarpments and divides produce striking changes in physiography. In Eastern Ohio, the Flushing Divide separates Ohio's two major preglacial (Teays-age) drainage basins, which contrast in relief, dissection and some surficial deposits. The north-flowing Teays system ceased to function once the earliest glaciers blocked water flow and caused a system of lakes to form, much like the TVA lakes on the Tennessee River. Teays-age valley bottoms and the lake depositis that fill them are still important

features in the modern landscape of unglaciated Ohio, shown as shaded areas on the physiographic map. East of the Flushing Divide, region 17.1, the Little Switzerland Plateau (the name borrowed from the most rugged area in Monroe County along the Ohio River), is the only unglaciated region without remnant Teays-age features to soften the topography. The area's rugged topography and nearly impermeable soil and rock give rise to the most dangerous flash floods in the state.

Ohio's largest region of surface-exposed bedrock, the Allegheny Plateaus (regions 14-17), is difficult to subdivide by geology alone. The most obvious bedrock control on physiography is in region 17, the Marietta Plateau, where fine-grained rocks of the Pennsylvania-age Conemaugh Group produce rounded hills, areas of reddish soil, and relatviely common landslides. Perhaps surprisingly, bedrock has more evident control in the glaciated part of the state. Large areas of the Berea Sandstone lie beneath thin drift on the Berea Headlands (regions 2.1 and 8.1). The Berea Sandstone is particularly resistant to glacial and shore erosion, which removed overlying softer rock units, leaving a relatively flat plain. The softer, more erodable units have been cut into the hilly Galion Glaciated Low Plateau (region 6); the contrast between these adjoining areas can be seen even from space.

The new physiographic map for Ohio is available from the Ohio Division of Geological Survey, 4383 Fountain Square Drive, Columbus, OH 43224-1362; phone (614) 265-6576. Source; Ohio Geology, Summer 1998, by C. Scott Brockman.

Ohio's new physiographic map divides the state into two major landforms: the Central Lowlands and Appalachian Plateau (see map p. 8). These are broken down into five distinct regions: (1) the Unglaciated Allegheny Plateaus; (2) the Glaciated Allegheny Plateaus; (3) the Till Plains, covered largely by unsorted and unstratified glacial deposits;

Glacial Grooves, Kelleys Island

7

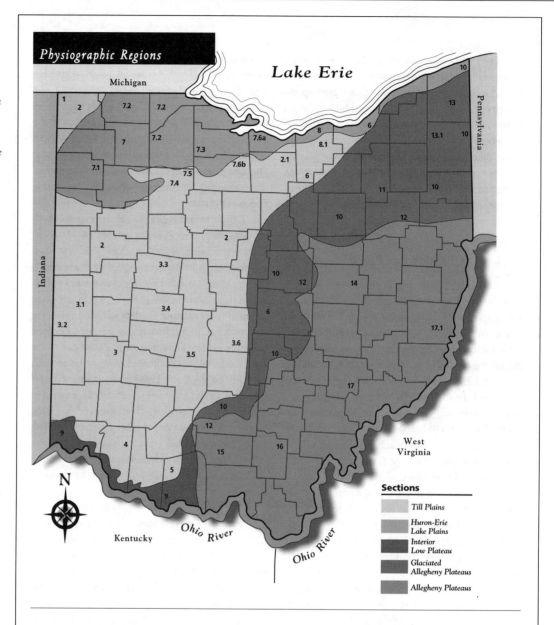

Physiographic Regions

Lake Erie

Michigan

Pennsylvania

Indiana

West Virginia

Kentucky

Ohio River

Ohio River

N

Sections

Till Plains

Huron-Erie Lake Plains

Interior Low Plateau

Glaciated Allegheny Plateaus

Allegheny Plateaus

1. Steuben Till Plain
2. Central Ohio Clayey Till Plain
   2.1 Berean Headlands of the Till Plain
3. Southern Ohio Loamy Till Plain
   3.1 Union City-Bloomer Transitional Terrain
   3.2 Whitewater Interlobate Plain
   3.3 Bellefontaine Upland
   3.4 Mad River Interlobate Plain
   3.5 Darby Plain
   3.6 Columbus Lowland
4. Illinoian Till Plain
5. Dissected Illinoian Till Plain
6. Galion Glaciated Low Plateau
7. Maumee Lake Plains
   7.1 Paulding Clay Bottom
   7.2 Maumee Sand Plains
   7.3 Woodville Lake-Plain Reefs

7.4 Findlay Embayment
7.5 Fostoria Lake-Plain Shoals
7.6a and 7.6b. Bellevue-
     Castalia Karst Plain
8. Erie Lake Plain
   8.1 Berea Headlands of the Erie Lake Plain
9. Outer Bluegrass Region
10. Glaciated Allegheny Plateau
11. Akron-Canton Interlobate Plateau
12. Illinoian Glaciated Allegheny Plateau
13. Grand River Low Plateau
    13.1 Grand River Finger-Lake Plain
14. Muckingum-Pittsburgh Plateau
15. Shawnee-Mississippian Plateau
16. Ironton Plateau
17. Marietta Plateau
    17.1 Little Switzerland Plateau

What's shallow at one end and deep at the other? Lake Erie.

(4) the glaciolacustrine area carrying the designation of Huron-Erie Lake Plains; and (5) a very limited portion of the Central Lowland which was never glaciated and which is usually referred to as the Interior Low Plateau. These five regions are summarized below. The big five have been further cut into 33 subregions.

Unglaciated Allegheny Plateaus

The southeastern quarter of the state, sometimes referred to as the Kanawha Plateau, is the truly hilly part of Ohio. Here a plateau of moderate elevation has been dissected by streams until it consists of narrow ridges and rounded hillocks separated by steep-sided valleys up to 300 feet in depth, with the larger valleys developing narrow floodplains. Generally, only the larger streams have narrow alluvial plains; the other streams, most of which are seasonal in character, are still actively engaged in downcutting. The interfluves, which tend to be elongated, are mostly in slope, although some suggestion of an earlier level surface is present. Also in this area, a high proportion of the natural forest covering has been removed, some because of mining and the rest as the result of the extension of cultivation; in some parts of the region a more extensive forest cover remains. Oil and gas wells are a common feature of the landscape.

Glaciated Allegheny Plateaus

Toward the west and especially toward the north, the Appalachian Plateaus surface has been modified by glaciation. Valleys are less deep than in the unglaciated portion as a result of glacial erosion, which has rounded and smoothed the hills, and glacial deposition, which has broadened and flattened the valleys. The original drainage has been displaced somewhat; small lakes and poorly drained swales have been added to the landscape. Interfluves in this region are broader and less dissected than those in the unglaciated plateaus; streams are more widely spaced and less deeply incised. Presence of a loose glacial rock covering is betrayed by the abundance of gravel pits in kame deposits along the larger valley bottoms and slopes. Kames are waterlaid sand and gravel features of glacial origin, generally forming irregular terraces along the sides of valleys. The recovery of sand and gravel is one of the more significant mineral activities of the glaciated plateau.

Till Plains

Over one-third of Ohio is covered by glacial deposits of low relief. Here in these Till Plains, upon a rock surface which had been well-eroded and largely leveled by streams, great ice sheets spread out deposits of loose glacial materials to depths of more than 100 feet in many places. The retreat of ice was erratic and halting, and where its edge remained for some time a ridge of material collected and formed ridges termed moraines by geologists.

The surface of the Till Plains is either gently undulating where morainic belts occur or where the underlying bedrock variations produce modest irregularities, or it is level. Relief is generally under 200 feet and over large areas well under 100 feet. However, in southwestern Ohio and in a narrow band diagonally across the state from Highland County to Richland County the glacial covering is thin and the effect of underlying bedrock is greater. In this area, which was covered only by early ice sheets, local relief is over 300 feet in many places.

Over the surface of most of the Till Plains glaciation has produced two results which are of special significance. First, topography has been smoothed, thus aiding accessibility and settlement. Second, the loose materials deposited over the plains have developed into excellent soils.

> *The soils of Ohio* **are the result of the** *weathering of the rock surface and its* **transportation by glacial** *ice, wind, and running*

Huron-Erie Lake Plains

In northwestern Ohio generally, and with a narrow extension along the shore of Lake Erie into northeastern Ohio, lie the Lake Plains. This essentially flat surface was created by the retreat of glacial ice northward; the released waters were trapped between the ice mass on the north, the glacial deposits left to the south, and the eastern continental divide. Sediments were deposited on the bottoms of these temporary glacial lakes. The ice retreat took place in several stages, resulting in various lake levels and surface extents, with a different outlet of the lake water in each instance. The first outlets were to the west; subsequent ones were to the east and included the present Niagara River channel. Once the waters were drained away the smooth lake bottoms were revealed.

A series of sandy beach ridges, each marking the edge of one of the early lakes, cross northern Ohio. On the flat Lake Plains the beach ridges, although only a few feet high, stand out as relatively prominent topographic features. Better drained than the lower lying areas, the beach ridges were the earliest settlement sites and the determinants for road locations.

Interior Low Plateau

Much of Adams County and small portions of adjacent Highland, Clermont, Hamilton and Brown counties lie within the Interior Low Plateaus. The present character of the surface in this unglaciated area is due largely to stream erosion of limestone bedrock, producing a topography quite unlike that of the rest of the state.

Evidence of underlying limestone bedrock in this region is betrayed by the irregularity of the land's contour and the large number of sinkhole depressions. Much forest cover remains on the numerous slopes and even along the valley bottoms. The flat-topped interfluves are cleared, however, and utilized for agriculture. Settlement has been primarily on the interfluves rather than along the valley bottoms. The road pattern is not as closely controlled by topography as in the unglaciated plateau, but some adjustment to landforms is noticeable. ᔷ

Sources: C. Scott Brockman, Ohio Division of Geological Survey; portions reprinted with the permission of the Ohio Department of Natural Resources from Ohio—An American Heartland, *by Allen G. Noble and Albert J. Korsok.*

That's rich: Ohio's soil is fertile, but not enough to grow the tuber that ate Toledo.

Dirty Politics

In May 1993, an Ohio House bill was introduced to make Miamian soil the official state dirt. Miamian soil, one of about 400 types found in Ohio, covers nearly 750,000 acres across 22 counties, mostly in central and western parts of the state. Then, and many times since, the resolution has been buried.

Soils

Characteristics

The soils of Ohio are the result of the weathering of the rock surface and its transportation by glacial ice, wind, and running water. At any place the particular soil characteristics are the result of an interaction of several factors: type of rock or parent material; topography or slope of the surface, which influences the water-holding character of the soil; vegetational covering, which contributes organic matter; and various aspects of climate such as amount and distribution of precipitation, temperature norms and variations, sunlight exposure, and depth of snowfall. Ohio's soils are grouped into eight categories, six of which cover large areas. The other two types, although they occupy small and widely scattered areas, are soils of such high agricultural productivity that they deserve special consideration. They are the peat and muck and the alluvial soils.

The principal areas of occurrence of peat and muck soils are the glaciated portions of the state in a band stretching obliquely across the state from Darke County to Ashtabula County. Within this region are deep accumulations of black or dark-reddish-brown soils of exceptionally high organic content. Artificial drainage generally must be provided and some application of fertilizer made before these soils can be used agriculturally. When these changes are made, such soils are among the most productive in Ohio. Well-known vegetable raising areas around Celeryville and Hartville are based upon muck and peat soils. However, there are some disadvantages associated with these soils. When artificially drained, the soils have a tendency to dry out and become powdery, and wind erosion is a serious problem. This can be combatted by the planting of poplar and other trees between the fields in rows perpendicular to the prevailing wind direction. Fire, which feeds upon the high organic content of the soil, is also a hazard.

Along major streams, especially in the well-developed valleys of eastern Ohio, ribbons of fertile alluvial soil have been laid down in the bottoms of the valleys or along the terraces that flank the bottoms. Although such soils are found along almost every stream and river, the largest occurrences can be found along the Ohio, Miami, Scioto, and Cuyahoga Rivers. Drainage tends to be somewhat poor on these soils, and flooding is always a potential hazard to their optimum utilization. Agricultural productivity varies from place to place, but is normally high.

The six most common soils fall naturally into three groups—residual soils, glacially transported soils, and lacustrine soils, each of which in turn can be subdivided into a limestone or a sandstone and

Pollution Penalties

Pollution killed 30,043 wild animals in Ohio in 1998, most of them fish. The Ohio Division of Wildlife collected $26,288 in fines from polluters.

shale sub-group on the basis of the parent material. Because limestone soils, which occupy the western half of the state, are fertile, it is that portion of Ohio which is most productive agriculturally. Sandstone and shale soils of eastern Ohio, where topography is generally rough, are not noted for their fertility. The lacustrine sandstone and shale soils are something of an exception, however; agricultural productivity here is relatively high.

Because of their complexity it is difficult to make generalizations about Ohio soils except under three headings—drainage character, organic matter content, and soil pH factor (the pH factor is concerned with the acidity and alkalinity characteristics of soils; acid soils require addition of lime to make them productive). As expected, general soils drainage characteristics correspond to topographic variations. Three general areas can be recognized. Those soils that are in general well-drained soils occupy roughly the glaciated plateau and the part of the Central Lowland covered only by earlier glaciations. Finally, the soils of western Ohio are characterized by generally poor drainage. Of course, within each of these regions there are wide variations of drainage conditions.

The pattern of organic matter content is quite simple. Except for muck and peat soils, the amount of humus ranges only between 1.5 and 3 per cent. In general, above-average concentrations of organic matter are found in those soils of the old Black Swamp region of northwestern Ohio; below-average amounts are most common in Appalachian counties. These differences illustrate the influence which topography and vegetation have had upon the development of Ohio soils. The soils of the northwest, developed in a humid region with dense vegetation growth, but on a level surface from which removal of decayed vegetation was extremely slow, still retain large accumulations of humus. Soils of the Appalachian counties, subjected to continual leaching as ground water percolates rapidly downward and as surface runoff drops quickly downslope, retain a lower proportion of original humic material.

Ohio was the number one importer among states in the transportation of hazardous waste in 1990, 1991, and 1993.

Except for some minor and highly restricted occurrences, Ohio soils are acid in reaction, ranging in pH from an average of 4.8 in Vinton County to an average of 6.7 in Ross County. It is interesting that the highest and lowest average values occur in adjacent counties. Three factors help explain this. First, the parent materials in Ross County are mostly limestone and in Vinton County mostly sandstone and shale. Second, most of Ross County was glaciated, whereas Vinton was not. Third, and perhaps most significant, large areas along the Scioto River are covered by alluvial soils high in lime.

Source: Reprinted with the permission of the Ohio Department of Natural Resources from Ohio—An American Heartland, *by Allen G. Noble and Albert J. Korsok*

Pollution and Landfills

As of 1996, there were 53 public-available and 23 industrial landfills in Ohio—where most of Ohio's municipal solid waste is deposited. Monitoring at 113 active and inactive landfills in 1993 found 38 with groundwater contamination and at 18 other sites, volatile organic compounds. Solid waste fills established earlier than 1976, when stricter regulations were enacted, pose greater risks to health and the environment. Most threats to groundwater are expected only at improperly run facilities and currently most of the facilities with groundwater contamination problems are unlined, inactive, municipal landfills.

In 1995, 35 Ohio counties had landfill facilities with five or more years of disposal capacity left. Even so, the Ohio EPA believes that the outlook is improving due to the regionalization of solid waste management. But it will continue to remain a problem due to new requirements and public opposition to locating new landfills.

Ohio has 1,180 unregulated (used prior to 1976) hazardous waste facilities in the state. Since 1980, 34 of these have been identified by the U.S. EPA on

Was this old rock fall at Seneca Caverns the work of crust faulting or water dripping?

No tread on me

Of the more than 850 million scrap tires in piles across the country, some 100 million of them are in Ohio—the state with the dubious distinction of being number one on the scrap tire chart. Wyandot County, meanwhile, is the state's epicenter; it has a tire pile with 20 million tires in one formidable place. Ohioans add an estimated 12 million tires to the mess each year.

—Ohio Environmental Protection Agency

the National Priority List or Superfund Sites.

At the end of 1993, 111 facilities generating hazardous waste were active, 92 percent of the facilities located in northern Ohio with 76 of the facilities reporting storage activities, 34 reporting treatment, and one reporting disposal.

Ohio was the number one importer among states in the transportation of hazardous waste in 1989, 1991, and 1993 but this trend appears to be declining. In 1989, Ohio imported 3.7 tons of out-of-state waste. The amount dropped to 1.9 million tons in 1990 and 1.6 million tons in 1993. Because of the many types of waste transported through and in Ohio, there is a risk to health and the environment coming from accidents. The number of vehicles transporting hazardous waste is about four percent of all shipping accidents and .02 percent of all crashes in Ohio.

Tire disposal in a state with over 7.3 million cars and 39 million tires is also a problem. Tires are not biodegradable and there is little use for recycled tires. Ohio's largest tire stockpile is in Wyandot County and contains 20 million tires in about 40 acres. Since tires were banned from landfills, illegal dumping has become a problem. Many are dumped in roadside ditches and illegally dumped tires may affect a wider group of people than those located in tire facilities. The population of mosquitoes may increase because scrap tires provide a good breeding habitat. La Crosse Encephalitis is one of the diseases associated with tire-breeding mosquitoes. From 1985 to 1993, the Ohio Department of Health reported an average of 21 cases per year. Tires were found at 80 percent of the exposure sites and were believed to be a secondary source in the remaining cases. There were also 51 fires involving tires reported to the Ohio EPA in 1992-1993. Exposure to smoke from burning tires may increase the risk of lung cancer from two in two million to two in ten thousand.

Source: Ohio Environmental Protection Agency

Superfund Sites

The U.S. EPA sites that are a priority for long-term investigation and cleanup are on the National Priorities List (NPL). The NPL is also known as the federal Superfund sites. There are currently 34 finalized, 16 construction complete, 39 proposed NPL sites in Ohio. ☜

SUPERFUND SITES

ASHTABULA COUNTY
Big D Campground
3678 Creek Road
Kingsville, OH 44048
Fields Brook
Water Bed of Creek
R3W T 13N
Ashtabula County 44004
Laskin / Popular Oil
717 North Poplar Street
Jefferson, OH 44047
New Lyme Landfill or
Ashtabula County Waste
SR 11 on Dodgeville
Road
New Lyme, OH 44066
Old Mill
Mill Road & Station
Rock Creek, OH 44084

BELMONT COUNTY
Buckeye Reclamation
SR 214
1 mile south of I-70
St. Clairsville, OH 43950

BUTLER COUNTY
Chem-Dyne Corporation
or Transenviron
500 Ford Blvd.
Hamilton, OH 45011
Skinner Landfill
8750 Cincinnati-
Dayton Road
West Chester, OH 45069

COLUMBIANA COUNTY
Nease Chemical Company
Benton Road (SR 14A)
Salem, OH 44460

DARKE COUNTY
Arcanum Iron & Metal
Pop-rite Lane off SR 49
Arcanum, OH 45304

FRANKLIN COUNTY
Air Force Plant 85
43 E. Fifth Ave.
Columbus, OH 43216 OH
**Rickenbacker Air National
Guard (USAF)**
7556 S. Perimeter Rd.
Columbus, OH 43217

GREENE COUNTY
U.S. Air Force
Wright-Patterson AFB
SR 144
Fairborn, OH 45324

GUERNSEY COUNTY
Fultz Landfill
CR 52
Byesville, OH 43723

HAMILTON COUNTY
Pristine, Inc.
Big Four & Smalley Road
Reading, OH 45215
**U.S. Dept. of Energy,
Fernald**
7400 Willey Road
Fernald, OH 45239

LAKE COUNTY
**Diamond Shamrock
Corp(Painesville Works)**
SR 535
Painesville, OH 44077

LAWRENCE COUNTY
**Allied Chemical
& Ironton Coke**
1130 South 3rd Street
Ironton, OH 45638
E.H. Schilling Landfill
US 52, Patrick Rd.
Ironton, OH 45638
**South Point Ethanol
Facility**
Old US 52
Southpoint, OH 45680

LORAIN COUNTY
Republic Steel Quarry
525 15th Street
Elyria, OH 44035

MIAMI COUNTY
Miami County Incinerator C
2200 North CR 25A
Troy, OH 45373
**United Scrap Lead
Company, Inc.**
1425 South Dixie Highway
Troy, OH 45373

MONROE COUNTY
Ormet Corporation
SR 7,
Hannibal, OH 43931
Cardington Road Landfill
1855 Cardington Road
Dayton, OH 45409
Powell Road Landfill
4060 Powell Road
Dayton, OH 45424
U.S. Dept. of Energy
Mound Facility
Mound Road
Miamisburg, OH 45342
**Valleycrest Landfill or
North San Landfill, Inc.**
200 East Valleycrest Drive
Dayton, OH 45404

MUSKINGUM COUNTY
UN Tech Auto
2200 Linden
Zanesville, OH 43701

PORTAGE COUNTY
Summit National
1240 Alliance Rd.
Deerfield, OH 44411

STARK COUNTY
Industrial Excess Landfill
1 mile south of SR 619 &
Cleveland Avenue
Uniontown, OH 44685
TRW Plant Miverva Plant
3860 Union Ave. South
Minerva, OH 44657

TUSCARAWAS COUNTY
ALSCO Anaconda
One Anaconda Drive
Gnadenhutten, OH 44629
Dover Chemical Company
15th & Davis Streets
Dover, OH 44622
Reilly Tar & Chemical Corp.
3rd Street
Dover, OH 44622

WASHINGTON COUNTY
Vandale Junkyard
Goose Run Road
Marietta, OH 45750

Source: Ohio EPA

14

Earthquakes

Although most people do not think of Ohio as an earthquake-prone state, at least 120 earthquakes with epicenters in Ohio have been felt since 1776. In addition, a number of earthquakes with origins outside Ohio have been felt in the state. Most of these earthquakes have been felt only locally and have caused no damage or injuries. However, at least fourteen moderate-sized earthquakes have caused minor to moderate damage in Ohio. No deaths and only a few minor injuries have been recorded for these events.

Ohio is on the periphery of the New Madrid Seismic Zone, an area in Missouri and adjacent states that was the site of one of the largest earthquakes to occur in historical times in the continental United States. Four great earthquakes were part of a series at New Madrid in 1811 and 1812. These events were felt throughout the eastern United States and were of sufficient intensity to topple chimneys in Cincinnati. Some estimates suggest that these earthquakes were in the range of 8.0 on the Richter scale.

A major earthquake centered near Charleston, South Carolina, in 1886 was strongly felt in Ohio. More recently, an earthquake with a Richter magnitude of 5.3 centered at Sharpsburg, Kentucky, in 1980 was strongly felt throughout Ohio and caused minor to moderate damage in communities near the Ohio River in southwestern Ohio.

Earthquake Regions

Three areas of the state appear to be particularly susceptible to seismic activity. Shelby County and surrounding counties in western Ohio have experienced more earthquakes than any other area of the state. At least 40 "felt" earthquakes have occurred in this area since 1875. Although most of these events have caused little or no damage, earthquakes in 1875, 1930, 1931, and 1937 caused minor to moderate damage. Two earthquakes in 1937, on March 2 and March 9, caused significant damage in the Shelby County community of Anna. The damage included toppled chimneys, cracked plaster, broken windows, and structural damages to buildings. The community school, of brick construction, was razed because of structural damage.

Northeastern Ohio has experienced at least 20 felt earthquakes since 1836. Most of these events were small and caused little or no damage. However, an earthquake on January 31, 1986, strongly shook Ohio and was felt in 10 other states and southern Canada. This event had a Richter magnitude of 5.0 and caused minor to moderate damage, including broken windows and cracked plaster, in the epicentral area of Lake and Geauga counties.

Southeastern Ohio has been the site of at least ten felt earthquakes with epicenters in the state since 1776. The 1776 event, recorded by Moravian missionary John Heckewelder, has a very uncertain location. Earthquakes in 1901 near Portsmouth, in 1926 near Pomeroy, and in 1952 near Crooksville caused minor to moderate damage.

Causes of Earthquakes

The origins of Ohio earthquakes appear to be associated with ancient zones of weakness in the Earth's crust that formed during continental collision and mountain-building events about a billion years ago. These zones are characterized by deeply buried and poorly known faults, some of which serve as the sites for periodic release of strain that is constantly building up in the North American continental plate due to continuous movement of the plates.

Seismic Risk

Seismic risk in Ohio, and the eastern United States in general, is difficult to evaluate because earthquakes are generally infrequent in comparison to plate-margin areas such as California and because active faults do not reach the surface and therefore cannot be mapped without the aid of expensive subsurface techniques.

A great difficulty in predicting large earthquakes in the eastern United States is that the recurrence interval—the time between large earthquakes—is commonly very long on the order of hundreds or even thousands of years. As the historic record in most areas, including Ohio, is only on the order of about 200 years—an instant, geologically speaking—it is nearly impossible to estimate either the maximum magnitude or the frequency of earthquakes at any particular site.

Earthquake risk in the eastern United States is further compounded by the fact that seismic waves tend to travel for very long distances. The relatively brittle and flat-lying sedimentary rocks of this region tend to carry these waves throughout an area of thousands of square miles for even a moderate-size earthquake. Damaging ground motion would occur in an area about ten times larger than for a California earthquake of comparable size.

An additional factor in earthquake risk is the nature of the geologic materials upon which a structure is built. Ground motion from seismic waves tends to be magnified by unconsolidated sediments such as thick deposits of clay or sand and gravel. Such deposits are extensive in Ohio. Buildings con-

A town like *Anna*

The Earthquake Capital of Ohio

Ohio during the twentieth century has had only a handful of earthquakes severe enough to cause significant property damage, but almost all of them were in Anna, the "Earthquake Capital of Ohio." During the 1930s alone, the ground in and around Anna moved 23 times. Two, on March 2 and March 9, 1937, were the most damaging earthquakes ever recorded with epicenters in Ohio.

About 9:45 a. m., on March 2, students in Anna's White Brick School were changing classes for third period. Former teacher Luther Fogt recalled, "The floor, the room, everything just quivered. The south wall of the room separated from the ceiling so that you could see the sky..."

There were no serious injuries, but Fire Chief Harry Cleaves' garage clock, broken for more than a year, started ticking again. The tremor was felt across six states, and made headlines in New York. Plate glass windows cracked in Wapakoneta, and Dayton office workers fled to the streets. At the Cincinnati Zoo, a gorilla named Susie screamed and beat her chest for twenty minutes. Billy, the secretary bird, frantically screeched and beat his wings. He was soon dead, his hasty exit attributed to the quake. "Billy," a newspaper reported, "had been ailing before the quake, and was in no condition to withstand shocks, earth or otherwise."

More intense than the one a week earlier, the March 9 quake was felt as far away as Milwaukee and Ontario. Buildings in Columbus wobbled, and there were reports of a roar in

structed on bedrock tend to experience much less ground motion, and therefore less damage. Geologic mapping programs in the state, geological surveys and the U.S. Geological Survey are therefore critical to public health and safety.

The brief historic record of Ohio earthquakes suggests a risk of moderately damaging earthquakes in the western, northeastern and southeastern parts of the state. Whether these areas might produce larger, more damaging earthquakes is currently unknown, but detailed geologic mapping and subsurface investigations will greatly help in assessing the risk. ⌒

Source: Reprinted with the permission of the Ohio Department of Natural Resources from "Earthquakes and Seismic Risk in Ohio"

the capitol rotunda. In Anna, all the chimneys tumbled down. Every house was damaged, with windows shattered and walls separated from the floors. All public buildings were declared unsafe. At St. Jacob's Lutheran Church, the organ pipes twisted and the 150-pound baptismal font lurched from its base. Chief Cleaves' clock stopped again, but so did every other timepiece in town, all frozen at 12:45. Though the beautiful White Brick school was now hopelessly riddled with cracks, the villagers managed to have their children back in class within a week. Fifteen people let the school board convert their parlors and dining rooms to classrooms. Streets were closed for traffic while students changed classes, played Red Rover, and had band practice on the pavement. Mr. Fogt unraveled the mysteries of active and passive verbs in Sophia Hagelberger's living room, and the superintendent set up his office in the home of physician Delphis Milliette.

During a 1931 tremor, Dr. Milliette had watched medicine bottles dance off a shelf, and promptly inquired about the school's earthquake coverage. When he learned that the White Brick had none, he insisted that the school board take out an unheard-of $30,000 policy. The school became the only one in Ohio with earthquake insurance. Only $90 had been paid on the policy when the quakes struck in 1937, and the good doctor became a village hero. Babies were named Delphis, and a new street in Anna was called Milliette. ⌒

—*Damaine Vonada*

Best known for inventing

scientific tools, Dr. John Locke

(1792-1856), a geologist,

completed the first study of

southwestern Ohio's geology for

the Ohio Geological Survey.

Locke's report gave the area its

reputation as the Mother Lode

of Ordovician fossils. His

geological map of Adams

County was Ohio's first county

map of its kind, and probably

the first in the U.S. Locke was

a keen observer, precise

practitioner and skillful writer.

*g*arden of Geological Delights

Berea Grit

Alias Berea sandstone, Ohio stone, Cleveland stone, and Independence stone: this cache of light sandstone in the Western Reserve not only made Berea the grindstone capital of the world in the 1800s, but also provided Ohio with some of its firmest foundations—including homes, courthouses, college buildings, the Garfield Memorial, the Soldiers' and Sailors' Monument, and Hope Memorial Bridge in Cleveland. Most of the sandstone found in Cleveland metroparks gets the Berea brand.

The railroad dynamited the actual petroglyph, but the name remains in Blackhand Gorge.

Blackhand Sandstone

Long ago, a black stain shaped like a hand decorated a 70-foot sandstone cliff above the Licking River. The best of several legends contends the petroglyph marked the boundary of a precious flint deposit mined by Ancient People. The "flint" region designated by the black hand was supposedly a neutral, or in modern parlance, a demilitarized zone. The "black hand" was destroyed during construction of the Ohio & Erie canal. The cream-colored sandstone, known as Blackhand sandstone, was quarried for buildings, bridges, and canal locks. Blackhand sandstone is the rock featured in the Hocking Hills, and at Blackhand Gorge State Natural Area, Licking County.

Blue Hole of Castalia

It is probably the only artesian well in the world with its own address, 502 North Washington Street, Castalia, Erie County, Ohio. At least forty-five feet deep, the Hole is so well fed by an underground source that the 7,519 gallons which flow through

every minute could supply a city of 75,000. The water is an even 48 degrees and dead—totally without the oxygen that sustains fish.

Cincinnati Arch

Not to be confused with any architectural marvel in Cincinnati, this "arch" refers to the crest of an elongated flex or bulge in bedrock stretching from Cincinnati to Toledo. The crash of tectonic plates that made the Appalachian Mountains rippled bedrock to the west. The slope of the arch is gentle and buried beneath glacial deposits, except around Cincinnati, the highest point in the arch. Here, erosion has worked fast to expose Ohio's oldest rock, fossil packed limestone from the Ordovician Period. In scientific circles, the Cincinnati Arch is the L'Arch de Triomphe for Ordovician critters.

Cranberry Bog

This is a wee bit o' Canada in Licking County where glaciers formed a swamp in which cold-loving northern flora thrive. Several thousand years old and barely holding out against erosion and Evinrude, Cranberry Island is an Ohio original—the only floating cranberry bog in the world. When the valley was dammed to make a canal reservoir, a 50-acre section of sphagnum moss broke from Cranberry Bog and rose with the water level, a veritable Noah's Ark on Buckeye Lake. Today, it is a state natural area and National Natural Landmark.

Concretions

The cliff that gives Highbanks Metropark, in Delaware County, its name, perversely looks like an old artillery range for all the cannonballs wedged in layers of shale. Think of a marble stuck in the pages of a book, or the famous pea beneath the princess. Actually, the orange or copper-colored globes are rock concretions. Scientists have not figured out how they form. They range in size from a few inches to nine feet in diameter. Concretion cores are typically calcite, surrounded by dolomite, then pyrite. One theory suggests that sediment grew like an onion or pearl around skeletal remains or bits of rotting plants. Concretions are found wherever Ohio shale is found. A good collection of them stands in a Columbus cloverleaf at the junction of I-270 and SR 315 (southbound ramp).

Copperas Mountain

Imagine disorderly, shoulder-to shoulder columns of long-playing records stacked 100 feet tall. The columns are slanting, fractured, shuffled, ready to topple. Remove the bottom disk, and the whole stack slides like an avalanche. Here and there, concretions (see above) bulge bug-eyed in the thin, brittle black shale layers. This gash across Copperas Mountain, in southwestern Ross County, is one of the weirdest, and most perilous cliffs in Ohio. The exposure faces Paint Creek and Seip Mound, an historical site off US 50 between Bourneville and Bainbridge, and straddles the Paxton-Twin township line. Mixed into this Devonian mess are layers of green mudstone, veins of barite, dolomite, calcite, breccia, and other crystals. All of it is crowned by hard Berea sandstone. Climbing the talus cliff can be fatal because loosened shale tablets cause rock slides and bring thousands of sharp shards onto the climber. Bluntly, climbers could be cut into stew meat. The cliff is on private property, but accessible from an unmarked, hard-to-find dirt road. From US 50, go southeast on Jones-Levee Road, right on Spargusville Road (CR 149), right on Storm-Station Road (TR 150, at a fork), left on a bumpy gravel lane (TR 530). It is easy to miss.

Flint Ridge

Nine thousand years ago, Indians from across the continent prized the red, blue, green, yellow, and pink flint that abounds in southeastern Licking and northwest Muskingum County. Elsewhere in Ohio, the flint is typically black or white, but elsewhere wasn't covered by a fortuitous sea 300 million years ago. Though white men today call this bonanza "Vanport" flint and seek it out for jewelry, the shallow quarries where Indians dug are still visible on the ridge. Go to Flint Ridge State Memorial for a look-see.

The Gap

The geological history for most places is seamless, with rocks of one era sleeping beneath the rubble of a younger period. Not the case in Ohio. The "gap" refers to an absence of 225 million years in Ohio's rock record. Ohio's youngest rocks are 250 million years old, products of the Permian Period. These Paleozic layers remain perched atop hills in southeastern Ohio. Where are the rocks and fossils from the Triassic, Jurassic, Cretaceous periods, and the recent Cenozoic Era? These younger rocks appear in the Rocky Mountains, but not here. Prolonged erosion probably dissolved these younger strata, and any dinosaur bones. That, or Ohio did not receive any more deposits for rock-making until the Ice Age glaciers covered it with gravel, sand, and clay.

Glacial Grooves

Between one and two million years ago, glaciers repeatedly advanced and retreated over all but the southeastern part of the state. Anything that big couldn't go away without leaving a calling card of sorts—erratics, moraines, kames, and the scarred rock that we call glacial grooves. Today the north shore of Kelleys Island displays the world's largest and most outstanding glacial grooves—deep trails etched in the limestone by the farewell performance of the Wisconsinan ice monster.

Grenville Mountains

Okay, so contemporary Ohio isn't blessed with mountains majesty above the fruited plain. But if we could rewind the geological tape a billion years, we would gawk at a line of lofty peaks called the Grenville Mountains running across Western Ohio between Lucas and Brown counties. How did they get there? Plate tectonics. What happen to them?

The snake marks the spot of Ohio's biggest bang: the Serpent Mound Cryptoexplosion.

Erosion reduced them to rubble. The mountains formed when the North American continental plate collided with another plate to the east. The crash uplifted rocks along other faults and old seams, such as the Grenville Front, which extended into Canada. Sediment from the eroded mountains filled in a rift valley to the west, sometimes to depths of 20,000 feet. All that's left of the mountains is the buried scar of the Grenville Front.

Gorge of the Little Miami River

To many eyes, this steep and unusual gorge is the prettiest natural area in Ohio. Start in Clifton Gorge State Natural Area (Greene County) and follow downstream trails through John Bryan State Park and Glen Helen Nature Preserve. Beautiful? Incredibly, at one spot, the Little Miami River's 130-foot plummet flosses through a skinny canyon that Olympic broad jumpers can bound. It is festooned with diverse and often unexpected plants. This is one of the few places in Ohio where the red baneberry grows, flourishing on the dolomite walls of the gorge. Historic? Of course. The area's natural history began with glaciers, whose meltwater carved the gorge and left behind a

trove of plant species. Human history here peaked during the last century when the rush of the river through the narrow gorge made it an ideal site for mills, and thus the industrial hub of Greene County. But before that, the gorge was the province of the Shawnee Indians, who late in the 1780s captured frontiersman Cornelius Darnell, a crony of Daniel Boone. Darnell escaped by jumping across the gorge, a death-defying feat that made him a local legend. Such leaps, of course, are discouraged today, as is climbing on the tall cliffs. In fact, the southern part of Clifton Gorge is such a hallowed preserve that even walking through it is by permission only.

Lake Tight

During the Ice Age, glaciers blocked the ancient Teays River watershed, forming a 7,000-square-mile impoundment known as Lake Tight. The lake, roughly centered where Ohio meets Kentucky and West Virginia, covered equal portions of the three states. Fine clay sediments, labeled Minford clay, settled in the sprawling lake. Eventually, meltwater made the lake spill over low divides and create new drainage routes. These new channels were the precursors of the Ohio River. The ancient lake is named after geologist William G. Tight, an early expert on the Teays River.

Meteorites

These are perhaps the rarest rocks in Ohio. Aside from the meteorites believed to have been imported from Kansas by Indians of the Hopewell culture, there have been only five meteorite "finds" (unwitnessed landing) and two "falls" (witnessed) in Ohio. The finds occurred in Clark, Hamilton, Montgomery, Preble, and Wayne Counties. The falls were witnessed on February 13, 1893, when a 1.98 pound meteorite came in from the Deep Cold near Pricetown, Highland County, and on May 1, 1860, when more than thirty fragments of a large meteorite fell near New Concord. The New Concord meteorite made one of the grandest entrances ever recorded in Ohio. A thunderous roar lasting about thirty seconds alerted citizens in two counties to the bright fireball that was racing across the noon sky. In the Earth's atmosphere, the meteorite split up into fiery fragments that scattered across thirty square miles. One of them struck and killed the day's only casualty—a calf. Folks picked up the pieces and found that all together they weighed 500 pounds. There probably are still undiscovered fragments of the meteorite around New Concord, but the largest one recovered (103 pounds) is owned by the Department of Geology at Marietta College. The most recent discovery occurred near Kossuth, Auglaize County in 1975. It weighed thirteen pounds. The Ohio Department of Geological Survey examines about ten presumed meteorites a year, but they turn out to be "meteorwrongs," usually industrial slag or peculiar looking native rocks.

Natural Bridges

Natural bridges, one of Ohio's best kept secrets, can be found at more than 40 locations in eastern and southern Ohio, but the largest is at Rockbridge State Nature Preserve in Hocking County. Centuries of erosion by rain and percolating groundwater have produced a stone arch that reaches 108 feet across a ravine and stands 55 feet above the ground. There are also spans along Archer's Fork Trail in Wayne National Forest and one that started as a crack in Fort Hill State Memorial.

Rock of the Ages

The biggest rock ever found in Ohio is the Brassfield erratic, a 430-million year old mass of limestone from five to seventeen feet thick that covers most of an acre. It was left by glaciers near the north fork of Olive Branch not far from Oregonia. In the 1840s, erratics were thought to be remnants of the Biblical Flood, but they are merely rocks that have been picked up and carried (by natural forces) from one spot to another.

Salt

Ohio has enough halite to supply the U.S. for the next 150,000 years. Formed from sea water 400 million years ago, the primary deposits are mined from tunnels 2,000 feet below Lake Erie or extracted via brine mines in northern Ohio. An average of 26 million tons is produced annually—forty percent of which goes to industry, thirty-five percent on roads, and five percent into America's salt shakers.

Serpent Mound Cryptoexplosion

Sometime during the Mississippian Period, 325 million years ago, a meteorite struck Earth where Adams, Highland and Pike counties converge. From cloud level, the impact area appears circular, about five miles in diameter and somewhat elongated, with noticeable rings and ridges radiating from a bullseye. The meteorite shattered and jumbled the horizontal rock layers. After the impact, the crust rebounded at the bullseye and pushed up Ordovician rocks (450 million years old) nearly 1,000 feet from their regular position. Broken chunks of the ancient rock stand vertically in places. Younger Mississippian rocks, 325 million years old, occupying an outer ring got punched down. Another explanation for this mysterious "disturbance" was a natural underground gas explosion along the scar of a tectonic collision (the Grenville Front). Something like a belch, or a bubble rising from the depths and breaking to surface. The event, whatever it was, derives its name from Serpent Mound State Memorial, which lies on its perimeter. And is it purely coincidental that Adena Indians built their effigy here? Wonders never cease. This unusual feature has been designated a National Natural Landmark by the U.S. Department of the Interior.

21

What we lack in peaks, we makeup in caves and rock formations. This is Old Man's Cave in Hocking Hills.

Sharon Conglomerate

Pimply, pebbly, abrasive and pocked characterizes conglomerate bedrock called Sharon, after the city in Pennsylvania just east of the state line. Milky white and rounded quartz pebbles, known as "lucky stones" and "poor man's pearls," decorate this resistant rock. Back in Pennsylvanian times, 300 million years ago, swift mountain streams north and east washed gravel into a sea then covering Ohio. The coarse deposit contained the tell-tale quartz stones, smoothed and rounded in the tumbling current. The gravel fanned in a delta larger than today's Mississippi River delta, then compacted into rock. Look for Sharon conglomerate in Nelson-Kennedy Ledges State Park, Cuyahoga Valley National Recreation Area, Gorge Metropark, Lake Katharine State Natural Area, Chapin Forest Reservation, and Holden Arboretum (Little Mountain).

Teays River

Before the Ice Age, the Teays River served as Ohio's main waterway. Starting in northwestern North Carolina, it flowed northwest through Virginia and West Virginia, coursing in the latter in the valleys now occupied by the New and Kanawha rivers. It entered Ohio near Portsmouth, continued north to Chillicothe in the opposite direction of the Scioto River, then swung northwestward. It left Ohio at Mercer County and swept west through central Indiana and Illinois, emptying into an embayment that became the Mississippi River. Some geologists believe the Teays drained north into the Erigan River, the predecessor of the St. Lawrence River. In either case, Ice Age glaciers blocked the Teays creating Lake Tight, then buried it with gravel. In Ohio, this interred valley is two miles wide and covered in some places by 500 feet of glacial debris. Other buried rivers include streams called Dover, Steubenville, Marietta, Groveport, Hamilton, Napoleon and Norwood.

Underground Forest

In 1991, miners in Jefferson County discovered curious 10-foot columns of coal in the Sterling North Mine. The miners thought they were hazardous, hollow "kettlebottoms," but geologists said they were the fossilized stumps of scaly lycopsid trees, which grew here during the Carboniferous Era some 300 million years ago. Scientists from the National Museum of Natural History have located 800 stumps in the mine, covering a distance of 1.6 miles. Spores taken from the coal indicate the presence of other ancient plants. The coal deposit was once a peat island located in a swampy delta. ✎

—SO

Bat
Cave

A Find of Rare Species Down Under

In February 1996 scientists contracted by the Ohio Division of Wildlife surveyed a 150-acre abandoned limestone mine in Preble County. What the team found in the mine amazed everybody: 25,319 bats, including 9,298 Indiana bats, a federally endangered species that has not hibernated in Ohio for 40 years. Five species of bats, North America's only flying mammal, huddled along 40 miles of underground tunnels. The congregation makes this "cave" Ohio's largest bat colony.

Bats live in natural caves, of course, but many habitats have become unfit for living due to human disturbances. For eons they have wintered in caves and old mines because they are dark, quiet, and nearly constant temperature. Human presence means light, sound, and a rise in temperature that could arouse the animals. Bat biologists figure that each arousal costs a bat 10-60 days of stored fat reserves. Aroused bats eventually go back to sleep, but some may not have enough stockpiled energy to last the winter. So abandoned subterranean mines may save bats.

—SO

Though Ohio has few natural caves, local bats find homes in a motherlode of underground mines.

*O*hio's Underworld

Ohio's underworld—caves, not crime—consists of 150 known caves existing in a 40-mile wide belt running from the Lake Erie Islands south to Adams County. South Bass Island in Put-In-Bay alone has 50 caves. There are other caves, dark secrets reserved for spelunkers, or preserved for wildlife found nowhere else in the world.

Absent a new discovery, Ohio won't ever be a cave capital, like Kentucky or New Mexico. Ohio has only seven natural caves open to the public, but frankly, none are worth driving across the country to see. Interest in them is largely local.

The hole of it all: from classic cavern to basic shelter, Ohio's got caves.

Cave scientists (speologists) are picky about defining a cave. To them a cave must be a naturally formed rock tunnel, underground, void of light, and with an ambient temperature of 54 degrees, eternally. Four ingredients are needed for a cave to form—rainfall, rock that acidic water dissolves (limestone and dolomite), rock with cracks, joints and openings, and an exit for water, such as a stream. Cave-making land, called karst topography, features alkaline bedrock such as limestone, dolomite, or gypsum.

Precipitation falling in karst topography percolates through a topsoil of organic material and becomes a diluted carbonic acid. This acidic water travels along cracks and bedding planes, dissolving calcium carbonate in the rock and carrying it downward and away. At a fast pace, the rock dissolves $1/32$ of an inch per year, but eventually the eroding crack enlarges into a cave. Sinkholes are surface depressions caused by collapsing cave ceilings. Surface water often empties into sinkholes and flushes through cave systems.

Stalactites, cave icicles, form when drops of water on cave ceilings evaporate and leave behind minerals. Successive drops add to the hanging formation. Drops that deposit minerals on cave floor, often directly below stalactites, form stalagmites. Stalactites that fuse with stalagmites become columns. Other ornate cave creations are similarly formed.

Bats and specialized tiny aquatic animals and insects can reside in the dark, humid and cool cave environment. Troglobites are animals that cannot survive outside the darkest niches of caves. Species of blind fish, flatworms, and salamanders comprise this highly adapted group. These fragile species are doomed if their cave is polluted or disturbed. Trogloxenes live temporarily in caves or near their lighted mouths. This latter clan includes raccoons, rodents, reptiles, insects, and even humans.

What follows can be considered a beginner's guide to Ohio's seven best cave attractions. All are privately-owned and open to the public for a fee. Call ahead for operating hours and opening dates.

Zane Shawnee Caverns

Now owned by the Shawnee Nation, United Remnant Band, this attraction features a basket of rare cave pearls, about 100 of them. The pearls are actually concretions that resemble moth balls. They start in cave pools when calcium carbonate precipitates on sand grains or pieces of rock. Also check out formations called soda straws, popcorn, sharks teeth, beehive, bacon and egg crystals, and the usual flowstone, stalagmites, stalactites, pools, and columns. The underground tour is nearly a half mile and descends to 132 feet below the surface. The site, open year-round, includes a small Shawnee-Native American Museum, and Southwind Park, a campground with five heated cabins. *SR 540, six miles east of Bellfontaine, Logan County. (937)592-9592.*

Ohio Caverns

Hands down this is the most delightful and largest cave in Ohio. In 1897, a curious boy probed a sinkhole and followed the cool air draft into a cave. Neon white spelotherms, stalagmites, and stalactites brighten the floor and the ceiling. They stand out like polished teeth against colorful walls iron-stained in tarnished yellows, magentas, and reds. The Crystal King is the biggest and most perfectly shaped snow white stalactite in Ohio. It has taken the "King" 200,000 years to grow five feet. Look for the Crystal Sea, drapes, and a formation resembling a spigot called the pump. *SR 245E, four miles east of West Liberty, near the Logan-Champaign county line. (937)465-4017.*

Seneca Caverns

Two boys and a hound chasing a hare found the opening to Seneca Caverns, originally the size of a half-bushel basket, in 1872. Technically, the cavern isn't a cavern at all but a high-angle reverse fault, or an earthquake crack, though it's impossible to determine if it was made by an earthquake. Think of the sliding and tilting walls of a carnival fun house. Adjacent slabs of limestone slipped about twelve feet horizontally. It is easy to see how the walls once fit together. The only other "crack" cavern of the high-angle variety is in Utah, but that one moved vertically instead of horizontally. *Northeastern Seneca County, four miles south of Bellevue. Take SR 269 south from Bellevue, then Thompson Township Road 178 west. (419) 483-6711.*

Olentangy Indian Caves

This cave, near the Olentangy River, actually was discovered by curious Wyandots who descended a steep shaft by rope knotted to trees. The constant 54 degrees made the limestone tomb a haven from fierce weather in summer and winter. The route leads to spacious rooms—Council Rock and Cathedral Hall—and through tight squeezes like "Fat Man's Misery." Wyandot chief Leatherlips was killed at the cave entrance by warriors. Whites called him a peacemaker, but Wyandots scorned him as a traitor. Small museum, frontier amusement park, and camping are available. *Southern Delaware County, on Home Road off SR 315 and US 23. (740) 548-7917.*

Perry's Cave

Storytellers say Commodore Oliver Hazard Perry stashed gunpowder here before his turning-point victory over the British in the Battle of Lake Erie in 1813. Gunpowder, doubtful; other stores, maybe. The cave is leaky and damp and Perry's gunpowder would have gone poof upon ignition. Still, the unlikely story keeps the uncomely cave alive. Perry's Cave is the largest of 50 caves on South Bass Island. Its big chamber is 280 feet long, 165 feet wide, seven feet tall, and 50 feet underground. A sickle-shaped pool is connected to Lake Erie, and rises and falls with the lake level. *Put-In-Bay, Catawba Avenue, follow the signs. (419) 285-2405.*

Crystal Cave

Crystal Cave is the geological heart of South Bass Island, metaphorically speaking. It's a giant geode forty feet below the surface in the center of the island. Geodes are round, hollow, grapefruit-sized (or smaller) rocks, which, when cracked like an egg, show tiny, glimmering crystals growing on the shells. Crystal Cave's geode is the size of a living room. Many of the bluish-white celestite (strontium sulfate) crystals lining the walls are supposedly the largest in the world. Some measure 24 by 18 by 10 inches, and weigh 300 pounds. Geologists suspect that Crystal Cave began when anhydrite crystals expanded like popcorn in dolomite cracks, then dissolved and left empty pockets; or when the interior of a gypsum dome collapsed and left hollowed fragments. *Put-In-Bay, 978 Catawba Avenue, across from Perry's Cave. (419) 285-2811.*

Give Me Shelter

Technically, many Ohio "caves" are shelter or recess caves, formed out of sandstone by surface runoff that has eroded less resistant rock that lays below resistant rock. Native Americans and early European settlers used the "caves" for shelter and gatherings, hence the name. They are a dime a dozen in Southeastern Ohio, the most famous in Hocking Hills State Park at Old Man's Cave, Rock House, and Ash Cave, the latter being the largest in Ohio. Others exist in state parks, state forests and state wildlife areas in the region, as well as Wayne National Forest.

Seven Caves

Picture a scenic dolomite gorge with 75-foot walls and a stream running down the middle. On one wall, a tributary called Cave Run has sliced a steep, V-shaped ravine. At one time it might have resembled a wedge cut from a wheel of Swiss cheese. In Cave Run Ravine, some 50 feet above the stream in the gorge, Rocky Fork, are the openings of caves: holes in the cheese. These are The Seven Caves, though actually there are eight of them. Geologists figure that 25,000 years ago the Wisconsinan glacier dammed Rocky Fork and forced its current to reverse direction. Melt-water from the glacier deepened the gorge below the level of tributaries (hanging valleys). Cave Run may have been a huge cave at one time. The house boulders at its mouth may have been the ceiling of such a cave. Outlaws used the caves for a hideout, and a captive frontiersman named Daniel Boone was tied to a tree and left overnight in the rain while his Shawanese captors snuggled in a cave. Admission to the caves lets you explore adjacent Highland Nature Sanctuary and Rocky Forge Gorge, an ace place. *Eastern Highland County, Cave Road off US 50, near the entrance to Paint Creek State Park. (937) 365-1283.* —SO

Down Deep

Why You Have That Sinking Feeling

At 526 feet, the Cadiz Portal Mine in Harrison County is the **deepest slope-cut mine** in Ohio. A 1980 study estimated that there are 20,823,512,000 tons of coal remaining under Ohio, about half of which can be mined. At the current rate of mining, that coal would take more than 200 years to recover.

The Barberton Limestone Mine, at 2,248 feet at the shaft, is **the deepest in the state**. Though out of operation for some 20 years, it remains singularly rare because limestone no longer warrants digging so deep.

In 1814 salt drillers struck oil in Noble County at a depth of 475 feet, making Ohio the **first state to discover oil** from a drilled well. By the end of the century, Ohio ranked first in the U.S. in oil production. Since 1888, Ohio has drilled 250,000 oil and gas wells, which puts it behind only three other states. The deepest well was 11,442 feet, drilled in Noble County in 1967.

John Cleves Symmes of Hamilton made a public declaration, backed up by a note from his physician that he was of sound mind: "I declare that the **earth is hollow**, habitable within; containing a number of solid, concentric spheres, one within the other, and that it is open at the pole twelve or sixteen degrees." He found no takers for his theory and a proposed expedition to the center of the earth, save his son Americus. During an 1849 lecture on the subject, Americus fatally injured both himself and the last chance for the Hollow Earth Theory when he fell from a Canadian stage.

—James Baumann

The Ohio River is more a web than a divider, more a circle than a line.

*W*hen we figure our addresses, we might do better to forget zip codes and consider where the rain goes after it falls outside our windows. We need such knowledge, need to feel as intimate with the branching and gathering of the Earth's veins as we do with the veins in our own wrists. The tilt of land that snares the rain also defines where we are more profoundly than any state line or city limit.

States often draw their borders along rivers, yet that is false to the land because rivers join rather than divide their two shores.

Nature ignores our political boundaries. Birds migrate up and down the valleys, seeds ride the currents, plants colonize outward from the banks and all manner of beasts—including humans—seek homes and food and one another along the paths of rivers. A true map of our continent would show a pattern of curving watersheds stitched together along high ridges, like a paisley fabric.

The watershed of the Ohio stretches into fourteen states, including ones as far afield as New York, Maryland and Alabama, draining an area that is roughly the size of France. The basin reaches from the Appalachian Mountains in the east to the Illinois prairies in the west, from the Great Lakes in the north to the Great Smoky Mountains in the south. Two sizable rivers, the Monongahela and Allegheny, give rise to the Ohio at Pittsburgh, and before it empties into the Mississippi at Cairo, almost a thousand miles later, it gathers in dozens of tributaries, including the Muskingum, Kanawha, Scioto, Big Sandy, Great and Little Miami, Kentucky, Green, Wabash, Cumberland and Tennessee. Its width varies from seven hundred feet in the upper reaches to nearly a mile at the mouth. In low stages, it pours twenty-two thousand cubic feet of water into the Mississippi every second, and in flood it pours 1.6 million per second, an amount that would cover a football field to the height of a four-story building. Those flood waters can be as muddy as the Old Man's but generally the Ohio is clearer, slow to mix with the "thick and yaller" current of the Mississippi, as Mark Twain observed. Depending on the light, the season, and the stage of the river, the water can remind you of coffee with cream, the amber of tobacco juice, the green of moss, the lavender of lilacs or robin's egg blue; or the surface can become a liquid mirror, doubling the islands and hills.

Swimming in the Ohio, I try to feel all the remotest creeks of that vast basin trickling through me. I like to imagine I can smell in the river the pines from the mountains, the oaks and hickories of the foothills, the blackberries and wildflowers of the bottomlands. What I'm likelier to smell is diesel oil, cotton poison, coal slurry, or sewage, because twenty-five million people live in the basin, and the watercourses are lined with towns, factories, mills, slag heaps, power plants, and refineries. Like the rest of our planet, the Ohio is caught in a tug-of-war between natural influences and human ones.

From bluffs along the river, you gaze down on a quintessential American landscape: A low island in mid-channel, half woods and half overgrown pasture surrounding the tumbled foundations of barns; coal-filled barges churning past, some headed for power plants whose cooling towers and smokestacks bristle around the next bend; other barges headed with corn or steel or automobiles, lashed to docks for unloading by conveyors and long-armed derricks; beyond the docks, a scramble of railroad tracks, high tension wires, gas lines, roads, our own channels of power following the river's; in the bottomlands, clapboard farm houses, some in ruins and some in restored glory; dented trailers with dish antennas and woodpiles and cannibalized cars in the yards; inlets marked by the white blaze of sycamores; fields of tobacco and soybeans; a chemical plant spewing gray smoke; hills illumined by redbud and the blue posers of larkspur; mud lots gouged by hogs, meadows grazed by cows; old cellar holes outlined by the persistent blooms of jonquils and forsythia; glacial sand and gravel pits; the spires and boxy shoulders of white frame churches; and on the ridge against the sky a whiskery fringe of trees. It is a landscape at once pastoral and industrial, wild and tame. The river is a sovereign power only half bound in the chains of our purposes. We exist as a people in that tension, loving wildness and fearing it, longing for contact with untrammeled nature and at the same time longing for control.

The Ohio has concentrated our desires and designs as it has concentrated the waters of a hundred streams. Because it was the principal avenue of settlement leading west from the colonies on the Atlantic seaboard, the history of our dealings with the Ohio epitomizes our dealings with the continent as a whole. By dumping our waste into the water, building dams and locks and bridges, raising levees, charting every point and riffle and bar, we have superimposed ourselves onto the river.

The Ohio carries for me the lights of the sky and the colors of the shore. It is the marriage of earth and air. Even in its chastened, diminished state, it holds out the promise of abundance, cleansing and renewal. ⮑

—Scott Russell Sanders

From "The Force of Moving Water," Staying Put, Beacon Press, *1995. Reprinted with permission.*

Water Resources

Ancient Waterways

LAKE ERIE

Lake Erie is the latest in a series of lakes occupying the Ohio-Canada frontier. After its makeover of Ohio's terrain 20,000 years ago, the retreating Wisconsinan glacier stalled in Canada. Its meltwater drooled south into a depression formed earlier by its own weight. Normally, the meltwater would drain via a river, but a lobe of the glacier blocking the eastern exit (the St. Lawrence River) created a huge lake instead. Lake Maumee once stretched across Northeastern Indiana, some 200 feet above the level of modern Lake Erie. As Maumee's shoreline shrank to lower levels, it successively formed lakes Whittlesey, Arkona, Warren, and Lundy, the latter staying for 8,500 years. Each lake left its mark—beach ridges (dunes), each successively lower. Lake Lundy became Lake Erie when a human felt an urgent need to rename the puddle shared by two countries and a lost Indian tribe.

TEAYS RIVER

Before the Ice Age, the Teays River served as Ohio's main waterway. Starting in northwestern North Carolina, it flowed northwest through Virginia and West Virginia, coursing in the latter in the valleys now occupied by the New and Kanawha rivers. It entered Ohio near Portsmouth, continued north to Chillicothe in the opposite direction of the Scioto River, then swung northwestward. It left Ohio at Mercer County and swept west through central Indiana and Illinois, emptying into an embayment that became the Mississippi River. Some geologists believe the Teays drained north into the Erigan River, the predecessor of the St. Lawrence River. In either case, Ice Age glaciers blocked the Teays, creating Lake Tight, then buried it with gravel. In Ohio, this interred valley is two miles wide and covered in some places by 500 feet of glacial debris.

Other buried rivers include streams called Dover, Steubenville, Marietta, Groveport, Hamilton, Napoleon and Norwood.

OHIO RIVER

The Ohio River is another product of the Ice Age. When the Kansan ice mass covered Ohio (the first of three or four continental glaciers), it dammed and buried the northwest flowing Teays River, the master stream in those days. The new main current, the Ohio River, drained along the margin of the ice. Glacial meltwater also cut new tributaries for the Ohio, and changed the direction of other channels—the Licking and Mohican rivers, for instance—that formerly fed the Teays.

After the American Revolution, the Spaylaywitheepi (the Shawandase word for the current) was a wild, unpredictable stream, with

It's Erie, *Dearie*

A Dark & Stormy Water

Familiarity breeds boredom, and even those who live close to Ohio's Great Lake forget their wet neighbor on dark nights. It's as if Lake Erie slips away, a party guest who can't stand the noise and smoke, preferring the quiet of the moonrise. We scarcely notice the lake's absence, so deafened are we by chatter and blinded by motion. Of course, that's crazy talk, more human egomania. The lake doesn't miss us. It doesn't wait up. It never writes.

We are the ones who drop in. Unannounced, we bring speedboats, loud radios and the wretched refuse of our teeming sewers. The lake maintains a tight-lipped silence. Vengeance is later. In February, the lake takes in a passing gale, feeds it up with moisture and gives it running room be-

fore steering it craftily ashore. Lake Erie extends her regards in ice, high water and howling wind. In August, its calling card is sudden lightning, jet-black skies and lines of vicious little whitecaps that swallow up, without a hiccup, the boats of electricians, dermatologists and retired school-teachers.

The lake comes looking on this wind. It scuds into shorelands it remembers as sopping wet and marshy out of the glacier time. It scours the uplands it remembers as unbroken forest. It whines along the rivers it once saw running clear. The lake wind doesn't see us. We are too impermanent and, at our present rate, don't look to be around that much longer. The lake doesn't go away.

—*John Fleischman*

Lake Erie Facts

Geologically speaking, Lake Erie is the oldest, shallowest, warmest, and most productive (for fish harvests) of the five Great Lakes. It also has the most species of fish.

The Ohio portion of Lake Erie represents 95 percent of the surface water in the state.

Average lake depth, 62 ft; maximum depth, 210 ft.

Lake Erie shoreline in Ohio equals 262 miles.

Eighty percent of Lake Erie's water comes from the Detroit River. The Maumee River is the second largest tributary. Other important tributaries flowing from Ohio are the Portage, Sandusky, Huron, Rocky, Cuyahoga, Chagrin, Vermilion, Black and Grand rivers.

Source: Lake Erie Fishing Guide, Ohio Division of Wildlife, Publication 276.

A River Or A Lake

Is the Ohio River really a river, or a chain of skinny lakes? After the American Revolution, the Spaylaywitheepi (the Shawandase word for the current) was a wild, unpredictable stream, with everchanging channels, shifting gravel bars, submerged snags, spinning eddies, and enormous sycamores shoulder-to-shoulder on the banks. Westbound emigrants attempting a summer run in a flatboat risked being grounded in shallows, and then massacred by defending warriors. Only dugout canoes could navigate it year-round. It coursed through a series of riffles and pools, split around cigar-shaped islands, and spilled over several waterfalls, the largest being the rapids at Louisville. Fords, in places, were waist high. Winter thaws and spring rains bloated the bath, but Indians knowingly built their villages inland and high above the highest water. Floods were never an enemy until Euro-Americans got in the way.

School kids in Ohio learn fast that their state's namesake starts at the confluence of the Allegheny and Monogahela rivers in Pittsburgh. From there it curls generally south and west 981 miles to the Mississippi River. After Pennsylvania, it forms the border between five states. Its tentacles drain portions of 11 states, representing 20 percent of the Mississippi River watershed.

Back then the Ohio dropped from an elevation of 700 feet in Pittsburgh to 250 feet at its mouth in Cairo, Illinois, an average of a half foot per mile. Travel was limited to a 3-4 month window in late spring and early summer. After that the river was too low, too icy, or too high.

In 1820 a commission of Ohio Valley states identified 102 obstructions to navigation between Pittsburgh and Louisville. The survey, partially funded by Congress, marked the start of federal tampering with water resources, and the end of the Ohio River's freedom. Five years later, the U.S. Army Corps of Engineers began civilizing the river, first by removing snags and sandbars that stalled and sank riverboats. A patriotic cry to deepen and regulate the river's flow rang during the Civil War when Union troops rushing to lift the Confederate siege at Chattanooga in September 1863 could not be ferried across the

everchanging channels, shifting gravel bars, submerged snags, spinning eddies, and enormous sycamores shoulder-to-shoulder on the banks. Westbound emigrants attempting a summer run in a flatboat risked being grounded in shallows, and then massacred by defending warriors. Only dugout canoes could navigate it year-round. It coursed through a series of riffles and pools, split around cigar-shaped islands, and spilled over several waterfalls, the largest being the rapids at Louisville. Fords, in places, were waist high. Winter thaws and spring rains bloated the bath. Indians learned to build their villages inland and high above the highest water. Floods were never an enemy until people got in the way.

Schoolchildren in Ohio learn fast that their state's namesake starts at the confluence of the Allegheny and Monogahela rivers in Pittsburgh. From there it curls generally south and west 981 miles to the Mississippi River. After Pennsylvania, it forms the border between five states. Its tentacles drain portions of 11 states, representing twenty percent of the Mississippi River watershed.

Back then the Ohio dropped from an elevation of 700 feet in Pittsburgh to 250 feet at its mouth in Cairo, Illinois, an average of a half foot per mile. Travel was limited to a 3-4 month window in late spring and early summer. After that the river was too low, too icy, or too high.

In 1820 a commission of Ohio Valley states identified 102 obstructions to navigation between Pittsburgh and Louisville. The survey, partially

Ohio at Bellaire due to shallow water. The first lock and dam, five miles below Pittsburgh, was finished in 1885. A dozen more locks accepted traffic in 1910, and channelization, or digging a trench for ship traffic, was done by 1929. Today, 20 locks and dams control the route. A sad sameness and drab uniformity now characterizes the river from start to finish. Even the Ohio River Fisheries Management Team, a six-state commission protecting the river's natural resources, admits, "The river is a series of slow-moving lakes, some as long as 100 miles and 50 feet deep."

The erstwhile river washes against Ohio for 451 miles. Within that span, nine locks and dams have created nine lakes, officially called "pools," totaling 91,300 surface acres of water. The interconnected "pools" are second in size in Ohio only to Lake Erie. Hence, the Ohio River's moniker as Ohio's Southern Coast. The Muskingum, Hocking, Scioto, Little Miami and Great Miami rivers empty into the Ohio.

Last count, 159 fish species live in the river. Of these, 25 varieties are considered sportfish, notably sauger, basses (largemouth, smallmouth, spotted, white, and hybrid striped), walleye, bluegill, crappie, and catfishes (channel and flathead). Fishers from shore and boat cast in the tailwaters below dams, the pools, or the embayments (the backwaters, and tributary mouths). A 1992 survey of anglers along the Ohio segment of the river, revealed that two-thirds of all fish catches were landed in tailwaters, a spot representing just one percent of the river's surface area. Bass captured most of the anglers' attention. Catfishers ranked the middle section between Huntington and Louisville their most popular area.

Six states cooperatively manage the river's fisheries through the Ohio River Fisheries Management Team. For Ohio anglers, this team approach means their fishing license is valid in Ohio River waters within Kentucky and West Virginia. And vice versa... Ohio River water ends at the first riffle or dam in tributaries. Reciprocity extends to shore fishing. The game laws of the state you are fishing in apply.

For more information consult these publications: *Ohio Fishing Regulations (available where fishing licenses are sold); Ohio River Fishing, Publication 124, Ohio Division of Wildlife; and Ohio River Fishing Guide, published by the Ohio River Fisheries Management Team, available from the wildlife division.*

funded by Congress, marked the start of federal tampering with water resources, and the end of the Ohio River's freedom. Five years later, the U.S. Army Corps of Engineers began civilizing the river, first by removing snags and sandbars that stalled and sank riverboats. A patriotic cry to deepen and regulate the river's flow rang during the Civil War when Union troops rushing to lift the Confederate siege at Chattanooga in September 1863 could not be ferried across the Ohio at Bellaire due to shallow water. The first lock and dam, five miles below Pittsburgh, was finished in 1885. A dozen more locks accepted traffic in 1910, and channelization, or digging a trench for ship traffic, was done by 1929. Today, twenty locks and dams choke the route. A sad sameness and drab uniformity now characterizes the river from start to finish. Even the Ohio River Fisheries Management Team, a six-state commission protecting the river's natural resources, admits, "The river is a series of slow-moving lakes, some as long as one hundred miles and fifty feet deep."

The erstwhile river today washes against Ohio for 451 miles. Within that span, nine locks and dams have created nine lakes, officially called "pools," totaling 91,300 surface acres of water. The interconnected "pools" are second in size in Ohio only to Lake Erie. Hence, the river's moniker "Ohio's Southern Coast." The Muskingum, Hocking, Scioto, Little Miami and Great Miami rivers all empty into the Ohio.

—SO

Gone Fishin' in Ohio

"Abounding with fine fish and wild fowl of various kinds, as also in most excellent meadows, in their present state, almost fit for the scythe."— *ad in Baltimore newspaper for homesteads along the Ohio, placed by George Washington,* ¹*773*

The vista of Erie from Lakeview is called Paradise (Island).

Lakes

There are more than 60,000 lakes, ponds, and reservoirs in Ohio. Almost all of these—about 200,000 acres of water—are manmade. A small number consists of natural bodies—about 6,700 acres of water.

Ohio's lakes, ponds, and reservoirs come in all sizes. They range from tiny ponds of only a fraction of an acre to huge reservoirs covering thousands of acres. Small farm ponds under two acres make up the majority of water areas in Ohio. Farm ponds are built by placing a dam across a small stream (onstream reservoir), by excavating into the ground (dug-out ponds), or by employing a combination of both methods. Farm ponds supply water for livestock and other uses at the farmstead while providing important benefits for wildlife and such recreational pursuits as swimming and fishing. In addition, pond water is sometimes used to fight fires in rural areas.

Since the passage of the first federal flood control legislation in 1936, the U.S. Army Corps of Engineers has built 28 dams in Ohio. Most of these are multipurpose reservoir projects involving flood control, water supply, stream flow augmentation, and recreation. The Ohio Department of Natural Resources often participates in these projects by developing recreational facilities around the lakes.

Some of Ohio's biggest lakes were built during the 1830s to supply water to the new canal system.

The canals were once vital transportation routes through Ohio. Today, canals are no longer used for transportation, but the large feeder lakes—Buckeye Lake, Grand Lake St. Marys, Indian Lake, Lake Loramie, Portage Lakes, and Guilford Lake— are now recreation areas.

The many other public and private recreation lakes cannot be overlooked. These include county lakes, metropolitan park lakes, real estate lakes, and private fishing lakes. The real estate lakes are relatively recent phenomenon. Increased affluence and leisure time have created a market for a second home, often a lakefront property. In a real estate lake development the developer buys land and builds the lake, then sells lots around the lake for urban development. Use of the lake is generally limited to lot owners. Lake Mohawk in Carroll County is the largest of these real estate development lakes in Ohio.

Groundwater

As rain and surface water soak into the ground, and after the soil, plants, grasses, and trees have taken a certain amount, the water filters down until it reaches the water table. The water table is the top of a zone below the Earth's surface in which all pores, holes, and cracks are filled with water. This collection of subsurface water is called groundwater.

Groundwater provides the base flow of streams. Base flow is the water that remains through the driest part of the year. When the water table is high enough to be exposed in the stream channel, groundwater discharges into the stream, making up the base flow. Many streams would dry up between rains if they were not fed by groundwater. The reverse is also true. Water in the streams and rivers feeds the groundwater supply by seeping through the stream bed or river bank. Groundwater and water in streams and rivers are interconnected parts of the same water resource. Hydrologists cringe when non-scientists mistakenly refer to underground rivers. The beasts just don't exist.

Source: excerpted with permission, Division of Water, ODNR, from Water: Ohio's Remarkable Resource.

Water Quality

Surface water pollution is divided into two categories: point and non-point. Discharges which come from a known source such as a pipe or sewer is a point source. Non-point sources come from a broader area, such as agricultural run-off or acid mine drainage.

The greatest threat to freshwater supplies in Ohio comes from non-point source pollutions as water runs off from broad land areas. Storm water is one of the most important sources of pollution while agriculture and urbanization are also contributors to such pollution. Because this type of pollution has a wide source, large portions of the environment may be effected but the threat is probably more of a direct risk to ecological systems rather than to human health.

More than 85 million tons of soil erode annually in Ohio and much of this ends up in lakes, rivers, and streams, degrading water quality and costing millions of dollars to remove. Agricultural run-off during and after rainstorms is also a way that ground water is affected, the run-off includes pesticides, fertilizer, and petroleum products that degrade water quality. Even though the use of pesticides on major crops in Ohio has been declining, approximately 75 percent of the ground water supply systems have detected levels of these pesticides although rarely do the concentrations in drinking water exceed standards set by the U.S. Environmental Protection Agency.

The northwest part of the state is at the greatest risk due to a higher use of chemicals in agriculture, although other areas of the state are sensitive due to the geology or season. Acute or chronic health effects are associated with contaminates in drinking water polluted from agricultural contamination. Nitrate, potentially fatal to children, is found in agricultural fertilizers. Between 1990 and 1994 seventeen violations for nitrate contaminations (eight in ground water / nine in surface water) were recorded and 2.5 percent of the wells tested had levels above U.S. EPA levels for drinking water.

Inactive or abandoned mines also pose risks to water quality. According to law, there is no acid mine drainage leaving an active mining site; all water must pass through a treatment facility. But erosion, sedimentation, flooding, and acid mine drainage from abandoned coal mines continues to severely affect the environment. High erosion rates at abandoned surface mines are at the highest of any land within the state. There are about 36,000 acres effected. Sedimentation in streams adjacent to mining activities affect approximately 3,435 acres.

Urban run-off, which far exceeds all other land uses in sediment produced per acre, brings with it non-agricultural storm water pollutants. With approximately 40 percent of private lawns being treated with pesticides, as well as the use of pesticides on golf courses and other public areas, it can increase the pollution in local lakes and streams. Storm water run-off, which contains road maintenance material, predominantly affects vegetation but does not pose a threat unless found in high concentrations.

Over the past 20 years in both the public and private sectors, Ohio has invested several billion dollars to control industrial and municipal waste water. While conditions have improved, discharges from waste water treatment plants are still a major source of pollution in 21.5 percent of the impaired streams in the state. By monitoring fish as an indicator of human health risk, samples collected from 1988 - 1992 indicated that 415 of them showed no sign of contamination from pollution, 24.6 percent showed moderate levels of contamination, and 27.6 percent showed high levels of contamination. Fish consumption advisories for all species had been issued for 6.8 percent of stream miles sampled in the state.

We are still paying the price for past practices. Even though Ohio has had permits for discharging waste water since 1972, many poor biological conditions can be traced to historical discharges as the release of chemical compounds continues to form sentiment that has settled on the bottoms of water bodies. ᕥ

MAJOR RIVERS & STREAMS

Name	Length in Miles	Flows into	Mouth in County	Drains Square miles
Ashtabula River	39.7	Lake Erie	Ashtabula	137.4 8.91 in PA
Auglaize River	101.9	Maumee River	Defiance	2,448.2 106.6 in IN
Big Walnut Creek	74.2	Scioto River	Pickaway	556.7
Black River	73.0	Lake Erie	Lorain	466.8
Captina Creek	38.6	Ohio River	Belmont	180.8
Chagrin River	47.9	Lake Erie	Lake	270.0
Conneaut Creek	56.8	Lake Erie	Ashtabula	191.2 153.5 in PA
Conotton Creek	38.7	Tuscarawas River	Tuscarawas	286.3
Cross Creek	27.4	Ohio River	Jefferson	128.1
Cuyahoga River	100.1	Lake Erie	Cuyahoga	813.3
Darby Creek	78.7	Scioto River	Pickaway	556.6
Deer Creek	67.1	Scioto River	Ross	408.4
Duck Creek	51.5	Ohio River	Washington	287.7
Eagle Creek	30.9	Ohio River	Brown	153.5
Grand River	98.5	Lake Erie	Lake	712.1
Hocking River	94.9	Ohio River	Athens	1,199.5
Huron River	59.7	Lake Erie	Erie	403.4
Indian Guyan Creek	31.5	Ohio River	Lawrence	76.5
Killbuck Creek	81.7	Walhonding River	Coshocton	612.9
Leading Creek	29.5	Ohio River	Meigs	151.08
Licking River	67.5	Muskingum River	Muskingum	780.5
Little Beaver Creek	51.0 1.5 in PA	Ohio River	Beaver (PA)	510.1 102.3 in PA
Little Hocking River	18.4	Ohio River	Washington	102.86
Little Miami River	105.5	Ohio River	Hamilton	1,755.3
Little Muskingum	69.7	Ohio River	Washington	314.5
Little Scioto River	41.3	Ohio River	Scioto	232.6
Mad River	60.2	Miami River	Montgomery	656.0
Mahoning River	108.3 11.2 in PA	Beaver River	Lawrence (PA)	1,132.8 55.2 in PA
Maumee River	105.4	Maumee Bay	Lucas	6,586.3 1,260.0 in IN 470.1 in MI
McMahon Creek	28.1	Ohio River	Belmont	91.2
Great Miami River	170.3	Ohio River	Hamilton	5,385.3 1,437.4 in IN
Mill Creek	28.1	Ohio River	Hamilton	166.2
Moxahala Creek	29.2	Muskingum River	Muskingum	300.7
Muskingum River	111.9	Ohio River	Washington	8,037.6

Name	Length in Miles	Flows into	Mouth in County	Drains Square miles
Ohio Brush Creek	57.1	Ohio River	Adams	435.0
Olentangy River	88.5	Scioto River	Franklin	536.3
Ottawa River Basin	41.6 0.6 in MI	N. Maumee Bay	Monroe (MI)	178.51 45.17 in MI
Paint Creek	94.7	Scioto River	Ross	1,142.7
Pine Creek	48.0	Ohio River	Scioto	184.7
Portage River	60.6	Lake Erie	Ottawa	601.78
Raccoon Creek	109.0	Ohio River	Gallia	683.5
Rocky River	48.0	Lake Erie	Cuyahoga	293.8
Salt Creek	45.4	Scioto River	Ross	553.4
Sandusky River	130.2	Sandusky Bay	Sandusky	1,420.7
Sandy Creek	41.3	Tuscarawas River	Stark	503.1
Scioto Brush Creek	36.0	Scioto River	Scioto	273.5
Shade River	38.2	Ohio River	Meigs	220.6
Shenango River	90.0 88.9 in PA	Beaver River	Lawrence (PA)	1,066.33
Short Creek	29.4	Ohio River	Jefferson	147.2
St. Joseph River	44.3	Maumee River	Lucas	1,060.4 603.2 in IN 219.2 in MI
St. Marys River	59.1	Maumee River	Lucas	816.7 359.0 in IN
Stillwater Creek	63.5	Tuscarawas River	Tuscarawas	485.1
Stillwater River	67.2	Miami River	Montgomery	673.2
Straight Creek	21.6	Ohio River	Brown	66.7
Sugar Creek	45.0	Tuscarawas River	Tuscarawas	356.2
Sunfish Creek (into Scioto R.)	26.5	Scioto River	Pike	144.6
Sunfish Creek (into Ohio R.)	31.4	Ohio River	Monroe	113.8
Symmes Creek	70.0	Ohio River	Lawrence	355.7
Tiffin River	59.2	Maumee River	Defiance	804.5 251.0 in MI
Tuscarawas River	129.9	Muskingum River	Coshocton	2,589.7
Vermilion River	58.7	Lake Erie	Erie	271.7
Wabash River (Ohio portion)	41.7	Ohio River	Posey (IN)	281.0
Walhonding River	23.5	Muskingum River	Coshocton	2,252.0
Wheeling Creek	30.2	Ohio River	Belmont	107.7
Whiteoak Creek	49.3	Ohio River	Brown	234.3
Wills Creek	92.9	Muskingum River	Muskingum	853.2
Yellow Creek	34.0	Ohio River	Jefferson	240.1

Source: Division of Water, ODNR

Scioto Sluice: Columbus O'Shaughnessy Dam

Water Tight Wisdom

"Just as astronauts must survive in a finite envronment, an environment containing only so much water, air, and space—so must man. We cannot poison the atmosphere, pollute drinking water, or tamper with the delicate natural processes without endangering our very existence."—
Samuel S. Studebaker, member Ohio Conservation Hall of Fame

Baptism of Water

High above Earth, Ohio looks wrinkled from thousands of water routes that erode away soil and stone en route to the Ohio River or Lake Erie. About 3,300 wrinkles have names; almost as many don't. The names we gave them say as much about us and the way we relate to the land as they do the quality of the water resources.

Many names reveal something about the wilderness experiences of Native Americans and pioneers, and the clashes between them. They reflect the wit of early settlers, their reverence for the land and their frustration in "conquering" it. Stream names describe the quality and abundance of Ohio's natural resources, locate family settlements, and delineate the boundary of cultural influences.

Judging from some names, pioneers didn't find a pristine nor bountiful land when they arrived to christen Ohio's currents. Thirty-nine rivulets carry the name "mud" or "muddy," and the number of currents named "dry" totals 52. In contrast, "clear" appears in the name of just 22 streams; and there is not a single "wet" creek.

Creek water apparently excited the taste buds of stream namers. The juice from 18 sugar runs, 16 sugar creeks, Sweet Run and Chocolate Run likely satisfied the pioneers' palette. Eighteen streams have "salt" in their names; and one can only cringe from the astringent flavor of nectar from Vinegar Run.

Pee Pee Creek produces giggles, but the name refers to another name, not water quality. In the autumn of 1785 Peter Patrick and three other pioneers ventured up the Scioto River Valley to claim land. Shawandase warriors chased the quartet away but not before Patrick tomahawked his initials in trees along a creek that emptied into the Scioto at Waverly. Later settlers, seeing Patrick's graffiti, dubbed the creek and township "Pee Pee."

Paving the way to heaven may have been on the minds of settlers who blessed streams with names like Christian Creek, Brimstone Creek, Priest Run, Temple Creek, River Styx, and Quaker Run. The devil's advocates, however, may have flavored the naming of Paramour Creek, Hellbranch Run, and Blackjack Branch. Moonshiners, or their patrons, probably were under the influence when Whisky Run, Grog Run, and Jug Run were christened. And what kind of

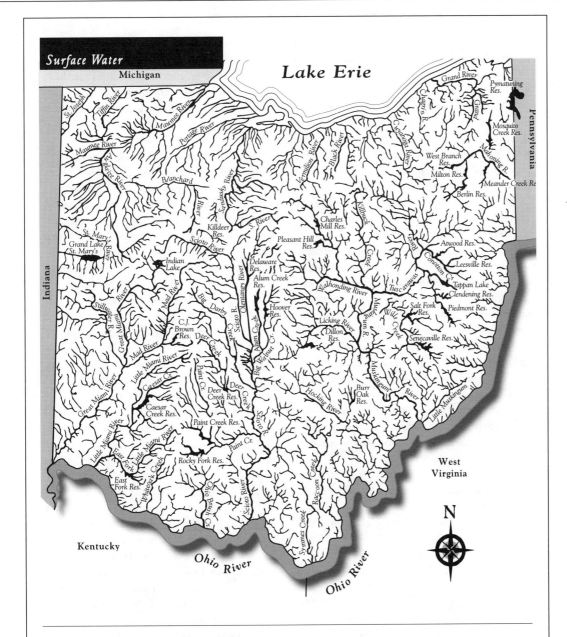

Surface Water

Michigan

Lake Erie

Indiana

Kentucky

Ohio River

Ohio River

West Virginia

Pennsylvania

N

From the Top

"The slightly rumpled surface....looking like a bedspread on which someone has taken a nap."

— John McPhee, writer, describing topography of Ohio

devilry lurked on the shores of Snooks Run? What rumors floated on Tattle Creek and Babble Brook?

By and large settling the Ohio wilderness was a peaceful affair. Sometimes, though, sudden inexplicable events sent shivers down the spine of the hardiest pioneers. Macabre stories of frontier hangings, rotting carcasses, murders and massacres lent a hand in titling Skull Creek, Scaffold Lick, Buzzardroost Creek, Bloody Run, Deadhorse Run, Death Creek, and Slaughterhouse Run.

Several streams recall bloody clashes between Native Americans and European Americans: Broken Sword Creek and Brokenknife Creek. Fallen Timbers, scene of the last major battle between Indians and whites in Ohio, is the namesake of two streams. The Auglaize River, which apparently means "fallen timbers" in some Indian dialect, also remembers that conflict.

Creekside homesteads did not always yield the promise of an endless supply of lifegiving water. Ponder the frustration of the farmer who named Lousy Run, or the despair and misery of the people naming Stingy Run, and creeks known as Blues, Dismal, Mosquito, and Roach.

The list of Ohio stream names also reveals the dichotomies of the human condition. There is an

Olive Branch and a Battle Creek; a Rich Run and a Poverty Run; a Chagrin River and a Bliss Run; Mad River and Joy Run; Perfect Creek and Mess Ditch; and The Inlet and The Outlet.

Many streams kept their Native American names, like the Cuyahoga River (meaning "crooked creek"), the Scioto River (Valley of the Deer), and the Maumee, Kokosing, Olentangy, and Hocking rivers. The state's most famous river, the Ohio River, comes from an Indian word Oeeeho, a reference (so we have been told) to the river's beauty and abundant fish life. Forty streams, runs, forks and creeks carry the title "Indian."

Nature also influenced early stream namers. Animals extirpated in the state—buffalo, elk, and bear (again resettling Ohio)—were memorialized with stream names. Other mammals commemorated in streams include skunk, snapping turtle, rattlesnake, raccoon, polecat, wolf, and wildcat. Birds and fish are remembered in creeks called sunfish, swan, crane, bald eagle, pike, sturgeon, turkey and salmon. To the trees some creeks belong, like beech, pine, spruce, red oak, willow, sycamore and walnut. There are two buckeye creeks, after the state tree. Streams named brush or brushy number 36. Not to be slighted, rocks and minerals received their due in streams called sand, stony, sulphur, salt, quarry, and limestone.

Tributaries entitled potato, vinegar, kitchen, pumpkin, spice, apple, potpie, turkey broth, and alum reveal our forebearers' concern for their stomachs. Frontier food fixing tools probably inspired the naming of Dinner Fork, Dirty Fork, Greasy Run, Lickskillet Run, Oven Lick, Spoon Creek and Butcherknife Creek. Waterways called Shot Pouch Run, Venisonham Creek, Hunter Creek, and Huntingcamp Creek recognize the frontier hunter, his weapon, and his prey.

Early use of streams for waterpower to grind corn and saw logs gave rise to 27 mill creeks or runs, plus several sawmill runs and miller creeks. The Industrial Revolution and the sudden growth of special industries and raw material production led to stream names like Potter Creek, Ax Factory Run, Pipe Creek, Lead and Steel runs, Iron Creek, Coal Run and Hydraulic Ditch.

Streams named with compass points, such as West Branch or North Fork, indicate the direction of tributaries from the main stem. And there are left and right forks, and brooks long and short. Names can represent the length of streams, like Fivemile Creek, though accuracy was not uppermost in the mind of some namers. For example, Fifteenmile Creek in the Little Muskingum River basin measures only 9.1 miles while Twomile Creek, a tributary of the Auglaize River, goes for 8.3 miles. From head to mouth Brown County's Big Run winds only three-fourths of a mile. Short Creek, on the other hand, empties into the Ohio River in Jefferson County after a 147-mile journey.

Sometimes just one name wasn't enough. Big Walnut Creek, which flows through Franklin County, once held the names Big Belly and Gahannah, the latter being an Indian name. Big Run, also in Franklin County, used to be called Adena Brook, and Buck Lick in Scioto County previously held the title of Steep Gut. Tenmile Creek in Lucas County becomes the Ottawa River after Sylvania; and Bean Creek becomes the Tiffin River somewhere in Fulton County.

The streams named after early settlers or families suggests a close relationship between pioneers and their land, and their need to recognize property rights. That practice created trouble among landowners who shared creeks with multiple names. Courts settled those disputes. Today, the U.S. Geological Survey is the final name-caller.

Stream names specify the people who have lived in Ohio—Shawnee, Huron, Ottawa, Delaware, Miami, Adena, Seneca, and Tuscarawas. Dutch Run, French Creek, Irish Run and German Creek refers to the European ancestry of creek dwellers. A close look at stream names reveals the distribution of white settlers from southern and northern states. In 1956, H.F. Kaup noticed that the use of "run" and "fork" was almost exclusively used in the southern two-thirds of Ohio. These terms, popular in southern states, point to the northernmost influence of southern culture and speech traditions. Usage of "branch" and "lick," even more southern in origin, shows up in the southernmost third of the state (with some notable exceptions, such as the west and east branches of the Cuyahoga River). The New England word "brook" is found in counties along Lake Erie, the area formerly comprising Connecticut's share of the Western Reserve

According to Kaup, the northern limits of "run" and "fork" roughly matches the divide that separates the Ohio River and Lake Erie watersheds. Southern culture prevailed in naming streams that eventually flowed into the Ohio River while northern culture predominated in the Lake Erie basin.

While headed either north or south Ohio's streams go along their rocky way, oblivious to labels.   *—SO*

Ohio's Water by the Numbers

PRECIPITATION

Statewide average precipitation (rain, snow, sleet, and hail): 38 inches a year, varying from as little as 26 inches to more than 50 inches from year to year.

Monthly average precipitation: 3.2 inches.

Driest month: February, 2.3 inches average.

Wettest month: June, 4.0 inches average.

Wet South: Southern Ohio, 44 inches per year average

Dry North: Areas closer to Lake Erie, 32 inches per year average.

Big Puddles: 43-45 inches of precipitation average per year. An area running southeast to northwest through central Clinton and Highland counties; area arching from southeastern Brown County across southern Adams County, southwestern Scioto County; and northern Geauga County

Dry Gulch: Ottawa, Lucas, northern Wood, and eastern portions of Fulton and Henry counties average less than 33 inches of precipitation annually, even though Fulton and Henry were once part of vast wetland known as the Great Black Swamp.

Rainfall: Most—Chardon, average 45.22 inches/year; Least—Put-in-Bay, average 30.96 inches/year; Heaviest short term—Sandusky, 9.54 inches in 8 hours, July 12, 1966.

Snowfall: Most—Chardon, average 106 inches per season; Greatest single—Steubenville, 36 inches in three days, November 1950.

STREAMS

Number: More than 3,300 named streams and probably as many smaller, unnamed tributaries.

Length: 44,000 miles, combined length of named streams: almost long enough to circle the Earth twice.

Surface Area: 41,000 acres or 64 square miles.

With the flow: Nearly three-fourths of the state's stream mileage flows toward the Ohio River, the rest to Lake Erie.

Length of Ohio River: 451 miles

LAKES

Erie: 2,250,000 surface acres; 262 miles of shoreline in state's jurisdiction.

Inland lakes and reservoirs: 200,000 acres, only 6,700 acres found in natural lakes.

SUPPLYING THE DEMAND

Wells: One million, withdrawing 720 million gallons of groundwater a day, just five percent of all used by state's human population. Forty percent of Ohioans get all their water from groundwater wells.

Public Source: Seventy-five percent of Ohio's 1,600 public water systems rely on groundwater for all or some of their supply.

Groundwater Pressure: Highest, more than 100 gallons a minute, in northwestern part of the state; lowest—less than five gallons a minute—in crescent of counties from Columbiana to Butler, and along the Lake Erie shore eastward from Erie County.

Irrigation: Only one percent of all withdrawn water is used to water farmland (in U.S., more than 50 percent). Croplands and golf courses use about 133 million gallons a day, which is less water than the city of Columbus uses in two days.

Power Plants: Use 8.2 billion gallons daily (1995), or 79 percent of all water used in Ohio—most of it in only 17 of the state's 88 counties.

Dam it: 60,000 water dams in Ohio.

Thirsty Ohioan: Average person uses 50 gallons of water a day.

Source: Ohio Environmental Protection Agency, Facts & Figures About Ohio's Environment, 1996.

MAJOR OHIO LAKES

Name	County	Surface Acreage	Public Boating Areas
Acton Lake	Butler	604	Yes
	Preble		
Alum Creek Lake	Delaware	3,387	Yes
Apple Valley Lake	Knox	485	No
Atwood Reservoir	Tuscarawas	1,540	Yes
	Carroll		
Bass Lake	Geauga	128	No
Beach City Lake	Tuscarawas	420	Yes
Berlin Reservoir	Mahoning	3,590	Yes
	Stark		
	Portage		
Bresler Reservoir	Allen	582	Yes
Buck Creek State Park	Clark	2,120	Yes
Buckeye Lake	Perry	3,136	Yes
	Licking		
Burr Oak Lake	Athens	664	Yes
	Morgan		
C.J. Brown Lake	Clark	2,120	Yes
Caesar Creek	Warren	2,830	Yes
	Clinton		
Charles Mill Reservoir	Ashland	1,350	Yes
	Richland		
Chippewa Lake	Medina	324	No
Clear Fork Reservoir	Morrow	1,010	Yes
	Richland		
Clendening Lake	Harrison	1,800	Yes
Cowan Lake	Clinton	688	Yes
Deer Creek Lake	Pickaway	1,277	Yes
Deer Creek Reservoir	Stark	313	Yes
Delaware Lake	Delaware	1,300	Yes
Dillon Reservoir	Muskingum	1,325	Yes
Dow Lake	Athens	161	Yes
East Branch Reservoir	Geauga	416	Yes
East Fork Lake	Clermont	2,160	Yes
Evans Lake	Mahoning	566	Yes
Ferguson Reservoir	Allen	305	Yes
Findlay Reservoir	Hancock	650	Yes
Grand Lake	Auglaize	12,700	Yes
	Mercer		
Grant Lake	Brown	181	Yes
Griggs Reservoir	Franklin	385	Yes
Guilford Lake	Columbiana	396	Yes
Hargus Lake	Pickaway	130	Yes
Hoover Reservoir	Delaware	3,000	Yes

NAME	COUNTY	SURFACE ACREAGE	PUBLIC BOATING AREAS
	Franklin		
Indian Lake	Logan	5,104	Yes
Jackson Lake	Jackson	243	Yes
Killdeer Reservoir	Wyandot	253	Yes
Kiser Lake	Champaign	380	Yes
Knox Lake	Knox	474	Yes
La Due Reservoir	Geauga	1,500	Yes
Lake Hope	Vinton	127	Yes
Lake Logan	Hocking	341	Yes
Lake Loramie	Shelby	785	Yes
Lake Milton	Mahoning	1,685	Yes
Lake Rockwell	Portage	539	No
Lake Vesuvius	Lawrence	105	Yes
Lake White	Pike	337	Yes
Leesville Lake	Carroll	1,000	Yes
Madison Lake	Madison	106	Yes
Meander Creek Reservoir	Trumbull	2,010	No
	Mahoning		
Michael J. Kirwan Reservoir	Portage	2,650	Yes
Mogadore Reservoir	Portage	900	Yes
Mosquito Creek Reservoir	Trumbull	7,850	Yes
Nimisila Reservoir	Summit	825	Yes
North Branch Kokosing Lake	Knox	154	Yes
O'Shaughnessy Reservoir	Delaware	920	Yes
Paint Creek Lake	Highland	1,190	Yes
	Ross		
Piedmont	Belmont	2,310	Yes
	Harrison		
Pine Lake	Mahoning	474	Yes
	Columbiana		
Portage Lakes	Summit	1,003	Yes
Punderson Lake	Geauga	101	Yes
Pymatuning Reservoir	Ashtabula	3,580	Yes
Rocky Fork Lake	Highland	2,080	Yes
Salt Fork Reservoir	Guernsey	2,952	Yes
Senecaville Lake	Guernsey	3,550	Yes
	Noble		
Stonelick Reservoir	Clermont	160	Yes
Tappan Lake	Harrison	2,350	Yes
Van Buren Lake	Hancock	53	Yes
Veto Lake	Washington	160	Yes
Willard City Reservoir	Huron	200	Yes
Wills Creek Reservoir	Muskingum	900	Yes
	Coshocton		

Source: Division of Water, Ohio Department of Natural Resources

After the Falls

Let's face it. Ohio's landscape is "vertically challenged." The waterfalls here won't ever top the misty heights of 2,565-foot Yosemite Falls, nor match the swagger and swallow of Niagara Falls. Not in a million years. But that doesn't mean we can't appreciate the good things that come in small packages.

Nobody has ever counted the hundreds of tiny cataracts in Ohio, nor calculated how much water spills over them. But, if you feel compelled to tally them, set some ground rules. Geologists define a waterfall as the flow of a stream over a vertical or steeply inclined wall of rock. However, they don't say how tall a waterfall must be, nor the angle of its decline. Do part-time waterfalls that dry up in summer count? And how do you measure falls that tumble down in levels or steps? Is each step a waterfall, or do you group them into one? Height is measured from where to where?

Ohio's Falling Water, in the Hocking Hills

Volunteer census takers, of course, can establish their own criteria.

Several of Ohio's loftiest waterfalls decorate gorges in the Hocking Hills. At 100 feet (thereabouts) Rock House Falls may be the highest spout in the state, though at times its flow drools and hardly seems worthy of being called a waterfall. Water trickles 90 feet off the lip of Ash Cave, and leaks 80 feet off ledges in Conkles Hollow and Cantwell Cliffs. Clearly, these falls are in their twilight years.

For year-round splashing and plumage try Brandywine Falls, one of a trio of scenic cascades in Cuyahoga Valley National Recreation Area. For roar (albeit modest) go to Clifton Gorge State Natural Area where the Little Miami River plunges through a narrow squeeze and over a 40-foot drop. During Christmas, Ludlow Falls gets 80,000 lights and a layer of ice, as if nature's fine touch was not enough.

Choosing a favorite waterfall, as selecting art, is a matter of taste. The typical Ohio waterfall is a ribbon of water falling from a cupped ledge, hanging over a gaping recess cave or amphitheater. Ash Cave in the Hocking Hills, and Charleston Falls in Miami County fit this mold. Some folks like the gentle flows that fan out like a bridal veil;

GUIDE TO KNOWN AND NAMED WATERFALLS

Name	Height (feet)	Nearest City	County
Ansel's Ledge Falls	30	Russell Center	Geauga
Ash Cave	90	South Bloomingville	Hocking
Berea Falls	30	Berea	Cuyahoga
Blue Hen Falls	20	Peninsula	Summit
Brandywine Falls	70	Peninsula	Summit
Buttermilk Falls	60	Peninsula	Summit
Buttermilk Falls	30	Georgetown	Brown
Buttermilk Falls	30	Madison	Lake
Cantwell Cliffs	80	Gibisonville	Hocking
Cascades, Birch Crk.	15-20	Yellow Springs	Greene
Cascade Falls	60	Painesville	Lake
Cascade Falls	60	Elyria	Lorain
Cedar Falls	50	South Bloomingville	Hocking
Cedar Falls	30	Cedar Mills	Adams
Chagrin Falls	25	Chagrin Falls	Cuyahoga
Charleston Falls	37	West Charleston	Miami
Conkle's Hollow Falls	80	South Bloomingville	Hocking
Crane Hollow Falls 1	55	Gibisonville	Hocking
Crane Hollow Falls 2	75	Gibisonville	Hocking
Crane Hollow Falls 3	60	Gibisonville	Hocking
East Monroe Falls	25	East Monroe	Highland
Falls Run	15	Layman	Washington
Forty-foot Falls	30	Hiram	Portage
Greenville Falls	25	Covington	Miami
Hayden Run Falls	35	Columbus	Franklin
Helena Falls	50	West Milton	Miami
Hemlock Falls	50	Butler	Richland
High Rocks Hollow		South Bloomingville	Hocking
Jenks Creek Falls	35		Geauga
Jerusalem Falls	30	Zanesfield	Logan
Lake Katharine Falls	15-25	Jackson	Jackson
Little Miami Falls	40	Yellow Springs	Greene
Little Miami Falls	15	Yellow Springs	Greene
Ludlow Falls	30	Ludlow Falls	Miami
Lulu Falls	25	Kingsville	Ashtabula
Lyons Falls, Upper	30-40	Loudonville	Ashland
Lyons Falls, Lower	30-40	Loudonville	Ashland
Minnehaha Falls	35	Hiram	Portage
Nelson Mills Falls	20	Nelson	Portage
Old Man's Cave, Upper Falls	40	South Bloomingville	Hocking
Old Man's Cave, Lower Falls	50	South Bloomingville	Hocking
Overlook Park Falls	30	West Milton	Miami
Paine Creek Falls	25	Painesville	Lake
Purgatory Hollow	45	Fredericktown	Columbiana
Rockbridge Falls	50	Rockbridge	Hocking
Rock House Falls	100	Gibisonville	Hocking
Rusty Run Falls	25	Yellow Springs	Greene
Sheepskin Hollow	15	Union Ridge	Columbiana
Sheick Hollow Falls	60	Gibisonville	Hocking
Stebbins Gulch Falls	50	Chardon	Lake
Stony Brook Falls	20	Kirtland	Lake
Sunderland Falls	40	Vandalia	Montgomery
Taylor's Falls	40	Bloomfield	Muskingum
Whispering Rock		South Bloomingville	Hocking

Editor's Note. Some waterfalls are on private property or restricted natural areas that require landowner permit for visitation. Also, rock surrounding waterfalls is slippery. Climbing can be perilous.

Rooting for the Falls

Nature Writer Steve Ostrander's Favorites:

1. *Brandywine*
2. *Ash Cave*
3. *Little Miami Gorge*
4. *Blue Hen*
5. *Lyons*
6. *Charleston*
7. *Cedar Falls*
8. *Helena*

Buttermilk Falls in the Cuyahoga Valley National Recreation Area and Paine Falls in Lake County are classic examples. Streams that bound down steps or cut zig zag trenches—Cedar Falls in Hocking Hills and Helena Falls in Miami County—have their adherents. Others prefer the classic horseshoe-shaped precipice with a frothy current, a type rare in Ohio. The setting is also important to connoisseurs. Does the waterfall accentuate the landscape or hide in it? Is it remote and wild or civilized and crowded in suburbia? And human-made falls don't count.

Native Americans regarded waterfalls as natural spigots for drinking water, bathing, and cleansing belongings. The mammoth caves behind some formations served as shelters, or as sites for large gatherings. Huge mounds of ash found on the floor of Ash Cave came from campfires tended by early Ohioans.

In their enthusiasm to record all of the natural wonders and assets in Ohio, Euro-American settlers and speculators noted the location of falls with commercial importance. To these entrepreneurs a waterfall was a beast of burden, as well as a pretty sight. Human-made waterfalls made for industry and flood control now hide once-celebrated natural waterfalls on all of Ohio's major rivers and streams. The rollicking falls at Cuyahoga Falls, once a tourist attraction, now sleeps behind a utility company dam. Other waterfalls died from natural causes—droughts, diversions, and changes in vegetation.

Cascades erode in an upstream direction. Backwash and spray from splashing current eat away at the fragile rock behind the waterfalls and forms a recess cave. This undercutting action, called sapping, weakens support beneath the precipice and causes chunks of the hard caprock to break off. This process repeats itself over and over as the falls retreats upstream.

Glaciers had a hand in making waterfalls, primarily by supplying enormous quantities water that eroded the rock. Hayden Run Falls in Franklin County is a "hanging valley" waterfall. This 35-foot tumble is a few hundred feet from the stream's confluence with the Scioto River. During the Ice Age the Scioto swelled with glacial meltwater and excavated the valley faster than the tributary. When the Scioto receded, Hayden Run was left flowing above the river. Since then sapping has moved the cataract up the steep walled gorge.

Some of Ohio's wet landmarks achieved their fame from the hermits who called them home. Tom Lyon, a Delaware, hid out between two falls that bear his name in Mohican State Park. Old Man's Cave in Hocking Hills State Park remembers Richard Rowe, its reclusive inhabitant after the Civil War. As refuge, Ohio's lack of verticality mattered little. ⌒

—SO

Nature, *Notable*

Julius F. Stone & John Wesley Powell

Only close friends knew that Julius F. Stone made history in 1869 by paddling the length of the Colorado River with his buddy and fellow Ohioan, John Wesley Powell. In 1925, Stone, chairman of Seagrave Corp,. gave his Gibraltar Island mansion, the former summer home of tycoon Jay Cooke, to Ohio State University. Today, Stone Lab, at Put-In-Bay, is a leading marine research institute. As chief of the Smithsonian's bureau of ethnology Powell was responsible for excavations of Hopewell and Adena culture sites in Ohio. Both men are members of the ODNR Natural Resources Hall of Fame.

GROTTOES
AT
ROCKY
FORK

Tree-phobes may pine, but Ohio's dark, dewy forests cause homesickness.

Ohio is topographically challenged, I confessed to a guide taking me on horseback through the foothills of the LaSal mountains in Utah. Long views are nonexistent, except from skyscrapers; and only on clear, dry days; and then all you see are rooftops mostly, except in Cleveland and Toledo where Lake Erie traces a soft line across an empty northern horizon.

That's partly why I'm in Utah, I told him, so I can stand on a mountain and look at another mountain; be enwrapped by a 180-degree night sky with touchable stars so bright they give me insomnia. I swear I hear them sizzle.

Yes indeed, Ohio lacks pointy peaks, lava piles, and all the spoils of recent volcanoes, avalanches, sun-stabbing heat, and kick-in-the-pants, call-the-cops geological rumbles. It also lacks bleached wilderness like Canyonlands National Park where the Green River collides with the Colorado River and fashions a naked, crinkled canyon as fierce and enchanting as the Grand Canyon. I reckon Canyonlands is one of the loneliest places on the planet for plants and animals.

"I drove across Southern Ohio once. Went to see a buddy at that college in Athens," the guide, Jeffrey, said, breaking the silence.

"What did you think of it—Southern Ohio that is?"

"It was pretty country awright, but I didn't see much," Jeffrey spoke politely. I chewed on his reply.

"What do you mean?" I finally asked.

"All those trees. I couldn't see passed those darn trees," he explained. "They made me edgy, and confined."

Jeffrey's "tree" phobia is forgiveable. He hails from a land of big skies, big canvases, big ditches, big ideas, big distances, big dramas, and big jokes. More space, than place. He knows only gnarly, prickly runt trees with 300 rings compressed into a trunk the size of my bicep; trees so scattered that each one constitutes a grove; trees skimpy with shade; beseeching trees gripping bare rock; trees that you can see over, see through, and see beyond. If it is true, what the Shoshones say, that people live like their trees, then it is no wonder that the fellow on the brochure for this place looks as bristly as the pines, shrubs and cacti that populate this pale plateau. Where open space and aridity made Westerners restless and searching, humidity and a closed canopy bound Ohioans to community and practicality. Westerners had horizons handed to them. Ohioans had to make theirs.

Suddenly, I got heartsick for the dark, dewy, deciduous forest of Ohio. Unbroken broad-leaved shade, and soft sod cushioned by a century of leaves. Comfortable trees. Rubenesque, oversexed, woodpeckered trees. Bathe me in all that suffocating, muscular, near-sighted, bewildering green. That claustrophobic, humid, duckweed green. Birth green; rot green. Green arising from the abundance of water. Give me that overcrowded green from ground to canopy, and the green driven by stamen and pistil. Oaks, maples, buckeyes and beeches, hickories and hemlocks, locusts and lindens, hornbeams and hawthorns, cottonwoods and cedars, elms and ashes, tulips, tamaracks, and tupelos, sassafras, sumacs, sycamores galore. Willows and walnuts and birches, oh my! Butternuts and bladdernuts, box elders and alders, sweetgums, smoketrees, and sourwoods, magnolias and mulberries, black cherries, hackberries and chokecherries, apples, aspens and arbor vitae, catalpas, paw paws, dogwoods, redbuds, planted pines and spruces. Gymnosperms, angiosperms and eager sperms. Viburnums, violets and vines. Electric green.

Ohio is green behind the ears, and green between the toes. We grow up amidst chlorophyll, and are envied for our green. Green grasses great and small. Green moss, green frogs, green salamanders, green grapes, green snakes, green herons, green beetles, green fish, green veggies, green algae, enough green seeds to fill a green sea. Green life grinning ear to ear!

Storytellers of yesteryears told of land hungry Easterners who swooned when they heard about the sylvan fecundity in Ohio Territory. To emigrating Euro-Americans the seamless thatch was simultaneously daunting and "luminous, youthful, supple...newborn out of the Ice Age," according to Ohio-born nature writer Rutherford Platt. Land boosters told them the hardwood forest was thick enough for squirrels to travel across the state without touching the ground. Pure buncombe, of course, since squirrels rarely stray beyond their birthplace. In spite of the innocent fiction, the enduring metaphor aptly characterized Ohio's thick and sprawling shag.

The Rolodex spinning in my mind stopped at Sayward Luckett, the pioneer heroine in Conrad Richter's novel *The Trees*, who encountered endless, voluptuous green from a fictional Ohio "bald" two centuries ago. "For a moment Sayward reckoned that her father had fetched them unbeknownst to the Western ocean, and what lay beneath was the late sun glittering on green-black water. Then she saw what they looked down on was a dark illimitable expanse of wilderness. It was a sea of solid treetops broken only by some gash where deep beneath the foliage an unknown stream made its way. As far as the eye could reach, this lonely forest sea rolled on and on till its faint blue billows broke against an incredibly distant horizon..."

If the Shoshones are right, it explains why early Ohioans sank deep roots, stayed focused, spaced settlements a day's horse ride apart, and felt safe behind enclosures. Because of the trees, there was no beckoning sunset to ride off into, no horizon to leap at, and no alluring peak to wonder about. No panoramas of purple mountains majesty, just millions of majestic trees.

By the dawn of the 20th century, though, Ohio's grand forest had dwindled to stumps and toothpicks, and Sayward's seamless and rounded horizon had become jagged, pitted, and sharp, like the blade of a bucksaw. Since then, Ohio's forest, under managed care, has reclaimed 30 percent of the state. But given a chance to go on a feeding frenzy, these temperate trees would cloak our cities in green in a score or two, the way a tropical jungle buried the best the Mayans built. The forest is simply biding its time.

Like Utah, Ohio once was a Promised Land, sought-after for its natural wealth rather than its isolation. It's the land that defined the Hopewell, Adena and all those who followed them. It's the holy land that will accept my manure when the time comes.

My horse shuttered, whinnied, shook his dusty mane, gyrations I took as cues to clam up and saddle up. The rest of the ride I silently pined for Buckeye green. ✑ —*SO*

Flora

Native Vegetation

The original landscape of Ohio was in large measure the result of various combinations of natural vegetation that developed in the different parts of the state. This original vegetation, however, has been almost completely altered by removal and disruption of natural balance. In 1800, primeval forests covered more than 25 million acres in Ohio; by 1940 the area of forest had been reduced to 3.7 million acres. The process of removal of forest vegetation has also produced modification in those areas remaining in natural vegetation.

The Great Black Swamp

Perhaps the most striking example of vegetation change has been in northwestern Ohio, where today there is little remaining evidence of the tangle of swamp forest, the Great Black Swamp, which originally stretched from Paulding and Van Wert counties to the marshy Lake Erie shore in Lucas and Ottawa counties. This great barrier to early east-west movement was slowly drained, cleared, settled, and turned to cultivation between 1860 and 1885. The extent of the Black Swamp approximates quite closely that of glacial Lake Maumee and occupies an area almost the size of Connecticut. Within this virtually level and naturally poorly drained area grew a dense forest dominated by elm and ash, but containing also oak, birch, cottonwood, and poplar. Elsewhere in the state, especially within the areas of glaciation, other patches of swamp forest developed, but were nowhere of large extent.

Nonforest Vegetation

Another type of vegetation which is widely distributed between those portions of the state subjected to glaciation is the sphagnum peat bog. The largest bogs are found in Crawford, Portage, and Fairfield counties.

Sphagnum peat bogs occupy the bottoms of kettle depressions and lakes formed by blockage of glacial meltwaters. Such areas, which have remained largely undrained since glacial time, provided a suitable environment for postglacial boreal forests. A thick accumulation of acidic organic matter, decomposing very slowly, produces a distinctive dark-colored soil. In addition to sphagnum moss, the vegetation includes tamarack, poison sumac, leatherleaf, sedges, and grasses.

Two other types of vegetation—freshwater marshes and fens and prairie grasslands—are associated in Ohio with high water tables and poor drainage. From a botanical point of view, the essential difference between the prairies of Ohio and the fens and marshes is the proportion of grasses to total vegetation cover; the grasses are less common in the case of marshes and fens and more common on the prairies. Marsh vegetation of bullrushes, cattails, giant reed grass, reeds, wild rice, and other aquatic plants is generously mixed with sedges and some woody shrubs. Fens are more restricted, have weakly alkaline waters in contrast to the neutral water of marshes, and have a vegetation of woody plants such as birch and willow. Marshes and fens are widely distributed throughout northern and western Ohio, although most areas of occurrence are small. The major exception is the marsh which stretches from Sandusky Bay to Maumee Bay.

Within Ohio natural prairies have come close to extinction. Although pioneer settlers considered the absence of trees in prairies to be a clear indication of soil infertility, most prairies were plowed and converted to fertile farmland. Almost from the beginning of settlement, prairies were overgrazed, with the result that the less palatable sedges began slowly to crowd out the prairie grasses. Sedge meadows are common today in northern and western Ohio.

Forest Vegetation

When the pioneers entered Ohio they found a nearly unbroken forest made up of many tree types. Variations in bedrock, topography, soil, and water supply created an intricate mosaic of forest types, each dominated by its own mix of species. Ohio originally supported at least six major forest types. Most extensive were the beech forests, often with a large number of sugar maple mixed in. This type occupied a broad swath of the state between its southwestern and northeastern corners, and most of the northwestern quadrant. Next most extensive was the mixed oak forest which covered much of hilly southeastern Ohio with outliers in both the Darby and Sandusky plains and in the Oak Openings region near

Symbol Status

≈ **State tree:** Buckeye *(Aesculus glabra), adopted 1953. According to pioneer historian S.P. Hildreth, the native audience to the first court of record in the Northwest Territory, convened in Marietta, greeted legal worthy Col. Ebenezer Sproat by shouting "Hetuck!" The Indian word for "eye of the buck" was supposedly in honor of Sproat's upright and manly appearance.*

≈ **State flower:** *Red carnation, William McKinley's lapel favorite, adopted 1904 as a "token of love and reverence" for the president's memory.*

≈ **State wildflower:** *White trillium (Trillium grandiflorum), adopted 1938*

≈ **State herb capital:** *Gahanna, designated 1972*

Two hardwood canopies in Mentor.

Toledo. Poorly drained areas were covered with an elm-ash swamp forest, while the rich, alkaline soils derived from limestone supported an oak-sugar maple forest. Certain favored parts of the state were dominated by mixed mesophytic forest. Nearly as rich in species were the bottomland forests that covered the floodplains of our larger rivers. Most of this magnificent variety is gone now, replaced by cornfields and housing developments. But here and there a tiny patch of old-growth forest remains—battered, usually, and hemmed in by "progress," but miraculously alive.

The original forests of Ohio were removed for crops to help feed a growing nation and to make room for the cities that contain a large part of the industrial might of the United States. But during recent years, the forest area of Ohio has been increasing. Some of this increase is accounted for by greater accuracy of recent surveys and the inclusion of some open woodlands not formerly classed as forest. Tree planting and natural re-seeding on abandoned agricultural lands probably account for the greater part of the increase.

Today, some 7 million acres of the 26 million acres of the state is woodland, encompassing about 26 percent of Ohio's land area. In the agricultural areas of the west and northwest, the

forests are in neat scattered patches of farm woods. Larger unbroken forests are characteristic of the hill country in the southeast where 65 percent of the forest area of Ohio is located. Every one of Ohio's 88 counties has some forest land—ranging from as much as 73 percent in Lawrence County to as little as about 3 percent in Fayette, Madison, and Wood counties. Eighteen of the counties are more than 50 percent forested and 32 more than 25 percent forested. All but 76,000 acres of forest land is commercial forest. Commercial forest is land that is capable of growing commercial crops of timber. The non-commercial forest land is in government parks and other areas that have been withdrawn from commercial use. Of forest acreage in Ohio, more than 90 percent is privately owned. Of this total only about 2 percent is held by the forest industry and the remainder is owned by private citizens or organizations like the Boy Scouts, Camp Fire Girls, and various churches. The remainder of the forest land, about 6 percent, is owned by federal, state, county, and municipal governments.

Ohio's forests are composed chiefly of hardwood species—trees with broad leaves that drop in the fall. Most numerous are the oaks. Also present in large numbers are hickory, ash, tulip tree, maple, beech, black walnut, sycamore, and cottonwood. Softwoods—needle-bearing trees——are not as common as the hardwoods. Pitch pine, short-leaf pine, and eastern red cedar are the chief softwood species in Ohio. Hemlock and eastern white pine occur naturally in some areas. About 150 species of trees are native to Ohio, and some others have been introduced as ornamentals or for reforestation. Not all of these species are commercially valuable. Most of the commercial forest products come from only about 35 species.

Trees usually grow naturally in mixture with each other in more or less definite patterns. These tree associations are termed forest types. There are eight forest types occurring in Ohio: oak-hickory, elm-ash-cottonwood, maple-beech, oak-pine, pitch pine-shortleaf pine, oak-gum, white pine and aspen. The names of the forest types indicate which species are predominant, but there are probably a few other species growing in the mixture. The oak-hickory type is the most common in Ohio's forests, occupying more than 47 percent of the commercial forest land. Next is the

maple-beech-birch type, which is found on almost a fourth of the commercial forest land. Next is the elm-ash-cottonwood type. None of the other types occupies more than 2 percent of the forest area.

In the commercial forests of Ohio, there were 20.2 billion board feet of sawtimber in 1978. In the forest growing stock—all trees of commercial species five inches and larger in diameter, measured 4.5 feet above the ground—there are 6.4 billion cubic feet of wood. It is from this growing stock that all forest products are harvested: pulpwood, sawlogs, posts, fuelwood, etc. The volume of Ohio's forest growing stock is the equivalent of 48 million cords of wood, enough to fill a freight train 16,500 miles long. Although the forest soils of Ohio are rich, and growing conditions for trees are good, the forest lands of the state are not growing as much timber as they are capable of growing. Forest fires, uncontrolled grazing, and lack of good management are a few of the reasons why Ohio forests have not yet reached full production.

Not only do Ohio's forests produce timber, but they also provide homes and food for wild

Green *Acres*

Ohio's Most Significant Stand of Trees

One of the prime stands of primeval forest in North America and certainly the most significant stand of trees in Ohio is Dysart Woods, located west of Centerville in Belmont County. Designated a National Natural Landmark in 1967, the 51-acre tract is a botanical dinosaur: Not only a living remnant of the endless, undisturbed forest that greeted humans, but also a reminder of what Ohio was like before the axes started swinging.

In 1998, mining shovels were scheduled to start boring in the area, much to the distress of the friends of Dysart.

Dysart Woods is considered an oak forest, but tulip poplars, white ash, black gum, beech, sugar maple, and hickory trees abound in various stages of growth from saplings to timbers a hundred feet tall, all of which are kept fiercely pristine and protected by Ohio University from any incursions by the hand of man. ⤶

49

Transeau Maps Ohio Primeval

If Ohio was once mostly trees, what sort of trees were they? The question was bothering scientists as early as 1904, when biologists at Ohio State University lobbied the legislature for a natural history survey, touting its usefulness in predicting soil fertility. It was clear that besides clearing millions of acres the farmers had also altered the mix of what remained, culling out "undesirable" species such as beech, favoring "valuable" trees such as sugar maple, introducing to Ohio complete strangers such as the Scotch pine. Even as abandoned fields were reverting to trees at the turn of the century, scientists were wondering about the exact composition and extent of the vanished primeval forest.

The question was still unanswered in 1915, when Edgar Transeau joined the faculty of Ohio State. A botanist from Illinois who counted himself a follower of the new discipline of "ecology," Transeau's chief interest was in prairies. He believed that the small Ohio prairies were the most easterly extensions of the great grassland that filled the bowl of North America when the settlers first came into the land.

Transeau wanted to map the Ohio prairies. Unfortunately, by 1915, the original prairies, along with the original Ohio forests, were largely destroyed. To map a forest or a prairie that no longer existed required some ingenuity. And OSU colleague, Paul Sears, hit on the idea of examining the earliest surveyors' records for clues.

The pioneers didn't keep botanical records, but they did employ surveyors to mark land boundaries. The surveyors created their own landmarks by blazing "witness trees," which were fully recorded in tract books. By plotting the witness trees, Sears produced the first map of "virgin" Ohio forest in 1925. The witness-tree method had flaws. No one knew what the surveyors were thinking when they blazed a particular tree. Was the witness tree typical of the area, or was it a "junk" tree a prospective owner wouldn't miss, or was it a unique specimen that stood out?

To refine the witness-tree map, Transeau began automobile surveys of the existing vegetation. His underlying assumption was that the native forest reflected deep-seated influences of climate, topography, and soil that humans could not alter. In Cincinnati, E. Lucy Braun, another pioneering ecologist, was using the same concept to map out the forests of eastern North America. Transeau was working on a much smaller scale and feeling frustrated by that. Equipping an observer with binoculars, Transeau cruised the backroads at forty miles per hour, identifying trees on the fly. This crude survey resulted in an updated map in 1927, but Transeau knew it wasn't thorough enough. Over the next thirty years, he set his graduate students to making county-by-county studies, comparing early surveyors' maps to their own intensive field observations. The county studies mounted up, but Transeau was unable to pull the pieces of the primeval puzzle together before his death in 1960.

It fell to former student, Robert B. Gordon, who returned to finish the Great Map after a long teaching career in Pennsylvania. Officially entitled "The Original Vegetation of Ohio at the Time of the Earliest Land Surveys," Gordon's map became a scientific and even popular sensation, the basis for similar maps today.

—*John Fleischman*

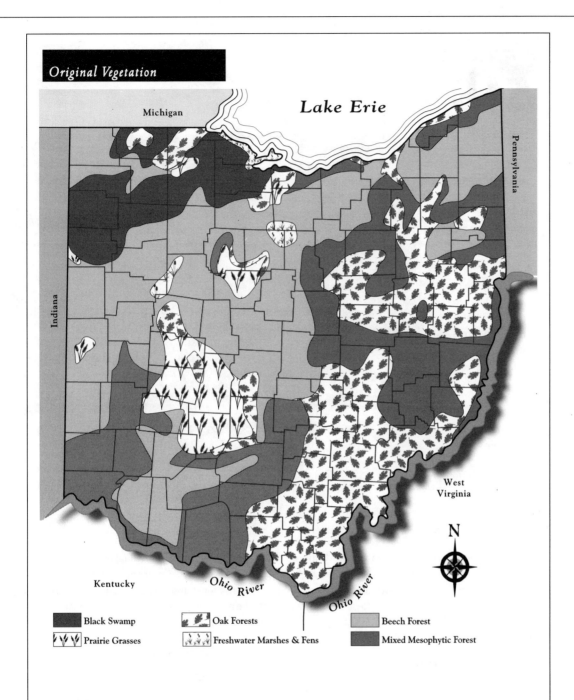

Original Vegetation

Michigan

Lake Erie

Pennsylvania

Indiana

West
Virginia

N

Kentucky *Ohio River* *Ohio River*

■ Black Swamp	🌿 Oak Forests	▨ Beech Forest
〰 Prairie Grasses	🌾 Freshwater Marshes & Fens	▦ Mixed Mesophytic Forest

animals and birds. They protect and help stabilize the precious water supply. Increasing numbers of people are taking to the forests in their leisure time for recreation and inspiration. Ohio's forest land-owners are learning that it is possible to enjoy all these benefits while at the same time growing crops of trees for the market. In Ohio, manage-ment of the forests for multiple uses is becoming the accepted principle. 🍃

*Excerpted with the permission of the Ohio Department of Natural Resources from "Ohio's Forests;" "Ohio's Original Woodlands," by Tim A. Snyder; and **Ohio—An American Heartland**, by Allen G. Noble and Albert J. Korsok*

On the Grow Again

Covering More Ground

Trees grow on 7.86 million acres, or thirty percent, of Ohio. A half century ago only 12 percent of Ohio was forested.

Woody Acres

Ohio boasts more than 65 billion trees and shrubs, or roughly 8,000 "woody stems" per forested acre.

Come fall berated, come summer appreciated: shade tree.

Hefty Harvest

Ohio woodlands grow nearly one billion board feet (189,200 miles) of wood annually. (A board foot is one foot long, a foot wide, and an inch thick.) Tree growth surpasses removal by a ratio of 2.4 to 1 for all trees (except white oak and beech) in all size categories.

Bumper Crop

Ohio's 2,200 tree farmers cultivate 421,000 acres of woodlands.

A Palletable Fate

Ohio harvests 300–400 million board feet of wood each year. According to the Buckeye Forest Council, 84 percent of Ohio's sawlogs (11 inches or more in diameter) is used for pallets. Roughly half of these pallets—trees from 18,000 acres—are used once and discarded.

Staking A Claim

Ninety-three percent of the state's forest land, or 7.19 million acres, is held by 329,000 private owners. Of this amount, individual owners control 56 percent, farmers 23 percent, corporations 11 percent, and forest industry companies three percent. The rest is public land, most of it managed by the Ohio Department of Natural Resources, Division of Forestry, 178,352 acres; and Wayne National Forest, 211,707 acres.

Tree Counties

Sixty-three percent of Ohio's forest grows on one-third of the land—the unglaciated hill country, a 28-county region anchored by Brown and Carroll counties.

If trees make the county, then Lawrence, Vinton and Scioto counties, each more than seventy percent forested, are Ohio's fashion plates. Paulding, Fayette, Pickaway, Defiance, Madison and Ottawa counties are less than one percent forested. Eighteen counties are more than 50 percent tree-covered, 32 counties more than 25 percent.

Decidedly Leafy

Deciduous (leaf-shedding) trees comprise 97 percent of Ohio's forests. Evergreens (conifers) make up the remainder. Three hundred species of trees and shrubs live in Ohio. Among these, there are a hundred hardwood tree species, and more than 25 softwood (conifer) species. Commercial forest products come from 35 species.

White and red oaks and hickory comprised 41.8 percent of the total wood volume in 1979, but only 33.3 percent in 1991. Meanwhile, percentages for sugar and red maples, white ash, yellow poplar and all others increased. This shift away from nut bearing trees adversely affects woodland wildlife dependent on mast trees for food.

A Forest by Any Other Name

Scientists have identified 43 different forest types in Ohio (oak-hickory, beech-maple, etc.) The oak-hickory forest rises on 47 percent of the commercial forest (timber) land; the beech-maple type on about 25 percent.

Little Sprouts

Division of Forestry nurseries at Marietta and Zanesville produce 7.5 million tree seedlings annually for reforestation. Between surveys conducted in 1979 and 1991, state nurseries sold more than 95 million seedlings.

Money Comes from Trees

Ohio's forest products industry is a $7 billion enterprise. The industry's 70,000 employees collect a $1 billion annual payroll.

Cash Crop

Landowners get 25 percent (maple) to 40 percent (cherry) of the final cost of lumber. The state's 200 sawmills employ 2,000 people.

Log Off

Opponents of logging in state forests claim that the Division of Forestry loses money in nearly every sale because the trees are sold at wholesale prices, roughly 25 cents to the dollar. Logging on public land is unnecessary because 93 percent of Ohio's woodlands are privately owned, they argue. Local governments receive half of the proceeds from timber sales in state forests.

Tree Top Dollar

In 1976 a single walnut tree in Williams County was sold for $35,000. Foresters estimated the veneer cut from the tree would cover more than two acres.

A Tree Grows in the City

In 1997, for the 16th straight year, Ohio led the nation in cities certified in the Tree City USA directory, a National Arbor Day Foundation program that honors effective management of city trees. That year Ohio's 212 Tree City USA communities planted 47,786 shade and ornamental trees, pruned 103,217 trees, cut down 21,249 trees. Volunteers contributed 49, 305 hours of work.

Supplanted by Nonnatives

For every urban tree removed, 2.5 trees are planted. However, most trees planted in cities and suburbs are not species from Ohio's original forest. ☜

Sources: U.S. Department of Agriculture, Forest Service; Ohio Department of Natural Resources, Division of Forestry; Buckeye Forest Council; Statewide Comprehensive Outdoor Recreation Plan, Ohio Department of Natural Resources (1993).

Life in the center lane: a giant faces a slow death by car.

"Yesterday, June 18, 1817, I measured a walnut almost seven feet in diameter, clean and straight as an arrow....I measured a white oak by the roadside which at four feet from the ground was six feet in diameter, and at seventy-five feet it measured nine feet around."

—Norris Birbank, in his diary

Giants Among Us

In a secluded pasture in Ashland County, a giant American sycamore presides over a creek that has nourished it for centuries. Every few years I sneak cross-lot to the shrine, and climb into its mossy lap, a pleasure I cannot partake with Abe at the Lincoln Memorial. Just above the ground four thick and gnarly limbs branch from a neck more than 48.5 feet around. I am a mere bug at the base of these boughs.

The elephantine appendages manage to reach skyward 129 feet, and fan out 35 yards. Imagine an up-side-down molar enlarged a million times. Another observer called them smokestacks.

By everybody's reckoning this megaton *Platanus occidentalis* is the largest flowering plant in North America, the largest living thing in Ohio, the champion of its species for now, and the second largest broadleaf tree in the country. Its life began in antiquity, before Shakespeare scribbled poetry and Columbus took to wandering. In the 1940s, its waist was a slender 35-feet, according to Clarence Briggs, the farmer who leased this land. It bulked up another 13.5-feet during the next three decades, then stopped growing apparently. Consider it a monument to one tree's luck and longevity, and nature's implacable fecundity.

The American sycamore goes unnoticed amidst the hoopla over Ohio's fabled (but daintier) oaks and buckeyes. Which is too bad, because the sycamore, a.k.a. plane tree, fills books with wide-eyed stories. The sycamores of yesteryear, presumably larger than the current king, were useful for their huge hollows. Before phone booths, youngsters packed themselves into sycamore trunks—ten, twelve, twenty towheads at a time. The record, if you believe it, is held by 40 settlers who squeezed into a two-story apartment tighter than bats in a belfry. Shawanese, Miamis, Mingoes camped and hid in their boles. Pioneers lived in them until cabins were built, then corraled livestock there. Frontier blacksmiths forged horsehoes and tools in

them. Here thieves stashed loot, be it cattle, nags, or gold. Dr. Manasseh Cutler, one of Marietta's founders, recalled six horsemen riding abreast through the hollow of a sycamore that bulged to 46-feet. Fallen behemoths have spilled lost love letters, stills, guns, toys, cached food, and other goodies from their bowels. In the natural world, sycamores are tenements for raccoons, herons, snakes, owls, squirrels, kingfishers, and others. Fishermen and hunters still retreat to sycamore caves when it rains.

Ohio lies smack dab in the middle of sycamore country. Look at how many arch over its rivers and streams. Thousands of them, perhaps millions, picnic along the parade routes. Beefy, puffy, arthritic, bumpy, shallow rooted things, as ancient-looking as Greek columns. Limbs and roots uncombed, pale, serpentine. Green-gray bark flakes as it expands, revealing an elastic, ashen skin that conjures images of marbled purity, or ghostly morbidity depending on your outlook on life. The lower branches appear reptilian, the topmost ones bone white. Mammoth leaves, big enough to hide a face, are mistaken for maple. Sapling sycamores, in contrast to elders, grow sleek and straight. No sagging abs for a century or two.

Humans chopped sycamore wood for butcher blocks, firewood, barrel staves, furniture and yokes. From leaf fall into pre-green spring, the sycamore's white splash broke the monotony of a gray landscape. To tiring migratory flocks a row of distant, pale-skinned sycamores means comfort, water, food, and shelter.

Like every heir awaiting its turn, Jeromesville's venerable sycamore became national champion in 1982 after a wheezing Kentucky monarch finally fell from its throne. Rot and rebellion almost threatened to toppled Ohio's king; one of its stacks crashed like a sword in 1997, thus thinning its armor. A new calibrating system being considered by the keepers of the National Register of Big Trees, a program of the American Forestry Association, may disqualify trees that branch near the ground. Crown or not, I'm still going to scamper into *P. occidentalis*' lap, as long as both of us are capable.

Ohio has other national and state champion trees. They are listed here, with their measurements. Go admire them, but don't forget the forest from whence they once came. Like human royals these have been pampered in cities, towns and farms. They have been given room to lounge and sprawl, not needing to economize. Their "owners" have been thoughtful, nurturing stewards who appreciate vintage flora. Among themselves, naturalists and foresters call these giants "wolf" trees, an unfortunate insult that assigns predation to plants that passively shade out rivals. In rarified circles, big trees are not necessarily healthy trees, commercially valuable, genetically desirable, nor beneficial to the forest. In a survival-of-the-fittest woods trees rarely reach championship proportion. Wilderness, by definition, means trees encountering competition, predation, and hardships such as disease, drought and habitat degradation. Winners in a real forest get to the canopy with straight trunks, compact crowns, and deep roots.

Detractors of tree stardom, there are a few, refer to the champs as freaks of nature, another injustice, and big trees programs as sentiment-building hype to hide the scars of industrial strength logging, species extinction, blah, blah, blah. Better to protect a forest, than mourn the loss of a regent disconnected from a forest. Point taken. But everyone loves a champion, where ever it might grow.

—SO

Making
the Cut

So Do You Think You Have a Winner?

The scoring system for national and state champion trees was based on measurements of the tree's circumference, height, and average crown spread. Circumference is taken 4-1/2 feet above the ground (breast height). If you think your tree is a contender, measure from the up-hill side if the tree grows on a slope. Take the measurement below this line if the tree forks or bulges at 4-1/2 feet. In that case, measure where the tree's size is normal. Each inch of circumference represents one point.

Height goes from ground level (uphill side if terrain slopes) to highest point of tree. Scout handbooks explain how to estimate an unknown height using a known height, such as a six-foot human. Each foot equals a point.

Average crown spread requires two measurements. Figure out the widest crown spread and the narrowest. Add these together and divide in half to get the average in feet. Each foot equals 1/4 point (or the average crown spread divided by four).

Nominations should include a photo of the tree, description of its health and shape (evidence of disease, broken limbs, etc.), exact location of the tree, property owner's name, address, phone, and nominator's address and phone number. Measurements will be verified by a professional forester.

Send nominations to the following locations, which can also provide exact locations of champions. American Forests, keeper of the National Register of Big Trees, recognizes champions for more than 700 trees in the U.S. The Ohio Forestry Association crowns 118 native and naturalized state champions, and 56 champions for non-native species. Booklet costs $6.

NATIONAL REGISTER OF BIG TREES
American Forests
P.O. Box 2000
Washington, D.C. 20013

OHIO'S BIG TREES
ODNR-Division of Forestry
3060 CR 939
Perrysville, OH 44864

Ohio Forestry Association
4080 S. High Street
Columbus, OH 43207
(614) 497-9580

CHAMPION TREES

Tree	Circ.	Height	Crown	Total	County	Nearest City
National Champs						
Slippery Elm, *Ulmus rubra* *	250	100	100	375	Huron	Monroeville
Slippery Elm, *Ulmus rubra* *	240	100	119	370	Fairfield	Sugar Grove
English Oak, *Quercus robur* *	187	88	91	298	Hamilton	North Bend
Shingle Oak, *Quercus imbricaria*	208	105	62	329	Hamilton	Cincinnati
Two-wing Silverbell, *Halesia diptera*	114	42	40	166	Hamilton	Cincinnati
Smoketree, *Cotinus obovatus* *	104	32	43	147	Hamilton	Cincinnati
Sycamore, *Platanus occidentalis*	582	129	105	737	Ashland	Jeromesville
Yellowwood, *Cladrastis kentukea*	276	72	73	366	Hamilton	Cincinnati

* National co-champion

Source: National Register of Big Tree, American Forests

Tree	Circ.	Height	Crown	Total	County	Nearest City
State Champs						
Arbor vitae, *Thuja occidentalis*	108	55	34	172	Greene	Yellow Springs
Ash, *Fraxinus*						
Black, *F. nigra*	58	96	31	212	Franklin	Columbus
Blue, *F. quadrangulata*	157	91	48	260	Hamilton	Cincinnati
Green, *F pennsylvanica*	220	96	110	344+	Warren	Waynesville
Green, *F pennsylvanica*	214	95	125	340+	Hamilton	Cincinnati
White, *F. americana*	252	115	90	390	Erie	Wakeman
Beech (Amer.), *Fagus grandifolia*	242	110	60	367	Ashtabula	Ashtabula
Birch, *Betula*						
River, *B. nigra*	159	87	72	259	Hamilton	Cincinnati
Yellow, *B. alleghaniensis*	111	87	63	214	Summit	
Black gum, *Nyssa sylvatica*	181	82	46	275	Meigs	Olive Twp.
Buckeye (Ohio), *Aesculus glabra*	162	82	67	261	Hamilton	North Bend
Buckeye (Yellow), *A. octandra*	135	100	62	251	Scioto	Portsmouth
Catalpa, *Catalpa speciosa*	226	80	66	303	Lorain	Oberlin
(Black) Cherry, *Prunus serotina*	219	87	47	353+	Highland	Hillsboro
(Black) Cherry, *Prunus serotina*	207	85	76	311+	Scioto	Portsmouth
Chestnut, *Castanea dentata*	52	64	43	127	Richland	Malabar Farm
Coffeetree, *Gymnocladus dioicus* (2)	196	80	70	294	Lake	Madison
Dogwood, *Cornus florida*	66	26	27	99+	Stark	Dalton
Dogwood, *Cornus florida*	43	38	35	90+	Huron	Norwalk
Elm, *Ulmus*						
American, *U. americana*	266	118	107	411	Ross	Chillicothe
Rock, *U. thomasii*	34	68	31	110	Fulton	Archbold
Hackberry, *Celtis occidentalis*	215	108	91	346+	Butler	
Hackberry, *Celtis occidentalis*	234	82	81	336+	Hancock	Findlay
Hawthorn, *Crataegus mollis*	108	35	57	157	Darke	New Madison
Hemlock, *Tsuga canadensis*	140	138	52	291	Ashland	Mohican SP
Hickory, *Carya*						
Bitternut, *C. cordiformis*	122	95	52	230	Hamilton	Cincinnati

Tree	Circ.	Height	Crown	Total	County	Nearest City
Mockernut, *C. tomentosa*	87	88	49	187	Morgan	Pennsville
Pecan, *C. illinoensis*	117	110	90	250+	Hamilton	Cincinnati
Pecan, *C. illinoensis*	137	120	85	278+	Hamilton	North Bend
Pignut, *C. glabra*	137	120	85	278	Franklin	Groveport
Shagbark, *C. ovata*	140	110	75	269	Gallia	Patriot
Shellbark, *C. laciniosa*	133	94	58	241	Vinton	US 50
Holly (Amer.), *Ilex opaca*	97	45	41	152	Vinton	Albany
Honeylocust, *Gleditsia triacanthos*	232	76	74	327+	Perry	Mt. Perry
Honeylocust, *Gleditsia triacanthos*	220	80	70	318+	Erie	Sandusky
Hophornbeam, *Ostrya virginiana*	90	69	41	169+	Trumbull	Warren
Hophornbeam, *Ostrya virginiana*	85	67	47	164+	Trumbull	Warren
Hophornbeam, *Ostrya virginiana*	82	70	35	161+	Mahoning	Salem
Hornbeam, *Carpinus caroliniana*	76	44	59	136	Hamilton	Cincinnati
Larch (Tamarack), *Larix laricina*	110	95	40	215	Cuyahoga	N. Royalton
Locust, *Robinia pseudoacacia*	210	86	38	306	Morgan	Stockport
Magnolia, *Magnolia*						
Cucumbertree, *M. acuminata* (2)	247	94	93	364	Stark	North Canton
Maple, *Acer*						
Black, *A. nigrum*	141	106	90	270	Franklin	Columbus
Boxelder, *A. negundo*	172	67	85	260+	Mahoning	Beloit
Boxelder, *A. negundo*	168	63	79	251+	Mahoning	Berlin Center
Red, *A. rubrum*	276	81	69	375	Carroll	Carrollton
Silver, *A. saccharinum*	273	79	81	372	Highland	Hillsboro
Silver, *A. saccharinum*	240	105	71	363	Shelby	Quincy
Sugar, *A. saccharum*	240	75	51	328	Trumbull	Vernon
(Red) Mulberry, *Morus rubra*	132	50	70	200	Huron	New London
(White) Mulberry, *Morus alba*	171	44	66	232	Hamilton	Cincinnati
Oak, *Quercus*						
Black, *Q. velutina*	205	100	94	329+	Erie	Berlin Heights
Black, *Q. velutina*	250	55	88	327+	Gallia	Cheshire
Bur, *Q. macrocarpa*	249	117	117	395	Hamilton	Wyoming
Chestnut, *Q. prinus*	179	129	109	335	Franklin	Groveport
Chinkapin, *Q. muehlenbergii* (2)	264	72	66	353	Ross	Frankfort
English, *Q. robur* (2)	187	88	91	298	Hamilton	North Bend
Red, *Q. rubra*	323	106	84	450	Ashtabula	Conneaut
Pin, *Q. palustris*	190	105	120	325	Stark	Canton
Pin, *Q. palustris*	217	75	97	316	Fairfield	Lancaster
Post, *Q. stellata*	120	67	63	203	Franklin	Grove City
Scarlet, *Q. coccinea*	218	107	91	348	Hamilton	Norwood
Swamp chestnut, *Q. michauxii*	148	81	92	252	Franklin	Hilliard
Swamp white, *Q. bicolor*	230	100	117	359	Adams	Sandy Springs
Water, *Q. nigra*	117	77	68	211	Hamilton	Cincinnati
White, *Q. alba*	257	104	130	394	Ross	Bainbridge
Willow, *Q. phellos*	194	94	81	308	Hamilton	Cincinnati

🐦 TOP POINTS

Sycamore, 737

Black Willow, 567

Cottonwood, 513

Red Oak, 450

Osage Orange, 426

🐦 GREAT GIRTH

(circumference in inches)

Sycamore, 582

Black Willow, 460

Cottonwood, 343

Osage Orange, 332

🐦 TALLEST (in feet)

Tuliptree, 164

White Pine, 152

Hemlock, 138

Cottonwood, 136

Sycamore, 129

CHAMPION TREES CONTINUED

TREE	CIRC.	HEIGHT	CROWN	TOTAL	COUNTY	NEAREST CITY
Osage Orange, *Maclura pomifera*	332	72	86	426	Hamilton	Cincinnati
Persimmon, *Diospyros virginiana*	122	66	40	198	Van Wert	Van Wert
Pine, *Pinus*						
White, *P. strobus*	105	152	46	269	Athens	Zaleski SF
Pitch, *P. rigida*	126	72	57	212	Hocking	Logan
Red, *P resinosa*	104	95	50	213	Huron	New London
Virginia, *P. virginiana*	106	56	54	176	Pike	Latham
Poplar, *Populus*						
Bigtooth aspen, *P. grandidentata*	80	117	51	209+	Hocking	Perry Twp.
Bigtooth aspen, *P. grandidentata*	84	106	39	200+	Hocking	
Cottonwood, *P. deltoides*	343	136	135	513	Delaware	Galena
Redbud, *Cercis canadensis*	84	33	34	126+	Lucas	Toledo
Redbud, *Cercis canadensis*	98	24	30	130+	Montgomery	Dayton
Red cedar, *Juniperus virginia*	83	80	12	166	Greene	Yellow Springs
Sassafras, *Sassafras albidum*	149	90	36	248	Franklin	Gahanna
Sourwood, *Oxydendrum arboretum*	70	98	35	177	Vinton	Zaleski
Spruce, *Picea*						
Norway, *P. abies*	127	113	47	252	Richland	Wthingtn. Twp.
White, *P. glauca*	55	45	25	106	Franklin	Columbus
Sweetgum, *Liquidambar styraciflua*	216	95	78	330	Scioto	Stout
Sycamore, *Platanus occidentalis*	582	129	105	737	Ashland	Jeromesville
Tuliptree, *Liriodendron tulipfera*	200	164	82	385+	Belmont	Dysart Woods
Tuliptree, *Liriodendron tulipfera*	262	100	73	380+	Scioto	Shawnee SF
Walnut, *Juglans*						
Black, *J. nigra*	174	105	93	302	Holmes	Millersburg
Butternut, *J. cinerea*	156	82	84	259	Ashland	Savannah
Willow, *Salix*						
Black, *S. nigra*	460	84	94	567	Columbiana	Leetonia
Weeping, *Salix babylonica*	244	58	73	320	Franklin	Groveport

KEY

(2)   Former national champion; +   State co-champion Source: Ohio Forestry Association

Reflections of amazing species: once lost, now found. Once gone, now we see.

Stalking the Wild Endangered List

Jim Bissell had put off looking at the property for five years. As the curator of botany at the Cleveland Museum of Natural History, he'd wasted too much of his valuable summer time following up on calls from people who thought they had unusual plants on their land. Such calls rarely led to something truly rare or special. Besides, this property was along Big Creek between Painesville and Chardon, an area where Bissell had already surveyed extensively. But the caller was persistent. So, one day in 1990, Bissell finally found time to visit the place.

It was a wooded hollow—probably an ancient, abandoned oxbow of the creek. He hiked through stands of hemlock and mixed hardwoods, cinnamon ferns and spicebush. The ground was surprisingly wet, as if the bottom of the hollow were a swamp perched above the creek. In the wettest part was a strange tree. It was a cottonwood, Bissell thought, although it had more rounded leaves and darker bark than the common Eastern cottonwood. When Bissell looked closer, he was shocked. It was the long-lost swamp cottonwood (*Populus heterophylla*).

The museum's herbarium, a collection of 60,000 pressed plant specimens, had a record of the tree being found "near Painesville" in 1892. Since then, it hadn't been sighted in that part of Ohio "I had looked for it on the lake plain for years and had just about decided I'd never find it," says Bissell, who informed the owner that her 30-acre property was unique. Her response to this news was to quickly donate the land to the museum for a nature preserve.

Until 1985, the swamp cottonwood was presumed extirpated from the entire state, meaning it hadn't been recorded in at least twenty years. Then a forester with the Ohio Division of Forestry happened to spot the tree in

59

Medina County. That inspired other botanists and naturalists to search again for the species. "Once somebody points out where something occurs, the rest of us go out looking," says Bissell. "When you find that little niche a plant needs, you go back to habitats you know are similar.

To date, the swamp cottonwood has been found in 23 places in Ohio. Far from being wiped out, the tree is not considered endangered or even threatened.

The "list" is actually a computer registry run by the Natural Heritage Program of the Ohio Division of Natural Areas and Preserves. The centralized database holds rare plant records, as well as records of rare animals, unusual natural communities and geological features. Although it is now a state project, the Heritage Program began in 1976 as a cooperative effort between the Ohio Department of Natural Resources (ODNR) and The Nature Conservancy, a nonprofit conservation organization that has pioneered the development of ecological databases. The idea behind the program was that by systematically keeping track of where rare things are found, it's easier to decide where to invest limited conservation dollars. Heritage Program information about Ohio and other states helps the U.S. Fish and Wildlife Service decide which plant and animal species deserve federal endangered or threatened status.

Botanists and naturalists report new plant findings to the Heritage Program staff, which records the information on topographic maps and in computer files. It lists the plant's scientific and common names, location, date found, name of the botanist and additional field notes. A precise location permits other researchers to check on the plants years later; old herbarium records were often frustratingly vague, giving locations such as "near a swamp in Ashtabula County." The botanist's

> *Every two years,*
> Jim Bissell joins the
> *other members of the*
> *Ohio Rare Plant*
> *Advisory Committee at*
> ODNR's Columbus
> *Headquarters for an*
> *all-day session ...*

name is also listed. If someone is known as a habitual mis-identifier, colleagues can quietly double-check the field work.

Every two years, Jim Bissell joins the other members of the Ohio Rare Plant Advisory Committee at ODNR's Columbus headquarters for an all-day session of adding and deleting species from the list. Generally, plants are listed because their habitats are being destroyed by development, pollution, drilling, mining or other human activities. Less frequently, plants are removed as their habitats recover. "Some aquatics that we think don't grow in Ohio anymore might have persisted through past years of polluted waters and may be starting to grow again," he says. "Maybe one of these days someone is going to spot a water-marigold."

More commonly, plants are removed from the list because a botanist simply gets good at finding them where they were previously overlooked. In 1984, hairy agrimony (*Agrimonia striata*) was found in just two places in the state and was listed as endangered. But Bissell started finding it in flood-plain meadows throughout Northeast Ohio, and now it's considered common.

Not everybody at the rare-plant advisory meetings will agree on what's common. "Lets say a plant is found all over the place in Northeast Ohio," Bissell says. "But if you're a botanist from the southwest part of the state and you've got only two habitats where it occurs, you'll come to the meeting and say 'Oh, it's so rare.' Meanwhile, I'm bored with it." The committee works by consensus before passing its recommendations to the director of the Natural Areas division, who is legally the keeper of the list. A committee recommendation has never been rejected.

While individual plants move on and off the list, the total number of listed species has remained relatively constant during recent years. The current list names 649 plant species in five categories: endangered (E), threatened (T), extinct in Ohio (X), potentially threatened (P) or recently added, status pending (A).

Once a plant is listed, is it truly protected? Unfortunately, from the point of view of most botanists, the Ohio endangered plant law itself is more advisory than protective. It's illegal to take endangered or threatened wild plants from their native habitats for commercial purposes. And you can't collect them for scientific purposes without a permit from the chief of the Division of Natural Areas and Preserves. The restrictions, however, don't apply to plants on your own land, or if you have written permission from the landowner.

"If you own the land, you own the plants," says Patricia Jones, data management supervisor for the Natural Areas division. You can take, possess, uproot, destroy or bulldoze your own plants, except perhaps if local zoning, federal wetlands regulations or public pressure can stop you. Endangered animals receive somewhat more protection. You can't shoot a bald eagle, for instance, even if it is roosting in your oak tree. You can, however, cut down the tree. "You can't possess the animal," Jones says, "but you can pave over its habitat for a parking lot."

Since ownership of habitat is the best protection, state agencies and private conservation organizations try to acquire key natural areas—oak savanna prairies, bogs and fens or beach dunes—that sustain rare plants and animals. If outright purchase is not possible, they offer conservation easements, which restrict use of the land in return for some tax advantages. Or the state simply tries to educate landowners, hoping that the people will become excited about preserving their ecological treasures.

After more than a century of botanical surveys, you'd expect the authorities to have a pretty complete accounting of the rare plants in the state. But new discoveries continue to be made, by professionals and amateurs alike. "The northwest and southeast parts of the state are understudied and are a gold mine," says Bissell. "Also the area just south of Youngstown. Every time I go to Columbiana County I find county records, and

> *Sometimes species are overlooked because they inhabit undesirable places — mosquito-infested swamps, dangerous cliffs, or boring places...*

some of them are Es or Ts.

"There's not enough field work being done," he continues. "The golden age of botany was the late 1800s. There were botanists at many universities and colleges throughout the country. They were out in the field, looking at the plants, learning about their region."

Field botanists are getting rarer themselves. In recent years, schools have built new laboratories for molecular biologists, while closing old herbariums. Retiring field botanists have not been replaced. "The experience is thin and decreasing," Bissell laments. "And even fewer people are out looking at insects. Who's looking for beetles?"

Nobody knows how many rare species are hiding in remote areas of the state. A recent statewide survey of butterflies and moths, for example, added about 20 species to the rare animals list. "It was the first time we had a survey of the biological status of those species," says David Ross, endangered species and wildlife diversity coordinator for the Division of Wildlife. "We're now doing a statewide dragonfly survey, which will probably discover more endangered species."

Sometimes species are overlooked because they inhabit undesirable places—mosquito-infested swamps, dangerous cliffs, or boring places that no hot-shot researcher wants to visit. Patricia Jones recalls the case of running buffalo clover (*Trifolium stoloniferum*), which is on the federal endangered list. "The information was that there were only a few locations left, until they spent some money to really look for it. They found it in Ohio in areas where botanists don't ordinarily like to go—old cow pastures where they think they won't find anything interesting."

And there's the story of spreading rockcress (*Arabis patens*). It hadn't been spotted in Ohio since 1910. Then it was found by accident along the Scioto River near Columbus in the late 1970s—ironically by a botany grad student collecting specimens for students to identify for an exam. "That was the problem," Jones says. "It blooms during exam time, and you have to get it when it's flowering, because otherwise it looks like any other mustard. The people who would normally be looking for it were either giving a test or taking a test. But there it was, exactly where it should have been, just a stone's throw from OSU."

The right person, the right place, the right time. All must come together if rare species are to be found. It happened to Bissell with the swamp cottonwood. And it happened to him again last year with the Louisiana sedge (*Carex louisianica*).

The only Ohio record of this small, grass-like plant was from Ashtabula County in 1960. Bissell had spent dozens of field days searching for it there, to no avail. Last October, he found it growing healthily near a park road in the Cleveland Metroparks-Bradley Woods Reservation—80 miles from Ashtabula County. It turned out he had been looking in the wrong habitat. His vision of the plant had been wrong.

"Now," he sighs, "I have to look in every damn swamp forest on the lake plain to see if I've been overlooking the Louisiana sedge." ✎

—*David Beach*

Source: The Greater Cleveland Environment Book, *ed.by* David Beach, *EcoCity Cleveland, 1998.*

Nature
Notables

For the Love of Blooms: William and Eliza Sullivant

He was the eldest son of Columbus founder Lucas Sullivant, heir to the family estate and businesses, and a gentleman of leisure. Eliza Griscom Wheeler was just 17 years old when she journeyed from New York City to marry Sullivant, a man nearly twice her age and once before married. But the love of botany conquered all. For the next 15 years the couple explored frontier Ohio and beyond, carefully collecting and cataloging its flora diversity.

While other naturalists concentrated on identifying flowers, the Sullivants became authorities on ferns, mosses, sedges, and grasses. Yale educated William did the taxonomic identifications, Eliza provided detailed illustrations. A circle of kindred spirits often accompanied the couple on field trips, notably Joseph Sullivant, William's younger brother who collected, recorded, and traded fossils, shells, minerals and zoophytes. The Sullivants shared (and traded) their specimens with leading East Coast botanists Dr. Asa Gray and Dr. John Torrey, thereby linking scientific communities and raising the prestige and interest in western flora. The Ohioans discovered 15 new plants. Some bear their names—*Sullivantia sullivanti* (for William), *Hypnum sullivantiae* (for Eliza), and *Carex sullivantii*, a sedge, are examples.

A cholera epidemic in Columbus sent the Sullivants packing to Mt. Vernon in the spring of 1850. Eliza, however, caught the contagion and died in August at age 33. Her stone portrait on the grave marker is trimmed in sullivantia. Though diminished, Sullivant's interest in botany continued until his death on April 30, 1873. His vast herbarium, believed to be the largest west of the Appalachians, was given to Harvard University and Ohio State University. Botanists still return to Sullivant's collection for a glimpse of Ohio's biological diversity in frontier times. —*SO*

OHIO'S ENDANGERED PLANTS (excludes threatened, rare and extirpated species)

Lichens
Baeomyces absolutus, Pink Dot Lichen
Collema coccophorum, Soil Pulp Lichen
C. conglomeratum, Dotted Pulp Lichen
Canoparmelia texana,
Buzzardroost Rock Lichen
Parmotrema madagascariaceum,
Madagascar Shield Lichen
Ramalina farinacea, Dotted Twig Lichen
R. intermedia, Sandstone Twig Lichen
Sticta weigelii, Weigel's Leather Lichen

Bryophytes
Buxbaumia minakatae, Ethereal Elf Cap Moss
Diphyscium cumberlandianum,
Cumberland Grain O'Wheat Moss
Fissidens hyalinus, Filmy Fissidens
Plagiothecium latebricola, Lurking Leskea
Tortella inclinata, Curved Tortella
Campylostelium saxicola,
Rock-loving Swan-necked Moss
Pytchomitrium drummondii,
Drummond's Ptychomitrium
Sphagnum riparium, Shore-growing Peat Moss

Pteridophytes
Filmy Fern Family
Trichomanes boschianum,
Appalachian Filmy Fern
Quillwort Family
Isoetes engelmannii, Appalachian Quillwort
Clubmoss Family
Lycopodiella appressum, Southern Clubmoss
Adder's Tongue Family
Ophioglossum engelmannii,
Limestone Adder's-tongue
Polypody Family
Polpodium polypodioides,
Little Gray Polypody
Selaginella Family
S. rupestris, Rock Spikemoss

Angiosperms - Monocotyledons
Water Plantain Family
Echinodorus rostratus, Bur-head
Sagittaria cuneata, Wapato
S. graminea, Grass-leaf Arrowhead
Sedge Family
Carex arctata, Drooping Wood Sedge

C. cephaloidea, Thin-leaf Sedge
C. crus-corvi, Raven Foot Sedge
C. decomposita, Cypress Knee Sedge
C. disperma, Two-seeded Sedge
C. echinata, Little Prickly Sedge
C. garberi, Garber's Sedge
C. limosa, Mud Sedge
C. longii, Long's Sedge
C. louisianica, Louisiana Sedge
C. lucorum, Fire Sedge
C. merritt-fernaldii, Fernald's Sedge
C. pseudocyperus, Northern Bearded Sedge
C. purpurifera, Purple Wood Sedge
C. retrorsa, Reflexed Bladder Sedge
C. siccata, Hay Sedge
C. striatula, Lined Sedge
Cyperus acuminatus, Pale Umbrella Sedge
C. dipsaciformis (C. retrofractus), Teasel Sedge
C. lancastriensis, Many-flowered
Umbrella Sedge
C. refractus, Reflexed Umbrella Sedge
Eleocharis caribaea, Caribbean Spikerush
E. engelmannii, Engelmann's Spikerush
E. ovata, Ovate Spikerush
E. parvula, Least Spikerush
E. wolfii, Wolf's Spikerush
Lipocarpha drummondii, Drummond's Dwarf
Bulrush
Rhynchospora globularis, Grass-like Beak Rush
Scirpus smithii, Smith's Bulrush
S. subterminalis, Swaying Rush
Scleria oligantha, Tubercled Nut Rush
Pipewort Family
Eriocaulon septangulare, White Buttons
Iris Family
Iris brevicaulis, Leafy Blue Flag
Sisyrinchium atlanticum, Atlantic
Blue-eyed Grass
S. montanum, Northern Blue-eyed-grass
S. mucronatum, Narrow-leaved
Blue-eyed Grass
Rush Family
Juncus diffusissimus, Diffuse Rush
J. greenei, Greene's Rush
J. platyphyllus, Flat-leaved Rush
Lily Family
Clintonia borealis, Bluebead Lily
Erythronium rostratum, Goldenstar
Streptopus roseus, Rose Twisted Stalk

ENDANGERED PLANTS CONT.

Water Nymph Family
Najas gracillima, Thread-like Naiad
Orchid Family
Arethusa bulbosa, Dragon's Mouth
Coeloglossum viride, Long-bracted Orchid
C. trifida, Early Coralroot
Cypripedium calceolus var. parviflorum, Small
Yellow Lady's Slipper
Isotria medeoloides, Small Whorled Pogonia
Platanthera blephariglottis,
White-Fringed Orchid
P. psycodes, Small Purple-Fringed Orchid
Grass Family
Aristida necopina, False Arrow-feather
Calamagrostis porteri spp.
insperata, Bartley's Reed Bent Grass
Cinna latifolia, Northern Wood Reed
Glyceria acutiflora, Sharp-glumed
 Manna Grass
Koeleria macrantha, Junegrass
Leersia lenticularis, Catchfly Grass
Melica nitens, Three-flowered Melic
Muhlenbergia cuspidata, Plains Muhlenbergia
Oryzopsis asperifolia, Large-leaved
Mountain Rice
O. racemosa, Mountain Rice
Panicum commonsianum,
Commons' Panic Grass
P. leibergii, Leiberg's Panic Grass
P. meridionale, Southern Hairy Panic Grass
P. perlongum, Long-panicled Panic Grass
P. spretum, Narrow-headed Panic Grass
P. villlosissimum, Villous Panic Grass
P. yadkinense, Spotted Panic Grass
P. saltuensis, Pasture Bluegrass
Schizachne purpurascens, False Melic
Schizachyrium scoparium
var. littorale, Coastal Little Bluestem
Water Hyacinth Family
Heteranthera reniformis, Mud Plantain
Pondweed Family
Putamogeton friesii, Fries' Pondweed
P. gramineus, Grass-like Pondweed
P. hillii, Hill's Pondweed
P. praelongus, White-stem Pondweed
P. robbinsii, Robbins' Pondweed
P. spirillus, Spiral Pondweed
P. tennesseensis, Tennessee Pondweed

Scheuchzeria Family
Scheuchzeria palustris, Scheuchzeria
Catbrier Family
Smilax herbacea var. pulverulenta,
Downy Carrion Flower
Yellow-Eyed Grass Family-Bur Reed Family
Xyris difformis, Carolina Yellow-eyed Grass
Maple Family
Acer pensylvanicum, Striped Maple
Amaranth Family
Froelichia floridana, Cottonweed
Cashew Family
Toxiodendron rybergii, Northern Poison Ivy
Carrot Family
Hydrocotlye umbrellata, Navelwort
Dogbane Family
Apocynum sibiricum, Clasping-leaf Dogbane
Milkweed Family
Aralia hispida, Bristly Sarsaparilla
Aster Family
Aster acuminatus, Mountain Aster
Chrysopsis graminifolia, Silkgrass
Conyza ramosissima, Bushy Horseweed
E. hyssopifolium, Hyssop Thoroughwort
H. longipilum, Long-bearded Hawkweed
Hymenoxys herbacea, Lakeside Daisy
Pluchea camphorata, Camphorweed
Prenanthes aspera, Rough Rattlesnake Root
P. crepidinea, Nodding Rattlesnake Root
Silphium laciniatum, Compass Plant
Verbesina occidentalis, Yellow Crownbeard
Vernonia missurica, Missouri Ironweed
Mustard Family
Arabis divaricarpa, Limestone Rock-cress
A. hirsuta var. adepressipilis, Southern Hairy
Rock-cress
A. hirsuta var. pycnocarpa,
Western Hairy Rock-cress
A. patens, Spreading Rock-cress
Cardamine pratensis var. palustris,
American Cuckoo Flower
Draba brachycarpa, Little Whitlow Grass
D. reptans, Carolina Whitlow Grass
Erysimum arkansanum, Western Wallflower
Pink Family
Arenaria patula, Spreading Sandwort
Sagina caroliniana var. wherri,
Wherry's Catchfly

Stafftree Family
Paxistima canbyi, Canby's
Mountain Lover (Cliffgreen)
Rockrose Family
Hudsonia tomentosa, Beach Heather
Lechea tenuifolia, Narrow-leaved Pinwood
Mangosteen Family
Hypericum boreale, Northern St. John's-wort
H. denticulatum, Coppery St. John's-wort
H. gymnanthum, Least St. John's-wort
Triadenum walteri, Walter's St. John's-wort
Dodder Family
Cuscuta coryli, Hazel Dodder
Sundew Family
Drosera intermedia, Spathulate-leaved
Sundew
Heath Family
Ledum groenlandicum, Labrador Tea

Rhododendron calendulaceum,
Flame Azalea
R. nudiflorum var. nudiflorum, Pinxter Flower
Spurge Family
Croton glandulosus, Northern Croton
E. purpurea, Glade Spurge
E. Serpens, Roundleaf Spurge
Phyllanthus caroliniensis,
Carolina Leaf Flower
Pea or Bean Family
Astragalus neglectus,
Cooper's Milk Vetch
Baptista australis, Blue False Indigo
Desmodium sessilifolium, Sessile Tick Trefoil
Galactia volubilis, Milk Pea
Lathyrus venosus, Wild Pea
Trifolium reflexum, Buffalo Clover
T. stoloniferum, Running Buffalo Clover

New
Growth

Hope for Two Ohio Originals

AMERICAN CHESTNUT
Reasons for leaving: Imported disease

Status: Endangered, but recovery possible with disease-resistant trees.

Stout American chestnuts stood trunk-to-trunk in Ohio's hardwood forests until this century. The tree could not fight off a fungus blight brought to the U.S. from Europe in 1904. The disease still attacks young chestnuts that sprout from infested stumps. Hope remains that this megaflora will rebound from clones being tested for disease-tolerance.

AMERICAN ELM
Reasons for leaving: Fungal disease

Status: Recovering via clones of disease-resistant survivors.

Dutch elm disease started in Ohio, and it may end here. Researchers at the U.S. Department of Agriculture labs in Delaware, Ohio and at the National Arboretum have developed disease-resistant trees from Ohio elms that withstood the plague.

—SO

Wildflowers Take Off in Toledo

Early in 1989, naturalist Guy Denny asked permission to inventory rare plants along the runways at the Toledo Express Airport. He was interested in the airport because it sits in the heart of Ohio's unique Oak Openings region and no survey had ever been done of plants. But Denny, later chief of the Division of Natural Areas and Preserves for the state's Department of Natural Resources, was not optimistic about finding rare plants. Airports normally dredge, bulldoze, spill fuel and plant aggressive ground covers.

So, that May, Denny drove up from Columbus with a botanist and a zoologist. The botanist, Allison Cusick, made an astounding find in the parking lot. A geranium on a traffic island caught his eye, and he went over for a closer look. There, beside the geranium, was a new plant for Ohio—the western rock jasmine, which usually grows in the Rockies. Only an inch-and-a-quarter high, it had adapted to concrete. Cusick started whooping and hollering.

The rock jasmine was just the opener; the Toledo Express Airport has turned out to be one of the best single havens for rare plants in Ohio. One reason is that the airport's normal maintenance practices happen to be just what these plants need. Like the Federal Aviation Administration, the plants can't stand trees in the way of their sunlight. Rare plants also are not necessarily frail plants; they may like to be jostled and have their seeds turned up in the soil by, say, a bulldozer.

But Toledo Express is also in the right place for rare plants: it is in the middle of the 150-square-mile Oak Openings, an unusual terrain that provides plant habitats that are virtually unique in Ohio.

At the time of the glaciers this area became a refuge for plants from other regions. The plants were left behind as conditions changed around the Oak Openings. Thus, the area still has many species that are rare in Ohio but common in far-flung places like the Jersey Shore or even, as the rock jasmine shows, the Rocky Mountains. Growing far from others of their species makes the Ohio varieties disjunct, which may mean they are genetically interesting, but definitely means they are historically interesting. Denny suggests that, just as human artifacts show human development, disjunct plants help us trace the landscape's past.

Around 1980, plagued by a herd of 27 whitetails, the airport cut down a lot of trees to deprive the deer of protective cover. After that, the seeds of the original sun-loving Oak Openings plants—seeds that lay dormant so long as shady conditions prevailed—sprang back to life.

When a two-acre rise was cleared of its trees, it came up in flowers—Ohio's largest collection of lupines, whose sky-blue flowers are succeeded in spring by yellow puccoons. The lupines and puccoons are rare and grow here along with the bird's-foot violet, the hairy pinweed and others.

The best place is a drainage ditch paralleling the main runway. This trough, which looks just like an ordinary weedy drainage ditch, contains hundreds of rare plants. It was discovered by Jim McCormac. At the crack of dawn on a June day, McCormac noticed a large-fruited cranberry growing on soil. It was another whoop-and-holler occasion, because, as McCormac knew, all the other large cranberries in Ohio grow in bogs.

But alas, the public can't see the rare plants. Airport security nowadays is a serious business. And that makes the plants safe from human terrorism.

—*Jane Ware*

ENDANGERED PLANTS CONT.

Beech Family
Quercus falcata, Spanish Oak

Gentian Family
G. puberulenta, Prairie Gentian
G. saponaria, Soapwort Gentian
G. villosa, Sampson's Snakeroot
Geranium Family
Geranium bicknelli, Bicknell's Crane's Bill
Gooseberry Family
Ribes missouriense, Missouri Gooseberry
R. triste, Swamp Red Currant
Water Milfoil Family
Myriophyllum heterophyllum,
Two-leaved Water Milfoil
M. verticillatum, Green Water Milfoil
Mint Family
Collinsonia verticillata, Early Stoneroot
Pycnanthemum verticillatum var. pilosum,
Hoary Mountain Mint
Trichostema dichotomum var. lineare,
Narrow-leaved Bluecurls
Bladderwort Family
Utricularia cornuta, Horned Bladderwort
U. geminiscapa, Two-scaped Bladderwort
Magnolia family
Magnolia macrophyla, Bigleaf Magnolia
Bayberry Family
Myrica pensylvanica, Bayberry
Waterlily Family
Nuphar variegata, Bullhead Lily
Olive Family
Evening Primrose Family
Epilobium angustifolium, Fireweed
Oenothera parviflora, Small-flowered
Evening Primrose
Plantain Family
Plantago cordata, Heart-leaf Plantain
P. patagonica, Woolly Plantain
Riverweed Family
Podostemum ceratophyllum,
Riverweed
Milkwort Family
Polygala cruciata, Cross-leaved Milkwort
P. curtissii, Curtiss' Milkwort
P. paucifolia, Gay Wings
Smartweed Family
Polygonum setaceum var. injectum,
Bristly Smartweed

Primrose Family
Hottonia inflata, Featherfoil
Shinleaf Family
Moneses uniflora, One-flowered Wintergreen
Pyrola chlorantha, Green-fowered Wintergreen
Buttercup Family
Aconitum noveboracense, Northern Monkshood
A. uncinatum, Southern Monkshood
Ranunculus pusillus, Low Spearwort
Trollius laxus, Spreading Globeflower
Buckthorn Family
Ceanothus herbaceus, Prairie Redroot
Rose Family
Amelanchier sanguinea, Rock Serviceberry
Crataegus uniflora, Dwarf Hawthorn
Potentilla arguta, Tall Cinquefoil
Sorbus decora, Western Mountain Ash
Spiraea alba var. latifolia,
S. virginiana, Appalachian Spiraea
Madder Family
Galium labradoricum, Bog Bedstraw
G. pallustre, Marsh Bedstraw
Willow Family
Salix pedicellaris, Bog Willow
Figwort Family
Agalinis auriculata, Ear-leaf Foxglove
A. purpurea var. parviflora,
  Small Purple Foxglove
A. skinneriana, Skinner's Foxglove
Aureolaria pedicularia var. ambigens,
Prairie Fernleaf False Foxglove
A. pedicularia var. pedicularia, Woodland
Fernleaf False Foxglove
Linaria canadensis, Old Field Toadflax
Penstemon laevigatus, Smooth Beard-tongue
Nettle Family
Urtica chamaedryoides, Spring Nettle
Valerian Family
Valeriana ciliata, Prairie Valerian
Violet Family
Viola missouriensis, Missouri Violet
V. nephrophylla, Northern Bog Violet
V. primulifolia, Primrose-leaved Violet
V. tripartita var. glaberrima, Wedge-leaf Violet
V. walteri, Walter's Violet

For a complete list of Ohio's imperiled plants, including threatened and extirpated species, contact the Ohio Division of Natural Areas and Preserves, 1889 Fountain Square Court, Bldg. F-1, Columbus, Ohio 43224-1388; (614) 265-6453

Beauty is in the Eyes of the Botanist

These botanists are a peculiar lot, the way they don hip boots and wade through mosquito clouds, and maggot-gagging marshes to verify a sundew, or cantilever over a cliff to inspect a Canby's mountain lover, or crawl on all fours to count the bracts on moss. Eccentric too, how they afix their dingy slouch hats, fuss over field guides and notebooks, and fastidiously organize specimens. Most of what they do in the field is low tech—eyes for observing, curiosity for hunches. Lined up beside jetsetters, glamorous film stars, or corporatos these chlorophyll counters may seem a few steps behind the times, but they are many places ahead of the rest of us, and richer for having rubbed against so much more life.

One of the ringleaders of this quirky bunch is Allison Cusack, chief botanist at the Division of Natural Areas and Preserves (DNAP). Much of what we know about Ohio's flora stems from Cusick's quarter century of research. His collection of 35,000 specimens, an assemblage that won him the 1998 Herbert Osborn Award from Ohio Biological Survey, sprouts in herbariums in Ohio and the Eastern U.S. For 15 years Cusick and Jim McCormac, another DNAP botanist, have faithfully published a yearly "Best Plant Finds" report in the division's newsletter. It salutes botanists who discovered new species in Ohio, new colonies of rarities, or rediscoveries of plants thought to have disappeared.

Okay, so maybe "Best Plant Finds" doesn't match Hollywood's "Best Picture" or NASA's snapshot of a new moon around Neptune. But among plant snoops, getting listed is like making the honor roll. Here are the kind of nuggets you'll find in "Best Finds." Cusick discovered the first community of dwarf dandelion in the Ohio River Valley and Ohio's second settlement of least St. John's-wort in 1994. Perennial headliners Jim Bissell and Beverly Danielson of the Cleveland Museum of Natural History, sniffed out Cleveland's evening primrose and early panic-grass in 1994. Both plants were new to Ohio's flora inventory.

Rediscoveries may be the most precious because they restore hope, and remind us that treasures lost can be found again. They pop up unexpectedly, like the birthday card Grandma sent when you were six and the $10 bill still inside, or a college sweetheart's love letter in an old biology text. In 1995, Cusick found Drummond's rock-cress growing on cliffs on Middle Bass Island, a tiny mustard that had not been seen in Ohio for 18 years. While exploring the banks of the Scioto River in 1997, Barry Weber of the Columbus Recreation and Parks Department bumped into the first rock elm to be seen in Franklin County since 1902. Wolf's bluegrass, last recorded in Ohio in 1965 and considered a goner, reappeared at Strait Creek Prairie Preserve in Ross County, thanks to the eyes of Dave Minney. Judy Dumke found the tiny blue scorpion weed in 1996, after a 44-year absence. Two year's later McCormac recorded the first small-flowered scorpion weed since 1904, and a smooth tick-trefoil, the first in more than a century.

Rediscoveries. Reappearances. Rebirths. Whatever. They prove that nature never quits diversifying, multiplying, persevering, mystifying, and reinventing itself. Coagulate all the weird and loving work of today's botanists and you have an idea of Ohio's amazing flora fecundity. Add it to the curios and revelations unearthed by their predecessors, from Bartram to Braun, and you have a sacred tome as alive and worthy and magical as any bible. And certainly a lot more useful than a moon around Neptune.

—*SO*

CHIPMUNK

I'm Nuts About Ohio!

Fur is cute while a shell is not, but Ohio's bivalves matter.

*W*aders are the mini-submarines of small stream biology, so when I sign on with Otterbein College biologist Dr. Michael Hoggarth's expedition to find the purple catspaw, he issues me a pair.

Clunky rubber boots welded to heavy, waterproofed canvas overalls that come up to my armpits, my waders turn out to be ideal for hunting a freshwater mussel once native to the Ohio River drainage basin that had not been seen alive in Ohio in well over a century.

Waders erase a river's sharp lines between wet and dry, between surface and stream. They give me the curious sensation of being the river. Thus they are perfect for exploring the bottom of Killbuck Creek, a soupy green, farmers' river that winds through rolling cropland in north central Ohio. It seems the last place on Earth to find a rare animal, which partially explains why it took Michael Hoggarth so long to find the purple catspaw.

In truth, the purple catspaw pearly mussel was little noted, nor long remembered after it disappeared from this part of the world. The last living or recently dead one was recorded in Ohio before the Civil War. That is, until Hoggarth found a small but healthy population of purple catspaws in the Killbuck, a hitherto undistinguished tributary of the Walhonding River. The Walhonding in turn flows to the Muskingum, which flows to the Ohio, which flows to the Mississippi and thus the world. And the finding of this rare animal has meaning for that wider world. Its survival may provide a clue for the fate of life on Earth, which is a lot of weight for a small Ohio bivalve to carry.

The purple catspaw first turned up again on the Walhonding itself in 1991. That's where Hoggarth first stumbled upon an unfamiliar but recently dead shell (both valves or halves of the bivalve were still attached by a ligament). The inside nacre of the valve was a distinctive purple, a key characteristic of the supposedly extirpated purple catspaw, a federally listed endangered subspecies (there is a related but distinct white catspaw that is even rarer). For two years, Hoggarth and his students scoured the Walhonding for more catspaws and found nothing. A year later while looking for rare fish

Nature Notable

When he was not busy cataloguing his patients' symptoms, Lakewood physician Jared Potter Kirtland (1793-1877) was counting every other Ohio lifeform. He compiled the state's first checklist of birds, mammals, reptiles, fish, shells and crustaceans. He also founded the Cleveland Academy of Natural Sciences (now the Museum of Natural History) and co-founded the American Association for the Advancement of Science. To show that Dr. Kirtland still counts, ODNR inducted him into their Hall of Fame in 1968.

in Killbuck Creek, Hoggarth found them.

Now Hoggarth is back at Killbuck in waders to guide his small expedition of the curious to a sight of a living purple catspaw. Even in its pre-settlement heyday, the purple catspaw was a relatively rare member of a vast family of native freshwater mussels, known as the Unionidae, that once flourished—infested the pioneers would have said—the great American inland rivers. Especially in the watershed of the mighty Mississippi, the Unionidae branched out in such variety and reproduced in such numbers that settlers called one variety "heelsplitters," regarding them as a menace to wading livestock and barefoot humans.

Still it must have been one of the breathtaking sights of early North America: imagine a clear-running Ohio River or an untamed Tennessee, tiled virtually from side to side with thick hedges of mussels. The scene is as impossible to visualize today as a wild herd of buffalo flooding unchecked across a prairie horizon. In one way, the Unionidae were more impressive, for the buffalo herds were but a single species. The Unionidae were a nation of species. Part of the richest freshwater mollusk fauna on earth, North American mussels alone accounted for over half of the species of freshwater mussels in the world. Today they have the dubious distinction of being one of the most threatened groups of animals on the planet.

Beaching the canoe on a sand bar, Hoggarth walks straight into the Killbuck and falls upon his knees as if in prayer. The water swells up to his waist. Along this reach, the Killbuck throws off its torpor and exhibits the classic riffle-run-pool sequence of a strong free-flowing river. Trees screen the fields on one bank and a small wetland buffers the other. In between, the Killbuck runs strong and cold. I follow him cautiously.

Alternating arms, Hoggarth begins "noodling" through the substrate of coarse sand and fine gravel to feel for mussels. Our companions, naturalist Dan Rice of the Ohio Department of Natural Resources, and Bill Gates, an Otterbein biology student, take station on their knees alongside. Gates pulls up all sorts of mussels that Rice and Hoggarth glance back to identify: *Flava, Postulosa, Complanata*. Rice and Hoggarth use the common names: Wabash pigtoe. Pimpleback. Fat pocketbook. Freshwater mussels sport a gaudy and downhome common nomenclature—monkeyface, pimpleback, pistol grip, three-horn warty back, mucket, hickory nut and squawfoot. But on this cool, rainy September morning, Hoggarth's expedition can't find a single *Epioblasma obliquata obliquata*, the purple pearly catspaw.

Still kneeling and noodling, Hoggart calls back, "I said we'd find a catspaw and I guaranteed it, gentlemen. It's still early. Don't panic. Besides they wouldn't seem so rare if you just pulled one out." Ten minutes later, Hoggarth has one, a male that he measures, photographs and "ages" based on the annular rings on its darkened green shell at 18-years-old. When he's done taking data, Hoggarth kneels in the water and carefully pushes the specimen back into the substrate to get on with his life. It's Hoggarth's 59th living purple catspaw. By day's end, he has three more for his records, thus increasing the world's known breeding population by roughly 5 percent.

Before Hoggarth's discovery, the purple catspaw was officially listed as a federal endangered species but it was, in reality, doomed. It survived only in two small non-breeding "terminal" populations in Tennessee and Kentucky. A fortunate mussel can live from 20 to 120 years, but once a species stops breeding, extinction is just a matter of time. Hoggarth's discovery of breeding purple catspaws in Killbuck Creek raised the survival chances of the subspecies from nil to merely bleak.

The purple catspaw and its Unionidae cousins are a classic example of what ecologists call "endemic species," species native to a particular place and found only there. Endemics are especially vulnerable to human disruption because their habitats are small "islands" in the environment. When that habitat—an island in the Pacific, a single hillside in a tropical forest or a free-flowing river in Ohio—is destroyed or drastically altered, the endemics disappear. And since they live no place else on Earth, they disappear forever.

The habitat of the Unionidae was trashed without a thought but with a terrifying thoroughness. They were driven out with silt, dams and pollution. Their beds were dredged up to get at the river gravel beneath their feet. They became a commodity in a ruinous shell trade, first for pearl buttons and, in recent decades, for "seeds"—plugs cut from the shell—to be used for

Continued on page 72 ➤

Bird Man
of Cincinnati

Audubon's Career Takes Flight

Jean Jacques "LaForest" Rabin Fougere Audubon strolled into Cincinnati in late 1819 the epitome of a poor, starving artist. He owned, exactly, the ragged clothes on his body, his trusty flintlock shotgun and sack full of bird pictures. Audubon did not expect his new job—taxidermist for the Western Museum—to profoundly change his life. Nor was he expected to profoundly change the world. He was like other rootless men on the frontier, looking for something—anything—that would clarify his life.

He found it when an acquaintance wrote a blind "Dear Sir" letter to the headmaster of Lancaster Seminary, the forerunner of the University of Cincinnati, suggesting that Audubon be hired to teach drawing or French. Dr. Daniel Drake, the seminary president, replied that he needed a taxidermist for his newly founded museum. The salary—$125 a month—was unbelievably generous. Drake also likely advanced Audubon the cash to rent a house at 414 E. Third St. and to fetch his wife and sons. (The residence, which stood until the 1930s, now lies beneath interstates 71 and 75.)

Word soon spread about Audubon's interest in birds. One day a woman brought him a least bittern bundled in an apron. Somehow the bird had tumbled down the chimney during the night and perched on her bedpost. The agreeable bittern posed two hours. But then the unsentimental Audubon killed and wired it for drawing and mounting. He once rescued an immature American kestrel that fell from its nest. The pet, named Nero, roosted behind his window shutter. The miniature falcon harassed the ducks and humored Audubon's wife and children on command. Nero's likeness appears in *The Birds of America*.

After just a short time, Drake let Audubon go, owing him $1,200. As consolation, he promised to exhibit Audubon's paintings of birds at the museum's opening in June 1820. The event would be Audubon's debut as an artist.

Audubon earned critical acclaim at the exhibition. The *Cincinnati Inquisitor* commented that "the style and execution of these paintings...are so superior that we believe...there have been no exhibitions west of the mountains which can compare with them." Indeed Audubon's birds looked alive, natural and wild, a refreshing and artful departure from the stiff, posed specimens in naturalist drawings of the times. Also, few in the field matched his astute observations and enthusiastic writing style.

Such approval emboldened Audubon, who finally declared himself a naturalist and artist and decided to publish a book. On Oct. 12, 1820, he left Cincinnati on a flatboat, determined to draw all the birds from the Ohio River valley to those residing in the Louisiana bayou.

His great masterpiece was published in 1838 in Great Britain.

—SO

culturing artificial Japanese pearls. They survived one invasion by an aggressive alien species, the Asian clam *corbicula*, only to face a new and possibly more damaging competitor, *Dreisseina*, or the European Zebra mussel, dumped into the Great Lakes by ships shedding water ballast and now spreading through the Mississippi drainage.

The fate of the Unionidae and related freshwater mussel family, the Margerterifidae, provide a sickening illustration of the vulnerability of endemics. The numbers are stark. Of the 297 native American freshwater mussel species identified in the last century, 21 are extinct and another 120 highly threatened today. That's 141 out of 297 species, nearly half of all species in this one family pushed to the edge of biological oblivion or beyond in less than 100 years. When groups of living things are going extinct at that rate, it raises some frightening questions. Is the diversity of life on Earth diminishing at a catastrophic rate? Is the Earth in the midst of another global mass extinction like the one that rang down the curtain on the dinosaurs?

So far, there have been five global mass extinctions; the last one 66 million years ago wiped out the Dinosauria. The scientific blame for that is currently fixed on a meteor strike or volcanism or both. If we are in the midst of a sixth mass extinction, the suspected agent is only too well known—us.

Enumerating life forms as Hoggarth does has been at the core of natural science since the 18th century when the Swedish naturalist Carl Linnaeus first proposed his classification system of kingdom-phylum-class-order-family-genus-species (or by one famous mnemonic memory aid, "King Philip Came Over From Germany Stoned."). Over time, as museum basements around the world filled up with bales of pressed plants, jars of pickled fish and drawers of delicately pinned insects, there have been great adjustments in his system. Yet more than 250 years into the explosion of biological science that followed Linnaeus, we still don't know how many distinct kinds of living things there are on Earth.

The total number of species scientifically described—that is, collected, characterized and assigned a scientific name—is only around 1 million, according to experts. The planetary total number could be 10 million to 100 million species. Nobody knows. Nobody is ever likely to know.

Once the renowned British ecologist J.B.S. Haldane was supposedly asked by the Bishop of Oxford, 'What do you deduce about the Creator from studying his creations?' And Haldane replied, "An inordinate fondness for beetles."

All belong to the great riot of life on Earth, what Psalm 104 calls, "things creeping innumerable, both small and great beasts." Animals, plants, monerans, protista and fungi, they swell the Earth's biodiversity. Detailing or even enumerating them all is probably well beyond the resources and brains of mere mortals. That leaves conservation biologists in a cleft stick. On the one hand, they can only be humbled by sheer variety of creation. On the other, if we can never know how many kinds of living things there are, how can we know if the diversity of life is narrowing at a catastrophic rate?

And that's where the freshwater mussels, the Unionidae and the Margerterifidae, come in. If we can't count the beetles, we can count the bivalves. For that, we can thank Thomas Say. one of the founding fathers of American natural history. He belongs to the heroic age of natural science when a continent opened not only to the European plow but to the new European scientific method. Say and a handful of other scientific pioneers rushed into the American wilderness to count up the unknown marvels of creation and to give them names. From them, we have the baseline data of "primeval" North America. From Say and his colleagues, we know how many species of freshwater mussels were in the great central basin of North America at the opening of the Ohio territory.

Behind the naturalists came the plowmen. The settlement of the interior of North America was one of the great migrations of world history. Westward-moving America was not merely a wave of people but a wave of botany and zoology. Old America brought with it Old Europe's crops, weeds, livestock, pests and sanitary customs. In a mere 200 years, the Ohio Valley was transformed into a new America, a land not of forest but of fields, pastures, mines, cities, and industry.

One of the first things to change was the water. Ohio's greatest modern icythologist, Milton Trautman, pointed out that as soon as the pioneers began hacking down the forest, erosion went wild. Humus-rich top soil poured into pristine streams, consuming the oxygen, and driving out fish that needed clear water and clean bottoms to breed. Trautman described his lifelong study of Ohio's declining native fish populations as "one long dirge." By the middle of the last century, oldtimers were wondering wistfully what had happened to the abundant waterlife and wildlife they remembered from the Ohio country's opening days.

They mourned the loss of the buffalo, the sturgeon and the passenger pigeon but the decline of one class of animals was practically unnoticed—the freshwater mussels. It's not that the pioneers didn't know they were there. They were impossible to miss, growing in thick shoals and in staggering variety. The pioneers gave them those colorful names. Yet in the early days of settlement, the naiades were not considered terribly useful. It took too much effort to get at their dubious tasting meat. The occasional pearls they contained were too few and too irregular to sustain an industry. The pioneers could not know that the freshwater bivalves in the Ohio and Mississippi drainage represented a different kind of treasure; collectively, the richest freshwater fauna on earth, accounting for over half of the species of freshwater mussels in the world.

Thomas Say knew they were remarkable for he knew more about the incredible abundance of unknown North American life forms including freshwater mussels than nearly anyone on Earth.

Webbed Wildlife

Ohio Division of Wildlife

www.dnr.state.oh.odnr/

wildlife/wildlife.html

U.S. Fish & Wildlife Service

Endangered Species List

www.fws.gov/~r9endspp/

statl-rs.html#LnkOH

Eco *Symbols*

Fauna Made Official

Animal magnetism is powerful in the state legislature because the adoption of feathered and fossilized friends as state symbols seems to be attractive to voters. Witness the almost rhapsodic additions to the Ohio Revised Code making it official.

STATE BIRD: the cardinal, adopted 1933. The adoption noted that the permanent resident of Ohio is known for its "clear, strong song and brilliant red plumage."

STATE ANIMAL: whitetailed deer, adopted 1987. "Naming the white-tailed deer as the official animal of the state does not relieve the division of wildlife of its duty to manage the deer population and its distribution," the bill noted.

STATE REPTILE: black racer, adopted 1995, thanks to Jacob Mercer, a fourth-grader who initiated the designation when he sent a letter to state representatives and senators. He and his classmates called the reptile the "farmer's friend" because it eats disease-carrying rodents.

STATE FOSSIL: trilobite, adopted 1985. "Isotelus, a genus of extinct marine arthropod of the class Trilobita, that lived in the seas that covered Ohio during the Ordovician period, about four hundred forty million years ago... is hereby adopted as the official invertebrate fossil of the state."

STATE INSECT: ladybug, adopted 1975. "The queenly Ladybug is symbolic of the people of Ohio—she is proud and friendly, bringing delight to millions of children when she alights on their hand or arm to display her multicolored wings, and she is extremely industrious and hardy, able to live under the most adverse conditions and yet retain her beauty and charm, while at the same time being of inestimable value to nature."

STATE FISH: proposed—smallmouth bass. Advocated by members of the Ohio Smallmouth Alliance who cite the billions of dollars sport fishing contributes to the local economy. ✎

Early on Say had seen more of the continent than almost any other scientist. Say was an intrepid explorer, a scientific Lewis and Clark, who'd accompanied Captain Stephen Long's 1820 Army expedition up the Platte River to the Rockies that reached the site of what became Denver, Colorado. Then in 1825, he shocked the finest scientific minds in Philadelphia by signing on with a hare-brained expedition down the Ohio River by keelboat to a new Utopian community planted in the heart of the western wilderness at a place to be called New Harmony, Indiana. New Harmony was the brainchild of the charismatic industrialist and would-be utopian Robert Owen.

The expedition assembled in Pittsburgh in the winter of 1825 and it was a motley crew of would-be utopians, educational reformers, two artists, a number of children, a hired crew, and the "father of American conchology, entomology, zoology and descriptive entomology." That was Thomas Say. With such distinguished company on board, the keelboat acquired the curious name of the "The Boatload of Knowledge," the claim being that never in America's still early history had so much knowledge been crowded onto one boat. For Thomas Say alone, the name of "Boatload of Knowledge" was correct.

On the crystal clear and very cold morning of December 8, 1825, the "Boatload of Knowledge" shoved off from Pittsburgh. Three days later, they ran hard aground on a sand bar. Unable to budge, the crew and passengers retired to bed and awoke the next morning to find themselves frozen in solid. They were stuck for the next nineteen days.

It sounds like a scene of pure American frontier comedy—a boatload of intellectuals stranded in a river that cared not a fig for theory. But Thomas Say was on board. When both the nominal leaders left the stranded keelboat, Say became captain. He was all the things frontier America was supposed to distrust—a scientist interested in bugs and shells, a gentle fellow of Quaker background, and a man totally indifferent to money. Yet Say took charge of the "Boatload" until the ice broke and then shepherded its human cargo downriver with little incident and great speed.

After guiding the "Boatload" to New Harmony, Say settled down quietly there to get on with his important work, a seven-volume description of American mollusks that he printed himself and had hand colored by the female students of the New Harmony school. He later married one of the young ladies who'd done the coloring. This book was the beginning of American "conchology," just as his earlier works on butterflies published in Philadelphia were the start of American entomology. He also published seminal works on fossils and zoology.

New Harmony, though, was anything but harmonious. The leaders were soon at each other's throats, exchanging vile allegations and eventually lawsuits. Most of the other intellectuals fled but Say stayed on with young wife, his pupils and his mollusks. The Duke of Saxe-Weimar met him there in 1826 and was struck by Say's unworldly demeanor and his blistered hands. Thomas Say died at New Harmony in 1834.

A lot has happened to the Ohio River and its tributaries since Thomas Say's time and most of it not good, at least from the rivers' point of view. I thought this might just be modern ecological nostalgia but in 1830, John James Audubon, retracing by steamer an 1808 flatboat voyage, was astounded at how fast the Ohio he remembered had vanished. "When I think of these times, and call back to my mind the grandeur and beauty of those almost uninhabited shores; when I picture to myself the dense and lofty summits of the forest, that everywhere spread along the hills, and overhung the margins of the stream, unmolested by the axe of the settler... all this grand portion of our Union, instead of being in a state of nature, is now more or less covered with villages, farms, and towns, where the din of hammers and machinery is constantly heard that the woods are fast disappearing under the axe by day, and the first by night—when I remember these extraordinary changes have all taken place in the short period of twenty years, I pause, wonder, and, although I know all to be fact, can scarcely believe its reality."

That change can be measured, thanks to the work of the pioneer naturalists like Thomas Say who described their variety at the dawn of civilization and to modern researchers like Dr. Hoggarth. Without having to put on a pair of waders, I went to the next best place to measure the reality of the change. It's in Columbus at the Ohio State Museum of Biological Diversity. It's not the sort of museum that would interest children but here are specimens of virtually all of the world's

1,000 known freshwater mussels species. They are kept in specially designed wooden cabinets, nestled in foam-padded drawers, row after row, aisle after aisle.

The driving force behind the museum is Dr. David Stansbery, an emeritus zoology professor who is an international guru of freshwater bivalvedom. He is the man everyone consults, his the museum everyone must check. Walking about with his hands buried in the pockets of his white lab coat, Dr. Stansbery showed me around his collection, pulling out tray after tray of seemingly identical mussel shells and pointing out tiny differences in shape that set them apart as species.

We came at last to the oldest specimen in the collection. Dr. Stansbery picked up the small cardboard box in which a shell sat on a cotton pad. It was a *Plethobasus cicatriciosis* and the label says it was collected at the mouth of the Wabash River where it empties into the Ohio in 1829. Once it was a common species in the Ohio River. Today it is only known from a small population in the Tennessee River just below Wilson Dam. I carefully turned the shell over to look at its pearly interior. Written there in the faintest of inks was a number, "10131,"

from the old Moores collection that is the core of this much larger holding. And there it said quite clearly, "From Thos Say." I was holding in my hand a piece of the wild Ohio, the free-flowing Ohio, a river through the Garden of Eden.

That's a staggering thought, almost like stepping backwards from a river's shallows into suddenly deeper water and feeling the strong channel current grab you round the middle. Even in waders on Killbuck Creek, there's a moment of fear. "Hey, be careful," says Michael Hoggarth looking up from examining the 62nd member of the world's last known breeding purple catspaw bed. "You don't want to get that wet."

Many of us have this pernicious notion that mass extinction is something happening Out There, something for dinosaurs in the dim past or rain forests in the near future. Forget the vanishing birds of Polynesia. Forget about the uncounted beetles of the South American rain forests. You can see the face of mass extinction in the American midwest. Across the North American heartland, an entire taxonomic order of endemics is facing its own biodiversity Armageddon. Why, fifty miles from Columbus, Ohio, you can wade right in. 🦅

—John Fleischman

Nature
Notable

Bird Bander Van Camp

Laurel Van Camp was counting and banding Ohio's bald eagles long before they became the conservation movement's poster critter. The raptor's reemergence on Lake Erie's shore started with Van Camp's careful observations and record-keeping back in the late 1940s. His defense of foxes, owls, hawks, and other "wanted" animals, beasts which were shot on sight half a century ago, reformed public opinion on predators.

Without fanfare and fuss, Van Camp banded 48,000 birds over 40 years, and planted thousands of trees in Northwestern Ohio. Although his big hands palmed 140 different kinds of birds, the screech owl was probably his favorite. He banded 4,000 of them, and 600 returned for new rings. He still handled owlets in his 80s, using a ladder to climb trees that he planted five decades earlier.

Another late bloomer, Van Camp became a state game protector in Ottawa County at age 42. He retired 23 years later, then became naturalist-emeritus at Magee Marsh State Wildlife Area. 🦅

—SO

Gone but not forgotten

Species "in memoriam" in Ohio:

PASSENGER PIGEON

Reasons for leaving: Unregulated hunting, habitat loss.

Status: Extinct.

The world's last passenger pigeon, a captive female named Martha, died at the Cincinnati Zoological Gardens on September 1, 1914. A Pike County farm boy reportedly gunned down the final wild bird on March 24, 1900. The passenger pigeon once was North America's most abundant bird. Stories of their immense flocks darkening the sky abound in nineteenth century stories and journals. While visiting Ohio in 1806, ornithologist and artist Alexander Wilson figured a flock he observed to be a mile wide, 240 miles long, and cruising at 60 miles per hour. That's two billion birds, in just one flock. Human gunners filled railroad cars with pigeon carcasses, and a family could gather a week's worth of squab by simply poking a shovel into a flock as it flew over their rooftop. Rapid deforestation along the bird's migratory route also speeded its decline.

CAROLINA PARAKEET

Reasons for leaving: Habitat loss, exterminated as farm pest, hunted for plumage.

Status: A goner.

Four years after the demise of the passenger pigeon, the lone surviving Carolina parakeet, a male, perished, also at the Cincinnati Zoo. In the wild, Carolina parakeets favored mast forests, especially sycamore nuts, and berries. When "civilization" arrived, the colorful bird got hooked on corn and green fruit, thus becoming the target of infuriated farmers. The parakeet's feathers adorned women's hats.

TIMBER WOLF

Reasons for leaving: Extermination policy, habitat loss.

Status: Extirpated (no longer present in Ohio), not a likely candidate for reintroduction.

Pioneers waged full-scale war against this wily livestock predator, and scary nocturnal howler. Back in those days the wolf was the devil incarnate, not the reincarnated noble beast of today. After wolves were blamed for 100 sheep deaths one night in Medina County, some 600 warriors gathered for a wolf hunt on December 24, 1818, an event called the Great Hinckley Massacre. The hunters encircled a township then closed a noose around their quarry, wiping out 300 deer (innocent bystanders), but only 17 wolves. The massacre was merely a prelude to the timber wolf's removal from Ohio.

MOUNTAIN LION

Reasons for leaving: Extermination policy, habitat loss.

Status: Extirpated, and not a likely candidate for reintroduction.

Known as cougar, catamount, wildcat, panther, painter, puma, but called much worse, *Felis concolor* was a threat to livestock and humans, and was eradicated with extreme prejudice by pioneers. Ohio's major zoos feature the beast, and that's as close as it will get to living here again.

PRAIRIE CHICKEN

Reasons for leaving: Someone stole their prairie.

Status: Extirpated.

Prairie chickens were common in Ohio until 1900. Though hunted commercially for dinner tables, the prairie chicken's main threat was the plow which converted its range into cropland.

WOOD BISON

Reasons for leaving: Habitat loss, unregulated hunting.

Status: Extirpated, not a candidate for reintroduction.

WHITEFISH

Reasons for leaving: Pollution, predation by exotic fish.

Status: Recovery possible as Lake Erie cleans up.

IVORY-BILLED WOODPECKER

Reasons for leaving: Habitat loss.

Status: Extirpated, probably extinct.

WAPITI (ELK)

Reasons for leaving: Unregulated hunting, habitat loss.

Status: Extirpated.

Day of the Dog

The Coyote Comes, But Not When We Call

The rustling rolled up the ridge and stuck in my ear like an arrow. I lurched as if poked by an electric prod. Frosty leaves crunched, dead twigs snapped, branches rattled. Whatever it was came charging toward me. Hot, red heartbeats boomed in my throat. I shouldered my shotgun, expecting a deer to spring out any second.

The crescendo quickened, but the racket did not resemble the prancing and thrashing of a fleeing buck on a zigzag course. No, this animal meant business. Suddenly to my right, just 30 yards away, two grayish-brown shadows bolted from the brush: coyotes!

Deer never appeared that day. No matter. The rare encounter with the state's most elusive canine resident was an unexpected gift, like finding five dollars in the pocket of a winter coat. I had heard the coyotes' plaintive, nocturnal howl before, felt their presence, too, and followed their tracks. But it was the first time I had seen them in Ohio, despite thousands of hours outdoors.

For scores of years, coyotes have been hounded by bounty hunters and blasted from pickup trucks. Fact is, I could have shot the "varmints" jogging through the woods; it's perfectly legal. Ohio has an open season on coyotes: no bag limit, no questions asked. But I have no taste for coyote, and it would be bad medicine to massacre a creature so wise, so fit and so much more defiant than me.

Adversity has toughened *Canis latrans* (which means "barking dog"). Not only has the predator survived ongoing holocaust, it has managed to expand its range and increase its population. Their realm now includes 48 states and all of Ohio's 88 counties. A few years ago a female with pups jogged down the runway at Burke Lakefront Airport, a mile or so from downtown Cleveland.

During a two-year span in the late 1980s, Ohio farmers blamed coyotes for 231 sheep kills. The rascals also take piglets, chickens, domesticated cats and dogs, squirrels, chipmunks, muskrats and fawns. But not all coyotes pounce on the innocent; five might pass up an easy meal before one strikes. More often, coyotes are accused of crimes when the true culprits are feral dogs; it is hard to picture Fido going wild, but it happens—often. Feral dogs are three times more likely to attack livestock, says the Ohio Division of Wildlife. Coyotes won't attack humans; wild dogs are another matter.

Novice eyes often confuse coyotes with gray foxes, wolves and dogs. Dogs and fox stride with their tails up (either parallel to the ground or skyward), but a coyote is never that overconfident. He keeps his tail down.

Coyotes are also unpredictable and secretive enough to elude study. Just when a den is found, the family relocates it. Released animals equipped with beeping radio collars have been tracked halfway across the state over a week's time, frustrating wildlife researchers trying to count them. So no one knows how many live in Ohio. They are everywhere and nowhere at the same time.

They are simultaneously scheming, foolish, opportunistic, sneaky, sociable among their own kind, vengeful, suspicious of others and learned. In other words, coyotes are us in canine cloth. And perhaps their most unforgivable sin is their snub of humanity. They avoid us, run from us and refuse to fetch a stick.—*SO*

Comeback Critters

WHITETAILED DEER

This abundant game animal had disappeared from Ohio by 1900, the victim of habitat loss due to agricultural expansion and poor land management. Unrestricted hunting played a lesser role in the ungulate's earlier demise. A successful reintroduction program managed by Ohio Division of Wildlife, coupled with improved habitat, had the deer population at 550,000 in 1996. Ohio has more deer today than 200 years ago.

WILD TURKEY

Loss of forest habitat and unregulated hunting had killed off Ohio's wild turkey by 1904. Restocking began in the 1950s, and today an estimated 120,000 turkeys roam in 72 of Ohio's 88 counties.

BALD EAGLE

The state's population of our national symbol had shrunk to just four breeding couples in 1979. Loss of wetland and shoreline habitat, and pesticide poisoning are blamed for the eagle's decline. Reintroduction programs, such as releasing captive-bred birds into the wild, have eagles soaring over Lake Erie again. The number of active nests has increased from four in 1979 to more than 30 in 1996. Thirty-five eaglets fledged that year. The statewide count in 1998 was a new record—a tally of 149 in mid-January. The bird remains an endangered species in Ohio though nationally its status has been downgraded to "threatened."

BEAVER

Unregulated trapping and draining of wetlands wiped out Ohio's beaver population for a century. Today, nature's "engineer" is busy building in two-thirds of Ohio, numbering more than 14,000. Humans and beavers are the only mammals that alter the environment to suit their purposes.

BLACK BEAR

Ohioans had exterminated black bears by 1850, and nobody expected to see them here again. Since 1981, however, bear sightings have increased in Eastern Ohio, and they have been seen in 36 eastern and south-central counties. The sightings include sows with cubs, indicating a permanent breeding population. The bruins migrated from West Virginia and Pennsylvania. Wildlife officials do not believe Ohio's woodlands will support a large bear population. Consider it an endangered animal in Ohio.

COYOTE

Though small colonies have always survived east of the Mississippi River, coyotes had been concentrated in the arid Western plains until the twentieth century. Their realm now includes 48 states and all of Ohio's 88 counties. They came en masse after wolves, their main canine competitor, were wiped out by the state's human population. Now they spurn humans but live suprisingly close to cities.

BOBCATS

There have been only 23 verified sightings of bobcats in Ohio since 1970. On the positive side, half of those spottings have occurred in the 1990s, raising hope that the poulation of this state endangered feline is increasing. All sightings have been in southeastern Ohio's forested hill country.

BROOK TROUT

Spring Brook in Geauga County may be Ohio's natural hatchery for brook trout, according to the Ohio chapter of the Nature Conservancy. Genetic studies by the U.S. Fish & Wildlife Service, Ohio Department of Natural Resources, and Ohio Environmental Protection Agency indicate that brookies from this spring-fed rill are descendants of ancestors that first appeared here at the end of the Ice Age some 12,000 years ago. These are not hatchery-reared nor transplanted swimmers. In fact, the tests suggest that the strain may be endemic (confined or specialized) to Ohio. Conservation groups, land conservancies, and the Geauga Park District are attempting to protect the stream. Also, a Division of Wildlife purchase of a trout hatchery in Castalia bodes well for the state's slowly resurging trout.

Fauna Fossils

MASTODONS & MAMMOTHS

Everybody has seen an elephant, but how many people know that five to ten thousand years ago and more, during the Ice Age, elephants of extinct types were common wild animals in Ohio? Their skeletal remains have been found in almost every county in the state.

There were actually two different kinds of Ice Age (Pleistocene) elephants: the mastodon and the mammoth. Judging by the number of fossil discoveries, the mastodon was the more common. Fossil remains of about 150 of these tusked megafauna, ancestors of elephants, have been found in the state, where they roamed the unglaciated southeast and fed in spruce forests; they, too, have been extinct for ten millennia. The famous Johnstown mastodon, unearthed in 1926 in Licking County, stands in the Cleveland Museum of Natural History. Recent evidence shows Ohio's first humans hunted and slaughtered mastodons, perhaps contributing to their demise.

The mastodon was the smaller of the two, with a stockier build and a back that was generally horizontal, while the mammoth was taller and had a back that sloped upward to his high, rather pointed head. The biggest difference, however, was in their teeth.

The mastodon's teeth were shaped a little like ours, though they were very much larger. A mammoth's tooth, on the other hand, was like that of a modern elephant. Like their contemporaries, mammoths and mastodons ranged on grasslands and forest edges. Both mastodons and mammoths used only one or two teeth at a time on each side of a jaw. As these teeth became worn down, they rotated upward (or downward) in the jaw, thus keeping a grinding surface in position. As the rotation took place, the teeth were pushed forward in the jaws. Thus, when a tooth was almost all worn away, it was so far forward, as well as up (or down) in the jaw, that it was simply pushed out of the mouth and the next tooth became the major tooth in action. A long-lived animal might lose as many as five teeth from each side of his jaws, both upper and lower, during his life and die with one left in each side. As a result of this unusual dental history, most mammoth and many mastodon finds in Ohio are single teeth. It is possible, in some cases, that several finds of single teeth came from a single animal; most of the Ohio finds, however, are considered to represent separate individuals because of the wide geographic distribution of the discoveries.

MAMMALS

Animals other than the mastodons and mammoths have also been reported from the Ice Age deposits of Ohio. One of the most interesting is the giant beaver, which was like the modern beaver, but two to three times larger. Another unusual animal was the ground sloth, a sloth so large (up to 8 feet tall), that, though his clawed feet were built for hanging upside down in trees like his modern cousins, the tree sloths, he had to walk on the ground, on the outsides of his feet because of his curled toes and claws. Others found in the Ice Age deposits of Ohio include the horse, bison, muskox, deer elk, caribou, peccary, tapir, turtle, muskrat, and some birds.

All of these finds are called fossils. This does not mean that the bones are now petrified, but simply that the animal lived in the geologic past. The majority of the bones found are still composed of bony material, though in many cases, some have been partly dissolved, so that when they are taken out of the ground and allowed to dry, they fall to pieces. As a result, many of the bones discovered need special care in order to be preserved.

—DR. JANE L. FORSYTH

Source: Reprinted with the permission of the Ohio Department of Natural Resrouces from the Ohio Conservation Bulletin

Dunk

Long before dinosaurs there was "Dunk," short for *Dunkleosteus terrelli*, the fiercest creature that ever swam in Ohio waters. Dunk was a bone-plated arthrodire who ruled the Devonian seas 400 million years ago. Though some of these shark-like predators may have reached lengths of 45-50 feet, Dunk averaged five meters from tooth to tail and weighed a ton. It jaws and long, sharp teeth were made for pulverizing crustaceans and ripping carrion. Twenty-two "dunks" have been uncovered from Cleveland shale. A vivid replica of Dunk is suspended from the ceiling in the nature center at Rocky River Reservation, a Cleveland Metropark.

Trilobites

The trouble with trilobites is their rarity. Finding a fossilized version of the ancient arthropod, Ohio's state invertebrate fossil, is a fossil collector's trophy.

Self-taught Ohio trilobite expert and hunter Tom Johnson has found more than 800 trilobites, including the world's largest, a flawless 16-inch specimen unearthed in Montgomery County in the 1970s. Trilobites (genus *Isoletus*) survived in Paleozoic seas for 500 million years ago, then disappeared 225 million years ago. ✒

Source: Ohio Department of Natural Resources, Division of Wildlife, May, 1996

Nonnatives

Endangering Native Species

PURPLE LOOSESTRIFE

Introduction method: Distributed as an ornamental flower.

Looks can be deceiving. This stunning purple blossom has taken over wetlands at the expense of cattails and other plants, some of them imperiled. Its thick colonies cannot provide cover, food, or nesting sites for waterfowl, frogs, turtles, muskrats, and other swamp creatures. It arrived on the East Coast from Europe and Asia in the 1800s and spread along ditches, canals and roads. It spreads rapidly on account of the two million seeds one adult produces each year. Purple loosestrife also has no bitter natural enemies on this continent, but several insects that attack the exotic are being considered.

ZEBRA MUSSEL

Introduction method: Ballast from ocean-going freighters.

Public enemy number one in the Great Lakes was discovered in Lake St. Clair near Detroit in 1988. The fingernail-sized mussel, a native of the Caspian Sea, accumulates in piles, much like a coral reef, on anything it can attach itself, including piers, water intake systems for power plants, rock levees, waste treatment plants, boats—even fish and native mussels. Females make a million eggs a year, each the size of a sand grain. Diving ducks and freshwater drum eat them, but not nearly enough to check the infestation. They threaten to alter the balance of aquatic wildlife in Lake Erie.

ROUND GOBY

Introduction method: Ballast of ocean-going freighters.

Like the zebra mussel, ocean-going freighters probably put this alien fish into the Great Lakes when they flushed ballast. It is a six-inch gray fish with black and brown markings, and a big head that boasts frog-like eyes. Gobies appeared in the St. Clair River in 1990. Right now, the invader does not threaten Lake Erie's sport fishery. Keep your fingers crossed.

RUFFE

Introduction method: Ballast of ocean-going freighters

The ruffe, not to me confused for orange roughy, is a small, spiny member of the perch clan from central and eastern Europe. It surfaced in Duluth harbor in 1985 and quickly spread through the Great Lakes. It seems to be reducing native populations of yellow perch and other forage fish. Like other pests, ruffe has a high reproductive potential (females lay 45,000 to 90,000 eggs annually), a ravenous appetite, and spiny fins that discourage attacks from predators such as walleye and pike.

SPINY WATER FLEA

Introduction method: Ballast of ocean-going freighters.

This tiny crustacean—a spike less than a half inch—may compete with young perch and other small fry for food, namely zooplankton. On a fishing line this Eurasian bugger resembles a tasty glob of yellowish jelly with pepper spots. Small fish cannot swallow its dagger-like body, so the spiny water flea population surges. That could mean less plankton for perch, and fewer perch for Lake Erie anglers. Get the picture?

WHITE PERCH

Introduction method: Erie and Welland canals.

This Atlantic Coast native competes with native species in Lake Erie and may cause a reduction in the Great Lakes walleye fishery.

SEA LAMPREY

Introduction method: Sneaked through the Welland Canal.

Sea lamprey, a predaceous, eel-like creature from the Atlantic coast, is partly responsible for the decline of lake trout and whitefish in the Great Lakes. They sneaked into the inland lakes in 1921 and began their feasting. ✒

STILL TIME TO SAVE

Critters classified endangered, threatened, of special interest (becoming rare), and extirpated (extinct in Ohio).

MAMMALS
Endangered
Indiana myotis (bat), *Myotis sodalis*
Eastern woodrat, *Neotoma floridana*
River otter, *Lutra canadensis*
Bobcat, *Felis rufus*
Black bear, *Ursus americanus*

Special Interest
Pygmy shrew, *Sorax hoyi*
Star-nosed mole, *Condylura cristata*
Southern red-backed vole, *Clethrionomys gapperi*
Woodland jumping mouse, *Napaeozapus insignis*
Badger, *Taxidea taxus*
Ermine, *Mustela erminea*

Extirpated
Snowshoe hare, *Lepus americanus*
Rice rat, *Oryzomys palustria*
Porcupine, *Erethizon dorsatum*
Timber wolf, *Canis lupus*
Marten, *Martes americanus*
Fisher, *Martes pennanti*
Mountain lion, *Felis concolor*
Lynx, *Felis canadensis*
Wapiti, *Cervus canadensis*
Bison, *Bison bison*

BIRDS
Endangered
American bittern, *Botaurus lentiginosus*
Least bittern, *Ixobrychus exillis*
Yellow-crowned night-heron, *Nyctanassa violacea*
Bald eagle, *Haliaeetus leucocephalus*
Northern harrier, *Circus cyaneus*
Peregrine falcon, *Falco peregrinus*
King rail, *Rallus elegans*
Sandhill crane, *Grus canadensis*
Piping plover, *Charadrius melodus*
Common tern, *Sterna hirundo*
Black tern, *Chlidonias niger*
Barn owl, *Tyto aba*
Yellow-bellied sapsucker, *Sphyrapicus varius*
Bewick's wren, *Thyromanes bewickii*
Winter wren, *Troglodytes troglodytes*
Sedge wren, *Cistothorus patensis*
Hermit thrush, *Catharus guttatus*
Loggerhead shrike, *Lanius ludovicianus*
Golden-winged warbler, *Vermivora chrysoptera*
Magnolia warbler, *Dendroica magnolia*
Kirtland's warbler, *Dendroica kirtlandii*
Northern waterthrush, *Seiurus noveboracensis*
Canada warbler, *Wilsonia canadensis*
Lark sparrow, *Chondestes grammacus*
Dark-eyed junco, *Junco hyemalis*
Osprey, *Pandion haliaetus*
Trumpeter swan, *Cygnus buccinator*

Threatened
Upland sandpiper, *Bartramia longicauda*

Special Interest
Snowy egret, *Egretta thula*
Little blue heron, *Egretta caerulea*
Cattle egret, *Bubulcus ibis*
American black duck, *Anas rubripes*
Sharp-shinned hawk, *Accipiter striatus*
Double-crested cormorant, *Phalacrocorax auritus*
Black vulture, *Coragyps attratus*
Red shouldered hawk, *Buteo lineatus*
Virginia rail, *Rallus limicola*
Sora, *Porzana carolina*
Common snipe, *Gallinago gallinago*
Long-eared owl, *Asio otus*
Short-eared owl, *Asio flammeus*
Northern saw-whet owl, *Aegolius acadicus*
Chuck-will's-widow, *Caprimulgus carolinensis*
Purple martin, *Progne subis*
Marsh wren, *Cistothorus palustris*
Henslow's sparrow, *Ammodramus henslowii*

Extirpated
American swallow-tailed kite, *Elanoides forficatus*
Greater prairie chicken, *Tympanuchus cupido*
Ivory-billed woodpecker, *Campephilus principalis**
Common raven, *Coryus corax*
Bachman's sparrow, *Aimophila aestivalis*

REPTILES
Endangered
Copperbelly water snake, *Nerodia erythrogaster neglecta*
Eastern plains garter snake, *Thamnophis radix radix*
Timber rattlesnake, *Crotalus horridus*
Massasauga rattlesnake, *Sistrurus catenatus*

Threatened
Lake Erie water snake, *Nerodia sipedon insularum*
Kirtland's snake, *Clonophis kirtlandii*

Special Interest
Spotted turtle, *Clemmys guttata*
Blanding's turtle, *Emydoidea blandingii*
Coal skink, *Eumeces anthracious*
Black king snake, *Lampropeltis getulus nigra*
Common garter snake (melanistic), *Thamnophis sirtalis*
Rough green snake, *Opheodrys aestivus*
Fox snake, *Elapha vulpina*

AMPHIBIANS
Endangered
Hellbender, *Cryptobranchus alleganiensis*
Blue-spotted salamander, *Ambystoma laterale*
Green salamander, *Aneides aeneus*
Cave salamander, *Eurycea lucifuga*
Eastern spadefoot, *Scaphiopus holbrookii*

Special Interest
Four-toed salamander, *Hemidactylium scutatum*
Mud salamander, *Pseudotriton montanus*

FISHES
Endangered
Ohio lamprey, *Ichthyomyzon bdellium*
Northern brook lamprey, *I. fossor*
Mountain brook lamprey, *I. areeleyi*
Lake sturgeon, *Acipenser fulyescens*
Shovelnose sturgeon, *Scaphirhynchus platorynchus*
Spotted gar, *Lepisosteus ocullatus*
Cisco, *Coregonus artedii*
Tongue-tied minnow, *Exoglossum laruae*
Popeye shiner, *Notropis ariommus*
Bigeye shiner, *N. boops*
Pugnose minnow, *N. emiliae*
Blackchin shiner, *N. heterodon*
Blacknose shiner, *N. heterolepis*
Mississippi silver minnow, *Hybognathus nuchalis*
Blue sucker, *Cycleptus elongatus*
Greater redhorse, *Moxostoma valenciennesi*
Longnose sucker, *Catostomus catostomus*
Blue catfish, *Ictalurus furcatus*
Mountain madtom, *Noturus eleutherus*
Northern madtom, *N. stigmosus*
Scioto madtom, *N. trautmani*
Pirate perch, *Aphredoderus sayanus*
Western banded killifish, *Fundulus diaphanus menona*
Channel darter, *Percina copelandi*
Spotted darter, *Etheostoma maculatum*

Threatened
Silver lamprey, *Ichthyomyzon unicuspis*
Paddlefish, *Polyodon spathula*
Rosyside dace, *Clinostomus funduloides*
Bigmouth shiner, *Notropis dorsalis*
Lakeshub sucker, *Erimyzon sucetta*
River darter, *Percina shumardi*
Bluebreast darter, *Etheostoma camurum*
Tippecanoe darter, *E. tippecanoe*

Special Interest
Shortnose gar, *Lepisosteus platostomus*
Goldeye, *Hipdon alosoides*
Mooneye, *H. tergisus*
Brook trout, *Salvelinus fontinalis*
Lake trout, *S. namaycush*
Lake whitefish, *Coregonus clupeaformis*
Speckled chub, *Hybopsis aestivalis*
River redhorse, *Moxostoma carinatum*
Eastern sand darter, *Ammocrypta pellucida*
Slenderhead darter, *Percina phoxocephala*
Iowa darter, *Eteostoma exile*
Spoonhead sculpin, *Cottus ricei*

Extirpated
Alligator gar, *Lepisosteus spatula*
Pugnose shiner, *Notropis anogenus*
Longhead darter, *Percina macrocephala*
Gilt darter
Crystal darter

CRAYFISHES
Threatened
Sloan's crayfish, *Orconectes sloanii*

Special Interest
Great Lakes Crayfish, *Orconectes propinquus*
Northern crayfish, *O. virillis*

ISOPODS
Special Interest
Caecidotea filicispeluncae
C. rotunda

BUTTERFLIES
Endangered
Persius dusky wing, *Erynnis persius*
Two-spotted skipper, *Euphys bimacula*
Frosted elfin, *Incisalia irus*
Karner blue, *Lycaeides melissa samuelis*
Purplish copper, *Lycaena helloides*
Swamp metalmark, *Calephelis muticum*
Regal fritillary, *Speveria idalia*

Threatened
Silver-bordered fritillary, *Boloria selene*

Special Interest
Grizzled skipper, *Pyrgus centaureae wyandot*
Olympia marblewing, *Euchloe olympia*
Edward's hairstreak, *Satyrium edwardsii*

Extirpated
Mitchell's satyr, *Neonympha mitchellii*
Mustard white, *Pieris napi*

MOTHS
Endangered
Unexpected cycnia, *Cycnia inopinatus*
Graceful underwing, *Catocala gracillis*
Pointed sallow, *Epiglaea apiata*
Spartiniphaga inops
Hypocoena enervata
Papaipema silphii
P. beeriana
Lithophane seiusta
Trichoclea artesta
Tricholita notata
Melanchra assimilis
Ufeus plicatus
Ufeus.satyricus
Erythroecia hebardi

Threatened
Wayward nymph, *Catocala antinympha*
The pink streak, *Fagitan littera*
Spartiniphaga panatela
Faronta rubripennis

Special Interest
Buck moth, *Hemileuca maia*
One-eyed sphinx, *Smerinthus ceriisyi*
Slender clearwing, *Hemaris gracills*
Purple arches, *Polia purpurissata*
Scurfy quaker, *Homorthodes f. furfurata*

Subflava sedge borer moth, *Archanara subflava*
Columbine borer, *Papaipema leucostigma*
Braken borer moth, *P. pterisii*
Osmunda borer moth/ *P. speciosissima*
Goat sallow, *Homoglaea hircina*
Macrochila bivittata
Phalaenostola hanhami
Paectes abrostolella
Capis curvata
Tarachidia binocula

Continued on page 86 ➤

Primitives Ply Our Water

Primitive fish whose ancestors swam around the legs of dinosaurs ply Ohio waters again. In 1996, 22 lake sturgeon were found in Lake Erie. Two years earlier, researchers netted 81 paddlefish in the Ohio River, at its confluence with the Scioto River. The exciting discoveries have prompted more restocking projects and research. Their reemergence also indicates that the quality of water in both hatcheries is improving.

Lake sturgeon are "prehistoric" fish that can grow to seven feet and 300 pounds, and live 100 years. Clad in bony plates on belly and back, sturgeon have sleek shark-like bodies and tails, and four whiskers (barbels) growing from its snout. They look frightening, but don't fret. Sturgeon lack teeth, and don't bite humans.

In 1885 commercial fishermen caught 531,250 pounds of sturgeon from Ohio waters. The filets were smoked and consumed. The eggs from the catch produced 237,155 pounds of caviar, the bladders made 277 pounds of isinglass, a gelatin used for glues and jellies, and the rest squeezed into 6,485 gallons of oil. By the 1920s, sturgeon had become rarities in the Great Lakes. It is an endangered species in Ohio.

The "paddle" of the paddlefish refers to its long, broad, flat snout. It also resembles a shark, although one with an elongated nose. Like the sturgeon, paddlefish numbers sank dramatically in the twentieth century. In 1994, Ohio State University researchers found larval paddlefish in the Meldahl Pool of the Ohio River, the farthest upstream they are known to spawn. Once listed as an endangered species, the paddlefish has been upgraded to a threatened species.

Paddlefish and sturgeon are throwbacks (and if you catch one, do just that!) to the Carboniferous (Pennsylvanian) to early Triassic times, 190-300 million years ago, when so-called Paleoniscoid fish ruled in fresh water. They represent our only links to these ancient animals. If you see either fish, report the location to the Ohio Division of Wildlife, 1-800-WILDLIFE. ⬳

—SO

$l$ooking Forward to Many Happy Returns

Monarch Butterflies

Monarch butterflies are one of nature's most fragile creatures, weighing only one-fiftieth of an ounce. Their wings look like scraps of orange and black silk tossed by the wind. Yet each year these delicate insects undertake one of the most arduous and fascinating journeys in nature. Beginning in late summer, monarchs throughout the northeastern United

The monarch of all it surveys dines on the queen's lace.

States and southern Canada travel up to 1,800 miles to reach their overwintering grounds in the mountains of central Mexico.

Flying at speeds of 10 to 30 miles per hour, the monarchs make this flight in just a few weeks, almost without stopping, according to Eric Metzler, an Ohio Department of Natural Resources' (ODNR) expert on butterflies and moths. Canadian butterflies gather by the millions at Point Pelee, Canada, before crossing the Great Lakes. The first wave of migrants usually reaches Ohio's north shore around the middle of August. Area residents say that some years the butterflies can be seen as far as 20 miles away, flying in orange clouds made up of thousands of butterflies. During migration, hundreds of monarchs can be seen feeding on the red and white clover planted in the "nectaring" field at Sheldon Marsh State Natural Area in Erie County.

As nighttime temperatures drop below 50 degrees-F the butterflies cling to the bark and leaves of the trees, huddling in large "clusters" to conserve body heat. The morning sun warms the wings of the outer layer of butterflies, which then fly away. The insects continue to fly away in layers until the innermost layer leaves the "clustering tree." If the trees are undisturbed by development, the butterflies may use the same trees year after year. Clustering trees are found all over Ohio, but the state parks and nature preserves along the north shore are some of the best areas to see monarchs roosting because of the concentration of butterflies crossing Lake Erie. According to Metzler, one tree may have thousands of butterflies clinging to it. Late afternoon or early evening is the best time to watch the monarchs settle into trees. In the morning, the butterflies take off in waves. Ohio's resident monarchs join the migration, which peaks in early- to mid-September. Stragglers will continue to cross the state until the first killing frost in October.

The butterflies begin to move north into Texas as early as February and reach Ohio in May or June. The northbound migration is less noticeable, Metzler said, because the butterflies filter back in small groups. The butterflies become sexually mature, mate, and die along the way, leaving the next generation to continue the journey north. Some sources say fewer than one percent survive the round trip.

—Jan Fields, Ohio Department of Natural Resources

BUZZARDS

It's not known how long the buzzards have been flying back to Hinckley, located just north of the I-71/271 split, each spring. No one even knows where they are coming back from (guesses range from Hocking Hills to Dade County, Florida). But for more than three decades, the town has made quite a spectacle about the ugly of face (yet soaring with grace) birds. Rokeby, a village along the Muskingum River in Morgan County, also celebrates the vultures return, albeit more modestly than Hinckley.

Each year in Hinckley, on the Sunday after March 15, sky-gazers gather to catch a glimpse of the buzzards flying overhead. While they wait, the crowds gorge themselves on a pancake breakfast whipped up in a local grade school by a host of volunteers.

Legend has it that the timeliness of the buzzards, officially known as turkey vultures, began in 1818 when the Hinckley townspeople decided to hunt down wolves by holding a giant circle hunt. Every available man and boy made a circle around

> *Each year in Hinckley, on the Sunday after March 15, sky-gazers gather to catch a glimpse of the buzzards flying overhead. While they wait, the crowds gorge themselves on a pancake breakfast...*

the woods and began closing in, driving out any animal until it teetered on the edge of a cliff. Then they opened fire. Spoils of this battle resulted in a feast for Hinckley residents and plenty of leftovers. Enter the buzzards, who now wing their way to town every March 15 hoping for a similar buffet, only to be disappointed by the smell of pancakes.

A more scientific explanation for the yearly fly-in might be that buzzards come to Hinckley because the rocky ridges outside of town are filled with caves and crevices that make perfect buzzard nests. As the rocks become more popular with hikers and climbers of the human persuasion, the buzzards have learned to make their homes high atop trees, in hollow logs or even on the ground.

Concerning their promptness, Harvey Webster of the Cleveland Natural History Museum said that the buzzards, as well as most other birds, are sensitive to photoperiods and can track the calendar by judging varying amounts of daylight. He goes on to add that the birds are driven north by their hormones and not any inherent need to impress a bunch of binocular-toting gawkers. The Ides of March is a good average date for the buzzards to arrive and still have time to find suitable nesting areas and a mate. Arriving exactly on the 15th, however, involves a good deal of luck because buzzards are not particularly strong flyers and bad weather or head winds can throw them off schedule.

Which is why it is said that Hinckley's official buzzard spotter spends much of early March looking at the ground, lest he catch a glimpse of an early arrival and spoil all the fun

—James A. Baumann

Apamea mixta
Agroperina lutosa
Chytonix sensilis
Amolita roseola
Brachylomia algens
Protorthodes incincta
Trichosilia manifesta
Euchlaena milnei

BEETLES
Endangered
Pseudanophthalmus krameri
P. ohioensis
Nicrophorus americanus

Special Interest
Cicindela hirticollis
C. ancocisconensis
C. marginipennis
C. cursitans
C. cuprascens
C. macra

MOLLUSKS
Endangered
Fanshell, *Cyprogenia stegaria*
Butterfly, *Ellipsaria lineolata*
Elephant ear, *Elliptio crassidens crassidens*
Purple catspaw, *Epioblasma o. obliquata*
White catspaw, *E. obliquata perobliqua*
Northern riffleshell, *E. torulosa rangiana*
Long solid, *Fusconaia maculata maculata*
Cracking pearly mussel, *Hemistena lata*
Pink mucket, *Lampsilis orbiculata*
Pocketbook, *L. ovata*
Yellow sandshell, *L. teres*
Eastern pond mussel, *Liqumia nasuta*
Washboard, *Megalonaias nervosa*
Hickorynut, *Obovaria olivaria*
Ring pink, *O. retusa*
White wartyback, *Plethobasus cicatricosus*
Orange-footed pearly mussel, *P. cooperianus*
Sheepnose, *P. cyphyus*
Clubshell, *Pleurobama clava*
Ohio pigtoe, *P. cordatum*
Rough pigtoe, *P. plenum*
Pyramid pigtoe, *P. rubrum*
Fat pocketbook, *Potamilus capax*
Rabbit's foot, *Quadrula cylindrica cylindrica*
Winged maple leaf, *Q. fragosa*
Monkeyface, *Q. metanevra*
Wartyback, *Q. nodulata*
Purple lilliput, *Toxolasma lividus*
Rayed bean, *Villosa fabalis*
Little spectacle case, *Villosa lienosa*

Threatened
Snuffbox, *Epioblasma riquetra*

Ebonyshell, *Fusconaia ebena*
Black sand shell, *Ligumia recta*
Three-horn wartyback,
Obliquaria reflexa
Fawn's foot, *Truncilla donaciformis*
Pondhorn, *Uniomerus tetralasmus*

Special Interest
Flat floater, *Anadonta suborbiculata*
Purple wartyback, *Cyclonaias tuberculata*
Wavy-rayed lamp mussel, *Lampsilis fasciola*
Round pig-toe, *Pleurobema sintoxia*
Salamander mussel, *Simpsonaias ambigua*
Deer toe, *Truncilla truncata*

Extirpated
Mucket, *Actinonaias l. ligamentina*
Rock pocketbook, *Arcidens confragosus*
Spectacle case, *Cumberlandia monondonta*
Scale shell, *Leptodea leptodon*
Western sand shell, *Ligumia subrostrata*
Ellipse, *Venustaconcha e. ellipsiformis*

* Possibly extinct

*Ohio entomologist "Battles" last
man-eating cricket. Not!*

White Herons In the Marshes near Port Clinton, Ohio

*n*ature preserves are expressways to the past, umbilical cords to the primeval world that we sometimes long for. They are the repositories of freedom, wildness, chaos, peace, and sanity. They represent the antithesis of regimented life in the city and home.

In the early 1960s, J. Arthur Herrick of Kent State University compiled an inventory of key natural areas for the Ohio Biological Survey. Herrick's list laid the foundation for a state nature preserve network, derived from the passage of the Scenic Rivers Act in 1968 and the Natural Areas Act of 1970. In early 1999, Ohio had 111 state nature preserves and more were in the works.

But what exactly are nature preserves? They are special places where endangered and threatened wildlife find refuge. What they are not are places designed for the human horde. Many preserves offer visitors little more than a hiking trail and a small parking lot. Rest rooms, if they exist, are often primitive. Drinking water, also iffy, may flow from a hand pump. Outdoor activities are limited to the "nonconsumptive" kind, such as hiking, birdwatching, and wildlife observation. Though not described here, more than half of the state's nature preserves are off limits to the public because they protect extremely fragile habitats harboring endangered species.

In nature preserves we begin to restore what Wendell Berry calls "charitable relations between humanity and nature." Here we accept natural processes and biological diversity, a discovery that will help us respect human diversity as well. —*SO*

Unless otherwise noted, further information about preserves can be obtained from the Ohio Department of Natural Resources, Division of Natural Areas and Preserves, 1889 Fountain Square, Building F-1, Columbus, Ohio 43224-1388, (614) 265-6453.
See "County & Metroparks" for state preserves located within parks.

Author's Favorite Preserves

- ◆Blackhand Gorge (*Licking*)
- ◆Clifton Gorge (*Greene*)
- ◆Highland Nature Sanctuary (*Highland*)
- ◆Conkles Hollow (*Hocking*)
- ◆Darby Plains Prairies (*Madison, Union*)
- ◆Eagle Creek (*Portage*)
- ◆Edge of Appalachia Preserves (*Adams*)
- ◆Flint Ridge State Memorial (*Licking*)
- ◆Fort Hill State Memorial (*Highland*)
- ◆Glen Helen Nature Preserve (*Greene*)
- ◆Goll Woods (*Fulton*)
- ◆The Holden Arboretum (*Lake*)
- ◆Lake Katharine (*Jackson*)
- ◆Old Woman Creek (*Huron*)   —SO

Nature Preserves

KEY

ADAMS COUNTY
1. Adams Lake Prairie
2. Caparral Prairie
3. Davis Memorial
4. Ege of Appalachia
5. Johnson Ridge
6. Strait Creek Prairie Bluff (also Pike Co.)
7. Whipple

ALLEN COUNTY
8. Kendrick Woods

ASHLAND COUNTY
9. Clear Fork Gorge

ASHTABULA COUNTY
10. Pallister
11. Pymatuning Crk. Wetlands

ATHENS COUNTY
12. Acadia Cliffs
13. Desonier

BELMON COUNTY
14. Emerald Hills

BUTLER COUNTY
15. Bachelor Game & Wildlife Reserve
16. Hueston Woods (Preble Co.)

CHAMPAIGN COUNTY
17. Cedar Bog
18. Davey Woods
19. Kiser Lake Wetlands
20. Siegenthaler-Kaestner Esker

CLARK COUNTY
21. Crabill Fen
22. Gallagher/Springfield Fen
23. Prairie Road Fen

CLERMONT COUNTY
24. Crooked Run Memorial Sanctuary

CLINTON COUNTY
  25. Culberson

COLUMBIANA COUNTY
  26. Sheep Skin Hollow

CRAWFORD COUNTY
  27. Carmean Woods
  28. Sears Woods

DARKE COUNTY
  29. Drew Woods

DELAWARE COUNTY
  30. Highbanks (also Franklin Co.)
  31. Seymour Woods
  32. Stratford Woods

ERIE COUNTY
  33. Erie Sand Barrens
  34. DuPont Marsh
  35. North Pond
  36. North Shore Alvar
  37. Old Woman Creek
  38. Sheldon Marsh

FAIRFIELD COUNTY
  39. Clear Creek (also Hocking co.)
  40. Christmas Rocks Nature Sanctuary
  41. Pickerington Ponds (also Franklin Co.)
  42. Rhododendron Cove
  43. Shalenberger
  44. Tucker (also Franklin Co.)
  45. Wahkeena

FRANKLIN COUNTY
  See 30. Highbanks (also Delaware Co.)
  46. Gahanna Woods
  See 41. Pickerington Ponds (also Fairfield Co.)
  47. Thomas

FULTON COUNTY
  48. Goll Woods

GREENE COUNTY
  49. Clifton Gorge Nature Sanctuary
  50. Glen Helen Preserve
  51. Travertine Fen
  52. Zimmerman Prairie

HAMILTON COUNTY
  53. Greenbelt
  54. Newberry Wildlife Sanctuary
  55. Sharon Woods Gorge
  56. Spring Beauty Dell
  57. Trillium Trails
  58. Warder-Perkins

HARDIN COUNTY
  59. Lawrence Woods

HARRISON COUNTY
  60. Mud Lake Bog

HIGHLAND COUNTY
  61. Fort Hill State Memorial
  62. Miller Nature Sanctuary
  63. Etawah Woods & Highland Nature Sanctuary

HOCKING COUNTY
  See 39. Clear Creek (also Fairfield Co.)
  64. Conkles Hollow
  65. Crane Hollow
  66. Little Rocky Hollow
  67. Rickbridge
  68. Sheick Hollow

HURON COUNTY
  69. August - Anne Olson

JACKSON COUNTY
  70. Lake Katharine

KNOX COUNTY
  71. Know Woods

LAKE COUNTY
  72. Hach-Otis
  73. Headlands Dunes
  74. Mentor Marsh

LAWRENCE COUNTY
  75. Compass Plant Prairie

LICKING COUNTY
  76. Blackhand Gorge
  77. Cranberry Bog
  78. Dawes Arboretum
  79. Flint Ridge State Memorial
  80. Morris Woods

LOGAN COUNTY
  81. Owens/Liberty Fen

LUCAS COUNTY
  82. Audubon Islands
  83. Campbell
  84. Irwin Prairie
  85. Kitty Todd

MADISON COUNTY
  86. Bigelow Cemetery
  87. Smith Cemetery

MAHONING COUNTY
  88. Kyle Woods

MEDINA COUNTY
  89. Swamp Cottonwood

MERCER COUNTY
  90. Baker Woods

MIAMI COUNTY
  91. Goode Prairie
  92. Greenville Falls

MONROE COUNTY
  93. Rothenbuhler Woods

OTTAWA COUNTY
  94. Lakeside Daisy

PICKAWAY COUNTY
  95. Stage's Pond

PIKE COUNTY
  96. Strait Creek Prairie (also Adams Co.)

PORTAGE COUNTY
  97. Beck, Evans Memorial
  98. Eagle Creek
  99. Flatiron Lake Bog
  100. Frame Lake Fen
  101. Gott Fen
  102. Cooperrider-Kent Bog
  103. Mantua Bog
  104. Marsh Wetlands
  105. Tinker's Creek (also Summit Co.)
  106. Triangle Lake Bog
  107. Tummonds

PREBLE COUNTY
  See 16. Hueston Woods (also Butler Co.)

RICHLAND COUNTY
  108. Fowler Woods

ROSS COUNTY
  109. Betsch Fen

SCIOTO COUNTY
  110. Raven Rock

SENECA COUNTY
  111. Collier
  112. Springville Marsh

SHELBY COUNTY
  113. Gross Memorial Woods

STARK COUNTY
  114. Jackson Bog

SUMMIT COUNTY
  115. Karlo Fen
  116. Portage Lakes Wetland
  See 105. Tinker's Creek (also Portage Co.)

UNION COUNTY
  117. Milford Center Railroad Prairie

WARREN COUNTY
  118. Caesar Creek Gorge
  119. Fort Ancient State Memorial
  120. Halls Creek Woods

WASHINGTON COUNTY
  See 12. Acadia Cliffs (also Athens Co.)
  121. Boord
  122. Ladd natural Bridge

WAYNE COUNTY
  123. Brown's Lake Bog
  124. Johnson Woods

WILLIAMS COUNTY
  125. Mud Lake Bog

NORTHEAST

Brown's Lake Bog Natural Preserve

Here you can clearly see the rings of vegetation that grow around the "eye" of a bog—in this case one of the last unmolested kettle lakes of the Ice Age. Amazingly, this National Natural Landmark was not drained like most of the surrounding land.

LOCATION
Southwestern Wayne County, Clinton Township.

OWNERSHIP
The Ohio Chapter of The Nature Conservancy.

SIZE & DESIGNATION
This 119-acre bog was registered as a National Natural Landmark in April 1967. Dedicated as a scientific state nature preserve in August 1980, it later became an interpretive site.

ACCESS
Starting from downtown Wooster, drive south on SR 3 about eight miles. Turn left (south) on Elyria Road then drive three miles and go right (west) on Brown Road to the small parking lot on the left .8 miles away. Look for the wooden sign.
Trails: There is only one way in and one way out of the bog. That is via a soggy path and boardwalk that travels from the parking lot to the bog and back. The walk to the bog is less than a half mile. The board-

walk splits into a "Y" at the bog.
The boardwalk "floats" on a sphagnum moss mat, which explains why it feels like you are walking on a water bed. While the mat feels strong and elastic its thickness may not be uniform. Do not step off the boardwalk (especially on the branches of the Y) because you may sink knee-deep or higher into the bog. You also may destroy fragile plants. Insect repellent, long pants, long-sleeved shirts, and ball caps are recommended for visits during the warm months.
The larger Brown's Lake, to the southeast, is off limits.
Information: Contact the Ohio Chapter of the Nature Conservancy, 6375 Riverside Drive, Ste. 50, Dublin, OH 43017, (614) 717-2770.

GEOLOGY
The bog (once a pond) and adjacent Brown's Lake are perfect examples of kettle lakes formed during the Ice Age. Thousands of years ago a couple of huge iceberg-sized chunks split from the retreating Wisconsinan glacier. The weight of these ice blocks created depressions. Sediment trapped in the glacier fell around the perimeter of the ice chunk, forming a lake bed which filled with melted water. Carbon 14 radioactive dating has concluded that the lakes were formed 10,000–11,000 years ago.
Scientists believe these particular ice blocks melted slowly, perhaps taking a century, because the ponds are framed by a variety of slightly elevated glacial deposits, such as eskers, kames, drumlins, and moraines. (See Siegenthaler-Kaestner Esker State Nature Preserve.)
The ponds benefited from these formations because they acted as a watershed and isolated them from other wetlands which were later drained or polluted.
The bedrock deep below the surface consists of Mississippian-era sandstone and shale some 320 million years old. The ponds are situated above an ancient valley that drained northward. The glaciers that swept across Ohio buried this waterway.
Precipitation running off higher ground fills the bog. Brown's Lake is likewise replenished but it drains southward into Odell Lake in Holmes County.
Scientists rightfully call the soggy, black soil in the bog, muck (Carlisle muck). It can be 40 inches deep in places, which is another reason for staying on the boardwalk. It also feels rubbery when you walk on it. A type of loam soil known as Alexandria silt has taken the higher ground.

WILDLIFE
If you were a migratory bird, say a Canada goose, flying over the preserve the bog would look like a target with concentric rings of vegetation emanating from a dark brown bulls-eye. The bog shows five distinct plant zones spreading from the

bulls-eye of open water.

The first ring is a dense mat of sphagnum moss, a rootless plant which floats on the water. The moss intertwines and accumulates into a carpet. It appears to rise and sink like a water bed or quake from the slightest disturbance on the water.

Sphagnum moss makes the bog water highly acidic because it takes in minerals from the water and expels hydrogen which combines with other elements to form acid. The dark brown, almost black, color of the water comes from the tannins that leach from dead leaves that hit the bulls-eye.

Plants that grow on the sphagnum moss mat comprise the next zone. Look for flowers like rose pogonia, marsh cinquefoil, and marsh trefoil. The carnivores—pitcher plant and tiny sundew—thrive here because they prefer acidic environments. They get their daily minimum requirement of nitrogen from the insects they trap.

The mat also supports willow, rosemary, cran-

Conserving
Preserves

Preserves Owned by the Ohio Chapter of The Nature Conservancy

NORTHEASTERN OHIO
Arcola Creek, Lake County *, **
Beck Fen, Summit-Portage counties
Brown's Lake Bog *
Crystal Lake, Portage County
Cuyahoga Wetlands (White Pine Bog Forest), Geauga County
Flatiron Lake Bog, Portage County
Herrick Fen, Portage County
Morgan Swamp, Ashtabula County
Stillfork Swamp, Carroll County

NORTHWESTERN OHIO
Kitty Todd Preserve, Lucas County
Bald Knob, Darke County

CENTRAL & SOUTH CENTRAL OHIO
Baker Swamp, Jackson County
Big and Little Darby Creeks, Franklin, Madison, Pickaway counties
— Commercial Point Riffles
— Fox Tract
— Richards Tract
Betsch Fen, Ross County
Edge of Appalachia Preserves, Adams County *, **, ***
Glade Wetland, Jackson County
Keystone Preserve, Jackson County
Strait Creek Prairie Bluff, near

junction of Adams, Pike, Highland counties

SOUTHWESTERN OHIO
Huffman Prairie, Montgomery County*
Redbird Hollow, Hamilton County
Richardson Forest Preserve, Hamilton County *
Withrow Nature Preserve, Hamilton County *, **

SOUTHEASTERN OHIO
Rothenbuhler Woods, Monroe County
Tefft Memorial, Washington County

INFORMATION
Ohio Chapter of The Nature Conservancy
6375 Riverside Drive
Suite 50
Dublin, OH 43017
(614) 717-2770

KEY: *— Managed by a park district
** — Open to public (permit not required)
*** — Joint ownership

berry, leatherleaf, and poison sumac. The roots of these plants spread and connect and have been known to support the weight of adult humans. (Testing this theory in the bog is not advised because people have become entangled in the roots.)

Shrubs like highbush blueberry, winterberry, chokeberry, poison sumac join trees such as alder and various willows on the shoreline, zone three. Behind it stands the swamp forest zone (swamp oak, ash, maples) adorned in the summer in waist-high ferns named royal, cinnamon and interrupted.

Skunk cabbage emerges from the muck of this wet forest in the early spring. Its name comes from the foul odor it dispenses. This member of the arum family can produce heat as high as 70° F, enabling it to melt snow at the surface, bake its own pollen and eggs to maturity quickly, and provide warmth for the bees and flies needed to pollinate the plant. Huge amounts of oxygen are consumed by the plant, and the colder the temperature gets, the more oxygen it uses.

The most distant ring is the mixed hardwood forest of oaks, hickory, maple, and other varieties.

Bogs live on borrowed time. If nature is allowed to pass through its stages, the bog will vanish beneath the hardwood forest. That is not likely to happen soon here. It has taken more than 10,000 years for the glacial kettle pond to become a bog, and an equal number of years may be needed for the forest to complete its task.

Bogs are archives that help scientists track the biological past. Things that fall into them rot very slowly. Some materials, like pollen, don't seem to decompose at all. Their long life lets them build layer upon layer of pollen.

Pollen found in a core sample removed from Brown's Lake Bog revealed several climate changes in the area since the Ice Age. A jack pine forest, similar to one found in Labrador today, thrived here on the heels of the retreating glacier. Elephant-like mastodons, elk, giant beaver, and bear probably resided in the area. A warm period 3,000–5,000 years ago brought prairie plants from the Great Plains, but cooler times later enabled a forest resembling a Northern Michigan woods of white pines, hemlock and oak to develop.

Swarms of airborne dragonflies snag mosquitoes loitering around the rim of the bog. During my visit on a hot, humid evening in June, few mosquitoes attacked me while I examined the bog from the left limb of the "Y." The dragonflies kept the pests away. The mosquitoes returned, however, when I reentered the forest where few dragonflies roamed.

HISTORY

Early white settlers considered this swamp land worthless. The muck, of course, could not be plowed, and nobody dared to graze here for fear of losing livestock in the mud. Timbering was impossible. The clouds of mosquitoes were almost as impenetrable as the undergrowth. And the place harbored bears, rattlesnakes, and wildcats.

Engineers tried but failed to build a road through the bog at the beginning of the century. A hunting and fishing club owned the land for many years. Naturalists exploring the bog before the boardwalk noted the density of the thicket, especially ankle-cutting plants like halberd-leaved tearthumb and stinging nettle, and swarms of mosquitoes.

In 1960 Oliver Diller and John Aughanbaugh published a booklet called *the Flora of Brown's Lake Bog,* listing an amazing constellation of 469 plant species. Their observations, and those of other scientists, heightened interest in preserving the property.

In 1966, The Nature Conservancy bought the site with a loan from the Citizens National Bank of Wooster. The conservation group retired the loan in 1967. The U.S. Department of the Interior listed the preserve as a National Natural Landmark in 1968. A 1980 survey that found the property protected 20 state endangered species prompted the Ohio Department of Natural Resources, Division of Natural Areas and Preserves, to dedicate the place a preserve in September 1980.

JOURNAL

June 19: This preserve is Ohio's Jurassic Park. It truly has a primordial, almost creepy, ambiance in the summer. Ferns reached my waist. Sudden, startling movements by unseen animals in the underbrush suggested beasts lying in ambush. Will I step into an enormous mutant pitcher plant and never be found?

The birdsong is especially melodious, simultaneously rapturous and haunting. The bullfrogs growled like sputtering outboard motors. Several of them advanced toward me. Their speech became bolder with each hop. These giants broke twigs as they approached. I reached the parking lot feeling exhilarated and relieved.

Clear Fork Gorge State Nature Preserve

Some 15,000 years ago a mighty wall of ice reversed the flow of a river and began creating this V-shaped gorge, Ohio's deepest canyon. The gorge is just one of the natural attractions in this scenic region of the state.

LOCATION

Southern Ashland County, Hanover Township.

OWNERSHIP

The state preserve, owned by the Ohio Department of Natural Resources, Division of Natural Area & Preserves, represents a small portion of the gorge. The remainder is held by the Division of Parks and Recreation, and that is the section we will explore.

SIZE & DESIGNATION

Clear Fork Gorge State Natural Preserve is 29 acres and located on the steep south bank of the Mohican river. The gorge can be viewed from trails in Mohican State Park and Mohican Memorial State Forest. The state park encompasses 1,294 acres and five miles of river front, while the state forest comprises 5,109 acres. Clear Fork Gorge was declared a National Natural Landmark by the U.S. Department of the Interior in November 1967.

ACCESS

Exit Interstate 71 at SR 97 and travel east through Bellville and Butler. SR 97 bisects Mohican Memorial State Forest. About a half mile into the forest (past the Memorial Shrine on the right), turn left on CR 939 (look for green park signs pointing to the forest headquarters, fire tower, youth camp, etc.). Immediately you come to a fork and must make a decision. The right fork goes to the state forest fire tower and a loop trail into Clear Fork Gorge State Nature Preserve, a path less than a mile. The left fork winds 1.2 miles to a striking covered bridge that spans the Clear Fork of the Mohican River.

Cross the bridge, turn right and park at the end of the road in the designated area (not the campgrounds). The distance from the interstate to the covered bridge is about 16 miles. Parking is available on the south side of the bridge, too. Trails from the covered bridge visit the gorge, but not the state nature preserve.

Trails: Hike the Hemlock Gorge, Lyons Falls and Pleasant Hill trails for the best views of the gorge. The covered bridge is a good point of departure.

Scenic overlooks offer quick views of the gorge. Winter is the ideal time to observe the formations. The best vista is east of the covered bridge. Retrace your route toward SR 97, but bear left at the fork, traveling past the youth camp and fire tower, and park in the next picnic area on the left. The gorge is extremely steep here, so stay in the designated area. Climbing the slope is dangerous and prohibited. The view from Pleasant Hill Dam is less spectacular but worth a peek if you are headed for Mohican State Park Lodge.

The state preserve is located on a precipitous, and densely wooded slope on the south bank. You must obtain written permission from the Division of Natural Areas and Preserves to visit the site.

Information: Mohican State Park, 3116 SR 3, Loudonville 44842; (419) 994-5125; Mohican Memorial State Forest, 3060 CR 939, Perrysville 44864-9791, (419) 938-6222; or the Division of Natural Areas & Preserves at (614) 265-6543.

GEOLOGY

A geological phenomenon called stream reversal created the beauty of the gorge. Long ago, two rivers originating from the same elevated area flowed in opposite directions. The plateau, in other words, acted like a divide between these two currents.

Around 15,000 years ago the massive wall of the Wisconsinan glacier blocked the flow of the river heading west. A huge lake containing glacial meltwater formed in front of this ice dam. Eventually, the lake water backed up over the divide and poured into the east-flowing river. The stream eroded through the divide, creating the new eastbound channel.

The hourglass shape of the gorge tipped off geologists to the stream reversal theory. Most river valleys widen as they travel downstream. Clear Fork gorge, however, narrows just east of the covered bridge then enlarges again. The divide is located at this pinched point, roughly a half mile downstream from the bridge.

Clear Fork Gorge shows its youth with "V" slopes, rapids, headwater (upstream) erosion, and slump rocks from river bank undercutting. It means the river continues to knife its way through the sandstone and shale bedrock that formed 300 million years ago.

Prominent formations of Blackhand sandstone can be seen in the gorge between the dam and bridge and around Lyons Falls. This thick layer may have been an offshore sand bar protecting part of the vast delta and ocean beach that once stretched for hundreds of miles through what is today eastern Ohio. (See Blackhand Gorge State Nature Preserve.) The marine life thriving in the calm muddy water between the sand bar and delta formed the Wooster shale seen downstream from the bridge.

Waves crashing into the sand bar carried heavier pebbles off the sand bar and deposited them on top of the shale resulting in three distinct strata of conglomerate sandstone. Above them lies a fat layer of Vinton sandstone. The overlook described above is perched on this rock.

WILDLIFE

See if you can find the various microhabitats in the gorge. The cool, shady lower portion of the south bank supports hemlocks and Canadian yew (relicts from the Ice Age) and red maple with a smattering of yellow birch, mountain maple, and black ash. The top is ruled by oaks, pines, and some black cherry and white ash. Just east of the covered bridge, on an eight acre plot, grows one of the last unmolested stands of hemlock and white pine in Ohio.

The sunnier north bank contains a panoply of hardwoods—red and white oaks, tulip tree, beech, maple, and sycamore. In the floodplain look for sycamore, hawthorn, various willows, buckeye, and dogwood.

A sample of the wildflowers includes mountain laurel (ridgetops), trailing arbutus, partridgeberry (uncommon), and some unusual hillsiders named shinleaf, wood lily, rattlesnake plaintain, and round-leaf orchis. Fifteen kinds of fern are found here, notably the rare walking fern.

Reptiles and amphibians are represented by box turtles (abundant), dusky salamanders, toads, black rat snake, and the poisonous copperhead.

Quiet hikers may spot a turkey along the Lyons Falls Trail. During my visit in spring, I spied two great blue herons, plus a kingfisher and an unidentified hawk. Fifteen species of warblers nest in the gorge, particularly the northern parula, hooded, cerulean, and American redstart.

HISTORY

The Delaware Indians settled here, hunting and fishing in the gorge. Some of their famous warriors were Janacake, Bill Montour and Thomas Lyon, who supposedly sought refuge near the waterfalls that bear his name.

The Indians were driven out by white settlers after the War of 1812. John Chapman, better known as Johnny Appleseed, visited here several times to look after his apple orchards. He carved his name in the sandstone wall at Little Lyons Falls, and for a time this graffiti was a tourist attraction. The name has since washed away.

The state began buying land for the state forest in the late 1920s. Pleasant Hill Dam is a flood-control project of the Muskingum Watershed Conservancy District. The impoundment flooded some of the most scenic portions of the gorge.

Clear Fork State Park was created from state forest land in 1949. The name was changed to Mohican State Park in 1966. The U.S. Department of the Interior declared the gorge a National Natural Landmark in 1967.

Eagle Creek State Nature Preserve

Some 12,000 years ago, this spot was shaped by the Wisconsinan glacier and the meltwater that poured from its snout. Today, beavers, once extinct in the area, are Nature's primary movers and shakers in this preserve.

Giant ferns, carnivorous plants, rare salamanders, even flying insects with names like bird-dropping moth and The Bride, are residents. Eagle Creek is a cornucopia and a kaleidoscope of life.

LOCATION

Northeastern Portage County, Nelson Township.

OWNERSHIP

Ohio Department of Nature Resources, Division of Natural Areas and Preserves.

SIZE & DESIGNATION

This 441.3 acre preserve was dedicated on April 18, 1974 as a state interpretive preserve.

ACCESS

From Garrettsville head northeast toward Nelson on Center Road for about 2.5 miles. Then go right (south) one mile on Hopkins Road. The parking lot will be on the right (west) side of Hopkins Road.

From SR 305 in Nelson go south, briefly, on Parkman Road, then almost immediately bear right (southwest) on Center Road, then left (south) on Hopkins Road.

The path from the parking lot across a field leads to the trailhead of two trails. Heading right at this "T" is the 1.5-mile, lasso-shaped Clubmoss Trail. The 2.5-mile Beaver Run Trail branches to the left and journeys to the Beech Ridge Trail, a .75-mile loop.

After heading north, the Clubmoss Trail reaches a fork, the start of its loop. Take the left fork, which traces the shore of a beaver pond and stops at an observation blind, an ideal spot for viewing wildlife. From here, the path continues along the edge of the pond then swings right, and wanders through a new forest and recovering field. A small bog appears on your right just before you reach the start of the loop. Look for skunk cabbage in the bog in late February.

The Beaver Run Trail heads south from the trailhead and stays on high ground as it follows one of the tributaries of Eagle Creek. Notice the swamp to your right as you start. One side trail stemming to the right leads to the mire. Don't attempt to walk across the swamp. Humans were not made for this terrain. Also, this path gets skinny in places. Watch out for roots!

Near the southeast corner of the preserve, the trail turns right (west), crosses two tributaries and Eagle Creek, itself. (The latter stream via a wooden bridge.) Take a breather on the bridge.

Continue ahead to the Beech Ridge Trail, which circles around a small buttonbush pond. Return to civilization via the Beaver Run Trail. This walk on flat, wooded terrain covers about 4.5 miles.

The preserve is open from sunup to sundown everyday. Restrooms and drinking water are not available at this site. Pack a canteen if you plan to hike all the trails. Preserve brochures, with a trail map, are stuffed in a wooden pocket on the bulletin board.

Nature education programs are regularly held at the preserve. Check the schedule at the bulletin board in the parking lot or contact the Ohio Department of Natural Resources.

GEOLOGY

Eagle Creek, once known as Silver Creek, flows off a sandstone escarpment located west and a little north of the preserve. The sandstone dates back some 330 million years, to the Mississippian geological period.

The current runs over this bedrock to just east of Garrettsville, a mile west of the preserve. Here, the creek begins a serpentine route across a wide, flat

Those Damn Beavers

The lustrous, soft, chestnut-colored fur of the beaver inspired European exploration into the interior of North America. Its pelts were highly-prized in Europe and in the New World.

In Ohio, the beaver was gone by 1830, the victim of two centuries of intense trapping and pioneering. Later, a ban on trapping enabled beavers to recolonize eastern Ohio. Today they live in just about every suitable watershed east of I-71 (with some exceptions, of course), and controlled trapping has resumed.

Rookie observers may confuse beavers and muskrats. Beavers have paddles for tails and webbed hind feet while muskrats have long, tapered, rat-like tails and unwebbed feet. These distinction, however, cannot be detected if the animal is swimming.

In their adult stage, beavers are bigger than muskrats, averaging 35 pounds and stretching more than two feet, compared to three pounds and 10 inches for the muskrat. Beavers build intricate dome-shaped lodges of twigs, branches, and mud (though on swift streams they may live along the bank). Muskrats use whatever vegetation is available, usually cattails and grasses.

The beaver's industriousness is famous. A life history on the critter, published by ODNR's Division of Wildlife, says, "Besides man, beaver are perhaps the only mammals able to alter the environment to suit their needs." One amazing beaver dam in Columbiana County measured 1,200 feet, almost a quarter mile. Most dams are much smaller, 50–200 feet long. Sometimes their dams flood cropland, an annoyance to farmers.

All you ever might see of other animals are their tracks. In contrast, the presence of beaver is obvious. Like human construction sites, the beaver's workplace is messy. Look for (1) gnawed and girdled trees with bite-sized wood chips strewn on the ground; (2) neatly clipped branches and sticks stripped of bark, either floating in water or laying beside fallen trees; and (3) grooves or troughs on pond banks where they slide into the water.

Beavers have been known to deforest shorelines of saplings and small trees. Sometimes they tackle huge trees 100 feet or more from shore. They feed at night, dining mainly on the bark and twigs of aspen, poplar, birch, willow, maple, cottonwood, and alder.

This swift swimmer is a cautious and alert plodder on land. To observe them you must move slowly and quietly to their habitat well before dusk and stay motionless in the bushes. If you are detected, they will slap their tail on the surface of the pond, a clap that will echo across the marsh.

—SO

floodplain. It now courses slowly over glacial till, an amalgamation of sand, gravel, silt, clay, and boulders deposited by the Wisconsinan glacier about 12,000 years old.

The abundance of life is indebted to the purity of water in Eagle Creek. After a heavy rain, however, the streams swell and the water becomes turbid with silt. During times of high water the stream may overflow its banks and carve new channels, or temporarily fill old ones. Silt settles in the calmer channels and pools and enriches the floodplain.

The indomitable beaver has influenced the course of Eagle Creek and some of its branches and tributaries. Their dams slow the pace of streams, and create ponds that collect silt and provide a new habitat for waterfowl.

Blocks of ice that split from the retreating glacier formed the small bogs. Till encircled the ice chunks as they sank into the ground. Water melting off the ice filled the depressions, or pools. Precipitation running off the surrounding higher ground refills the bogs.

WILDLIFE

The beaver is not the only celebrity at Eagle Creek. The list of protected plants includes the bug-eating pitcher plant (threatened) and round-leaved sundew (potentially threatened), which both snare insects. Buckbean (threatened), catberry, tawny cottongrass, Virginia chain-fern, long sedge, large cranberry, and grass-pink (the latter all potentially threatened) find refuge in the preserve.

Cottonsedge, common in the arctic tundra, grows here at its southern limit. Winterberry holly, another northerner, likes the sphagnum bogs. Try to find Venus' looking-glass, partridgeberry, yellow fawn lily, cardinal flower, arrow-leaved tearthumb, purple trillium, golden saxifrage, and hawkweed. All totaled, 93 kinds of wildflowers and grasses grow at Eagle Creek.

Ostrich ferns rise to heights of five feet. It is one of 20 ferns (and allies) recorded here. Fern fanciers should search for the crested wood fern. Clubmoss, or creeping pine, is abundant along the Clubmoss Trail. It spreads like a net in the litter layer, the bed of accumulated leaves on the ground.

Don't forget the woody plants—100 varieties en masse. North-facing slopes sponsor the members associated with a beech-maple forest, while the south-facing ridges, warmer and drier, favor the oak community. Less common hardwoods include cucumber magnolia and yellow birch. Basswood (linden), American elm, black maple, white ash, and dogwood fill out the roster.

Eagle Creek protects the blue-spotted (endangered) and four-toed (potentially threatened) salamanders, and the spotted turtle, also potentially threatened.

A survey done by Tom S. Cooperrider of Kent State University in the mid-1970s turned up hundreds of moths and butterflies (lepidoptera) flitting around Eagle Creek. Here are a few. Enjoy their colorful names, as well as their colorful wings:

Galium sphinx—only the second sighting in Ohio at the time; agreeable tiger moth—content when eating dandelion, pigweed; smeared dagger moth—a flying assassin; the herald—winters in caves; old-wife underwing—better than being underfoot; the sweetheart—loves willows and poplars; girlfriend underwing—rubs her boyfriend's antennae in oaks; bird-dropping moth—named for its diet, not what it drops; lost owlet—eats woolgrass when not disoriented; the bride—honeymoons at Eagle Creek; the penitent—repentant smeared dagger moths.

Eagle Creek gets its name from the bald eagle, an endangered bird that may have lived in the swamp at one time. These days, you are much more likely to see geese, ducks, herons, hawks, owls, and songbirds. And you might get a glimpse of deer, raccoon, opossum, skunk, and fox.

HISTORY

The Ohio Chapter of The Nature Conservancy bought 328 acres of this property, much of it cropland, for $36,000 in 1972. The Ohio Department of Natural Resources designated it a scenic preserve on April 19, 1974, but upgraded it to an interpretive preserve on August 29, 1977.

Using federal funds, ODNR purchased the site from the conservancy, plus additional acreage.

JOURNAL

Mid-October: I have trekked every trail but have found no fresh evidence of beavers. That's like going to Disneyland and not seeing Mickey Mouse. Unlike the Disney star who answers every curtain call, the beavers at Eagle Creek can come and go as they please, punch their own clock, and build at their own pace.

Fowler Woods State Nature Preserve

Beeches and maples, a hundred feet tall and a century old, have raised the roof of this shady, old swamp forest. But in the heart of this wildness, in dark and murky waters, an impenetrable buttonbush swamp uses its power to keep the tall timbers at bay.

LOCATION
Northeast Richland County, Butler Township.

OWNERSHIP
Ohio Department of Natural Resources, Division of Natural Areas and Preserves.

SIZE & DESIGNATION

Fowler Woods totals 148 acres. It became an interpretive preserve on May 16, 1973, the first state-designated preserve.

ACCESS

From downtown Mansfield, go north 16 miles on SR 13, then east 1.1 miles on Noble Road, and finally south .2 mile on Olivesburg-Fitchville Road. The parking lot will be on the right.

Trails: Two trails traverse the grounds, and an observation tower, hidden in the trees, overlooks the buttonbush swamp. Total mileage—two miles.

The Beechdrop Trail is a 1.3-mile boardwalk, making it one of the few preserves accessible to disabled visitors.

The 40-foot observation deck stands at the end of a cul-de-sac that extends from Beechdrop Trail. If that is your first destination, go straight (right) from the bulletin board, which stands just beyond the parking lot, and head into the woods. To walk a perimeter, continue on to the Beechdrop Trail, then turn right on the Crataegus Trail.

Built-in benches promote a slower pace and serve as peaceful viewing and listening platforms. Fowler Woods, far from towns and major highways, was a quiet place before a regional landfill became a reality on neighboring property.

GEOLOGY

As you drive here, you'll probably note the flat to gently undulating terrain. This typography was shaped by the Illinoian and Wisconsinan glaciers, the last one covering Ohio about 15,000 years ago.

As they melted, the glaciers left behind a mixture of clay, sand, gravel and rocks called till, which served as the base for soil. This deposit buried valleys, rerouted streams, and gave the land its definition.

One type of glacial formation is an end moraine, marking the spot where the wall of the glacier stalled for awhile and left till piled up in a long ridge. Much of Fowler Woods grows atop the St. John's moraine, a mile-wide, hummocky belt stretching across the northern part of the county. The area explored by the Crataegus Trail, however, lies on a ground moraine, where a finer till has been evenly spread by an advancing glacier. Ground moraines create flatter terrain. Just a mile south of the preserve the Mississinewa end moraine rises.

You will not find extreme topography in the preserve, just little rises and almost imperceptible changes in elevation (30–40 feet). The bedrock 100–150 feet beneath the surface is shale and sandstone made some 330 million years ago during the Mississippian geologic period.

The preserve contains blends of two kinds of soil—the Pewamo-Bennington and Bennington-Cardington types. Pewamo-Bennington soil, high in clay, occupies most of the preserve, except along Noble Road. The dark, poorly-drained Pewamo soil sustains the swamps, with the light-colored Bennington soil on the knolls and ridges. Cardington

soils are found on a few slopes.

WILDLIFE

Spring brings wave after wave of wildflowers, blossoming on nature's ingenious staggered schedule. Almost 200 varieties have been counted, notably marsh marigold, golden saxifrage, watercress, and yellow water crowfoot. Look for the beechdrop (hence the name of the trail) rising from the roots of beech trees from August to October. Dwarf ginseng, unusual in Ohio, thrives here in thick communities. Gifted nature-lovers, though, will search for these miracles: yellow fawn lily, stitchwork, henbit, common cleavers, king devil, enchanter's nightshade, and moonseed vine.

Now turn to ferns. Last count, sixteen varieties covered the forest floor.

American beech and sugar maple dominate the scene, sinking their roots on higher ground. Some of these giants are two centuries old. Ash and red maple have spread out in the poorly-drained swamp forest. An amazing assortment of trees and shrubs flourish here, 58 kinds, including four species of oak, and three types of dogwood and ash. Fowler Woods is the only state preserve protecting a grove of balm-of-Gilead, a rare poplar whose offspring sprout from roots.

About 80 acres of the 133-acre preserve is forested, with 50 acres classified as mature. The rest is former farm land in the various vegetative stages of reverting to a forest, a process called natural succession.

The forest abounds with common furry critters and popular songbirds and warblers. Sharp eyes might spot a red-tailed, sharp-shinned (potentially threatened), or Cooper's hawk. At dusk, listen for the hoot of a barred owl. Turkey vultures, commonly seen circling overhead during the day, may roost in the tall beeches in the evening.

A good birding spot is the observation tower overlooking the buttonbush swamp. From this podium, you can conduct the revelry of spring peepers and chorus frogs (two of eight species of frogs and toads) whose song echoes through the preserve.

In the good old days of the 19th century, Fowler Woods boasted a great blue heron rookery of 150 nests, one of the biggest nesting areas in the state. Unfortunately, the birds abandoned the site many years ago.

The place also once overflowed with massasauga rattlesnakes, but these also have disappeared. Eight kinds of snakes live there now, such as the rare northern copperbelly (not to be confused with the poisonous copperhead).

Four kinds of woodland salamanders have found a rich life in the woods. The giant among them is the spotted salamander, which can grow to seven inches.

HISTORY

Clouds of mosquitoes and swampy terrain have kept Fowler Woods safe from human development. It is the only place left in the region to remind us of the immense forest that greeted the first humans.

Though much of the surrounding area had been settled, these woods were not claimed until August 1832 when John Dobbin bought the tract from the government. The deed carried President Andrew Jackson's signature. For many decades the intersection of Noble and Olivesburg-Fitchville roads was known as Dobbin's Corners.

Chester and Hettie Fowler acquired the farm in 1917, and lived there until 1962. They left 50 acres of the woods untouched, the section referred to as the old growth forest, and resisted several lucrative bids from lumber companies. In 1970 the Fowlers asked ODNR forester Jack Basinger to examine the woods. Basinger recommended that the forest be preserved, so in 1971 the state bought the farm from the Fowler family. ODNR dedicated the site as an interpretive preserve on May 16, 1973, the first state nature preserve.

Though Fowler Woods has avoided the ax it might not miss the cutting odor of rotting garbage thanks to a 280-acre regional landfill right next door to the preserve.

JOURNAL

May 13: Imagine a landfill beside this ancient woods. Trees trimmed with litter clinging to their limbs. Bird nests made from coffee stirrers, dental floss, and tissue. The roar and gas fumes of bulldozers and dump trucks. I see dust rising from the tires of these earth shakers and coating the autumn leaves of sugar maples, changing their bright, translucent orange hue into a chalky pastel. Instead of smelling the fresh salad scent of the forest, the fart of human plunder will taint the air.

I went back into the woods, closed my eyes beneath a beech, and dreamed I was in the Modern Museum of Art in New York City surrounded by the masterpieces of impressionist painters. When I removed the roof and walls of the gallery, the clamor, dirt and distractions of Manhattan rushed in to ruin the dream.

Fowler Woods is a living museum and a sacred place. Its roof and walls have been the silent open spaces that surround it. The landfill will pierce these walls and raise the roof. It cannot remain blessed unless it remains whole. Our ancestors did not encounter the stench of garbage, hills of refuse, nor clouds of dust when they entered this domain. Nor should we.

Frame Lake Fen—J. Arthur Herrick State Nature Preserve

A Nature Conservancy naturalist called this preserve a "mosaic of wetland com-munities." Indeed, a rare tamarack fen, a cattail pond, a lake, and a moist sedge meadow are all bunched together in this sanctuary. Some of Ohio's rarest plants and animals reside here. Oddly, acid-loving flora sprout from hummocks right beside plants that thrive in the alkaline water that trickles from mounds of dirt deposited by a glacier.

LOCATION

Western Portage County, Streetsboro Township.

OWNERSHIP

The preserve is owned jointly by Kent State University and the Ohio Chapter of The Nature Conservancy. The conservancy manages the site.

SIZE & DESIGNATION

The preserve encompasses 137 acres. Some 110 acres has been designated an interpretive preserve by the Ohio Department of Natural Resources, Division of Natural Areas and Preserves.

ACCESS

From Streetsboro head south on SR 43. A quarter mile south of the intersection of SR 43 and SR 303, go right 2.2 miles on Seasons Road. Just beyond a railroad crossing, turn left on a gravel road that serves as the northern boundary of the preserve. Pull into the small parking lot on the right. From Kent, go north on Hudson Road, left (west) on Ravenna Road, and right (north) on Seasons Road. Leave the RV at home because it might sink deep into the sod of this small, sloped, sometimes soggy parking lot. Motorists should inspect the lot before parking, and drive slowly at the narrow bridge just before the preserve.

Trails: A trail leads from the parking lot across a meadow to the marsh that surrounds Frame Lake. The path continues east and loops around a beech-maple forest in the northeast corner of the preserve. Backtrack from the start of the loop to return to the parking lot.

A boardwalk covers part of the trail, but expect wet, muddy shoes because the path is soggy most of the year. Please stay on the path! Summertime visitors should expect swarms of mosquitoes.

Information: The Nature Conservancy schedules field trips to the preserve. Contact the Ohio Chapter of The Nature Conservancy, 6375 Riverside Drive, Ste. 50, Dublin, OH 43017, (614) 717-2770.

GEOLOGY

The preserve lies atop an ancient river valley buried by till, a mixture of unsorted gravel, sand, silt, and clay, dumped by the Wisconsinan ice sheet about 12,000 years ago. The hills are called kames, which formed when till poured through a hole on the top of the glacier like sand through an hourglass.

Water bleeding from the base of the kames created the fen that wraps Frame Lake. Since groundwater is not affected by sun or wind its temperature stays constant, around 54° F. The kames contain limestone (calcite) deposits, which accounts for the alkalinity of the water.

Fens are spring-fed wetlands that flush, or flow. Water leaves this fen through a natural outlet that flows toward the parking lot. (See Cedar Bog State Nature Preserve to learn more about a fen.)

Frame Lake and the small ponds or bogs scattered throughout the wetland are man-made, constructed by previous property owners.

WILDLIFE

The tamarack, or American larch, is a rare and potentially threatened plant in Ohio. It is a common resident in the northern woods of Canada, but in northern Ohio it lives at the extreme southern edge of its natural range.

Like hemlocks and arbor vitae, tamaracks probably marched south in the vanguard of the Wisconsinan glacier. Although the glacier eventually withdrew, a few clusters of tamaracks stayed behind, having found suitable cool habitats. The tree likes an open wetland where it will not be crowded out by encroaching maples or black ash.

Unlike pines and spruces, a tamarack (also a conifer) drops its needles in autumn. A tamarack's cones (thumbnail-sized) and needles (rarely more than an inch) are smaller than those of the European larch, a non-native tree more widely distributed.

Various sedges (marsh grasses) took root in the marly water, along with sphagnum moss, a spongy moss that spread as the fen matured. As it accumulated, the moss built acidic hummocks that attracted round-leaved sundew (potentially threatened) and large cranberry. These acid-loving plants also share the fen with alder-leaved buckthorn (growing in thickets) and shrubby cinquefoil. Both seek alkaline soils.

A healthy stand of wild calla, a potentially endangered member of the arum family, thrives in a bog in the northeast corner of the preserve. The endangered bayberry survives here at the western edge of its range. Pioneers boiled the berries, then skimmed the wax that floated to the top of the kettle for candles.

The wetland is a paradise for the spotted turtle and four-toed salamander (both potentially threatened), as well as the smooth green snake, a rarity. You might see muskrat lodges among the cattails, but the animals themselves are reclusive. Waterfowl—notably Canada geese, wood ducks, and mallards—head for the lake.

HISTORY

J. Arthur Herrick was one of the founders of the modern nature preservation movement in Ohio. For 16 years, beginning in 1958, Herrick, a biologist at Kent State University, compiled lists of natural areas for the Ohio Biological Survey.

Herrick's 1965 inventory included 212 areas. It grew to 580 sites in 1974. Most of the areas are now protected.

Frame Lake, located a few miles north of the KSU campus, was one of Herrick's favorite sites. He persuaded the university and conservancy to buy the land from H.C. Frame.

Frame purchased the place in 1940, and sometime in the early 1950s deepened and enlarged an existing man-made pond to create a lake for waterfowl.

Hach-Otis State Nature Preserve

A trail meanders through a land of giants—100-foot tall oaks, beeches, maples, and hemlocks, all of them surpassing two centuries of life on Earth. The mammoth tulip trees are all straight as a board. Their limbs branch far above any human's reach, none lower than 50 feet from the ground. Suddenly the land opens to a commanding view—a living diorama. Slithering below, like a mud-colored snake, the Chagrin River slides along its tortured, wrinkled, and gouged riverbank littered with fallen trees, boulders, and some errantly tossed beer cans. Looking deep and faraway, other clay-packed bluffs trace the zigzag course of this eternal reptile.

LOCATION

Western Lake County, Willoughby Township.

OWNERSHIP

The Cleveland Audubon Society owns the preserve but the Ohio Department of Natural Resources, Division of Natural Areas and Preserves manages it.

SIZE & DESIGNATION

The 80-acre site was designated an interpretive nature preserve on July 1, 1977. Audubon members call it a sanctuary.

ACCESS

From I-90, exit at SR 91 and travel south .8 miles to US 6. Take US 6 east 1.2 miles, then go north on SR 174 just a few hundred feet to Skyline Drive, which deadends at the preserve's parking lot in .3 miles.

Trails: Two loop trails branch from a boardwalk that originates in the parking lot. One footpath explores the north half of the preserve (to the left), while the other, slightly longer path, curls to the south.

Both trails travel on relatively flat terrain through the tall trees, along the edge of ravines, and to the bluffs overlooking the river. A stairway assists hikers across one ravine on the South Trail, the most challenging of the paths.

Warning! The rim of the cliff, composed of clay and loose soil, is unstable, especially in late winter thaws and after heavy rains. Do not lean on the "loose tooth" trees whose exposed roots dangle over the rim. They could fall into the valley with you clinging to the roots. Climbing the riverbank is perilous and prohibited.

The parking lot will accommodate 28 autos, so there's plenty of room for the RV. Toilets and picnic tables will not be found here. A bulletin board at the trailhead describes the preserve.

Special Places & Events: Hach-Otis is open every day from sunup to sundown. Nature programs on wildflowers, trees, and other topics are held here by Audubon members and ODNR naturalists.

GEOLOGY

The Chagrin River is re-excavating a valley that was entombed by the debris (clay, sand, boulders, etc.) of the last continental ice mass, the Wisconsinan glacier. Meltwater flowing off the retreating glacier (roughly 12,000 years ago) took the path of least resistance, in this case the ancient river system. Since then, it has been eating away the glacial gravel and underlying bedrock.

The 150-foot bluff smiles on a gallery that reveals the erosive energy and artistry of the Chagrin River. The current already has swept away the glacial spread of sandy, gritty topsoil and the thick layer of clay beneath it. The flaky, blue-gray bedrock underneath the clay is Chagrin Shale, a product of the Devonian period some 350–370 million years old. This rock, once the bed of a shallow and murky sea, appears in thin-plated layers and erodes rather easily, too. (The shale disappears beneath the bluff midway around the bend).

Precipitation assists the arching arm of the Cha-

grin. Rain and melting snow make the bluff more unstable by undermining the lip and carving gullies enroute to the river. Each year a little more of the bluff falls into the river.

Notice how tributaries also have cut steep V-shaped ravines into the riverbank. These smaller and intermittent streams break down the bluff from other angles.

All of these activities show a tortured landscape along the slope of the bluff. Mudslides, gaping gullies, turret-like detached columns, and knife-edged ridges of turf balancing a tree or two are characteristic of the terrain. Trees entangled like pickup sticks block the mouths of the ravines.

The bluff at Hach-Otis preserve faces east, at the bottom of a horseshoe-shaped bend in the river. Trace the course of the river upstream and downstream, and see that more bluffs, looking in other directions, rise in the distance. Directly across the river, however, the land is flat and occupied by homes. Some residences rest on stilts because the lowland is washed by floodwater.

Someday, perhaps, an enraged Chagrin River will carve a new channel across the points at the top of the horseshoe. The current below the bluff would then become a mere trickle, or a pond, or a marsh, or a dried up, abandoned river channel. Speculation, of course, but possible.

WILDLIFE

Except for coltsfoot and a few weeds, not much grows on the harsh, unsettled slope of the river bluff. Behind the precipice, though, resides a luxuriant forest of husky beeches, sugar maples, oaks, tulip trees, and hemlocks, the latter hiding in the shady and cool ravines. Many of these giant specimens rise 100 feet, well above the canopy of the understory trees.

Astute observers can detect the hand of man in this mature woodland. The forest was last timbered in the 1870s, and the few remaining stumps attest to the size of those fallen trees. The veterans mentioned above mostly grow near the ravines—a landscape too difficult for the lumberjacks.

Many sugar maples were tapped for their sap in the 1920s. Some of the aged beeches near the rim of the bluff still show the initials and blazes (trail signs) of pioneer trappers.

John Lillich of Willoughby Hills, an Audubon member and the local expert on the sanctuary, once counted 36 different kinds of warblers in the sanctuary (and he doesn't consider himself a devoted birder). During the spring migration these boisterous beauties accumulate in the ravines and wait for the wind blowing from Lake Erie to subside before continuing their flight to Canada.

Birders should be at the east-facing bluff at sunrise, says Lillich, because many species like to bask in the early morning sun. You may see barred and great horned owls, sharp-shinned hawks (potentially threatened), kingfishers, and pileated woodpeckers (who feast on ants).

As you might imagine, wildflowers put on quite

a show. See if you can spot red trillium (toadshade), squirrel corn, wild leek, trailing arbutus, jack-in-the-pulpit, foam flower, partridgeberry (an evergreen shrub), fringed gentian (potentially threatened) and Wood's hellebore, a threatened species. Squawroot, a scaly, pine cone-like parasite that rises above the roots of the red oak, populates the floor in great numbers in early June.

On scheduled night hikes during a full moon, Lillich often takes his charges to see a luminous fungus called foxfire.

Another character to spot is the mourning cloak, a butterfly with purplish-black wings fringed with blue dots and yellow lace. In June, look for the male sunning himself on a fallen log or tree limb. He may begin a spiralling courtship flight to the treetops. At that altitude he folds his wings and dives back to his perch and waits for a mate.

Most mourning cloaks hibernate during the winter, though some may migrate. They may leave their cozy quarters on balmy winter days. This popular bug may be the longest living butterfly in its adult stage—10 months.

HISTORY

Back in the 1940s, Mr. & Mrs. Edward Hach, longtime members of the Burroughs Nature Club, decided they did not want the cherished woodlot on their farm to fall into the wrong hands. So, in 1944 they gave 26 acres to the Cleveland Bird Club, the predecessor of the Cleveland Audubon Society. The sanctuary has been open to the public since 1944.

A few years later, C.W. Shipman, a naturalist who participated in the Hach transaction, persuaded Harrison G. Otis to sell about 55 acres of his Beech Hills Farm to Harold T. Clark. The local philanthropist (Clark) then donated the property to the bird club, completing the dimensions of the sanctuary.

The Ohio Department of Natural Resources dedicated the site as an interpretive preserve on June 23, 1977.

Headlands Dunes State Nature Preserve

Headland Dunes is the beach we all dream about—tall, windswept sand dunes, grasses rustling in the sea breeze, shorebirds tiptoeing at the edge of a wave. It is all that we have left of an ocean shoreline, which long ago edged into the heartland of North America. Today, Headland Dunes is the last and best beach resort in Ohio—for wildlife.

LOCATION

Lake County, Painesville Township. Ownership Ohio Department of Natural Resources, Division of Natural Area and Preserves.

SIZE & DESIGNATION

Headlands Dunes is a 25-acre ecological research preserve, dedicated on May 13, 1976.

ACCESS

The preserve is located at the east end of Headlands Beach State Park. From SR 2, travel north on SR 44, which ends at the state park entrance. Turn right and drive to the easternmost end of the parking lot and park near the beach. To the right of a park concession and bathhouse look for the sign designating the entrance to the preserve. Near this sign is another marking the northern terminus of the Buckeye Trail. There are several paths. Follow the one with the interpretive sign.

The preserve is open daily during daylight hours. Drinking water, rest rooms, and picnic grounds are available at the state park. Please observe the preserve from the beach (defined below) or along paths originating from the parking lot.

From the state park, you can reach the preserve by simply walking east along the shore toward the lighthouse.

Please do not walk across the fragile dunes, or make new paths. Sunbathing, picnicking, and recreation activities are prohibited in the preserve (essentially the dunes and grassy area behind them). Pursue those activities at the longest, and best state park beach in Ohio.

Trails: A few unmarked paths (not really trails) wander through the preserve. Officially, these paths are off limits, but visitors unknowingly follow them anyway. Walk lightly and in single file if you take these paths.

The pier roughly marks the east boundary of the preserve. And if you have hiked to the pier you might as well explore the Coast Guard lighthouse. Children will enjoy this little adventure and challenge. Two cautions: the rocks are uneven; and don't become a statistic by diving from the lighthouse where the currents are unpredictable.

GEOLOGY

Around 12,000 years ago, this beach was part of the Atlantic seacoast. At that time the mile-high Wisconsinan glacier rested north of the Lake Erie shoreline. Its weight caused the land to sink. Northeast of here a lobe of the ice mass held back the ocean. However, when this ice dike broke saltwater rushed through the St. Lawrence valley and filled the basin. The new body of water was called the St. Lawrence Sea.

It did not take long for Atlantic seacoast plants to colonize the beach of this new sea. Eventually, though, the glacier melted and the land rebounded, probably around 10,000 years ago. The sea went out the same way it came in—through the St. Lawrence valley—and left its coastal plants to fend for themselves on the shore of a freshwater sea.

Natural shaping of the Lake Erie shoreline by wind and waves was interrupted in 1827 when the federal government built piers at Fairport Harbor, at the mouth of the Grand River. The piers acted as big sand traps. Sand transported on eastbound currents parallel to the shore (longshore currents) got caught by the west pier and enlarged the beach. Today's shoreline, west of the pier and lighthouse, is a half mile farther into Lake Erie than its 1827 position. The breakwater will continue to "beach" sand until the shoreline reaches its tip.

Ecologically speaking, the beach is located between open water and sand dunes. It changes daily due to the forces of waves, currents, wind, and humans.

Scientists have divided the beach into three zones. The wet, packed sand constantly washed by waves is the lower beach. Human footprints left on the lower beach are well-defined and provide clues about the size, age, gait, direction, and pace of the walker until they are erased by a wave. The middle beach remains undisturbed until a thunderstorm rolls waves upon it. The sand here is dry and loose; footprints lose their shape and speak fewer truths. Only the severest storms touch the third zone of a beach where the sand is looser, and finer than the middle zone, and probably warmer. Your feet sink in this sand. The footprint is a mere depression.

The line of debris that has washed upon the shore marks the end of the boundary between beach and dune, between two habitats.

WILDLIFE

Science puts things into categories, and makes distinctions. Dunes are no exception. Like beaches, dunes have zones; the foredune, interdunal, secondary, and backdunes.

The foredune, or primary zone, located just above the drift line (debris), is inhospitable, and rather desert-like. Only plants that can tolerate scorching sun, dry wind, blowing sand, and arid, infertile soil survive here.

Species like beach grass and beach pea (isolated from the Atlantic shore), switchgrass, winged pigweed, sand dropseed, purple sand grass, and wild bean will be the first squatters on the foredune. Characteristically, these plants have deep-spreading roots (perhaps 20 feet into the soil), succulent (sacs) stems or leaves, leathery textures, and leaves that curl or fold to retain moisture. They trap blowing sand, and thus build up the dune. The grasses grow skyward quickly (several feet high) ensuring they are not buried by the sand they capture.

These pioneers stabilize the dune, provide some shade, and enrich the soil when they die. They set the stage for poison ivy, grape vines, and wafer ash (a shrub).

Canada wild-rye, and wild bean, plants uncommon in northeastern Ohio grow thickly here. Western xerophytes (varieties used to dry habitats such as clammy weed, four-o'clock, winged pigweed, sand dropseed) have staked their easternmost range at Headlands Dunes. And other Atlantic coast species—sea rocket, seaside spurge, purple sand grass—recall the ancient salty sea that once bathed this shore.

Typically, the interdunal area behind the foredune is a marsh, followed by secondary dunes and backdunes. Eventually, willow, cottonwood and black oak move into the back zones.

Other creatures live in the dunes. Fowler's toad, one of only two toad species native to Ohio, hops around here. You will see them in great numbers near the interdunal ponds during the spring breeding frenzy. In early June, the little buggers leave the water and head for the woods.

In good years, monarch butterflies flock to the beach. Like many waterfowl, these migrants rest and refuel on the dunes before venturing across Lake Erie.

HISTORY

Not many sandy beaches and dunes existed along Lake Erie's southern shore, between Sandusky Bay and Dunkirk, New York, when white settlers began to colonize the Great Lakes. After nearly two centuries of "beach improvements" only a handful of these precious habitats survive. Headlands Dunes is one of the last. Mentor Headlands, west of the preserve, has a small beach-dune community.

The effort to save the dunes from "beach improvement" became more urgent when scientists discovered its plants live isolated from their kin on the Atlantic coast.

Jackson Bog State Nature Preserve

This tiny wetland, a slim relict of the Ice Age, safeguards 23 rare plants and one protected reptile. One rarity, the carnivorous pitcher plant, prefers acidic bogs, but here, and in only one other place in Ohio, it thrives in an alkaline fen. Jackson Bog also may be the only place in Ohio where the hooded ladies' tresses still survives.

LOCATION

Northwestern Stark County, Jackson Township.

OWNERSHIP

Jackson Bog is the property of the Jackson Local School District. The site is managed by the Ohio Department of Natural Resources, Division of Natural Areas and Preserves.

SIZE & DESIGNATION

This 6-acre fen became an interpretive nature preserve on December 12, 1980.

ACCESS

From Canton, go about eight miles northwest on SR 687. A half mile west of the intersection with SR 241, turn into a driveway to the Jackson Township community park and the offices of the Jackson Local Board of Education. Follow signs to the new recreation facility and park the car on the left side of the parking lot.

Trails: Two routes to the bog are now open. Face the playground in the park. To your left, at the bottom of a slope, you will find a path along the edge of the mowed park. Follow this path a few hundred yards, past a natural pool, to the wooden signs at the entrance of the preserve. Ignore, for now, the trail to the right.

The journey is hardly a mile-long walk with two small swells to ascend. In fact, the walk through the preserve is so short you are apt to ask yourself, "Is that all there is?" Force yourself to travel slowly and to study details.

You can also explore the trails through the community park west of the preserve. Those trails, as you face the preserve entrance sign, are to your right.

A longer path to the preserve begins at the edge of the woods beyond the picnic shelter in the park. In the second small picnic area along this trail (marked by a tall white oak), take the trail that bears left down the ridge.

GEOLOGY

Try to imagine two enormous lobes of a continental glacier draped like a stage curtain over northeastern Ohio some 14,000 years ago. Jackson Bog is tucked right in the crotch of these looping lobes.

For decades, torrents of water carried tons of gravel and sand to the edge of these melting lobes. Here the sediment in the meltwater, called till, poured into holes, pits, and crevices at the front of the stationary glacier (like sand falling in an hourglass). When the ice finally disappeared the till formed mounds and conical-shaped hills called kames. The bumpy terrain in the Akron–Canton area is a broad band of glacial kames.

Water melting off the retreating glacier kept the ground saturated. The newly deposited gravel deposits showed an amazing capacity to retain water in underground aquifers. Jackson Bog is situated right where this groundwater surfaces as a spring, in this case at the base of a kame.

Actually, Jackson Bog is a fen, which is a spring-fed wetland, usually with alkaline soil. Water in a fen flows, though imperceptibly. In contrast, precipitation recharges a bog, and water leaves by evaporation.

The water that seeps into Jackson "Fen" is alkaline because the gravel it passes through before surfacing contains limestone. As the groundwater percolates through the gravel it dissolves some of the limey substances in the limestone and becomes enriched with calcium and magnesium bicarbonates. At the surface, calcium carbonate precipitates (separates from water) and makes an ash-colored mud called marl.

The rain and snow that permeate through the glacial gravel replenishes the aquifer, which, in turn, feeds the fen. Prolonged drought, pollution of the aquifer, or further human development could disrupt this natural cycle and ruin the fen environment.

WILDLIFE

During the Ice Age, plants that typically grew in Canadian bogs colonized this cool, wet area. Temperatures warmed after glaciation and plants from southern climes (the ones we commonly see today) gradually replaced the northern (boreal) vegetation. However, in a few pockets of suitable habitat some northern bog plants held on. One of these microhabitats is Jackson Bog.

A fen is a rather difficult environment for plants. Few plants can flourish in high alkaline (pH 8–9) soil, plus the spring water is always cool (54°F) and low in oxygen. Scientists called these inhospitable characteristics "limiting factors." The limiting factors in the preserve resemble those found in a glacial environment.

This fen is subtly divided into vegetation zones, defined by their proximity to the alkaline seeps.

The open marl zone lies closest to the springs and only tough low-growing sedges and grasses seem to thrive there. Some specialized plants flourish, notably false asphodel (potentially threatened), round-leaved sundew (potentially threatened), pitcher plant (threatened), grass-of-Parnassus, and Kalm's lobelia. Supposedly, Ohio's largest pitcher plant patch persists in this preserve. The flower usually dwells in an acidic environment.

The sedge-meadow zone, farther from the springs, has developed a thin layer of sedge peat that supports taller plants and shrubby cinquefoil, a common shrub in a fen. The peat layer seems to float or quake.

As the sedge peat accumulates, a shrub-meadow zone develops. It is farthest from the spring and appears to be a transition area between fen and shrub-swamp habitats. This zone has clusters of tall shrubs like alder, willow, poison sumac, and dogwood, with a few elms or red maples.

The preserve may be the only Ohio home for the hooded ladies' tresses. That species, plus another rarity living here called the small purple foxglove, are endangered plants.

Other protected plants sinking roots include threatened species like the round-fruited pinweed, highbush-cranberry, flat-leaved bladderwort, and variegated scouring-rush; and potentially threatened species such as tall manna-grass, tufted hairgrass, Baltic rush, small fringed gentian, long-beaked and autumn willows, Leggett's pinweed, marsh arrow grass, and six sedges (little yellow, twig-rush, Crawe's, yellow, fen, prairie).

HISTORY

The wetland has been known as Stewart Bog, Kettle Lake Bog, and Timken Bog, depending on the property owner. In 1975 Jackson Township unveiled a master plan for a park near the wetland. This prompted the ODNR and others to protect the fen. In 1980, the Division of Natural Areas and Preserves dedicated less than six acres of Jackson Bog as an interpretive preserve.

Johnson Woods State Nature Preserve

Clela Johnson could have lived high off the hog, anywhere in the world. But she didn't have the heart to squander the woods her late husband held so dear. Not even for the million dollars loggers offered for her ancient white oaks. Most of us aren't sorry at all. What she did was give one of the biggest and healthiest old-growth forest in Ohio to the people of Ohio.

LOCATION

Northeastern Wayne County, Baughman Township.

OWNERSHIP

Ohio Department of Natural Resources, Division of Natural Areas and Preserves.

SIZE & DESIGNATION

This interpretive preserve is 206 acres.

ACCESS

From Orrville, head north on SR 57 four miles then turn east (right) on Fox Lake Road. Slow down at the thicket of tall trees and park in the lot on the north side of the road.

Trails: A 1.5-mile, double-loop boardwalk trail winds through the Big Woods, starting across the road from the parking lot. The boardwalk is made of a composite from recycled plastic and wood. Visiting hours are dawn to dusk.

GEOLOGY

The woods grows on flat, swampy ground drained by a rill that joins Little Chippewa Creek, a tributary of the Tuscarawas River. Granite boulders from Canada, known as erratics, tell of a glacier's gentle pawing here 12,000 years ago.

WILDLIFE

Big trees preside over this pristine place. The celebrated white oaks, most three or four centuries old, rise 100 feet and higher. Their trunks expand to three or four feet in diameter, and their posture stays perfectly straight and branchless for more than half their heavenward journey. Here, too, grow swamp oaks, red oaks, American beeches, sugar maples, and shagbark hickories of similar proportions, the latter with bark peels the size of toboggans. Before it fell, a 154-foot pignut hickory at the southern edge was Ohio's tallest tree. Thirty years ago a tulip here had a 30-foot girth. The current state recordholder has a circumference just shy of 22 feet. Wild black cherry, ironwood, yellow birch, elderberry, and others stand in the understory. Together, 35 varieties of trees inhabit the woods.

In 1959, Dr. C.V. Riley, a biologist at Kent State University, "discovered" the forest, then known as Graber Woods, for the Ohio Biological Survey at Ohio State University. The woods' fame grew when Dr. Emma Lucy Braun, Ohio's preeminent botanist and ecologist at the time, called it a "virgin white oak forest" edging towards a "mesophytic" (mixed species) stand in her 1964 classic Deciduous Forests of Eastern North America. Her recondite depiction still prevails, though a few detractors have characterized the spot as a beech-sugar maple forest.

Perspicacious observers might see the struggle between the veteran oaks and hickories and the upstart beech-maple tide. The invaders have the edge because they can thrive in the shade, whereas an infant oak cannot. Beeches even grow defiantly from stumps of putrefied oaks. With two types of mature forests intermingling, Johnson Woods may be at its peak in diversity.

Though just a shred of the former seamless, primeval forest, Johnson Woods is substantial enough to behave like an organism. The size makes it less vulnerable to severe storms and disease. It's packed with woodland birds—wood thrush, pileated woodpecker, scarlet tanager, Acadian flycatcher, ovenbird, and warblers. In the 1990s scientists from the Smithsonian Institution studied the nesting success of the preserve's forest birds.

Buttonbush swamp communities have developed in clearings. Spring and summer brings an ejaculation of wildflowers like trout lily, spring beauty, rue anemone, monkeyflower, partridgeberry, coltsfoot, cardinal flower, anise root, cut-leaved toothwort, hairy Solomon's seal, aster, ragwort, watercress, mayapple, and others. Ginseng is present along with ferns called rattlesnake and lady. Flabby moss entombs pillars of rotting oaks.

Squirrels, raccoons, fox, and deer rate this a paradise, judging by their abundant tracks.

HISTORY

Jacob Conrad found a lush, unbroken forest when he arrived here from France in 1823. We can only guess why he didn't clear this woodlot. Maybe it was too wet and wild to farm, which was Andrew Johnson's theory. Maybe he kept it for hunting, barn lumber, or "banked" it for timber cash in case of lean times. Whatever his reasons, they made sense.

Luck has played a role in saving this forest, too. Its owners have been frugal, hardworking folks, wise land managers and, consequently, better off than many people. The Grabers (Conrad's successors) struggled through the Depression, and the Johnsons raised nine children; both families were able to resist shedding the oaks.

Andrew Johnson died in January 1994. Clela Johnson fulfilled her husband's wish in November 1994 by donating 155 acres to the state, and selling 51 acres on the north side of the road. The boardwalk trail replaced a muddy path in 1997.

JOURNAL

August: Descriptions like "natural cathedral" and "majestic forest" and "precious jewel" apply here; so do "poison ivy jungle," and "mosquito market." The virulent pests are just doing their part in the web of life—the part that drives humans crazy. Jillions of the tiny kamikazes dove into my children and me on our hike. Although we've learned to take precautions (and to endure them), a few penetrate our defense. There's a lesson in that, too. Just when I feel secure, nature always bites me in the buttocks, puts me back in line, reminds me that I am merely a fragile fiber in its immortal web. Suffering the mosquito's sting and the ivy's itch are as necessary for long-term human fitness as grief, triumph and boredom, I tell myself.

Near the trail's end I paused beside an oak and let my charges sprint to the car ahead of pursuing swarms of bugs. The mosquitos drilling my chin and cheek remind me of my part in the world—the part that must leave this place alone, for its sake and mine.

Kyle (Arthur) Woods State Nature Preserve

Except for maple sugaring, this hardwood forest, a remnant of the original Ohio woods, has hardly been disturbed by humans since the turn of the century.

LOCATION
Central Mahoning County, Canfield Township.

OWNERSHIP
Ohio Department of Natural Resources, Division of Natural Areas and Preserves.

SIZE & DESIGNATION
This 81.9-acre woodlot was dedicated as an interpretive nature preserve on May 14, 1983.

ACCESS
Kyle Woods borders the eastbound lane of the Ohio Turnpike, but you cannot get to the preserve from this four-laner. Instead, exit SR 11 at US 224 (Canfield). Go east on US 224 (Boardman-Canfield Road) a little more than three miles, then turn right (south) on Tippecanoe Road at a traffic light. Just beyond the spot where the Ohio Turnpike passes overhead, turn right and take your first left, a driveway that climbs to the preserve parking lot.

Trails: The mile-long, lasso-shaped Sugarbush Trail that visits a meadow and mature forest begins at the parking lot. Sections of the woods remain swampy year-round, so wear appropriate footwear. Rest rooms and drinking water are not available at this site.

Special Places & Events: Loghurst Farms, once part of the Kyle estate, is located next to the preserve. This Western Reserve Historical Society site is open to the public from Memorial Day through October.

Information: Call (330) 533-4330 or the Western Reserve Historical Society at (216) 721-5722.

GEOLOGY
This lush forest grows atop a thick layer of glacial till, a salad of sand, gravel, boulders, silt, and clay. The Wisconsinan ice mass deposited the dirt when it scoured this landscape about 12,000 years ago.

The preserve lies on flat terrain above the Mill Creek Valley. The tiny rills that trickle from the site fill tributaries of Mill Creek, which joins the Mahoning River in Youngstown.

WILDLIFE
The Ohio Department of Natural Resources says the "Big Woods" part of the preserve is "representative of the original forest in Mahoning County." In other words, Kyle Woods is about the best forest you are going to find in this heavily-populated, highly industrialized county. Supposedly the "Big Woods" has hardly been disturbed since the mid-19th century, and not at all since 1903 (except for tapping maples for syrup).

Though American beech and several members of the maple clan dominate the scene, some 25 types of trees actually thrive here, making the preserve a more complex habitat than it seems. Some sources call this woods a mixed mesophytic forest because of the diversity of species.

The preserve also protects sizable specimens of tulip tree, cucumber magnolia, wild black cherry, black gum, ash, white and red oak, sourgum, and shagbark hickory. Apple trees also grow in the meadow.

Spring begins with the joys of large-flowered trillium, spring beauties, Solomon's seal, trout lilies, and others. The striking pale green-yellow blossoms of the cucumber magnolia tree open in May-June, but the scent of these beauties can be foul. Just as attractive (if you are open-minded), are the tree's scaly, dark red cones, seen August to October.

The meadows brighten with wildflowers, especially asters, goldenrod, milkweed, thistle, and berry patches attract birds. Here, in late summer, you might catch a buck deer polishing his new antlers by rubbing them against the trunk of a sapling. He has hundreds to choose from for the task. Another meadow inhabitant, the eastern bluebird may streak by, its blue flight contrasting with an overcast sky.

Fox, fox squirrel, deer, opossum, and raccoon are among the forest dwellers. Great horned owls and red-tailed hawks nest in the tall trees. The usual cast of warblers occupies the canopy in the spring. When the tree canopy closes in late spring and shades the woods in a greenish tint, you are more apt to hear these songbirds than see them.

HISTORY

In 1803, Conrad Neff built a sturdy stagecoach inn on this site using black walnut logs from the forest. The inn became a stopover on the Cleveland-to-Pittsburgh road. Later, Jacob Barnes, an abolitionist, bought the place. It became a "station," an inn of sorts, on the Underground Railroad, a network of safehouses for runaway slaves seeking freedom before the Civil War.

Arthur Kyle purchased the log house in 1903. Though he farmed much of the property, the "Big Woods" was left alone, except for the late winter extraction of maple syrup. This activity continued into the 1950s, and relics of the sugarhouse can still be seen in the woods by keen observers. The northwest corner of the preserve was farmed until the 1970s.

In February 1977, about the time sap begins to flow in the sugarbush, Miss Josephine Kyle, a retired physical education teacher, donated 53 acres of "Loghurst Farm" to the Ohio Department of Natural Resources, in memory of her father. She gave the family's log home, the oldest and largest structure of its kind in the area, to the Western Reserve Historical Society in 1978. The historical site is open for visitors during the warm months.

Kyle Woods preserve opened to the public in October, 1981, but was not formerly dedicated until May 14, 1983. With the help of the Ohio Chapter of The Nature Conservancy ODNR purchased an additional 29 acres.

Marsh Wetlands State Nature Preserve

Let's face it. You've got to love swamps to come here. It's no place for humans. I could not shake the uneasy feeling that a dozen pair of eyes observed my every footfall. This trackless, dense, and impenetrable swamp filters water headed for the Cuyahoga River, and shelters an abundance of plants and animals. It is the realm of the noble beaver, and creatures that live in the murky waters.

LOCATION

Northern Portage County, within the Mantua city limits.

OWNERSHIP

Ohio Department of Natural Resources, Division of Wildlife.

SIZE & DESIGNATION

Marsh Wetland totaling 152 acres, is open to the public. Though managed by the Division of Wildlife, hunting and trapping are prohibited in the preserve, because it is in the city limits of Mantua.

ACCESS

Take SR 44, which links the county seats of Chardon (Geauga County) and Ravenna (Portage County) and bisects Mantua. At the traffic light in Mantua, go east on High Street. Just past a large brick structure, the Mantua Service Department, look for a mowed field on the right. A buried tile over a ditch serves as the driveway. Drive into the field and park near the wooden sign at the edge of the grass. If you drive to the crossroads with Peck Road, you have gone about 100 yards too far.

Marsh Wetlands often is mistaken for Mantua Bog State Nature Preserve. The two preserves are neighbors. Marsh Wetlands lies at the southwestern corner of the intersection of High Street and Peck Road, while Mantua Bog is located in the southeastern corner. Mantua Bog, a National Natural Landmark, can be visited only with written permission from the Division of Natural Areas and Preserves.

Trails: Frankly, only come here if you have no other place to go, or if you want to seek a special wetland habitat. Trails have not been constructed in Marsh Wetlands. You can venture along the northern edge of the swamp on an elevated, abandoned railroad bed, serving as a bike-hike trail. Head west, parallel to High Street, toward the center of Mantua.

I recommend side trips off the rail bed for closer views of the wetland. Wear rubber boots and pants to safeguard against water, bugs, and briars. Look for gaps in the thickets and follow deer trails. The rail bed will serve as the route of a bike and hike trail (and petroleum pipeline).

You can follow the railroad bed all the way to a park in Mantua and back to the car for a mile or so ramble. Or wander into the marsh via the Cuyahoga River (upper portion), which is a state scenic river.

GEOLOGY & WILDLIFE

In this area the Cuyahoga River flows over flat to rolling terrain and washes glacial till (sand, gravel, silt, boulders) deposited here 12,000 years ago by the Wisconsinan glacier.

The wetlands that flank the river on its journey through Mantua provide refuge for many rare and protected plants and animals. Beavers have built numerous lodges in Marsh Wetlands Preserve. Waterfowl, reptiles, snakes, muskrats, are common. Tracks indicate the presence of whitetailed deer and raccoons.

ODNR has yet to conduct an indepth plant and animal survey of this preserve.

Mentor Marsh State Nature Preserve

Once a lake bed then a river channel, Mentor Marsh thrives as one of the last freshwater marshes in northeastern Ohio. Soggy soil and dense plant life have kept humans out of this wetland. Now it serves as a perfect home for a wide assortment of swamp creatures.

LOCATION

Lake County, City of Mentor.

OWNERSHIP

Mentor Marsh is jointly owned and managed by the Ohio Department of Natural Resources, Division of Natural Areas and Preserves, and the Cleveland Museum of Natural History.

SIZE & DESIGNATION

This swamp-forest encompasses 646.5 acres. It has been designated a state interpretive nature preserve, Ohio's first, and is a National Natural Landmark, designated by the U.S. Department of the Interior in 1964.

ACCESS

Exit SR 2 at SR 44 and travel north toward Lake Erie. SR 44, which forms the eastern boundary of the preserve, ends at Headlands Drive, the northeast boundary. SR 283 roughly forms the southern boundary. Corduroy Road, off SR 283, crosses the marsh and takes visitors to the Marsh House, the preserve's visitor center.

Trails: Hiking is permitted on four trails during daylight hours. Trail maps can be found beside the parking lot. The longest and most challenging trail, the two-mile Zimmerman Trail, runs from a parking lot on Headland Drive (west of SR 44) to another parking lot at the end of Rosemary Lane (Morton Park) in Mentor. It follows the path of the ancient river, first southerly then westerly, passing through hardwood stands, around hummocks, and along the edge of the marsh. It crosses shallow ravines and rills. Portions of the path could be flooded.

The one-third mile, boardwalked Wake Robin Trail goes straight into the marsh from a parking lot on Woodbridge Drive. This path will keep you dry and take you deep into the marsh. A few paces west, also on Woodbridge Drive, is the Carl and Mary Newhous Overlook, a paved path just one-tenth of a mile long. Folks in wheelchairs or pushing strollers might fancy this view.

The Kerven Trail starts at Marsh House, the nature center on Corduroy Road. This .75-mile lasso-shaped trail leads through a forest and a field and traces the south shore of the marsh. Portions of this trail also can be soggy.

Special Places & Events: Nature programs are held for groups by appointment.

Information: About nature programs, contact the Mentor Marsh Nature Center, 5185 Corduroy Road, Mentor, Ohio 44060, (440) 563-9344.

GEOLOGY

Just within the last 12,000 years or so, this area has been a lake bed, a dry plain, a river, and now a marsh. A marsh is a wetland found beside a large lake or an ocean, usually with lagoons wide enough for a canoe and featuring many plant and animal habitats.

About 10,000–12,000 years back, east of here, an enormous dam of ice blocked melting Wisconsinan glacier water from escaping through the Niagara-St. Lawrence valleys. The water backed up behind this ice dike and formed Lake Warren, whose shoreline was 100 feet higher that Lake Erie's. (US 20 in Northeastern Ohio follows the beach ridges of this ancient lake.)

One day the ice dam collapsed and Lake Warren drained into the Atlantic Ocean, leaving the Mentor area high and dry. Now comes the Grand River. The current starts in the high ground (the Allegheny Plateau) to the east, then heads across a flat lake plain, curling, bending, and snaking its way to Lake Erie.

Back then, Lake Erie drew its shoreline farther north. The Grand River meandered in the flatlands close to that shoreline. At present-day Fairport, the river S-hooked west, then south for a mile, and west again for three miles through a neck to Lake Erie. Gradually, wind and waves eroded the shoreline southward, choking the neck and river mouth. Meanwhile, the big west-to-south riverbend near Fairport kept eroding the bank northward, toward the approaching lakeshore.

Nobody knows exactly when, but one day (before white settlement) the riverbank at the big bend collapsed, either run over by a flood, or beaten down by waves during a violent storm. In either case, the Grand River had a new outlet to Lake Erie.

The abandoned river channel filled with silt and sediment from decaying plants, and evolved into a lush marsh abounding with plants and animals preferring an aquatic environment. Black Brook and Heisley Creek, former tributaries to the Grand River, freshen the marsh. Though plugged at the surface, water from the marsh still seeps westward through sand into the lake.

WILDLIFE

The mask of the marsh has changed several times since the rerouting of the Grand River. Had it been left alone, the marsh might have been a woods today.

Shortly after its abandonment, submerged plants (the stringy weeds that stick to oars and paddles), water lilies, and water lotus moved into the shallows. The ruins of these plants and the silt they collected set the stage for cattails, bulrushes, and sedges (grasslike plants), which grew inward from the shore and shrunk the ponds. This is probably how the marsh looked in the 1850s when disappointed settlers reported that the area lacked trees.

Meanwhile, buttonbush, alder, and willow took root in the soggy soil at the edge of the marsh. Then elm, ash, red maple and pin oak—the swamp forest trees—colonized the old river banks and marched into the swamp itself. By the 1950s, only a small pool of the open marsh had not been overwhelmed by the trees. The natural process that transforms a wetland into a woods was on the road to completion.

However, in the late 1950s, the forest beside Black Brook began to die. Soon, some 225 acres of forest had been wiped out and cattails made a comeback. Naturalists discovered that pollution (run-off) from a nearby salt mine, and higher Lake Erie water levels killed the forest. The stumps protruding above the water like funereal statuary remind us of the former woodland.

The saltier water enabled the long-stemmed plume grass, which reaches heights of 10 feet, to become the dominate marsh flora. Beavers colonized the marsh in 1973. Their dams raised the water level, choking a red maple-pin oak community along the northeast shore. A few clusters of these trees survive on higher ground.

Buttonbush, alder, and black willow continue to thrive near open water in the northeast section. On the old river banks look for beech and sugar maple. A small mixed oak swamp forest,

uncommon in the Lake Erie region, still exists along the eastern border of the preserve.

The marsh is a bird-admirers' paradise. Some 200 different kinds of birds—both permanent residents and migratory species—have been counted at Mentor Marsh. Expert birders might record as many 125 species during peak days of the spring and fall migrations. You are more apt to hear some birds than to see them, so thick is the vegetation and so shy the birds. These recluses include the long-billed marsh wren, and the Virginia and king rails.

Migratory waterfowl such as ducks, coots, teals, and gallinules feast in the calm, shallow water, while geese and others dine in deeper channels. Great blue herons tiptoe on the edges for frogs and small fry. The dead stumps mentioned above serve as homes for bluebirds, wood ducks, red-headed woodpeckers, and the prothonotary warbler. Bitterns, killdeer, and varieties of shorebirds also can be seen. And everywhere, red-winged blackbirds perch on cattails while marsh wrens scurry among the reeds. Swallows perform their aerial acrobatics above the pond. Northern harriers (marsh hawk) and an occasional osprey fly in higher patterns over the preserve.

And what would a swamp be without snakes—queen, ribbon, and northern water snake—but none are poisonous. Spring peepers and bullfrogs share their melodies. Careful observers might see a mink, red fox, weasel, raccoon, or opossum on an evening food binge. The dome-shaped dwellings of cattails and grass belong to muskrats, sometimes seen near trails.

HISTORY

In the 1930s, Charles Shipman, a chemist, advocated saving the marsh and nearby Headlands Beach. Shipman's message laid the groundwork for the 1951 state purchase of 125 acres for Headlands Beach State Park. A portion of this acquisition included a tip of the marsh (Shipman Pond) and was dedicated Shipman Wildlife Memorial in 1956.

In the early 1960s, local conservation groups hooked up with the Cleveland Museum of Natural History and the Ohio Chapter of The Nature Conservancy (TNC) to block plans for a boating and water skiing park at the site.

In 1965 the Morton Salt Company gave the state surface rights to 320 acres, followed by a 90-acre donation by Diamond-Shamrock Company. Later, the local Mentor Marsh Committee and TNC bought 80 acres of swamp forest targeted for logging.

The Cleveland Museum of Natural History later became custodian of this "living museum." Daily management of the preserve is the bailiwick of the Mentor Marsh Committee.

Mentor Marsh was one of the nation's first National Natural Landmarks, a designation granted by the U.S. Department of the Interior in 1964. On May 10, 1973 the marsh became a state nature preserve.

North Kingsville Sand Barrens

The chilly waves of ancient Lake Warren once rinsed this sand ridge. Today, Lake Erie's shore is a half mile away, but the dune remains a secret garden for a bouquet of imperiled plants, and home for an endangered songbird and some rare beetles.

LOCATION

Northeastern Ashtabula County, Kingsville Township. From I-90 travel north on SR 193 to US 20. Follow US 20 east, then turn north (left) on Poore Road. The preserve is on the left side (westside) of Poore Road just across the Conrail railroad tracks.

OWNERSHIP

Cleveland Museum of Natural History

SIZE & DESIGNATION

118 acres

ACCESS

The preserve is open daily fron dawn to dusk. For information contact the Cleveland Museum of Natural History, Natural Areas Division, 1 Wade Oval Drive, Cleveland, OH 44106, phone (216) 231-4600.

GEOLOGY

Go back 12,000 years when the Wisconsinan ice mass was parked a dozen or so miles north of here. Picture an inland sea, called Lake Warren, swelling in front of the glacier with its southern shore, beaches, and dunes farther inland than Lake Erie's current coast. The sand ridge in this preserve marked the shore of old Lake Warren. The big pond shrunk to Lake Erie's current dimensions after an ice lobe

More Preserves

Preserves Owned by the Cleveland Museum of Natural History (2,679.7 acres)

ASHTABULA COUNTY
Blakeslee-Barrows Preserve, 132 acres

Cathedral Woods, 15 acres

Grand River Terraces, 546 acres

Kolff Riffle, 50 acres

North Kingsville Sand Barrens, 118 acres (open to public)

Pymatuning Creek Fen, 215 acres

ERIE COUNTY
(all on Kelleys Island, 116.5 acres)

Coleman Tract

The Glade

Long Point Preserve

Scheele Preserve

Sweet Valley Preserve

Woodford Woods

GEAUGA COUNTY
Fern Lake Bog, 14.5 acres

Koelliker Fen, 13.6 acres

Soubusta Woods, 59 acres

HOCKING COUNTY
Joyce Preserve, 300 acres

LAKE COUNTY
Mentor Marsh, 691 acres (open to public)

Cottonwood Hollow, 30.6 acres

MEDINA COUNTY
Medina Sanctuary, 33.5 acres

TRUMBULL COUNTY
Groves Woods, 155 acres

Chamberlin Woods, 110 acres

Contact: The Cleveland Museum of Natural History
1 Wade Oval Drive, University Circle
Cleveland, Ohio 44106-1767 (216) 231-4600 or toll free (800) 317-9155
TTY: use Ohio Relay Service, +1 (800) 750-0750 "email to:info@cmnh.org"

blocking the Niagara-St. Lawrence drainage melted. That left the shore of Lake Warren high and dry. (Also see Erie Sand Dunes State Nature Preserve.)

Museum botanists discovered the significance of the site while cataloging the county's sand barrens in 1986. They dubbed it an oak savanna, a rare habitat in northeastern Ohio. Subsequent trips confirmed that small-flowered primrose, southern hairy panic-grass, and bluebeard lily, all endangered plants, colonized the ridge, along with the imperiled racemed milkwort, pale green panic-grass, and a flourishing settlement of wild lupine. Other prairie progeny thrive here, such as wild pea, and various goldenrods and asters. Botanists figure the periodic fires ignited by railroad sparks abetted the survival of the prairie patch.

The north side of the preserve has a dark swamp forest with hardwoods, hemlocks, and rare blossoms called yellow clintonia (known to exist in only two other locations in Ohio), and showy orchis. Here you will find the slender striped maple, an endangered tree in Ohio, distingushed by vertical white stripes on its bark. The swamp also supports red salamanders, and skunk cabbage, a late winter-early spring bloomer known for its fetid odor. The "barrens" is the only known site in Ohio of a moss named bug-on-a-stick.

Harry Lee Jr., the museum's "beetle" man and a self-taught entomologist, found rare beetles called dry-adapted, darkling, and ground (Xestonotus lugubris) in the preserve, along with unusual bees and wasps. These invertebrates will be closely monitored to gauge the impact of preservation efforts.

Birders may spot a white-throated sparrow because the preserve is the only known nesting location for the species in Ohio. Keep eyes peeled for the grasshopper sparrow, another rarity.

HISTORY

The museum purchased half the site, formerly owned by Jacoba Fisk, in December 1990. Three years later William C. McCoy donated 50 acres, followed by an eight-acre donation by Ron Kister in 1998.

Portage Lakes Wetland State Nature Preserve

Just south of Akron, amidst wall-to-wall suburbia, a speck of Ohio's post-glacial natural history survives.

LOCATION

Southern Summit County, Coventry Township.

OWNERSHIP

Ohio Department of Natural Resources, Divi-

sion of Natural Areas and Preserves.

SIZE & DESIGNATION

This interpretive preserve is only six acres.

ACCESS

From I-277/US 224, go south on SR 93, east (left) on Portage Lakes Drive (CR 75) one mile. Park at the Kiwanis Senior Center.

Trails: Put on high boots to tramp around in this wet, shrubby site. Follow your instincts, for trails are missing at this triangular-shaped parcel.

GEOLOGY

Here, another iceberg calved from the backpedaling Wisconsinan glacier 12,000 years ago. The ice melted into a self-made depression, became a kettle pond, then a bog as vegetation and sediment encroached. This is a spring-fed wetland. The rest is natural history.

WILDLIFE

Portage Lakes Wetland is a tall shrub-carr sphagnum bog sprinkled with speckled alder and arrowwood. The largest specimen is the tamarack (or larch), a potentially threatened species, accompanied by swamp birch, alder-leaved buckthorn and smooth gooseberry (the latter being uncommon). Plants here are common in the colder, boreal habitats of Canada—and the climate here after the Ice Age.

Other residents are red maple, highbush cranberry, blueberry, Canada mayflower, burnet, marsh marigold, nannyberry, swamp saxifrage, and poison sumac. Sphagnum moss covers hummocks. Skunk cabbage and ferns called royal and cinnamon are present. Naturalists are trying to reseed Labrador tea, pitcher plant, and spreading globeflower here.

HISTORY

The state acquired the location (and the property of Portage Lakes State Park) in 1926. Originally part of the state park, nine acres of wetland were transferred to the Division of Natural Areas and Preserves in 1978. Three acres were sold to the Portage Lakes Kiwanis Club for a senior citizens center in 1981.

Sheepskin Hollow State Nature Preserve

Just a few miles from Pennsylvania, this preserve shelters a hidden gorge in the watershed of a national and state scenic river. The soon-to-be-enlarged site enriches the value of nearby park land

and the outdoor experiences of visiting humanity.

LOCATION
Eastern Columbiana County, Middleton Township.

OWNERSHIP
Ohio Department of Natural Resources, Division of Natural Areas and Preserves.

SIZE & DESIGNATION
This 457-acre site was dedicated in 1991. Completion of a purchase that would more than double the preserve's size was expected in 2000.

ACCESS
From Lisbon, follow SR 154 east to Negley, then go three miles south (right) on SR 170, and 1.5 miles east (left) on Pancake-Clarkson Road to the railroad overpass serving as a parking area. Walk south on the abandoned rail bed. Enter the preserve on the left by crossing beneath the track through a stone culvert.

A railroad trestle used by local visitors has been removed. The preserve is open daily dawn to dusk.

GEOLOGY
A tributary of Little Beaver Creek washes through narrow and scenic Sheepskin Hollow and forms a pair of waterfalls tumbling over impressive outcroppings of sandstone and shale of the Pennsylvanian Era.

WILDLIFE
Towering eastern hemlocks crowd both banks of steep Sheepskin Hollow. These shade-loving boreal trees give way to a mixed hardwood forest of beech, maple, and oaks on the sunnier ridges. The preserve protects rare blossoms called pipisissewa, Bicknell's panic-grass, pink lady's slipper (orchid), and Canada fly honeysuckle.

HISTORY
A portion of the preserve, formerly Little Beaver Creek Preserve, derives from the large, private Vodrey Preserve in Fredericktown. In 1998, the Division of Forestry was expected to transfer a large adjacent tract to the Division of Natural Areas and Preserves.

Swamp Cottonwood State Nature Preserve

The wet pockets in this small preserve support Ohio's healthiest community of swamp cottonwood, a potentially threatened tree species.

LOCATION
Southwestern Medina County, Homer Township.

OWNERSHIP
Ohio Department of Natural Resources, Division of Natural Areas and Preserves.

SIZE & DESIGNATION
Just 21 acres.

ACCESS
Exit from I-71 at Lodi and go west on US 224. A mile west of Homerville, turn south (left) on Camp Road (TR 36), then west (right) a half mile on Williams Road (TR 79) to an unmarked pull-off on the south side of the road.

The place lacks hiking trails, but you can snoop around anyway.

GEOLOGY
The site could be an old kettle lake that formed about 12,000 years ago when a slab of ice broke off the vanguard of the retreating Wisconsinan glacier and melted into a depression. Accumulating sediment and vegetation has transformed the pond into a swamp forest.

WILDLIFE
Swamp Cottonwood, a bottomland tree common on the Carolina coast, survives only in scattered colonies in the Ohio River Valley and Midwest. At maturity, it is smaller than its cousin, the eastern cottonwood. Pin oak, silver maple, swamp white oak, basswood, and poison sumac also grow here. Ferns are represented by varieties called royal, sensitive, cinnamon, Christmas, and marginal wood. Several kinds of sphagnum moss flourish, along with false hop sedge, a threatened plant.

HISTORY
The Division of Natural Areas and Preserves bought the place, the former Giar Farm, in 1986.

Tinker's Creek State Nature Preserve

Like meandering Tinker's Creek, the serpentine trail snaking through this isolated wetland takes you into the realm of beavers, waterfowl, dragonflies, and bullfrogs. It's a cornucopia of pond, marsh, forest, and stream creatures.

LOCATION

Border of Summit and Portage counties, Aurora and Streetsboro townships.

OWNERSHIP

Ohio Department of Natural Resources, Division of Parks and Recreation owns the land. The Division of Natural Areas and Preserves manages the site.

SIZE & DESIGNATION

This 786-acre marsh became a scenic nature preserve on Dec. 27, 1974.

ACCESS

From Hudson or Aurora, motor down the Hudson-Aurora Road to Old Mill Road and head west 1.6 miles to the preserve.

Exit Interstate 480 at Frost Road and take an immediate left across from the filling station. Turn right at the next intersection (half mile away) on to Hudson-Aurora Road, go past the entrance to Tinker's Creek State Park, then turn left (west) on Old Mill Road. The parking lot is located on the north side of the road. Seven Ponds Trail begins across the street, near the railroad tracks.

Trails: Seven Ponds Trail parallels the railroad at first and cuts through a pine plantation. In the pines the trail splits. The trail to the left is the half-mile Lonesome Pond Loop Trail. Hikers with limited time can take this route to get a taste of the preserve.

To see all seven ponds, stay on the Seven Ponds trails.

Though insect repellent, long pants, long-sleeved shirts and ball cap are recommended for summer hikes, I was never bothered by mosquitoes (late June) thanks to thousands of hungry dragonflies who cleared the air of the pests. The daring buggers even buzzed under the brim of my hat, literally snagging mosquitoes heading for my brow.

Seven Ponds Trail measures 1.75 miles and is easy to follow. Keep in mind that the terrain, though flat, can be muddy and slippery.

GEOLOGY

Tinker's Creek originates from higher ground in northern Portage County and snakes across a plateau leveled by a glacier 15,000 years ago. Consequently, water flows and drains slowly here, and much of the land is a fertile, sprawling peat swamp and marsh. (After this slow start, Tinker's Creek boils through a deep gorge in the Bedford Reservation a few miles downstream, creating one of the nation's natural landmarks.)

Human handiwork enlarged an existing wetland. The railroad grade built a century ago along the western boundary of the preserve acted as a dam and turned fields into shallow ponds and mires. Tinker's Creek is a remnant of that large swamp.

Much of the wetland has been drained for farming and other enterprises. The seven ponds in the preserve all are man-made.

Beavers also have tampered with this oasis. Their projects slow the current of the creek. These incessant builders can transform a landscape faster than any other animal, except humans.

WILDLIFE

Tinker's Creek preserve teems with life. Around the time the place became a nature preserve, Dr. David Waller of Kent State University identified 188 species of birds, proof of the swamp's value as a habitat. Waller's sightings included rarities such as the bald eagle, the American and least bitterns, loggerhead shrike, and king rail, all endangered; the sharp-shinned hawk, red-shouldered hawk, Virginia rail, purple martin, and sora, all "special interest" or potentially threatened. Others have seen the endangered black tern. Some of these protected birds can still be observed here.

You may also spot several varieties of flycatchers, the Louisiana waterthrush, wood duck, scarlet tanager, yellow, cerulean and blackburnian warblers, common loon, osprey, American coot, and great horned owl. The preserve is a perfect location to view the spring and autumn migrations of birds.

The preserve safeguards three threatened plants (spotted pondweed, highbush cranberry, and crinkled hairgrass) and five potentially threatened—prickly bog sedge, long sedge, prairie sedge, catberry, and swamp oats.

Fifty-five kinds of wildflowers have been identified. Test your skills looking for dwarf St. John's-wort, lesser toadflax, wild licorice, hog peanut, Canadian dwarf cinquefoil (five fingers), mad dog skullcap, turtlehead, bottle gentian, northern arrowwood, pickerelweed, meadow sweet, and wild cucumber.

Another Kent State researcher, Dr. Tom S. Cooperrider, reported that ferns named ground-pine, bracken, sensitive, rattlesnake, and marsh grew here in the mid-1970s. You might see royal fern, too.

The preserve protects snapping turtles, four-toed salamanders, and snakes. Deer, fox, mink, weasel, raccoon, squirrel and chipmunk live here. Several cottontail rabbits bounced into the underbrush on my approach.

Lepidopterists are rewarded by the 241 species of butterflies and moths counted here in 1986 by Dr. Roy W. Rings of the Ohio Agricultural Research and Development Center in Wooster. The red admiral, little wood satyr, promethea moth, and the rare hesitant dagger moth have been observed flitting about. (Is the latter moth rare because he hesitates to use his dagger?)

Trees have not been forgotten. They are represented by white pine (planted), hawthorn, ash, slippery elm, alder, red osier, willows, aspen, beech, black cherry, red maple, oaks (swamp white, red, pin, and chinkapin), dogwood, and others. Cattails as big as trees are prolific, and buttonbush are everywhere.

HISTORY

This abundant area has been heavily trapped (beaver, muskrat, and mink being the main targets), hunted, and fished. Recently-fired shotgun shells found along the trail attest that hunting, an illegal activity in the preserve, still occasionally occurs here. The land also has been drained for cultivation and grazing. Two oil pipelines cross the property.

The preserve land once was part of the adjoining state park. Two decades ago 786 acres of the state park became a designated nature preserve.

JOURNAL

June: Just as I entered woods on a narrow strip of land a loud clap echoed through the preserve. It was the alarm of a beaver. The creature had slapped the still marsh waters with his paddle-like tail. Ripples on the pond next to the railroad tracks revealed the location of the sentry. I searched for the beaver through my binoculars.

A second, louder crack sounded, the splash about 100 yards from the first one. A few ducks scattered, then a heron, then silence fell upon the marsh again.

The by-products of the beaver's work—gnawed saplings and shrubs, stripped branches, girdled trees, piles of wood chips—litter the banks of Tinker's Creek and the ponds. Two beaver lodges (perhaps abandoned) clung to the east bank of the pond just north of the observation platform.

After this commotion I glimpsed a group of blue-winged teal. They had not fled after the beaver's splash, and remained calm in my presence. From the viewing deck, I observed a pair of olive-sided flycatchers, several warblers (too quick to identify), numerous red-winged blackbirds (one shrieks above my head protecting a nest), and in the distance the nests of bald eagles, perhaps, or ospreys in the tops of dead trees.

In mid-June, the bullfrog's raspy croak sounds like the growl of a dying outboard motor. Each footstep sends a croaker into the drink; a few squeal before splashing.

Judging from a chat I had with a local fellow (who packed a 12-gauge shotgun on a rack in his pickup) turkeys might be settling into this sanctuary. He had seen some in there the previous winter.

Tummonds (Charles A.) State Scenic River Preserve

Charley Tummonds paddled many of the country's great rivers, but the Upper Cuyahoga River was dearest to his heart. Tummonds traveled down the current a final time, a short time after he died in 1984, when friends sprinkled his ashes in the stream at a bend in the river south of Mantua. At that spot a nature preserve remembers his spirit and his name.

LOCATION

Northern Portage County, Mantua and Shalersville townships.

OWNERSHIP

Ohio Department of Natural Resources, Division of Natural Areas and Preserves.

SIZE & DESIGNATION

This 86-acre refuge became the first state scenic river preserve in March 1986. The designation means the site protects a state scenic river.

ACCESS

The preserve protects 1.5 miles of the Upper Cuyahoga State Scenic River, beginning a half mile downstream from Mantua.

Visit the place by canoe, launching at the Mantua village park. By car, travel south from Mantua a half mile on SR 44 and park off the road. The preserve is on the west side of the highway. You have gone too far if you reach Goodell Road. There is no trail system.

GEOLOGY

Around Mantua (say MAN-too-ay), the upper section of the Cuyahoga River washes across glacial till and marshland. The two branches of the Crooked River (the Cuyahoga's nickname) converge in Burton, then the main stem meanders southerly to Akron where its strikes a summit and rushes north into Cleveland and Lake Erie.

WILDLIFE

The preserve is an excellent woodland corridor packed with husky beech, sycamore, basswood, green ash, silver and red maples, wild black cherry, and oak trees. The site features a dry kame woods, swamp forest, and a small sphagnum moss bog. Bewick's wren, an endangered bird, has been observed here.

HISTORY

Charles A. Tummonds of Mantua was a river activist. He was a founding member of the Upper Cuyahoga Association, a conservation group; national commodore of the American Canoe Association; and a member of the 1980 U.S. Olympic Committee. In 1975, he won the U.S. national kayaking championship, senior division. He died before his time in November 1984.

SOUTHEAST

Boord (Falls Run) State Nature Preserve

The waterfall here is a wide sandstone slab, an altar across the gorge. It tilts slightly to the west, so that Falls Run drools comically from only one side of its lip during low water. The shady ravine is cool and quiet, a haven for evergreens and ferns. Bird song harmonizes with water song in Washington County's best hemlock ravine.

LOCATION
Southern Washington County, Fairfield Township.

OWNERSHIP
Ohio Department of Natural Resources, Division of Natural Areas and Preserves.

SIZE & DESIGNATION
This preserve, open to visitors, comprises 89 acres.

ACCESS
Head west from Marietta on SR 550, which branches from SR 7 south of the city. Go through Barlow and a hamlet called Layman. Turn left (south) on CR 6, then right (three-quarters of a mile) on TR 69. In a half mile the preserve sign will appear on the left (east). The preserve stays on the east side of the road. CR 6 is 4.5 miles east of Bartlett.
Parking is a problem. There is not enough room off the narrow road for most cars. There is more off-road room ahead, where the road paralle Falls Run. Unmarked trails begin here, too. Do not block access to farm fields.

GEOLOGY
Falls Run cuts through a thick slab of 250 million-year-old (Permian Era) sandstone and carves a gorge 60-80 feet deep. True to its name, the gorge's center-piece is a handsome, though modest, waterfall framed by cliffs and overhanging outcrops. Falls Run empties into West Branch, which zigzags to the Ohio River.

WILDLIFE
Naturalist Marilyn Ortt stumbled on this gem, considered the best hemlock and white pine ravine in Washington County. Indeed, the gorge is deep enough, cool and moist enough for shade-loving hemlocks to crowd the slopes. Trees and shrubs typical of the Appalachian hardwood forest—oak, walnut, hickory, mountain laurel—have also staked a claim.
State-imperiled rock skullcap, narrow-leaf tooth-wort and golden knees flourish, along with rattle-snake plantain, partridgeberry, Canada mayflower, barren strawberry, maidenhair spleenwort, Christmas and polypody ferns, and teaberry. The county's only colony of pink mocassin flower grows here.
Sixty species of birds have been observed, notably the pine siskin, slate-colored junco, ruby-throated hummingbird, red-breasted nuthatch, blue-winged warbler, crossbill, warbling vireo, bobwhite, and common whip-poor-will.

HISTORY
The preserve is named in honor of the Boord family of Dayton, which made a partial gift of this preserve to ODNR in 1986.

JOURNAL
Summer: Remove shoes and socks. Go creeking in Falls Run, whose water is chilly in July. I slip twice on algaed rocks, before falling and soaking my shorts. I didn't come prepared with towels and change of clothes. That means the car seat will become wet—and stay wet for several days. And I'll have to sit in it. I make a mental note to repeat the Boy Scout oath before departing on my next trip.

Compass Plant Prairie State Nature Preserve

The leaves of the compass plant are said to align themselves in a north-south direction, hence the name. In Ohio, though, the endangered plant has taken

a different bearing, for here marks its
easternmost range.

LOCATION
    Eastern Lawrence County, Mason township.

OWNERSHIP
    Ohio Department of Natural Resources, Division of Natural Areas and Preserves.

SIZE & DESIGNATION
    The prairie preserve totals 16 acres.

ACCESS
    From Ironton, travel northeasterly (compass direction) on SR 141. The preserve is 1.5 miles northeasterly from the hamlet of Aid, on the east side of the highway.
    There are no designated parking areas, nor trails. Pull off the road, and do not block driveways. The preserve can be visited any day from dawn to dusk.

GEOLOGY
    The compass plant and its associates arrived several thousand years ago when a prolonged heat spell allowed prairie plants from the Great Plains to probe into Ohio. The return of cool and damp weather revived the deciduous hardwood forest. The prairie peninsula disappeared except for a few scattered island communities.

WILDLIFE
    The preserve protects Ohio's only colony of compass plant, which consists of some 800 plants. The flower is easy to spot July-September. It stands 10 feet and opens a yellow blossom reminiscent of prairie dock and and other tall sunflowers. Its leaves are deeply clefted, and finger-like, and pointing north-south. The resinous sap in their stem was supposedly used by Indians as a chewing gum.
    These plants actually may be latecomers to the site, which might have been a forest at the time of Euro-American settlement. The surrounding land was farmed for oats, sorghum, hay, and pasture in this century, and this "clearing" may have sponsored this prairie community. Other prairie species grow here, including partridge pea, big bluestem, little bluestem, Indian grass, butterfly weed, and tick seed. Look for rose-pink gentian, early ladies'-tresses, dwarf sumac, green milkweed and hairy (Carolina) ruellia, the latter two also imperiled in Ohio. Best time to visit is August.

HISTORY
    The Ohio Chapter of The Nature Conservancy acquired the property and later transferred it to the Division of Natural Areas and Preserves. The site is also referred to as the Ora. E. "Andy" Anderson Preserve, which honors a former state senator and local conservationist.

Conkle's Hollow State Nature Preserve

Something pulls me into the gorge at Conkle's Hollow. Maybe it's the bold, massive cliffs, the noble hemlocks or the misty caves. Conkle's Hollow, tucked away in a crease of the scenic Hocking Hills, conjures up a fairy-tale place of dragons and armored princes. Once captured by its spell, you'll learn why this hollow is hallowed ground.

LOCATION
    Southwest Hocking County.

OWNERSHIP
    This preserve is co-owned by the Divisions of Forestry and Parks and Recreation, both in the Ohio Department of Natural Resources. The Division of Natural Areas & Preserves manages the facility.

SIZE & DESIGNATION
    This 87-acre scenic nature preserve was dedicated on April 22, 1977.

ACCESS
    The preserve straddles the border of Benton and Laurel townships, some 18 miles from your starting point on SR 33. The easiest route is to head south from Rockbridge and follow SR 374 as it zigzags and snakes through Hocking State Forest and Hocking Hills State Park. From SR 374, turn left on Big Pine Road (look for the sign), which takes you to the preserve's entrance about two-tenths of a mile away.
    From Logan, take SR 664 south to SR 374. Head west on SR 664/374, past Old Man's Cave in Hocking Hills State Park. Stay on SR 374 when it splits from SR 664 west of the park's lodge, then turn right on Big Pine Road.
    Trails: Indulge your first impulse and walk into the gorge. From the parking lot, cross the iron foot bridge, visit the information board (where brochures may be tucked into a box), then take the Gorge Trail straight ahead along the stream.
    For a hawk's view into the hollow, take the rim trail to some of the most splendid views in Ohio, and I highly recommend it. But remember to stay on the trail! You are probably tired of hearing that warning, but here it may save your life.
    Conkle's Hollow is open every day, from first to last light. Drinking water (well), latrines, and picnic tables can be found in the parking area and along the driveway. Please throw away your litter

in a container. Read the interpretive trail signs to learn more about the ecology of the preserve.

GEOLOGY

Let's back up some 350 million years when rivers and streams ran off steep Alps-like peaks (today's rounded Appalachian Mountains) in the east and emptied into an inland sea that covered most of Ohio. These swift mountain streams deposited coarse sand and finer sediment in a long, irregular shaped delta that went across much of what today is eastern Ohio.

Later, the ocean vanished and the land heaved upward. The sand in the delta dried and compressed into a rock called Blackhand sandstone. (See Blackhand Gorge State Nature Preserve.) The thickness of the sandstone layer ranges from 85–250 feet, but in the gorge at Conkle's Hollow it measures 200 feet. In the ensuing years, erosion has removed overlaying sediment and shaped the sandstone into the gorges, rock shelters (recess caves), knobs, and natural bridges typical in the Hocking Hills.

The Blackhand formation has three zones in Conkle's Hollow. The rim layer is firmly cemented and withstands erosion better than the middle layer, which is crossbedded (see explanation below) and more susceptible to erosion. Notice the gouged out caves at this level. Another firmly cemented stratum, about 100 feet thick, comprises the lower zone.

Beneath the towering, cream-colored cliff in the gorge, you may notice a bluish-gray rock in the stream. This is Cuyahoga shale, a product of the Mississippian geological period, 345–320 million years ago. A thin layer of coarse, pebbly sandstone, called conglomerate, lies above the Blackhand sandstone in places.

The cascades in Conkle's Hollow let you visualize a process called undercutting, which has carved waterfalls as diminutive as the one at the end of the Gorge Trail and as mighty as Niagara Falls. For thousands of years the nameless rill that has tumbled southward through the hollow and into Big Pine Creek (near the trailhead) has fallen over a ledge of Blackhand sandstone into a pool. Spray and backwash from the splashing current ate away the rock behind the waterfall and formed a recess cave.

For undercutting to work the rock layer behind the pool must be "less resistant," meaning it erodes faster than the "resistant" strata on the top. Though most of the rock in the gorge is Blackhand sandstone, some layers are less resistant than others. That explains the series of waterfalls at the crotch of the gorge. A well-cemented, resistant layer sits above a less resistant strata. Beneath that plane is another resistant layer, and so on.

Also, observe the cross-bedded layers in the big cliffs. Cross-bedded refers to the archlike layers (typical of delta deposits) that lie at acute angles beneath the horizontal layer. The angles in cross-bedded rock show the direction of the water current at the time of deposition. These cross-beds are less resistant to erosion.

Undercutting, or sapping, weakens support beneath the precipice and causes chunks of the resistant cap to break off and crash into the valley. Some of the flat slabs of rock piled in the creek bed are the victims of undercutting.

Study the coarse sand beneath the waterfall at the end of the Gorge Trail. It will give you some idea what the beach and delta of the inland sea must have looked like 350 million years ago.

Along the Gorge Trail look for rock shelters (caves) in the walls, car-sized boulders (Slump Rock) detached from the cliffs, and the pitted facades. These show erosion at work.

Conkle's Hollow is a box canyon—or an open-ended ravine enclosed by steep, vertical walls. The only way out is the way you got in.

WILDLIFE

If you step into the gorge after working up a sweat walking the rim trail, a shiver might run down your spine. The temperature is cooler here because the cliffs and tall trees shade the valley floor.

In the cool nooks and crannies, plants commonly found in chillier northern climates, such as hemlock, Canada yew, teaberry, and partridgeberry, have thrived for thousands of years. They arrived like pioneers some 14,000 years ago in the vanguard of the Wisconsinan glacier, which drove to within six miles of the preserve.

Sections of the gorge look like some Greek god dumped a box of giant pickup sticks on the scene. These hemlocks and hardwoods fell in 1982 and 1985, the victims of violent storms that uprooted hundreds of trees. They will be left there to provide shelter for critters and to slowly decay and return nutrients to the soil, as nature intended. In the gaps opened by the fallen trees, young tulip trees and sweet birch stretch skyward.

Ferns and mosses, several varieties, spread out on the gorge floor. One type found here is the endangered triangle grape fern.

Four plants listed as threatened can be found on the grounds: radiate sedge, pale green panic grass, pipsissewa (a relative of wintergreen), and a wildflower called round-leaved catchfly. Ten species are potentially threatened, notably the long-beech fern and the rock club moss (both reasons enough for not climbing the rocks, their preferred habitat).

Atop the sun-exposed ridges where drier and thinner soil prevails, chestnut oak and Virginia pine grow in clusters. You also will find large specimens of tulip tree, beech, and assorted hardwoods. Blueberry, black huckleberry, and mountain laurel have wedged their way into cracks on exposed walls. Deerberry, sourwood, serviceberry, and three kinds of hickory (shagbark, mockernut, and kingnut) also grow in the preserve.

The footbridge leading from the parking lot to the trailhead crosses Big Pine Creek whose fertile floodplain sponsors one of the best stands of river birch in Ohio.

The preserve is home for many creatures typical of the Ohio woods. The northern copperhead, a poisonous snake, has been seen slithering in these parts, but your chances of spotting one are remote.

HISTORY

Hunters of the ancient Adena and Fort Ancient cultures probably camped under the overhangs, or cornered their quarry in the box canyon. Wyandots and Shawnees shared these hunting grounds, which were situated close to a trail that connected Central Ohio and West Virginia.

The preserve takes its name from W.J. Conkle who carved his name into the west wall in 1794 or 1797. The inscription "A.O. Cow 1898" appeared beneath it, and both names were reportedly framed in a rectangle of stars. Unfortunately, the engravings were pilfered or dissolved by erosion.

A descendant claims W.J. Conkle came to Ohio from Germany at his father's request. Generations of the Conkle family have inhabited, toiled and died in the area. Several descendants still live nearby, two centuries after W.J. Conkle left his mark on the rock of ages.

The state bought the prize for its scenic beauty in 1925. During the Depression years the Civilian Conservation Corps planted pines on the grounds. You can see them, now mature, on the rim trails. The gorge was dedicated as a scenic nature preserve on April 22, 1977.

Dysart Woods

This is one of only a few places in Ohio that looks anything like the primeval forest that nourished the Indians and greeted the first white settlers 300 years ago. Much of the land surrounding these woods has been strip-mined for coal, clear-cut for timber, and grazed by livestock making the ancient trees more precious. How did the lumberjack's axe and farmer's plow miss these woods?

LOCATION
Central Belmont County, Smith Township.

OWNERSHIP
Ohio University.

SIZE & DESIGNATION
The property consists of 455 acres, though the virgin woods comprises about 50 acres. Dysart

Woods was designated a National Natural Landmark by the U.S. Department of the Interior in 1967.

ACCESS
From Exit 208 on I-70 head south on SR 149 for about 2.5 miles. Turn left on SR 147, which goes through Belmont. Continue on SR 147 southeast about four miles then turn right when you see the Dysart Woods Laboratory sign. That road is TR 234, but you will bear right immediately on TR 194, and travel past the caretaker's residence on the left into the preserve. Park in the designated area on the left (east side).

Trails: The two virgin woods stand in ravines, separated by a ridge of younger hardwoods. Township Road 194 bisects this ridge. One trail (blue blazes) departs from the corner of the parking lot; the other (red blazes) sneaks into the woods across the road.

The narrow trails here are less-developed, or more natural (take your pick) than paths in other preserves. Behemoths that have fallen across trails remain whole, uncut by chain saw. These huge trunks and limbs that block the path like twisted dinosaurs may challenge adults, but kids will like climbing over them. The obstacles add to the adventure and let you feel the size of the slumbering giants.

Seekers of solitude and silence will enjoy this remote place. You will hear forest sounds mostly, and the activities of nearby farms. You will not find rest rooms or other human comforts in the grassy parking lot. Not a bad place—the parking lot—to spread out a blanket for a picnic or snooze. Just make sure you take all your belongings with you.

Information: Contact Ohio University, Department of Environmental and Plant Biology, Athens, Ohio 45701-0869, (740) 593-1120.

GEOLOGY
Dysart Woods grows atop shales and sandstones formed during the Permian geologic period, 285–225 million years ago. Deposits of coal, some near the surface others hundreds of feet below, also run through here.

The coal seams recall another great primeval forest, known as the Carboniferous Forest, which reigned here about 310–280 million years ago, during the late Pennsylvanian and early Permian geologic periods. The Carboniferous Forest was a luxuriant swamp woods growing on the coast of a warm, shallow sea. The dead leaves and branches of this forest accumulated in thick layers. Eventually, the ocean level rose, and buried and choked the forest under water, clay and sand. These heavy sediments squeezed the decaying vegetation into "black gold." Ironically, the nuggets of that ancient forest may undermine Dysart Woods. In 1998 a local coal company gained permission to mine coal close to the edge of Dysart Woods.

WILDLIFE
Dysart Woods is one of the best places in the

Eastern U.S. to study forest life and plant succession, or the changes in the types of plants living at a specific location. Biologists call Dysart Woods a mixed mesophytic forest, meaning that a kaleidoscope of trees—in this case, various oaks, beech, tulip tree, sugar maple, and other hardwoods—will share the site.

Some white oaks reach skyward to 170 feet and boast 48-inch diameters. You will also see stout wild black cherry, white ash, beech, and sour gum trees.

When these hardwoods fully leaf in late spring they will close the canopy, and virtually block sunlight from reaching the forest floor. Shade tolerant beech and maple seedlings can grow in this dark environment but not sun thirsty oaks and tulip trees.

When old trees fall, sunlight rushes to the ground faster than water leaking from a corrupted dam. The seedlings and saplings who bathe in this light race to fill the vacancy in the sky.

Earlier stages of plant succession are underway at this refuge. Notice how pioneer shrubs and trees (raspberry, chokeberry, redbud, hawthorns, alder, sassafras) have invaded meadows. These will be replaced by other species, followed by the blend of oaks, hickories, and the beech-maple stands.

Colonies of mushrooms and fungi are ubiquitous, especially at the base of trees and rotting giants. Besides adding beauty and color to the forest, they advance the life-cycle of the forest by breaking down the life-giving nutrients in the decaying vegetation. Look at their delicate features, but do not trample them.

The woods provide shelter for the birds and furry animals typical in these parts. As you enter the woods listen for woodpeckers tapping on trees. Pay special notice to the holes in trees. You might see a wood duck, raccoon, or some other critter peeking at you.

History

The Dysarts descend from Miles Hart who moved to Belmont County from Pennsylvania in 1813. Hart's granddaughter married Henderson Dysart. The succeeding generations cleared much of their land slowly, all except two woodlots, which were allowed to stay in their pristine state. (The fact that logging on steep ravines was difficult was probably a factor in the decision.)

The Ohio Chapter of The Nature Conservancy bought the 455-acre farm from the Dysart family when it learned the forest might be logged. When funds ran low, Ohio University agreed in 1966 to pick up the remaining payments and to protect the parcel as a nature preserve and field research laboratory.

In April 1967 the U.S. Department of the Interior recognized Dysart Woods as a National Natural Landmark because it contained one of the last virgin deciduous forests in the Eastern U.S. The commemorative plaque is set in a stone on the caretaker's lawn.

The preserve has become an outdoor education and nature study facility for local high school and college students, as well as scientists. Scientists from around the world make pilgrimages to Dysart Woods.

Coal mining—or the removal of the carboniferous forest that previously grew here—has been the biggest threat to Dysart Woods recently. Although the creation of a buffer zone around the preserve in 1970 has halted the encroachment of surface strip mining, underground mining, particularly long-wall mining, may irreversibly harm this priceless habitat.

Extracting the coal could alter the water table in the area and parch the soil. Surface disturbances associated with underground mining—higher dust levels, truck traffic, vibrations in the ground, and unnatural water runoff—could put stress on the vegetation.

Worse yet, long-wall mining (the PAC-Man-like burrowing through underground coal seams) causes the ground to actually sink or collapse into the earth. This sudden shifting, called subsidence, could uproot 300-year old trees and reduce Dysart Woods to a pile of pickup sticks.

Journal

June 4: Deer again. I spot two does as I reach the crest of a ridge on the Red Trail. They loitered for 10 minutes then high-tailed it. I continued on the trail thinking about the deer, occasionally looking over my shoulder for them in case they doubled back.

When I reached I-70 I realized that the deer had distracted me from my business of locating the champion tulip tree on the Red Trail. I never did see it. For all I knew the famous tree was the one I hid behind to watch the whitetails. Next time I'll find it, deer or no deer.

Lake Katharine State Nature Preserve

A lost colony of endangered bigleaf magnolia, separated from its Kentucky kin by several hilly counties, struggles on the banks of Salt Creek. It is an oddity, a survivor, found nowhere else in Ohio. Altogether the sprawling Lake Katharine Preserve guards 20 endangered species, including a diminutive petal called roundleaf catchfly, and the seldom seen bobcat. Lake Katharine has some of the most rewarding hiking trails in the state.

LOCATION
Western Jackson County, Liberty Township.

OWNERSHIP
Ohio Department of Natural Resources, Division of Natural Areas and Preserves.

SIZE & DESIGNATION
Boasting 1,850 acres, Lake Katharine is the second largest state-owned preserve. Half of it has been designated interpretive for public visits. The remaining half has been reserved for scientific study. The preserve also is known as the Edwin A. Jones & James J. McKitterick Memorial Wildlife Sanctuary, named after the previous owners of the land.

ACCESS
From Jackson, travel two miles west on State Street (which becomes CR 76 outside of town), then turn right on CR 85 (Lake Katherine Road). The road ends at the parking lot where you will find the buildings of old Camp Arrowhead.

To reach the boat launch (see fishing and boating restrictions below), travel north on US 35, go left on CR 84, then immediately right on CR 59 (Rock Run Road). Turn left on CR 59A, which ends at the preserve manager's home. Park in designated areas. You will not find destination signs on this route.

Trails: Three well-designed trails wind through the preserve. However, only one of them, the Pine Ridge Trail, follows the lakeshore, although only for a few paces. Stop at the information board near the parking lot for a brochure and trail map.

From time to time, winter storms and flooding have closed trails. The closures will be posted at the information board.

Fishing & Boating: Lake Katharine's bulky bass (seven pounders) and her bluegills and crappie have been exciting fishermen for years. Some anglers claim they have snagged panfish as big as a dinner plate.

Katharine, however, plays hard to get, which adds to her mystique as a fishing hot spot. Only five permits are issued per day for Friday, Saturday, Sunday or Monday, from April to October. The lake remains boat-free the rest of the year. Call the preserve office at (740) 286-2487 on the last Friday of each month between 8 a.m. and 5 p.m. to make a reservation. You are entitled to only one reservation per call, and only one reservation per month. The permit is good for only one boat, and one day. If you change your plans and fail to cancel your permit within 24 hours, you will forfeit lake privileges for a year.

The boat launch area has 10 parking spaces but you must carry (not drag) the boat down a steep 110-yard path to the lake, a strenuous task for solo anglers. Motorized watercraft are not allowed. Non-fishing boaters can certainly use the lake. Call the preserve office for the rules governing lake use.

Information: Call the preserve at (740) 286-2487 or the Ohio Department of Natural Resources.

GEOLOGY
The cliffs at Lake Katharine preserve are composed of Sharon conglomerate, a type of sandstone studded with round, white quartz pebbles called lucky stones.

During the Pennsylvanian geologic period, some 300 million years ago, swift rivers and streams rushing off high peaks to the east (the predecessors of the Appalachian Mountains) washed gravel into the inland sea that inundated most of Ohio at the time. This deposit accumulated in a broad delta that stretched across Eastern Ohio. After the land uplifted and the sea dried this conglomerate compressed into rock. Iron-rich water that washed over and seeped into the deposits firmly cemented them.

You can easily see the quartz pebbles embedded in the cliff walls along the Salt Creek Trail. Their roundness resulted from the agitation in the ancient streams. The beds of these gravel deposits were never uniform.

Study the bedrock carefully for awhile. (Trail post #5 on Calico Bush Trail offers a close-up). The sculpting has been done by the process called differential weathering. It works when water soaks into the rocks and dissolves the areas not permeated with iron cement. Pebbles weakened by weathering pop out of the facades and lay in piles beneath the walls, and sometimes on the trails.

In winter the water that has seeped into the rock freezes and expands, thus creating cracks. Some cracks enlarge and eventually break slabs off the cliff. The cracks and pocks provide homes for lichens, mosses, and ferns, which assist erosion.

Differential weathering occurs fastest where the iron is weakly concentrated in the rock. The lumps, burls, swirls, and knobs on the rock indicate iron-saturated spots that have defeated weathering.

Over time Little Salt Creek and Rock Run have worn down the formations. The walls also show other scars of erosion—recess caves and honeycombs. The powerful forces of erosion that formed these gorges established habitats that enabled some plants to extend their range of existence.

WILDLIFE

The ravines, ridges and floodplains are sanctuaries for some 20 plants listed as endangered, threatened, or potentially threatened. An endangered wildflower called Sampson's snakeroot lives here, along with butterfly pea, a threatened species. Several grasses, and a spiny shrub bearing black berries called devil's walking stick (or Hercules-club) are among the potentially threatened. The latter plant, like others in this choice habitat, thrive at the northern edge of their range.

Two snakes observed here, the rough green snake and the black king snake, are rare in Ohio.

Although the Wisconsinan glacier never reached Jackson County (its deepest local penetration being southeastern Ross County) plants from northern regions that marched ahead of the ice mass, notably hemlock, found a suitable microclimate in the cool, shaded ravines.

Lake Katharine marks the northern boundary of the endangered bigleaf magnolia, a flowering tree commonly found in the southern Appalachian highlands but only in one location in Ohio. A colony of about 2,000 bigleaf magnolias, a remnant flora of the ancient Teays River Valley, grows along the Salt Creek Trail. Only about 50 have reached seed-producing maturity.

The tree's kissing cousin, the umbrella magnolia, is more abundant here, but still potentially threatened in Ohio. This tree also reaches the fringe of its range in the preserve.

Leaf design distinguishes them. Umbrella magnolia leaves taper at the stem and are slightly smaller than the "bigleaf," which has twin lobes at the base of the leaf.

You cannot miss these beauties when their creamy-white and fragrant petals unfold in the spring. Later, they will drop seed pods resembling pine cones. In late autumn and winter their huge tobacco-sized leaves cover the floodplain. The bigleaf has green buds; the umbrella brown buds.

The preserve boasts a prominent collection of hardwoods—tulip tree, oaks (chestnut, white, red, black, scarlet, shingle), sycamore, cottonwood, some beech, hickory, and others.

Ferns brighten the cool, shady places. Christmas fern, so-called because it stays green in winter and sports an ear resembling a yuletide stocking on its leaf, appears everywhere. You also find common polypody (cliff faces), as well as wood, fancy, evergreen wood, and maidenhair (horseshoe-shaped frond) ferns.

The interpretive guide for the Calico Bush Trail encourages you to focus on the work of lichens and mosses. These hardy pioneers inhabit rocks and rotting logs, places where no other plants chose to live. Slowly, they decompose rocks and rot, and prepare the ground for larger plants.

The calico bush, better known as mountain laurel, blooms in June along the Calico Bush and Pine Ridge trails. Also look for these uncommon blossoms along this path: mountain watercress, starflowers, puttyroot, and stemless lady's slipper.

Another rarity found here, the potentially threatened roundleaf catchfly, struggles at the base of the cliffs. Blueberries and wintergreen, an evergreen with white flowers and red berries, cling to the lip of the cliffs.

Quiet, slow walkers may see deer, turkeys, and perhaps the bobcats (an endangered critter) known to live here. Spotted salamanders may dart across the boardwalks or race on top of the rocks. Years ago a timber rattlesnake was spotted but you are unlikely to find this reclusive critter.

Look for the telltale signs of a beaver colony along the lakeshore—gnawed tree branches stripped of their bark, girdled trees, inch-long chips near stumps, sticks chiseled to pencil points. The lake contains prize bass and panfish.

HISTORY

The preserve is named for Katharine M. Jones, wife of Edwin Jones, a former owner of the property. Jones, president of the Globe Iron Company in Jackson, and his partner, James McKitterick bought the land during the mid-1940s. The duo constructed a 260-foot long earthen dam across Rock Run Gorge in 1946, and a lodge, blockhouse, and residence, all for the opening of Camp Arrowhead in 1947. The summer camp for boys operated for 18 years.

The Girl Scouts last used Camp Arrowhead in 1970. The Ohio Department of Natural Resources acquired it in August 1976 and dedicated it as a nature preserve in July 1977.

Leo Petroglyph State Memorial

There are two kinds of petroglyphs (rock writing) in this little gorge—the ones carved by humans, and the ones sculpted by nature. And two kinds of creatures—real and imaginary.

LOCATION
Northern Jackson County, Jackson Township.

OWNERSHIP
Ohio Historical Society

SIZE & DESIGNATION
The site encompasses 12.3 acres.

ACCESS
From US 35 north of Jackson, turn left (northeasterly) on CR 28 (a.k.a. Sour Run and Coalton roads) and go to the hillside hamlet of Leo. There turn left on CR 29 (Raysville Road), and an immediate left (heading northwest) on Park Road (TR 224). The parking lot for

the historical landmark is on the left.

First stop, of course, is the pavilion that shelters the famous petroglyph. After admiring the ancient human art, follow the path into the rocky gorge. The trail traces a creek, climbs above the ravine, and circles back to the pavilion. Roundtrip is a half mile, tops.

Information: Ohio Historical Society, 1982 Velma Avenue, Columbus, Ohio 43211, (614) 297-2300

GEOLOGY

The water erosion that created the striking gorge also exposed the fine-grained sandstone slab that became a canvas for the early graffiti artists. In the ravine, the cliff walls become pebbly and gritty. This formation is Sharon conglomerate, which appears in nearby Lake Katharine State Nature Preserve and in a broad band reaching into northeastern Ohio. The small, white stones embedded in the conglomerate are quartz pebbles. Their roundness indicates they once were tossed in swift streams and deposited in a deltaic beach. The deposit later compacted and was buried by overlaying layers. Nature's petroglyphs are the ledges and honeycombs that erosion sculpted in the rock.

WILDLIFE

Snakes, fish, birds, and animals tracks appear in the petroglyph. Some of these creatures survive in the preserve. Hemlocks keep the gorge shady year-round, and in summer tulip trees, white oaks and beeches spruce up the place. I heard woodpeckers, saw hawks, and discovered raccoon tracks.

HISTORY

Petroglyphs are etchings in rock. The 20 by 16-foot slab here displays 37 figures, represented by snakes, human effigies, birds, fish, small mammals, and footprints of humans and animals. Their meaning and significance (to the artist) remains unknown. Flint spear points and other artifacts uncovered at the site indicate the carvers were early native Ohioans called the Fort Ancient people, who lived in Southern Ohio from 100 A.D. to 1500 A.D. Some of the objects have faded over time.

JOURNAL

Winter: After hiking the ravine, I examine the petroglyphs again, this time for answers. This tale appeared: the ravine was well-known, a hunting camp perhaps, a place where people stayed long enough to scratch figures into rocks. I see the hand of many carvers spanning centuries. The "writers" were individuals with idle time, or doodlers at the campfire. The figures don't seem organized for reading or decoding, which would be expected if the objects had religious importance. They might represent clans, game animals, or wild dreams. Maybe a bird etching told the next visitor that members of the Hawk clan had been there, or the animal track encourages the next hunter. We will never know, and perhaps that's best.

Marie J. Desonier State Nature Preserve

This is a place of silence, far from any city. If you seek solitude and quiet you have come to the right place. This remote preserve in the hills of southeastern Ohio protects several kinds of habitat, and hikers will find the trails challenging.

LOCATION

Southeastern Athens County, Carthage Township.

OWNERSHIP

Ohio Department of Natural Resources, Division of Natural Areas and Preserves.

SIZE & DESIGNATION

The preserve encloses 491 acres. It was designated an interpretive site on March 26, 1975.

ACCESS

The closest village is Coolville. From there, head west on US 50 for nearly four miles and turn right on CR 56, the second right after the split of routes 50 and 7. (The road destination sign was not standing when I visited.) Travel .3 of a mile and turn left on CR 65 (also known as Jordan Run Road). The gate to the preserve will be on your left in .7 of a mile. A sign says to park beside the gate if the parking lot gate is closed.

Trails: The two-mile Oak Ridge Trail climbs steep terrain and takes you through various habitats, from recovering farm fields to woods of tall timbers.

Though there is little chance of getting lost, a trail map posted on the bulletin board in the parking area would be helpful for visitors who like to know the lay of the land. Hiking is forbidden in the portion of the preserve which lies on the east side of CR 65.

Desonier benefits from its remoteness and steep terrain. It is one of those rare places where the sounds of nature can be heard without distractions.

GEOLOGY

Study the winding course of Jordan Run and its feeders. Notice how the current erodes the outside bank of the stream and piles gravel and sand on the inside bank, making bigger loops. All sorts of beach-combing critters—deer, raccoon, fox, turtles, snakes—patrol on these pebbly pads.

Jordan Run, which bisects the preserve, straightens when it hits bedrock. The preserve lies atop layers of shale and sandstone of the Pennsylvanian and Permian periods (225–320 million years ago).

After a heavy rain a half dozen small rivulets tumble 30 feet over ledges in the ravine on the north side of site. You can hear the hollow echo of these little wonders (but cannot see them) from the Oak Ridge Trail. It has taken these tiny creeks many centuries to create the steep terrain and ravines. The topography in the preserve varies from 680–900 feet in elevation.

WILDLIFE

The preserve is noted for its diverse vegetative habitats, ranging from abandoned farm fields in various stages of succession (the continuous restorative process of one species being replaced by another) to lush beech-maple stands in the deep hollows and oak-hickory woods on the higher and drier slopes. Dense areas covered by young trees (hawthorn, dogwood, redbud, sumac), competing hardwoods and shrubs surround the mature wood-lots. Open lots and crop lands border the property.

The cornucopia includes 81 varieties of wildflowers (notably, "at risk" species like Virginia meadow-beauty, green adder's mouth, weak aster, American mistletoe), and 54 species of woody plants, according to a mid-1970s inventory. Ferns are also abundant.

As you would expect amidst such diversity, songbirds are abundant—29 species counted back in 1975. Numerous ruffed grouse have found a home here. Dusky salamanders and red-spotted newts reside in the creek beds.

HISTORY

The preserve is named after its former owner, Marie Josephine Desonier, who as a World War II Army nurse known as Captain Stein or Stone, served on General Dwight Eisenhower's staff as a public health and refugee advisor. She was the first Allied woman soldier to see the horrors at Buchenwald concentration camp. Later, she served as a consultant to General Douglas MacArthur, head of the Allied occupation forces in postwar Japan.

After the war she married an Army officer named Desonier, settled down in Athens County, and held administrative and teaching posts in local hospitals. She was crowned Mrs. Nelsonville in 1955 and competed for the Mrs. America title. A newspaper story appearing at the time reported that her maiden name was Isselstein.

Marie Desonier bought 301 acres (about 60 percent of the land that became the preserve) in 1930 for $2,000. She sold it to her brother, Henry Stein, in 1966. She died in 1968. Henry Stein gave the tract to ODNR for a nature preserve in his sister's honor in 1974. The preserve was dedicated in 1975, and ODNR purchased four adjoining parcels totaling 189 acres in 1980.

A threat to the preserve's quietude in 1986 drew local conservation groups out of their silence. The preserve's advocates protested a plan to reroute US 50 to within a few hundred yards of the refuge. Petitions condemning the plan (400 signatures) were sent to ODNR and other government agencies. Route 50 stayed on its old course.

JOURNAL

April 28: The remains of a fox, reduced to a skeleton and a few patches of fur, lay right in the middle of the Oak Ridge Trail, just a few paces from Jordan Run. The carcass had been there awhile, judging by how the bones had begun to sink into the soft earth and the lack of flesh. Scavengers usually scatter the bones of dead animals, but not this one. This skeleton remained intact, frozen like a fossil, posed in the middle of a stride.

How did it die? No signs of a scuffle, every bone in its place. A gunshot from the road? Disease? Did a flood drop it there? Could it have just died on the trail of old age, starvation, or weariness?

I have sometimes felt like this fellow looks.

Rockbridge State Nature Preserve

When the spring wildflowers bloom in early May, the natural arch becomes a rainbow, glowing like some half-buried celestial halo. A thin thread of water, working at its eternal pace, chiseled Rockbridge in the Hocking Hills.

LOCATION

This jewel is found in Hocking County, on the border of Good Hope and Marion townships, near the village of Rockbridge (about five miles northwest of Logan).

OWNERSHIP

Ohio Department of Natural Resources, Division of Natural Areas and Preserves.

SIZE & DESIGNATION

This 99.3-acre geological wonder was designated as an interpretive nature preserve on June 21, 1978.

ACCESS

Exit US 33 at Crawford-Starner Road (TR 504) and immediately turn right onto Dalton Road (TR 503), which curves left and dead-ends at the preserve parking lot.

Trails: The Natural Bridge Trail gently ascends from the parking lot, following an old fencerow. Read the preserve rules on the information board before trekking. Upon entering the corner of a meadow the Natural Bridge Trail turns left (north) along a ridge. The Beech Ridge Trail goes straight. Either trail leads to the stone arch.

Canoeists paddling on the Hocking River can beach their boats at the designated landing and walk to the arch.

Tempting as it may be, do not walk across the rock! Falling from it will cause injury or death. There also is a chance that your weight will damage or weaken the span.

Climbing the rock walls also is prohibited and risky to you and wildlife. Remember that wildflowers, small animals, fungi and tree roots thrive on the cliffs. Footing can be slippery and hazardous at the bank of the Hocking River, especially during the spring when the current is high and swift.

The cold, leafless months are best for studying the geological features. But the setting may be at its best at two times during the year—spring (late April and early May), and autumn.

Special Places & Events: Naturalist programs are held here periodically. Check the information board in the parking lot.

GEOLOGY

Rockbridge is the largest of 40 known natural bridges in Ohio. It measures 100 feet in length, and arches 50 feet across a narrow hollow. The width varies from 5–20 feet, with a thickness of around five feet. Rockbridge's only rival is Ladd natural bridge, also a state preserve, located in Washington County. The Ladd preserve is not open to the public.

The Rockbridge stone arch, comprised of 300 million year-old Blackhand sandstone, started as a typical recess cave, like Ash Cave or Old Man's Cave in Hocking Hills State Park, with water falling over its overhanging lip. (See Conkle's Hollow and Blackhand Gorge.) The sandstone on the top, tightly cemented by iron and silica, has resisted erosion. The lower strata, on the other hand, were weakly cemented enabling the backsplash of the waterfall to hollow out a cave beneath the caprock.

The woodland stream also ate away the cement along a north-south running seam, or crack, in the caprock behind the lip. Eventually, the rock behind the fracture weakened and collapsed, creating a hole. Erosion by the stream widened the gap, leaving a solitary band of sandstone to bridge the ravine.

A 50-foot cascade still tumbles over the recessed ledge, though during the dry summer months the current shrinks to a thread. The tributary ends its journey at the Hocking River, which forms the eastern boundary of the preserve just 100 yards from the bridge.

WILDLIFE

Elderberry groves and pawpaw trees (noted for their banana-shaped fruit) line the path from the parking lot (along with other species). The meadow shows the typical characteristics of an open area changing into a forest, a transition called succession. As you might expect, Beech Ridge Trail traverses a knoll dominated by beech, oak, maple and hickory. The land was logged during the 1930s, so this woodlot is called a second-growth forest.

Careful observers may spot deer, ruffed grouse, turkey, beaver and fox in the preserve. Tracks indicate that raccoons and skunks live here, too.

Dozens of common wildflowers carpet the floor, including creeping trailing arbutus, pale Indian pipe, dwarf iris, stonecrop, Joe-pye weed, and Roman ragweed. Great rhododendron and the green adder's mouth, its habitat diminishing, offer a few blossoms.

HISTORY

The rock bridge has been a favorite destination for picnickers. In the 1840s, passengers traveling on the Hocking Valley Canal, which ran beside the river between Lancaster and Logan, insisted on stopping here. Some families rented boats, paddled to the river landing, and dined under the arch. In the early 20th century, the Columbus, Hocking Valley and Toledo Railroad, operating on the opposite river bank, stopped at Rockbridge. Canoeists still land here to enjoy the scenery.

Zora Crawford, a former owner, reported that his son once drove a tractor over the bridge (but only once), and that another daredevil crossed it with a horse and buggy. Performing those feats today could cost you your life, a stiff fine, or jail time.

The Ohio Department of Natural Resources, Division of Natural Areas and Preserves bought half of the site in 1978 and quickly designated it a scenic preserve. Another forested tract, east of the Beechwood Trail and bordering the river, was added in 1990.

CENTRAL

Blackhand Gorge State Nature Preserve

The Licking River has scoured a "lick" through dense layers of ancient sandstone creating a steep-walled gorge that's been a landmark for prehistoric Indians as well as canalboat, trolley, and railroad passengers.

LOCATION
Eastern Licking County, Hanover Township.

OWNERSHIP
Ohio Department of Natural Resources, Division of Natural Area & Preserves.

SIZE & DESIGNATION
Blackhand Gorge became an interpretive nature preserve on September 20, 1975. It comprises 981 acres.

ACCESS
Start in Newark and go east on SR 16 to its intersection with SR 146 (about eight miles). Travel southeast on SR 146 just .25 miles then turn right on CR 273, heading south. CR 273 dead ends at TR 275 (Rockhaven Road) near the village of Toboso.

Here you have a choice. Turn right (northwest) on TR 275 and park in the lot a half mile away to explore the foot path on the north side of the Licking River. Or, turn left, cross the river and pull into the main parking lot. Bicyclists and wheelchair visitors use the latter entrance.

Reaching the preserve from I-70 is complicated. Westbound travelers exit at Gratiot, cross US 40 and head north on Poplar Forks Road (TR 339). Turn right (east) on Flint Ridge Road, then shortly go left (north) on TR 278. Where TR 278 joins TR 277 bear left on TR 277, but then take your next right, continuing north on TR 278. In Toboso, turn left on TR 275 and park in the lot at the left.

Eastbound I-70 travelers exit at Brownsville and go north on SR 668, right (east) on Flint Ridge Road, left on TR 291, right on TR277, and finally left on TR278 to Toboso.

Trails: Blackhand Gorge has seven hiking trails and is one of only a few nature preserves with a bicycle and wheelchair trail. Five trails stem from the main parking lot, where you also will find latrines, picnic tables, information board, and a log cabin. The main trail is the North Central Bikeway, a four-mile, paved path that clings to the south shore of the Licking River. It used to be the bed of a railroad track. At one point the path goes through a man-made gorge called the "Deep Cut," a path blasted through sandstone for the railroad. At this spot follow the short path to your right that leads to the river. The rock wall on the north bank (not actually in the preserve) once held the "Black Hand." More on that later.

The dirt hiking trails are easy to follow, but expect brief, steep climbs up a few ridges. Being a former railroad grade, the paved bikeway is flat. Bikers are asked not to race or speed down the bikeway, nor ride their cycles on other trails. Rock climbing is forbidden. Again, stay off the railroad trestle.

GEOLOGY
The exposed rock walls reveal the timeless tread of the river, and the temporary toil of man.

A vast inland, shallow ocean, called the Waverly Sea, covered much of Ohio around 325 million years ago (late Mississippian Period). It was refreshed by fast-running rivers and streams descending from heights today known as the Appalachian Mountains. These waterways deposited coarse sand and finer sediments into this sea in huge, interlocking deltas roughly stretching from Wayne County to the Ohio River. It some places, these layers of sand were 250 feet thick. Strata more pebbly than others (indicating they were closer to the base of the highlands) are called conglomerates.

Overlaying layers of mud and sediment compressed the sand, and water enriched with iron oxide cemented the grains into rock called Blackhand sandstone.

Like the rest of eastern North America, the land gently rose, or uplifted, probably during the Permian geological period some 285–225 million years ago. The sea also may have shrunk. During the ensuing millions of years rain, wind and sun feasted on the softer strata above the sandstone, and then the sandstone itself, creating the rocky knobs, gorges, cascades, caves, outcrops, and rock bridges characteristic of eastern and southeastern Ohio.

As it has for many millennia the Licking River and its tributaries continues to cut a path through this sandstone. The river started as a meltwater stream tumbling from the Wisconsinan glacier, which left this area about 16,000 years ago.

The slow work of the river cannot compare with the pace of humans, who, armed with explosives and rock-breaking tools, removed tons and tons of this ancient beach for canal locks, railroad trestles, glassworks, and gravestones during the last two centuries. Slowly, though, nature is covering up the human disturbances.

WILDLIFE

Follow the succession of tree species from the heights to the river. On the formerly deforested ridgetops, Virginia pine, oaks, hickories, and mountain laurel grow in dry soil. Various hardwoods (oaks, maples, beech) and an extravagance of wildflowers carpet the slopes, but in the floodplain, sycamores, willow, box elders, and cottonwoods hold sway.

The Licking River forms the boundary between two major types of forest, though only a trained eye can detect the differences. The north bank favors what scientists call the mixed mesophytic forest species—a melting pot, or stew, of oaks, hickory, chestnut, tulip tree, beech, maple, even hemlock. Trees characteristic of a mixed oak forest—white, black, chestnut oaks with sourgum, dogwood, Virginia pine, and others—prevail on the southern slopes.

Various surveys show that the preserve harbors 73 different trees and shrubs, 150 kinds of wildflowers, and 15 varieties of ferns. Mosses (including the rare rock clubmoss) and liverworts wrap many boulders and rock walls.

Animals common in these parts—deer, raccoons, squirrels—live in the gorge. Red-tailed hawks and vultures often hover above the valley. Sixty-four bird species have been counted here, as well as nine species of toads and frogs, and six categories of salamanders.

HISTORY

Long ago, a large petroglyph (a carving, etching or painting on rock) shaped like a hand, and black in color, appeared prominently on a gorge wall above the river. Pioneers who saw it claimed it was twice the size of a man's hand.

The origin of the "black hand" inspired many legends. Some say it pointed to the valuable nearby flint quarries where native people manufactured arrowheads, axe heads and other essential tools (See Flint Ridge State Memorial below.) The symbol also may have been an early "peace" sign, marking the boundary of sacred grounds (like contemporary neutral or demilitarized zones). The tribal leaders of various nations may have sanctified the area so that nobody controlled the strategically important quarries upstream.

Other tales claim the hand was the blood-stained hand of a murder victim, or that it marked a lover's leap. Floods failed to erase the blackened stain.

Unfortunately, the black hand was blasted away by dynamite during the construction of the Ohio-Erie Canal. The current flowing through the "Licking Narrows," at first too skinny and shallow for canal boats, was fattened by a dam downstream. Quarries on the south side of the river provided stone for canal structures still visible on the Canal Lock Trail.

The completion of the Central Ohio Railroad through the gorge in the 1850s signaled the end of the canal era. The railroads built tracks through the narrows and a trestle across the river. Later, an electric, interurban trolley line running between Newark and Zanesville blasted a tunnel through the sandstone on the north side. The last interurban steamed through the narrows in1929). Relics of the bygone transportation systems can be seen in the preserve.

The former Rock Haven Park resort, located on Rockhaven Road east of the Marie Hickey and Oak Knob trails, became a popular destination. When trolley service ceased, autos carried tourists to the park on the old interurban right-of-way, but even this pleasure ended with the advent of bigger cars, paved highways, and new pasttimes.

Flint Ridge State Memorial

For hundreds of years, the Ancient People (prehistoric Indians) converged at this spot to gather flint, a stone more valuable to them than gold. The Great Spirit required all who entered the sacred region to pledge peace and harmony, a pact apparently respected for centuries. A hardwood forest has buried the quarries, leaving us to ponder the peace and serenity that still prevails.

LOCATION
Southeast Licking County, Hopewell Township.

OWNERSHIP
Ohio Historical Society.

SIZE & DESIGNATION
Flint Ridge is a state memorial totaling 520 acres.

ACCESS
Eastbound travelers leave I-70 at the Brownsville

exit and take SR 668 north about four miles. The site is at the intersection of SR 668 and Flint Ridge Road.

Westbound visitors must exit I-70 at Gratiot, go north (right) a quarter mile to US 40 (National Trail), then west (left) on US 40 to Brownsville. Turn right on SR 668, and right on Flint Ridge Road.

Trails: Several trails snake through the hardwood forests of this nature preserve. All trails, except the Overlook Trail, begin in the picnic area. Handicapped explorers can take the .25-mile paved trail with handrails and Braille interpretive signs from the picnic area to the museum. The hiking trails ramble through wooded ridges and ravines and are sometimes challenging.

The depressions or small black pools you see along the trails are the ancient flint quarries. Soil eroding off the sides closed the abandoned mines. Some have become permanent ponds, filling up with water that runs off the slopes.

Colorful blue-gray flint boulders and chips can be seen everywhere along the trails. Go ahead and examine the chips, but please leave them in the preserve. Also, don't dislodge or move flint boulders, nor chip them. These are historical artifacts! The ridges were sacred grounds!

The museum, built above a quarry, features a diorama of Indians mining and shaping flint. Rockhounds can buy flint and other souvenirs in the gift store. Rest rooms and drinking water also are located in the museum. You will find picnic tables and latrines in the picnic grounds.

Information: Call (740) 787-2476 or contact the Ohio Historical Society, 1982 Velma Ave., Columbus, OH 43211-2497, (614) 297-2300, (800) 686-1545.

GEOLOGY

This area is one of the few places in the country where flint is so bountifully seen on the surface. This deposit, known as Vanport flint, sits on top of ridges covering an area of six square miles. The thickness of the layer varies from one to 12 feet.

Though many flint deposits date back to Silurian times (440 million years), the rock at Flint Ridge is younger, a mere 300 million years old, formed during the Pennsylvanian geologic period. Though it resembles limestone, flint is a type of quartz, mainly composed of silica (silicon dioxide).

Back in the Pennsylvanian times, a warm, shallow sea covered this part of Ohio. The ocean was tropical because Pangea, the huge land mass that later would split and separate into the continents we know today, rested at the Equator. The marine life that died fell to the ocean floor, creating a soft, limey soup. The silica needed to make flint probably came from the skeletons of sponges, specifically their spiny spicules. The sponges must have been abundant in this particular spot. The silica was compressed into flint by the weight of several layers of clay and other sediments that fell on top of it.

Chemical impurities trapped in the soggy stew gave flint its shades and streaks of red, green, yellow, pink, blue, black, and white. About 200 million years ago the land rose, or uplifted. Erosion carried away the soft surface layers and exposed the flint bedrock.

Though heavy and hard, flint is brittle enough to crack and chip. The flint that Indians found on the surface sometimes flaked, weakened by the weathering of rain, sun and wind. They also discarded an inferior form of flint, called chert. The good stuff was found in seams beneath the surface.

Mining flint with primitive tools was backbreaking work. After removing surface obstacles like dirt and trees, the ancient people split open the flint by pounding wooden wedges into natural cracks with granite or quartzite rocks weighing 25 pounds or more. These heavy hammering stones were brought here from Canada by the glaciers.

Large chunks of flint were carried to worksites and cut into smaller pieces roughly matching the size of the desired implement. Some implements were manufactured at the mine, but most intricate toolmaking was done at locations beyond the ridges.

Today, flint is collected for its beauty, not its utility. Its hardness, color, and glossy polish make it a favorite gemstone of jewelers and collectors.

WILDLIFE

The flint ridges may have been one of the few places in prehistoric Ohio that showed the wear and tear of constant human habitation. The ancient people who assembled here probably blazed a network of trails. The tread of miners beat down the grounds around the quarries. The surrounding woods must have been vigorously hunted, and trees were felled to support mining activities as well as for shelter and fires. But their impact on land was comparatively minor compared to that of those who lived here for the last two centuries.

Though white settlers cleared the ridges for farming, a mature, mixed hardwood forest has grown back during the 60 years that the land has been protected The emerging forest has begun to conceal the hand of man. Even the ancient quarries have filled in with natural debris. In the spring they become black pools sponsoring aquatic life and quenching the thirst of animals. By autumn most have dried up.

The plants and animals typical in this type of forest reside here. Tracks on the shore of one "black pool" revealed the presence of deer and raccoons. Streaks of yellow—threads of gold—in the forest canopy revealed the beauty of warblers.

HISTORY

The Ancient People, called Palaeo-Indians, arrived here about 10,000 years ago, near the end of the Pleistocene Era or Ice Age. Maybe they noticed the colorful rocks while hunting for mastodon or bison, and quite by chance discovered that the rock could be chipped into durable tools and arrowheads.

Word got around about the rock in them thar' hills, and soon a prehistoric version of a gold rush ensued. Indians from faraway lands showed up for flint. To avoid territorial disputes, bloodshed, and covetousness the flint ridges were declared sanctified grounds, or neutral zones. The Great Spirit, tribal leaders decided, made the flint for all the people.

A few miles east of the flint ridges, a "black hand" once appeared in a sandstone cliff above the Licking River. Many believe the black hand marked the eastern boundary of this demilitarized zone. (See Blackhand Gorge State Natural Preserve.)

Smaller flint deposits also were mined by Indians in Vinton, Jackson, Coshocton, Hocking and Perry counties.

Indian traders distributed the gem widely. Artifacts carved from the local flint have been uncovered in Kansas City, Louisiana, and on the Atlantic coast.

Flint lost its luster when European explorers brought iron tools and weapons into the continent. White settlers utilized a lesser grade of flint for buhrstones to hone tools or grind grain. The sparks produced by striking flint started fires. The famous rifle of the frontier, the flintlock, got its name from the flint used to detonate the gunpowder.

Flint chips gathered from the ridges formed part of the roadbed of the National Road (U.S. 40) through Licking and Muskingum counties.

The Ohio Historical Society purchased the historic and geologically unique ridges in 1933. The museum opened in 1968.

JOURNAL

May 21. I sit beside the trail and stare through the shiny black pool into the ancient mine. I envision miners intent on their task, but mostly I wondered how the Ancient People managed to make these ridges a realm of nonviolence.

Did peace come after a period of strife and killing among the groups, or before war occurred? Were they practicing an honored, common tradition, or ritual, of sharing the vital and divine gifts of the cosmos? Questions bubble to the surface of the black pool. How did people reach truces then? By balancing power, or by balancing interests? Did their communal lifestyle make it easy for them to share strategic resources? How did they enforce the neutral zone? How long did it last? Did they control the terms of trade?

Did they worry, as we modern people do about oil, that the flint mines someday would be exhausted? Did they practice conservation, or limit the amount of flint quarried by groups?

Were the Ancient People better at making peace than us?

Can we learn from them? Is the reward of these ridges the flint itself or the peace it made?

Tell me dark water. What do you say? What does your silence mean?

The Darby Plains Prairies

In these seed-sized patches of land the survivors of the great tallgrass prairie now grow like a wreath over the pioneers who plowed the "flower nation" into cornfields. When you visit these remnants of the Darby Plains prairie in July and August you become bewitched by the exploding hues of the flowers. Come here in the winter and the ghosts of Lucinda Smith and Lucy Bigelow will do the same.

LOCATION

These three preserves are located a few miles apart in Madison and Union counties.

OWNERSHIP

The respective township trustees own the Bigelow and Smith preserves. Dayton Power & Light Co. owns the Milford Center site. All three locations are managed by the Ohio Department of Natural Resources, Division of Natural Areas and Preserves.

SIZE & DESIGNATION

Bigelow Cemetery, .5 acre; Smith Cemetery, .6 acre; Milford Center Railroad, 7 acres.

The pioneer graveyards, each measuring about a half acre, have been designated as interpretive nature preserves. Bigelow was dedicated on October 3, 1978; Smith on December 6, 1982. Milford Center Prairie, also an interpretive preserve open to the public, stretches for 1.3 miles along the right-of-way of a former rail line. It joined the state preserve system in 1986.

ACCESS

To reach Smith Cemetery (Northern Madison

County, Darby Township) head west from Plain City on SR 161. In about two miles, go south (left) on Kramer Road, then west (right) on Boyd Road. Look for a patch of oak trees and tall grass 100 feet off the road to the right. Park alongside the road or off to the side of the small farm lane leading to the cemetery. Do not block the potholed lane nor drive to the site.

Bigelow Cemetery is in Pike Township, Madison County. Continue west on SR 161 about five more miles, then go south one mile on Rosedale (formerly Weaver) Road. Again, look for trees surrounding a cemetery. You will have to park your car on the berm.

Milford Center Prairie is in southwestern Union County (Union Township), just north of the intersection of SR 4 and US 36. From Bigelow Cemetery, return to SR 161 and travel west to the hamlet of Irwin, nearly five miles, then go north (right) on SR 4. About two miles up SR 4, a little north of US 36, you cannot miss seeing the broad-shouldered towers of an electric power line intersecting with the road. Park the car in the grassy area on the west (left) side of SR 4. Walk north (toward Milford Center.

You will have to park on the side of the road at all three locations, so don't bring the RV. Consider turning on your flashing emergency lights if your car partially juts into the road, especially at dusk. This may be distracting, but better safe than sorry.

Trails: Bigelow Cemetery lies right beside the road—you cannot miss it. Smith Cemetery is 100-feet off the road but is reachable by a path. Mowed paths serve as trails in these preserve. The trail at Milford Center, also a mowed path, follows the power line.

These sanctuaries are at their natural best when the prairie blooms in July and August. However, folks who like to visit old bone yards should come in the winter, when the stones and the ghosts are easier to see.

Keep in mind that some of the gravestones are nearly 180 years old and fragile. Need I say that picking flowers and gathering seeds is prohibited?

GEOLOGY

Though prairies may have existed in Ohio before the Ice Age, scientists are rather certain that about 4,000–6,000 years ago (long after the last glacier) the land experienced a long warm and dry spell called the Xerothermic Period. The heat wave triggered the eastward migration of the Great Plains tallgrass prairie. A finger, or peninsula, of the western prairie overwhelmed the forest and probed as far east as Pennsylvania and north into Michigan.

Scientists suspect that the climate cooled again, and drove back the frontier of the prairie (the French word for meadow) to the Illinois-Indiana border. Some 300 prairie islands, however, withstood the reemergence of the forest. These patches of prairie ranged in size from a few acres to several square miles. One of these outposts was the Darby Plains of Central Ohio.

The Darby Plains is located between Big and Little Darby creeks. Though a slight summit, or divide, separates the watersheds of these creeks, the flat terrain drains slowly. Consequently, the grassland stays swampy in the spring and early summer, deterring the sprouting of tree seedlings.

By late August or early September, however, the soil becomes parched and cracked. Any tree seedlings that survived the soggy spring would be wiped out by summer drought or fires ignited by lightning or Native Americans. Likewise, sprouts that make it through the summer drown next spring. The Darby Plains would remain a prairie as long as this wet and dry cycle continued.

Fires are essential for the survival of the prairie. While the infernos wreak havoc on the encroaching hardwoods, they did little harm to the fire-tolerant prairie plants whose underground life processes avoid the flames. The fires, then, help the prairie in its turf fight by suppressing the forest.

The blaze also destroys the thick mat of dead grass on the surface, and returns nutrients (ash) to the soil. With the suffocating mat gone, the spring's rain and warm sun reach the seedbeds faster, and trigger rapid growth.

Cinders spewing from passing railroad engines set the Milford Center prairie (and nearby fields) ablaze. During dry months farmers feared for their crops every time a train roared through the countryside. Few of them realized the fires they extinguished abetted the prairie they had suppressed.

The plains Indians called the fires "red buffalos." They torched the tallgrass following an ancient hunting strategy of stampeding game to awaiting marksmen. They also knew the fires opened the grassland for the grazing animals (bison) they hunted. Some researchers suggested that these first Americans "managed" the land by torching the prairie.

Following nature's cue, naturalists revive prairie remnants and new meadows with periodic burnings, which are said to be good for the prairie's soul as well as for its seed.

WILDLIFE

Who can resist their names? Ox-eye, whorled rosinweed, flowering spurge, black-eyed Susan, royal catchfly. Some 30 types of flowers and grasses have been counted at Smith Cemetery, a fewer number at Bigelow Cemetery.

In July and August the "rainbow" blooms. Bring your field guides, but remember that prairie flowers often go by several names. Keep in mind that the plants you see represent only a portion of the varieties that once flourished on the Darby Plains.

You are likely to find big bluestem ("big" because it soars to 10 feet), Indian grass, Canada anemone, wild bergamot, purple and gray-headed coneflowers, and stiff goldenrod at both sites.

Little bluestem grass, wild garlic, smooth aster, New Jersey tea, gray dogwood, gray willow, guara, ox-eye, prairie false indigo, Virginia mountain-mint, prairie cord grasses, skunk meadow-rue, and golden Alexanders nearly conceal the gravestones in Smith Cemetery.

At Bigelow Cemetery look for the potentially threatened royal catchfly (once thought to be the only colony in Ohio), plus hazelnut, wax-leaved meadow-rue, wild petunia, sainfoin (also called scurf pea), tall coreopsis, pale-leaved sunflower, and prairie dock (sometimes reaching 10 feet).

Milford Center has the greatest variety of plants (57 different species in the last count). Its cache of royal catchfly is the largest in the state, and its small community of vetchling, or veiny pea, a rare legume, may be the only one left in Ohio.

Here butterflies and dragonflies, hundreds of them, collide and bounce about in reckless flights. Bees, their flights focused and determined, dive for nectar. Their bodies tremble like the struck tines of a tuning fork. These insects are the pollinators and propagators of the prairie. Birds and bugs make up part of the day watch at a prairie cemetery.

At sunrise in the summer hundreds of spider webs glisten like diamond necklaces. Shortly, though, the sun's rays evaporate the dewdrops and the spider at the edge of the now-invisible web waits for a victim.

Bison, elk and the prairie chicken (grouse) once lived on Ohio's prairies. Their departure, however, benefited the cow, the groundhog and the meadowlark, the residents of more cultivated landscapes. Early morning visitors may see matted grass where a deer had slept.

The wood bison that once roamed here was larger than its cousin on the Great Plains. It carried the "wood" prefix because it could graze in the forest and in grassy openings. Indian and white hunters preyed on the beast. The last one in Ohio was killed in Lawrence County in 1803. Only a couple thousand of them survive in Canada.

HISTORY

Native Americans harvested prairie plants for food, medicines, and fibers. The white pioneers, however, came here to plant corn and wheat. Their plows, more than any other factor, destroyed the prairie.

The first shipment of settlers arrived between 1810 and 1820, mostly from New England and Pennsylvania. They traveled down the old "post road," what we call State Route 161 today, to an area they called the "barrens," paying from 40 cents to $2 an acre.

The prairie proved formidable at first, being either too wet, too thick, or too dry (late summer) for the plow. Swarms of mosquitoes sometimes darkened the sky.

Some pioneers gave up and went home. Benjamin Hough bought 172 acres of the barrens on Oct. 21, 1815, but a year later he sold the tract (cemetery and all) to Russell and Lucy Bigelow who toiled there for at least six years. Lucy and four of her children are buried in the cemetery. The land has had many owners, but the cemetery always carried the name of these early settlers. Bigelow Cemetery received its last body in 1892, for a total of 78 markers. It became a state preserve in 1978.

Samuel Smith, a Methodist minister and a Revolutionary War veteran, brought his family from Vermont to the area in 1818. In 1824 his son, Samuel Smith Jr., married a 14-year-old orphan named Lucinda Andrews, whose sister and parents were among the first occupants of what became known as Smith Cemetery. Samuel Jr. bought the land containing the graveyard shortly after Lucinda died at age 22 on February 11, 1832. Other family members were buried there, too.

Two years later, however, Samuel Jr., and his second wife, deeded the cemetery to the Darby Township trustees and said good riddance to the Darby Plains. A century and a half after Lucinda Smith's death, the graveyard holding her bones became a sanctuary for the prairie's soul as well.

A railroad crossed the plains in the 1850s, connecting Milford Center with Delaware and Springfield. The line had several owners, the most famous being the Cleveland, Cincinnati, Chicago and St. Louis Railway Company, a.k.a. The Big Four. Dayton Power & Light Company bought the railroad right-of-way in 1962 and constructed a power line.

It is remarkable, given the historical record, that these tiny botanical jewel boxes survived at all. During the last two centuries, the prairie has been drained and cultivated, its fertility unlocked to feed a hungry nation. Weed killers, insecticides, and chemical fertilizers shrunk the prairie even more.

Amazingly, specks of the original prairie held on—as accidents, as oversights, in neglected, overgrown pioneer cemeteries, along untidy fencerows, and beside abandoned railroad tracks.

JOURNAL

July: As I walked through these little gardens I recalled an observation by William Least Heat-Moon, author of PrairyErth. Heat-Moon recommended visiting old prairie graveyards to rediscover what the Indians called the "flower nation." He also wrote, "But if you stay in a white man's old burial ground long enough, this darkness must come to you: his way of life is the land's death and his way of death is the land's life."

Like short-lived pioneer plants, pioneer people usually died young. One exception was Solon Harrington, now a resident in Smith Cemetery. His survivors noted on his stone that he died on May 15, 1855, having lived 99 years, four months, and 19 days.

Gahanna Woods State Nature Preserve

If you can block out the roar of jets landing and leaving nearby Columbus airport you will hear the plaintive song of spring peepers, or the ominous croaking old trees make when they sway in the wind. Be careful staring into the swamp. The polished glass surface of the forest pond has been known to hypnotize. Fortunately, most victims emerge from the trance when a skimming dragonfly or water strider disturbs the water.

LOCATION
Northeastern Franklin County, Jefferson Township.

OWNERSHIP
Ohio Department of Natural Resources, Division of Natural Areas and Preserves. Managed by the Gahanna Department of Parks and Recreation.

SIZE & DESIGNATION
Gahanna Woods, comprising 54 acres, was dedicated an interpretive nature preserve on January 10, 1974.

ACCESS
Exit I-270 at SR 16, go east .25 mile and turn left (north) on Taylor Station Road for about three miles.

This preserve, open everyday from sunrise to sunset, is next to a city park that has a parking lot, picnic area, a short nature trail, and a small playground.

Trails: Look for the sign pointing to the nature preserve trails on the south side of the parking lot. Stop at the information board for a brochure that contains a trail map and a list of all the plants found in the preserve.

Gahanna Woods is a swamp forest, so remember that the trails may be wet year-round. Boardwalks have been built over soggy areas. When hiking it is a good idea to protect your body against insect attacks.

GEOLOGY
The large boulders you see in the woods are chunks of granite from Canada left behind by the Wisconsinan glacier that swept across central Ohio some 15,000 years ago. The ice mass also deposited a layer of unsorted soil composed of sand, gravel, clay, boulders, and silt, a mixture called glacial till.

Now imagine that this layer of till is chunky peanut butter unevenly spread across a slice of bread. The bread represents the bedrock and the chunks in the peanut butter (till) are the blocks of granite (known as erratics). In some spots the layer of till will be thin, sunken, or pitted. The rain that filled these shallow depressions and potholes formed ponds and made the land ready for the plants and animals you see in the preserve.

WILDLIFE
On Earth, water sponsors life. In the glacier-made ponds at Gahanna Woods plants quickly took root. Grasses and shrubs appeared along the edge. The remains of these plants accumulated in the ponds and shrunk them. That enabled trees fit for wet soil to invade, dump more debris (leaves, dead trees), and begin taking over the area.

So, in the soggy shallows of the swamp forest at Gahanna Woods, pin oak, swamp white oak, silver maple, black cherry, elm, and ash have sunk their roots. On higher and drier ground (and here it is only a few feet) beech and sugar maple muscle each other for space.

The old farm fields that make up much of the preserve are in various stages of succession—a naturalists' term referring to the slow transformation of open areas to forests. In that transitional area between the forest and the field, trees such as hornbeam, sassafras, hawthorn, honey locust, as well as impenetrable thickets of black raspberry and multiflora rose, are common. A stand of prickly ash grows here, too. It offers its branches to caterpillars that change into the striking swallowtail butterflies.

All totaled some 40 woody species can be found here, and about 160 different varieties of herbaceous plants (get out your field guides), even characters such as bedstraw, rattlesnake fern, hog peanut, skunk cabbage, mad-dog skullcap, Philadelphia fleabane (say that one fast 10 times), tick-trefoil, heal-all, and Indian tobacco (put that in your pipe and smoke it).

Some of the pastures here remain quite grassy and open because they have been cleared by ODNR. The mowing controls succession and maintains the preserve's diverse habitat for the numerous birds, insects and mammals who prosper in a mixed environment.

Though you may never see them, it is still worth knowing that four rare moth species reside here. One of them—the winter moth—owes its existence to the controlled habitat of the meadow.

The uncommon and reclusive four-toed salamander, an amphibian designated "special interest" (or potentially threatened), lives in the rotting logs on the forest floor, and an endangered sedge called Cypress-knee sedge may sprout beneath the lowest limb of the buttonbush. False-hop sedge, a threatened plant, may be growing nearby.

According to a 1987 bird survey, woodcocks, belted kingfishers, wood ducks, Acadian flycatchers, ruby-throated hummingbirds, blue-gray gnatcatchers, scarlet tanagers, downy woodpeckers, and the great horned and barred owls were some of the birds nesting in the preserve. Visiting birds included the dark-eyed junco (an endangered species), ruby-crowned kinglet, great blue and green-backed herons, veery, Eastern meadowlark, and the Canada (endangered), hooded, Nashville, Tennessee, black-throated green, bay-breasted, and prothonotary warblers.

Gahanna Woods is at its best in the spring,

summer and early fall. Focus on the forest in the spring when wildflowers and bird song are abundant, then switch to the fields in the summer for the butterflies, bugs, birds, and bloomers common in this habitat. The ponds will be their fullest in the spring, but by July some will dry up.

Mosquitoes can be bothersome in the swampy forest in the summer; less so in the fields. On the plus side, mosquito-eating dragonflies are abundant by the ponds. Those who like to watch nature's unfolding details will enjoy this preserve more than the recreational hiker and seeker of sensational scenery.

HISTORY

The Ohio Chapter of The Nature Conservancy bought 101.5 acres in 1972 with private funds matched by federal dollars from the U.S. Department of the Interior, Land and Water Conservation Fund. The ownership of some of the purchase was given to the Ohio Department of Natural Resources and City of Gahanna. ODNR designated 50.7 acres as an interpretive nature area on January 10, 1974.

JOURNAL

April 4: The primordial, collective song of spring peepers rose above the bird song and echoed throughout the woods. Each pond had its own chorus, its own calendar and score, and its own conductor. Sometimes only one chorus chirped, other times all of them clamored in one big jubilant and hysterical crescendo. The Ohio countryside must have sounded like this when the church bells rang in every village to announce Lee's surrender at Appomatox Court House in April 1865.

After a spell of silence, a soloist offers a plaintive, scratchy aria. Others soon offer their voices, then the choir, then all choirs, repeating rapture.

Hoover Nature Preserve

This is a preserve built for birding, by birders, for birds. Bring binoculars, and bird checklist.

LOCATION
Southern Delaware County, Genoa Township.

OWNERSHIP
Columbus Recreation and Parks Department.

SIZE
This rectangular slice of land comprises 37 acres. It is sometimes called the Hoover Meadows Preserve.

ACCESS
From I-270 in northeastern Columbus, take SR 161 (Dublin-Granville Road) east, then immediately go north on Sunbury Road toward Hoover Reservoir.

Sunbury Road hugs the west bank of the lake but midway crosses to the east side via a causeway. After crossing the lake bear left, going northbound on Sunbury Road. Just past Harlem Road, bear right at a fork, staying on Sunbury Road. The preserve entrance is a half mile on the right. From Delaware, take US 36/SR 37 to Sunbury, Sunbury Road to Galena, Sunbury Road to the preserve.

Trails: The trails that loop, twist, and journey through this ribbon of land were made possible by the Columbus Foundation, the Edwin & Nellie Rousenberger Family and a corps of volunteers. The paths visit meadows, woods, shrubland, and wetland, as well as more than 40 bird houses, or nesting boxes. The boxes are spaced far enough apart for bird privacy and safety. Eventually, observation boxes will be built for humans with binoculars.

The preserve is a bluebird wildlife sanctuary and its managed to attract this colorful meadow bird.

Information: Contact the Columbus Parks and Recreation Department, 420 W. Whittier St, Columbus, OH 43215, (614) 645-3337.

GEOLOGY
Big Walnut Creek, which provides the water for Hoover Reservoir, starts just south of Mount Gilead in the Glaciated Plateau then travels southerly along the eastern edge of the Till Plains physiographic region.

WILDLIFE
Birders keep close tabs on the goings-on at the artificial nests and elsewhere. Twenty bluebirds fledged here in 1995, the best being box 210B accounting for five youngsters. Tree swallows fledged 136 babes that year. Boxes 406, 407 and 105, located near ponds, yielded six each. Herons have roosted here, and prothonotary warblers have been spotted.

On December 9, 1995, a snowy owl—the bird pictured on "White Owl" cigar boxes—paid a rare visit. Visitors will find printed updates in a box by the parking lot. A November 1996 update says to watch for the golden-crowned kinglet hanging around chickadees, titmice and nuthatches along fencerows and thickets. December's update asks eyes to be on the lookout for the state-endangered dark-eyed junco, a.k.a. common snow bird and tomtit, described as "leaden skies above, snow below," referring to the bird's plumage. Seeing this hemlock-beech loving junco in Hoover Meadows would be extraordinary. But one never knows.

HISTORY
This preserve opened in 1988. Another sanctuary, called Mud-hen Marsh, was developed in 1994 at the southeastern corner of Hoover Reservoir. Find the entrance to it, and a wheelchair accessible trail and observation deck, at its entrance near the intersection of Big Walnut and Sunbury roads.

JOURNAL
Best place to set up watch is the easternmost

section, by a marsh, at closing. Besides birds, you are apt to see dragonflies, frogs, and deer.

Knox Woods State Nature Preserve

It is said, and I believe it, that two men hugging the same ancient tree in this woodlot will never touch their fingers. This is how the forest must have looked when white settlers arrived, or something very much like it The woods has towering sugar maples, beeches, black oaks, shagbark hickories, red oaks, and black walnuts for cabins, barns and fences; and a forest floor free of thickets, briars, vines, easy enough to clear for roads. Indeed, Knox Woods is a rarity and one of the last healthy and undisturbed forests, albeit small, in Ohio.

LOCATION
Knox County, Monroe Township.

OWNERSHIP
The Knox County Commissioners own the site, but it is managed by the Ohio Department of Natural Resources, Division of Natural Areas and Preserves.

SIZE & DESIGNATION
This 30-acre woodlot was dedicated a scenic nature preserve on October 11, 1973.

ACCESS
Knox Woods is just a mile northeast of the Mt. Vernon city limits on US 36. Park behind the Knox County Opportunity Center.

Trails: A grassed-over lane lined by stately walnut, oak and hickory trees leads to an information board at the edge of the woods. Study the trail map and description of the preserve before starting.

Two loop trails totaling 1.5 miles—the Shawnee and Mingo trails—make a complete circuit of the preserve and snake along ridges and creek beds. The Shawnee Trail wanders through the northern two-thirds of the property, while the Mingo Trail covers the southern third. The trail names pay tribute to the first Ohioans who saw this forest.

A T-shaped ravine lies in the middle of the preserve, but the trails winding up and down this feature remain gentle. Knox Woods is open daily during daylight hours.

GEOLOGY
Glacial till (gravel, sand, rocks and other sediments) left here by the Illinioan ice mass, which invaded Ohio about 125,000 years ago, rests above sandstone 345 million to 325 million years old. The woods are just six miles east of the reach of the Wisconsinan glacier, the last ice mass passing over Ohio some 20,000 years ago.

Intermittent streams have washed away some of the glacial drift to form ravines, but this erosion has not reached the bedrock so don't look for outcrops and ledges here.

WILDLIFE
Knox Woods is a good place to study the life cycle of a forest. For a moment divert your eyes from the big trees and observe small wonders, like a patch of ground recently scraped by browsing deer. These "scrapes" are easy to find. Just look for areas where the leaves have been kicked up or scratched to expose the dark forest soil. I spotted several scrapes on the Mingo Trail.

During the spring you are apt to find tiny, pale sprout uncurling in a scrape. A deer searching for acorns tossed off the leaves above this sprout, giving it an advantage, perhaps, over others struggling through the mat.

Wildflowers common in a mixed hardwood forest thrive on this forest floor, notably trillium, violets, bloodroot, hepatica, and toothwort. However, by mid-June the forest's canopy closes and little sunlight strikes the ground. That explains the absence of multiflora rose and wild grape vines, plants that seem to choke trees in the woods. There isn't enough light for these invaders. A 1990 survey, however, found 34 herbaceous plants (species whose stems wither every year) growing in the preserve.

Holes in the canopy appear when dead trees fall or fail to "green." Sunbeams streaming through these openings energize the sprouts and saplings struggling beneath the canopy. The forest rejuvenates where the giants rot.

Also, notice the colorful fungi and mosses growing on the fallen trees. These breakdown the old trees, and speed up the return of the nutrients back into the soil for the young ones.

Besides the varieties mentioned above, this strip of forest, surrounded by cornfields, harbors huge specimens of tulip tree, black gum, black cherry, sugar maple, various oaks, and white ash.

HISTORY
Many years ago, orphans found homes faster if they could milk cows, harvest corn, and split wood. So it made sense for the Knox County commissioners to have a farm and a woodlot at its children's home. The tree-lined path to the preserve once was a farm lane that led from the barn to the pastures and woods, which

was then as much a refuge for children as for trees.

Eventually, the children's home was converted to the county social services office (farm chores no longer carrying weight with prospective parents) and the highest bidding farmer leased the cornfields. Though the woods remained undisturbed, they were also unprotected.

When funds ran low, the county commissioners considered leasing the woods to lumber companies, according to Dick Mavis, who has been commissioner since 1975. A state forester made an inventory of the lot and marked it for timber. But nobody got to the point of swinging an axe.

Instead, Mavis said his predecessors—Lester Bennett, Charley Cole, and Harry Daily—decided to preserve the forest, and let it be seen "through the eyes of a child rather than the roar of a chain saw," according to the preserve's dedication paper. That set the stage for the 1973 designation of the woods as a state scenic nature preserve. The woods bears the county's namesake, General Henry Knox, the nation's second secretary of war.

The county still leases the cornfields straddling the preserve, and from time to time somebody suggests thinning out the woods. But, Mavis said, the commissioners are just going to let nature take its course in Knox Woods.

JOURNAL

April 4: Near the entrance to the woods, a man in a catcher's crouch carefully pulled back matted leaves at the base of a shagbark hickory. He summoned his children, a girl about 14 and a boy, I'd say, age eight. They stopped playing with a puppy and obeyed (or indulged) their father.

The man gently lifted the blanket of leaves, the way a new father would present a sleeping infant to his parents. The children leaned over and peaked, but the father said, "You'll have to get down on your knees to see."

"What is it, Dad?" the boy asked.

"You tell me," answered the father. The children inspected the scene silently for 15 seconds or so.

"Ladybugs! There! Look at all of them!" The girl exclaimed.

"What are you looking at?" I wondered aloud.

"Ladybugs!" the boy said, like he had found gold. The father nodded to join them.

I watched the trio again in the woods beside the brook, where the father searched for salamanders beneath the rocks. These scenes reminded me that you sometimes have to scratch the surface to find magic, wonder, and answers. Maybe one of these children will return with their children to the ladybug tree at Knox Woods.

Morris Woods State Nature Preserve

Birders, raise your binoculars. The former owners converted this farm into a wildlife sanctuary then gave it to the state for everybody to enjoy.

LOCATION
Northwest Licking County, Liberty Township.

OWNERSHIP
Ohio Department of Natural Resources, Division of Natural Areas and Preserves.

SIZE & DESIGNATION
This 104-acre site became a scenic nature preserve on Feb. 5, 1980.

ACCESS
From Johnstown take US 62 northeast, then east on Dutch Lane Road for a half mile. Leave Newark west on SR 16, then north on SR 37 to Alexandria. Just beyond this village turn right (north) on Northridge Road for about 5.5 miles, then left on Dutch Lane Road.

Trails: Four trails traipse for about four miles past a couple of ponds, through a luxuriant forest, and across an open meadow. Review the trail map on the information board before departing. Two trails start at the parking lot.

Information: Check the information board for a schedule of these programs, or contact the Ohio Department of Natural Resources.

GEOLOGY
The terrain around here is generally flat, thanks to the bulldozing action of several glaciers. The last ice mass (Wisconsinan glacier) left behind till, or unsorted gravel, rocks, sand and other sediments. The till and the flat landscape sponsored the growth of the enormous beech-maple forest that dominated the land in pre-settlement days. The gentle slopes posed no obstacle to the pioneers who cleared the forest for farming.

James Abbott, the former owner, altered the course of creeks to create the ponds.

WILDLIFE
Wildlife surveys done in the mid-1980s counted 42 species of birds, including rose-breasted grosbeaks, Kentucky warblers, redstarts, veery, pileated woodpeckers, and barred owls. The ponds attract waterfowl common to Ohio. Birdhouses can be spotted throughout the property.

Moth and butterfly types numbered 300, and 85 kinds of wildflowers have been observed. American ginseng, a rare plant, grows here. Harvesting the plant in the preserve is illegal.

A mature beech and maple forest, interspersed with oaks, cherry and hickories, rules the forest. Elsewhere, saplings compete in thickets, and briar patches provide habitat for birds and rabbits. Abbott's Pond Trail cuts through a grove of planted pines and across a grassy meadow kept trim by ODNR.

HISTORY

James Abbott, owner of a Columbus auto parts store and a passionate birdwatcher, bought this old livestock farm in the 1950s and transformed it into a wildlife sanctuary. He planted trees, dug a pair of ponds, installed birdhouses, and built trails and a home. He invited schools groups and nature clubs to the sanctuary.

Abbott called the estate Morris Woods, a tribute to his father Morris Abbott, supposedly an active member of the Audubon Society. Lake Helen honors James Abbott's mother.

James Abbott died in 1979. Local school districts were offered the refuge, but they lacked the funds to maintain the grounds. The Ohio Department of Natural Resources received the property as a gift in 1979, and designated it a scenic preserve on February 5, 1980.

Originally, the Abbott home was to be converted into a permanent nature education center, but this plan has been abandoned due to a shortage of money. Nature programs occasionally are staged there.

JOURNAL

April 4: Three turkey vultures circle overhead. Their pterodactyl-sized shadows ran across the forest floor and up tree trunks, adding menace to the primordial mood of the woods.

Ominous as they appear, buzzards do not do their own killing. They are scavengers who rip the flesh from dead animals. Nature's clean up crew.

Humans have given vultures a bad rap, viewing them with distaste or as comic and clumsy creatures. Our disgust for buzzards stems from their unsightly looks (a face that only a mother could love), and their eating habits. We shudder to think of them mistakenly pecking out our eyeballs while we nap under a tree. To us, they represent doom and avarice, working in league with body snatchers.

Vultures, of course, are graceful flyers who ride thermals and trace figure-eights for what seems like hours. We should no longer hold these gentle, long-suffering bone pickers in low esteem, but instead grant them the nobility and high status we give to predators like hawks, eagles and falcons.

If nature has been partial in this matter (which it has not, of course) then perhaps it is the migratory vulture, more abundant and adaptable than buteos, harriers and owls, who has won its favor. Maybe the vulture's face is the one nature loves.

Seymour Woods State Nature Preserve

"City people like to be neat," James O. Seymour once said. "Mother Nature is not neat." Seymour Woods is not neat either, and it's going to stay that way—as its former owner intended.

LOCATION

Southern Delaware County, Liberty Township.

OWNERSHIP

Ohio Department of Natural Resources, Division of Natural Areas and Preserves.

SIZE & DESIGNATION

106 acres.

ACCESS

From Delaware, take US 23 south, and turn right (west) on Winter Road (past the Boy Scouts camp). The preserve entrance is .75-mile on the right. A small off-road parking area is available.

Trails: The main northbound path stem leads to an old stone lodge. Loop trails branch east and west of this main route. The east loop visits recovering fields, woods, and small streams (the best for birding). The west loop is wooded. The trails total less than two miles. Trails stay open dawn to dusk every day.

GEOLOGY

Examine the creek beds at crossings on the eastern loop. The round rocks resembling bowling balls are "concretions." Geologists suspect concretions began as pieces of organic matter (a twig perhaps), which secreted minerals, such as iron, and attracted sediment. Concretions grow in concentric layers, like pearls or onions. You'll see fragments, looking like pottery shards, in the creeks. Concretions also can be seen at nearby Highbanks State Nature Preserve, a Columbus Metropark, and in Camp Lazarus, the adjacent Boy Scouts camp.

WILDLIFE

Seymour Woods is a mixed hardwood forest of oaks and maples with black cherry, black walnut, black locust, box elder, and hackberry. The former owner reforested a pasture in the early 1980s, and these are beginning to take hold.

Wildflower lovers can look for Miami mist, dame's rocket, white baneberry, Solomon's seal, green dragon, Solomon's plume, mayapple, and others.

HISTORY

Records indicated that James Seymour of Bexley, a founding partner of the Columbus law firm of Vorys, Sater, Seymour, and Pease, owned this property in 1944. He donated it to the state, which dedicated it a state nature preserve in November 1982. A 1997 ballot issue that would have turned preserve management over to the Preservation Parks of Delaware County failed to win voter approval in Delaware County.

JOURNAL

Late spring: After Seymour Woods, I explored

the limestone ruins of Bieber's Mill on the shore of the Olentangy River, along Chapman Road. The site is owned by ODNR as a scenic river something-or-other. James Bieber had a mill here in the 1870s, but he followed mills erected at the location in 1804 and 1843. There's been talk of restoring the historical landmark, but not much action. The state worries a wall some day will collapse on a snoop like me. In spite of the risk, I poked around, and waded in the Olentangy, which is shallow here in summer.

Shallenberger State Nature Preserve

The hills around Lancaster look as if a fist, deep within the Earth, punched rock through the crust and left the rubble in dome-shaped piles. These are called knobs. One of them, Allen Knob, crowned by chestnut oaks and mountain laurel, presides over Shallenberger State Nature Preserve.

LOCATION
Central Fairfield County, Hocking Township.

OWNERSHIP
Ohio Department of Natural Resources, Division of Natural Areas and Preserves.

SIZE & DESIGNATION
The "knob," comprising 87.5 acres, became a scenic nature preserve on May 15, 1973.

ACCESS
From Lancaster, go 4 miles southwest on US 22, then .25 mile north (right turn) on Beck's Knob Road.

Trails: The trails to the summits become steep. Nevertheless, they are worth the exertion because the views of the surrounding farmland are splendid. Rock climbing is prohibited and can be dangerous to humans and the fragile plants clinging to the rocks.

GEOLOGY
Forces above the surface, not a powerful subterranean fist, actually created these knobs. Some 325 million years ago (near the end of the Mississippian geological period) a shallow inland sea covered the area. Rivers and streams filling this ocean deposited sand in a huge delta at the western margin of the Appalachian Plateau. In some places these layers of sand were 500 feet thick. Overlaying layers of mud and sediment compressed the sand, while water rich in iron oxide glued the grains. The product was a rock commonly called Blackhand sandstone. (See Blackhand Gorge.)

Eventually, the land gently uplifted, the ocean disappeared, and rivers changed current. During the next 300 million years rain, wind, and sun beat down the layers above the sandstone, then the sandstone itself, creating the rocky knobs, gorges, cascades, caves, outcrops, and rock bridges characteristic of southeastern Ohio.

Stop along the Arrowhead Trail to feel the gritty texture of the boulders that have rolled off of the knob, and notice the cracks in the facades caused by weathering. The iron oxide that cemented the sand gives the rock its orange tint. A curious depression on the top of Allen Knob, suggesting a quarry at one time, becomes a tiny pond during the spring.

Though the summits of the knobs narrowly avoided a collision with the mile-thick Wisconsinan glacier some 12,000 years ago, the ice mass did bulldoze gravel and sand around the bases of the knolls. This glacial feature, called an end moraine, has influenced the plant life at Shallenberger preserve.

WILDLIFE
On the tops of the unglaciated knobs, where the soil is skinny and dry, chestnut oaks reign beside mountain laurel, a flowering shrub typical in the Appalachians. Here it grows on the south and west sides. The mountain laurel's pinkish blossoms appear from late May to mid-July. Also on the crest, look for ferns like polypody, ebony spleenwort and walking fern.

Below the rocky tops, in the fertile moraine deposits, grows a forest of white and red oaks, red and sugar maples, American beech, wild black cherry, hickory, elm, white ash, tupelo, tulip tree, honey locust, and black walnut. Wildflowers commonly seen in this type of forest (mixed mesophytic) brighten the floor in the spring and summer. Some of them are foam flower, purple dead nettle, small-flowered crowfoot, cut-leaved toothwort, and mouse-eared chickweed.

Tracks in the snow after an all-night storm showed that deer, squirrels, fox, mice, and raccoons had been active at sunrise. Birders can find tanagers, vireos, warblers, hawks, owls, the horned lark, and other common species.

HISTORY
Local Native American tribes no doubt had explored the knobs. One of their major trails, just four miles north of the park, became Coonpath Road.

Hunter's Run honors a Kentucky-born Revolutionary War captain named Joseph Hunter, believed to be the first permanent white settler in Fairfield County in 1797. (Some 800 people attended an outdoor drama reenacting Hunter's settlement, staged in the preserve in September 1988).

Pioneers following Hunter cleared this land in the early 19th century. Their gravestones in a nearby cemetery may have been quarried from these knobs.

The Fairfield County Commissioners received

the property when its owner and preservationist, Jay M. Shallenberger, died in 1971. Grazing continued on several acres near the parking lot until 1973 when the commissioners turned over the site to the Ohio Department of Natural Resources. Remnants of an orchard still stand in the northwest corner of the preserve.

Journal

March: When I reached the crest of Allen Knob, two days after a snowstorm, a pair of turkey vultures took wing and hovered on thermals for 20 minutes. They took turns eyeing me, and tracing figure-eights in the wind. One had lost a couple of wing feathers.

They flew toward another knob, but returned to their roost when I reached Ruble Knob. The gap in the wing span of one bird identified them as the pair I had seen earlier.

On the ride home I listened to a radio broadcast about the throngs of people who had attended Hinckley's annual celebration for its returning buzzards. (See Hinckley Reservation.) I wondered if their encounter with the vultures was as close as mine.

Stage's Pond State Nature Preserve

Binoculars and telephoto lens are a must because the observation deck is one the best spots in central Ohio for viewing the antics of migratory birds.

Location
Pickaway County, Walnut Township.

Ownership
Ohio Department of Natural Resources, Division of Natural Areas and Preserves.

Size & Designation
Stage's Pond, totaling 178 acres, has been a state interpretive nature preserve since August 23, 1974.

Access
From Circleville head north on US 23 about five miles, then go east two miles on Haggerty Road (also known as Red Bridge Road). Look for the parking lot on the north (left) side, just east of Ward Road.

Stage's Pond, the larger of two ponds on the premises, is ideal for a quick glimpse of birds, and for a longer walk. If you are coming here for a fast gander at the geese, an observation blind is just a couple of hundred yards from the parking lot. Your approach to the lookout is concealed by white pines bordering the path.

Trails: The unhurried will find the Moraine Trail worthwhile. It starts at the information board (trail maps may be available here) and heads north (a sign points the way). The Moraine Trail crosses a field and enters a wooded area where the Kettle Lake and Multiflora trails branch off to the left. Ignore these for now and continue ahead of the Moraine Trail. This path ends where the White Oak Trail begins. The White Oak Trail, a thinner and less defined path, loops through the northeastern section of the preserve. It returns to the Moraine Trail.

On the way back follow the Multiflora Trail, named for the multiflora rose thicket the path cuts through, to the Kettle Lake Trail. (A bench on the Multiflora Trail offers a peak of both ponds during the "leafless" months.)

The Kettle Trail goes downhill from the woods into the meadows. Resist the temptation to run down this hill because you will spook the critters on the ponds, and those living at the edge of the forest. This trail runs between the ponds, up a knoll, then traces the wooded southwestern shore of Stage's Pond. The trail ends at the northwestern corner of the property, at Ward Road. (Bicyclists and hikers will find an entrance here, but its use is discouraged by ODNR.)

The terrain is relatively flat, with a few gentle knolls. The trails are usually wet year-round, and some spots hold ankle-deep water. Boardwalks have been constructed across rills, and swampy places, and benches along the trail serve as rest spots and observation points.

Geology
Stand on a knoll overlooking the ponds and try to imagine the size of the ice chunk that formed the 64-acre depression below. That's what happened about 15,000 years ago when the Wisconsinan glacier covered the area. Geologists believe a huge block of ice broke off from the glacier and parked here. Water melting from the receding glacier piled sediments like sand and gravel around the ice block. The knoll you are standing on is made of that glacial debris. Eventually, the ice melted into the pit and formed what geologists call a kettle lake.

At one time the water level may have been much higher, so that one large pond flooded the lowland. The ponds swell and shrink depending on the rainfall. After heavy spring rains, the two ponds may briefly merge, but by summer they have shrunk to separate bodies of water. Water from the shallow and smaller pool, the one beneath the observation blind, flows toward the larger and deeper pond.

A drought in 1988 reduced the ponds to muddy puddles. Such an event, of course, requires all species to survive on less of this vital resource, and some animals may abandon the site altogether in search of water.

Wildlife
The waterfowl poster on the back wall of the observation blind helps you identify the various migratory birds that visit the preserve. Common tenants include the great blue heron, pintail, mallard, green and blue-winged teal, canvasback, red-billed grebe. A great blue heron swept

away when I emerged from the woods on the Kettle Lake Trail, followed by a hawk that had been perched atop a lifeless tree a couple hundred yards away. Less skittish was a pair of red-winged blackbirds, guarding their territory from the branches of saplings.

The meadows host many songbirds (eastern meadowlark included), plus pheasant, quail and rabbits. ODNR manages a habitat for woodcock near the parking lot. Robins and cardinals were abundant during my March visit. Deer and fox tracks crisscrossed through the uplands woods in the White Oak Trail section.

The forested areas, once heavily lumbered and grazed, sponsor the wildflowers common among oak, hickory, walnut, and maple. You'll find multiflora rose suffocating the understory in some areas, and raspberry patches along the trail. Meadow flowers bloom in the summer and attract butterflies.

Specimens of an endangered aquatic plant called featherfoil, resembling a cluster of floating upright stalks 3–8 inches tall, were planted here in 1981 from a colony in Scioto County. Their survival, however, is suspect because they will be abundant one year then disappear for 6–7 years before reappearing again.

HISTORY
A Scot named Richard Stage originally settled on this land, payment for his service in the Revolutionary War. At first, Stage was given land in Adams County, but he sold that parcel and staked his family's future on the Pickaway Plains.

When the Stage family sold their holdings in 1970, stories circulated that a housing development was on the way. Though Stage's Pond showed the scars of grazing and the plow, the Pickaway County Garden Club believed the land was worth rescuing and began its "Save the Stage's Pond" campaign in the early 1970s. In 1973, the club raised $20,204 (the amount needed to reserve $62,000 in matching state and federal funds) with the help of the Columbus Regional Council of the Garden Club of Ohio, other conservation and garden clubs, news media, school groups, and businesses. The Ohio Chapter of The Nature Conservancy negotiated the 123-acre sale and transferred the property to the Ohio Department of Natural Resources when federal matching funds were approved.

Surveys taken in 1973–74 concluded that 60 percent of the property had been cultivated in row farming, 25 percent was classified as grazed woodlot, while 15 percent was open pasture. Seventy wildflower species, and 20 different kinds of trees and shrubs were counted.

Stage's Pond was the first preserve established by a grassroots money-raising effort. You'll find a tribute to that conservation work stamped on a granite boulder near the parking lot. The Pickaway County Garden Club also has contributed money for construction of the bird blind and for more land. An additional 54.7 acres were purchased in 1980 by ODNR.

There is still work to be done. The northern half of Stage's Pond belongs to a property owner who allows hunting and fishing. The state agency hopes to acquire this property someday to fully protect this valuable kettle lake.

JOURNAL
March 28. As I started up the White Oak Trail, I was certain I would spot deer. The woods here provided food and cover for them and was surrounded by fields. Hunters' blinds on the property line, and fresh tracks raised my expectations.

Sure enough, I startled a pair of whitetails from their bed behind the branches of a fallen tree near the northernmost turn in the trail. They snapped branches and tossed leaves as they fled, and my heart raced after them.

Wahkeena Nature Preserve

This place was not "wahkeena" (a Yakima word meaning "most beautiful") when Carmen Warner received it as a wedding present in 1931. Except for a few whiskers growing on a wart (trees surviving on a rocky knob) the property suffered from deforestation and neglect. But Carmen (Hambleton) Warner was a determined gardener and birdwatcher. In no time, she transformed this treeless farmland into a sanctuary befitting its name.

LOCATION
Southeastern Fairfield County, Berne Township.

OWNERSHIP
Ohio Historical Society.

SIZE & DESIGNATION
Wahkeena (say Waw-KEE-nuh) Nature Preserve totals 150 acres. It is a state historical site.

ACCESS
From downtown Lancaster, travel on US 33 southeast about six miles. Turn right at the "Wahkeena" sign onto Old Logan Road (CR 86),

Gifts of Life

In 1999, Ada Burke donated a glacial era wetland in Pickaway County to the Columbus Audubon Society. Calamus Swamp was expected to be dedicated a state natural area and open for visits in the summer of 2000.

then take the second right in one mile to Pump Station Road (TR 274). The preserve will be on your right in about 1.5 miles.

First stop should be the lodge, the former Warner residence, which has been converted into a nature education center with permanent exhibits. Pick up a trail guide while you are there.

Trails: The brief Shelter Trail (just a half mile) follows a hemlock-lined path and creek to a shelter house built by the Warners. Here you can cross a foot bridge and return to the lodge on the other side of the creek or continue on the mile-long Casa Burro Trail.

From the shelter house the Casa Burro Trail passes an impressive stand of tulip trees and other hardwoods. The trail circles left and climbs a steep ridge, then descends the hill. The journey ends with a walk through a pine grove. Signs along the trail warn that a rifle range is not far away! Stay on the trail.

Also, walk the boardwalk trail through a marsh (west of the lake), visit the observation blind overlooking Lake Odonata, and study the marsh (once a pond) and old gardens east of the lodge. These latter paths wander through the backyard of Wahkeena.

Special Places & Events: A fulltime, on-site naturalist offers education programs for schools and nature groups in this open-air classroom. Scientists also use the preserve as an outdoor laboratory.

Information: Contact the preserve manager at (740) 746-8695 or the Ohio Historical Society, 1982 Velma Avenue, Columbus, Ohio 43211, (888) 909-6446.

GEOLOGY

Wahkeena is another preserve located at the "edge" of glaciation. (Also see Chestnut Ridge and Clear Creek metroparks and Shallenberger State Nature Preserve.) The various glaciers that scoured much of Ohio during the Ice Age just missed this spot. A lobe of the last mighty ice mass, the Wisconsinan glacier (about 12,000 years ago), extended down the Hocking River Valley but quit at the village of Sugar Grove, just a mile east of the preserve.

The cliffs and bedrock outcrops in the preserve are made of Blackhand sandstone. Some 350 million years ago sand deposited here by the waves of an inland sea and by streams rushing off mountains to the east became compressed into rock. Later, the land rose and exposed the sandstone to the erosive power of water, sun, and wind. These forces carved the rock into the formations typical in the Hocking Hills. (Also read Blackhand Gorge and Conkle's Hollow.)

The house-size boulders near the lodge are called float rocks. Erosion split these chunks of sandstone from the outcrops. They rolled down the ridge and rested where you see them.

Look for the natural springs where groundwater surfaces and flows into creeks.

WILDLIFE

This once naked land now teems with wildlife.

During a recent spring 100 species of birds and 15 different mammals were spotted. Warblers favor Wahkeena's woods, and even the rare prothonotary warbler has been seen, its golden breast streaking through the brush like a sunbeam. Lucky observers may find a pileated woodpecker. I observed a cerulean warbler above boardwalk trail.

Thirty species of fern, the most common being Christmas fern, carpet the ground. Search for the delicate maidenhair fern during your visit.

Eight varieties of orchids thrive here, including some favorites like showy orchis and pink lady's slipper. Rhododendron and mountain laurel also grace the grounds.

The trees in the forest are young, say 60–65 years old. Many were planted by the Warners, who also let natural succession takes it course, too. The hemlocks that line the Shelter Trail probably were transplanted from another location in the preserve. These are relicts from the last glacier, which promoted the migration of trees and plants common in Canada to Ohio.

Graceful dragonflies and damselflies hover over Lake Odonata whose name honors the taxonomic order of these insects. Frogs and turtles are abundant on the shores of the lake and marshes.

A bird checklist and brochures explaining Wahkeena's geology, ferns, trees, and wildflowers are available at the nature center for a small fee.

HISTORY

Wahkeena pays tribute to the creative forces of Carmen Warner, as well as nature's. She was a devoted gardener and an avid ornithologist, the latter interest inherited from her father James Chase Hambleton, first president of the Columbus Audubon Society.

After buying the tired 94-acre farm in 1931, the Warners planted trees, and built a lodge, three lakes, a footbridge, a corral and barn for pet burros, bird feeders, and a shelter house in the woods. Additional land purchases increased the holding to 150 acres. Topsoil was dumped on newly-constructed garden terraces, and a hog barn was converted into a quaint guest house. Visitors said the estate had a country club look to it.

Mrs. Warner named the grounds Wahkeena after admiring Wahkeena Falls in the Columbia River Gorge in Oregon.

Dr. Warner, a noted surgeon and instructor in Columbus, passed away at age 88 in 1943. Carmen Warner died in 1956, and bequeathed the estate to the Ohio Historical Society "for nature study and as a preserve for birds and other wildlife."

In the early 1960s, the historical society and the Ohio Association of Garden Clubs, whose many members made pilgrimages to Wahkeena, set up a trust fund for nature education programs. The association also advises the owner on preservation matters.

Log on to www.ohiohistory.org/ for more information on Wahkeena Nature Preserve.

SOUTHWEST

Adams Lake Prairie State Nature Preserve

It is said that Dr. Emma Lucy Braun, Ohio's foremost botanist-ecologist, knew every flower and tree in Adams County—and that they knew her. She believed that the shortgrass prairie growing on the thin soil of her native county was much older than the tallgrass prairie of Central Ohio. Adams Lake Prairie is a remnant of that early prairie invasion.

LOCATION
Central Adams County, Tiffin Township.

OWNERSHIP
Ohio Department of Natural Resources, Division of Natural Areas and Preserves.

SIZE & DESIGNATION
This 22-acre prairie became an interpretive nature preserve on May 16, 1973.

ACCESS
Enter the preserve from Adams Lake State Park, located a mile north of West Union on SR 41.

Trails: The double-loop trail begins across the street from the parking lot. In a few places the Post Oak Trail splits. Take the left fork, heading east into the forest. After crossing several small creek beds, the path swings south and up a hill. At the summit the path veers west and comes to a clearing—the prairie opening.

Here, on a boardwalk, the path forks. Turn left onto the Prairie Dock Trail, which traces the periphery of the prairie and rejoins the Post Oak Trail. Go left at this junction to return to the parking lot.

This 1–1.5-mile walk can be shortened by a half mile by bearing right on Post Oak Trail (near the entrance), and walking the Prairie Dock Trail. The latter route bypasses the forest on the eastern half of the preserve.

The best time to view the prairie blossoms is mid-July through Labor Day.

GEOLOGY
The prairies in Adams County are older and different than their counterparts in the Darby Plains, which grew on moist flatlands 4,000–6,000 years ago, a span of time called the Xerothermic Period. (See the chapter on the Darby Plains prairies). The shortgrass prairie here is a leftover of an earlier western prairie invasion, perhaps predating the Illinoian glacier that came within a stone's throw of this site 125,000 years ago.

The tallgrass prairie on the Darby Plains has flourished on thick beds of glacial till deposited by the Wisconsinan glacier roughly 12,000 years ago. In contrast, the prairies in unglaciated Adams County struggle on dry and thin soil derived from bedrock.

Beneath Adams Lake Prairie lies a layer of Crab Orchard shale. It is made of mud and silt that settled to the bottom of an ocean more than 455 million years ago (Ordovician geological period). When the sea retreated this goo, now exposed, turned into shale.

Once exposed, Crab Orchard shale does not stay shale for long. Rain, sun and wind cause it to disintegrate into a cream-colored mud filled with bits of dolomite, giving it a calcareous flavor. When moist it once again becomes sticky, and easily erodes away. When baked it becomes hard as a brick. Trees have difficulty sinking roots in this kind of soil, but not the members of the shortgrass prairie. They arrived during some other long-term heat wave, either before or after the Illinoian glacier. Nobody knows for sure.

Eventually, though, the climate changed and the forest took over much of the land. By the time white settlers reached central Adams County, the shortgrass prairie had been reduced to isolated islands on rocky promontories, gullies, and eroded conical-shaped hillsides called "bald hills" and "buffalo beats." These treeless places did not favor the farmer's plow so livestock grazed on these meager fields.

Adams Lake Prairie appears to be an offspring of a remnant patch of prairie. Prairie vegetation (shortgrasses, red cedar, wildflowers) often spreads into abandoned farm fields (former forests). That is what happened here sometime in the 1920s, according to the Ohio Department of Natural Resources. The prairie continues to struggle against the surrounding oak-hickory forest, which also has taken back some of this hillside, too.

WILDLIFE

In his journal, Dr. John Locke wrote that the "buffalo beats" of Adams County were "a paradise for the botanist." Locke, then assistant state geologist, had been commissioned to prepare a geological survey of Adams County in the mid-1830s. His description of the prairie still rings true.

Folks who have visited a lush, thick-matted tallgrass prairie are going to see a different kind of prairie at Adams Lake. The vegetation here is sparse, clumped together, and shorter. Some of slopes in gullies are barren, and erosion continues its dirty work. Observe the details. Look how the vegetation is thicker at the base of the handful of trees that have managed to sink their roots. The roots of these trees grow on clumps, or little earthen islands, a foot or so higher than the surrounding turf. Grasses and wildflowers also flourish on these mounds because the tree roots have trapped the moisture and soil needed for their survival. The herbaceous clump-dwellers, in turn, retard erosion and add nutrients to the soil.

There are plenty of the familiar prairie flowers. Prairie dock, nodding onion, pale-spiked lobelia, flowering spurge, golden Alexanders, and long-leaved bluets survive better than others on the barren spots. The endangered Sampson's snakeroot, little bluestem (a grass), shooting-star, prairie rose, downy wood mint, stiff gentian, three-lobed violet and green milkweed (potentially threatened) grow on more fertile sections.

Almost 100 wildflowers and grasses are listed in ODNR's preserve brochure. Downy skullcap, prostrate tick-trefoil, madder, king devil, self-heal, featherfleece, gall-of-the-earth, are some.

The preserve sponsors 27 shrubs (shrubby St. John's-wort) and trees (notably red cedar and juniper) that grow slowly in shallow soils. Other trees, usually on the fringe of the prairie opening, have established themselves, including shingle oak, post oak, white oak, sassafras, black locust, flowering dogwood, and redbud.

The shade of these trees inhibits the spread of the sun-hungry prairie and prepares the land for the return of the trees of the deep forest. In the preserve these latter species are represented by white, red, and black oaks, and shagbark and pignut hickories.

Critters are not fond of this hostile habitat. The one that stands out, or rather crawls out, is the notorious red mound builder ant, or Allegheny mountain ant, said to be the most aggressive of its clan east of the Mississippi River.

As their name suggests, these busy bugs build mounds, perhaps 12–18 inches high, composed of unearthed dirt with a sprinkling of twigs, bark, leaf scales. Beneath the mound is a maze of tunnels (think of a bowl of spaghetti) that may house 100,000 laborers.

These fearless ants will attack almost anything with their pinching mandibles. Humans are safe unless they stand beside an anthill too long. They secrete formic acid when they bite.

The mounds are scattered throughout the pre-serve. Leave the anthills alone. Disturbing an ant nest is just as harmful and disrespectful as teasing a caged tiger to hear it growl.

HISTORY

As noted above, the beauty of this prairie was first reported by Dr. Locke in the 19th century.

In 1947, Adams Lake was created when the Lick Branch of Ohio Brush Creek was dammed. The water in the 47-acre lake quenched the thirst of nearby West Union. In 1950 the lake became the centerpiece of Adams Lake State Park.

Later, Dr. Braun, who knew the flora and fauna of the region better than the back of her hand, brought the Adams Lake prairie to the attention of her colleague at the University of Cincinnati, Dr. Richard H. Durrell.

In 1971, Durrell, then a member of the newly-formed Ohio Natural Areas Council, raised the idea of protecting this prairie. ODNR purchased the site in 1972, and dedicated it as an interpretive preserve on May 16, 1973.

JOURNAL

September: Just wish Lucy Braun was alive to show me around this place. I picture her dressed in khaki pants, cotton blouse rolled up to the elbows, floppy hat shading her tawny, bespectacled face. With a pencil, she lifts petals with her pinky, then jots down a note on a clipboard. She moves about the prairie randomly, instinctively, flower to flower, a course not unlike a butterfly's.

Bachelor Wildlife and Game Preserve

Joseph M. Bachelor, a professor at Miami University for 20 years, started a preservation effort by bequeathing 535 acres in 1947. Other faculty and friends followed his example, and the sanctuary comprises 10 tracts totaling nearly 1,000 acres.

LOCATION

Northwestern Butler County, Oxford Township.

OWNERSHIP

Miami University.

SIZE & DESIGNATION

The nearly 1,000-acre preserve is managed by the Bachelor Reserve and Other Natural Areas Committee. Hiking trails wander through Bachelor Wildlife and Game Reserve (535 acres), Reinhart Reserve (44 acres), Silvoor Biological Sanctuary

(2.5 acres), Kramer Woods (14 acres), Brown Glover Tract (100 acres), Western Woods (120 acres), Peffer Memorial Park (80 acres), and Four Mile Woodlands (20 acres).

ACCESS

From Oxford, home of Miami University, drive on Bonham Road, which branches northeasterly from the corners of Talawanda and Sycamore streets on campus. Turn right on Oxford-Milford Road where Bonham Road deadends. There is a parking lot on the northside of Bonham Road, about 1.5 miles from Oxford. Trailhead parking also is found on SR 73, just east of the college's stables and Four Mile Creek, and on Oxford-Milford Road. Access to Peffer Memorial Park is on US 27 just south of town.

Trails: Hiking trails branch north and south from the Bonham Road parking lot. The Pine, East and Reinhart loops, and the path along Harker's Run, all on the south side, are the best because they offer several habitats, woodland ponds, varying terrain, excellent creeking, and quietude. Put them all together for a walk five or more miles. Take the Pine Loop (1.4 miles) or the East Loop (1.8 miles) for short walks. Swaying steel cable bridges cross Harker's Run, though in summer you may prefer to wade across the shallow stream.

On the north side, the North Loop tracks the perimeter of the north section of Bachelor Preserve, and a connecting trail leads to Kramer Loop. Though metal signs at trail intersections are helpful, a trail map in the parking lot (or printed maps) would make the paths more user friendly.

Other trails in the system feel crowded by the village and college, but they can be rewarding.

Information: Contact the Bachelor Reserve and Other Natural Areas Committee, Miami University, Department of Zoology, Oxford, OH 45056, (513) 529-3100.

GEOLOGY AND WILDLIFE

A melting pot of habitats and wildlife thrives in this collection of natural areas that ring Miami University. Oak groves stand above unshaven cedar glens carpeted by clubmoss. Elsewhere, maturing pines are giving way to beeches. Woodland ponds with sycamores on their lips drip into Harker's Run where the outlines of entombed Ordovician animals sparkle in water. Deer have worn rutted trails; raccoon tracks scribble creek beaches.

HISTORY

While he taught at Miami University, Dr. Joseph M. Bachelor stockpiled land just outside the orbit of the campus. He lived on the land, worked as a gentleman farmer, and left 535 acres of it to the university when he died in 1947. In his will, Bachelor stipulated that the woods was to be kept as a nature preserve and research area in perpetuity.

Faculty and friends followed suit, and the university bought tracts to link the properties. Dr. Robert A. Hefner and Mr. and Mrs. Stuart Fitton

donated the Silvoor Biological Sanctuary in 1978, Paul and Edith Kramer gave their mature woodlot in 1987, and in 1991 the college received 44 acres from Dr. and Mrs. Roy Reinhart. Peffer Memorial Park remembers G. Maurice Peffer, whose uncle, Fred C. Yager, paid for development of the park facilities. William Amos and Dorothy Amos also donated money for park development.

JOURNAL

February: I'm standing in one of the preserve's open, cedar meadows, an island encircled by hardwoods, shrubs, and aging conifers. Spongy and shaggy clubmoss, or what I knew in my youth as creeping pine, spreads in every direction and intensifies the evergreeness. The tangle seems to be a single, reaching, creeping organism. The morning's light snowfall sweetens the scene like powdered sugar. Only one human, wearing waffle-soled size 10s, has passed this way before me. Deer have worn criss-crossing runs decades deep around the cedars, but none has been trodden today. A cedar stand just cannot offer enough cover, midday in the middle of February. In hardwoods a quarter-mile ahead I stumbled up on a whitetail staring at me fifty yards portside: a skinny buck who has shed his rack I suspect. The deer strikes a "deep freeze" pose hoping I pass without noticing him. Injured deer employ this "wait and see" strategy, too. But I know the trick, and act nonchalantly. I even looked away, showed disinterest, and thereby fooled the deer into thinking his deception had worked. We played this game for two or three minutes before the deer hobbled away on three legs. I doubt it would survive the winter.

Caesar Creek Gorge State Nature Preserve

All diffidence aside. First, a torrent of water gushing from the last glacier widens a crack in 440–500 million-year-old limestone and sculpts this gorge. Then, two centuries ago, a former black slave adopted by the Shawnees, names the creek after himself—Cizar. And just two decades ago, nature persuades new human arrivals to preserve this splendid place as Ohio's third state natural area. How lucky can you get?

LOCATION

Northwestern Warren County, Wayne Township.

Ownership

Ohio Department of Natural Resources, Division of Natural Areas and Preserves.

Size & Designation

Dedicated as a scenic nature preserve on January 2, 1975, this preserve encompasses 461 acres. The Little Miami River, which forms the west border of the preserve, is a state and national scenic river.

Access

Exit I-71 at SR 73 and go west toward Corwin. Just before SR 73 crosses the Little Miami River, turn right on Smith Road, which bends left and empties into Corwin Road. Turn left on Corwin Road and travel south for about two miles. The parking lot for the hiking trails will be on the left after crossing Caesar Creek bridge.

From Waynesville, where US 42 and SR 73 meet, travel east on SR 73 across the Little Miami River (a half mile), turn left on Smith Road and left on Corwin Road.

Trails: The trail network in the preserve is known as Caesar's Trace. The eastbound trail emerging from the parking lot briefly ascends an old farm lane before dropping into the floodplain of Caesar Creek.

The path heads upstream, following the south bank of the creek beneath the rim of the gorge. The creekside trail is the most scenic part of the journey, and you will not be branded a slacker if you backtrack to the car when the trail swings away from the stream.

The Little Miami Scenic Park Trail cuts through the preserve, hugging Corwin Road. After the hike, drive north on Corwin Road, take your first left, and visit the new covered bridge (the Corwin M. Nixon Covered Bridge) stretching across the Little Miami River. You also can view the river up close by parking in the lot for canoe access on the right before the bridge.

Vegetation hides the gorge walls in the summer. To see them, come back in the winter. The trail along the creek and floodplain is often soggy and slippery. Rest rooms are found at the parking lot, which is large enough for school buses and recreational vehicles.

Interpretive nature programs are conducted here throughout the year by naturalists.

Geology

Raging torrents of water gushing from the melting Wisconsinan glacier some 12,000 years ago created this picturesque gorge and stream. Meltwater from the glacier's brow cut a path through the loose glacial till, composed of gravel, clay, sand, boulders. Then it scoured limestone and shale bedrocks dating back to the Ordovician geological period, roughly 470 million years ago.

These fossil-rich ancient rocks reveal the creatures who lived in the broad shallow sea that inundated Ohio at that time—brachiopods, bryozoans (corals), trilobites, crinoids. Their remains made the limey soup that became limestone. Look, but do not collect the fossils. (Author Edward Abbey called these precious stones "leavem-rites," or leave-em-right where you found them.)

Caesar Creek runs into the Little Miami River, which forms the western boundary of the preserve. Come here in the winter when the trees have dropped their leaves to see the geological features. The gorge wall reaches a height of 180 feet.

Wildlife

Several varieties of bass, plus suckers, bullheads, sunfish, carp, catfish, black crappie, and rare brook pimpernel swim in Caesar Creek. The creek's abundance of darters, minnows, shiners, frogs, and crayfish attracts great blue herons and kingfishers.

In the floodplain forest, flickers screeched at me while other woodpeckers, less alarmed, continued their excavations. Driving in, I noticed two hawks (species unknown) flying separate routes up the Little Miami River.

I know the preserve has a healthy red fox. I saw it jogging up the old farm lane. Its bushy tail stiffened and its eyes bulged in panic when it saw me. Judging by tracks along the trail and shore, white-tailed deer and raccoons reside here.

More than 110 kinds of wildflowers blossom in the preserve. Notables include rarities like shooting star, large summer bluets, plus Miami mist, wild ginger (roots taste like ginger), cleavers, golden ragwort, among many. Prairie species and pokeweed (with its distinctive black berry clusters) grow conspicuously in the recovering meadows.

A late 1970s, inventory found 63 woody species in this mixed deciduous forest—sycamore, cottonwood, walnut, beech, several oaks, sugar maple, hickory, flowering dogwood, box elder, black maple, tulip tree, burning bush, American elm (now gone), etc.

Except for the steep gorge wall, the entire preserve has been subjected to farming, lumbering, or grazing. Now natural succession, nature's slow process of changing the meadows back into hardwood forests, is reworking its wonders on this land.

History

Humans have been visiting this gorge for 8,000 years. The first group of ancient people, conveniently classified by archeologists as the Paleo Indians, gave way to the Mound Builders, and then the so-called Fort Ancient Indians by 1200 A.D. These latter hunters and gatherers supposedly built several villages near here. They grew corn, beans, and squash in the floodplain to supplement a diet of animals killed by a bow and arrow. Later, the Wyandot, Miami, and Shawnee people used this area.

In 1776, Shawnee warriors defending their territory attacked a flatboat on the Ohio and captured a black slave named Cizar. Some might say the Shawnees freed Cizar. Anyway, Cizar enjoyed hunting near this stream, and named it after himself, so the story goes. It could be that the Shawnees referred to the stream as Cizar's because he had chosen it as his hunting ground.

Supposedly, Cizar advised Simon Kenton, Ohio's Daniel Boone, to follow Caesar Creek to the east bank of the Little Miami River when he escaped from the Shawnee village at Oldtown. A major Indian trail followed the west bank of the river. A lesser Indian trail on the Caesar Creek side of the river was dubbed Bullskin Trace by white settlers. Runaway slaves followed this branch of the Underground Railroad to safe houses owned by Quakers.

In spite of its designation as a state nature preserve in January 1975, the U.S. Army Corps of Engineers dammed Caesar Creek a mile upstream in 1978. The corps' action (supposedly to control flooding in the Little Miami Valley) flooded a hamlet called Henpeck, the entire town of New Burlington, and several ancient Indian sites. Caesar Creek State Park and State Wildlife Area were the byproducts of the impoundment, too.

Cedar Bog State Memorial

"Welcome to the Ice Age," says Site Manager Terry Jaworski, beginning his tour for visitors at Cedar Bog State Nature Preserve. The greeting is appropriate. Cedar Bog beckons you back in time, to a chilly period when Ohio was covered by ice. In spite of its name, this 428-acre preserve in Champaign County is not really a bog, but a rare and fragile fen.

Location

Southern Champaign County, Urbana Township.

Ownership

The site is jointly owned by the Ohio Historical Society and Ohio Department of Natural Resources, Division of Natural Areas and Preserves. It is managed by the Ohio Historical Society.

Size & Designation

Fifty-three acres of this boreal-prairie fen remain protected as a scientific preserve, while 90 acres is designated interpretive. The rest of the property, 285 acres, is a scenic nature preserve open to the public at scheduled times. The historical society has dedicated the refuge as a state memorial. Cedar Bog also is a National Natural Landmark.

Access

From Urbana, travel south on US 68 about 4 miles, then one mile west on Woodburn Road. Look for the entrance and parking lot on the right, just past the railroad tracks. The preserve is a little more than 9 miles north of Springfield on US 68.

Trails: The fragile ecosystem of the fen requires careful protection—and careful explanation. That's why the resident site manager leads you on a tour along a boardwalk trail measuring .8 miles.

A rest room is located in the parking lot, but drinking water is not available. Carry a small canteen. The fen water sometimes rises above the boardwalk trail, so be advised that the path can be wet and slippery in places.

It is always best to make an appointment to visit this preserve, but it isn't necessary.

Information: Contact Cedar Bog State Nature Preserve, 980 Woodburn Road, Urbana, Ohio 43078 (937) 484-3744 (site manager); or (888) 909-6446 at the Ohio Historical Society, 1982 Velma Avenue, Columbus, Ohio 43211-2497.

Geology

Cedar Bog's special geological history creates the unique habitat for the wildlife thriving here. It is a remnant of a series of fens, swamp forests, and wet prairies that once stretched across the broad Mad River Valley, which itself was formed by the runoff from the Wisconsinan ice sheet 12,000–18,000 years ago. The Wisconsinan was the last of at least three (possibly four) continental ice sheets that blanketed Ohio during the Ice Age.

The melting glacier removed hilltops, rerouted streams, and scoured bedrock. In southern Champaign County, it dumped hundreds of feet of gravel into the abandoned tributaries of the ancient Teays River, a northwesterly flowing stream which, in its preglacial heyday, rivaled the potency of the Ohio River. (The Teays River was long gone before the arrival of the Wisconsinan glacier). Two long ridges of this gravel debris, or moraines, flank a valley where Cedar Bog is situated.

The groundwater that seeps down the Mad River Valley and the smaller Urbana Outwash percolates through the calcium and magnesium-enriched gravel and surfaces as springs northeast of the preserve. These fountains—cool because they have not been warmed by the sun—keep the water flowing through the fen year-round, and at a relatively constant temperature (54° Fahrenheit) and volume.

The "hard" water is charged with dissolved bicarbonates of calcium and magnesium. These compounds combine with mud to form a lime-rich soil called marl. Only specialized plants can survive in this rather harsh habitat of cool water and marl.

The spring water "flushes" the fen and refreshes Cedar Run as it meanders throughout the preserve. This flushing action is the trademark of a fen. In contrast, a bog sits in a basin and catches precipitation. Water leaves a bog through evaporation.

The water supports the site's delicate ecosystem. The fen shrinks whenever the flow has been interrupted by prolonged drought, mining of the gravel, or diversion (draining or ditching) for farming, transportation, recreation, or housing developments.

Cedar Bog is now just $\frac{1}{16}$ its original size. Long ago it swamped 7,000 acres. Scientists have figured that 15 of Ohio's 52 original fens have vanished, and that the survivors, like Cedar Bog, are tiny shadows, mere relicts, of their former glory. Ohio has lost 95 percent of its wetlands since the settlement of white people.

Left to nature's slow pace, fens and bogs eventually would fill with natural debris (soil and plant matter) and turn into forests. Somewhere else, new wetlands would emerge and continue the life cycle. However, human activities have severely disturbed this process of regeneration. We can say

reliably that a new bog will not be born when one meets its natural death. Consequently, Cedar Bog and other rare fens must be "saved" from natural forces, and managed for preservation.

WILDLIFE

At first, the fen's saline water (calcium carbonate) and cool temperature discouraged plant life. Eventually, though, sedge (a marsh grass) took root on the marl flats. Repeated growths of sedge formed a peat-like deposit and sponsored the encroachment of northern white cedar, which gives the preserve its name. Northern white cedar, or arbor vitae, a common tree in colder, northern climes, came into Ohio in the vanguard of the glacier. This

Bogged
Down

How to Know Your Fen from a Bog in the Ground

For years the words bog, marsh, fen, swamp, and quagmire were used interchangeably (except by astute students of wetlands). Now we know each has a special place in the natural process.

BOG BASICS
•Starts as a pond, formed when a chunk of ice broke from a glacier and melted in a depression.
•Water enters as precipitation and leaves through evaporation.
•Water is acidic (3.5–5.5 pH); oxygen and nitrogen deficient.
•Generally circular-shaped, and vegetation grows in rings from an "eye."
•Water temperature is usually around 54 ° F.
•Northern plants like red maple, birch, hemlock, blackgum, pines may find a habitat here.
•Most bogs in Ohio are in the northeast, but a few occur in the northwest. See Brown's Lake Bog.

FEELING LIKE A FEN
•Lies in shallow areas near gravel ridges (moraines) formed by glaciers. The gravel is rich in calcium and magnesium.
•Groundwater travels through the marly gravel, surfaces as a spring, and leaves via another body of water. Though a current may be imperceptible, water flows through and flushes a fen.
•Water is slightly acidic to alkaline (5.5–8 pH); lacks oxygen and nitrogen.
•Water temperature remains fairly constant at 54 ° F.
•Sedge grass and arbor vitae are common plants.
•Usually "meadowy" in shape; and plants grow in clusters, not concentrically.
•In Ohio, fens are found in the northeastern and western parts of the state. Besides Cedar Bog, visit Jackson Bog (another misnomer) and Frame Lake-Herrick Fen state nature preserves.

—SO

tree, designated as potentially threatened in Ohio, survives in pockets that encourage its growth. These sturdy specimens were prized for railroad ties and as Christmas trees.

Oddly, the fallen needles of the cedar produce an acidic soil enabling partridgeberry, bulblet fern, Canada mayflower, starflower, and green woodland orchid (potentially threatened species) to flourish.

Thirty-two other Ice Age imports dwell here, including shrubs like the scrubby cinquefoil and the state-threatened northern dwarf or swamp birch, which survives to the Arctic Circle but reaches its southern extreme here. Some eastern hardwoods have gained a foothold on the periphery, notably butternut, a potentially threatened tree whose nut attracts deer.

Other shrubs are represented by the common spicebush, ninebark, willows, huckleberry, and alder-leaved buckthorn. These communities, once more numerous, are being crowded by the arbor vitae.

Wild orchids from the temperate areas—small yellow lady's slippers (endangered) and grass-pink (potentially threatened)—mix with prairie blossoms, such as blazing star and prairie dock, which entered the scene during a dry, warm spell, the so-called Xerothermic Period, about 4,000 years ago. Like Ohio's wetlands, the state's prairie meadows enjoyed a greater range and collection of flora.

As you hike, look for large-flowered trillium, marsh marigolds, Johnny jump-ups, rue anemone, three kinds of Solomon's seal, round-leaved sundew (potentially threatened), Riddell's goldenrod, coreopsis, prairie valerian (endangered and at its eastern limit), dog violets, queen-of-the-prairie, bellflowers, skunk cabbage, Canadian burnet (a.k.a. white swamp candles), grass-of-parnassus, Kalm's lobelia, and the potentially threatened fringed gentian, a late summer and autumn bloomer.

All totaled, 59 protected species (endangered or otherwise) have taken up residence at Cedar Bog. One of them is the venomous massasauga rattlesnake, known to nest in a field of Kentucky fescue, a hybrid grass. Another is the spotted turtle (look for spots on its shell), an elusive reptile that dives to safety when it senses danger. Both of these critters are designated "special interest" by the Division of Wildlife, a listing roughly equal to "potentially threatened."

Several butterflies commonly seen flitting about at Cedar Bog are rarely found anywhere else in Ohio. These are the swamp metalmark (endangered), Milbert's tortoise shell, and silvery checkerspot.

Cedar Bog provides a habitat for more than 100 bird species. One rarity that has been observed here is the yellow rail, which breeds only in tiny, widely scattered areas in the Great Lakes and Canada.

Eighteen kinds of fish swim in Cedar Run. Two rare swimmers are the endangered tongue-tied minnow and the brook trout, the latter designated "special interest." The cool waters of spring-fed Cedar Run is one of the few places the brook trout survives in Ohio. The Mad River sponsors trout, too, but most other Ohio streams are too warm for this prized game fish. Other unusual fish include the American brook lamprey, mottled sculpin, brook stickleback, and central mudminnow. Of course, fishing in the preserve is unlawful.

HISTORY

Though much of the original fen—known at various times as Cedar Swamp, Urbana Bog, Dallas Cedar Swamp, and Dallas Bog—became farmland, a few landowners protected this unique land. One of them was Russell Randall, who guarded his showy lady's slippers (wild orchids) with a shotgun in the 1920s.

In 1922, wildflower artist and Cincinnati Tree Council founder Florence Murdoch, owner of some of the wetland, tried to get the fen protected by the Ohio Department of Forestry. Others took up the cause later, notably the Urbana Women's Club. Finally, the state set aside $10,000 to buy the fen in 1938, but just as the transaction started, Governor Martin L. Davey (Davey Woods preserve in Champaign County is named after him) vetoed the deal.

Florence Murdoch, who had sold her share of the fen to a relative, early in 1941, carried the torch again later that year when she discovered that one of the owners planned to drain the bog and fatten cattle in it. She enlisted the support of Edward Sinclair Thomas and Erwin C. Zepp, both curators at the Ohio Archeological and Historical Society, the precursor of the Ohio Historical Society.

Thomas talked with the new governor, John W. Bricker, who agreed not to block the purchase. Thomas and others finagled $5,000 from the state to buy an 88-acre tract of Cedar Bog for the state's first nature preserve. The purchase killed the cattle ranch scheme. The title was transferred to the historical society in 1942.

Later, the Ohio Chapter of The Nature Conservancy helped to acquire some 200 acres to form a buffer zone beside the fen. Additional land has been acquired over the years.

Greater protection came in April 1967 when the U.S. Department of the Interior declared Cedar Bog a National Natural Landmark. On February 28, 1979 the fen was designated a state nature preserve by the Ohio Department of Natural Resources.

Conservation groups led a successful campaigns in 1959 and again in 1972 against widening US 68, the main drag between Urbana and Springfield. However, those so-called highway "improvements" resurfaced again in the early 1990s.

Chaparral Prairie State Nature Preserve

It is a wonder anything grows at all in this dry, skinny soil, which, until 1984, had cows tearing out its grass. But Chaparral Prairie's rehabilitation has been remarkable under state protection. It looks like a shortgrass prairie opening again. Come here in the middle of summer and see attractions like rattlesnake master (a non-poisonous prairie plant), and a butterfly named Edward's hairstreak.

LOCATION
Central Adams County, Tiffin Township.

OWNERSHIP
Ohio Department of Natural Resources, Division of Natural Areas and Preserves.

SIZE & DESIGNATION
Chaparral Prairie is an interpretive preserve protecting 67 acres.

ACCESS
Starting in West Union, take SR 247 north about 2.5 miles, then go west (left) on Chaparral Road. In 5–6 miles Chaparral Road (CR 22-C) bends sharply left. However, you bear right on Hawk Hill Road (TR 23). The entrance will be on the left in about 200 yards. The small parking lot only can handle a few autos.

Trails: Follow the mowed Hawk Hill Trail that begins just to the left of the stout barn at the end of the lane. The trail heads straight to the back of the meadows, curves left through a grove of cedars, ascends an oak ridge, then returns to the starting point for a .75-mile hike. The other paths that stem from this main trail are firebreaks.

Special Places & Events: Interpretive nature programs held during the year point out the highlights of this area. Visit from mid-July until Labor Day when the prairie flowers bloom in their full majesty.

GEOLOGY
One of the world's top ecologists, the late Dr. Emma Lucy Braun, believed that the dry, shortgrass prairies in her beloved Adams County were much older than the lush, tallgrass of Central and Northern Ohio.

The latter prairies (see Darby Plains Prairies) arrived during a warm spell 4,000–6,000 years ago and sprouted in a fertile soil deposited some 12,000 years ago by the Wisconsinan glacier.

That ice mass never reached into central Adams County. Dr. Braun concluded that the Adams County prairies came during an earlier warm or Xerothermic Period, perhaps even before the Illinoian glacier covered most of Ohio and the northwestern

corner of Adams County 125,000 years ago.

Another authority on Ohio prairies, K. Roger Trautman, believes 300 prairie openings, perhaps covering 1,000 square miles, broke the endless carpet of Ohio's hardwood forest at the time of European settlement of the New World.

Lacking the repeated dumpings of glacial topsoil, the soil at the dry Chaparral prairie is thin, less fertile, and it washes away easily. These factors make a difficult environment for wildlife.

WILDLIFE
Technically, this preserve is a "shortgrass blackjack/post oak-red cedar shale glade prairie." Though a mouthful to say, the description reveals some of the trees you will find here.

The blackjack oak growing here at the northern edge of its range, is a potentially threatened species in Ohio. The leaves of both the post oak and the blackjack oak feel leathery with hairy undersides. These adaptations enable the trees to retain water during hot days in this scrubby landscape.

Eastern red cedar is a typical tree in abandoned fields (so is post oak). Since it prefers calcium-rich soil, its presence usually indicates limestone or shale. Earthworms also like calcareous soil, and their numbers swell in red cedar meadows.

The major attractions at Chaparral Prairie, of course, are the flowers and grasses of the shortgrass prairie. Rattlesnake master, a potentially threatened plant in Ohio, grows abundantly here. Its thistle-like burry head produces tiny greenish-white florets in mid-July.

Prairie dock is the tall, yellow flower that seems to be watching your movements in the field. It is well-represented on this site, as is pinkish-blue spiked blazing star. An uncommon white variety of the latter species lives alongside the trail.

The endangered Carolina leaf-flower finds refuge here along with prairie false indigo and pink milkwort (both threatened), Carolina buckthorn, hairy wingstem, and narrow-leaved summer bluets. All potentially face extinction in Ohio.

Fifty-nine kinds of butterflies and moths (lepidoptera) have been observed here, including the rare Edward's hairstreak (listed as a "special interest" insect). Try to spot beauties called confused cloudy wing (more common in southern states), banded hairstreak, cross line skipper, northern broken dash, and imperial moth, among others.

As you might suspect, the cedar trees attract cedar waxwings and robins, the latter gobbling up the earthworms in the cedar soil. At the start of my walk a dozen goldfinches exploded from the shrubs and briars behind the barn. They scattered widely and dove into the meadow flora until I passed. They must have reunited because they all flushed again when I reached trail's end.

HISTORY
This land was heavily farmed and grazed until 1984. Philip and Margarite Hahn sold the land to

the Ohio Department of Natural Resources, which designated it an interpretive preserve on December 19, 1986.

Clifton Gorge State Nature Preserve—John L. Rich Nature Sanctuary

The Little Miami River, boiling through a narrow chasm of steep dolomite walls, makes Clifton Gorge State Nature Preserve one of the most impressive natural areas in Ohio. The site is famous for its spectacular geological formations, rich diversity of plant life, and local legends.

LOCATION
  Northern Greene County, Miami Township.
OWNERSHIP
  Ohio Department of Natural Resources, Division of Natural Areas and Preserves.

SIZE & DESIGNATION
  The preserve comprises 269 acres. The portion north and west of the Little Miami River was designated an interpretive preserve on October 2, 1973. It is open to the public daily from sunrise to sunset. The biologically unique southern section (75% of the preserve) is reserved for scientific study, and written permission must be obtained to explore it.
  Clifton Gorge also is a National Natural Landmark. The Little Miami River is a national and a state scenic river.

ACCESS
  Located just a quarter mile west of the Village of Clifton on SR 343, the preserve is the easternmost link of a three-mile-long chain protecting the canyon of the Little Miami River. To the west are John Bryan State Park and Glen Helen Nature Preserve in Yellow Springs. From I-70 go south on SR 72 eight miles to Clifton, then west a half mile on SR 343.
  Trails: From a roomy parking lot, a clearly marked trail leading from the parking lot splits into three paths at the edge of the gorge. The most popular is the John L. Rich Trail, which descends from the rim to the bottom of the gorge where its winds around boulders once attached to the cliff, and trees that reach to the top of the gorge. The path hugs the Little Miami River whose abrasive action and fresh mist are best experienced from this vantage.
  Heading west (downstream) you pass features like Steamboat Rock, the squared boulders of an old

dam and paper mill, a calm pool called Blue Hole, and a plaque commemorating the site as a National Natural Landmark.
  The portions of the trail that climb the gorge wall are somewhat challenging, though aided by sturdy stairs. Boardwalks and decks have been built over rocky sections of the rich trail. Several interpretive signs add spice to the visit.
  Stay on the trails! Hiking on the rim, especially The Narrows, can be dangerous if you leave the trail. Keep an eye on small children. Don't let teenagers test their invincibility and immortality by reenacting Darnell's Leap (see History). And stay out of places marked as restoration areas where rare, and fragile plants are protected. Rock climbing and swimming are not permitted.
  Special Places & Events: A small picnic area and latrines are located in the parking lot. A water well is found here, too, but it is not always in service.
  Attend one of the nature programs to learn more about the gorge. The programs usually begin at The Bear's Den, a small amphitheater at the trailhead. Look for a trail map at the spot.
  Information: Phone the preserve manager at (937) 964-8794.

GEOLOGY
  The cliffs that you see are made of thick layers of dolomite (60 feet or more) lying above a vein of shale (Massie shale). Their formation began more than 400 million years ago (Silurian Period) when Ohio was flooded by a shallow, murky inland sea. Successive blankets of sediment, including marine life, fell to the bottom of this sea. Eventually the land lifted above the water surface and the latest layers of rock eroded away leaving the bedrock exposed.
  In the more recent Pleistocene times, the last two million years or so, a series of continental glaciers sculpted the land. The last glacier, the Wisconsinan, left its deep mark in Clifton Gorge, carving the 80-foot high cliffs 16,000 years ago. Meltwater from the retreating ice mass poured into the newly-formed Little Miami River Valley and began cutting through cracks in the bedrock.
  In this part of Ohio, Cedarville dolomite (35-feet thick) lies above Springfield dolomite (in thin layers about seven feet thick in the gorge). Cedarville dolomite resists erosion more than Springfield dolomite. Consequently, the Springfield stratus, which you see at the level of the river or just above it has worn away faster than the Cedarville strata, creating recesses (undercuts), overhangs, and eventually gorges.
  The house-sized chunks of rocks in the riverbed, like Steamboat Rock, once loomed as precipices of Cedarville dolomite. They fell into the valley when the Springfield dolomite beneath them eroded away.
  The conical-shaped formations in the cliffs are giant potholes formed by swirling water during the glacial period. Notice how the turbulence has formed a pothole at the base of the Falls of the Little Miami along The Narrows Trail (heading upstream).
  The cutting of the Little Miami River continues

today. Downstream in the gorge, and into John Bryan State Park, the river has carved into deeper layers of bedrock, revealing more shale, another dolomite layer (Euphemia) and limestone (Brassfield formation). These strata look like benches on the sides of the river. Springs bubble out from between the shale and dolomite.

WILDLIFE

The 80-foot high gorge and preserve boasts an extraordinary assemblage of plant life—some 343 kinds off wildflowers, 105 species of trees and shrubs, and 16 types of ferns.

The hemlocks, ferns, Canadian yew, and arbor vitae clinging to the dolomite walls remind us of those long ago years of glaciation. These plants from the northern woods survive here, along with mountain maple and red-berried elder, on the cool, shaded south wall. Clifton Gorge also in one of the last refuges in Ohio for the red baneberry bush.

Various micro-habitats have emerged on the darker south bank of the gorge. Life in these fragile communities depends on the intensity of sunlight, soil moisture, and steepness of the cliff. Some of the flora here is "disjunct," or separated from its natural range, which partly explains why this section of the preserve is designated scientific and closed to the public. Several groups grow on slump rocks (boulders), which partly explains why rock climbing is prohibited.

Chinkapin oaks flourish on the steeper slopes enriched by calcareous (calcium enriched) soils, while other oaks and sugar maples grip the gentler grades beneath cliffs. Along the river grow sycamore, cottonwood, willow, silver maple, box elder and elm. Species typical of prairies can be found in clearings and outcroppings at the top of the gorge, an area once heavily farmed.

Ten species of snakes and five types of turtle represent the reptile collection in the preserve. Salamanders (eight species) and frogs and toads (seven kinds) reside here.

The preserve shelters many common mammals, but the most reclusive are mink, weasel, skunk, short-tail shrew, and red fox.

HISTORY

Clifton Gorge is famous for its lovers and leapers. The Indians knew the Blue Hole as the Spirit Pool in honor of an Indian maiden who drowned there after a warrior rejected her love. Legend says the girl's spirit mingles with the mist on a midsummer's night and moans sorrowfully. Later, the pool became a favorite spot for artists.

In 1799, Daniel Boone and a party of white frontiersmen were captured for trespassing by the Shawnee chief Black Fish and taken to the Shawnee village near Old Town. One of the men in Boone's party, Cornelius Darnell, escaped by outrunning his captors and leaping across the chasm at The Narrows, a death-defying, 22-foot jump, ill-advised today.

The river and gorge were prized for their water power in the 19th century. The evidence of several dams and mills can be seen along the trails. The overgrown, faint ruins of a stagecoach inn lie beside the Orton Trail (named for pioneering geologist Edward Orton, past president of Antioch College and Ohio State University). Travelers, of course, could not resist peeking into the gorge.

In December 1924, the state finally accepted a 500-acre parcel bequeathed by John Bryan, an inventor and conservationist. Three governors had rejected the gift because Bryan had placed a ban on the land's use for public religious worship. Much of this land became the state park.

Hugh Taylor Birch, who gave Antioch College land for nearby Glen Helen Nature Preserve, also left 161 acres around the gorge to the state.

The Ohio Chapter of The Nature Conservancy purchased a portion of the upper gorge in 1963 with an anonymous gift in memory of Dr. John L. Rich, a geology professor at the University of Cincinnati and member of the Ohio Natural Resources Commission from 1952 until his death in 1956. In 1968, the conservancy raised $38,000, and transferred its holding for inclusion in the state park. Cincinnati garden clubs held fund-raisers to help the state buy more land. The purchases stopped residential and recreational developments planned for the gorge.

The gorge also was designated a National Natural Landmark in 1968 by the U.S. Department of the Interior. A year later the Little Miami River became a state scenic river, followed in April 1973 by national scenic river designation. Clifton Gorge was protected as a state nature preserve in October 1973.

Culberson (Dean A.) State Nature Preserve

The last glacier of the Ice Age, the Wisconsinan, flattened the forest that grew on the till deposited by its predecessor, the Illionian glacier. The Wisconsinan overlapped the Illinoian's range except in a few places in Southwestern Ohio. The woods in the Culberson preserve is one of those exceptions. It is the largest remaining example of "an Illinoian plains forest" in Ohio (and perhaps North America).

LOCATION

Southwestern Clinton County, Vernon Township.

OWNERSHIP

Ohio Department of Natural Resources, Division of Natural Areas and Preserves.

SIZE & DESIGNATION

This preserve totals 238 acres, and is bigger than it looks from the highway.

ACCESS

From Wilmington, travel southerly on SR 730. About a mile south of the intersection with SR 350, still on SR 730, look for a large stand of trees off the road on the left (east). That's the preserve.

There is no preserve sign, nor visitor facilities. Roadside parking is difficult, but possible. An unmarked fencerow-ditch is your only access route.

Trails: Once in the forest, you can follow old woods roads and animal trails through the refuge. The preserve is oddly shaped like two squares touching at a corner. The woods seen from the access point comprises the first block. The eastern corner of this small tract funnels into the much larger woods. The terrain is flat and soggy.

GEOLOGY

The Illinoian till soil beneath this forest was deposited about 125,000 years ago, compared to Wisconsinan till just 20,000 years old. So, this Illinoian soil has been exposed to the elements longer than Wisconsinan dirt. Beneath this old till is fossil-laden limestone bedrock, dating back 450 million years to the Ordovician Period. Now add water to the mixture. The result is a whitish, limey marl soil, heavy in magnesium and calcium carbonate, and very slippery.

WILDLIFE

This woods, formerly known as Villars Chapel Woods, is a remnant of a vast white swamp oak forest that once spread across the southern counties of Ohio, Indiana, and Illinois. In 1994 this wet woods had 26 tree species, notably mature swamp white oaks, plus oaks called pin, bur, black, shingle, white, and Shumard. Beech, sugar and red maples, shagbark hickory, cottonwood, wild black cherry, bigtooth aspen, sycamore, sweet gum, and white elm also filled the canopy. American hornbeam, ironwood, dogwood, and spicebush stood in the understory. Pumpkin ash, a potentially threatened tree in Ohio, is represented here.

The study counted 13 varieties of fern (grape, rattlesnake, ebony spleenwort, crested, others); 11 sedges, and plants called three-seeded mercury, bulbous bittercress, cardinal flower, false nettle, and partridgeberry. Rarities include northern fox grape, bristly scorpion grass, purple fringed orchid, and tiger salamander.

HISTORY

Old timers say this forest was damaged by fire in the mid 1930s, and lightly grazed and logged by farmers. Stuart Anliot, a Wilmington College biologist, was influential in saving the woods. Myra Culberson donated the original tract for the preserve, which honors her husband. The preserve was dedicated in October 1979.

JOURNAL

Late winter: Someday I'll be an old timer with wild stories. Local old timers tell stories (recent in their memories) of "buck" sheep entering the woods, and never returning. And of bobcats howling at night (just a few years ago, some of them swear). And of coon hunters getting "confused" until they are found, the flatness and sameness causing disorientation. I slogged through this forest one March day—didn't see hide, hair, scat, or tracks of a bobcat. Heard no howling nor growling, except a faraway semi-truck. But I'm not sure I'd recognize those clues if I saw them. I reckoned "old timers" tales aren't for scientific consumption anyway. Like old wives' tales, there's a bit of truth wrapped by mystery, myth, and innocent exaggerations. Instead, they represent the wildness of youth, and serve as warnings about entering strange places, like dark swampy forests.

Davey Woods State Nature Preserve

Davey Woods protects one of the largest and richest stands of old growth forest in west central Ohio. An impressive 40-acre parcel of tulip trees, many reaching a height of 100 feet and a diameter of four feet, is the hallmark of this preserve.

LOCATION

Western Champaign County, Concord and Mad River townships.

OWNERSHIP

Ohio Department of Natural Resources, Division of Natural Areas and Preserves.

SIZE & DESIGNATION

Davey Woods, dedicated as an interpretive preserve on May 2, 1990, comprises 103 acres.

ACCESS

From Urbana, go seven miles west on SR 36, then north (right turn) a mile on Neal Road to Smith Road (TR 65). Travel .4- mile on Smith Road, turn right on Lonesome Road (TR 66) for .2- mile to the parking lot on the left. Lonesome and Smith roads serve as two boundaries of this triangular-shaped preserve.

Trails: Two connecting trails basically trace the perimeter of the preserve. The paths were blazed by members of an archery club that used the grounds. Study the trail map posted on the information board before heading off. Walk both of them for a two-mile journey.

GEOLOGY

The undulating plains of the area are characteristic of glaciated Ohio (referring to the two-thirds of Ohio whose surface was shaped by glaciers). The surface essentially is composed of glacial till, a blend of clay, silt, sand, and small rocks, deposited by the retreating Wisconsinan glacier, some 12,000–18,000 years ago. Ohio's fertile agricultural soils developed in this Ice Age sediment. Beneath the till lies Silurian-age dolomite and limestone, formed some 410–440 million years ago. Limestone and dolomite, made of compressed marine life, signal the presence of an ocean here long ago.

The preserve is drained by two intermittent streams that merge near the parking lot and flow into nearby Nettle Creek. Intermittent means water does not always flow in them year-round, perhaps only seasonally or after heavy rain. Nevertheless, the erosive power of these diminutive currents has sculpted the hollows in the woods.

WILDLIFE

Though by no means a virgin forest, much of Davey Woods has reached maturity (meaning the trees have reached their full size and are naturally and somewhat evenly spaced). Other portions are recovering from agricultural use, and struggle in various stages of succession. This growth, found at the start of the Conrad Trail shows itself in thickets of young trees competing for dominance.

Besides the towering tulip trees, some 50 species of trees and shrubs thrive in Davey Woods, notably large beech, sugar maple, shagbark hickory, red oak, white ash, basswood, white oak, cherry, blackgum, and Ohio buckeye. Wildflowers carpet the grounds in the spring.

Numerous birds reside in the woods, including such favorites as the cerulean, Kentucky and hooded warblers. Deer find refuge here. Four of them tiptoed past me on the Conrad Trail.

HISTORY

The woods, known locally for years as Conrad Woods, survived because the Grayson Conrad family resisted the temptation to log it. The main trail honors the four-decade conservation effort of the former owners, who in the mid-1980s announced they were looking for a buyer.

Dr. Louis Laux, a biology professor at Wittenberg University in Springfield, took the cause to the Ohio Chapter of The Nature Conservancy who purchased the land in 1988, aided by a $55,000 donation from the Davey Tree Expert Company of Kent. The gift amounted to half the purchase price.

ODNR agreed to pay off the remaining half of the loan and to acquire the property from The Nature Conservancy.

Davis Memorial State Natural Area

This ecological anomaly straddles two physiographic regions, and, consequently, contains 15 rare plants found in only a few other places in Ohio. Here you will find Ice Age survivors, delicate rarities that sprout only from alkaline bedrock, and abandoned prairie blossoms whose ancestors invaded the region eons ago. Here in 1928, Ohio's legendary field botanist, Dr. Emma Lucy Braun, cut her academic molars by establishing the site's national importance in a publication called "Vegetation of the Mineral Springs Area of Adams County, Ohio." Rock quarries now pock Braun's old stomping ground. The company doing all the digging—Davon Stone Inc.—donated this unique slab to the Ohio Historical Society in 1967. You decide if the charity was an act of pennace, or of good intentions.

LOCATION

Northeastern Adams County, Meigs Township.

OWNERSHIP

The Ohio Historical Society owns the site, but in 1993 the Division of Natural Areas and Preserves took over its management.

SIZE & DESIGNATION

This state historic memorial is 87 acres and has been declared a National Natural Landmark by the U.S. Department of the Interior.

ACCESS

From the junction of SR 32 and SR 73, go southeasterly on SR 73 several miles, then turn right on Jaybird Road (CR 18). Follow this road through the hamlet of Jaybird to the gate of a General Electric Company facility. Bear right here onto Beaver Pond Road (TR 129), though the dirt road is not marked. A few miles ahead the alternating gravel and asphalt road forks, each prong being Davis Memorial Road. Take the right fork (TR 129) and immediately turn into a small parking lot on the left with a monument to

Edwin Davis. From Peebles, go south on SR 41, left on SR 32 (Appalachian Highway), right on Steam Furnace Road, then first left onto Davis Memorial Road (TR 129 and unmarked). Another small parking lot is found on the south fork of Davis Memorial Road (TR 126, not the picnic shelter).

The blue-blazed Buckeye Trail bisects the preserve and anchors two loop paths, the Sullivantia and Agave Ridge trails.

GEOLOGY

Geological diversity gives this place its botanical diversity. The most prominent feature is Peebles dolomite, a magnesium fortified limestone that lines the rock walls of Cedar Fork Glen. This, and overlying Greenfield dolomite, formed at the bottom of a Silurian Period sea, some 440 million years ago. Because Peebles and Greenfield dolomites derive from the remains of sea creatures, they contain high concentrations of alkaline substances. Soil above this bedrock supports alkaline-tolerant vegetation, such as the prairie plants described below. Higher up, Ohio black shale crowns the ridges producing the acidic soil for the oaks and their associates. This thin, brittle layer started 375 million years ago, during Devonian times.

Cedar Fork and percolating, naturally acidic runoff has produced a karst-like landscape of small caves, rock sculptures, and sinkholes in the alkaline dolomite layers. Cedar Cave, located at the merger of the Buckeye-Agave Ridge trails, contains stalactites and cave creatures. The top is Greenfield dolomite, the floor Peebles dolomite. Lost Comb Cave is easily seen on the southern leg of Sullivantia Trail where it nearly touches TR 126. Note: Caves are rare geological formations and fragile wildlife habitats. Probing, exploring, defacing, or disturbing this cave, without permission from the Division of Natural Areas and Preserves, is illegal.

Educated eyes will detect sinkholes, depressions caused by the collapse of underlying bedrock, and a sizable fault in the dolomite layers. The best example of a sinkhole is on the Buckeye Trail at the south edge of the preserve. The hard-to-detect fault along the northwest wall of Cedar Fork shows Peebles and Greenfield dolomites side by side. Long ago, Greenfield dolomite slid about 30 feet down a crack in the bedrock to the level of Peebles dolomite.

WILDLIFE

As a "tweener" area located on the western edge of the unglaciated Appalachian Plateau and the northeastern limit of the Lexington Plains (Bluegrass Region), Davis Memorial preserve hosts a broad diversity of floral wildlife, along with holdovers from the Ice Age and a prairie probe that swept by 120,000 years ago.

Examine the cliff along the Sullivantia Trail. The top is trimmed with arbor vitae, or white cedar, which arrived ahead of the Wisconsinan glacier 20,000 years ago. The shady, and cool microhabitat enables this boreal plant to survive in southern Ohio. This environ-ment also benefits sullivantia, the delicate and endangered cliff-dweller growing from cracks and pits on the wall. The plant is named for its discoverer, William Starling Sullivant, a pioneer botanist and son of Columbus founder Lucas Sullivant. Sullivantia shares the facade with ferns called walking, bulblet, and purple cliffbrake. Liverwort, a scaly rock-hugging plant resembling moss, grows near the base.

In the past, Great Plains prairie vegetation has migrated into Ohio during warm and dry periods. The Adams County prairies were established about 120,000 years ago, while prairies in Central and Western Ohio arrived 4,000 to 6,000 years ago. Dr. Braun documented the tiny prairie openings in her beloved Adams County, including the one here along the Agave Ridge Trail. Though shrinking in size, the microhabitat sponsors tall larkspur, hoary puccoon, limestone adder's tongue fern, flowering spurge, gramma grass, hairy wing-stem, and the trail's namesake Agave virginica, or American aloe. Prescribed burnings and control of invasive alien plants enable these colonies to continue.

Oaks named white, chestnut, black and scarlet dominated the acidic ridgetops. Huckleberry and blueberry occupy the shrub level, and sassafras and dogwood stand in the understory. Trees rise slowly in this austere spot. Several are 200 years old, but their size is diminutive compared to their contemporaries. Elsewhere, tulip tree, black cherry, sycamore, Virginia pine, basswood, and black walnut grow above wild hydrangea, blackhaw, wild gooseberry, maidenhair fern, common cinquefoil, downy rattlesnake plantain, and hawkweeds typical of Ohio hill country. Another specialty of the house, a canebrake, survives at the terminus of the Sullivantia Trail. This eight-foot plant is common in the southern states.

Other plants include shrubs called ninebark, spicebush (host for the spicebush swallowtail butterfly), bladdernut, and leatherwood, groves of paw paw (nursery for zebra swallowtails), chinquapin oak, and dwarf hawthorn. The slopes blush with spring wildflowers. Look for Walter's violets and bluecurls.

HISTORY

Mineral Springs, the geographic reference in Dr. Braun's research, lies a few miles south of Davis Memorial. The little gorge along Cedar Fork, the glen preserved by the state memorial, figured in the realm of Braun's booklet. Her detailed field study of the area provides a baseline, think of a snapshot, of the flora in residence at the time. Such a baseline enables today's botanists to decipher the ecological changes at the location, and to maintain the diversity that caught Braun's eyes and still makes the place scientifically valuable.

A Cincinnati contingent of The Nature Conservancy persuaded the Davon Stone Inc. to donate the site to the Ohio Historical Society in 1961. The preserve remembers Edwin H. Davis, former board chairman of the company. The Ohio Division of Natural Areas and Preserves took over management of the site in 1993, the year it was dedicated a state nature preserve.

JOURNAL

October: Fall has shed this preserve's summer splendor, but not all of it. While admiring sullivantia dangling from dolomite, I glimpsed a whitetail deer drinking from Cedar Fork. The doe splashed to shore but did not flee far, figuring she was safe in this sanctuary. Squirrels overpopulated the hardwoods. I have never before seen so many of them in such a small area. Dozens scattered as I hiked. Judging by their puny size, and extremely skittish behavior, it will be a tough winter for them.

Davon-owned Plum Run quarry butts against the state memorial, the huge pit reminding us how lucky Davis preserve did not suffer the same fate. The company should consider donating the wetland upstream from the preserve.

Edge of Appalachia Preserves

Here, in the rugged hills of Adams County, ecosystems influenced by several geological epochs present a botanist's paradise, as well as some of the most prodigious topography in the state. One stout incisor, ominously called Buzzardsroost Rock, stands sentry over one of the state's best natural panoramic views. The Richard and Lucille Durrell Edge of Appalachia Preserve System protects about 100 rare or endangered plants and animals that cling to life at the "edge" of the Appalachian Plateau.

LOCATION

This group of preserves lies about 10 miles east of West Union, near the village of Lynx. It roughly forms a 12-mile long corridor on the east bank of Ohio Brush Creek from the Ohio River to north of SR 125.

OWNERSHIP

Ohio Chapter of The Nature Conservancy and Cincinnati Museum of Natural History.

SIZE & DESIGNATION

Nearly 13,000 acres are protected, making the Edge of Appalachia the largest preserve in Ohio. Lynx Prairie (some 100 acres) is a National Natural Landmark registered by the U.S. Department of the Interior. Two other preserves in the system—Buzzardsroost Rock and The Wilderness—carry the same distinction. Only Lynx Prairie and Buzzardsroost Rock are open to the public.

ACCESS

The climb to Buzzardsroost Rock begins at the parking lot on the south side of Weaver Road, off SR 125, and east of Ohio Brush Creek. Weaver Road is a staple-shaped loop road that begins and ends at SR 125.

Trails: The trail heads south, crosses SR 125, and enters the woods. After crossing the footbridge that spans Easter Run (look for the small waterfall at the right) the path zigzags through a thick, new growth forest and a cedar grove. Just beyond a group of house-sized dolomite boulders, the trail turns left and begins a steep and strenuous climb to the promontory.

An oak forest crowns the top of the ridge. The trail dips into a hollow, bends right, then proceeds along the edge of a ridge. Finally you reach the prow of this rock formation. A boardwalk on the summit leads to an observation deck where the beauty of Adams County unfolds below.

I rate this one of the best overlooks in the state. Besides the wonderful view, you experience the harsh environment, especially the brisk wind, on the rock. In spite of their ungainly appearance and undeserved notoriety, the turkey vultures (or buzzards) are a joy to watch soaring on thermals. This spot also served as a lookout for Indians.

Simply backtrack to reach the starting point. The round trip is about 3 miles. The path is easy enough to follow. It is narrower than many paths and blocked in places by fallen trees, but these features add to the excitement and challenge of the journey. Small children easily bound over obstacles for adults.

To reach Lynx Prairie, travel to Lynx on SR 125, then south on Tulip Road for a half mile to East Liberty Church. Turn left into the church parking lot and park by the white fence at the end of the driveway. The trail begins at the southeast corner (to the right) of the church cemetery. Here you will find a plaque commemorating Lynx Prairie and Buzzardsroost Rock as National Natural Landmarks.

The double-loop trail is flat, narrow, and wet in spots. Visit in July, August and September when the prairie blooms.

The red and white blazed trails stem from the main path. The trails visit 10 disconnected prairie islands surrounded by cedars, shrubs, and hardwoods.

Information: Contact the Cincinnati Museum of Natural History, Union Terminal, 1301 Western Avenue, Cincinnati, OH 45203, (513) 287-7020; or the preserve director at Edge of Appalachia Preserves, 19 Abner Hollow Road, Lynx, OH 45650, (937) 544-2880 for a schedule of educational programs, information on group outings, or permission to visit the other preserves. Or contact the Ohio Chapter of the Nature Conservancy, 6375 Riverside Drive,

Ste. 50, Dublin, OH 43017, (614) 717-2770.

Geology

The secrets of the rich diversity of plants here are locked in the rocks below. Three dramatic geological events have made the "Edge" a remarkable place.

As its name implies, the preserves straddle the boundary of the Appalachian Plateau (or Appalachian Escarpment) east of Ohio Brush Creek, and the Interior Low Plateau to the west. This geological border, which runs diagonally through Ohio from northeast to southwest, and as far south as Alabama, also acts as a biological demarcation. In the eastern third of Adams County, the "edge," or brink, of the plateau travels north-south facing Ohio Brush Creek. This is the only place in Ohio where the escarpment is dramatically exposed.

Now board a time capsule and go back 410–440 million years ago to the Silurian geological period. During this time forces in the Earth's crust

---

Sisterhood of Science

It Took Braun to Study Bushes and Bugs

Their peers said Emma Lucy Braun (1889-1971) knew every plant in southwestern Ohio, and her sister, Annette (1884-1978), every bug.

The sister-scientists, born in Kansas, shared a snug home in the Mt. Washington section of Cincinnati, where they cultivated a two-acre garden of weird and rare plants. They called the outdoor lab the "science wing." An old photo taken by a student on a field trip shows them wearing blousy riding khakis tucked into high boots. Visor caps nest atop grey buns; and their wire-rimmed spectacles seem permanently affixed on tanned faces. They are seated on the ground, sharing an apple and a joke. Though diminutive in stature, their stature blossomed far beyond Ohio, and their teachings at the University of Cincinnati pollinated a generation of naturalists.

Lucy Braun was Ohio's foremost botanist in the 20th century, bar none. She remains influential a half century after publication of her monumental book, *Deciduous Forests of Eastern North America*, a pricey volume still available in the "local interest" section of large bookstores. Dr. Braun published three other books and 120 articles in 20 different journals. She identified four new plants for the world, and was a pioneer in advocating for nature preserves. The prairie pockets she found near Lynx in Adams County became national natural landmarks in 1967. (See Edge of Appalachia Nature Preserve). In the course of excelling at what she did, the University of Cincinnati scholar scored many "firsts" for women—first woman elected president of the Ohio Academy of Science, first woman chosen president of the Ecological Society of America, and first woman selected to the Ohio Conservation Hall of Fame.

Annette Braun, the first woman to earn a doctorate degree from the University of Cincinnati, was an entomologist and an international expert on microlepidotera, or moths. She often accompanied her younger sister on university field trips, or those sponsored by the Ohio Academy of Sciences and conservation groups. While Lucy studied flora, Annette eyed the insects.

—SO

created a fold, or roll, known as the Cincinnati Arch. Imagine that Cincinnati sits on the crest of this arch with the rock sloping gently west and east (also northward).

Erosion over many millennia washed away much of the crest, exposing ancient limestone and shale of the Ordovician Period (450 million years ago) as well as formations of Silurian and younger Devonian (350–410 million years ago) rock. The Edge of Appalachia preserves sit on the eastern "edge" of this erosion.

So, in this compact area, you will find the plants that grow in soils derived from Ordovician, Silurian and Devonian rocks. An educated observer can trace the borders of these soil-rock types by reading the vegetation lines.

Another influence, the ancient Teays River, explains why some plants have been orphaned from their relatives in the southwestern Appalachians. The Teays River flowed through Ohio from southeast to the northwest. Tributaries feeding this preglacial river drained the area. An endangered plant like cliff-green, also called Canby's mountain lover, migrated up the tributaries. This rare evergreen grows at the Edge.

Successive glaciers bulldozed everything in their path, even the great Teays River. However, the ice sheets stopped about 10 miles north of the preserves, and cut off the southern plants from their kin.

Buzzardsroost Rock, separated from the main wall by a 50-foot cleft (hence its other name, Split Rock), boasts the steepest topographical relief in Ohio. This tarnished rock molar from the Siluran geologic period (420 million years ago), measures 81 x 75 x 36-feet. The slump rocks you pass on the trail, and Buzzardsroost Rock itself, are composed of Peebles dolomite (whitish color). This stratum lies above a thinner layer of Bisher dolomite (yellowish), Crab Orchard shale, Brassfield limestone (exposed at Easter Run Falls), and Richmond formation (beds of limestone and shale). Ohio Brush Creek (at the right from the overlook) flows over this latter formation in this area.

The rock creating the whale-back, or swelling, behind the promontory is Ohio black shale, a younger, Devonian-aged formation. The roots of toppled trees grip shards of this shale.

WILDLIFE

As noted above, the preserves support plants growing at the outer limits of their range. You will also find odd plant communities competing in the same locale—the eastern deciduous (hardwood) forest, the prairie, the north woods or boreal forest.

At Lynx Prairie, for example, red cedars ring one prairie opening and mark the border between soils derived from Devonian black shale (for the cedars) and Silurian dolomite (for the prairie). Pines and other "acid-tolerant" plants (blueberry, huckleberry) also appear in the "sour" soil derived from shale, both at Lynx Prairie and Buzzardsroost Rock. False aloe, an agave plant common in the Southwest,

grows in the prairie, too.

Note the prairie grasses—big and little bluestem, Indian grass and side-oat grama—as well as the wildflowers like purple coneflower, blazing star, rattlesnake master (potentially threatened), obedient plant, lobelia, prairie dock, and others.

There may be as many 100 patches of prairie in the preserves, allowing 250 plant varieties to bloom. These prairies are remnants of a larger prairie that swept into Ohio long ago. Exactly when the Adams County prairies arrived, and what areas they occupied, are still being debated.

Dr. Emma Lucy Braun thought the prairie patches in Adams County were relics of early prairie invasions, perhaps 100,000 years old. Lynx Prairie and nearby Adams Lake and Chaparral prairies are examples of the ancient prairie. (Also see the Darby Plains for a discussion on younger prairies.)

The prairies in the Edge may have stretched to SR 125 in the 1910s, according to Dr. Braun. The extensive farming being practiced then kept the forest at bay and actually may have helped the prairie survive. Red cedars also dotted the prairie landscape 80 years ago.

Dr. Braun named each of the 10 prairies in the preserve. The names describe the wildlife you will see and three describe shape and location . One site is Annette's Prairie, named after her sister, a zoologist who helped in all field work. Another is called Elizabeth's Prairie.

Buzzardsroost Rock also harbors a small prairie of roughly 20 species. Trees have not taken root because of severe exposure to sun, heavy winds, and lack of water.

Elsewhere, a rare saxifrage and wall rue spleenwort (a threatened fern) cling to some cliffs. Northern white cedars (arborvitae), stowaways on the last (Wisconsinan) glacier, have migrated into the preserves. This potentially threatened species is found in only three other places in Ohio—Cedar Bog, Davis Memorial and Clifton Gorge nature preserves.

The cliff-dwelling sullivantia, a rare plant in Ohio, thrives in a few cool gorges, and in the dolomite cracks. Tiny rock gardens grow in the pocked Peebles dolomite (a good reason for not climbing the slump rocks beside the trail). Here, struggles wild columbine, purple-stemmed cliff-brake (a rare fern), and rock cresses (four species are endangered in Ohio). The potentially threatened Carolina buckthorn encroaches on the edges of the prairies, along with redbud and dogwoood.

The green salamander and the Allegheny wood rat, both endangered, reside here. In mature forests look for the pileated woodpecker, several kinds of hawks, warblers, and vireos. Turkey and black vultures, or buzzards, soar above the cliffs, inspiring the name for Buzzardsroost Rock. The black vulture carries the "special interest" designation, meaning it is a potentially threatened bird. Blue grosbeaks, Henslow's sparrows, and indigo buntings have been spotted, too.

HISTORY

In 1959, the Ohio Chapter of The Nature Conservancy purchased its first land in Ohio, the 53 acres comprising Lynx Prairie. Officially, this preserve is the E. Lucy Braun Preserve, honoring the University of Cincinnati botanist, author, ecologist, and conservationist whose studies brought national attention to this unique natural area.

Buzzardsroost Rock also known as the Christian and Emma Goetz Nature Preserve, was acquired by the conservancy using contributions from three Cincinnati garden clubs.

Due to Dr. Braun's work, Lynx Prairie was dedicated a National Natural Landmark by the U.S. Department of the Interior in April 1967. That distinction also is held by Buzzardsroost Rock and The Wilderness preserves (December 1974).

Richard and Lucille Durrell, whose names appear in the title of the preserve system, have been long-time champions, organizers, and benefactors of this "ark" in southern Ohio. Both are retired geologists from the University of Cincinnati. The Kenney Preserve, is a gift from Ray and Margaret Kenney, the latter a student of the reknowned Dr. Braun.

Edge of Appalachia may be the largest museum land holding in the United States.

JOURNAL

September 2: A hiker I meet on the trail tells me I will not be disappointed by the view at Buzzardsroost Rock. A half dozen buzzards swirled above the cliff, he said.

When I arrived, the buzzards were not flying (my luck) but the view was splendid. The tops of oaks and tulip trees, rooted in the valley below, almost reached the brow of the rock.

Then I saw a shadow paint a black line across the canopy. A pair of buzzards hovered above, appearing on cue for the latest visitor. Altogether, five vultures winged around the cliff—soaring, dipping, circulating. They performed for 20 minutes, then vanished—my cue to leave.

Drew Woods State Nature Preserve

In the early 1980s some of the monster old-growth trees here got an "X" painted on their trunk—a mark indicating their destiny was soon to be horizontal in a sawmill. Informed of its ecological importance, the Indiana lumber company that owned these straight stalks gave them to state preservationists.

LOCATION

Northern Darke County, Brown Township.

OWNERSHIP

Ohio Department of Natural Resources, Division of Natural Areas and Preserves.

SIZE

Just 15 acres.

ACCESS

From Greenville, go north on SR 118. Past Ansonia turn left (west) on Brown Road, north (right) on Michael Road, and left (west) on Zumbrun Road. The preserve is the woodland on the left (southside) before Woods Road.

Visitor facilities are absent, so you will have to park off the road and tramp around. The woods is open to humans daily during daylight hours.

GEOLOGY

The terrain is flat, poorly drained, and holder of three small woodland ponds. The Wisconsinan glacier that passed over this area 12,000 years ago acted like a road grader.

WILDLIFE

In his letter to Pike Lumber Company in Akron, Indiana, Richard Moseley, first chief of the Division of Natural Areas and Preserves, noted that 79 trees in the small grove had circumferences greater than six feet. One oak's girth measured 13-feet, two inches. The point being, Moseley said, Drew Woods might be the last oak-maple upland forest left in Ohio. Word of the woods reached scientists in Columbia University in New York. In 1985 they took core samples from some giants to study climate changes during the past several centuries.

Somebody counted 27 different species in the canopy and understory. White oak and sugar maple dominate the big trees with silver maple, hickory, and beech in supporting roles. Providing ground cover are sessile bellwort, mayapple, jewelweed, fleabane, bottlebrush grass, and others. The place is a haven for the grove sandwort, a threatened plant.

HISTORY

Biologist J. Arthur Herrick alerted the land preservation community about Drew Woods in 1961.

The preserve name honors the decendants of former owner Eliza Drew Miller of Ansonia.

Fort Ancient State Memorial

Human history meshes with natural history at this historic site. The precision-cut 2,000-year-old earthworks here suggest that the clever builders understood destiny, their place in the universe, and the advantages of recording time. Their structures—even ponds and ditches—seem planned, scripted. Did these ancient people set their sights high, or close to the horizon? Were they out to conquer nature, manage it, worship it? Did they foresee their doom? The book on the Hopewell moundbuilders closed around 500 A.D. After a big gap in time, and seemingly in knowledge, the Fort Ancient people opened theirs 400 years later.

Archeology is a lot like the army. Digging trenches yonder, moving dirt from here to there and back. For more than a century, archeologists have been sifting through Fort Ancient's dirt to find out why the Hopewells piled it there in the first place. Maybe the reasons 2,000 years ago weren't any different than the army's.

LOCATION
Central Warren County, Washington Township.

SIZE & DESIGNATION
This state memorial, totaling 764 acres, is listed on the National Register of Historic Places. Fort Ancient is bordered by the Little Miami River, a national and state scenic river.

OWNERSHIP
Ohio Historical Society.

ACCESS
Southbound travelers on I-71 exit at Wilmington Road and take Middleboro Road south then SR 350 west (right) to the entrance. Northbound motorists take the SR 123 exit and follow that road east. Just after exiting turn left on SR 350, heading east to the entrance.

Trails: The nature trails and scenic overlooks are found in the South Fort section of the landmark. Park in the lot close to the North Overlook, a promontory looking north into the Little Miami River valley. After admiring the view, follow the Earthworks Trail south beside a line of earthen mounds. At a marked gap, turn right and descend to the half-mile, forested Terrace Trail, which hooks back north toward the North Overlook. Terrace Trail meets the River Trail, which goes to the Little Miami Scenic Trail (left) or to the overlook and parking lot (right). The mile-long Earthworks Trail visits other mounds atop the ridge, and a southern facing overlook.

The Little Miami Scenic Trail is a rail-to-trail hike and bike trail along the Little Miami River. The Buckeye Trail shares this river route. Hikers descend 275 feet in elevation from the North Overlook to the riverside path. Little Miami State Park serves as a corridor for the path This section of the route journeys through the wide, gaping gorge of the Little Miami River.

A stop at Fort Ancient is not complete without seeing the landmark's new $3.5 million museum, which contains American Indian artifacts, dioramas, interactive exhibits, and outdoors garden. Picnic tables and rest rooms are available.

Information: Contact Fort Ancient State Memorial at (513) 932-4421 or 800-283-8904; or the Ohio Historical Society, 1982 Velma Avenue, Columbus, OH 43211-2497, (614) 297-2300, (800) 686-1545.

GEOLOGY
From the South Fort and I-71 overlooks the southbound Little Miami River seems to be flowing the wrong way. Panning south to north a narrow, deep valley broadens beneath the Jeremiah Morrow Bridge, Ohio's tallest span. A hawk notices that the valley continues to widen heading north. That topographic structure suggests a river moving north—into the enlarging, terraced valley. Indeed, Little Miami's ancestral current headed north and cut a traditional, expanding valley. However, at the end of the Ice Age some 20,000 years ago, the Wisconsinan glacier dammed the river about three miles north of Fort Ancient (near Caesar Creek State Park) and created a lake. Eventually, the lake overflowed and chiseled a new southbound route.

The bedrock beneath Fort Ancient and exposed in the gorge is fossil-laden limestone and shale dating back to the Ordovician Period, 450 million years ago. Among fossil collectors, the locale is celebrated for its trilobites, Ohio's state fossil. The soil atop the bedrock derives from the Illinoian glacier, which arrived about 125,000 years ago. When wet, these older, weathered soils produce a slick and very slippery mud, tabbed gumbo till. Hiking trails become slimy after rain.

WILDLIFE

Though most people come here for a lesson in human history, the site's natural history can be instructional. About 87 percent of Fort Ancient is forested, though most of the trees are relatively young. It is a mixed thatch of oaks, ashes, beech, sycamore, elm, tuliptree, and Ohio buckeye. Woodland wildflowers such as jack-in-the-pulpit, hepatica, mayapple, Ohio spiderwort, columbine, showy orchis, jewelweed, smooth Solomon's seal, bluebells (floodplain) and several varieties of trillium are present.

The limestone bedrock allows a long-living rarity American columbo (a.k.a wild cabbage) to fill our hearts. The plant's life process feeds romantic yearnings. Each spring the columbo grows a rosette of rabbit-ear shaped leaves, and a single stalk that rises 4-5 feet. Botanists blessed with patience enough to observe the flower say it matures (ripens) at age 25-30, then opens a yellowish blossom for one day and perishes.

A 1982 inventory of the site's flora mentioned state-imperiled residents called water avens and white wood sorrel, and creatures called goat's beard, blackhawk, red-dead nettle, scorpionweed, one-flowers cancer root, angelica, yellow rocket, gooseberry, and yellow corydalis.

Crawling critters include the eastern newt, Jefferson salamander, box turtle, queen snake, and spring peeper. Birds seen here include the wild turkey, brown creeper, red-bellied woodpecker, belted kingfisher, scarlet tanager, worm-eating and cerulean warblers, and vireos red-eyed and white-eyed.

A 35-acre tract north of I-71 protects Ohio's westernmost grove of old-growth chestnut oaks. Some specimens are estimated to be 300 years old.

HISTORY

Fort Ancient State Memorial is the largest and best preserved "prehistoric" Indian hilltop enclosure in North America. The landmark features 3.5 miles of earthen walls enclosing 100 acres. The intricate earthworks were built by the people of the Hopewell culture 1,500 to 2,000 years ago. Builders chose a ridge 235 feet above the Little Miami River.

The Hopewell culture lasted from 100 B.C. to 500 A.D. People of the Fort Ancient culture came later, from 900-1650. Fort Ancient Indians established villages inside the South Fort earthworks, and in the valley below South Fort. They were not moundbuilders, and may have been clueless about the meaning of the ancient piles.

Modern humans have suggested three reasons, the three "Cs," for the earthworks—citadel, cathedral, and calendar (or celestial). Earlier thinkers believed the structures were "forts," hence the name, but investigators today reason the enclave had religious and cultural significance. Recently, scientists figured out that the Hopewells probably had developed a calendar based on the alignment of celestial bodies along gaps in the wall and with a set of mounds in the North Fort grounds.

During the last two thousands years, the site has served as a ceremonial complex (Hopewells), a village and farmland (Fort Ancients), a state park (1891), Civilian Conservation Corps camp, and state historical memorial, the latter being 20th century uses. The historical society says archeologist Warren K. Moorehead, lead digger at Fort Ancient in the late 1880s, convinced the Ohio legislature to make Fort Ancient Ohio's first state park in 1891. That disputes another claim that Buckeye Lake became the first state park in 1894.

Exhibits in the memorial's new museum explain the life and activities of Ohio's earliest settlers. Collecting artifacts and plants at Fort Ancient is prohibited.

JOURNAL

Summer: I'm standing on a small mound by Route 350, the westernmost of four lumps arranged roughly as compass points, and imagine that I'm a Hopewell celestial observer making his rounds. If this were dawn on June 21, I would see the sun climbing through the first gap in the earthen wall north of SR 350. From this spot at a different time, I would note the minimum northern moonrise through the gap used by the highway. In 9.3 years, again from the same spot, I would note the maximum northern moonrise through the second gap north of SR 350. That's how the Hopewell's set their watch, read the Earth's pulse, knew when to plant, pray, dance and make love.

Fort Hill State Memorial

We can imagine what inspired the Hopewell people to build the astonishing earthworks on this lofty site. Its elevation offered protection and the extravagant forest and creek provided nourishment. Perhaps, though, they were just struck by its simple, natural beauty, and saw it as a sacred place.

LOCATION

Southeastern Highland County, Brush Creek Township.

OWNERSHIP

Ohio Historical Society.

SIZE & DESIGNATION

This state memorial encompasses 1,200 acres.

ACCESS

From Hillsboro, the county seat, travel east 10 miles on US 50, then south (right) seven miles on SR 753. Go right (south) on SR 41. The entrance will appear on the right in a half mile. From Chillicothe travel west on US 50.

Drive past the museum, cross the narrow bridge, and park at the right of the loop-shaped parking lot. Look for wooden signs to the trailheads. Picnic tables ring the parking lot. You also will find rest rooms, a shelter house, and a soda pop machine. Check out the information board and trail map before departing. Brochures might reside in the mailbox at the board.

Trails: Decisions. There are 11 miles of nature trails at Fort Hill. If your primary interest is the Indian embankment then you will want to walk the two-mile Fort Trail, which begins at the information board, ascends the steep hill, and loops around the ridge before returning to the parking lot. The hike up the hill certainly makes you appreciate the effort required to build the earthworks. The overlook at the top (best viewed in the winter when the vegetation is gone) is a small reward for your strain.

Another trail visits Baker Fork Gorge and the earthworks. Four trails depart from the northeast corner of the parking lot—the Gorge Trail (yellow metal blazes), the American Discovery Trail, the Deer Trail (blue metal blazes), and a section of the Buckeye Trail (blue-painted markers).

The Deer and Buckeye trails split from the Gorge Trail about a mile into the adventure and head west (right) across Baker Fork. They strain up to Reed's Hill, then turn south into a hollow and up to Jarnigan's Knob, elevation 1,273 feet. From here they descend to Baker Fork and rejoin the Gorge Trail.

Though recognizable year-round, the mounds and surrounding countryside are best seen during the winter. Stop at the overlook at the north end of the "fortress" before dropping off the ridge and returning to the parking lot.

Protect yourself with insect repellent if you come here in the summer. Winter hikes will offer better views of the geological features and rugged terrain.

Special Places & Events: The Fort Hill museum, boasting exhibits on the archeological and natural features in the preserve, has irregular hours.

Information: Contact the Ohio Historical Society, 1982 Velma Avenue, Columbus, Ohio 43211, (888) 909-6446, or Fort Hill State Memorial at (937) 588-3221.

GEOLOGY

Like the Edge of Appalachia Preserve to the south, Fort Hill lies on the "edge" or boundary of different geological regions. It stands as one of the westernmost outliers of the Appalachian Plateau, which rises to the east. The Central Lowland spreads out to the west. The preserve also marks the border between glaciated and unglaciated Ohio. The Wisconsinan glacier flattened the lowlands to the

north and west, but never touched the highlands (hence the county name) here.

A finger of the glacier did probe into an area known as the Beech Flats, northeast of Fort Hill. The ice dammed the Paint Creek valley and created a new divide. Two new streams, fed by the melting glacier, drained into different systems. Heads Branch entered Rocky Fork Creek while Bakers Fork cut through a gap west of Fort Hill and refreshed Ohio Brush Creek.

The cliffs above Bakers Fork and along the Gorge Trail consist of Peebles dolomite, whose origin dates back about 410 million years ago to the Silurian geological period. Similar to limestone, dolomite contains large amounts of calcium derived from marine life whose remains fell to the floor of an ocean that covered Ohio. This ocean bed later hardened into bedrock.

Ohio shale of the Devonian era (375 million years ago) rests above the dolomite and comprises the thickest layer on the hill. This is topped by thinner layers of Bedford shale and Berea sandstone, both products of the Mississippian geologic period (320–345 million years ago). The shales and sandstone represent the floors of later oceans, only these were much shallower seas. The forest mat covers these younger bedrocks, so few outcrops appear.

Three natural rock bridges can be seen from the Gorge Trail on the west wall of Baker Fork. Two of them may be hard to spot behind vegetation in the summer, but only the most self-absorbed hiker would fail to be impressed by the formation found near the intersection of the Gorge and Deer trails. The rill that sculpted this little masterpiece still drools through the pore and down a waterfall. A recluse named David Davis lived in one of the recess caves on the west wall in the mid-19th century.

Be ready for rugged terrain. The summit of Fort Hill stands more than 420 feet above the water level of Baker Fork, and reaches an elevation of 1,280 feet.

WILDLIFE

Because of its unique geographic position, geological history, and difficult terrain, the state memorial protects one of the most botanically diverse areas in southwestern Ohio.

The soils derived from the various bedrocks support their favorite plants. The flora thriving on the cool, moist north and east hillsides differs from the plants rooted on the warm, drier south and west facing slopes.

Several plants and animals listed as rarities in Ohio find refuge here. One of these is Canby's mountain lover, or cliff-green, an endangered plant in Ohio, which clings to life on the edge of the dolomite cliffs. This creeping survivor entered Ohio from the south along the ancient and abandoned Teays River valley. It lives in only one other location in the state, the Edge of Appalachia preserve in neighboring Adams County. Fort Hill's remnant community lies at the northwestern frontier of this plant's range.

Sullivantia (potentially threatened) and the rare Canada yew, both plants from northern climates, came here in the vanguard of the glacier and found a habitat in the gorge. Sullivantia was collected and studied for the first time in 1839 by William Starling Sullivant, an early Ohio botanist whose father, Lucas Sullivant, founded Columbus.

This unusual walking fern, sullivantia's other name (though it is not actually a fern), rises from the moss on rocks then spreads its slender stems along the surface. The tips take root when it finds a suitable habitat. Purple cliff-brake, another uncommon plant and a real fern, grows in crevices on the sunny side of the rocks.

Some treasures struggle at the top of the dolomite cliffs. Here the overlying shale pans out creating a narrow, harsh, and thin-soiled environment. But that's where you will find Walter's violet, an endangered wildflower that went undiscovered north of Kentucky until the 1960s. And here survives the potentially threatened dwarf hackberry, so-named because it rarely exceeds eight feet in height; and plantain-leaf pussytoes and moss phlox, somewhat rare, both of them, but unprotected.

On the sun-baked acidic upper slopes look for rock chestnut oak (at its western limit in Ohio), with purple wood-sorrel growing beneath it. Chinkapin oaks thrive in the alkaline soil of these exposed areas. Other familiar plateau species sink roots here, such as huckleberry, round-leaf greenbrier, low blueberry, and veined hawkweed.

Elsewhere, the forest boasts large specimens of tulip tree, sugar maples, red and white oak, among others. Many American chestnut trees filled out to diameters of five feet before they were felled by disease.

Other flowers begging for your glance include wild geranium, wood-poppy, black cohosh, Solomon's plume, zigzag goldenrod, and purple spring-cress. Bulblet fern is tucked away in the nooks and crannies of the cliffs.

With so many different habitats colliding, the state memorial sponsors a rich assemblage of birds. Scan the treetops for scarlet tanager, red-bellied and hairy woodpeckers, crested flycatcher, wood pewee, tufted titmouse, white-breasted nuthatch, blue-gray gnatcatcher, yellow-throated vireo, and cerulean warbler.

In the tree canopy look for warblers (14 kinds such as the Kentucky, black-and-white, worm-eating, redstart, and hooded), red-eyed vireo, ovenbird, wood thrush, Acadian flycatcher, and the downy woodpecker.

Near streams see if you can glimpse the Carolina wren (the largest of Ohio's wrens and one of its most memorable singers), the yellow, parula and so-called sycamore warblers, and phoebes and rough-winged swallow (tucked in the dolomite cliffs along Baker Fork). Clearings in the forest attract the yellow-billed cuckoo, flicker, and ruby-throated hummingbird.

The thickets of saplings at the edge of the forest and field conceal towhees, yellow-breasted chat, indigo bunting, goldfinches, and the omnipresent cardinal.

Hikers might flush ruffed grouse or whip-poor-will. Great horned and barred owls, red-tailed hawks, turkey and black vultures cruise the airways above the forest. The rare black vulture (listed as a special interest bird in Ohio), here at the northern edge of its range, is distinguished from its commonly seen cousin, the turkey vulture, by a splash of white on the wing tips.

Butterflies are plentiful. Test your powers of observation by seeking rarities named brown elfin (feeding on redbud trees), olive hairstreak (red cedar eater), and the extremely rare early hairstreak, seen by the historical society's natural history curator in April 1947.

Daring nature lovers can find the rare wood-eating cockroach in the caverns of rotting logs. These peculiar critters care for their offspring, one of only a handful of insects who do. The preserve is the northwesternmost limit of its habitat.

Another miracle, Sanborn's crawfish, reaches its westernmost influence in the waters of Baker Fork.

HISTORY

The stone and earthen embankment on the top of Fort Hill was constructed by the Ancient People (probably the Hopewell Indians) long before Europeans migrated to North America. Excavations did not turn up artifacts to identify the builders. Nevertheless, scholars figure the "fort" was erected by the same people who constructed nearby circular earthworks, namely the Hopewell Indians whose heydey ranged from 300 B.C.–600 A.D.

"Fort" implies an earthwork for military defense. Earlier witnesses concluded it must have been a defensive structure because of its location on high ground near known villages. More likely, the enclosure was a ceremonial site, perhaps a place for crowded religious gatherings, though this is an educated guess. Nobody can explain the absence of artifacts, nor the actual goings-on atop this knob.

The embankment is an amazing accomplishment, considering the primitive tools used back then. The earthwork encloses 40 acres. Three borrow pits, where dirt for the mounds was excavated, have become intermittent ponds.

The wall measures a little more than 1.5 miles, and has 33 irregularly spaced gateways, or gaps. The reason for the gaps remains a mystery to archeologists. The height (perhaps uniform long ago) ranges from 6–15 feet, and the width at the base is about 40 feet.

The embankment lies just below the actual summit level of the hill. In some places it descends more steeply than the natural slope of the hill. Slabs of Berea sandstone mined from the summit serve as a foundation.

A cross-section of the wall indicates the builders had an elaborate blueprint, proof of their skill as planners and organizers. First, they raised the natural slope slightly with dirt and topped it with flat stones.

Then they piled on more soil and capped it with more rock. The slabs retarded erosion, strengthened the walls, and gave builders solid stepping stones.

It is not known if the native civilizations succeeding the Hopewell Indians knew the significance of the earthworks. When white settlers arrived in the late 18th century an ancient forest of towering trees concealed the embankment. John Locke, an early naturalist, estimated in 1838 that one chestnut standing on the wall and a tulip tree beside it were 600 years old.

The area was part of the Virginia Military District, land set aside between the Scioto and Little Miami rivers for veterans of the Revolutionary War. John Wilcoxson established a settlement in 1795 near Sinking Spring (though he did not stay long), and Jacob Hiestand owned a nearby tavern in 1807.

Settlers usually traveled along Limestone Road (now State Route 41), which joined Wheeling, West Virginia, and Limestone (today's Maysville), Kentucky. This rugged road, following Zane's Trace laid out in 1797, supposedly was one of the earliest stage routes in the Northwest Territory.

Sawmills and gristmills appeared on Baker Fork in the early 1800s. Reed's Mill (actually built by Henry Countryman in 1802) operated on the north side of the grounds, hence the name of Reed's Hill. The sawmills, of course, had ample supples of virgin timber. A 1860 tannery, in Lincolnville, used the bark of chestnut oaks in the tanning process.

Baker Fork sheltered a hermit named David Davis in the mid-19th century. Davis reportedly made a paint from a rose-colored mineral and sold it in the area.

The state established the preserve in 1932 with the help of local citizens. More land has been acquired over the years, bringing the total to 1,200 acres. Trails and facilities have been constructed with the help of the Civilian Conservation Corps and National Park Service. A museum featuring archeological and natural history exhibits was constructed in 1968.

JOURNAL

Sitting on a log and studying the slender, snaking mound, I am tempted to write my own story about the builders of the Fort Hill earthworks. I suspect the Hopewell Indians moved to a better site before completing the enclosure. That could explain the gaps in the wall and the absence of artifacts.

The gateways are simply unfilled openings in the wall, perhaps paths for workers treading be-

> *John Locke, an early naturalist, estimated in 1838 that one chestnut standing on the wall and a tulip tree beside it were 600 years old.*

tween the interior and exterior slopes. It certainly is easier to carry tools, rock, and dirt through level gaps than over mounds, even slight elevations. Though erosion has randomly worn down the earthwork to odd heights, one could argue the original height of the embankment also was irregular because it was not finished.

Because of its unfinished state, no group ceremonies had been held and no permanent settlements were established on the summit, so the debris of large-scale human gatherings would not have been uncovered. Vital building tools were removed to a more promising site, or left to rot and hide in the humus.

I cannot reckon why they abandoned the site. Perhaps they found a better hilltop with more earth and rocks that broke easily from their solid foundations? Who knows?

Glen Helen Nature Preserve

Glen Helen has it all—babbling brooks, a scenic river, fountains of golden spring water, glens, caves, moving rock pillars, summer nature camps, a hospital for hawks, covered bridges, a school forest, a pine forest and prairie, a butterfly preserve, a swinging cable bridge, historic sites, cool cascades, a forest, an Indian mound, an abundance of birdsong and wildflowers, a handsome visitors center and museum, cliffs, trails going every which way, a national following, a cadre of protectors, a quarterly newsletter, plenty of land and money, and so many shrines that the place has a mythical life of its own.

LOCATION
Greene County, Yellow Springs.

OWNERSHIP
Antioch College, Yellow Springs.

SIZE & DESIGNATION
Glen Helen is a privately-owned 1,000-acre nature preserve and outdoor education center. The U.S. Department of the Interior designated some 200 acres of the preserve a National Natural Landmark in October 1965. The Little Miami River is a national and a state scenic river.

ACCESS
Central Ohio travelers take I-70 west, then south 6.5 miles on US 68 to Yellow Springs. Turn left at the first traffic light onto Corry Street. The parking lot to the main entrance will be a half mile away on your left. Dayton and Cincinnati area travelers take I-675 to the Dayton-Yellow Springs Road exit. Go east six miles to Yellow Springs. Turn right on Corry Street, beyond US 68, to the parking lot.

Trails: Glen Helen offers a complex web of interconnecting nature trails, adding up to 20 miles. They are open during daylight hours. The paths briefly described below will whet your appetite, but I recommend just letting your eyes and curiosity be your guide. Trail maps are found at the Glen Helen Building (visitors center) and the Trailside Museum.

Folks interested in geology might trace the path outlined in booklet entitled "Teaching Geology in Glen Helen," available at the visitors center. Starting at the preserve's Outdoor Education Center (off SR 343), the Geology Trail visits features in the western portion of the glen, such the Cascades on Birch Creek, Helen's Stone, the Yellow Springs, Bone Cave, a travertine mound, Pompey's Pillar, and the Blue Hole.

The most challenging walk might be a 10-miler established by local Boy Scouts. This one starts at the Visitors Center, descends into the ravine, follows Yellow Springs Creek downstream to its confluence with the Little Miami River. Here you cross to the south shore of the river and hike into the south glen. Turn around at Jacoby Road, bear right at the next fork, and climb a ravine. The trail returns to the North Glen, passing Grinnell Mill (a national historical landmark), and memorials to Horace Mann, founder of Antioch College, and Erastus Birch, one of the first college trustees. Turning north the trail marches through a pine forest, passes the Cascades of Birch Creek, and returns to the starting point.

Numbered signposts on the trails designate locations along the historical trail. Pick up a "Guide to Historical Spots in Glen Helen" at the visitors center. Consult your trail map as you proceed, and mark your progress and location as you walk.

Special Places & Events: Children usually hurry to the Swinging Bridge, an elevated cable footbridge across Yellow Springs that recalls those scary rope bridge scenes in Tarzan or Indiana Jones movies.

The Glen Helen Building, 405 Corry Street, has rest rooms, gift shop, meeting rooms, and exhibits. The Trailside Museum and Visitors' Center, 505 Corry Street, (937) 767-7375 is a favorite children's hangout; it has natural history exhibits and hands-on curiosities. A blind for observing wildlife is located on the trail between the buildings.

Since 1956, the Glen Helen Outdoor Education Center has held summer camps and weekend nature programs for groups of people of every age. Injured and sick birds of prey repair at the OEC's Raptor Center, open for visitors.

Fishing is allowed in the preserve only in the Little Miami River south of Grinnell Road. Additional parking is located in the Yellow Springs lot off SR 343.

GEOLOGY
The creeks that have gouged ever-deepening ravines in the glen expose rock created about 500 million years ago. To see all the layers, go to the crossing on Birch Creek known as the Stepping Stones and walk upstream. You start off standing on bedrock called Dayton limestone. Rising from the creek the west bank shows alternating layers of shale (Osgood), limestone (Laurel), shale, three types of dolomite (Euphemia, Springfield and Cedarville), topped by glacial till (a blend of clay, sand, gravel that serves as the foundation for soil).

The dolomite and limestone deposits signal the presence of marine animals. The remains of these ancient creatures sank to the bottom of oceans that inundated the continents. Shale is essentially compressed mud (clay and fine-grained quartz) also deposited in sea floors.

The youngest strata, the dolomites, were formed a mere 400 million years ago. But not all dolomites are alike. Notice that the top layer, Cedarville, appears dense and chunky, while the ones below it are thinner and brick-like. It also is important to know that Cedarville dolomite resists erosion more than the other dolomites. (See Clifton Gorge State Nature Preserve.) And of all the strata here, shale is the least-resistant to erosion, meaning it wears away faster than limestone and dolomite.

Knowing this gives you insight into the formation of the cascades and the Blue Hole below the falls. The turbulence and spray behind the cascade erodes the less-resistant Euphemia and Springfield dolomites, creating stairs and ledges beneath the lip of resistant Cedarville dolomite. This undercutting action eventually weakens the support beneath the cap, causing it to fall into the stream.

A short distance downstream is the Blue Hole, where Birch Creek tumbles over a small ledge of Euphemia dolomite into a round pool. The creek has washed away the shale beneath the dolomite creating the crescent-shaped falls.

The village derived its name from the "yellow springs" found in the glen between Yellow Springs Creek and Birch Creek. The spring bubbles from a dolomite outcrop and flows at the brisk pace of 68–80 gallons a minute. The water temperature is always around 55°F.

The "yellow" (actually rust-color) in the water comes from iron pyrite (also known as fool's gold) deposits in the rock. The water is much clearer than the orange-colored rocks let you think; nevertheless, don't drink from the spring.

Nearby is an unusual travertine mound some 75 feet high and 500 feet across. It began growing as the continental Wisconsinan glacier retreated from Ohio about 15,000 years ago. Water flowing from the Yellow Spring has given the soil on the mound its orange tint. The mound is mostly composed of calcium carbonate (85 percent), iron oxide (6 percent) and organic material.

Pompey's Pillar looks like a lonely chess piece awaiting nature's next move. It split from the wall long ago and has been sliding downhill ever since. Geologists call this slow slide "creeping." During a freeze the earth expands and lifts up the pillar, but during a thaw gravity takes over and pushes it ever so slightly down the slope.

Careful observers will find cavities in the cliffs. These lead to small caves in limestone formations. Water that became acidic when it seeped through the dead vegetation of the hardwood forest dissolves through cracks in the limestone. As erosion occurs these slits grow into crevices and holes in the bedrock. These subterranean water vessels dry up when the water, for any number of reasons, stops flowing. Passages that open at the ground are called caves. The most famous one in the preserve is Bone Cave. Supposedly, a dozen fourth graders can be stuffed into this hole. But don't try it!

Boulders of igneous rock, called erratics, dumped here from Canada by the glaciers, are strewn throughout the grounds. An example is Helen's Stone, located near the Yellow Springs parking lot.

WILDLIFE

Few places are more blessed and enriched with wildflowers and birds. Seventy-four varieties of blossoms have been counted in the late winter and spring, and 76 species during the summer.

Mayapples and trilliums are easy enough to spot in spring but can you find squirrel corn, stonecrop, golden Alexander, corn salad, dwarf larkspur, showy orchis, or jack-in-the-pulpit? This summer look for flora named enchanter's nightshade, dogbane, boneset, beggar's ticks, flower-of-an-hour, moneywort, selfheal, bouncing bet, and sweet flag. Pick up checklists at the visitors center before exploring.

The Glen Helen Association Birding Group keeps track of the feathered animals in the preserve.

In the summer, butterflies rise in flocks at the Ralph Ramey Butterfly Preserve in the south glen.

The group has recorded sightings of 145 different species in the glen. Some of them are rare or occasional visitors. Year-round residents include the red-tailed hawk, belted kingfisher, pileated woodpecker, cedar waxwing, and American goldfinch. The gift shop has a checklist.

In the summer, butterflies rise in flocks at the Ralph Ramey Butterfly Preserve in the south glen. Ramey, director of Glen Helen from 1973–1990, was the second director of the Division of Natural Areas and Preserves at the Ohio Department of Natural Resources.

HISTORY

Native Americans enjoyed the cool waters in the glen for centuries. A mound built by the Hopewell people is located between the cascades and spring. The glen fell within the stomping grounds of the Miami and Shawnee nations. The latter tribe built its central village on the banks of the Little Miami River just six miles away at Oldtown. The Indians considered the water from the yellow spring a health potion and a major trail near this landmark.

The first white settlement in the early 19th century was a stagecoach tavern. Later, came water-powered mills, Antioch College, and railroad tracks The yellow spring also attracted tourists seeking scenery and medicinal water. By the second half of the 19th century, the glen had become a vacation resort.

The glen's popularity as a tourist destination faded by the turn of the century. It now was sought as a nature sanctuary. Chicago attorney and Antioch alumnus, Hugh Tayor Birch, bought many parcels and gave them all to the college in 1929.

He called the place Glen Helen, in honor of his daughter. A commemorative plaque embedded in a glacial erratic, called Helen's Stone, rests near the Yellow Spring parking lot. Birch Creek remembers the benefactor, not the tree.

Over the years, more land has been acquired, and facilities such as an outdoor education center (1956), visitors center, museum, and raptor center have been added.

The pine forest in north glen was planted by the Ohio Department of Natural Resources in the 1920s. For many years, local high school students have been growing and selling Christmas trees for the preserve's school forest.

Some 200 acres of the preserve was designated as a National Natural Landmark in October 1965.

JOURNAL

May 7: Near the yellow spring a large boulder orphaned from its northern origin lies beneath a mam-

moth white oak. Locals call this shrine Helen's Stone because a plaque bearing a poem written by Helen Birch Bartlett, the preserve's namesake, is stamped to the rock. The rock and tree speak her words.

The verse echoes through the glen. Her father's name—Hugh Taylor Birch. I've heard that name before. The Rolodex in my brain spins— Hugh Taylor Birch State Park. The same man donated oceanfront property for a state park in the Sunshine State.

Halls Creek Woods State Nature Preserve

Canoers of Little Miami River should add this place to their itinerary. The place being Stubbs Mill, a mile downstream from Morrow, three miles upstream from South Lebanon. It's a good spot to rest weary paddler's elbow. Stretch the legs with a walk along Halls Creek. Nap on a sun-baked limestone outcrop beside a waterfall. Pet the 450 million-year-old critters embedded in the crusty rock.

LOCATION
Southern Warren County, Union & Salem townships.

OWNERSHIP
Ohio Department of Natural Resources, Division of Natural Areas and Preserves.

SIZE & DESIGNATION
The preserve guards 278 acres along Halls Creek.

ACCESS
Southbound travelers on I-71 take SR 123 southeasterly, go right (south) on Waynesville Road, right on Halls Creek Road to its merger with Mason-Morrow Road (CR 38). Northbound motorists exit I-71 at South Lebanon (SR 48). Take Mason-Morrow Road east out of South Lebanon, along the Little Miami River. A parking lot for the preserve is on the south side of Mason-Morrow Road, near its junction with Halls Creek Road.

From the parking lot, which also serves as a canoe access, head upstream on Halls Creek. There are no marked trails, but paths exist as well as animal lanes. The preserve is open every day, sunrise to sunset.

GEOLOGY
The Wisconsinan glacier, the last in the Ice Age, largely overlapped the area covered by its predecessor, the Illinoian glacier. Halls Creek is an exception. The stream washes over a thin layer of Illinoian till deposited about 125,000 years ago. In several places, the creek tumbles over refreshing waterfalls that expose limestone dating back to the Ordovician Period, 450 million years ago. Grey Run, a small tributary of Halls Creek, also reveals fossil-laden Ordovician rock.

WILDLIFE
Mature oaks, hickories, beeches, and maples enwrap Halls Creek. This forest nurtures a luxurious bouquet of wildflowers and ferns, including wild hyacinth, dwarf larkspur, hepatica, and spring beauty. Old field habitats, openings in the forest, let other species flourish, notably running buffalo clover, one of only two Ohio-endangered plants also listed as endangered in the U.S. The small flower resembles common white clover, so watch where you step. Other survivors finding sanctuary here are wild kidney bean, prickly pear (a cactus), and Virginia dayflower, all potentially threatened.

HISTORY
Halls Creek Woods became a state scenic river preserve in February 1989.

Highlands Nature Sanctuary & Etawah Woods

Before it collides with Paint Creek, Rocky Fork passes through one of Ohio's most enchanting gorges, a place the best minds at Disney World could never improve. Caves have been naturally drilled into the gorge's limestone walls, well-above Rocky Fork's water level. Rare plants and trees that survive on the cliffs are absent a half mile away. Rough-winged swallows dive for insects in criss-crossing patterns that humble the most daring aviators. The creek's clean water feeds an array of freshwater mussels, including a beauty nicknamed pocketbook.

LOCATION
Eastern Highland County, Paint Township.

OWNERSHIP

Highlands Nature Sanctuary is a non-profit land preservation and natural history education organization.

SIZE & DESIGNATION

The sanctuary totals 919 acres.

ACCESS

From US 50, near the Highland-Ross County line, go southwesterly on Cave Road (following signs to Seven Caves attraction). Park in the lot for Seven Caves.

Trails: To visit Etawah Woods, a state nature preserve in the sanctuary, visitors must arrange for a guided hike. The trail into Etawah (pronounced etta-wa) Woods begins at the parking lot. Local legend says an Indian maiden by that name dove into the chasm to join a lost love. The spot of her "lover's leap" is marked on the trail. Stairways descend into the gorge where rock formations called Steamboat Rock and Three Sisters are viewed.

Along the route you will pass a cave that comfortably sheltered Shawnees who were guarding a captive named Daniel Boone. The frontiersman endured a rainy night tied to a tree. A trail sign remembers a local thug named Bob McKimie who hid out in the caves. Later in life, McKimie reformed and became a respected citizen. The path is about a mile long.

Information: Contact Highlands Nature Sanctuary, 7629 Cave Road, Bainbridge, OH 45612, (937) 365-1363, E-mail: Lhenry@bright.net. Call Seven Caves for hours at (937) 365-1283.

GEOLOGY

Think of Highlands Sanctuary as a border town—geologically speaking. It is located on the border of land covered by ice during the Ice Age, and the southeastern third of Ohio that remained unglaciated. The junction of Cave Road and US 50 near Paint Creek State Park is located in the glaciated plateau of Ohio. Drive a few miles west on US 50 to enter a physiographic region called the Till Plains, a vast area massaged and enriched by the glaciers. The ascent up Cave Road to the sanctuary marks the foothills of the Appalachian Plateau. These particular rounded hills were probably gently pawed by the edge of the glaciers. Go east several miles to see hills unmolested by an ice blanket. Directly south a handful of miles, the Lexington Plains, or Bluegrass Region, pokes into Highland County. This eco-region is characterized by its karst topography of limestone cliffs, caves, and sinkholes, and unusual plants that survive in impoverished soil.

The preserve also straddles the line where the ancient limestone and dolomite bedrocks of western Ohio meet the younger sandstone and shale strata to the east. The caves, cliffs, and walls in the preserve are Silurian-age dolomite (Peebles Formation), roughly 400 million years old. The same magnesium-fortified formation is found at Clifton Gorge and Davis Memorial nature preserves. A few miles east, in Pike State Forest, the bedrock exposed in ravines and streams is sandstone and shale of the Devonian Period, 370 million years old.

Highlands Sanctuary is in cave country. Somebody has counted 23 caves. The Seven Caves, a park soon to become part of the sanctuary, owns seven of them, the largest —787 feet in depth. Most of the caves are perched above the water level of Rocky Fork, roughly at the same elevation. Scientists suspect the separate caves were once joined to a larger cave system whose underground water refreshed Rocky Fork. Glacial meltwater, however, accelerated erosion and quickly deepened the gorge. Rocky Fork chiseled across and below the cave network. When the water level subsided, the caves were abandoned high and dry.

Disney could never improve Rocky Fork's magical charm. Features named Steamboat Rock and the Three Sisters are house-sized slump boulders that calved from the gorge facade and landed in the stream bed at odd angles. One tilting boulder kisses the wall, and Rocky Fork flows into this tunnel of love. (The feature also is known as Eye of the Needle). Other walls assume human and animal profiles.

WILDLIFE

Rocky Fork Gorge is also a border town, botanically speaking. The pitted cliffs are hanging gardens of flashy wildflowers, showy ferns, and buxom trees. Columbine, sullivantia (potentially endangered), bulblet fern dangle from the pocked walls. On the rim look for alkaline-loving orchids called large yellow ladyslipper (potentially endangered) and crane-fly. Colonies of shooting star and snow trillium (potentially endangered) spread on the forest floor along with celandine poppy, miterwort, and American columbo (or century plant). The latter grows stalks 5-6 feet high, and at age 30 blooms hundreds of yellowish lily-like flowers, then dies.

Leftovers from the Ice Age, notably hemlock and arbor vitae (potentially endangered), grow abundantly in this cool, sheltered gorge. Another resident, Canada yew (a rarity in Ohio), spreads beneath the hemlocks. Delicate boreal wildflowers called grass of parnassus and wand lily survive here also.

Two plants common in the southern U.S., but endangered in Ohio, live at their northernmost limit in Highland Sanctuary. Walter's violet is the diminutive violet struggling on the thin soil that glazes boulders and ledges. One colony of little gray polypody, a fern, lives high on one limb of one ancient ash in the ravine. Naturalists identified this state-endangered plant only after a strong breeze tossed a frond to the ground.

Pockets of prairie probably decorated the location once. Several prairie "indcator" plants persist, namely big bluestem grass, nodding wild onion, side-oats gramma grass, and little bluestem grass.

Tree communities run into each other, creating

a forest represented by beech, maples, oaks, hickories, tulip, cucumber magnolia, butternut, and Kentucky coffee tree. The understory is dominated by blue ash, bladdernut, wild honeysuckle, and leatherwood.

Birders can keep busy observing nesting warblers named ovenbird, cerulean, parula, Louisiana waterthrush, and yellow-breasted chat. Broad-winged and red-shouldered hawks soar above the gorge, joined by the turkey and black vulture. The red-bellied and pileated are the most common woodpeckers. At dusk, listen for the plaintive cries of the whip-poor-will, and owls known as barred, great horned, and screech.

One day of field study found that Rocky Fork supported 13 species of freshwater mussels, including the wavy-rayed lampmussel (potentially threatened). Other species are expected to be discovered in later creeking adventures. The small creek boasts more mussel species than Europe (eight) or North America west of the Rocky Mountains (six). Eastern North America, with 350 species, is the freshwater mussel capital of the world. Ohio has 80 varieties.

HISTORY

Highlands Nature Sanctuary started by accident in 1976 when naturalists Larry and Nancy Henry were doing research in Highland County. They pooled their resources, bought four tracts in 1991, and started a land preservation project. In 1995, the sanctuary purchased Etawah Woods (47 acres) from Lewis Miller, owner of Seven Caves. The next year it bought a 75-acre logged site known as Ten Thousand Trees Preserve and Barrier Ridge Preserve (250 acres). Loans from the Ohio Chapter of The Nature Conservancy helped in some cases.

In May 1996, the Henrys' neighbors on Cave Road, the Waddells (George, Bud and Ann), invited them to tea at their 1912 hunting lodge-home, Beechcliff. After greetings, the Waddells surprised their guests by announcing that Beechcliff and six acres would be donated to the sanctuary as a nature education center. The John M. Waddell Learning Center opened in October 1996.

The sanctuary acquired the rest of the Seven Caves (13 acres with seven caves and cliffside lodge) and 500 acres upstream along the creek.

JOURNAL

Spring: Putting in the canoe at Barrett's Mill Road, we head down Rocky Fork. The ride through the gorge was enchanting and challenging—probably the prettiest stretch of paddling water in Ohio. We threaded through the Eye of the Needle, washed by the Three Sisters, waved to hikers at Seven Caves, waded off a gravel beach, and explored a side cut canyon. Entering Paint Creek we hooked a right, danced through a long section of testy rapids, and finished at US 50 just shy of Copperas Mountain. Everybody wants to do that again.

Hueston Woods State Nature Preserve

Set a spell beneath an ancient beech and let the primeval world enter your soul. This is the mammoth beech-maple forest that greeted Matthew Hueston when he arrived here in the late 18th century.

LOCATION

Preble County, Israel Township, and Butler County, Oxford Township. The nature preserve lies within Hueston Woods State Park.

SIZE & DESIGNATION

This 200-acre forest became an interpretive nature preserve on October 2, 1973. The U.S. Department of the Interior added the site to the National Registry of Natural Landmarks in March 1967.

OWNERSHIP

Ohio Department of Natural Resources, Division of Parks and Recreation owns the preserve, and co-manages it with the ODNR Division of Natural Areas and Preserves.

ACCESS

From Oxford travel north about four miles on Brown Road, which dead ends in the preserve. Traveling southeast on SR 732 and SR 177 (temporarily sharing the same road bed), turn right on SR 732 (going toward Oxford), then right at the park entrance in a half mile. Turn left at the first fork, marking the start of the state park loop road. Drive beyond the Acton Lake Dam, and two picnic areas. Turn right into the next parking lot labeled for the preserve and the Blue Heron Trail. (If you reach Brown Road, you have gone too far.)

Trails: The Blue Heron Trail begins on the right side of a paved circle at the end of the parking lot. The path descends a gentle slope toward Acton Lake, an intermittent stream to your left. Other trails include the West Shore Trail, which originates in a nearby state park, the Sugar Bush and Big Woods trails. The Big Woods Trail leaves the preserve, crosses the state park loop road, and joins the Hedge Apple Trail. The state park also offers a number of other hiking trails. Maps are available at the state park lodge.

GEOLOGY

Some 450 million years ago (Ordovician geological period) this area was covered by a sea teeming with small creatures. The accumulated remains of the animals (brachiopods, gastropods, trilobites, cephalopods, etc.) mixed with the mud and sand on the sea floor. This soup later turned into limestone and shale.

Sometime during the Silurian times (395–430 million years ago), the land heaved and formed what is known as the Cincinnati Arch, a gentle roll, or wave, stretching from Toledo to Kentucky. The movement probably occurred in response to the uplifting that created the Appalachian mountains to the east. Hueston Woods lies just a little west of the arch's crest.

The swelling lifted the Ordovician and Silurian rock layers toward the surface. For the next 300 million years, or so, weathering and erosion, removed overlaying sediment, flattened the crest, and exposed the rock layers.

During the Ice Age, which started about a million years ago, at least three and possibly four continental glaciers covered much of Ohio. The last glacier, the Wisconsinan, visited the area roughly 15,000 years ago and covered it with a thick layer of till, a blend of gravel, sand, clay, silt, and boulders.

Streams fed by the meltwater of the withdrawing glacier immediately began to wash away the till and excavate new valleys. One of these currents was Four Mile Creek, which runs through the state park. Over many millennia the creek, and some of its tributaries, reached the Ordovician bedrock of the Cincinnati Arch.

This ancient rock is exposed in the tiny rill alongside the Blue Heron Trail. Notice the fossilized remains of the marine life embedded in the rock. Supposedly, more than 250 species of sea life have been counted in the fossil rocks around Hueston Woods.

Look, but do not collect. Please leave the rocks in place. The state park has established two fossil collecting areas, near Acton Dam and on Hedge Row Road.

The glacial till spread across this landscape became the host for the verdant forest preserved at Hueston Woods.

WILDLIFE

Hueston Woods is one of only a few forests in Ohio that has been left in its original, primeval state. Here giant-sized American beeches and sugar maples are the kings of the forest. This type of woods, the beech-maple forest, is near its southwestern most limit in Ohio. Just a few miles down the road these trees will no longer hold sway over their brethren.

Beech trees occupy 44 percent of the forest canopy (treetop level), sugar maples 28 percent, and white ashes 19 percent. The tulip tree has had some success, and so has black walnut, red oak, sycamore, shagbark hickory, and honey locust but their numbers are small. Beneath these grow spicebush, pawpaw, hackberry, elderberry, and prickly gooseberry.

There is more to this old forest than old trees, of course. Numerous brands of wildflowers brighten the forest floor. Scientists who have compiled lists over the years have reported seeing three-birds orchid and harebell, both threatened species, and jack-in-the-pulpit.

It is no surprise that beechdrops are plentiful in this forest. This parasitic flower blooms beneath beech trees from August to October, and gets its nourishment from tree roots.

See if you can find showy orchis, climbing nightshade, low larkspur, field pussytoes, Venus' looking-glass, hoary puccoon, and yellow corydalis (yellow harlequin). One researcher counted 20 kinds of lichens and 80 varieties of bryophytes (mosses), signs of a healthy forest.

Birders can search for some 150 different species that have been sighted in the area. These include the pileated and redheaded woodpeckers, the cerulean and Kentucky warblers, the red-eyed and yellow-throated vireos, the great horned and barred owls, scarlet tanager, yellow-billed cuckoo, rufous-sided towhee, Louisiana waterthrush, great crested flycatcher, indigo bunting, and others. Acton Lake attracts several species of waterfowl.

The black racer, eastern milk, fox, garter, black rat, and northern water snakes slither in the area. The usual group of mammals—deer, raccoon, skunk, fox, opossum—roam the woods.

Hueston Woods' purity has inspired scientists and students from many disciplines to conduct research here. Their studies enhance our understanding of the natural forces at work in the forest.

HISTORY

Though most stories on the history of Hueston Woods begin with Matthew Hueston, he was not the first human inhabitant in the area. Artifacts such as arrowheads, tools, and corn grinders point to a Native American settlement at the nearby confluence of Four Mile and Talawanda creeks. An Indian mound also rises about a mile south of the dam. The Miami people lived here when white settlers arrived.

Hueston's tale begins in 1794 when he marched as a soldier in General "Mad" Anthony Wayne's frontier army. Hueston remembered the vast forest and rich soil in southwestern Ohio as the army journeyed north to the Battle of Fallen Timbers. Wayne defeated the Indians and made the frontier temporarily safe for more white settlers. After completing his service, Hueston began buying land in the area. This particular woods was part of a 310-acres tract he acquired in 1797.

Hueston has been called Ohio's first conservationist because he refused to clear the tall trees along the west bank of Four Mile Creek. It could be, however, that the creek valley was simply too steep for farming and logging, and perhaps the sugar maples were more valuable as syrup producers than as timber products. Or, it could be that Hueston considered himself prosperous enough to leave part of his holdings wild (the part too tough to clear).

Whatever the reason, the Hueston clan, generation after generation, kept this forest standing. When the last family member died in 1935, Morris Taylor, a Hamilton banker, purchased the acreage and held it in trust until the state could buy it.

In 1940, State Representative Cloyd Acton of Eaton persuaded the state legislature to begin acquiring the Hueston estate. Taylor sold the land to the state in 1941. The parcel was first designated as a state forest. More land was purchased in 1945.

The Oxford Honor Camp, which housed honor prison inmates, operated here for 12 years beginning in 1952. A 1,200-foot earthen dam was built across Four Mile Creek in 1956, a major step toward establishing the state park. The impoundment created Acton Lake, named after the legislator, the following year. The water filled in a portion of the steep and scenic Four Mile Creek valley.

The state park opened a short time later. The lodge was finished in 1967. That year, in March, the U.S. Department of the Interior listed Hueston Woods on the National Registry of Natural Landmarks. The 200-acre site became the state's 14th nature preserve on October 2. 1973.

Johnson Ridge State Nature Preserve

In recent years the preserve has been called a woods, a barrens, a prairie, and a ridge. Though its name has changed, the place has stayed the same. The "place" being a rare "blackjack-post oak barrens prairie" that protects ten state-imperiled plants and a bouquet of prairie and woodland wildflowers.

LOCATION
Central Adams County, Oliver and Tiffin townships.

OWNERSHIP
Ohio Department of Natural Resources, Division of Natural Areas and Preserves

SIZE & DESIGNATION
The refuge protects 200 acres.

ACCESS
Take SR 247 northerly from West Union for several miles, then turn right on Unity Road (CR 10). The preserve is on the right at the junction of SR 247 and Johnson Road (a.k.a. Allsgood Road, TR 192)

A tiny parking spot is available on Unity Road (CR 10), a bit north of Robinette Road (TR 85), near some ponds.

Trails: The site lacks a designated trail system, but you are free to roam any day, dawn to dusk.

GEOLOGY
The prairie openings in Adams County are believed to be remnants of a larger prairie that arrived 125,000 years ago. That makes them older than the ones on the Darby Plains, the latter coming 4,000 to 6,000 years ago. Prairie pockets here missed the last load of fertile topsoil deposited by the Ice Age. Consequently, the soil in these patches is thin, dry, impoverished, and it washes away easily. The harsh habitat, however, suits plants that adapt to these "barrens."

WILDLIFE
The preserve is hardly barren. Second-growth oaks and hickories occupy most of the ravines and ridges. Naturalists zero in on the prairie barrens, the thin, balding spots dominated by scraggly post and blackjack oaks, the latter a potentially endangered species. Both oaks are smaller than their white and red oak cousins. Carolina buckthorn, a potentially threatened tree, also stretches on the ridge along with the redbud, dogwood, sassafras, black locust, tulip tree, and red cedar.

Prairie barrens support one of the largest populations in Ohio of prairie false indigo (potentially threatened). Imperiled plants called spider milkweed, large summer bluets, grooved flax, false scurf pea, few-flowered nut rush, starved panic grass, and blue-green sedge live here, too.

Elsewhere in the preserve look for blazing star, pale spiked lobelia, butterfly weed, mountain mint, hoary puccoon, wild ginger, mayapple, false Solomon seal, green dragon, moth mullein, and wild geranium.

HISTORY
This public land has had several names in its

short history. It was known as Johnson Woods when the Ohio Chapter of The Nature Conservancy acquired it from Marjorie Johnson and J. Howard Dawson in 1987. After the TNC transferred the tract to the Division of Natural Areas and Preserves, the name was changed to Unity Woods because another state preserve in Wayne County was called Johnson Woods. Unity Woods was dropped in 1996 and replaced by Indigo Barrens to avoid confusing the preserve with a nearby campground with the same handle. The next year, Johnson Ridge replaced Indigo Barrens to honor the gift of the previous landowner.

Kiser Lake Wetlands State Nature Preserve

Two surviving prairie fens, remnants of larger glacial wetland, allow rarities like Ohio goldenrod, queen-of-the-prairie, shrubby cinquefoil and small fringed gentian to stay alive.

LOCATION
Western Champaign County, Johnson Township, adjacent to Kiser Lake State Park. The nature preserve is split into two sections. The Headwaters area at the east end of the lake on CR 19 (Kiser Lake Road) is open to the public. The Grandview Heights section near the state park boat launch requires a permit.

OWNERSHIP
Ohio Department of Natural Resources, Division of Parks and Recreation owns the site, but it is managed by the Division of Natural Areas and Preserves.

SIZE & DESIGNATION
The preserve protects 51 acres of wetlands.

ACCESS
From Urbana, the easiest route to the Headwaters area is US 36 west to St. Paris, then north (right) on Kiser Lake Road (A small parking area and boardwalk trail are present at the Headwaters section.

GEOLOGY & WILDLIFE
Only two vestiges remain of Mosquito Lake Bog, now called Kiser Lake. The bog actually is a fen, fed by spring-water that leaks from nearby glacial mounds and flows down the creek. A bog, in contrast, captures precipitation and usually has no outlet. (See Cedar Bog State Memorial.)

Specifically, the lake (trending northwest-southeast) divides the Farmersville moraine, which lays

northeast-southwest. The moraine, a glacial deposit shaped like a long rolling hill or low ridge, marks the spot where the vanguard of the last Ice Age glacier stalled and let sand, gravel, and boulders accumulate. The dome-shaped hills in the area are kames, where sediment drained through holes in the ice (think of sand flowing through an hourglass).

As you stroll along the boardwalk look for queen-of-the-prairie, shrubby cinquefoil, Kalm's lobelia, grass-of-parnassus, smaller fringed gentian, big bluestem (a grass), Ohio goldenrod, poison sumac, and other unusual marsh flora.

HISTORY
Mosquito Lake Bog was in the stomping grounds of Tecumseh, the celebrated Shawandase warrior, and frontiersman Simon Kenton, whose bones rest in a graveyard near Urbana.

Blame the lake on John W. Kiser. He and his family envisioned a shallow, spring-fed lake for wildlife and recreation. In 1932 the state acquired several hundred acres of Kiser's land. Seven years later a dam built across Mosquito Creek flooded the fen and created Kiser Lake, the main facility for the latter state park. A memorial at the end of Kiser Road remembers the park's namesake.

Siegenthaler-Kaestner Esker State Nature Preserve

This sausage-shaped ridge was once a creek flowing beneath a mountain of ice, a veritable glacial storm sewer, that left behind a sinuous mound of clay, sand and gravel.

LOCATION
Champaign County, Harrison Township.

OWNERSHIP
Ohio Department of Natural Resources, Division of Natural Areas and Preserves.

SIZE & DESIGNATION
This interpretive preserve of 37 acres was dedicated on June 21, 1978.

ACCESS
Starting from Urbana, travel north on SR 29 about 10 miles. Turn right on Calland Road for 2.5 miles, then right on Couchman Road for a half mile. Park on the south side of the road.

Trails: The trail from the parking lot heads straight south along a fencerow for several hundred yards, then turns right down a slope and up to the spine of the esker. The short loop trail begins and ends here. Go in either direction, for the path follows the ridge then circles along the base of the formation and back up the ridge. You'll walk about a mile.

Stay within the fenced area. The preserve is open from sunup to sundown every day.

GEOLOGY

Few vantage points in Ohio offer such a variety of glacially-shaped features. The footpath leads to a 15-foot tall esker, a glacial deposit composed of sand, clay and gravel. A stream flowing through a tunnel at the base of the Wisconsinan glacier (15,000 years ago) gave this esker its shape. When the ice mass dissolved, glacial till (clay, rocks, sand and silt) carried in the current filled the stream bed. The esker traces the course of the meltwater creek.

Look south to see another esker made by the same south-flowing glacial stream. (This ODNR-owned esker is off limits to the public). The combined length of these twin formations is 2,000 feet. To the west rises another esker, this one created by a different stream.

Impressive as these eskers seem, they are comparatively small. An esker west of New Richmond in Logan County is more typical. It measures two miles in length and soars to 25 feet.

The dome-shaped knolls north of the esker are kames, created when gravel carried by meltwater running on top of the glacier fell into openings in the ice. Picture sand streaming through an hourglass to get an idea how a kame came about.

Scientists think that eskers and kames show that the glacier's retreat had stalled or slowed, and that it was melting down (shrinking), as well from its face.

The marshy area to the east is an old kettle lake formed when a block of glacial ice melted in a depression. Though you cannot see it from the esker, a larger and deeper kettle lake lies to the east, on the other side of the ridge.

The flat terrain west and south of the eskers is another meltwater creation called an outwash valley, a feature resembling interconnected, fanlike alluvia. Here the meltwater flowed slowly in a broad, shallow delta.

On the walk back to the car, notice the huge boulders beside the trail in the grazed woodlot. These are erratics, foreign rocks, brought here from the north by the glacier.

WILDLIFE

Livestock grazed on these glacial formations for decades. The few hickories and oaks that stand on the summit remind us of the forest that once

The preserve honors Vaughn and Freida Seigenthaler who donated these 37 acres of geological history to the Ohio Department of Natural Resources.

covered the esker. Nowadays, hawthorns, various berry patches, and honeysuckle are trying to take over the ridges. These plants provide ideal habitat for the many small birds darting across the ridge.

When I visited in mid-April, a small herd of deer grazing on the west esker bounded away to the woods that covered the southern esker. Canada geese nested in the soggy kettle lake.

With binoculars I watched the courtship antics of a pair of eastern meadowlarks in the grass at the base of the kames. While the female waddled and fanned her tail feathers, the male extended his wings halfway and broad-jumped 10 feet. After five or six leaps the lovers disappeared into a thicket.

Tiger salamanders, a potentially threatened amphibian, were found at the base of the esker in 1988. They did not appear when I visited their domain.

HISTORY

The preserve honors Vaughn and Freida Seigenthaler who donated these 37 acres of geological history to the Ohio Department of Natural Resources.

Whipple (Robert A.) State Nature Preserve

Robert A. Whipple was somewhat eccentric. He died penniless in an Indiana nursing home in July 1988 and had to be buried with tax money. Whipple had one possession—title to 187 acres of wooded land in Adams County—and he willed it all to the Division of Natural Areas and Preserves. The gift was a big surprise, because nobody knew about Whipple and his hidden treasure. It was decided not to look this gift horse in the mouth.

LOCATION
Southern Adams County, Monroe Township.

OWNERSHIP
Ohio Department of Natural Resources, Division of Natural Areas & Preserves

SIZE & DESIGNATION
The interpretive preserve comprises 187 acres.

ACCESS
From US 52 (along the Ohio River), go north a mile on SR 247. A pulloff parking area with a sign is present. Travelers from West Union take SR 247 south.

Trails: There are no designated trails, but don't let that stop you. Bear east from the preserve sign, up a ridge then down to Cummings Creek. Explore the creek. It is open every day, dawn to dusk.

GEOLOGY
Cummings Creek has formed a box canyon at its headwaters in the preserve. The canyon walls, some 50 feet high, are made of dolomite, a magnesium-rich limestone. Dolomite is susceptible to cracking (fracturing) that can be miles long. Precipitation soaking through leaf litter and soil becomes a mild carbonic acid capable of dissolving the alkaline dolomite. The acidic water gradually widens the crack and weakens its walls. Eventually, forest debris collapses into the fractures, creating linear, symmetrical sinkholes. Sinkholes often indicate an underground cave network. The sinkholes at Whipple preserve, however, are enlarged fractures and probably do not block the entrance to caves.

Water that eats away the walls of the cracks makes overhanging ledges. These precipices later break off the wall and fall into a ravine as slump rocks.

WILDLIFE
The dolomite slump rocks create a rare mini-habitat called the calcareous cliff community where the walking and bulblet ferns, wild columbine, and bishop's cup (miterwort) thrive in abundance. Elsewhere, look for twinleaf (find it fast for its petals last a day or two), wild ginger, moonseed, black snakeweed, cliffbrake, Indian hemp, clearweed, white trout lily, wild licorice, wild petunia, lance-leaved loosestrife, and shooting star. Christmas and rattlesnake fern also occur.

Carolina buckthorn and southern (rusty) blackhaw, both potentially threatened in Ohio, survive here at the most northern extent of their range. Bladdernut, ailanthus, silky cornel, blue and green ash, paw paw, spicebush climb skyward with oaks, tulips, maples and beech. In the early 1990s, someone counted 40 types of woody plants and 69 herbaceous varieties.

HISTORY
Robert Whipple worked at an auto plant in Cincinnati before moving with his mother to Holten, Indiana. He inherited the place from his mother in 1971. She bought it in 1958. Previous owners farmed it, and the ruins of that industry—barn, fenceposts, lanes—are rotting in the woods. To their everlasting credit, the Whipples let nature restore the land. Whipple apparently participated in animal welfare causes.

Zimmerman Prairie State Nature Preserve

Penned by a busy urban highway, a utility easement, and two abandoned railroads, this three-acre fen is one of the last strongholds of the Ohio goldenrod, a potentially threatened wildflower.

LOCATION
Western Greene County, Beavercreek Township. The site is wedged between US 35, two old railroad lines, and Research Boulevard (SR 835), all a bit west of a settlement called Zimmerman.

OWNERSHIP
Ohio Department of Natural Resources, Division of Natural Areas and Preserves

SIZE & DESIGNATION
Just 3.5 acres.

ACCESS
There is no convenient parking spot, nor trails. Park along US 35 carefully.

Trails: Another entry is along the railroad bed, now a hiking and biking path called the H Connector Trail.

GEOLOGY
The preserve is one of Ohio's southernmost fens, a type of wetland fed by alkaline spring water. This one is a remnant of a larger prairie fen that spread across the valleys of Beaver Creek and Little Beaver Creek.

WILDLIFE
Besides the Ohio goldenrod, prairie plants such as prairie dock, Riddell's goldenrod, queen-of-the-prairie, oxeye, whorled rosinweed, saw-toothed sunflower, yellow-seeded spikerush, Indian grass and big bluestem flourish here. The reclusive spotted turtle, a rare reptile, finds sanctuary here.

HISTORY
The site, originally acquired by the Ohio Chapter of The Nature Conservancy, became a state nature preserve in August 1985. As a bonus, the Native Plant Society of the Miami Valley has saved an adjacent 14-acre prairie.

NORTHWEST

Audubon Islands State Nature Preserve

Maumee Valley birders who acquired these islands unofficially renamed them after America's greatest nineteenth century birdman, a Frenchman named John James Audubon. The river islands offer prime nesting and wildlife habitat for the wild creatures dearest to Audubon's heart.

LOCATION
Lucas County. The preserve is comprised of Ewing and Grape islands, which are located in the Maumee River between Maumee and Perrysburg.

OWNERSHIP
Audubon Islands is part of Side Cut Metropark owned by the Metropolitan Park District of the Toledo Area.

SIZE
The island bird sanctuary totals 170 acres.

ACCESS
You can only get there by boat, which you dock at a primitive landing on Ewing Island in the channel between the islands.

Trails: From the boat landing, a one-mile trail loops through old field habitat and re-established prairie. Naturalist-led programs with boat transportation are occasionally scheduled.

Information: Contact the Metropolitan Park District of the Toledo Area, 5100 West Central Avenue, Toledo, OH 43615, (419) 535-3050.

GEOLOGY
Nobody knows exactly how these islands formed. The river begins to slow, widen, and thin out here, so sediment gets a chance to settle. Ewing Island, the larger one, has a backwater finger poking into its midsection, indicating an abandoned channel.

WILDLIFE
The preserve is a bird sanctuary consisting of woods, successional areas, restored prairie, meadows, thickets, and former farmland. It attracts migratory waterfowl, shorebirds, songbirds, and specimens like the belted kingfisher.

HISTORY
The islands were acquired by the Maumee Valley Audubon Society and donated to the Toledo metropark district. It was dedicated a state nature preserve in November 1988.

Collier (Howard) State Scenic River Preserve

Originally acquired for a canoe access, Collier Preserve may now be better known for its outstanding spring wildflowers that decorate floodplain and ridgetop alike.

LOCATION
Southern Seneca County, Seneca Township.

OWNERSHIP
Ohio Department of Natural Resources, Division of Natural Areas and Preserves

SIZE
The site occupies 200 acres along the Sandusky River, a state scenic waterway.

ACCESS
From Tiffin, head southwesterly on SR 53. About six miles past the junction with US 224, turn left (east) on TR 26. At the Sandusky River, turn right on TR 131, then left on TR 38 a quarter mile.

Visitor facilities include a large parking lot, rest rooms, picnic tables, canoe access, and a 1.5-mile trail, portions of which are a boardwalk. The trail starts on a ridgetop then plunges to the floodplain of the Sandusky River.

GEOLOGY
The Sandusky River snakes over cave country. The northeast area of the county features Seneca

Caves, and an attraction called Indian Trail Cave (closed) punctuates the northwestern corner of Wyandot County. The latter is a true cave, descending 45 feet below the surface with a 100-foot passage 4-10 feet wide.

Seneca Caverns is actually a long crack in the limestone bedrock, perhaps caused by an earthquake. A tiny stream at the bottom of the crack supports half-inch shrimp-like crustaceans known as troglobites, or amphipods.

WILDLIFE

The colonies of marsh marigolds and skunk cabbage make striking and bold visual statements in early May. These are complemented by displays of Dutchman's breeches, sharp-lobed hepatica, white and yellow trout lily, squirrel corn, twinleaf, and three brands of trillium.

The bottomland canopy is closed by sycamore, cottonwoods, ash, with oaks, tulips, and beeches occupying higher ground.

HISTORY

The site is named in honor of former state Budget Director Howard Collier.

Erie Sand Barrens State Nature Preserve

To the casual summer visitor, this seemingly God-forsaken place looks like some overgrown, weed-infested field a farmer forgot to plow. There aren't many shade trees, no boulders to climb, and no water in sight. So, what gives? Well, 12,000 years ago, this barren land was Lake Erie's beach. Geologically, it was called Lake Warren. Later, plants of the western tallgrass prairie rooted themselves in the harsh sandy ridges, and have somehow survived for 4,000 years.

LOCATION

Southwestern Erie County, Oxford Township.

OWNERSHIP

Ohio Department of Natural Resources, Division of Natural Area and Preserves.

SIZE & DESIGNATION

Erie Sand Barrens is a 32-acre interpretive preserve.

ACCESS

From SR 4 (about 1.5 miles north of the Ohio Turnpike), in a hamlet appropriately called Sandhill, head east on Mason Road. About .7-mile down the road, in a village called Bloomingville, turn left on Taylor Road. A mile ahead the narrow road reaches an unmarked fork. Take the right fork, known as Scheid Road. (Taylor Road dead ends ahead.) Look for the wooden preserve sign on the right and park in the small allotted space or on the berm (especially if you are driving an RV or another oversized vehicle).

Trails: The mowed loop trail starts at the parking lot. You can't miss it. Figure on a half-mile walk.

Summer visitors will be treated to wildflowers, butterflies, and mosquitoes, so bring insect repellent. Wear a cap and long pants. A canteen might come in handy because there is no drinking water nearby. Come here in the winter if you want to study the sand ridge.

GEOLOGY

To appreciate this preserve you have to go back about 12,000 years. At that time the Wisconsinan ice mass sat in a basin today occupied by Lake Erie.

Try to imagine a series of interrelated geological events. First, north-flowing water blocked by the glacier forms a new body of water called Lake Warren. Water melting from the glacier also fills the lake.

Meanwhile, a small drain opens at the eastern end of the lake, either through a gap in the ice or over a low lake bank. The shoreline of the lake, however, stays relatively constant for years because the amount of water entering the lake equals the amount escaping.

Picture the melting glacier and northbound streams carrying sand and gravel into the lake. Waves and currents produced by a cold, north wind then distribute the sand onto beaches, sand bars, and sand spits.

As the glacier melts, more water escapes through new outlets, like the St. Lawrence valley. The lake shrinks and leaves its former shoreline high and dry.

About 4,000 years ago the climate in Ohio became warmer and drier than the present climate. Scientists call that heat wave the Xerothermic Period. The existing deciduous forest shriveled and the tallgrass prairie of the Great Plains moved into Ohio. When the climate cooled again, the prairie retreated westward. The forest returned, except in scattered pockets where local conditions made it possible for the prairie to survive.

This sandy beach ridge was one of these pockets. Here plants of the prairie and the beach survive on the ancient shore of Lake Warren.

WILDLIFE

Plants that tolerate dry, well-drained, windswept, sandy soil thrive in the preserve. These include, in wet depressions, Ohio's only colony of least St. John's-wort, an endangered species. Here lives variegated scouring rush, flat-leaved rush, olivaceous spikerush, dwarf bulrush, twisted yellow-eyed grass, and field sedge, all threatened plants; and potentially threatened specimens named grooved flax, tall St. John's-wort, lance-leaved violet, and Virginia meadow-beauty. The latter plant has few kin in Ohio—one community in Gallia County, another in Jackson County. Sand panic grass,

Why We Are Bugged by Mosquitos

Like coyotes, mosquitos are despised, cursed, hunted, and pursued. But in spite of a full-scale, global war against them, they keep turning up in staggering numbers and inventing strains of disease that kill their hosts. Although their brains amount to only a few hundred cells, mosquitos continue to outsmart humans.

Dr. Don Dean is one of Ohio's experts on mosquitos. While most of his colleagues gather glamorous creatures of the insect world—butterflies, beetles, dragonflies, and moths—Dean tracks down a serial killer. Using a contraption called a "mister" (think of a Rube Goldberg setup linking a vaporizer to a mosquito net), he traps the little kamikazes in different settings with a goal to collect the nearly 60 species of mosquitos that sting and slurp in Ohio.

The state's abundance of water, humidity, vegetation, and unseemly shelters, notably ridges of used tires, enables mosquitos here to prosper virulently. It is no wives' tale that aggressive females give mosquitos their bad reputation because they must suck protein-rich mammalian blood to produce fertile eggs. Meanwhile, wimpy, non-biting males fatten themselves on nectar and plant fluids so they can be swallowed by any of a hundred creatures higher on the food chain.

Aedes vexans is the most common mosquito in Ohio (and perhaps the nation), accounting for about half of the state's bedaggered banditi. The pesky night flyers buzzing around the yard, and your ear, are probably *Culex pipiens*, a.k.a. the house mosquito. Though their itch is worse than their bite, these species are relatively harmless compared to *Aedes albopictus*, alias Asian tiger mosquito, so-named, said Dean, because "it is quite remarkably striped," as if anybody cares to study the foe closely. This bugger can transport deadly St. Louis encephalitis, which took a handful of Ohioans a few years back. It arrived from Asia in 1986 in a boatload of used tires, of which Ohio, to its everlasting disgrace, has accumulated millions.

Tire domes and other unnatural habitats also shelter species that spread the nasty Eastern equine encephalitis and La Crosse encephalitis, the latter a rather mild bug. Only a few mosquitos transport the germs, so your chances of getting sick are slim. ⌐

—SO

common in the Great Plains, grows here at its easternmost limit.

Specimens like the striking partridge pea, prairie milkweed, and sand panicgrass occupy the driest and highest ground. Other rarities growing here are western ironweed, variegated horsetail, slender knotweed, arrow-leaved violet, and hairy milkweed. See if you find sweet everlasting, heath aster, and boneset.

In August, the time of my visit, butterflies swirled about like wind-tossed confetti. The orange, black-veined monarch butterfly was numerous. This beauty winters in one concentrated area of Mexico and migrates north in the spring. It would not survive without the milkweed, the host plant for the monarch's summer life cycle—from egg laying to caterpillar to full-fledged butterfly.

In spite of its bright coloring and slow, clumsy flight, which appears to make it an easy target for predators, the monarch population is wholesome. That's because it is toxic to predators. The monarchs have learned to tolerate and store cardiac glycosides, a mild poison absorbed from its host plant.

Birds that mistakenly eat a monarch caterpillar or butterfly get sick. The striking orange wings of the monarch alert predators to leave the insect alone.

The nonpoisonous viceroy butterfly mimics the monarch to survive. It hopes that predators think it is a distasteful monarch. Viceroys are not as abundant as monarchs. If they were equal or greater in number than monarchs, birds would not become trained to avoid the orange and black flyers.

Cows shun milkweed because of its ill effects. Digitalis, another cardiac glycoside, can be extracted from purple foxglove, another plant found in the preserve.

History

Early white settlers thought this "barren" land was worthless, and unfit for the plow. But as the population grew, even this "barren" land got farmed and grazed.

The Erie sand barrens owe their preservation to a local botanist and the U.S. Army. Turn-of-the-century botanist, E. L. Moseley, discovered the geological and botanical importance of the land he called Oxford Prairie. During World War II, the U.S. Army bought most of the prairie, then largely under the plow, for an ammo dump. The army, now holding the land, stopped farming and let unused portions of the land grow back into a prairie.

The National Aeronautics and Space Administration acquired the 6,000-acre tract in 1958 and established the Plum Brook Station, a research facility still occupying neighboring land. (Taylor Road stops at the fence that surrounds this NASA site.)

In the early 1980s, 1,600 acres of the station became government surplus. The U.S. Department of Defense, with the help of the Ohio Chapter of The Nature Conservancy, transferred 32-acres to the Division of Natural Areas and Preserves in May 1983.

Goll Woods State Nature Preserve

We are indebted to five generations of the Goll family who resisted the temptation to flatten the luxuriant forest they called the "big woods." Some of Ohio's oldest oaks preside over Goll Woods, a virgin thatch of hardwoods and a remnant of the vast Great Black Swamp. The woods is now an isolated island, and Fulton County's only link to its original natural past.

Location
Western Fulton County, German Township.

Ownership
Ohio Department of Natural Resources, Division of Natural Areas and Preserves.

Size & Designation
In December 1974, Goll Woods joined the National Registry of Natural Landmarks, administered by the U.S. Department of the Interior. A month later, in January 1975, it was dedicated as a state scenic nature preserve by the Ohio Department of Natural Resources. The preserve protects 321 acres. The Society of American Foresters also has declared Goll Woods a natural area.

Access
From Archbold, go 2.5 miles north on SR 66, then west (left) on County Road F for three miles. At the intersection with TR 26, head south (left turn) for .25 mile and pull into the parking lot on east side. TR 26 runs through the middle of the woods. Another smaller parking facility is located on CR F, west of the intersection with TR 26.

Trails: Tree lovers get ready. For the next 3.5-miles you will journey through a cathedral of tall timbers the likes of which you will not find in many places in Ohio. You are going to see trees the size of smokestacks. One giant oak is believed to be 500 years old. The adventure begins at the parking lot of TR26. Study the bulletin board and its maps of several trails beside the parking lot before departing; the best route follows the perimeter of the preserve, roughly the Cottonwood and Tulip Tree trails. A plaque commemorating Goll Woods as a National Natural Landmark hangs on the flip side of the board.

Goll Woods is a swamp forest growing on horizontal land. Consequently, the trails are often muddy and slippery, so wear appropriate footwear.

All of the paths are wide and easy to follow. Insect repellent is recommended during the summer. I regretted wearing shorts during my early September visit because of nettles at the edge of the paths.

Special Places and Events: Rest rooms are located in the TR 26 parking lot, which easily accommodates school buses. You can spread a picnic blanket on the lawn, but remember to dump your trash in the garbage barrel near the toilets. A drinking water pump is located at the bulletin board. Interpretive nature programs are held at the preserve throughout the year.

GEOLOGY

The story of Goll Woods begins 12,000 years ago, when the latest continental ice sheet, the Wisconsinan glacier, was parked in the neighborhood of Canada. The frozen mass had recently covered two-thirds of Ohio. With climate now warming, it was retreating northward at a snail's pace.

A huge lake refreshed by glacial meltwater and northbound runoff filled the basin south of the glacier. The lake level swelled to 200 feet above the current level of Lake Erie and once boasted a shoreline that reached into Allen and northeastern Mercer counties.

The shoreline of this lake fluctuated. Whenever the glacier temporarily advanced the lake inundated and submerged the existing beach ridge. A new beach then would form, but its contour depended on the position of the glacier. Names have been given to each stage of the lake: Maumee, Whittlesey, Warren, and Erie.

The three major natural phenomena of Northwestern Ohio—the Great Black Swamp, the oak openings, and the marshes of Lake Erie and Sandusky Bay—trace their origins to these glacial lakes and the ensuing events. Goll Woods is a remnant of the Great Black Swamp, our interest in this chapter.

The water reached its current level (Lake Erie) after the Niagara-St. Lawrence outlet opened through the wall of ice. That left the old sandy shorelines high and dry. Much of the former lake bottom became a great, exposed plain. It measured about a 120 miles in length and 30–40 miles in width, roughly parallel to the Maumee River.

The powdery clay deposit that sifted to the old lake floor, now serving as an impervious subsoil beneath a more porous topsoil, refused to let water soak deep into Earth. The poor drainage on this flat terrain did not help matters. Muddy, flooded, gooey conditions prevailed and gave rise to the "Great Black Swamp," as it was called beginning in 1812. The "black" referred to either to color of the soil, the shadow beneath the forest canopy, or the fortunes of those who ventured into it.

WILDLIFE

Though still affected by the glacier, vegetation quickly occupied the chilly swamp. Lichens, mosses and sedges appeared first, but they gave way, as the climate warmed, to conifers (spruce, pine, tamarack, hemlock) and eventually to the familiar deciduous trees (oak, beech, birch, maple, etc) that dominate today.

Humans began draining water from the swamp as a goal of public policy in the mid-19th century. The former forest wetland, converted to cropland, shrank to a few isolated islands of tall timbers. Goll Woods is one of the last vestiges of that primeval realm. An 80-acre section of the East Woods is considered an undisturbed, virgin woodland. It is this woodlot that draws the most attention.

A booklet on the preserve claims the forest probably evolved from a reed swamp to a sedge meadow, then to a dogwood-cottonwood community, and eventually to a swamp forest. Goll Woods continues to evolve. A discerning eye will notice four types of forest in the preserve: the swamp forest; a community supporting a mixed bag of species (called a mixed mesophytic forest); a beech-maple forest; and a plantation of maturing pines, sowed in rows back in the mid-1960s. The pine forest did not occur naturally.

Pockets of the swamp forest exist throughout the woodlot. Water lies on the surface most of the year, thanks to the subsoil of impenetrable clay. Trees that can tolerate wet ground live here, such as black ash, red and silver maples, and swamp oak. Scientists refer to this grouping of trees as the elm-ash-soft maple swamp forest. Dutch elm disease killed the elms that once stood shoulder to shoulder in the canopy. Shade-tolerant, moisture loving pawpaw and spicebush grow in the understory.

The mixed mesophytic forest is most apparent on the west side of the East Woods. Long ago it was a swamp forest, but as the land drained new species entered the scene. Today, it is a collection of oaks (burr, white, chinkapin), walnut, shagbark hickory, basswood, tulip tree, and some white ash and sugar maple.

One behemoth burr oak from this assemblage, estimated to be 500 years old, measures five-feet, two inches in diameter. Foresters have calculated that a pair of huge white oaks from this grove would provide enough lumber to build a small house.

Towering, erect specimens of tulip tree (a.k.a. whitewood and yellow poplar) rise in these woods. Pioneers often built log cabins from tulip trees because the young tree prunes itself resulting in a straight trunk.

A beech-maple community thrives in a cluster in the eastern part of the East Woods. These trees reside on what remains of a beach ridge formed by old Lake Whittlesey around 11,000 years ago. (See geology section above.) Though barely discernible, this slight elevation provides enough drainage for these species to gain a foothold. Naturalists call this stable condition a climax forest. The beeches and maples may enlarge their domain if the woods continues to drain.

You will have to look above the top of the understory trees and the saplings to find the limbs of most of these giants. The branching starts about 50–60 feet above the ground.

Goll Woods also safeguards blue and green ash, bigtooth aspen, black gum (black tupelo, sourgum), black maple, two types of dogwood, ironwood, Ohio buckeye, bitternut and pignut hickories, redbud, hackberry, hophornbeam, box elder, and others. Sycamores and cottonwoods arch over the Tiffin River.

Wildflowers steal your eyes from the trees in the warm months. These include appendaged waterleaf, false spikenard, nodding trillium, perfoliate bellwort, avens, bastard toadflax, jimsonweed, and turtlehead. Three protected plants hide in the preserve—three-birds orchid (threatened), spotted coral root and jack-in-the-pulpit (both potentially threatened).

Prominent ferns found here include Christmas, Goldie's, rattlesnake, fragile, lady, sensitive, glade, maidenhair, and spinulose woodfern. During the Carboniferous Period (280–345 million years ago) ferns grew as tall as trees.

Birds, plenty of them, nest in these peaceful woods. For a challenge, look for the Baltimore orioles, eastern wood pewee (listen for its pee-a-wee song), red-bellied woodpecker, redstart, rose-breasted grosbeak, scarlet tanager, towhee, and barred owl. The endangered hermit thrush might be seen here, too.

Dr. Roy W. Rings of the Ohio Agricultural Research and Development Center in Wooster collected 213 insect species from Goll Woods in 1988 (the year ODNR stopped limited insect hunting in the preserve). One common insect was the tiger swallowtail butterfly. Another carried the name, olive-shaded bird dropping moth.

Elk roamed in the area until the 1830s. Mountain lions disappeared in the 1840s, while bears and wolves lasted into the 1870s, and ravens into the 1880s. Deer, raccoons, and red fox are the biggest furry critters found here now. The latter's tracks resemble a small dog's. Note the direction of the tracks. If they go straight they probably belong to a fox. Dog trails tend to zigzag, and the tracks appear to be staggered or out of line (hence, dogtracking).

The forest ponds harbor fairy shrimp, crayfish, scud, frogs, and salamanders, a food source of raccoons, skunk, and opossums.

History

The Ottawa, Chippewa, Delaware, Potawatomie, and perhaps Wyandot Indians hunted in the Great Black Swamp. These were Indians living in the region explored in 1679 by Chevalier Robert de la Salle, a French fur trader.

In 1834, more than a half century after the American Revolution, German pioneers settled in the area, hence German Township. Arriving in 1836, among a second wave of immigrants, was Peter Goll and his family from Dobs, France. Goll purchased 80 acres for $1.25 an acre the following year. Over time his acquisitions grew to 600 acres.

In the 1960s, the preservation of Goll Woods became a goal of the Northwestern Ohio Natural Resources Council, Toledo Naturalists Association, and the Ohio Chapter of The Nature Conservancy. The Ohio Department of Natural Resources bought the property from the Goll family in 1966, and dedicated it as an interpretive preserve in January 1975. A month earlier, in December 1974, the U.S. Department of the Interior listed Goll Woods on the National Registry of National Natural Landmarks.

Gross Woods State Nature Preserve

For generations, this thick mat of trees was called "Grandpa's Woods." Grandpa was Samuel Gross, who vowed to keep this 40-acre swamp forest looking exactly as it did when he inherited it from his father, Nicholas. Grandpa's descendants continued that conservation ethic. Now the Ohio Department of Natural Resources is entrusted to keep the place looking as Nicholas Gross first saw it.

Location
Northeast Shelby County, Jackson Township.

Ownership
Ohio Department of Natural Resources, Division of Natural Areas and Preserves.

Size & Designation
This 49-acre woodland became a state interpretive preserve on May 4, 1982.

Access
Leave I-75 at the Botkins Road exit and travel on Botkins Road about six miles to the preserve parking lot on the left side of the road. It is the largest patch of woods around.

Trails: A 3,000-foot boardwalk trail built in 1985 loops through the wet preserve. The path begins and ends at the parking lot, which can accommodate several vehicles, including recreational vehicles.

Since this site is a swamp forest, visitors should protect themselves from insect pests in the summer. Please don't ride bicycles on the boardwalk. Splinters await the feet of barefooted strollers.

Geology
This part of Ohio is as flat as plywood, though a few rolling hills break the monotony. Gross Woods lies atop poorly-drained till, a rich mixture of clay,

176

gravel, sand and rocks deposited by Wisconsinan ice sheet some 12,000 years ago. In the spring, shallow, black pools form in the depressions.

To the northwest, outside the preserve, stretches the Mississewa end moraine, a slightly elevated till ridge showing us where the glacier stalled and unloaded sediment in its vanguard.

If you dig down deep enough you will uncover dolomite, a sedimentary rock made of marine life that settled to the bottom of an ocean during the Silurian geological period, some 420 million years ago.

WILDLIFE

Gross Woods is one of the last mixed-species swamp forests in Western Ohio. By "mixed" scientists mean the diversity of trees in the woods is unusual and extraordinary. And, you won't find many (if any) 40-acre mature wood-lots standing in these parts.

Gross Woods is a burr oak-basswood swamp forest, though 25 varieties of trees grow here. Buxom specimens of these deciduous hardwoods dominate the wettest spots. Mammoth beeches and red oak grip the higher ground, here, measured in inches.

Some of the trees are more than 200 years old. Notice how the trunks of these giants rise straight above the canopy of understory species, such as sugar maple. The branches on some of the tall ones don't appear until the 50-foot mark, evidence of the maturity of this woods. Trees that grow in open areas sprout branches much closer to the ground.

Healthy groups of shagbark hickory, black walnut, white oak, and ash are easily found here, too.

Some 150 kinds of wildflowers have been identified, notably the delicate miterwort (bishop's cap), swamp buttercup, wild geranium, toadside trillium, cleavers (used by pioneers for bed ticking), and bloodroot. Come here in the spring for this floral show.

A group of great blue herons once had a rookery (nesting area) along the western edge of the preserve. They abandoned the woods a few years ago, perhaps moving to a site closer to their feeding spot at Indian Lake.

The usual cast of four-legged forest critters frolics in the forest. And a normal bevy of songbirds sprinkles the air with merriment in the spring and summer.

HISTORY

The preserve honors Samuel Gross (1852-1937) and his seven children who kept this woodlot as near to pristine as could several farming generations. Their "disturbance" amounted to removing several oaks for barn timbers, and collecting some downed wood for warmth. Grandpa Gross also harvested game in his woods and gathered edible mushrooms.

In 1972 the Gross family donated the parcel to the Ohio Chapter of The Nature Conservancy, which turned it over to ODNR in 1976.

Irwin Prairie State Nature Preserve

Five distinct plant communities thrive in this preserve, variously described as a wet prairie, and an oak savanna. The rare wildflowers and grasslike plants make this a special place—one of the last sedge meadows in the state.

LOCATION
Northwest Lucas County, Spencer Township.

OWNERSHIP
The Ohio Department of Natural Resources, Division of Natural Areas and Preserves.

SIZE & DESIGNATION
This 223-acre prairie was dedicated as an interpretive nature preserve on December 27, 1974.

ACCESS
From I-475, head west on US 20 about four miles, then go south on Crissey Road to Bancroft Street. Turn right on Bancroft Street and travel west about 1.5 miles (past Wolfinger and Irwin roads) to the parking lot on the left.

Trails: A boardwalk trail starts from the parking lot and heads south through a stand of mixed oaks (around the parking lot, actually), a shrub swamp, and a edge meadow. The walk bends left (east), crosses Irwin Road, and snakes through another sedge meadow, a small pin oak forest, and finally to a viewing platform that gazes upon a grassland. There is a fork in the trail just before you reach the observation tower. Choose either leg of this loop—each leads to the platform.

Exit by retracing your steps. This easy, flat ramble covers a little more than two miles. Summer hikes require precautions against insects. You may be tempted to walk barefooted in the summer. Don't! The hot boards can scorch your feet.

Signs tell visitors not to ride bicycles on the boardwalk. But I discovered, during my tour of the preserve, that adult and teenaged bicyclists ignore the sign. Walkers should be careful but assertive. After all, the boardwalk was designed for foot travel. Please keep two-wheelers off the boards.

Irwin Prairie can be visited during daylight hours every day. Drinking water and rest rooms are located in the parking lot.

Information: ODNR has published a booklet on the natural history of Irwin Prairie. To obtain a copy, and for other information (such as nature programs) contact the Ohio Department of Natural Resources, Division of Natural Areas and Preserves, Fountain

Square, Building F-1, Columbus, Ohio 43224-1331, (614) 265-6453.

GEOLOGY

Irwin Prairie lies in a yellow-brown sand belt known as the Oak Openings, which once stretched from Detroit, Michigan, into Lucas County, and parts of Fulton and Henry counties. In Ohio, the Oak Openings region measures 25 miles in length, and anywhere from 3.5–7 miles in width.

Geologists think the sand came from Michigan on the heels of the retreating Wisconsinan glacier, around 10,000–12,000 years ago. A river fed by the meltwater of this glacier transported the sand (a glacial deposit) into Lake Warren, the Ice Age ancestor of Lake Erie.

The shore of Lake Warren reached much farther inland than today's Lake Erie because the glacier blocked the water outlet (the Niagara-St. Lawrence valleys) to the sea. The longshore currents of Lake Warren, moving westward and parallel to the shore, carried the sand to the southwestern shore, building beaches and sand bars.

When the outlet finally unplugged, Lake Warren shrank roughly to the size of the current Lake Erie. The abandoned beaches and sand bars became windswept sand dunes. (See Oak Openings, Sheldon Marsh.)

The sand deposits varied in depth. Above thick deposits, a few scrubby plants, like black oak (thus the name "oak openings"), survive on the dry earth. At Irwin Prairie, however, the sand layer is thin, and the surface water is trapped above an impervious strata of clay. Consequently, wet conditions prevail year-round, allowing the vegetation of a wet prairie to grow in this unique habitat. The swampy, flooded environment also discourages encroachment by most trees, which tend to settle on the higher ground.

WILDLIFE

Irwin Prairie is one of the last and largest of the wet prairies in what is left of the Oak Openings in Ohio. A century and a half ago this timberless wetland may have been a mile wide and seven miles long. But extensive drainage since the last half of the 19th century has bled the land so that farms and villages could be established.

The siphoning ditches lowered the water level, and let cottonwoods and aspens march into the meadows. Only about 50 acres of the original Irwin Prairie remains.

The stroll along the boardwalk takes you to five of the six distinct plant communities. (Botanists debate the boundaries and classifications of these groups.) The parking lot is surrounded by oaks, mostly pin oaks. The branches of this sturdy tree "pinned" or bound barn timbers—hence the name. A shrubby swamp of willows and dogwoods is followed by a clearing that boasts characters typical of the western tallgrass prairie.

A large sedge meadow lies on the east side of Irwin Road. Visually, the spot briefly recalls the savannas of Africa and South America. The main plant, twig-rush (potentially threatened in Ohio), is really a sedge. A sedge has a triangular, solid stem (especially at the top), while a rush stem is hollow and never three-sided.

Ahead, you venture through a tiny stand of pin oaks, another thicket of shrubs, and then a field of blue-joint grass and northern reed grass. In the spring, this field becomes a shallow pond that attracts waterfowl, thousands of frogs, and the dainty fairy shrimp.

You may also see elm (American and red), red maple, swamp white oak, sassafras, and black cherry trees on the way. Check out the shrubs named ninebark, meadowsweet, prickly ash, and bristly greenbrier.

Forty-four wildflowers are listed in ODNR's booklet on the preserve. The prairie collection boasts spiked blazing star, tall coreopsis, wild bergamot, and big bluestem (a grass). Five kinds of goldenrod wash the meadow with "gold." Look for butterflyweed, white beardtongue, ladies' tresses, mermaid weed, small-fringed gentian (potentially threatened), swamp candles, and wild carrot (a.k.a. Queen Anne's lace).

Lucky observers might spot a least bittern (an endangered bird), a Virginia rail or sora (a "special interest" bird, or potentially threatened), a pied-eyed grebe, and a common snipe. Find a marsh wren (becoming a rarity in Ohio) in your binoculars, or an endangered sedge wren.

Muskrat, mink, raccoons, opossums, red fox, skunk, and deer live or browse here. The rare spotted turtle (perhaps resting beside a drainage ditch) and ribbon snake (seen by the author slithering between the planks of the boardwalk at the trailhead) represent some of the reclusive reptiles.

HISTORY

Native Americans found a rich bounty of wildlife in this verdant savanna. Canoes could slide into its nook and crannies during periods of high water, but at other times the swampy conditions made hunting, fishing, and gathering strenuous.

Early French explorers may have trapped fur-bearing critters in the area. Later settlers found the land too waterlogged and treeless for settlement. That changed in 1859 when the Lucas County Commissioners began draining the wetlands for farming. The slow work of bleeding the area continued well into the 20th century.

In 1960, John Stophlet, a local naturalist, persuaded Dr. J. Arthur Herrick, boss of the Natural Areas Inventory Project for the Ohio Biological Survey, to visit this place. Herrick declared it, "one of the rarest of gems in Ohio."

In June 1964, members of the Toledo Naturalists Association began a study of the site they named Irwin Prairie (after a pioneer named William Irwin who settled here in 1865). Their findings confirmed Herrick's conclusion, and led to the creation of a grassroots organization.

In 1971, the Ohio Chapter of The Nature Conservancy started raising money to buy the prairie. By 1974 the conservancy and the Ohio Department of Natural Resources had acquired the funds to buy Irwin Prairie. On December 27, 1974 Irwin Prairie became a state nature preserve.

Lakeside Daisy State Nature Preserve

The Lakeside daisy is the rarest of the 206 endangered species in Ohio. It survives naturally, and barely, in only three places on Earth—in a limestone quarry on the Marblehead Peninsula, and in two spots on Ontario's Lake Erie shore. In Ohio, humans can view this rare jewel in its preserve only once a year—in May—when its yellow blossoms religiously obey the sun's golden rays.

LOCATION
Ottawa County, Danbury Township, near Lakeside on the Marblehead Peninsula.

OWNERSHIP
Ohio Department of Natural Resources, Division of Natural Areas and Preserves.

SIZE & DESIGNATION
The endangered flower lives in a 19-acre scientific preserve which is off-limits to humans, except in May.

ACCESS
Driving west on SR 2, exit northbound on SR 269, and take this road over Sandusky Bay, through Danbury to its junction with SR 163. Turn right (east) on SR 163 and travel to Lakeside. Turn right on Alexander Pike (town hall and firehouse on the corner) to the preserve.

The preserve is open to visitors only in May. A permit must be obtained from the Division of Natural Areas and Preserves to visit the preserve any other time. Visitors must park on the berm and stay in designated areas. There is no trail for May visitors, so you are free to roam about—only be careful not to step on the plants.

GEOLOGY
The tough Lakeside daisy has chosen to live on bare, limestone rock that 375 million years ago (Devonian geological period) was an ocean floor. When the ocean receded this bottom stew of sea creatures and mud hardened into a rock that geologists call Columbus limestone. It contains the fossils of ancient shellfish and fish, some of which grew to lengths of 25 feet.

In Ohio, this slab of limestone stretches from Columbus to the Lake Erie Islands. In places it's 100 feet thick. The top half of the strata, almost pure calcite, is quite valuable, and has been extensively mined throughout its range.

WILDLIFE
The Lakeside daisy's existence in Ohio is a conundrum. The plant belongs to the genus Hymenoxys, which claims 14 native species in North America. Thirteen members of this clan reside in the southern Rocky Mountains and western Great Plains, south as far as South America. Why, then, does one isolated species live east of the Mississippi River? How did it get here? When did it arrive?

Scientists do not really have answers. While some attribute its appearance to traveling Indians or to early 19th century cattle drives (seeds transported in cow manure), others believe it arrived several thousand years ago with the tide of the tallgrass prairie and got left behind.

The Lakeside daisy lives in a harsh and fragile environment—on bare, windswept, sun-baked, storm-pounded limestone or dolomite rock.

In early May, the bright yellow petals of the perennial flower open atop a solitary, leafless stem measuring 6–11 inches. The leaves of the plant form a tight, fleshy rosette on the rock surface. Each community of daisies blossoms about the same time.

The daisies are heliotropic, meaning all the flower-heads obediently follow the path of the sun in unison. At sunset, the double-notched petals point west, and at dawn they salute the eastern rays. The blossoms pay homage to the sun for about a week, then begin to drop their petals.

Though the plant disperses seeds in mid-June, it also reproduces by spreading its underground stem (called a rhizome) from the rosette.

The Lakeside daisy has been called the four-nerved starflower, the stemless rubberweed, and the mountain sunflower. The latest name was adopted by Clarence M. Weed, a researcher at the Ohio Experimental Station who conducted the first studies of the plant in May 1890. He named it after the nearby village, Lakeside, and the name stuck.

The common name aside, scientists continue to wrestle with the plant's precise scientific name. This taxonomic tug-of-war has produced a half dozen

Latin names since Clarence Weed's day. ODNR has settled on one chosen by a veteran naturalist, Allison Cusick, who believes our rare daisy is a species all its own, called Hymenoxys herbacea.

Although Hymenoxys herbacea is the floral star attraction, the small preserve also protects 11 other rare plants, such as rock sandwort, balsam squawweed, and Great Plains ladies'-tresses. Other prairie favorites—notably spiked blazing-star and stiff goldenrod—grow here, too. Most of these wildflowers blossom two months after the Lakeside daisy (mid-July) when the preserve is closed to the public.

HISTORY

While Clarence Weed is credited for naming the daisy and bringing it to the attention of the scientific community, it was Ruth E. Fiscus of Cleveland Heights who carefully observed the plant and crusaded for its protection for more than 40 years. Later, Marblehead resident Colleen "Casey" Taylor led a statewide effort to preserve the quarry.

In 1988, ODNR bought 19 acres of abandoned quarry from Standard Slag Company, now a subsidiary of Lafarge Corporation of Paris, France. The following year, the state agency began monitoring the plant's growth, and transplanted a few flowers to a quarry in nearby Kelleys Island State Park.

Other research avenues are being traveled in Illinois, which lost its last natural daisy habitat in 1981. Fortunately, biologist Marcella DeMauro rescued a few plants and reestablished them in protected sites. Later, she crossbred the Illinois and Ohio survivors and planted the offspring in selected locations.

Lawrence Woods State Nature Preserve

Centuries old mammoth hardwoods preside over this thousand-acre kingdom. This newly-acquired realm includes diminutive rarities, such as the heart-leaf plantain, an imperiled blossom found in only two other places in Ohio. A mile long boardwalk fashioned from recycled shopping sacks and other discards routes visitors through the swamp forest.

LOCATION

Southern Hardin County, Taylor Creek Township. From Kenton drive southerly on US 68 a few miles, then go east (left) on CR 190. Look for the preserve entrance lane on the south (right) side of CR 190, just east of CR 155.

OWNERSHIP

Ohio Department of Natural Resources, Division of Natural Areas and Preserves

SIZE & DESIGNATION

The preserve protecting this old-growth forest is 1,059 acres.

ACCESS

Slow down after you pass CR 155, and turn right on a gravel road (an old farm lane) next to a barn. Park in the designated area and take the 1.2-mile boardwalk trail. The "lumber" is made of recycled shopping bags and wood fiber. Though more expensive, the recycled material has a longer lifespan than treated lumber, an important consideration in a swamp forest.

GEOLOGY

Hardin County is farmland and flatland. Raked and smoothed by the Wisconsinan glacier, pimples and dimples make a difference in this topographically-challenged till plain. Dimples in the preserve stay soggy most of the year and support plants and critters acclimated to wet habitats. Upland vegetation collects on the drier pimples, which rise just a few feet above the water table. These slight changes in elevation produce great diversity and several microhabitats. All life survives above glacially deposited till—no bedrock outcrops here. Water in the preserve trickles into nearby Taylor Creek, a tributary of the Scioto River.

WILDLIFE

Lawrence Woods is the most impressive and biologically diverse forest in its neck of the woods. More than 1,500 species have been counted so far. Gargantuan specimens of red maple and sycamore (these in soggy spots) share the canopy with giant red, white and burr oaks, sugar maple, American beech, white ash, and shagbark hickory which occupy the slightly higher and drier sites.

Wildflowers, more than 100 kinds, thrive in every niche. Common spring bloomers like large-flowered trillium, trout lily, cut-leaved toothwort, wild geranium, bloodroot, spring cress, Dutchman's breeches, spring beauty, jack-in-the-pulpit, yellow and blue violets, and wild blue phlox are abundant. Moist areas boast marsh marigold, jewelweed, golden ragwort, turtlehead, cardinal flower, and heart-leaf plantain, whose relative, common plantain, is judged a weed. However, this rare wetland plantain, with only three widely disjunct colonies in Ohio, is being considered for federal protection. Grove sandwort, another state-listed plant, grows alongside the trail.

Look for the scaly-barked buttonbush swamp along the trail. The shrub grows in thickets at the edge of swamps and wetlands. Their round seed heads burst open into bristling balls of tubular flowers (similar to hydrangea) whose sweet fragrance attract bumble-bees and butterflies. Promethea and sphinx moths spend their larval time beneath buttonbush leaves.

Vernal ponds are breeding grounds for several kinds of secretive mole salamanders. Except for a nocturnal orgy in spring, these reclusive amphibians spend their time burrowed in forest duff. Salamanders named four-toed, smallmouth, spotted, and tiger, which can grow to a foot in length, breed in the puddles. The pools also swarm with the spring peeper, chorus frog, wood frog, and gray treefrog.

The boardwalk opens the woods to more birders, who undoubtedly will add to a growing checklist. Search or listen for the pileated woodpecker, scarlet tanager, veery, cerulean warbler, hooded warbler, ovenbird, acadian flycatcher, downy woodpecker, eastern pewee, and red-eyed vireo. Come dusk, the barred and great-horned owls sound off. Tracks indicate that squirrels, raccoons, deer, and wild turkey live here.

HISTORY

William Lawrence, the preserve's namesake, was a noted statesman, author, banker, and agricultur-alist. The Division of Natural Areas and Preserves bought this treasury from his descendents just in the nick of time in 1997. Hundreds of husky hardwoods got logging stripes (blue paint) just months before the sale. The preserve was formally dedicated on May 1, 1999.

North Shore Alvar State Nature Preserve

The rare and specially-adapted plants exposed on this rocky habitat—dubbed an "alvar" by scientists—endure the fierce winds, waves, and ice dished out by Lake Erie, as well as intense sunlight which heats the limestone floor to frying-pan temperatures in summer. Twelve millenium ago, the Wisconsinan glacier scratched claw marks here as it returned to its Arctic origin.

LOCATION
Erie County, Kelleys Island.

OWNERSHIP
Ohio Department of Natural Resources, Division of Parks and Recreation. Jointly managed by the Ohio Divisions of Parks and Recreation and Natural Areas and Preserves

SIZE & DESIGNATION
This preserve comprises only .7 acre.

ACCESS
From the Village of Kelleys Island on the south shore of the island, head north on Division Street. Continue passed Glacial Grooves State Memorial to the boating launch in Kelleys Island State Park (end of the road).

Stay on the state park loop trail, trickling from the northwest corner of the parking lot, to avoid disturbing endangered plants. The site is open daily dawn to dusk. For information contact Lake Erie Islands State Park, 4049 E. Moores Dock Road, Port Clinton, OH 43452; phone (419) 797-4530.

GEOLOGY
Rubble at the bottom of the northbound, retreating Wisconsinan glacier scored and gouged the exposed limestone bedrock about 20,000 years ago. Later, meltwater pooling in front of the glacier created a great lake that spread to Fort Wayne, Indiana, and flooded Kelleys Island. When a lobe of the ice mass (near Buffalo) finally collapsed, ancient Lake Erie gushed northeasterly through the Niagara-St. Lawrence valley. As Lake Erie shrank to its current size, the limestone-dolomite outcrops clawed by the glacier reappeared as islands off the southern shore.

Columbus limestone, an ocean floor 370 million years old, armors the northwestern brow of Kelleys Island. Abandoned nearby quarries remind us of the past mining of this carbonate rock.

WILDLIFE
"Alvar" is a Swedish word to describe similar landforms in the Baltic Sea area. Alvars are limestone or dolomite slabs uncovered by glaciers. They remain exposed and inhospitable to woody plants for a variety of natural reasons. Soil buildup is slow due to constant pounding by waves, wind, and ice. Water escapes through porous limestone, and summer heat bakes the rock.

In North America, alvars are found in the Great Lakes basin, most of them along the coast of Ontario, Canada. Ohio has three known alvars. Two "disturbed" alvars are located on the Marblehead Peninsula at Lakeside Daisy State Natural Area and Marblehead Lighthouse. The Kelleys Island alvar is the most natural and best preserved of the three.

The alvar here protects hardy floral refugees from various habitats. It boasts Ohio's only extensive settlement of the northern bog violet, an endangered boreal plant found in the moist, shaded rock crevices. Big bluestem, a prairie grass, and balsam squaw-weed, another westerner, thrive here, too. Rarities called Pringle's aster, usually found in New England and the Appalachians, and Kalm's lobelia have anchored roots.

HISTORY
The "alvar" became a state natural area in early 1999.

North Pond State Natural Area

This natural wetland is one of the last remaining freshwater estuaries along the Lake Erie shore. A narrow channel acting like an embilical cord links Ohio's "great lake" to the pristine marsh, home for the endangered wapato and rare waterbirds.

LOCATION
Erie County, Kelleys Island.

OWNERSHIP
The Division of Natural Areas and Preserves leases the location from the Division of Parks and Recreation; the two entitites jointly manage the site.

SIZE & DESIGNATION
30 acres.

ACCESS
Take Division Street north from the Village of Kelleys Island. A little more than a mile from town, go east (right) on Ward Road for a half mile to a parking lot on the right.
A path to the preserve's 1,400-foot boardwalk trail and observation tower begins across the road, in North Bay area of the island.

GEOLOGY
When Lake Erie receded at the end of the Ice Age (see Geology in North Shore Alvar State Natural Area) the pond was abandoned atop newly exposed Kelleys Island. Runoff filled the pond and created the outlet to Lake Erie. North Pond remains a natural wetland, managed by natural forces, not by dikes, dams, and manmade channels.

WILDLIFE
An estuary is a body of water where different kinds of water mix. Here, freshwater from the pond, essentially runoff, churns and bonds with Lake Erie freshwater to produce a unique chemical soup.
Vegetation packs into the preserve. The boardwalk passes a colony of wapato, a state-endangered arrowhead plant, so-named for its distinctive arrowhead-shaped leaf and white summer blossom. Its tubers are eaten by ducks and muskrats. Also search for swamp rose mallow, bulrushes, pond lilies, and other wetland species.
Birding can be productive at the observation tower. Migrating waterbirds, especially numerous species of ducks, use the pond before and after flights across the lake. Rarities in Ohio, such as the white pelican and Eurasian wigeon, have been spotted here.

HISTORY
Originally part of Kelleys Island State Park, North Pond became a state natural area in early 1999.

Old Woman Creek State Nature Preserve

Here, the waters of Old Woman Creek and Lake Erie churn together to make a chemically different body of water—an estuary—and a habitat filled with creatures who live in the deep, the creek, the swamp, and the woods.

For 9,000 years, the first Ohioans occupied a village on a nearby bluff and harvested the bounty from the estuary. Today, scientists housed on a different bluff, try to uncover the secrets of the estuary, the most studied natural area in Ohio.

LOCATION
Erie County, Berlin and Huron townships, just east of Huron.

OWNERSHIP
Ohio Department of Natural Resources, Division of Natural Areas and Preserves.

SIZE & DESIGNATION
The site is an interpretive preserve of 571 acres. The estuary also is protected as a national estuarine reserve. Scientists studying the estuary's ecology hope to better understand the function and importance of this kind of coastal marsh.

ACCESS
The preserve is about two miles east of Huron city limits on US 6. Look for the main entrance on the right, just after you cross a stream, which happens to be Old Woman Creek.
Trails: After the visitor center, follow the paved path, the Edward Walper Trail, that leaves the northwest corner of the parking. This wheelchair and stroller accessible trail descends a quarter mile through woods to an observation deck that gazes up on the estuary. Please stay on the trail, and discourage kids from climbing on trees that have fallen into the estuary. Besides the obvious dangers, their sudden

appearance "out on the limb" may force wildlife to flee from their feeding or nesting places.

The pavement ends at the observation deck. The continuing gravel trail, unfortunately, is too difficult for wheelchairs. This path traces the edge of the estuary for awhile (go slow and look for herons and other beasties on the far shore) then enters a marshy woods. Here the trail splits. A left turn climbs a brief slope and returns to the parking lot and visitor center. I recommend that you bear right and stay on the Walper Trail, which winds through a wooded area, old farmland in various stages of succession (look for the rusting farm equipment along the way), a wet meadow, and back to the parking lot. The whole journey measures about a mile.

There is more—the barrier beach at the mouth of Old Woman Creek. Turn left (west) onto Route 6 at the end of the drive, heading toward Huron. Immediately after crossing the bridge over Old Woman Creek, turn right into the first driveway. Park in the small designated lot at the left. A white building will be at the right. Backtrack a bit and walk around the barn to the creek then stroll to the barrier beach. The homes that you see on the grounds are dormitories for visiting researchers.

Go ahead and take off your shoes and wade along the shore. That's it, though. Swimming is forbidden. Also, please refrain from collecting natural artifacts and picnicking. Keep this beach as natural and as undisturbed as possible. One more rule: don't wander onto private beaches. To the west, the preserve beach ends where the sand ends. Signs posted on the trees behind the beach mark the boundary of the preserve. To the east, a wooden sign designates the location of a private beach.

Special Places & Events: If it's open, the visitor center should be your first stop. The nature exhibits, including an aquarium, and other displays will give you a great picture of the geology, history, and wildlife of the estuary. Children love the "living stream" aquarium featuring the fish that live in the estuary. Fresh water actually flows through this aquarium, and recreates the habitat of the fish.

You also will find various brochures on the preserve, and a bird checklist. Rest rooms and drinking water also are available.

Special education programs and workshops are available for individuals and groups.

Information: Old Woman Creek State Nature Preserve, 2514 Cleveland Road East, Huron, Ohio 44839; (419) 433-4601. You can also contact the Ohio Department of Natural Resources.

GEOLOGY

Old Woman Creek is a special kind of estuary. Traditionally, an estuary holds brackish water, a mixture of saltwater from the sea and freshwater from a stream. In this type of estuary the salinity of the water depends on the amount of freshwater flowing into the estuary, and the water's distance from the sea. The water level of a saltwater estuary fluctuates daily according to the strength of lunar tides.

Old Woman Creek estuary, however, is a freshwater estuary. Though Lake Erie (actually an inland sea) and Old Woman Creek are both freshwater, their chemical compositions are not the same. A different chemical mixture is produced where these waters meet. Estuarine water near the mouth of the creek is more like that of Lake Erie, but inland its characteristics are closer to those of the creek. Precipitation and other weather conditions, far more than tides, influence the water level at Old Woman Creek. The changes in the water level are subtler than those experienced in saltwater estuaries.

The estuary filters out sediment and pollution headed for Lake Erie (though there are limits to how much purification the estuary can accomplish). It also can hold floodwater after heavy rains.

As its name suggests, the barrier beach at the mouth of the creek acts as a barrier that separates the lake from the creek. In a sense, it regulates the flow of water. Take away the beach, and the estuary disappears.

Spring rains swell Old Woman Creek, flush the estuary, and force creek water over the barrier beach. Storm waves breach the beach and spill lake water into the estuary. The waves also push sand back on the beach.

By midsummer, the beach has closed the creek's mouth. Still, lake water percolates and seeps through the sand and into the estuary.

The beach fattens and shrinks, and this affects the water content in the estuary. In the last dozen years, the beach has been thicker, and thinner, than its current size.

WILDLIFE

Like nearby Sheldon Marsh State Nature Preserve, Old Woman Creek teems with life. Many species, dwindling in numbers in Ohio, find refuge in the preserve including a nesting pair of bald eagles.

Let's start with the critters best viewed under a microscope—plankton. These tiny plants and animals—billions of them—serve as the foundation of the life cycle in the estuary. They are consumed by small fish that like to spawn in the warm shallows around lotus beds. Bigger fish (bass, walleye, etc.), as well as herons and egrets, eat the small fry. Eagles, terns, and gulls then feast on the game fish.

The estuary, beach, meadows, and woodlands attract almost 300 species of birds, including ducks, herons, raptors, shorebirds, and warblers. A bird checklist for Old Woman Creek and Sheldon Marsh is available at the visitor center. (Also see the chapter on Sheldon Marsh).

As you can imagine, amphibians and reptiles are abundant. Amphibians are represented by the American toad (able to eat 10,000 bugs in a three-month span), spring peeper (known for its spring melody and the "X" mark on its back), leopard frog (like the cat this frog is spotted), and red-backed salamander (which breathes through its skin, not lungs).

Reptiles commonly seen are the eastern fox snake (mistaken for the venomous copperhead), eastern garter snake (the most widely distributed snake in the U.S.), northern brown snake (likes snails, slugs, worms), northern water snake, snapping turtle (don't try to pet it), eastern box turtle (distinctive yellow and brown patterns), midland painted turtle (plain looking except for the painted red design on the edge of its shell), and Blanding's turtle (potentially threatened, look for a yellow chin).

Forty kinds of fish live in the estuary, an ideal spawning location for many. They include the largemouth bass, carp, sunfish, perch, shiners, and shad.

Enriching the largesse of the estuary are 14 protected plants, such as the endangered clasping leaf dogbane, bushy aster and narrow-leaved bluegrass. The following residents are threatened species—beach wormwood, leafy tussock sedge, Bebb's sedge, slender sedge, plains frostweed, and Lake Erie pinkweed. Five are potentially threatened—inland sea rocket, seaside spurge, early buttercup, Great Plains ladies' tresses, and purple sand grass.

Nature occupies every niche. On open water you'll find American lotus (mistaken for water lily) in abundance, along with pond and water lilies, arrow arum, pondweed, and swamp rose mallow.

HISTORY

Around 11,000 years ago ancestors of the First Ohioans reached the shore of Lake Erie. The continental ice sheet known as the Wisconsinan glacier had withdrawn into Canada. These settlers, the Paleo-Indians, hunted mastodon (an elephant), caribou, and probably elk. They also fished the waters of Lake Erie, its marshes, estuaries, and streams.

Just north of where State Route 2 crosses Old Woman Creek (south of the visitor center) Kent State University researchers uncovered artifacts of the First Ohioans at excavations called the Anderson site. Archeologists figured the Paleo-Indians lived there 9,000–10,000 years ago. The camp was occupied at various times during the past 10,000 years, the last native people perhaps being the Ottawas.

The Anderson site was carefully selected. It is located on a bluff where the creek empties into the estuary. The rich resources of the estuary, the lake,

Northwest
Web

Log On For More In Northwest Ohio

AUDUBON ISLANDS
www.dnr.state.oh.us/odnr/dnap/location/audubon_islands.html

COLLIER
www.dnr.state.oh.us/odnr/dnap/location/collier.html

GOLL WOODS
www.dnr.state.oh.us/odnr/dnap/location/goll_woods.html

GROSS WOODS
www.dnr.state.oh.us/odnr/dnap/location/gross_woods.html

IRWIN PRAIRIE
www.dnr.state.oh.us/odnr/dnap/location/irwin_prairie.html

KENDRICK WOODS (Metropark)
www.dnr.state.oh.us/odnr/dnap/location/kendrick_woods.html

LAKESIDE DAISY
www.dnr.state.oh.us/odnr/dnap/location/natural_areas/lakeside.html

OLD WOMAN CREEK
www.dnr.state.oh.us/odnr/dnap/location/oldwoman_creek.html

SEARS WOODS
www.dnr.state.oh.us/odnr/dnap/location/sears_woods.html

SHELDON'S MARSH
www.dnr.state.oh.us/odnr/dnap/location/sheldon.html
www.dnr.state.oh.us/odnr/dnap/location/natural_areas/sheldon.html

SPRINGVILLE MARSH
www.dnr.state.oh.us/odnr/dnap/location/springvill_marsh.html
www.dnr.state.oh.us/odnr/dnap/location/natural_areas/springville.html

and the forest were within arm's reach.

As the climate warmed, the evergreen forest of the cold, glacial era was replaced by the deciduous (leaf-losing trees) hardwood forest that moved in from the south. This ecological transformation inspired technological changes among the Archaic Indians, the people who lived here between 9,000 and 3,000 years ago.

The last 3,000 years, the Woodland Period, produced profound changes. The Indians began to cultivate plants to supplement the food they secured from hunting, gathering, and fishing. As they became more dependent on agriculture (around 900 A.D.) native crops were abandoned for corn, beans, and squash, all of which originated in Mexico.

A major settlement was established at the Anderson site during the 15th century. Though these Ohioans (late Woodland Indians) planted maize (corn), hunting, fishing, and gathering still seemed to be more important.

The whitetailed deer was the most important game animal, providing meat, clothing, tools, utensils, and other items. Elk, turkey, bear, raccoon, and rabbit also were hunted. The wetlands gave them waterfowl, beaver, and muskrats.

The Treaty of Green Ville in 1794 marked the end of the Indian culture in northwestern Ohio. The people who valued the land were replaced by immigrants (Europeans and Americans) who valued what they did to the land, like cut down the dense forest.

In 1805, Almon Ruggles surveyed this neighborhood for the government. This region became known as the Firelands, land reserved for Connecticut Yankees displaced during the American Revolution. J.K. Thompson constructed the first gristmill on Old Woman Creek near Berlin Heights. Soon there were six sawmills, two more gristmills, and five sandstone quarries.

The giant oaks along the creek fell. They were transported to Huron, which, in the 19th century, became a large shipbuilding city. Strawberries, raspberries, grapes and other fruits became important agricultural crops.

Fortunately, several landowners in the 20th century—the Anderson and Hartley families—resisted offers to build homes and recreational developments on the shores of Old Woman Creek. Oberlin College has protected part of the beach and east shore since 1913.

Old Woman Creek estuary became a state nature preserve on September 5, 1980. Much of the property is designated for scientific research. It also is protected as a national estuarine sanctuary.

Research is partially funded by the National Estuarine Reserve Research Program, created by Congress to help the state save the last few natural estuaries. The program is administered by the National Ocean Service, Office of Ocean and Coastal Resource Management, an agency of the National Oceanic and Atmospheric Administration of the Department of Commerce.

The buildings above the barrier beach are living quarters for researchers studying the waters, wildlife, and wonders of Old Woman Creek estuary.

JOURNAL

Spring: A female bald eagle nested atop a dead tree at the edge of the estuary—a perfect location, far enough from humans, ringside seat beside a supermarket. From the rim of the nest, she dove down on spawning fish and brought them to the nest. I watched her white head bob in the nest, presumably feeding her young.

Sears (Paul B.) & Carmean Woods State Nature Preserves

Good forests also make good neighbors. Paul Sears and Fred Carmean, who shared an interest in nature and trees, were good neighbors. Hearing that Sears was selling his cherished 99-acre woods to the state for $163,000, Fred Carmean figured he would outdo his long-time friend. Carmean decided to donate his 39-acre beauty to the state preservationists.

LOCATION

Southwestern Crawford County, Bucyrus Township.

OWNERSHIP

The sites are owned by the Ohio Department of Natural Resources, Division of Natural Areas and Preserves. The Crawford County Park District manages them.

SIZE & DESIGNATION

Sears Woods is 99 acres; Carmean Woods, 39 acres.

ACCESS

The preserves are neighbors, side-by-side on Mt. Zion Road. From Bucyrus, go south on SR 4 a few miles, then turn right (west) on Mt. Zion Road. In less than two miles the signs for the preserves will appear on the right. Use the parking lot by the sign for Sears Woods.

Trails: A mile-long loop trail enters Sears Woods from the parking lot. (Ignore the short paths in the meadow). The west leg of the loop crosses two footbridges before following the Sandusky River. The northern turn in the loop goes across a forest opening. A connector trail branches from east leg of the Sears Woods Trail, crosses a gravel lane separating the preserves, and enters Carmean Woods. After a .75-mile loop through Carmean Woods, retrace your steps to Sears Woods and complete the walk to the parking lot.

GEOLOGY

In eastern Crawford County, a terminal moraine, an elongated mound at the vanguard of the Wisconsinan glacier, serves as the divide between two major watersheds and the source of two rivers. The Sandusky River begins its journey just a few miles from the headwaters of the Olentangy River, a tributary of the Scioto and Ohio rivers. By tracking the route of rivers, you can trace the trend of the moraine and watershed divide.

The Sandusky snakes along the north side of the moraine west to the northside of Bucyrus, where it turns southwesterly through Sears Woods. At the Crawford-Wyandot county line it veers north and empties into Lake Erie. The Little Scioto River begins at the southern edge of Bucyrus (not two miles from the Sandusky) and goes southwesterly parallel to SR 4 and the Sandusky River. However, where the Sandusky bends north, the Little Scioto turns south into the Scioto and Ohio rivers.

Sears and Carmean woods are located just north and west of the hump dividing the Lake Erie and Ohio River watersheds. Mt. Zion Road rides over the summit of the divide, roughly at its intersection with Denzer Road. Downtown Bucyrus is on the bubble between the watersheds.

WILDLIFE

Though they stand side-by-side, Sears and Carmean woods are not exact twins. Naturalists describe Sears Woods as a former mixed oak forest that has evolved into an impressive old-growth beech-maple forest. Carmean Woods is mixed forest very much on the swampy side. Both forests birth splendid wildflowers in spring, and keep alive old codgers who have been around for a couple of centuries. Ohio's former state champion butternut tree grew in Sears Woods.

The spring festival includes large-flowered trillium, bloodroot, wild ginger, tall bellflower, meadow rue, and Solomon's seal, and a profusion of ferns called maidenhair, sensitive, New York, broadbeech, grape and fragile.

Carmean Woods contains vital vernal ponds—woodland wetlands that "pond" in late winter and spring, but dry up in summer and fall. In May, these ponds get as busy as African waterholes.

HISTORY

In his time, Paul Sears was considered one of the nation's foremost ecologists, botanists, and conservationists. He authored 11 books, dozens of papers, researched and mapped Ohio's vegetation, bogs, prairies and forests, and taught at six universities, including Ohio State, Oberlin and Yale, during a 99-year lifespan.

Sears' ancestors arrived on the third voyage of the Mayflower. His grandfather bought the "woods" in 1870, though the family lived closer to Bucyrus. The Division of Natural Areas and Preserves purchased the Sears tract in 1986, four years before Sears died in Taos, New Mexico. Carmean "one-upped" his buddy that year.

Sheldon Marsh State Nature Preserve

The locals once called this place Sheldon's Folly. They just couldn't figure out why a Sandusky doctor would spend his money on a slim, spit of sand that attracted bugs and, half the time, was washed over by Lake Erie. And those pretentious iron gates at the entrance were eerie, as if a dowager's vine-covered estate lay in ruins behind a row of creaking oaks. But Dr. Dean Sheldon was more interested in wildlife than local gossip. He knew that his marsh was an important stopover for migratory birds flying across Lake Erie, and that the spit was one of the last undisturbed barrier beaches along Ohio's north coast.

LOCATION

Sheldon Marsh is located a few miles west of Huron in Erie County, Huron Township.

OWNERSHIP

Ohio Department of Natural Resources, Division of Natural Areas and Preserves.

SIZE & DESIGNATION

The state dedicated this 463-acre marsh and barrier beach an interpretive nature preserve on February 5, 1980.

ACCESS

From Huron, head west on SR 2, exit north on Rye Beach Road to the intersection of US 6, then go west on US 6 about .5 mile to the preserve (northside). Look for the iron fence on the right.

Trails: From the parking lot off US 6, follow the paved path at the left, which once was the driveway to Cedar Point amusement park. At the former Sheldon home, the pavement ends but the trail remains wide and smooth. It appears to be manageable for folks in wheelchairs or pushing strollers.

The marsh will soon appear on the left. Ahead, the trail joins a paved lane (from the right) and continues north toward the beach. The road leads to an observation deck on the left and to the National Aeronautical & Space Administration pump station at the beach. The observation deck, with benches, offers an excellent panorama of the marsh all year.

At the pump station, look for the narrow trail heading into the woods. This wild, narrow path through a dense thicket of reeds ends at the barrier beach. I strongly recommend that you walk this brief trail in the summer to experience the jungle-like vegetation growing on the sand spit. The barrier beach stretching to the west is a good place to rest a spell and soak in the sun, listen to the waves, and search the sky for bald eagles.

Backtrack to the exit. You might want to take the blacktopped left fork back to the start. If so, follow the trail to the end, then take the path at the right. It leads across a lawn to the parking lot.

If you took the right fork, along the marsh and through the forest, consider a short loop trail to the right just past the ranger's house. It returns to the driveway.

The site is open daily from sunrise to sunset, April–October. Permission is required for visits from November–March.

Information : Contact the preserve manager,

American *Ornithology*

Nesting Instincts

Genevieve Jones learned about birds by accompanying her physician father, Nelson, on his calls around Circleville. Nelson and "Gennie" collected nests and eggs, but identifying them proved difficult for lack of a book. Still, Gennie sketched the specimens with the eyes of an artist and scientist.

In 1876, Gennie saw John James Audubon's "Birds of America" (see page 71) at the Philadelphia Centennial Exhibition. Audubon's tome inspired her to begin "Illustrations of the Nests and Eggs of the Birds of Ohio." The book became a family project. Childhood friend Eliza Shulze helped Gennie with the illustrations; brother, Howard, provided samples and field notes; Nelson managed the project; and Virginia Jones, Gennie's mother, colored the plates. Critics who got proofs marveled at the girls' talent and precision. Early subscribers included Rutherford B. Hayes and Teddy Roosevelt. Midway through the project, however,

Genevieve succumbed to typhoid fever at age 32 in August 1879. Then Shulze abruptly quit to attend art school. The grief-stricken family vowed to finish Genevieve's life work. Watercolorists Josephine Klippart, Nellie Jacobs, and Kate Gephart were hired to help Virginia Jones with the plates. The family spent more than $25,000, a vast sum in those days.

When it finally appeared in 1886, the 329-pager contained detailed notes of eggs and nests and 68 elegant lithographs. Elliot Coues, a leading ornithologist, wrote "there has been nothing since Audubon in the way of pictorial illustrations of American Ornithology to compare with the present work." But critical acclaim and a bronze medal at the World's Columbian Expostion in Chicago in 1893, did not make the costly book a hit. Only 10 had been sold by 1901. Today, the finest one is owned by the Cleveland Museum of Natural History. Valued at $80,000, it was Virginia Jones' personal copy.

Old Woman Creek State Nature Preserve, 2514 Cleveland Road East, Huron, OH 44839, (419) 433-4601 or 443-7599. Or, get in touch with the Ohio Department of Natural Resources, Division of Natural Areas and Preserves, Fountain Square, Building F-1, Columbus, OH 43224-1331; (614) 265-6453.

GEOLOGY

The narrow finger of land stretching west into Lake Erie is a sand spit. It acts as a barrier beach and protects the wetland marsh from the heavy waves of the lake.

Geologists suspect this sand spit began to develop about 4,500 years ago when the water level of the lake increased and flooded the shore. The sand and mud of the old shoreline that washed into the lake during this inundation was later hurled back toward the land by waves and deposited as an offshore sandbar—the foundation for the spit.

In western Lake Erie the close-to-shore current that transports sand and other sediment (called a littoral drift) flows from east to west. When littoral drift is slowed by an obstruction—the shore, a bay, the mouth of a river, a sand bar, a shallow basin, or a beach—the sand it carries begins to settle.

At this spot on the coast the drift moves toward the shore at an oblique angle. The spit was born where the current struck land. It grew into the lake in the direction of the littoral drift, toward the west. A marsh evolved in the calm water between the spit and land.

Like a desert sand dune, a sand spit shifts position. It widens toward the lake when the water level drops, but during high water it thins out and heads for land.

Twenty years ago the western tip of the spit was connected to the eight-mile long Cedar Point spit. During a furious storm in November 1972, waves crashed through the barrier and created a channel. Since then, Lake Erie's waves have shoved the Sheldon Marsh spit landward some 1,000 feet. A January 1993 storm breached the barrier again, about 1,000 feet east of the tip.

The breakthroughs occur because a series of longwall piers constructed east of the preserve in Huron traps sand heading for the spit. Barrier beaches and spits weaken if they are not replenished with sand. They dissolve when big storm waves pound the beach and open passages.

Plants trying to gain a toehold on the spit face a tough environment of high waves, strong winds, and burning sun. The eastern end of the spit, anchored to the mainland, is more stable because driftwood, and vegetation stop the waves, collect sediment, build up the sandy soil with their roots and rotting material, block the wind, and provide shade for plants that need it.

Still, the spit rises only six feet above the lake level at its highest point.

Small lobes growing southward from the tip actually are tiny deltas created by the runoff of waves that wash over the beach. This erosion by waves explains how the spit has curled inward and drifted toward land.

Under present circumstances the spit is doomed. So is the marsh, which shrinks as the beach drifts toward land. Eventually, waves will push the beach into the mainland, and kill the marsh. Human intervention might save the spit. Jetties and offshore barriers would slow down waves and capture much needed sediment for the sand-starved beach. However, such "beach nourishment" projects could harm a new residential development and marina on the nearby Chaussee Road/Cedar Point causeway. Developers have deepened the channel opened by the 1972 storm for pleasure boats.

WILDLIFE

Few places on the Lake Erie coast can match Sheldon Marsh's accommodations for wildlife, especially its various wetlands, which include a large lake (Lake Erie), a bay, a cattail and sedge grass marsh, woodland swamp, and a pond. These moist habitats, and the barrier beach, serve as sanctuaries for a vast assemblage of birds, fish, amphibians, reptiles, and plants, many of them endangered or threatened.

For the birds who must journey across Lake Erie every equinox, Sheldon Marsh is a welcomed stopover for rest, food and shelter. More than 300 species of birds, most of them migratory, have been spotted here, ranging from the majestic and endangered bald eagle to the diminutive ruby-throated hummingbird.

An ODNR checklist of birds indicates that you might see 23 of the 25 birds listed as endangered in Ohio, including: the peregrine falcon, bald eagle, common and black terns, magnolia, Kirtland's and Canada warblers, northern waterthrush, and dark-eyed junco.

Fifteen of the 18 species listed as "special interest" (roughly meaning potentially threatened) by the Division of Wildlife have been spotted here. These include double-crested cormorant, and northern saw-whet owl

Twenty-six varieties of waterfowl (notably the white tundra swan) and 35 kinds of warblers have been counted. Carefully located bird boxes attract wood ducks, bluebirds, kestrels, and tree swallows.

Some 44 members of the fish world live around the preserve, such as walleye, perch, catfish, bullhead, minnow, shiner and bluegill. Fishing, of course, is prohibited.

Reptiles and amphibians, represented by 32 species, are abundant here. This population includes turtles (Blanding's — special interest), salamanders (red-backed, Jefferson), frogs and toads (American toad, bullfrog, spring peeper, leopard), and snakes (blue racer, northern water, northern brown, eastern garter).

Keen observers might see some of the 22 mammals that have resided here, like deer, raccoon, least weasel, muskrat, mice and moles.

In the forest, look for oaks and shagbark hickory on higher ground; elm and ash closer to the marsh. These are joined by cottonwood, willows, mulberry, silky dogwood, maples, basswood, bald cypress, dawn redwood, aspen, and ginko, the last introduced by Dr. Sheldon.

Many endangered, threatened or potentially threatened plants live in the preserve. The list, partly based on a 1990 survey, includes beach wormwood, inland sea rocket, low umbrella sedge, Engelman's umbrella sedge, Schweinitz's umbrella sedge, matted spikerush, seaside spurge, bushy cinquefoil, jack-in-the-pulpit, sand dropseed.

From mid-April through June, wildflowers such as trillium, marsh marigolds, cut-leaved toothwort, wild geranium, trout lily, and cardinal flower color the forest floor. Marsh mallow, American lotus and water lily are abundant in late summer.

HISTORY

The gates at the entrance to the preserve are all that remain of the original car entrance to Cedar Point Amusement Park. The drive was abandoned in the 1930s because the lake too often washed away the road on the narrow spit. The park entrance was moved farther west, but the gates stayed.

The marsh, bay, and beach became a favorite waterfowl hunting and fishing spot for local sportsmen. The site was one of only a few undisturbed coastal properties.

In 1954 Dr. Dean Sheldon, a Sandusky physician and conservationist, purchased 56 acres of this tract and managed some of it as a nature sanctuary. He and his family built the farm pond near the entrance, planted trees (some of them exotic species), and placed birdhouses throughout the property.

The Ohio Department of Natural Resources acquired the Sheldon land in 1979 and combined it with adjoining tracts to create the nature preserve in 1980.

An adjoining marsh recently purchased by the Ohio Chapter of The Nature Conservancy (TNC) more than doubles the wetland area now protected for nature. This TNC preserve (not open to the public) will be known as the John B. and Mildred A. Putnam Memorial Preserve, honoring the family that bequeathed $37 million to the conservation group.

According to ODNR's brochure, the U.S. government gave much of the Big Spring Prairie (16,000 acres) to the Wyandot Indians in 1818 because it suited their traditional hunting and gathering ways.

Springville Marsh State Nature Preserve

Springville Marsh is the largest remnant of the Big Spring Prairie, a sprawling wetland that once stretched 15 miles from Carey to Fostoria. Forty years ago the marsh was stripmined for its muck, but nature has largely concealed that human intrusion.

LOCATION
Southwest Seneca County, Big Spring Township.

OWNERSHIP
Originally purchased by the Springville Marsh Committee and the Ohio Chapter of The Nature Conservancy, the property was turned over to the Ohio Department of Natural Resources, Division of Natural Areas and Preserve.

SIZE & DESIGNATION
The Ohio Department of Natural Resources dedicated the 201-acre wetland as an interpretive nature preserve on August 1, 1981.

ACCESS
From Carey, travel north on US 23/SR 199 for 3.5 miles, then head west (left) on TR 24. Look for the parking lot on the south side after crossing railroad tracks.

Trails: Half of the distance of the one-mile loop trail is a boardwalk that begins at the parking lot and leads to a viewing platform and an observation tower. The remaining half of the trail visits a woodland along the west edge of the preserve. Look for a preserve brochure and trail guide at the information board at the trailhead.

The observation tower presents the best view of the marsh. This is especially true in the summer when tall sedges and grasses block your vision at the ground-level platform. Visitors riding in wheelchairs and pushing strollers can probably manage the boardwalk trail.

Though wildlife can be seen any season, bird life is especially abundant during the spring and fall migrations. Visibility is best at these times because vegetation is low.

Summer hikers should guard against mosquitoes by wearing insect repellent, a ball cap, sunglasses, and long pants. Marsh plants will soar above your reach in the summer. The vegetation is so thick in July and August, I cannot imagine a human crossing the marsh without assistance.

GEOLOGY

The terrain in this part of the world is flat to gently rolling, thanks to the scouring action by the Wisconsinan glacier some 12,000 years ago. The ice sheets, in other words, prepared the land for the wet prairie and unique ecology that came later.

Dolomite (the same bedrock found at Niagara Falls) lies near the surface of the slight ridges surrounding the preserve. The ridges also contain the water for the marsh and ponds. This cool, spring water (hence the names of the marsh and prairie) carries calcium derived from the bedrock. The calcium-rich, marl soil, composed of sedge peat mostly, was mined by fertilizer companies.

Technically, Springville Marsh is a fen because it is refreshed by alkaline spring water from underground sources. Cedar Bog State Memorial, described in this book, is another spring-fed fen.

WILDLIFE

In this dense cattail-bulrush-sedge marsh live some of Ohio's most precious plants and critters. The American and least bitterns, each endangered, find refuge here. The spotted turtle, listed as a special interest (potentially threatened) reptile, might be seen in spring basking on a log protruding from the marsh or pond. "Special interest" birds like sora and Virginia rails, and the marsh wren, are counted among the population of birds.

Grass-like pondweed, an endangered plant, attracts waterfowl, and grows near few-flowered spikerush, a threatened specimen. Little yellow sedge, twig-rush (typically found on the Atlantic coast), long-beaked willow, Ohio goldenrod, white beak-rush, and shining ladies'-tresses, all potentially threatened species, thrive in this verdant wetland. Also look for the blossoms of bittersweet nightshade, Kalm's lobelia, yellow avens, and nodding ladies' tresses among the numerous fen orchids.

See if you can spot the Ice Age relicts, the small clusters of plants more common in the north—shrubby cinquefoil and grass-of-parnassus (white, green-striped flowers). Ferns are represented by the royal, northern marsh, adder's-tongue, and sensitive.

Several rarities have been planted in Springville Marsh to extend their range—swamp birch (threatened), fringed gentian (potentially threatened), small white lady's slipper, and spiked blazing star.

Cottonwoods dominate the swamp forest, which is low enough to be seasonally flooded. Big-toothed aspen, hackberry, wild cherry, and dogwood also grow here.

The marsh, forbidding to humans, is luxuriant for the 136 species of birds who live here or pass through. The nesting birds include the above-mentioned rails, common gallinule, American coot (not the human kind), blue-winged teal, wood duck, and willow flycatcher. You also might see the great blue heron, other varieties of ducks, the pileated woodpecker, and the merlin, a jay-sized falcon often mistaken for the larger peregrine falcon. The wooded areas attract warblers, gold-finches, sparrows, and other common residents.

The dome-shaped piles of cattails that you see from the observation tower are muskrat dens. Mink, fox, weasel, rabbit and deer also reside here.

Springville Marsh preserves an extraordinary collection of wildlife living in five distinct habitats: pond, stream, cattail marsh, swamp forest, and sedge meadow.

HISTORY

Native American and early white pioneers successfully hunted and trapped in the marshland.

According to ODNR's brochure, the U.S. government gave much of the Big Spring Prairie (16,000 acres) to the Wyandot Indians in 1818 because it suited their traditional hunting and gathering ways. A more likely explanation is that pioneer farmers found the marshland unsuitable for agriculture—so they gave it to the Indians.

The Hocking Valley Railroad put a rail line through the marsh in 1877. Ditches drained the swamp so that more crops could be sowed. By 1900 the place known today as Springville Marsh was an onion farm.

The Smith Agriculture Chemical Company bought the swamp in 1937 and began dredging the calcium-rich muck from the bottom. The muck was loaded into the cars of a small-gauge railroad and transported to the nearby main rail for shipment to fertilizer companies. The mining ended in 1956, and the land quickly reverted to a marsh.

Naturalists have flocked to the marsh. At the turn of the century, Dayton-born naturalist Thomas A. Bonser documented the flora and fauna of the Big Spring Prairie in his master's thesis.

H. Thomas Bartlett, a local science teacher, has been studying the birds at Springville Marsh since 1978. In his 1990 report, he observed 205 species, representing 77 percent of all types seen in the region.

In the late 1970s, local concerned citizens organized the Springville Marsh Committee and with the help of the Ohio Chapter of The Nature Conservancy bought the marsh. Some of the land was acquired through a gift in memory of Charles and Bertha Krejci Vanek, former landowners. The title was transferred to the Ohio Department of Natural Resources, Division of Natural Areas and Preserves in 1981.

JOURNAL

August 17: I am struck by the height and density of the cattails and phragmites (cane-like grasses). They grow beyond my reach—eight feet tall or so.

Cruise control: for those who take the trail well-traveled, all roads lead to Ohio's nature centers.

*n*ature centers bridge the chasms that separate many humans from the natural world. Think of them as gathering and connecting places, reminding humans that they are bonded to forces as old and true as the planet itself.

If life is a game of tag, nature centers are the designated "safe" places.

The nature centers hereafter described are privately-owned, nonprofit organizations dedicated to natural history education and preservation. (Nature centers in public parks are noted elsewhere.) Most started after a deceased wealthy benefactor left large land tracts, country estates, and seed money for nature education programs. Founding members fixed up the fledgling sites and, when money became handy, hired a professional staff to run them, with the support of volunteers.

Membership and program fees, endowments, gift shop profits, and grants keep nature centers "green," in a manner of speaking.

Typically, nature centers have been "improved" with hiking trails, human-made habitats (ponds, prairies, etc.) that diversifies the wildlife, and accommodations for people (parking lots, boardwalks, observation decks, bird feeders, and the like). They have exhibits and educational programs for all ages, small research libraries, wildlife windows, and perhaps gardens. Geology, botany, butterfly, outdoors photography, astronomy, birding, hiking, horticulture, and ecology clubs gather in nature center meeting rooms.

Each center seems to have a specialty. Brukner Nature Center, for example, patches up injured animals, and The Wilderness Center protects a patch of 300-year old trees. All nature centers have year-round appeal and activities, and comforts like toilets and drinking fountains for those who need them.

Envision them as divine sanctuaries—everlasting monasteries for nature and kindred spirits—and enjoy.

—SO

The Web of Nature Centers

Aullwood Audubon Center
www.audubon.org/local/
sanctuary/aullwood
www.dayton.net/audubon/
aullwd.htm

Brukner Nature Center
www.tdn-net.com/brukner/

Dawes Arboretum
www.dawesarb.org

Holden Arboretum
www.holdenarb.org

Nature Center at Shaker Lakes
www.efohio/NCSL.htm
www.natucenter-cleveland.com

NORTHEAST

Holden Arboretum

This cultivated setting of neatly-trimmed lawns and carefully manicured gardens also protects national natural landmarks, a fairy-tale forest, and a river valley buried and rerouted by a glacier.

LOCATION

Lake County, near Kirtland.

OWNERSHIP

The Holden Arboretum, an independent, not-for-profit institution.

SIZE & DESIGNATION

The Holden Arboretum encompasses more than 3,100 acres, including Stebbins Gulch (425 acres) and Little Mountain (190 acres). Stebbins Gulch, Bole Forest, and Hanging Rock Farm, sites owned by the arboretum, have been listed on the National Registry of Natural Landmarks by the U.S. Department of the Interior.

ACCESS

Leave Interstate 90 at Exit 193 (Mentor) and travel south on SR 306. At the bottom of the hill (less than a mile), cross the East Branch of the Chagrin River and turn left on Kirtland-Chardon Road. Go about 3.5 miles (past the Newell Whitney Museum and Penitentiary Glen Metropark) then turn left on Sperry Road. The entrance to the arboretum will be on the left in 1.5 miles.

The arboretum has blazed more than 20 miles of trails, some easy walks through gardens, others strenuous journeys through off-premises gorges.

I recommend four trails. The Pierson Creek valley loop (3 miles) and Bole Forest Trail (.75 miles) begin on the main grounds. Access to Stebbins Gulch and Little Mountain is restricted to naturalist-led hikes, usually held on weekends. These gems are not located on the main grounds, and a fee is charged for the hikes. Call or write for a schedule of these interpretive walks.

First stop should be the Warren H. Corning Visitor Center to pick up a trail map and guide to the plant collections. The visitor center offers refreshments, the Treehouse gift shop, rest rooms, nature exhibits, a 7,500-volume natural history library, and classroom for the numerous educational programs held year-round.

Visit the various gardens while you are here. The staff at the visitor center can tell you the blooming schedule of the collections, and point you in the direction.

INFORMATION

Holden Arboretum, 9500 Sperry Road, Kirtland, Ohio 44094; phone (440) 946-4400 or 256-1110.

GEOLOGY

Little Mountain owes its appeal to the geological and dramatic forces that first built the bedrock, and then began tearing it down. These natural forces continue to work their magic on this precious place.

The summit is an enchanting maze of warty ledges, narrow cracks, and dark and sonorous passages, topped by lofty, pointed pines. You half expect to be startled by a gnarly troll or a pebble-faced dragon on the trail.

Little Mountain consists of three rocky knobs in an L-shaped formation. The tallest and southernmost knob (1,266 feet in elevation) rests in Geauga County. Directly north, partly on the county line, is the middle-sized knob, elevation 1,244 feet. The shortest (1,247 feet) and smallest one lies to the northeast in Lake County.

The "mountain" stands on the northern edge of a peninsula-shaped ridge jutting from the Appalachian Plateau. Gildersleeve Knob (Chapin Forest Reservation) and Thompson Ledges also form this

192

Lake Erie

Michigan

Indiana

Pennsylvania

Kentucky

Ohio River

Ohio River

West Virginia

N

WILLIAMS | FULTON | LUCAS

OTTAWA

DEFIANCE | HENRY | WOOD | SANDUSKY | ERIE

PAULDING | PUTNAM | HANCOCK | SENECA | HURON | LORAIN

VAN WERT | HARDIN | WYANDOT | CRAWFORD | RICHLAND | ASHLAND | WAYNE

MERCER | AUGLAIZE | MARION | MORROW | KNOX | HOLMES

SHELBY | LOGAN | UNION | DELAWARE | COSHOCTON

DARKE | MIAMI | CHAMPAIGN | LICKING

PREBLE | MONTGOMERY | GREENE | CLARK | MADISON | FRANKLIN | FAIRFIELD | PERRY | MORGAN

BUTLER | WARREN | CLINTON | FAYETTE | PICKAWAY | HOCKING

HAMILTON | HIGHLAND | ROSS | VINTON | ATHENS

CLERMONT | BROWN | ADAMS | SCIOTO | PIKE | JACKSON | MEIGS | GALLIA

LAWRENCE

LAKE | ASHTABULA

GEAUGA | TRUMBULL

MEDINA | SUMMIT | PORTAGE | MAHONING

COLUMBIANA

STARK | CARROLL

TUSCARAWAS | HARRISON | JEFFERSON

GUERNSEY | BELMONT

MUSKINGUM | NOBLE | MONROE

WASHINGTON

Cleveland

Holden Arboretum

The Nature Center of Shaker Heights

CUYAHOGA

Canton

The Wilderness Center

Brukner Nature Center

Troy

Aullwood Audubon Center

Dayton

Newark

Dawes Arboretum

Cincinnati

Cincinnati Nature Center

Nature Notable

R. Henry Norweb, Jr., director of Holden Arboretum for 24 years, was inducted into the Ohio Natural Resources Hall of Fame 1983.

edge. Because all three cobbles are now isolated from their main geological formation they are called outliers. Each is capped by a speckled band of sandstone called Sharon Conglomerate.

The origin of the conglomerate dates back to the Pennsylvanian geological period, roughly 300 million years ago. Swollen and speedy streams falling from a mountain range to the north and east (the predecessor of the Appalachian Mountains) transported massive amounts of gravel and sand into the sea that spread across Ohio at the time. The sediments formed a broad delta with extending fingers, supposedly larger than the modern Mississippi delta.

The streams were swift enough to toss quartz pebbles in their currents. These are the white pebbles, called "lucky stones," found in Sharon Conglomerate.

Later, the ocean withdrew, the land uplifted, and the exposed delta hardened into a rock. The layer of Sharon sandstone is about 100 feet thick on the tallest knob, but it was probably much larger before erosion began its work. Sharon Conglomerate is classified a resistant rock because it withstands erosion better than softer, or less resistant, layers like shale.

Shale and siltstone, members of the Cuyahoga Formation that date back to the Mississippian period

Date with Nature

"Anyone of them who feels within his bosom, that he holds an appointment, to make a correct survey of nature... let such a one move onward and fame and glory will follow his labors. No governor will appoint him, nor Legislature pay him. The Creator will reward him."

— *Caleb Atwater,* A History of the State of Ohio, Natural & Civil, *1838*

some 330-335 million years ago, lay beneath the conglomerate caprock. These layers remain hidden beneath the gentle slope that you climb to reach the ledges on Little Mountain. Still deeper are Berea sandstone, Bedford shales and siltstone, and Ohio shale. These layers once served as the floors of ancient oceans.

Younger Pennsylvanian-era rock once capped the conglomerate (as it still does in southern Geauga County) but erosion has slowly and patiently washed it away. The water which kept flowing off the Appalachian Plateau (feeding the Grand, Chagrin, and Cuyahoga rivers) eventually cut through the resistant Sharon and Berea sandstone. Then the river systems removed the softer shales and widened their valleys. Little Mountain and the other knobs, situated between these preglacial rivers, either missed or withstood the full fury of the currents.

The continental ice sheets that followed chipped away at Little Mountain, too. They scoured and leveled off its top, drove ice wedges into thin cracks to make gaping crevices, and lifted boulders 30-feet in diameter and deposited them several miles away. The last glacier, the Wisconsinan, coated the outliers with a layer of till (unsorted rock debris) as it withdrew some 12,000 years ago. Its meltwater probably flossed through the crevices and channels in mad torrents. In the ensuing years much of the glacial till has washed away.

Though resistant to erosion, Sharon Conglomerate soaks in water like a sponge. The liquid slowly seeps through the sandstone, but when it gets to the impenetrable Cuyahoga shale it flows laterally to the surface. That explains the appearance of little springs at the base of Little Mountain.

Because of its higher elevation (nearly 700 feet above Lake Erie) Little Mountain receives a heavy dose of snow, nearly twice as much as Cleveland. The snow hastens erosion and nourishes the ground for wildlife.

Stebbins Gulch sounds like its belongs in some God-forsaken, parched piece of desert in the Old West. I like to think some ornery conservationist purposely called this green, pristine place a gulch to scare away developers.

Gulch refers to a steep-sided, V-shaped valley, what we Ohioans would call a gorge or ravine. It got to be a gulch because of Stebbins Run, the waterway that "runs" through it.

Stebbins Run has been on the job since the retreating Wisconsinan glacier began spewing melt-

water here some 12,000 years ago. The meltwater first washed away till—the gravel, sand, and clay deposited here by the ice sheet—then tackled the bedrock.

In the arboretum's section of the gulch, it has sliced through 300-million-year-old Orangeville shale (Cuyahoga Formation) of the Mississippian Period, and older Berea sandstone, also of the Mississippian Period. Now it is working on still older Bedford (Mississippian) and Cleveland (Devonian Period) shales, and if it gets through them it will reach Chagrin shale, some 370 million years old (Devonian Period).

All of these bedrocks were formed beneath the ancient oceans that covered Ohio. The sediments that compose these layers (mud, silt, and sand) were carried into the shallow seas by streams falling off a mountain chain, the predecessor of the Appalachian Mountains.

The creek descends 100 feet through the preserve, a gradient rivaling the mountain streams in the Appalachians. Hikers will be treated to a pair of small waterfalls tumbling over shale, splendid sights anytime of the year.

When you hike through this gorge look for the round or elliptical concretions embedded in horizontal layers of shale. Scientists think concretions started as pieces of organic matter (a piece of a tree branch perhaps) that attracted minerals, such as iron, and other sediments. They grew in layers, like pearls or onions. Weathering and erosion loosens them and they roll into the creek bed.

Stebbins Run has cut beneath the groundwater table in places. Water "bleeds" from the cliffs, or trickles out as springs, and refreshes the stream.

In summer the steep walls of this gaping abyss retain cool air and shade the creek. The temperature hardly ever goes above 75 degrees. The cliffs block the Arctic wind in the winter, thus moderating temperatures.

Bole Forest lies on a thick bed of glacial till deposited here about 12,000 years ago by the Wisconsinan glacier. The land gently slopes eastward to the East Branch of the Chagrin River, which brushes one corner of the 70-acre preserve.

Although there are no enchanting ledges here, and no slit exposing bedrock, the rich humus soil that has accumulated makes this ground a perfect site for the propagation of giant trees.

Some 75,000 years ago **Pierson Creek Valley** was part of a larger, swifter river system that flowed northward into a lake that preceded Lake Erie. Back in those days the valley was deeper and wider, and boasted higher waterfalls. Then the monstrous Wisconsinan glacier filled the valley with gravel, boulders, and other rubble, then sealed it in ice for centuries.

When the monster began to withdraw to its polar origins, about 12,000 years, its meltwater followed the easiest path, the buried valleys. The glacier that entombed the river also renewed its life.

Several rivulets that fall and merge at the southern edge of the arboretum's land form Pierson Creek. The creek drops swiftly now (120 feet per mile) and builds up enough steam to shape the land. Tributaries running in steep "V" gullies feed the northbound stream. The mouths of some of these feeders are choked with sand and clay, evidence of the rapid and relentless pace of erosion.

Notice the "slumping" in the valley. Gravity and groundwater combine to detach huge blocks of earth from valley (or gully) walls and slide them toward the stream. This is called slumping. The trees and plants growing on these clay-sand slumps go along for the ride. Most of the time the trees topple into the stream, but occasionally one will keep its balance and grow on the moveable, miniature mudslides.

Pierson Creek is elastic and everchanging. Spring rains, fallen trees, slumping, debris dams and the like, reroute the course of the channel, sometimes dramatically.

The absence of waterfalls (except near the headwaters) and bedrock outcrops in the valley proves the stream still tosses over till (glacially transported sediment). It also reveals its age, just a puppy at 12,000 years old, thereabouts. The current curls around granite boulders (delivered by the glacier from Canada) and foams over fallen trees, but these cannot be considered waterfalls. The mud-stained water tells us that erosion is working fast. Nobody knows, though, when Pierson Creek will reach rock bottom.

WILDLIFE

A number of micro-habitats defined by geology and climate makes Little Mountain a remarkable place for nature study.

Rock outcrops, ledges, and shallow soil usually make an austere environment for vegetation, but Little Mountain's heavy year-round shower of rain and snow enables plants to thrive.

Warty rock faces and cracks, nourished by the abundant water, sponsor the growth of clubmosses and ferns such as shining clubmoss, Christmas fern, hayscented fern, and common polypody fern.

Most striking are the eastern hemlocks, white pines, and yellow birches, species much more typical in the woods north of Ohio. Notice how the roots of these trees have slithered over the ledges, grasped boulders and cracks. Some roots have even bridged a crevice by snaking over a toppled mate. The origin of the white pines has inspired debate. They are the same size and age, suggesting that they sprouted as a group simultaneously after a natural disturbance, such as a fire or a terrific storm, cleared a space for them on the hill. This theory cools the claim that the pioneering pines, like the hemlocks (represented by seedlings to giants), are remnants of the Ice Age surviving in this colder micro-environment.

A beech-maple forest grows on the lower slopes of Little Mountain. This community is more typical in the surrounding region. Other trees live here, too, including black gum, white ash, cucumber magnolia, oak (chestnut, red, scarlet and white), tuliptree, and alternate-leaved dogwood.

Botanists in the 19th century listed several rare species growing here—trailing arbutus, mountain maple, one-sided pyrola, pipsissewa, and rattlesnake plantain—but they are no longer residents. Disease wiped out the American chestnut community, though shoots still pop up from rotting stumps.

Some of the wildflowers are wild sarsaparilla, fairybells, wintergreen, Solomon's plume, wild oats, and white snakeroot. Look for blueberry, witch hazel, and huckleberry, and let your nose take you to honeysuckle (two kinds).

The winter wren (endangered), Acadian fly-catcher, solitary vireo, indigo bunting, and black-throated green warbler offer challenges for birders.

195

The usual collection of four-legged creatures populate the peaks—deer (overabundant), fox, raccoon, opossum, woodchuck, squirrel, and chipmunk. Two centuries ago the woods still harbored elk, bear, wolf, and panther (a.k.a. mountain lion, wildcat, cougar, puma). The last bear on Little Mountain, a 400-pound beast, was killed by hunters in 1825.

The cool microclimate of Stebbins Gulch (totaling 425 acres) allows trees more typical of forests farther north to survive. These plants include eastern hemlock, yellow birch, and rarities like mountain maple and Canada yew (dwindling in number because it is a favorite snack of the overpopulated deer colony). These tend to grow on the slopes, terraces, and ravine edge.

Elsewhere, you will find chestnut oak dominating the drier bluffs, beech and sugar maples on the level uplands, as well as basswood, wild black cherry, and tupelo.

Because of its ruggedness, much of Stebbins Gulch missed the effects of ax, plow, and grazing livestock. The northern side of the gulch retains fragments of the old growth forest that greeted Native Americans and white settlers.

Folks fond of wildflowers can brighten their eyes on wild columbine clinging to rocks, shinleaf pyrola (a wintergreen containing a pain reliever), miterwort, Canada mayflower, partridgeberry (creeping on the ground), turtleheads (it looks like its name), and others.

Like Little Mountain, Stebbins Gulch abounds with ferns. Some kinds, like polypody fern and walking fern, stick to boulders. Other ferns, notably silvery glade and fancy, grow just about everywhere.

Three Ohio-endangered birds—the dark-eyed junco, winter wren, and Canada warbler—reside here, along with the eastern wood pewee, Louisiana waterthrush, eastern phoebe, and others.

While you are tramping along the stream try to spot the mountain dusky salamander and brook lamprey, the latter endangered in this state.

In Bole Forest towering sugar maple and American beech dominate the setting. Many are more than 30 inches in diameter at breast height and sport crowns of 100 feet.

Not to be outdone, individual tulip trees, tupelos, and oaks (mostly red) reach similar proportions. Buxom examples of wild black cherry, basswood (also called linden), white ash, cucumber magnolia, eastern hemlock, sycamore, black walnut, eastern cottonwood, yellow birch, and American elm also are present if you look carefully.

As you walk through the forest notice the straightness of the giants. Many do not have branches below the 75-foot mark. In a mature forest competition among seedlings is fierce. Theirs is a race to the sky. Those who grow erect earn the most sunlight and blossom quickly. In Bole Forest, a corps of seedlings and saplings, representing all species, stands ready to replace the veterans who fall.

Wildflowers bloom in their staggered schedule from April to October. Many varieties carpet this forest floor, such as wild chervil, cleavers, barberry, Virginia waterleaf, spotted touch-me-not, great lobelia, wood sorrel, bouncing bet, Indian pipe, and blue cohosh.

The flora and fauna of the valley unfolds at the Boardwalk in Pierson Creek Valley, an offshoot of the Pierson Creek Loop. Obtain a plant checklist at the Visitors' Center. Many of the plants are labeled for easy identification.

Fifteen kinds of ferns and their allies can be examined, such as scouring rush, ostrich, silvery glade, and Goldie's wood ferns. Some of these are tucked in nooks and crannies.

Wildflowers—42 varieties on the checklist—brighten the valley throughout the warm months. Bring your field guides and look for fairy candles, great merrybells, spotted touch-me-not, false mermaid weed, wake robin trillium, yellow mandarin, and others.

Several kinds of hardwood communities face the creek. The oak-maple group dominates in some places with towering sugar maples, white and red oaks, and hickories (shagbark, pignut, and bitternut). You'll find white ash, American basswood (linden) and some sourgum in this collection too.

The floodplain forest contains a blend of sugar maple, black walnut (creekside), tulip tree, some beech, basswood, ash, cucumber magnolia, and sassafras. Beech, sugar maple, eastern hemlock, and red oak populate the beech-maple woods.

HISTORY

The arboretum is "beholden" to Albert Fairchild Holden, a mining engineer who at his death in 1913, at age 46, was president of the Island Creek Coal Company, and managing director of both the U.S. Smelting, Mining & Refining Company and the American Zinc, Lead, and Smelting Company. He was the son of Liberty E. Holden, one of the founders of the Cleveland *Plain Dealer* newspaper.

After the death of his wife, Katharine, and 12-

year-old daughter, Elizabeth, Holden established a memorial fund to finance an arboretum. Holden had a keen interest in geology, botany, and ornithology. His sister, Roberta Holden Bole, persuaded him to establish the arboretum in Cleveland. Holden had thought of donating the money to the Arnold Arboretum at Harvard University. In 1931, after two original sites proved unsuitable, the arboretum took root on 100 acres donated by Benjamin P. and Roberta Holden Bole, namesakes of Bole Forest.

Since its founding, the arboretum has received enthusiastic and generous support from contributors, neighbors, and volunteers. The arboretum now manages more than 3,100 acres, presides over 4,801 different plants, pays a staff of full- and parttime employees, holds more than 240 education programs and 105 hikes a year, and claims a membership of more than 7,200 families.

The Warren H. Corning Visitor Center honors a contributor and lifetime volunteer. The Thayer Center remembers Holden's daughter, Katharine Holden Thayer.

No evidence has been uncovered to suggest that Native Americans settled on Little Mountain, nor that they considered it a spiritual sanctuary. Doubtless, many of them explored the rock formations and hunted on the slopes.

Capt. Truman Griswold of Mentor supposedly was the first known white man on Little Mountain, probably in 1810. Ashbel Messenger built a cabin here in 1815. One time he reached his home just ahead of pursuing wolves who caught the scent of his blood-stained foot.

For awhile early settlers eked out a living by farming, milling, or lumbering. In 1831, Simeon Reynolds, a pioneer, turned Little Mountain into a resort when he built a hotel on his property. More hotels and private clubs attracted tourists to the site during the next 90 years.

The Little Mountain Club, founded in 1872 by Cleveland millionaire Randall P. Wade, boasted John D. Rockefeller, U.S. Senator H. B. Payne, and soon-to-be U.S. president James A. Garfield as members.

The hotels were gone by the mid-1920s, and Ralph T. King, a member of the club, bought most of the mountain. Over the years, his descendents, and other landowners, have donated land encompassing Little Mountain to The Holden Arboretum. A sign at the trailhead honors Fanny and Ralph King. The arboretum owns 172 acres of Little Mountain, but the preserve is surrounded by new homes.

Charles S. Prosser of the Ohio Geological Survey reported on Stebbins Gulch in 1912. "This glen is the most interesting geological locality in Chardon Township and one well worthy of careful study." The gulch was added to the National Registry of Natural Landmarks in 1968 by the U.S. Department of the Interior.

Pierson Creek takes its name from a local family whose descendents were early settlers. The creek supposedly originates on Pierson Knob, another Sharon Conglomerate outcrop located outside the arboretum.

The Nature Center at Shaker Lakes

This green gash in urban Cuyahoga County commemorates a precious valley and the memory of the humans who preserved it. In the mid-1960s, local conservationists stopped construction of a highway and established a nature center that provides environmental education programs to 250 schools each year. The residents here say they have survived nicely without the freeway, and won't trade their nature center for anything.

LOCATION
Cuyahoga County, City of Shaker Heights.

OWNERSHIP
The Nature Center at Shaker Lakes, a nonprofit group, leases 280 acres from the city of Cleveland. A separate six-acre lease covers the nature center building and grounds.

SIZE & DESIGNATION
In 1971 the U.S. Department of the Interior, National Park Service, designated the 280-acre site a National Environmental Education Landmark, and National Environmental Study Area.

ACCESS

From I-271, go west on Chagrin Blvd. (US 422 & SR 87), right (north) on Richmond Road (SR 87), left (west) on Shaker Blvd., right (north) on South Park Blvd. Bear left at fork and follow signs to nature center on left. Accessible from Rapid Transit Authority's Green Line, South Park stop. Walk north on South Park Blvd. Bear left at fork. From Downtown Cleveland, take Carnegie Ave. to Stokes Blvd. (Fairhill Rd). Turn right. Turn left on Coventry Rd., then right on to North Park Blvd. Follow Nature Center signs to South Park Blvd.

Hiking trails begin at the nature center on South Park Blvd. The easiest one is the barrier-free All-Peoples' Trail, a one-third mile elevated boardwalk leading to a marsh, stream, small waterfall, bird blind, and observation deck. Another showcase trail is the staircased Stearns Trail, a mile-long loop that starts at the wildflower garden and traipses to a woodland, marsh, and Doan Brook ravine. Other routes go east through Doan Brook Gorge and around Horseshoe Lake (between North Park and South Park boulevards), and northwest around Lower Lake, off the All-Peoples' Trail. A U-shaped path for bikes and walkers lies between Shaker Blvd. and South Woodland Road, and West Park Blvd., and South Park Blvd. Trails are open daily from 6 a.m. to 9 p.m.

The Nature Center building has classrooms, Duck Pond Gift Shop, some exhibits, rest rooms, offices, and meeting rooms. It is the gathering place for educational programs run by staff naturalists and volunteers, and for the Explorer's Club, sponsoring outings for teens. A picnic shelter built by The Friends of the Nature Center at Shaker Lakes is available for groups. The newsletter of the center is called "The Rookery."

INFORMATION

Contact The Nature Center at Shaker Lakes, 2600 South Park Blvd., Cleveland, OH 44120; phone (216) 321-5935.

GEOLOGY

The forks of Doan Brook converge near the nature center. It is a young creek, born at the end of the Ice Age, roughly 12,000 years ago. Melting glacial water and centuries of natural runoff created a deep, scenic gorge walled with shale and sandstone. Small cascades trickle from sidecuts and flow into the shallow brook. In the early 19th century Shaker settlers dammed the stream to form Horseshoe Lake and Lower Lake. The rill empties into Lake Erie.

WILDLIFE

The preserve is a haven for birds and their human watchers. More than 245 species have been spotted, and at least 45 brands reside here, including the endangered peregrine falcon. Warblers zero in on the place in spring. The Tennessee, Cape May, Canada, and prothonotary are some of the nesters. Red-shouldered, red-tailed, Cooper's, and northern harrier hawks frequent the site. Waterbirds are abundant. Look for the common loon (on migration), great egret, mergansers (both hooded and red-breasted), and great blue heron. Ring-necked pheasant and wild turkey have become established in this suburban setting. Inside the center is the Jean Eakin Bird Observation Station, a viewing window with field glasses and speakers delivering birdsong.

Mammals include muskrat, deer, squirrels, and bats. Representing reptiles are the map, box, painted, and snapping (common and alligator) turtles, and the milk, garter, and black snakes. Bluegill, carp and sunfish swim in the lakes.

Trees grow in predictable locations. Sycamores and cottonwoods line the brook. Hemlock thrives in shady ravines with beech and maple nearby. Oaks tend to occupy higher and drier ground, with sassafras and flowering dogwood in reverting areas. Look for witch hazel blossoms, September through November, on the sides of ravines and the edge of the woods.

Dwarf crested iris blooms abundantly in spring, along with columbine (several colors), large-flowered (white) and wake robin trilliums, mayapple, and violets. Summertime brings Joe-Pye weed and ironweed into color.

HISTORY

Never underestimate the grit of garden clubs. In the mid-1960s, a four-lane freeway through the Shaker Lakes Park looked like a "done deal." The road, called the Clark Expressway, or I-290, even appeared on state road maps. The Ohio Department of Transportation, however, could not detour the determination of thirty-five garden clubs, and a half dozen grassroots groups, that dug in their trowels.

Activists organized two groups, the Park Conservation Committee and the Committee for Sane Transportation and Environmental Policy. The committees led tours through the park, appealed to schools and communities for a nature center, commissioned the National Audubon Society to survey the site for its nature education potential, and began a letter-writing campaign. Audubon reported that the site was perfect for a nature center.

The Shaker Lakes Regional Nature Center was established in September 1966. It immediately began raising funds to build a nature center building on six acres leased from the City of Cleveland. The center opened in 1969. In 1970, Governor James Rhodes heard the opposition to the freeway during a meeting at a local school. A short time later the road became a dead deal.

The Doan Brook Valley has always been a reverred place. The Shakers who settled here in 1822 called it "The Valley of God's Pleasure." To enrich their pleasure the religious sect established mills and dammed Doan Brook, creating Horseshoe and Lower lakes. The utopian community had disintegrated by the 20thcentury.

Nathaniel Doan later owned the property. It became parkland shared by Shaker Heights, Cleveland Heights, and Cleveland upon his death. The nature center leases land from those communities.

The Wilderness Center

This restive land of deep silence is becoming a wilderness again after serving as farm, timber lot, coal mine, pasture, and roadway. The trails in this recovering place wander through woodlots of 300-year-old hardwoods, by groves of sweet-scented pines, across floodplains, around duck ponds and forest pools, beside tallgrass prairies, and the remnant of an Ice Age lake.

LOCATION

Southwestern Stark County, Sugar Creek Township.

OWNERSHIP

The Wilderness Center is a nonprofit nature education and research center supported by memberships, donations, and bequests.

SIZE & DESIGNATION

The Wilderness Center comprises seven tracts of land totaling 883.5 acres in four counties. Sigrist Woods has been designated an Ohio Natural Landmark.

ACCESS

From Wilmot, the nearest village, drive northwesterly on US 250. After crossing the bridge over Sugar Creek (about a mile out of Wilmot) turn right (north) on Alabama Avenue. The entrance to the center's headquarters will be on the left. Park in the lower lot if you intend to stay beyond 5 p.m.

Although the Sigrist Woods, Sugar Creek, and Fox Creek trails, and Pioneer Path can be reached from paths leaving from the Interpretive Building, you can continue north on Alabama Avenue to small parking lots for these trails.

The road becomes gravel beyond the entrance to the center. The parking lot for the Sigrist Woods, Fox Creek, and Sugar Creek trails is on the right, with the lot for the Pioneer Path ahead on the left.

One of the center's satellites, Zoar Woods, is open to the public. Located in northern Tuscarawas County, exit Interstate 77 at Bolivar, travel east on SR 212 to Zoar, south on CR 82 about three miles, then west (right turn) on TR 380 to a lane that leads to the parking lot. Look for a sign at the entrance of the driveway.

Please drive carefully. Amish residents traveling by horse-drawn buggy, or on foot, have a right to the road. Proceed slowly at the top of hills, and around blind curves.

Six trails at the main site (578 acres) offer seven miles of hiking pleasure. They are open daily from dawn to dusk.

Trail maps are available in the lobby of the Interpretive Building. The building has restrooms, wildlife exhibits, a wildlife window (bird feeders), gift shop, planetarium, meeting rooms, and administrative offices.

The Wilderness Center is also a popular magnet for cross-country skiers. It hosts several special interest clubs (birding, photography, astronomy, woodcarvers, etc.) for members. A small, fulltime staff is bolstered by volunteer members.

INFORMATION

The Wilderness Center, 9877 Alabama Ave.,

SW, P.O. Box 202, Wilmot, Ohio 44689-0202; phone (330) 359-5235.

GEOLOGY

The holdings of The Wilderness Center have a split personality, geologically speaking. The headquarters site and four smaller tracts (not open to the public) are located at the edge of a region that has been covered by one or more continental glaciers in the last million years or so. These lie in "glaciated" Ohio, which comprises about two-thirds of the state.

Zoar Woods (Tuscarawas County) and the center's Doughty Property (Holmes County, no trails) had not been frozen by glaciers. These are found in "unglaciated" Ohio, largely eastern Ohio south of this location, as well as Pike County and parts of Adams and Brown counties.

The last glacier, the Wisconsinan (12,000 to 15,000 years ago) deposited thick bands of debris called till (sand, gravel, boulders, silt, clay) over the land. It brought with it large boulders from Canada, called erratics. You can see them laying alone in the forest. Most of these orphans are composed of igneous rock, such as granite.

In northeastern Ohio the glacier's influence dipped halfway into Holmes County, covered all of Stark County except the southeastern quarter, and blanketed the northern half of Columbiana County.

The torrents of meltwater that poured from these ice masses created rivers and streams, the erosive agents that have shaped this land. Today, the currents are mainly refreshed by precipitation that runs off the neighboring hills and slopes.

The primary streams in the main preserve are Sugar Creek, forming the southeast boundary, and Fox Creek, which bisects the main site and runs southeasterly into Sugar Creek.

One spot is the marsh located east of the Wilderness Walk and north of the prairie. This former Ice Age lake used to be recharged by water descending from surrounding slopes. Silt carried by the runoff filled the lake and enabled vegetation to gain control. Water and silt still collect in the basin.

Wilderness Lake, the pond south of the Interpretive Center, is manmade. An earthen dike on the east shore contains the water and serves as a footpath.

As noted above, coal was mined from the Zoar Woods property. Coal is a fossil fuel, meaning it originated from accumulated vegetation that grew here during the Pennsylvanian and Mississippian geological periods some 285-345 million years ago. Coal, in other words, is an old forest (the so-called Carboniferous Forest) compacted into black, combustible rock.

Scientists depict the Carboniferous Forest as a lush swamp forest. Trees that fell into the stagnant swamp quickly became waterlogged and sank to the bottom where rotting ceased. The trees piled up in this swamp.

The bottom layer is first pressed into peat, then lignite, bituminous coal, and in rare instances anthracite coal. Each form becomes more compact and contains less and less water. For instance, peat is about 40 percent water, while coal is five percent. After compression, anthracite may be only 1/25th its original size. Bituminous coal, the kind found in Ohio, is 80 percent carbon.

Coal cannot form without accumulation and compression (the latter occurring because of the former). Other ancient swamp forests did not transform into coal because bacteria immediately decayed the fallen vegetation. As a result, there was no accumulation, no compression, and no coal.

According to a brochure published by the center, Zoarites, members of the nearby Zoar utopian settlement (1817-1898), also extracted iron ore from the mine for handmade crafts and tools.

WILDLIFE

Sigrist Woods is the crown jewel of the center. It is one of this state's few unbroken links to its natural, or primeval, past. Its existence is an eccentricity, an appropriate description considering the personality of its former protector (see History).

This 30-acre woods is a climax forest, meaning it has fully matured and become self-perpetuating. Barring any major human or natural disturbances, the characteristics of the woods should not change much over time.

Three-hundred-year-old oaks (red and white mostly), sugar maples, beeches, hickories, and sycamores stand erect over the woods. Their intertwining branches high above the ground close the forest canopy by late spring, leaving the floor in perpetual shade for nearly five months.

Beneath them rise stately basswoods, black walnut, wild black cherry, sourgum, and white ash. Still lower, hornbeam, dogwood, ironwood (also known as blue beech and musclewood), spice bush, and maple-leaved viburnum occupy the understory. Buxom specimens of willow and elm grow beside huge sycamores in the nearby floodplain.

In all honesty Sigrist Woods cannot be called a virgin woods because humans have soiled the spot with saws and livestock—though not enough to substantially alter its natural integrity. Soon the signs of earlier selective logging (sawed stumps) and grazing will disappear.

Elsewhere in the preserve, a "second growth" forest is reaching maturity. Second growth refers to a woodlot previously logged. Here oaks and hickories claim the higher and drier ridges, with beech and maples dominating the slopes. Groves of various pines, planted years ago, offer some refreshing green in the winter.

Due to past woodland grazing, the wildflower show is not especially spectacular. Still, count large-flowered trillium, dogtooth (trout) lily, Solomon's seal, and Virginia bluebells among the collection. The center is planning a wildflower restoration program.

The Wilderness Center, so it claims, was the second preserve in Ohio to plant a tallgrass prairie. The meadows total 20 acres and feature floral beauties called blazing star (abundant), coreopsis, sunflower, and prairie coneflower. An amazing collection of ferns (and their associates), some 37 varieties, grows at Zoar Woods.

At dusk listen for the hoots of great horned, screech, and barred owls. Once in awhile a barn owl (endangered) appears. Long-eared owls, designated a special interest (potentially threatened) bird in Ohio, have been seen hiding in the pines, both at the main site and at Zoar Woods. They probably come here during the winter.

Ruffed grouse and wild turkey live in the woods but are seldom seen. Canada geese, various ducks, and a occasional swan settle on the pond, mostly during spring and autumn migration times.

The usual cast of creatures reside in woods and meadows—squirrels, deer, raccoons, skunks, foxes, and ground hogs (where the center's property borders farmland). Muskrat and beaver hide in the wetlands, and coyotes have been spotted. A river otter (endangered in this state) released by the Ohio Department of Natural Resources has been seen once, but there is no evidence that it has become a permanent resident. The bobcat, another endangered animal, roams in the neighborhood, but has not yet appeared at the preserve.

HISTORY

The Wilderness Center was established in 1964, largely on abandoned farmland and recovering woodlots.

Arrowheads and fragments of other artifacts found on the property indicate that the Ancient People (paleo and woodland Indians) probably hunted here, but no camp or village has been discovered.

White settlers began trickling in around 1810. By 1830 most of the land had been purchased and cleared for cultivation and grazing.

Religious separatists from Germany sought refuge and isolation in northern Tuscarawas County in the second decade of the 19th century. In 1817 they established the village of Zoar, a communal settlement. As noted above, they mined iron ore and coal from mines at Zoar Woods. They also paid for their land, some 5,000 acres, by contracting sections of the Ohio-Erie Canal. Ironically, the commune's isolation ended when the canal opened in 1832.

The community fell into a slow decline following the 1853 death of its leader Joseph Bimeler. The last members sold their remaining holdings in 1898.

Sigrist Woods takes its name from its former owner, Charles Sigrist, a bonafide and likeable eccentric, who lived, as eccentrics do, alone. Sigrist's pecularities fed many tales. Folks still wonder why he preserved a sheep's head in a jar.

Another curiosity is why he never chopped down the woods. Of course, his contemporaries who asked that question never sat in the shade beneath one of Charley's giant trees. Once, apparently, he did sign away the trees, but when the loggers arrived he changed his mind and chased them away. Bless the eccentrics!

JOURNAL

October 1993. I watch the low-angled rays of the sun brighten the autumn leaves that float motionless on a small woodland pond. The steady beams, thinned to ribbons by hundreds of trees that stand between the pond and the light source, briefly turn the leaves into chards of gold. This treasure dissolves when the sun falls behind a flat, gun-blue cloud on the horizon.

The scene reminds me that the best is yet to come to The Wilderness Center. The prairie promises to ripen fuller next year, and the forest will continue its task of reclaiming its former glory, both here at the main site and at Zoar Woods.

CENTRAL

Dawes Aboretum

Folks searching for a pastoral, manicured setting to study nature will discover it on this cultivated landscape, more a series of exquisite gardens than a wild natural area. Still, you can easily spend a day wandering around this living horticultural museum.

LOCATION

Southern Licking County, about six miles south of Newark on State Route 13.

OWNERSHIP

The Dawes Arboretum.

SIZE & DESIGNATION

The arboretum encompasses 1,149 acres, two-thirds of which is open to the public. One-third is farmland, another third a forest plantation and natural area and the rest plant collections.

The owners define arboretum as "a place where trees, shrubs, and other woody plants are grown, exhibited and labeled for scientific and educational purposes."

ACCESS

From Interstate 70, exit at SR 13 and head north. Traveling distance from the interstate to the entrance on your left—about 2.5 miles.

To familiarize yourself with the grounds stop at the visitors center for a guide and map, then drive the 4.5-mile auto tour. Return to the visitors center and begin your hike.

To explore the Deep Woods, a hardwood forest of oak, maple, beech, black cherry, and hickory trees, follow the Maple and Oak trails, and return via the Holly Trail. Distance—about 1.5 miles. Pick up brochures on the Maple and Holly trails at the visitors center (though both are written for elementary school students). The trails, wide and smooth enough for small vehicles, are marked by their leaf designs.

Visit the log cabin and pioneer cemetery along the way. The cabin and surrounding woods present a picture of what Ohio looked like around the time of statehood. This route passes through Holly Hill, where more than 100 kinds of holly grow, forestry test lots (7,000 trees planted in 1930 are studied for growth and survival), and back to the visitors center.

Ambitious hikers can stay on the Oak Trail for a 2.5-mile journey to the many nooks and crannies of the grounds.

Small parking lots off the auto route allow visitors to see plant collections and special features. Children will insist on climbing the observation tower at the southeast corner of the grounds to look at the nearly half-mile long arbor vitae hedge spelling out Dawes Arboretum.

The auto route also visits:

The Famous 17, a grove of Ohio buckeye trees planted to form the number 17. The design commemorates Ohio's admission to the United States as the 17th state.

Dawes Memorial, a Grecian-style mausoleum in the northeast corner of the property where Beman and Bertie Dawes, the former owners, are buried.

Daweswood House, the former home of Beman and Bertie Dawes, serves as a museum, and exhibit hall for the arboretum shovel collection (see History section).

Education Center, a renovated barn used for classrooms, meetings, and workshops.

The Henry Dawes Visitors Center has a nature center (a favorite place for kids), gift shop, information desk, Bonsai collection, library, classrooms, rest rooms, drinking water, and administrative offices.

The natural area located across the highway can be explored with written permission. Inquire at the visitors center. A tunnel safely carries visitors to the area.

Ball playing and other recreational games are prohibited. Pets must be kept on a leash. Swimming, wading, boating, and ice skating are forbidden at Dawes Lake. (Members of the arboretum can fish there, however.)

INFORMATION

Dawes Arboretum, 7770 Jacksontown Road S.E., Newark, OH 43056-9380; phone (740) 323-2355, 1-800-44-DAWES, or on the Internet at www.dawesarb.org. The grounds of the arboretum are open every day from dawn to dusk, except on Thanksgiving, Christmas, New Year's Day, or when threatening weather strikes. There is no admission charge.

WILDLIFE

As you would expect, the arboretum exhibits fine examples of exotic and native plant communities. Collections of maples, oaks, crab apple, pines, apples, and holly grow in special groves. Scientists study their growth, adaptability, and resistance to diseases. Elsewhere on the property, the Ohio Department of Natural Resources manages plots of test trees for future seed production.

Rare trees, such as the Japanese stewartia, lacebark pine, and paperbark maple, thrive in special areas at the edge of the Deep Woods. A Japanese garden is just a stone's throw away from the visitors center.

A unique cypress swamp, accessible by a boardwalk, gives visitors a feel for this tropical ecosystem. In the winter and spring, black, murky water reaches the knobby "knees" of the cypress, but by July the water has vanished. The arboretum sponsors one of the northernmost plantings of this tree.

Birdwatchers should polish the lenses of their field glasses because 173 species of birds have been observed on the grounds. Get a checklist at the nature center before eyeing the sky.

Count the sharp-shinned hawk (special interest), northern harrier (endangered), northern bobwhite, American kestrel, red-headed woodpecker, bluebird, cedar waxwing, and brown-headed cowbird among the year-round residents. These beauties also have been seen—pine siskin (winter), northern oriole, northern parula, bobolink, summer tanager, whippoorwill, and ruby-throated hummingbird.

Migratory waterfowl visit Dawes Lake and Tripp Higgins Pond in the spring and fall. Warblers,

31 kinds, arrive in the spring and summer, even the yellow-breasted chat and the blackpoll warbler.

HISTORY

Beman Gates Dawes and Bertie O. Burr, both descendants of Revolutionary War era personalities, made their mark in history by founding The Dawes Arboretum in 1929 with oil company profits.

Dawes, born in Marietta in 1870, is a descendant of William Dawes who shouted "The British Are Coming!" on that midnight ride with Paul Revere. (Staffers at the arboretum say Dawes never got much credit for riding farther and alerting more colonists than the reverred Revere.) In his lifetime, Beman succeeded as an engineer, businessman, and as a politician.

Bertie O. Burr, born in Lincoln, Nebraska in 1872, could reportedly trace her line to Aaron Burr, Thomas Jefferson's vice president. (Burr is better known as the duelist who killed Alexander Hamilton, and as a political schemer linked to a western secessionist plot.) At age 20, Bertie received a gold lifesaving medal from the U.S. Treasury for her bravery in saving two girls from drowning in a flooded Nebraska river.

Dawes was toiling in the coal and coke business in Lincoln when he met Bertie Burr. The couple married in Lincoln in 1894.

Beman brought his bride to Central Ohio in 1896 and began making a fortune in the oil and natural gas business. They also raised five children—four boys and a girl. He served in the Ohio House of Representatives from 1905-1909, and bought 140 acres and a large brick house (Daweswood House) south of Newark in 1918. The couple lived in Columbus but used the Licking County home as a weekend and summer residence. Dawes established the Pure Oil Company in 1920. They founded the arboretum on June 1, 1929.

An endowment for the arboretum was created from the oil company's profits. Over time the arboretum grew in size and reputation. The Dawes died in the 1950s.

Beman's well-known brother, Charles Gates Dawes, also contributed generously to the endowment. Charles Dawes, a brigadier general, won the Nobel Peace Prize in 1925 for his Dawes Plan, establishing the framework for German reparations after World War I. He served as vice president of the United States from 1925–29.

Almost 100 famous people have dedicated

trees at the arboretum. The list includes John Pershing, commander of U.S. military forces in World War I, heavyweight boxing champion Gene Tunney, airplane inventor Orville Wright, astronaut and U.S. Senator John Glenn, explorer Admiral Richard Byrd, and Olympic gold medal athlete Jesse Owens.

The shiny, nickel-chromium plated shovels used by the dedicators hang in the rathskeller of Daweswood House Museum. Brass plates identify the trees they have planted along the Tree Dedicators Trail in the Old Arboretum section (northeast) of the grounds.

Pershing Avenue, flanked by twin rows of trees representing the typical species planted alongside U.S. streets, marked the visit of "Black Jack" Pershing in 1929. It is located in the southern section of the property, west of Dawes Lake.

JOURNAL

June 1993. Strolling through the Deep Woods I am wondering if "history-making" is somehow genetically stored and transferred. Did Charles, a vice president and celebrated diplomat, and Beman, an oil company president and arboretum founder, inherit some of William's seeds? Was it some leftover spark of Aaron Burr, who raided British supply lines and pickets in New Jersey in 1777, that spurred Bertie Burr to risk her life on a Nebraska river?

I reached an intersection on the trail. To my left a trail led to a pioneer cemetery in a trimmed clearing. Here rest the bones of the Beard and Green families, descendants of John Beard and Benjamin Green, the first permanent white settlers in the area.

Like William Dawes, Beard and Green were patriots too, only they were common soldiers who received this land in the Ohio wilderness for their service in the Revolution. I can only conclude that the descendants of Dawes and Burr must have felt a historic bond with Beard and Green and pre-  *served the cemetery in their memory.*

SOUTHWEST

Aullwood Audubon Center & Farm

Thoughtful stewardship has transformed this once tired land into a wildlife sanctuary teeming with life. Children and grown-ups find this hands-on, living nature lab an exhilarating experience.

LOCATION
Montgomery County, Butler Township

OWNERSHIP
National Audubon Society.

SIZE & DESIGNATION
The grounds at the Aullwood Center comprise 70 acres.

ACCESS
Leaving Dayton, take Interstate 75 north, then Interstate 70 west. Exit northbound on SR 48. Travel a mile, turn right (east) on US 40 and cross Englewood Dam. Just past the dam, take the first right onto Aullwood Road and bear right as you round a bend. Park in the lot on your left to go to the Audubon Center. The entrance to the Aullwood Farm is on

Frederick Road. Stay on US 40 after crossing the dam. Turn right to Frederick Road.

A web of interconnecting trails journeys through the sanctuary. Pick up a trail map when you pay your admission charge at the center.

Specialty trails such as the Wildflower Trail, Geology Trail and Discovery Trail travel to particular areas in the refuge. The Center-Farm Trail links the nature preserve with the adjacent farm.

Natural history exhibits fill the nature center. You'll discover poisonous snakes and animal skulls and other hands-on exhibits: a must-see place for kids. A gift shop and rest rooms are located here. Naturalist-led tours begin here, too.

INFORMATION

Contact the Aullwood Audubon Center and Farm, 1000 Aullwood Road, Dayton, Ohio 45414-1129; phone (937) 890-7360. Admission is free to the members of the National Audubon Society and Friends of Aullwood.

GEOLOGY

Aullwood is not noted for grand geological landmarks, but it does have one thing many preserves lack—fossils.

Fossils are pictures in rocks. The tiny drawings are the remains of plants and animals that sank to an ocean floor and became encased in the rock. Study the large stones beside Aullwood Brook and find the fossils. A magnifying glass might be helpful.

The plants and animals frozen in these rocks tell us that this part of Ohio once was covered by a warm, shallow ocean because their relatives live in that type of environment today.

About a half mile from the center, on the west side of the spillway at the base of the Englewood dam, lies a pile of 450 million-year-old (Ordovician Period) limestone rocks with fossils in them.

You can walk to the fossil bed, about 20 minutes, or drive. Turn left from the center, then take your first right to the river parking lot. Climb around the spillway to the other side of Stillwater River.

A guide you can purchase at the center ($1) describes fossilized and extinct animals—brachiopods (fanlike shells), bryozoans (spotted twigs), crinoids (mop head), pelecypod (clam shell), horn corals (ice cream cone), cephalopod (ringed cylinder), gastropods (snail-shaped tube), and trilobites (beetle, or crab-shaped), the official state fossil.

WILDLIFE

Being an Audubon-owned refuge, Aullwood is a birder's paradise, attracting numerous species, especially warblers, thrushes, woodpeckers, woodcocks, and owls.

Between 1959 and 1960 the Aullwood staff planted a 2.5 acre tallgrass prairie, using seeds collected from an Adams County prairie. Reportedly, it was the first prairie restoration project in Ohio. Now more than 74 various prairie residents thrive here, notably big bluestem, Canada wild rye (both grasses), and flowers like foxglove beard tongue, blazing star, bergamot, prairie and purple coneflower, compass plant, and tall tickweed. July and August are the peak months for prairie viewing. You will also find this meadow swarming with bees, birds and butterflies.

Prairie plants are perennials, meaning their roots stay alive after the above ground stems wither away in the fall. Because most of a prairie plant lives underground it is able to survive harsh winters, ground fires, and temperature and water extremes.

In its first year of life a prairie plant may sink roots a foot deep but grow only an inch above ground. An eight-foot tall plant, like prairie dock, may have a root system equally deep in the earth. Early farmers found it nearly impossible to plow prairies because the roots would entangle their wooden plows. However, the steel plow, invented in 1840 by John Deere, ripped through the prairie sod and led to the demise of the prairie that for awhile stretched from Pennsylvania to the foothills of the Rocky Mountains.

The Aullwood Center manages its prairie by burning it every so often. Burning allows spring rain and sun to nourish new shoots without killing the forbs and underground root system.

Most of the common woodland and meadow animals live in the Aullwood sanctuary. Astute observers might see a meadow jumping mouse, foxes, a bog lemming (like a vole), muskrat, mink (a rarity), and the endangered Indiana bat.

At Muskrat Marsh look for the snapping turtle and common musk turtle, sometimes called a stinkpot turtle because it sprays a foul odor when pestered. The eastern box turtle crawls in fields and wooded areas, and the map turtle, with whorled and striped patterns on its shell, lives at Bluegill Pond.

Queen snakes may be curled around tree limbs over Aullwood Brook looking for frogs, crayfish and salamanders. Blue racers and black rat snakes, both can be five feet long, lurk in the woodlands. These two constrict, or squeeze, their victims (mice, shrews, birds) before swallowing them.

Turning over a rock or log may reveal a red-backed salamander (the most common type at Aullwood), or the colorful spotted salamander, introduced to Muskrat Marsh in 1965. Various kinds of frogs raise their voices in the spring and summer. During the spring breeding season you will see their frenzied splashing and jumping in the shallows.

History

A plaque in the parking lot of the nature center and farm reminds visitors that the preserve and adjacent farm is a gift from John and Marie Aull. John Aull, a businessman, bought this former farmland in the early 1900s. Over the years he and his wife, Marie, transformed it into their country residence, a nature preserve, and landscaped gardens.

Mrs. Aull, gave the land to the National Audubon Society and established a fund for an outdoor education complex. The center was dedicated in 1957, and claims to be the Midwest's first community nature center.

Bruckner Nature Center

This preserve, powered by the memory of its founder and members, boasts trails that wander through wooded floodplains, ravines, pine groves, and ridgetops. When you tire of hiking you can browse through the nature center, a 190-year-old restored log house, and a wild animal hospital that treats 1,500 patients a year.

Location

Southwestern Miami County, Newton Township.

Ownership

The Brukner Nature Center is a nonprofit organization dedicated to environmental education and wildlife rehabilitation, chiefly supported by its members.

Size & Designation

The grounds total 165 acres. The Stillwater River,

which borders the preserve, is a state scenic river. Iddings Log House, a refurbished pioneer home, is listed on the National Registry of Historic Places.

Access

From Troy, the county seat, travel west on SR 55. Turn right (west) on Horseshoe Bend Road (roughly three miles from the SR 55 and SR 718 split), then right (north) on the preserve's driveway. Park at the nature center. Horseshoe Bend Road also joins SR 48 just north of Ludlow Falls. Head east from that point to reach the center.

Ten well-marked trails measuring nearly seven miles entice hikers to every habitat in the preserve. They are open (and free) year-round during daylight hours. Pick up a map and trail guide at the nature center, the starting point.

The connector trail behind the nature center descends into the floodplain of the Stillwater River and leads to a number of paths. One of them, the Stillwater Loop (.75 mile) traces the edge of the creek and the bottom of Bluebell Hill, so named for the showy April display of mertensia, Virginia bluebells, or Virginia cowslip. A bluebell by any other name is still a bluebell.

Another path, the half-mile Swamp Boardwalk Trail, zigzags across a marsh to an observation tower. This soggy trail could be impassable during spring floods.

The Buckeye Valley-Wilderness Ridge Trail (1.4 miles) is the longest and most rugged ramble in the preserve. This lasso-shaped path stems from the Wren Run Trail (north of the observation deck) and visits the ravines and ridges in the north section.

Folks who prefer flat terrain and the scent of conifers should make a bee line for the half-mile Pinelands Trail, starting at the totem pole on the east side of the parking lot. The Trillium Valley Trail (.3 mile) branches north from the Pinelands Trail then swings west and joins the connector trail at the confluence of two intermittent brooks. As the name suggests, trillium abound along this trail.

The Interpretive Center features nature exhibits, a wildlife viewing room, an auditorium, classrooms, 1,000-volume natural history library, gift shop, rest rooms, and one of only a few wildlife rehabilitation centers in the state. School-age children and adults can participate in the numerous nature programs held at the center.

Please respect some rules. Plant picking, picnicking, and pets are prohibited. Trails are for foot travelers, not for horses and vehicles, including trail bikes.

INFORMATION

Contact the Brukner Nature Center, 5995 Horseshoe Bend Road, Troy, Ohio 45373, (937) 698-6493.

GEOLOGY

During times of high water, the Stillwater River cannot decide which way to flow around an oxbow, or horseshoe-shaped, bend in this preserve. When I visited one autumn day this swelled river bend masqueraded as a delta, with a maze of tangled currents flowing helter-skelter, like panic-stricken animals fleeing a forest fire.

Of course, on gentler days the meandering creek stays on course as it sweeps the banks and trickles around shifting sandbars. This leaner current, now easier to follow with the human eye, continues to reshape its path but at a much slower pace.

You won't find bedrock protruding from the Earth's epidermis in the preserve. Stillwater Creek and its dissecting tributaries still wash away glacial till, an unsorted mixture of dirt (gravel, sand, silt, clay, and boulders) deposited by the Wisconsinan ice mass around 12,000 years ago. Some day, perhaps, they will reach rock bottom.

Clayton Brukner, the center's founder, dammed a couple of small brooks with a bulldozer to make Cat Face Pond and Cattail Pond, both located along trails south of the Interpretive Center.

WILDLIFE

This natural area protects the habitats of 360 kinds of wildflowers; the staff and members conduct an annual blooming count. Look for skunk cabbage and squirrel corn along the Swamp Boardwalk Trail. Try to find rose gentian and Crane's orchid (both rarities), false hellebore, showy orchid, butterfly weed (meadows), snow trillium, marsh marigold (also called cowslip), and large bellflower.

Close to 50 species of trees and shrubs have been counted, such as white and red oak, sassafras, tuliptree, sugar maple, witch hazel, black walnut, shagbark hickory, and wild black cherry. The softwoods are

> *The emergency room* of the wild animal *hospital attends to as many as 1,500* patients a year. *Veterinarians try to patch them up and...*

represented by non-native white and red pines, planted in the 1950s.

The center publishes an annual birdlist and conducts a census at Christmas time. So far, 170 varieties have been sighted. Red and white-winged crossbills (uncommon), pine siskins, and red-breasted nuthatches favor the pines. Owls (great horned, barred, and screech) and pileated woodpeckers prefer the deep hardwood stands.

Evening and rose-breasted grosbeaks, ruby-throated hummingbirds, and little green herons (creek) are regular visitors. Countless species of warblers brighten the forest canopy in the spring with their colorful feathers and rich songs.

The northern harrier, an endangered species in Ohio, and the saw-whet owl and sharp-shinned hawk, both poentially threatened birds, have been spotted here, but they flew off to other locations. More common are the red-tailed and Cooper's hawks.

The regular cast of four-legged furry beasts appear—deer, red and gray fox, mink, muskrat, ground hog, muskrat, and others. Amphibians are represented by the two-lined, red-backed, and tiger salamanders; reptiles by the painted and box turtles, and black rat, northern water, and northern ring-necked snakes.

Several injured animals, such as a bald eagle, can be observed in a "zoo" of sorts between the Interpretive Center and log house. These captive animals would perish if released into the wild.

The emergency room of the wild animal hospital attends to as many as 1,500 patients a year. Veterinarians try to patch them up and return them to their natural habitat. Some orphaned or injured critters become traveling actors for nature programs in the center or at schools. The center also offers loaner pets, or companions, for people recovering from strokes, and other ailments.

HISTORY

Clayton J. Brukner, a bachelor known to be a bit ornery, was a self-taught aviation designer and manufacturer in Troy. He is remembered as the innovative builder of the WACO airplane in the 1920s.

Brukner bought this farmland in 1933, the darkest year of the Great Depression, and simply let nature takes its course. The 50,000 red and white pines planted in the 1950s have grown into the lush evergreen forest east of the Interpretive Center.

In the early 1960s, Brukner learned to his dismay that the popular Aullwood Center, the National Audubon Society's nature education center near Dayton, had to turn away school groups. Conservation organizations, notably the National Audubon Society, assisted Brukner in determining that the area could support another nature center.

In 1967, Brukner and a small group of followers began building trails, ponds, and facilities for a nature center. They completed their work in the spring of 1974, and opened the center in May. Brukner died in 1978.

Some 20,000 school children and 90,000 others visit the grounds yearly. And that restored log house, built in 1804 by the Iddings family, sits in its original location on a bluff overlooking the Stillwater River.

Cincinnati Nature Center

Just beyond the eastern reach of Cincinnati's extending thorn lies this place of softness, solitude, and silence. Here the seasons unfold, undisturbed. The words collaboration and consent better describe nature's behavior than competition and contention, the latter terms more appropriately applied to humans. And we owe this gift to a 17-year-old boy who a century ago spent all his earnings to save a beech forest that was about to be felled for tobacco.

LOCATION

Western Clermont County, Union Township.

OWNERSHIP

The Cincinnati Nature Center is a private, non-profit environmental education organization.

SIZE & DESIGNATION

The center protects 1,425 acres set aside for nature.

ACCESS

From Interstate 275 travel east on US 50 (one of the Milford exits). At the traffic light in the small village of Perintown, turn right on Round Bottom Road. Follow the signs. A mile up the road go left on Tealtown Road. The entrance will appear on the right. After paying a $3 entrance fee (non-members), drive to the parking lot.

From Batavia, the county seat, head north on State Route 222, west on US 50, then left at the light in Perintown.

Wanderers have their pick of 15 trails, totaling almost 15 miles. Pick up a trail guide at the Rowe Building (visitors center) and take a few minutes to familiarize yourself with the detailed map and legend. The paths are easy enough to follow with the trail map—the best map of its kind among all the large preserves I have visited. The center even marks the location of benches with astericks on the map. Because of the complexity of the trail system, I recommend that you trace your path and check off each numbered intersection as you reach them.

Folks with physical limitations can enjoy the preserve on the paved all-persons' trail. Children will especially enjoy viewing wildlife from the boardwalks that rim the edge of ponds, most a short walk from the Rowe Building.

The nature center (Rowe Building) offers exhibits, a gift shop, library, rest rooms, drinking water, meeting rooms, and a cozy fireplace on cold days. The center schedules numerous educational programs for children and adults during the year, even safaris (North American and overseas nature trips).

INFORMATION

Contact the Cincinnati Nature Center, 4949 Tealtown Road, Milford, Ohio 45150; (513) 831-1711.

GEOLOGY

Imagine entering a time capsule that goes back 450 million years, to the Ordovician geological period. Back then Ohio was located near the Equator and covered by a shallow sea that teemed with sea creatures on the ocean floor.

Eventually, the sea withdrew and the remains of the animals became entombed in exposed layers of bedrock we call limestone and shale, the former ocean floors. Other sediments then buried the rock.

Later, the land now called southwestern Ohio swelled, or arched, probably when the Earth wrinkled and formed the Appalachian Mountains, roughly 250 million years ago. Think of Cincinnati sitting on the peak of the arch, and the nature center on the eastern slope. The shrug also brought the ancient limestone and shale to the surface again.

Nobody knows for sure what happened during the next 249 million years. Maybe the sediments that topped the bedrock got washed away by erosion. Maybe the arch was a lonely, torpedo-shaped island, or an archipelago of islands, surrounded by another sea. Perhaps a primeval forest stretched out across the area. Maybe dinosaurs browsed here.

The story resumes about a million years ago when the second of four glaciers, this one the Kansan glacier, put down a layer of till (sand, gravel, boulders, clay, silt) over the Ordovician rock. Milky-colored meltwater laden with silt and pebbles rushed from nostrils in the snout of the glacier.

The next glacier, the Illinoian, spread a blanket of till over Clermont County about 400,000 years ago, but the Wisconsinan ice sheet, the most recent glacier dating back just 12,000 to 15,000 years, did not extend into the area.

Avey's Run has removed hills of glacial dirt and uncovered the alternating layers of Ordovician limestone and shale. The creatures who lived in that long ago marine environment—brachiopods, bryozoans, gastropods, trilobites, criniods, cephalopods, and the like—are imbedded in the rock. The best place to see this slice of ancient life is along the half-mile Geology Trail (see numbered trail landmarks 6-9 on the trail map).

In spots the fossils are so abundant that I was reminded of modern shell-crowded beaches, like those on Sanibel Island in Florida. By straining your imagination maybe these locked-in-rock bottom feeders will wiggle a little or jettison into Avey's Run.

Fossil observing is certainly encouraged, but digging and collecting them is not allowed. Consider these finds "leavem-rites," short for "leave them right there" for the next beachcomber.

Avey's Run tumbles over a trio of petite waterfalls along the Geology Trail. Notice that the strata of limestone and shale alternate. When water long ago began flowing across these exposed layers the softer (less resistant) shale washed away faster than the harder (resistant) limestone, creating steps. The current and backsplash at these cascades gnaws small caves into the shale, a process called undercutting. Eventually, the unsupported limestone layer, whether it is a precipice jutting from the bank or a protruding lip of the waterfall, collapses into the stream.

WILDLIFE

The founder's beloved beeches share this second-growth (previously logged) forest with maples (especially sugar maple), seven varieties of oak, hickories, sycamore, tulip tree, ashes, and an occasional black cherry, walnut, and elm. In ravines some individual trees boast enormous girths and heights.

Dogwood, hackberry, Ohio buckeye, staghorn sumac, catalpa, pawpaw, persimmon, ironwood, hornbeam, black locust, basswood, Kentucky coffee-tree, magnolia, pines, red cedar, and cottonwood round out the tree list.

A checklist and blooming schedule printed by the center lists 237 different flowers, an extraordinary number, growing on the grounds. The blooming period lasts nine months.

Christmas rose and snowdrops, appropriately named, appear in January followed by bloomers called spring snowflake and windflower in February. These winter species represent a group of 39 plants introduced on the property by the Krippendorfs.

The forest floor explodes in color with 35 plants emerging in March, including toothwort, yellow adder's tongue, twinleaf, and wild stonecrop. April brings 35 more flowers into view, such as blue-eyed Mary, butterbur, henbit, dame's rocket, and jack-in-the-pulpit.

Green dragon, common speedwell, thimbleweed, and lily-leaved twayblade are among the 31 plants that blossom in May. Look for yellow goat's-beard, king devil, birdfoot trefoil, and foxglove beardtongue (containing digitalis) in June.

You can count 41 flowers in July—ragged fringed orchis, moonweed, bouncing bet, and American lotus, among them. August introduces 39 beauties, like sharp-winged monkeyflower, virgin's bower (a clematis-type vine), flower-of-an-hour, and dodder, followed by five in September—knapweed, asters, and goldenrods.

The diversity of birds (153 varieties) almost matches the flower list. (Birders can get a checklist at the Rowe Building.) Six endangered birds—yellow-bellied sapsucker, winter wren, hermit thrush, northern waterthrush, Canada warbler, and dark-eyed junco—have been observed here. Seven birds designated "special interest" (potentially threatened) have caught the eye of astute watchers. These include the sharp-shinned and red-shouldered hawks, saw-whet and long-eared owls, sora, purple martin, and Henslow's sparrow. All totaled, 32 species of warblers and 11 kinds of sparrows might be seen.

The preserve offers sanctuary to the Indiana bat, an endangered animal, and one of five bat species found in the area. Another endangered critter, the blue-spotted salamander, succeeds along with seven others from the salamander clan. Nine types of toads and frogs (Fowler's, gray treefrog, etc.) find habitats on the grounds.

Snakes are represented by nine species, notably the rough green snake, designated special interest (potentially threatened). Five kinds of turtle, and two brands of skunk are found here.

Badger, a rarity nowadays and designated a special interest animal, and coyote enjoy the safety of the refuge along with weasels, fox, mink, flying squirrel, and others.

HISTORY

Carl Krippendorf, the son of a shoe manufacturer, was a sickly child. But his long summers of fresh air at the Clermont County home of Dr. Colin Spence restored his health and emboldened his heart.

When he learned that the beloved beech forest that he tramped through as a boy was going to be flattened for a tobacco farm, Krippendorf, just 17 years old, swiftly bought the parcel with the cash he earned at his father's factory. He added tracts to his domain when he could, and with his father's help built a stately lodge, a wedding gift for his bride.

Krippendorf and his wife, Mary, lived at "Lob's Wood" from Easter to Thanksgiving for 64 years. In the early years Carl commuted to Cincinnati every day, an exertion that required Mary to shuttle him to train stations by buggy. Over the years, the Krippendorfs planted trees and flowers (39 varieties), mostly around the lodge, built a pond, a pumping station, and Clermont County's first swimming pool. And they farmed some. They died within a month of each other in 1964.

Rosan Krippendorf Adams, their daughter, told

> *In the early years Carl commuted to Cincinnati every day, an exertion that required Mary to shuttle him to train stations by buggy.*

friends that her parents had no intention of ever developing the estate. That prompted Stanley Rowe, a businessman and arboretum founder, and Karl Maslowski, an outdoors photographer, to revive their idea of establishing a nature center. The pair had been unable to acquire a neighboring property, now an outdoor education center called Wildwood.

National Audubon Society planners reported that the Krippendorf site was ideal for a nature center. The 175-acre preserve was purchased by the newly-formed Cincinnati Nature Center Association on January 17, 1966. The Interpretive Center, named for Rowe, opened in the early 1970s, and wings and improvements have been added since then.

More land has been acquired, too—Long Branch Farm in 1973, Fox Rock in the mid-1970s, and Gorman Heritage Farm in 1995. The property now totals 1,425 acres. The center has more than 5,000 members, and more than 6,000 school children attend nature programs here.

JOURNAL

October 27, 1993. Standing on the heights above Avey's Run and Fox Rock, a jet of cool polar air, the first of the season, enters my nose. It is sweet, refreshing, tinged with the sting of ice crystals.

Leaves that last week clung to the uppermost, frayed branches of the canopy—here being oaks, tulips, and maples mostly—have been liberated by the recent winds and bone-chilling rains. Autumn is past its prime here. Nature requires tiny icy tempests, working like wild sabers, to loosen the tenacious grip of the leaves from the understory. These sudden, cold blasts stir the litter on the forest floor.

In still air, I watch leaves randomly, aimlessly float. Most reach the ground, but some become impaled or entangled by twigs, and others rest softly on ferns, shrubs, and rocks.

Each flake delivers a message to the earth. By late October the forest floor has a winter's worth of information to digest. I wonder, does the maple sapling who spears the topmost autumn leaf from an ancient red oak learn the secret of longevity?

Early 20th Century Fox. Yesterday's vermin are today's wildlife.

*n*ational wildlife refuges and state wildlife areas are semantic kin. They are indeed places celebrating "something wild," but many of the similarities end there.

America's 500 national wildlife refuges, including one in Ohio, are scattered sanctuaries preserving a kaleidoscope of habitats and creatures, mammoth and microscopic, that make this planet go. The U.S. Fish and Wildlife Service, a division of the Department of the Interior, pilots this leaky ark, a 92 million-acre land mass a tad bigger than Ohio, Indiana, Kentucky and West Virginia combined. Wildlife preservation and nature education are the primary missions of a national refuge. Most human visitors go to national refuges for nature observation, hiking (restricted to marked trails), and outdoor photography. Though hunting and fishing are employed as wildlife management tools in more than half of the refuges, these activities are restricted and tightly controlled by the FWS.

State-owned wildlife areas, on the other hand, serve primarily as game preserves for fishers, hunters, and trappers. But visitors are by no means restricted to these groups. Fact is, the Ohio Division of Wildlife, who administers and manages these areas, encourages so-called non-consumptive outdoorsmen to get wild. When they arrive, birders, hikers, and wildlife watchers find few rules to hinder their adventures off-trail save the common courtesies of environmental friendliness. ✑

211

Managing the the country's widely scattered refuges is never easy because wildlife cannot be corraled and never will flourish in one big Eden. Nature prohibits a moose from playing in the same marsh with manatees, and alligators dare not hunt alongside their reptilian relatives in the Mojave Desert. So the FWS must stake out claims where wildlife roams. And then there are the incomplete humans, still covetous of wildlife's diminsihing land (and their hides), and still clueless about the intimacies that bind us together and power the Earth.

Refuges guard habitats as varied as Alaska's tundra, Maine's pine forest bogs, Hawaii's tropical atolls, Nebraska's prairie wetlands, New Mexico's cactus desert, and Florida's swamps. All that adds up to more than 220 species of mammals, 600 kinds of birds, 250 reptiles and amphibians, 200 fish, and several thousand plants. The bean counters haven't even started on insects.

Ohio has been shortchanged in national refuges. At the dawn of the millenium, it had only one refuge, Ottawa National Wildlife Refuge, within its borders. However, as this book was going to press, the FWS had proposed the Little Darby National Wildlife Refuge, some 25 miles northwest of Columbus (see sidebar). The early 1990s saw the creation of Ohio River Islands National Wildlife Refuge, which preserves an archipelago of riverine islands technically in the boundaries of West Virginia and Kentucky.

Money for federal refuges trickles from taxes on the purchase of sporting goods, items like binoculars, tent stakes, shotguns, canoes, sleeping bags, and pitons. Note that national wildlife refuges differ from state wildlife areas (described later).

Don't expect landscaped grounds, overnight accommodations, nor elaborate services. As their titles proclaim, wildlife refuges are for wildlife—and except for a handful of eccentrics, humans are not considered wildlife.

SOUTHEAST

Ohio River Islands National Wildlife Refuge

The Ohio River is allowed to go wild here, and nobody is going to call the cops nor the Corps of Engineers. This little known linear wildlife refuge protects the islands and backwaters that nurse and feed migratory birds, freshwater fish, and rare mussels. The refuge is perfect for island hopping boaters, wanna-be Huck Finns, and adventuresome hunters.

LOCATION

The refuge comprises 19 islands along 362 miles in the Ohio River channel from Phillis Island in Pennsylvania downstream to Manchester 2 Island, Kentucky. Although 17 of the refuge's islands are a stone throw from Ohio, none is within the state's boundary.

SIZE & DESIGNATION

The refuge currently totals more than 1,100 acres. Sixteen entire islands and portions of Wheeling, Manchester 2, and Neal islands are owned and administered by the Department of the Interior, Fish & Wildlife Service. The boundaries extends from river mile 35 to mile 397.

Wildlife Areas

Michigan

Lake Erie

Ottawa National Wildlife Refuge

Magee Marsh State Wildlife Area

Lake La Su An State Wildlife Area

Shenango State Wildlife Area

Grand River State Wildlife Area

Killbuck Marsh State Wildlife Area

Salt Fork State Wildlife Area

Spring Valley State Wildlife Area

Waterloo State Wildlife Area

Cooper Hollow State Wildlife Area

Tranquility State Wildlife Area

Indiana

Pennsylvania

West Virginia

Kentucky

Ohio River Islands National Wildlife Refuge

Ohio River

N

Counties: ASHTABULA, LAKE, GEAUGA, TRUMBULL, MAHONING, COLUMBIANA, CUYAHOGA, LORAIN, MEDINA, SUMMIT, PORTAGE, STARK, CARROLL, JEFFERSON, HARRISON, BELMONT, GUERNSEY, NOBLE, MONROE, WASHINGTON, MORGAN, MUSKINGUM, COSHOCTON, TUSCARAWAS, HOLMES, WAYNE, ASHLAND, RICHLAND, KNOX, LICKING, PERRY, FAIRFIELD, PICKAWAY, FRANKLIN, DELAWARE, MORROW, MARION, UNION, MADISON, FAYETTE, ROSS, HOCKING, VINTON, ATHENS, MEIGS, GALLIA, JACKSON, SCIOTO, LAWRENCE, ADAMS, PIKE, HIGHLAND, BROWN, CLERMONT, HAMILTON, BUTLER, WARREN, CLINTON, GREENE, CLARK, CHAMPAIGN, MONTGOMERY, PREBLE, DARKE, MIAMI, MERCER, SHELBY, AUGLAIZE, LOGAN, HARDIN, VAN WERT, ALLEN, PAULDING, PUTNAM, HANCOCK, WYANDOT, CRAWFORD, SENECA, HURON, ERIE, SANDUSKY, WOOD, OTTAWA, LUCAS, FULTON, HENRY, DEFIANCE, WILLIAMS

Plans call for the refuge to protect 35 islands, covering 3,500 acres.

ACCESS

A small boat is the best and only way of reaching most islands. Wheeling Island, however, is connected to Wheeling, West Virginia by a bridge.

Boaters won't find docks or such on shores. Beach the boat or anchor it to explore the islands. The refuge is open daily from sunrise to sunset.

Accommodations: Fishing, nature study, bird watching, photography, hiking (no marked trails), and picnicking are permitted. Restricted hunting is allowed on most islands (see below). Camping, over-night boat mooring, archeological collecting, and campfires are not permitted in the refuge.

Hunting and Fishing: Hunters can pursue deer (archery only), waterfowl, coots, rails, gallinules, snipe, woodcock, dove, rabbit, and squirrel in the refuge during applicable state seasons. Sportsmen must be licensed in the state in which they hunt.

Game laws in that state apply. For example, a hunter going for game on Williamson Island must have a West Virginia hunting license and respect the state's regulations. Shotgunners must use steel or bismuth (non-toxic) shot in the refuge for waterfowl and small game. Repeat. Lead shot is not allowed.

Hunters should contact the refuge headquarters

for site rules and restrictions before visiting. Wheeling, Crab, Middle and Neal islands are closed to hunting. Paden and Mill Creek islands allow only archery deer hunting.

Reciprocal agreements allow Ohio, Kentucky, and West Virginia anglers to fish in the river with their home state license. Game laws of the state you fish in apply.

Information: Ohio River Islands National Wildlife Refuge, P.O. Box 1811, Parkersburg, WV 26102, (304) 420-7586.

GEOLOGY

Islands aren't forever, as the refuge's pamphlet notes succinctly. Sixteen have been lost in this century, and the Ohio River isn't making replacments.

"The glacial transport of sand and gravel that formed these islands no longer occurs. Those [islands] that remain are irreplacable."

At the start of the 20th century, 57 islands existed within the refuge's boundaries. The next century begins with 41 islands, and six of those are fully humanized (developed). Blame sand and gravel mining, development, and alterations for navigation (dams, dredging, locks, etc.) for the loss of 16 islands.

The Ohio River islands were formed by the natural accumulation of flood deposits on gravel and rock bars to the level of the flood plain. Surviving islands are either football-shaped or elongations that parallel a river bank. Navigational improvements removed the river's island-building depositions and its island-making capabilities. Islands, rapids and waterfalls vanished beneath the navigational "pools" (lakes) rising behind dams. Sedimentation has fused Grape and Bat islands. A palustrine wetland (emerging shrubs, trees in swamp) exists between them.

Within the refuge's boundaries—362 river miles—the Ohio River descends a half-foot per mile and averages 1,350 feet in width. It flows through the

National
Wildlife

The Darby Gets a Little Refuge from Uncle Sam

The U.S. Fish and Wildlife Service was expected to decide by 2000 whether to establish a 50,000-acre national wildlife refuge in the headwaters of Little Darby Creek, some 25 miles northwest of Columbus.

Little Darby Creek, a national and state scenic river, is a priceless, biological treasure, and the realm of many endangered mussels, fish, and plants. Scientists and naturalists rate the Darby watershed the best freshwater-warmwater habitat in the Midwest, bar none.

The refuge, dubbed the Little Darby National Wildlife Refuge, would straddle Union, and Madison counties, a region nearly bereft of public recreation land, and an area targeted for intense residential and commercial development. Suburban growth is the biggest threat to Little Darby Creek.

Refuge land would be acquired only from willing sellers, and would not interfere with local agriculture and governments. Money for wildlife refuges comes from taxes collected from the sale of hunting and fishing equipment and related items. The FWS plans to establish prairie wetlands, prairie pastures, and recreation opportunities (wildlife watching, fishing, hunting, hiking, nature study, etc.) in the refuge.

Appalachian Plateau physiographic province, except at the downstream end (last three islands) which is located in the Interior Low Plateau (Bluegrass or Lexington Plains) region.

WILDLIFE

Here's the list of goodies: 351 species of plants (33 trees, 25 shrubs, 293 herbaceous treats), 133 kinds of birds, 55 fish species, and 30 varieties of freshwater mussels.

The shallow waters around the islands, especially the back channels, are rich nurseries and feeding areas for game fish, such as freshwater drum, channel catfish, spotted bass, white bass, largemouth bass, and sauger.

Forage fish like gizzard shad and emerald shiner hang out here, and so do the sand shiner, river shiner, and bluntnose minnow. Fish found in the refuge's water—goldeye, mooneye, silver chub, black buffalo, and river redhorse—are considered rare in Ohio.

Biologists found the federally endangered pink mucket mussel near Lesage Island. The refuge preserves mussels listed as imperiled in Ohio—the wartyback, monkeyface, bullhead, Ohio River pig-toe, butterfly, and Ohio heelsplitter.

Plant life shows diversity because of numerous wetland habitats. The usual cast of bottomland hardwoods—sycamore, cottonwood, black willow, black walnut, silver maple, black locust, slippery elm—crowds the riverbanks and island shores. Ohio rarities in the refuge include Turk's-cap-lily, mountain bindweed, snow campion, reflexed umbrella sedge, staminate burreed, lyre-leaf rockcress, and two-leaved water milfoil.

The avifauna in the refuge is diverse because of the collision of open water, terrestrial, and wetland habitats. Passerine birds on the edges of the Mississippi and Atlantic flyways use the chain of islands as rest stops.

Waterbirds (35 species) are the most abundant and conspicuous residents. Shorebirds called spotted sandpiper and killdeer stay year-round, while the semipalmated sandpiper and semipalmated plover stick to wetland cover. Waders include great blue and green herons, and some of them establish nests. Fourteen kinds of waterfowl have been seen, the most common being the Canada goose, wood duck, and black duck. Osprey (endangered), red-tailed hawk, and American kestrel are also frequently spotted, and bald eagles fly by from time to time. (Ospreys like dam tailwaters where fish mass.) Warblers often stay through early June because caterpillars and other food morsels are abundant.

Island isolation and the mixing of aquatic and land habitats has created a high carrying capacity for mammals, says the refuge managers. Mammals are thick because their habitats are compressed and supercharged. The mammalian cast consists of deer, woodchuck, cottontail rabbit, raccoon, mink, opossum, muskrat, and beaver. Riverine furbearers are especially abundant in back channels and wetlands. The nocturnal pipistrelle, big brown and red bats feast on summer insects and spend their daylight beneath loose bark and in tree cavities.

HISTORY

Throughout human history, the Ohio River islands provided temporary shelter, hunting and fishing grounds, and cover for the Native American and European Americans who explored, exploited, and settled in the valley. In the 19th century, fugitive slaves were known to hide on the islands during their escapes to freedom. Today, anglers in major bass tournaments use the islands as landmarks and hotspots.

Over the years the islands have been used for Indian encampments, farming, logging, dredging, sand and gravel mining, mooring, oil drilling, hiding contraband (booze during Prohibition) and illegal trash dumping. Artifacts of all these activities can still be found, though collecting any artifact is unlawful.

Ohio River Islands National Wildlife Refuge was established from 19 islands in 1990.

JOURNAL

We take for granted that the Ohio River has always looked the way it does today. Compare a modern Ohio River map with one a century old. There's a difference. In the early 1900s, island hoppers could stop at 49 islands within West Virginia's jurisdictional waters. Since then, navigational and industrial developments killed 14 islands. Gone, but not totally forgotten, are islands named Line, Baker (one of two by this name remains), Cluster (one of two remains), Black, Beach Bottom Bar, Pike, French, Willow, Blennerhasset Towhead, Belleville, Goose, Towhead (Old Town), Letart (one of two remains), and Raccoon.

NORTHWEST

Ottawa National Wildlife Refuge

Endangered bald eagles rule as the titular monarchs over this flat realm, which harbors more protected birds than any other place in Ohio. More visible than the scarce eagles are the waterfowl, shorebirds, and warblers who populate and propagate in this marsh at the edge of the "Great Black Swamp," a vast and formidable wetland that once stretched from Sandusky to Detroit. Thousands of migratory birds use the refuge as a roadside rest area during their annual journeys on the great Mississippi Flyway.

LOCATION

Ottawa National Wildlife Refuge complex encompasses five sites in Lucas and Ottawa counties, but only one is open for people. Visitors can hike at the Ottawa headquarters located off SR 2 in Ottawa County near the border with Lucas County. Permission is required to visit the other four sites: West Sister Island, Cedar Point, Navarre Marsh, and Darby.

SIZE & DESIGNATION

8,316-acres. West Sister Island is Ohio's only national wilderness area.

The U.S. Department of the Interior, Fish & Wildlife Service (FWS) owns the Ottawa, Cedar Point, West Sister Island, and Darby sites. Navarre Marsh, next to the Davis-Besse nuclear power plant, belongs to the Centerior Energy Corporation, but the FWS administers it.

ACCESS

Don't come here if you are seeking shade, waterfalls, big trees, a gorge, rugged terrain, or a babbling brook for skinny-dipping. They don't exist.

But if birds are your passion (or you are looking for a change of place), this is your destination. Though the refuge is primarily a haven for waterfowl, shorebirds, raptors, and other wildlife, it also is a paradise for birders toting binoculars, field guides, and checklists. A small, illustrated checklist of birds appears on the back of the trail guide. A complete checklist is available at the refuge office (or write for one before you visit).

Trails: The Ottawa site offers four, interconnecting hiking trails, totaling seven miles. The refuge is open every day from sunrise to sundown. The terrain is flat, and open, and the trails are easy to follow. You will find maps at an information board in the parking lot, or at the headquarters beside the parking lot. Rest rooms (vault toilets) are located a few paces west of the parking lot.

The Swan, Yellowlegs and Mallard trails are rectangular-shaped and follow levees that crisscross the marshes. The Blue Heron Trail traces levees, too, but it also traipses through fields, woodlots, and a marsh. An observation deck equipped with a permanent telescope is located on the north loop of the Blue Heron Trail (south leg of the Swan Loop).

The Swan Loop (1.75 miles) gives folks with limited time a good view of this unique wetland. Walk the Yellowlegs and Mallard loops to improve your chances of glimpsing a bald eagle.

The levees act as observation mounds, allowing you to see for thousands of yards across this expanse. (This is the place to go if you like that "big sky" feeling.) Binoculars are essential because the wildlife, given tons of space, simply will not cooperate by staying close to the trails.

Though the terrain is easy, the sun and wind can

be your biggest challenge in the summer. Pack insect repellent, sun screen lotion, visor caps, sunglasses. Water canteens are strongly advised for summer hikes. I don't recommend a long walk for kids who are mosquito magnets. Hike to the observation deck and back—less than mile roundtrip. Though the trails stay on top of levees and remain relatively dry, sections of the path can get soggy and slippery.

Hunting: Controlled hunting and trapping manages the populations of geese and muskrats. Hunters and trappers are selected through annual drawings.

Information: Refuge Manager, Ottawa National Wildlife Refuge Complex, 14000 W. SR 2, Oak Harbor, OH 43449, (419) 898-0014.

GEOLOGY

Lake Maumee, the forerunner of Lake Erie and one of a series of glacier-fed lakes that occupied the basin, swamped much of northwestern Ohio some 13,000 years ago. (The lake actually stretched from western New York to Fort Wayne, Indiana.) The Wisconsinan glacier, whose meltwater refreshed the lake, blocked drainage outlets. Eventually, the ice mass retreated northward and unplugged outlets. Lake water drained northeast through the Niagara-St. Lawrence valley.

Lake Maumee shrunk roughly to the current size of Lake Erie. The former lake bed, smoothed out by wave action and gentle currents, became the Great Black Swamp, a flat plain measuring 120 miles in length and 30-40 miles in width (some 1,500 square miles). Two factors kept the area wet—flat terrain slowed drainage to a snail's pace, and a clay subsoil stopped water from soaking into the earth.

Marshes emerged between the swamp and Lake Erie. The water level of the lake determined the size of the marsh. The marsh moves inland during periods of high water, and retreats when the water level falls. Ottawa refuge protects remnants of the Great Black Swamp and the Lake Erie marshes.

Today, man-made dikes (doubling as hiking trails) control water levels according to a long-term wildlife management plan. The pools are drained in the summer, and flooded in autumn.

Viewed
the Best

What is Watchable?

The goal of the National Watchable Wildlife Program is simple. Find the best places in each state to see critters, then tell everybody about them. The Defenders of Wildlife coordinates the program nationally, but lets local sponsors run the show. In Ohio, the sponsors were the Ohio Department of Natural Resources, Division of Wildlife, the Defenders of Wildlife, and the U.S. Department of Defense.

Sponsors picked a 24-member steering committee to select locations in Ohio. Committee members represented conservation and hunting groups and government agencies.

Everybody's work led to the designation of 80 "Watchable Wildlife" sites and publication of the *Ohio Wildlife View Guide*, by W.H. (Chip) Gross, author and project manager. For more information read Gross' book (Falcon Press, 1996) and site specific chapters in this volume.

WILDLIFE

Ottawa National Wildlife Refuge is the kingdom of birds:

• Eighteen of the 25 birds listed as endangered in Ohio, one threatened bird, and 14 of the 18 birds designated as being of "special interest" (SI), roughly meaning potentially threatened, have been observed here.

• Seven endangered, eight SI, and one threatened species nest here.

• Seven endangered species (bald eagle, northern harrier, common tern, magnolia warbler, Canada warbler, northern waterthrush, and dark-eyed junco) are listed as "commonly seen" or "fairly commonly seen" on the refuge's checklist. Six SI birds (double-crested cormorant, American black duck, sharp-shinned hawk, sora, common snipe, purple martin, marsh wren) are similarly listed.

All totaled, 274 species of birds are regular visitors at the refuge, which lies beneath a branch of the Mississippi Flyway, one of those invisible highways-in-the-sky that birds have instinctively followed for millenia. Another 49 varieties have been seen only a few times and are classified "accidentals."

One of the most dramatic arrivals in late winter and early spring is the all-white tundra swan (or whistling swan), returning to its Arctic nesting ground after wintering in the Chesapeake Bay. In a good spring, as many as 5,000 of these graceful birds may be seen in the marshes of southwest Lake Erie. They return in the fall, but their numbers are fewer and less concentrated. The call of the tundra swan, also known as the whistling swan, is a shrill bark resembling "wow, wow-wow."

The area north and east of the refuge office is called the Goosehaven because Canada geese assemble here in March en route to their northern nesting areas. Some Mother Geese, however, do bed down and raise their young here. Before flying across the lake the geese beef up on grass shoots, pondweeds, and crops such as corn, sorghum, and buckwheat, which have been sowed here just for them.

Songbirds also arrive in the spring. Look for these little beauties, all warblers, in the woods—the Tennessee, Kentucky, Connecticut, yellow-rumped, blackpoll, Wilson's and palm.

Though eagles are seen year-round they are best viewed from February, when nesting begins, until the fledging of eaglets in July. The nest re-sembles a platform of branches and sticks atop a tall tree. While one adult hunts, the other stays in the nest with the young until they have fledged. Look for these noble birds flying above treelines (nest sites). They have white, or "bald," heads, and striking white tail feathers. Listen for their distinct, piercing screech. They dine on fish, but may attack small animals if hungry.

Bald eagles were once numerous on the Lake Erie shoreline. Lakeshore development, logging, and pesticide use reduced the flock to just four nesting breeding pairs statewide in 1979. In 1992, the number of nests statewide reached 20 with 31 eaglets in the baskets, thanks largely to a restoration program by the Ohio Department of Natural Resources. As many as 25 to 30 eagles were seen at a time that year at the refuge.

Though the news has been heartening, the bald eagle still faces extirpation in Ohio. Further lakeshore development is reducing habitat, and the level of toxic chemicals affecting reproduction in eagles (DDT and PCB) remains high in spite of laws outlawing their use. Oddly, young birds appear to be more skittish than their parents when humans enter their domain.

Besides eagles, ducks, geese, and swans, the refuge attracts the great blue heron and great egret, both commonly seen, plus pheasant, deer, rabbits, owls, hawks, and muskrats (abundant).

HISTORY

Though Native Americans found the Lake Erie marshes foreboding, they managed to feed and clothe themselves on the game found here, and no doubt acquired valuable eagle feathers. Those who exchanged furs for the white man's tobacco and corn called themselves "ottawas," their word for trader.

Driven from their homes in Canada and northern Michigan, the Ottawas settled in the southwestern Lake Erie area in the 1740s, living at the edge of the Great Black Swamp. French trappers also journeyed into this area. In 1763 the great Ottawa chief, Pontiac, organized regional tribes but failed to drive out the British.

For awhile the Great Black Swamp proved impenetrable to white settlers. Eventually, the vast swamp and marshes were drained and subdued for agricultural, industrial, commercial, and residential developments. Only pockets of the Great Black Swamp survive (see Oak Openings Metropark, Goll Woods) and the marshland, once more than 300,000

Bird hunter and best friend take the field.

acres, has been shrunk to 15,000 acres, much of it protected by federal and state governments.

In 1938, President Franklin Roosevelt declared 82-acre West Sister Island a national wildlife refuge. This patch of land in Lake Erie is a priceless rookery for black-crowned herons, great blue herons, and great egrets. The island became Ohio's only national wilderness area in 1975. It is closed to the public. The federal government began acquiring marshland for a refuge in the 1960s. More than 8,000 acres have been protected so far.

FIELD NOTES

If you can choose your day, by all means come in the spring (March-April) and autumn (October-November) when the populations of winged migratory creatures peak. The weather is apt to be more pleasant, too.

Nature education programs are held at the refuge headquarters throughout the year. A few stuffed animals are displayed in the lobby of the office.

JOURNAL

August 18. I scan the treeline along Crane Creek hoping to see a bald eagle—even for just a second. No luck. I head back to my car disappointed but recall a much sadder (and spooky) story about eagles near Vermilion on November 22, 1963.

Following his routine, biologist John M. Anderson, manager of the Winous Point Club, drove his car on the long, dusty driveway to the mailbox. And following habit, he glanced at the abandoned eagle's nest atop a dead elm tree. (Secretly he hoped the national bird would return to the nest.) When he reached the mail box, news of the assassination of President Kennedy came over the car radio.

Anderson lingered at the mail box awhile, motor idling, paralyzed by the shocking news. He drove back slowly, listening to the radio. Acting on reflex his eyes drifted to the old elm. The nest was gone! "The eagle's nest had fallen from the tree and crashed to the ground in the same hour that President Kennedy was shot," Anderson said later.

State Wildlife Areas

Wildlife areas are perfect for souls (or soles) who cannot stay on a beaten down track. You don't have to stay on trails. You can trail a scent, zigzag around shrubs, snoop around a woodchuck hole if you want. You can get snagged in briar patches, stuck in a swamp, or lost on a look-alike ridge if you want. Climb a tree, crawl through a hollow log, rest in a recess cave, trip over a fence.

Though most of the money to purchase them comes from license fees paid by sportsmen chasing game, others—bird watchers, hikers, wildlife observers, photogra-

A creek runs through it; wading and casting

phers, boaters and outdoors enthusiasts—can get their kicks in them, too. You don't need a hunting, fishing or trapping license to enter a wildlife area, unless you are engaged in those activities. In fact, 29 wildlife areas have been recently designated Ohio Watchable Wildlife Areas.

Game animals comprise a tiny fraction of the critters in wildlife areas. Many areas support endangered plants and animals. Sites managed for a certain game animal also allow creatures who share that habitat to survive. What's good for the turkey, in other words, is also good for the squirrel, the wood warbler, the oak and the spring beauty.

Wildlife areas are not for everybody. Camping is not allowed in them, though some areas are adjacent to state parks with campgrounds, or just a few miles away from private camping areas. Forget about latrines and drinking water. Trails, if they exist, tend to

be old farm or logging roads. The trails may not appear on area maps, and they usually don't make convenient loops nor take easy routes. Hiking is not recommended during deer hunting season when eager hunters fill the woods. Play it safe: Wear bright clothes (orange, yellow, light blue) and stick to trails and jeep roads. Harassing animals and hunters is unlawful.

Horses are prohibited, except at sites with bridle trails originating in state parks and designated for that purpose. In these cases, horse and rider must stay on the trail. Off-road vehicles and mountain bikes must stay on public roads.

Boaters will find launching areas, nothing fancy, and parking spaces. Check on horsepower limits before launching. Restrictions on hunting, fishing and trapping apply at several areas. The Division of Wildlife prints fishing and hunting maps of most wildlife areas. The hunting maps have property borders, roads, facilities, roads, vegetation, streams, phone numbers, and a helpful narrative about the location and the game available. Fishing maps for lakes show lake depth, structure, location of ramps, currents, roads, etc. These are available from wildlife area headquarters, district offices, or from the Ohio Division of Wildlife, 1840 Belcher Drive, Columbus, OH 43224-1329. Go to the directory of public hunting and fishing areas to find out which map to obtain.

The "special" wildlife areas on the next page were chosen for their overall appeal to sportsmen and the "non-consumptive" crowd. Each is an Ohio Watchable Wildlife Area, and open year-round.

OHIO "WATCHABLE WILDLIFE" SITES

NORTHEASTERN REGION
- Fowler Woods State Natural Area, *Richland County*
- French Creek Reservation, *Lorain County*
- Lake Isaac Waterfowl Sanctuary, *Cuyahoga County*
- North Chagrin Reservation, *Cuyahoga and Lake counties*
- Penitentiary Glen Reservation, *Lake County*
- Headlands Dunes-Mentor Marsh state natural areas, *Lake County*
- Big Creek Park, *Geauga County*
- Shenango State Wildlife Area, *Trumbull County*
- Mosquito Creek State Wildlife Area, *Trumbull County*
- Grand River State Wildlife Area, *Trumbull County*
- Tinkers Creek State Natural Area, *Summit and Portage counties*
- Cuyahoga Valley National Recreation Area, *Summit and Cuyahoga counties*
- Spencer Lake State Wildlife Area, *Medina County*
- Mohican Memorial State Forest, *Ashland County*
- Funk Bottoms State Wildlife Area, *Wayne and Ashland counties*
- Killbuck Marsh State Wildlife Area, *Wayne and Holmes counties*
- The Wilderness Center, *Stark County*
- Mill Creek Park, *Mahoning County*
- Zepernick Lake State Wildlife Area, *Columbiana County*
- Tappan Lake Park, *Harrison County*
- Jay D. Proctor Wildlife Education Center, *Tuscarawas County*

SOUTHEASTERN REGION
- Woodbury State Wildlife Area, *Coshocton County*
- Salt Fork State Wildlife Area, *Guernsey County*
- Egypt Valley State Wildlife Area, *Belmont County*
- Senecaville State Fish Hatchery, *Guernsey County*
- The Wilds, *Noble County*
- Scioto Trail State Forest, *Ross County*
- Cooper Hollow State Wildlife Area, *Jackson County*
- Shawnee State Forest, *Scioto and Adams counties*
- Kincaid Fish Hatchery, *Pike County*
- Blue Rock State Forest, *Muskingum County*
- Wayne National Forest, *Athens, Lawrence, Washington, other counties*
- Waterloo State Wildlife Area, *Athens County*
- Hocking State Forest, *Hocking County*
- Tar Hollow State Forest, *Ross, Vinton, Hocking counties*

CENTRAL REGION
- Hebron Fish Hatchery, *Licking County*
- Blacklick Woods Metro Park, *Franklin and Fairfield counties*
- Pickerington Ponds Metro Park, *Franklin and Fairfield counties*
- Blendon Woods Metro Park (Walden Waterfowl Refuge), *Franklin County*
- Stage's Pond State Natural Area, *Pickaway County*
- Deer Creek State Wildlife Area, *Pickaway and Fayette counties*
- London Fish Hatchery, *Madison County*
- Delaware State Wildlife Area, *Delaware County*
- Big Island State Wildlife Area, *Marion County*

NORTHWESTERN REGION
- Kendrick Woods, *Allen County*
- Killdeer Plains State Wildlife Area, *Wyandot County*
- Indian Lake State Park, *Logan County*
- Springville Marsh State Natural Area, *Seneca County*
- Lake La Su An State Wildlife Area, *Williams County*
- Maumee State Forest, *Fulton County*
- Farnsworth Metropark, *Lucas County*
- Oak Openings Preserve Metropark, *Lucas County*
- Irwin Prairie State Natural Area, *Lucas County*
- Maumee Bay State Park, *Lucas County*
- Mallard Club Marsh State Wildlife Area, *Ottawa County*
- Magee Marsh State Wildlife Area, *Ottawa County*
- Metzger Marsh State Wildlife Area, *Ottawa County*
- Ottawa National Wildlife Refuge, *Ottawa County*
- Toussaint State Wildlife Area, *Ottawa County*
- Little Portage State Wildlife Area, *Ottawa County*
- Pickerel Creek State Wildlife Area, *Sandusky County*
- Resthaven State Wildlife Area, *Sandusky and Huron counties*
- Sheldon Marsh State Natural Area, *Huron County*
- Old Woman Creek State Natural Area, *Huron County*
- Grand Lake, *Mercer and Auglaize counties*

SOUTHWESTERN REGION
- Paint Creek State Park, *Highland and Ross counties*
- Tranquility State Wildlife Area, *Adams County*
- Crooked Run Memorial Sanctuary, *Clermont County*
- Indian Creek State Wildlife Area, *Brown County*
- Cincinnati Nature Center, *Clermont County*
- Miami Whitewater Forest, *Hamilton County*
- Gilmore Ponds Interpretive Preserve, *Butler County*
- Caesar Creek State Wildlife Area & State Park, *Warren and Clinton counties*
- Spring Valley State Wildlife Area, *Warren and Greene counties*
- Beaver Creek State Wildlife Area, *Greene County*
- Germantown Reserve, *Montgomery County*
- Hueston Woods State Park, *Butler and Preble counties*
- Aullwood Audubon Center and Farm, *Montgomery County*
- Brukner Nature Center, *Miami County*
- Garbry's Big Woods Sanctuary, *Miami County*

NORTHEAST

Killbuck Marsh Wildlife Area

Killbuck Marsh is Ohio's largest surviving inland marsh, and its loaded with wetlands wildlife. Birders gather here for the parade of migratory birds every spring and fall. Floating lazily on Killbuck Creek is the best way to see the mysteries in the marsh, but if bobbing is not your bag, several hiking trails show the way.

LOCATION

Southwestern Wayne County, Franklin and Clinton townships; Holmes County, Prairie Township.

SIZE & DESIGNATION

Land—5,483 acres; water—11 acres. This state wildlife area is an Ohio Watchable Wildlife Area.

ACCESS

Park along state routes 83 and 226, which pass through the wildlife area, or in small lots on side roads named County Line (area headquarters), Force, Clark, Kimber, Cemetery, Valley, and Messner.

Trails: A foot trail usually packed with wildlife goes between parking on Force Road (east side of Killbuck Creek) to Clark Road, and northward to parking on Willow Road (near Kimber Road). Figure on a one-way walk of two miles. Another mile-long trail travels south from County Line Road (east of Killbuck Creek) to a tributary called Tea Run. Back-

track, or bushwhack up Tea Run to SR 83. An easy and elevated path (three miles) is the abandoned railroad grade between Messner and Force roads. Hikers are not allowed in the refuge between Force and County Line roads. Be prepared for soggy trails and swarming bugs.

Boating: Canoers take Killbuck Creek from Valley Road (TR 76) to Paint Valley Road (CR 320), west of Holmesville, a run of six miles on easy water. Contact the Area Manager before paddling. The mile-long section between Force and County Line roads is a wildlife refuge, and canoers must stay in their boats and navigate the main current. The only obstacles are sections of shallow water in late summer, and a ganglion of channels in the marsh. Expect to take a wrong turn or two. The stream can usually be paddled to its junction with the Walhonding River.

Hunting & Fishing: Waterfowl hunters will find wood ducks, mallards and blue-winged teal plentiful here. Trappers take muskrats and raccoons, and frog and turtle hunters have success in the marsh pools. Northern pike, carp, bullheads, largemouth bass, and suckers await fishers. Panfish are stocked in ponds.

Shotgun shooters will find a hand trap range for clay and paper targets on Kimber Road.

Information: Ohio Division of Wildlife, Wildlife District Three, 912 Portage Lakes Dr., Akron, OH 44319, (330) 644-2293.

WILDLIFE

Killbuck Marsh is a great place to study the spring and fall migrations of birds, especially waterfowl. Rarities such as the bald eagle, peregrine falcon, black rail, Eurasian wigeon, cattle egret, and prothonotary warbler are seen here. More common are the great blue heron, northern harrier, moorhen, sora, willow flycatcher, marsh wren, northern oriole, swamp sparrow, cedar waxwing, and rough-winged swallow.

Beavers are colonizing the marsh, and so is the river otter, an endangered animal released here in 1991. The eastern massasauga rattlesnake, also endangered, inhabits the marsh but your chances of encountering one are remote. Deer, rabbit, bobwhite quail, pheasant, fox squirrel, woodchuck, and skunks are represented here.

HISTORY

Land acquisitions for Killbuck Marsh started in

1969. Dikes and sluiceways have been constructed to control water flow. Ducks Unlimited, a conservation organization, was a partner in restoring 350-acre Wright's Marsh as a waterfowl habitat at the north end of the wildlife area. Members of other conservation groups have planted trees and shrubs to improve habitats for other wildlife.

FIELD NOTES

Killbuck Marsh is one of only a few nesting sites in Ohio for the sandhill crane, an endangered stork-like bird often confused with the great blue heron. Sandhill cranes have gray bodies and red crowns. While herons coil their neck in flight, cranes extend theirs like geese.

Learning to See

Other Suggested Wildlife Areas

Tranquility. Northern Adams County, wedged between SR 770 and CR 100. This hilly wildlife area of woodland, creeks, shrubland, and meadows has plenty of game for hunters, and migratory songbirds for birders. This Ohio Watchable Wildlife Area straddles eco-regions and hosts plants found in both glaciated and unglaciated soils. Shooting range, parking areas, fishing ponds, 4,254 acres.

Spring Valley. Greene and Warren counties, access via US 42 and Roxanna-New Burlington Road. A 2.5-mile trail and viewing tower overlook the marsh offer excellent encounters with 230 species of birds and other wildlife. Bordered by the Little Miami River, a national scenic river, the site has a boat ramp for fishing, rifle range, and canoe access to the Little Miami bike path. 842 acres.

Beaver Creek. Greene County, Fairground Road between Trebein and Beaver Valley roads. An amazing assembly of rare plants and animals inhabits six types of wetlands. Follow a boardwalk trail across a unique freshwater fen from Fairgrounds Road. Look for a bog lemming, massasauga rattlesnake, spotted turtle, and sedge wren, all endangered. Plant species number more than 300. Parking also available on New Germany-Trebein Road. 380 acres.

Grand River. Trumbull County, state routes 88 and 534. The Grand River and five tributaries create a site of diverse habitats. A boardwalk trail from CR 213, south of SR 88, wanders through a wetland noted for beavers, waterfowl, shorebirds, and aquatic plants. At dusk, you might glimpse a river otter, reintroduced here in the late 1980s. The 6,799-acre site features a dog training area, many parking places, lots of roving room.

Waterloo. Western Athens County, entrance at intersection of state routes 56 and 356. Heavily forested like adjacent Zaleski State Forest and Lake Hope State Park, Waterloo features dozens of trails and gravel roads for hikers, and a fire tower for wildlife observing. The site houses the state's research station for turkey, grouse, deer, squirrel, bear, songbirds, and birds of prey. Excellent location for woodland birds. 1,521 acres.

SOUTHEAST

Cooper Hollow Wildlife Area

Cooper Hollow straddles the Kanawha Trail, a route first trodden by bison herds and their American Indian pursuers. Later, Colonial militia used it, pursuing Indians, and finally came white settlers pursuing wealth and freedom on the American frontier. Logging, iron making, intensive farming, and mining exhausted the land during the ensuing 150 years. Today, these hills are reclaiming their natural luster and again becoming abundant ground for humans pursuing game, solitude, and encounters with wildlife.

LOCATION

Southeastern Jackson County, Madison Township.

SIZE & DESIGNATION

Land—5,421 acres; water—9 acres. A Watchable Wildlife Area.

ACCESS

From Jackson, head south on SR 93. In a hamlet called Clay, turn left (east) on Pyro Road (CR 47). Look for the roadside sign. In two miles, go left on CR 2 (CH&D Road). The driveway to the area headquar-

ters will be on the left (about two miles) just after a bridge. The small parking lot just past Madison Furnace might be your first stop. From here, take the trail north of the swamp to a beaver pond, and explore the furnace.

From US 35, turn southwesterly on Moriah Road (CR 5), right on Joe Evans Road, right on CR 2. Designated parking lots are found along (or off) TR 119, TR 122, CR 5, and CR 2. Pull offs are scattered throughout the area.

Trails: Skilled hikers should try the hilly foot trails—basically old logging and farm lanes—that roam through the various habitats and provide great opportunities to see wildlife. Like most state wildlife areas, the trails here are not marked (blazed), and the DOW map doesn't show the many paths that branch from the main trails. Nevertheless, carry the DOW map (and perhaps a topo map) and at each trail fork verify your route with a compass. The main trail is usually the widest, the one cleared of trees, and which shows the tread and evenly spaced grooves of tractors.

The best trails in Cooper Hollow stem from a parking area off Cooper Hollow Road (TR 119). Refer to the DOW map. From the Madison Furnace pull over, backtrack over the bridge and immediately turn left (east) on Vega Road (TR 130). Turn right (south) at the next intersection onto Cooper Hollow Road (TR 119). Drive two miles southeast (past several parking spots) to a gravel lane on the left (east side of road) leading to a parking area on top of a ridge. (The site is a mile northwest of the junction with Moriah Road).

One path heads southeast to Moriah Road just east of its merger with TR 119. Follow TR 119 back to your car. A more challenging two-mile path goes northwest through fields and forests. This path bends east, then north, and west (after an intersection with a dead end trail), north again, and southwest. It stops in hardwoods, but don't panic. Take a northwest heading, and bushwhack (200 yards) until you reach a gravel lane, or Sugar Run. Go left (west) at either landmark until you reach TR 119. Turn left to get back to the driveway and your car.

A path on the west side of TR 119 goes up the hill. In a few hundred yards, walk across the field on your right and follow the trail that funnels out of it. The "main" trail ends in 1.5 miles at a designated parking place on Joe Evans Road. Backtracking is recommended over tramping on township and counties. Be quiet and alert. Turkeys, deer, and songbirds are abundant along this segment.

Hunting & Fishing: Hunters find good populations of squirrels, deer, turkeys, and grouse. Wood ducks, mallards, blue-winged teal, hawks, snapping turtles, snakes and frogs frequent the swamp near Madison Furnace. Warblers and other songbirds reside in the upland hardwoods. An observation deck behind the area headquarters gives you chances to watch field birds, especially the eastern woodcock in spring, woodchucks, and other critters. Look for beaver and muskrats in the marshes and along streams.

Largemouth bass, bluegill, and channel catfish swim in Symmes Creek and the beaver ponds, but don't expect big catches.

Information: Ohio Division of Wildlife, District Office, 360 East State St., Athens, OH 45701, (740) 594-2211. Also, Cooper Hollow State Wildlife Area, Area Manager, 5403 CH&D Road, Oak Hill, OH 45656, (740) 682-7524.

WILDLIFE

Cooper Hollow is one of 80 Watchable Wildlife sites in Ohio, selected for its rich diversity of habitats and wildlife. Oak-hickory groves comprise 1,250 acres, and 1,800 acres is considered "reverting" farmland with second growth hardwoods, crabapple, hawthorn, dogwood, sassafras, sumac, honeysuckle, and pines. The remaining acres are fields, beaver-made wetlands, and corridors carved by Symmes Creek and Sugar Run.

HISTORY

The ruins of Madison Furnace recall the once-proud industrial might of the region, and the resultant ecological disaster. In the nineteenth century, loggers shaved immense hardwoods off these slopes to make charcoal for the Madison Furnace and nearby Limestone Furnace (the two a mile apart). Farmers dependent on the iron furnaces also cleared the land. The furnaces operated in the Hanging Rock iron manufacturing district in Southeastern Ohio.

Madison Furnace glowed from 1854 to 1902, but Limestone Furnace lasted only from 1855 to 1860. Iron manufacturing declined as supplies of local ore and wood depleted. New iron ore discoveries in the Upper Great Lakes doomed the industry. Supporting industries, such as farming, failed, too. The business bust left the hills naked and the soil used up, but nature is slowly returning the hills to their former glory.

ODNR began buying this land for a wildlife area in 1953. The public land is being restored to support upland forest wildlife and species that prefer meadows and reverting land, such as grouse.

JOURNAL

January 30. I paused atop an oak ridge and heard the sound a breeze makes when it kicks up leaves on a forest slope. The sound grew, subsided, and rose again followed by a quiet interval. Odd, I thought, nothing else stirred in the deep calm forest.

I froze in my tracks as the sound approached. A flock of turkeys marched 40 yards ahead. An unknown boss bird must have been issuing silent commands because the birds halted as a group, scratched the ground together, tramped on in step, stopped and scratched again, in a loose formation. One neck suddenly stiffened like a periscope. I remained inert, held my breath and blinked, stared so my eyes watered. It didn't work. The nervous jake sprinted and winged skyward. A second later the whole flock flushed. Two dozen birds rose like a wave, crested over treetops, and glided down the hollow. When the commotion died, I topped the ridge and saw a dozen more fleeing on foot. A moment later the woods got calm again.

Salt Fork Wildlife Area

Salt Fork encourages the free flow of hyperbole. Its myriad of habitats, some carefully managed for hunter and fisher, houses an amazing array of creatures. The menu of outdoor activities cannot be consumed in just a few days. There are 20,000 acres of playland and dozens of quiet coves. So leave the crowds that collect at the state park lodge, beach, marinas, and clubhouse and really get wild.

LOCATION

North-central Guernsey County.

SIZE & DESIGNATION

Land—12,000 acres (17,229 with state park);

water—2,952 acres, 74 miles of shoreline. A state Watchable Wildlife Area.

ACCESS

From I-77, head east on US 22 and follow state park and state wildlife roads. The wildlife headquarters is off US 22, east of the turn for the state park lodge.

Accommodations: Visitors should obtain the Salt Fork Wildlife Area brochure (Publication 155) from the Division of Wildlife before departing. The brochure map shows the sections open and closed to hunting (and restrictions), lake depths, vegetation (woodland, grassland, etc.), marshes, facilities, parking areas, fishing access, and other useful landmarks.

The resort state park offers overnight accommodations at its 148-room lodge, lakeshore cabins, campgrounds (family, horsemen's, and group camping), plus fine dining, a half-mile swimming beach, and an 18-hole golf course favored by deer at dusk. (See Salt Fork State Park, page00) Anglers can launch boats at Salt Fork and Sugartree Fork marinas, both full-service, or at six other spots (Park roads 65, 11, 3, 23, 14, and 5). Consult the area wildlife map for fishing access sites.

Trails: The Buckeye Trail passes through the state park. Hikers can bushwhack through the wildlife area, or follow 34 miles of trails designated for hooves and feet.

Hunting & Fishing: Hunters can practice at a shooting range, located on Park Road 59 (Parker Road or TR 587).

Numerous streams have cut gently rolling terrain to create steep-sided hollows and ravines. The place is loaded with deer, though unlucky hunters dismay that many find refuge in the state park where hunting is not permitted. Rabbits, squirrels, woodcocks, raccoons, grouse, and turkeys are bagged here, too. Trappers pursue muskrat, mink, beaver, and raccoon. Beaver lodges ring the shoreline. Embayments and marshes support waterfowl such as mallard, teal, bufflehead, goldeneye, wigeon, Canada goose, and wood duck.

The Division of Wildlife stocks Salt Fork Lake with muskies, largemouth bass, walleyes, channel and flathead catfish, bluegills, sunfish, and crappies. Smallmouth bass, suckers and bullheads also swim in the pond. Cast for muskies near the dam, and on the north shore below the lodge. Try the calm coves with heavy vegetation for summer bass.

Information: Ohio Division of Wildlife, District Four Office, 360 East State Street, Athens, OH 45701, (740) 594-2211. Also Salt Fork State Park, 14755 Cadiz Road, Lore City, OH 43755, (740) 439-3521.

WILDLIFE

Few places in Ohio match Salt Fork's habitat diversity, which includes oak-hickory woodlands, croplands, open water, marshes, pine plantings, reverting meadows (shrubland), stream bottomlands, and grasslands. Roughly, one-third of the wildlife area is forested with oaks and hickories on the dry ridges and maples, beech, ash, willow, elm, and sycamore on the moister slopes and bottomlands. Cropland and pastures make up a third of the area, with the remainder dominated by shrubs and small trees, like dogwood, hawthorn, sassafras, and crabapple.

Besides waterfowl, birders can look for bitterns, rails, and waders in the shallow marsh areas at the tips of the lake. Herons also appear in summer, and the woods feature the pileated woodpecker (listen for its telltale pecking), scarlet tanager, barred owl, Kentucky warbler, black-billed cuckoo, and American redstart.

HISTORY

The place gets its name from the salt licks that attracted Native Americans and white settlers to the southeastern corner of the park. Zane's Trace, a pioneer trail built in 1797, runs a few miles south of the park. The route was topped by the National Road, US 40, and I-70. In 1837 David B. Kennedy built a majestic sandstone house overlooking Sugar Tree Fork. The home is listed on the National Register of Historic Places and stands at the end of the Stone House Trail in the state park.

Salt Fork still has a new look. The earthen dam to impound Salt Fork was finished in 1967. The state park lodge opened in 1972.

FIELD NOTES

Walk along the lakeshore in winter and listen to the moans, whoops, whines and belches of heaving ice. You'll swear the water is a beast trying to crack the shell. One summer evening we counted 62 deer in the fields, and believed that millions of fireflies fled into the heavens. In mid-April turkey gobbles echo down hollows. To get closer you might have to inch across a meadow of blooming redbuds and dogwoods.

NORTHWEST

Lake La Su An Wildlife Area

Ordinarily, the Division of Wildlife doesn't put human first names on its lakes and ponds. But to get ponds bulging with bass and bluegills it had to keep the names. Start your visit at Lake Mel, then go to Jerry's Pond, and Clem's Pond, and to lakes Ann and Sue.

LOCATION

Northwestern Williams County, Northwest and Bridgewater townships.

SIZE & DESIGNATION

Land—2,100 acres; water—134 acres. Lake La Su An is an Ohio Watchable Wildlife Area.

ACCESS

From Montpelier, go north on SR 576 then west on CR R or CR S. From US 20, head north on CR 7, left on CR R. Parking is located on county roads R, S, and 8, as well as the access road into the wildlife area from CR S.

Trails: Service roads closed to vehicles act as hiking trails. A two-mile loop around ponds starts at the parking area between lakes Ann and Sue.

Boating: Ramps for small boats are available at lakes La Su Ann, Lavere, Ann, and Sue. Motor boats up to 10 horsepower are allowed on Lake La Su An, all others electric motors or paddles. A game checking station is located on CR R.

Hunting & Fishing: Just keep saying bass and bluegills. Little fishing pressure prior to the state's purchase of the site in 1981 meant ponds teeming with these two varieties. In many of the area's 14 ponds, largemouth bass densities per acre rank the highest in the Midwest. And bluegills 8 to 11 inches long are landed 70 percent of the time in the premium ponds.

Fishing is restricted here so that the naturally abundant populations of those game fish continue. Special permission and reservations are required. Other restrictions may apply, too. Call the area headquarters or district office before a fishing trip. The West Branch of the St. Joseph River flows through the area, east of the ponds. Rock, largemouth and smallmouth bass, northern pike and crappie inhabit the stream. Special restrictions do not apply to the river.

Waterfowl hunting is restricted to Monday, Wednesday, Friday, and Saturday, from dawn to noon. Hunters also score on rabbits, squirrels, deer, and pheasants. Trappers have success snaring muskrats.

Information: Lake La Su An State Wildlife Area, Area Manager, Rt. 1, Box 88, Montpelier, OH 43543, (419) 636-6189 (checking station) or (419) 459-4676. Also Ohio Division of Wildlife, District Two, 952 Lima Ave., Box A, Findlay, OH 45840, (419) 424-5000.

WILDLIFE

Bring binoculars for closeups of waterfowl and shorebirds, which flock here during spring and autumn migrations. Some of the drop-ins include the protected sandhill crane, marsh hawk and short-eared owl. Ponds called Teal and Wood Duck (off CR R) attract birds of those names.

HISTORY

Ed Broadbeck insisted that his friends and daughters be remembered when he donated his ponds and property to the state in 1982. The Division of Wildlife agreed. Lakes La Su An, Ann and Sue honor his daughters, while ponds named Lavere, Clem, Mel, Lou, and Jerry memorialize his friends. Ed named one puddle after himself, and another US (Uncle Sam). The origin of Hogback Pond remains a mystery.

Broadbeck built the ponds in the 1960s, intending to put them to work as "pay" fishing lakes. But Ed stayed most of the year at his home in Florida, so the pay lake idea faded. Meanwhile, the bluegills and bass that Ed dumped into the ponds multiplied without pressure and predation. The fish management program keeps these populations healthy and wise.

FIELD NOTES

Watch your step. The northern copper-belly snake, a rarity not to be confused with the venomous northern copperhead, lurks in the area.

Magee Marsh Wildlife Area

Magee Marsh is the end of the road for birds who may be at the end of their line. Twenty of the 25 bird species listed as endangered in Ohio, and 16 of 18 birds designated as "special interest" (potentially threatened) have been observed in this fertile wetland. Here is your chance to see them, too.

LOCATION

This area straddles the border of Lucas and Ottawa counties.

SIZE & DESIGNATION

Land—2,000 acres; Water—80 acres. This refuge is an Ohio Watchable Wildlife Area.

ACCESS

From SR 2, take the entrance road to Crane Creek State Park. Magee Marsh sprawls out on both sides of the road. Stop at the contemporary rustic lodge serving as the Sportsmen Migratory Bird Center and Crane Creek Wildlife Experiment Station. The road continues to the state park.

The road to the state park beach offers rewarding views of the marsh and its inhabitants. Hint: Stay in your car when observing the birds. Parking and unloading, noisy and intrusive actions, almost always causes the critters to flee. The birds near the road are used to cruising cars, but the approach of humans harasses them. For best results, roll down the windows, drive slowly, avoid loud talking, and keep the motor idling if you must stop.

Keep other autos in your sights, too. Cars behind you may not be interested in watching a great blue heron wade in the water. Wave those cars ahead. Also, geese and ducks frequently cross the road. Give them plenty of room. Driving up closer often confuses them, and delays their crossing and your progress.

Trails: You can view the marsh from the porches (two levels) of the Sportsman Migratory Bird center. A boardwalk trail (wheelchair and stroller accessible) along the edge of a marsh pond leads to a three-story observation tower. The Magee Marsh Bird Trail, a boardwalk measuring .6 miles, begins at the beach entrance of Crane Creek State Park. Look for the wooden sign on the left, and park in the lot. Folks in wheelchairs and pushing strollers can negotiate this flat trail. Keep bicycles and tricycles off the path, please. Roundtrip is 1.2 miles.

Boating: A ramp for small boats, located on the northside of SR 2 east of the state park entrance, provides access to Turkey Creek and Lake Erie. Boating in the ponds and bays is not allowed. The water level may not be deep enough for some boats. Boating in Magee Marsh is not allowed, unless special permission is granted.

Hunting & Fishing: Waterfowl hunting is limited to a small number of hunters selected in a drawing. Likewise, trapping for muskrats is restricted. Applications are available at wildlife district offices. Special waterfowl hunting days are held for young hunters.

There is parking here for anglers and wildlife watchers who roam on the dikes.

Special Places & Events: The Sportsmen Migratory Bird Center is a must stop. It has some excellent exhibits of the wildlife that thrives in the Lake Erie marshes. Hunters will enjoy the duck hunting displays and the center's collection of decoys. A "touch table" challenges children to handle bones, skulls, feathers, fur, etc. of marsh animals. A state wildlife officer is usually on duty to answer questions, and you will find written information about the marsh at the information desk. The center has rest rooms, and on hot summer days its air-conditioned atmosphere and cold drinking fountain are refreshing. In winter, the center is closed on weekends.

The Crane Creek Wildlife Experiment Station, the state headquarters for wetlands wildlife research, is housed in the nature center. Some of the station's numerous duties are developing and managing the wetlands habitats, increasing wildlife populations (Canada geese, bald eagles and beavers, for examples), and to study wetlands ecology. Magee

Marsh was a site for Ohio's goose restoration program in the 1960s.

Information: Ohio Department of Natural Resources, Division of Wildlife, District Two, 952 Lima Avenue, Box A, Findlay, Ohio 45840, (419) 424-5000 or (419) 898-0960 (area manager). Sportsmen Migratory Bird Center, 13229 W. SR 2, Oak Harbor, 43449, (419) 898-0960.

Geology

Magee Marsh is part of a once enormous marshland called the "Great Black Swamp." The swamp stretched from Detroit, inland to Fort Wayne, Indiana, and eastward to Sandusky, roughly the shoreline of old Lake Maumee, the precursor of Lake Erie.

Lake Maumee was formed by the meltwater of the Wisconsinan glacier, about 12,000 to 10,000 years ago. As the glacier retreated northward, water rushed through the Niagara-St. Lawrence valleys and shrunk Lake Maumee approximately to the size of Lake Erie today. The poorly-drained plains south and west of this new shoreline became the Great Black Swamp, a paradise for wildlife but a place largely unsettled by Native Americans.

The size of the marsh now depends on the water level of Lake Erie, which derives 90 percent of its water from the upper Great Lakes (Huron, Michigan, and Superior). The water level, of course, fluctuates seasonally (lowest in February, highest in June), and decade to decade. A record peak level was reached in 1973, followed by a period of recession, then increases in the late 1980s.

During periods of high water the marsh swells inland, but it shrivels up again when the level drops.

Barrier beaches (sand spits and sandbars) protect marshes by impounding water and absorbing Lake Erie's crashing waves. The beach at Crane Creek State Park serves as a barrier beach. However, these natural dams sometimes lose their effectiveness when the lake level rises, or during violent storms.

Learning to See

Watching Wildlife 101

- Remember the two Ds, dawn and dusk. These are the best times to see wildlife.
- Binoculars bring wildlife closer to you. They let you to study critters from afar without harassing them.
- Birders should consider calling refuge offices before a visit. Staffers usually know the lowdown on migratory birds in the refuge.
- Wetlands support more life than deep woods. Wildlife also is generally more abundant along "edges," the zones between woods and meadows, or between swamps and woods.
- Walk slowly and silently. Tiptoe a few paces, stop and observe for several minutes, then repeat the gait. Focus your gaze 50-100 yards into the forest, the likely distance to see deer, etc.
- Wear hats to shade eyes, trousers to deny insects and prickers, and comfortable shoes that you don't mind scuffing. Natural colors improve your chances of observing wildlife. (Bright colors should be worn during hunting season.)
- Hiking sticks are great for balance, support, leaning on, probing, poking around, and companionship. Carry a trail map (a must for first time visits), small canteen (especially with kids), pocketknife, empty fanny pack, and toilet tissue (just in case).

All but a small fraction of the Great Black Swamp and marshland has been drained for agricultural and human developments. Still, nature may have the last laugh. Geologists have discovered that the land in the southwestern end of Lake Erie is gently sinking about two feet per century. If left undisturbed, Lake Erie's shoreline and the marsh will be located farther inland in the 23rd century.

WILDLIFE

For many years humans viewed marshlands as barren, featureless, and lifeless wastelands. As we have learned, just the opposite is true. Acre for acre, marshes and other wetlands produce more wildlife than any other kind of habitat.

The most visible representative of this bounty are the migratory birds who come here in the thousands every spring and fall. Magee Marsh is one of the important stops for waterfowl and warblers winging on the Mississippi Flyway, the highway-in-the-sky that birds have flown for millenia. It also is a vital habitat for the following protected birds who have been seen in Magee Marsh. During a bird count in autumn 1994, all four federally-endangered birds found in Ohio—peregrine falcon, bald eagle, Kirtland's warbler, and piping plover—were scoped at Magee Marsh on the same day. The place hides 156 kinds of songbirds, including 35 species of warblers.

The cast of characters includes the state endangered American bittern, least bittern, yellow-crowned night heron, northern harrier, king rail, sandhill crane, common tern, sedge wren, winter wren, black tern, yellow-bellied sapsucker, loggerhead shrike, hermit thrush, golden-winged warbler, Canada warbler, magnolia warbler, northern waterthrush, and dark-eyed junco. Other protected birds are the snowy egret, little blue heron, cattle egret, American black duck, sharp-shinned hawk, red-shouldered hawk, double-crested cormorant, Virginia rail, sora, common snipe, upland sandpiper, long-eared owl, short-eared owl, northern saw-whet owl, purple martin, and marsh wren.

Altogether, ODNR's checklist includes 303 birds. In season, you will likely see the pied-billed grebe, tundra swan, dunlin, Bonaparte's gull, common nighthawk, bay-breasted warbler, and snow bunting. Sharp eyes may spot the snow and blue goose, willet, glaucous gull, whippoorwill, ruby-throated hummingbird, Brewer's blackbird, and lapland longspur.

Muskrat are abundant. Deer, skunk, mink, raccoon, fox, rabbit, woodchuck, and opossum also flourish here. Look for these snakes—fox, northern brown, common water, garter, Kirtland's and queen. Turtles are represented by the snapping (some up to 50 pounds), painted and Blanding's. Listen for these frogs—bullfrog, green, leopard, striped chorus, cricket and spring peeper. Salamanders include the mudpuppy, Jefferson, spotted, and red-backed.

Wildflowers bloom in summer, notably pink rose mallow, Joe-Pye weed, arrowhead, water lily, blue skullcap, pickerel weed, American lotus, and burr marigold.

HISTORY

The successive tribes of Indians who have lived in this area relied on the rich marshland for food and furs. The Ottawas, who moved to the shore in the 1740s, swapped furs for European goods with French and other traders.

A French explorer named Etienne Brule was probably the first white man in these parts. He landed at the mouth of a nearby stream on All Saints Day (November 1) in 1615, and named the stream Toussaint Creek (All Saints Creek). The few French who settled here built primitive bark huts, lived off the land, doing little, fortunately, to civilize the marsh.

Later settlers drained the wetlands for farms, and allowed livestock to graze in the marsh in dry years. A different kind of harvesting began in the 1850s when hunting clubs started "waterfowling," or shooting ducks and geese for market. Members of the Crane Creek Shooting Club traveled from Cleveland, Pittsburgh and Detroit to enjoy the hunt. The ducks were salted and shipped to market in wooden barrels.

When attempts to convert the marsh to farmland in the early 1900s failed, the land was allowed to return to marshland for waterfowling and muskrat trapping. From the late 1920s through 1950 hunters in the private club here bagged 2,500 ducks a year. Trapping yielded 97,000 muskrats from 1939 to 1951.

Maintaining the marsh habitat became too costly for the hunting club. ODNR bought the place in 1951, including the beach, and started controlled waterfowl hunting. The Crane Creek Wildlife Experiment Station was established in 1956. The Sportsmen Migratory Bird Center was constructed in 1970.

Conservations clubs, notably Ducks Unlimited and the Ohio Decoy Collectors and Carvers Association, have been helpful in providing money, and support for marsh development and the exhibits at the nature center.

Scouts honor circa 1940: Chop a tree, plant a tree.

Ohio's forests started on land spoiled by mining, fire, erosion, wasteful logging and farming, or neglect. Remarkably these forests now have plenty of trees, though most are 20th century trees, young by old-growth standards. Whether these treed places continue to rebound depends on a careful balancing act by their stewards—us.

State forests—Shawnee, Zaleski and Tar Hollow especially—and Ohio's only national forest, known affectionately as "The Wayne," are as close as the state gets to wilderness. But recreational and commercial demands on these lands are often at odds. Are they a tree farm for the paper industry, or a backwoods playground for rugged individualists—or both?

The Ohio Division of Forestry, the administrative steward of state forests, is a state agency within the Ohio Department of Natural Resources. It is run by a chief forester, who is appointed by the director of ODNR. Forestry is responsible for the operation and maintenance of Ohio's 178,500-acre state forest system, which includes 19 state forests and two state tree nurseries. This system is managed under a multiple-use concept to provide timber, backcountry recreation, wildlife habitat, resources for education and research, and protection of soils, watersheds, aesthetics, and other environmental qualities.

The Forestry Advisory Council makes management recommendations about state forests to the chief of the division. The council consists of eight members appointed by the governor with the advice and consent of the state senate. Each serves a four-year term and not more than four are permitted from the same political party.

What with three separate management units and holdings scattered like confetti across 12 counties the Wayne National Forest is a migraine to administer for a staff stretched thin and trying to please all interest groups and visionaries. Only some of the land is managed by the U.S. Forestry Service; the rest is privately owned. It is a forest still in its adolescence. Only time will tell how and if it will grow up.

—*SO*

NORTHEAST

Fernwood State Forest

Forty-years ago strip mines scarred this landscape, but since the 1960s the place has been on the mend. The wizened, tall trees on ridges and in ravines survived the holocaust; the smaller ones on gentle slopes, put there in reforestation projects, hide the scars of strip-mining. Nature's landscaper, the indomitable beaver, masterminded the chain of ponds and wetlands seen along the hiking trails. With any luck you'll see one of these furbearers at sunset.

LOCATION
     Central Jefferson County, Cross Creek Township.

SIZE AND DESIGNATION
     2,107 acres.

ACCESS
     Fernwood State Forest is composed of three separate blocks. From US 22 in Wintersville, follow Bantam Ridge Road (TR 34) south to Fernwood, then go in a southwesterly direction on CR 26, and left on Douglas Applegate Road (TR 181). On this road you will find the forest headquarters, trailheads, and Little Round Top Picnic Area. Continue west on CR 26 to reach the campground and target ranges. Another chunk flanks the north side of McIntyre Creek, west

of New Alexandria (accessible via TR 177).
     Accommodations: Camping is available at Hidden Hollow Campground, located off CR 26 west of the ranger station. It offers twenty-two sites. The accommodations include picnic tables, fire rings, drinking water, and vault toilets. A forest officer collects the fee after you choose your site. The campground and hiking trails are open from 6 a.m. to 11 p.m..
     Trails: Deer Run Trail heads south from a parking area on TR 181, just before the campground road. The path goes alongside a mining drainage ditch that beavers have transformed into slender ponds beneath cliffs of shale and limestone. To stay on course, ignore the side trails branching left.
     After 1.5 miles, Deer Run Trail crosses a stream and joins Beaver Dam Trail, the primary route turning right. Beaver Dam Trail tracks northwest, through another alley of beaver dams and marshes, to CR 26. Return via TR 181, passing the forest headquaters and a panoramic view en route. The walk measures four miles. If Beaver Dam Trail is flooded due to beaver excavations, backtrack along Deer Run Trail.
     A nature trail also ambles through the "land lab" next to the campground. The land lab is an environmental education project sponsored by the Division of Forestry, the Jefferson Soil & Water Conservation District, and the Jefferson County Conservation Education Committee.
     Hunting & Fishing: Gun enthusiasts sharpen their aim at target ranges for rifle, shotguns (trap shooting), and handgun. Riflemen will find a 100-yard range and seven benches, while pistol shooters practice at a 25-yard range with eight benches. Shotgunners have two benches and a range for clay birds. The ranges, open daily a half hour before sunrise to a half hour after sunset, are located on the road to the campground, off CR 26. Shooters must supply their own targets (paper or clay), and remove their empty casings.
     Hunting and fishing are allowed, except in restricted areas (check at the headquarters). The ponds, stocked with bluegill, bass, and channel catfish, are good places for beginners. Hunters chase deer, grouse, rabbit, and squirrel.
     Two vistas, with parking, on Douglas Applegate Road have views of the Cross Creek Valley.
     Information: Available from Fernwood State Forest, Route 1, Box 186A, Bloomingdale, OH 43910-9726, (740) 264-5671.

HISTORY
     Two centuries ago, Fernwood served as the hunting ground for Mingo Indians, a catchall name for a group of displaced Indians representing several nations. A major Indian trail, connecting Mingo Town (south of Steubenville) and Toledo, followed Cross Creek, which flows through the northern edge of the

State & National Forests

Lake Erie

Michigan

Maumee
State
Forest

Pennsylvania

Indiana

Mohican-Memorial
State Forest

Yellow Creek
State Forest

Harrison
State Forest

Fernwood
State Forest

Blue Rock
State Forest

Sunfish
Creek
State
Forest

Tar Hollow
State Forest

Perry
State Forest

Hocking
State Forest

Gifford
State
Forest

E

F

C

Scioto Trail
State
Forest

Zaleski
State
Forest

B

West
Virginia

Pike
State Forest

Shade River
State Forest

Brush
Creek
State
Forest

Richland
Furnace
State Forest

Shawnee
State
Forest

Dean State
Forest

Wayne National Forest

A. *Ironton District Office*
B. *Athens District Office*
C. *Marietta District Office*
D. *Lake Vesuvius Recreation Area*
E. *Leith Run Recreation Area*
F. *Burr Oak Cove/Wildcat Hollow*

D

A

N

Ohio River

Kentucky

Ohio River

Little Round Top section of the state forest.

Coal mining in the 1930s left the site a lunar landscaped pocked with small ponds and mounds of dirt. However, a limestone basement enabled trees and shrubs to reoccupy the hills. In 1961, the state purchased 2,000 acres from the North American Coal Company, originally for public hunting. The Division of Forestry acquired the site from the Division of Wildlife in 1968. Reforestation and recreation facilities arrived later, thanks to funding by the Appalachian Regional Development Act of 1965 and the Ohio Capital Improvements program. Originally called the Jefferson Reclamation Area, Fernwood became Ohio's eighteenth state forest in 1973.

FIELD NOTES

Fortunately, the limestone in the cliffs above the beaver ponds helped to neutralize the acid in water running off mines. Listen for barred owls at dusk. Hawks are often seen hovering above the beaver ponds and ravines.

Harrison State Forest

Like its nearby twin, Fernwood, Harrison

State Forest offers camping, scenic trails,

and target ranges on reclaimed mining land. It is a popular hang-out of local hunters, trail riders, and pond fishers.

LOCATION
Central Harrison County, Archer Township.

SIZE AND DESIGNATION
1,345 acres.

ACCESS
From Cadiz, head north on SR 9 a couple miles. Turn right on CR 13 (Clearfork Road), and left on TR 189 to reach Ronsheim Campground (follow signs). Continue north on SR 9, then right on TR 185 (Camp Road) to the trail riders camp.

Accommodations: Seven family campsites comprise the Ronsheim Campground. The trail riders camp has 20 sites. Each campground has picnic tables, fire rings, drinking water, and latrines. The camping fee is collected by a forest officer.

Trails: Equestrians and hikers share 24 miles of paths that visit meadows, woods, ponds, and high ridges. Get a trail map before departing. The main route, Deep Hollow Trail, connects the Ronsheim Campground and trail riders camp, and crosses two roads. Follow the blue blazes. Four loop trails lure

travelers off this trail. From Ronsheim Campground, hikers and riders can visit a trio of woodland ponds via the Lakeview and Lakeside trails, or head north on the Hilltop Trail to meadows and viewpoints. The latter path crosses Hanover Ridge Road (CR 17), makes a loop, and returns to the start. Hunters enjoy these trails too, so everybody should stay alert. Trail parking also is located on TR 182, roughly midway between the camping areas on Deep Hollow Trail.

Hunting & Fishing: Try the three stocked ponds east of Ronsheim Campground, and the one at the horse camp.

The shooting range on TR 182, south of road's junction with the Deep Hollow Trail, is open everyday from a half hour before sunrise to a half hour after sunset. Youngsters under age 16 must be accompanied by an adult.

Information: Contact Fernwood State Forest, Route 1, Box 186A, Bloomingdale, OH 43910-9726; (740) 264-5671. The state forest is open daily. Campers, hunters, and anglers can be present during other hours.

HISTORY
Harrison State Forest started with the purchase of stripmined land in 1961. Recreation facilities were developed with funds from the Appalachian Regional Development Act of 1965. More than 100,000 trees were planted on 186 acres in 1992 and 1993.

They Have *it All*

Ohio State Forest Features

State forests with...
- **Most trail miles**: Shawnee, 142 miles; Zaleski, 73 miles; Tar Hollow, 52 miles.
- **Backpack trails:** Shawnee (60 miles), Zaleski (23 miles)
- **Horsemen's campgrounds:** Shawnee, Tar Hollow, Hocking, Zaleski, Harrison
- **Family campground** (fee): Fernwood and Harrison
- **Primitive camping**: Mohican, Shawnee, Zaleski
- **All-purpose vehicle areas:** Perry (16 miles), Pike (15 miles), Richland Furnace (9 miles); Maumee (5 miles).
- **Scenic auto trail:** Shawnee
- **State parks:** Shawnee, Blue Rock, Tar Hollow, Zaleski, Hocking, Mohican Memorial, Scioto Trail, Pike, Shade River.

Mohican Memorial State Forest

Think of the state forest as a green expanse that anchors and steers the rest of Mohican Territory, and as a primitive playground for outdoor recreation enthusiasts. A well-tended shrine to Ohio's war dead makes this sacred ground for humans. Clearfork Gorge, enshrined as a National Natural Landmark, and the forest over its rim makes this a sacred place in all other ways.

LOCATION
Southwestern Ashland County, Hanover Township.

SIZE AND DESIGNATION
Mohican Memorial State Forest is an Ohio Watchable Wildlife Area, all 4,506 acres. The forest helps protect Clear Fork Gorge, a National Natural Landmark.

ACCESS
From Loudonville, travel south on SR 3, then turn right on SR 97. Drive about three miles, turn right, bear left at the fork and follow Forest Road 8 (toward covered bridge). A mile or so passed the covered bridge, take a sharp right to the ranger station. The bridle trail staging area is on SR 97, and fire tower and gorge lookout are on Forest Road 1. A state forest map is a must for newcomers.

Accommodations: The state forest reserves ten primitive (and free) "park and pack" campsites for backpackers and overnight hikers. The tent spots are located on trails. Contact the state forest office for permits and directions. Primitive camping is also available in the state park at the covered bridge. These sites along the Clearfork would be ideal except for the occasional foul odor wafting from latrines.

Go to the Mohican State Park campground (SR 3) or Pleasant Hill Lake Park (SR 95) for fancy camping accommodations (showers, toilets, hookups, etc.), though on summer weekends these places fill quickly. Don't fret, though, because Mohican Territory is loaded with private campgrounds.

Trails: Combined, the state forest and state park offer 36 miles for hiking. Of this, 22 miles is available for trail riding, and 10 miles for snowmobilers. Trail users usually begin at one of four places in these public land units. Hikers congregate at the covered bridge (Forest Road 8) because all trails radiating from this landmark are foot paths. The bridge itself

stands in the state park. From here, trails head east through Clear Fork Gorge, and west to Big Lyons and Little Lyons falls and Pleasant Hill Dam, all across state park land. Hog Hollow Trail, white arrows, begins on the east side of the bridge and parallels forest roads to the fire tower on Forest Road 1. Hikers also depart from Pleasant Hill Dam, managed by the U.S. Army Corps of Engineers (CR 3006 or Goon Road), for walks on the Lyons Falls and Clearfork Gorge trails.

Horseback riders start at a staging area on SR 97, east of the War Memorial Shrine. Hitching posts and latrines are available. Trail riders should follow trails blazed red, blue, yellow and green. The Mohican Fire Tower on Forest Road 1 is a convenient starting point for snowmobilers. (Other motorized vehicles and bikes are not allowed on the snowmobile trail.) The snowmobile trail is for experienced drivers because it winds through forests and steep ravines, crosses creeks and roads, curves sharply in places. Parking is found at each of these trailheads.

Notably, Mohican Territory lies in Ohio's snow belt. When the white stuff arrives cross-country skiers head for the bridle trails. Don't ski on the snowmobile trail, however.

The guide map for the forest shows the trails, staging areas, and parking spots on township roads. The latter facilities are popular with hunters. Detailed maps of the bridle and snowmobile trails are available from the state forest headquarters.

Hunting & Fishing: Hunters and trappers can pursue their favorite game animals in the state forest, except in Memorial Forest Park (boundary marked in red), Mohican State Park, and Clear Fork Gorge State Natural Area. State forest property lines are marked in yellow paint. Clearfork is one of a handful of Ohio streams cool enough to support trout. Fishing is permitted.

Special Places & Events: The Memorial Shrine, the stone chapel overlooking SR 97, is worth a peak. Established by the Ohio Federation of Women's Clubs, the memorial honors Ohioans who lost their lives in military conflicts since 1940. Behind the shrine is 270-acre Memorial Forest Park, which is designated a nature preserve.

Youngsters like to climb the Mohican fire tower located on Forest Road 1. Winter visitors should inspect the stairs for snow and ice before climbing.

Information: Mohican Memorial State Forest, 3060 CR 939, Perrysville, OH 44864-9791, (419) 938-6222.

HISTORY
The state began buying land for this state forest in 1928. The thick groves of mature white and red pines seen along roads were planted by workers of the Civilian Conservation Corps during the 1930s. The CCC had a camp in the state forest. Clear Fork State Park (renamed Mohican State Park in 1966) was created from state forest land in 1949. In 1967, Clear Fork Gorge was designated a National Natural Landmark by the U.S. Department of the Interior.

Look for the plaque certifying the designation at the covered bridge. Later, the Ohio Department of Natural Resources established Clear Fork Gorge State Natural Area.

The "Memorial" in Mohican Memorial State Forest refers to a 1945 act passed by the Ohio Legislature to create a 3,500-acre forest to remember Ohioans killed in military service. Their names are inscribed in books inside a glass case. General Curtis LeMay, a Columbus native, delivered the dedication speech on April 27, 1947. The Ohio Federation of Women's Clubs maintains the shrine. Ohio Gold Star Mothers hold a memorial service here the last Sunday in September.

FIELD NOTES

Besides pine plantations, Mohican has native hardwoods—oaks, hickories, beech, maples, aspen, sweet gum, ash, wild black cherry, walnut, sycamore. Home-grown white pine and hemlock thrive here, too.

In the early 1990s Mohican Memorial State Forest served as a field lab for a Smithsonian Institution study of neotropical migratory songbirds (warblers, thrushes, flycatchers, vireos, etc.). Mohican still attracts large numbers of these popular birds. Additional research is underway to determine the diversity and population of these species. Bring binoculars for peeks at the cerulean and black-and-white warblers, American redstart, ovenbird, and northern parula (which likes hemlocks).

The gorge trail produces herons, kingfishers, painted turtles, ducks in summer. Hawks and turkey vultures are usually soaring overhead, and occasion-

Tree Stewards

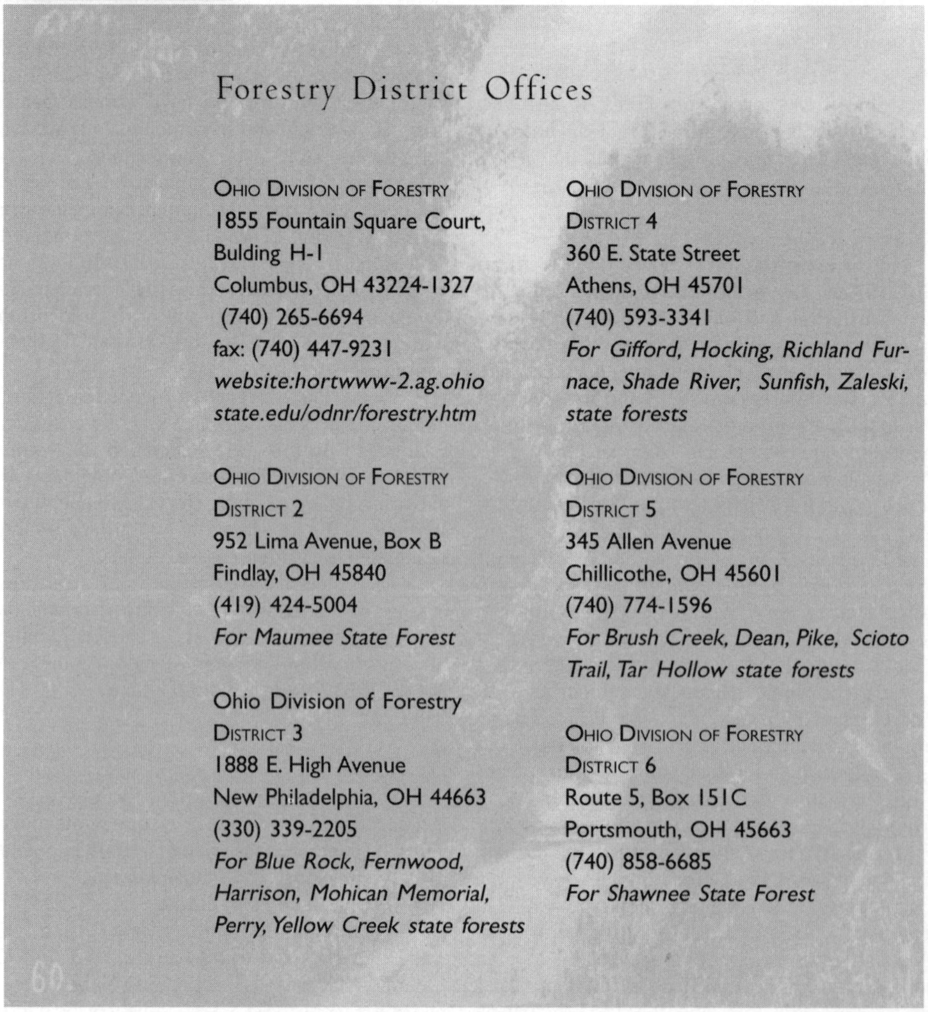

Forestry District Offices

OHIO DIVISION OF FORESTRY
1855 Fountain Square Court,
Bulding H-1
Columbus, OH 43224-1327
(740) 265-6694
fax: (740) 447-9231
website:hortwww-2.ag.ohio state.edu/odnr/forestry.htm

OHIO DIVISION OF FORESTRY
DISTRICT 2
952 Lima Avenue, Box B
Findlay, OH 45840
(419) 424-5004
For Maumee State Forest

Ohio Division of Forestry
DISTRICT 3
1888 E. High Avenue
New Philadelphia, OH 44663
(330) 339-2205
For Blue Rock, Fernwood, Harrison, Mohican Memorial, Perry, Yellow Creek state forests

OHIO DIVISION OF FORESTRY
DISTRICT 4
360 E. State Street
Athens, OH 45701
(740) 593-3341
For Gifford, Hocking, Richland Furnace, Shade River, Sunfish, Zaleski, state forests

OHIO DIVISION OF FORESTRY
DISTRICT 5
345 Allen Avenue
Chillicothe, OH 45601
(740) 774-1596
For Brush Creek, Dean, Pike, Scioto Trail, Tar Hollow state forests

OHIO DIVISION OF FORESTRY
DISTRICT 6
Route 5, Box 151C
Portsmouth, OH 45663
(740) 858-6685
For Shawnee State Forest

Ohio Forest reality: The sap also rises, 1930's.

ally an osprey or bald eagle lingers to catch fish. Orioles and warbling vireos are common in the sycamores. Early spring, just as buds open, look for spawning fish in the shallows.

Yellow Creek State Forest

Yellow Creek State Forest consists of two rectangular blocks attached to Highlandtown State Wildlife Area. The forest protects the watershed of Little Yellow Creek, which empties into the Ohio River at Wellsville.

LOCATION
　Southwestern Columbiana County, Wayne Township.

SIZE AND DESIGNATION
　756 acres.

ACCESS
　Yellow Creek lacks accommodations for visitors, but can be reached from designated parking areas in Highlandtown State Wildlife Area, along TR 773 (Sharp Road) and TR 876.
　Accommodations: The nearest camping can be found at Beaver Creek State Park.
　Trails: No marked trails have been constructed, but hunters and wildlife have blazed some.
　Hunting & Fishing: Hunting and trapping are allowed in the state forest lands.
　Information: Contact Fernwood State Forest, Route 1, Box 186A, Bloomingdale, OH 43910, (740) 264-5671.

FIELD NOTES
　Planted conifers keep the lower slopes green year round, and hemlocks stand in the shady ravines. Birds to look for include the sharp-shinned hawk, long-eared and great horned owls, whip-poorwill, brown creeper, and the worm-eating and cerulean warblers.

SOUTHEAST

Blue Rock State Forest

Seventy years ago very little wildlife and few trees survived here. Blue Rock State Forest reminds humanity that the land can heal, returning to its former grandeur.

LOCATION
Southern Muskingum County, Salt Creek and Blue Rock townships.

SIZE AND DESIGNATION
4,579 acres. An Ohio Watchable Wildlife Area.

ACCESS
To reach the forest headquarters follow Cutler Lake Road, which branches from SR 60 south of Duncan Falls. Trailhead parking is a quarter mile away on Forest Road 8.

Twenty-six miles of combined bridle and hiking trails wind through the woods and along state forest roads. Refer to the state forest guide and map. Note the thirteen parking spots throughout the grounds.

Accommodations: For camping go to Blue Rock State Park on Cutler Lake Road, or nearby private campgrounds.

Trails: My favorite route, and the most woodsy one, starts at the trailhead on Forest Road 8. Starting northwest, parallel to Cutler Lake Road, the path curves westerly to the junction of Forest Road 8 and Poverty Ridge Road. Follow the latter lane south about a mile, and re-enter the woods eastbound (look for the trail marker at a parking area). This path circles easterly toward the trailhead, but before you reach the start, take a southeast-heading trail that crosses Salt Creek and Cutler Lake Road. Here, the trail swings easterly and crosses Ridgeview Road, then it

hooks northwest and crosses Browning Road, then trends southwest to Cutler Lake Road, near Forest Road 8. You also can start this journey from the fire tower on Ridgeview Road.

Special Places & Events: Climb the fire tower at the picnic area on Ridgeview Road (branching from Cutler Lake Road). Legal hunting and trapping are allowed. The Zanesville Rifle Club manages a range on Sugar Grove Road (not on public land).

Information: Contact Blue Rock State Forest, 6665 Cutler Lake Road, Blue Rock, OH 43720-9740, (740) 674-4035.

HISTORY
Like Tar Hollow and Zaleski state forests, Blue Rock started as marginal farmland acquired by the federal government in the 1930s under the Resettlement Administration. Ownership was later transferred to the Ohio Division of Forestry, though the federal government retained three-fourths of the oil and gas rights. Reforestation, land management and erosion control practices transformed exhausted farmland into a beautiful and productive forest.

The Cutler Lake section was given to the newly created Division of Parks and Recreation in 1949. That parcel became Blue Rock State Park.

FIELD NOTES
Blue Rock has premium spring and fall colors, especially along Browning and Poverty Ridge roads. Besides turkeys, look for deer, warblers, grouse and salamanders in the woods.

The forest gets its name from the blue-colored shale found along the banks of the Muskingum River.

JOURNAL
A flock of tom turkeys, having gleaned a cornfield, assembled at the edge of a hardwood stand that marked the border of Blue Rock State Forest and a private farm. I paused on Cutler Lake Road and watched them enter the woods in single file, like a procession of penitent monks. The trailhead was a mile ahead, on a gravelly, washboard forest road. The sights and sounds of a new trail made me forget the turkeys. But just as I crowned a ridge, about half a mile from our last encounter, they scattered wildly, noisily, every tom for himself. They gobbled warnings from treetops, then one by one they melted away into cover.

Brush Creek State Forest

On a map, Brush Creek State Forest looks like wind-tossed leaves scattered on the ground. It comprises twenty separate patches strewn across the formidable hill country of Scioto and Adams counties. The trees are hardwoods, the land hard to manage.

LOCATION

Northwestern Scioto County, Rarden and Morgan townships; Northeastern Adams County, Franklin and Bratton townships.

SIZE AND DESIGNATION
12,610 acres.

ACCESS

The ranger station and bridle trail terminus is on SR 73 near the Scioto and Adams county line. This state forest comprises widely scattered tracts.

Accommodations: No camping is permitted in the state forest. Go to Pike Lake or Shawnee state parks, or a private campground.

Trails: The best route for hiker and rider is a bridle trail between the forest headquarters on SR 73 west of Rarden in Scioto County and a parking area on Coffee Hollow Road in Adams County, a linear distance of 6-7 miles. The trail forms a triangular loop at the Coffee Hollow Road terminus, which adds a mile to the journey. Park at either end of the trail, and be aware of deadend trails that stem from the main drag.

A shorter bridle trail, about four miles, loops around a tower off Fire Tower Road (also called Crabtree Cemetery Road in Scioto County). A 1.5-mile linear path for foot travelers runs off Douglas Road in Franklin Township, Adams County.

Hunting & Fishing: The people aimlessly roaming through the woods in spring, heads to the ground, are hunting for mushrooms. Folks also harvest nuts, ginseng, and berries here. Hunters will find deer, turkeys, grouse, and squirrels in the woods.

Information: Contact Brush Creek State Forest, 275 SR 73, Peebles, OH 45660-9592, (740) 372-3194.

HISTORY

Brush Creek State Forest sprouted in 1928 as a section of Shawnee State Forest. By the early 1950s it was detached from Shawnee and called Scioto Brush Creek State Forest. Additional purchases have raised the forest's size to more than 12,600 acres, making it the fourth largest state forest.

FIELD NOTES

Most of the forest consists of steep hillsides, deep hollows, and skinny ridges protecting the northern watershed of Scioto Brush Creek—an ideal location for hardwoods.

Dean State Forest

Dean State Forest commemorates the aptly named Forest W. Dean, whose survey of forests in southern Ohio in 1920 resulted in more land purchases for woodlands. This state forest can rightfully claim to be the father of the woods that surround it today—Wayne National Forest.

LOCATION

Western Lawrence County, Decatur Township.

SIZE AND DESIGNATION
2,745 acres.

ACCESS

SR 373 departs from SR 93 and winds through Dean State Forest before rejoining its parent highway. At the northernmost junction of SR 93 and SR 373 (north of Center Station) follow SR 373 south (east on a compass), then go easterly on Forest Road 1 to the headquarters. You'll find a small parking area on SR 373 (Howe Hollow Road) for the Periscope, Tar Kiln, School House and Pinkston trails.

Accommodations: No camping here. Lake Vesuvius Recreation Area, part of Wayne National Forest, is nearby.

Trails: Twenty miles of trails for horseback riders and hikers track through these furry hills. The Periscope, Tar Kiln, and Schoolhouse paths branch from the east side of SR 373, near a parking area for trail users. Across the road, a redesigned Pinkston Trail begins its loop through the southwest section of the parcel.

A connector trail from Long Hollow Road (Forest Road 2) into Wayne National Forest has been closed to protect an endangered plant. A path connecting the Tar Kiln and Periscope trails, shown on the state forest brochure, does not exist. Instead, follow Forest Road 1 to complete a loop. Easter Hollow Trail goes east from Long Hollow Road, and may be connected to the former trail to Wayne National Forest to create a loop.

Hunting & Fishing: One popular activity here is hunting for deer, wild turkey, grouse, squirrel and rabbits. Several small ponds are used by anglers. Mushroom and ginseng hunters find success here.

Information: Contact Dean State Forest, 149 Dean Forest Road, Pedro, OH 45659-9740, (740) 532-7228.

HISTORY

The first white settlers here were Pennsylvanians who traced their ancestry to Holland and Ireland. In the nineteenth century the original hardwood forest was logged for charcoal, the fuel for the region's iron blast furnaces. Later, fires started by sparks from the Cincinnati, Hamilton and Dayton Railroad kept the forest low and charred.

A parsimonious Ohio General Assembly let foresters at the Ohio Agricultural Experiment Station spend $10,000 for land in June 1916. One naked chunk, acquired for $4.50 an acre in Lawrence County, became Dean State Forest, then totaling 1,500 acres. A smaller tract, called Waterloo Forest, became the seed for Zaleski State Forest.

The denuded land became a reforestation laboratory after its purchase by the state in 1916. Foresters planted several species to find out which ones grew best in the region. The white pine, red pine, and tuliptree stands along SR 373 (Texas Hollow Road) are the products of those plantings. A Civilian Conservation Corps camp here built roads, improved timber stands, and designed trails in the 1930s. Today, Dean State Forest is an unbroken block of forested land.

FIELD NOTES

This is forested hill country with steep ravines recently ravaged by flash floods. Look for woodland warblers such as cerulean, prairie, yellow, black-and-white, worm-eating, and Kentucky, plus oven-bird and yellow chat.

Gifford State Forest

Gifford State Forest is a small rectangle of woods, 320 acres, offering small hiking and hunting pleasures. A master race of trees may rise from seeds born here.

LOCATION
Northeastern Athens County, Bern Township.

SIZE AND DESIGNATION
320 acres.

ACCESS
From Athens, travel east on SR 550 about 17 miles. In Sharpsburg, take SR 377, heading toward Chesterhill. In half a mile, forest roads on the left lead to picnic tables and trails. From McConnellsville, follow SR 377 south. There are two small parking areas on SR 377—one north of the main entrance, one south of it.

Accommodations: No camping is allowed within the forest. The forestry division manages part of Gifford as a seed farm. The guide states, "Trees planted here are genetically superior plants that produce superior seeds, which are made readily available to the citizens of Ohio for reforestation."

Trails: The Indian Stone and Vista loop trails,

totalling three miles, branch from the parking lot. The trails start just a few steps southwest of the small fishing pond. The Vista loop is the shorter loop. The trails are wide, easy to follow, and muddy when wet. Be prepared for long, steady climbs and descents. A side trail leads to a so-so overlook of pine plantations, and the intersection of state routes 377, 550 and 329. Horses are not allowed on these trails, though some riders do not yield to this prohibition. The state forest guide shows the trails.

Hunting & Fishing: Deer, grouse, rabbit, and squirrel collect here for hunters.

Special Places & Events: The forest guide indicates where experimental seed orchards have been planted. The species include black walnut, white pine, red oak, pitlolly pine, autumn olive, sweet gum, loblolly pine, black alder, cottonwood, and others.

The "Indian Stone" landmark is a sandstone outcrop at the head of a formerly scenic ravine. I say "formerly" because this northernmost portion of the state forest was recently clear cut. Indian Stone lacks a trail marker, but you will see it, after passing it, if you look back.

Information: Gifford State Forest, 17221 SR 377, Chesterhill, OH 43728-9604, (740) 554-3177.

HISTORY

In 1959 William Gifford Selby donated the tract to the state for experimentation and research. The name honors his mother, Virginia Gifford, and family members.

FIELD NOTES

The trail wanders past several charming and intriguing boulder-strewn ravines. Linger in these slits for wildflowers and mosses such as purple-stemmed cliffbrake and several kinds of spleenwort.

Gifford still shows the signs of coal mining and other abuses. Much of the location is land on the mend, however.

Hocking State Forest

The deeply cleaved gorges here are buttressed by 300-million-year-old sandstone walls and 300-year-old hemlocks. Trickling waterfalls echo in the shady ravines; pine trees flourish where corn once stood. The best way to see this inscrutable landscape, the largest public holding in the Hocking Hills, is on foot or hoof. The state forest and nature preserves enrich the attractions of the fabled state park.

LOCATION

Southern Hocking County, Laurel and Benton townships.

SIZE AND DESIGNATION

Hocking State Forest, 9,267 acres, has been designated an Ohio Watchable Wildlife Area.

ACCESS

Forest headquarters is located on SR 374, which zigzags between US 33 (at Rockbridge) and SR 56. Pick up a state forest map to reach other destinations in this checkerboard forest.

Accommodations: Horses and humans can bed down at the trail riders campground (23 primitive sites) on Keister Road. Others must use the campground at Hocking Hills State Park, or nearby private facilities.

Trails: The Buckeye Trail, the major foot path, runs north-south across the state forest and state park. Try the segment (blue blazes) from the rock climbing area on Big Pine Road to Old Man's Cave, Cedar Falls, and Ash Cave in Hocking Hills State Park.

Four color-coded bridle trails totaling forty miles twist inside the state forest and on township roads. Main trails have red, orange and purple blazes, while all side trails are green. The staging area is the horsemen's camp on Keister Road (TR 231) off SR 374. A separate bridle trail map (available from the forest headquarters) outlines the routes and distances between lettered landmarks. Hikers can also follow these trails.

Ninety-nine acres of forest on Big Pine Road, east of Conkle's Hollow State Natural Area, have been set aside for rock climbing and rappelling. Climbers must supply their own equipment. Climbing elsewhere on state-owned property is unlawful, and dangerous.

Hunting & Fishing: Hunting, trapping and fishing are permitted. Outdoorsmen should get a state forest map to avoid trespassing on private land and nature preserves. State forest property is marked by yellow signs, or yellow blazes on trees. White or red marks show the borders of nature preserves, which prohibit hunting, trapping and fishing.

Information: Hocking State Forest, 19275 SR 374, Rockbridge, OH 43149-9749, (740) 385-4402.

HISTORY

The Division of Forestry's predecessor, the Ohio Agricultural Experiment Station, began purchasing tracts in Hocking County in 1924. Since then, worn out farmland has nursed tree seedlings into a mature forest, erosion has been checked, and DOF management plans have refreshed the land. Uncontrolled logging was banned, and replaced with regulations that assure that the harvest does not exceed the rate of tree growth.

During the Depression, relief workers built trails, planted trees, developed recreation facilities, and made roads. Hocking State Forest provided the seed land for the state park and three nature preserves. The state forest is also managed for wildlife. For example, released beaver and wild turkey stayed, and deer returned.

FIELD NOTES

The Division of Forestry's brochure notes that "One of the special attractions of Hocking State Forest is the natural vegetation. Plant species commonly found farther north mix with typically southern species to provide an unusual variety of native plant life and associated wildlife.

"Virginia and pitch pines, sassafras, and black, scarlet, white and chestnut oaks grow on the generally dry ridge areas. Hemlock, beech, black birch, red and sugar maples, yellow poplar, white ash, red oak, basswood and hickories grow in cool gorges, moist coves and on slopes. Flowers, shrubs and ferns commonly associated with these site conditions also abound.

"Plantations of red, white and shortleaf pines have developed from plantings of seedlings on abandoned farm fields. These stands of native and planted pines often indicate where corn and wheat once grew on subsistence farms in the 19th and early 20th centuries." Some old growth trees in the forest are believed to be 400 to 500 years old.

Birds congregate in large numbers in the region. Keen eyes should look for the veery, hermit thrush, Blackburnian warbler, solitary vireo, and brown creeper which have stretched their range to include the Hocking Hills. At night, listen for the whippoorwill and barred owl. Warblers and hawks reward birders during spring and autumn migrations.

Though the most impressive geological landmarks reside in the state park and nature preserves, the state forest still claims enchanting ravines, and secret waterfalls.

Perry State Forest

Perry State Forest boasts popular trails for all-terrain vehicles—sixteen miles of track across hilly land stripped of its trees and coal. There are quieter, less celebrated trails for humans and horses, too.

LOCATION

Perry County, Clayton Township.

SIZE AND DESIGNATION

4,579 acres.

Second forest hardwood produced miles of veneers.

ACCESS

From New Lexington, head north four miles on SR 345 to Rehobeth, then go west (left) on CR 48 to the parking area beside Miles Lake for hiking and bridle trails. About 1.5 miles farther north on SR 345, turn left on TR 154 to reach the parking lot for all-purpose vehicle users.

Trails: Mountain bikes, motorcycles, and all-terrain vehicles (less than 40 horsepower and 48 inches in width) have eight color-coded trails to ride. The state forest guide shows the trail system and prints the rules for operation. Vehicles are allowed on these trails April through November, and latrines and picnic tables are present then. Hikers, hunters most, walk on the trails in winter.

Hikers and horsebacker riders will have better experiences on the eight-mile, double-loop bridle trail at Miles Lake. The perimeter loop is roughly six miles. There is ample parking beside Miles Lake, and a couple of pull-over spots west of the lake, near the trail head. Horses can drink the water in Miles Lake, but neither hikers nor horses can stay overnight.

Hunting & Fishing: Hunting and trapping are permitted. However, Miles Lake, Lake Buckeye and Lake Essington will disappoint most serious anglers.

Information: Contact Blue Rock State Forest, 6665 Cutler Lake Road, Blue Rock, OH 43720-9740, (740) 674-4035.

HISTORY

This barren, torn up land looked like it had been in a brawl when the state got it in 1961. Reforestation is greening it up, albeit slowly.

FIELD NOTES

This is land on the mend, so don't expect extravagant forests. Note instead the reforestation effort, particularly the Global ReLeaf Heritage Forest planted beside Miles Lake in 1994.

The bridle trail section south of CR 48 is the most rewarding in the state forest.

Pike State Forest

Autumn here is as good as it ever gets in Vermont, but closer to home. A section of Zane's Trace, a pioneer trail, courses over these ridges.

LOCATION

Northwestern Pike County, Mifflin, Perry, Benton townships.

SIZE AND DESIGNATION

11,960 acres.

ACCESS

The forest headquarters is located on Lapparell Road, just off SR 124 in Latham. The trails for all-purpose vehicle users lie several miles west of the ranger station on SR 124. To reach parking areas for bridle and hiking trails, travel east from Latham on SR

124, north on Morgans Fork Road, left on Auerville Road in Morgantown.

Accommodations: Pike State Park is one of the author's favorite campsites.

Trails: Thirty miles of interconnecting and underrated trails for riders and hikers wander through the state forest. Horseback riders have three starting points: Auerville Road, a mile west of Morgantown; at the end of a gravel road off Auerville Road, two miles west of Morgantown; and atop a hill on Greenbriar Ridge Road, which branches north from Auerville Road a mile or so west of Morgantown. Hikers can access trails from these spots, or in Pike State Park. The trail through Tobacco Barn Hollow, and the loops branching from it like butterfly wings, are especially rewarding.

The Buckeye Trail crosses through the state forest and state park along a northeast-southwest axis. The historic segment between Auerville Road and the Kincaid Fish Hatchery on SR 124 overlaps Zane's Trace, the overland trail marked by Ebenezer Zane in 1797. (Trail riders on the Buckeye Trail are encouraged to follow the side trail that loops around the state park.) The state forest brochure shows the direction of trails and parking places.

On a separate tract of land, about two miles east of Sinking Spring on SR 124, trail bikers, all-terrain vehicle (ATV) drivers, and mountain bikers, can play on 15 miles of trails. The ATV trails are closed December through March.

Hunting & Fishing: Hunters and trappers can pursue their favorite game animals here, and mushroom gathering is becoming more popular. Fishers looking for a quiet, secluded spot should try Anderson Lake (a pond really) off Dry Bone Road. The location is starred on the forest map. The roads through the forest will bring joy, but they aren't joy rides for the driver. Be ready for winding, slanting, rocky, narrow, corrugated, muffler-scraping dirt roads. Don't take low-riding RVs on these difficult passages.

Information: Available by contacting Pike State Forest, 334 Lapparell Road, Latham, OH 45646-9722, (740) 493-2441.

HISTORY

Check out the Eager Inn at the intersection of Morgantown and Pike Lake roads. It is one of the first hostelries built on Zane's Trace, which brought settlers to this area around the turn of the nineteenth century. The stretch of the Buckeye Trail from Auerville Road to SR 124 is as close as you can get to reliving a walk on the actual trace. Between Chillicothe and Aberdeen, Ebenezer Zane followed a military path blazed earlier by Kentuckians on a revenge raid against Shawandase. During the Civil War, Zane's old road served Confederate raiders commanded by John Hunt Morgan. The remains of an unknown Union soldier supposedly killed in a skirmish with Morgan rests beside Pike Lake in the state park.

Land purchases for the state forest started in 1924.

Much of the area was used-up hill farms and fire-damaged timber stands. Civilian Conservation Corps laborers reforested the slopes, and constructed recreation facilities for what became Pike Lake State Park. Today, the state forest comprises 13 separate tracts.

FIELD NOTES

Birdwatchers stay alert for woodland species—pileated woodpeckers, white-eyed vireo, worm-eating warbler, American redstart, among others. Barred owls are heard at night in the state park campground and sometimes whip-poor-wills. I have spotted a scarlet tanager near the abandoned fire tower. Also, go to Latham and visit the 30 ponds at the Kincaid fish hatchery, where the Division of Wildlife raises muskellunge and steelhead trout. Look for waterfowl and shorebirds.

JOURNAL

I remember most the first of many trips to this neck of the Ohio woods. It was May, and trillium, dogwood, and other wildflowers speckled the slopes. The birdsong was as loud and busy and diverse as any Manhattan marketplace. It is enchanting here in the summer too, especially tramping on old Zane's Trace, now the route of the Buckeye Trail.

Richland Furnace State Forest

Nature knows not retribution. It simply spreads a green garment to heal the wounds, and hide the scars of Ohio's first smokestack industry. The iron furnace at Richland, idle for more than a century, crumbles like a Mayan temple under the weight of the chlorophyll.

LOCATION
Northeastern Jackson County, Washington Township.

SIZE AND DESIGNATION
2,448 acres.

ACCESS
Take SR 327 from Wellston, turn right on CR 32 (Loop Road). Bear left at the fork, and park in the lot for all-purpose vehicle users. SR 327 crosses other blocks of forest land, but there are no "official" parking spots.

Accommodations: There is no camping available on forest land.

Trails: Nine miles of woodland trails (orange blazes) are designed for APVs, though hikers can use the trails too. APVs include cross-country motor-cycles and all-terrains vehicles, or "quads," less than 40 horsepower and 48 inches wide, and mountain bikes. Motorized vehicles must display a valid APV license.

Hunting & Fishing: Hunting and trapping are permitted.

Information: Available from Zaleski State Forest, P.O. Box 330, Zaleski, OH 45698-0330, (740) 596-5781.

HISTORY

During the 19th century, Richland was a bustling company town in the heart of the Hanging Rock Iron District, the second largest producer of iron ore in the nation. Today, it's a busted ghost town. The stony ruin of the iron furnace (north of the state forest on TR 6) reminds us of those halcyon days of temporary prosperity.

The good old "iron" days was a holocaust for the oak-hickory forest. While miners dug out iron ore under layers of sandstone and limestone, loggers mowed down trees for charcoal for Richland Furnace. Several old ore pits can be seen on state forest ridges.

Land for Richland Furnace State Forest was acquired between 1945 and 1950.

The harder they fall

FIELD NOTES

The Division of Forestry explains Richland's rebound this way. "The oak-hickory forest vegetation that currently exists on Richland Furnace State Forest is a direct result of the past land use. During the iron era all the vegetation was removed (clearcut) for the production of charcoal. This allowed for direct sunlight to reach the forest floor and regenerate species that require full sunlight to reproduce, such as the oaks. After areas were logged for charcoal, the remaining slash was allowed to burn repeatedly. Wildfires were common and were not of concern unless they threatened human health or safety. Because of this, the thinly barked trees were eliminated from the regenerating forests, which allowed the present day thicker barked oak-hickory stands to develop.

"The railroad on the north and east sides of

the forest also played a significant role in the present day composition and condition of the forest. Before the 1950s railroad engines did not have spark arrestors. As a result, during the spring and fall, railroad-ignited forest fires were very common and damaged many trees. Today, many of the taller trees at Richland Furnace State Forest are of poor health or low vigor. The Division of Forestry is nurturing these stands back to health. Silvicultural treatments employed include removal of unhealthy individual trees through selective harvests, to the reestablishment of an entire stand through regeneration harvests. The result is a healthier forest for future generations."

Scioto Trail State Forest

The state forest is a green, hilly refuge wedged between the Scioto River corridor shared by the river, a rail, and a road, and Route 23, which tracks an old Indian route known as the Scioto Trail. This overlooked spot surrounds a quiet state park, and features fine trails for feet, horses and bikes.

LOCATION

Southeastern Ross County, Franklin and Huntington townships.

SIZE AND DESIGNATION

Scioto Trail State Forest encompasses 9,390 acres, and is an Ohio Watchable Wildlife Area.

ACCESS

From US 23 south of Chillicothe, take SR 327 to

the ranger station beside the fire tower. Straight ahead, Stoney Creek Road (Forest Road 1) leads to trails and the state park campground.

Accommodations: Scioto Trail State Park has 57 sites (20 with electric) at Caldwell Lake; and primitive sites at Stewart Lake.

Trails: Twenty-seven miles of trails for hikers, horses, and mountain bikers, illustrated on the state forest guide, wind through the woodlands. The Buckeye and American Discovery trails go through the forest, too. The trails here are well-designed, and well-marked and do not match the severe topography of the landscape.

Long-distance trekkers should try the Long Branch Trail. Best place to start is from a tiny parking spot on North Ridge Road (Forest Road 2) about 200 yards north of Stoney Creek Road (Forest Road 1). Follow the blue blazes of the Buckeye Trail east a short distance to a T junction. The Long Branch Trail heads northwest (left), the Buckeye Trail goes south (right). Long Branch Trail goes northwest/north several miles. At the intersection with another bridle path, bear right, staying northbound. (Remember this junction because you will take the southwesterly route home.)

After crossing Moss Hollow Road (TR 196) you will reach the southern tip of a double loop trail. From here, whichever way you go, you can hike, bike, or ride the perimeter loop, one or the other loop, or a figure-8. Homeward, recross Moss Hollow Road, and at the next intersection take the right fork (southwest) to North Ridge Road. Go southeast (left) on the road a mile, then south (right) on a bridle trail, and east (left) on the Buckeye Trail to the car. Take water and snacks.

Hunting & Fishing: Hunting, trapping, horseback riding, and mushroom gathering are permitted.

Special Places & Events: The fire tower is always a treat for people who like heights. It is located beside the forest office, near the US 23 entrance. The view is obscured by trees now matching the height of the lookout. But this benefits birders seeking an eye level peek at feathered minstrels.

A Mountain Bike Family Campout is held each summer to encourage this activity.

Information: Scioto Trail State Forest, 124 North Ridge Road, Waverly, OH 45690-9513, (740) 663-2523.

HISTORY

The hills now occupied by the state forest served as hunting grounds for the ancient moundbuilders and Shawandase people who established a large settlement at Chillicothe. The warrior path known as the Scioto Trail ran to the Ohio River, and points north.

The site was an artillery range during World War I. Six-inch howitzers and 75-millimeter guns from nearby Camp Sherman fired from the mouth of Stoney Creek (intersection of Stoney Creek and Three Locks roads) at targets near the state park lakes.

The state purchased this bombed-out and burned-out place from 1922 to 1937. The first 9,000 acres went for an average of $7.70 an acre. The roads, lakes, and recreational facilities were developed by the Civilian Conservation Corps in the 1930s.

FIELD NOTES

Scioto Trail is a bonanza for spring blossoms and morel mushrooms, especially along North Ridge and South Ridge roads. Look for blooming dogwoods and redbuds, Dutchman's breeches, wild geranium, white trillium, and blue phlox. Come back in the fall for the hardwood fireworks display. The forest has 35 species of trees.

This is good habitat for woodland birds. Look for arriving warblers—notably the ovenbird, blue-winged, northern parula, cerulean, Kentucky, worm-eating and hooded—as you admire the wildflowers. Other nesters are scarlet tanager, flycatchers, vireos, Louisiana waterthrush, and Eastern pewee.

Deer, turkey, and grouse test hunters. Occasionally, an endangered bobcat or a black bear is spotted. The raccoon, red fox, gray squirrel, opossum, and skunk also prowl the grounds.

Shade River State Forest

Nineteenth century iron furnaces used up the old growth hardwoods that once presided above Forked Run near this state forest. Today, planted pines named white, red, loblolly, Virginia, shortleaf, and pitch provide most of the "shade" in this forest. Native oaks and hickories are returning, and colonies of hemlock and mountain laurel linger in secret gorges.

LOCATION
Northeastern Meigs County, Olive Township.

SIZE & DESIGNATION
2, 475 acres.

ACCESS
Shade River State Forest, comprised of four tracts and attached Forked Run State Park are wedged among state routes 248, 124 and 681. Parking areas are found on township roads 265, 270 and 277, forest roads 5 (off TR 272), 4 (off TR 276), and 10 (off CR 46). To reach the few parking spots, take TR 277 north from SR 124, and TR 265 off SR 248 and CR 46.

Accomodations: Camping is available at Forked Run State Park, which also offers boating, swimming, fishing and picnicking opportunities.

Trails: There is just one hiking trail in the state forest, a mile long loop on TR 277, south of the intersection with TR 265. However, hunters, trappers, berry pickers, nut gatherers, mushroom collectors, and ordinary sightseers can freely roam in the woods. Forked Run State Park also has footpaths.

Information: contact either Gifford State Forest or Forked Run State Park, P.O. Box 127, Reedsville, OH 45772-0127, (740) 378-6206.

HISTORY

Although the state forest shelters the watershed of Forked Run, it derives its name from the Shade River that curls across Meigs County and joins the Ohio River at Long Bottom. Captured white settlers knew the dark, rocky mouth of the Shade River as Devil's Hole because Indians crossed the Ohio River here after raids into Virginia. To them, walking through Shade River gorge was akin to hiking in Hell.

At the height of the Industrial Revolution in the late nineteenth century, coal mining, iron blasting, and salt furnaces brought brief prosperity to the region. To the forest, the Industrial Revolution was

Hell. In the early 1950s, pines were planted on abandoned fields, and a chunk of land was transformed into a state park.

FIELD NOTES

The forest and state park serve up plenty of wildflowers, blossoming trees, and critters. Dogwoods and redbuds sprinkle color on drab slopes in late April. These are followed by wildflowers such as blue phlox, dame's rocket, spring beauty, cardinal flower, fleabane, and aster. The cast of quadrupeds includes raccoon, opossum, gray squirrel, deer, and gray fox. Turkey and grouse head the list of game birds. The whippoorwill, scarlet tanager, wood thrush, and pileated woodpecker reside here, too.

Shawnee State Forest

No wonder Shawnee is called The Little Smokies. It is as close as Ohio gets to having a wilderness, though less than a

Old
Flame

Last of the Red Hot Spotters

In 1978, Marian Sanders' final descent from Green Ridge Tower in Pike State Forest marked the end of an era. She was Ohio's last fire tower spotter.

Armed with equipment considered crude today—maps, binoculars, an alidade, telephone, and radio—Sanders surveyed the countryside for telltale signs of smoke. For six years, climbing the towers at Scioto Trail and Pike state forests was a daily activity during the fire-prone months of March, April, May, October and November. In a 1982 interview she said that her hours in the towers gave her a "quiet closeness with nature." Her favorite month was October, when nature's autumn plummage danced in brilliant warm colors. Pro-

tecting the woods also made her feel important and accomplished.

Some days an epidemic of fires kept her busy on the radio or telephone. High winds and thunderstorms shook the tower and sent shivers up her back. Spotters were sitting ducks for lightning. Sometimes they had to sit tight in the observation deck until the storm passed.

"You had to hang on for dear life when the wind whipped up during a storm. It wasn't the kind of job for someone afraid of heights, either," she said.

Today Sanders stays more down to earth, as a secretary in the division's district office in Chillicothe.

—SO

century ago the angled slopes lay barren from logging and fire. Recovery has been swift. Today, you can get lost—actually, figuratively, and willingly—in Shawnee's scrunched terrain. The state's toughest, loneliest, and orneriest trails snake through the hills and hollows. If you wander off the path, and stumble into dark hollows called Dead Man's or Cut Lip, you might run into a timber rattler, or a black bear, or a backpacker who looks like one of those creatures.

LOCATION

Southwestern Scioto County, Nile, Union and Brush Creek townships; Southeastern Adams County, Green Township.

SIZE AND DESIGNATION

At 62,502 acres, Shawnee is the largest state forest in Ohio. It also is a Watchable Wildlife Area and boasts the state's only wilderness area. The designation protects the 8,000-acre location from logging and development.

ACCESS

SR 125, branching from US 52 in Friendship, bisects the state forest. The Panoramic Scenic Drive, Shawnee State Park, and most trails stem from this state highway. Backpackers will find parking at the intersection of SR 125 and the road to the state park lodge. To reach the horse camp from SR 125, follow Forest Road 1 (Shawnee Road) and Forest Road 4 (Bear Lake Road). Forest Road 6 (Copperhead Road) branches from Forest Road 4 to the Copperhead fire tower. Get a map at the state forest headquarters on US 52, a half mile east of SR 125, before exploring.

Accommodations: See specific trail descriptions. Also, Shawnee State Park offers more than 100 campsites (electric, showers, toilets) at Roosevelt Lake, plus vacation cabins and rooms at the resort lodge.

Trails: Shawnee has 142 trail miles, more than any state forest. Although the 60-mile backpack trail gets most of the acclaim, hikers and horses share 75 miles, some of it in the wilderness area. Trails are shown on the state forest guide, a must for each trail user.

The backpack trail system (foot travelers only) has been carefully reproduced on a topographical map in the state forest guide. Lettered points and distances on the map help hikers plan their journey, which can last six to eight days. Eight primitive campsites are spaced along the route. Each has a privy, and all but Camp 6 has drinking water nearby

(within a mile). (Camp 7, not shown on the map, is a little west of Point T.) Consider the entire network to be strenuous.

Some sections of the trail—between intersections with forest roads, for instance—provide great day hikes. Some forest roads have small pull-offs near these intersections for day trippers. Rely on the forest guide and discover your own day-hike segments.

The official staging area for backpackers is the parking lot at the intersection of SR 125 and the road to Shawnee State Park lodge. Register at the kiosk and grab a map for each hiker. The North Loop (Point A) begins on the other side of SR 125. The South Loop starts near the swimming beach, a quarter mile down the park road, and takes a well-worn, southwesterly route. Backpackers with small children might consider this path to Camp 8, about 6.5 miles. The first 4.5 miles (points A to R) is considered moderate by Shawnee standards. Hikers also can park at the Civilian Conservation Corps Camp on Pond Lick Road, and pick up the main trail at the western tip of Pond Lick Lake (Point J). Camp 4 is less than a mile northwest bound, and Camp 5 is five miles south. You also can start at Camp Oyo, a Boy Scout Reservation, located on Forest Road 1 off SR 125 near Point H. Just after making the turn, look for the parking lot on the left, and the scout camp on the right side.

Camp Oyo is also the trailhead of a 14-mile loop called the Silver Arrow Trail, Shawnee's first backpack trail built by scouts in the 1960s. The eastern arm of the Silver Arrow (also a bridle path) meets the North Loop a little east of Camp 1. Overnight hikers on the Silver Arrow should register at the backpackers kiosk near Point A before departing. The Silver Arrow route is shown on the state forest guide.

Horseback riders congregate at the 58-site Bear Lake Horse Camp, equipped with tie-up posts, drinking water for human and horse, and rest rooms. Hikers cannot camp here, but they can walk on any bridle trail in the state forest. Several horse trails converge at Bear Lake, including the Silver Arrow. The Cabbage Patch Bridle Trail leaves Sunshine Ridge Road (Adams County) for destinations in the Shawnee Wilderness Area. A popular day ride is the Mackletree Trail between the Roosevelt Lake state park beach and the Panoramic Drive. Riders should not overlook nearly 100 miles of scenic forest roads.

The Panoram Scenic Loop Drive is the only "official" auto trail in the state forest system. Be ready for a roller coaster ride into The Little Smokies. The 25-mile gravel route begins at Pond Lick Road (also Forest Road 1) off SR 125, several miles east of Roosevelt Lake. You can also take Panoram Road (Forest Road 2) from US 52, near the state park marina. Stop at Picnic Point for refreshments and the view of the Ohio River Valley. Set aside an hour for the journey.

Hunting & Fishing: Hunting, fishing, trapping, and mushroom collecting are permitted in these woods. Most fishing occurs at four ponds created by Depression-era dams. Turkey Creek Lake, and Roosevelt Lake are in the state park along SR 125.

Bear Lake is near the horse camp, while Pond Lick Lake lies beside the CCC camp. And don't forget the Ohio River as a source of angling adventure.

Special Places & Events: For another great panoramic view, drive to Copperhead Fire Tower on Forest Road 6, near the horseman's campground. Golf and boating also are available at the state park.

Information: Contact Shawnee State Forest, 13291 US 52, Portsmouth, OH 45663-8906, (740) 858-6685.

HISTORY

In the eighteenth century, Native Americans who called themselves Shaawanwaaki, meaning "people from the South," established a major settlement at the confluence of the Scioto and Ohio rivers, the site of Portsmouth today. The forested hills west of the village, the state forest land, was an abundant hunting ground with black bear, beaver, wolf, river otter, wild turkey, and deer. Warriors scouted the river from these heights. White settlers shortened the tribe's name to Shawnee, which became the forest's namesake.

After destroying the Indians, the pioneers took on the wilderness. Shawnee's forests soon fed the furnaces of the Industrial Revolution. Building stone was removed from Vastine and Cabbage Patch hollows (in the wilderness area) during this time. Railroad cars lugged the rock to the Ohio River where it was loaded on barges for destinations such as Cincinnati. By the dawn of the twentieth century, the slopes had been cleared, burned, and abandoned. Shawnee State Forest started in 1922 when the state purchased 5,000 acres for reforestation, and another tract for what became the Theodore Roosevelt Game Preserve. Roosevelt Lake honors Teddy Roosevelt, not Franklin Roosevelt. Six Civilian Conservation Corps camps were located here in the 1930s.

In 1949, portions of forest along SR 125 were transferred to the Division of Parks and Recreation for Shawnee State Park. Scouts built the Silver Arrow Trail from Camp Oyo in the 1960s. Construction of the backpack trail was finished in 1974. The wilderness area was designated that year. In 1981, arson charred 500-acres between Camp 8 and Point R on the backpack trail.

FIELD NOTES

Black bears have been seen in Shawnee, and the secretive and endangered bobcat resides here. For deep woods songbirds Shawnee's unbroken vastness is a paradise. However, clear-cut logging, a practice akin to strip-mining, punctures the sublimity, harms neotropical birds, and stirs heated debate. Birders find rewards year-round, as upward to 100 species have been recorded. Rarities include the golden-winged warbler, long-eared owl, and fox sparrow. Orioles and eastern meadowlarks hang out in overgrown fields.

Several kinds of oak and hickory occupy the ridges along with red and sugar maple, sassafras, basswood, tuliptree, buckeye, black gum, white ash, red elm, hackberry and aspen. Sweet gum, beech, black cherry, black walnut, sycamore, birch, cottonwood, and butternut (rare) stand in the bottomlands. Pines (red, white, shortleaf, and pitch) and hemlocks also survive.

Shawnee has dazzling fireworks displays of spring wildflowers—find the showy orchis and tiny whorled pogonia—and autumn leaves.

The Division of Forestry practices both selective and clearcut (or regeneration cutting) logging in Shawnee. Selective harvesting means individual trees or small colonies are taken to poke holes in the forest canopy. Trees that thrive in shady environments, such as beech and sugar maple, benefit from this strategy. Forest integrity is generally unchanged from selective cuts.

Clearcutting removes all trees in a large prescribed area. This enables light to reach sun-soaking species, such as white oak, white ash, and tuliptree. Critics argue that clearcutting ruins the forest ecology of the location, adds stress to adjacent stands, and reduces forest diversity. Whereas deer, grouse, and some songbirds benefit from clearcuts, deep woods mammals and birds survive better with selective cuts.

JOURNAL

When fog sleeps thick and low in the Ohio River Valley, Shawnee's furry ridges resemble a pack of humpbacked sea creatures cresting at the surface of an ocean of clouds.

Sunfish Creek State Forest

Sunfish Creek State Forest does not straddle its namesake, which empties into the Ohio River at Clarington, four miles south. Names aside, the highlands here become stages to view the curvy Ohio River, circling turkey vultures, and soaring hawks. Don't let the lack of human comforts forestall a visit.

LOCATION

Northeastern Monroe County, Salem and Switzerland townships.

SIZE AND DESIGNATION

637 acres.

ACCESS

On SR 7 between Clarington and Powhatan Point.

Trails: There are no formal hiking trails or campsites here. Hunters and trappers bushwhack or follow game trails. Views of the Ohio River are available from forested elevations.

Information: Contact Gifford State Forest (see page 246).

FIELD NOTES

Hawks and buzzards gracefully glide on the heights above the Ohio River. Phoebes nest along Blair Run, and the woods caters to both the yellow-billed and black-billed cuckoos.

Tar Hollow State Forest

Overlooked by Hocking Hills–bound travelers, Tar Hollow remains off the beaten track, but we're not complaining. The small, no-frills state park within the forest discourages luxury campers and boaters, so that leaves the steep, thickly wooded place largely to hikers, hunters, horseback riders, and "flexible" campers.

LOCATION

Eastern Ross County, Colerain and Harrison townships; Northwestern Vinton County, Eagle Township; Southwestern Hocking County, Salt Creek Township.

SIZE AND DESIGNATION

Tar Hollow State Forest, an Ohio Watchable Wildlife Area, totals 16,120 acres.

ACCESS

SR 327 runs along the eastern border of the state forest. From SR 327, take Clark Hollow Road (Forest Road 2) to the headquarters and fire tower; Poe Run Road (Forest Road 8) to the horse camp; Forest Road 10 to the state park. From Chillicothe, follow the Charleston Pike to Tucson, then Piney

State Nurseries

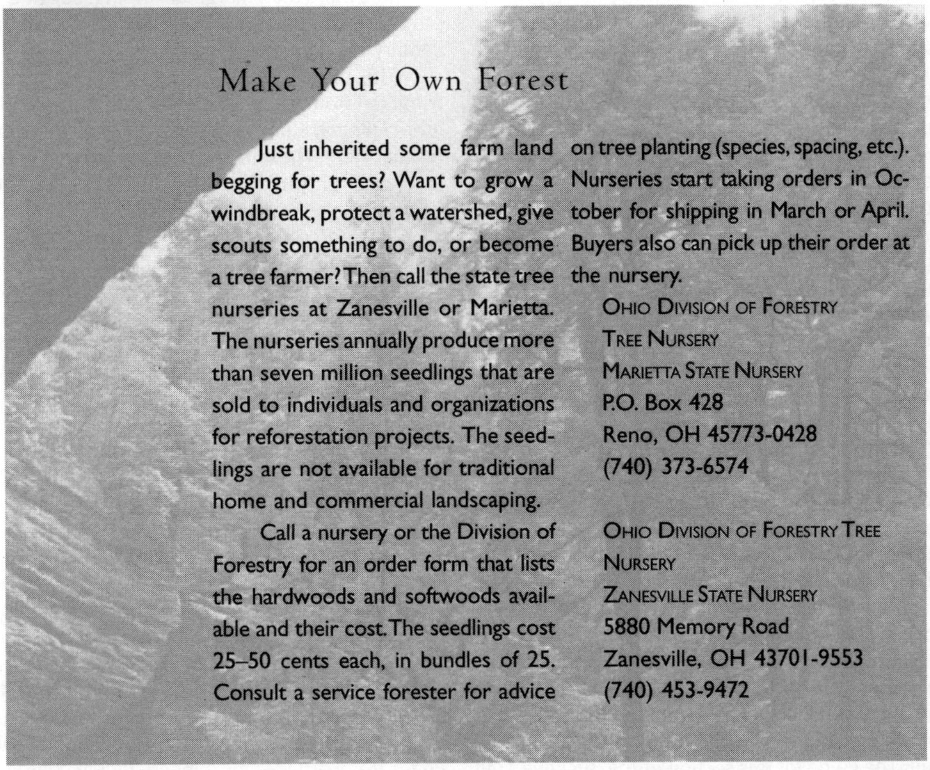

Make Your Own Forest

Just inherited some farm land begging for trees? Want to grow a windbreak, protect a watershed, give scouts something to do, or become a tree farmer? Then call the state tree nurseries at Zanesville or Marietta. The nurseries annually produce more than seven million seedlings that are sold to individuals and organizations for reforestation projects. The seedlings are not available for traditional home and commercial landscaping.

Call a nursery or the Division of Forestry for an order form that lists the hardwoods and softwoods available and their cost. The seedlings cost 25–50 cents each, in bundles of 25. Consult a service forester for advice on tree planting (species, spacing, etc.). Nurseries start taking orders in October for shipping in March or April. Buyers also can pick up their order at the nursery.

OHIO DIVISION OF FORESTRY
TREE NURSERY
MARIETTA STATE NURSERY
P.O. Box 428
Reno, OH 45773-0428
(740) 373-6574

OHIO DIVISION OF FORESTRY TREE
NURSERY
ZANESVILLE STATE NURSERY
5880 Memory Road
Zanesville, OH 43701-9553
(740) 453-9472

Creek Road to the ranger substation.

Accommodations: Trail riders can camp at the 50-site, primitive horse camp, scouts at Camp Dulen with permission, backpackers and others must sleep in the state park or at a nearby private campground.

Trails: The Chief Logan Trail is the chief hiking trail. It is a strenuous, steep, ankle-twisting path not meant for hikers out-of-shape, out-of-breath, nor out-of-mind. It measures nearly 23 miles, but thoughtful trail designers divided it into north and south loops, so the adventure can span two days.

Boy Scout Troop 195 in Columbus blazed the trail and named it after Mingo Indian Chief Logan. The original 1958 trail followed forest roads, but it was reconfigured through the woods in 1965. The scouts still maintain the trail with red blazes, signs, and checkpoints. Each loop has named segments, or trail legs, such as the grueling Hocking Segment at the start of the North Loop, or the Vinton Segment on the South Loop. The segments give hikers their bearings and make the walk memorable.

The trailhead is in Tar Hollow State Park, in the parking area for the Pine Lake Picnic Area below the dam. The conventional route, the North Loop, starts at the southeast corner of the lot, and goes across the park road and takes a sharp ascent—the notorious Hocking Segment, so-named because this leg is in Hocking County. (Scout discipline must have dictated the "one-way" orientation of the Chief Logan Trail for the red blazes are painted only on one side of marked trees. Still, fit hikers preferring to go against the grain—to avoid noisy groups departing ahead of them or the state park campground—should have no trouble following the trail the wrong way.)

The North Loop meanders twelve miles, over segments called Hocking, Ross, Sawmill, Lookout, Slickaway Hollow, Fire Tower, and Pine Lake (a.k.a. Brush Ridge Trail). The South Loop goes ten miles with segments named Butcher, Tucson, Powerline, and Vinton. Add two miles if you take the Camp Dulen side trail off the South Loop. The loops pinch to a narrow waistline at the Brush Ridge Fire Tower, roughly the midpoint of the entire hourglass trail system. The fire tower has a picnic area and toilets, and can serve as a day-use trailhead, especially for the South Loop. The state park campground is just a few miles from the tower.

The state forest map shows the Logan Trail, but it does not distinguish the loops nor label the segments and Dulen Trail. Officially, the trail to Camp Dulen (off the Powerline Segment) is reserved for scouts on overnight hikes. Scouts should check in at the ranger station first.

The Buckeye Trail (blue blazes) takes a jacknife-shaped route through Tar Hollow. From SR 327 it follows Clark Hollow Road past the ranger station, then goes on the Vinton Section of the Logan Trail to the fire tower. Here it veers south to Blue Lick Road and points beyond. Hikers and trail riders can use the trail. The guide for this section of the Buckeye Trail says backpackers can tent at Camp Dulen.

Thirty-three miles of trails radiate from the 50-site, primitive horse camp on Poe Run Road (Forest Road 8). The camp has water for horses, hitching posts, and latrines. Drinking water and electricity are not available. Trails are marked with white blazes and outlined on the forest guide. Riders also have 15 miles of forest roads at their disposal, with departures from the fire tower and the picnic area on Forest Road 3 south of the powerline. While horses cannot travel on the Logan Trail, humans on foot can hike on the bridle trails.

Hunting & Fishing: Deer, squirrels, turkey and grouse await and elude hunters. Some 1,700 acres in Coey Hollow (northwestern chunk) is a special ruffed grouse management area. The Ohio Division of Wildlife and Ruffed Grouse Society are participating in the habitat restoration project.

Special Places & Events: Brush Ridge Fire Tower is climbable—a hundred steps to the top—and offers panoramic views of the landscape. It's a great spot for an autumn picnic.

Information: Tar Hollow State Forest, Route 1, Box 387, Londonderry, OH 45647-9632, (740) 887-3879.

History

The Hopewell and Shawandase people who established large settlements at today's Chillicothe considered these steep, forested hills as hunting grounds. White settlers came late to this spot, largely because the land was too rugged and the soil too thin for much more than marginal farming. Logging was profitable for awhile but by the early twentieth century the hills were bald.

The place gets its name from the pitch tar extracted from local pine trees and processed into lubricants and elixirs. Pitch was not the only product distilled here. The hills and hollows hid stills making "moonshine," which local producers boasted "stuck to yer ribs like tar."

Like Zaleski and Blue Rock state forests, Tar Hollow is a Depression delight. During the 1930s, marginal farmland was purchased by the federal government for recreation, reforestation, and erosion control projects. Displaced farmers (in some cases, squatters) were resettled, and relief workers under the Civilian Conservation Corps toiled on roads, dams, buildings, bridges, and planting trees. Tar Hollow State Forest, and the state park, grew from this conservation effort.

Field Notes

Tar Hollow is known statewide for its great hunting, but on the last Saturday in April, a different brand of hunters gathers there. They comb the slopes unarmed, toting sacks, eyes searching the leaf litter for the most elusive and tastiest morsels in the forest—morel mushrooms. They come from all points of Ohio, and beyond, for the annual mushroom hunt. The rules are simple. Whoever gets the most *edible* morels wins. Prizes are awarded to the winners, though a basketful of plump morels constitutes the richest reward.

Autumn's palette has no inhibitions here. Spring brings forest flora to the forefront, and hundreds of morel mavens.

Zaleski State Forest

Say "Zaleski" to a devoted Ohio back-packer, and watch a grin form. Then the eyes wander wistfully away. You get the same reaction hearing a mother's lullaby, or smelling the neighbor's barbecue, or whispering "Monte Carlo" into the ear of a high roller.

LOCATION
Northeastern Vinton County, Brown, Madison, Elk and Knox townships; Athens County, Waterloo and York townships.

SIZE AND DESIGNATION
26,824 acres.

ACCESS
SR 278 splits the state forest. The headquarters and sawmill is on SR 278, a few miles north of Zaleski, and the backpackers' parking area is off the highway,

Father *forest*

Dr. Warder Prescribed Shade

Ohio has had more than its share of notable tree surgeons. But Dr. John A. Warder was a Cincinnati "human" physician, who decided the American Forestry Association would be good for what ails us all. In 1875 Dr. Warder organized the group and became the association's first president. With fellow Cincinnatians, Judge Alfonso Taft, Alfred Springer, and Colonel William L. DeBeck, Warder planned the AFA's first national event in 1882, a gathering called the American Forestry Congress, which fused academic lectures with splashy public relations.

The congress, held in Cincinnati, was the largest forestry meeting ever held in the United States. It coincided with Arbor Day, the original "earth day." Highlight of the five-day congress was a tree planting party in Eden Park that attracted more people than trees. Here's how a newspaper reporter saw it.

"Twenty-five thousand people gathered in Eden Park to witness the ceremonies attending the planting of trees in memory of many famous men. Public schools were closed and thousands of children were among the spectators. A procession marched from the city to the park, and as it entered the grounds, a salute of 13 guns was fired."

Warder's leadership inspired members of the Cincinnati Forestry Club to form the Ohio State Forestry Association in 1883, which two years later lobbied successfully for state legislation creating the Ohio State Forestry Bureau, the great-grandfather of the Ohio Division of Forestry. Today, Ohio's largest English oak spreads its shade at Warder's former estate in North Bend.

—SO

251

across from Hope Furnace in Lake Hope State Park. From SR 278, south of Zaleski, follow Atkinson Ridge Road to the fire tower and hunters camp. The easiest route to the horse camp is TR 20 off SR 356.

Accommodations: Day-use visitors can camp at Lake Hope State Park. The road to the campground is off SR 278, a bit north of Hope Furnace. As noted above, backpackers have their choice of the three off-trail, primitive camping areas (points C, D, and H). They are miles apart, deep in the woods, and free of charge. The backpacker's map shows their locations. Drinking water (Baker pump) and a latrine are provided at each location.

A primitive campground for trail riders has water for horses and latrines (for humans). Primitive camping for hunters is located on Atkinson Ridge Road (TR 5), a few miles northeast of Zaleski. Your driving target is the fire tower. In both cases campers should bring their own drinking water.

Trails: Think of the 23.5-mile backpackers' trail as three fused loops that can be hiked individually as long day hikes, or as an extended ramble. Backpackers must register at the information board before hiking. Maps are usually available here. First time hikers, or backpackers who have not been to Zaleski for several years, should not leave without one. The main trail is blazed in orange, the side trails in white. Plot your hike by noting the distances between lettered points. Zaleski has the only interpretive backpacking trail, with numbered posts on the route. The numbers correspond to brief stories in the trail guide. The stories enhance the walk, and give reasons to pause. Read the trail rules before hiking.

The backpack trail runs over hills and hollows and is considered strenuous. Wear sturdy and comfortable shoes. Each hiker should leave with a full canteen. Trousers and caps are strongly recommended for summer hikes. Poisonous copperhead and timber rattlesnakes inhabit the woods, but you are more likely to be struck by a car at a road crossing than being attacked by one of these reclusive creatures. Still, you have been warned.

Numbered landmarks on the south loop include abandoned stagecoach roads, the ruins of a mining town, glimpses of the spooky Moonville railroad line, an Adena Indian mound and flint quarry, a turkey restoration area, former iron mines, and tree plantations. Landmarks on the Central Loop include abandoned mines, old roads, farms, and mills. Though it lacks water and campsites, the trail is deserted (of humans) most of the time, and a good choice for solitude seekers. For total oblivion and transcendental experiences take the North Loop. Backpacker and author Robert Ruchhoft found the "pine basilica" on this route to be "one of the most beautiful of the living world I know for silent meditation."

The backpack trail winds through northeastern third of Zaleski. Trails for horseback riders (and hikers) journey on a separate trail system in the southeastern third of the property. The abandoned railroad bed running along Hewlett Fork and Raccoon Creek (and through the haunted Moonville Tunnel) divides the trail systems. Equestrians cannot travel on the backpack trail.

Riders have six, color-coded, overlapping trails adding up to nearly 50 backcountry miles. The 16.4-mile dark-blue blazed path, the longest of the six, travels to Lookout Rock, a sandstone promontory overlooking Raccoon Creek and the Moonville Tunnel. For a quickie, take the 3.2-mile yellow trail from the horse camp.

Hunting & Fishing: The northeastern boundary of the state forest abuts Waterloo State Wildlife Area (1,361 acres) and Wayne National Forest. Hunters and trappers can enter Waterloo from the North Loop camping area by hiking southeast from Point H (toward J) a bit and taking an abandoned logging road on the right, where the trail bends left. The old road goes south into the wildlife area. (The road is the main drag through the wildlife area.) Fact is, several old lanes, barely discernible in places, merge here and thread through the forest and the turkey management area. The backpack map shows them as thin dashes. A compass and map of the wildlife area are recommended.

Special Places & Events: Much of the backpack trail is routed through a turkey wildlife management area, a project shared by the divisions of forestry and wildlife to restore the forest habitat for wild turkeys. Similarly, the Atkinson Hunters' Camp lies within a ruffed grouse management area. In spring, the woods resounds with the startling gobbles of tom turkeys, and the drumming of grouse.

Ruchhoft's cathedral of pines is the old Carbondale Forest (a.k.a. Doolittle, Enderlin or York forest), a shaggy, mixed conifer plantation started in 1906. Botanists found 197 species of vascular plants here during a study in the mid-1960s. The specimens were put in the Bartley Herbarium at Ohio University. Only sixty of the original two hundred acres remains. It is the most distant spot from the staging area (about eight hiking miles), and indeed, an enchanting place (see Field Notes).

Information: Zaleski State Forest, Division of Forestry, Zaleski, OH 45698, (740) 596-5781.

HISTORY

It is hard to believe that this verdant, majestic backcountry, so thick now in forest and history, had once been fleeced of its hardwoods and bedrock to fuel a gluttonous iron industry. Not surprisingly, the local state park and state forest trace their names to the blast furnaces that briefly brought prosperity. Hope Furnace, the namesake of Lake Hope State Park, started producing top quality iron in 1853. To the south, Zaleski Furnace was founded in the 1850s by a consortium led by Count Peter Zaleski, a Paris banker acting as the financial agent for Polish exiles in France. The entrepreneur never stepped into Vinton County. These and other furnaces in southern Ohio and neighboring states comprised the Hanging Rock iron manufacturing region.

The Zaleski area furnaces slowly died out after the Civil War. A handful of hardy farmers survived on marginal land, but mostly the shorn hills were left to rejuvenate themselves on their own. Zaleski's vast woods now supports eco-tourists of diverse pleasures, and a resurgent lumber industry. Today, the ruin of Hope Furnace marks the start of the Zaleski backpacker's trail.

Stop for awhile at the donut-shaped Indian mound on the South Loop (signpost 5). The ceremonial earthwork indicates the presence of the Adena people, who roamed across southern Ohio between 800 B.C. and 700 A.D. They came here for the blackish rock, called Zaleski flint. The stone made fine tools and projectile points. Though the more durable flint from the Licking River Gorge was preferred, Zaleski flint was an excellent second choice. Try to envision Adena craftsmen chipping the flint. Try chipping a piece yourself.

This beleaguered land snoozed after white settlers exploited it for sandstone, millstones, game animals, iron ore, trees, coal and clay. That changed in the 1930s when federal funds were used to buy marginal farms for reforestation and resettlement. Zaleski, Blue Rock and Tar Hollow were areas selected for these programs. Zaleski became the site of a Civilian Conservation Corps camp. Relief workers reforested the hills, constructed roads and trails, and built the state's first resort lodge at Lake Hope State Park, dedicated in 1949. Today, the CCC camp operates in similar fashion for disadvantaged youths.

Zaleski expanded in 1969 when the Division of Forestry swapped 5,649-acre Raccoon State Forest in Vinton County for 6,216 acres adjacent to the state forest held by the Mead Corporation. The wildlife management areas and backpack trail were established in the 1970s.

FIELD NOTES

The vast Zaleski–Lake Hope–Waterloo region has abundant wildlife. Besides game animals, 80 species of birds have been identified, including cedar waxwing, various warblers, vireos, hawks, owls, indigo bunting, and wood thrush.

Aquatic life in streams is sparse due to lingering "yellow dog," a pollutant from past mining that increases the acidity of the water.

JOURNAL

Zaleski gives your soul elbow room, and a chance to catch up on forgotten places and lost time. The forest inspires big, bashful, sweaty men to write verse.

On a autumn day several years ago, I rested beneath some buxom oaks along the South Loop backpack trail, and scribbled some thoughts on a pad. The pocket pad disappeared after unpacking, but it turned up again recently. Its rediscovery rekindled a memory.

"Planks of sunlight, widening, narrowing, probing, building a day; rebuilding a planet. Acorns fall as meteorites and leave thumb-sized depressions."

NORTHWEST

Maumee State Forest

Looking at the map, noting that this is the only state forest west of Interstate 71, I just long to push the sixteen separate,

straight-edged segments of Maumee State Forest into a large green block neatly squared off like the rest of this topographically challenged region.

LOCATION

Eastern Fulton County, Swan Creek Township; Western Lucas County, Swanton Township; Northeastern Henry County, Washington Township.

SIZE AND DESIGNATION

Maumee State Forest is 3,068 acres in scattered tracts. It has been chosen as an Ohio Watchable Wildlife Area.

ACCESS

In this neck of the woods, they designate roads sequentially with impersonal letters and numbers. Think of roads A, B, C as latitude lines, and roads 1, 2, 3, etc. as longitude lines. Trees here grow like roads

Forestry futures in 1954: From woods to farms to woods once more.

and crops, in rows clearly marked.

Forest Headquarters is on Fulton County Road D (Archbold Lutz Road). Parking for bridle trails is found at Jeffers Road, off SR 64 in Lucas County, and Washingtown Township Road V in Henry County. All-purpose vehicle trail parking is on Fulton County Road 2.

Accomodations: There is no camping here.

Trails: Maumee has fifteen miles of bridle trails, divided between two locations. Parking for the Lucas County trailhead (near Oak Openings Preserve) is on Jeffers Road. The Henry County trails start on TR V. Trails cross flat terrain, wet in places. Hikers also can use these paths.

Five miles of trails for all-purpose vehicles (mountain bikes and hikers permitted) begin on Road 2 in Fulton County. Observe the rules of the road, especially the one-way routing of traffic. Parking and latrines are available. Overflow parking is offered on Road C.

Hunting & Fishing: Hunting, trapping and fishing are permitted in the state forest. Some local restrictions apply.

Special Places & Events: Just west of the All-Purpose Vehicle (APV) area are the windbreak arboretum and progeny test site. Established in 1990,

the arboretum tests various trees and shrubs for use as windbreaks. Planted in rows, windbreak trees reduce erosion of agricultural topsoil by wind. Genetic superior trees grow in the progeny test site. Stems from progeny trees are grafted to stock trees, then seeds are collected from the hybrids and planted in state nurseries.

Information: Maumee State Forest, 3357 CR D, Swanton, OH 43558-9731, (419) 822-3052.

HISTORY

Maumee State Forest was among eight state forests created between 1945 and 1950. The APV area was developed in 1973.

FIELD NOTES

Think of Maumee as an extension of Oak Openings Preserve, which protects one of the nation's most unique ecosystems: an oak savanna. A wet sedge meadow on Henry CR 2 is Maumee's contribution to the novel region. Birding can be rewarding, especially in heavily wooded, undeveloped tracts. Look for the northern saw-whet owl; red-breasted nuthatch; broad-winged hawk; common snipe; and pine, blue-winged, and chestnut-sided warblers.

Forest Sentinels of Bygone Days

They once stood tall on their hilltop outposts, guardians of all that surrounded them as early warning systems against forest fires. Today, Ohio's retired fire towers, stripped of their original importance, serve as tourist attractions. They have become, like lighthouses, relics of bygone days.

Nationwide, some 5,000 towers once stood on promontories from Maine to California. The spotters in them were the eyes of the federal and state forest services. At one time spotters at 39 towers in Ohio scanned for puffs of smoke rising above the treetops. Today, the National Forest Service keeps just a handful on active duty.

Ohio's first tower, a 60-foot steel frame, was built atop Copperhead Hill in Shawnee State Forest. Later models reached 100 feet so they could peak over foreground trees. All of the towers held a glass-enclosed observation deck where lookouts equipped with binoculars, maps, radio, telephone and alidade (a straightedge device used to pinpoint fires) scanned the hilltops and valleys for smoke signals.

Spotters stood guard in March, April, May, October and November, the months most prevalent for fires. They stayed especially alert in the early afternoon when the temperature rose and wind speed accelerated.

Most forest fires in Ohio are started by careless people, with the leading cause attributed to unattended trash burning. Next leading cause is arson, then tobacco ashes, campfires, railroad sparks, and electric fences.

Lightning, a major cause of fires in Western states, rarely ignites a fire in humid Ohio. Women comprised half of the fire detection force.

When a fire was sighted the lookout contacted another tower and together they pinpointed the location of the smoke. One of the spotters then called a "smoke chaser," usually a forest service employee, who rushed to the scene and determined the intensity of the blaze. Local fire departments put out the fire. From their perch, lookouts tracked the progress of firefighters and noted changes in wind, and fire movements.

Aircraft did a better job of this, however. Pilots circled above a blaze, described the terrain and the fire's strength, then notified firefighters of the fire's speed and path. They stayed in radio contact with ground units and steered crews to the hot spots.

Aerial surveillance in Ohio began in the 1940s. For 30 years pilots and tower lookouts shared the job. Slowly, the Division of Forestry acquired more airplanes, and by the mid-1970s had enough to retire the towers.

Aerial spotters were busiest in 1981, when 1,774 forest and brush fires torched 9,300 acres. The worst fires occurred in Shawnee State Forest and in Lawrence County. In the early 1990s, the expense of airborne spotting, and improved communications in rural areas, grounded planes. Today finding and fighting forest fires on 5.8 million acres of woodlands is the responsibility of the public and rural fire departments.

—SO

WAYNE NATIONAL FOREST

Wayne National Forest eludes definition, perhaps even comprehension. It sprawls across Southeastern Ohio on land ravaged, rescued, recovering, and regal. It is a land of leisure and litigation, a red flanneled playground and a white-collared battle-ground. The trees here are old and new and ages in-between. A national forest with shrubland and fields too; and decorated with pit ponds and luxuriant lakes. Though it is land that has several times been stripped and shaved of its natural resources, it is still "working" land that yields some of its wealth—timber, natural gas, oil—to industrialized society. These extractions draw protests from environmental and conservation groups who rightfully say that enough is enough. For outdoorsmen, there are fewer rules, and richer rewards. It is a wilderness of wonder for weekenders.

What with three separated management units and holdings scattered like confetti across 12 counties, The Wayne is a migraine to administer for a staff stretched thin and trying to please all interest groups and agendas. Oddly, most of the land within its jurisdictional boundary is privately owned, and Congress has placed a moratorium on more public purchases in some counties. On Forest Service maps the administrative realm is white covered with green patches that represent the land actually managed by the service. Beyond the national forest border, Ohio is painted pale yellow. This national forest is unfolding, enlarging, taking shape. Nobody can say what it will be when it grows up.

For millenia a vast, pristine oak-hickory forest covered the region. In this wilderness, small bands of Native Americans established villages along rivers, farmed in clearings, hunted for elk and deer, and cut thin trails through the woods. Europeans arrived in the 1700s—first explorers and adventurers, then trappers, traders, and pioneer farmers. By 1800 the Indians who had lived in harmony with this land had been replaced by settlers poised to squeeze all its

wealth. Ohio led the nation in iron manufacturing in 1850, and ranked fourth in lumber production. The natural resources of the area—timber, iron ore, and limestone—fueled this boom, including the 69 blast furnaces in the Hanging Rock Iron District, centered in Lawrence County. Concurrently, oil and gas drilling, coal mining, and clay manufacturing also had runs of fortune. In the early twentieth century the iron ore ran out. One by one the furnaces closed and left behind a land deforested, polluted, and worth about $1 an acre.

In 1932, the third year of the Depression, taxes were owed on 36 percent of the land now comprising the national forest. Two years later, the Ohio legislature passed a bill allowing the federal government to buy land for a national forest. Between 1935 and 1942, some 77,000 acres were bought for $4-5.50 an acre. The forest service started a tree nursery near Chillicothe. A large Civilian Conservation Corps camp at Vesuvius Furnace employed hundreds for dam construction, reforestation, recreation projects, roads, and other programs. In 1951, when Wayne filled out to 97,000 acres, it officially became a national forest. During the Reagan Administration (1983), Wayne was targeted to shed 63,800 acres of its then 169,000 acres. However, public protest protected those acres, and sparked more acquisitions.

The Wayne remains a mystery to most Ohioans. It lacks an identity and cohesiveness. Those who have heard about it wonder where it is located (the three separate management units don't help), and what they can do when they get there. To some, a national forest is a faint idea, an obscure place, a bit rough on the edges and wild at heart. Better not chance it. There's no lofty lodge in The Wayne, no lakeshore cabins, and no restaurants with a view. You're pretty much on your own there.

Few places in Ohio can match The Wayne's abundant solitude, isolation, and room for roughing it without a knapsack of regulations. Here are the activities you can pursue anywhere on national forest land—free, without much hassle, and usually without company.

* Backpacking and cross-country hiking. Hikers can use trails if they want, or just take off into the bush. Carry water and maps. Presumably, you can find your way home. Fourteen days is your max stay.

* Primitive camping. Anywhere on national forest land, anytime of the year. Over by that little pond if you like. Even under the stars on Archers Fork Trail. Rangers encourage campers to use cleared sites. Small campfires are permitted, though stoves are preferred. Just two exceptions to this policy. Freelance camping is not allowed near developed campgrounds (such as Lake Vesuvius Recreation Area), nor in ecologically-sensitive "special areas."

* Rock climbing. Everybody hopes you climb within your ability, and stay off unique landmarks,

such as rock shelter caves and natural bridges.

* Hunting, trapping and fishing. Obviously, Ohio laws apply. Hunting and trapping are prohibited in "recreation areas." Got questions? Call the nearest forest service office.

* Collecting small amounts of forest products for personal use, such as blackberries, mushrooms, pine cones, herbs, rose hips, etc., is still allowed anywhere. However, when collecting becomes harvesting, or a cottage industry, you will need a permit. To protect plants (ginseng comes to mind) from overcollection, Wayne National Forest developed a permit system several years ago. Collectors now must pay $10 for a permit, and stay in designated areas. Permits are available at the forest offices listed below. Ohio laws apply. If you are wondering if you need a permit, contact the forest service.

If botany is your bag there is plenty to keep you busy here. Starting in 1991 a team of scientists from Ohio State University began counting the plant species in The Wayne. So far, they have found 344 species in the Athens Unit, 324 species in the Marietta Unit, and 279 varieties in the Ironton Unit. Some plants are rare and protected. The inventories will improve land use decisions in the national forest, preserve fragile habitats, and enlighten humanity. Awhile back forest officials began designating certain locations "special areas." These remote locations may contain endangered plants, rare plant communities, waterfalls, historical ruins, or unique scenery, all of which could be ruined by uninvited exotic plants, erosion, trampling, over-harvesting, overloving. Humans can visit most of these spots, but not with their horses, motorized vehicles, bikes, and pets. Most don't have trails, parking, nor facilities for humans. These Special Areas are listed below, but their exact locations must be obtained from a forest office.

According to a study, some 689,000 visitors came to Wayne National Forest's 227,000 acres in 1996, not many when compared to visitations to Cleveland Lakefront or Salt Fork state parks. Fifty-five percent were "nonlocal" visitors living outside the Ohio counties in its realm, and neighboring Ohio River counties in Kentucky and West Virginia. Nevertheless, these outdoors tourists sweetened the regional economy by $45.7 million. The Wayne supported more than 1,000 jobs and generated nearly $25 million in salaries. The national forest is vital to the economy of Southeastern Ohio.

Because of the forest's scattered holdings and remoteness, maps are highly recommended for backcountry activities. Topographical maps showing national forest land and other features are available from any forest office. Each quadrangle map costs $4, plus $3.50 shipping charge per order. A hiking and backpacking trail map ($1) shows the routes of the footpaths described below. The trails are shown on sections of topo maps. Forest Service maps of the Athens District (and Marietta Unit) and Ironton District are available for $4 each. These picture forest holdings, roads, waterways, commu-

nities, landmarks, and include recreational information (not topographical). Maps of horse trails, off-road vehicle trails, and Hanging Rock Fishing Area are free.

The outdoor guide of Wayne National Forest describes the campgrounds and picnic areas, attractions, trails, special areas, and other fun stuff in the Ironton, Athens, and Marietta units. The Ironton District is subdivided into activities at Lake Vesuvius Recreation Area and elsewhere in the district. The Marietta Unit, though officially part of the Athens District, is handled as a separate entity here.

IRONTON DISTRICT - LAKE VESUVIUS RECREATION AREA
Southwestern Lawrence County
Information
Wayne National Forest
Ironton Ranger District
6518 State Route 93
Pedro, OH 45659
Phone: (740) 532-3223; TTY (740) 532-0424

ATHENS DISTRICT
Portions of Athens, Hocking, Morgan, Washington, Perry, and Vinton counties
Information
Wayne National Forest
Athens Ranger District
219 Columbus Road
Athens, OH 45701
Phone (740) 592-6644; TTY (740) 594-4175

MARIETTA UNIT
Portions of Washington, Monroe, and Noble counties
Information
Wayne National Forest
Marietta Unit/Athens District
Rural Route 1, Box 132
Marietta, OH 45750
Phone: (740) 373-9055; TTY (740) 373-4138

CAMPGROUNDS & PICNIC AREAS
Oak Hill Campground. Ironton District, Lake Vesuvius Recreation Area, seven miles north of Ironton off SR 93. Follow CR 29 into the recreation area (look for entrance). Take road (CR 20) to campground, boat ramp, beach. Facilities include 24 sites, some with electric hookups, flush toilets, showers (fully accessible), picnic tables. Sites 1-18 can be reserved. Three sites accessible for disabled campers. Open April 15 to October 15. Fee is $10 per day, $2 extra for electricity. Reservations available, but not necessary, by calling toll-free, 1-800-280-CAMP (2267); TTY 1-800-879-4496. Service charge for a reservation is $7.85. Swimming beach, hiking trails, boat ramp and rental nearby.

Iron Ridge Campground. Entrance to Lake Vesuvius Recreation Area, Ironton District, from SR 93. Stay on CR 29 and follow forest signs to camp. Choose from among 41 sites, 21 with electric hookups. Water, trailer parking, vault toilets, and tent pads are available. Three sites accessible for disabled visitors. Campground is open year-round, but water flows April 15-October 15. Fee is $8 a day, $2 extra for electricity. Reservations available, but not necessary, by calling toll-free, 1-800-280-CAMP (2267); TTY 1-800-879-4496. Service charge for a reservation is $7.85. Close to horse trails, hiking trails, Vesuvius Furnace.

Two Points Group Campground. Take Lake Vesuvius Recreation Area (Ironton District) entrance from SR 93, left on CR 20 following signs to Two Points, Oak Hill Campground, beach. Two large sites are available. One has a shelter and handles 100 people, while the other (no shelter) accommodates 25 campers. Open April 15-September 15. The shelter site costs $35 a night; the shelter-less site $15. Vault toilets. Reservations required at 1-800-280-CAMP (2267); TTY 1-800-879-4496. Service charge for a reservation is $7.85.

Burr Oak Cove Campground. Athens District, Athens County. From SR 13, take CR 107 east. Burr Oak Cove is first campground on right. Road continues to state park camping and beach. Nineteen sites (some walk-in) with drinking water, latrines, picnic tables, fire rings. Lakeview Trail, one mile, leads to Burr Oak Lake. Access to Buckeye Trail, North Country Trail, Burr Oak Backpack Trail, Wildcat Hollow Backpack Trail, Burr Oak State Park. Fee is $5 a night May 15-September 30. Sites are free (no water) October 1-December 7. Closed December 8-May 14.

The Ohio River is just a "stone's throw" away from *Leith Run Recreation Area* (Marietta Unit), 18 miles north of Marietta on SR 7. The area is open April 15 to October 15. Eighteen campsites have electricity, water, grills, fire rings, picnic tables, and lantern posts. Hot showers, flush toilets, and dump station are available. A campground host will collect the nightly $18 during the summer. Campsites can be reserved (add $7.50 service charge). Discounts available for seniors. The day use area, open 6 a.m. to 10 p.m., features fishing piers, a spacious boat ramp and dock at the Ohio River, two reservable picnic shelters, picnic tables, volleyball, horseshoe pits, wildlife observation decks, access to the Scenic River and North Country hiking trails, and playground. Daily parking cost is $2. The picnic shelters ($25 day) accommodate 65 people and come equipped with water, electricity, grills, and picnic tables.

Lamping Homestead is a small, remote "back-to-nature" campground in Southern Monroe County (Marietta Unit). From the Monroe-Washington county line, go north on SR 26, west on SR 537 two miles, left on TR 307. This quiet location is perfect for initiates to primitive camping. The site has six walk-in tent sites (free), eight picnic spots, rest rooms, and a group picnic shelter. Stocked bluegills, bass, and catfish swim in a two-acre fishing pond. Nearby Clear Creek is great for wading and creeking. Lamping Trail for hikers offers forested loops of 1.8 miles and 3.2 miles. The land was once the home of the Lamping Family, who settled here in the early

1800s. An Indian mound also rises on the property. The site is open year-round.

Lane Farm, three miles north of Marietta on SR 26 (Marietta Unit), has four primitive campsites, picnic tables, rest rooms, and fishing and canoe access to the Little Muskingum River. The site serves as a trailhead for the North Country Trail. Open year-round; no fee.

Hune Bridge (Marietta Unit), twelve miles north of Marietta off SR 26. Cross the Little Muskingum River on historic Hune Covered Bridge to reach three primitive campsites, parking for canoe and fishing access, and rest rooms. The southern terminus of the Covered Bridge Trail is located here. Open all year; no fee.

Haught Run fourteen miles north of Marietta along the Little Muskingum River (Marietta Unit). Cross the river on CR 406. The site has three campsites that double as picnic spots, canoe and fishing access, and rest rooms. Access to Covered Bridge Trail. Open all year; no fee.

Ring Mill has three camping/picnic sites off CR 68 at Poulton in Southern Monroe County (Marietta Unit). CR 68 branches from SR 26. It is a great place to begin a canoe trip on the Little Muskingum River. Rest rooms and a picnic shelter are available. The old stone house was built by the Ring Family in 1846. Open all year; no fee.

Stone Church Horse Camp. See Stone Church Horse Trail below.

Vesuvius Furnace Picnic Shelter, located on CR 29 behind Vesuvius Furnace, is a picnic area for groups up to 200 people. The shelter has electricity and a ball field. Cost is $35 a day. Reservations required at 1-800-280-CAMP (2267); TTY 1-800-879-4496. Service charge for a reservation is $15.75.

Roadside Picnic Shelter, CR 29 near Vesuvius Furnace, handles groups up to 200. No electricity. Cost is $25 daily. Reservations required at 1-800-280-CAMP (2267); TTY 1-800-879-4496. Service charge for a reservation is $15.75.

Rock House and *Pine Knob* picnic grounds are located on the road to Oak Hill Campground. They offer picnic tables on a first-come basis at no charge.

Sand Run Picnic Area, Hocking County. Located on Dawley Road (TR 28) between SR 595 and SR 278. Six shaded picnic sites, parking, fishing pond, vault toilets accessible for disabled, trash pickup. Open May 15-December 15.

Utah Ridge Pond & Picnic Area, Athens County. TR 295 near Doanville. Six picnic tables, four parking spaces, grills, fishing pond, trash collection.

Capital Christmas Tree Picnic Area is a two-table picnic area on SR 7, a mile north of Leith Run Recreation Area. Rest rooms are available; no camping. The Christmas tree that decorated the Statehouse ground in Columbus in 1987 was cut down here. Open all year; no fee.

SWIMMING

Big Bend Beach, Lake Vesuvius Recreation Area, at the end of CR 20 has a sandy, roped-off beach, changing rooms with toilets, snack bar, drinking water, and parking. Beach is open from May 31 to September 1. Daily fee is $1. Location has some shaded, grassy sites and tables for picnics. Lakeshore Trail passes through the site.

Lake Vesuvius Recreation Area Boat Dock & Rental. Entering from SR 93, turn left at Vesuvius Dam (CR 20). Boat dock is the first driveway on the right. The ramp is open all year for launching small boats (electric motors only). Private boats can be moored for $1 a night, or $50 a season (April 15-September 9). Rowboats, canoes, and paddleboats can be rented from a concession booth during the summer. Drinking water, rest rooms, snacks available in summer. The boat dock parking lot also serves as a trailhead for the Lakeshore, Backpack, and Rock House trails.

ATTRACTIONS

The ruins of *Vesuvius Iron Furnace* stand near Vesuvius Dam at the intersection of county roads 29 and 44N. Actually, the sandstone stack, erected without mortar, remains. Park across the road from the furnace. The furnace was named after the volcano in Italy. A museum and nature center next to the furnace is open Saturday 10 a.m. to 5 p.m., and Sunday 1-5 p.m. Performances of a play called "The Ironmaster's Daughter" are held at an amphitheater between the museum and furnace.

Vesuvius Dam across the road from the iron furnace was constructed by the Civilian Conservation Corps in the 1930s. A CCC camp was located nearby. The dam impounds Storms Creek.

The Lake Vesuvius Recreation Area's *Visitor Center* (Ironton District) at the entrance on SR 93 has information on trails, sites, facilities, and activities.

To escape the rat race, go to *Timbre Ridge Lake Recreation Area*, a 100-acre lake enwrapped by 1,200 acres of woodland near the Lawrence-Gallia county line (Ironton District). It's purely primitive—no water, no toilets, no designated campsites. From Ironton go north on SR 141, then north on SR 775 at Wilgus. At a spot on some maps called Greasy Ridge you got two choices. Boaters and anglers usually go right (easterly) on TR 213, left on TR 217, left on CR 37, and left on the entrance road (across from Okey Church). The road leads to a boat ramp above the damp, parking below it. (From Gallipolis take SR 141, SR 775 to Lecta, CR 37 to the entrance.) Campers, hikers, and misanthropes should continue north on SR 775 a tad. Just passed Mt. Pleasant Church, look for a small parking area on the right side of the road. Start walking east on the old dirt road, now reserved for foot travelers. It leads to Timbre Ridge Lake. The second trail branching from the main stem follows the north shore to the dam. Camping is allowed anywhere, and it is okay to swim in the lake (at your own risk). Camping, hunting, or swimming are not allowed at the dam, boat launch, or private property on the north shore. Deer, turkey, squirrels, rabbits, waterfowl, and grouse await hunters. Fishermen try for large-mouth bass, bluegill and channel catfish from shore or boat (electric motors only). Bass between 12-15 inches must be released. A leaflet with a map is available from the Ironton district office.

Shawnee Lookout Tower, Eastern Hocking County, Ward Township. From New Straitsville, take SR 216 south. Just before the Hocking County line, turn right on TR 393 (Sand Run-New Straitsville Road). The lookout stands at the X-shaped intersection of TR 393 and TR 22 (Jobs-New Pittsburgh Road). Just before that junction, look for a dirt driveway on the right which goes to the tower. From SR 78, south of Murray City, take TR 22 (Jobs-New Pittsburgh Road), heading northwest, to its merger with TR 393. You also can park off the road.

Tinkers Cave, Eastern Hocking County. A quarter mile from Shawnee Tower. From the X junction mentioned above, go 100 yards southeasterly on TR 22 (towards Murray City). Park in a small pullover (by a forest service sign) on TR 22. A short trail leads to the cave. Combine this visit with the tower. The rock shelter cave was allegedly the hideout of legendary horse thief Seth Tinker in the mid-nineteenth century. Debate continues on whether Tinker was a Civil War patriot or a wily profiteer who sold stolen nags to both sides. Mystery surrounds his disappearance around the village of Monday. Leaflet available.

Payne Cemetery, border of Perry and Hocking counties, off the westside of SR 595. (From Shawnee Lookout continue north on TR 393 and SR 216 to New Straitsville then turn south on SR 595.) Burial site of several Civil War veterans of the U.S. Colored Troops. Paynes Crossing was settled by free blacks from Virginia in the early 1800s. The hamlet disappeared after coal companies bought the land in the early twentieth century. The site was restored in the early 1990s by historical groups and the forest service. A monument now stands at the historic cemetery, and research continues. Call for a leaflet.

Greendale Wetland. Wildlife watchers take note. From Payne Cemetery continue south on SR 595 about two miles to a parking area one-tenth of a mile north of Greendale. You also can begin the trip from the merger of SR 595 and US 33. Follow an abandoned railroad grade across the wetland. So far, 79 bird species have been seen, including the pied-billed grebe, sharp-shinned hawk, blue winged warbler, hooded merganser, double-crested cormorant, wood thrush, yellow-rumped warbler and Lincoln's sparrow. Beaver and muskrat have colonies here. Also look for the black racer (the state snake), stinkpot turtle, bullfrog and red-spotted newt. Site improvements are planned.

Stone Church, Southern Perry County. At the junction of CR 38 (Old Town Road) and CR 39, north of New Straitsville. A plague after the Civil War supposedly wiped out the people who attended St. Peter's Catholic Church. The ruins of the 1845 church and tombstones (both on private land) are all that remind us of the settlement. The site marks the trailhead of the Stone Church Horse Trail.

The *Ring Mill House* is listed on the National Historic Register. The historic, sandstone home is located on CR 68, three miles from SR 26. Primitive camping, picnicking available.

Back in the 1880s, the residents at *Hune House*, SR 26 at Hune Bridge, could spend summer evenings chatting on the big porch. Built by William Hune in 1885, locals called it Hune Inn because the owner accepted boarders.

Irish Run Natural Bridge is only one of seven natural rock bridges in Ohio. The western leg of Archers Fork Trail goes right by the landmark, which is 51 feet long, 16 feet thick, and 39 feet tall. For directions see Archers Fork Trail.

HIKING TRAILS

Wildcat Hollow Backpack Trail. This premier, well-designed woodland path straddles the Perry-Morgan county boundary, north of Burr Oak Lake (Athens District). A trailhead with ample parking and latrines (summer) is located on Morgan County Road 58, which stems from SR 78. From SR 13, north of the road to Burr Oak Cove, go east on TR 298 (follow signs). Access is possible from Irish Ridge Road (TR 295) and other roads, though parking is not patroled. The trail (white squares) has loops of five and fifteen miles. Day hikers often camp near the trailhead. Backpackers can camp anywhere along the trail, but consider already established camps to save forest resources. The trail connects with the Burr Oak Backpack Trail. A topographic trail map and brochure are available from the Athens office. Hiking only.

North Country & Buckeye trails. For 43 miles these long walks share the trail bed across the Athens unit, though only 23 miles actually passes over national forest property. The eastern terminus for both is Morgan County at the junction of SR 78 at CR 58. From here the trail follows the shore of Burr Oak Lake (Burr Oak State Park backpack trail) to Burr Oak Cove (11.7 miles), then west to Trimble State Wildlife Area and northwest to Tecumsey Lake (30.4 miles). It continues to the Stone Church Horse Trail and to the western terminus on SR 668 at TR 690, near the Hocking-Perry county line. Portions of the trail trace public roads, but the route will be moved off-road as national forest land is acquired.

Some 40 miles of the *North Country Trail* also snakes through the Marietta Unit, along country roads, logging lanes, and backcountry trails. The northernmost terminus is Ring Mill House. You also can start at Knowlton Bridge Park. Trails from these termini join and go to a community called Glass (7.6 miles). The trail (star blaze on a triangle) continues southwesterly to the Archers Fork Trail, southerly to German Cemetery on CR 9 (meeting the Scenic River Trail), westerly to Bear Run (28.1 miles), then downstream along the Little Muskingum to Lane Farm, the southern terminus. The forest service has a map and mileage chart upon request.

Interpretive signs along the easy *Rock House Trail* (red blazes) tell the story of Ohio's iron industry.

The paved, 3/4-mile, wheelchair-accessible path begins at the north end of the Lake Vesuvius boat dock parking lot (CR 29) and concludes at a large recess cave long ago inhabited by American Indians. A wood boardwalk enters the cave. The landmark also can be reached via side trails from the Oak Hill Campground and Rock House Picnic Area. Drinking water, refreshments, and rest rooms are found at the boat dock (summer only).

The half-mile *Whiskey Run Trail* (red blazes) begins a loop at the Iron Ridge Campground (campsite 35) and visits the shore of Lake Vesuvius. The name comes from a whiskey still that once made moonshine beneath a rock shelter near the path. A section of the this is shared with the Lakeshore Trail.

Lakeshore Trail is a great adventure along the banks of Lake Vesuvius. Just follow the blue dots for eight miles around the lake. Start at the boat dock, beach, Vesuvius Furnace, Iron Ridge Campground (via Whiskey Run Trail), or Oak Hill Campground (via Rock House Trail). Fishermen use the path for shore fishing. In summer, follow the route to the beach, or take a dip at one of the "unofficial" swimming holes. Camping (backpacking) is allowed along Lakeshore Trail beyond the boundary of the recreation area, generally the northeastern third of the lake. Folks at the visitor center can point out the area, if you have doubt. A topo-hiking map printed by the forest service ($3) also shows the border. Sections of the trails are strenuous, and children should be warned about cliffs, especially north of the beach. The backpack trail branches from the Lakeshore Trail at three spots. The segment from Vesuvius Dam to the boat dock follows county roads. Hikers only.

Vesuvius Backpack Trail snakes for 16 miles across hilly, forested terrain in remote areas. The trail is not divided for shorter day hikes. Hikers should be fit, though novices can tackle the trail. Camping is allowed outside the boundaries of the recreation area. A handy topo-hiking map (entitled "Hiking and Backpacking Trails") printed by the forest service ($1) also shows the border and the route. Start the hike either at the Lake Vesuvius boat dock (CR 20) or at Vesuvius Iron Furnace. If you start at the boat dock (by the concession), follow the Lakeshore Trail toward the beach. In a mile (midway to the beach) the backpack trail (marked by yellow dots) breaks off to the left. The trail stays somewhat close to Lake Vesuvius for the first four miles, then it twists away northeast of the lake. It touches the Lakeshore Trail briefly at mile 12, then branches left (southwesterly) and finishes by the picnic shelter at Vesuvius Furnace. The trail also is accessible from TR 245, the road off CR 29 that goes to the Paddle Creek horse trail parking lot. TR 245 starts north, but near a sharp right (east) turn look for a pullover and connector trail northbound. to the backpack trail. At this point you are about 11.5 trail miles from the boat dock, and 4.5 miles to Vesuvius Furnace. You park here at your own risk. Day hikers shuttling between trailheads might find this spot convenient terminus.

Two excellent hiking trails straddle Symmes Creek in Western Gallia County. *Symmes Creek Trail* stays north of Symmes Creek while *Morgan Sisters Trail* wanders south of it. Symmes Creek Trail, six miles, has two unmarked, half-hidden trailheads on Symmes Creek Road. From Gallipolis or Ironton take SR 141 toward hamlets called Gage and Cadmus. Halfway between these burgs turn onto Woodside Road (CR 12, a.k.a. Vernon Woods Road). After a sharp right turn, the road runs into Symmes Creek Road (no signs at the junction). Go left here onto Symmes Creek Road (CR 15). Bear left at all mergers ahead, paralleling the creek. Heading westerly, the first trailhead is a small pullover a half mile east of the first bridge over Symmes Creek. The better trailhead is a half mile west of the bridge, at the end of short driveway. Follow the white diamonds with orange dots.

Morgan Sisters Trail has challenging loops of two, four and eight miles. The designated trailhead is located on a deadend gravel lane (TR 16) off Greenfield Township Road 25. To get there, take SR 233, which branches from SR 141 north of Cadmus, about 3-1/4 miles, then turn right on TR 25. Look for the trailhead on the right in a half mile or so. The Coal Branch Loop begins here, marked by white diamonds with yellow dots. To the east are the Ridge Loop and Schoolhouse Loop, blazed similarly. Unofficial trailheads are found at the ends of Bethel (TR 22) and Morgan Sisters (TR 17) roads, both off SR 233. Half of the trail ambles through Morgan Sisters Woods, a designated Special Area believed to be uncut beech-maple and oak-hickory forests.

A connector trail links the two trails at the bridge over Symmes Creek noted above. The bridge is midway between the two Symmes Creek trailheads on Symmes Creek Road. Several cars can park here. This is the best trailhead for hikers hoping to walk both trails. Overnight camping is allowed along these trails, preferably at spots already cleared. The "Hiking and Backpacking Trails" broadsheet printed by the forest service ($1) is helpful.

One of the most rugged and scenic foot trails in the national forest, *Archers Fork Trail*, travels over Irish Run Natural Bridges and alongside rock shelters. The loop totals 9-1/2 miles. Located in remote Washington County, Independence Township, trailheads are found on TR 14 (along Jackson Run) and TR 34 (west of TR 411). The North Country Trail shares the northern and western legs of this path. Where Archers Fork Trail meets CR 36, hikers can take a connector trail (three miles) to the Covered Bridge Trail. Camping is permitted in clearings along the trail. Horses and motorized vehicles prohibited.

Most folks traveling between Rinard Covered Bridge and Hune Covered Bridge ride in a canoe on the Little Muskingum River, or in a car along SR 26. The *Covered Bridge Trail,* five miles, also links these landmarks for hikers. The trail is also accessible at the Haught Run campground.

Behind *the trees*

The Annotated Wayne

Owner/Manager: U.S. Department of Agriculture, National Forest Service

Acres: 227,086 (June 1997)

Trails: 314.65 miles (October 1996)

Visitors: 689,000 (1996)

Five Most Popular Activities: Hunting (37 percent of visitors), camping (14 percent), off-road vehicles (11 percent), hiking (seven percent), and fishing (six percent).

Eco-Regions: Unglaciated hill country

Fossil Fuel Wells: Nearly 5,500

Ohio Watchable Wildlife Areas: Wildcat Hollow trailhead (Athens District), Symmes Creek trailhead and Lake Vesuvius (Ironton District), Leith Run Recreation Area (Marietta Unit).

Try hiking upstream from Hune Covered Bridge, then canoeing from Rinard Covered Bridge. A connector trail joins this route to the Archers Fork and North Country trails. Horses and motorized vehicles prohibited.

Ohio View Trail traces steep sandstone cliffs above the Ohio River, presenting sprawling views of the valley and close looks at a second-growth forest. The well-designed path crosses creeks, slides across slopes, visits shady glens, and high points above the river. This end-to-end (linear) trail has termini on SR 7 at Beavertown (three miles north of Leith Run Recreation Area) and SR 260 at Yellow House. Park on the river side berm of SR 7, and the south berm of SR 260. The walk measures seven miles one direction. Horses and motorized vehicles prohibited.

Scenic River Trail starts at Leith Recreation Area and goes 3.4 miles north to a small parking spot at German Cemetery on CR 9. Hikers can continue on the North Country Trail at CR 9. Switchbacks climb the steep slopes overlooking the Ohio River. Roundtrip, the trail covers 6.8 miles. Horses and motorized vehicles prohibited.

Lamping Homestead Trail. Refer to Lamping Homestead campground above.

HORSEBACK RIDING TRAILS

Backcountry bridle trails total 46 miles in the Lake Vesuvius neighborhood. The *Main Loop* winds for 31 miles across forests, shrubland, open fields, streams and ridges. Shorter routes include the *Kimble Loop*, 5.25 miles, and *Paddle Creek Loop*, three miles, and abbreviations of the Main Loop using connector trails and legs of the Kimble and Paddle Creek loops. The easiest access to the Main Loop (gray diamonds) is at the *Sand Hill Trailhead*, located on CR 29, the main entrance road to Lake Vesuvius Recreation Area from SR 93. Follow signs to the Sand Hill staging area. To reach the *Paddle Creek Trailhead,* continue east on CR 29, then go left (north) on TR 245 to its end. Follow the white dots (on gray diamond) of the Paddle Creek Loop north to reach the Main Loop. In a quarter-mile or so the trail forks. Both prongs head north to the Main Loop. Take the left fork to go westbound on the Main Loop. The right fork is for riders heading eastbound on the Main Loop or to Kimble Loop (blue dots on gray diamond). The *Johns Creek Trailhead* serves the northern section of the trail system. From the main entrance (CR 29) travel north on SR 93 a mile, then turn right on CR 4. Go five miles on CR 4, following signs to the trailhead. From here, take the *Dean State Connector* (red dots) south to the Main Loop. The northbound trail leads to Dean State Forest. Small portions of the Main Loop and half the Kimble Loop use public township road. The *Vesuvius Connector Trail,* accessible from Johns Creek or Sand Hill, divides the Main Loop in half. Camping in small clearings is permitted along the trail. Hikers are allowed on the bridle trails, but horses

are not permitted on hiking trails. Carry water, or purify it. Pick up a trail map before saddling up.

Stone Church Horse Trail. Located in Southern Perry County, Salt Lick and Monday Creek townships, this 21-mile twisting loop trail has trailheads on CR 38 (Old Town Road, off SR 93 north of New Straitsville) and TR 190, the latter serving as the trailhead for the North County Trail. The trail can be divided into two shorter loops. Overnight camping is permitted along the trail or at a new riders' camp on CR 38. The eight camp sites have spacious parking (45'x15'), covered paddocks, fire pits, grills, tent pads, vault toilets, and drinking water (in tank, bring pails and jugs). Fee is $8, payable in a self-service kiosk. The old trailhead on CR 38 is for day use (6 a.m. to 10 p.m.), though overnight parking is allowed during deer hunting season. Horse and rider must stay on the wide trail, blazed by gray diamonds. A trail guide is available. A nine-mile section of this trail is shared by the Buckeye and North Country trails. Hikers and equestrians only.

The Wayne's newest horse trail is the *Kinderhook Horse Trail*, Washington County, Newport Township. To reach the trailhead, go north on CR 25 from SR 7 in Newport, then east (right) on CR 244. The double-loop path provides 10 miles of riding, some of it on the steepest slopes in the national forest. Follow the gray diamonds. Keep horses and riders out of Kinderhook Cemetery, the trail's namesake located on private land. Leaflet available.

Hikers are welcomed on all bridle trails.

FISHING

The Ironton District has the most fishing opportunities in Wayne National Forest. Lake Vesuvius (143 acres) supports largemouth bass, bluegills, channel catfish, crappie, and saugeye. Timbre Ridge Lake has 100 acres inhabited by largemouth bass, bluegills, and channel catfish. Stream fishing is allowed in Symmes Creek and Pine Creek.

Locals around Ironton hang out at the *Hanging Rock Fishing Area* where 51 small ponds challenge (or frustrate) human fishers. The ponds reside in an unreclaimed (but recovering) mining and logging area, so expect high walls and thick vegetation. From Ironton take US 52 west to Hanging Rock, SR 650 north a half mile, left on Forest Road 105. Most ponds are passed the ORV trailhead. The forest service and Izaak Walton League has published a guide and map of the ponds. The guide shows the location and accessibility (drive-to or walk-in) of the numbered ponds, foot trails, size of pond (acres), and fish species in each pond. Pond 25, for example, is a "drive-to" five-acre pond containing bass, bluegill, catfish, and sunfish. Some ponds contain no fish. The guides help fishers decide where and what to fish. There are a dozen or so unnumbered ponds which have fish, but getting to them may be difficult.

A Little Miami music: the scenic river near Clifton.

a *scenic river used to be defined by the eyes of the beholder. Nowadays, though, a waterway crowned as "scenic" must be more than a pretty face. These beauty queens must also have squeaky clean reputations and a talent for keeping them.*

Designation is based on the amount (or lack) of human development that has influenced the flow, water quality, natural diversity, use, and riparian habitat of the stream. In most cases, only portions of a river's length meet the qualifications. Rivers designated "wild" boast heavily forested river corridors, little human intrusion, high water quality, and thriving aquatic communities. The "scenic" designation goes to streams whose corridors are less pristine in most categories than wild rivers.

"Recreational" rivers have significant cultural, historical, and natural attributes worth preserving.

So far, 11 waterways, totaling 683 miles, have been designated state scenic rivers by the Ohio Department of Natural Resources, Division of Natural Areas and Preserves (ODNR). Three rivers have earned national scenic river status from the U.S. Department of The Interior.

In fact, Ohio wrote the book on protecting and improving the scenic and historic value of designated rivers, as well as their natural wealth, water quality, watershed and riverine environment. That state's first scenic rivers act was also the nation's first, enacted in 1968. Since then the programs Ohio has created to preserve and restore its rivers and streams have become models for other states.

Scenic river designation does not alter land ownership nor restrict use of the stream for boating (canoeing), fishing, photography, nature study, etc. However, these activities are subject to local restrictions.

For details on river designation, preservation programs, and use of designated streams contact Ohio Department of Natural Resources, Division of Natural Areas and Preserves, 1889 Fountain Square Court, Columbus, OH 43224-1331, (614) 265-6453. —*SO*

NORTHEAST

Chagrin River

Though surveyor and explorer Moses Cleaveland was chagrined to discover this river was not the Cuyahoga River, the river's name does not reflect his disappointment. Actually, the name supposedly comes from an Indian word "shagarin" meaning "clear water."

SIZE & DESIGNATION

Scenic. The Chagrin River became Ohio's ninth scenic river on July 2, 1979. Total miles designated—49.

WATERSHED

The main stem of the river originates in northern Geauga County. It flows southwest into Cuyahoga County, then north through Cuyahoga and Lake counties. The Aurora Branch arises in northwest Portage County and joins the main stem in southeastern Cuyahoga County. The East Branch snakes across northern Geauga County and meets the main stem in Lake County (Willoughby). The river empties into Lake Erie.

DESIGNATED PORTIONS

Main stem, 23 miles, from its confluence with the Aurora Branch downstream to the US 6 bridge; Aurora Branch, 11 miles from the SR 82 bridge to its merger with the main stem; East Branch, 15 miles, from the confluence with the main stem upstream to the Heath Road bridge at the Lake-Geauga county line.

Grand River

The Grand River wears two faces. It lolls and plods through Ashtabula County, then rides a wild roller-coaster around steep banks in Lake County.

SIZE & DESIGNATION

The Grand River was designated scenic and wild on January 17, 1974. Total designated miles—56 ; 23 wild, 33 scenic.

WATERSHED

The Grand River starts in southeastern Geauga County, swings into northwestern Trumbull County and north into Ashtabula, then west through Lake County and into Lake Erie.

DESIGNATED PORTIONS

From US 322 in Ashtabula County to the covered bridge in Harpersfield (Ashtabula County) the river is designated scenic, but from the covered bridge to the Norfolk & Western railroad trestle south of Painesville (Lake County) it is wild.

Little Beaver Creek

Ohio's first wild river also may be its most pristine and primeval. The first Ohioans arrived in this green valley 10,000 years ago. Those who have ever canoed this creek find its currents tricky.

SIZE & DESIGNATION

Little Beaver Creek became Ohio's first wild river on January 15, 1974. It became the state's second national scenic river (34 miles) in October 1975. Total designated miles—36 ; 20 wild, 16 scenic.

WATERSHED

Little Beaver Creek comprises three forks. The North Fork travels in an arch from southeastern Mahoning County into Beaver County, Pennsylva-

Muskingum River, Ohio

nia, and Columbiana County, and joins the main stem at Fredericktown. The Middle Fork flows southerly from southern Mahoning County and joins the West Fork, coming from Guilford, in Williamsport. The creek spills into the Ohio River, just east of the Ohio-Pennsylvania state line.

DESIGNATED PORTIONS

A portion of each fork is designated wild and scenic. The wild portions include West Fork from Y-Camp Road downstream to the confluence with the Middle Fork; North Fork from Jackman Road to the main stem (east of the confluence of the west and middle forks); and main stem from the confluence of the west and middle forks to .75 miles north of Grimm's Bridge.

The scenic sections are comprised of North Fork, from the Ohio-Pennsylvania border to Jackman Road; Middle Fork from Elkton Road to the merger with the West Fork; and main stem from .75 mile north of Grimm's Bridge to the state line.

UPPER CUYAHOGA RIVER

Some 2,500 years ago ancient people called Mound Builders inhabited the upper Cuyahoga River, but they suddenly and inexplicably vanished after living there a century or so. Another mound building culture—beavers—arrived later, only to be exterminated by white settlement. The beavers, however, have returned and resumed their mound building in the wetlands and swamps that recharge this river.

SIZE & DESIGNATION

The Upper (upper meaning close to the river's source) Cuyahoga River was designated a state scenic river on June 26, 1974. Total designated miles—25 scenic.

WATERSHED

The west and east branches of the Cuyahoga River begin in northern Geauga County. Both branches flow south through the county and join south of Burton. The river continues south, cuts a swath across northwestern Portage County, then swings west and north through Summit County, Akron, and Cuyahoga County. It concludes its journey at Lake Erie in Cleveland.

DESIGNATED PORTIONS

The river is designated scenic from the Troy-Burton township line in Geauga County to US 14 in Portage County, a 25-mile stretch.

265

SOUTHWEST

Little Miami River

Rich in human and natural history, the Little Miami's currents have bathed the likes of the Fort Ancient Indians, Daniel Boone, Tecumseh, and Simon Kenton. The waters also have carved the spectacular ancient dolomite walls in Clifton Gorge. It is Ohio's first state-designated scenic river and its first national scenic river.

SIZE & DESIGNATION

The entire length of this river is designated scenic. It was dedicated in stages from April 23, 1969 to October 21, 1971. National designation got underway in August 1973 and was completed in January 1980. Total miles dedicated—105 state scenic; 92 national scenic.

WATERSHED

The source of the Little Miami River is in rural southeastern Clark County. From there it flows through Greene, Warren, Clermont, and Hamilton counties into the Ohio River, east of Cincinnati.

DESIGNATED PORTIONS

The entire length of the river, and part of its north fork, is designated scenic. It is a national scenic river from Clifton to its confluence with the Ohio River.

Stillwater River & Greenville Creek

For most of its journey the Stillwater River, as its name implies, meanders so gently that its water appears motionless. In places, the stillness is solid enough to reflect the sycamore branches that lazily arch over the current.

During his military campaign to wipe out Indians, General "Mad" Anthony Wayne built a fort on a tributary of the Stillwater River. He called it Fort Greene Ville. The treaty signed at the fort in 1794 opened much of Ohio to white settlers.

SIZE & DESIGNATION

The rivers were dedicated in stages from July 1975 to April 1982. Total designated miles—93; 83 scenic, 10 recreational.

WATERSHED

Stillwater River originates in western Darke County near the Indiana border and flows eastward. Greenville Creek begins in Indiana and proceeds east to its meeting with the Stillwater at Covington in Miami County. The Stillwater River continues southeast and merges with the Great Miami River in Dayton.

DESIGNATED PORTIONS

Greenville Creek is a scenic river from the Ohio-Indiana border to its merger with the Stillwater River. From the Riffle Road bridge in Darke County to the Englewood Dam (Montgomery County), the Stillwater River is scenic. It is designated recreational from the dam to its demise in Dayton.

Big Darby Creek tiptoes around Columbus.

CENTRAL

Big and Little Darby Creeks

The watershed is one of the most valuable freshwater habitats in the country. Many endangered fish and mollusks live in waters cleansed by the prairies of the Darby Plains. The habitat is so valuable that The Nature Conservancy, a leading land preservation organization, has declared this watershed one of its "Last Great Places."

SIZE & DESIGNATION

These streams became state scenic rivers on June 22, 1984. The U.S. Department of the Interior made it a national scenic river in 1995. Total miles dedicated—82.

WATERSHED

Big Darby Creek starts in southeastern Logan

County and journeys through Champaign, Union, Madison, Franklin and Pickaway counties. From southeastern Champaign County, Little Darby Creek goes through Union and Madison counties before connecting with Big Darby Creek in western Franklin County.

DESIGNATED PORTIONS

Big Darby's scenic designation runs from the Champaign-Union county line to its confluence with the Scioto River in Circleville. Designation for Little Darby begins at Lafayette-Plain City Road (CR 5) in Madison County to its merger with Big Darby in Franklin County.

Kokosing River

The Kokosing River is the first, and so far only, waterway in the vast Muskingum River watershed to earn scenic river designation. The name derives from anglicized Native American expressions. The Lenni Lenape word "kokosink" was translated by whites to mean "river of many Delaware villages." Indians who spoke an Algonquian dialect supposedly called it "kokoshing," meaning "river of little owls." Pioneers preferred the latter version and sometimes referred to the stream as Owl Creek.

SIZE & DESIGNATION

The Kokosing River became a state scenic river in 1997. Total designated miles—47.6, all classified scenic.

WATERSHED

Headwater tributaries reach into Morrow, Richland, and Ashland counties. Overall, the river drains 482 square miles and its main stem splits Knox County. Some 57 miles from its source, the Kokosing joins the Mohican River to form the Walhonding River in western Coshocton County. The Walhonding and Tuscarawas rivers fuse in Coshocton to create the mighty Muskingum River, a tributary of the Ohio River.

DESIGNATED PORTIONS

The scenic designation applies to the main stem from its mouth in western Coshocton County upstream 41.1 miles to the Knox-Morrow county line. The same classification goes for the North Branch of the Kokosing from its confluence with the East North Branch at Fredericktown to the Kokosing River northwest of Mt. Vernon, a distance of 6.5 miles.

Olentangy River

This river briefly slices a path along the border of 350 million-year-old shale and limestone, and below a steep bluff it washes mysterious, round "ironstones" (concretions), some the size of wrecking balls, that have rolled into its current.

SIZE & DESIGNATION

The Olentangy became Ohio's third scenic river on August 24, 1973. Total miles designated— 22.

WATERSHED

This stream runs from the Crawford-Richland county line, through Crawford, Marion, Delaware, and Franklin counties. It empties into the Scioto River in Columbus.

DESIGNATED PORTIONS

Twenty-two miles of the river are designated scenic from the Delaware State Park dam in Delaware County to Wilson Bridge Road in Worthington, Franklin County.

NORTHWEST

Maumee River

The blood of American, Indian, British, and French soldiers stained this river during the frontier wars of the 18th and

19th centuries. The Maumee flowed beside a vast wetland known as the Great Black Swamp, but like the mighty warriors' blood, the swamp has been reduced to a mere memory.

SIZE & DESIGNATION

The Maumee River earned scenic and recreational river status on July 18, 1974. Total designated miles—97; 53 recreational, 43 scenic.

WATERSHED

The St. Joseph and St. Marys rivers converge in Ft. Wayne, Indiana, to form the Maumee River, which then shoots northeast through Paulding, Defiance, Henry, Wood, and Lucas counties, and into Lake Erie.

DESIGNATED PORTIONS

The scenic portion of the river runs from the Ohio-Indiana border to the US 24 bridge, west of

Like salmon, humans swimming upstream cannot surmount the dam.

Defiance. From that spot to the US 20 & SR 25 bridge in Perrysburg the river is designated recreational.

Sandusky River

Like their Seneca and Wyandot predecessors, modern and better outfitted fishermen gather along this river's banks during the migration of walleye and white bass from Sandusky Bay. The river winds through some of Ohio's most fertile farmland, a product of the glacier that deposited rich soil 12,000 years ago and the litter of the forest that once grew on the surface.

SIZE & DESIGNATION

The Sandusky River was declared a state scenic river in January 1970. Total miles designated—70.

WATERSHED

From its headwaters in southeastern Crawford County, the Sandusky River heads west across Crawford County, then north into Wyandot, Seneca, and Sandusky counties. It drains into Sandusky Bay.

DESIGNATED PORTIONS

Scenic river designation runs from US 30 in Upper Sandusky (Wyandot County) to Roger Young Memorial Park in Fremont, Sandusky County.

Notable Quotables

Thick Grasses That Were Emerald Green

"For those of the army who had never before seen the Sandusky Plains, their first view of it yesterday was breathtaking. The heavily forested hills through which they had been riding for the better part of a week had abruptly leveled out into high plains, with vast fields of grass as far as the eye could see. Their guides told them this type of terrain would continue all the way to the Sandusky towns, still some 30 miles distant: deep thick grasses that were emerald green in their lush new growth and so high that the early morning dew soaked their horses and bathed the riders themselves to their waists. There was a deceptive sense of peace to the vista and a strong illusion that they had entered upon an expansive green sea where the surface was calm and smooth except where breezes touched down and rippled the grass in pleasant waving swaths all the way to the western horizon. The illusion of a sea was further enhanced by, here and there in the distance, great isolated groves of trees projecting above the grasses, appearing to be a series of lovely islands. So strong was this sense, in fact, that almost immediately the men referred to these groves as islands and dubbed them with colorful names based on their size or shape or color. Smaller groves, hazy and indistinct in the distance, loomed above the grasses like ships traversing the sea from one of the larger islands to another."

— Allan W. Eckert, historical novelist, describing the Sandusky Plains (Crawford and Wyandot counties) in the spring of 1782, from **That Dark and Bloody River**, page 342.

The cure for 90 °F, 10 feet of Ohio lake water.

*h*umans give words life, and all life evolves. Take the word "special." Twenty years ago it simply meant something inherently prized and esteemed (like a special friend), or an uncommon bonus or extra.

In these more sensitive (or politically correct) times, "special," as a nuance, also boosts or empowers things once deemed different, peculiar, or common. But in all senses of the word, the following recreation sites are special. The 10 parks of the Muskingum Watershed Conservancy District offer extraordinary fishing, boating, and camping behind earthen dams in hilly Eastern Ohio. Euphemistically called Big Muskie, Ohio's second-largest park system is run by a quiescent and quasi-government agency that blends flood control and recreation responsibilities. The parks are located in the Muskingum River watershed, covering one-fifth of the state.

The Cuyahoga Valley National Recreation Area, a dagger-shaped, riparian "green space" bridging the Cleveland and Akron suburbs, is Ohio's only national park—almost. Though the National Park Service makes distinctions between "national park" and "recreation area," they are lost here. To most Ohioans, CVNRA looks like a national park (absent camping), feels like a national park, smells like a national park, so the 33,000-acre place must be a national park.

And there's ReCreation Land (not my spelling) a big patch of turf in Southeastern Ohio's coal country owned by American Electric Power. The utility holding company lets humans play on its 30,000-acre reclaimed coal-mined area, whose boundary changes amoebic-like year to year, depending on mining. And it's all free. Now when was the last time you got something free from a utility company?

The only way to find out for certain if these areas fit your definition of "special" is to make a special trip to one or all to see for yourself.

—SO

AEP ReCreation Land

Put this place in the best kept secret category. Remember it like a fiver found in a coat pocket. Imagine an outdoors playground of 30,000 acres making a comeback after being pocked and scarred by coal mining. The land boasts forests of hardwoods and pines, undulating and razorback hills, 350 ponds packed with fish. Hiking trails and campgrounds are there if you need them. All of it is open, public, and free. Put a New Age name on it —ReCreation Land—and locate it in Ohio's Outback.

LOCATION

AEP ReCreation Land currently overlaps the borders of Morgan, Muskingum, and Noble counties.

SIZE & DESIGNATION

AEP turned three vast tracts—49,700 acres—into public recreation playgrounds. The Avondale mining land, 4,200 acres, was designated a state wildlife area in 1957. Four years later, the Ohio Power Recreation Lands (now called ReCreation Land) dawned, providing campgrounds, hiking, hunting, trapping, fishing, and wildlife watching on 30,000 acres. Another 15,500 acres south of Coshocton, called the Conesville Coal Lands, opened in 1985 as public hunting, trapping and fishing grounds.

ACCESS

State routes 78, 83, and 284 form the main arteries. County and townships roads branch from these roads into more remote sections.

Avondale Wildlife Area straddles the Perry-Muskingum county lines between state routes 93, 345 and 669 and U.S. 22. Three tracts comprise the Conesville Coal Lands, which flank the Muskingum Watershed Conservancy District's Wills Creek area on the Muskingum-Coshocton county boundary. State routes 83, 93 and 541 snake through the place.

AEP is not finished mining in ReCreation Land.

Modern earth diggers can scoop up coal seams unreachable in the past. Consequently, areas open today may be closed next year and for five years after that. ReCreation Land's boundary recreates itself, depending on mining, but roughly 30,000 acres stays available for outdoors fun.

Mining noise can disturb the peace, but not often. The campsites stay quiet and placid. Restricted areas are marked in red on the map, and posted in the field.

A permit is required to visit ReCreation Land, Avondale Wildlife Area, and Conesville Coal Lands. Permits are free and must be carried at all times on the sites. Family permits are available but children over age 18 must have an individual permit.

Accommodations: Twelve primitive "parksites," offering hundreds of campsites, are scattered throughout ReCreation Land. Campgrounds have picnic tables, latrines, drinking water, and parking. Nothing fancy. But nobody comes here expecting resort accommodations. Several camps rest beside calm lakes or streams, notably Sand Run, Sawmill Road, and Keffler Kamp. Camping is free on a first-come basis. Maximum stay is three weeks. Look for the self-registration locations in each camp. Campers must have a permit with them. Ohio wildlife laws apply to hunters, trappers, and fishers. From time to time, a campground is temporarily closed because of nearby mining, so campers should call ahead before heading out. Below, each "parksite" is identified by a letter on the brochure map, available at the address below:

• Hook Lake (A), off SR 83, north of its junction with SR 284 and SR 78. Picnic shelter, fishing ponds on site. Open as a horse camp. Check on its status.

• Sand Hollow (C), Camp Site Road off SR 284, north of the SR 284 and SR 83 intersection. Extras include picnic shelter, shoreline sites.

• Sawmill Road (D), off southside of SR 83 (south of Renrock). Features a covered bridge, picnic shelter, and beaver dams.

* Windy Hill (E), a small picnic site off SR 83 at junction with CR 27. RV campers sometimes park here. Telephone, information center, scenic overlook available.

• R.V. Crews (F), on SR 78 south of the merger of state routes 83, 78, and 284. Has picnic shelter, telephone, information center, ponds, scenic overlook, trails.

• Maple Grove (G), small camp on SR 284, just north of the intersection of state routes 83, 78, and 284.

• Woodgrove (H), off CR 27, which branches from SR 78 north of Reinersville and SR 83 south of

ReCreation Areas

Michigan

Lake Erie

Indiana

Kentucky

West Virginia

Pennsylvania

Ohio River

N

American Electric Power Public Lands
A) Recreation Land
B) Conesville Coal Lands
C) Avondale Wildlife Area

Cuyahoga Valley National Recreation Area

Muskingum Watershed Conservancy District Lakes

1) Charles Mill		8) Clendening	
2) Pleasant Hill		9) Piedmont	
3) Wills Creek		10) Seneca	
4) Beach City		11) Mohicanville Dam	
5) Atwood		12) Bolivar Dam	
6) Leesville		13) Dover Dam	
7) Tappan		14) Mohawk Dam	

ReCreation Story

According to AEP, ReCreation Land has

• *Hosted more than 3.3 million visitors since opening in 1961, most driving an average distance of 100 miles.*

• *Sheltered some 25,000 campers per year.*

• *Contributed $2 million to the local economy.*

Renrock. Access to the Buckeye Trail.

•Bicentennial (K), Noble County Road 20 branching from SR 83 north of the Noble-Morgan county line. Recently reopened with lakeshore sites.

•Horse Run (L), off SR 83 north of SR 83-284-78 intersection.

•Keffler Kamp (N), off CR 27 which runs between SR 78 and SR 83. Lakes at the pine-shaded sites.

•Beaver Run (Q), off SR 83 near turn for Sawmill Road area.

•Renrock (S), off SR 83 north of Morgan-Noble county line. Picnic area with shelter, used by RV campers.

Camping is not allowed at Avondale Wildlife Area and Conesville Coal Lands. These tracts also lack rest rooms, drinking water, and developed parking areas.

Trails: Dozens of unmarked, abandoned mining roads serve as foot trails in the AEP lands. Follow them to your heart's content, only keep track of your progress and mark your backtrack route. These paths tend to follow ridges parallel to ponds and creeks.

In ReCreation Land, the best maintained route is a 10-mile segment of the Buckeye Trail, which runs along the eastern edge of the property. The northern

273

The "compleat" Ohio angler, complete with fish.

trailhead begins on the west side of SR 78 near the Morgan-Noble county line, and about a quarter mile west of Sharon Township Road 27. If parking on SR 78 is a problem, try the berm on TR 27. Southbound from here, the blue-blazed trail crosses CR 27. Woodgrove campground is short walk west on this road, and serves as a trailhead. It passes ponds and follows Dyes Fork to SR 78/83 where a grassy parking area with picnic table serves as a trailhead. Look for entrance signs. The trail continues for three more miles, and exits AEP land at TR 944.

The current ReCreation Land map shows an old haul road, now serving as a trail in the horse riding area, tracking near the western boundary. It runs from Morgan CR 11 at the south end to the northern terminus on Bristol TR 952. Midway, it crosses SR 78, about 2.5 miles west of its junction with SR 83. The haul road south from this point may be open to motorized traffic.

Park officials constructed four trails in the 1970s, but they are no longer kept cleared, blazed nor otherwise maintained. Nevertheless, they exist and get trampled by hunters, trappers and fishermen. Look for the Bicentennial Trail going north from Keffler Kamp along the pond to SR 83 and continuing to the Bicentennial Parksite. It also heads south to CR 27. The R.V. Crews Memorial Trail starts at a crushed stone parking spot on SR 78, west of the R.V. Crews parksite. The path loops around ponds and connects with offshoot trails that wander around more ponds to the northwest. AEP is considering opening this trail to mountain bikers (check first). The Maple Grove Trail curls around ponds from Maple Grove Parksite to Sand Hollow Parksite. From there, the Sand Hollow Trail drifts north, parallel to SR 284. Again, these trails are not marked.

Inactive haul roads, now foot trails, spread like the veins in a leaf in Avondale Wildlife Area. A clever (or obsessed) land reader can connect the segments for a continuous hike from the hamlet of Avondale (north) to SR 669, seven to 10 trail miles. Old mining lanes also run every which way in the Conesville Coal Lands.

Generally, AEP is liberal-minded toward foot travelers. Off-trail hiking is permitted and pleasurable.

Restrictions are posted at parksites. Hiking is not allowed on active haul roads and railroad tracks, private property, nor in restricted mining areas. Motorized all-terrain vehicles are forbidden on AEP trails. Swimming, target shooting, and rock climbing are not allowed.

Horseback riders can now roam in a large area on the western side of ReCreation Land, thanks to a pact between AEP and the Morgan County Chapter of the Ohio Horse Council. The section is bordered by SR 78, CR 11, CR 91, TR 952 (Carmel Ridge Road) and TR 940.

Hunting, Fishing & Trapping: Parksites in ReCreation Land get crowded during deer hunting seasons. The place has a reputation for producing big bucks. Hunters can also bag turkeys, fox and gray squirrels, grouse, raccoons, bobwhite quail, and cottontails. Though not prime waterfowl territory, gunning for Canada geese, mallards, wood ducks, black ducks, and blue-winged teal can be productive near ponds and swamps. Trappers gather here for beaver (special permit required), muskrat, raccoons and other pelts.

Some ReCreation Land ponds tremble with fish. Stories of 10-pound largemouth bass are not fiction. Dreams of a dozen largemouths before noon have come true. The waters have been stocked with largemouth and smallmouth bass, northern pike, bluegill, crappie, sunfish, chain pickerel, and channel and shovelhead catfish. Some anglers spend a three-day weekend casting and hiking a string of ponds. Remote ponds harbor sunnies and bluegills in the nine-inch category. Though most folks fish from shore, small boats and inflatables can be launched on the ponds near access roads (six horsepower limit). First-timers usually have strikes on ponds next to campgrounds. Connoisseurs of frog legs can spear a bounty here.

Information: For a permit or further information, contact any American Electric Power (Ohio Power and Columbus Southern Power) office, any Ohio Department of Natural Resources, Division of Wildlife office, or American Electric Power, P.O. Box 328 (59 West Main Street), McConnelsville, OH 43756, (740) 962-4525. Permits also are available in local stores. Ask also for the latest foldout brochure and map of the areas.

History

Fifty years ago this place was anything but a recreation paradise. In 1945 earth-moving machines began skinning and scraping "black gold" that had slept near the surface in Southeastern Ohio for 300 million years. Coal seams here were four feet thick, and yielded a whopping 5,000 to 5,800 tons an acre. Trucks, conveyors, and railroad cars carried the fuel to electric power plants in the Muskingum River Valley. In its heyday, coal mining employed thousands of people, and injected millions of dollars into the local economy.

All good seams eventually play out, or the best machine cannot reach them. Some coal companies took a powder and left the land naked, cratered, trenched, tattooed, sterile, and unsightly. A few wooded ridges and groves of oaks were spared, but not much else. To its credit, American Electric Power, parent of the Ohio Power and Columbus Southern Power companies and subsidiary coal firms, began restoring the landscape right from the start. Since 1945, the utility has planted 41 million tree seedlings—black locust, alder, sycamore, cottonwood, silver maple, oak, ash, black walnut, tulip tree, and tons of pines. Ponds were created where groundwater settled in mining holes. Limestone strata beside coal veins naturally took the bite out of "yellow dog," an acidic pollutant from surface mining that nuked streams and lakes. The ponds are near perfect for panfish and bass. Campgrounds and picnic areas were built, and the dirt roads that once conveyed coal trucks faded into overgrown foot trails.

Granted, AEP gets public relations mileage with these patched up parcels. Be that as it may, harvest the utility's goodwill anyway. Remember, AEP didn't have to recharge the land to this extent, nor turn it public. Second, these tracts, like wine, will improve with age.

Field Notes

Keen observers will notice two kinds of land restoration. Mines closed and reclaimed since passage of a tough reclamation law in 1972 mimic their original topographical contours and tend to be open, grassy areas. The Conesville tracts, and portions of ReCreation Land, represent this type. Pre-1972 coal lands show the high walls and pits resulting from unreclaimed mining, and are predominately forested. Avondale and most of ReCreation Land are examples. Tiny ponds, mere puddles some of the them, dot ReCreation Land and Avondale Wildlife Area.

Beavers are everywhere in ReCreation Land. Look for their dams, lodges, slides, and wood chips beneath gnawed trees and shrubs. You might see these nocturnal creatures at dusk. Opossum and skunk also live here. Birders won't be disappointed in the field and forest habitats. Great blue herons appear on the pond shores.

Cuyahoga Valley National Recreation Area

On Ohio's ever-shrinking official road map (the version printed by the ever-enlarging Department of Transportation), the Cuyahoga Valley National Recreation Area looks like a green caduceus between the orange-yellow smears of Cleveland and Akron. Each year, several million human pilgrims come to the "park" for its healing power, brew of trails, history, wildlife, and charming villages. The setting is pastoral, somewhere between unshaven suburbia and upscale small town. Picture farmhouses, covered bridges, Hale Farm, Blossom Music Center, ski slopes, restored canal locks, scenic railroad, photogenic waterfalls, youth hostel, hikers and bicyclists, sandstone ledges, hemlocks, ponds, and antique shops.

LOCATION

Along the banks of the Cuyahoga River as it flows from Bath Road in Summit County to Rockside Road in Cuyahoga County. From I-77, go east from exits (north to south) at Rockside Road, Independence, Brecksville (SR 82), Boston Mills (SR 21), Wheatley Road (SR 176), and Ghent Road. From I-271, exit at SR 303 (Peninsula), and SR 8. Also Accessible from the Ohio Turnpike (exits 11 and 12), and state routes 82, 303, 8 and 21.

SIZE & DESIGNATION

About 22 miles of the Cuyahoga River twists through federal property totaling 33,000 acres. Several sites in the recreation area have been designated as national historic locations. They are described below. A beaver marsh seen from the Towpath Trail has been declared an Ohio Watchable Wildlife Site.

Technically, CVNRA is a "national recreation area," not a national park. The bureaucratic distinction is lost or ignored by visitors, and Ohioans consider it a national park. The National Park Service administers the place, they reason, so it must be a national park. No one argues that the park was established largely to protect valuable "green space." It blends in seamlessly with metroparks created earlier by Cuyahoga and Summit counties. In fact, it links the park systems, and serves as a trail hub for long paths, such as the Buckeye and Towpath trails.

ACCESS

Best place to begin your adventure is at one of three visitors' centers. Canal Visitors Center, 7104 Canal Road, Bath, is found at the north end of the park. From I-77, go east on Rockside Road over the river, south on Canal Road to its merger with Hillside Road. During warm months, the center features free demonstrations (weekends in the afternoon) of Lock 38 on the old Ohio & Erie Canal. Exhibits inside explain canal history, and lock operations. The center is open year-round and has information on trails and natural history. Phone: (216) 524-1497 or (800) 445-9667.

Happy Days Visitor Center serves the central portion. It is located on the south side of SR 303, east of Peninsula, and a mile west of the junction with SR 8. Parking for the center, however, is on the north side of SR 303. Take the tunnel to reach the center. The building was constructed by the Civilian Conservation Corps in the 1930s as a day camp for city kids. The joyful name comes from the popular tune "Happy Days Are Here Again." Today the center has exhibits, publications, meeting rooms for slide shows and nature programs, rest rooms, picnic tables, and hiking trails. Phone: (440) 650-4636.

Hunt Farm Visitor Center, open seasonally, has information, rest rooms, telephone, drinking water, and parking for towpath trail users. Look for an old farmhouse at the corner of Bolanz and Riverview roads, south of Peninsula.

The Park Service headquarters occupies old mill buildings in an abandoned company town called Jaite at the merger of Riverview and Vaughn roads. Riverview Road runs along the west bank of the Cuyahoga River from Independence to Bath

Road. The restored park offices were once company stores and homes for papermill employees, built in 1906. The structures are on the National Register of Historical Places.

Accommodations: The only sleeping places within CVNRA borders are Stanford Farm, a farmhouse converted into an American Youth Hostel (AYH), located on Stanford Road, Boston Mills (440) 467-8711; a campground at Dover Lake Park (440) 467-SWIM, a water theme park on Highland Road; and The Inn at Brandywine Falls (216-467-1812 or 650-4965), a bed & breakfast place at 8230 Brandywine Road at Stanford Road. None of these are owned by the park service. Other nearby privately-owned campgrounds and lodgings offer accommodations.

Picnic Areas: Picnic spots are scattered throughout the park and in adjacent metroparks. In CVNRA you will find tables at the visitors' centers, Kendall Lake, the Ledges, Brandywine Falls, Octagon Shelter (off Truxell Road), Rockside Road, Sagamore Grove (Sagamore Road near Frazee House), at Riverview and Columbia roads, Station Road Bridge, Boston Store, Indigo Lake (Riverview Road near Hale Farm), Oak Hill, Pine Hollow Parking Area on Quick Road, and Ira and Indian Mound trailheads. Picnic areas operate on a first-come basis. Large groups can reserve picnic shelters at the Ledges, Octagon, and Kendall Lake Locations. Reservations (fee) for the current year begin January 2.

Trails: With 180 miles of blazed trails, the Cuyahoga Valley playground—an area comprised of CVNRA and adjacent metroparks—has become a mecca for hikers, bicyclists, Nordic skiers, and horseback riders. The longest and featured trail is the Ohio & Erie Canal

Sometimes catching 40 winks is the point of going fishing.

Towpath Trail. Only a handful of trails in Ohio brings together nature, history, and humanity as well as the 20-mile towpath, which follows the full length of the park. Think of this multipurpose path as a stem with other trails leafing from it. The celebrated Buckeye Trail also wanders for 34 miles in the valley, sometimes in CVNRA, sometimes in adjacent park land.

Other trails range from a half mile to nearly five miles and most are interconnected so that users can travel various lengths. CVNRA's trail system will continue to grow, thanks largely to a partnership between the Park Service and the Cuyahoga Valley Trails Council, 1607 Delia Avenue, Akron, OH 44320. The council has designed and built trails, and printed trail handbooks. All trails are free and open year-round during daylight hours with the exception of the Order of Arrow Trail, a 13-mile Boy Scouts path. For permission to hike this trail, contact the Boys Scouts Akron Area Council by phone at (330) 773-0415. Maps for most trails are available at the main visitor centers.

Nearly 21 miles of horseback riding trails snake through the southern half of the recreation area. Five trails straddling Wetmore Road on the east side of the Cuyahoga River connect with two trails across the river off Everett Road via the Valley Trail. By combining paths equestrians can travel a 16-mile circuit through pine and hardwood forests, across creeks and meadows, and along roads and wetlands. The northern half of the park has a three-mile trail for horse and rider. Though designed for horses, hikers can use these trails too.

Trails of all kinds are also available in bordering metropolitan parks. See Bedford and Brecksville reservations (Cleveland Metroparks), and Furnace Run, Hampton Hills, O'Neil Woods and Deep Lock

Quarry metroparks (Summit County parks).

Attractions and Special Events: Along the Towpath Trail, look for the remains of locks, dams, aqueducts, and feeder channels that regulated the *Ohio & Erie Canal.* A working lock remains at Canal Visitor Center. The ruins of an aqueduct are present at Tinkers Creek near Mile 13. Good examples of locks are Lock 29 in Peninsula, Fourteen Mile Lock (Lock 37), and Lock 28, a.k.a. Deep Lock, because it had the deepest chamber. Most of the canal channel has filled in, but with some imagination you can picture its path and purpose.

The *Cuyahoga Valley Scenic Railroad* is a popular scenic railway on the west bank of the Cuyahoga River between Independence and Akron. Passengers ride in historic coaches pulled by diesel locomotives. In CVNRA, the train has authorized stops at Lock 39, Canal Visitor Center, Station Road Bridge, Boston, Peninsula (headquarters), and the Ira and Indian Mound trailheads. Roundtrips range from 16 miles to 52 miles, and reservations are highly recommended. Operates June to December. For ticket information and schedules contact Cuyahoga Valley Scenic Railroad, P.O. Box 158, 1630 West Mill Street, Peninsula, OH 44264, (216) 467-8711 or (800) 468-4070. The attraction is not affiliated with the Park Service.

The *Cuyahoga Valley Environmental Education Center* off Oak Hill Road is a year-round nature study campus for area school children and adults run by the Park Service. This is a reserved area, not a drop-in nature center. The former Gilson home serves as a dormitory. In 1877, the patriarch of the family died trying to cross Furnace Run during high water. The incident prompted construction of the Everett Covered Bridge.

The once-booming canal town of *Boston*, now Boston Mills Road east of the river, is wrapped in history and legend. Ottawa planters cultivated apple trees here long before Johnny "Appleseed" Chapman arrived in the early 19th century. During canal days, Boston became an overnight stop between Cleveland and Akron. The launching of the canal boat *Allen Trimble,* built at a Boston boatyard, announced the start of the canal on July 3, 1827. Counterfeiter James Brown (1800–1865) and his horse-thieving brother, Dan Brown, based their illegal industries in Boston. They distributed their "products" to unwitting canalers. Both eventually went to prison. President Zachary Taylor commuted James' sentence. He later served as a local justice of the peace. *Boston Store* on the towpath is a museum on canal history. A few miles

south is a village called *Peninsula*, a National Historic District known for its shops, galleries, and restaurants. The name derives from the peninsula-shaped curve formed by the Cuyahoga before canal days.

The homes in the canal-era village of *Everett* are being restored by the Park Service for the teaching staff at the Cuyahoga Valley Environmental Education Center, and for administrative offices, library, and historic artifacts. The U.S. Department of the Interior designated the hamlet a national historic district in 1974. Check out the *Everett Covered Bridge,* open for feet and bicycles, just a half mile down the road. A flood in 1975 wiped out the 1870s version. The Park Service matched the original design for its 1986 replacement.

Frazee House, Canal Road at Sagamore Road, shows federal-style architecture typical of fancy homes in the Western Reserve of 1826. Restored by the Park Service in 1995, it is open seasonally with exhibits. The Frazee and Jonathan Hale homesteads are the oldest brick homes in the valley. *Hale Farm and Village* (admission fee), Oak Hill Road, reenacts life in the Cuyahoga Valley in the 1820s. The Western Reserve Historical Society owns and operates the site. Artisans demonstrate their crafts at the village. For information contact Hale Farm and Village, 2686 Oak Hill Road, Bath, OH 44210-0296, (330) 666-3711 or (800) 589-9703.

Other historic homes along the towpath include the 1854 *Edmund Gleason Farm*, a Greek revival house and English-gambrel barn at Canal and Tinker's Creek roads, and the *Abraham Ulyatt House* (private), built in 1849 at Canal and Stone roads.

Wilson's Mill, originally Alexander Mill, diverted water from canal to power its grinding wheel from 1853 to 1972. Electric power was used until the mid-1990s. The mill, located on Canal Road south of Alexander Road, remains open as a grain and feed store.

Pinery Narrows refers to the stretch of the Cuyahoga between Frazee House and Station Road Bridge. Towering white pines and hemlocks once thickened on the sharply angled slopes, hence the name. In the early nineteenth century, the straightest ones were cut for masts and floated to Lake Erie shipyards. None of the giants survive, though second-growth hemlocks appear in side cut ravines.

Blossom Music Center, 1145 West Steels Corner Road, Cuyahoga Falls, is the summer home of the Cleveland Symphony Orchestra. Bring a picnic lunch and listen to Beethoven in a natural grass

What would be hardship at home is happiness in the woods.

amphitheater. The site is owned and managed by the Musical Arts Association (not affiliated with the Park Service). Nearby *Porthouse Theater* is owned by Kent State University. Admission is charged for both.

Boating: The Cuyahoga River would be a great canoe ride, except for unhealthy pollution entering from an Akron wastewater treatment plant. Pollution means sewage stuff, fecal matter, high levels of bacteria. In spite of this, some river rats put in canoes and rafts. The garbage is diluted and less of a health threat during times of high water. Lowhead dams at Peninsula and Station Road Bridge (above SR 82) require portage. There are no "official" put-ins in the park, but if you must paddle, try the parking lot for Lock 29 in Peninsula (north of SR 303 and west of railroad) and at the end of Pine Hill Road, off Aurora Road (SR 82) on east side of river. The latter access is across from Station Road Bridge and Brecksville Reservation, and below the low head dam. Distance from Peninsula to SR 82 is seven miles. Be sure to take out at SR 82, before the dam.

Hunting & Fishing: Shore fishing is allowed at Kendall Lake, Indigo Lake, Averill Pond (Stanford Trail), Sylvan Pond (Oak Hill Trail), Meadowedge Pond (Plateau Trail), Horseshoe Pond (Major Road),

Goosefeather Pond (Scobie Road off Oak Hill Road), Coonrad Pond (Ranger Station on Riverview Road). Fishing the Cuyahoga is unproductive and not recommended due to poor water quality.

Hunting is not allowed in the CVNRA.

Information: For more information, contact Superintendent, CVNRA, 15610 Vaughn Road, Brecksville, OH 44141, (216) 524-1497 or (800) 445-9667.

HISTORY

Nomadic humans inhabited the area 10,000 to 12,000 years ago, as the Ice Age melted into history. They hunted bison, mammoth, elk, and caribou, and gathered the fruit of the forest. They were succeeded by people who had learned to farm, trade, and establish permanent settlements. A hillock at the southern end of the park is believed to be an earthen mound of an ancient civilization. So-called "historic" people—Lenni Lenape (Delaware), Ottawa, Erie, Seneca (Iroquois), and Mingo—inhabited the area. The Cuyahoga Valley may have been neutral territory among the tribes because of its importance as a route from Lake Erie to the Ohio River.

Moravian missionaries established a European

settlement in 1786 on Tinkers Creek, near its confluence with the Cuyahoga. Their village, called Pilgerruh, was short-lived. Ten years later, Moses Cleaveland led Connecticut pioneers to the valley, another Moses delivering pilgrims to the promised land. By treaty, the Cuyahoga served as the western boundary of the U.S. until 1805.

By the second decade of the 19th century agricultural production exceeded the subsistence level. Farmers and business interests seeking more prosperity pushed for construction of canals to link Ohio to markets on the East Coast (via the Erie Canal) and Gulf of Mexico. By the mid-1820s, Ohio had begun work on the Ohio & Erie Canal, going more than 300 miles from Cleveland to Portsmouth. The July 3, 1827 launching of the *State of Ohio*, a canal boat built in Akron, marked the opening of the canal between Cleveland and Akron. Gov. Allen Trimble led the procession, which included a Boston-built boat inscribed with his name. The entire length was completed in 1832. It was the West's engineering marvel at the time. The canal brought prosperity to the valley. Towns, mills, stores, liveries, depots, and trading houses sprouted. By 1840, Ohio was the country's largest agricultural state.

The canal's glory years were short. Privatization led to maintenance problems, but the canal's killer was the railroad that replaced it in 1888. The locks and towpath became historical relics after a 1913 flood. The Cuyahoga Valley transformed into an escape place between burgeoning Cleveland and Akron. In this century, the establishment of metropolitan parks, scout camps, Blossom Music Center, Hale Farm in the valley started a revival that led to CVNRA in 1974. Park creation, and its continued managing, has been a cooperative effort among local, federal and state governments, citizens groups, and volunteers. The National Park Service opened the entire length of the Ohio & Erie Canal Towpath Trail in 1993.

GEOLOGY

As rivers go, the Cuyahoga is a puppy, born a mere 12,000 years ago at the end of the Ice Age. Characteristic of young streams, it is short (100 miles), shallow, sluggish, and mud-banked. The last Ice Age glacier, the Wisconsinan, buried, rerouted, and reversed drainage systems as it pawed across northeastern Ohio. The Cuyahoga is a consequence of that glacial manipulation, and some of its flow stretches 500 feet above an ancient riverbed.

Although Native American did not assign names to rivers, the Cuyahoga derives its name from the Lenni Lenape (Delaware) word for "crooked." Indeed, the river is crooked, or rather, V-shaped, parabolic. From its swampy source in Geauga County, its flows southerly into Akron then veers north off the summit that gives Summit County its name. A few miles south, the Tuscarawas River bounces off the summit and streams south to the Muskingum River. Eons ago the two rivers flowed as one stream, the ancient Dover River. But now the Cuyahoga turns north and empties into Lake Erie at Cleveland. Between Akron and Cleveland, the river twists through the national recreation area.

The Ritchie Ledges, or simply The Ledges, behind Happy Days Visitor Center, is Sharon conglomerate, roughly 300 million years old. It formed after strong mountain streams, flowing from the north and east, deposited immense piles of gravel on the coast of an ocean then covering Ohio. The churning water gave the quartz pebbles their rounded shape. This gravel beach fanned out in a wide delta, bigger than the delta at the mouth of the Mississippi. After the sea receded, the sediment compacted into the coarse rock you see here. Water eroding through joints in the rock created the maze of passages characteristic of the ledges. Tree roots growing and expanding in the cracks hastened the erosion. Remnants of Sharon conglomerate ledges also appear along the Bike & Hike Trail between SR 303 and Boston Mills Road. Much of the Boston Ledges area, however, was buried during construction of the railroad grade. Caution: Climbing the ledges is unsafe for humans, destructive for nature. Human abuse can ruin fragile mosses, lichens, and plants that grow on the rock cliffs.

FIELD NOTES

Department stores do inventory to take stock of the business. So do naturalists. Its exhaustive and tedious grunt work but important for land management. At the CVNRA, now 60 percent forested, 923 plant species grow, including rarities such as yellow lady's slipper, thin leaf sedge, Greene's rush, fringed gentian, and juniper. Somebody identified 77 kinds of moss, 17 types of liverwort and hornwort, and 66 varieties of lichens.

The Cuyahoga River serves as a flyway for migratory birds—waterfowl, warblers, swallows, wrens, flycatchers, etc.—every spring and fall. More than 230 species assemble here, and the birding improves yearly as the forest recovers and wetland habitats are constructed. Among warblers look for the palm, yellow-rumped, Nashville, pine, and orange-crowned. Good eyes will find the black-crowned and yellow-crowned night herons, the cattle egret, and least bittern. Dusk brings the melodies of whippoorwills and barred owls to visitors' ears.

The bald eagle, peregrine falcon, and osprey—all endangered—occasionally visit. Red-headed and red-bellied woodpeckers reside here, as do the wild turkey, bobwhite and ring-necked pheasant. Winter birders might spot common goldeneye, tundra swan, winter wren, Lapland larkspur, and rufous-sided towhee. Visitor centers sell bird checklists for thirty cents.

Mammals are represented by 32 species. The cast includes the beaver, coyote, long-tailed weasel, hairy-tailed mole, meadow jumping mouse (sometimes mistaken for frogs), mink and southern flying squirrel. Twenty-two types of amphibians have been seen. Look for the spotted and four-toed salamanders (rare), tree frogs called pepper and greater green, and the omnipresent bullfrog. Red-eared slider (a snake, not a curve ball), stinkpot turtle, five-lined skink, and ringneck snake are on the roster of 18 reptiles.

Ponds, creeks and the Cuyahoga River (somewhat) host fish called northern hog sucker, brook stickelback, stoneroller minnow, Johnny darter, and southern redbelly dace. Anglers cast for black and white crappie, bullhead (black, brown, and yellow), sunfish (redear, pumpkinseed, Warmouth), bass (largemouth, rock, and smallmouth), bluegill, and sucker.

A survey at two locations in the park in 1996 uncovered 41 kinds of butterflies. Monarchs, great spangled fritillaries, European skippers, and wood nymphs were abundant, but the coral hairstreak, little glassy wing, comma, and painted lady were soloists. Butterfly collecting is not permitted.

Attractions & Special Events: CVNRA has outdoors summer concerts, festivals, and large group activities at its Special Events Area, off Riverview Road, 1.5 miles north of Ira Road and 4.5 miles south of SR 303. Park staffers and volunteers lead nature and recreation programs all year from various locations. Write or call (1-800-445-9667) for a "Schedule of Events," published by the park.

JOURNAL

In the spring of 1996, I hiked north from Station Road Bridge to see a great blue heron rookery in the Pinery Narrows. After a short mile-long walk, I was rewarded with the sight of big, gawky shorebirds uncomfortably nesting in piles of sticks atop sycamore trees. They fidgeted, flapped their wings for balance, stretched to work out stiffness. Then I spotted the source of their agitation: the scenic train had backed up to the rookery to let adolescent school kids have a five-minute look. As the train pulled away, the pilot blasted the train horn (a silly safety precaution, I suppose). The explosion flushed the herons off their nests, shaking loose all the fine china and glassware in the riparian forest. Anger swelled my throat. If a terrorist heron had awakened a nursery of peaceful newborns with a foghorn, it would have been destroyed with extreme prejudice. Small disturbances, compounded daily, lower nesting success, and possibly send the herons packing.

MUSKINGUM WATERSHED CONSERVANCY DISTRICT

Politicians, planners, and countless committees had been talking about changing the shape of Eastern Ohio since the murderous flood of 1913. The disaster took 50 lives in the Muskingum River Valley, and ruined property totaling $300 million. It took the powers that be 20 years to finally move a spadeful of dirt. Since its creation in 1933 the *Muskingum Watershed Conservancy District (MWCD) has subdued the convulsive river (at least for now), and managed a string of lakes and recreation areas that rival Ohio's state parks.*

LOCATION

The Muskingum begins in Coshocton where the Tuscarawas River, descending from the northeast, joins the Walhonding River from the northwest. From here, it slides 112 miles to Marietta and empties into

The Muskie is Wide

• *MWCD contains Ohio's two largest public campgrounds at Tappan and Seneca lakes.*

• *It's lakes count for 342 miles of shoreline, more than Lake Erie*

• *Ohio's largest muskellunge and sucker fish were caught in MWCD waters.*

the Ohio River. En route it is refreshed by Wills Creek and the Licking River at Zanesville.

SIZE & DESIGNATION

The watershed is the largest within Ohio, encompassing 8,051 square miles, roughly one-fifth of the state, or an area bigger than New Jersey. It drains parts of 18 counties from Akron to Marietta, and Mansfield to Cadiz.

After the state park system, "Big Muskie" is Ohio's largest outdoor playground. It boasts 38,000 acres of public land, more than 3,000 campsites, 342 miles of shoreline (more than Lake Erie), some of the best fishing in Ohio (including state record fish catches; for details, see park descriptions and page 526 [fishing chapter]), plus boat ramps, cabins, marinas, hunting, trapping, resort lodge, boat and bike rentals, golf courses, swimming, hiking trails, picnic areas, two airfields and a heliport, and nature centers. All 10 lakes, and three dry dams are designated state wildlife areas.

ACCESS

See individual areas and parks for details.

Information: To learn more, and unless otherwise noted in descriptions that follow, contact the Muskingum Watershed Conservancy District, 1319 Third St., NW, P.O. Box 349, New Philadelphia, OH 44663-0349, , (330) 343-6647; fax, (330) 364-4161; web site, http://www.mwcdlakes.com.

HISTORY

A previous makeover of the region occurred near the end of the Ice Age, roughly 20,000 years ago. Although the thick ice sheet only covered the northern and western fringes of the basin, meltwater that poured off the glacier reconfigured the rest of the landscape. Sprawling lakes at the vanguard of the glacier breached divides and created new watersheds. Ancient river systems vanished, or reversed directions, or occupied new channels. The Muskingum River and its tributaries spawned from the Ice Age.

Native Americans paddled the Muskingum to reach Lake Erie and the Ohio River. They supplemented their diet with mollusks and fish from its water. One fabled muskellunge caught back in those good

> *One fabled muskellunge... measured six feet and weighed 100 pounds.*

old days measured six feet and weighed 100 pounds. White settlers plied the river in flatboats, and later in steamboats. In the late 1830s, the state constructed a canal of eleven locks and ten dams along the river as a branch of the Ohio & Erie Canal. (See Muskingum River State Park.) By the mid-1850s railroads had made canals obsolete.

Flooding has always been part of life in the Muskingum Valley. This recurring natural event restored nutrients to bottomland soils, reconfigured channels, and performed other beneficial and mysterious chores. High water becomes a problem, however, when people get in its way. The deforestation that brought prosperity to human enterprises in the 19th century hastened soil erosion and aggravated flooding. Five severe floods ransacked the basin from 1850-1900. Besides the loss of fifty souls, the powerful 1913 flood ruined the canal and washed away every bridge, dock, and pier between Zanesville and Marietta.

From 1935 to 1938, the MWCD and U.S. Army Corps of Engineers built 14 dams on headwater tributaries with $41 million in federal funds and thousands of workers employed by the Public Works Administration. The project also involved buying land, organizing agencies, and relocating roads, railroads, pipelines, and families. The MWCD, a political subdivision of the state, owns and manages the public land in the district. It pays for itself through visitor fees (small day-use charges, camping, lodging, etc.), residential and commercial leases, and vendor contracts. An 18-member Conservancy Court, composed of a common pleas judge from each county in the district, governs the MWCD. The U.S. Army Corps of Engineers operates the dams and flood control systems.

Permanent reservoirs—Atwood, Beach City, Charles Mill, Clendening, Leesville, Piedmont, Pleasant Hill, Seneca, Tappan, and Wills Creek—swell behind 10 impoundments. The gates at Bolivar, Dover, Mohawk, and Mohicanville "dry" dams close only during floods. The new lakes, comprising 16,000 acres, doubled Ohio's inland water resources, and became valuable recreation areas that attract more than five million visitors annually.

Atwood Lake and Park

"It's another lovely day at Atwood Lake Resort and Conference Center. How can I help you?" That's how the receptionist answers the resort's toll-free phone line, even when it's raining torrents. Atwood is the flagship park—the luxury liner—of the Muskingum Watershed Conservancy District, with resort lodge, great sailing, modern campground, two golf courses, lakeshore cabins, jacuzzi, the whole nine yards. You can even rent an aquacycle at the beach, a tricycle with balloon tires that floats on water. I'll stick to my canoe and cast for largemouths in a peaceful lake cove.

LOCATION

Carroll County, Monroe Township, and Tuscarawas County, Warren Township.

SIZE & DESIGNATION

Land –3,000 acres; water –1,540 acres. MWCD owns the lake and surrounding land, except for the dam, spillway, and picnic area, which is owned and managed by the U.S. Army Corps of Engineers. The Ohio Department of Natural Resources, Division of Wildlife has designated the property a state wildlife area.

ACCESS

From Interstate 77 (Exit 93), travel on SR 212 southeasterly 11 miles, then take CR 93 (Atwood Lake Road) to the west marina and park entrance. Turn right on CR 114 (Lakeview Road) to reach the campground. Other facilities, notably Atwood Lake Resort and Conference Center, are on SR 542, which branches from SR 212 and SR 39. From New Philadelphia, follow SR 39 to Dellroy.

Accommodations: Choose among the 104 room Atwood Lake Resort and Conference Center (a.k.a. Atwood Lodge), three types of cabins, or primitive to full-hookup camping.

The lodge (off SR 542) also has a restaurant, lighted tennis courts, indoor and outdoor swimming courts, meeting rooms (up to 400 people), jacuzzi, lounge, and two golf courses (an 18-holer measuring 6,007 yards, and a lighted nine-hole, par 3 course with a driving range). There's also an airfield for small planes and a helicopter pad just a few miles away.

Atwood Lake has vacation cabins outfitted for year-round cooking, eating, and sleeping (no linens). Seventeen, four-bedroom cabins dot the shoreline near the resort. These cabins can handle 10 people comfortably. For information on lodge rooms and the four-bed cabins contact Atwood Lake Resort and Conference Center, 2650 Lodge Road, Dellroy, OH 44620, (800) 362-6406 or (330) 735-2211.

Ten, two-bedroom vacation cabins are located near the campground (off Lakeview Road, or CR 114). Each has a lake view and accommodates six people. Three are heated for year-round pleasure, five have screened porches, two have decks. Five rustic "camper" cabins are scattered in the campground. Rustic means your basic cottage: wood floor, roof, three windows, one electric outlet, a fluorescent lamp.

The campground has sites for travelers with huge RVs (full hookups) or "pup" tents (primitive spots). All 500 sites are available on a first-come, first-served basis. Many head for Section F, at the tip of a peninsula jutting into the lake. Campground amenities include an activity center featuring nature exhibits, laundry, camp store, and snack bar; plus basketball, volleyball, bike trail, showers, toilets, dump station, and playground. Four group campsites, picnic shelters, group picnic areas are also available. To find out more contact the park above.

Picnic Areas & Swimming: The sandy swimming beach near the camping area has changing rooms, concession stand, playground, water, and picnic tables. Here you can also rent bumper boats, pedal boats, and big-wheeled aquacycles.

Trails: Seven miles of foot trails depart from the campground and cabin area. The most popular walk goes from the amphitheater to an observation tower—a short hike. A bike trail runs alongside Atwood Lake Road near the Atwood Marina West. In the winter cross-country skiers can ski on the golf courses, and trails.

Boating: Two full-service marinas cater to boaters. Atwood Marina West, located on Atwood Lake Road near the campground, has docks, ramps, rental boats, boat sales, fuel, store, restaurant, and gift shop. It stays open daily, all year. Contact Atwood

Marina West, 9298 Atwood Lake Road, Mineral City, OH 44656, , (800) 882-6339 or (330) 364-4703.

The Sail & Power Marina East, off SR 542, is open daily March 1-November 1. Here boaters find docks, ramps, fishing supplies, sales and rentals, and snack bar. Write to P.O. Box 57, Dellroy, OH 44620, (330) 735-2323. The U.S. Army Corps of Engineers also has a boat launch and picnic area near the dam it owns and operates at the western tip, off SR 212.

Explore 28 miles of shoreline with a maximum depth of 41 feet. The Atwood Yacht Club, a private sailing club, stages races here. Waterskiing (horsepower limit 25 hp) is popular, too. Sightseers can view the lake in scheduled cruises. The pontoon boats stop at the marinas and lodge.

Hunting, Trapping & Fishing: Atwood Lake boasts good catches of saugeye (a hybrid of sauger and walleye), channel catfish, bullheads, largemouth bass (try the shore near the cabins), crappie, bluegill, yellow perch, walleye, and northern pike. The Ohio Department of Natural Resources stocks the lake. In 1995, 155,631 saugeye fingerlings fortified these waters. Call the marinas for current catch reports. Ice fishing is highly recommended here.

Hunting and trapping are permitted in designated areas. Some archers consider Atwood a hot spot for early season bucks. Hunters should get a park map before entering the woods. Stay clear of the many private cottages around the lake.

Attractions & Special Events: The park hosts the annual Atwood Area Fall Festival held on the first weekend in October. You'll find Civil War reenactments, primitive weapons, crafts, food, antique engines, classic cars, haunted hayrides, and other attractions.

Information: Contact Atwood Lake Park, 4956 Shop Road, NE, Mineral City, OH 44656, (330) 343-6780.

FIELD NOTES

Birders keep their eyes peeled for nesting greenbacked herons, clans of ducks, great horned and barred owls, six brands of woodpeckers (notably pileated), and grouse.

Beach City Lake

Beach City Lake, developed primarily for flood control, is a local fishing hole in Amish Country. Pike and bass swim here, but most settle for panfish. The nearby Beach City State Wildlife Area is a hunter's haven for waterfowl.

LOCATION

Northwestern Tuscarawas County, Franklin and Wayne townships.

SIZE & DESIGNATION

Land –930 acres; water–420 acres.

ACCESS

At the junction of SR 93 and SR 250.
Accommodations: None.
Trails: None designated.
Boating: No motors faster than 10 horsepower, please. Shoreline measures 18.8 miles with an average depth of four feet and a maximum depth of 13 feet. A public boat ramp, the only MWCD development, is located on SR 93, south of its merger with SR 250.

Trapping & Fishing: Northern pike, channel catfish, bullhead, largemouth bass, crappie, bluegill, and saugeye swim here. Some 42,300 saugeye "one-inchers" were stocked in 1995. Hunting and trapping are allowed in designated areas. Adjacent Beach City State Wildlife Area offers additional opportunities.

Charles Mill Lake and Park

The first time I saw Charles Mill Lake was out of the corner of my eye, while hurrying to Wooster on Route 30. On the way back to Columbus, I slowed down for a longer look. Next time, I drove in, lingered awhile, tossed a few pebbles into the water, watched a bass jump for a bug, vowed to spend a day or two here next time. And I did come back here for a day or longer; and I said to myself then that next time I'll probe the coves in my canoe, trying to catch the bass that teased me way back when.

LOCATION

Five miles east of Mansfield, straddling Richland and Ashland counties.

SIZE & DESIGNATION

Land–2,000 acres; water–1,350 acres. The U.S. Army Corps of Engineers owns and operates the dam, spillway, and picnic area at the south end of the park. The Ohio Department of Natural Resources, Division of Wildlife lists the sites as a public hunting area.

ACCESS

From I-71, go east on US 30, then south on SR 603, and west on SR 430. Travelers on US 30 exit at SR 603 (east of I-71). The park entrance is on SR 430, west of SR 603. Follow park signs to the campground, marina, and cabins.

Accommodations: More than 500 camp sites occupy a finger pointing south in Charles Mill Lake. Some sites have electricity, some don't. Most can handle RVs up to 35 feet. Five camper cabins, several patio cabins with screened porches, and tepees (4-6 people) can be rented. Frills include hot showers, playground, flush toilets, game courts, swimming beach, picnic shelters, and amphitheater for nature programs. An activities leader prepares games and crafts for kids and parents in summer.

Boating: Boaters launch their craft at the Charles Mill Marina in the camping area. Open daily from mid-March to mid-October, the marina offers docks, ramps, boat sales, rentals, supplies, fuel, fishing gear, licenses, bait, and snacks. Pontoon boats can be dry docked here during winter. Contact Charles Mill Marina, 1277 SR 403, Mansfield, OH 44903, (419) 368-5951. The private Mohican Yacht Club operates a marina at the south end. Pontoon boats are popular here.

Although the lake is relatively shallow, averaging 5.5 feet and no deeper than 16 feet, boaters have 34 miles of shoreline to navigate. Horsepower limit is 10. Sightseeing cruises on pontoon boats ply in warm weather.

Trails: There is a short, not-very-exciting trail off SR 430 (west of the entrance). Go to Mohican State Park or one of the Richland County metroparks instead.

Hunting, Trapping & Fishing: There is plenty of room to cast for catfish (channel and flathead), bull-head, largemouth bass (late summer especially), crappie, bluegill, and saugeye (147,000 stocked in 1995). Call the marina for catch report. Ice fishing is permitted.

Hunters and trappers should obtain a park map at the entrance to familiarize themselves with the areas off-limits to hunting.

Attractions & Special Events: The Charles Mill Boat Parade, a fleet of whatever floats in the lake, assembles for thousands of participants and spectators in August.

Information: Contact Charles Mill Lake Park, 1271 Rt. 4, SR 430, Mansfield, OH 44903, (419) 368-6885.

FIELD NOTES

Keep binoculars ready for the spring and autumn migrations of ducks—canvasback, redhead, gadwall, American wigeon, ring-necked, scaup, bufflehead, and mergansers (hooded, common, red-breasted). The scarlet tanager, northern oriole, red-headed woodpecker, cerulean warbler, great-crested flycatcher, and wood thrush are common in woodlots.

Clendening Lake

Clendening is Big Muskie's "quiet child," a solitary spot with unwrinkled water, and shy, beguiling beauty. Its master proudly claims that soft-spoken Clendening is the "largest undeveloped lake in Ohio," meaning the 41-mile shoreline is cottage-free and uncluttered. No carry-outs, pizza parlors, nor bait sheds litter the shore. No beach, bumper boats, nor bike path. Clendening Lake hatched when the U.S. Army Corps of Engineers plugged Brushy Fork Creek at Tippecanoe in 1937. It has matured into one of the state's most photogenic lakes—a picture perfect snake of a lake.

Camp Ohio — drive off, drop in, camp out, drop out.

LOCATION

Southwestern Harrison County, Washington and Nottingham townships.

SIZE & DESIGNATION

Land–4,800 acres; water–1,800 acres. MWCD has designated the lake as a "natural wildlife area" with limited development and human intrusions. The U.S. Army Corps of Engineers owns and maintains the dam, spillway, picnic area, and playground near the village of Tippecanoe. The place also is a state wildlife area.

ACCESS

You get there via SR 800 or SR 799 (Clendening Lake Road). The campground and marina are located on Bose Road, off SR 799.

Accommodations: A campground with 80 sites (with and without electricity) can accommodate tenters and RVs up to 35 feet. Hot showers, flush toilets, and playground are available. The nearby marina rents four motel units, and two camper trailers March through October. Boaters can sleep in their craft in marked areas. Check at the marina.

Trails: A section of the Buckeye Trail wanders through the eastern end of the park, roughly running along the lakeshore between SR 799 (near the junction with Long Road) and Brushy Fork Road (CR 1). You are free to roam in untrodden areas around Clendening Lake.

Boating: Clendening Marina offers docks, a ramp, boat sales and service, fishing supplies, rental boats, fuel, and a lunch counter. It is open every day March 2 through November 1. Another boat launch is off CR 6, east of Tippecanoe.

Average water depth is 16 feet; the deepest spot is 41 feet. Boat motors cannot exceed 10 horsepower. Boaters can swim in the area marked by buoys (inquire at the marina or check park map).

Hunting, Trapping & Fishing: Clendening is an angler's paradise, whether or not you catch fish. Reknowned for catfish, Ohio's largest flathead catfish was snagged here on July 28, 1979. The beast weighed 76 pounds, eight ounces, and measured 53.6 inches. Gear-stripping cats in the 45–60-pound category are landed yearly. Clendening is also a hot spot for smallmouth and largemouth bass. The "regulars" head for Hefling

Bay or Coleman Run Bay (Long Bay). Also try for muskellunge (in May), bullhead, crappie, bluegill (summer), and saugeye (spring, fall). ODNR dumped 180,000 tiny saugeye into the lake in 1995.

Deer, turkeys, squirrels, and grouse inhabit the land. Insiders say MWCD land along SR 800 is ripe with deer. The marina and campground areas are off-limits. Be careful hunting near the YMCA and Boy Scout camps on the east shore, and the scout camp south of the marina.

Contact Clendening Marina, 79100 Bose Road, Freeport, OH 43973, (740) 658-3691.

Leesville Lake

Leesville Lake put the "musk" in Big Muskie, especially in July. Many whoppers (fish and stories) have originated here. Though celebrated for its mighty muskellunge, Ohio's biggest sucker (referring to the fish) came from Leesville's depths. So, at Leesville you can catch a whopper of a sucker, or be a sucker for a whopper.

LOCATION

Southwestern Carroll County, Perry, Orange, Union, and Monroe townships. The lake is boxed in one three sides by state routes 212, 164, and 332.

SIZE & DESIGNATION

Land–2,709 acres; water–1,000 acres. The dam, spillway, and surrounding picnic area are owned and managed by the U.S. Army Corps of Engineers.

ACCESS

Follow these routes to reach the marinas and campgrounds. From Carrollton take SR 332 (Scio Road) south, then turn right (west) on Azalea Road (CR 22) to reach the Petersburg Boat Landing (also called the North Fork Marina and Campground). To find Clow's Marina and Campground (South Fork facilities), continue south on SR 332, then take SR 164 west, SR 212 north, and Deer Road (right turn).

Accommodations: The campgrounds at the two marinas have a total of 200 sites, some with electric hookups. RVs up to 35 feet can fit in a site. Cabins and motels rooms are also available at marinas. Campground amenities include a playground. Atwood Lake Park staffers operate the campground at Clow's Marina. (Don't confuse the marina campgrounds with the several youth camps that ring the lake.)

Boating: The full-service marinas have docks, public ramps, fuel, fishing licenses and supplies, boat rentals, and food. Both stay open daily March 1 through November 1. Hours change depending on the season. Summer hours are roughly sunrise to sunset.

A horsepower limit of 10 hp is in effect. Boaters can explore 28 miles of shoreline. The deepest spot is 47 feet; the average depth is nearly 20 feet , the deepest among MWCD lakes.

Hunting & Fishing: Fishers, wildlife officers, and outdoors writers rank Leesville the top muskie lake in Ohio. It recently led Ohio with 41 "Huskie Muskie" catches (42 inches or longer), and 469 trophies (30-42 inches), according to the Ohio Huskie Muskie Club, a conservation group founded in 1961 to support muskie sport fishing. To maintain that ranking the Ohio Department of Natural Resources put 2,000 fish (averaging 10.5 inches) into the lake in 1995. Hot spots include the deep water along the dam (especially in August at dusk) and the North Fork between Camp Muskingum and the dam. Crappie in the three-pound class have been pulled out of Leesville, where they gather in shallows at both tips of the lake. Big catches of pike, channel catfish, bullhead, largemouth bass, bluegill, and yellow perch have also been reported.

Heavily forested sections have wild turkey, squirrel, grouse, and deer (especially the South Fork, along SR 164). In fact, Leesville is a "sleeper" hot spot for whitetails. Beside this MWCD site, sportsmen can pursue game in nearby Egypt Valley (14,300 acres) and Leesville state wildlife areas. Some state game land abuts MWCD boundaries.

Information: Contact Clow's Marina, 4131 Deer Road SW, Bowerston, OH 44695, phone (740) 269-5371; Petersburg Boat Landing and Campground, 2126 Azalea Road SW, Carrollton, OH 44615, (330) 627-4270.

FIELD NOTES

Osprey, an endangered raptor, has been spotted over the shore, but it does not nest here. Gulls are plentiful at times. Great blue herons have settled on some ridges above the lake. In the woods, listen for pileated woodpeckers, black-billed cuckoos, and warblers.

Piedmont Lake

Scotland's Loch Ness has its fabled freshwater monster, Nessie, the prehistoric "something" seen by a handful, sought by hundreds, doubted by thousands. Piedmont Lake has freshwater monsters, too: giant-sized muskellunges. One old-timer swears he saw a seven-footer pull up alongside his 14-foot boat! The mighty beast lifted the boat as it swam away. Occasionally, a cagey (or lucky) angler reels one to the surface: the state-record monster was caught by Joe Lykins on April 2, 1972—55 pounds, 50.25 inches! Anglers scored 29 in the "Huskie Muskie" category (42 inches or longer) in 1996. Some 260 trophies (30 inches or longer) were taken here in 1995. Loch Ness, eat your heart out.

LOCATION

Northwestern Belmont County, Flushing and Kirkwood townships; Southwestern Harrison County, Moorefield Township, Northeastern Guernsey County, Londonderry Township.

SIZE & DESIGNATION

Land–4,416 acres; water–2,270 acres. The U.S. Army Corps of Engineers owns and operates the dam and spillway.

ACCESS

From I-70, travel north on SR 800. Turn right on Marina Road (just south of the junction with US 22) to reach the campground and marina at the north end of the lake. The south boat ramp is on TR 803 off SR

800. US 22 touches the northern tip. SR 800 branches from US 22.

Accommodations: Piedmont Marina has 87 campsites, 17 with electricity, 16 with full hookups. Showers, flush toilets, and a playground are available. It also runs a four-room motel (unheated) April 1 to November 1.

Picnic Areas: Look for the picnic tables in the US 22 roadside rest area near the dam, a facility of the Ohio Department of Transportation.

Trails: The Buckeye Trail traces the northwest shoreline from US 22 to the marina. You are free to roam on the rest of the trail-less property.

Boating: Boat owners can launch from two ramps: one at the marina, the other on TR 803, off SR 800. The full-service marina has docks, boat sales and service, fuel, fishing gear and licenses, boat rentals, and snack bar. It is open April 1 to November 1, hours varying with the season. A boater's swim area is located a mile southeast from the marina. A 10-horsepower limit on a boat motor is enforced.

The deepest pool is 38 feet; the average depth, 14.8 feet.

Hunting & Fishing: The Ohio Huskie Muskie Club puts Piedmont Lake near the top of its list of hot spots. Stringers of bluegill, bass (largemouth and smallmouth), crappie, yellow perch, saugeye, bullhead, and catfish (channel and flathead) come easily to veteran lakers. Insiders recommend Sixmile Run Bay and Indian Run Bay for June bass. For the latest hot spots, call the marina or cozy up to one of the members of the sportsmen's camps on the lakeshore.

The Ohio Department of Natural Resources keeps feeding Piedmont with future champions. In 1995, 231,536 saugeye, 2,310 muskellunge, and 23,215 channel cat fingerlings were released here.

There is lots of space for deer, squirrels, turkey and ruffed grouse, and hunting pressure is weak because the rugged terrain of ridges and hollows deters many hunters. I hear that grouse are abundant and that turkey roam in large flocks in the southern half of the lake.

Information: Contact Piedmont Marina, 32281 Marina Road, Freeport, OH 43973, phone (740) 658-3735.

FIELD NOTES

Hardwoods cloak the slopes—beech, maple, oak, hickory mostly. The pines you see have been planted for reforestation and erosion control. Nesting birds include red-tailed and Cooper's hawks, whippoorwill (listen for its distinctive song in the evening), screech, barred, and great horned owls, Arcadian and great-crested flycatchers, warblers (worm-eating, yellow, Kentucky, cerulean, and others), scarlet tanagers, orchard and northern orioles, ruby-throated hummingbird, belted kingfisher (along shore and streambanks), rufous-sided towhees, and black-billed cuckoo. Waterfowl assemble during the spring and autumn migrations. Sometimes tundra swans linger in mid-March.

Pleasant Hill Lake and Park

This place has an identity problem, but some misunderstandings are easily corrected. The lake you see from the lodge at Mohican State Park is Pleasant Hill Lake, not Mohican Lake. Most of the land around the lake (except for the lodge) is part of Pleasant Hill Lake and Park. The campground on the north shore (across from the lodge) resides in Pleasant Hill, not Mohican Memorial State Forest nor Mohican State Park, which each have campsites below the dam, along the Clear Fork of the Mohican River.

Pleasant Hill Lake and Park represents more than 22 percent of the recreation land that most Ohioans simply call "Mohican." Pleasant Hill Lake has more campsites than the better-known state park and state forest combined, and runs the only public swimming beach and marina on the lake. And it is just as close to all the other attractions—ski slopes, canoe liveries, etc.—in Mohican Territory.

LOCATION
Southeastern Richland County, Worthington and Monroe townships; Southwestern Ashland County, Green and Hanover townships.

SIZE & DESIGNATION
Land–1,345 acres; water–850 acres. The U.S. Army Corps of Engineers owns and maintains the dam, spillway, and parking lot to hiking trails into Clearfork Gorge.

ACCESS
The park entrance is on SR 95, which passes north of the lake. From Loudonville (crossroads of state routes 3, 60 and 39), take SR 39 heading westerly, then SR 95 westerly (left).

Accommodations: Pleasant Hill Lake has 380 campsites with electric hookups and space for RVs up to 35 feet. Some 20 sites on a separate loop can handle bigger campers requiring full hookups. Camp sites are available on a first-come, first-served basis. Two areas have been set aside for group camping.

Campground comforts include hot showers, toilets, shelterhouse (reservation required), nature center, amphitheater, playgrounds, dumping station, and an activity center for games, programs, crafts, and family fun. Follow park signs to the public swimming beach with, concession stand, changing rooms and toilets. (The park is open year-round, but fully operational Memorial Day to Labor Day.)

Reservations are recommended for the 10, two-bedroom vacation cabins, and four camper cabins. The vacation cabins can sleep six people, and come with cooking and eating utensils, and bedding (no linen). Camper cabins provide no-frills shelter for four.

Some campers and visitors arrive in Piper Cubs. Pilots can land small planes at an MWCD airfield and hike less than two miles to the campground and marina via Covert Road.

Trails: Two tiny trails in the campground—Blue Heron and Deer Run trails—serve as nature education labs, or as brief walks between activities. Go to the state park and state forest for real hikes.

Boating: Unlimited horsepower makes Pleasant Hill Lake popular for water skiing, rooster-tailing, and flat-out racing. You'll find a public boat ramp off Covert Road, near the marina; though some use the launch operated by the Pleasant Hill Boat Club east of the campground. The park brochure map shows two boater swim areas.

The marina is full-service, meaning it features

docks, boat sales and rentals, full, lunch counter, fishing supplies, licenses, and bait. It is open April 15 to October 15. Contact Pleasant Hill Marina, (419) 938-6488.

Probing Pleasant Hill Lake's 13-mile shoreline is not as thrilling as other Big Musky lakes. This one lacks the jaggedness, and the numerous roots and branches because the reservoir occupies a deep, smoothed-out gorge. Water of the Clear Fork of the Mohican River plunges to 54 feet in spots (the deepest pool among MWCD lakes) but it evens out to 16 feet.

Hunting & Fishing: One snowy day in February 1994 I found a half-dozen hearty "eskimos" throwing baited lines into frothy water below the plug containing Pleasant Hill Lake. A few "keepers," a species unknown to me, bobbed in one guy's pail. "Saugeyes," said a smiling angler with icicles clinging to a graying beard. Both fish and fisherman enlivened in the icy weather. Bluegill, crappie, yellow perch, bass (small-mouth, largemouth, and white), catfish (channel and flathead), and bullhead also patrol the lake.

The public lands all run together—MWCD property, the state forest, state park—making a contiguous hunting ground of about 9,000 acres. Plenty of room

Muskellunge 101

The Fish Who Would be King

The name of Ohio's largest game fish, muskellunge, comes from an Ojibway Indian word meaning big fish or great pike. Like all members of the pike family, the muskie has large teeth and a soft dorsal fin located far back near the forked tail. It differs from the other members of the pike family (northern pike and pickerels) in having cheeks that are half scaled; the others have fully scaled cheeks. The upper body of a muskie is greenish, yellowish, or brownish olive; the sides are light olive-green, yellow, or golden with some dusky spots on the rear third. The belly is white or yellowish.

Females muskellunge grow faster and live longer than males. By age 3, females are larger than males, and they continue to grow faster in later years. The largest muskie caught in Ohio since 1982 was an 11-year-old female 55 3/4 inches long and 47 1/2 pounds; the oldest was a 13-year-old female.

Muskellunge have a decided preference for clear, cool waters with sandy bottoms and aquatic vegetation or submerged brush. Males become sexually mature at three years of age, females at four. Spawning occurs in April and May when water temperatures reach the low 50s. The eggs are small, about 50,000 to 60,000 per quart. A single female may produce as many as 200,000. The eggs are dropped on soft shallow bottoms, where they adhere to vegetation and other debris.

The hybrid or tiger muskie is an artificial cross between a northern pike male and a pure muskie female. The hybrid looks like the pure muskie except that it has five or six pores on the bottom of the chin bone instead of seven to nine. The hybrid also normally has dark-and light-colored bars on its sides and back and spots on the caudal, dorsal, and anal fins. Muskies are ambush feeders, taking anything that moves if it will fit in their mouth. Suckers are probably the most common food in streams; in lakes, shad and carp are frequently eaten.

—SO

for game and its pursuers.

Information: Contact Pleasant Hill Lake and Park, 3431 SR 95, Perrysville, OH 44864, (419) 938-7884.

Seneca Lake and Park

Seneca Lake is the MWCD's biggest lake and its biggest recreation site. Statewide, Seneca Lake is third largest in Ohio, and with 576 campsites it has the state's second biggest public campground, topped only by Tappan Lake.

LOCATION

Northern Noble County, Wayne, Seneca, and Beaver townships; Southern Guernsey County, Richland Township. The lake is wrapped by state routes 313, 147 and 574.

SIZE & DESIGNATION

Land–4,060 acres; water–3,550 acres. The site also is considered a state wildlife area. The U.S. Army Corps of Engineers owns and operates the dam and spillway. The U.S. Fish and Wildlife Service runs the Senecaville National Fish Hatchery below the dam.

ACCESS

All facilities are located in the northwest corner of the park. From I-77, drive eastward on SR 313 to Senecaville. The Marina Point campground and marina will be on the right, just past the intersection with SR 574. Take SR 574 southbound (across the dam) about two miles to the park campground and beach.

Accommodations: The 576-site campground is divided into two locations. Both spots have showerhouses and toilets. All sites have electricity, and can handle RVs up to 35 feet. Some accommodate longer campers.

The Marina Point campground (SR 313) offers 320 sites (20 with full water and sewage hookups). Families favor the Seneca Lake Park campground (SR 574) which boasts 256 sites, 106 full hookups. The latter camp (in full service from Memorial Day to Labor Day) has a swimming beach (with concession stand and changing rooms), several playgrounds,

three picnic shelters, a nature center, amphitheater, boat and bike rentals, miniature golf and daily activities for families. Five unfurnished camper cabins (sleep four), and five two-bedroom vacation cabins (sleep six) provide other camping choices. Cabins should be reserved in advance.

Trails: The intrastate Buckeye Trail follows the paved highways through the park—state routes 313 and 574. You won't have to battle traffic and noise on the two-mile Nature Trail in the Seneca Lake Park camping area.

Boating: There is plenty of room for speedy motor boats (up to 180 horsepower) with skiers in tow. Slower-paced sailors can cruise into the Seneca's many crooked coves, and isolated inlets. Boat ramps are located at Marina Point, and at the roadside rest stop off SR 574 near the dam.

Docks, boat sales and rentals, restaurant, bait, fuel, and fishing licenses are found at the marina, open daily February 1 through November 1. Contact Seneca Lake Marina, P.O. Box 128 Senecaville, OH 43780; (740) 685-5831. Note the location of boater swim areas on the park brochure map. The lake has a maximum depth of 31 feet; an average depth of 12.25 feet.

Hunting & Fishing: Like its MWCD brethren, Seneca Lake is an anglers' paradise. Walleyes top the list of prize catches. No wonder. More than 357,000 walleye fingerlings were released here by the Ohio Department of Natural Resources in 1995, along with 3,000 striped bass. Fishers also catch their limit of bass (white, striped, and largemouth), catfish (channel and flathead), crappie, bluegill, and bullhead. Some yellow perch and muskellunge may inhabit the water.

Hunting is permitted except in restricted areas. All of Ohio's premier game targets reside here. The Guernsey County Fish & Game Association, Noble Fish & Game Club, and Seneca Sportsmen's Club have headquarters along the lake.

Information: Contact Seneca Lake Park, 22172 Park Road, Senecaville, OH 43780, (740) 685-6013.

Tappan Lake and Park

Just name it—fishing, water skiing, paddling quiet coves, hunting big and small game, snoozing in a camp hammock, swimming at a sandy beach, hiking deep into the woods, viewing wildlife—Tappan Lake and Park has got it. You'll need a map to find your way around Ohio's largest public campground.

LOCATION

Western Harrison County, Franklin and Stock townships. Tappan Lake lays northwest-southeast midway between Cadiz and Urichsville along US 250.

SIZE & DESIGNATION

Land–5,000 acres; water–2,350 acres. Tappan Wetland Area (See Field Notes) is designated a Watchable Wildlife Area. The U.S. Army Corps of Engineers owns and operates the dam and spillway.

ACCESS

From Cadiz, take US 250 northwesterly to the southeastern tip of the lake. Turn left on Deersville Road (CR 55) then right (west) on Deersville Ridge Road (CR 2). The park entrance will be on the right, just before Deersville, about 3.5 miles from US 250. From Urichsville travel on US 250 to Eslick Road (TR 280) which crosses the Seneca Lake dam and ends at CR 2 (Moravian Trail Road). Turn left on CR 2, and go through Deersville to the park entrance. Tappan Lake Marina is on US 250.

Air travelers can land small planes at Tappan Airpark, at the southern tip of the lake, off US 250. The park and marina are 5-6 miles away.

Accommodations: Tappan Lake has Ohio's largest public campground—989 sites each with electricity (25 for RVs requiring full hookups), plus modern rest rooms and showers, camp store, laundry, activity center (nature exhibits, game room), playgrounds, amphitheater, nature programs, swimming beach (changing rooms, lifeguards, concession stand), dumping station, picnic areas and shelters, and group camping. Naturalists lead educational programs during warm months.

Campers who need a roof can choose among 11 vacation cabins (two-bedrooms), and four camper cabins. Reservations are required for cabins and group camping.

Trails: Tappan Lake has the best and longest designated hiking trails in the MWCD system. You'll find the trailheads in the camping area. Get a park brochure before departing. At six miles, the Fox Trail is the longest, but the four-mile Deer Trail may be the most scenic because half its route follows the lakeshore. A combination of these paths produces a 3-4 hour hike of eight miles. The two-mile Pine Tree Trail is a more modest hike, and as the name suggests rambles through a pine plantation.

Turkey Ridge Trail connects the park campground with Tappan Wetlands (two miles roundtrip). Shorter hikes are located between the beach and vacation cabins.

The famous Buckeye Trail runs between the dam and CR 2, roughly along a pipeline access. Start hiking at the dam or TR 288. The trail heads north to Leesville Lake, and south to Clendening and Piedmont lakes, also MWCD areas.

A summer mountain bike race is held on some hiking trails at Tappan Lake; bicycles are prohibited on foot paths all other times.

Boating: Campers can launch their craft at the small marina in the campground. The roadside rest on US 250 (half mile from the dam) also has a boat ramp.

The full-service Tappan Lake Marina is across the lake, off US 250. Services there include boat sales and rental, bait and licenses, restaurant, docks, fuel, ramps. Four cabins also can be rented (not open in winter). The marina is open daily March 1 to early December. Contact Tappan Lake Marina, 33315 Cadiz-Dennison Road, Scio, OH 43988, (740) 269-2031.

Motor boats up to 120 horsepower can speed across the water with skiers in tow. Sailing and pontoon boating are popular too. Tappan Lake has 41 miles of shoreline and many coves (especially east of US 250) for boaters seeking peaceful water. Maximum depth is 34 feet; average depth is 15 feet.

Hunting & Fishing: Though fishing remains the primary pursuit here, hunters drive to Tappan Lake for deer, too. The place is considered a top spot, especially for early season bow hunting. Lately, hunters have set their sights on woods around Bontrager Bay (end of TR 288) and Willis Run Bay (accessible from the roadside rest on US 250 and Willis Run Road). Turkey, partridge, rabbits, and squirrels are plentiful, too.

Shore fishing around the campground, beach, and Deer Trail can be productive for catfish and sunfish. Tappan Lake boasts saugeye two-feet long, though most keepers average 14-16 inches. The saugeye trend should continue because the 238,000

A jig of line, a loafer, and thou, fishing in the wilderness.

fingerling released in 1995 are reaching maturity. Large walleyes have recently been landed in Lower Beaverdam Bay and near causeways. Bass (large-mouth and white), crappie, yellow perch, bluegill, and bullhead also inhabit the water.

Information: Contact Tappan Lake and Park, P.O. Box 29, Deersville, OH 44693; (740) 922-3649.

FIELD NOTES

Tappan Wetlands Area, two small ponds en-circled by a hardwood forest, attracts ducks, geese, great blue herons, belted kingfishers, as well as deer. Follow the Turkey Ridge Trail from the park and set your sights on the observation tower between the ponds. Bring binoculars. Wild turkeys, red-tailed hawks, turkey vultures, pileated woodpeckers, yellow-shafted flickers, and songbirds have been seen or heard in this preserve (crossed by Beall Road).

Wills Creek Lake

Located in a triangle formed by Coshoc-ton, Cambridge, and Zanesville, this undeveloped, skinny lake is ideal for the pursuer of fin, fur, and feather.

LOCATION

Northeastern Muskingum County, Adams and Monroe townships, and southeastern Coshocton County, Linton Township.

SIZE & DESIGNATION

Land–4,846 acres; water–900 acres. The loca-tion is also a state wildlife area.

ACCESS

From Coshocton (SR 16), go south on SR 83 (Coshocton Road), which bisects the lake. From Zanesville, travel east a few miles on I-70, then go north on SR 93 (Adamsville Road). SR 93 merges with SR 83 and forms the east boundary of the lake. TR 143 (Wills Creek Road) acts as a south shoreline drive, connecting the state highway.

Accommodations: None.

Boating: A public boat ramp is available off SR 83, north shore. A 10-horsepower limit is in effect. Canoes can reach shallow, remote areas of the lake and swamp—the places waterfowl and trophy fish reside. This narrow impoundment has a 52.8-mile shoreline, an average depth of 6.5-7 feet, a maximum depth of 22 feet.

Hunting & Fishing: Muskies, channel catfish, largemouth bass, bluegill, crappie, bullhead and saugeye swim in the water. In 1995, more than 271,000 saugeye were released in Wills Creek Lake.

Wild At Heart

Big Darby Public Hunting Area, just 20 miles from Downtown Columbus, is my special "wild" area. Wild because I can be wild at heart, go where whim takes me, and poke around if I choose. Wild because the critters act like wild critters; and ninety percent of the time I'm alone, or think that I am. Wild because I can howl like a beast here, shoot a shotgun, or plunge into a creek.

Although I've been here more than a hundred times, I keep going back, rain and shine, in every season and mood. Mostly, I come here for a dose of Big Darby Creek, a national scenic river and the prettiest vessel in these parts. In case you haven't heard, and accuse me of bragging, Big Darby Creek is one of the most valuable and fecund freshwater streams in the eastern United States because it supports 94 species of fish, and 35 kinds of mollusks (more than Europe and Australia combined), the most endangered group of animals in the U.S. One noted scientst, Dr. Tom Watters, believes Big Darby and its tributaries has the greatest diversity of freshwater mussels in North America, and perhaps on Earth. The Nature Conservancy has dubbed it one of the "Last Great Places," a distinction the conservation group has given to a mere handful of sites in the whole wide world. Biologists note that 74 imperiled plants and animals live in its watershed, the rarest and most elusive being the Scioto madtom, a tiny sucker indigenous to this creek. Of course, I cannot tell a madtom from a minnow, but knowing they are there gives me comfort and power.

The place is 800 acres of abandoned farmland—not too small, never big enough—mostly upland meadows and bottomlands cultivated for corn and soy-beans (wildlife food). Forested stream banks, groves of mature hardwoods, and shrub land trim these open areas. There are a couple of ponds, one manmade and one that might be Ohio's southernmost glacial pothole. That's guessing on my part. A hulking powerline, which cuts diagonally across the place, and a family cemetery, my favorite spot for a picnic, remind visitors of the land's human presence.

Old farm lanes make hiking easy, but I usually follow my quadruped brethren along deer trails as far as I can. That's the advantage of public hunting and state wildlife areas. You can trail footprints, zigzag around shrubs, or snoop around a woodchuck hole if you want; or get snagged in briar patches, stuck in a swamp, or lost on a look-alike ridge. You can climb a tree, crawl on a limb stretching over the creek, nap in a tree hollow, trip over a fence. Two pieces of advice: Always leave the beaten track, and pack toilet paper.

I explore here, hunt here, watch wildlife, putter around. I toss a fishing line into Big Darby, swim in it, glide a canoe over it, snooze on its sycamored shores, search for arrowheads and mussel shells. Come autumn, I follow golden leaves down the current. In spring, Big Darby's swollen and incorrigible current scrambles elephantine trees like socks in a dryer. Canada geese bravely nest on its islands and shores. In July, a platter-sized sycamore leaf becomes a raft for a pulsing, electric-blue colony of breeding green darner dragonflies. In January, I have followed a coyote's tracks across ice packs to hoar-frosted gravel bars. I bring a camera here more often than a gun, because the images I capture for my mind, chase away nightmares.

—SO

Before state parks, Ohio public recreation (here circa 1913) was not always egalitarian.

*i*t's 1949. The first flock of postwar Baby Boomers is enjoying their "terrible twos." The nation has begun to rebound from two nightmarish decades of economic depression, dissension, and international war.

While it rebuilds Western Europe, westernizes Japan, and draws an Iron Curtain around a Red menace, America seeks stability, progress, and peace and quiet at home. America is awakening from a coma, and gasping for mind-clearing fresh air.

Ohio's state parks grew from the ashes of worldwide war and poverty. In 1949, following a national trend, Ohio legislators hatched the Department of Natural Resources, which in turn sprouted the Division of Parks and Recreation.

The organizational skill that breached the Great Depression and won WW II now could be applied to redemptive peacetime progress. Public recreation land held by several, disjointed state agencies were assembled under the administration of the nascent division. Portions of state forests and lakes that rose behind flood control dams were transformed into grand egalitarian parks. Other parks grew from wilderness.

Seventy-two state parks ranging in size from one acre to 17,000 acres, and each with its own identity, had blossomed by 1998. That year more than 70 million humans visited Ohio's state parks, making them the most popular "sports arenas" in Buckeye land.

State parks remain the best recreational bargains in the state. Egalitarian, frontier principles like the "first-come, first-served" applies in most places, at most times. We come and go when we please.

There's probably a state park within an hour's drive wherever you live in Ohio. No admission charge, no membership fees. Once the car is packed—the hard part—there are no other excuses. ☜

SOUTHEAST

Barkcamp

The distinctly human urge to leave a mark on the land is portrayed in two unusual landmarks here. Belmont native Harvey Warwick Jr., the longtime Mail Pouch chewing tobacco sign painter, put his broad brushstrokes on an 1800s barn built here by apple grower Isaac Bentley. Near the barn, frontiersman Lewis Wetzel, a psychopathic killer who took sport in murdering innocent Indians, paused after scalping a victim to carve his surname in a boulder.

LOCATION
Belmont County, Union Township.

SIZE & DESIGNATION
Land: 1,232 acres; water: 117 acres.

ACCESS
From I-70, drive south on S.R. 149 a couple of miles, then turn east (left) on Township Road 92 to the park entrance on the left. Follow park signs to your destination.

Accommodations: The picturesque 150-site campground always has vacancies. No frills here. The shower house (wheelchair accessible) near the amphitheater is a plus. Pets can camp at designated sites. Five Rent-A-Camp spaces, and two wheelchair sites are available. A horseman's campground accommodates 25; the group camp, 15.

Picnic Areas: Seven picnic areas (with rest rooms) rim the lake. The Lake and Overlook picnic areas have lake views, and are the most popular.

Trails: Equestrians take heart. Fifteen miles of trails thread through the park—the longest follows the park perimeter. Get a park map before saddling up. Besides the campground, riders will find picnic tables and rest rooms at a trailhead in the northeast corner of the park (off Park Road 6).

Hikers have four choices. The Lakeview Trail on the east shore is the longest and most gratifying. This two-mile loop, as its name suggests, traces the lakeshore for a mile. It branches from Park Road 3, about a quarter mile from the Overlook Picnic Area. The half-mile Woodchuck Trail circles within the Lakeview Trail.

On the west shore, the .6-mile Hawthorn Trail begins near the equestrian camp; the half-mile Hawk Trail starts near the Antique Barn (a.k.a. Mail Pouch Barn). Another option is the bridle trail along the western shore.

Swimming: The 700-foot beach is popular with the local crowd in summer. Plenty of parking, changing booths, drinking water, and rest rooms. Sometimes a concessionaire sells snacks and beverages.

Boating: Belmont Lake is skinny and shallow. Boats propelled by oars, paddles, and electric motors are your choices here. Bear left at the park entrance and follow signs to the boat ramp and docks on the north side of the park.

Hunting: More than 900 acres of parkland can be hunted. Whitetails, grouse, and squirrels are plentiful some years.

Fishing: They say there's big bass in Belmont Lake. Check the slot limit before casting. The Division of Wildlife dumps thousands of rainbow and golden trout into the lake. These captive-bred, no-brainers chase worms, cheese bits, and other fast food delicacies. Stick to the bass, bluegills, and crappie. Wheelchair anglers can throw in lines at the fishing access near the Lake Picnic Area. The dam is a popular spot.

Information: Contact Barkcamp State Park, 65330 Barkcamp Park Road, Belmont, OH 43718, (740) 484-4064.

HISTORY
Loggers ripped the bark off trees at a "bark camp" before sending the logs to the sawmill. The park derives its name from this activity. The stream dammed in 1963 to create Belmont Lake is called Barkcamp Creek.

Quakers arrived here in 1800. They resettled emancipated slaves in the county in the 1820s, and helped fugitive slaves reach Canada via the Underground Railroad before the Civil War.

The notorious Lewis Wetzel, honored by a plaque near the barn, hardly merits the same

An inland lifeboat drill at Blue Rock State Park.

affection. This member of the Wetzel gang was a cold-blooded, unrepentent Indian killer. Almost all of his victims (more than seventy) were non-combatants, or friendly Indians, whom he assassinated from ambush. He preferred "hunting" alone, and shunned fighting Indians as a soldier. Wetzel should never be on the same pedestal as Simon Kenton and Daniel Boone.

FIELD NOTES

Rate Barkcamp a quiet retreat off the beaten track. The Antique Barn displays old farm equipment and period bric-a-brac. It's worth a peek. It also is a stop on the paved Pioneer Trail for the handicapped. Another point of interest on this path is an outhouse with a traditional half-moon cutout.

Blue Rock

The "blue rock" isn't turquoise but a unique shale that looks bluish when wet. However, there's not much blue rock at Blue Rock—just a little at the lake's spillway. You'll see more of it along the Muskingum River (at the village of Blue Rock) and its tributaries. Certainly, Blue Rock is a better name for a state park than Oil City, the previous name of this locale.

LOCATION

Southern Muskingum County, Blue Rock Township.

SIZE & DESIGNATION

Land: 335 acres; water: 15 acres.

ACCESS

From SR 60 in Gaysport (Blue Rock), go east on Buttermilk Road (follow signs), left on CR 45 (Cutler Lake Road). At Duncan Falls (on SR 60) take winding Cutler Lake Road, through the state forest, to the park.

Accommodations: This is another unheralded campground with 101 non-electric sites on two loops. The camp has toilets, water, tables, fire rings, playground, dump station, three Rent-A-Camp spots, three camper cabins (with campstove, lantern, and cooler) in the group camping area, and warm showers (coin) at the beachhouse. Another amenity, a small camp store, has snacks, supplies, souvenirs, etc. Pets are welcomed in designated areas. Kids gravitate to the brook that cuts across the upper loop—good creeking.

Campers who want to rough it can hike a half-mile to a walk-in campground (tents only) off the Ruffed Grouse Trail. Register at the park office before hiking. Group camping for 32 people also is available. Private campgrounds border the state forest north of the state park.

Picnic Areas: Follow signs to the park's four picnic areas. Two of three shelterhouses (reservations) offer electricity.

Trails: Seven trails totaling three miles wander through the park. From the beach, take the path across the earthen dam, then go left on the Hollow Rock (lakeshore) and Ruffed Grouse trails for a 1.5-mile hike. Equestrians and hikers can also wander the bridle paths in adjacent Blue Rock State Forest for longer, quieter, and more challenging journeys.

Swimming: The 250-foot swimming beach is located at the northwest corner of the lake. The beachhouse has restrooms, showers, changing booths, phone, lockers, and snacks.

Boating: Rowboats and canoes outfitted with oars, paddles, or electric motors can cruise on shallow Cutler Lake. Launch at the ramp off Cutler Lake Road, east of the beach. Rowboats can be rented.

Hunting: None here. Go to the state forest.

Fishing: Cast for bass, catfish, bluegills. The shallow east end is turning into a cattail marsh.

Information: Blue Rock State Park, 7924 Cutler Lake Road, Blue Rock, Ohio 43720, (740) 674-4794.

HISTORY

White Eyes presided over the Shawandase village near Duncan Falls, named for a white trapper whose mutilated body was discovered on a gravel bank in the Muskingum River.

During the 1930s, the federal Resettlement Administration bought tired land in the Blue Rock, Tar Hollow, and Zaleski areas of Southeastern Ohio. The impoverished former landowners were resettled in nearby cities. Proponents of this noble action claimed that it cut local government spending, but critics complained it was just a government land grab. Anyway, relief workers planted trees and designed roads and trails, thereby preparing the marginal farmland for forests, recreation, wildlife and timber. WPA laborers excavated Cutler Lake with horses and drags in 1938. A year later, ownership was transferred to the Ohio Division of Forestry, which opened the spot for swimming, camping, and other outdoor activities. Reforestation continued to restore the emaciated slopes. Blue Rock State Park, a spinoff of the state forest, was dedicated as a state park in 1949.

FIELD NOTES

Climb the old state forest fire tower on Ridgeview Road. From the campground drive northwesterly (toward Zanesville) on Cutler Lake Road, then right on Ridgeview Road. Turn right on the driveway to the fire tower 1.25 miles on Ridgeview. Picnic tables and shelter are available. Climb the tower for the view—but at your own risk.

In winter look for flocks of wild turkeys in surrounding cornfields and wooded ridges. Hawks like to hover above Salt Creek, the stream dammed to make Cutler Lake.

Burr Oak

Come October, there's gold in these hills. The gold being autumn's vibrant colors— the doubloons of oaks, the coppers of beech, the patina of sycamore, and the purple baubles of dogwood and sumac. The lodge rests by a ridge road called the "Rim of the World," a rollercoaster ride for any roadster.

LOCATION

Southwestern Morgan County, Homer and Union townships; Northern Athens County, Trimble Township.

SIZE & DESIGNATION

Land: 2,592 acres; water: 664 acres.

ACCESS

Burr Oak is roughly midway between Nelsonville and McConnelsville. The lodge, cabins, marina, three boat docks, and backpacker camp are located off SR 78, a scenic drive nicknamed the "Rim of the World." The park's campground, main swimming beach, and office are found on CR 107 branching from SR 13, north of Glouster.

Accommodations: Take your pick—resort lodge, cabins, or camping. The lodge, located off SR 78 north of Glouster, offers 60 rooms (modern with rustic charm), restaurant, indoor and outdoor pools, small swimming beach, tennis courts, basketball, gift shop, TV lounge, nature center, and meeting rooms that can handle 200 people. The centerpiece is the timber-framed, cathedral-ceiling sitting lounge or quiet area with windows looking into the forest canopy and lakeshore. Autumn colors turn these into stained-glass windows. It is a great room for reading, quiet games, and sitting beside the fireplace.

Thirty two-bedroom cabins sit atop a forested ridge about a mile from the lodge. Consider yourself lucky to book one during the peak season running from Memorial Day to the end of deer hunting season. Cabin guests have access to lodge amenities and the Buckeye and Burr Oak backpack trails.

Ninety non-electric, wooded sites are ready for campers on the west shore of the lake, on CR 107 off SR 13 (north of Glouster). The main campground has showers, flush toilets, laundry, dump station, three Rent-A-Camp sites, and pet sites. Wayne National Forest also has a small, primitive camping area, called Burr Oak Cove, just before the state park facility.

Backpackers and boaters can rough it at

Lake Erie

Michigan

Oak Point/
South Bass Island

Headlands
Beach

Geneva

Pymatuning

Harrison
Lake

Maumee
Bay

Kelleys Island
Marblehead Lighthouse
East Harbor

Punderson

Pennsylvania

Crane Creek

Cleveland Lakefront

Mosquito

Independence
Dam

Mary Jane
Thurston

Tinker's Creek

Nelson Kennedy

Findley

Van Buren

West Branch

Lake Milton

Portage Lakes

Quail
Hollow

Guilford Lake

Malabar Farm

Beaver
Creek

Indiana

Grand Lake
St. Marys

Mohican

Mount
Gilead

Jefferson
Lake

Indian Lake

Delaware

Lake
Loramie

Alum Creek

Kiser Lake

Dillon

Salt Fork

Barkcamp

Buck Creek

Madison
Lake

Blue Rock

Sycamore

Buckeye
Lake

Wolf Run

Hueston
Woods

John Bryan

Muskingum
River

A. W.
Marion

Deer
Creek

Lake Logan

Burr Oak

Little
Miami

Caesar Creek

Hocking Hills

Strouds
Run

Cowan Lake

Great Seal

Tar Hollow

Lake Hope

Paint Creek

Scioto
Trail

Lake
Alma

Forked
Run

West
Virginia

Stonelick

Pike Lake

East
Fork

Rocky Fork

Lake White

Adams Lake

Jackson
Lake

Shawnee

Kentucky

Ohio River

Ohio River

N

First and Last

First state lands dedicated
as parks — Buckeye Lake,
1896; Indian Lake, Grand
Lake (St. Marys), Lake
Loramie, Guilford Lake,
Summit (Portage)
Lake, 1902.

Newest state park —
Marblehead Lighthouse, 1998

lakeshore primitive camps at boat docks 2 (15 sites) and 3 (eight sites), both on the east shore off SR 78. Drinking water and latrines are available. Good locations for those traveling on the Buckeye Trail, or boaters who want to park and camp. Group camping is located near Boat Dock 3, CR 14 off SR 78.

Picnic Areas: Tables and grills are located at key facilities. The largest picnic area is behind the main swimming beach.

Trails: Hikers rate the trails in and around the state park among the best in the state. The 29-mile Burr Oak Backpack Trail is the main drag. It wraps around the lakeshore, and serves as the host route for most of the Buckeye Trail's journey through the park. The trails split for several miles between Boat Dock 3 and the cabins. Except for some grueling climbs on the east side, the path ranges from easy to moderate in difficulty. The official trailhead is Boat Dock 1 off SR 78 in Bishopville. Walkers can jump on the trail at each boat dock, the campground, beach, dam (Buckeye Trail west terminus), CR 15 (Buckeye Trail north terminus), CR 58 (near Wildcat Hollow Backpack Trail in Wayne National Forest), and near the cabins. Camping is permitted at the main campground, and at boat docks 2 and 3.

Except for the .33-mile Chipmunk Trail near the

lodge, the park's Lakeview, Buckeye Cave, Ravine, and Red Fox trails overlap the route of the backpack trail. The park brochure shows the orientation of these trails. Long-distance hikers can walk to the Wildcat Hollow Backpack Trail in Wayne National Forest at the north tip of the Burr Oak backpack trail. At CR 58 walk north (right) a few hundred feet to the Wildcat Hollow trailhead. Camping is permitted anywhere along this national forest trail.

An eight-mile bridle trail runs on the west side between the park office (CR 107) and CR 58. A couple of horseback riding liveries near the park offer rides on private trails.

Swimming: Burr Oak's 1,000-foot swimming beach is located on the west shore between the campground and Boat Dock 4. Showers, snack bar, changing area, and flush toilets are available. Lodge pools and a small beach below the lodge are reserved for lodge and cabin guests.

Burr Oak Lake holds some interest for scuba divers. Water now covers seven covered bridges left

standing when the lake formed in 1950. The Division of Wildlife's fishing map of the lake offers clues to their location. Also consult old county road maps. Diving is not allowed near the dam.

Boating: Burr Oak Lake's narrow, jagged shape and quiet coves make it fun to explore in small boats propelled by motors ten horsepower or less. Five boat launches, four off SR 78, provide access to the 50-year-old lake. Boat Dock 1 in Bishopville (CR 15 off SR 78) has a marina, commissary, boat rental (canoes, jonboats, pontoons), concrete ramps, rental docks, and fuel. Docks 2 and 3, off SR 78, are your basic, no-frills gravel ramps, and they provide primitive camping, drinking water, and latrines. A modest, unnumbered launch is located near the resort lodge. Dock 4 on the west shore (CR 107 and CR 63 from SR 13) has concrete ramps, docks, and a boat rental. All totaled, the park has close to 175 dock slips, and nearly 400 boat tie-ups.

Hunting: Consider the Burr Oak area a hunting hotbed. Deer, turkey, squirrel, grouse, raccoon and

Bed Roll,
Please

So Many Ways to Park and Sleep Over

- Number of state park overnight visitors — 846,000 (1996)
- Number of family campsites in park system — 9,285
- Number of state parks with campsites — 57
- Biggest family campgrounds
  East Harbor, 570 sites
  Hueston Woods, 491 sites
  East Fork, 416 sites
- Number of parks with group camping — 34
- Parks with horsemen's camps — 11
- Parks offering seasonal campsites (1-6 month stays) — 13
- Best (and only) fly-in campground — Wolf Run
- Best lakeshore campground for boaters — Burr Oak
- Most unusual overnight accommodation — The hexagonal "cabent,"
  half-cabin and half-tent cabin at South Bass Island
- Number of parks with Rent-A-Camp sites — 36
- Parks with Rent-A-RV — East Fork, Alum Creek, Geneva, Punderson
- Parks with Rent-A-Tepee — Indian Lake, Jackson Lake, Mohican
- Parks with houseboat rentals — Alum Creek and Paint Creek
- Biggest state park resort lodge (rooms) — Salt Fork, 148 rooms
- Smallest lodge — Punderson, 31 rooms
- Number of parks with cabins — 16
- Parks with the most cabins— Lake Hope, 69; Hueston Woods, 59

fox are plentiful in the park and nearby national forest and state wildlife areas. Check at the park office or ranger station for restrictions. Burr Oak becomes a hunter's headquarters during deer gun season.

Fishing: Burr Oak Lake is best known for its largemouth bass in the eight-pound category. Stocked saugeye are taking hold, and walleye (stocked earlier) are still present. Crappie, bluegill, sunfish, carp, and channel catfish keep anglers busy. Hotspots are the dam and northern coves (catfish). Burr Oak is perfect for summer evening boat casters—calm, clean water, quiet coves, shoreline camping.

Information: Burr Oak State Park, 12000 Burr Oak Road, Glouster, OH 45732-9570, (740) 767-3570. Burr Oak Lodge, Route 2, Box 159, Glouster, OH 45732, (740) 767-2112 and (800) 282-7275.

HISTORY

Some of the mining towns around here had a reputation. In Santoy, a bit north of the park, two men faced off in a gunfight over a $20 debt. Both took slugs; one died. Then there was the time the coal company payroll was robbed by mounted bandits. The boys made a clean getaway by vanishing in the hollows and recess caves of the area. A fire that took the coal tipple and several shops, and the ensuing economic depression, turned Santoy into a ghost town by the mid-1930s.

The hamlet called Burr Oak survived until 1950 when the U.S. Army Corps of Engineers dammed the east branch of Sunday Creek for the lake. Most of the town's buildings and seven covered bridges were drowned. The impound serves as a water supply, flood control structure, and recreation lake. The state park was dedicated in 1952.

The area's fabled burr oaks, some reached heights well above 100 feet, were wiped out by logging companies. A new stand of burr oaks, called the R.J. Miller Memorial Grove, was planted near the cabins in 1968.

FIELD NOTES

Lucky park visitors might catch Park Naturalist Lynn Barnhart talking about wildlife at the lodge, or better yet, conducting a bird banding experiment. Barnhart uses seeds and berries to lure birds into a feeder-cage-trap located behind the ranger station. He gently cups each nervous captive in a gloved hand, slides it into a "breathable" cloth bag, and knots the top. Back at the lab (the nature room at the lodge), Barnhart weighs, measures, identifies, and examines each bird. He keeps the information in a journal. Captives with a ring or band on a leg have been here before.

Beavers have established colonies along the lakeshore, especially in the secluded northern reaches. Spring wildflowers include Dutchman's breeches, bloodroot, trillium, and violets galore.

The park's two namesakes, the tree and village, have disappeared from the scene—the former to the axe a century ago, the latter to the mid-twentieth century dam and lake builders.

Dillon

Dillon is a "tweener" park with scenery between spectacular and so-so, facilities between resort and no-frills, and terrain somewhere between hills and flatlands. It's a passable camping destination from which to explore sites around Zanesville and Newark.

LOCATION

Muskingum County, Falls, Hopewell, Licking townships.

SIZE & DESIGNATION

Land: 5,888 acres; water: 1,660 acres (summer). The U.S. Army Corps of Engineers owns the property and leases it to the Ohio Department of Natural Resources. The Corps still operates the dam and spillway.

ACCESS

From Zanesville, take SR 146 west to the park entrance (Clay Littick Drive). Interstate travelers take the "Dillon State Park" exit in Zanesville.

Accommodations: The park brochure says Dillon's 29 family cabins overlook the north shore. Not quite. The best you can hope for are glimpses and peeks of the reservoir. Nevertheless, there is plenty of tree foliage in summer for shade lovers. These modern accommodations boast air conditioning and cable television, and nine cabins have porches aimed at the lake.

Dillon's 192-site campground gets crowded in the summer, even though most sites lack shade. Get here early if you intend to stay the weekend. Electricity is available at 180 sites; the rest are primitive walk-in spots for tenters. Facilities include showers, flush toilets, commissary (laundry and camp store open Memorial Day to Labor Day), dump station, court games area, and nature center.

Picnic Areas: Picnic areas are located at the beach, near the park office and at the end of Park Road 36. The best one overlooks the lake, north of the park office, off Park Road 7. Two picnic shelters in the park can be reserved. The 118-foot earthen wall provides an uneasy backdrop in the Corps' picnic area beneath the dam. I keep imagining the dam collapsing.

Trails: The longest path is the Licking Bend Trail, a lakeshore trace between the beach and marina. The park brochure claims it is six miles in length, but that is generous. Four shorter, branch trails twist through the campground. The Hickory Ridge and Kingridge trails are the most challenging.

Bicyclists (and hikers) can enjoy the lakeshore and state wildlife area on park roads 7, 8, and 9, west of the park office. Get a park map before departing. Park Road 7 westbound ends at SR 146. Dismount and walk on the berm to SR 8, just 50 yards ahead on the left.

Swimming: Locals and campers swarm on the park's 1,360-foot beach, which features a bathhouse, showers, snack bar, wading pool, lockers, and a game area for volleyball, basketball, tennis, handball, shuffleboard and other activities. Shade is scarce around the beach.

Boating: Dillon Reservoir has something for every boater. Boats with unlimited horsepower are allowed on about half the lake. The remainder—the shallow western section and extremities branching north and south—is a no wake zone for paddlers in the slow lane. Wildlife observation is best in these calm waters.

Most motorboaters head for the marina (east of the cabins) where they will find fuel, ramps, seasonal docks (70 for rent, 28 for cabin residents and campers), and snacks. Various watercraft, from pedalboats to pontoons, can be rented here. Canoe trips on the Licking River can be arranged at the marina.

Smaller boats launch from three ramps in the no wake zone. The Big Run ramp is off SR 146 east of the park entrance. Park Road 7 takes you to the Nashport ramp. Pleasant Knob, located at the end of Park Road 17 off Pleasant Valley Road (CR 408), is the only park ramp on the south shore.

The reservoir is deepest near the dam (30 feet), and shallowest in the western third, about seven feet. When the water depth is lowered three feet in winter, the lake basin looks more like a river winding across a mudflat.

Hunting: Although hunters favor the state wildlife area that enwraps the western half of the reservoir, some pursue game, especially ducks, in designated areas in the state park. Deer, grouse, squirrel and rabbits also wander into range. Several duck blinds are available through the park office. Maps of the lake and wildlife area are available from the Division of Wildlife.

The Dillon Sportsmen's Center, operated by the League of Ohio Sportsmen, offers skeet and trap shooting (fees charged), and target ranges for rifles and handguns. Competitions are scheduled during warm months, and hunter safety classes are held here.

Fishing: Cast for bluegill, perch, crappie, largemouth bass, channel catfish (plentiful), and walleye (occasional). Tipsters say bass fishing is best in May in the Poverty Run and Big Run coves. Carp and bullhead are found in shallow marshes at the west end.

The tailwater below the dam is considered a hot spot for walleye, muskellunge, largemouths, and cats. Scout the shoreline in winter for stumps, fallen trees and other natural debris that in spring attract fish.

Information: Dillon State Park, P.O. Box 126, 5265 Dillon Hills Drive, Nashport, OH 43830-0126, (740) 453-4377 park office, (740) 453-0442 campground, (740) 454-2225 U.S. Army Corps of Engineers, (740) 454-6784 Dillon Sportmen's Center.

HISTORY

The Licking Valley has been a human highway for centuries. The Adena people lived here in semi-permanent villages. The Nashport Mound attests to their residency. These and successive native people traveled upstream on the river to reach Flint Ridge where they mined priceless flint for tools and weapons. En route they passed through a sandstone gorge famous for its large petroglyph of a black hand. The "black hand," either a natural stain or drawing, marked the boundary of the sacred flint quarries. Although the black hand was blasted off the gorge during construction of Ohio & Erie Canal, the Licking Narrows is protected in Blackhand Gorge State Nature Preserve. Farther west, Flint Ridge State Memorial preserves remnants of the celebrated flint quarries. After canals, a railroad—today's B&O line—ran through the valley.

In 1803, Moses Dillon, a Quaker missionary from Maryland, came here to spread the gospel among the natives. Instead, he stumbled on iron ore and coal and built one of the world's largest iron works at a village known as Dillon Falls. Iron from his foundry went into Zanesville's famous "Y" bridge.

The Flood Control Act of 1938 authorized construction of a flood control dam at Dillon Falls, but World War II, insufficient funds, and the Korean War delayed construction for 20 years. The $30 million project was finished in September 1961. Besides the dam and spillway, railroads, villages, roads, cemeteries, and utilities had to be relocated. The state park opened in August 1968.

FIELD NOTES

Persistent and curious nature lovers will be rewarded by Dillon's diversity. Birders should scout for abundant populations of great blue and green herons. Other marsh birds include the great and cattle egrets, black-crowned night heron, sora rail, Wilson's snipe, osprey and bald eagles (during migrations), and marsh hawks. Also look for the common loon, pied-billed and horned grebes, double-crested cormorant and tundra swan.

Twenty-seven species of ducks appear at Dillon. The most common are mallard, wood duck, blue-winged teal, pintail, baldpate, ring-necked, and scaup. Canada geese nest here. Bobwhite quail and eastern woodcocks like the fertile bottomlands along the river. At night listen for whippoorwills and owls. Wild turkey, introduced in the 1980s, are seen around the cabins.

Forked Run

Put Forked (say For-ked) Run in the best kept secret category. On a map, the barbed Forked Run Lake looks poised to attack the mighty Ohio river. You can launch a boat into the river, or into the lake. There's no lack of trees. This forested park has Shade River State Forest for a northern neighbor, and the woods of Southeastern Ohio beyond that.

LOCATION
Northeastern Meigs County, Olive Township.

SIZE & DESIGNATION
Land: 815 acres; water: 102 acres. Adjacent Shade River State Forest is 2,600 acres.

ACCESS
From SR 124, the highway along the Ohio River, follow the park entrance road to campground, office, beach, boat ramp, and hiking trail. The park's Ohio River access is a short distance downstream, off SR 124.

Accommodations: Imagine 200 campsites located on forested ridges overlooking a lake and the Ohio River. Your choice of shade or sun on five loops. Always a vacancy. The campground has showers, 35-foot slips for RVs, four Rent-A-Camp sites, dump station, two camper cabins, and sites for pet owners. No electric hookups, however, which might explain the vacancies. Swimming beach, park office, hiking trails, and concessions are nearby.

Picnic Areas: Three picnic areas and two reservable shelters are available. Look for tables along the entrance drive, at the beach parking lot, and above the beach, the latter a small, shady site beside a cove.

Trails: Lakeview Trail, 2.5 miles, is the best of two trails in the park. Start at the beach, and follow the wooded lakeshore. This somewhat tough trail loops to the camping area and back to the beach. Honeysuckle Trail is a half-mile interpretive trail that begins at the park office.

Swimming: The park's 800-foot sandy beach is heavily used on hot summer weekends, largely because it's the only beach for many miles. Changing booths, picnic tables, and parking are available.

Boating: Launch into the Ohio River or Forked Run Lake. Take your pick. Lake boaters have a paved ramp at the dam, or a gravel ramp for the upper lake on TR 272, off SR 248. The main ramp has a concession that rents rowboats, canoes, pedalboats and sells refreshments, ice and bait (May through September). A 10 horsepower limit keeps the lake fit for fishing and swimming.

The park's two-lane, concrete Ohio River ramp is downstream, a mile from the park entrance road. The facility is lighted for 24-hour service, and it boasts rest rooms, courtesy docks, and access for disabled anglers. No horsepower limits on the Ohio River. The Belleville Lock and Dam is several miles upstream.

Hunting: Hunting is allowed in designated areas. Check in at the park office before going into the woods. Hunters going to the state forest often camp at Forked Run. Deer, squirrels, wild turkey, and grouse are the main targets.

Fishing: Largemouth bass weighing in at five to six pounds are common from the lake. Anglers report good catches of flathead catfish, crappie, and bluegill. The lake gets a yearly delivery of rainbow, golden and brown trout, and saugeye. And there's the Ohio River fishery awaiting your line.

Information: Forked Run State Park, P.O. Box 127, Reedsville, OH 45772, (740) 378-6206.

HISTORY
After raids into Virginia (now West Virginia), Shawnee warriors crossed the Ohio River at the mouth of the Shade River, a rocky spot dubbed the Devil's Hole by captives. The winding, heavily forested (and shady) valley covered the natives' escape to their villages in the Scioto River valley. The park entrance begins on a wide, flat and fertile bottomland referred to as "long bottom" by young George Washington, who surveyed this land for Virginia. The name stuck, and the town of Long Bottom is downstream from the park. The rich soil here still yields tomatoes, cabbage, melons and sweet corn.

The nearby villages of Reedsville and Belleville became boat-building towns in the previous century. Park construction started in May 1951, and the lake was completed in October 1952.

FIELD NOTES
A black bear cub, a refugee from West Virginia, wandered into the park in 1990. Bald eagles have been seen in the upper reaches of the park, but none has stayed to nest.

Great Seal

This state park, located a few miles north of historic Chillicothe, derives its name from the Great Seal of the State of Ohio painted inside the dome of the Statehouse in Columbus. The story goes that after an all-nighter at Adena, Thomas Worthington's nearby estate, Governor Edward Tiffin, Worthington, and Secretary of State William Creighton watched the sun rise over hills to the east, the scene depicted in the seal. Although the real "seal" hill is Mt. Logan, just south of the state park, the summits in the park—Mt. Ives, Sugarloaf, Bald Hill—inspired the vision, too.

Many have gorged on the spectacle of Old Man's Cave.

LOCATION

Ross County, Greene and Springfield townships. From Chillicothe, travel north on SR 159.

SIZE & DESIGNATION

Land: 1,862 acres.

ACCESS

Just past the junction with US 35, go right on Marietta Road to the park access road. To reach the park office and trail to Rocky Knob, take Rocky Road off Marietta Road. Trails and parking to Mt. Ives are on Lick Run Road, off Rocky Road. The campground entrance is farther north, off Marietta Road. Trails to Sugarloaf Mountain and Bald Hill start here. Southbound travelers follow US 23, then Delano Road to Marietta Road.

Accommodations: The 15-site primitive campground has water and vault toilets. Campers with horses are permitted in sites 1-5. Pets are allowed.

Picnic Areas: The park's picnic area is located in the Sugarloaf section, off Marietta Road. Latrines, water, shelterhouse (first-come basis) and a playground are available.

Trails: By Ohio standards Great Seal's 20 miles of woodland trails are challenging because of their steep climbs and descents up and down rocky knobs. Wear sturdy, sensible shoes (especially adults), carry water, use a walking stick, and have fun. The park brochure shows the trail routes.

The easiest of six trails are the Picnic Loop (one mile), starting and finishing at the shelterhouse in the picnic area; Spring Run (3.4 miles), branching from the Picnic Loop; and Grouse Rock (less than a mile), looping from the Park Office on Rocky Road. These paths are reserved for foot travelers.

Experienced hikers and horsemen prefer the color-coded bridle trails, such as the 2.1-mile Sugarloaf Mountain Trail (yellow blazes), rising from the campground at the north end of the park. The Mt. Ives loops (orange), straddling Lick Run Road, anchor the southern portion of the park. Look for parking on Lick Run Road near trailheads. (Other trail guides and maps refer to Mt. Eyes, but longtime local residents insist the ridge is Mt. Ives, so the latter name has been adopted.)

Shawnee Ridge Trail (blue) measures 7.8 miles and connects the Sugarloaf and Mt. Ives trails. Rocky Road bisects Shawnee Ridge Trail east of the Park Office. You can pick up the trail at this intersection for a shorter hike, just be certain you park off the road. The northern half of this trail offers loops around Bald Hill and Sand Hill, while the southern route traipses across Rocky Knob.

Hunting: Hunting is allowed in designated areas. Check at the park office before departing. Deer, squirrel, turkey and grouse are the primary targets.

Information: Great Seal State Park, 825 Rocky Road, Chillicothe, OH 45601, (740) 773-2726.

HISTORY

The Scioto River Valley, a major Native American thoroughfare, hosted the great moundbuilding cultures and later the Shawandase. Both nations chose Chillicothe as their headquarters, and the city served as Ohio's state capital from 1803-1810 and 1813-1816.

The celebrated Mingo leader, Tahgajute (Chief Logan), supposedly delivered his famous "lament" speech north of the park. He stopped his vengeful raids on whites thereafter. Logan's prominence faded under drunkenness, and he was assassinated by another Indian in 1780.

Following the Indian wars, Nathaniel Massie established the first permanent white settlement at Chillicothe in 1797. That year Ebenezer Zane carved his trace, Ohio's first national road, to Chillicothe, beginning a flood of emigration. The natural neighborhood then fell into ruin.

FIELD NOTES

Bring binoculars for the vistas atop Sugarloaf, Mt. Ives, and Rocky Knob, which form the escarpment of the Appalachian Plateau running south and east. Glaciated plains lay north and west of this line of hills.

Crooked chestnut oaks occupy the rocky slopes, and sometimes you will see maples on higher elevations. Usually chestnut oaks reside on the highest, driest, and most impoverished sites. Woodland creatures abound in the park.

Hocking Hills

In spite of its decline, Hocking Hills remains a top spot for year-round natural wonder. It's a must see for all Ohioans. The sandstone sculptured and hemlock-shaded gorges still sparkle. The massive recess caves are still massive. The trickling waterfalls still enchant visitors. Exploring the nooks and crannies, and the less-favored sites can bring lasting rewards. There's more to the Hocking Hills than Old Man's Cave.

Cedar Falls, Hocking Hills

LOCATION

Southeastern Hocking County, Benton, Laurel and Good Hope townships.

SIZE & DESIGNATION

Land: 2,331 acres; water: 17 acres.

ACCESS

The park has six separate sites located between US 33 and SR 56. Start at US 33 at Rockbridge and take SR 374, which zigzags southerly to attractions called Cantwell Cliffs, Rock House, Old Man's Cave, Rose Lake, and Cedar Falls. Ash Cave is on SR 56, a little west of its junction with SR 374. The campground, dining lodge, and cabins are found at Old Man's Cave on SR 374/664. The park is accessible from US 33 via SR 664 (Logan) and SR 180. Follow signs to destinations.

Accommodations: The state park has two camping areas near Old Man's Cave. The main camp, with 172 sites, is situated on a wooded ridge above the gorge. Open year-round, the entrance is near Upper Falls, on SR 374. Electricity runs at 159 sites. Amenities include a showerhouse (April through October), toilets, water, playground, dump station, laundry, and amphitheater. Winter campers use latrines. A small group camp (10 tents) can be reserved. During warm months, the main place fills up fast, sometimes by sunset on Friday.

If that happens, drive another mile or two on SR 374 to the walk-in campground for tent campers. Thirty primitive sites are available, but you will have to tote your gear. Plenty of privacy and quiet here, and water and latrines are available. A reservable camp for large groups (160 people) is located near Ash Cave, off SR 374. Hocking State Forest offers a horsemen's campground near Rock House, or try one of several private campgrounds in the area.

Forty, two-bedroom cabins stand near the dining lodge. The entrance road is a tad west of Old Man's Cave, off SR 374. The popular housekeeping cabins sleep six and come loaded with gas heat, full kitchen, TV, fireplace (gas), and microwave oven. Reservations are necessary. The dining lodge (open April through October) features a restaurant, TV lounge, meeting room (up to 300 persons), game room, snack bar, and outdoor swimming pool. The park office, open all year, is found here.

At Old Man's Cave, check out the Hocking Hills Visitor Center for educational exhibits on natural history, rest rooms, snack bar and gift shop.

Picnic Areas: Each site (except Rose Lake) offers picnic areas with grills, tables, drinking water, and latrines. All but Cedar Falls and Rose Lake have shelterhouses on a first-come basis. Old Man's Cave and Ash Cave have the largest picnic places.

Trails: Oodles of them. Long ones, short ones, tough ones, easy ones. A paradise for hikers who can come here on uncrowded days. The longest one, the six-mile Grandma Gatewood Trail, happens to be the best path, too. Consider it the park's signature trail, for it includes the geological structures, waterfalls, and heavy vegetation that makes the Hocking Hills famous. It runs between Old Man's Cave and Ash Cave, with a stop midway at Cedar Falls. These three sites are the most popular places in the park. The trail, part of the Buckeye Trail and designated a National Recreation Trail, honors Emma "Grandma" Gatewood, the legendary Ohio pathfinder and the first woman to hike the Appalachian Trail alone. The park's annual Winter Hike follows the Gatewood Trail. Roundtrip it is 12 miles, though most hikers have a vehicle awaiting at one of the termini.

Here's a summary of trails at six park sites (north to south).

Cantwell Cliffs. Come here to avoid the crowds accumulating at other locations. A path from the parking lot splits at the picnic shelterhouse. The left fork quickly descends via steps into a gorge carved by Buck Run. The right fork traces the gorge rim to waterfalls, then drops into the canyon. Various paths wander through the valley, one favorite being a narrow passage called Fat Woman's Squeeze. The trail goes to a charming U-shaped rock wall, roughly 150 feet tall. All hiking trails stay within the site.

Rock House. Halfway up a 150-foot cliff of Blackhand sandstone is a dark cave, called the "House of Rock," a spot reminiscent of the cliff dwellers in the Southwest U.S. The cave, supported by sandstone columns, is 200 feet long, 25 feet tall in places, and 20-30 feet deep. Long ago, Native Americans lived here. So did thieves, murderers and bootleggers, who dubbed the spot "Robbers Roost." The loop trail to the attraction starts at the shelterhouse, finishes at a park road east of the trail entrance. You'll climb 200 steps on the journey. For fun, look for the pioneer rock inscription bearing the letters "ITFBRBAR-ITFFAWMTAW." Translated, it means, "In the fall, Buck Run bananas (slang for paw paw fruit) are ripe—in the frosty fall, a wise man takes a wife."

Old Man's Cave. A network of trails compressed in a half-mile long gorge visits fabled Old Man's Cave, Upper Falls, Lower Falls, Broken Rock Falls, Eagle Rock, Whale in the Wall, Devil's Bathtub and Sphinx Head. The trail through the gorge, along Queer Creek, is the most scenic, though crowded and noisy on weekends. The rim trails offer easier walking, but less scenery. An A-framed bridge crosses the gorge and has a great view. Caution: Do not walk at the cliff edges. The ground may be loose and slippery. Serious injury or death occurs when a hiker falls off the edge. Hikers venturing into the gorge will climb many steps and a few tunnels. These "aids" become icy and slippery in winter. Be prepared to manage them on your fanny. Please do not climb the cliffs. Endangered plants, such as the round-leaved catchfly, grow on the walls, not to mention fragile mosses, lichens, and liverworts which take decades to recover.

Rose Lake. Only one way in and out. Park on the southbound side of SR 374. Follow the half mile "improved" path to the lake. Follow lakeshore paths blazed by anglers.

Cedar Falls. Settlers mistook the hemlocks here for cedars, but the name stuck. One of Ohio's most photogenic (and most photographed) falls, Cedar Falls is midway on the Gatewood Trail between Ash Cave and Old Man's Cave. A loop trail (less than a mile) visits the attraction from a parking area off SR 374. Stay awhile, but don't climb the falls, nor the cliffs.

Ash Cave. The mildest and most dramatic trail in the park is the quarter-mile, handicapped-accessible gorge path to the entrance of Ash Cave, a 90-foot high recess cave measuring 200 feet end-to-end, and 100 feet in depth. Like an unruly strand of hair, a ribbon of water falls off the cliff ledge into a pool at the cave entrance. The cave's name comes from a huge mound of ash left by Native Americans who regularly camped here. The Salt Creek (which runs through the Ash Cave picnic area) and Queer Creek valleys served as trails between Shawandase villages along the Scioto River and Kanawha River in West Virginia. Take the rim trail above Ash Cave to travel on the Gatewood Trail to Cedar Falls.

Hocking State Forest has bridle and hiking trails. Hiking is also permitted in Conkles Hollow State Natural Area, a few miles from Old Man's Cave.

Swimming: An outdoors swimming pool at the dining lodge is free for cabin guests and to other visitors for a fee. Campers can use a pool in the campground. The pools are open Memorial Day to Labor Day. Wading is tolerated but diving in the pools beneath waterfalls is prohibited and dangerous. Rose Lake is not for swimming either.

Fishing: Spring-fed Rose Lake, the park's water supply, contains largemouth bass, bluegill, catfish and stocked golden and rainbow trout. Fisherman's parking is on the west side of SR 374, north of Cedar Falls. From there, you have to hike a half mile to reach the lake. The short hike is worth the catch in beauty and fish. No boats allowed.

Special Places & Events: The biggest event of the year is the Winter Hike on the third weekend in January, regardless of weather. An army of hikers, sometimes 5,000 souls, takes the Grandma Gatewood Trail from Old Man's Cave to Ash Cave. Refreshments are available midway at Cedar Falls. Buses return hikers to the starting point. Folks seeking solitude should go elsewhere this weekend.

Slide shows, movies, nature talks entertain visitors at the campground amphitheater. Guided hikes often begin at the Naturalist's Cabin near the Visitors Center.

Information: Hocking Hills State Park, 20160 SR 664, Logan, OH 43138, (740) 385-6841.

HISTORY

The gorges and caves in the Hocking Hills have been harboring humans for centuries. The Paleo Indians were probably here 7,000 years ago. The Adena (moundbuilders) people arrived 2,000 years ago followed by the so-called Fort Ancient people from the 1300s to 1600s. Wyandots, Lenni Lenape, and Shawandase used the area in the 18th century. The Wyandots, who had a settlement in modern Logan, called the river "hockhocking," referring to the stream's bottle-shaped gorge north of Lancaster.

Whites who trickled into the area after the Treaty of Green Ville in 1795 found abundant game. However, in 1799 the last local wood bison was killed on the banks of Queer Creek. Two brothers, Nathaniel and Pat Rayon, built a cabin at Old Man's Cave in 1795. Both were buried in or near the cave. The recess gets its name from another trader-trapper-frontiersman named Richard Rowe (or Roe), who moved his family from Tennessee in 1796 to the Ohio River Valley to establish a trading post. While exploring Salt Creek, Rowe stumbled into the Hocking Hills. He lived the rest of his long life in the area and, like the Rayon boys, was supposedly interred in the cave, date of death unknown. Other accounts have Rowe fleeing from West Virginia, or Virginia, or the Cumberland Mountains, after the Civil War, and living quietly as a hermit.

Mills grew over Cedar Falls, Upper Falls, and Rock House. Colonel F.F. Rempel of Logan put up a 16-room tourist hotel at Rock House in 1835. By 1870, the region had become a well-known scenic attraction. In 1924, the state forestry department bought 126 acres to protect Old Man's Cave. More purchases enlarged the park in the 1920s; and trails, structures, roads, and other improvements were constructed by laborers for the Works Progress Administration in the 1930s. The state park was created from forest property when the Ohio Department of Natural Resources started in 1949. The dining lodge and cabins were added in 1972.

Out of Jefferson's furnace, into the campfire.

FIELD NOTES

The remarkable Blackhand sandstone walls in Hocking Hills started as a delta deposit at the edge of a shallow sea 350 million years ago. Keen observers notice that the topmost and bottom sandstone layers are more resistant (harder) than the middle layers. The recess caves and formations at Rock House have been chiseled from this loosely cemented (softer) midsection.

Many rock facades are pitted due to honeycomb weathering. This occurs when water soaks through porous sandstone and erodes loose sand grains on the exterior wall. The removed sand forms pits and tiny tunnels that resemble bee honeycombs. (See Conkles Hollows State Natural Area, for more geological history.)

Although the Wisconsinan glacier stopped north of the Hocking Hills, it affected the shape of the land and its vegetation some 20,000 years back. Meltwater from the glacier engorged local streams and accelerated the erosion that carved region's unique gorges and rock formations. The cool, deep ravines later provided sanctuary for boreal vegetation—hemlock, Canada yew, yellow and black birch—that arrived at the end of the Ice Age. Rarities struggling in the park include round-leaved catchfly, lady's slipper orchids, devil's walking stick, and sullivantia. Rock ledges hide snakes called copperhead (venomous), black rat and ring-necked, and the dusky and red-backed salamanders. Sunfish, darters, the black-nosed dace, least brook lamprey, and mottled sculpin swim in the creeks.

Some of the hemlocks at Cedar Falls and Old Man's Cave reach heights approaching 150 feet, making them among Ohio's tallest trees. Hocking Hills has good populations of woodland birds. Springtime birding for warblers can be rewarding.

JOURNAL

I write about this park with reservations and misgivings. The more its beauty is celebrated, the more its beauty is ruined. Ohio's most reknowned park, frankly and sadly, has lost its luster, largely because it has been loved to death. Pestled trails, gorge walls defoliated by unthinking climbers, caves crumbling to dusty sand under human tread, hemlock trunks rubbed raw by hiking boots or polished by human buttocks, more litter and graffiti, traffic jams and impatient drivers in parking lots, sometimes noisy campground, on and on. Nothing neolithic anymore. Less hype in the hyperboles.

Jackson Lake

Loggers stripped the hillsides surrounding the nearby Jefferson Iron Furnace for charcoal. A "second-growth" forest rose on the naked slopes after the furnaces closed.

Jackson Lake preserves a bit of industrial history, and shows a landscape on the mend.

LOCATION
Southern Jackson County, Jefferson Township.

SIZE & DESIGNATION
Land: 92 acres; water: 242 acres.

ACCESS
From Jackson, the county seat, take SR 93 south to Oak Hill, then head west on SR 279. Jefferson Furnace is on SR 279 (west shore). Camping, park office, and swimming are found on Tommy Been Road.

Accommodations: All 34 camping sites have electricity; 10 sites are reserved for tenters. Vault toilets, drinking water, dumping station are the facilities. Pets are welcome. Ask about the Rent-A-Tepee.

Picnic Areas: Picnic tables and shelters (3) dot the west shore.

Swimming: A small swimming beach adjoins the campground.

Boating: This is a thin, shallow lake. Nothing faster than a 10 horsepower engine. You'll find two launches off SR 279, one on each side of the lake.

Hunting: Not here. Go to Cooper Hollow State Wildlife Area (5,339 acres), just six miles away.

Fishing: Think bass in the 10-pound range, and lesser catches of 4-5 pounds. And don't think it's coincidence that these biggies hang out at the northern end of the lake, around Rhodes Island, owned by former Governor James Rhodes. Muskie, bluegill, catfish, and carp are caught here too. Three fishing access spots branch from Tommy Been Road, and a 50-foot fishing easement encircles the lake. A private concessionaire outside the park rents boats.

Information: Jackson Lake State Park, 935 Tommy Been Road, P.O. Box 174, Oak Hill, OH 45656, (740) 682-6197

HISTORY
Jefferson Furnace operated from 1854 to 1916, the longest running forge in the Hanging Rock Iron Region. It produced excellent iron from the ore mined in Southeastern Ohio. Its iron was favored for cannons during the Civil War. At its peak, the foundry made 10 tons of iron a day.

The ruins of the Jefferson Iron Furnace remind me of two disconnected events—the Civil War naval battle between the *Monitor* and the *Merrimac*, and nature's regenerative power. Top quality iron produced at the furnace outfitted the Monitor, the Union ship in naval history's first ironclad clash.

The nation's iron industry relocated to the Lake Superior Region in the late 19th century; and the Hanging Rock area went into decline. Coal and salt also has been extracted from the area.

Laborers with the Civilian Conservation Corps

hand dug the lake basin during the Depression. In 1938 Black Fork was dammed to create Jackson Lake. The state took possession of the recreational spot a short time later, but the park was not dedicated until 1979.

Lake Alma

C.K Davis, a local coal baron, dammed Little Raccoon Creek in 1903 and named the 60-acre lake behind it Alma, after his wife. An island off the western shore became an amusement park with a merry-go-round, dance hall, outdoor theater, rides, food, and side shows. The fun and games ceased in 1910, and Lake Alma became a city water reservoir and state park.

LOCATION
Vinton County, Clinton Township, and Jackson County, Milton Township.

SIZE & DESIGNATION
Land: 290 acres; water: 60 acres.

ACCESS
The park entrance is on SR 349, a half mile north of the Vinton-Jackson county line. The park is four miles north of Wellston.

Accommodations: Lake Alma's quaint and popular family campground has 60 sites, most of them located in wooded ravines. From the park entrance on SR 349, follow Park Road 1 past the beach and boat launch, then go left on Park Road 2 to the camping area. Campground has electricity, latrines, self-registration, fire rings, dump station, drinking water, playground, but no showers. Campers with pets have a designated area. Some sites are a tight squeeze for RVs. A group camp, accessible via a footbridge, is located on the seven-acre island, former location of the amusement park.

Picnic Areas: Local folks come for summer picnics along the lakeshore. Most have grills. Three first-come, first-served shelters are available for groups. Favorite spots are the three picnic areas on the southeastern shore off Park Road 1, and the tables beside a pine grove near the swimming area.

Trails: Old Pine Trail, .5 mile, links the campground and swimming area. From the camp, hikers angle up to a ridge of hardwoods then descend through planted red and white pines.

Acorn Trail, one mile, wanders from the campground (start at Site 25) to ridges and hollows, into Jackson County, to a park road and along the south shore to SR 349. The easiest trail is a paved, mile-long jogging/bikeway trail, which occupies the left edge of one-way Park Road 1.

Swimming: Two beaches, totaling 550 feet, flank a concession area on the north shore. Change booths, parking, and picnic tables are available. Lifeguards are on duty on summer weekends at the larger beach. Follow Park Road 1.

Boating: Lake Alma is a water supply for Wellston, so boaters are limited to electric motors. The boat launch, on Park Road 1, is east of the swimming area. Boats can be rented from a concession at the beach.

Hunting: Hunters can pursue game in two areas of the park land. The largest block of land is west of SR 349 and the parallel railroad, and north of the Vinton-Jackson county line. This area is open October 15 to March 1 for all hunting and trapping. An area south and west of the campground, and bisected by the Acorn Trail is open during deer archery season only. Hunters should stop at the park office for a map and guidelines. Ohio game laws apply. Deer, turkeys, squirrels, and grouse challenge hunters.

Fishing: Throw lines here for largemouth bass, crappie, bluegill, and channel catfish. Panfish hang out near the footbridge to the group camp. Bass lull near the beds of lilies and coontail that are taking over portions of the lake. ODNR has stocked the water with several hundred white amurs, or grass carp, to munch on the unwanted vegetation. Release the monster if it takes your hook.

Information: Lake Alma State Park, Route 1, Box 422, Wellston, OH 45692, (740) 384-4474.

HISTORY

The City of Wellston bought Davis' lake for a backup water supply in 1926. It leases the park land to the Ohio Department of Natural Resources.

FIELD NOTES

Lake Alma's second-growth woodlands serve up spring wildflowers named large-flowered trillium, hepatica, wild geranium, and bloodroot. Birders can listen for wood thrush, pileated woodpecker, barred, great horned owls, and various waterbirds.

Lake Hope

Lake Hope is another "tweener" park— something between a fancy resort and a rustic, no-frills park. Snug in the rugged, hilly terrain of unpeopled Vinton County, the place approaches paradise for folks who like to poke around in the great outdoors. It's got great trails (including the Zaleski backpacking trail) for hikers, pioneer boneyards, ghosts in a railroad tunnel, old iron furnaces, cabins with fireplaces, wildlife galore, and a dense state forest.

LOCATION
Northeastern Vinton County, Brown Township.

SIZE & DESIGNATION
Land: 3,103 acres; water: 120 acres.

ACCESS
SR 278 (connecting Zaleski and Nelsonville) runs through the park. The park headquarters is located on SR 278 between the turnoffs to the dining lodge and beach.

Accommodations: Lake Hope has more cabins (69) than any other park, and some of the most romantic ones too. Its 23 "sleeping" cabins (1-4 bedrooms) around the dining lodge have fireplaces, as well as central heating. The sleepers near the beach only have fireplaces. Reserve these popular year-round cabins well in advance. (The firewood for sale is sometimes green, so bring your own supply.) Large groups (up to 24 people) gather at Laurel Lodge, also near the dining lodge. This dwelling, open year-round, has a fireplace and a kitchen. Call 6-12 months ahead for a reservation. Standard cabins (near the beach) and deluxe cabins are also available.

A wooded, 223-site campground on hilly Furnace Ridge Road has 46 electric hookups, latrines, heated showerhouses, three Rent-A-Camp slips, playgrounds, and a laundry. Two camper cabins can be rented in summer (reservations). Pets are allowed in designated areas.

Organized campers (up to 100) can reserve the Lake Ridge Group Camp, located at the end of Lake Ridge Road (Park Road 20). From SR 278, take Park Road 15, or Irish Ridge Road (just east of the campground road), then go left on Long Ridge Road (still Park Road 15), left on Park Road 20. Pick up a park map for visual directions.

Adjacent Zaleski State Forest offers free primitive campsites and drinking water along its celebrated 21-mile trail for backpackers. (See Zaleski State Forest, Register at the trailhead across from Hope Furnace.

Stone Terrace Restaurant [(740)596-4117] in Lake Hope Lodge serves full-course meals, and a gourmet peek at the lake. After eating, warm up by the fireplace, or admire the stone-timber interior, or enjoy a peaceful after-dinner ambience. The restaurant stays open year-round on weekends, but the weekday schedules changes with the seasons. The Sycamore Room on the ground floor can seat 100 people for meetings.

Picnic Areas: You will find picnic areas on SR 278 at Hope Furnace, at the beach (with shelterhouses) and dam, and along Cabin Ridge Road (branching west at the beach). Try the Grouse Point and Oak Point areas off Cabin Ridge Road.

Trails: Fifteen miles of trails lead hikers along a calm lakeshore, across rugged hills, and down hollows with pock-marked, sandstone ledges, and into densely wooded forests. The Hope Furnace (3.5 miles) and Peninsula (a three-mile loop) trails, trace the lakeshore, and are especially striking at dusk. (You might glimpse a beaver at that time.) The Olds Hollow Nature Trail, a shorter (1.5 miles) and more challenging path, goes to a pioneer cemetery, traverses hills and hollows, and visits Olds Cave (a recess cave) and a pine forest. This trail links to the Zaleski backpacking trail. The Hebron Hollow Trail (1.5 miles) and its limbs connect campers to the Hope Furnace Trail. It departs from the end of the campground drive. Upland game birds (turkeys and ruffed grouse) and beavers might be spooked along the Little Sandy Trail (two miles) connecting Grouse Point Picnic Area and SR 278. Mountain bikers also can use Little Sandy Trail from a trailhead on Cabin Ridge Road. The park brochure marks the routes of these trails.

The park has six miles of bridle trails, but horsemen may be better off at Zaleski State Forest where they will find 33 trail miles and an equestrian's campground.

Swimming: The 600-foot beach at the west end of the lake cools hundreds of bathers on a summer day. Youngsters especially enjoy jumping from the dock. Here you will find rowboats, pedalboats, and canoes to rent, food and beverages, a bathhouse with showers and toilets, and picnic tables and shelters. Lifeguards are usually on duty in summer.

Boating: Lake Hope is calm and restful; and being kept that way. Only watercraft propelled by human muscles or electric motors (3 horsepower maximum) can ply this surface. The concession at the beach rents boats, and sells bait and tackle. From May to September, the shop stays open daily from 8 a.m. to sunset; and at odd, unpredictable hours through November.

Hunting: Hunting is banned on state park land, but allowed in the state forest.

Fishing: Years ago Lake Hope's clear water was deadly to fish and risky for some bathers, due to the iron and sulfur pollutants from nearby coal mines that seeped into the Big Sandy Run watershed. Telltale orange stains on creek banks once revealed the contamination. Happily, a reclamation project plugged the mines and freshened the lake that now nurtures catfish, largemouth bass, crappie, and bluegills.

Information: Lake Hope State Park, Rte. 2, Box 3000, McArthur, OH 45651, (740) 596-5253

HISTORY

The young forest that cloaks the hills today conceals the deforestation that occurred more than a century ago. Thousands of loggers cut down thousands of acres of ancient trees to fuel the iron industry that once flourished here. Hope Furnace, constructed in 1853 from sandstone quarried from the ridge behind it, stood in the Hanging Rock Iron Region, the nation's chief iron manufactory. Laborers whacked down huge trees—325 acres a year, or 13,000 cords—to make charcoal for the iron furnaces. Charcoal pits smoldered continuously. Miners extracted iron ore found in sandstone, and hauled it to the furnace in mule-driven carts. Local legend has it that remnant iron deposits account for a high number of lightning strikes at Lake Hope. At its peak Hope Furnace produced 15 tons of iron a day.

Before 1860 the furnaces overproduced, causing prices to decline and debt to increase. Demand soared during the Civil War and so did prices. Shortly after the war, however, richer deposits of iron ore were discovered in Minnesota, Michigan and farther west. Also, the Ohio forests became depleted. By 1900 the furnaces in Ohio had closed. Coal mining, once a big deal in Vinton County, played out early in the 20th century, too.

Native Americans prized the flint—called Zaleski black flint—found in outcrops beside SR 328 northwest of the lake. They fashioned the hard stone into projectile points. A lower grade of flint was quarried by white settlers and used in the making of millstones. A seven-foot diameter millstone fetched $500. Washington Keeton, the farmer who once owned this land, and other family members are buried in the cemetery above the beach.

Zaleski, Tar Hollow, and Blue Rock state forests developed from a New Deal program in the 1930s. Federal funds bought big blocks of played out farmland in these areas and converted the properties into forest and recreation areas. The former landowners were resettled in nearby towns. At Zaleski, laborers toiling for the Depression-era Civilian Conservation Corps (CCC) built the dam across Big Sandy Run, and most other facilities. The Zaleski CCC Camp, now a state-run operation, still provides service in the park. Lake Hope grew from the state forest and became a state park in 1949.

FIELD NOTES

Look for yellow lady's slipper, a rare and delicate woodland orchid, blooming in secret hollows. Blue-eyed Mary, bloodroot and wild geranium show their beauty here, and summer hikers note the colonies of jewelweed where trails cross creeks.

SR 278 twists beside Big Sandy Creek, which in preglacial times was Zaleski Creek. It drains into Raccoon Creek just below the dam. The creek and road squeeze through a striking sandstone gorge at the north end of the park. Beaver dams occasionally cause the highway to flood, so be careful. Cruise the charming gravel backroads through the state forest if you stay awhile. They are "challenging" indeed—narrow, washboard surface, pocked, curving, unstable edges. Pure joy. And tiptoe through spooky Moonville Tunnel, supposedly inhabited by the ghost of a railroad brakeman who collided with a train.

Believers see the brakeman's lantern in the tunnel. To get there go a quarter-mile south of the park office, take Hope-Moonville Road, or T18. Stay left at the first fork, and travel about two miles to the tunnel. I dare you to walk through the tunnel at night. Officially, this section of the track is abandoned. Unofficially, I have my doubts.

JOURNAL

The lily pads lured us to a half submerged tree where we tied up the canoe and swam among acres of floating blossoms. Okay, so maybe swimming outside a "designated" area is not permitted, maybe it is. And I suppose getting entangled in lily roots and drowning was a possibility. No matter, we chanced it. My sleek daughter, imagining herself a mermaid or manatee, sniffed a flower, then dove and nosed up to another. My son, more a playful otter, squirmed away from the fish (a largemouth bass perhaps?) that tickled and nuzzled his legs. My wife and I simply bobbed among the blossoms, and doing so became lily pads ourselves. We lingered here until something inside told us to paddle on. We eased past beaver lodges, waved to shoreline fishers, flushed herons, watched crows and hawks circle, but that night the lilies filled our dreams.

Lake Logan

Tourist hordes heading for the Hocking Hills overlook this day-use park, but not cagey fishers. They come here to top the state record saugeye pulled from the lake, or to land another trophy largemouth bass, like the former state champ ten-pounder caught here 30 years ago. Locals know Lake Logan has the only decent beach in the whole Hocking Hills. Anyone can wet their line or splash here, just don't expect to camp overnight.

LOCATION
Central Hocking County, Falls Township.

SIZE & DESIGNATION
Land: 319 acres; water: 400 acres.

ACCESS
Lake Logan is a few miles west of Logan, off US 33 and SR 664. From US 33, go southerly on SR 664 a quarter mile, then right (west) on Lake Logan Road (CR 3). Most park facilities line CR 3. Lake Logan Road also meets US 33, a few miles northwest from SR 664.

Accommodations: None, unfortunately. Try local private camps.

Picnic Areas: Picnic areas ring the lake. There's one at the beach, at the boat rental, by the spillway (SR 664), and at the end of Blosser Road (off SR 664). The latter, located on south shore, has the most appeal for picnickers seeking privacy. Areas at the beach, boat rental, and Blosser Road have drinking water; all have latrines.

Trails: The Buckeye Trail goes across the northwest section of the park. Pine Vista Trail, not a quite a mile, loops around a hill north of the beach. You can also stroll along the lakeshore; the full circuit is 10 miles.

Swimming: The park's 525-foot swimming beach is on the north shore on Lake Logan Road. Amenities include concession/snack bar (mid-May to Labor Day), drinking water, changing boots, rest rooms, and picnic tables.

Boating: Lake Logan has a loyal cadre of sailboaters, but most watercraft on the lake carry fishing tackle and bait. The boat motor cannot be stronger than 10 horsepower, nor go faster than 10 miles per hour. The chief boat launch, with two ramps and walk-out dock, is at the east side of the lake. Here, a concessionaire rents pontoon boats, rowboats, canoes, dock slips, small bass boats (with electric motors), and pedalboats. A smaller ramp is north of the beach. Both locations offer boat tie-ups.

Hunting: Deer, turkey, ruffed grouse, squirrels, and woodcock can be bagged by hunters in the eastern and northeastern sections of the park. Waterfowl hunting is permitted in some of the skinny upper sections of the lake. Check boundaries at the park office.

Fishing: Lake Logan is largely managed for fishing, and with trophy results. The state's biggest saugeye—a 31-inch beauty that weighed 12.4 pounds—came from these waters in March 1993. For awhile the catch was a world record. Expect excellent chances for catfish (channel, flathead, and yellow bellied), and decent hauls of muskie, bass, bluegill, crappie, and northern pike.

Lake Logan has an average depth of 25 feet. Over the years several hundred Christmas trees have been submerged to give the lake bottom structure. Several stores along the way have bait and tackle.

Information: Lake Logan State Park, 30443 Lake Logan Road, Logan, OH 43138, (740) 385-3444 (park office), (740) 385-6727 (boat rental).

HISTORY
Duck Creek was dammed to create Hocking Lake in 1955. The Division of Wildlife managed it as a wildlife area until 1964, when the property was transferred to the Division of Parks and Recreation.

The lake also was renamed Lake Logan, so it would not be confused with Hocking Hills State Park and Hocking State Forest.

Lake White

Tell the kids, or unsuspecting adults, that Lake White was created by Pee Pee water. No kidding. Water from Pee Pee Creek, that is. The creek was dammed in the early 1830s to be a reservoir for the Ohio and Erie Canal. The creek's giggly name has nothing to do with water quality. Crooked Creek runs into Pee Pee Creek just below the dam. At this confluence and elsewhere, pioneer Peter Patrick carved his initials into trees to mark his claim. Pee Pee Creek takes its name from Peter Patrick's pioneer pictograph.

LOCATION
Northern Pike County, Pee Pee Township.

SIZE & DESIGNATION
Land: 107 acres; water: 337 acres.

ACCESS
From Waverly, go three miles south on SR 104, then turn right (northwesterly) on SR 551. Park facilities are located at this intersection on the south side of lake.

Accommodations: As another outdoor writer put it: You must have an urgent reason to camp at Lake White. Not exactly a slum, but far from an ideal campground. Twenty-three primitive, shadeless, and sometimes soggy sites stretch across a filled-in depression once serving as the channel of the Ohio & Erie Canal. Latrines and water are available, but no electricity, dump station, flush toilets. It borders SR 104, a sometimes busy highway with noisy nighttime trucks. It is rarely full. Enough said.

Picnic Areas: A scenic, reservable picnic shelter, halfway up a hill, overlooks Lake White. It features a fireplace and room for 75 people. Another shelterhouse stands near the campground, and picnic tables are scattered throughout the place. If not reserved, the shelters are available to the first takers.

The second floor of the lakeshore building serving as the park headquarters is a reservable meeting room with a balcony for viewing the lake. The facility, ideal for reunions, holidays, and groups, has a kitchen and fireplace.

Swimming: A small, 50-foot beach, usually uncrowded, is just north of the park headquarters. Changing booths are available near SR 551.

Boating: Most humans come here to water ski, and sail. There are no horsepower limits. On summer weekends, lake traffic becomes heavy. Park visitors cannot use the personal docks in front of private homes that line the shore. The public boat launch is near the park headquarters on SR 551. Folks in the slow lane might enjoy the upstream, backwater coves.

Fishing: A majority of anglers cast from boats because most of the shore is privately owned. Stay away from the high-speed areas. Head for backwater coves for bass, saugeye. catfish, crappie and bluegill. The state-record spotted bass was caught here in 1976 by Roger Trainer of Waverly. The 21-inch beast weighed five pounds, four ounces.

Information: Lake White State Park, 2767 State Route 551, Waverly, Ohio 45690, (740) 947-4059

HISTORY
Where to put the channel of the Ohio & Erie Canal? Through Piketon, on the east side of the Scioto River, as planned? Or through Waverly, hometown of Robert Lucas, then Speaker of the Ohio House of Representatives? Waverly won, for reasons that should be obvious.

On the morning of September 6, 1832, Waverly residents crowded along the canal waiting for it to fill with water from Pee Pee and Crooked creeks. Nine o'clock came, no water. Ten o'clock, no water. Eleven o'clock, still no water. Finally, at noon water trickled into the canal to the great relief of public officials and a restless crowd. Creek water had been temporarily blocked by a gravel bar upstream. The canal was in decline by 1860; and officially closed in 1913.

The lake became a make-work recreation project for laborers of the Works Progress Administration in the 1930s. It became a state park when the Department of Natural Resources was created in 1949.

FIELD NOTES
Don't expect much furbearing wildlife. Quiet coves and shorelines hide waterfowl and shorebirds. Flocks of Canada geese gather on the water in winter. Lucky eyes might catch migrating tundra swans, snow geese, common loons, and grebes. Nesters include orioles, Eastern wood pewee, rufuos-sided towhee, warblers (Kentucky, blue winged, yellow and prairie), and assorted vireos.

Muskingum River

Ohio's oddest state park comprises 93 miles of sidewinding and sycamored river, and a restored, historic canal system built 160 years ago. The "parkway" reconnects the state's first perma-

nent city, Marietta, with Zanesville, once the state's capital and a hub for pioneer travelers, riverborne or overland.

LOCATION
Muskingum River as it flows through Muskingum, Morgan, and Washington counties.

SIZE & DESIGNATION
Land: 120 acres; water: approximately 93 miles of river.

ACCESS
Park jurisdiction goes from Ellis Lock in Muskingum County to Devola Lock in Washington County.

Accommodations: The park system manages two campgrounds along the river. Lock 11 (Ellis Lock), north of Zanesville, has 20 sites (CR 49 off SR 60). Luke Chute (Lock 5) has eight free sites for boaters only. Water, fire rings, latrines, picnic tables are provided. Privately-owned campgrounds line the river. Camping also is available at Blue Rock and Dillon state parks.

Picnic Areas: Locks have a picnic table or two, and latrines (except Lock 9 at Philo).

Trails: The Muskingum River is the trail. Those who cannot walk on water will find hiking trails at Blue Rock State Park, Blue Rock State Forest, and Dillon State Park.

Swimming: There's no park beach, and swimming is not allowed at the locks and dams. Private property owners control swimming along their shores. Many people swim at their own risk in the river—you decide.

Boating: Boating is the main event. Boats of all sizes and shapes ply these waters on summer weekends. The slow current created by the dams suits houseboats and pontoons, and these are the most prominent crafts on the river. Unlimited horsepower means power boats, water skiers, and other flotation contraptions in tow. Rowboats and canoes also bob on the sluggish water.

Go through at least one of the park's ten historic locks, regardless of your kind of boat, to see how you "lock" through on the river. Signal the lockmaster as you approach and navigate between the red and green buoys. Boats with horns sound one short blast, though rowboaters and canoers often resort to whistles or yells. Boaters with marine radios can reach the lockmaster on channel 13. Stay 300 feet from the lock gates until the lockmaster motions you to proceed. Follow the lockmaster's instructions. You will have to tie-up and cushion your boat. Big boats should have 150 feet of mooring line, others 75 feet. When the boat is secured, the gates are locked and water is pumped in or out to achieve the desired water level. Wait for the lockmaster to signal you to leave the lock, and depart slowly. Locks 3, 4, 7, and 10 have canals. Contact the park office for annual pass applications.

Plan your outing when locks are open. Locks operate from mid-May to the third weekend in October. Other times you are locked between locks. From time to time a lock is closed for repair. Contact the park office for hours, which vary depending on the season, and status of locks.

Locks are found on either bank. Large watercraft must worry about bridges with clearances at normal level ranging from 11 feet to 35 feet. Check mileage and clearance charts. Public launch ramps are located at Beverly (Lock 4), Luke Chute (Lock 5), Stockport (Lock 6), Malta (Lock 7), Zanesville (Riverside Park), and Ellis (Lock 11). Private launches are available at McConnellsville (Lock 7), Devola (Lock 2), and Zanesville (Lock 10). Buoys mark the river's navigational channel from Ellis to Marietta. A navigation chart of the river is available for $5. Fuel and food are available at private marinas.

Fishing: Cast for largemouth, smallmouth and spotted bass from shore, boat, or along tributaries. Channel catfish and saugeye also swim in the Muskingum. Once abundant, muskellunge are few and far between nowadays. Fishing is allowed at lock sites, but not on lock walls.

Special Places & Events: Canal lockmasters show visitors how America's last hand-operated locks work every Sunday from Memorial Day through Labor Day weekends. An annual Lock Festival is held in Beverly (Lock 4) in June. Activities include locking demonstrations, boats races, antique boats, and canoe rodeo.

Information: Muskingum River State Park, P.O. Box 2806, Zanesville, OH 43702-2806, (740) 452-3820, (740) 452-3147.

HISTORY
The Muskingum River has been a river of conquest and vital transportation route for the humans—Native and European—that have used it. Though Indians didn't name rivers, this one possibly derives from the Lenni Lenape (Delaware) utterance "Moos-kin-ging" meaning "elk eye river." It probably referred to a spot along the river where elk herds gathered. The stream could have been called Sycamore River, for the mammoth trees arching over the banks, but white settlers preferred to name rivers after noble mammals.

The establishment of Marietta at the Muskingum's mouth in 1788, began the transformation of the river from wild, unpredictable current to stable, productive citizen. Steamboats joined flatboats and keelboats on the river in 1824, but only when the river swelled to nearly flood stage. In 1836, river settlements celebrated the Ohio Legislature's approval of a capital improvement bill for a canal from Marietta to the Ohio and Erie Canal at Dresden, north of Zanesville.

Major Samuel Curtis, a West Point graduate, configured a system of 10 locks and 110 dams, which opened in October 1841. For the next 40 years, the "golden age" for steamers, paddlewheelers monopolized freight and passenger service. Improvements continued in the nineteenth century. Bridges replaced ferries, and a state road along the

Future Ohio-born presidents might claim they "slept" in a log cabin, at Pike Lake.

east bank (predecessor of SR 60) was opened in 1837. The first train between Zanesville and Marietta ran on June 30, 1888.

Steamboat traffic declined over the next 30 years, and so did revenue for the canal. Floods in 1884, 1898 and March 1913 strained the system, but it was the steamboat, not the swamped railroad, that brought flood relief to victims. Flood control projects in the Muskingum's headwaters came next (see Muskingum Watershed Conservancy District). The river's last steamboat, *Richland,* was dry docked in Zanesville on September 12, 1934.

The federal government closed the Muskingum canal locks in 1951, and the railroad quit passenger service between Marietta and Zanesville two years later. By the early Fifties, people traveled between the cities in a car. Still, the canal and rail closings produced a disconnected and empty feeling, the way the closing of an interstate highway or major airport does today. In November 1958, however, the canal was reborn when Ohio Department of Natural Resources took control. Since then the department periodically repairs the locks and dams to keep pleasure boats running from Ellis Lock south of Dresden to Devola Lock in Marietta.

FIELD NOTES

The Muskingum once supported freshwater mussels the size of dinner plates, whose contents provided meals for its harvesters. The creatures built their enormous shells from dissolved limestone released by bank erosion or tributaries. The usual culprits of pollution, overharvesting, and sedimentation led to their decline. Still, the Muskingum is the last Ohio refuge for mussels known as monkeyface shell,

fan shell, butterfly shell and Ohio pigtoe. Several rare fish continue to live here, notably northern madtom, sand darter, mooneye, and channel darter.

Pike Lake

All the hyperbole for this pocket-sized park applies—charming, quaint, rustic, sublime. Friendly park staffers keep the showpiece tidy and casual. Early risers are treated to mist on Pike Lake, fawns at the water's edge, droplets on trillium petals, and warblers in a hazy forest canopy. The beach is really a country swimming hole where lanky kids in cutoffs feel right at home.

LOCATION
Northwestern Pike County, Benton Township.

SIZE & DESIGNATION
Land: 600 acres; water 13.

ACCESS
From US 50 east of Bainbridge, go south on Potts Hill Road, south (right) on Pike Lake Road (TR 348).
Accommodations: Pike Lake's cabins and

lodge stand along a tree-lined park road that climbs a ridge beside Pike Lake. A dozen family cabins (two bedrooms, sofa-bed, kitchen, shower, bath, screened porch) are open year-round. Built in 1972, each sleeps six comfortably. The Civilian Conservation Corps built the 13 "standard" cabins in the 1930s. These updated cabins bed down 4-6, but lack a porch. Utensils and dishes are provided in both.

Pike Lake Lodge, originally a CCC bunkhouse, handles groups up to 20 in two bedrooms, and a second-floor dormitory with seven bunks. A large porch peeks on Pike Lake. It has a full kitchen, central heat, and air conditioning.

Shady, quaint, clean, private describes the 112-site campground on Pike Lake Road. All but 10 sites have electric hookups. Although showers and flush toilets are not available, latrines, drinking water, wheelchair sites, playground, horseshoe court, basketball, softball field, nature center with amphitheater, pet sites, dump station, and camp commissary meet your needs.

A creek spilling from Pike Lake runs besides the camp for those who enjoy creeking. A reservable group camp for 60 people is offered.

Picnic Areas: Family gatherings are popular at the park's picnic areas. Two are located north of the lake on Pike Lake Road, and there are tables on Egypt Hollow Road, and between the lake and campground. Water and latrines are nearby.

Trails: Five footpaths total a 3.8-mile journey through park land, including a section of the Buckeye Trail shared by the North Country, and American Discovery trails. The park brochure marks the trail routes.

Greenbrier Trail, a half mile, is a self-guided interpretive trail starting by the Nature Center on Egypt Hollow Road. Brochures are available at the park office. Mitchell Ridge Trail, 1.2 miles, is a tough woodland loop that begins nearby the dam spillway. The Buckeye Trail splits from the east leg of the loop. Wildcat Hollow, 1.2 miles, explores rough terrain with trailheads on Pike Lake and Egypt Hollow roads. Lake Trail, .4 mile, goes along the east shore of Pike Lake, and the half-mile CCC Trail links the Greenbrier Trail.

Swimming: A 155-foot sandy beach and new bathhouse create an almost Norman Rockwell setting. They are situated on a tiny island at the north end of the lake. You'll cross a footbridge to get there. Water, snacks, and rest rooms are available. An off-shore anchored deck in water five feet deep collects kids of all kinds. Perfect for "cannonball" and "belly flop" dives, and tossing screaming siblings into the water. Lifeguards control the action.

Boating: Thirteen-acre, tear-shaped Pike Lake is ideal for rowboats, canoes, and inflatables (not tubes) propelled by paddles and electric motors (up to 4.5 horsepower). This is where you teach youngsters navigation. The camp commissary on the west shore rents rowboats, canoes, and pedalboats. The store is open daily from Memorial Day through Labor Day and weekends April,

Wide Acres

Ohio's Largest State Parks

Combined land and water acres
1. Salt Fork, 20,181 acres
2. Pymatuning, 17,500 acres
3. Grand Lake, 14,000 acres
4. Mosquito Lake, 11,811 acres
5. East Fork, 10,580 acres

Land acres
1. Salt Fork, 17,229 acres
2. Paint Creek, 9,000 acres
3. East Fork, 8,420 acres
4. Caesar Creek , 7,941 acres

5. Dillon, 6,030 acres

Water acres (excepting Lake Erie)
1. Grand Lake, 13,500 acres
2. Mosquito Lake, 7,850 acres
3. Indian Lake, 5,800 acres
4. Pymatuning, > 4,000 acres
5. Alum Creek, 3,387

Longest (linear)
1. Muskingum Parkway, 93 miles
2. Little Miami, 50 miles

May, September, and October.

Fishing: Shore anglers have plenty of places, even a floating fishing pier near the commissary. Cast for largemouth bass, bluegill, channel cat, bullhead, and crappie. The lake, originally dug by CCC workers with shovels, was recently drained, dredged, and restocked.

Special Places & Events: Drive south on Pike Lake Road to a stone house called Eager Inn on the left at the intersection with Morgan's Fork Road. A placard explains the place, built in 1797, was one of the original roadhouse inns along Zane's Trace. The pioneer road continued south on Morgan's Fork Road. If you want to retrace the Trace, turn right on Auerville Road, left on Fire Tower Road, left briefly on Green Ridge Road, and an immediate left on Latham Road to Latham. Continue straight on Grassy Fork Road.

Morgan's Fork remembers the Confederate General John H. Morgan and his daring raid across Southern Ohio in 1863. Morgan and his troops apparently holed up at the Eager Inn and fought a brief skirmish with Union pursuers. Soon after the battle, farmers found a fatally wounded Union soldier in a field now claimed by Pike Lake State Park. The fellow could not be identified. Casualty of Morgan's Raid? Deserter? Confederate spy impersonating a Yank? Pine Lake's "Tomb of the Unknown Soldier" is an unmarked headstone beneath an oak tree by the dam.

The state park hosts a Harvest Moon Campout in the last October weekend. This is preceded by a Fall Festival of Leaves in Bainbridge, with the usual rides, craft stands, carnival food on Main Street.

Information: Pike Lake State Park, 1847 Pike Lake Road, Bainbridge, OH 45612-9640, (740) 493-2212

HISTORY

Park and state forest facilities were constructed initially by laborers in the Civilian Conservation Corps in the 1930s. The workers made the lake and earthen dam, built cabins, roads, fire towers, and planted thousands of pine trees. Following formation of the Division of Parks and Recreation in 1949, a portion of Pike State Forest became Pike Lake State Park.

FIELD NOTES

Much is said of the autumn colors here. Pike Lake's spring wildflowers deserve attention too. The park's nature center doubles as a wildlife rehab center. Injured critters are housed in two fenced areas along Egypt Hollow Road. They are released when they have repaired.

Salt Fork

Salt Fork has it all, from lodge luxury to rugged ravine. There's 20,000 acres of outdoors playland, rolling hills clothed in green and packed with critters, and a lake pleasing to speedster, paddler, and swimmer. The lakeshore cabins rank high on everyone's list, and a short, torturous golf course usually humbles the loftiest hackers. There's space enough for those who want to get lost, and for those who want to find themselves.

LOCATION

North-central Guernsey County.

SIZE & DESIGNATION

Land: 17,229 acres (includes state wildlife area); water: 2,952 acres.

ACCESS

From I-77, head east on US 22 roughly seven miles to the park entrance road on the left. The park office is the first building on the right. Carefully follow state park signs to your destination. The campground is on Park Road (PR) 3, the beach on PR 2, Salt Fork Marina on PR 14 (first left), the lodge, cabins and golf course on PR 3, and Sugartree Fork Marina on PR 17.

Accommodations: You can bed down at a lodge, cabin, family campground, or primitive group camp. Salt Fork's resort lodge has 148 rooms, the largest in the state park system. The ambience is a casual blend of breezy modern resort and rustic living, the latter flavor seasoned by stone fireplaces and vaulted wood-beam ceilings. Amenities include pools indoors and outdoors, sauna, fitness room, game room, gift shop, volleyball, tennis, shuffleboard, basketball, playground, dining room, snack bar, lounge, and large meeting rooms.

The park's 54 scenic cabins may be the most sought-after shacks in the system. Nearly all of them are just steps away from the lakeshore. Those not exactly on the shore usually have broader lake views. Book these choice digs far in advance. A paved boat ramp with docks accommodates boaters, and a short hiking trail starting at the boat launch ascends to the lofty lodge. The cabins are also within walking distance of the golf course.

The road to the cabins descends from Park Road 3, the first left after registering at the lodge. This road soon forks. I prefer cabins along the left fork, directly below the lodge. Hikers will find woodland and shoreline trails stemming from the end of the right fork.

The family campground features 212 sites with electricity. Shady and open sites are available. Campers will find showerhouses, flush toilets, sites for folks in wheelchairs, pet sites, drinking water, amphitheater, nature programs, and dump station. The showerhouse in Loop A is heated and stays open year-round. The camp fills up fast on weekends between

Memorial Day and Labor Day.

Organized groups up to 150 can tent at a rustic group campground. To get there continue east on US 22 passed the park entrance road. Turn left on TR 587, a.k.a. Parker Road, to the camp on the left. The Buckeye Trail also follows Parker Road. Campers with horses use a 20-site camp off PR 1, near the parking areas for the Stone House and Hosak Cave trails.

Picnic Areas: Picnic areas are scattered in scenic locations around the lake. The primary areas are the main beach and along Park Road 14. A top-notch site for wheelchair visitors is located on Park Road 1, near the horsemen's camp. It features three shelters, extended tables, toilets, paved paths, and water. A shelterhouse is available on a first-come basis.

Trails: Salt Fork offers 14 trails totaling 14 miles for hikers and two courses covering 20 miles for horse riders. Ten trails branch from Park Road 5, which leads to the campground and beaches. The most trodden among these are the two-mile Shadbush Trail running from the campground to the lodge, and Gunn's Glenn, also two miles, looping from the campground to the shore.

More adventurous walkers go north on Park Road 1 and take the Stone House Trail, a 1.8 mile journey along an arm of the lake to a recently restored stone farmhouse (see History). Beaver lodges and deer are likely to be seen. Nearby is Hosak's Cave Trail, a dinky but scenic half-mile loop path to a shelter cave. The park brochure rates the latter path "potentially dangerous" to discourage amateur rock climbers. The Buckeye Trail crosses the northeastern corner of the park, paralleling PR 59. Bushwhackers can roam freely in public hunting areas. Trails are shown on the park brochure.

Two five-mile bridle trails depart in opposite directions from the horsemen's camp. The Orange Loop heading northwest tends to be favored by riders because it largely follows the lakeshore. Riders taking the Blue Loop see woods and fields but no lake. Hikers can use these paths too.

Swimming: Salt Fork's main swimming beach is 2,500 feet, making it one of the largest inland beaches in the state. A modern bathhouse has showers, lockers, toilets, and snack bar. Picnic tables are sprinkled around the beach. Many campers choose the smaller and more private campground beach at the end of PR 5. Boaters can swim off this latter beach and in other designated areas.

Boating: With 74 miles of shoreline, Salt Fork Lake has plenty of room for water recreationists of all speeds. Two full-service marinas offer fuel, boat rentals, fishing gear, food and beverages, 470 dock slips, parking and paved launches. Salt Fork Marina, boasting 364 docks, serves the east side of the lake, while Sugartree Fork Marina attracts boaters on the west side. Other improved boat ramps are located by the park cabins, behind the park office (PR 23), the shore opposite Sugartree Fork Marina (end of CR 831), and at the campground beach. Primitive launches for canoes and small boats are found at the north end at Hosak's Cave (PR 29), and north of the dam on PR 64 (off Old Twenty One Road), and off US 22 on the east edge of the lake.

Salt Fork Lake is an unlimited horsepower reservoir, except in no wake zones shown on the park brochure map. Water skiers and jet skiers flock to the pond. Sightseeing cruises lasting an hour and 15 minutes depart daily (seasonal) from Sugartree Marina in a 65-foot passenger boat. Boaters may camp on their boats in no-wake zones within 50 yards of shore.

Golf: Salt Fork's 18-hole golf course is the shortest in the park system, just 6,036 yards, but it is the toughest. Hilly terrain means steep, uneven fairways, terraced greens, and many greens unseen for approach shots. Golfers who walk this par 71 nightmare can expect a workout. The clubhouse has a snack bar and pro shop. Call far ahead for weekend tee times.

Hunting: Deer, turkey, squirrels, ruffed grouse, rabbits, woodchuck, raccoon, beaver, muskrat, mink, quail, woodcock, and waterfowl are pursued here by hunters and trappers. Check boundaries of restricted areas at the park office. Some portions are open only to primitive weapons. The state wildlife area has a shooting range on PR 59.

Fishing: Anglers cast for muskellunge, small and largemouth bass, channel catfish, walleye, bluegill, and crappies. The Division of Wildlife stocks Salt Fork Lake with muskies, largemouth bass, walleyes, channel and flathead catfish, bluegills, sunfish, and crappies. Smallmouth bass, suckers and bullheads also swim in the pond. Cast for muskies near the dam, and on the north shore below the lodge. Try the calm coves with heavy vegetation for summer bass.

Information: Salt Fork State Park, 14755 Cadiz Road, Lore City, OH 43755, (740) 439-3521 (park office, (740) 432-1508 (campground), (740) 432-7185 (golf course), 1-800-282-7275 (lodge and cabin reservations. Salt Fork State Park Lodge, P.O. Box 7, Cambridge, OH 43725, (740) 439-2751.

HISTORY

The park name comes from a salt well used by Native Americans and early European settlers. The latter group called the creek beside the briny well, Salt Fork.

In 1837, Benjamin Kennedy, an Irish immigrant, bought 80 acres along Sugar Tree Fork and built a massive mini-manor house from locally mined sandstone. The two-story manse measured 40 by 18 feet, and cost a mere $600. Some of the stones in the finely crafted home are nine-feet long, and 14 inches wide. Kennedy's descendents lived there until 1966. The following year the state bought the property and park construction began. The earthen dam impounding Salt Fork and Sugar Tree Fork was finished in 1967, and the lodge opened in 1972.

Although Kennedy's home was listed on the National Register of Historic Places in 1975 it slowly fell into ruin, and occasionally rising lake water flooded the basement. Several years ago the limb of a tall white pine planted by Benjamin Kennedy crashed on the roof. Park staffers and community volunteers rallied to save the home. Benefactors donated cash and lumber. The proceeds of a pontoon boat cruise to the home help fund the restoration. The 1.8-mile roundtrip stroll to the stone house is one of the park's best hikes.

FIELD NOTES

Deer watching is a favorite pasttime here. Herds appear on the golf course, and smaller groups slink along park roads. Dusk and dawn are the best times to see deer. Shining lights on them for a better view is unlawful.

Few places in Ohio match Salt Fork's natural diversity of woodlands, croplands, open water, marshes, pine plantings, reverting meadows (shrubland), stream bottomlands, and grasslands. Roughly, a third of the area is forested with oaks and hickories on the dry ridges and maples, beech, ash, willow, elm, and sycamore on the moister slopes and bottomlands. Cropland and pastures make up a third of the area, with the remainder dominated by shrubs and small trees, like dogwood, hawthorn, sassafras, and crabapple.

Numerous streams have cut gently rolling terrain to create steep-sided hollows and ravines. Wildflowers like wild geranium, large-flowered trillium, violets, asters, and goldenrod rise in the woods and meadows. Rabbits, squirrels, woodcocks, raccoons, grouse, turkeys, muskrat, mink, beaver, and raccoon are permanent residents. Beaver lodges ring the shoreline. Embayments and marshes support waterfowl called mallard, teal, bufflehead, goldeneye, wigeon, Canada goose, and wood duck.

Besides waterfowl, birders can look for bitterns, rails, and waders in the shallow marsh areas at the tips of the lake. Herons also appear in summer, and the woods feature the pileated woodpecker (listen for its telltale pecking), scarlet tanager, barred owl, Kentucky warbler, black-billed cuckoo, and American redstart.

Scioto Trail

In 1824 William Hewitt forsook the world and holed up in a cave beside an Indian path that whites adopted and called the Scioto Trail. Atop furry bluffs a few miles east, Hewitt watched a steady procession of settlers; everybody was in a hurry to reach their destination. But not Hewitt the Hermit, who lived here in splendid solitude until death at age 70 in 1834. The small sandstone obelisk (circa 1842) at the park's entrance commemorates Hewitt's shy behavior.

LOCATION

Southeastern Ross County, Franklin Township.

SIZE & DESIGNATION

Land: 218 acres; water: 30 acres. Scioto Trail State Forest has 9,151 acres.

ACCESS

Hewitt's haven is still bypassed by travelers speeding on US 23 (the old Scioto Trail). Maybe it's best they keep going. Scioto Trail State Park won't sit well with people in a hurry.

The park and state forest entrance—SR 372—is midway between Chillicothe and Waverly, on the east side of US 23. Consider the state park and state forest as inseparable entitities with the same name. To reach state park facilities (divided into two areas), take the right fork at the fire tower and follow Forest Road 1 (Stoney Creek Road) or signs to camping and the park office. This road cuts through the Stewart Lake section of the state park. Ahead, turn left (northbound) on Forest Road 3 to reach the Caldwell Lake area.

Accommodations: For the reclusive campers, Scioto Trail has two primitive, walk-in tent campgrounds at Stewart Lake. One campground (wooded) sits above and north of the lake and offers drinking water and latrines. The other sprawls out in the field west of the lake (latrines only).

The campground at Caldwell Lake has 77 sites (20 with electric hookups). Not many comforts here, just latrines and a dump station, but then you are here to get away from it all. There is usually a volunteer here in the summer to assist campers.

Picnic Areas: You'll find picnic areas at the state forest fire tower (shelterhouse too), Stewart Lake, and Caldwell Lake (at the dam and beside the campground). Early birds will claim the picnic tables on an island in Caldwell Lake (accessible by footbridge). Latrines and play areas are found at the lake sites.

Trails: Stick to the trails in the state forest, notably the DeBord Vista Trail, 2.5 miles from the main campground to the fire tower; the Long Branch Trail, running northerly about four miles from Stoney Creek Road (1.5 miles east of the turn to Caldwell Lake) to Moss Hollow and Toad Hollow roads; and the Buckeye Trail, with connector trails from Stoney Creek Road, just east of Stewart Lake and at the terminus for the Long Branch Trail. The American Discovery Trail runs through the forest (on the Buckeye Trail). Next try these state park paths: the two-mile Church Hollow Trail (rugged), branching from the campground; and the CCC Trail (one mile) from the Log Church at Caldwell Lake.

The state forest maintains 26 miles of bridle trails for travelers on horses, feet, and mountain bikes. Pick up guides for the state forest and park for a complete picture of local trails.

Boating: The small lakes cannot take anything faster or noisier than an electric trolling motor. Boaters with canoes, rowboats, and johnboats (small rowboats) will find launches at the lakes.

Fishing: The lakes fall short as fishing meccas, but bass, bluegills, and catfish lurk beneath the surface.

Information: Scioto Trail State Park, 144 Lake Road, Chillicothe, OH 45601-9478, (740) 663-2125.

HISTORY

Scioto Trail was overlooked by the First Ohioans. People of the Adena and Hopewell cultures built numerous mounds and earthworks in the Scioto and Paint Creek valleys, none has been uncovered in Scioto Trail. Perhaps Native Americans limited their presence to keep it rich in game?

The spot was still a wilderness when Hewitt camped in the cave. Hewitt became a legend to the locals, who erected the monument beside his hovel in 1842. The construction of US 23, which tracks the old Indian Trail from Chillicothe to Portsmouth, ruined Hewitt's cave, and required relocation of the marker 1,000 feet south of its original site.

Artillery blasts shattered the peace of Scioto Trail during World War I. Gunners from Camp Sherman in Chillicothe fired missiles from the confluence of Stoney Creek and the Scioto River at targets near Stewart and Caldwell lakes.

The state began buying up the former artillery range—for a mere $7.70 an acre—in 1922; the intent being to develop a forest. Land purchases ended by 1937. During the 1930s, the Civilian Conservation Corps built the roads, lakes, and trails for recreation. The state park took shape later on two parcels within the state forest.

A replica of a pioneer log church stands in the Caldwell Lake campground.

FIELD NOTES

Climb the 60-foot state forest fire tower near the park entrance. The view is still worth trudging up 72 steps to the top platform, though it is somewhat obscured by mature trees. When the tower was still

For The *Birds*

Top 10 State Parks for Bird Watching

Crane Creek — Waterfowl haven next to Magee Marsh State Wildlife Area and Ottawa National Wildlife Refuge on Lake Erie shore.

Hocking Hills — Look deep into the woods for nesting warblers. The bird song becomes rapturous in late April.

Mohican — Clear Fork Gorge and surrounding state forest attract birds year-round.

Maumee Bay — The boardwalk across a marsh, and meadow trail are hot spots.

East Fork — Rich variety of habitat and plenty of room offer homes for wild turkey and the rare Henslow's sparrow. Plenty of trails for birding.

Hueston Woods — The Big Woods Trail through an old growth beech-maple forest is a must. Raptors on the mend can be seen close up at the nature center.

Lake Hope — A sleepy lake crowded by a thick forest is paradise for hawks, songbirds, and herons.

Salt Fork — Ohio's biggest park has a full menu of habitats for birds, including endangered ospreys.

Headlands Beach — Flanked by Headlands Dunes and Mentor Marsh state nature preserves, this park gets shorebirds, migrants, and piping plovers, an endangered critter.

Shawnee — The huge state forest in league with the resort park cradles a large population of birds in this rugged, forested hill country.

—SO

used, foresters trimmed nearby trees so that lookouts could see the horizon.

The park and state forest are at their best during the peak weeks for spring wildflowers and fall colors. Mushroom harvesters flock to the forests in early spring.

Shawnee

Here's a resort park smack in the middle of Ohio's "Little Smokies," a destination encircled by a 60,000-acre state forest that comes close to being a wilderness. A few miles from the lodge, just over a dozen rugged ridges, the Ohio River sweeps southwesterly burdened with water from the Scioto River.

LOCATION
Southwestern Scioto County, Nile Township.

SIZE & DESIGNATION
Land: 1,100 acres; water: 68 acres. The park is surrounded by 60,000-acre Shawnee State Forest.

ACCESS
From Portsmouth, head west on US 52 about seven miles, then turn right (northwest) on SR 125. Roughly five miles ahead, the campground at Roosevelt Lake will appear on the left, followed by Turkey Creek Lake, and the park road (on the left) to Shawnee Lodge, the cabins, and park office. The golf course and marina are off US 52, west of SR 125.

Accommodations: Shawnee has accommodations ranging from rustic to resort. The 50-room lodge blends modern conveniences with rusticity expressed with Native American artifacts, large fireplaces, and seemingly endless forest. One artifact, an attractive birch bark canoe, is not a native product of Southern Ohio. White birch, the donor tree, does not grow here. Rooms have furnishings made by local artisans. Lodge amenities include a restaurant (with views of Turkey Creek Lake), fitness center, lounge, gift shop, indoor and outdoor pools, sauna, jacuzzi, game room, tennis and basketball courts. Seven meeting rooms can handle 400 people attending a conference.

Twenty-five two-bedroom cabins perch atop a ridge near the lodge. Each has a screened porch and can sleep six people. Cabin guests can use lodge facilities.

The campground at Roosevelt Lake has 107 sites, and all but three offer electricity. Two showerhouses have coin laundries and flush toilets. One shower is available from mid-April through most of January (for hunters). Pets are welcomed at 33 sites. A short walk takes campers to a swimming beach at Roosevelt Lake. The place usually fills up for the annual trout derby (third Saturday in April), holiday weekends, and the Fall Hike and Campout on weekend three in October. Horseback riders can bed down at a 58-site horsemen's camp in the state forest. Backpackers can settle down at primitive tent sites along the state forest backpackers trail (see Shawnee State Forest, page 246).

Picnic Areas: Picnic tables with grills are clustered at Roosevelt Lake and at opposite ends of Turkey Creek Lake. Two shelters are available at Roosevelt Lake on a first-come basis. Take a picnic lunch to an overlook on the Panoram Scenic Loop Drive (see below) through the state forest.

Trails: Several of Ohio's premier hiking and horseback riding trails wander through Shawnee State Forest. The state park itself serves up small potatoes—the Lampblack Nature Trail, a mile loop departing from the lodge parking lot; the Turkey Creek Nature Trail, a mile loop starting near the boat ramp at the south tip of Turkey Creek Lake; and the Look-Out Trail, a rigorous half-mile walk to a panorama leaving from the south side of Roosevelt Lake. Consider these teasers for the state forest trails.

Motorists can take the Panoram Scenic Loop Drive, a 25-mile backroads ride through Shawnee Territory, or make their own loops among 160 miles of roads.

Swimming: Bathers have a choice of beaches at Turkey Creek Lake or Roosevelt Lake, named for the first Roosevelt president. Each has changing booths and picnic sites. Turkey Creek Lake has a snack bar and boat rental. Guests at the lodge and cabins can swim in the indoor and outdoor swimming pools.

Golf: Although the park lodge resides in "Ohio's Little Smokies," the 18-hole Shawnee Golf Course sprawls across flat bottomland beside the Ohio River. Rating the difficulty of the par 72, 6,400-yard course is challenging, and depends, really, on your score for the round. The pro shop (next to the marina) offers burgers, sandwiches, beverages. The Marina Cafe has more grub, including ribs. The Ohio River and "Little Smokies" create an attractive backdrop for the course.

Boating: Boaters in the slow lane go to Turkey Creek Lake (55 acres) and Roosevelt Lake (13 acres) where electric motors can propel craft. A two-lane ramp awaits boats at the south end of Turkey Creek Lake, off SR 125. Small boats can be rented at a concession near the beach for this lake, off the park lodge road. Take Mackletree Run Road to reach the one-lane launch for Roosevelt Lake.

Bigger motor boats and sailboats use the park's marina on the Ohio River, off US 52. The site has a trio of two-lane ramps, plus fuel, parking, 150 docks with electric and water hookups (fee), restaurant (seasonal). There's unlimited horsepower on the river, and plenty of room to explore.

Fishing: Spring-fed Turkey Creek Lake stays cool enough for trout, specifically rainbows, browns, and a hybrid from both. The lake gets truckloads of trout just before a fishing derby on the last Saturday in April. Largemouth bass, catfish, bluegill and crappie reside in both lakes.

Roosevelt Lake is ideal for youngsters. Take them to the bridge going to the campground, a hot spot for panfish and bass. The Ohio River fishery is a few miles away.

Information: Shawnee State Park, 4404 State Route 125, Portsmouth, OH 45663-9003, (740) 858-6652 (park office), (740) 858-4561 (campground), (740) 858-6681 (golf course), (740) 858-5061 (marina)

Shawnee State Park Lodge, P.O. Box 189, Friendship, OH 45630-0189, (740) 858-6621 (lodge and cabins), (800) 282-7275 (reservations for lodge).

HISTORY

The park name honors the Shawnee nation whose people occupied much of Southern Ohio at the time of the European invasion. This particular area was a primary hunting ground. In their native language the Ohio River was known as Spaylaywitheepi. White settlers displaced the Shawnees, or Shawandase, by 1800.

The state acquired the park land in 1922, and originally called it Theodore Roosevelt State Game Preserve. In the 1930s, a half dozen Civilian Conservation Corps camps were established in the recovering forest. CCC workers built roads, dams, trails, and the future park's infrastructure. The area became a state park and state forest when the Ohio Department of Natural Resources was founded in 1949. The park got a new name, Portsmouth State Park, but this was replaced by Shawnee to fit the architectural theme of the lodge that opened in 1973. The golf course accepted hackers in 1980.

FIELD NOTES

The park and state forest comprise one of Ohio's richest, wildest, and largest unbroken forest tracts. Old growth trees survive in ravines: In quiet recessess, rare woodland wildflowers, such as whorled pogonia and showy orchis, emerge in spring. Shawnee is one of the last strongholds for the state endangered bobcat, black bear, and timber rattlesnake. Poisonous copperheads slide in the woods, but you are more likely to be struck by lightning than the fangs of a rattler or copper; furtive and secretive critters these. Hard to get to know, not that I want to meet one face to face. Don't let them keep you from exploring the park.

JOURNAL

If only I could have been here two centuries ago when Shawnee warriors hunted in this furry forest. Even then the terrain was too formidable for permanent villages. And even for them this was a place to get away from it all—away from war, away from the Southern and Eastern invaders poised to overtake them. You might glimpse spectral forms in these misty woods, not angels, but painted, sleek warriors chasing other restless spirits. The solitude and silence of the deep woods serves as a sacrament.

Strouds Run

The pleasant, seven-mile hike along the shore of Dow Lake is worth the trip. Beyond that, Strouds Run, just a few miles northeast of Athens, rests in a thick forest, and sleeps beneath a lullaby lake. Hikers also have challenging, steep climbs, rewarded by panoramas. While out-of-towners head to the more celebrated nearby parks—Burr Oak, Lake Hope, and Hocking Hills, Strouds Run attracts loyal followers.

LOCATION

Athens County, Canaan Township.

SIZE & DESIGNATION

Land: 2,606 acres; water: 161 acres.

ACCESS

Southbound on US 33, exit onto SR 550 a few miles northwest of Athens. Take SR 550 toward Athens. Go left on North Lancaster Road which becomes Columbia Avenue. After crossing US 33, turn right on Strouds Run Road (CR 20), heading east. Once inside the park, look for signs to the campground, beach, park office, etc. The south end of the park is accessible from the north lane of the US 50 bypass (where the highway narrows to two lanes).

Accommodations: Eighty semi-primitive campsites line the semi-wooded bank of Strouds Run, north of Dow Lake. The entrance is off TR 212. Semi-primitive meaning no showers, no flush toilets, no hookups. Ten sites are reserved for pet owners, three for Rent-A-Camp occupants. A camper cabin sits on one site. The group campground, also off TR 212, can handle 150 campers.

Picnic Areas: Picnic places are found along the park road on the north shore, and by the dam at the south end. Large groups can feast beneath three shelters located at the entrance, beach, and boat ramp. Vault toilets are nearby. Picnic tables go fast on weekends.

Trails: A seven-mile Lakeview Trail winds around the wooded shoreline of Dow Lake, passing through cool pine groves, hardwood groves, and areas reduced to shrub height by indomitable beavers. You can pick up the trail at several spots. Eastbound travelers on CR 20 will find trailhead parking on the right at the northeast tip of the lake. You also can start near the beach (at the end of Lake Road near boat tie-ups) or at the parking lot for the dam off the US 50 bypass.

For a short distance from any terminus, the trail is well-trodden. Eventually, the path narrows, indicating the range of most pedestrians. The trail is full of small delights. It pokes into ravines, crosses brooks guarded by arching sycamores, and tracks beside an utopian colony of old growth oaks. Plenty of shady spots for shore fishing. Smaller sibling trails lead to overlooks, a pioneer graveyard, and an Adena Indian mound. The only demerit for the trail is the sound of traffic on the nearby US 50 bypass.

Broken Rock Trail (two miles) should be renamed Broken Body Trail, because its steep climb strains knees, ankles, backs, and (in my case) tailbone. It loops from the Lakeview Trail, along Lake Road. An un-named (and unnecessary), precipitous path bisects the loop. The park map shows a scenic overlook where the trail crosses a bridle path. The spot is scenic enough, but a profound, sprawling view it is not.

The one-mile Indian Mound Trail loops off Lakeview Trail east of the dam. As the name suggests, it visits an Adena Indian earthwork. West of the dam is Sycamore Valley Trail (half mile). The old growth colony is just beyond this trail's western terminus with the Lakeview Trail. A half-mile path at the northwest corner of the lake goes to a pioneer cemetery.

Homestead Trail, a 1.5-mile loop, is a favorite of campers because it climbs to Vista Point, an honest-to-goodness scenic overlook above Dow Lake. The trailhead near the camp amphitheater is the shortest route to Vista Point.

A tangle of bridle trails reconstructed by the Ohio Horse Council branches from a horseman's parking area in the northeast corner of the park (TR 21).

Swimming: College students from nearby Ohio University and Hocking Technical College, and the local crowd, gather on the 900-foot beach on weekends. The beach has changing rooms, water, and rest rooms. Scuba divers (buddy system) can explore Dow Lake, except near the beach.

Boating: Boats with a 10 horsepower limit are permitted on Dow Lake. You'll find a ramp, rental office, and tie-up stakes near the beach.

Hunting: Hunting is permitted in designated areas, which are explained at the park office. Deer, turkey, and squirrel are your best bets.

Fishing: Cast for largemouth bass, bluegills and catfish. Dow Lake is nearly 40 feet deep at the dam. The northeastern section is shallower and muddier. A trout derby is held in mid-April shortly after several thousand golden and rainbow trout are released. The Division of Wildlife has published a fishing map of Dow Lake. Lakeview Trail is boon for shore anglers.

Information: Strouds Run State Park, 11661 State Park Road, Athens, OH 45701, (740) 592-2302.

HISTORY

Storytellers say the park was the brainstorm of Clarence Dow, a professor at Ohio University in Athens, who stumbled upon the old-growth oaks above Strouds Run just after WWII. Dow persuaded the state to purchase land along the creek for reforestation and preservation. The Division of Parks and Recreation acquired the land soon after its creation in 1949. The park opened in 1960 following construction of the lake that bears Dow's name.

The park gets its name from the Stroud family who settled here in the early 1800s. Like other settlers, they journeyed in a flatboat on the Hocking River to Athens, then found suitable farm land in the surrounding hills. The Adena Mound near the dam reminds us that the Strouds were not the first pioneers in the valley. The Shawandase lived in the area before whites arrived.

FIELD NOTES

The second-growth forest around Dow Lake is luxuriant. Here and there in the thatch, colonies of "old-growth" oaks survive with specimens more than 200 years old. Though not considered a prime sight by avid birders, the park has its high times. A pair of ospreys arrive about the time trout are released in April. Warblers gather in spring, and owls seem plentiful judging by the calls I heard at dusk.

Look for Linscott Spring, a local landmark, near the park office. It gushes 200,000 gallons of fresh groundwater daily into Strouds Run and the lake. Strouds Run empties into the Hocking River.

Tar Hollow

Tar Hollow State Park is a great place to get lost. The hard part is finding a reason to leave. Trees denser than raccoon fur now coat ridges and ravines that a century ago were nude and impoverished. Fifty years ago moonshine was the cash crop in them thar' hills, but these days humans search the hollows for delectable morel mushrooms. Come in autumn, and let winds scatter confetti of gold, orange, russet, red, and purple leaves on your parade through the woods.

LOCATION

Tar Hollow State Park straddles the border of Northeastern Ross and Southwestern Hocking counties. The state forest of the same name reaches into Vinton County.

SIZE & DESIGNATION

Land: 619 acres; water: 15 acres. The surrounding state forest comprises 16,000 acres.

ACCESS

Take SR 327, which twists along the boundaries of these counties, then turn westbound on Tar Hollow Road (Forest Road 10) to the park facilities. The park office is located on Tar Hollow Road (Forest Road 10).

Accommodations: Twenty of the park's 88 campsites now have electric hookups. The sites (shady and open) are divided into the Ross Hollow and Logan Hollow loops. The showerhouse and playground are located at the Ross Hollow loop. Groups up to 75 people can camp in a designated area in Logan Hollow (reservations two weeks in advance). Tent campers should check out the primitive walk-in sites atop a nearby grassy knoll on Tar Hollow Road (Forest Road 10).

Tar Hollow's special Four Hills Resident Camp can entertain 175 people for conferences, retreats, environmental groups, youth groups, etc. Each of the 28 cabins handles eight guests, and leaders can lodge in three staff cabins. The recreation and dining hall has a modern kitchen, and visitors can stroke rowboats and canoes, or swim in Pine Lake at a private beach. Contact the state park to reserve this facility.

Picnic Areas: For pure picnicking, Tar Hollow may have no peers. Family reunions are popular. Eight shelterhouses stand in hollows and ridgetops and are surrounded by picnic tables. Stake a claim early because the "first-come, first served" principle applies. Four have lights and electricity. Latrines and drinking water are close-by. The big shelterhouse in the Logan Hollow camping area can be reserved up to a year in advance.

Less crowded picnic areas are found in the state forest along South Ridge Road (Forest Road 3).

Trails: The state park only has the Ross Hollow Trail, a two-mile route departing from the Ross Hollow campground loop. Long distance hikers and backpackers go to the state forest where they face a formidable challenge in the 16-mile Chief Logan Trail, a difficult and exhausting double loop path that journeys across ridges and up and down steep, wooded, and loose slopes. A section of the northern loop passes through the state park below (southeast of) Pine Lake. Backpackers can camp at the state forest fire tower, where both loops, and the Buckeye Trail, converge.

Horse riders should gather at the horseman's camp (Forest Road 8) in the state forest and explore its 25 miles of bridle trails.

Swimming: The public beach measures 200 feet; maximum depth of six feet. Sorry, no changing rooms, just latrines. Lifeguards patrol during the summer.

Boating: Canoes and rowboats (electric motors, 4 hp maximum) can be launched from a ramp near the beach.

Hunting: Two kinds of hunters take to these fields and forests. Animal hunters find plenty of wild turkey, deer, squirrel, rabbit, and ruffed grouse in the state park and state forest. In spring, mushroom marchers hunt for morels, the tasty, spongy marvels that may colonize entire slopes. The hills and hollows here will test the fitness of hunters.

Fishing: Don't expect much from shallow, smooth-bottomed Pine Lake. Maybe a bluegill, bass, crappie, or catfish will bite. Maybe not.

Special Places & Events: A morel mushroom hunt is held in Tar Hollow State Forest in April. The amphitheater near the beach is the site of weekend nature programs (movies, walks, talks) from Memorial Day to Labor Day.

Information: Tar Hollow State Park, 16396 Tar Hollow Road, Laurelville, OH 43135, (740) 887-4818.

HISTORY

Hunters from the Hopewell settlements (200 B.C. to 500 A.D.) in Chillicothe, and later Shawandase and Mingo warriors, probably chased deer, turkeys, and other game in these steep hills. Tar Hollow kept its wilderness intact longer than other places because its rugged terrain discouraged farming. Eventually, settlers cleared it for lumber and farming. The pitch pine forest here yielded pine tar, a necessity on the frontier, hence the name. Pioneers made balms, liniments, and lubricants from pine tar.

In the Depression of the 1930s, the federal government bought chunks of marginal farmland in Southeastern Ohio under a New Deal program called the Land Utilization Program. Some former landowners favored a fresh start in cities, but many Tar Hollow folks resettled on farms just outside the park boundary. Relief crews developed the land into a forest and recreation area. The Ohio Division of Forestry took control of Tar Hollow Forest Park in 1939. The state park dedicated in 1949 sprouted from this state forest.

FIELD NOTES

Don't ever pass up a chance to see Tar Hollow's colorful autumn performance. A hike through the woods, or a drive on state forest roads will be rewarding. Come here in spring for blossoming trees (dogwood) and wildflowers such as bloodroot, Solomon's seal, cardinal flower, and wild geranium.

The area swarms with warblers in spring, notably the Kentucky, pine, yellow-throated, cerulean, worm-eating, American redstart, and hooded. Other nesters include turkey vulture, eastern bluebird, northern bobwhite, scarlet tanager, and Henslow's sparrow.

Hikers should stay alert for the state-endangered timber rattlesnake, which hangs on here, though you are more likely to be struck by lightning than a rattler. Bobcats, also endangered, are occasionally spotted. Look for the painted turtle at Pine Lake, or the five-lined skink, a blue-tailed amphibian.

Wolf Run State Park

Another week running in place in the human rat race? Grab your fishing gear and fly a Piper Cub to the Noble County Airport. Park the plane at the south end of the runway. Pitch a tent. Start a fire. Watch the sun subside over Wolf Run Lake. Maybe hook a 30-pound catfish in the morning.

LOCATION
North-central Noble County, Noble Township.

SIZE & DESIGNATION
Land: 1,118 acres; water: 220 acres.

ACCESS
Wolf Run also caters to vehicles that stay on terra firma. Leave I-77 at Exit 28 (Belle Valley) and go east on SR 821. After Belle Valley, turn left on SR 215, then left (a mile or so) on Wolf Run Road (TR 126) to the park road that leads to the office and campground. Continue east on SR 215 two miles to reach the beach and boat launch. From Caldwell take SR 821 north, SR 215 east.

Accommodations: Some campers rate Wolf Run one of the most scenic campgrounds among state parks because several of the 138 campsites (no hookups) that sit high above the lake shore have splendid vistas. A few shoreline sites are available to boaters. Showerhouses, latrines, dump station, and a laundry round out the facilities.

Only the pilots of planes and boats can camp at Ohio's only fly-in campground on the sloping north shore. Boaters must tie up their crafts at the shore and hike uphill to the 20-site camping area. Flat sites are few, but the privacy, uniqueness and scenery compensate for any discomfort. There is no corral here for cars, RVs, etc., and the only "facilities" are latrines, fire rings, and picnic tables.

A primitive, walk-in camp for youth groups of up to 150 is located at the tip of the lake's northern fork. Make reservations two weeks in advance.

Picnic Areas: The main picnic spot is on TR 126 near the dam and west of the campground. The shaded site features a playground and a shelterhouse (first-come, first-served basis). Picnic tables dot the beach area too.

Trails: About 2.5 miles of the Buckeye Trail traces the wooded western shore of the V-shaped lake. Pick up this "intrastate footpath" at the dam, then ramble north to the group camp and back. The Cherry Tree Trail, a half-mile loop, is located near the park entrance (north side of Wolf Run Road) beside a nature center.

Swimming: A small swimming beach (150 feet) borders the boat launch on the east side of the park. Not a beach to brag about, but refreshing enough on a hot summer day. It has changing sheds, latrines, and lifeguards (part time).

Wolf Run's relatively clear water (most of the time) enables scuba divers to explore its depths (beyond the beach area). Solo diving is not allowed. Divers must mark their diving area.

Boating: Wolf Run's eight-mile shoreline wrinkles with shady coves and calm inlets—perfect for canoes and motor boats (10 horsepower limit). You'll find a launch and tie-ups beside the beach (off SR 215). Boaters also can park by sites at both campgrounds.

Hunting: Hunters can tramp for deer, ruffed grouse, squirrels, and wild turkey on roughly 700 acres. Pick up a map of the hunting area before starting.

Fishing: This is the home of the whoppers. Consider the 65-pound shovelhead catfish snagged in a net survey by state wildlife officers, and the 45-pounders reeled in by fishers in the early 1990s. Scary. Largemouth bass weigh in at 10 pounds or more. A slot limit requires the release of bass between 12-15 inches.

Now the trout. ODNR dumps 4,000 rainbows, browns, and goldens (resembling large goldfish) into the lake in March. These untested, couch-potato hatchery fish like cheese, Colby or Swiss preferred. Wolf Run is also good for crappie and bluegill.

Information: Wolf Run State Park, 16170 Wolf Run Road, Caldwell, OH 43724-9503, (740) 732-5035.

HISTORY
Noble County, the last of Ohio's 88 counties to be established, became the center of the nation's nascent oil industry—accidentally. While drilling for brine in 1814, Robert McKee of Caldwell struck oil instead. The "black gold" was considered worthless until commercial uses were discovered. Wells and derricks then sprouted all along the Duck Creek Valley, America's first oil boom. (Pennsylvanians argue that Colonel Edwin Drake's well near Titusville in 1859 marked the start of the world's oil industry.) When oil prices fell during the Civil War, drilling ceased, and the boom busted. McKee's "accident" still stands at the intersection of state routes 78 and 564.

In 1963, the state began buying land for the park, part of the West Fork Duck Creek Watershed Project for flood control, drinking water and recreation. The dam and spillway creating the lake were finished in 1966, and three years later the site became a state park. Curiously, the park is named after the Wolf family, earlier white settlers, not for the impounded creek, nor the wild canine that once prowled here.

FIELD NOTES
The needs of local industries—farming, coal mining, petroleum, iron and salt mining—and villages led to the deforestation of the area. Hardly a stick stood by the turn of this century. A new "second growth" forest cloaks 70 percent of the region. This forest features mixed species of white and red oak, tuliptree, beech, sugar maple, wild black cherry, and white ash.

NORTHWEST

Catawba Island

Think of Catawba as a port to Lake Erie. Your basic boat launch, fishing pier, picnic grounds, and parking lot.

LOCATION
   Northeastern Ottawa County, Catawba Island Township.

SIZE & DESIGNATION
   Land: 18 acres.

ACCESS
   From SR 2 east of Port Clinton, take SR 163 westerly, then north on SR 53, west on West Catawba Road, left on Moore's Dock Road (TR 146) to the entrance.
   Picnic Areas: Check out the picnic area with a lake view.
   Swimming: Yes, at a tiny pebble beach, and at your own risk.
   Boating: The park's four-lane boat launch provides boaters with quick and easy access to Lake Erie. A parking lot for 200 vehicles fills up fast on summer weekends.
   Fishing: The Western Basin of Lake Erie is straight ahead. The park is a major rendezvous for boaters heading for the walleye fishery around the Lake Erie islands. There's a lighted fishing pier with benches for shore casters. Yellow perch is the main catch, followed by largemouth bass, catfish, and an occasional walleye. In winter, Catawba becomes an ice fishing haven.
   Information: Lake Erie Islands State Parks, 4049 E. Moores Dock Road, Port Clinton, OH 43452, (419) 797-4530

HISTORY
   The name of the island and park derives from the Catawba grape grown here for sweet wine.

Crane Creek

Sun, sand, and Lake Erie's gentle waves bring people to Crane Creek. The great blue herons and graceful egrets that beautify the surrounding marsh may have been mistaken for "cranes," which give the park and a nearby creek their names. The park is smack dab in the middle of one of Ohio's best birding locations.

LOCATION
   Eastern Lucas County, Jerusalem Township, and Northern Ottawa County, Benton Township.

SIZE & DESIGNATION
   Land: 79 acres (lakeshore).

ACCESS
   From SR 2, midway between Port Clinton and Toledo, follow the road to the state park and Magee Marsh State Wildlife Area.
   Swimming: Crane Creek's 3,500-foot sandy beach along Lake Erie is the main reason for coming here. Latrines, changing booths, lifeguards are available. Visitors can walk along the beach in Magee Marsh State Wildlife Area (west of the main beach), but swimming and picnicking are not allowed there.
   Picnic Areas: Tables and grills are scattered beneath tall cottonwoods. One picnic shelter is available on a first-come basis.
   Trails: The Magee Marsh Bird Trail, a mile long boardwalk at the verge of the state wildlife area, attracts thousands of birders. The wheelchair-accessible path has trailheads from the east and west ends of the parking lot. The path journeys through woodlands at the edge of Magee Marsh. It is an excellent location to see waterbirds and bald eagles that nest at the marsh and nearby Ottawa National Wildlife Refuge. (For more information see "Magee Marsh State Wildlife Area", and "Ottawa National Wildlife Refuge".
   Hunting: Hunting is not permitted in the state park. Hunters should go to the nearby state wildlife areas instead.
   Fishing: Shoreline fishing is allowed from the breakwall at the east end of the park. Crappie, yellow perch, walleye, freshwater drum, bluegill, and channel catfish swim in the offshore water. Ice fishermen gather at Crane Creek, which provides a ramp for

lakebound snowmobiles. The public fishing spot at Turtle Creek, east of the park off SR 2, offers access to Lake Erie.

Special Places & Events: On the last Sunday in September the Lake Erie Waterfowlers have a "festival" featuring waterfowl decoys, bird dog trials, skeet shooting, woodcarving, and exhibits at the Sportsmen's Migratory Bird Center, Magee Marsh State Wildlife Area.

Information: Contact Crane Creek State Park, 13531 West State Route 2, Oak Harbor, OH 43449, (419) 898-2495.

HISTORY

At the time of European settlement, Crane Creek leaked into Lake Erie from the Great Black Swamp, a mammoth wetland stretching from Ft. Wayne, Indiana to Lake Erie. The swamp blocked settlement until an 1859 "improvement" bill fostered construction of ditches to drain the land for agriculture. The marshlands along the Lake Erie shore became popular havens for waterfowl hunters. By 1950, some 30,000 acres of prime waterfowl land between Toledo and Sandusky was held by private clubs. That changed in 1951 when the Ohio Department of Natural Resources purchased 650 acres along the lakeshore for duck hunting and park development. The swimming beach opened in 1955.

FIELD NOTES

Zebra mussel shells, an unwanted exotic animal that has infested Lake Erie, became a nuisance here in the early 1990s. The "empties" piled up knee-high on the beach and its retaining walls. An eradication program has removed the pest, except for an occasional flare up.

East Harbor

East Harbor is a prime destination for folks harvesting the ripe fruits of Lake Erie's western basin; the fruits being sun, fish, waves, birds, and campfires. Ohio's wine country is just beyond this park's entrance.

LOCATION
Eastern Ottawa County, Danbury Township.

SIZE & DESIGNATION
Land: 1,152 acres.

ACCESS
From SR 2 east of Port Clinton, go north on SR 53, east on SR 163, north on SR 269 (Buck Road). The entrance to the campground and beach is on the right in a mile. Continue north another mile to find the marina.

Accommodations: East Harbor's campground is the largest in the state park system with 570 non-electric sites. In spite of its size, the place usually fills by Friday evening during the summer. The camp comes ready with three showers and laundries, paved sites, flush toilets, nature center, amphitheater, commissary, pet sites, dump station, two boat ramps, fish cleaning station, playground, and ball field. The downsides are tightly spaced sites (you will hear your neighbors snore, smell their "smores") on largely open ground. Not much shade. There are two reservable group camps—a 50-site spot for youngsters, and a 100-site location for adults. Campers can be stored in a fenced area at the marina.

Picnic Areas: Picnic tables are strewn along both the "new" north beach beach and the "old" south beach (swimming prohibited), and near the park exit. The Harbor View (beach road before causeway) and Lockwood (by Park Office) picnic areas have reservable shelters.

Trails: A seven-mile trail system journeys to all of the park's natural habitats. The South Beach and Wetlands trails visit the barrier beach that once held the swimming beach before its destruction by storm in 1972. Red Bird Trail goes along the shore of East Harbor in the campground. West Harbor Trail arcs from the tip of the North Beach swimming area to the marina. Middle Harbor Trail explores the Middle Harbor, which is a game sanctuary. A wildlife observation blind overlooks the wetland sanctuary. Blackberry Trail goes from the ranger station to the West Harbor Trail by the water tower.

Swimming: Hundreds of thousands of people refresh themselves at the park's 1,500-foot sandy beach. The park system built the north beach after a storm ruined the south beach in 1972. In summer, shuttle buses transport visitors from the south beach parking lot to north beach swimming area.

Boating: Fleets launch from East Harbor's marina, a mile north of the park entrance. The location has two launches (fee charged for one), fuel, boating and fishing supplies, restaurant, mechanic, year-round boat storage, and 123 dock slips for day and seasonal use. The slips are assigned by lottery. Call the park office for information on dock rentals and boat storage. Boats departing from the marina enter West Harbor.

A small boat ramp in the campground is used by campers. This ramp delivers boats into East Harbor. Lake Erie has no horsepower restrictions, but speed and wake limits may apply in West Harbor and East Harbor. Boats are banned in Middle Harbor.

Hunting: Waterfowl hunting is permitted on the east side of the off-shore islands by the north swimming beach. (The season occurs during cold weather.) Five duck blinds in the park are awarded through a lottery drawing held in August.

Fishing: Lake Erie, which Ohio's officialdom calls the "Walleye Capital of the World," can be seen, scented, heard, and experienced at East Har-

A shallow lake is a changeable lake proves western Lake Erie at Crane Creek.

bor. The Western Basin of Lake Erie also contains yellow perch, smallmouth and white bass, and catfish. East Harbor and West Harbor have bluegill, bass, crappie and carp. Shore anglers have plenty of opportunities to cast into East Harbor, West Harbor, and Lake Erie. Parking lots are provided on the causeway between East and Middle harbors, a popular spot for panfish. East Harbor is also a gathering area and staging ground for Lake Erie ice fishermen.

Special Places & Events: Get up before sunrise. Go to the beach. Face east. Watch the sunrise.

In summer the park has an arts and craft festival, fishing derby for kids, and hayrides (September).

Information: East Harbor State Park, 1169 N. Buck Road, Lakeside-Marblehead, OH 43440-9610, (419) 734-4424 park office, (419) 734-5857 campground, (419) 734-2289 marina.

HISTORY

Wyandots and Ottawas occupied the area before French trappers arrived in the eighteenth century. All three groups used the celebrated Scioto Trail which merged with a lakeshore path that passed through the park. Later, the British displaced the French, then Americans booted out everybody at the end of the War of 1812.

On Marblehead Peninsula to the east, Marblehead Lighthouse, one of the oldest on the Great Lakes, has become a historical landmark and tourist destination. On the bay side of the peninsula, Confederate soldiers rest in a cemetery on Johnson Island. Captured Confederates were imprisoned there during the Civil War.

East Harbor has been a park and vacation destination since the late 1940s.

FIELD NOTES

Middle Harbor Trail is tailor-made for birders and wildlife watchers. The sanctuary is a refuge for black-crowned night herons, great blue herons, egrets, and other shorebirds and waterfowl. Bring binoculars and checklists.

Note the parking area just before the park entrance road. Stop here and examine the glacial grooves carved in limestone by the Wisconsinan glacier some 12,000 years ago. Not as impressive as the grooves on Kelleys Island, but interesting nevertheless.

Grand Lake

Ohio's largest inland lake once quenched the thirst of the Miami & Erie Canal, which brought success to humans. Today, it delights boaters who end the day where they started, and anglers seeking a stringer of panfish. It is one of the original state parks founded in 1949, and the only inland lake with a lighthouse.

LOCATION

Western Auglaize County, St. Marys Township; Eastern Mercer County, Center and Franklin townships. (continued on page 330)

he Happy Haunting Grounds

BY STEPHEN OSTRANDER

For those who dare, state parks offer a chance encounter with the spectral characters of campfire ghost stories.

The Last of the Lyons at Mohican

The legends of Paul and Tom Lyons grow warts and bone spurs with each recitation. Lyons Falls, a cavernous ravine tucked deep in Mohican State Park, is named after Paul Lyons, the peaceable but hapless white recluse who lived here. The tales of his demise vary. One has him crushed by a falling tree while building a neighbor's cabin. Another says he accidentally stumbled 80-feet over the falls one dark and stormy night while collecting a stray steer. Believers hear the cow bell, and glimpse Lyons' ghost swinging a lantern atop the cliff.

Tom Lyons was not kin to Paul Lyons, that much is known. His true identity remains obscure, and his legend could be a giant sin initiated by his persecutors. My guess is fearful locals gave the fellow this nom de plume to identify his hermitage and redoubt. Some storytellers say he was a renegade Lenape (Delaware) warrior returning to ancestral hunting grounds, but others derisively called him a "half-breed" squatter or a "white gone Injun." Hideously scarred, Tom flavored his grotesque appearance with a necklace of 99 withered human tongues. Vigilantes ambushed him on a stagecoach road passing through the forest before he could claim his 100th victim. Killbuck Swamp became Tom's happy hunting ground, but his ghost returns to Clear Fork Gorge to finish his "tongue lashing."

The story could be a bloody lie to excuse a crime, too. It could be that Tom Lyons (or whoever he was) had a legitimate claim to the land, that he had retreated there to live in peace. Could be his dreadful face showed the wounds of war, torture,

Log cabin postcard is the Schoenbrunn school house New Philadelphia, Ohio

and the rigors of wilderness. Could be the tongues belonged to deer (no inspection was made), and that he strung them as a talisman or trophy. Could be his native tongue and wild ways aroused suspicion and contempt. Could be he defied harassment, threats, and insult. Could be he was simply the last Indian for bigots to kill. Could be his evil personna was the foul product of his killers.

The Women Scorned of Malabar

Ceely Rose was pitifully plain, pleasantly plump, and played with broken toys in her attic (catch my drift?). She lived on a farm in Richland County, on the grounds of what became Malabar Farm State Park. Like all lonely farm girls in 1896-days, she longed for a knight in shining armor to carry her off to Camelot. Her "prince" was a local gent named Hugh Fleming. He talked politely with Ceely, but she mistook his kind words for earnest statements of love. Teased by rival girls, Ceely announced her engagement to Fleming. The news upset Fleming, but he let Ceely down easy, saying that her parents disapproved of the match. The fib spared Ceely's feelings, but not the lives of her family.

Ceely promptly disposed of her parents and brother with arsenic, a common agent in rat poison. Some stories claim she dispensed small doses of the poison in food over three months, but other reports suggest Ceely put lethal doses in the breakfast coffee. Rebecca Rose, Ceely's mother, fell first. David Rose, the father, went to fetch help but succumbed in the doctor's office. Brother Walter left to do chores but never returned. Amazingly, Rebecca, who had only sipped her coffee, survived and told authorities she had served breakfast. During her recovery, Ceely fed her another dose, and this time succeeded.

Ceely remained free because police lacked direct evidence of guilt. Also, Fleming supposedly departed, raising suspicion about his involvement (though he may have fled from the girl's revenge). Anyway, months later Ceely's closest friend tricked her into confessing the crime within earshot of concealed detectives. Ceely spent her remaining days in an asylum for the criminally insane, dying at age 83.

Park visitors have seen candles burning in the Rose house (Bromfield Road), and Ceely looking out the window for her lost love.

Playful Poltergeists of Punderson

Lodgers and staffers swear they have seen playful phantoms in the manor house at Punderson State Park. A recumbent guest awoke to hear the romp and laughter of children, but she found the noisy room empty. Park rangers report sudden drafts in hallways and echoing peals of laughter. A night staffer on her rounds saw the dining hall lights shut off, and the vision of a woman garbed in a bonnet, cloak, and gown. Another time, the figure covered two children with her cape before vanishing. Bearded male ghosts have walked through beds and walls, another locked a guest in a bathroom. A man hanging from a rope (for three hours!) terrified lodge employees. A giggling girl in a pink nighty wanders upstairs and on the staircase, but only when no living children are around. Spectral mischief—rattling pots and chandeliers, flying objects, metal fire doors ajar, footsteps, doors opening and closing, TVs and faucets coming on full blast at 3 a.m.—seems commonplace.

The inexplicable activities probably relate to tragic events that occurred in and around the Tudor-style mansion, now a state park lodge. Lemuel Punderson, who settled the land here in 1808, was preparing for a secret business meeting when he died of fever (though servants whispered he committed suicide by drowning in the lake). In 1928, W.B. Cleveland was about to sell the prop-

erty (and recover his fortune) when he also succumbed to ague. The next owner, Karl Long, who bought the place for $250,000 and started building the Tudor mansion in 1929, became an overnight failure in the 1929 stock market crash. Busted and distraught, Long may have dangled himself from a tree on the grounds (or in the attic), but this, too, may have been a servants' tale. The Punderson "children" may be the spirits of children who perished in a tavern fire across Punderson Lake in 1885.

Headless But Hopeful

On certain nights a headless man waves a railroad lantern inside the Moonville Tunnel near Lake Hope State Park (Hope-Moonville Road, TR18). He is the spirit of a murdered railroad conductor who "lost" his head over a woman. The woman happened to be married to a Baltimore & Ohio engineer. The husband uncovered the affair and tricked the unwitting conductor into inspecting train brakes. When the prostrate conductor stretched his neck across the tracks to check the wheels, the engineer jerked the train forward and decapitated the bugger.

Unlucky at Locks

Double-dare you to hike the Beaver Creek State Park's Vondergreen Trail to Gretchen's Lock on any August 12. Gretchen was the daughter of Gill Hans, the Dutch builder of the lock. When she died on August 12, 1838, her father temporarily buried her in the lock until she could be reinterred in her beloved Holland. On the trip to the homeland, however, Gretchen's remains and her father were swallowed by the sea. She is said to reappear at the lock on the anniversary of her death.

August 12 is also the night the crumbling walls of Hambleton's Mill rattle and groan with reported hauntings. Yard spinners think the eerie noises come from the spirit of Esther Hale, a Quaker preacher in Sprucevale, now a ghost town. Esther was supposed to be wed on August 12, 1837, but her betrothed left her standing alone at the altar. Neighbors found Esther dead just before Christmas still in her wedding gown.

Another spirit labors at the park's so-called Jake's Lock; the illuminated lantern of a former lock keeper who was struck by lightning has been seen in the water. This ghost knows no particular calendar, though naysayers insist that the eerie light has other celestial origins, appearing only when the moon shines on the water.

—SO

Size & Designation
Land: 500 acres; water: 13,500.

Access
The large lake with the recently shortened name (for years known as Grand Lake St. Marys), Grand Lake is bounded by state routes 703 (north), 127 (west), 219 (south), and 364 (east). From I-75, take US 33 west, SR 29 west, Riley Road south to SR 703. Park office, campground, marina are off SR 703.

Accommodations: The park's campground boasts 206 sites on six loops, of which 135 locations have electric hookups. Facilities include two bathhouses, five latrines, dump station, playground, and swimming beach for campers only. The area is beside the northeast corner of the lake, off SR 703.

Picnic Areas: Shelterhouses, tables, and latrines line SR 364, on the east shore. Picnic areas also are located at Montezuma Bay on the south shore, Windy Point Road; SR 127 on the west shore; Harbor Point Area on the north shore, Harbor Point Drive; the north shore and the end of Anderson Road (off SR 703); and at the park marina, northeastern corner.

Swimming: Public swimming beaches are located near the marina, Harbor Point Area (off SR 703 east of Celina), and Windy Point, on the south shore off SR 219. Boaters can swim in designated areas, including the Anderson Road picnic area, and off an island east of Windy Point in the "no ski zone."

Boating: Thousands of boats, all sizes and shapes, some with motors some with sails, bob along the 52 miles of shoreline containing Grand Lake. The park has five boat ramps, the best one located at the full service marina on the east shore, off SR 364 and 703. Ramps also are found north of the picnic area on SR 364 (east shore), Windy Point (south shore), another south of Celina on SR 703, and at the Celina waterfront. Boats and dock slips (100) can be rented at the marina.

Most of the lake allows unlimited horsepower boating, though pilots must observe a no wake zone 300 feet from shore. Water skiing is prohibited on roughly a third of the lake off the south shore.

This lake is "grand" because of its surface area, not for its depth. It's deepest spots are 7-8 feet, and it is said the tallest NBA basketball players can cross it flat-flooted. Boaters should stay alert for tree stumps and other obstacles in the shallows.

Hunting: Waterfowl hunting is permitted in Mercer State Wildlife Area in the southwestern corner of the lake. The Division of Wildlife has an annual lottery for 90 duck blinds. Contact the wildlife area at (419) 268-2020 for more information.

Fishing: Extensivie shore access and submerged structure make this an excellent fishing hole. Crappie fishing is par excellence, and catches are good for bluegill, catfish, and yellow perch. Largemouth bass are being pursued with vigor, too.

Special Places & Events: Check out the Ohio's inland lake lighthouse on the Celina waterfront. The Celina Rotary Club built it in 1986.

Star Spangled Celebration in August features a day of crafts and games followed by fireworks over the lake. The Celina Lake Festival in late July has rides, games, Civil War reenact, and fireworks.

Information: Grand Lake State Park, 834 Edgewater Drive, St. Marys, OH 45885, (419) 394-3611 (park office), (419) 394-2774 (campground).

History
Simon and James Girty, frontiersmen who sided with Native Americans, established a trading post at an outpost that grew into St. Marys.

Construction of the Miami & Erie Canal included several reservoirs to keep the canal channel five feet deep. To that end, German laborers toiling for 30 cents a day and a swig of whiskey started digging the lake. State government was not always a prompt paymaster in those days. Farmers who had not been reimbursed for land lost to the reservoir, and local nascent environmentalists disturbed by the foul odor of disintegrating vegetation, vandalized the embankment in May 1843. The repairs cost $17,000. At its completion in 1845, Grand Lake was the world's largest human-made lake, covering 13,500 acres.

The area experienced an oil boom in the 1890s, and for several years oil derricks protruded above the surface. A mound of rocks in the middle of the lake marks the site of the last oil well. The Ohio Department of Natural Resources designated Grand Lake one of its original parks in 1949.

Field Notes
There was a time when great blue herons had a rookery here of 175 nests in 39 trees. Bald eagles, hundreds of them, nested here before 1900. Neither of those grand birds nests here today. Still, you can see ducks, grebes, geese, swans, egrets, loons, cormorants and ospreys during the spring and fall migrations.

Harrison Lake

Just a few miles from the state line, Harrison Lake State Park gets as many Michiganers as Ohioans. Maybe those stubborn foreigners believe it's still part of their state, which it was (in their minds) until Congress settled a boundary dispute in 1836.

Location
Northwestern Fulton County, Gorham Township. From US 20 & 127, go south on CR 27 (a.k.a. Reynolds Road and Knauer Road).

Size & Designation
Land: 142 acres; water: 105 acres.

Grand Lake: When the name was longer, so were skirts.

Take SR 66 north from Archbold, then turn left (west) on CR M (Dutch Ridge Road). Park office and family camping are off CR 27.

Accommodations: Take your pick of two family camps. The Class A campground with 126 sites on the north shore (CR MN) has the works: electric hookups, showers, flush toilets, paved parking pads, three Rent-A-Camp sites, pet sites, sites for physically challenged campers, small nature center, volleyball, basketball, horseshoe pit, and small beach.

Fifty-two Class B sites on the south shore (CR M) are primitive and private. Latrines are available. Some have lake views. Group camping, up to 50 people, is located along the lake, off CR M near the Class B campground. Reservations are required for group camping.

Picnic Areas: Picnickers will find 370 picnic tables and 70 grills along park roads on the south and north shores. Two shelterhouses, one on each shore, are available on a first-come basis.

Trails: An easy 3.5-mile lakeshore trail encircles the lake and joins all the park's facilities. (Just two hills to climb). Another, less scenic trail goes along the perimeter of the north campground.

Swimming: There's a 150-foot beach by the north shore camping area. Adequate, but nothing special. Day-users reach the beach on the park road off CR 26.

Boating: This salamander-shaped lake accepts small boats powered by arms and electric motors. The boat ramp is on the south shore (west side), off CR M or CR 27. Latrines and parking available.

Fishing: Test your luck on largemouth bass, bluegill, crappie, bullhead, catfish, and northern pike.

Information: Harrison Lake State Park, Route 1, Fayette, OH 43521, (419) 237-2593.

HISTORY
For ten years Ohio and Michigan argued about their mutual border. Michigan wanted it drawn from the mouth of the Maumee River straight across to Indiana, about 11 miles south of the current line. Ohio claimed the present border line. Congress sided with Ohio in 1846, but had Michigan won, Harrison State Park would be theirs.

The park is located in what was formerly a vast wooded wetland called the Great Black Swamp, which long ago was a lake bed. Ottawas settled in this "undesirable" place, and some lived there until forced out in 1842, about the time swamp drainage technology was being introduced. The new settlers siphoned the swamp and plowed its rich black soil. A remnant of the Great Black Swamp forest still stands at nearby Goll Woods State Natural Area.

In 1941, Mill Creek was dammed to make Harrison Lake, at first a public hunting and fishing area. It became a state park in 1950.

FIELD NOTES
Birders should keep their scopes clean for vesper sparrows, common yellowthroats, great blue herons, and brown thrashers. Also look for the thirteen-lined ground squirrel, a rare mammal.

Independence Dam

Though named for a dam across the
Maumee River, the old Miami & Erie

Canal is the featured human-made attraction. The park threads along the river and canal, and is only 100 feet wide in one spot.

LOCATION
Eastern Defiance County, Richland Township.

SIZE & DESIGNATION
Land: 604 acres; water: Maumee River

ACCESS
This skinny park lies between the Maumee River and SR 424, three miles east of Defiance. The park entrance is a bit east of Independence Road, the marina entrance and park office a bit west of it.

Accommodations: Forty non-electric sites can accommodate tenters and trailers. The area has drinking water, latrines, pet sites, dump station (at marina), tables and fire rings. The campground is about 2.5 miles from the park entrance.

Picnic Areas: Four shelters, 125 tables, eight latrines, and 40 fire grills meet the needs of picnickers. Drinking water and playground equipment is provided at the picnic area near the campground.

Trails: An easy, 2.5-mile hiking trail extends from the park road at eastern edge of the park. Like the park road, it lays atop the towpath of the Miami & Erie Canal. The Buckeye and North Country Scenic Trail follow this route.

Boating: The marina consists of four ramps, the park office, rest rooms, picnic tables, and dump station. It is located a half mile above Independence Dam. There are no horsepower restrictions on the Maumee River. Canoers traveling downstream can easily portage around the dam, or begin their trip below the dam. Parking is available at picnic areas. Perhaps someone will petition ODNR to build a small ramp below the dam.)

Fishing: Smallmouth bass, northern pike, catfish, walleye, and crappie are landed along the shore. The deeper, boiling water below Independence Dam attracts fish and is the park's hotspot. Shore angling and picnicking are popular activities here.

Information: Independence Dam State Park, 27722 State Route 424, Defiance, OH 43512-9085, (419)784-3263.

HISTORY
Independence Dam lies in the path of history. In 1794 General Anthony Wayne marched troops along a military route, erstwhile Indian trail, now occupied by SR 424. Wayne's soldiers beat combined Indian forces downstream at the Battle of Fallen Timbers. The defeat opened Western Ohio to white settlement.

The ruins of Lock 13 on the Miami & Erie Canal can be seen at the park entrance. The canal, built in the first half of the nineteenth century, brought prosperity to the region. Water drawn from the impoundment behind a wooden dam kept the water in the lock and canal at a serviceable level. Railroad development doomed the canals in the later decades of the century. A devastating flood finished it off in 1913.

A concrete dam replaced the wooden one in 1924. The Ohio Department of Public Works bought the park land. In 1949, the property was transferred to the Ohio Department of Natural Resources.

FIELD NOTES
The Maumee River is the largest stream in Northwestern Ohio and the second largest flowing into Lake Erie. It delivers an average of 4,700 cubic feet per second.

Kelleys Island

Most people come to Kelleys Island to see the rock grooves, or to be a rock groupie at a groovy village hangout. Getting there via ferries can be as much fun as being there, especially if Lake Erie misbehaves. The out-of-the-way state park occupies a peaceful bluff on the north shore, a few miles from a bustling tourist depot. To date, Kelleys Island is gentler and quieter than South Bass Island and Put-In-Bay, and the regulars hope it stays that way. Be ready for great sunsets, hovering and plaintive gulls, and perch or walleye sizzling on a campfire grill. If you can't stand the heat, take a dip in the lake.

LOCATION
Erie County, Kelleys Island.

SIZE & DESIGNATION
Land: 661 acres

ACCESS
Ferries to the island leave from the Marblehead Peninsula and Sandusky. From the ferry landing take SR 575 (a shoreline road) or Division Street to the state park.

Accommodations: The camping area has 129 non-electric sites, showers, flush toilets, dump station, pet sites, playground, and two Rent-A-Camp sites. Ask for a shoreline site. A reservable camp for youth groups handles 50 campers. Sites disappear fast in summer. Signs posted at ferry docks in Sandusky and Marblehead indicate if the campgrounds are open or closed.

Trails: Most of the park's five-mile trail network is found in the East Quarry area bordered by Ward, Woodford, and Monagan roads, and Division Street. The 3.5-mile web visits an abandoned limestone quarry, and Horseshoe Lake. The main trailhead is located on Ward Road, two others on Monagan Road. The park office has a trail guide for the East Quarry trail.

North Shore Trail, 1.5 miles, departs from the camping area and makes a loop to the west. Glacial Grooves State Memorial is a short walk from the campground.

Bike riding is a popular past-time on slow-paced Kelleys Island. Bring your own wheels or rent them from vendors.

Swimming: A 100-foot sandy beach below the campground serves as a swimming area.

Boating: The boat launch has two ramps protected by a paved L-shaped breakwall. There is a loading dock, but no facilities for overnight mooring. The ramps serve Lake Erie fishermen and pleasure boaters who enjoy cruising the island's shore or visiting nearby islands.

Hunting: Small sections of park are available to hunters. Check at the park office.

Fishing: Lake Erie's vast fishery surrounds the island. All those walleyes, yellow perch, smallmouth bass, and so little time. A breakwall at the marina is paved for shore fishing. For a change of place (or if the lake is too choppy) try Horseshoe Lake in the park East Quarry section.

Special Places & Events: Glacial Grooves State Memorial, a geological landmark maintained by the Ohio Historical Society, is a short walk from the campground. Think of the "grooves" as the Ice Age's signature as it departed Ohio. They were formed in limestone bedrock by the scouring action of the advancing Wisconsinan glacier about 32,000 years ago. Mining a century ago destroyed grooves 2,000 feet long. The 400-foot formations on Kelleys Island are believed to be the largest in the country.

Another famous carving on Kelleys Island is Inscription Rock on East Lakeshore Road. Indians with time on their hands (probably fishermen) drew pictographs on a limestone slab 300-400 years ago. Seth Eastman, an Army officer, copied their likeness for posterity. Natural forces and human tread have erased many etchings, but Eastman's faithful copy has itself been copied for display at the landmark.

Information: Lake Erie Islands State Parks, 4049 E. Moores Dock Road, Port Clinton, OH 43452, (419) 797-4530; (419) 746-2546.

HISTORY

The entire island is listed on the National Register of Historical Places. First known human settlers were the Erie Indians, who left behind evidence of villages, earthworks, and petroglyphs. A Euro-American settlement started in 1833 when Datus and Irad Kelley bought land here for $1.50 an acre. Wine making started 150 years ago and several island vintners still squeeze fermented grape juice into bottles. Abandoned limestone quarries remind us of that extractive industry. Kelleys Island became a state park in the 1950s.

FIELD NOTES

Fossil hunters can add to their collections at East Quarry and North Quarry. Eighteen species of gastropods, coral, brachiopods, and pelecypods have been uncovered here. You must get a collecting permit at the park office before exploring.

Lake Loramie

The park is steeped in human and natural history. Once the site of a wilderness trading post, Indian battle, frontier fort, and canal town, it is now the scene for odd-ball trees, enchanting wetland and prairie flowers, and a trail formerly traveled by "Hoggies."

LOCATION

Western Shelby County, McLean and Van Buren townships; Southern Auglaize County, Jackson Township.

SIZE & DESIGNATION

Land: 400 acres; water 1,665 acres.

ACCESS

From Sidney, head northwest on SR 29. About six miles out of town, go left on Ft. Loramie-Swanders Road, then right (north) on SR 362. The camping area, park office, canal towpath, and beach are located on SR 362 at the west end of the lake.

Accommodations: The park's campground has 166 sites, all with a paved parking spot. Roughly 130 sites have electric hookups, and 40 sites sit beside the lake (some with boat tie-ups). Campers will find showers, flush toilets, dump station, nature center, playground, and three Rent-A-Camp sites. Two of three reservable group camping areas cater to tent campers. The family camp fills fast on summer weekends.

Picnic Areas: There are oodles of picnic tables—400 around the beach alone. Great spots are located on peninsulas and islands off SR 362, north of the dam. On the east end, picnic areas are located at the end of Luthman Road and at Siegle's Bridge (SR 119).

Trails: The best known and most popular trail is the Miami & Erie Canal Towpath, which cuts across the west end of the park. This flat, easy path continues to Delphos, 48 miles north. It also serves as the route of the Buckeye Trail and North Country National Scenic Trail.

Smallest State Parks

1. Oak Point—1 acre

2. Marblehead—3 acres

3. Catawba Island—18 acres

4. South Bass Island—35 acres

5. Adams Lake—95 acres

6. Nelson Kennedy Ledges—167 acres

Inscription Rock at Kelleys Island: No bright lights, no apostrophe.

Youngsters especially enjoy the 1.5-mile nature trail around Blackberry Island, reached by a footbridge (take Eilerman Road off Ft. Loramie–Swanders Road). Campers can walk to the island path via the 1.5-mile Lakeview Trail at the south end of the campground. Upper Loramie Trail explores a bit of the northeast shore from Siegle's Bridge parking lot.

Little Turtle Trace is a figure-eight cross-country skiing trail on Ft. Loramie–Swanders Road, east of SR 362. Hikers and hunters also use the path.

Swimming: The park's popular sandy beach measures 600-feet, and it gets packed on summer weekends. There are plenty of picnic tables, a playground, all conveniently placed near the campground and towpath.

Boating: Although Lake Loramie allows unlimited horsepower motors, 90 percent of the water is a no wake zone. Speedsters have a small area of the lake north of the beach and west of Blackberry Island. Water skiing is prohibited.

Boaters access the west end at a ramp off SR 362, at Black Island, north of the spillway. Fishers tend to launch from two east side ramps at the Luthman Road access (south of SR 119). You'll find picnic tables and latrines at the latter location. Canoers and other slow boaters have plenty of quiet coves and sheltered spots to explore.

Hunting: Hunting is permitted in designated areas shown on the park brochure.

Fishing: Think largemouth bass, especially along the western shore and upstream shallows. Local bait and tackle shops usually know where they are biting, but the owner might send you where they aren't. Lake Loramie sometimes hosts professional bass tournaments. Crappie, bluegill, catfish, bullhead, and carp provide challenges.

Information: Lake Loramie State Park, 11221 SR 362, Minster, OH 45856-9311, (937) 295-2011.

HISTORY

Lake Loramie and the nearby village of Fort Loramie commemorate Peter Loramie, a French-Canadian Jesuit missionary who preached Christianity to Wyandots and Shawnee. He later became a trader who set up an outpost nearby in 1769. Euro-American settlers accused Loramie of fomenting unrest on the frontier and providing sanctuary for warriors. During a raid into the Great Miami River Valley in 1782, General George Rogers Clark destroyed the outpost and an Indian village. Loramie fled westward with the Shawnee. In 1794, General Anthony Wayne built a fort on the site of Loramie's homestead.

Loramie Creek was dammed in 1824-25 to make a feeder reservoir for the Miami & Erie Canal, then under construction. The canal stretched for 249 miles and included three reservoirs, 19 aqueducts, 103 lift locks, three guard locks, and 36 miles of side cuts and feeders. Mule teams driven by "Hoggies," or drovers, pulled boats along elevated towpaths that paralleled the canal.

Lake Loramie was acquired by the newly-formed Ohio Department of Natural Resources in 1949 and became a state park.

FIELD NOTES

Lake Loramie is stocked with little wonders, such as meadows supporting bluebirds, a great blue heron rookery on Blackberry Island, a stand of bald cypress trees, a grove of sweet gums in the campground, patch of prairie (Eilerman Road), and rafts of water lily and American lotus on the lake.

Mary Jane Thurston

This park is a good place to cast for fish and frontier history. The Maumee River is just beyond the tent flap for boating and fishing pleasure. Indian warriors and American militia spilled blood here in a prelude to a decisive confrontation. Two rowdy towns competed for canal trade here, but only one survives today.

LOCATION
The main part of the park is along the Maumee River where Henry, Wood, and Lucas counties meet.

SIZE & DESIGNATION
Land: 555 acres

ACCESS
The main entrance is on SR 65, which traces the south bank of the river. US 24 follows the north bank; cross at the bridge in Grand Rapids. The park's North Turkeyfoot Area, 450 acres, is on US 24 on the north bank, upstream (west) five miles from the main area.

Accommodations: A 34-site campground (non-electric) has separate areas for tenters and RV campers. Three sites have water hookups. Latrines, drinking water, and flush toilets (seasonal) are available.

Picnic Areas: Native American warriors led by Blue Jacket and American soldiers commanded by General Anthony Wayne supposedly skirmished on the main picnic area in 1794. The confrontation was a warmup for the Battle of Fallen Timbers downstream. The park's shelterhouse was built by the Civilian Conservation Corps in 1936. It's a popular place for group outings (reservations required), and presents a striking view of the river.

Trails: The best hiking in the main park area is actually downstream in Providence Metropark. Take the Gilead Side Cut Trail toward Grand Rapids to get there, then follow the Miami & Erie Canal Towpath. This route also serves the Buckeye and North Country National Scenic trails, which leave the park at the Wood-Henry county line.

Mosquito Loop Trail, .75-mile, wanders through a bottomland forest near the campground. The trail's name is self-evident in summer.

Six miles of trail have been blazed in the North Turkeyfoot Area. Horseback riding is permitted on these paths. Parking lots are located on US 24.

Swimming: Swimming in the Maumee River is prohibited. Park employees don't like to fish drowned humans from the churning water below the dams. Fishermen can wade in the river; being mindful of slippery rocks and sudden deep pools.

Boating: The park's up-to-date marina (off SR 65) serves much of the boating crowd on this section of the Maumee, which is navigable for 20 miles upstream. There's a two-ramp launch here, plus 116 dock slips and some tie-ups for shallow draft boats (season rental), and four docks for drop-in boaters (two-hour parking limit). Fuel and other sundries are available at a private marina a half mile upstream.

First-time boaters should note that the river is impassable downstream because of dams at the east end of the park. Several large rocks just above the dams await distracted pilots.

Unlimited horsepower means that powerboats, water skiing, and pleasure craft will be in the water. Sailboats also launch here.

Fishing: Come April, anglers cast for spawning walleyes from shore or while wading. The Maumee teems with walleye at this time, mostly downstream from the Providence Dam. White bass reach the dam in May, salmon (coho and chinook) arrive in autumn. Channel cats, northern pike, smallmouth bass, and crappie also swim in the Maumee.

A fishing pond in the main park contains bluegill, largemouth bass, and crappie. It's a good place to teach kids.

Information: Mary Jane Thurston State Park, 1-466 SR 65, McClure, OH 43534, (419) 832-7662.

HISTORY
In August 1794, General Anthony Wayne marched his troops over this land en route to the Battle of Fallen Timbers, where he overwhelmed Blue Jacket's combined Indian forces and opened the region for white settlement. Skirmishers from both sides dueled and died here before the historical battle.

The Miami & Erie Canal was constructed down the Maumee River in the 1830s, and Providence on the north bank, and Grand Rapids (then known as Gilead) on the south bank competed for the canal trade. Dams were built here to refresh the canal. The Gilead Side Cut Canal enabled canal boats to bypass the dams and trade in Grand Rapids. A major fire and cholera epidemic wiped out Providence, but its glory days as a canal town have been revived thanks to restoration efforts at Providence Metropark. A visit to Thurston should include the canal lock, mill, and steamboat at the metropark.

The state park is named after Mary Jane Thurston, a school teacher, whose 14-acre posthumous donation to the state in 1928 became the nucleus for the park.

FIELD NOTES
In early spring millions of walleye struggle up the Maumee River to spawn. Before European settlement, Native American fishers netted and speared walleyes in rapids and shallow riffles. The practice was repeated in autumn during the salmon runs.

Marblehead Lighthouse, the oldest beacon in continuous service on the Great Lakes, became Ohio's 73rd state park in 1998. The 67-foot landmark has been beaming since 1822. The U.S. Coast Guard, its operator since 1946, passed the "torch" to the Ohio Department of Natural Resources after it was declared surplus property, meaning its light would soon be extinguished. Renovations to improve the site for tours (summer weekends and holidays) are underway. The 1880 lighthouse keeper's home serves as a park residence.

Dams and other human obstacles impede the progress of these fish today.

Maumee Bay

Northwestern Ohio felt cheated not having a state park resort. That changed in 1991 when an existing state park opened anew with a lodge, cabins, nature center, and golf course. Ohio's ultra-modern state park resort, in suburban Toledo, has all the recreational venues and comforts for bipedal animals, though it sorely lacks the remoteness found at other resorts in the fleet. Maumee Bay is a great introduction to wetlands nature, and resort living.

LOCATION
Central Lucas County, Oregon Township.

SIZE & DESIGNATION
Land: 1,450 acres; water: 72 acres, plus Lake Erie.

ACCESS
From Downtown Toledo, travel southerly on I-280. Exit at SR 2 (Navarre Road) and go east a half dozen miles. Turn left (north) on North Curtice Road, which ends at the main park entrance. The campground is a mile west on Cedar Point Road.

Accommodations: The cabins here are called cottages because their attactive beachhouse design (octagonal) differs from the cabins in other parks. Though lacking shade, these are the most architecturally appealing cabins in the state park system. There are 20 of them, some with two bedrooms, others with four. Sorry, no lake views. Some, however, overlook ponds, back against the golf course, or peer into a swamp forest. All have full kitchens and bathrooms, central heat, air conditioning, gas fireplace, TV, microwave, telephone. All are widely scattered for privacy, and each has a driveway and parking spot. Two sets of cottages are uniquely connected by walkways. Cottages have to be booked for a week between Memorial Day and Labor Day. Other times weekend and one-day bookings are available. Cottages guests can use all the frills at the lodge. Roll-away beds are available.

Quilter Lodge is the latest showpiece of the park system. It features 120 deluxe rooms with balconies, dining room, lounge, snack bar, indoor and outdoor pools, three racquetball courts (one usually set for

"wallyball," sauna, exercise room, whirlpools, conference rooms, ballroom, meeting rooms, games electronic and old-fashioned, gift shop, and TV room. Most lodge rooms peek at Lake Erie. Outside you will find tennis courts, picnic tables, and easy access to the shoreline, nature center, fishing area, and stepped retaining wall behind the lodge.

The modern campground is no slouch, except for a total lack of shade. Choose from among 256 spacious sites, each with electric hookups (30 and 20 amp plugs), accessibility for disabled persons, and room enough for large RVs. Amenities include four showerhouses with hot water and flush toilets, a laundry, dump station, water tanks, fishing ponds, three Rent-A-Camp sites, and pet sites. The place fills up fast on summer weekends.

Picnic Areas: The only picnic area is found by the swimming beach at Inland Lake. Someday there might be bayside tables and grills. A couple of attractive shelters are located on the knoll between the beaches. One overlooks the amphitheater.

Trails: A must is the two-mile Boardwalk Trail, which begins at the Trautman Nature Center, near the lodge. The double-loop six-foot-wide interpretive path tracks across a cattail marsh, swamp forest, and a grassland (savanna). Side paths on the eastern side of the far loop lead to an observation tower ideal for birdwatching, and a wildlife blind. The short loop near the nature center caters to visitors with disabilities. Youngsters working for the Ohio Civilian Conservation Corps built the trail in the early 1990s. Another trailhead is located by cabin ten.

Asphalt trails for bicyclists, joggers, rollerbladers and walkers connect the Inland Lake with the lodge and campground on the west side. Much of the flat, six-mile course goes through a recovering meadow between the lake and camp, and joins a track encircling Inland Lake. Bicycles can be rented at the lodge or the boat concession at Inland Lake. Several miles of bridle trails begin at a staging area (no amenities) on Cedar Point Road, a bit west of the park entrance. Bring your own horse. Hikers can use these paths too.

Swimming: Lodge and cabin guests take advantage of indoor and outdoor pools at the lodge. Campers and day-trippers gather at the beaches. The 2,000-foot beach at Inland Lake has two showerhouses, boat concession, snack bar, parking, picnic tables, and an amphitheater with stage big enough for a symphony orchestra.

Half-mile Erie Beach, facing Maumee Bay, offers bigger waves, and rentals of parasails, jet skies, and "banana" boats. A half dozen offshore rock piles civilize the waves. The beach by the western three walls is used by anchoring boaters, jet skiers, windsurfers; the eastern half by waders, sunbathers, and daytrippers. Folks at this beach use a showerhouse next to the amphitheater. Pollution closes Erie Beach occasionally, and in spite of eradication efforts, zebra mussels pile on the shore. Warnings may be posted.

Boating: Boaters have two choices: Lake Erie or Inland Lake. Slow boaters and novices should stick to 60-acre Inland Lake or 12-acre Canoeing Lake, a lagoon-like pond off Inland Lake. Both are open to non-motorized craft such as sailboats, canoes, rowboats, pedalboats, etc. Boats of these types can be rented from a concession at the beach. Launching areas (not ramps) are located west of the park office on Park Road 1 and the west side of Canoeing Lake. If the state park has a weakness (accommodation-wise) it is the lack of a boating facility for Lake Erie bound boats. These boaters have to launch elsewhere.

Golf: The park's 6,941-yard, 18-hole, par 72 course is well-bunkered, well-watered (meaning obstacles), rolling, treeless, and windy, just like a Scottish seacoast links course. Fairways have bent Bermuda grass, greens are relatively small, multi-tiered and windblown. Lodge and cabin guests can get tee times

Nature Notable

Madame Butterfly

Once upon a time, close to midnight, Doris Stifel got a phone call from an acquaintance who reported that thousands of monarch butterflies were roosting in a suburban Toledo tree. During their late summer migration, southbound monarchs from Canada sometimes rest en masse on the Ohio shore after crossing Lake Erie. When Stifel arrived at the tree at dawn, neighbors were seated in lawn chairs, with coffee cups steaming, donuts on a table, and cameras loaded on tripods. After all, seeing a frisky septuagenarian climb a tree to tag delicate insects is a once-in-a-lifetime experience.

Stifel is the queen among monarchs—one of the country's leading experts on *Danaus plexippus.* The energetic 76-year-old Toledo biologist labors in places a thousand miles apart, all to save the habitat of the migratory monarch butterfly. In Ohio, she tags more than 4,000 of the wanderers a year, and tracks their route from Lake Erie to Central Mexico, where 30 million monarchs winter in a fifty-acre oyamel fir forest.

In November 1997, Stifel participated in an international monarch conference in Mexico, with scientists from the U.S., Mexico, and Canada. Conferees focused on the insect's winter sanctuary. Though seemingly abundant, scientists worry that destruction of the insect's small winter digs could cause its population to crash. Meanwhile, Stifel has observed a decline in Ohio's monarch population due to roadside cutting, widespread application of weed killers, and adoption of no-till farming. The latter practice saves vital topsoil but eliminates clover that nourishes butterflies and bees.

Stifel raises monarchs in milkweed gardens, an activity she shared with the naturalists at Maumee Bay State Park. The park's nature center now has a monarch nursery that releases hundreds every year. The monarch queen also lectures and writes on the butterfly. She keeps in touch with lepidopterists from Panama to Toronto via the Internet.

—SO

when they reserve rooms, but others should call a week in advance (Wednesday for weekend times). Lessons and group outings are available. Call the pro shop at (419) 836-9009. Pro tip: keep approach shots to greens low. Wind can be the biggest challenge.

Hunting: At times the park allows archers to hunt deer, and shotgunners to aim at waterfowl in designated areas. Golfers are always free to shoot birdies at the links. Rabbits are abundant in the western half of the park, but hunting was not permitted.

Fishing: There are all those walleyes, freshwater drum, smallmouth bass, and yellow perch in Lake Erie, from shore or boat. Inland Lake contains panfish mostly, and a few walleye. The fish stocked in the pond next to Big Hill in the early 1990s are maturing nicely, and good catches await campers at ponds in the campground.

Concrete porches have been built for anglers on both sides of a ditch that drains into the lake between the lodge and Erie Beach. Perfect spot for fishers with special needs.

Special Places & Events: A 500-seat amphitheater between the swimming beaches is the site of events as varied as popular nature programs (movies, talks, etc.) to mini-concerts by members of the Toledo Symphony. It is also a favorite hangout for young park visitors. Contact the park office for special events.

The Trautman Nature Center commemorates Ohio naturalists Dr. Milton B. Trautman, author of the monumental *Fishes of Ohio,* and his wife, Mary. Exhibits explain the natural history of Maumee Bay and Lake Erie marshes. Wildlife observers take advantage of the viewing windows and video cameras that peer into the marsh. The center also has an auditorium that offers a list of films for viewing (just ask the naturalist), and research facility.

Come here in June and you are likely to see mosquito-net tents beside the center. For several summers monarch butterflies have been hatched, tagged and released. Six hundred flew from the coop in 1997. In late summer, thousands of monarchs may rest in the park after fluttering across Lake Erie. The beauties are en route to their winter haven in Central Mexico.

When it snows, Big Hill, a human-made sledding hill west of Inland Lake, becomes the center of activity. It might be the best sledding hill in northwestern Ohio because it is the only one of appreciative altitude. Skating is permitted on the pond next to the hill. Ice fishermen can put tip-ups atop frozen Inland Lake and Lake Erie. Hiking paths become trails for cross-country skiers. Skis can be rented at the lodge. Erie Beach attracts kite flyers in winter, and a hardy group that rigs sails to unmotorized sand buggies.

Information: Maumee Bay State Park, 1400 Park Road 1, Oregon, OH 43618, (419) 836-7758 (park office), (419) 836-8828 (campground), (419) 836-9117 (nature center), (419) 836-1466 lodge, 1-800-282-7275 (lodge and cabin reservations).

HISTORY

The Western Basin of Lake Erie's predecessor stretched as far west as Ft. Wayne, Indiana. When the lake receded to its current configuration, the former lake bed became a vast wetland known as the Great Black Swamp. Euro-American settlers considered the swamp, comprising the Lake Erie marshes and inland swamp forest, wild and inhospitable, a sanctuary for mountain lions, elk, wolves, and a handful of Indians. Their attitude changed when engineers with new gizmos showed them how to drain and ditch the place into farmland and valuable real estate. By the 1870s, half the swamp had been lumbered, drained, and cultivated.

The state started buying park land here in the mid-1970s. Maumee Bay opened in 1975, atop a location formerly known as Niles Beach. It reopened as a resort park in May 1991, following construction of the golf course, and cottages, and Quilter Lodge, named after State Representative Barney Quilter. In 1992, 400 acres at the east end of the park were transferred to the Division of Wildlife for creation of Mallard Club Marsh State Wildlife Area.

FIELD NOTES

Of all habitats, wetlands provide the greatest diversity, largely because they offer an abundance of life's necessities—water, food, and shelter on easy flat terrain. The wetlands in the park and nearby state and national wildlife areas attract more than 300 species of birds, including shorebirds, waterfowl, woodland songbirds, and raptors such as the bald eagle and osprey. The park is a stopover for many migratory species. Ring-necked pheasants bed down in the park's meadows. For several years a family of peacocks (escapees from a nearby farm) have camped by the nature center. The resplendent male is not shy about running up his colors.

Reptiles and amphibians slither and sing everywhere. An early spring walk along the Boardwalk Trail prompts chorus frogs to trill. Look for the fox snake, painted turtle, northern water snake, spotted salamander, bullfrog, and green frog too.

Floral residents include cattails, several kinds of reed grass, cottonwoods, willows, buttonbushes, swamp white oak, and clumps of native prairie grasses and flowers. Wild rice once grew prolifically in the Lake Erie marshes, which long ago measured a quarter million acres. A few stalks of this imperiled plant survive today. In summer squadrons of dragonflies dive on misty clouds of mosquitoes and gnats. You are likely to see the tracks of the ubiquitous raccoon and whitetailed deer.

JOURNAL

For 10 straight winters we have shared a state park resort cabin with Ken, Sally, Kirsten and Alex Rider of Columbus. This winter's gathering (1998) was at Maumee Bay (Sally's choice). We delayed Saturday's supper to hike the Boardwalk Trail at dusk (my insistence), and view the flights of geese returning to the marsh. En route we watched separate herds of buck and doe deer casually browsing. One group crawled beneath the elevated boardwalk, a leap over the structure from unstable muck being risky.

We arrived at the observation tower in time for the rush hour performance. From all horizons Canada geese arrived in waves. Thousands of birds angled across purple eastern skies. Thousands descended from amber, golden western skies. A few flocks kept formation, but most broke rank, approached in strings resembling an unfastened, dangling necklace, their discipline apparently disheveled, and deteriorated at day's end. Their enchanting and plaintive honking echoed across the marsh, their quick-flapping wings recalled the rustle of gowns on prom night. I swear I heard them pant. They settled in moonlit midnight marsh ponds east of the park, state-protected wetlands serving as their precious habitat.

South Bass Island & Oak Point

These tiny toehold parks serve as gateways to Put-In-Bay, a festive tourist town, boater's hangout, and angler's port. Commodore Perry ambushed the British from this harbor in 1813. Today, fleets armed with fishing poles and bait depart from the sheltered cove to ambush walleyes and such.

LOCATION
Both parks are on South Bass Island, Ottawa County.

SIZE & DESIGNATION
South Bass Island comprises 35 acres; Oak Point, one acre.

ACCESS
South Bass Island is reached by ferries from Catawba Island and Port Clinton. Oak Point is on the north side of the island, off SR 357. To reach South Bass Island State Park, take Catawba Avenue from Put-In-Bay.

Accommodations: Four times I have tried to camp at South Bass; four times I've struck out. The place is packed by noon Friday, and the "no vacancy" signal posted at the ferry dock gives me the bad news. I end up at a private camp on the island or mainland.

Thirty of the camp's 135 sites (non-electric) spread atop a cliff overlooking Lake Erie. These are reserved for tenters. Open the tent flap, watch the sun draw down the night. Amenities include showers, latrines, pet sites, and group camp for 50 people.

South Bass has the only hexagonal "cabents" in the park system. Part cabin, part tent—cabent. The four sites are located on the south side of the park. These are rented by the week from Memorial Day to the last weekend in September. Applications for reservations are available at Catawba Island State Park (see above) and must be submitted by January 31. A drawing in early February determines who gets one.

Oak Point has no overnight facilities. Try privately-owned lodgings on the island.

Picnic Areas: Lake Picnic Area at South Bass is at the end of Catawba Avenue and has tables, grills, water, a shelterhouse, and playground.

S. Bass's Perry's Monument: always glad to see you.

Happy Trails To You

Miles of hiking trails in park system — 640

Best state parks for hiking (based on foot trail miles in park)
* East Fork, 71 miles
* Little Miami, 50 miles
* Caesar Creek, 43 miles
* Burr Oak, 28 miles
* Tar Hollow, 27 miles

Number of parks with mountain bike trails — 13

Most popular state park hiking trails — Hocking Hills Parks

Parks with snowmobile trails — 19; Total miles of snowmobile trails — 142 (est. does not include lakes)

Picnic tables, water, and latrines are maintained at Oak Point.

Swimming: South Bass Island has a pebble beach. Oak Point has zilch.

Boating: South Bass has a single-lane ramp and a loading dock at the end of Catawba Avenue. Docks that can handle 22 boats are maintained at Oak Point on a first-come basis. Commercial and private marinas also cater to your boating needs.

Hunting: None, unless you count those looking for a different sort of game at the numerous beer halls in town.

Fishing: Lake Erie's vast fishery awaits. You can't miss it. An L-shaped pier beside a single-lane ramp provides shore fishing at the south end of South Bass. Perch, crappie, smallmouth bass, and walleye are the main catches. Anglers can also throw lines at Oak Point.

Information: Lake Erie Islands State Parks, 4049 E. Moores Dock Road, Port Clinton, OH 43452, (419) 797-4530, (419) 285-2112.

HISTORY

The phallic column towering over Put-In-Bay is the Perry's Victory and International Peace Memorial, commemorating Oliver Hazard Perry's naval victory over a British fleet on September 10, 1813. The battle was fought off the northern shore of South Bass Island.

For 40 more years the island remained sparsely settled by humans. In 1854, J.D. Rivers bought South Bass and four other islands. Put-In-Bay was the location of his 2,000-head sheep ranch, but he gradually switched to growing grapes and fruit, which became the agricultural mainstays. Vineyards still cover much of the island.

Tourism took off in the late nineteenth century and is the top industry today. South Bass Island State Park occupies the grounds of the old Victory Hotel, gutted by fire in 1919. The ruins are located in the center of the park.

FIELD NOTES

Tear your eyes away from the lake to examine the glacial grooves beside the camp's showerhouse. The gouges were fashioned by the claws of Wisconsinan glacier about 12,000 years ago. Many campers bring bicycles to the island, or rent them from vendors. Bicycles outnumber motor vehicles on this small resort island.

Van Buren

Van Buren is a tiny mudhole park in Ohio's flatlands. Its only attributes are a lakeshore hiking trail, some semi-attractive primitive camp sites alongside a still, skinny lake, and oceans of calm and silence. Van Buren unwinds busy people, unnerves busybodies.

LOCATION

Northern Hancock County, Allen Township.

SIZE & DESIGNATION

Land: 251 acres; water: 45 acres

ACCESS

From Findlay, take I-75 north and exit eastbound on SR 613. After crossing railroad tracks at the edge of Van Buren, turn right on TR 218, and right at the park entrance.

Accommodations: Campers who can rough it have 40 rustic sites on the north shore. Latrines handle the basic necessities. A dozen sites line Van Buren Lake. A primitive, walk-in group camp for organized groups can accommodate 100 people. Reservations are required for groups.

Picnic Areas: Tables and grills are scattered throughout the park. The north and south shore each have a shelterhouse (and latrines) available to the first arrival. The latter, off TR 229, is accessible to physically challenged visitors.

Trails: Lake Shore Trail, 2.5 miles, encircles the lake. Two short loops branch from this path on the wooded south shore.

Boating: Modest boats propelled by paddles or electric motors are allowed on shallow Van Buren Lake. A small ramp is provided.

Hunting: Park land east of TR 229, more than half the acreage, is public hunting ground. Parking is found on the west side of TR 229, north shore.

Fishing: Van Buren is perfect for shore fishing. The hiking trail provides access, trees the shade. It's a great lake for beginners. Cast for largemouth bass, catfish, bluegill, carp, crappie, and bullhead.

Information: Van Buren State Park, P.O. Box 117, Van Buren, OH 45889-0117, (419) 299-3461.

HISTORY

In 1939, a dam plugged Rocky Ford Creek and made Van Buren Lake, originally a wildlife preserve. The site became a state park in 1950 when it was turned over to the Division of Parks and Recreation. Yes, the park and nearby town honor Martin Van Buren, eighth president of the United States.

FIELD NOTES

A large campground is next to the park for those who need fancier accommodations. Second-growth beech and maple are maturing in the park. Great blue herons, horned larks, bluebirds, and great crested flycatchers entertain birders.

SOUTHWEST

Adams Lake

Don't drive across the state to this day-use park. No camping, no swimming, and the hiking trails through the prairie preserve total .75 miles, if that. Picnickers, though, will find shady sites; and the fishing is decent. Originally built for a potable water supply, Adams Lake became a recreation lake in 1950 after suspended sediment muddied the water, so to speak.

LOCATION
    Central Adams County, Tiffin Township, a mile north of West Union on the west side of SR 41.

SIZE & DESIGNATION
    Land: 48 acres; water: 47 acres

ACCESS
    A single park road on the west side of SR 41 leads to picnic areas, a boat ramp, and nature preserve.
    Picnic Areas: The picnic shelter, available on a first-come basis, can handle 120 diners; otherwise stake a claim to picnic tables scattered along the shore. Kids can entertain themselves on the wood-beam playground near the park entrance. The park has vault toilets and drinking water.
    Boating: Launch small crafts at the ramp across from the park office. Propulsion by paddles and electric motors only.
    Fishing: Largemouth bass, bluegill, crappie, channel catfish, bullhead and carp swim in the often cloudy water.
    Information: Write c/o Shawnee State Park,

4404 SR125, Portsmouth, OH 45663-9003, (740) 858-6652. Adams Lake State Park, 14633 State Route 41, West Union, OH 45693, (937) 544-3927.

FIELD NOTES
    Adams Lake is the only state park in the Lexington Plains, a finger of Kentucky's Bluegrass Region that pokes into Adams and Highland counties. Consequently, many plants here have more relatives south of the Ohio River than in the rest of the state. Floral rarities named blazing star, agave, prairie dock rise in adjacent Adams Lake Prairie State Natural Area, a sanctuary for older prairie stock.

Buck Creek

Being right next to Springfield, and midway between Dayton and Columbus, Buck Creek attracts more than a million visitors. The C.J. Brown Reservoir, a U.S. Army Corps of Engineers project, is the centerpiece of this new, busy state park.

LOCATION
    Central Clark County, Moorefield and Springfield townships.

SIZE & DESIGNATION
    Land: 1,910 acres; water: 2,120 acres

ACCESS
    From I-70, head west on US 40. Turn right (north) on Bird Road which becomes Buck Creek Lane. Continue north to the park entrance and beach. Follow the main park road to the right to reach picnic area, the marina, campground, and cabins.
    Accommodations: Buck Creek's 26 two-bedroom cabins offer shady privacy on a peninsula elbowing from the east shore. Several open toward the lake. Reservations are required far in advance for these popular cabins. Each sleeps six and comes with kitchen, bath, screened porch.
    The 101-site campground is nearby. The sites provide little shade, though 89 have electric hookups. Comforts include showers, flush toilets, dump station, and pet sites. Rarely filled, and only a few lake views.
    Picnic Areas: Three large picnic areas branch left from the main park road on the east shore, near the marina. Two shelters here are available to those who stake the first claim. On the west side, a picnic area by the U.S. Army Corps of Engineers Visitor Center is heavily used by summer fishers. There's

another spot, just before the Visitor Center, at the terminus of the Buckhorn Trail. To get there from the park entrance, follow Robert Eastman Road west, then Croft Road. Look for the signs.

Trails: Hemmed in by railroad tracks and roads, Buck Creek has a measly (and easy) five miles of hiking trails, though none of them is especially interesting. The Buckhorn Trail, the longest on the west side of the lake, parallels railroad tracks for most of its three miles to Moorefield-Catawba Road (access there). Lakeview Trail, used by shore anglers, starts in the cabin-campground area and follows the east shore.

Snowmobilers can use a six-mile loop on the east side when conditions permit. Staging area is the picnic area pointing left off the main road, north of the marina. Hikers can also use this trail, which largely tracks across shrub land.

Swimming: Buck Creek's 2,400-foot sandy beach near the entrance is one of the largest in the park system. It has a bathhouse, concession area, and lifeguards. It's a busy and noisy place in the summer, with power boats and water skiers speeding nearby. Sunbathers seeking a snooze might want to go the campground, which is open and quiet.

Scuba divers head for the no wake zone by the campground-cabin area. Buddy system recommended.

Boating: Most people come here for boating, not for whitetailed bucks. The attraction is the large zone in the southern half of C.J. Brown Reservoir for power boats (unlimited speed) and water skiing. The modern, full-service marina on the east shore has four ramps, fuel, seasonal docks, snack bar, bait shop, accessories, licenses, and rest rooms. Boatless visitors can rent a fishing boat, pontoon, jet ski, canoe, or a pedal boat here. There's another ramp by the beach. The northern half of the reservoir and the east shore between the campground and beach is a no wake zone, perfect for slow boaters.

The Ohio Division of Watercraft has its District 2 office next to the park office.

Hunting: Hunters can pursue that big buck and other game in designated areas posted at the park office.

Fishing: Buck Creek, entering from the north, loads the reservoir for largemouth bass, black crappies, bluegills, carp, suckers, bullheads, and sunfish. The Division of Wildlife loads it with walleye, channel catfish, and white crappie. For tips consult the division's fishing map, or ask for advice at the marina or Visitor Center.

Special Places & Events: U.S. Army Corps of Engineers Visitor Center on the east shore (Overlook Drive) has exhibits explaining the natural history of the area, and operation of the dam. The site has an overlook, picnic area, and fishing access area. Call for hours.

Crabill House on the west side of the park is a restored 1820s home listed on the National Register of Historic Places. For tour information contact the Clark County Historical Society at (937) 324-0657.

Information: Buck Creek State Park, 1901 Buck Creek Lane, Springfield, OH 45502, (937) 322-5284 park office, (937) 323-1582 watercraft office, (937) 322-5992 marina.

U.S. Army Corps of Engineers, 2630 Croft Road, Springfield, OH 45503-2515, (937) 325-2411.

HISTORY

After contributing to the removal of the Native American population, celebrated frontiersman Simon Kenton and six other Kentucky families settled along Buck Creek, a short distance downstream from the dam. David Crabill built a Federal-style home on the west bank of the creek in the 1820s. The Clark County Historical Society leases the eight-acre homestead from the Corps of Engineers and offers public tours. The road to the park entrance branches from US 40, the original National Road, which reached Springfield in 1838.

Construction of the flood control dam spanned from September 1966 to 1974 (three years delay from 1968-71). The state park opened in June 1975. The reservoir's namesake honors C.J. Brown Sr., a newspaper publisher who served Ohio as lieutenant governor, secretary of state, state statistician, and member of Congress.

FIELD NOTES

The northern extreme of the reservoir is shallow and good for waterfowl watching. Here, you might glimpse the endangered spotted turtle, and rare round-leaved sundew and horned bladderwort. In meadows, listen for the dicksissel and Henslow sparrow, also rarities.

JOURNAL

A sudden snowfall met us at the park entrance one early November afternoon. Snowflakes splattered on the windshield the way bugs do in the summer. "Watch for deer, son. This snow storm will make them move to shelter fast." I told 11-year-old David, more an instruction to momentarily freeze his fidgety body than a sharing of wisdom. But sure enough, seconds later, a thick-necked eight-point buck with weightlifter shoulders and linebacker haunches bolted across the road, just 25 yards ahead.

David's eyes popped. The rogue's bulky body disappeared in a thicket, but for awhile we followed his cream-colored rack, swinging and bouncing above bushes like ocean whitecaps.

"Did you see him, Dad?" he said, giving me the look of awe that little boys reserve for their father after watching him belt the game-winning homer at the company picnic.

"Now you know why they call this place Buck Creek," I said with certainty.

Caesar Creek

The park's namesake never led Roman legions into battle, but storytellers say Caesar, a runaway slave, followed Shawandase war chief Blue Jacket on raids against his former oppressors south of the Ohio River. Caesar supposedly "ruled" this valley, as a resident or a hunter. An ancient trail on the east side of the creek used by Caesar was renamed Bullskin Trace by the white settlers, many of them Quakers, who replaced the Shawandase.

LOCATION

Northeastern Warren County, Massie and Wayne townships.

SIZE & DESIGNATION

Land: 7,940 acres; water: 2,830 acres. The Ohio Department of Natural Resources leases the property from the U.S. Army Corps of Engineers.

ACCESS

From I-71 travel westerly on SR 73 to reach park facilities on both shores of Caesar Creek Lake. Turn right (north) on Brimstone Road and Mills Road, then left on Center Road to get to the campground. Go left (southwesterly) to find the Nature Center, Pioneer Village, and U.S. Army Corps of Engineers Visitors Center (Clarksville Road). From US 42, follow SR 73 easterly to park locations.

Accommodations: Electric hookups are available at each of the 287 sites in the family campground, on Center Road. This is a modern, lightly shaded camp with showerhouses, rest rooms, flush toilets, pet camping, playground, boat ramp, and four Rent-A-Camp sites. Vacancies are usually available on summer weekends. There's a youth hostel (not a park facility) just before the campground entrance on Center Road.

Horse riders take advantage of a 25-site campground on Furnas-Oglesby Road.

Picnic Areas: Family reunions, company summer picnics, and the like are held at the Hopewell Day Lodge off Clarksville Road (north of the Visitor Center). The rental place has a kitchen, meeting area, outside grills and tables, and access to the Perimeter Hiking Trail. Four picnic shelters with lake views are available near the Pioneer Village off Oregonia Road. Also try the Fifty Springs Picnic Area, off SR 73 west of Harveysburg. The Corps of Engineers has picnic facilities at its Flat Fork Ridge Recreation Area near the dam and spillway. A reservable shelter there handles 100 picknickers.

Trails: Caesar Creek has trails for hikers, bikers and horseback riders. Equestrians have trails ranging from two miles to twenty, the latter being the Solidago Downs Trail along the western shore between the horseman's campground and Spring Valley–Paintersville Road and on the eastern side between Spring Valley–Paintersville Road and Roxanna–New Burlington Road. The northern loop of this trail journeys through Caesar Creek State Wildlife Area, a public hunting area. Riders saddle up at their campground. Hikers also can use this route.

The Perimeter Trail (a collection of trails known by other names) traces the shoreline of the lake south of SR 73. Start at the Corps of Engineers Visitor Center, which offers exhibits on the region's natural history and the dam. The northern route, from the Visitor Center to SR 73 (passes the day lodge and Furnas Shores boat launch) measures 7.2 miles. The southern route (east shore) goes from the dam to SR 73, a distance of 4.3 miles, with stops at Pioneer Village and the nature center. The Buckeye Trail overlaps portions of the Perimeter and Solidago trails. Shorter trails exist at the Corps' Flat Fork Ridge, Visitor Center, and below the dam, the latter being the mile-long Gorge Trail (the prettiest in the park for some). Also go to nearby Caesar Creek Gorge State Natural Area and Spring Valley State Wildlife Area. Get trail maps at the park office or COE Visitor Center.

Hiking difficulty ranges from easy to moderately-difficult, the biggest obstacles being slippery clay and a few steep ravines. Trails pass through young woods, meadows and shrub land. Give the place a couple more decades to heal.

A five-mile mountain bike trail exists near the campground between Center Road and Harveysburg Road. A good departure point (other than the above) is a parking area at the end of Ward Road. The Little Miami Scenic Trail, a hike and bike trail, can be picked up by pedalers in Corwin.

Swimming: The centrally-located beach off SR 73 measures 1,300 feet. Bathers will find a concession area and changing booths.

Boating: Water skiing and power boating are popular in Caesar Creek Lake because it allows unlimited horsepower. Five ramps serve boaters.

Two large and busy ramps branch from SR 73 on the west shore. At the park office (SR 73) turn south to find the Furnas Shore ramp, or north to reach the North Pool ramp. Another west shore launch, Haines Ramp, is located at the end of Compton Road. The east side has ramps at the campground, and off Oregonia Road (Wellman Meadows Ramp).

Slow boaters have plenty of quiet coves to explore, especially in the northern reaches of the lake. Wildlife viewing is best there.

Fishing: The park brochure reports great crappie fishing here, but other observers say the catches are, frankly, crappy these days. Better off casting for white bass, stocked walleye and saugeye, bass (largemouth and smallmouth).

Special Places & Events: The Corps of Engineers leases a tract of land to the Caesar Creek Pioneer Village Association, the group of volunteers that runs the Pioneer Village (off Oregonia Road). The site includes a restored log cabin and barn, circa 1807, and other Quaker-made buildings relocated here. Think of the village as a living history museum with monthly programs. For information on tours and programs, contact the park office or Pioneer Village, 3999 Pioneer Village Road, Box 1049, Waynesville, OH 45068; phone (937) 897-1120.

The Visitor Center run by the Army Corps of Engineers has hands-on natural history exhibits, dioramas, and explanations on the "plumbing" of the dam, spillway, and lake.

The park's nature center, across from the Pioneer Village, is the site of nature programs, organized hikes, and outdoor skills demonstrations.

Information: Caesar Creek State Park, 8570 East SR 73, Waynesville, OH 45068-9719, (937) 897-3055 park office, (937) 488-4595 campground.

U.S. Army Corps of Engineers, Caesar Creek Lake, 4020 N. Clarksville Road, Waynesville, OH 45068-9408, (937) 897-1050.

HISTORY

Seven centuries ago native people known as Fort Ancient Indians (they didn't called themselves that) were the lords of Caesar Creek and Little Miami River valleys. In 1978, the U.S. Army Corps of Engineers occupied Caesar Creek, and in the name of flood control choked it with a dam. Behind the dam grew a state park and wildlife area which in summer and fall is overrun by recreation tourists.

The Corps of Engineers is a maker and a breaker. In 1978, its flood control dam made the lake (technically a reservoir), but it broke (by flooding) the lives and homes of settlers around New Burlington. People destined to be flooded were uprooted and resettled; the tradeoff being a lake and park that will presumably improve with age, a nature preserve protecting a gorgeous gorge, a clean water supply that the Corps claims will "augment natural low flow conditions downstream of the dam in the interest of water quality," meaning the quality of the Little Miami River, a national and state scenic river.

FIELD NOTES

Ordovician era fossils can be collected below the dam by obtaining a free permit at the Corps of Engineers Visitor Center. Observe property boundaries. Fossil collecting in bordering Caesar Creek Gorge State Natural Area is not allowed.

Cowan Lake

Some humans come here for the living freshwater fish, others for the "frozen" swimmers of an ancient salt sea. Still, others come to sail, camp, relax and explore.

LOCATION

Southern Clinton County, Vernon and Washington townships.

SIZE & DESIGNATION

Land: 1,076 acres; water: 700 acres

ACCESS

Cowan Lake is wedged between US 68, SR 350 and SR 730, southwest of Wilmington. To find the north shore campground, cabins, boat launch, and beach from Wilmington, travel south on SR 730, and turn left on Osborne Road, right at the park entrance. The marina on the south shore is accessible from SR 730, a left turn just passed the dam. The fastest route from Wilmington to the south shore public beach, park office and boat ramp, is US 68 south from Wilmington, SR 350 west (right), then right on Beechwood Road to the park office and docks, or right on Yankee Road to the swimming beach.

Accommodations: The campground has 237 campsites, all with electricity. Amenities include two showerhouses, flush toilets (nine rest rooms total), laundry, pet sites, dump station, commissary, amphitheater, playground, camper's beach, boat ramp, and hiking trails. Each site is paved to handle RVs up to 35 feet. The place fills fast on summer weekends. Call ahead to find out if vacancies exist.

Just as popular are the park's 27 family cabins, open year-round. Each has a lake view and sleeps six. Many are reserved a year in advance.

Picnic Areas: The Maples, Hilltop and Pine Tree picnic areas straddle Yankee Road, south side. A reservable shelterhouse and dance pavilion are available. The camp commissary can be rented for receptions and meetings in the off-season. It features a fireplace, rest rooms, and lake view.

Trails: Cowan Lake's 4.5 miles of trails are not especially interesting. The best is the .7-mile Lotus Trail which offers a pier for observing wildlife. Trails named Lakeview, Beechnut Loop, Dogwood, Oldfield, Emerald Woods are shown on the park brochure.

Swimming: Day visitors gather at the 1,000-foot beach on the south shore, off Yankee Road. There's a bathhouse, shower, picnic area, and snack bar at the location. Campers bathe at the beach near the campground and north shore boat ramp.

Boating: Cowan Lake caters to boaters and sailors in watercraft 10 horsepower or less. The South Shore Marina [(937)-289-2656] at the end of SR 730 has ramps, canoe and small boat rentals, supplies, fuel, bait, food, docks, tackle and fishing tips. The boat launch at the end of Beechwood Road, south shore near the park office, has eight ramps, docks, and parking. Boaters also launch from north shore ramps near the campground. Docks are available there too.

Cowan Lake Sailing Club operates a private harbor near the marina.

Hunting: There are designated areas. Don't expect much.

Fishing: Cowan Lake is noted for bass, and veterans claim a daily catch of 20 is common. Most, however, are smaller that 15 inches and must be released. Muskies over 20 pounds, and shovelhead cats more than 50 pounds have been pulled from the lake. Lucky anglers can harvest largemouths in the six-pound class, smallmouths at four pounds, and crappie at two pounds. Fishing piers on the south shore near the park office offer ideal shore fishing.

The Division of Wildlife's fishing map of Cowan Lake is helpful. Regulars know there are secrets and tips to be caught at the marina.

Information: Cowan Lake State Park, 729 Beechwood Road, Wilmington, OH 45177, (937) 289-2105 park office, (937) 289-2656 marina.

HISTORY

William Smalley arrived in 1797, and was the first white settler to settle along a creek later called Cowan Creek. The creek and park name derives from John Cowan, a pioneer surveyor.

The state started buying the land in the late 1940s. Cowan Creek got dammed in 1950, and the park opened in 1968.

FIELD NOTES

Fossils are abundant in the limestone along Cowan Creek, below the dam. But don't wander beyond park boundaries. The prize find is a trilobite. Lotus Cove Trail leads to acres of American lotus, a lily-like flower not common in small inland lakes.

East Fork

Southwestern Ohio's largest state park boasts 10,000 acres of land and water, 70 miles for hikers, 55 miles for horse riders, habitat for endangered species and surviving prairie wildflowers, 416

habitats for humanity, a 3,000 year-old Indian mound, and five fancy boat ramps for the summer fleet. Given a few more decades to green, and East Fork will be the bauble of the region.

LOCATION

Central Clermont County, Batavia, Tate and Williamsburg townships.

SIZE & DESIGNATION

Land: 8,420 acres; water: 2,160 acres. The Ohio Department of Natural Resources leases the property from the U.S. Army Corps of Engineers.

ACCESS

The park lies between SR 32 (north) and SR 125 to the south. The campground and bridle trail are located on the north shore. To reach these from I-275 or Batavia, take SR 32 (Appalachian Highway) east, then Half Acre Road (Afton) south to Old SR 32. Here, turn left on Old SR 32, then right at the park entrance. At the road fork, go left to the camp, right to the horse trails.

To reach the swimming beach, backpack trail, and boat ramps on the south shore, take SR 125 from I-275 to the entrance at Bantam. From Batavia, follow SR 222 south to SR 125 and turn left.

Accommodations: East Fork has the fourth largest campground in the state park system. The entrance is on the north shore off Old SR 32. It has 416 sites on 12 loops, all with electric hookups. The area features showers, flush toilets, a 200-foot beach, boat ramp, six Rent-A-Camp sites, pet sites, amphitheater for nature programs, and a horsemen's camp on Loop A. The Buckeye Trail passes through the campground.

East Fork introduced Rent-A-RV in 1997. A home on wheels, only you don't have to drive and park this 29-footer. These six rentals come with bathroom and kitchen (even a coffee-maker), sleeping for six (two queen-size beds and two bunks), furnace, air conditioning, color TV and audiocassette, and a fire ring and picnic table. Campers provide their bedding. Reservations are accepted after March 1 for sites open April–October.

Picnic Areas: Tables are clustered at a dozen sites around the lake, most on the south shore off park roads 1-3. The Corps of Engineers maintains some nice spots near its Visitors Center on the west shore, Slade Road off SR 122.

Trails: East Fork's trails are just growing whiskers and accumulating stains on hatbands. Consider them excellent paths for beginning backpackers, and so-so for experienced wanderers seeking a new adventure.

The most trodden route is a portion of the blue-

Hoofing It

• *Miles of bridle trails in park*
system — Almost 399

• *Best state parks for horseback*
riding (based on bridle trail
miles in park)

1. East Fork, 55 miles

2. Alum Creek; Little Miami,
*   50 miles*

3. Paint Creek, 25 miles

4. Beaver Creek, 23 miles

blazed Buckeye Trail from the campground westerly to an abandoned gold mine, less than two miles roundtrip. The trail is shared with horseback riders. It continues west to the East Fork of the Little Miami River (below the dam) and leaves the park at Greenbriar Road. Eastbound from the campground it goes to Williamsburg.

The Steve Newman Worldwalk Perimeter Trail honors Steve Newman from nearby Bethel, who circumnavigated the landed portions of Earth on foot, a journey the hiker-writer dubbed his Worldwalk. The Perimeter Trail traces the perimeter of the park for 31 or 37 miles, depending on the route. Hikers and riders must carefully follow green blazes because the path overlaps with the Buckeye Trail, American Discovery Trail, North Country Trail, East Fork Backpack Trail, and park side trails in places. Start at the campground on the north shore, or the access for the East Fork Backpark Trail on Bantam Road (south shore). Other than the state park camp, the Perimeter Trail features three primitive camping spots with lean-to bunkrooms and rest rooms (tenting allowed). One site is a bit east of the south shore trailhead, and perfect for weekenders arriving on Friday after work. Others are found south of Clover Road (southeast), and on the north side, between Park Road 4 and Greenbriar Road.

East Fork Backpack Trail is a less remote backpacking path that starts at the trail access on Bantam Road and stays on the south side of the park for 14 miles. Red painted blazes mark this trail. White-blazed side trails lead to overnight camps, one shared with the Perimeter Trail.

Bridle Trails: Riders can follow the Perimter Trail and a network of interlocking loops bisected by Park Road 4 on the north side. Daytime riders can park at a staging area on Park Road 4. Campers start from Loop A at the campground. The Perimeter Trail is accessible from the campground and near Greenbriar Road.

The park's five-mile mountain bike trail starts a little west of the park entrance on SR 125.

Swimming: Campers use a beach on the north shore. Others go to a 1,200-foot beach on the south shore with a concession and picnic area.

Boating: Full speed ahead on unlimited horsepower William H. Harsha Lake, named after the Portsmouth Congressman who served from 1960 to 1981. Six boat ramps serve boaters. They are located at the Corps of Engineers dam (Slade Road), at the end of Park Road 4 (north shore), at the campground, at the end of Tunnel Mill Road (northeast), end of Park Road 1 and Reisinger Road (south shore).

Hunting: Gunners can go for game in designated areas posted at the Park Office.

Fishing: Toss a line for largemouth and smallmouth bass, bluegill, crappie, and hybrid striper (stocked).

Special Places & Events: In summer William H. Harsha Lake (the name slowly being replaced by East Fork Lake) attracts rowing crews from around the country for the National Collegiate Rowing Championship. Visit a pair of abandoned gold mines during the Gold Rush Days program in May. Also check out the Storytelling Campout in June, and Christmas in July Campout.

The park has its own version of Mounties—called the East Fork Mounted Search and Rescue Team. Park volunteers created it in 1994 to assist hikers, hunters and park rangers on the backcountry and bridle trails. The squad consists of 40 experienced volunteer riders and six ground support members. The Mounties have not used their training so far, but they are ready when duty calls.

Information: East Fork State Park, P.O. Box 119, Bethel, OH 45106, (513) 734-4323,

HISTORY

Discovery of a 3,000-year-old Indian mound indicates occupancy by Adena people. Erie tribesmen supposedly used the area until their removal at the start of the 18th century.

Gold mines opened here in 1869. The one near Elk Lick, off the Buckeye Trail, consisted of a flume for separating and washing gravel containing gold flakes. An underground mine in the Twin Bridges Road area had gold embedded in rock.

Old Bethel Church by the south park office was constructed in 1818 on the site of an 1807 log cabin church.

The reservoir called William H. Harsha Lake or East Fork Lake was formed behind a dam built for flood control by the U.S. Army Corps of Engineers in 1978.

FIELD NOTES

Prairie wake robin, a wildflower thought to be extinct in Ohio, was rediscovered here in the 1970s, along with prairie rarities called scorpion grass and potato dandelion. Another imperiled critter, Henslow's sparrow, lives in the park's meadows. Its high-octave chirp is difficult for humans to hear.

Almost everywhere the Wisconsinan glacier overlapped the spread of its predecessor, the Illinoian glacier. In East Fork, deposits of the earlier glacier can be examined.

Hueston Woods

Hueston Woods today is one of Ohio's busiest resort parks, the flagship in the southwestern corner of the state. It is also overdeveloped, graying, and a bit frayed because it is trying to do too much.

LOCATION

Southwestern Preble County, Israel Township; Northwestern Butler County, Oxford Township.

SIZE & DESIGNATION
Land: 3,596 acres; water: 625 acres.

ACCESS
From Eaton or Oxford travel on SR 732 to the park entrance road. That leads to the park loop road and all facilities. Follow signs.

Accommodations: Let's start with the lodge, famous for its 100-foot sandstone fireplace and Indian artifacts in the lobby. It stands on a bluff on the east shore, providing a commanding view of Acton Lake. The spot supposedly was a council site for Indian tribes. Accommodations include 96 rooms, indoor and outdoor pools, dining room, lounge (bar), snack bar, game room, TV lounge, exercise area, sauna, whirlpool, tennis, volleyball, basketball, gift shop, shuffleboard, courtesy boat docks, and easy access to hiking trails. The largest of four meeting rooms handles 300 people.

Two types of cabins are available. Twenty-five, two-bedroom family cabins sleep six and are open all year (heated, full kitchen, screened porch). One-bedroom standard cabins, 36 of them, are located on a separate road. These "efficiency" cabins sleep four, available April through October. Both types are rented on a weekly basis in summer.

Hueston Woods offers two kinds of family camping at the northwest corner of the park. The Class A campground with 255 sites features electricity, pads for 30-foot RVs, showers, laundry, flush toilets, shade and open sites, pet sites, and a camp store. Tenters and large family groups prefer the Class B "rustic" campground with 236 sites, absent electricity and other amenities. Class B sites are more spacious, shadier, and less crowded.

Organized groups can pick from several spots, the best one being close to the north shoreline. There's one primitive campsite site for horse and rider at a staging area off Four Mile Valley Road.

Picnic Areas: Nine picnic areas—all with latrines, eight with water—make Hueston Woods a picnickers paradise. Areas named Locust Grove and Acton Lake are near the dam (south end). Pine Grove and Maple Grove on the west side are between the nature preserve and nature center. Hedge Row and Quarry area are along Hedge Row Road, beside the Class B camp. Launch Ramp and Deer Pen flank the marina, and Sycamore stems from the loop road on the north side.

Trails: Thirteen trails, each less than two miles, provide hikers with quick outings. Loop trails named Cabin, Pine Loop and Sycamore branch from the road leading to the standard cabins. Cedar Falls Trail wanders around the Sycamore Picnic Area. Equistem Loop and Gallion Run trails twist between the Class B and Class A camps; Indian Mound Trail loops around the Class A camp, and Hedge Apple Trail is squeezed between the park loop road and Butler-Israel Road on the west side. The Mud Lick Trail, a series of three loops, connects the family cabins and the lodge.

Unquestionably, the best trails snake through Hueston Woods State Natural Area, a National Natural Landmark located on the west side of the lake. This suggested route requires a shuttle. Start at the parking lot for the Big Woods Trail and take that trail southerly, across Brown Road, to another parking lot, then walk the Blue Heron Loop toward the lake. Here, follow the West Shore Trail southbound to the Acton Lake Picnic Area by the dam. It's about four miles, and you can look for fossils in the gorge below the dam.

Horseback riders head for the bridle trails, six miles total, stemming from a staging area on Four Mile Valley Road. A guide is available at the park office. Park officials will make hikers happier by extending the shoreline trail to the lodge, thus connecting park facilities on both shores for foot travelers.

Swimming: A 1,500-foot beach awaits bathers and sun-soakers on the west shore. There's a bathhouse there, along with a concession and picnic tables. An unmarked trail goes south along the shore to the nature preserve and a fishing pier. Swimming pools at the lodge are reserved for lodge and cabin guests.

Boating: Sailboat is the preferred water vehicle on Acton Lake, largely because motors are restricted to 10 horsepower. The marina on the west shore has eight ramps, 234 dock slips, plenty of parking, a snack bar and bait shop. Here you can rent boats ranging from canoe to pontoon. Courtesy docks enable boaters to visit or stay at the lodge, but a ramp does not exist there.

Golf: Day visitors and overnighters swing their niblicks at the park's 18-hole golf course on the west shore, off Brown Road. The par 72 course measures 7,005 yards, the second longest links in the park system. Call the pro shop at (513) 523-8081 to schedule a tee time March until November.

Fishing: Casting for bluegill, largemouth bass, and catfish is considered good to excellent (once you find them). Crappie fishing is so-so, but improving. A slot limit is in effect. Check at the park office or marina before reeling them in.

A wheelchair accessible fishing pier is located on the west shore, at the end of Brown Road near the Sugar House. Shore fishers have established spots along the West Shore Trail and by the dam.

Special Places & Events: Pioneer Farm Museum, at the corner of Doty and Brown roads near the golf course entrance, features the restored 1820s farmhouse of the Doty Family and a Pennsylvania-style barn. The former park office now is leased to the Oxford Museum Association, which opens the home for interpretive programs during the warm months.

In late February and early March maple syrup pours from the Sugar House at the end of Brown Road. Syrup from local trees is made with primitive contraptions and modern equipment. Park at the beach and follow the crowd on the Sugar Bush Trail.

Injured critters such as bald eagles, hawks, owls, and deer receive special treatment at the park's Wildlife Rehabilitation Center, located near the park office. Large outdoor cages enable you to see these repairing animals. Inside the adjoining nature center, snakes, owls, rodents, and other woods and wetlands residents entertain visitors. The park's natural history is explained via exhibits. The nature center is open April through October, daily Tuesday–Sunday.

Fossil collectors search for Ordovician marine life along Four Mile Creek below the dam at the south end, and above its merger with Acton Lake. Parking is provided on the loop road by the impoundment. Park in the Quarry Picnic Area on Hedge Row Road to explore the upstream, north side fossil bed. Fossils are abundant at both locations. Ask for a fossil guide at the park office or nature center.

Information: Hueston Woods State Park, Route 1, College Corner, OH 45003, (513) 523-6347 park office, (513) 523-6381 lodge, 1-800-282-7275 lodge and cabin reservations.

HISTORY

Matthew Hueston is remembered because his land became a state park and nature preserve. Hueston signed up with General Anthony Wayne's army in 1794 and marched through the area en route to the Battle of Fallen Timbers, where Wayne decisively defeated combined Indian forces commanded by Blue Jacket. While camped at Fort St. Clair, near Eaton, Hueston noted the fertility of the soil. He returned in 1797, staked a large claim to land along a stream later called Four Mile Creek, and prospered.

The old growth beech-maple forest on the west bank of Four Mile Creek proved more important than Hueston's heroics. Just why the pioneer and his successors didn't cut down this ancient grove is unclear. We're glad they didn't because it saved the place for park development.

Morris Taylor, a Hamilton conservationist, bought this land in the late 1930s when the last of the Hueston clan perished. Morris held it in trust until Preble County legislator Cloyd Acton persuaded the state to buy it as a state forest in 1941. Acton Lake commemorates the lawmaker's effort.

The Ohio Board of Corrections established a camp here for honor inmates in 1952. These men worked to build the 1,200 foot earthen dam that created the lake in 1956. Hueston Woods became a state park the following year. Campgrounds, cabins, marina, lodge and golf course were developed in the 1960s.

JOURNAL

I come here, frankly, only for the fossils and ancient forest. The limestone below the dam is thick with fossils. A rock the size of a dinner plate will contain as many brachiopods as that large bag back at camp contains potato chips. Take one home. Look at it from time to time, and remember that long, long ago Ohio was crawling with life beneath a sea that breathed at the Equator. Remember, too, that the old forest three miles upstream contains the quiet, accumulated wisdom of several centuries. If it perishes, so does its wisdom. At Hueston Woods you can stand in worlds ancient, old and new.

John Bryan

Wedged between two celebrated and popular nature sanctuaries, John Bryan State Park protects a geological masterpiece, the gorge of the Little Miami River, a national and state scenic river. Trails along the river explore dolomite cliffs more than 130 feet tall, and trees named beech, hemlock, sycamore, and cottonwood just as impressive. Winter's ice and snow adds to the majesty of this park for all seasons.

LOCATION

Northern Greene County, Miami Township.

SIZE & DESIGNATION

Land: 755 acres. Some 2.2 miles of the Little Miami River, a national and state scenic river, passes through the park. Clifton Gorge State Natural Area east of the park is a National Natural Landmark.

ACCESS

From US 68 in Yellow Springs (midway between Xenia and Springfield) travel east on SR 343, then south (right) on SR 370 into the park.

Accommodations: A hundred non-electric sites, most shaded, await family campers. Latrines, playground, drinking water and dump station are available, but not showers nor flush toilets. A reservable group camp handles 100 people.

Picnic Areas: The park's Lower Picnic Area along the river may be the most popular in the park system. Three other areas—the Upper, Wingo, and Orton area—stand atop the cliffs. Lower and Orton areas offer shelters to picnickers who stake the first claim. Drinking water is available.

The park has a day lodge for large groups. Two fireplaces keep the place warm in winter, a screened porch cools it off in summer. The lodge comes equipped with a kitchen, a coffee-maker, stove and refrigerator. Call the park office for a reservation.

Trails: Three main trails track through the gorge and connect with paths in Clifton Gorge State Natural Area east of the park. The two-mile North Rim Trail departs from the Upper Picnic Area and goes upstream, into the nature preserve and terminating in the Village of Clifton Mill. Rock climbers will find five sites designated for their sport on this trail, including one for rappeling. The Pittsburgh-Cincinnati Stagecoach Trail begins at the park road beneath the cliff and heads upstream along an old stagecoach lane. At the eastern park border this 1.3-mile trail becomes the John L. Rich Trail in the nature preserve and eventually merges (via a staircase) with the North Rim Trail. Footbridges in the Lower Picnic Area and at the eastern border lead to the 1.2-mile South Gorge Trail. An easy walk is the 1.2-mile Arboretum Trail, which begins near the Day Lodge and passes by a star-gazing observatory run by the Miami Valley Astronomical Society.

Shorter trails wander through the Lower Picnic Area, and connect picnic area to the main trails.

Boating: To canoe the Little Miami River you must leave the park and launch downstream at Jacoby Road or at the US 68 bridge (below the dam).

Fishing: Smallmouth bass, rock bass, and panfish swim in the river. Shore fishing is permitted.

Special Places & Events: From time to time the Miami Valley Astronomical Society opens the observatory for public shows and demonstrations. Call the park office for infomation.

Information: John Bryan State Park, 3790 SR 370 Yellow Springs, OH 45387, (937) 767-1274.

HISTORY

The park's namesake, John Bryan, was a prosperous inventor and businessman who purchased this site (and adjoining Clifton Gorge) in 1896 and called it Riverside Farm. In 1918, he bequeathed the marvelous place to the state "to be cultivated by the state as a forestry, botanic and wildlife reserve park and experiment station." Three governors, however, rejected the gift because Bryan stipulated the land could not be used for public religious worship. Finally, in December 1924 it was accepted, and in May 1925 the site became a park under state forest jurisdiction. A portion was transferred to the Division of Parks and Recreation in 1949, the rest ended up as a nature preserve managed today by the Division of Natural Areas and Preserves.

FIELD NOTES

John Bryan is one of a trio of places protecting the Little Miami River. The park's natural inventory includes 105 tree species, 343 varieties of wildflowers, 16 kinds of ferns and rarities called Canada yew, redberry elder, mountain maple, and arborvitae. Birders have counted 90 species of birds living or visiting the park. Reptiles number five species of turtles, and ten snakes. Amphibians are represented by eight kinds of salamander and seven frogs and toads. See also the chapters on Clifton Gorge and Glen Helen Nature Preserve.

The park is one of only a few "public" locations in Ohio for rock climbing. The designated climbing sites are located on the North Rim Trail. This is usually a group activity, though solo climbers may be present. Beginners should have a few lessons before scaling the 130-foot walls. Rapeling equipment is allowed at one spot. Climbing is unlawful in the nature preserves.

Large stump blocks that have detached from the cliff are habitats for rare plants. Climbing these harms the plants, and may harm humans.

Kiser Lake

They just couldn't leave well enough alone. "They" being the humans who decided to dam a perfect Ice Age fen to create a damned imperfect state park. The dam, built in 1939, transformed 360-acre, glacier-made Mosquito Lake Bog into 396-acre, bulldozer-made Kiser Lake. If "they" had it to do over today, would this place be a fen or foe?

LOCATION

Western Champaign County, Johnson Township.

SIZE & DESIGNATION

Land: 474 acres; water: 396 acres.

ACCESS

From US 36, roughly between Urbana and Piqua, go north on State Route 235 a bit more than three miles, then east on Possum Hollow Road. At Kiser Road, turn left (north) and follow signs to facilities (camping, beach) on the east side of the lake. To reach sites on the west side, continue north on SR 235 and turn right at your destination.

Accommodations: The campground, 115 sites (no electricity), is located at the eastern end of the lake. The grounds have picnic tables, playgrounds, fire rings, latrines and a dump station. Pets are permitted in designated spots. Two Rent-A-Camp sites are available. The camp gets crowded on summer holidays, otherwise its easy to find sites. Large groups can reserve a campground (250 capacity) on the south shore (eastern side).

Picnic Areas: Outdoor diners enjoy the lake from five areas—most with lake views. Picnic shelters at the end of Kiser Lake Road and off SR 235 (south shore, west end) serve on a first-come basis. Two picnic areas are located between the family and group campgrounds off Kiser Lake Road, another near the park office (north shore, west end).

Trails: Easy trails (4.5 miles total) through slightly wooded and rolling terrain branch from the campgrounds and hug the lakeshore. Try the 1.5-mile North Bay Trail, which traces the north shore between park roads.

Swimming: A 600-foot swimming beach (with refreshment stand) on the north shore (east side) stays open from Memorial Day to Labor Day. Lifeguards patrol the beach daily during summer. Scuba divers can explore the water (buddy system) except near the beach.

Boating: Pilots in small sailboats ply Kiser Lake, which measures 2.5 miles in length. Sailors launch their craft from north shore boat ramps at each end of the lake. The launch at the west side rents aluminum boats. Rowboats and canoes also ride the surface. Motors are not permitted. Boats can be tied up at seasonal docks (45 maximum) off Park Street in the village of Grandview Heights.

Hunting: Put your sights on the migratory waterfowl that stop here. All other game is off limits.

Fishing: Five fishing piers makes Kiser Lake popular with shore anglers. Cast for bass, catfish, bluegill, and crappie.

Information: Kiser Lake State Park, Box 55, Rosewood, OH 43070, (937) 362-3822.

HISTORY

Mosquito Lake Bog was in the stomping grounds of Tecumseh, the celebrated Shawandase warrior, and frontiersman Simon Kenton, whose bones rest in a graveyard near Urbana.

Blame the lake on John W. Kiser. He and his family envisioned a shallow, spring-fed lake for wildlife and recreation. In 1932 the state acquired several hundred acres of Kiser's land. Seven years later a dam built across Mosquito Creek flooded the fen and created Kiser Lake, the main facility for the latter state park. A memorial at the end of Kiser Road remembers the park's namesake.

FIELD NOTES

Only two vestiges remain of Mosquito Lake Bog, now called Kiser Lake Wetlands State Natural Area. The Headwaters Section of the preserve at the eastern end of the lake features a boardwalk for an easy stroll through this unique wetland. The bog actually is a fen fed by spring-water that leaks from nearby glacial mounds and flows down the creek. A bog, in contrast, captures precipitation and usually has no outlet. (See Cedar Bog State Memorial)

Specifically, the lake (trending northwest-southeast) divides the Farmersville moraine, which lays northeast-southwest. The moraine, a glacial deposit shaped like a long rolling hill or low ridge, marks the spot where the vanguard of the last Ice Age glacier stalled and let sand, gravel, and boulders accumulate. The dome-shaped hills in the area are kames, where sediment drained through holes in the ice (think of sand flowing through an hourglass).

As you stroll along the boardwalk look for queen-of-the-prairie, shrubby cinquefoil, Kalm's lobelia, grass-of-parnassus, smaller fringed gentian, big bluestem (a grass), Ohio goldenrod, poison sumac, and other unusual marsh flora.

Little Miami

Imagine a river and a parallel trail stitching together time, places, and people. That's the role of Little Miami State Park, a 50-mile trail corridor connecting parks, preserves, historical landmarks, wildlife areas and towns in four counties. It's a place for bicycling, hiking, cross-country skiing, horseback riding, rollerblading, time traveling, and canoeing. The park encourages adventures on land and water.

LOCATION

Little Miami State Park is a 50-mile linear park along the Little Miami River from Hedges Road in Southwestern Greene County to Terrace Park in Clermont County.

SIZE & DESIGNATION

This linear park is a 50-mile trail corridor. The Little Miami River is a national and state scenic river.

ACCESS

The park is accessible from exits off I-71 and I-275, US 22/SR 3, state routes 50, 126, 350, 73 and 42, and county roads that span the Little Miami River.

Picnic Areas: Picnic tables, parking, phones, and rest rooms for park users are found at trail staging areas in Spring Valley, Corwin, Morrow, and Loveland. Shelters at Loveland and Morrow are available on a first-come basis.

Trails: The Ohio Division of Parks and Recreation manages a 50-mile section of the Little Miami Scenic Trail, the stretch from Hedges Road south of Xenia to the confluence with the East Fork of the Little Miami River near Terrace Park. The rail-to-trail route continues north through Xenia to Yellow Springs. Now it reaches Springfield. Primary staging areas are found in Loveland (Adams Road), Morrow (US 22/SR 3), and Corwin (north of SR 73). Other departing points are Fort Ancient State Memorial (SR 350), Spring Valley State Wildlife Area (Roxanna-New Burlington Road), Oregonia (Oregonia Road) and Mathers Mill (Wilmington Road).

The Buckeye Trail utilizes the path from Caesar Creek Gorge to Milford. Portions are paved, portions are gravel. Being an abandoned rail grade, the trail is flat, wide, and easy to follow. Keep in mind, though, that the trail serves many recreationists. Horseback riding is permitted but no overnight facilities are provided. Bicycles can be rented from shops along the trail.

Swimming: Officially, swimming is prohibited in the state park. However, wading and floating in life preservers and inflated tubes is usually okay. Tubing, in fact, is a popular pasttime in summer. Do these activities at your own risk.

Boating: The Little Miami River allows canoes and inflatables on 86 of its 105 miles. Though not especially challenging for thrill-seeking paddlers (except during high water), the river offers an abundance of scenery and wildlife, a curvy current, clean water, and plenty of access areas. It is a great, wholesome family adventure. The current gets crowded on summer weekends. Paddle weekdays if possible, or off season.

Within this state park canoers, rafters, and tubers can put-in at Spring Valley State Wildlife Area (Roxanna-New Burlington Road bridge), Corwin (below lowhead dam), at Caesar Creek Gorge State Natural Area (Corwin Road), Mathers Mill, Fort Ancient State Memorial (SR 350 bridge), Halls Creek access in Morrow (below dam), Kings Mill (Grandin Road), Glen Island in Foster, and Lake Isabella Park. Canoe and raft rentals are available along the river.

Fishing: Largemouth bass, white bass, sauger, and panfish entertain anglers in canoes and floats, or from shore at canoe access points.

Information: Little Miami State Park, c/o Caesar Creek State Park, 8570 East State Route 73, Waynesville, OH 45068-9719, (937) 897-3055.

HISTORY

Stop at Fort Ancient to explore the amazing earthworks of the Hopewell culture people who inhabited the area from 300 B.C to 600 A.D. At the time of European settlement the Miami and Shawandase lived in the valley. (North of Xenia the Little Miami Scenic Trail passes through Shawnee Park in Oldtown commemorating the birthplace of Tecumseh, war chief of the Shawandase.)

Farmers and millers inhabited the valley in the nineteenth century. Towns named Kings Mill and Mather Mill recall the early industrialization of the region. The trail follows the raised bed of the abandoned Little Miami Railroad, built in the 1840s. Little Miami Park became a state park in 1979.

FIELD NOTES

Little Miami River Valley becomes a panorama for 340 species of wildflowers, and almost as many birds, in the spring and summer. Look for Virginia bluebells, wild columbine festooned on dolomite cliffs, and mammoth sycamores anchored on banks. Sheltered gorges are shaded by hemlocks and rare Canada yew. The section by Fort Ancient State Memorial is one of Ohio's deepest gorges, and perhaps its most luxurious for natural growth.

Paint Creek

A river, to be a river, is supposed to be 100 miles long (the East and Harlem rivers in New York City being two notable exceptions). Paint Creek is three miles shy of being a river, so its loyalists call it the country's longest creek.

LOCATION

Eastern Highland County, Paint Township; Southwestern Ross County, Paint Township.

SIZE & DESIGNATION

Land: 9,000 acres; water: 1,200 acres. The Ohio Department of Natural Resources leases the property from the U.S. Army Corps of Engineers, which manages the flood control dam and spillway at the southeastern tip of the reservoir.

ACCESS

The park entrance is on the northside of US 50, near the Highland-Ross county line.

Accommodations: The 199-site campground sits on a scenic bluff overlooking Paint Creek Lake. Located on Taylor Road, north of US 50, the all-electric camp has hot showers, flush toilets, pet sites, laundry, dump station, commissary, boat ramp, amphitheater, three Rent-A-Camp spots, and a nature trail. Horseback riders use a primitive camp at a staging area on Upp Road, off US 50.

Paint Creek recently became the second state park to offer rental houseboats. These are equipped with a bathroom, shower, galley (sink, stove, refrigerator, microwave), television and VCR, air conditioning, furnace, and sundecks. The cabin sleeps six. Houseboats are available at the Deer Park marina.

Picnic Areas: Picnic sites are located north of the dam off Rapid Forge Road, at the marina, swimming beach, and Rattlesnake boat ramp off Snake Road.

Trails: Paint Creek features trails for travelers on foot, hoof, mountain bike, and snowmobile (snow permitting, of course). Horse and riders can explore 25 miles of bridle trails on the west side of the lake. The trail system has three connected loops comprising an 18-mile Main Loop, a 13-mile Middle Loop, and a seven-mile Short Loop. A staging area with camping, trail maps, latrines, and water is located near the Pioneer Farm on Upp Road, north of US 50. Snowmobilers and cross-country skiers can explore these routes in winter, and hikers can tread upon them at anytime.

Four hiking trails ranging from a half-mile to 2.5 miles depart from various locations. Milkweed Meadow Nature Trail starts at the campground, Falls Trail and Fern Hollow Trail near the Rattlesnake boat ramp, and Little Pond Trail from Rapid Forge Road.

The trailhead for the park's double loop mountain bike path is located on Taylor Road, east of the campground. Hikers can use it too.

Swimming: Paint Creek's underused 1,000-foot swimming beach lines the southern shore north of US 50. A bathhouse with rest rooms is available. The quiet cove also serves folks swimming from boats too.

Boating: The southern half of Paint Creek Lake is reserved for water skiing and power boating (unlimited horsepower). Most of these boaters launch from the Deer Park Marina, just south of the dam and spillway. North of the "speed zone," boaters launch from a small ramp at the end of Taylor Road (campers mostly), or at the Rattlesnake Boat Access off SR 753. Speed is restricted in the branching north arms and secluded coves. Slow boaters have plenty of spots to discover where motorboats dare not propel.

Hunting: Land flanking the northern antlers of Paint Creek Lake is managed by the Division of Wildlife as Paint Creek State Wildlife Area. Ohio's largest non-typical whitetail was harvested here several years back. Most of Ohio's other game species will be found here also.

Fishing: Paint Creek hosts an annual "crappiethon," which attracts hundreds of anglers and offers prizes totaling hundreds of thousands. The reservoir is indeed an excellent natural fishery for white and black crappie, as well as rock bass, channel cats, bluegill, and suckers. The lake also is a saugeye hot spot. A seven pounder landed in 1988 was a world record for awhile. Stocked tiger muskie and northern pike complete the angling inventory. Tailwater fishing is above average. Fishing maps are available from the Division of Wildlife and Corps of Engineers office.

Special Places & Events: Summer visitors should snoop around the Pioneer Village on the west shore (Upp Road) where replicas of a log cabin, and farm buildings, vintage early 1800s, can be enjoyed. Programs and activities relating to the village theme are held throughout the year. The Annual Sweet Corn Festival is the last week in July.

Information: Paint Creek State Park, 14265 US 50, Bainbridge, OH 45612, (937) 365-1401 park office, (937) 981-7061 campground.

U.S. Army Corps of Engineers, 504 Reservoir Road, Bainbridge, OH 45612, (937) 365-1470.

HISTORY

Vengeful Euro-American settlers sometimes killed the first Indian they met to even a score. Storytellers remember the sad ending of a peaceful Shawandase called (phonetically) Waw-will-a-way, who was wrongly blamed for scalping a paleface. The warrior killed one white ambusher and wounded two others before dying of a gunshot in his chest. Waw-will-a-way was buried at the confluence of Paint and Rattlesnake creeks. The site, as well as early mills, is now underwater.

Earlier Native Americans inhabited the fertile valley. Seip Mound State Memorial in Bainbridge and the earthworks at Mound City Group National Monument in Chillicothe recall the civilizations of the Hopewell culture.

Periodic flooding in the Scioto River Valley resulted in flood control dams across contributing creeks called Paint, Alum, Deer, Big Walnut, and the Olentangy River.

In the early 1970s, the U.S. Army Corps of Engineers put a plug at this bend, concealing a natural centerfold gorge and creating Paint Creek Lake, for better or worse. Oldtimers remember the stunning gorge before it was filled by the lake. Even the state park brochure mourns the loss, "Before Paint Creek was impounded to form a reservoir, the creek valley was unrivaled in the state for scenic beauty and its display of wildflowers." Though the reservoir ended the stream's uninterrupted flow, it formed a fishing and boating attraction that punctuates a scenic auto route, US 50, across western Ross County. It became a state park in 1972.

FIELD NOTES

The Corps of Engineers did not erect the first dam in this area. During the Ice Age, the Illinoian glacier advanced as far as Bainbridge and blocked a northbound tributary of Paint Creek's ancestral stream. The ice plug flooded the valley as far as Fort Hill State Memorial, an impoundment known as Cynthiana Lake. The lake drained when the ice mass retreated.

Venture into Paint Creek Lake's nooks and crannies to catch a glimpse of the old valley.

Rocky Fork

Park promoters call Rocky Fork a paradise for boaters. Indeed, park facilities cater to boaters of all speeds. Fishers have plenty of water and shore space to catch muskies, bass and walleyes.

LOCATION

Eastern Highland County, Paint and Marshall townships.

SIZE & DESIGNATION

Land: 1,384 acres; water: 2,080 acres.

ACCESS

From Hillsboro travel southeasterly to its junction with North Shore Road (TR 274) at the western edge of the lake. Turn left on North Shore Road to reach the campground, hiking trails, and north beach docks and concession. To find the South Beach and East Shore marinas, Fisherman's Wharf, and dam, stay on SR 124. Turn left (east) on Chestnut Road (TR 194). Turn left (north) on White Lane to Fisherman's Wharf, and left on Blue Ribbon Road to the South Beach Marina. Continue east on TR 194, now Spruance Road, then north (left) on CR 51 to arrive at the East Shore Marina. US 50 passes north of the park. From here, take SR 753 or North Beach Road south to the park.

Accommodations: This 190-site campground in the northwest corner of the park fills fast on weekends during the warm months. About 130 sites offer electricity, and 20 include water. Facilities at the camp include showers, flush toilets, dump station, pet sites, camp store, laundry, amphitheater, recreation barn (reservable game room, meeting area) and campers' beach. The Highland County Airport on North Shore Road is less than a mile walk from the campground. A group camp can be reserved through the park office.

Picnic Areas: Picnic areas are located on the north shore, Blinko Area, along East Shore Drive, and at South Beach Marina.

Trails: Four trails totaling four miles aren't much to write home about. All of them—Deer Loop, Paw Paw Trail, Bee Loop, and Pumpkin Path—begin near the campground. Pumpkin Path (park in a grassy area across from the campground entrance) leads to the Belden Saur Memorial Bird Observation Station, a wetland bird blind funded by the Appalachian Front Audubon Society and built by the Highland County Manpower Program.

Swimming: The North Beach's gravel-sand beach, located at the south end of North Beach Road, measures 200 feet. Boaters can swim here at the mouth of a cove, or in a no wake zone on the east shore. An activity center above the beach is a large gathering pavilion with a kitchen, grills, and screened-in dining area. Across the lake, South Beach Marina has a 600-foot beach with changing rooms and picnic areas. Both beaches have marinas.

Boating: The center of Rocky Fork Lake is an open zone for unlimited horsepower boats. In the summer this lane attracts water skiers, jet skiers, and fast pleasure craft. Slow boaters stay in no wake zones at the east and west ends of the lake, and 300 feet from shore.

Two marinas and five launches make it easy to enter Rocky Fork. You will find the East Shore Marina and Restaurant at the end of Lucas Lane (off CR 51) and the South Beach Marina at the end of Blue Ribbon Road. Launches are also found at North Beach (off North Shore Road), on East Shore Drive, at Fisherman's Wharf (end of White Lane). Campers enter from a ramp at the campground.

The North Beach ramp has pontoon boats for rent, fuel, and supplies. It is preferred by pleasure boat owners and anglers. The U.S. Coast Guard has a station near the East Shore Marina.

Hunting: Hunters can pursue game in designated areas only. Check at the park office.

Fishing: Rocky Fork gets stocked with 100,000 walleyes yearly, and 4,000 muskies in the 10 to 12 inch category. But it is crappies that fill stringers. Bass and bluegill are plentiful, too.

Rocky Fork's grassy shoreline offers plenty of opportunities for land casters. Blinko Picnic Area is popular with anglers. Fisherman's Wharf has a pier for wheelchaired fishers.

Special Places & Events: Boaters decorate their boats for an annual boat parade in August. Hydroplane competitions have been held in the lake's fast lane.

Information: Rocky Fork State Park, 9800 N. Shore Drive, Hillsboro, OH 45133, (937) 393-4284.

HISTORY

Millwrights saw the promise of Rocky Fork in the 19th century. Mills grinding grain, sawing lumber, carding wool, and weaving blankets occupied sites along the stream. The last mill, McCoppin's (formerly Costello's) Mill, stands below the spillway on the east side. A town to be called Lodore was planned at McCoppin's Mill in 1897. Lodore was to be a railroad town built for the Black Diamond line. The deal lost steam, however.

At the start of the 20th century, Colonel Walter H. Hutchins, a Cincinnati native who vacationed here, came up with the idea of damming Rocky Fork for a recreational lake. Hutchins lived to watch construction of that dam begin in 1949. The park opened in 1953.

FIELD NOTES

Birders can observe their favorite wetland birds at the observation blind built by Audubon members. Rocky Fork becomes one of Ohio's most scenic canoe rides. Put in at Barrett Road in spring below the dam and paddle through the gorge to Paint Creek, then navigate the rapids below the confluence.

Stonelick

Stonelick Creek has coughed up some gold dust, but the real reward is the out-of-the-way park itself. Put Stonelick in the Prozac category with a campground that never fills, a calm lake for smooth sailing and drifting, lonely fish hankering to be caught, and a low decibel level.

LOCATION
Northern Clermont County, Wayne Township.

SIZE & DESIGNATION
Land: 1,058 acres; water: 200 acres.

ACCESS
Exit I-275 at Milford and head east on SR 131, then go left (northeasterly) on SR 727 to the park. The beach and family campground are found on Lake Drive, branching from SR 727 on the south shore. Stay on SR 727 to reach the boat ramps on the north shore.

Accommodations: Stonelick's shady, uncrowded campground on the south shore has 115 sites

Making Concessions

Total collections (1996) from

state park concessions (bike

rentals, T-shirts, camp stores,

etc.) and fees : $22 million,

41 percent of division's budget.

with electricity. Amenities include a showerhouse, laundry, flush toilets, dump station, pet sites, and an amphitheater for nature programs. Fifteen lakeside sites are perfect for campers with canoes. Just slide the boat into Stonelick Lake whenever. Stonelick was the first park to offer Rent-A-Camp sites, and four of these are available.

A primitive group camp (latrines only) on the north shore can handle 200 campers. Reservations are required.

Picnic Areas: Picnic areas are clustered along the lakeshore. Tables are abundant on the south shore, off Lake Drive. All areas offer lake views, most have shade.

Trails: Seven miles of marked trails await hikers on the south shore. All track across relatively flat terrain, and visit woods, prairie-like meadows, creeks, and lakeshores. Four trails converge on Lake Drive (before the campground), but parking is lacking. Take the Red Fox Trail, two miles, or Southwoods Trail, less than a mile, from the camp check-in station. The latter leads to the 1.5-mile Beechtree Trail.

Swimming: A swimming beach on the south shore, separated from the campground, measures 500 feet, but the sand band is narrow. A lifeguard patrols the place on busy summer weekends. Changing booths and picnic tables are available, but shade is scarce.

Boating: Stonelick Lake is great for small sailboats, canoes, and tiny craft propelled by electric motors (power limit). Canoers can launch from selected lakeshore sites in the campground. Others must use the ramps on the north shore off SR 727. One is located on the west end near the intersection with Newtonville Road, the other close to Edenton on the east side.

Hunting: Designated areas only. Don't expect much.

Fishing: The former state-record spotted bass was landed at Stonelick Lake. The stumpy, weedy, shallows still conceal whoppers, they say. Crappies and bluegills are taken from shore locations. Catfish roam here, too. Stonelick is perfect for beginners and kids. ODNR is improving the habitat with regular plantings of shore forage.

Information: Stonelick State Park, 2895 Lake Drive, Pleasant Plain, OH 45162, (513) 625-7544.

HISTORY

A landmark noting the first white settlement in Wayne Township is located near the group camp on the north shore. A Civil War era cemetery, also on the north shore, remembers the William Sloan family. Frontiersman Simon Kenton and Shawandan War Chief Tecumseh supposedly fought against each other in a battle along Grassy Fork, east of the park, in 1792.

The state started buying land here in the late 1940s, originally for a public hunting and fishing area. A dam creating Stonelick Lake was finished in 1950. The Division of Parks and Recreation eventually acquired the site and turned it into a state park.

FIELD NOTES

Traces of gold—the real thing—have turned up in Stonelick Creek, but finds are rare. Still, Stonelick Creek below the dam is good for creeking, though officially discouraged.

Prairie flora grows along some of the hiking trails in July and August. The calm, uncrowded water gives waterborne birders peeks at migratory waterfowl. Songbirds arrive in spring, depart in autumn. Catch their flight as they form flocks.

Sycamore

This beacon for trail users—hikers, horse riders, bicyclists, skiers, and snowmobilers—will improve with age. The park straddles Wolf Creek, which gets my vote for an alternative park name.

LOCATION

Montgomery County, Madison and Perry townships.

SIZE & DESIGNATION

Land: 2,368 acres; water: five acres.

ACCESS

From Dayton, head west on US 35 and exit north on Diamond Mill Road which bisects the park and leads to the park office.

Accommodations: Two camping areas cater to organized groups. Camp A offers primitive sleeping shelters, rest rooms and a large activities barn with electric and wheelchair accessibility. Camp B, reserved for tent campers, has electric service, picnic tables and fire rings. Both camps are located off Snyder Road on the east side of the park.

Picnic Areas: The Overlook Picnic Area off Providence Road has tables scattered around ponds and a large enclosed pavilion that can be reserved or claimed by the first arrival. The shelter has two big fireplaces (you supply the wood) enabling it to stay open year-round.

Trails: Sycamore has trails for hikers and three kinds of riders. Most foot travelers stick to eight miles of interconnecting loop trails that journey along wooded Wolf Creek. Carefully follow the trail map on the park brochure, available at the park office. The staging area for hikers is on Wolf Creek Pike, west of Snyder Road. From here, head west on the south leg of the Ghost Hedge Nature Trail. The path crosses Seybold Road and continues west. At Nolan Road, go to the north side of Wolf Creek. Here you can return to the trailhead via the north leg of the Ghost Hedge Trail (eastbound to complete a 4.5-mile walk), or trudge west on the double-loop Beech Ridge Trail, which circles a pond in the Overlook Picnic Area and returns to Nolan Road. The latter route is an eight-mile adventure. You can also begin the hike at the picnic area.

Horseback riders can also depart from the staging area on Wolf Creek Pike. Consult the trail map at intersections because the bridle paths cross the hiking trails at several locations. Horsemen can also ride on the snowmobile trail in the northwest corner of the park. Note the side trail on the map joining trail systems on both sides of Diamond Mill Road. The Ohio Horse Council keeps the trail fit.

The Overlook Picnic Area has a staging area for the snowmobile track, a twisting, eight-mile course framed by Providence, Diamond Mill, Airhill, Heckathorn roads, and Wolf Creek Pike. There's a small gravel parking area on the northside of Providence Road not shown on the park map. Horsemen and hikers should stay off the snowmobile path when vehicles are using it. Dirt bikes and four-wheel drive vehicles cannot use this trail.

The Wolf Creek Bikeway touches the northern border of the park. This bike and hike trail follows an abandoned rail bed for 13 miles between Trotwood and Verona. It crosses Snyder Road by the entrance to the group campground, and Diamond Mill Road, north of the park office.

Boating: Canoes and rowboats can float on three small ponds in the Overlook Picnic Area. No ramps.

Hunting: The western two-thirds of the park is open for hunting, roughly 1,500 acres. The terrain is flat with reverting farmland and woods—good habitat for deer, rabbits, and squirrels.

Fishing: The ponds in the picnic area are perfect for beginners casting for largemouth bass, bluegill, and catfish. Wolf Creek yields largemouths reluctantly.

Information: Sycamore State Park, 4675 N. Diamond Hill Road, Trotwood, OH 45426, (937) 854-4452.

HISTORY
This land became a state park when a developer's bubble burst. Purchased in the 1970s for a housing tract, the underfunded project fizzled before bulldozers arrived and the state picked it up for a sweet price. Sycamore became a state park in 1979. The park derives its name from the tall sycamore trees lining Wolf Creek. A family campground is planned for the future.

FIELD NOTES
It's nearly impossible to sneak up within 10 yards of a pileated woodpecker while he's working his jack hammer. Sycamore State Park yielded that rare moment for me. The bird was busying pecking on the backside of a fallen sycamore along the Ghost Hedge Trail. I could only see the top of his bobbing head, and chips flying. This went on for a couple of minutes. Behind me a female jogger approached. I signaled her to stop and be silent, but she shrugged and kept pace. At the tree the startled bird squawked and flushed; the jogger shrieked and jumped off the trail. I gave her my "I told you so" expression. She gave me her "buzz off" face. Each of us went our separate way.

Best Features

Special State Park Attractions

• *Longest fishing platform—Cleveland Lakefront*

• *Star gazing observatories—John Bryan, Portage Lakes*

• *On Underground Railroad route—Alum Creek, Caesar Creek*

• *Best fossil finds—Caesar Creek, Kelleys Island, Hueston Woods*

CENTRAL

Alum Creek

The southern half of this claw-shaped park gets most of the attention, and most of the five million people who come here annually. Alum Creek Reservoir's 3,000-foot beach, Ohio's longest inland beach (and one of its busiest), attracts thousands of bathers on a hot summer weekend. Heading north, human clamor tapers off. Shady coves, calm water, good fishing, long hiking and bridle trails, and rocky cliffs provide softer and quieter outdoor experiences.

LOCATION
    Delaware County, Orange, Berlin, Brown townships.

SIZE & DESIGNATION
    Land: 5,213 acres; water: 3,387 acres. The U.S. Army Corps of Engineers owns the land and leases it to the Ohio Department of Natural Resources.

ACCESS
    Traveling north from Columbus on US 23 turn east (right) on Lewis Center Road for about two miles. Go north (left) on Lackey–Old State Road to the park office, marina, and campground. Continue straight to the Corps of Engineers Visitors Center, multi-purpose trail and mountain bike trail. Take US 36 & SR 37 west from I-71 to reach the horsemen's camp and hiking trails on the north side of the park.

Accommodations: Campers have their choice of 297 sites (all electric) on the west shore of Alum Creek Lake. Enter the campground from Lackey–Old State Road (CR 10) south of Cheshire Road. Water showers, latrines, waste station, water, playground and horsehoe pits are available. The park's five Rent-A-Camp sites and unique Rent-A-RV (recreation vehicle) should be reserved far in advance. Swimmers can splash at the small campground beach instead of driving three miles to the large public beach. A primitive campground (latrine and water) for equestrians (permit required) is located at the north end off Howard Road.

Picnic Areas: Picnic areas are found at the marina, public beach, New Galena boat ramp (east shore off Africa Road), Cheshire Road boat ramp, and near the dam. The Corps of Engineers offers two shelterhouses at its recreation area below the dam.

Trails: Horseback riders and long-distance trekkers head for the three lakeshore bridle trails in the peaceful northern half of the lake. Combined, these trails total 27 miles.

    The wooded paths on the east shore are among the best in Central Ohio. Park near the entrance of the Howard Road boat launch, located on the east shore. Walk east on Howard Road until you find trailheads on each side of the road (just a few paces beyond the guardrails). The forested northbound trail on the left is the Winterhawk Trail, the longest path in the park (figure fifteen miles). Take it north to SR 521, cross the bridge, and return along the west shore, this segment mostly crossing fields and shrub land. It also is accessible from parking lots on Hogback Road and SR 521. On this journey, Winterhawk Trail ends at the horsemen's day use camp on Howard Road. Walk eastbound across the bridge to the starting point.

    Hunter's Hollow Trail goes south from Howard Road. It crosses ravines, winds around inlets, and finishes with two loops that visit shale cliffs that overlook the lake. Maple Glen Trail departs from the horsemen's camp, travels south across open areas, hooks around the lower claw, and stops shy of Cheshire Road and the campground. You can hop this trail at a parking area on US 36/SR 37. Equestrians should start their adventures at the designated location on Howard Road, where they will find water and latrines. These trails wander through areas open to hunting, so be careful during hunting season. Wear some bright orange clothing to be safe.

    Campers who prefer a short hike should try the Deer Run Trail, a one-mile loop branching from the northernmost campground road (M Road). An interpretive guide is available at the park office. Four brief trails—Pine Loop, Pond Loop, Field Loop, and Lake View trails—twist around the park office. Each is less than a mile. Get a trail map at the park office before departing.

    The park's popular mountain bike trails test

novice and advanced riders. Trailhead parking is found on Lewis Center Road, at the southeast corner of the park between Africa Road and I-71. Only experts should peddle on the hilly, forested North Trail. Beginners stick to the open, flat South Trail (two miles). Two connecting trails challenge intermediate bikers. Foot travelers are not allowed on these paths. The trails remain open year-round.

Hikers, skiers, joggers, snowmobilers can use the Multi-Purpose Trail at the New Galena boat ramp (off Africa Road). This trail also goes through hunting areas.

Swimming: Alum Creek's 3,000-foot beach is the longest inland beach in the park system. Just 20 miles from Columbus, it gets downright crowded here on summer weekends. The beachhouse has changing rooms and a concession stand. Boaters can swim in designated areas near the US 36/SR 37 bridge. Small beaches at the campground are reserved for campers.

Boating: Speed demons, power boats, water skiers, and jet skiers own the southern half of the lake, where unlimited horsepower motors make wake (10 mph at night). The marina on the west shore (off Lewis Center Road) has a boat ramp, boat rental, fuel and supplies, dock rental, and rest rooms. Launches and latrines are also

Best Bets

Pick of the Parks

Lake Hope — Kids love this beach. Excellent trails in nearby state forest, charming horseshoe-shaped lake, quiet location, plenty of wildlife, beaver colonies, park restaurant bails out wet campfires, so-so camping.

Shawnee — Hilly terrain is otherworldly. Backpacking trail through wilderness area gets A+ for solitude and challenge. If Ohio has an outback, this is it.

Headlands Beach — Best Lake Erie beach in the state. Surrounding nature preserves are a bonus.

John Bryan/Little Miami — Top-notch, four-season scenic trails in the gorge of the Little Miami River. Good staging area to explore adjacent natural areas. The bike trail along the river in latter is always memorable, even on rainy days.

Beaver Creek — Park is rich in natural wonders, historical sites, and haunting spirits. Canoeing is rewarding on the national scenic river.

Burr Oak — This resort park maintains its casual, understated, backwoods ambience. Lakeshore camp sites for boaters are unique.

Excellent hiking trails. Surrounding Wayne National Forest and wildlife areas are extras.

Mohican — Combined with state forest, Clearfork Gorge, Malabar Farm State Park, Pleasant Hill Lake, it is an ideal destination for exploring Mohican Country. Canoeing and biking add to the adventure.

Pike Lake — Think of it as a "best kept secret," or a coin found under the chair cushion. Charming, shady, forest, quaint lake, nice people, rustic locale. Nature preserves, canoeing nearby.

Alum Creek — The crooked and secluded inlets along the northern half of the lake remain irresistible and enchanting to slow boaters. The interconnected bridle-hiking trails around the northern lakeshore are the longest and best foot paths in Central Ohio.

Maumee Bay — Ignore the fancy lodge if you can, and hone in on the natural setting. Go from this departing point to explore wildlife refuges to the east.

—SO

Where Life's A Beach

Longest natural beach —

Headlands Beach, one mile

Most crowded beach —

Cleveland Lakefront

Longest inland beach — Alum

Creek, 3,000 feet

Best small beaches for

youngsters — Pike Lake; Lake

Hope

Swimming beaches in park

system — 76

Park with longest boardwalk

— Maumee Bay

located at the New Galena ramp (off Africa Road near the Multi-Purpose Trail), and at the Cheshire ramp (off Africa Road, north of Cheshire Road).

Slower paced boaters (sailboats, canoes, rowboats, trollers, etc.) favor the more scenic northern half of the reservoir with its quiet coves and ledges. To avoid the pandemonium in the open zone, slow trollers launch from the east shore off Howard Road. Campers with small boats can put in at the campground.

The popular marina offers boat docks on a lottery basis. Boaters apply for slips in August, and learn the results in September. Contact the park office for details.

During the summer, the lake is 65 feet deep at the dam. The level is lowered three feet in the winter to later capture spring runoff.

Hunting: Sportsmen can pursue rabbits, deer, waterfowl, grouse, and pheasants in designated areas. Trapping also is permitted. Hunters and trappers should pick up a map showing the designated areas at the park office. Use caution because equestrians and hikers could be traveling on trails during hunting season. Hunters and trappers should stop at the park office for a map showing areas designated for their sport.

Fishing: Cast for bass, bluegill, channel catfish, crappie, and walleye in the reservoir's many quiet, shady coves. Angling for saugeye, introduced in 1988, is good in the tailwater below the dam. Recently, 3,000 tiger muskie were released for new fishing challenges. The Division of Wildlife's fishing map of the lake will be helpful.

Special Places & Events: The Fantasy of Lights brightens Alum Creek's campground in December. Local sponsors illuminate the grounds for an evening, drive-thru Christmas light show. The admission charge benefits charities.

During the summer, the park naturalist leads nature programs at the campground amphitheater. Also, stop at the Corps of Engineers' visitor center on Lewis Center Road for exhibits and programs.

Information: Alum Creek State Park, 3615 South Old State Road, Delaware, OH 43015, (740) 548-4631.

U.S. Army Corps of Engineers, 5905 Lewis Center Road, Lewis Center, OH 43035, (740) 548-6151.

HISTORY

Settlers fearful of an avenging Indian horde "as thick as blackbirds" built Fort Cheshire in 1812. It was one of four, two-story log fortresses erected in Delaware County during the War of 1812. The Indian attack never materialized, so Fort Cheshire served as a schoolhouse until the Civil War. Look for the commemorative plaque in the campground.

Mound building natives of the Adena culture built seven mounds along Alum Creek. Archeologists excavated six sites before all were flooded by the Corps of Engineers' impoundment "mound" in 1974. The residents in a pioneer cemetery, however, were

relocated to a nearby cemetery.

In the 1700s Lenni Lenape (Delaware) people resettled here after the Iroquois forced them from Pennsylvania's Delaware River valley. Their occupation was brief, however. Colonel Moses Byxbe, a Revolutionary War veteran, built a home along Alum Creek in 1805, and one time owned some 38,000 acres in the county.

Before the Civil War, fugitive slaves traveling on the Underground Railroad left the Hanby House, a safehouse in nearby Westerville, and followed Alum Creek northward to freedom in Canada. Africa Road on the east shore recalls the settlement 30 freed slaves from North Carolina established there in 1854. A proslavery neighbor, Leo Hurlburt, called the village Africa, and the name stuck.

Alum Creek dam forms part of the Ohio River Basin flood control system, administered by the Corps of Engineers. Construction lasted from 1970 to 1974. The earthen impoundment is 93 feet tall and 10,200 feet in length. Besides controlling floods in the Scioto River watershed, Alum Creek Reservoir is a water supply for Columbus.

FIELD NOTES

The cliffs of Ohio shale that line the banks of Alum Creek were formed hundreds of millions of years ago. Its dark color is due to decayed plant life that mixed with clay.

The park has diverse habitats of woodlands, shrubs, and meadows. The second-growth beech-maple supports wildflowers like trillium, wild geranium, bloodroot, and spring beauty. Look for deer, woodchuck, fox squirrel, and rabbit.

Birders should look for the Henslow's, grasshopper and savanna sparrows, dickcissel, horned lark, eastern meadowlark, and bobolink in recovering meadows, shorebirds at the beach, waterfowl in the northern shallows.

A.W. Marion

A. W. Marion, the park's namesake, was a Pickaway County soul and the first director of the Ohio Department of Natural Resources. The place could easily have been called Devil's Backbone State Park, after the ridges that run across the landscape. The "backbone," a prominent terminal moraine, marks the edge of the Wisconsinan glacier, here 12,000 years ago.

LOCATION

Eastern Pickaway County, Washington Township.

Once upon a time, manmade Buckeye Lake was as lovely as it is still beloved.

SIZE & DESIGNATION
Land: 307 acres; water: 145 acres.

ACCESS
From Circleville take US 22 east a few miles, north (left) on East Ringgold-Southern Road (TR 42), west (left) on Warner-Huffer Road (TR 77) to the campground and east side of Hargus Lake. Boaters and anglers head for the west side of the lake via US 22 east, north (left) on Bolender-Pontius Road (TR 66), east (right) on Warner-Huffer Road (TR 77). Turn left at the intersection to reach the boat ramp and boat rental; turn right for picnic tables.

Accommodations: The woodland campground offers 60 sites (no electric hookups) year-round. Latrines, playground, and drinking water are available. Pets are welcome. Call the park for group camping reservations. A privately-owned campground near the boat ramp (west shore) has 300 sites with electricity and other amenities.

Picnic Areas: The best picnic tables and grills overlook the lake on the west shore. Look for the table on a small island. Use a boat to get there.

Swimming: Sorry, no beach. Boaters, however, can take a dip in a designated area (look for buoys) in the southeastern corner of the lake.

Trails: The five-mile Hargus Lake Trail, your typical follow-the-lakeshore path, passes through woodlands, creeks, and ravines. It is exerting in spots, but not especially strenuous overall. The trail starts in the campground, and goes to the boat docks, and A.W. Marion Memorial. The .75-mile Squawroot Nature Trail begins and ends at the campground.

Boating: Boats must be powered by humans or electric motors. Public docks, ramp, and boat rentals (some with motors) are available on the west shore. Some camping gear, food, beverages can be purchased at the concession, open April through September.

Warning: zebra mussels infest Hargus Lake. The prolific pests probably came here via a boat. Boaters should remove the small shellfish from their craft before leaving the lake. Don't spread the plague to another lake.

Hunting: The park permits hunting in mid-October. Deer, squirrels, rabbit, pheasant, and waterfowl are the main targets.

Fishing: Hargus Lake's main channel reaches a depth of 50 feet. Drained and improved in 1956 and 1986, Hargus Lake keeps bluegill, muskies, largemouth bass, and catfish happy.

Information: A.W. Marion State Park, 7317 Warner-Huffer Road, Circleville, Ohio 43113, (740) 474-3386.

HISTORY
Construction of the dam across Hargus Creek began in 1948. In 1950, the newly formed Division of Parks and Recreation took over the site, then known as Hargus Creek Lake State Park. The park was renamed the A.W. Marion State Park in 1962.

Buckeye Lake

Traffic on Interstate 70 sometimes slows to a crawl 30 miles east of Columbus because straining cars and pickups pulling heavy boats are easing on and off the highway. They all are heading for or leaving Buckeye Lake, a water playground for more than a century. Water sports and fishing are pursued with vigor here, even in winter.

LOCATION

Northeastern Fairfield County, Walnut Township; Licking County, Bowling Green, Union and Licking townships; Perry County, Thorn Township.

SIZE & DESIGNATION

Land: 175 acres; water: 3,382 acres.

ACCESS

Buckeye Lake is boxed by I-70, and state routes 13, 37 and 204. At the Buckeye Lake exit on I-70, go south on SR 79 to the boat launch in the village. To reach the park office in Millersport from I-70, go south on SR 37 (west of SR 79), east (left) on Hebron Road, south (right) on Millersport Road, left on Liebs Island Road.

Picnic Areas: Look for tables, grills and shelters at Picnic Point in the Village of Buckeye Lake (north shore), on Liebs Island near the park office (west shore), Brooks Park Area off South Bank Road (southwest shore), and in a settlement called Fairfield Beach, south shore. Shelters go to the first arrival.

Swimming: Two public swimming beaches are open from Memorial Day to Labor Day. A 100-foot beach is available on the south shore at Fairfield Beach. The west side is served by the park's Brook Park Area on South Bank Road. Both beaches are small and lightly used. Boaters can take dips at buoyed locations at both ends of the lake.

Boating: Someone estimated that 3,000 boats bob on Buckeye Lake's shore, and on nice summer weekends all of them seem to be on the lake. The lake measures seven miles in length, and a mile or more in width, so there's usually room enough for everybody. Two large open zones allow powerboats (unlimited horsepower), jet boats, and water skiing. The middle section of the lake, south of the Village of Buckeye Lake, is a no wake zone to protect Cranberry Bog, a National Natural Landmark. No wake areas exist 300 feet from land and at each end of the reservoir. Speed is reduced to 10 mph between sunset and dawn.

The Buckeye Lake Yacht Club, a hang-out for the sailing clan, brags that it is the largest club on an inland lake in the U.S. The boast stands until another club bothers to challenge. Sailing is best on weekdays, and early Saturday morning before the motorboats arrive.

Pontoon boaters often spend the day creeping along shore and visiting friends and the lakeshore villages of Millersport, Fairfield Beach, Thornport, Avondale Park, Harbor Hills, Buckeye Lake, and Roby Beach.

Liebs Island at the west end has a pair of two-lane ramps designed for the big boys. That's true for the modern two-ramp launch at North Shore in Buckeye Lake (end of SR 79). Older and smaller ramps in Fairfield Beach and in Brooks Park Area are more appropriate for small boats. The state park rents 40 seasonal dock slips. Commercial marinas have boat rentals, supplies, and docks.

One in three winters is cold enough to permit ice boating. These hardy sailors can use the same facilities as summer pilots.

Hunting: Duck hunting is allowed from boats or blinds assigned by the Division of Wildlife.

Fishing: For more than a century boatloads of fish and anglers have been brought to Buckeye Lake. In 1891 a state-owned railroad car called the "Buckeye Fish Car" transported crappie and bass from Lake Erie to Buckeye Lake. Leftovers from the nearby Hebron Fish Hatchery also get dumped into Buckeye Lake. These days, there's a fishing tournament here every week from March to July, including several for the pros.

The average depth of the lake is 4.5 feet. Even so, large muskies exist (try the deep pools) complementing catches of yellow perch, bluegill, crappie, channel cats, bullhead, and largemouth bass. Wheelchair fishers can cast from a pier near the north shore ramp. Ice fishing, when conditions permit, is best on the east side.

Special Places & Events: The island south of the Village of Buckeye Lake is actually a floating mat of sphagnum moss called Cranberry Bog. The unique location is a National Natural Landmark and a state natural landmark. When the water level rose after impoundment in 1830, the acreage you see detached from an existing bog and became a floating island. The lake's midsection is a no wake zone to protect the sanctuary. In spite of this, the island shrinks a little each year. The place is off limits to the public, except for an open house one weekend in June. Registrants are ferried to the island to see blooming orchids and other bog rarities, including cranberry. Call the Ohio Division of Natural Area and Preserves at (614) 265-6453 to sign up for the tour.

Information: Buckeye Lake State Park, Box 488, Millersport, OH 43046, (740) 467-2690.

HISTORY

In 1751, explorer Christopher Gist camped at the edge of a bog he dubbed Buffalo Lick and the Great Swamp. Seventy-five years later construction workers began building dikes, thus turning this inhospitable swamp into a reservoir that would supply the Ohio & Erie Canal with water. They finished the Licking Summit Reservoir, the lake's original name, in 1830. Additional dikes enlarged the lake. Canal boats plied across the western edge of the canal. A bike path called the Ohio Canal Greenway runs along the canal's towpath from Hebron to Buckeye Lake (follow SR 360).

The canal declined after the Civil War. In 1894, the Ohio Legislature turned feeder reservoirs into public parks. At that time, Licking Summit Reservoir was dropped for Buckeye Lake. By 1900, cottages and amusements cluttered the lakeshore. Buckeye Lake Amusement Park, located in the north shore area in Buckeye Lake, was a popular destination in the 1940s and 1950s, especially for big band stars. The lake became one of the original state parks when the Ohio Department of Natural Resources was created in 1949.

FIELD NOTES

Buckeye Lake grew from a swamp that once was a lake. About 12,000 years ago icebergs broke off the face of the retreating Wisconsinan glacier and melted into depressions. These lakes and pond were called kettleholes. Vegetation and sediment reduced the lakes to swamps. The Great Swamp described by Christopher Gist had been a kettlehole. If natural processes took over again, Buckeye Lake would likely revert back to a swamp.

Birders should look for the large heron rookeries on adjacent land. The birds visit the shallows frequently.

Deer Creek

Flat, unforested farmland is not the best locale for a resort. Puny, implanted trees and shrubs line a well-groomed golf course that features soft, catcher's mitt greens. Hiking trails are short, unconnected, and uninteresting, especially when the meadow plants die and lay down in fall and winter. It's a good enough place to exercise your legs and pony, but not your eyes and mind.

LOCATION

Southwestern Pickaway County, Perry Township; Northeastern Fayette County, Madison Township.

SIZE & DESIGNATION

Land: 3,617 acres; water: 1,277 acres. The adjoining state wildlife area comprises 3,710 acres. The U.S. Army Corps of Engineers owns the land and leases it to the Ohio Department of Natural Resources.

ACCESS

From US 22 and US 62/SR 3 take SR 207 to Dawson-Yankeetown Road, then go easterly to the park entrance. Follow park signs to the campground, golf course, lodge, cabins and horsemen's camp. The

park marina is off SR 207, south of Pancoastburg. The beach is located on Crownover Mill Road, off SR 207. The U.S. Army Corps of Engineers has a visitor's center on Deer Creek Road.

Accommodations: Deer Creek's showcase lodge taps the sun's rays to boost its central heating system. It boasts 110 rooms (half with a lake view), indoor and outdoor pools, whirlpool, sauna, exercise room, restaurant (ask for a lakeside table), lounge, game room, TV lounge, gift shop, attractive and spacious sitting area with fireplace, putting green, tennis courts, volleyball court, basketball, and courtesy docks. Six meeting rooms can handle conferences. The largest accommodates 600 humans. Twenty-five two-bedroom deluxe cabins are located within easy walking distance of the lodge. The "sort of" historic Harding Cabin, several miles from the lodge, sleeps 7-9 people. This unique facility is rented by a lottery. Call the park office for details. Harding Cabin was not a presidential retreat. It was actually owned by the former president's attorney general Harry M. Daugherty. The nation's top lawman built the place here in 1918. President Warren G. Harding "was said to have visited this cabin," but no one claims that he ever snoozed there. Harding's name was put on the cabin to pump up its historic importance, as well as park revenues.

The plush campground offers heavily shaded, lightly shaded and open sites. All 232 spaces have electricity and take RVs 35 feet long. Facilities include four showerhouses, flush toilets, two playgrounds, pet sites, bike rental, camp store, dump station, amphitheater, latrines, hiking trails, five Rent-A-Camp locations, and volunteers to offer assistance. A group camp for 60 (reservable) and horse riders' camp with three sites (water and latrine) are available elsewhere.

Picnic Areas: A large picnic area with latrines is located along the park road west of the beach. Other tables are located below the dam (Deer Creek and Williamsport-Crownover Mill roads), marina (off SR 207), and on a park road off SR 207, south of Pancoastburg.

Trails: Four hiking trails provide exercise. The relatively new three-mile Rolling Hills Trails departs from the north side of the lodge parking lot and goes to the campground (site 224). Hawkview Meadow Trail is a mile interpretive loop near the camp check-in station. Ridge Trail is a mile loop by the cabin with a wildlife observation blind. Lodgers at Harding Cabin take the Ghost Tree Swamp Trail, one mile, to visit naked trees killed by floodwater.

Horseback riders and snowmobilers (if and when it snows) share a double-loop, fourteen mile track that wraps around the lodge, campground and Harding Cabin. The staging area is near the campground check-in station where the loops meet. Riders can also start at the horseman's camp.

The park's new mountain bike trail, just 1.2 miles for novices, begins at the end of the park going west at the beach.

Swimming: Deer Creek's broad sandy beach of 1,700 feet draws big crowds in summer. There's open space for play, a concession selling snacks and beverages, changing booths, and lifeguards. Boaters may swim in a cove jutting north at the lodge.

Boating: Unlimited horsepower on the lake brings power boats, jet skis, and water skiers to Deer Creek Lake. Most of these activities occur in the southern part of the lake, from the dam to the marina. A modern, full service marina has ramps, fishing supplies, food, docks, and a menu of rental boats (canoes, boats with 25 hp motors, pontoons, pedalboats, johnboats, etc.) A large boat launch with ample parking is located by the Harding Cabin, Road D-1 off McCafferty-Crownover Mill Road.

Golf: Deer Creek's 18-holer is the longest in the park system—7,134 yards, par 72. And it's well-bunkered with 52 traps and 10 ponds. It's nicely manicured, but topographically-challenged. Fairway trees eventually will grow, but will they ever separate the golf course from the overgrown meadows beyond the rough? Weekend golfers must have tee times (call in advance), and tee times are recommended other days. The pro shop (740)-869-3088] has golf accessories, club rentals, and a snack bar.

Hunting: Deer, rabbit, grouse, quail, and pheasant can be hunted in designated areas of the park. Woodchucks are abundant on this old farmland. Hunters usually have better luck at Deer Creek State Wildlife Area. The Division of Wildlife hunting map for the site shows the public hunting areas. Trappers have success with fox and raccoon. Gunners can sight-in and practice at a shooting range (fee) on Yankeetown Road (CR 17).

Fishing: Deer Creek is a top-rated fishery for saugeye, which have been heavily stocked since 1978. The Corps of Engineers' tailwater fishing area (wheelchair access) below the dam is a late-winter hot spot for this fish. They also swim in the stream above the lake. Crappie, bluegill, largemouth, smallmouth, rock and white bass, carp, bullhead and flathead catfish are also landed. Use bright lures in this lake's turgid water.

Special Places & Events: The U.S. Corps of Engineers headquarters on Deer Creek Road has information on the operation of the flood control dam and an overlook. It's okay to walk on top of the dam.

Information: Deer Creek State Park, 20635 Waterloo Road, Mt. Sterling, OH 43143, (740) 869-3124 park office, (740) 869-3508 campground, (740) 869-3088 golf course, (740) 869-3728.

Deer Creek Resort Lodge, 22300 State Park Road #20, Mt. Sterling, OH 43143, (740) 869-2020, 1-800-282-7275 lodge and cabin reservations.

U.S. Army Corps of Engineers, 21897 Deer Creek Road, Mt. Sterling, OH 43143-9505, (740) 869-2243.

HISTORY

The park's cabins perch atop Tick Ridge, but 4,000 years ago nomadic native people camped here while they hunted and gathered in the valley. Burial sites by the camp suggest it was regularly visited or served as an outpost for a lengthy period.

Congress gave the okay to dam Deer Creek in 1938 but it took 30 years to finish it. The state park opened in 1974; the lodge in 1982.

FIELD NOTES

Note the fields and meadow flowers like teasel, thimbleweed, goldenrod, daisy fleabane, jewelweed, and chicory, whose dried roots can be ground to make a coffee-like drink.

Like a snake shedding skin, Deer Creek changes its appearance in late September. The U.S. Army Corps of Engineers drains the lake 15 feet leaving a muddy bath tub ring on the shore. Powerboaters and water skiers flee to land, swimmers disappear, and Deer Creek starts to hibernate, like an amusement park after Labor Day. Hunters and anglers arrive, but they are a quiet lot who prospect for a game dinner in secret places.

Delaware

Thickening woodlands, expansive prairie-like meadows, productive shrubland, and developing wetlands are making Delaware State Park a natural wonder and recreation destination. The setting indulges the speed boat and water skiing crowd, and those seeking a quiet cove filled with naive fish.

LOCATION

Northern Delaware County, Troy and Marlboro townships.

SIZE & DESIGNATION

Land: 1,815 acres; water: 1,330 acres. The wildlife area totals 4,670 acres. The U.S Army Corps of Engineers owns the land occupied by the state park and state wildlife area, and leases it to the Ohio Department of Natural Resources.

ACCESS

The park entrance is on US 23, about six miles north of Delaware. Follow park signs to your recreation destination. The state park is on the west shore of Delaware Reservoir, while the Delaware State Wildlife Area takes up the eastern shore and the northern point of the west shore.

Accommodations: The campground on Park

An umbrella for two is ready at Indian Lake.

Road 27 features 214 campsites (164 with electricity) in four loops. Loop A lacks hookups. Amenities include showerhouses with toilets, dump station, nature center, vending machines, bike rental, youth camp (50 capacity), and trails. Three Rent-A-Camp sites can be reserved.

Picnic Areas: Six picnic areas fill up fast on summer weekends. The five lakeshore areas—Buckeye Grove, Walnut Grove, Cardinal Grove, Elmwood Grove—are the most popular. Buckeye Grove has a shelterhouse. The Corps of Engineers has a nice picnic area (off US 23) near its headquarters at the southern tip of the reservoir.

Trails: Five trails totaling 7.5 miles depart from the campground. The park guide shows their routes. No bridle trails have been blazed. ODNR should consider a long lakeshore path through the park and wildlife area for hikers and riders.

Swimming: The 800-foot beach is at the south end of the park, at the end of Park Road 28. Facilities include a bathhouse, showers, and snack bar. Boaters can swim in a west shore cove across from the beach, and beside campground Loop C in the no wake zone.

Boating: The southern two-thirds of the reservoir is a speed zone for power boaters and water skiers (unlimited horsepower). North of campground Loop B and the youth group camp the lake is a no wake zone.

Delaware's full-service marina has fuel, food, fishing and boating supplies, rest rooms, seasonal docks (275 slips in the park), and rental of pontoons, wave runners, fishing boats (with and without engines), canoes, and pedalboats. Launches and docks are also located at the Cardinal Grove and Elmwood Grove picnic areas (Park Road 22), and on the east shore at the end of Park Road 6, off Horsehoe Road.

Experienced canoers and kayakers ride swollen Olentangy River when the Corps of Engineers opens the floodgates in autumn to draw down the lake for winter. Novices should not try this stunt.

Delaware Reservoir has numerous coves and pockets to explore, especially the northern section which forks above the campground. The left branch continues north to the Olentangy River, while the right fork goes to Whetstone Creek.

Hunting: Hunting is not allowed on state park land, stretching from the north loop of the campground to the Corps of Engineers headquarters on the west shore. There's 4,670 acres of public hunting land on the eastern shore and northern reaches. A wetland on the south shore offers waterfowl hunting. Duck blinds are awarded by lottery. The Division of Wildlife has a public shooting range on SR 229 and an archery range and target trail at the intersection of Cline and Prospect-Mt. Vernon roads.

Fishing: Delaware has become a great saugeye fishery due to repeated stocking since 1989. The tailwater below the dam is productive in late winter. White bass begin migrating into Whetstone Creek and Olentangy River in April. Muskellunge, crappie, largemouth and smallmouth bass, catfish, walleye (stocked since the 1960s), and bluegill are also landed. The Division of Wildlife stocks 55 artificial ponds in the wildlife area, which largely serve as wildlife habitats.

Special Places & Events: The U.S. Army Corps of Engineers office on US 23 has information on the operation of the dam, as well as a small recreation site consisting of picnic tables, shelterhouse, rest rooms, basketball and volleyball.

Information: Delaware State Park, 5202 US 23 North, Delaware, OH 43015, (740) 369-2761 office, (740) 363-4561 campground, (740) 363-6102 marina.

U.S. Army Corps of Engineers, Delaware Lake, 3920 US 23 North, Delaware, OH 43015-9708, (740) 363-4011.

HISTORY

Delaware State Park commemorates its home county, the nearby city, and the native people who once lived here. The Indians called themselves Lenni Lenape, but other tribesmen referred to them phonetically as *Na-Be-Naugh-a*, meaning "people from the east." Indeed, the Lenni Lenape fled to Ohio from the Delaware River Valley and Eastern Pennsylvania to escape Iroquois expansion.

Around 1812, Fort Morrow was built around a brick tavern that overlooked the Olentangy River, near today's lakeshore. Settlers feared British-inspired Indian attacks during the War of 1812-14. A few scares sent settlers to the palisades, but no battles occurred. The fort dissolved after the war. Limestone used for the Ohio Statehouse was quarried nearby.

Another army appeared after World War II, the Army Corps of Engineers. Construction of an earthen levee below the confluence of the Olentangy River and Whetstone Creek was built from 1947 to 1951. Delaware State Park opened that year.

The U.S. Department of Agriculture, Forest Service has a research lab at the south end of the lake, and the Division of Wildlife operates the Olentangy Experiment Station on Horseshoe Road.

FIELD NOTES

Delaware State Park and State Wildlife Area have become premium birdwatching areas, thanks to development of wetland habitats. Watch for migrating waterfowl and rarities such as the bald eagle, osprey, northern goshawk, northern harrier, sandhill crane, king rail, short-eared and long-eared owls, snowy owl, and cattle egret. Soaring hawks and turkey vultures are common. Wild turkeys were introduced in 1994. The state park has a bluebird trail near the camp.

> *Delaware State Park and State Wildlife Area have become* premium birdwatching areas, thanks to development of wetland habitats.

Indian Lake

From humble origins as a glacial teardrop, Indian Lake swelled to become a canal feeder reservoir then a state park for water enthusiasts. Dubbed the "Midwest's Million Dollar Playground," cottages encrusted on the lakeshore and islands attest to Indian Lake's enduring popularity. Fishing and camping add to its recreation opportunities.

LOCATION

Northwestern Logan County, Stokes and Richland townships.

SIZE & DESIGNATION

Land: 648 acres; water: 5,800 acres.

ACCESS

The park is framed by US 33, and state routes 366, 235 and 117. SR 366 and US 33 run along the southern shore through Russells Point and Lakeview. The park office, campgrounds, and Old Field swimming beach branch from SR 235, which breaks from US 33 in Lakeview. Go north and east on SR 235 from Lakeview. Islands called Fox (park land), Orchard and Wolf can be visited on SR 708 from Russells Point. SR 368 branches north from SR 366 and leads to Moundwood Marina and west side islands.

Accommodations: Indian Lake's huge campground, third largest in the park system, offers 443 sites, 370 with electricity. Beyond this, campers have heated showerhouses, flush toilets, laundry, a camp commissary that features games, bait, food, a playground, dump station, two designated pet areas, two Rent-A-Camp spots, two Rent-A-Tepee sites, amphitheater, nature center, and 20 dock slips with electricity for overnight boaters. On summer holidays, the place is booked by Thursday; Friday evenings other weekends.

Picnic Areas: Picnic tables line the South Bank

(along SR 366) and West Bank (beside SR 235). They can also be claimed at the swimming beaches, Pew Island, Moundwood Marina, and scattered places.

Trails: The Cherokee Trail is a cakewalk measuring three miles west of the camping area. Pew Island, accessible via causeway off SR 368, has a mile-long trail encircling the island.

Swimming: Two small beaches pack in people during summer. Old Field Beach is a 900-foot sandy beach off SR 235/366 north of Lakeview. Fox Island Beach, SR 708 north of Russells Point, measures 500-feet but is equally busy. A small beach in the campground is reserved for campers. Boaters can swim in designated areas near Old Field Beach, Hermit Island, and Walnut Island.

Boating: Boating is the reason most people come here. The western half of the lake is an open zone for water skiers and power boaters who want full throttle. There is no horsepower restriction here. Lighted buoys 1–5 (west of the lake islands) mark the open zone. Boaters should consult the latest state park map, which marks the open zone, the location of buoys, speed channels, no wake and no ski zones, islands, shallow areas, and stump areas. Indian Lake is the only inland lake with lighted buoys for night-time navigation.

Public boat ramps are located at Chippewa Marina near the campground, Moundwood Marina, off SR 368, near Old Field Beach, and in Lakeview. Some 510 seasonal dock rentals are available. There are plenty of commercial launches and docks, if public facilities are crowded. Slow boaters can explore 68 islands and shallow, marshy areas.

Hunting: Waterfowl hunting is permitted in certain areas. Find out where at the park office.

Fishing: The best time to fish is in spring and fall, when the lake isn't busy. Bass tournaments seem to be weekly events, sometimes 45 in a year. Largemouths reside around an excellent habitat provided by the lake's 68 islands. White bass school along the south bank in spring.

Millions of saugeye have been stocked since 1988, and this fish represents the main catch. Bluegill, crappie, yellow perch, catfish, and walleye fill daily limits too.

Special Places & Events: A Maple Syrup Festival is held in late February or early March.

Information: Indian Lake State Park, 12774 State Route 235 N., Lakeview, OH 43331, (937) 843-2717 park office, (937) 843-3553 campground.

HISTORY

In 1850 the Ohio Legislature approved money to impound Indian Lake as a feeder reservoir for the Miami & Erie Canal. Construction lasted from 1851 to 1860, most of it done by Irish laborers with picks, shovels, and carts. Ironically, the canal was already in decline when the reservoir was finished.

On April 9, 1898, state lawmakers dedicated Indian Lake a state recreation area. This sparked Indian Lake's rise as a resort. Two railroads brought vacationers to what became known as the "Midwest's Million Dollar Playground." Indian Lake became a state park in 1949 with the creation of the Ohio Department of Natural Resources.

FIELD NOTES

Before its impoundment, Indian Lake was one of a cluster of kettlehole lakes in the area. These formed when the chunks of ice broke from the retreating Wisconsinan glacier about 12,000 years ago. The blocks melted in depressions, creating small lakes and ponds. Indian Lake sits by the divide of two Ohio rivers. Water released at the spillway in Lakeview becomes the Great Miami River. The source of the Scioto River is just a few miles north.

Migrating waterfowl following ancient air routes gather at Indian Lake in spring and autumn, though not as many as a century ago. Herons still have a rookery on some of the islands. Scout for ducks, grebes, swans and egrets. Bald eagles used to nest here.

> *The best time to* **fish is in spring** *and fall, when the lake isn't busy.* **Bass tournaments** *seem to be weekly events, sometimes 45 in a year.*

Madison Lake

Don't drive across the state for this park. Somebody deeded the place to the state after WW II, so it was turned into a mudhole state park in topographically-challenged terrain bereft of forest. Possibly the loneliest park in Ohio.

LOCATION

Madison County, Union Township. The park sits between state routes 665 and 56.

SIZE & DESIGNATION

Land: 80 acres; water: 106 acres.

ACCESS

From SR 665 (east of London) turn right (south) on Spring Valley Road, then left (east) on Cheseldine Road to the park entrance on the east shore. From SR 56, go east on Big Plain-Circleville Road, left (north) on Spring Valley Road, right on Cheseldine Road. To reach pack facilities on the west shore take Wood Lane (CR 307) off Spring Valley Road.

Picnic Areas: Picnic areas are located on each shore of the lake. The shelterhouse in each area is available on a first-come basis.

Trails: A .75-mile loop called the Sugar Maple Trail is the only path in the park. It begins near the shelterhouse on the west shore.

Swimming: Swimming here can be risky, but not because the water is deep or crowded with humans. Sometimes signs are posted at the small 300-foot beach warning of high levels of bacteria in the water due to farm runoff. It also lacks lifeguards. Changing rooms and latrines are available at the beach.

Boating: Madison Lake is perfect for small sailboats, row boats, and canoes (electric motors only). There is a boat ramp and dock south of the beach, and a concessionaire rents boats in the summer.

Hunting: Hunters can pursue ducks and geese at the north end of the lake.

Fishing: Shore and boat fishing for bass (try the shallow north end), bluegill, crappie, channel catfish, and bullhead is pursued here by local regulars.

Information: Madison Lake State Park, c/o Deer Creek State Park, 20635 Waterloo Road, Mt. Sterling, OH 43143-9501, (740) 869-3124.

HISTORY

Park development began in 1946 when a small parcel of the land was deeded to the state. A dam built across Deer Creek in 1947 created the lake. The lake became a state park in 1950.

FIELD NOTES

Beavers have built prominent lodges along the shore. The park supports speckled alder, a slender tree more common in northern climates.

Mount Gilead

This quaint, pint-sized park offers a charming setting for campers, change of pace trails for hikers and pleasant picnicking beside twin ponds.

LOCATION

Northbound travelers on I-71 exit at SR 95 and bear northwest toward Mt. Gilead.

SIZE & DESIGNATION

Land: 140 acres; water: 32 acres.

ACCESS

The park entrance is just a mile from the town. From US 42 in Mt. Gilead, go east on SR 95 to the park.

Accommodations: A little jewel of a campground nestles beneath tall red pines. All 60 sites have electricity. Latrines and a dump station are provided. Four Rent-A-Camp sites are available, and several spots are designated for pet owners. This attractive campground is rarely full. Group camping is available at the west end, by the park office.

Picnic Areas: Two tidy and generous picnic areas overlook the south shore of Mt. Gilead Lakes. The ridgetop area has three shelters, many tables, and latrines. A smaller spot hugs the lakeshore by the boat ramp.

Trails: Central Ohio hikers looking for a refreshing change should try the three loop trails above the north shore. Combining trails (and some overlapping) produces a journey a little shy of six miles. West to east the loops are named Piney Woods (for its conifers), Fern Ridge, and Sam's Creek. The western trail head (to Piney Woods) is by the park office, while the Sam's Creek terminus starts in the campground. Kids love the side trail at the lower picnic area. An interpretive trail guide is ready at the office.

Boating: Small boats propelled by paddles or electric motors are allowed. A boat ramp is provided on the south shore.

Fishing: Mt. Gilead consists of two lakes (ponds) separated by a dam. The higher eastern pond flows into the western pond. There's another dam at the far west side. Cast for panfish and bass. Good place for beginners.

Special Places & Events: Apple Butter Festival is held in early October. Popular monthly events are held by an active staff.

Information: Mt. Gilead State Park, 4119 State Route 95, Mt. Gilead, OH 43338, (419) 946-1961.

HISTORY

The first Mt. Gilead Lake was constructed in 1919 by damming Sam's Creek. The second arrived, below the first, on July 10, 1930. The resulting recreation area was managed by the Ohio Bureau of Engineering until it was turned over to the Ohio Department of Natural Resources in 1949.

FIELD NOTES

Refreshing pine scent lingers in the campground and conifer forest traversed by the Piney Woods path. The park also has a mature stand of second-growth beech. The rolling terrain in the area results from terminal moraines, or ridge deposits, left behind by the Wisconsinan glacier about 12,000 years ago.

NORTHEAST

Beaver Creek

The gorge of Little Beaver Creek, a national and state wild and scenic river, offers a wilderness experience, and challenging canoeing and hiking trails. The park protects several state-imperiled plants and perhaps a black bear or two. And cancel your expensive trip to Vermont for autumn leaves. Come here instead.

LOCATION
Eastern Columbiana County, Middleton and St. Clair townships.

SIZE & DESIGNATION
Land: 3,038 acres; water: four miles of river.

ACCESS
From East Liverpool go north on SR 7. (US 30 west shares the road bed for several miles.) Turn right (east) on Bell School Road, then left (north) on Echo Dell Road. Pick up a map at the park office near Gaston's Mill.

Accommodations: Pine scent spreads through one loop of the 55-site family campground off Leslie Road. All are "rustic" sites, meaning no electricity, no flush toilets, no showers (but there is a dump station). Pets are permitted.

Primitive camping for groups (reservations) and horse riders (100 capacity) is available in separate locations off Sprucevale Road.

Picnic Areas: Three of the park's four picnic areas are located near the mill and pioneer village. Two areas are clustered around the pioneer village on the south bank of the creek; another overlooks the stream on the north side. The spots have tables, grills, vault toilets, play areas. Another picnic ground is found near the primitive group camp off Sprucevale Road.

Trails: Some rate the creek side trails the most scenic in Ohio, especially in autumn. A "must" for foot travelers is the five-mile Vondergreen Trail on the north bank from Echo Dell Road (Pioneer Village is across the creek) to the primitive camp in Sprucevale. You'll pass cliffs, canal locks, and natural wonders. This trail is part of the 21-mile Sandy Beaver Backpacking Trail (Elkton to East Liverpool) maintained by the Boy Scouts. The state park is roughly midway on this journey.

Vondergreen Trail connects with the family campground via the northside picnic area and a spur of the 2.2-mile Dogwood Trail. The latter loop path also traces the creek for a mile. Pine Ridge Trail, just a half mile, leaves from Leslie Road near the campground. The Fisherman's Trail goes downstream from Sprucevale Road, at Hambleton's Mill, to the park border.

Beaver Creek is popular with equestrians because of its 23-mile trail system. Most trails depart from the horseman's camping area. Hoof Beat is the longest trail—16 miles—and most exciting, crossing the creek several times and tracing ridges and tough terrain. Shorter rides are Whispering Pine Trail (seven miles) and Leisure Loop (one mile). Bring your own mount, or saddle up at a private riding stable on Sprucevale Road.

Swimming: Sorry. Though swimming is "officially" prohibited, hikers can cool off by "creeking," and canoers have been known to tie up for a dip in Little Beaver Creek.

Boating: The creek's cool, crystal-clear water awaits canoers. For a three-mile paddle through the gorge, put-in at the Echo Dell Road bridge (near Pioneer Village) and take-out at the Sprucevale Road bridge. Easy, Class I riffles on this stretch. Continue downstream for challenging rapids, such as Class III rapids in Fredericktown. Bring your own canoe, or rent one from a local livery. Canoes, rafts, and sturdy tubes on the stream, please.

Hunting: Designated areas only. Better off going to Highlandtown State Wildlife Area off SR 39.

Fishing: Beefy bass (smallmouth and rock) hide in the creek. Most anglers take creekside hiking trails to favorite spots.

Special Places & Events: Demonstrations of pioneer skills and crafts highlight the annual Pioneer Craft Days at Gaston's Mill in early October.

Information: Beaver Creek State Park, 12021 Echo Dell Road, East Liverpool, OH 43920, (330) 385-3091.

HISTORY
There's plenty. Humans of the so-called Fluted Point Culture arrived 10,000 years ago. Their fluted arrowheads, pottery and flint knives have been uncovered nearby. Wyandots and Mingos resided

here later. Frontier renegade Simon Girty probably hid (or gathered forces) in the gorge.

The relicts of eight locks of the Sandy and Beaver Canal still stand in the park. Lusk Lock (1836), the most ornate (double staircase) and largest along the canal, is definitely worth a stop. It is located on separate park land upstream from Gaston's Mill. Continue north on SR 7, turn left on CR 419 (Middle Beaver Road). Park in the designated area and climb the steps. Lock 36, restored in 1991 for re-enactments, is at the Pioneer Village, and Lock 42 (a.k.a. Hambleton's Lock) lingers at Sprucevale. Moving upstream are Gretchen's Lock (Lock 41), locks 40 and 39, Vondergreen's Lock, and Grey's Lock.

Built from 1828 to 1848, the 73-mile canal had 90 locks and 30 retention dams between Bolivar and Glasgow. The canal closed in 1853 after going bankrupt on lawsuits stemming from a reservoir project. No matter, the railroad was driving it under anyway.

Gaston's Mill, erected in 1837 by Samuel Conkle, reminds us of the creek's importance as a power source. Volunteers from the Columbiana County Forests and Parks Council and the Columbiana County Historical Association now run the mill. Pioneer Village is open 1–5 p.m. on most weekends.

The ruins of Hambleton's Mill crumble in old Sprucevale, once a bustling canal town at the Sprucevale Road bridge. The howls and hoots heard at night here may be the spirits of former residents. Local legends say the ghost of Esther Hale, a jilted bride, haunts the mill.

FIELD NOTES

Rare plants such as Canada yew and mountain laurel survive in the valley, alongside trees commonly found in colder climates—hemlock, yellow and black birch. Jewelweed lines the stream in midsummer. Wild turkey has re-established itself; and black bears have been sighted. Birders look for warblers, scarlet tanager, Cooper's hawk, and others in the gorge.

Cleveland Lakefront

This is not exactly the place to get away from it all. The city presses against you wherever you go. Lake Erie's shore attracts the 8-10 million annual visitors who put up with crowded beaches, busy boat ramps, and populated piers.

LOCATION

This park is comprised of six separate sites: a collection of orphaned city parks and shore resorts stretching 14 miles along Cleveland's lakefront.

SIZE & DESIGNATION

Land: 476 acres; water: Lake Erie.

ACCESS

To find Edgewater Park, head west from downtown Cleveland on SR 2 (West Shoreway). After crossing the Cuyahoga River, take the Edgewater Park exit and follow signs to the facility of your choice.

East 55th Street Marina and Gordon Park is accessed from Downtown Cleveland by going east on I-90/SR 2. Leave the freeway at the East 55th Street exit (Interchange 175) for the marina. Continue east to the East 72nd Street ramp (Interchange 176) for Gordon Park (westbound travelers can exit at Martin Luther King Boulevard, Interchange 177). The state park office is at Gordon Park.

Visitors access Euclid Beach, Villa Angela and Wildwood Park by travelling eastbound, leaving I-90/SR 2 at Exit 179 and following SR 283 (Lakeshore Blvd.) north (east). All three spots are located off roads branching north from Lakeshore Blvd. Take Neff Road north to Wildwood Park, the easternmost site.

Picnic Areas: Euclid Beach, Edgewater, Wildwood, and Gordon parks have picnic areas. Seven shelters are available (some reservable). Edgewater offers a pavilion.

Trails: Just a 1.6 mile fitness trail at Villa Angela.

Swimming: Three beaches cool off millions of humans each summer. Edgewater Park boasts a wide, 900-foot beach with concession stand, rest rooms. Bathers can splash on beaches at Villa Angela (900-feet and bathhouse) and Euclid Beach (650 feet).

Boating: Armadas sail from the docks and three boat launches in the park. Edgewater has 10 boat ramps and some docks on its eastern edge, while the Gordon (some docks) and Wildwood launches each have six ramps. Seasonal docks with electric and water hookups, 335 of them, can be rented at the East 55th Street Marina. The concessionaire there has bait, fuel, tackle, and food. Wildwood rents boats, and has a concession.

Fishing: Plenty of lakeshore fishing is available. Try the platforms at East 55th Street Marina (concession available) and Gordon Park, the piers at Edgewater and Villa Angela (wheelchair accessible), or the breakwalls at Wildwood. In spring, coho salmon return to Euclid Creek, via Wildwood Park. Not to mention all the fish in Lake Erie.

HISTORY

The Cuyahoga River used to wind around Whiskey Island and spill into Lake Erie at Edgewater Park until the navigation channel was dug in the 1820s. The spot became a city park in 1894 after its purchase from J.B. Perkins, son of a railroad magnate. The bluff on the west side of Edgewater Park (known as the upper park) has been a popular panorama of downtown Cleveland. That fellow frozen as a statue near the pavilion is Conrad Mizar, the founder of park concerts. In 1893, William J. Gordon bequeathed his estate to Cleveland, which turned it into a 105-acre park. Back in the Roaring 20s, you could "cut a rug" all evening for just three cents in the dance hall at Wildwood. The former resort featured lakeshore cabins for tired hoofers and amusement park tourists.

Euclid Beach once was more famous for its rides than its beach. The amusement park lasted from 1895 to 1969. Its popularity peaked in the 1920s. Financially-strapped Cleveland leased four sites to the Ohio Department of Natural Resources in 1977, and these formed the state park in 1978. Euclid Beach was acquired in 1982; Villa Angela in 1984 and 1991.

Information: Cleveland Lakefront State Park, 8701 Lakeshore Blvd., N.E., Cleveland, OH 44108-1069, (216) 881-8141.

FIELD NOTES

Lakefront is a scene to be "seen" (meaning humans) in summer. Not the spot for folks seeking quiet, secluded, uncrowded, natural settings. Shorebirds hang out at the beaches.

Findley

Findley State Park's speck of fame is its second-growth forest and small lake amidst a landscape cultivated for cows. The Civilian Conservation Corps planted a half million trees here when the place was a state forest. Come see the fruits of its labor.

LOCATION

Southern Lorain County, Huntington and Wellington townships.

SIZE & DESIGNATION

Land: 903 acres; water: 93 acres.

ACCESS

The park is four miles south of Wellington on SR 58. Follow park roads to the beach and camping areas.

Accommodations: Findley's sprawling campground has 272 sites in the shade and sun. None offer electricity. Comforts include showers, flush toilets, commissary, laundry, playground, dump station, pet camping, and three Rent-A-Camp sites. From the entrance on SR 58, follow Park Road 3 to the camping area.

Picnic Areas: Day trippers will find tables and grills on the west side of the lake at the end of Park Road 1, by the boat launch on Park Road 4, and at Picnic Pines, Park Road 3.

Trails: Ten miles of paths wander through the park, including a section of the Buckeye Trail. You can hike around Findley Lake by combining (from camp) the Spillway, Hickory Grove, Larch, Buckeye, Creekbank, and Lake trails. The Hickory Grove and Wyandot Self-Guided trails begin at the park office and visit the west side of the park. The Wyandot Trail is the Black River Audubon Society's 15-station interpretive trail. Pick up a trail guide at the park office.

Swimming: Not much sand at this 435-foot swimming area., though there is a concession available for snacks.

Boating: There's a marina, boat rental (canoes, rowboats, pedalboats), loading dock, and concrete ramp near the west shore picnic area on Park Road 4, and a smaller launch near the campground, south shore. Electric motors only.

Hunting: Waterfowl hunting (and nothing else) is allowed in designated areas. Check at the park office.

Fishing: Cast for largemouth bass (slot length in effect), crappie, and bluegill in this busy body of water.

Information: Findley State Park, 25381 SR 58 , Wellington, OH 44090-9208., (440) 647-4490.

HISTORY

The state park's namesake was Guy B. Findley, a Lorain County Common Pleas Court Judge. Findley bought this agricultural land in 1936 and 1937. He later donated it to the state for use as a state forest. The half million trees mentioned above were planted by the Civilian Conservation Corps for the Ohio Division of Forestry. Findley Forest was transferred to the Division of Parks and Recreation in 1950. An earthen dam constructed from 1954-56 formed Findley Lake.

FIELD NOTES

A spot in the park is a nature sanctuary to protect Duke's skipper butterfly, a rare insect. Birders are likely to see the pine siskin, common redpoll, red and white-winged crossbills, and evening grosbeak.

Geneva

Geneva's excellent marina harbors a fleet of sailboats, fishing boats and pleasure craft that plies the tempestuous waters of Lake Erie's Central Basin. During storms, Erie's full fury pounds Geneva hard, bringing the fleet back to the safe harbor.

LOCATION

Northwestern Ashtabula County, Geneva Township.

ACCESS
    From US 20 in central Geneva, take SR 534 north, then Lake Road West. Follow park signs to the beach, marina, campgrounds, and cabins. The park office is found at the corner of Padanarum Road and Lake Road West.
    Accommodations: The 91-site, all-electric campground is located at the west side of the park on two loops off Lake Road West. Sun seekers stick to sites on the open first loop. The second loop has shade. Campground features include a showerhouse, dump station, flush toilets, laundry, three Rent-A-Camp sites and pet area. Campground usually fills every weekend between Memorial Day and Labor Day.
    Geneva's 12 lakeshore cabins go fast via a lottery held in February. Reservations are accepted in January. Each cabin has three bedrooms, full kitchen, screened porch facing the lake, and cable television.
    Picnic Areas: Crabapple Grove Picnic Area, south of the marina off Service Road, has tables and grills scattered along No Name Creek. Two shelter houses for groups are available on a first-come basis. Chestnut Grove Picnic Area, located on SR 534, sits in old white oak woodlot. Rod & Gun Club is on Padanarum Road, north of the park office.
    Trails: Three miles of easy hiking trails link the Crabapple and Rod & Gun Club picnic areas, visit small ponds, and straddle the west bank of Cowles Creek.
    Swimming: Lake Erie's fierce wave bombardment wiped out the old swimming beach at the Chestnut Grove Picnic Area in 1991. The new 300-foot beach straddles the shore and breakwall west of the marina. Lifeguards are on duty during the summer. Swimming off the east breakwall, which is topped with a sidewalk for strolls and fishing, is not allowed.
    Boating: Geneva's modern, top-shelf marina, built by the U.S. Corps of Engineers and Ohio Department of Natural Resources in 1989, is the heart of this park. An armada docks here in summer. Catch this—six ramps, four loading docks, illuminated, parking for 200 autos, fuel pumps, fish cleaning area, rest rooms with showers, full service store, bait and tackle, fishing licenses, charter boats, and, saving the best for last, seasonal slips for 383 boats. Breakwalls provide a calm chute into Lake Erie.
    Fishing: Lake Erie's Central Basin is straight ahead, and so are the steelhead trout, yellow perch, smallmouth bass, and summer walleye in deep water. Shore anglers cast from the east breakwall and from the marina. Ice anglers have a snowmobile staging area, west of the marina, off Lake Road West. Supplies are available at the marina.
    Information: Geneva State Park, P.O. Box 429, Padanarum Road, Geneva, OH 44041, (440) 466-8400 park office, (440) 466-7565 marina.

HISTORY
    Chestnut Grove Picnic Area was the first park

property, acquired in 1964. Parcels were purchased through 1972, the last being the cabin and campground areas.

FIELD NOTES
    The beaches and freshwater marshes in the park support seaside plants rare in Ohio, such as sea rocket, sea spurge, beach pea and silverweed. Swamp smartweed, leafy sedge, and other aquatic plants fill the marshes at the mouths of Cowles, Wheeler and No Name creeks. Waterbirds can be seen at these wetlands.

Guilford Lake

Guilford Lake has been almost every kind of wetland. First, it was a woodland swamp, an old glacial lake perhaps, near the headwaters of the West Fork of Little Beaver Creek, then a canal feeder lake, then drained farmland, now a sleepy state park lake. Fishing is the big draw in this slow-paced park.

LOCATION
    Central Columbiana County, Hanover Township.

SIZE & DESIGNATION
    Land: 92 acres; water: 396 acres.

ACCESS
    From Lisbon, head west on US 30, turn right (west) on SR 172. To reach the park office, campground and beach on the east and north shores, turn right on Baker Road, left on East Lake Road (TR 745), left on Teegarden Road (CR 411), left on Camp Boulevard. Continue on SR 172 for boat ramps on the south shore and picnic areas on Lakeview Road.
    Accommodations: The camp's 42 non-electric sites are located in an old pine grove on the north side of the lake. Amenities include drinking water, showers, toilets, fishing dock, playground, boat ramp, picnic tables and fire rings. Try for shady lakeside sites peeking at tiny Pine Island.
    Picnic Areas: Picnic areas stand along the western shore on Lakeview and Teegarden roads and Camp Blvd. A picnic shelterhouse, located at the junction of the latter roads, is available on a first-come basis. The beach, boat rental, and spillway also have picnic tables.
    Trails: A half-mile lakeshore path, called the Education Trail, starts at Teegarden Road, near the campground.
    Swimming: Camp Boulevard, which branches

from Teegarden Road, leads to the 600-foot sandy swimming beach set in a cove on the north shore. The beach has changing booths and latrines.

Boating: Boaters can launch their craft from ramps at the campground, East Lake Road (east shore), and at the end of Shore Lane (south shore, off Hanna Drive and SR 172). Motors cannot exceed more than 10 horsepower. A private concessionaire rents boats from a south shore marina on Spillway Drive, off SR 172.

Fishing: Cast for bluegills, crappie, northern pike, and stocked largemouth bass and channel catfish. The lake can get thick with fishers on summer weekends. Shore anglers toss at the spillway and along the north shore, and west side picnic areas.

Information: Guilford Lake State Park, 6835 East Lake Road, Lisbon, OH 44432, (330) 222-1712.

HISTORY

A spelling error on an application for Grange membership changed Gill's Ford into Guilford. Town folks accepted the mistake so the process would not be halted. The mistake stuck. The place derives its name from E.H. Gill, chief engineer of the Sandy and Beaver Canal. Gill led the construction of an elevated road across the swampy spot known as Gill's Ford (or Gillford).

Guilford Lake started as a reservoir for the canal, a private venture that opened in 1834. Though just 73 miles in length, the canal needed 90 locks, 30 dams, three reservoirs, two tunnels, and a 400-foot aqueduct. The canal was short-lived. By 1874, date of the Grange application, the company had drowned. Farmers unplugged the dike and cultivated the fertile lake bottom for awhile. The state bought the land in 1927 and five years later had reconstructed the dam and lake. Guilford Lake was one of the original parks turned over to the newly established Ohio Department of Natural Resources in 1949.

FIELD NOTES

Guilford Lake's swampy origin suggests it was once a natural glacial lake. At the end of the Ice Age, roughly 12,000 years ago, huge blocks of ice broke off the edge of the retreating Wisconsinan glacier. The ice melted into depressions, forming kettle lakes. Encroaching sediment and vegetation transformed the lakes into swamps, like the one encountered by the builders of the Sandy & Beaver Canal.

Headlands Beach

Headlands kicks sand in the face of all other beaches in Ohio. The eastern half preserves a few acres of Lake Erie's original shoreline. Migrating birds and butterflies loiter in the park's trees after flights across the lake.

LOCATION

Lake County, Lake Erie shore near Fairport Harbor.

SIZE & DESIGNATION

Land: 126 acres.

ACCESS

Get to SR 2, then take SR 44 north to its end at the state park.

Picnic Areas: Picnickers will find a large area with tables and grills between the parking lots. A shelterhouse near the beach is reservable by calling Cleveland Lakefront State Park.

Trails: The best trail is a stroll along the mile-long beach to the breakwall and back. The northern terminus of the Buckeye Trail starts here, and hikers can follow paths in nearby Headlands Dunes and Mentor Marsh state natural areas.

Swimming: Headlands Beach has the largest (a mile long) and most natural swimming and tanning beach in Ohio. It's wider than a football field in spots. The dunes at adjacent Headlands Dunes State Natural Area make this site a haven for naturalists too. The beach has nearly 4,000 parking spots for its million annual visitors, two concession stands, changing booths, and rest rooms.

Boating: Jet ski recreational boats may be rented at the beach. No other boating facilities are available.

Hunting: None.

Fishing: The usual Central Basin catches await shore anglers, who can cast from the breakwall at the eastern edge of the park. Anglers also wet lines from a fishing dock at Shipman Pond, located south of the west beach. Catches usually are bass (largemouth, rock and smallmouth), yellow perch, bluegill, walleye, coho salmon, steelhead trout, sucker and bullhead.

Information: Headlands Beach State Park, 9601 Headlands Road, Mentor, OH 44060, (440) 257-1330. Mailing address: Cleveland Lakefront State Park, 8701 Lakeshore Blvd., NE, Cleveland, OH 44108-1069, (216) 881-8141.

HISTORY

The state began buying park land west of Fairport Harbor in the early 1950s. Painesville Beach State Park opened in 1953, but the name was changed to Headlands Beach two years later. Large flocks of bathers came immediately. Strong waves and undertow closed the beach in 1957, but it reopened the following year after repairs.

FIELD NOTES

Monarch butterflies heading for their winter quarters in Central Mexico sometimes accumulate by the thousands in September. They may rest in the trees for a day before continuing their journey.

Plants common on the Atlantic coast grow in the sand dunes here. Sea rocket, beach pea, seaside spurge, beach grass and purple beach grass are imperiled creatures in Ohio.

Geneva On the Lake is summer payback for winter's lake effect.

Jefferson Lake

Jefferson Lake may be the loneliest state park in Ohio, because fewer than 100,000 humans annually leave their tracks here. The campground is never full, and solitude, scenery, and stars are abundant.

LOCATION
Northwestern Jefferson County, Ross and Salem townships.

SIZE & DESIGNATION
Land: 945 acres; water: 17 acres.

ACCESS
From SR 43, head north on Park Road (CR 54). The park entrance is at the intersection of CR 54 and TR 219. Continue north on CR 54 to the campground entrance.

Accommodations: The park features 100 restful and well-spaced campsites (no electricity) on two loops. Oaks and hickories shade the second loop (sites 54-100). The first loop has some open areas and paved slips for recreational vehicles. Two sites are reserved for Rent-A-Camp visitors. Creature comforts are limited to latrines and water fountains. The bathhouse at the beach has showers.

Picnic Areas: Look for picnic areas throughout the park—notably near the beach (shelterhouse), nature center, and the dam (on CR 54). A secluded picnic spot (and shelterhouse) is tucked in the southwestern corner of the park, on TR 219, just north of SR 43. Shelterhouses are available on a first-come basis.

Trails: Fifteen miles of paths await hikers. The park brochure, available at the camp check-in station, marks the trails. The longest treks are the three-mile Beaver Dam Trail (trailheads at the beach and campsite 16), and the Lakeside & Trillium route (two miles) which connects the dam to picnic area 3 (southern shelterhouse). Horseback riders can use the trails, too.

Swimming: A small beach (200 feet) straddles the western shore below the campground. Campers reach the beach via the Downhill Trail branching from the first loop. Day-use swimmers park at the parking lot branching west from CR 54. The bathhouse has showers and toilets.

Boating: Only non-motorized boats and crafts with electric motors (four horsepower limit) can float on Jefferson Lake. Boaters will find a paved launch at the parking lot for daytime visitors (off CR 54).

Hunting: Hunting is permitted in designated areas. Check at the park office.

Fishing: Cast for largemouth bass, channel catfish, bluegill, and sunfish in shallow Jefferson Lake. Stocked carp must be released.

Information: Jefferson Lake State Park, Route 1 Richmond, OH 43944-9710, (740) 765-4459.

HISTORY

The famous Mingo chief, Logan, lived in the neighborhood of Town Fork (the creek impounded to form Jefferson Lake) in the 18th century. Town Fork flows into Yellow Creek. The massacre of Mingo's family at Yellow Creek's confluence with the Ohio River sparked Lord Dunmore's War in 1774.

During the Depression, the National Park Service began developing the spot for recreation. Laborers for the Civilian Conservation Corps (and its state equivalent) finished the dam in 1934, but 12 years passed before water filled the basin to create Jefferson Lake. The park was given to the newly-created Division of Parks and Recreation in 1950.

FIELD NOTES

Jefferson County borders the Ohio River, a lure for anglers and boaters. You will find access ramps at the New Cumberland Lock and Dam, Steubenville Marina, and Indian Short Creek.

Lake Milton

One of Ohio's newest state parks, partly founded on the site of an old amusement park, amuses boating, swimming, and fishing enthusiasts.

LOCATION

Northwestern Mahoning County, Milton Township.

SIZE & DESIGNATION

Land: 1,000 acres; water: 1,685 acres.

ACCESS

I-76 splits this park. Recreation facilities are found on both sides of the north-south trending lake. Leave I-76 at the SR 534 exit east of the lake. Go south on SR 534 a mile, then turn west (right) on Mahoning Avenue. Picnic area and boat ramp are located on Milton Avenue, branching from Mahoning Avenue. Miller's Landing boat ramp, fishing access (causeway), and rest rooms are located on Mahoning Avenue. A swimming beach, boat launch and rental, and other facilities are found on the northwest shore, on Grandview Road and Jersey Street.

Picnic Areas: Four shelterhouses are offered on a first-come basis. The best tables are located at the swimming beach on the west shore, and at the end of Milton Avenue, on the eastern shore.

Swimming: Lake Milton's new 600-foot beach, called Craig Beach, has changing rooms, showers, rest rooms, playground, picnic tables, basketball court, sand volleyball court, cruises (for a fee) and ski boat rentals. The beach is on Grandview Road, which runs on the west shore between Mahoning Avenue and Pricetown Road. Convenience stores

are conveniently located across the street.

Boating: Lake Milton attracts boaters of all speeds. Unlimited horsepower boating is allowed north of I-76, and from the Mahoning Avenue causeway to a settlement called Scotts Corners. No wake zones are between I-76 and Mahoning Avenue, the southern quarter of the lake, and 300 feet from the shore. Boaters can ply partly up the Mahoning River at the southern tip.

The park has two modern boat ramps at Miller's Landing, on Mahoning Avenue, and Robinson's Point (wheelchair access), on Jersey Street. Follow park signs. Seasonal rental docks (72 spots) are available at the Milton Avenue marina. Applications for boat slips are accepted in August for the following year.

Hunting: Waterfowl hunting is permitted in restricted areas. Check at the park office.

Fishing: Lake Milton offers good catches of stocked walleye, bluegill, largemouth bass, crappie, and channel catfish. You might hook a smallmouth bass, bullhead, yellow perch, white bass, and muskellunge. Lake Milton usually gets cold and thick enough for ice fishing. The Division of Wildlife has force-fed Lake Milton with more than three million walleye yearlings. Walleye and bass keepers must be fifteen inches (check at park office for length changes). Most of the shoreline is privately owned. Non-boating anglers will find a nicely developed access on the Mahoning Avenue causeway, with parking and toilets.

Information: Lake Milton State Park, 16801 Mahoning Avenue, Lake Milton, Ohio 44429-9998, (330) 654-4989.

HISTORY

In 1910, to quench the thirst of Youngstown's growing population and industries, the city bought 3,416 acres in Milton Township along the Mahoning River for a reservoir. A few years later a 2,800-foot dam had impounded Lake Milton. A small amusement park operated awhile at Craig Beach, site of the new swimming beach. Saloons, skating and dance halls cluttered the east shore.

The lake was emptied in 1986 for dam repairs. During reconstruction, the state park system acquired sections for park development. Lake Milton was dedicated a park in 1988.

FIELD NOTES

Migratory waterfowl can delight birders during spring and autumn migrations.

Malabar Farm
State Park

This state is more a shrine to Pulitzer Prize winning novelist Louis Bromfield's pioneering conservation

Imagining Malabar

"The adventure of Malabar is by no means finished but I doubt that the history of any piece of land is ever finished or that any adventure in Nature ever comes to an end. The land came to us out of eternity and when the youngest of us associated with it dies, it will still be there. The best we can hope to do is to leave the mark of our fleeting existence upon it, to die knowing that we have changed a small corner of this earth for the better by wisdom, knowledge and hard work."

—Louis Bromfield, Pleasant Valley

ethics than to his considerable literary exertions. Bromfield bought the played out pastures with book royalties, then restored its fecundity, and created a model farm that became an enduring legacy.

LOCATION
Southeastern Richland County, Monroe Township.

SIZE & DESIGNATION
Land: 914 acres; water: three acres.

ACCESS
Leave I-71 at Exit 169 (SR 13). Drive on SR 13 to the northwest side of the freeway overpass. Here, turn onto Hanley Road heading east. In a couple of miles go right on Little Washington Road, then, shortly, left on Pleasant Valley Road The park entrance is about seven miles away.

Accommodations: Equestrians and family campers share a primitive 15-site campground at the end of Bromfield Road, the park entrance lane. Nothing fancy—fire rings, picnic tables, latrines, drinking water. Malabar Youth Hostel on Bromfield Road offers comfortable, but modest lodging in a 1919 "mail order" farmhouse where Bromfield stayed while the mansion was built. The place has 24 beds (males in one dorm, females in the other), a kitchen and dining area. Call (419) 892-2055 for reservations.

Picnic Areas: You'll find a grassy picnic area beside the campground with tables, grills, latrines and water pump.

Trails: Doris Duke Woods Trail starts by the entrance road to the Sugar Shack. The Butternut Nature Trail branches west by the Sugar Shack, and Junglebrook Trail stems from the Farm Complex Road, east of the main parking lot. Each trail is a mile loop path.

The park's 12-mile Horse Trail starts at the horseman's camp on Bromfield Road, west of the mansion. It visits Malabar Inn, Mt. Jeez and the sawmill.

Swimming & Boating: Go to nearby Pleasant Hill Lake Park.

Fishing: The five farm ponds have bluegill and catfish, but don't expect much.

Special Places & Events: A guided tour of The Big House—a must for grownups—features Bromfield's library, the bric-a-brac of his life, and the rooms where he threw parties for his Hollywood friends. Screen stars Humphrey Bogart and Lauren Bacall tied the knot and honeymooned at Malabar Farm in 1945. The 32-room residence is a "blend of Western Reserve architecture" designed by Bromfield and architect Louis Lamoreaux. It was purposely built

to look like wings were added over the years. Tours occur Tuesday through Sunday year-round for a small fee. Check on the hours when you arrive. The Silo Gift Shop next to the Big House is one of only a few places still selling Bromfield's books.

Children head for the "farm complex" comprising a dairy barn with cows, smoke house, corn crib, chicken coop, carpentry shop and greenhouse, and pastures. Barnyard critters are friendly at a petting farm off Bromfield Road. Wagon rides around the farm go from April through October, every day except Monday. Tours depart four times a day. The journey takes 45 minutes.

Malabar Farm has many farm-related activities and demonstrations during the year, usually on weekends. The biggies are the Maple Syrup Festival held at the Sugar Shack on two weekends in March; Spring Plow Days in May when draft horses and mules plow furrows the old fashioned way; Ohio Heritage Days in late September, featuring crafts, vintage farm machines, music; and Christmas at Malabar in December (the place gets decked out for the holiday). Barn dances are held several times a year.

Pugh Cabin, near the Sugar Shack, is a day-use place for group meetings of up to 50 people. Reservations are necessary. The Ceely Rose House (not open to public), below the Big House, may be haunted by the murderess Ceely Rose. (See "Happy Haunting Grounds")

Bromfield set up a produce stand next to the Malabar Inn to sell surplus veggies and bend ears on the virtues of conservation and contour farming. The restored stagecoach inn, built in 1820, serves home-cooked meals, Tuesday-Sunday, May through October and weekends in March and April. It is now state-owned and available for group reservations (419) 892-2784. From the park entrance, drive east on Pleasant Valley Road less than a mile.

Information: Malabar Farm State Park, 4050 Bromfield Road, Lucas, OH 44843, (419) 892-2784.

HISTORY
In 1926, Mansfield native Louis Bromfield won the Pulitzer Prize in Literature for *Early Autumn,* but the next year he followed the "lost generation" of American writers to France. There he stayed until World War II, whereupon he purchased four played out farms in Richland County's Pleasant Valley. He called the place Malabar Farm, derived from his book, *The Rains Came,* set in India's Malabar Coast. Bromfield entertained America's literati and Hollywood stars in the mansion he called simply "The Big House."

Bromfield made his mark as a conservationist and agricultural reformer. Using natural fertilizers and new techniques he restored the farm's fertility. His books on the farm's recovery broadened his appeal and made Malabar Farm seem like an Eden. The writer-farmer, 6'1" in bare feet, talked with the conviction of a crusader. Often, he gave lectures on conservation farming atop Mt. Jeez because it was the only place his audience could see his entire empire. The bald hill at the north end of the property got its name from Bromfield's first utterance on the summit—"Jeez!" You can get there via a road off Pleasant Valley Road (a few hundred yards east of the park entrance) or on the hiking and bridle trail.

When Bromfield died in 1956 the farm was entrusted to the Malabar Farm Foundation. In 1972, the state rescued the place from foreclosure and for the next four years the farm was operated jointly by the Ohio departments of agriculture and natural resources. ODNR took over the place in 1976 and designated it a state park.

Tobacco company heiress Doris Duke, a Bromfield friend, saved a woodlot on the property after the author's death. The nature trail through the woods carries her name.

FIELD NOTES

The woodlands behind "The Big House" protect mature stands of beech and maple. Ferns and moss decorate sandstone outcroppings, and cool, shady ravines support hemlocks. Spring hikers will find trillium, spring beauties and blue phlox on the ground, and the yellow warbler, indigo bunting and scarlet tanager in the trees.

Mohican

The state park is just one piece of a pie called Mohican Territory. This slice provides a resort lodge and protects Ohio's deepest gorge. Thousands of acres of state forest, nature preserves, and a water conservancy park surround the state park.

LOCATION

Southwestern Ashland County, Hanover and Green townships.

SIZE & DESIGNATION

Land: 1,294 acres. The state park is a corridor protecting Clearfork Gorge, a National Natural Landmark.

ACCESS

The campground is on SR 3, a few miles south of Loudonville. To reach the lodge from the camp, go

Nature
Notable

Farmer and the Swells

Louis Bromfield could have kept writing the novels that made him rich, won him a Pulitzer Prize, and kept him on the social pages in Hollywood and New York. Instead, he bought four exhausted farms near his hometown, Mansfield, and restored them to their full bounty using conservation farming, a revolutionary concept at the time.

The writer-conservationist made Malabar Farm a showcase for contour plowing, erosion control, organic farming, crop diversification, and water conservation. Bromfield first stopped the erosion and siltation of remaining topsoil. Huge gullies vanished and diversion ditches carried away runoff water. Plows followed the natural contour of the land to reduce erosion—contour plowing. Grass and legumes planted between strips of row crops promoted water absorption and halted erosion. Bromfield overcame the need to use chemical fertilizers and pesticides, without declines in crop yield and nutritional value.

Bromfield didn't invent conservation farming, but he made it a cause celebre. Hundreds of folks gathered atop Mt. Jeez for Bromfield's frequent preaching on conservation. Hundreds of famous folks piled into the mansion for parties and feasts. The Bromfield Estate gave Malabar Farm to the state in 1972. As Malabar Farm State Park, it operates as a working education farm.

—SO

south on SR 3 a half mile, then turn right (westbound) on SR 97. Go north on McCurdy Road, right on CR 3006, left on the park road leading to the lodge. From Exit 165 on I-71, take SR 97 to SR 3, and left (north) a half mile to the campground-cabin entrance. To reach the lodge, follow SR 65 northeast in Butler, then go right on Pleasant Hill Road, left on McCurdy Road, left on CR 3006.

Accommodations: At Mohican you can sleep in the lap of luxury or on a lump of leaves. Mohican Lodge offers comfort in 96 air-conditioned rooms. Frills in the lodge include indoor and outdoor pools, restaurant dining (request window seats for lake views), sauna, whirlpool, lounge, game room, gift shop, tennis, basketball, shuffleboard, horseshoes, and exercise room. Meeting rooms handle banquets up to 450 people. The lodge stands on a bluff overlooking Pleasant Hill Lake.

The cabins and family campground are lumped together, along the Clearfork of the Mohican River, a 10-mile drive from the lofty lodge. The entrance is on SR 3, a half mile north of its intersection with SR 97, and a few miles south of Loudonville.

Twenty-five deluxe family cabins line the shady river, and their spacing favors privacy. Each cabin sleeps six and comes with kitchen, utensils, bedding, screened porch, and showers.

The 177-site riverside campground fills fast on summer weekends. Electric hookups are ready at 153 sites. Wooded and grassy sites are available. The place has a showerhouse, flush toilets, laundry, camp store, dump station, playground, and a swimming pool. Nature programs are nightly features at the amphitheater during the summer.

Hemlock Grove Campground is a 24-site primitive location three miles upstream from the busy main camp. To get there from the family campground entrance, turn right on SR 3, right on SR 97, right onto State Forest Road 8, then left at the fork, following signs to the forest headquarters and covered bridge. After crossing the bridge, turn right and pick a spot. From the lodge entrance, turn left on CR 3006 (Goon Road), cross the dam and bear right at the next merger. A mile ahead turn right on CR 939, then bear right at the next junction, left before the bridge. These are beautiful, peaceful, creekside sites with picnic tables and latrines. One morning I found a happy camper snoring on a bed of leaves. I guess tents are optional here.

A group camp for 100 people is located around the bend from the Hemlock Grove Camp, near the state forest office. All sites go fast on weekends, but there are zillions of private campgrounds in the neighborhood.

Picnic Areas: Mohican has five picnic areas. The best is the Overlook Area, which features a shelter and tables that peek into steep Clearfork Gorge. From SR 97 a half mile or so west of the park office, travel northerly on Forest Road 1. On the north side of the river, you find tables and a shelter near the covered bridge and at Vista Point Picnic Area, near the forest office. There are tables at the dam and a shelter near the campground entrance. Latrines and

water are available at some locations.

Trails: Try this route from the campground. On the north side of the river, by the bridge separating the cabins and campground, go upstream on the Hemlock Grove Trail. This scenic path goes through Clearfork Gorge to Hemlock Grove Campground and the covered bridge. Take the bridge to the south bank, then find the plaque commemorating the gorge at the start of the Lyon Falls Trail. In a half mile, go left on the moderately difficult loop that visits Big Lyons Falls, Little Lyons Falls, and Pleasant Hill Lake dam. Here, cross to the other stream bank, run down the embankment and take the easy Pleasant Hill Trail (.75-mile) to the covered bridge. Return to camp via the Hemlock Grove Trail which is always worth repeating. The route covers all the trails in the state park, except for a half mile section few take between the dam and Lyons Falls turnoff. Figure on walking five miles. You can start these paths at the covered bridge and dam.

The state forest has great trails for hikers, horseback riders, Nordic skiers, and snowmobilers.

Swimming: Mohican lacks a swimming beach. (Better go to adjacent Pleasant Hill Lake Park.) The lodge has pools for lodge and cabin guests. Campers use a pool in the campground.

Boating: Canoers, kayakers, and floaters in inflatables journey down the scenic gorge of the Clearfork of the Mohican from the covered bridge at the entrance to the primitive campground. You can take out at the bridge by the cabin area, or by the SR 3/97 bridge just above the confluence with the Blackfork, or points downstream in Holmes and Knox counties. To reach the covered bridge follow directions to the primitive campground above.

Boaters can enter below Pleasant Hill Lake dam if they are willing to carry their boat and gear down a steep embankment and rocky stream bank. Doing so adds nearly a mile to the trip.

Pleasant Hill Lake is managed by the Muskingum Watershed Conservancy District. The entrance to its park and marina is on SR 95.

Fishing: Clearfork Gorge is gaining a reputation as a fair trout stream. This tributary of the Mohican River also has smallmouth bass, largemouth bass, crappie, carp, catfish, perch and bluegill. Saugeye are sought in the tailwater below the dam in late February and March. Fishing opportunities exist at Pleasant Hill Lake.

Special Places & Events: The fire tower in the state forest is an irresistible landmark. Climb it and enjoy the view. Follow Forest Road off SR 97 until you get there. The Memorial Shrine along SR 97 was built by the Ohio Federation of Women's Clubs to honor Ohio's war dead of World War II. The 270-acre site in the state forest is a nature sanctuary.

Information: Mohican State Park, 3116 State Route 3, Loudonville, OH 44842, (419) 994-5125, (419) 994-4290 campground and cabin reservations.

HISTORY

The park is named after the river, not the extinct Indian tribe that was centered in New York. The spot was a Lenni Lenape (Delaware) hunting ground, and some of that band—warriors named Janacake, Bill Montour, Thomas Lyon, and James Smith—resided in the area. John Chapman, a.k.a. Johnny Appleseed, planted apple trees in Mohican Territory and reportedly carved his name on the ledge at Big Lyons Falls. Vandals or erosion removed the evidence. Mohican State Park grew out of the state forest of the same name in 1949. Originally Clear Fork State Park, the name was changed to its current one in 1966.

State Park
Websites

The Web Of It All

Ohio State Park websites begin with the following prefix—**http://www.ldnr.ohio.gov/odnr/directory/**—followed by the park suffix printed below.

NORTHEASTERN OHIO
Beaver Creek - **beaverck.htm**
Cleve. Lakefront - **clevelkf.htm**
Findley - **findley.htm**
Geneva - **geneva.htm**
Guilford Lake - **guilford.htm**
Headlands Bch. - **headlands.htm**
Jefferson Lake - **jefferso.htm**
Lake Milton - **lkmilton.htm**
Malabar Farm - **malabar.htm**
Mohican - **mohican.htm**
Mosquito Lk - **mosquito.htm**
N-K Ledges - **nelsonk.htm**
Portage Lake - **portage.htm**
Punderson - **pundrson.htm**
Pymatunign - **Pymatung.htm**
Quail hollow - **quailhlw.htm**
Tinker's Creek - **tinkers.htm**
West Branch - **westbrnc.htm**

SOUTHWESTERN OHIO
Adams Lake - **adams.htm**
Buck Creek - **buckck.htm**
Caesar Creek - **caesarck.htm**
Cowan Lake - **cowanlk.htm**
East Fork - **eastfork.htm**
Hueston Woods - **hustonw.htm**
John Bryan - **jhnbryan.htm**
Kiser Lake - **kisrlake.htm**
Little Miami - **lilmiami.htm**
Paint Creek - **paintcrk.htm**
Rocky Fork - **Rockyfrk.htm**
Stonelick - **stonelck.htm**
Sycamore - **sycamore.htm**

SOUTHEASTERN OHIO
Barkcamp - **barkcamp.htm**
Blue Rock - **bluerock.htm**
Burr Oak - **burroak.htm**
Dillon - **dillon.htm**
Forked Run - **forkedrn.htm**
Great Seal - **grtseal.htm**
Hocking Hills - **hocking.htm***
Jackson Lake - **jacksonl.htm**
Lake Alma - **lakealma.htm**
Lake Hope - **lakehope.htm**
Lake Logan - **lklogan.htm**
Lake White - **lkwhite.htm**
Muskingum R. - **muskngmr.htm**
Pike Lake - **pikelake.htm**
Salt Fork - **saltfork.htm**
Scioto Trail - **sciototr.htm**
Shawnee - **shawnee.htm**
Strouds Run - **strouds.htm**
Tar Hollow - **tarhollw.htm**
Wolf Run - **wolfrun.htm**

CENTRAL
Alum Creek - **alum.htm**
A.W. Marion - **awmarin.htm**
Buckeye Lake - **buckeye.htm**
Deer Creek - **deerck.htm**
Delaware - **delaware.htm**
Indian Lake - **indianlk.htm**
Madison Lake - **madison.htm**
Mt. Gilead - **mtgilead.htm**

NORTHWESTERN OHIO
Catawba Is. - **lakeerie.htm**
Crane Creek - **cranecrk.htm**
East Harbor - **eharbor.htm**
Grand Lake - **grndlake.htm**
Harrison Lake - **harrison.htm**
Independ. Dam - **indpndam.htm**
Kelleys Is. - **lakeerie.htm**
Lk Loramie - **lklorame.htm**
M.J.Thurston - **mjthrstn.htm**
Marblehead - **marblehead.htm**
Maumee - **maumebay.htm**
South Bass - **lakeerie.htm**
Van Buren - **vanburen.htm**

Clear Creek Gorge is packed with birds, from great blue herons and kingfishers on the shore to fifteen kinds of woodland warblers, notably northern parula, hooded, cerulean, and American redstart. Turkey vultures seemingly hover for hours on thermals rising from the gorge.

The Mohican River used to flow in the opposite direction. The Wisconsinan glacier, however, stopped a little north of the spot and blocked the river. A large lake formed in front of the ice, and eventually it topped its bank and reversed direction. Geologists figure the river's flow was 100 times stronger than the current current. The view of the lake at the Pleasant Hill Lake dam helps visualize the scenario.

JOURNAL

No spectral vision, no phantasms of the forest, appeared during my late-night visit to Lyons Falls, a purported haunt of spirits Tom and Paul Lyons. Giving up on the ghosts, I crept to the silvery strand of water that passed as a cascade, its trickle amplified by the cave and hollow. Suddenly, I slipped, got drenched; and then, making the best of it, stripped to skinny-dip. Under the spray I got elbowed, bumped by some "thing" unknown, unheard, and unseen. The blow tripped me again; and I rose, stick in hand, ready for combat. Retrieving a mini mag light from my fanny pack (okay, so I cheated), I panned the ravine. Nothing, not even wind. Nor had anything heavier than a leaf splashed into the pool. Dressing quickly, I scrambled up the ledge, and checked Paul Lyons' grave beside the trail. The burial stone seemed unmoved. No disturbance, though a deer had stood there recently. The flashlight found a ghoulish gargoyle! But it turned out to be just a knotty tree hollow and not Tom Lyons' face!

Never mind. I'll keep seeking out ghosts and other artifacts of a forgotten world—fossils, tracks, arrowheads, pebbles, bones, feathers, gossamer wings—until I, too, become an artifact.

Mosquito Lake

It spite of its unpleasant sounding name, Mosquito Lake is an attractive place, especially for anglers waving wands for walleye and boaters pulling skiers.

LOCATION
Central Trumbull County, Bazetta and Mecca townships.

SIZE & DESIGNATION
Land: 3,961 acres; water, 7,850 acres.

ACCESS
The state park is boxed by state routes 88, 46, and 305, and Hoagland-Blackstub Road. The park office is located on SR 305 at the south end of the reservoir.

Accommodations: The park's spacious and wooded campground has 234 non-electric sites, a few along the lakeshore. Amenities include a boat launch with tie-ups, showerhouse, flush toilets, dump station, latrines, playground, horseshoes, volleyball. Always a vacancy, rarely a wait in line to register. Enter from Hoagland-Blackstub Road.

Picnic Areas: Prime picnic areas flank the beach and by the boat ramps on SR 305. Grills and tables are provided. The U.S. Army Corps of Engineers provides picnic facilities at a recreation area near the dam, south end off SR 305.

Trails: Hikers, horse riders, and snowmobilers share the 10 mile West Side Trail, a lakeshore trail between Everett-Hull Road and SR 88. The staging area is on Hoagland-Blackstub Road, north of SR 305. On the east shore, hikers and snowmobilers have an eight-mile network called the East Side Trail; the trailhead is at the end of Main Street, west of Cortland. Beaver Trail is a 1.5-mile loop departing at the campground boat launch.

Swimming: A 600-foot sandy swimming beach is located at the south end of the reservoir, off SR 305. There are changing booths, rest rooms, and picnic tables nearby.

Boating: Mosquito Lake's ample girth and straight north-south orientation make it ideal for power boating and water skiing. The southern two-thirds of the lake, south of the SR 88 Causeway, allows unlimited horse-power motors. Slow boats should stay within the no wake zone, 100 yards from shore. Traffic here must slow to 10 mph after sunset.

Speed limit is 15 mph from the SR 88 causeway north to Mahan-Denman Road (TR 240). Water skiing is prohibited in this area, which falls within Mosquito Creek State Wildlife Area. Boats cannot enter the wildlife refuge north of Mahan-Denman Road.

The south end boat launch near the beach and park office has six ramps, several docks, and parking for hundreds of vehicles. If it is congested, go to launches on the east shore off SR 305 or at the end of Main Street in Cortland. Fishermen often depart from ramps on each side of SR 88, also on the east shore.

Hunting: Hunting is permitted in designated areas. Check at the park office. Regulated hunts, by drawing, are conducted at Mosquito Creek State Wildlife Area at the north end.

Fishing: One year somebody figured 60,000 walleyes were hooked in Mosquito Lake, and half were keepers. The survey merely confirmed the lake's fecundity for fish. Insiders say walleye fishing is best in spring and fall when these gamers move toward shore. You also can cast for northern pike, bluegills, bass, and crappies (white and black).

The Corps of Engineers provides shore fishing opportunities at its facilities off SR 305 at the south end, and in the tailwaters below the dam.

Fishing in the waters comprising the wildlife refuge, north of Mahan-Denman Road is a no-no. Do it and you'll get the hook.

Information: Mosquito Lake State Park, 1439 SR 305, Cortland, OH 44410-9303, (330) 637-2856 park office, (330) 638-5700 campground, (330) 637-1961 U.S. Army Corps of Engineers.

HISTORY

Congress authorized the Mosquito Creek project in 1938 to control flooding of the Mahoning, Beaver, and Ohio rivers. The $4 million project was finished in 1952, and the Corps of Engineers figures it has saved $59 million in flood damages. Water can be released from the reservoir to improve downstream water quality, and to supply water to Warren. The Ohio Department of Natural Resources has leased the site from the Corps since the early 1950s.

FIELD NOTES

Mosquito Creek's two-way flow is an anomaly, accordingly by the Corps. "A feature unique to Mosquito Creek Lake is its use of an uncontrolled natural spillway. The natural spillway is located at the upper end of the lake in a low-lying reach of the Mosquito Creek–Grand River Divide. The elevation of the spillway at the point of divide is such that if an impoundment of flood water should fill the lake to an elevation of 904 feet above sea level, the southerly outflow of the lake would be reversed. The overflow would then be discharged through the natural spillway into a tributary of the Grand River, which flows north into Lake Erie."

Nelson-Kennedy Ledges

Here you can wander through a Pleistocene world of rock walls draped with hemlocks, pitted with caves, and cluttered with boulders as big as a house: an imaginary place of hideouts, romantic trysts, and furtive creatures. The Ice Age returns every winter, promoting the wild growth of ice beards on ledges, and glass shields on facades.

LOCATION

Northeast Portage County, Nelson Township.

SIZE & DESIGNATION

Land: 167 acres.

ACCESS

The park entrance, to the Nelson Ledges, amounts to a parking lot on the east side of SR 282, which runs between US 422 and SR 305. The Kennedy Ledges, northwest corner of Kennedy Ledges and Fenstmaker

roads, remains "undeveloped" and off-limits unless you obtain a permit at Punderson State Park.

Picnic Areas: North of the parking lot, you'll find picnic tables, grills, latrines.

Trails: Three miles of trails twist around the Nelson Ledges, and the accompanying boulders, caves, waterfalls, rock passages (crevices), and tight squeezes affectionately known as Dwarf's Pass and Fat Man's Peril. You can follow the route recommended below or make your own way with the park brochure map.

Start at the trailhead for the Yellow Trail on the west side of SR 282 north of the park's parking lot. Trace the trail to features called Cascade Falls and Gold Hunter's Cave, the recess behind the falls. From here, go southerly on the Yellow Trail to Old Maid's Kitchen, Dwarf's Pass, and to the White Trail. Turn left on the White Trail but soon go right (south) on the Red Trail, a somewhat difficult trail through Fat Man's Peril, Indian Pass and Devil's Icebox. The Red Trail hooks east along Sylvan Creek to meet the Blue Trail. The path to the right is a short loop, returning from whence you started. Better to go left (north) beside ledges to Shipwreck Rock and the White Trail. Now turn left and follow the white blazes across The Narrows to Minnehaha Falls and Devil's Hole. The White Trail loops back to the ledges and returns to SR 282 at the south end of the parking lot.

These trails through moss-covered passages can be exciting. Be prepared for rocky, tree-rooted trails, however. Don't climb the dangerous and slippery ledges, which protect rare plants. From time to time litter accumulates in hard to reach places, giving the park and the unknown litterers a black eye. Beverage containers are now banned from the trails.

Information: Nelson-Kennedy Ledges State Park, c/o Punderson State Park, 11755 Kinsman Road, Box 338, Newbury, OH 44065, (440) 564-2279.

HISTORY

The area surrounding the park was crisscrossed by important Indian trails. Ohio's cheesemaking center, called "Cheesedom," emerged here in the 1830s. James A. Garfield, the 20th president of the U.S., was educated at nearby Hiram College, called Western Reserve Electric Institute in Garfield's time. He was president of the college at age 26.

The former vacation spot was picked up by the state in the 1940s and became a state park in 1949.

FIELD NOTES

The park's rock formations are made of Sharon Conglomerate, a pebbly sandstone formed eons ago. (See Lake Katharine State Natural Area, page 118, for the geological origins of this layer.) Wind and water, aided by thawing and freezing, eroded less resistant rock, leaving the conglomerate exposed.

The beech-maple forest is intermingled with trees from northern climes—hemlock, Canada yew, and yellow birch. Notice how their roots creep into rock cracks and contribute to the erosion of the ledges. This is also a haven for ferns called maidenhair, Christmas, grape, wood, and common polypody, the latter often growing like whiskers in rock pocks and cracks.

Woodland wildflowers are abundant. A rarity called red trillium clings to the edge of the ledges. Climbing the rocks and ledges can destory their fragile habitat, and injure the climbers.

Portage Lakes

The original glacial lakes were strung along a portage path used by Native Americans traveling from the Lake Erie and Ohio River watersheds. Later, the lakes provided water for the Ohio & Erie Canal, which passed north of Nesmith Lake. Today, the thirteen Portage Lakes serve as a recreation playground for Akron and Canton.

LOCATION
Southwestern Summit County, Coventry and Franklin townships.

SIZE & DESIGNATION
Land: 1,000 acres; water: 2,520 acres.

ACCESS
The park is accessible from I-277, SR 93 (Manchester Road), and I-77. The facilities at Turkeyfoot Lake are located off SR 93, about 10 miles south of Akron. From Canton, travel north on I-77. Leave at Exit 118 and go north on SR 241 and west on SR 619. The campground overlooks Nimisila Reservoir. To reach it, journey south from the Turkeyfoot Lake entrance on SR 93, then left (east) on Center Road. At South Main Street turn left (north), right on Caston Road, right on Christman, right into the camping area. Follow state park signs.

Accommodations: The "rustic" campground (rustic meaning primitive) occupies a peninsula that juts into Nimisila Reservoir, though none of the 74 sites has a lakeview. And there is no separate beach for campers. Camping for pet owners is available. A "rustic" boat launch adjoins the camping area and shore anglers take advantage of a day-use parking lot.

Picnic Areas: Five picnic areas crowd the Turkeyfoot area. Choose from among the Big Oaks (the biggest with a shelterhouse), Latham Lane, Bay Side, High Point, and Turkeyfoot Beach areas. Old

Park Picnic Area, off SR 619, has a boat ramp and shelterhouse. Shelterhouses are available on a first-come basis.

Trails: Five miles of easy, interconnected paths weave around the Turkeyfoot area off SR 93. The longest is Shoreline Trail, 3.25-mile loop from the beach to Big Oaks Picnic Area.

Swimming: Bathers splash and tan at an ample, 900-foot sandy beach at the Turkeyfoot Lake area. There's plenty of parking, plus changing booths, drinking water, lifeguards (summer) and latrines.

Boating: Boating is big here, but regulated to please all users. Turkeyfoot Lake and East Reservoir have high speed zones for skiing and speed boats (400 horsepower max). These areas have designated hours and days for "speed" activities, and for sailboating. These regulations are posted at the launches and park office. All other areas, including Mud Lake, Rex Lake, Long Lake, Nesmith, North Reservoir, Cottage Grove, and Miller lakes, are no wake zones. Electric motors can ply Nimisila Reservoir, now a beacon for wind surfers.

Turkeyfoot's marina has four-lanes, loading docks and plenty of parking. Other boat launches are located at Long Lake (Cove Road off SR 93), North Reservoir (State Mill Road), Old Park Picnic Area, and Nimisila Reservoir (campground, two on Christman Road, South Main Street).

Hunting: Shotgunners aim at waterfowl in designated areas. Check at the park office.

Fishing: Chain pickerel can be landed from Portage Lakes —not many lakes in Ohio can boast that. The state-record pickerel, six pounds and 26 inches, was pulled from Long Lake in 1961. Turkeyfoot Lake, the deepest in the chain, regularly gets a load of state-raised walleye and saugeye. Nimisila Reservoir, among the shallowest, is stocked with northern pike. Muskellunge, catfish, bluegill, crappie, largemouth bass, bullhead and carp tug at lines.

North Reservoir has a fishing platform for anglers with disabilities (Portage Lakes Drive). Nimisila Reservoir is ringed with fishing access points.

Special Places & Events: The Astronomy Club of Akron leases land near the park office to operate a small observatory. Programs are scheduled seasonally, or during an important celestial event.

Information: Portage Lakes State Park, 5031 Manchester Road, Akron OH 44319, (330) 644-2220.

HISTORY
The Portage Lakes region played a key role in Ohio's early history. Native Americans plied the waters as they portaged from the Cuyahoga River to the the Muskingum watershed and the Ohio River. Indians and settlers gathered at this landmark to trade. American troops mustered here during the War of 1812.

Some of the lakes and runs were built exclusively to keep the Ohio & Erie Canal at the required four-foot level. When the canal died in 1913, local industries siphoned water from the lakes via runs and channels.

The Ohio Department of Public Works, which

took over the canal system, built Nimisila Reservoir in 1939 to maintain the level of existing lakes. The Ohio Department of Natural Resources took over the lakes for recreation in 1949.

FIELD NOTES

Vegetative survivors of the Ice Age are sprinkled throughout the park, namely tamarack (larch) trees and cranberry. The lakes and wetlands bring Canada geese, mallards, wood ducks, and other waterbirds to the park. Woodcock, great blue heron, various hawks and owls, beaver, and muskrat are residents.

Punderson

Some winters 70 inches of snow falls on Punderson's trails, making it a frosty paradise for cross-country skiers, sledders, and snowmobilers. All that white fluff serves as camouflage for the ghosts said to haunt the park's lodge, a quaint, restored Tudor-style mansion.

LOCATION

Central Geauga County, Newbury Township.

SIZE & DESIGNATION

Land: 846 acres; water: 150 acres.

ACCESS

The entrance is on the south side of SR 87, about five miles west of Burton.

Accommodations: Punderson Lodge has 31 rooms, some with fireplaces, some with full-length picture windows overlooking the lake, some with ghosts (See page 328). The staff dusts and polishes the Old English bric-a-brac that makes the place charming. Other lodge features are a restaurant, lounge, shuffleboard, horseshoes, outdoor pool, game room, three meeting rooms, tennis and basketball courts.

The park's 26 deluxe cabins (all ghost-free) offer more privacy. Each sleeps six, and now comes with a television. Reservations for the lodge and cabins are recommended.

The campground (201 all-electric sites) fills fast on summer weekends, partly because of its close proximity to Sea World and Six Flags of Ohio amusement parks. Early birds get the private, wooded sites, latecomers usually get uneven, hilltop spots on crowded loops. Campers who need frills have three showerhouses and laundries, four Rent-A-Camp sites, and flush toilets. Pets are permitted in designated areas. Youngsters can climb on playground equipment.

Punderson's raccoons are notorious campground invaders. The most clever bandits know how to open

coolers. So, stow your food out of their reach (the car is perfect).

Picnic Areas: Picnic areas are situated on a bluff above the swimming beach, and at the marina. You'll find picnic tables at the tennis courts and off Park Road 2 beside the Mushers Trail.

Trails: In the warm months, foot travelers trample on 14 miles of trails, but these are shared in winter (snow permitting) with cross-country skiers and snowmobilers. My favorite is the 1.5-mile Erie Trail, which departs from the campground and circles Stump Lake. The Iroquois Trail traces the west shore of Punderson Lake and connects the lodge with the beach and marina.

Punderson gets packed with cross-country skiers, snowmobilers, and sledders after a snow storm. Families head for the lighted sledding and toboggan hill north of the marina. Nearby is the heated winter sports chalet, which sells snacks, hot beverages, and rents cross-country skis. Snowmobilers generally take trails east of Park Road 1 (main road from entrance to the lodge), while cross-country skiers favor trails on the west side.

Swimming: The swimming beach (600 feet) is north of the lodge. There is plenty of parking. The pool is reserved for lodge and cabin guests.

Boating: The camp store and marina at the north end of Punderson Lake rents canoes, pedal boats, and rowboats. You can launch your own craft, too, (electric motors only) at the marina. Try Stump Lake (half the size of Punderson Lake) if you seek a more primitive setting. Also, paddle the Water Nature Trail to numbered sites along the shore.

The marina also rents bikes, and sells camping goods, food, some fishing tackle, and firewood. During the summer it is open daily.

Fishing: The Division of Wildlife dumps several truck loads of golden trout into Punderson Lake. Largemouth bass, bluegills, catfish and crappie also swim here. The Iroquois Trail leads to ideal casting spots along the western shore of Punderson Lake, such as the fishing pier midway between the lodge and beach. Campers favor the fishing pier branching from a trail at site 26. Ice fishing is permitted.

Golf: Punderson's tightly-packed 18-hole golf course rounds out the resort facilities. For tee times dial (440) 564-5465.

Special Places & Events: Punderson hosts the Ohio Championship Cross-Country Ski Race and the Buckeye Classic Sled Dog Race in January (weather permitting).

Information: Punderson State Park, Box 338 11755 Kinsman Road, Newbury, OH 44065-9684, (440) 564-2279 park office, (440) 564-1195 camping, (800) 282-7275 lodge, (440) 564-5465 golf.

HISTORY

Indians once burned campfires on the land occupied by the campground. Lemuel Punderson, Newbury Township's first permanent white settler and the park's namesake, built a dam and grist mill at the south end of the lake in 1808. The lake grew into a small resort. Cottages, taverns, and a hotel

No man is an island when there's a kid with pole, longing for lunkers.

accommodated weekenders from Cleveland.

Karl Long started building the Tudor-style manor house in 1929, then lost his fortune in the stock market crash that year. The estate was finally finished in 1948, but that year the Ohio Division of Wildlife acquired the property. The grounds became a state park in 1951. The mansion was renovated in 1956 and 1982.

FIELD NOTES

Punderson Lake is Ohio's largest (90 acres) and deepest (75 feet) glacial kettle lake. Some of the stocked golden trout survive year-round in the cold depth. At the end of the Ice Age, about 12,000 years ago, enormous blocks of ice broke off the face of the Wisconsinan glacier. The ice made depressions, and sediment carried by glacial melt-water enwrapped it. As the temperature warmed the ice melted into a basin, or kettle, created by its own weight and surrounding piles of dirt. Stump Lake and Pine Lake (western edge of the park) are kettle lakes too, but these are filling in with natural debris faster than Punderson. Ohio once had hundreds of glacial puddles, but most have either been swallowed up by encroaching vegetation, shrunk naturally to bogs and fens, or altered (drained, dammed, etc.) by humans.

Pymatuning

One of the best locations in the nation for walleye and muskie has camping and park facilities for water enthusiasts in two states. The state wildlife map of the lake points to hot spots for crappies, bass, and bluegills, and there's a place on the Pennsylvania side, says the map, "where ducks walk on fishes backs."

LOCATION

Southeastern Ashtabula County, Andover and Richmond townships.

SIZE & DESIGNATION

Land: 3,500 acres; water: 14,650 acres. Ohio's share of the lake amounts to 4,000 acres.

ACCESS

This hook-shaped lake straddles the Ohio-Pennsylvania border. The southern end of the lake is accessible from US 322, the middle section via SR 85 (off US 6), the north from Leon Road, off US 6 and SR 7. Most state park facilities stem from Pymatuning Lake Road, which runs along the Ohio shore.

Accommodations: A large family campground with 373 sites is located off Pymatuning Lake Road (near Slater Road), at the south end of the park. The park office is three miles north. Some 352 sites have electric hookups, the best one being the lakeshore spot on the northern loop. Amenities include a tent-only area, four showerhouses with flush toilets, laundry, commissary, playground, nature center, amphitheater, boat launch, and small swimming beach.

Sixty cabins are clustered south of the park office.

Twenty-seven, two-bedroom family cabins sleep six and are heated for year-round enjoyment. These recently modernized units include gas fireplaces, cable TV, and microwave ovens. Thirty-three standard cabins sleep four. These unheated units are available May through October. A small beach for cabin guests is nearby. These extremely popular units are rented by the week June-August. Reservations can be made a year in advance by calling (440) 293-6684.

Picnic Areas: Five picnic areas are scattered along the shore. Poplar Grove, north of the campground, offers lakeshore views and a shelter to the first arrivals. Tables with grills are found at Birches Landing, the main swimming beach, and Padanarum Area (north), the latter with a shelter.

Trails: Beaver Dam Trail is a mile loop near the picnic area for the main swimming beach. As the name suggests, the activities of beavers are evident along the interpretive trail. Whispering Pines Trail is a mile long path breaking from Fishing Point near the cabins. The name recalls the tall white pines that once grew here.

Swimming: The main public beach, just south of the SR 85/ PA 285 causeway, measures 1,000 feet and features a bathhouse with showers, toilets, and snack bar. Campers and cabins guests have separate beaches.

Boating: To maintain the lake's integrity as a fishing destination, boats cannot be souped up beyond a 10 horsepower motor. The Ohio shore has five launches, all off Pymatuning Lake Road. Ramps at the Padanarum Area (north, at the end of Leon Road) and Birches Landing, north of the campground, offer fuel, fishing and boating supplies, snacks, and boat rentals ranging from canoes to pontoons. Campers and cabin guests have ramps in their areas. Another serves the main beach, near Gibbs Road.

Boaters are wise to heed three precautions: Pymatuning gets very choppy, very fast when wind freshens and before storms. There are hundreds of submerged stumps just below water level, which partly explains the 10 hp limit. Pymatuning is a big lake and cruising pontooners should give themselves plenty of time to return.

Hunting: Designated areas only. Waterfowl mostly. Check at the park office.

Fishing: In Indian times Pymatuning meant "a crooked man's dwelling." Nowadays, it means "walleye." Some years, the crooked man's dwelling yielded 50,000 walleyes, many of them 10 pounders, sleek and shiny. Crappiethons (tournaments) held here attest to the lake's bulging population of this panfish. Some manage to grow to a foot or 14 inches. Bluegill fishing is considered excellent, and smallmouth bass good (though overlooked). Other catches are yellow perch, white bass, and channel catfish. Pennsylvania stocks the lake with walleyes and muskies, but the latter fish has not taken to the water as hoped. Ohio planted 5,000 muskies in the lake in late 1997. Keep your fingers crossed, and line untangled.

The lake is jointly managed by Ohio and Pennsylvania. An Ohio fishing license is valid in Pennsylvania water if fishing from a boat. Anglers casting from a Pennsylvania shore or island need that state's fishing license. Reciprocal rules apply to Pennsylvanians fishing in Ohio. Check size restrictions for walleye (minimum usually 15 inches), bass (12 inches) and muskies (30 inches).

Being in the snow belt, Pymatuning Lake gets blasts of snow and lake-freezing temperatures. The lake usually permits ice fishing, snowmobiles, and ice boats. Obviously, you check conditions before venturing upon the ice.

Special Places & Events: The spillway in Pennsylvania, on PA 3011 (Linesville Road between US 6 and PA 285), is the place "Where ducks walk on fishes backs." Thousands of tourists stop here to feed bread crumbs to ducks and carp whose numbers are so great that ducks actually climb atop the carp to retrieve a morsel. In spite of its appeal, the practice should be stopped because wildlife dependent on human handouts is not wild any more.

Information: Pymatuning State Park, P.O. Box 1000, Andover, OH 44003-1000, (440) 293-6030 park office, (440) 293-6684 campground.

HISTORY

For decades the only whites venturing into Pymatuning Swamp were trappers collecting beaver and mink pelts. Later, loggers hauled out tall and straight white pines for sailing masts. Little by little, settlement edged into the swamp and ruined all but a sliver of its wilderness. Farmers prospered by growing onions at the edge of the swamp, the headwaters of the Shenango River.

In 1933, the outlet for the swamp was cleared and dammed by Pennsylvania to regulate the flow of the Shenango and Beaver rivers. Pymatuning Lake swelled behind the impoundment. Ohio began buying park land along its shore in the mid-1930s, and by the 1950s the Division of Parks and Recreation started building recreation facilities.

FIELD NOTES

Pennsylvania has a visitors' center with wildlife exhibits, fish hatchery, and birding tour on Ford Island, Linesville Road. Bald eagles can be seen from the visitors' center.

Quail Hollow

The name Quail Hollow sounds pretentious. Maybe Harry Bartlett Stewart flushed a covey of quail the day he bought the place in 1914. Maybe it was wishful thinking on his part. The park lies at the northern edge of the bird's range. A few may have lived here in the early 1970s, but after several devastating winters the bobwhites retreated to scattered locations in Southern Ohio. Today, this pastoral park serves as a conference center and quiet, day-use facility.

LOCATION
Northern Stark County, Lake Township.

SIZE & DESIGNATION
Land: 698 acres; water: two acres (pond).

ACCESS
From Canton, follow SR 43 northward to Hartville, then travel on Congress Lake Ave. to the entrance. From I-77, go north on SR 241, east on SR 641 to Hartville, north on Congress Lake Ave.

Accommodations: Just a primitive group campground for 25 people that can be reserved by incorporated groups. Parking, water, and rest rooms are a quarter mile from the campsite.

Picnic Areas: There are a two picnic areas (first-come basis). The best one, called Shady Lane, is beside a small fishing pond, off the driveway. Spruce Grove Picnic Area is near the former Stewart manor.

Trails: Eight interpretive hiking trails, totaling 8.75 miles, wander over the grounds. The interconnecting, color-coded trails carry the names of the habitats they visit—Coniferous Forest, Deciduous Forest, Tallgrass Prairie, Sedge Marsh, Meadowlands, Beaver Lodge, and Peat Bog. A perimeter walk, combining trails, measures 5-6 miles and visits most habitats. Consult the trail map on the park brochure. Trails depart from the pond, and Natural History Study Center. The fishing pond has an observation deck for wildlife viewing. Feel free to stroll through the herb garden and restored manor grounds.

Four miles of bridle trails start near the pond and journey through forest and field. Foot travelers can also use the horse trails.

Fishing: Toss a line into Blackberry Hill Pond, but don't expect much. Fishing is not permitted in the beaver ponds.

Special Places & Events: The Natural History Study Center, formerly the Stewart manor, hosts nature education and community activities. The small conference center has a library, kitchen, dining hall, basement rathskeller, and meeting rooms. Incorporated groups can reserve the place for workshops and special events. Natural history and outdoor education programs for schools and groups are available upon request. Ten rooms in the manor serve as a Visitor's Center, open 9 a.m. to 5 p.m. The center features natural history and historical exhibits. Volunteer staffers may be present in the afternoon.

Information: Quail Hollow State Park, 13340 Congress Lake Avenue, Hartville, OH 44632, (330) 877-6652.

HISTORY
Conrad Brumbaugh came to this spot in 1811. He hacked away the wilderness and built a square log house measuring 24 feet a side. Bears killed his livestock, rattlesnakes leaped from the mire, and people reportedly disappeared in his dense wild berry patches. Brumbaugh, however, stuck it out. A wooden frame home replaced the pioneer dwelling in 1842. In it he raised 11 boys and four daughters. Fire later took this home. The Brumbaughs held their ground. The family cemetery is located off the park entrance drive.

Harry Bartlett Stewart, head honcho of the Akron, Canton & Youngstown Railroad, started buying the Brumbaugh tract, and adjoining properties, in 1914. The manor house, combining Greek Revival and Federal architectural designs, was finished in 1929. Harry Jr. and his family lived here from 1937 to 1975, then sold the property at half price to the Ohio Department of Natural Resources.

FIELD NOTES
Some of the habitats—the tallgrass prairie and pine plantation—are contrived, but enjoyable nevertheless. Beaver, fox, deer, skunk, and raccoon find refuge here. Poison sumac thrives in the sphagnum peat bog. Nearby Congress Lake is a natural kettle lake that formed at the end of the Ice Age. A bird blind at the end of the Woodland Swamp Trail attracts human wildlife watchers.

Tinker's Creek

Owners of this place come and go, and none has named the lake. Awhile ago the place was a private park called Colonial Spring Gardens. The state bought the land in 1966 as a wildlife area. In 1973, it opened as a state park, but the following year the western half was dedicated as a state nature preserve. Tinker's Creek is your basic day-use park with a twist for nature enthusiasts—a wetland worth exploring. Three-quarters of the park acreage is wetland.

LOCATION
Northwestern Portage County, Streetsboro Township.

SIZE & DESIGNATION
Land: 354 acres; water: 15 acres.

ACCESS
From Gate 13 of the Ohio Turnpike, go north on SR 14/I-480. Exit at Frost Road heading east. Immediately turn left on a road leading to a T intersection. Here, go right on Aurora-Hudson Road. The park entrance is one mile on the left.

Picnic Areas: Two picnic areas are shaded by towering white oaks. A shelterhouse with electricity is available near the beach on a first-come basis.

Trails: Four short and sweet trails amounting to 3.5 miles wind through the park. The best path, a 1.5-mile journey on Pond Run Trail, visits two ponds, bottomland woods, and the manmade lake with no name. Other trails are the one-mile Whitetail Loop, the half-mile Gentian Trail, and Lakeview Trail, a .75-mile path around the lake with no name.

Swimming: A 200-foot beach is located on the south shore of the manmade lake with no name. The park provides changing booths and flush toilets.

Fishing: The manmade lake with no name yields little, just a few bluegills, bass, crappie, and catfish. The large fish wallowing in the shallows are grass

carp, put there to control vegetation. Throw it back if you catch one.

Information: Tinker's Creek State Park, 10303 Aurora-Hudson Road, Streetsboro, OH 44241, (330) 296-3239 or (330) 562-5575.

Mailing Address: c/o West Branch State Park, 5708 Esworthy Road, Rte. 5, Ravenna, OH 44266-9659, (330) 296-3239.

HISTORY
The park gets its name from Joseph Tinker, a surveyor for the Connecticut Land Company who arrived with Moses Cleaveland in 1797.

FIELD NOTES
The state park and adjacent nature preserve offer chances to see the wildlife in wetlands, a world belonging to beavers, rails, waterfowl, dragonflies, sedges, egrets, bitterns, and loggerhead shrikes. Hundreds of frogs will splash into the ponds as you approach. Osprey and bald eagles drop in occasionally.

The wetlands in the state park and nature preserve started as kettle lakes formed during the Pleistocene Ice Age. Chunks of ice that broke off the face of the retreating Wisconsinan glacier melted into depressions, creating the kettleholes. Small, spring fed ponds exist in the park and preserve.

The unnamed lake in the state park, however, is human made, constructed during the time the property was a private park.

> *The state park and adjacent nature preserve offer chances to see the wildlife in wetlands, a world belonging to beavers, rails, waterfowl, dragonflies,...*

West Branch

Back in 1812, Captain John Campbell mustered militia volunteers here then marched them to Cleveland to fight the British. Today, the lake's jagged shore and crooked coves muster fishers and boaters.

LOCATION
Eastern Portage County, Ravenna, Charlestown, and Paris townships.

SIZE & DESIGNATION
Land: 5,352 acres; water: 2,650 acres. The

Ohio Department of Natural Resources leases the area from the U.S. Army Corps of Engineers.

Bordered on the north by SR 5, and accessible from SR 14 and SR 225. To reach the park office, bridle trail, and campground from SR 5, go south on Rock Spring Road, left on Copeland Road and onto Esworthy Road. The swimming beach and marina are at the end of Cable Line Road, off SR 225. Park signs point the way.

Accommodations: The 103-site campground is on a peninsula that juts from the north shore of Michael J. Kirwan Lake on Esworthy Road. The campground has drinking water (pumps), rest rooms, waste water receptacles, playground, dump station, and amphitheater. Sites do not have electricity. Several lakeshore sites have boat tie-ups. Two Rent-A-Camp sites are available. A reservable group camp handles 60 people. Horseback riders can get permission to camp in a small campground near the camp office.

Picnic Areas: Picnic tables and shelters are scattered in the park—all on a first-come basis. The beach, marina, and boat ramps have shelters. Two picnic areas line the lakeshore between the marina and beach.

Trails: An eight-mile section of the Buckeye Trail is the best footpath through the park. From trailheads on Rock Spring and Industry roads, the trail splits to form a loop that travels on the west end of the park on both sides of the lake. The map on the park brochure shows the route. Three easy trails—Deer Run, Clubmoss, and Black Cherry—depart near the park office. They total 2.8 miles. The Corps of Engineers has the mile-long Little Jewel Run Nature Trail below the dam. The trail starts on Wayland Road.

Twenty miles of bridle trails start at a staging area on Esworthy Road. The trails snake along the north shore, mostly east of Rock Spring Road. A small horse camp is available with a permit. Go to the park office for a trail map and permit.

Snowmobile trails twist for some 20 miles on the south side of the lake. The West Boat Ramp off Rock Spring Road serves as a staging area and trailhead. From here, the trails wind eastward to Silver Creek Bay. Maps are available at the park office.

Swimming: The park's swimming beach measures 700 feet and includes showers, changing rooms, and food concession. From the campground backtrack to Rock Spring Road and turn right. Go east (right) on SR 5, south (right) on Wayland Road, west (right) on E. Cable Line Road, north on road to the beach. From SR 225 take E. Cable Line to the beach road. Boaters can swim in Silver Creek Bay, south and west of the beach.

Boating: Michael J. Kirwan Lake sprawls for 10 miles and points west from its dam off Wayland Road. Boats with unlimited horsepower can ply the water east of the Rock Spring Road causeway. No wake zones extend 300 feet from shore, and west of the Rock Spring Road causeway. Sailboat flotillas decorate the water in summer.

A marina at the end of Alliance Road has fuel, boat rentals, supplies, and seasonal dock rentals for 200 boats. Two other launching ramps on the south shore are located on Gilbert Road (East Boat Ramp) and off Rock Spring Road (West Boat Ramp), near the causeway. Small boats can depart from the fishermen's access on the north shore at Rock Spring Road.

Hunting: Hunters can pursue small game, waterfowl, and deer on the south shore west of Gilbert Road, and on the north shore west of Rock Spring Road. A no-hunting zone extends 400 feet from developed buildings. Contact the park office for details.

Fishing: Monster muskies might be lurking in the deep pools by the dam. The state's largest tiger muskie— 45 inches, 26.5 pounds—was caught here in 1984. But anglers usually have better luck casting for walleye, crappie, largemouth and smallmouth bass, bluegill, and catfish. The Ohio Division of Wildlife publishes a fishing map of the lake. Ice usually covers the lake, offering the winter tip-up clan a chance to catch their limit.

Fishermen can park and launch canoes and rowboats at an access area on the north shore, west side of Rock Spring Road.

Information:

West Branch State Park, 5708 Esworthy Road, Rte. 5, Ravenna, OH 44266-9659, (330) 296-3239.

U.S. Army Corps of Engineers, Michael J. Kirwan Dam & Reservoir, P.O. Box 58, Wayland, OH 44285, (330) 358-2247

The current dammed to create Michael J. Kirwan Reservoir is the West Branch of the Mahoning River. The river's name derives from the Lenni Lenape (Delaware) expression "mahonink," meaning "at the salt lick." Indians and white settlers gathered salt from the banks of the Mahoning River near Warren.

The U.S. Army Corps of Engineers finished the $20 million, 9,900-foot flood control and water supply dam in 1965. The impoundment has prevented more than $75 million in flood damage, according to the Corps. The state park opened in 1966.

Before its impoundment, the West Branch of the Mahoning River flowed easterly at the base of the Kent terminal moraine, a ridge of glacial sediment marking a pause in the retreat of the Wisconsinan glacier about 12,000 years ago. Much of the land around the lake is recovering farmland, and young forest. Spring wildflowers include bloodroot, Dutchman's breeches, skunk cabbage, and trillium. Red fox and raccoon prowl at night, the latter a campground visitor.

The usual cast of migratory waterbirds appear— geese, loons, grebes, ducks, coots and cormorants. Warblers include prairie, Nashville, magnolia, and Connecticut. The bald eagle has been seen, and good eyes might glimpse a short-eared owl.

The Beach at Century Park Lorain, Ohio

many of the best out-
door recreation play-
grounds and nature education
facilities in Ohio are found in
county parks, or what big city
folks call "metroparks."

The state's big metropark districts cater to suburban and urban visitors, and typically are found at the edge of the swelling metropolis. However, some, like Dayton's Island Park or Cleveland's Ohio & Erie Reservation, are surrounded by skyscrapers or factories, while others, like Clear Creek Metropark, are more than an hour's drive from "downtown." Whereas "city" parks generally concentrate on facilities for organized team sports and indoor recreation, county parks usually focus on individual outdoor recreation opportunities, such as hiking, picnicking, wildlife observation, bicycling, etc. More often than not,

county park districts set aside more than half the acreage of each park for nature. In some cases, 80 percent of the property is a nature refuge. With some exceptions, most parks are "day use" sites.

The metropark movement started in Ohio's big cities after legislation in 1915 gave counties the authority to establish park districts. Now "suburban" counties like Lake County, and rural ones like Monroe County offer outdoor experiences for their residents. It is safe to say, that most of Ohio's growth in park land in the last two decades has been accomplished by county park districts. Consequently, it is wise policy to visit and support your local park system.

The metroparks come all sizes, shapes and conditions. They have been formed from pristine parcels and from tortured turf, such as quarries, or reclaimed land.

Here is a guide to selected county and metropark park districts in Ohio. Parks featured in my previous book, *Natural Acts*, or those that double as state nature preserves get better descriptive treatment than other parks because natural history information on those sites is more abundant. ◠

NORTHEAST

◆◆◆ ASHTABULA COUNTY ◆◆◆
Ashtabula County Park District, 25 W. Jefferson St., Jefferson, OH 44047, (440) 576-0717.

◆◆◆ COLUMBIANA COUNTY ◆◆◆
Columbiana County Park District, 130 W. Maple St., Lisbon, OH 44432, (330) 424-9511.
Scenic Vista Park, 235 acres, Wayne Ridge Road, Center Township, picnic area, nature programs, trails.

◆◆◆ COSHOCTON COUNTY ◆◆◆
Coshocton County Park District, 23253 SR 83, Coshocton, OH 43812, (740) 622-7528.
Lake Park Recreation Area, 457 acres, SR 36 & SR 83. Roscoe Village, canal boat rides, swimming, playground, camping, picnicking, fishing, bike and hike trails, golf, Walhonding River.

◆◆◆ CUYAHOGA COUNTY ◆◆◆
The state's first metropark district started with no money and just three acres of bottomland straddling Rocky River, a parcel donated by a brewer. A revised state law in 1915 enabled counties to fund park districts and to acquire property for park lands. Later that year, the Cuyahoga County park board hired William Stinchcomb and Frederick Law Olmstead, the son of America's foremost landscape architect in the 19th century, to develop a park plan. The two designers envisioned an interconnecting ring of parks and boulevards around fast-growing Cleveland—a chain of green that has become known as the Emerald Necklace. Today, Cleveland Metroparks comprises 14 reservations totaling more than 19,000 acres.
Information about the following and other parks can be obtained by contacting Cleveland Metroparks, 4101 Fulton Parkway, Cleveland, OH 44144-1923, (216) 351-6300.

Bedford Reservation

Tinker's Creek has been tinkering in this valley for many millennia. The awesome hemlock-lined, severely sloped gorge sculptured by the creek became a National Natural Landmark in 1968. In summer, the mist churned by the boiling creek stays in the cavity of the canyon until late morning. The forest climbs above the thinning vapors, spills over the rim of the deep cut, and seems to flow, grasp, and grope toward the horizon. For a moment, it is easy to forget that miles of concrete, and a million people have got this place surrounded.

LOCATION
Southeastern Cuyahoga County, encircled by the cities of Bedford, Bedford Heights, Oakwood, Walton Hills and Valley View.

SIZE
2,109 acres. Tinker's Creek Gorge is a National Natural Landmark.

ACCESS
From downtown Cleveland, travel south on I-77, east on I-480, and south on I-271. Exit at Broadway and head north about a mile. Turn left on Northfield Road, right on Union Street, left on Egbert Road, then right at the entrance. Drive on the Gorge Parkway to the Tinker's Creek Scenic Overlook parking lot on the right. Drive past the tiny overlook between the Egbert and Lost Meadows picnic areas.
Trails: A three-mile trek begins at the scenic overlook and goes east to the Egbert Picnic Area. The trail heading east (right), along the edge of the woods to the wide, gravel bridle trail leads to the picnic area, a small gorge created by Deer Lick Creek and a run behind Bridal Veil Falls. This path is also the famous Buckeye Trail, which circles the state. A paved All-Purpose Trail is across the street from the trailhead.
Facilities: Rest rooms are located at the picnic areas and Shawnee Hills Golf Course (off Egbert

Road), where golfers can try to shoot featherless birdies and eagles on an 18-hole course.

GEOLOGY

It has taken Tinker's Creek thousands of years to scour through mounds of till (sand, gravel, clay, etc.) dumped by the Wisconsinan glacier 12,000–15,000 years ago, and through three layers of bedrock ranging from 330-370 million years old, all of them the former floors of shallow, ancient saltwater seas.

The stream falls more than 200 feet on its 1.9 mile passage through the park. The overlook at the start of our trail rests on a cliff 200 feet above the water.

The youngest exposed rock is Berea sandstone, composed of tiny quartz crystals cemented by clay. The crystals shine like diamonds in the sunlight. About 330 million years ago (Mississippian geologic period), currents washing off higher ground to the east and north distributed sand along an ocean shore in a wide fan. This delta dried and compacted into rock when the sea receded. Huge chunks, or slump rocks, of this sandstone have rolled into the creek, the victims of undercutting, a force where water erosion removes softer rock layers beneath a harder layer causing pieces of the harder rock to split off. Other blocks of slump rock are found along the trail in the ravines of tributaries that flow into Tinker's Creek.

Cleveland shale (350 million years ago), made

More metroparks

Other Cleveland Metroparks

Bradley Woods, 785 acres, North Olmstead and Westlake on the Lorain County line. Picnic area and fishing pond.

Brookside Reservation, 135 acres, John Nagy Boulevard next to Cleveland Metroparks Zoo. Ball fields, picnic areas, and open spaces.

Euclid Creek Reservation, 346 acres along Euclid Creek. Picnic areas, creekside trail.

Garfield Park Reservation, 177 acres, in Garfield Heights between Broadway and Turney Road. Nature center, wetland, picnic areas, and hiking trails.

Huntington Reservation, Bay Village on the shore of Lake Erie. Lake Erie Nature & Science Center,

Schuele Planetarium, Huntington Playhouse, Baycrafters, Huntington Beach, picnic areas.

Ohio & Erie Canal Reservation, 280 acres. A 12-mile extension of the Ohio & Erie Canal Towpath Trail from the Cuyahoga Valley National Recreation Area to Harvard Avenue.

of extremely small bits of quartz, clay and mica, lies beneath the sandstone. Waves washing the shore carried these fine sediments into the sea. The rock's black color comes from the murky decayed material of shoreline plants that fell into a late Devonian sea. In Central Ohio, geologists call this formation Ohio shale. Fossils rarely turn up in Ohio shale, but here geologists have found a rewarding fishing hole.

In 1979, Bob Burns, a geologist from Maple Heights, uncovered a chunk of pyrite (a.k.a. fool's gold) shaped like a shark's skull. The 360 million-year-old beast still had its teeth. The find was a dunkleosteus, an armored fish that grew to lengths of 20–30 feet. A replica of "Dunk" hangs in the nature center at Rocky River Reservation.

At Bridal Veil Falls notice the "ripple" rock, small ridges in shale formed by lapping ocean waves. Please leave the rocks in the stream. Observe, but do not collect.

Downstream, beyond the gorge, the creek has begun to reveal Chagrin shale, bluish-gray and opaque, formed 360 million years ago.

Part of the buried valley of the ancient Dover River runs through the northeast part of the reservation. Like the Cuyahoga River, the Dover River flowed northward, except it refreshed an ocean. In its heydey, the Dover was supposedly deeper than the Cuyahoga River and was one of two major drainage routes in the region. The glaciers that slid over the landscape rerouted the river and filled the valley with glacial till.

WILDLIFE

Oaks, beech, maples and their associates dominate the woods on both sides of Tinker's Creek. All totaled, 29 kinds of native trees have sunk their roots here. Others found in the woods include ash, tulip tree, cucumber magnolia, and basswood on the gradual slopes; shagbark hickory joins the oaks on the rim.

The cool, shady gorge allows hemlock and American yew, trees more common in colder climates, to thrive. These arrived in the vanguard of the Wisconsinan glacier. Ohio's gorges and ravines are the only habitats suitable for hemlock and other immigrants from the north woods. Yellow birch also survives on the slopes.

A rare cluster of mountain maple, living at the southernmost extent of its range, grows on a steep slope in the northeast corner of the park. Another tree reaching its northern limit is the redbud, common in Central Ohio and farther south but unusual in Northeast Ohio.

Some winged sumac, also near its northern limit, stands here, too. Its leaves become brilliant red in autumn.

The woods also shelters a few old stands of red and white pine, supposedly remnants of an ancient pine forest. Most pines that you will see, however, were planted by humans in this century.

Sycamores, beech, sugar maples, willows—all common inhabitants—prevail in the bottomland.

The reservation protects a number of threat-ened, rare or uncommon wildflowers, grasses and ferns: (flowers) hellebore, fringed gentian, large round-leaf orchid (potentially threatened), dwarf crested iris, round-leaf violet, yellow ladies' slippers, twinleaf, tall tickseed, swamp thistle, Indian cucumber root, whorled rosinweed; (grass) scouring-rush; and (ferns) Goldie's, fragile, silvery, rattle-snake, and cutleaf grape.

HISTORY

A petroglyph, drawing on rock, found at Poet's Cave along Deer Lick Creek, proves that ancient people once inhabited the land.

The creek's namesake, Joseph Tinker, arrived with Moses Cleaveland's surveying party in 1796. He helped plat the holdings of the Connecticut Land Company east of the Cuyahoga River. Tinker's groundwork led to the construction of grist, woolen, and chair-making mills that utilized the creek's water power.

Tinker's Creek was one of the first scenic areas chosen for a park by the newly-commissioned Cleveland park board in 1915. Bedford Glens Park, located on the north bank, became a popular playground before World War II, featuring dances, bowling, picnicking, and sightseeing. It was destroyed by fire in 1944. Tinker's Creek almost became Lake Shawnee in the early 1960s, but a plan to dam the creek was opposed by the park board and conservation groups.

Lake Isaac Waterfowl Sanctuary (in Big Creek Reservation)

Birds and other creatures find a safe haven in the ponds, marshes, thickets, and bottomland woods that comprise the Lake Isaac Waterfowl Sanctuary in Big Creek Reservation.

LOCATION

Southwestern Cuyahoga County, near Middleburg Heights.

SIZE & DESIGNATION

Big Creek Reservation is 566 acres. Lake Isaac is an Ohio Watchable Wildlife Area.

ACCESS

Exit I-71 at US 42/Pearl Road. Head north on Pearl Road (toward downtown Cleveland), then turn left (west) on Fowles Road, which goes under I-71. Turn left (south) on Big Creek Parkway and almost immediately Lake Isaac appears on the right. Park in the designated area.

Trail: Many visitors contentedly view the lake and its waterfowl from the benches behind a long, roadside observation area. But if you get restless, try out the mile-long lasso-shaped trail that starts to the right of the observation platform.

For most of its distance, the gravel path is open, wide, and flat. There's lots of trail room for restless kids. Just try to keep their volume down. Residential subdivisions surround Lake Isaac, and roads choke it from all sides. Busy railroad tracks serve as the western border, and high-flying power lines cut across the property. Try to ignore these distractions. Focus on the details, small scenes, and little miracles when visiting this park.

GEOLOGY

Lake Isaac is a glacial pothole created around 12,000 years ago when a huge chunk of ice split from the Wisconsinan ice mass and formed a depression in the land. Water from the melting glacier cube filled the lake. A dam was later constructed to enlarge and stabilize the lake.

WILDLIFE

Lake Isaac is a haven for waterfowl. Metropark observers have counted as many as 800 birds on the lake—wood ducks, black ducks, mallards, and Canada geese mostly. Great blue herons and green herons are seen occasionally. Other transients such as blue-winged teal, gadwall, pintail, and wigeon fly in during the spring and autumn migrations.

Please observe the signs at the observation platform that urge visitors not to feed the birds. The geese and ducks are not pets.

Fox, deer, mink, raccoons, opossum, rabbits reside here, along with what sounds like a boat load of bullfrogs. Carp, bluegill, and others swim in the water but snagging them with hook, line and sinker is unlawful.

Brecksville Reservation

Chippewa Creek fashioned a fairy tale, mist-filled gorge of precipitous rock walls before it emptied into the Cuyahoga River. Like mercenary sentries on a castle wall, tall and straight hemlocks, more accustomed to the boreal forests of Canada, protect the crown jewel of this reservation.

LOCATION
Southern Cuyahoga County, near Brecksville.

SIZE
3,392 acres.

ACCESS
Leave I-77 at the exit for SR 82/Brecksville. Travel east on SR 82, past the intersection with SR 21 to the entrance on the right. Turn left at the T intersection to Chippewa Creek Drive and park in the lot for the Harriet Keeler Memorial Woods on the right. The trails described below are accessible from here.

Trails: Curiosity compels visitors to head for the scenic overlook first. From the parking lot, go across the street, turn left on the paved all-purpose trail to the overlook. After ogling the gorge, walk east (downstream) on the gravel hiking trail that traces the rim of the gorge. Follow the green blazes of the Chippewa Gorge Trail.

The gorge measures .6 miles, and after walking that distance, the trail descends into the floodplain, exchanging the habitat of hemlock and white oak for the soggy environs of willow and marshland. At the bottom of the hill, a bridle trail joins from the left. A slight detour left down this bridle path takes you to a ford across the creek and an excellent place for wading, photographs, or napping.

The gorge path crosses a suspension bridge built by the Ohio National Guard and returns to the Chippewa Creek Parkway near its intersection with the Valley Parkway. Cross the road to the Chippewa Creek Picnic Area.

Here you have a choice of three trails. The Buckeye Trail also enters the area (blue blazes) near the Oak Grove Picnic Area. A trail marker notes the distances to Cincinnati—441 miles via the western loop, or 552 miles through Eastern Ohio. Headlands Beach, its northern terminus, is a mere 65 miles away.

A bridle trail crosses your path before you reach Deer Lick Cave, a sandstone shelter cave. After crossing Meadows Drive the trail turns north between Sleepy Hollow Golf Course and the road. (The Buckeye Trail splits and continues west.) The path again crosses the road and snakes northward, through the Meadows Picnic Area to the nature center.

Special Places & Events: Visit the exhibits at the historic nature center before following the yellow then white blazes to the Keeler Memorial and the parking lot. Rest rooms and drinking water are available at the nature center. During July and August, visit the park's planted tallgrass prairie (with viewing deck) just west of the nature center. For information, call (216) 526-1012.

Less ambitious hikers, or folks pressed for time, can visit Deer Lick Cave by car. Park at the designated spot on Valley Parkway and walk to this site on the foot trails. Frankly, the trail may be at its best in May and October, when wildflowers and autumn leaves puts hikers into a trance. Other treats include eight picnic areas, golf, museum, stop on Cuyahoga Valley Scenic Railroad, and connecting trail to Cuyahoga Valley National Recreation Area.

GEOLOGY
Chippewa Creek washes over bedrock rich in

Buzz on Buzzards

🦅 Buzzards dine on death, picking flesh from the corpses of raccoons, ground hogs, snakes, skunks, turkeys, birds, fish, mice.

🦅 If starving, vultures may attack live small animals, but never humans.

🦅 They can live as long as 20 years.

🦅 They usually soar at altitudes less than 200 feet when hunting, but when migrating they have been observed at 5,000 feet.

🦅 They do not have a voice box, communicating instead by hissing and grunting. While hawks screech while flying, buzzards fly silently.

🦅 To distinguish turkey vultures from hawks while they are airborne, look at the shape of their wing span. A buzzard's six-foot wing span forms a shallow V, whereas the wings of eagles and most hawks lie flat.

geological history. The waterfall seen from the scenic overlook tumbles over Berea sandstone, a mere 330 million years old (Mississippian geological period). This gray, tightly-packed rock contains tiny quartz crystals (sand) that were deposited near the shore of a shallow sea. Streams falling from uplands to the east and north brought the sand to the sea. Waves tossed the grains and redistributed them along the shore. Ripple marks (small ridges) showing wave action are often found in Berea sandstone.

Beneath Berea sandstone lies three layers of shale comprising what geologists call the Bedford formation (345 million years old). Color reveals the Bedford layers. Look for the chocolate red strata (iron oxide gives it the rusty tint), followed by a gray layer, then an opalescent shale called Euclid bluestone. The creek runs over a long slab of this beautiful bluestone just upstream from the ford on the bridle trail (the detour from the Chippewa Creek Trail that I described above). Walk barefooted across the bluestone and admire its polished appearance.

Blackish Cleveland shale, also known as Ohio shale, can be seen in the creek. This rock is made of dust-sized particles of quartz, mica, and clay. Scientists think that the black color comes from rotting plants washed into a brackish, shallow ocean and carbonized around 350 million years ago (Late Devonian period). The decay explains the almost black color of the rock.

Near its confluence with the Cuyahoga River, the creek has exposed Chagrin shale of Middle Devonian vintage, 360 million years old. The unstable slopes are littered with huge boulders called slump rocks, and tortured by narrow and steep ravines cutting perpendicular into the gorge walls. When the creek removed the softer shales, blocks of erosion-resistant sandstone, now unsupported, fell into the valley.

The ancient Dover River used to flow in this area. It drained northeastward into what is now the Atlantic Ocean. During the Ice Age this river system became dammed by ice and its current was reversed into the south-flowing Tuscarawas River. Retreating glaciers dumped dirt into this abandoned valley and its tributaries. This glacier debris, called till (a mixture of sand, gravel, clay and other stuff), is especially thick around here.

The terrain above the gorge is flat and poorly drained due to a high amount of clay in the soil. (Clay soil does not allow water to seep through it as fast as sandy soil.) Consequently, several marsh ponds have emerged behind the ledge, providing a habitat for aquatic wildlife.

WILDLIFE

The gorge and creek sponsor a variety of ecosystems that support a number of rare and unusual plants.

The ancestors of the hemlocks rooted on the rim and slope came here from Canada during the Ice Age when the climate was colder. They thrive here today because the gorge provides the cool, shady environment they need to survive.

Mountain maple, trailing arbutus, and yellow birch, also more common in northern climes, grow in the gorge, too. Another rarity found in the gorge is a wildflower called round-leaved orchid (a potentially threatened flower). A small stand of American chestnuts reportedly grows on the north bank.

Some comely white and red oaks, real hunks stretching more than 100 feet into the sky, reside on the flat-topped ridge, sprinkled with black cherry and hickory. Beech and sugar maples prefer the moister slopes. The floodplain downstream from the gorge boasts a marsh and a riverine thicket dominated by sycamore, cottonwood, and willow.

Several types of ferns grow in the gorge—silver glade, royal, lady, devil's bit, broad buck, crested, and walking fern, a rarity in these parts.

The Deer Lick Trail is surrounded by your favorite hardwoods, spiced here and there by pines and spruces planted during the 1930s by laborers for the Works Progress Administration.

The ponds behind the gorge serve as breeding areas for salamanders and frogs in the spring. Jefferson salamanders, reclusive critters, reside at the Oak Grove Picnic Area pond. When early spring rains fall these tiny creatures leave their burrows for a 2–3 week breeding orgy. They hide in their tunnels for the rest of the year, regaining their strength for the next March downpour.

Look for red-spotted newts and spotted salamanders in the pond across the road from Deer Lick Cave, a good place, I hear, to listen to spring peepers.

From mid-July to Labor Day the flowers in the reservation's "prairie zoo" burst into color. The stars of the show are dense blazing star, prairie dock, coreopsis, bergamot and boneset. Altogether, some 50 plants grow in this planted prairie.

Birders will find an abundance of feathered friends flying about the woods and fields. A 1979 survey found 41 species nesting here, including the cerulean warbler, wood thrush, redstart, red-eyed vireo, cuckoo, belted kingfisher, red-breasted grosbeak, great horned owl, cedar waxwing, Louisiana waterthrush, and three varieties of flycatcher.

HISTORY

The men who built the nature center in the 1930s left their mark in the wood. Roman numerals on the beams helped them assemble the building, also known as the trailside museum. Notice the leaf carvings in the black walnut and cherry. Test your observation skills by finding the "ghost leaf," a modified tulip leaf carving.

The trailside museum opened on June 11, 1939. It was built under the auspices of the Works Progress Administration and Civilian Conservation Corps, two federal agencies that hired unemployed men for public works projects during the Depression years. More than 17,000 people visited the museum in 1939. Millions have passed through the doors since then.

Author, teacher, and nature lover Harriet L.

Keeler (1846–1921) is remembered by a plaque embedded in a glacial erratic, a granite boulder dropped here by a glacier. The memorial lies along the trail in the 390-acre forest that carries her name. The forest, dedicated in 1990, is bounded by the park roads. Near the tribute a local garden club has erected a deck overlooking the prairie.

Just outside the park on SR 21 is the Squire (Charles) Rich Home and Museum, managed by the Brecksville Historical Society (for hours call (216) 526-6757). Rich bought 160 acres here in 1835 and 150 acres later. The house he built for $600 was made from trees felled in the nearby forest.

A humbler man lived on the land before Rich. Just north of the museum stands the gravestone of Benjamin Waite, a private in Mosley's Massachusetts Regiment during the Revolutionary War. He died in February 1814.

Hinckley Reservation

San Juan Capistrano has its famous swallows, but Hinckley is renowned for its buzzards—turkey vultures. On a Sunday in mid-March, flocks of birdwatchers, tourists, and curiosity seekers outnumber the buzzards who annually return to their ancient roosts in the ledges, caves, and cliffs of this sanctuary.

LOCATION
Northeast Medina County, Hinckley Township.

SIZE
2,275 acres.

ACCESS
Leave I-71 at the Brunswick exit and travel east on SR 303. Go to the village of Hinckley (about 3 miles), turn right (south) on SR 3 for a little more than half a mile, then left on Bellus Road. The West Drive entrance to the reservation will be about two miles on the right. After a mile on West Drive, turn left at the sign pointing

A Strange
Bird

Noble Carvings Make Ohio's Mount Everest

Hinckley Reservation harbored another kind of "buzzard," an eccentric named Noble Stuart, a bricklayer, stone mason, and ledge sculptor. Nettie Worden, the daughter of the original landowner, Hiram Worden, was 82 years old when she took Noble Stuart as her third husband.

From 1945–55, in the ledges behind the Worden house, Stuart carved the faces of George Washington, Thomas Jefferson, and baseball great Ty Cobb, as well as a clipper ship, a sphinx, and a Bible with the inscription "IS ALL." Back at the house, he carved a crucifix, an Indian toting a tomahawk and knife, as well as Romulus and Remus, the mythical founders of Rome.

Everybody thought Nettie's brother, Frank Worden, a monument maker, did the carving, and for awhile the bashful Noble did not let on that he was the artist. Nowadays, such artistry would land you in jail. A trail to the ledges starts at the Worden Heritage Homestead, managed by the Hinckley Historical Society. To get there, turn right from West Drive on to State road, then right on Ledge Road.

The bathing beach on Lake Erie

to the Boathouse and Johnson's Picnic Area. Park at the end of this drive in the picnic area.

Trails: One route goes to Whipp's Ledges, one of the destinations of the buzzards. The blacktopped All-Purpose Trail can be used by visitors in wheelchairs or pushing strollers and is not a recommended route for undisturbed nature study.

The trail to the ledges begins to the right of the shelterhouse, built in 1938 by the Works Progress Administration. The hike to the top of the ledges is short, moderately strenuous, but worth the effort. At the bottom of the ledges, the trail veers left and takes you through the cracks and crevices of the sandstone formation. The rim of the ledge is 350 feet above Hinckley Lake.

Facilities: The park has eight picnic areas (three reserved), swimming beach, bridle trail (also good for hiking), ballplaying fields, fishing, sledding, cross-country skiing, ice skating, and boating facilities.

GEOLOGY

The rock at Whipp's Ledges is made of Sharon conglomerate, a coarse, pebbly sandstone. Some 300 million years ago (during the Pennsylvanian geologic period) swift-flowing streams originating from mountains to the north and east deposited gravel into the sea covering Ohio. This sediment of quartz pebbles piled up in a huge delta bigger than the modern Mississippi River delta. When the ocean receded, the deposit compacted into this rock conglomerate.

The pebbles became smooth and round because they were constantly being tumbled in the streams.

Notice the pebbles that litter the ground, changing back to the loose gravel deposit of millennia ago. Humans speed up erosion when they climb the rocks and free pebbles.

Though Sharon conglomerate resists erosion, the East Branch of the Rocky River has eroded through it. Water also has seeped through hairline seams to create the cracks and crevices characteristic of the ledges. Trees growing in the cracks also have widened some of the gaps. House-sized boulders, called slump rocks, have split from the ledge and rolled down the slope. They fell off because softer rock layers (less resistant strata) beneath them eroded away and no longer supported them.

The streams running through the Johnson Picnic Area and north of Worden's Ledges contain rocks with fossils. Maybe you will find the outline of a 300 million-year-old critter at the bottom of this brook.

WILDLIFE

The buzzards are the main feathered attraction. They begin to arrive in early March (not all at once on Buzzard's Day) from their winter homes, which may be as close as Kentucky or as far away as South America.

The Hinckley Reservation provides an ideal nesting and feeding habitat for this bird. Buzzards lay their eggs on the bare ground of ledges, in recess caves, in hollow trees or at the base of trees growing on the walls of cliffs, or in thickets. The open fields and forest here make suitable hunting grounds. Buzzards fly on warm currents of rising air called thermals, which develop above fields.

Beside buzzards, pheasant and bobwhite quail nest in the meadows. Hinckley Lake and two other ponds attract various species of waterfowl. I observed a great blue heron, wood ducks, mallards, gulls, a yellow warbler, and a belted kingfisher on my walk. White-eyed vireo and the parula warbler, uncommon in northeastern Ohio I have been told, have been identified here.

Hinckley Reservation is 73% forested, a much larger percentage of woods than when it was established more than 60 years ago. Oak, hickory and white ash grow on the drier, higher ground on top of the ledges, but on the slopes you will find beech and sugar maple communities (mixed with some black cherry), followed by red maple on lower slopes, and sycamore and cottonwood (some huge specimens) in the floodplain.

An impressive stand of chinkapin oak grows on the northeast bank of Hinckley Lake. Stands of various pines and spruces have been planted throughout the reservation. Ginseng, a threatened plant in Ohio, and ostrich fern, uncommon in these parts, thrive here.

Hinckley Lake supports largemouth bass, northern pike, channel catfish, bluegill, white and black crappie, bullhead and sucker.

HISTORY

Today, the Hinckley Reservation is known as a place that protects animals. But for more than a century the area was remembered for the Great Hinckley Hunt, a massacre really, that occurred on Christmas Eve in 1818 when 600 armed men and boys killed just about everything that moved on four legs (except hunting dogs) or flew. Some versions of the story claim the famous buzzards feasted on the carcasses in the spring.

A different, but equally gruesome, tale of attempted murder surrounds Whipp's Ledges. Robert Whipp came to Hinckley from England in 1848, and, bit by bit, purchased 2,000 acres in the township, including the sandstone cliffs that take his name. However, Whipp's second wife (30 years his junior), her lover, and her brother tried to strangle Whipp with a rope one night. The wife, who had just married Whipp, and her conspirators probably sought the title to his vast land holdings. Whipp survived the attack. His wife and her brother went to jail; the unidentified lover stayed free.

In the 1920s, Hinckley resident George Emmett sought to preserve "the Switzerland of America," an enthusiastic description of the land that he wanted to include in the Emerald Necklace. John F. Johnson joined Emmett's cause and donated 236 acres, 100 of which comprised Hinckley Lake. The East Branch of the Rocky River was dammed in 1926 to create the lake.

Cleveland Press reporter Robert Bordner is credited as Hinckley's first buzzard booster. He observed the annual return of the birds in 1957 and inspired hundreds of humans to see them in the park. Watching the vultures soon became a tradition.

Mill Stream Run Reservation

Mill Stream Run, once known as The Gully, has sliced a small, and not-so-scenic gorge through ancient sea beds on its way to the East Branch of the Rocky River. Once the trees leaf, you hardly see the ravine on the hard-to-follow, fast-eroding, and poorly-designed trails in this metropark.

LOCATION
Southwestern Cuyahoga County, near Strongsville.

SIZE
3,177 acres.

ACCESS
The Royalview Picnic Area part of the reservation is located off I-71 at the Strongsville/SR 82 exit. Travel east on SR 82 about a mile, turn right on Valley Parkway, and then right on Royalview Lane (look for the sign) and park in the small two-car lot just over the bridge, on the left, before Royalview Lane bends right.

Trails: Several trails wander through the Royalview section of the park. The two best trails (meaning the easiest ones to discern) begin at the parking slips near the entrance. Mountain bike ruts tell you are on the right track, though some of them stray off the beaten path. Sturdy boots are recommended because the trails are muddy and cross ravines. The terrain, however, is not difficult (though climbing some ravines requires exertion).

Special Places & Events: A favorite winter attraction at the reservation is The Chalet, a pair of 1,000-foot long toboggan chutes that operates with and without snow. In summer, swimmers head for Wallace Lake. Both attractions are north of these hiking trails. Other attractions are a music mound, fishing, boating, archery range, ballfields, and nine picnic areas

GEOLOGY
Mill Stream Run is one of many currents running perpendicular from the East Branch of the Rocky River. The run has washed away glacial till dropped here 10,000–12,000 years ago by the Wisconsinan ice mass, and exposed bedrock layers of shale and sandstone that began as ocean floors more than 300 million years ago during the Mississippian geologic period.

A slice of this gritty layer cake can be seen on a steep bank of the run about 200 hundreds yards behind the rest rooms in the picnic area. Here thin bands of blue-gray siltstone, called Meadville Shale, sit atop a stratum of Strongsville sandstone, named after the nearby city. Downstream in the reservation, Rocky River scours over Orangeville shale, a soft, gray crumbly rock. Look for this formation near the Bagley Road (north) entrance.

Winter is the best time to see how the river and the runs have worked the terrain. The floodplain is wide and flat, and when the water rushing down the hillside in tributaries reaches the bottom land, it loses velocity and lets fine grains of sand and clay settle. This erosive action enables wildlife, which thrives in sandy, wet floodplains, to move in.

During the spring flood season the river and the runs overflow their regular banks and follow new channels. Look for these auxiliary channels in the floodplain stage (exposed, dusty tree roots are clues). Large trees that fall into tiny tributaries trap sediments and create a diversion that could change the course of the rill and the distribution of soil and wildlife.

WILDLIFE

The reservation is a quilt of fragments: here a mature forest of tall oaks; there a habitat for cottonwoods and sycamores; yonder, pines planted decades ago losing their turf to encroaching hardwoods; and elsewhere, saplings of many species compete for space on a hillside that has been hunted, lumbered, farmed, and grazed over the last two centuries.

Fields that were once farmed by human pioneers now sponsor the plant pioneers who will begin the task of changing the land back into a forest. These meadows are undergoing succession, nature's eternal process of returning the land, in stages, to its original state as a hardwood forest.

Mill Stream Run safeguards a threatened wild-

Nature
Notable

Late-blooming Hardwood Lover

Arthur B. Williams was 56 years old when he became the first naturalist for the Cleveland Metroparks in 1930. Before that the Yale-educated Williams, a New Jersey native, had toiled in the real estate business, perhaps for 20 years. He also had studied law.

But nature became his game later in life. In 1931, Williams opened what is believed to be the first trailside museum in the U.S. in the middle of the ancient forest that now carries his name. Two years later he told the park board, "Here on the very edge of the old Appalachian plateau, under these great beech and sugar maple trees, are to be found perhaps a greater profusion of early spring wildflowers than in any other of the park reserves. The fact that the forest has been left undisturbed, means also that birds and other animals live here in great numbers—at certain times seeming to occupy every available niche..."

In 1935, he received his Ph.D. from Western Reserve University. His thesis was based on his in-depth study of the beech-maple-hemlock forest at North Chagrin. (You might obtain a copy from the Cleveland Museum of Natural History.)

Williams retired in 1950 and died the next year. The park board immediately dedicated a portion of the beech-maple-hemlock forest in his honor. Twenty-three years later Williams again was saluted when the U.S. Department of the Interior designated his beloved forest a National Natural Landmark.

View at Rocky River, Cuyahoga County

flower, blunt mountain mint, found in the meadows. North of the run's "run in" with the river, near a grove of pawpaw trees (themselves uncommon in northeastern Ohio), a rare blossom called green dragon, often confused with jack-in-the-pulpit, grows in soggy soil. A green dragon fully unsheathes its pointed "tongue" and extends it several inches, whereas jack-in-the-pulpit just slightly reveals his bitter barb beneath its hood.

You must walk through the meadows during the summer for the butterflies—dozens of varieties, flying about as if confetti rained from the sky. A two-tailed swallowtail landed on me by mistake by the picnic ground. It did not stay long. I had little to offer in the way of food, and my fragrance resembled a livestock pen more than a shadbush blossom, its eventual target.

If you are lucky you might see a woodcock rising in a field. This game bird, remembered more for its springtime aerial acrobatics than its taste, is trying to make a comeback in northern Ohio.

HISTORY

Farmers and woodsmen found artifacts in these ravines left behind by Indians who lived here 1,000 years ago. The Indians probably hunted game on the hillside and fished in the river. The Erie nation inhabited the area until marauding Iroquois warriors drove them out in 1660. In the mid-18th century Shawnee, Delaware, and Wyandot Indians shared the forests and streams.

White settlers arrived in the early 19th century—families named Sanderson, Southard, Wheller, and Clement. They built farms, a canal, a hamlet, and mills for sawing wood, and making wagons, furniture and baskets. For awhile, the town that grew up at the crossroads of Drake and Hunt road was called Sanderson's Corners, honoring Allison Sanderson, a mill owner. Another small mill town, Slab Hollow, on Howe Road, took its name from the slabs of rock that littered the creeks in the hollows. By the Civil War, steam had replaced running water as a source of power and the mills closed.

Local folks knew this tributary of the Rocky River simply as The Gully. But this name was not suitable for a park in a pastoral suburban setting, so officials came up with Mill Stream Run (ignoring the redundancy of using stream and run in the name). It became a gem in the "Emerald Necklace" in 1976. The park honors the early mill owners.

JOURNAL

Birdwatchers know the Rocky River valley is a major corridor for migratory waterfowl and forest birds (warblers). But I had more fun watching some permanent residents engaging in one of nature's jousts. Halfway down the hillside on Trail 2 a bunch of crows shrieked and fussed in the treetops. They were harassing a barred owl. I watched for a moment and saw that the owl was getting the worst of it. So, I clapped my hands. The crows scattered west, the owl, wisely, chose an easterly flight pattern.

North Chagrin Reservation

Diversity and abundance preside here. The trails in this reservation journey to hemlock-lined ravines, a castle built by a wanna-be English "squire," a beech forest designated a national treasure, a marsh and a river lagoon, a virgin white pine forest, a wildlife sanctuary, oxbows, and the ruins of the nation's first outdoor nature center.

LOCATION

The reservation straddles the boundaries of Cuyahoga and Lake counties and is bounded by the Chagrin River (east), and US 6 (Chardon Road) and SR 91 (SOM Center Road).

SIZE & DESIGNATION

1,986 acres. The Dr. Arthur B. Williams Memorial Woods has been designated a National Natural Landmark by the U.S. Department of the Interior.

ACCESS

Leave I-90 at the exit for Willoughby and SR 91. Travel on SR 91 south for about a mile, then turn left (east) on US 6 to the entrance on the right. Take the Buttermilk Falls Parkway to the parking lot at North Chagrin Nature Center.

Trails: North Chagrin Nature Center is centrally located for trails that explore both the northern and southern halves of the reservation. Exhibits in the center explain some of the natural history in the park. Grab a trail map there and guides to certain trails. Rest rooms, drinking fountains, and a bookstore called "Earthwords" are located at the center.

The reservation map shows a tangle of trails that only the swiftest sprinter could cover in a day. Visitors with limited time can stroll on a trio of brief loop trails—Sanctuary Marsh, Buttermilk Falls, and Wildlife Management—in the Sunset Wildlife Preserve, all near the nature center. (A detailed map of these paths is on the flip side of the Reservation map.) The Sanctuary Marsh Trail, and All-Purpose Trail (which traces the perimeter of Sunset Wildlife Preserve) are accessible to folks traveling in wheelchairs and strollers.

Folks with big chunks of time should go to Buttermilk Falls, a bridal-veil-type cascade sprawling over black Cleveland shale. Take the Boardwalk across Sanctuary Marsh to Buttermilk Falls Trail, which ends at the parkway. Across the road, follow the Hemlock Trail into the gorge for 1.75 miles to Squire's Lane Trail, a .75-mile patch used

by Feargus B. Squire when he supervised the construction of his weekend retreat. It ends at the Squire's Castle, a good place to rest, picnic, and stretch out on the lawn in front of this miniature English-style castle. Of course, you should snoop around the "castle." (An offshoot from the Squire's Lane Trail, the White Pine Trail, visits one of the last virgin white pine stands in Ohio.)

The interconnected Overlook and Sylvan trails wander through the A.B. Williams Memorial Woods in the southern half of the park. A bronze plaque stamped into a granite boulder that was orphaned by the Wisconsinan glacier 10,000 years ago, commemorates the landmark and Dr. Williams, the first naturalist for the Cleveland Metroparks. Notice that hemlocks also grow in this beech-maple community. Just beyond this, at a right turn in the trail, the Castle Valley Trail enters the woods. Ahead, look for a log shelterhouse that faces a ravine formed by a tributary of the Chagrin River.

For those who want to walk the Buckeye Trail, it travels through the southern half of the park. Beginning at the parking lot near the Wilson Mills Road entrance to the reservation, the Buckeye Trail shares a bridle path that runs alongside Buttermilk Falls Parkway as far as the Forest Picnic Area. Then it goes east through the A.B. Williams Memorial Forest, turns north at Ox Lane, then leaves the park via Rogers Road.

All the trails are easy to follow, wide, smooth, and only moderately challenging.

Special Places & Events: Nature programs for all age groups are held throughout the year at the nature center and adjacent nature education building. Call the nature center at (216) 473-3370 for a schedule. The reservation has five picnic areas (two reservable), and winter sports areas.

GEOLOGY

The Chagrin River winds northward along the east boundary of the preserve. When you explore the reservation, drive along the Chagrin River Road and notice the sweeping turns in the river. The pond at Squire's Castle and the lagoons across the road once formed an "oxbow," or a bend in the river shaped like a thin-necked human head. One day the current breached the neck and formed a new channel. The abandoned, or decapitated, oxbow became a pond, recharged every so often by a flood or runoff from nearby slopes. Other oxbows are along the road, though most are marshes.

For centuries the river and its ravine-forming tributaries have been eating away till (gravel, sand, clay, etc.) left behind by the Wisconsinan glacier some 12,000 years ago. The soil is known as Volusia clay loam, an unproductive turf for agricultural crops, which may explain why the big trees here still stand.

At Buttermilk Falls, the creek has gnawed down to the bone—black Cleveland shale—and shaped a charming, bending, and steep gorge visible from the Buttermilk Falls, Hemlock, and

Hickory Fox trails. The gorge is maybe 100–120 feet deep. Other trails visit east-running ravines, too, but the one at Buttermilk Falls is the most dramatic.

The Cleveland (or Ohio) shale washed by the falls is about 350 million years old. It is made of tiny bits of quartz, mica and clay, as well as decayed plant material that gives the rock its black color. The deposit once was the bed of a shallow sea, perhaps a few feet deep and prone to receiving fallen and rotting plants.

WILDLIFE

North Chagrin Reservation may be best known for its huge hardwood trees. It also protects one of only a handful of untouched white pine forests in the state. (Take the White Pine Trail off the Squire's Loop Trail to see it.) This "softwood" was prized for ships' masts in the 18th and 19th centuries, but somehow, to our good fortune, the axemen missed this stand.

The park, of course, attracts the usual collection of birds—owls, hawks, warblers, bluebirds, woodpeckers, etc. I have learned on the sly that the prothonotary warbler, which every birder wants to mark off on the checklist, is often seen in a spot the locals call "The Swamp", south of the merger of Ox Lane and Chagrin River Road. Look for tree swallows there, too.

Geese, ducks, and other waterfowl favor Sanctuary Marsh and Sunset Pond near the nature center. The boardwalk that spans the marsh is a great lookout, as is the observation deck on the southeast shore of Sunset Pond. You are apt to observe frogs, turtles, water lilies, and all sorts of dragonflies from these vantage points.

HISTORY

The pint-sized palace called Squire's Castle was supposed to be the digs of the gatekeeper who would guard the real mansion Feargus B. Squire wanted to build in the forest out back. Squire's Lane Trail traces the path to this would-be castle.

Instead, the stone house became a weekend retreat for Squire, an English-born oilman whose rags-to-riches determination earned him a vice-presidency at Standard Oil of Ohio, along with Frank Rockefeller, brother of company founder John D. Rockefeller. The "castle" had several small bedrooms, living areas, a large kitchen with a porch, and the master's library or "hunting" room. The stone for the castle was quarried from the 525 acres he had acquired.

Squire, a quiet and aloof man, was rumored to enjoy the solitude of his country rookery but his wife refused to establish a home so far from the social and cultural world of Cleveland. Anyway, Squire gave up the place after he retired in 1909. But he did erect that dream castle—Cobblestone Garth—in Wickliffe next to all the others on Millionaire's Row. Squire sold the property in 1922. Three years later Cleveland Metroparks bought it as the focus for North Chagrin Reservation.

Rocky River Reservation

The Rocky River has spent the last 12,000 years carving an Olympic bobsled trail through this reservation. In doing so, it has unearthed the creatures that lived here long before the dinosaurs.

LOCATION

Western Cuyahoga County, stretching from Lake Erie to the Ohio Turnpike.

SIZE

2,540 acres.

ACCESS

To get there, exit I-480 at Grayton Road and go south toward Hopkins Airport. Turn right at the traffic signal on to Brookpark Road, then drive past the Lewis Research Center and the across the bridge. Continue on Brookpark Road, turn left on Clague Road, then right on Mastick Road. The entrance to the reservation, Shepard Lane, will appear on the left in about a half mile. Shepard Lane descends into the valley and ends at Valley Parkway. Turn right on this road, then right again into the parking lot of the nature center.

Trails: Start your visit at the nature center, which has exhibits on wildlife, fossils, and geology. Kids will especially enjoy "Dunk," the 20-foot long reproduction of a dunkleosteous, a prehistoric shark. Step onto the observation deck for an introduction to the steep cliffs and the river, which flows beneath the porch. Rest rooms and drinking water are available.

Before leaving, pick up the Woodlands Trails brochure describing four nearby trails, and the Fort Hill guide if you intend to hike this trail. Both are at the reception desk.

I also recommend the bridle trail, running along the river east of Valley Parkway. Take off your shoes and wade in the river. (Swimming is forbidden, but wading is okay.) Many folks park at nearby Cedar Point Picnic Area and strike out for Arrowhead Island, seen from the deck at the nature center. Visitors in wheelchairs can negotiate the trail through the Ron Hauser Memorial Wildflower Garden, located between the nature center and the parking lot, or the paved All-Purpose Trail. Energetic hikers can traipse south several miles via the All-Purpose or bridle trails to Berea Falls, or you can drive there.

GEOLOGY

The Rocky River is a ribbon of erosion, neatly exposing chunks of ancient ocean beds and more than 300 million years of geological history from its source in Summit County (East Branch) to its mouth at Lake Erie.

At Berea Falls (Rocky River South Reservation), the river falls over a fat layer of gray Berea sandstone composed of tiny quartz grains cemented by clay. The sand was probably deposited in a shallow sea in a delta-like pattern by currents washing off higher ground to the north and east. The formation is cross-bedded (arc-like, or criss-cross deposits), and shows the direction of the shifting currents that carried the sediments to their positions.

Berea sandstone resists erosion. That cannot be said of the reddish shale (Bedford formation) beneath it. The backsplash of the waterfall keeps eating away the softer shale, a process called undercutting, and forms a recess cave beneath the sandstone. Eventually, huge chunks of unsupported sandstone will fall into the river. Undercutting occurs on the banks of the river, too. The river earned its name from the sandstone boulders at the bottom of Berea Falls.

Alongside the nature center, the current flows over Cleveland shale, flaky and almost black in color because it holds a lot of decayed matter. The floor of the shallow sea that covered this area 350 million years ago (late Devonian Period) must have been a black, slimy ooze. Before it empties into Lake Erie, the river washes over older rock called Chagrin Shale, created perhaps 360 million years ago.

Today, the east and west branches of the Rocky River merge at Cedar Point Road, a half mile south of the nature center. Years ago, however, the west branch looped westerly and joined the east branch a little farther downstream, probably near Shepard Lane. West Channel Pond and the ponds and marshes that you see along the Wildlife Management Trail were once the path of the west branch.

WILDLIFE

Long before dinosaurs there was "Dunk," a bone-plated bottom feeding arthodire. Dunk, short for *Dunkleosteous terrelli*, was king of the Devonian sea some 400 million years old. Dunk, a shark-like creature measuring 45–50 feet, feasted on crustaceans. Dunk's fossilized remains turned up in the Cleveland shale cliff upstream from the nature center and others like him in other locations in northern Ohio. A replica of the beast hangs in the nature center.

The Rocky River valley is an important corridor for migrating birds—various ducks, and warblers. Green, great blue, black-crowned, and yellow-crowned herons have been observed here, along with spotted sandpipers and red-breasted nuthatches, the latter a rarity in these parts. The bluffs on the Fort Hill Trail and the meadow and marsh on the Wildlife Management Trail are prime birding spots.

In the Ron Hauser Memorial Wildflower Garden, named for a local resident who was fond of the wildflowers in the reservation, look for red and white baneberry, foam flower, turtlehead, Soloman's seal, false rue anemone, Jacob's ladder, and seven types of ferns. The garden is located next to the nature center.

Elsewhere, you will find blossoms such as bittersweet nightshade, Dutchman's breeches, wild ginger, Virginia bluebells, jack-in-the-pulpit, blue cohosh, yellow adder's tongue, and others.

Trees typically found in the floodplain grow in abundance here. Ohio buckeye trees and black maple, uncommon around here, also grow in the bottomland. Pines and spruces planted 60 years ago have matured and live in groves scattered throughout the reservation. Wild black cherry and various locusts thrive in large numbers.

HISTORY

Native Americans (Whittlesey Tradition) lived on this site, perhaps from 1000–1640. They lived in the valley, farmed the floodplain, and used the river for fishing and transportation. Numerous arrowheads, bannerstones, and other artifacts of these people have been unearthed in the area.

Fort Hill and Mt. Pleasant became places for defense, worship, and perhaps, burial. Fort Hill may have been impregnable for a time. The fortifications on the hill are located where the two branches of the river pinched. The strip of land between the streams may have been only 30–50 feet wide. Because the hill was nearly surrounded by 90-foot vertical slopes, attackers had to advance up this heavily defended, steep-sided isthmus. Battles also may have been fought on Mt. Pleasant, where a suspected burial mound is located.

The Erie tribe also settled here. They may have abandoned the site after stream piracy made Fort Hill vulnerable; or when Iroquois warriors drove them off during the colonial period.

White settlers attracted to the river's water power began arriving in the early 19th century. The names of nearby roads remind us of these pioneers. James Ruple (Ruple Road) and seven brothers dug in here. Calvin and Charlotte Spafford (Spafford Road joins Ruble Road south of the nature center) were related to Amos Spafford, a member of Moses Cleaveland's surveying team. The ruins of Joel Lawrence's grist mill, built in 1832, can be seen across the street from the Cedar Point Picnic Area. Lawrence was a constable in 1827.

The Frostville Museum on Cedar Point Road depicts the life of these early settlers. You can walk to the museum, run by the Olmsted Historical Society, on a service road from the southeast corner of the Wildlife Management Trail.

Gen. William Tecumseh Sherman visited the valley after the Civil War and declared it was as beautiful as the most scenic valleys in Europe. In the 1910s, businessmen with homes overlooking the river began a campaign to protect the area from commercial and industrial exploitation. This led to the creation in 1912 of a county park board, the predecessor of the Cleveland Metropolitan Park Board of 1915. That year Frederick Law Olmsted, son of the country's most reknowned landscape architect, explored Rocky River for the board.

South Chagrin Reservation

Late at night, when nobody was looking, Henry Church, a blacksmith and spiritualist, crept down to the Chagrin River and chiseled figures in a sandstone wall that faced the river. Was he talking to the ghost of an Indian maiden, or just retouching the gorge with a few strokes of his file? Try as he did, this early graffiti artist could not improve on the beauty the Chagrin River has sculpted over the millennia.

LOCATION
Southeastern Cuyahoga County, near Bentleyville.

SIZE
1,398 acres.

ACCESS
Leave I-271 at the exit for US 422 and travel east. Turn left on the Hawthorn Parkway, which dead ends at the Squaw Rock Picnic Area.
Trails: The mile-long journey to Squaw Rock, the site of clandestine, Henry Church's carving, slides down a hemlock-rimmed gorge with high sandstone walls to a charming waterfall, and through dark and secluded ravines and shelter caves once used by ancient people.

GEOLOGY
The walls lining the river gorge and perpendicular ravines in the Squaw Rock area are made of Berea sandstone, a compressed, gray rock composed of miniscule quartz crystals bonded by clay. This thick stratum originated in the Mississippian geologic period, 320-340 million years ago, when a sea covered Ohio.
Squaw Rock is a chunk of Berea sandstone that fell off the wall. These huge boulders are called slump rocks. Berea sandstone (named after the nearby Cuyahoga County city) was extensively quarried for buildings, canals, bridge foundations, and gravestones (one of Henry Church's specialties). Quarry Rock Picnic Area, as you might have guessed, was the site of a sandstone mine when Henry Church was a boy.
Here the sandstone lies atop shale—specifically Chagrin shale—a flaky, blue-gray bedrock created

back in the Devonian days, roughly 375 million years ago. A warm, clear, skinny sea glistened over Ohio in those days. Chagrin shale is made of the extremely fine particles of quartz, mica, and clay, as well as dark organic matter, essentially decayed trees and plants that give the rock its dark complexion.

WILDLIFE
The hemlocks are remnants of the Ice Age. Another orphaned tree of the north woods, the mountain maple, also flourishes around Squaw Rock.
South Chagrin also protects the only known stand of sweet birch in the metroparks system as well as these species considered uncommon in Ohio— yellow birch, river birch, cucumber tree, bigtooth aspen, and American chestnut (potentially threatened species in Ohio).
Of course, you will see various other trees in these woods. A small arboretum, off Arbor Lane, sponsors a collection of native and naturalized trees.
Perspicacious birders should keep their eyes peeled in the hemlocks for a chance glimpse of the black-throated warbler, a bird more common in the northern boreal woods. Also try to spot the red-shouldered hawk, pileated woodpecker, American redstart, downy woodpecker, red-eyed vireo, northern oriole, Louisiana waterthrush, and chestnut-sided warbler.
A 1980 survey found 36 varieties of wildflowers in the park, though there may be more. These include harbinger of spring, red trillium, yellow mandarin, squirrel corn, and bishop's cap.
Sulphur Springs Brook is the only trout stream in the park district. The waterway is stocked and managed by the metroparks and University School.

HISTORY
The sandstone rock that reveals the ancient seas also holds the secrets of some humans.
In 1885, Henry Church could chisel an Indian woman in a slump rock. Today, of course, he would be thrown in jail for defacing park property. Church was born in Chagrin Falls in 1836. One newspaper account said he was only the second white child born in that community. His father taught him to be a blacksmith, a practical trade, but Henry had the inclinations of an artist, too. He played the bass viola and harp in an orchestra, and taught himself to sculpt and paint. Part of his self-education was journeying on a train to Cleveland to watch Archibald Willard paint "The Spirit of '76."
Contemporaries called the folk artist a philosopher, even though he did not publish a book of his thoughts, nor announce any great idea. The moniker probably stems from his pursuit of spiritualism (he went to seances in Chagrin Falls), and his reputation among locals as an eccentric.
Around 1885, so the story goes, Church sneaked down to the river at night (two miles distance) and carved figures in sandstone boulders. It was difficult work by the dim light of a lantern. On one face of the rock he chiseled what appears to be a serpent, a

quiver of arrows, wildcat, skeleton, eagle, shield, flag, and the most discernible figure—an Indian woman, or squaw.

He started on the east face of the boulder with a log cabin and U.S. Capitol. When two neighbors discovered his secret, he abandoned the project and never gave anybody a clue about the significance of the figures. One critic surmised that "Squaw Rock" represented the "rape of the Indians by the white man." Others suggested a historical theme, depicting life in America from the time of Indians and ravenous beasts, to the coming of civilization and democracy.

Church did finish sculptures and show them to admirers. Some are displayed at the Western Reserve Historical Society in Cleveland. The sandstone probably came from local quarries. His most famous in the collection shows a small child leading a lion and lamb. It was his tombstone, and he was buried beneath it in 1908.

Cleveland Metroparks acquired the land containing Squaw Rock in 1925. A trail to the attraction was built in 1931, and the rock was been reinforced with a concrete support. Still, it faces the vagaries of the Chagrin River and the elements. In 1980, Church received the recognition he tried to avoid in his lifetime when the Whitney Museum in New York City featured his work in an exhibit with other American artists.

As noted, Dr. David Brose, a Case Western Reserve University and Cleveland Museum of Natural History archeologist, did unearth the bones and teeth of a small woman a short distance from Squaw Rock in 1975. Radiocarbon tests put the woman's age at 8,000–10,000 years. She was laid on hemlock boughs at the back of a shelter cave, suggesting that she had died during child birth and been placed there by comrades who eventually moved on. The discovery indicates that the climate and habitat of the area, which was still influenced by the glacier to the north, could support humans—and their spirits. Brose also discovered arrowheads, tools and other artifacts dating back to 3500 B.C. These items were probably used by hunters who established temporary camps in the caves.

The Cleveland Natural Science Club built Look About Lodge in the reservation off Miles Road. In 1967, a former Boy Scout camp was added to the park.

JOURNAL

July. It dawned on me when I read a news clip about Dr. Brose's archeological investigations of South Chagrin Reservation. Brose found a native skeleton; Church, it's soul. I suggest that Church, a spiritualist, was communicating with the spirit of the ancient woman while he tapped on the rock. The Stone Age lady was telling the Industrial Age man her story.

Church stumbled on the spirit while he was hiking to the nearby quarry. His nosy, non-believing neighbors interrupted the seance, requiring Church and the apparition to flee and be silent. I rest my case! Is the spirit still there, hovering in the

ravine, restlessly searching for the bones that have been removed?

◆◆◆ GEAUGA PARK DISTRICT ◆◆◆
For information, write or call Geauga Park District, 9160 Robinson Road, Chardon, OH 44024, (440) 286-9504.

Big Creek Park

Scenic Big Creek, its slopes coated by a fur of beeches, hemlocks, and maples, bisects this 642-acre wooded tract. The Donald W. Meyer Center, a natural education facility, is the focal point of the park.

LOCATION
Northern Geauga County, a few miles north of Chardon.

SIZE
642 acres.

ACCESS
Choose from entrances on Robinson Road (main entrance), Woodin Road, and Ravenna Road.

Trails: A network of 11 trails (6.4 miles) and a section of the Buckeye Trail carry visitors to the natural attractions in the park.

Special Places & Events: The Donald W. Meyer Center features nature exhibits, classrooms, and a wildlife feeding area. Campground (permit), three fishing ponds, horseback riding trails, and four picnic areas are available.

GEOLOGY
The tributaries feeding Big Creek have cut impressive ravines, giving the park some steep relief and bedrock outcrops.

WILDLIFE
A beech-maple forest covers most of the park. However, hemlocks populate the cool, shady slopes where the Big Creek valley pinches. The spring wildflower show in this forest is especially colorful.

The place also attracts, like a magnet, the warblers and songbirds who spend their winter in the tropics.

HISTORY
The Great Depression ruined Samuel Livingston Mather's dream of building a posh resort at this place. In 1955, he donated 505 acres (of his original 1,000-acre holding) to the state. The park district began leasing the land in 1965, and obtained title in 1990.

Swine Creek Reservation

Oldtimers say the creek was named by pioneer farmers who slept easy knowing their foraging hogs would not run away from this valley. First, no sensible beast—and a hog is an especially sensible critter—would ever stray far from the Mother Lode of acorns and other mast crops that rained upon this landscape. Second, not even an athletic hog could reach the rim of the ravines after pigging out on the nuts. The muddy, slippery cliffs cradling the creek corraled the prosperous swine.

LOCATION

Southeastern Geauga County, Middlefield Township.

SIZE

331 acres.

ACCESS

Leave Middlefield, heading south on SR 608. A couple of miles outside of town, SR 608 ends at SR 528. Drive straight across SR 528 onto Old State Road, then immediately turn left to Swine Creek Road. Turn left on Hayes Road, and another left at the park entrance. Bear right (north) at the first intersection and park at the Woods Edge Picnic Area.

Trails: Ten trails totaling six miles visit nearly every nook and cranny in the reservation. Look for trail maps at a parking lot next to the trailhead for the Siltstone Trail.

Fishing: Anglers can fish for bass and bluegill at Killdeer and Lodge ponds. Swimming and wading are not allowed, however.

Special Places and Events: Swine Creek Lodge opens on Sunday afternoons during the winter. Stop by for a hot beverage and a warm fire. Cross-country skiers can slide on the Gray Fox, Wagon, Squaw Root, Walnut, Meadowlark, and part of the Siltstone trails. If you get tired of hiking or skiing hop on the wagon pulled by a team of Clydesdale horses (weekends only). Nature programs are held yearround.

Some 30 acres of the forest is a sugarbush where maple syrup drips into buckets in March. Visitors can watch the sugar making process at the Sugarhouse,

More
metroparks

Other Geauga County Parks

Walter C. Best Wildlife Preserve, 101 acres, SR 44 (Painesville-Ravenna Road), Munson Township. Wildlife observation blind, trails, fishing, lake.

Whitlam Woods, 100 acres, Pearl Road, Hambden Township. Wooded ravines, creeks.

Headwaters Park, 926 acres, SR 608 and US 322. East Branch Reservoir, Buckeye Trail, Crystal Lake Picnic Area, boat ramp, hike and bike path, shore fishing.

Beartown Lakes Reservation, 149 acres, Quinn Road, between SR 44 and SR 306. Lakes, pond, Spring Creek, fishing, beaver lodges, observation deck, trail for hikers and riders, picnic areas.

Bessie Benner Metzenbaum Park, 65 acres, 7940 Cedar Road, Chester Township. Woodland, swamp, creek, observation platform, trails, picnic area, playground.

Eldon Russell Park, Rapids Road, Troy Township. Cuyahoga River canoe access, fishing, nature trail, picnic area.

Burton Wetlands, 663 acres, Burton Township. Forty imperiled wetland plants thrive here.

The West Woods, 792 acres in Newbury-Russell townships.

The Rookery, 443 acres in Munson Township.

open on March weekends. Just follow the path to the Sugarhouse from the Woods Edge Picnic Area.

Please drive slowly and carefully, especially at bends and crests in the roads. Amish folks on foot and in horse-drawn carriages own the road, too. Also, be wary of pets and livestock in the road.

GEOLOGY

There go those oldtimers again: this time talking tall about diamonds that fell into Swine Creek during a hailstorm. Actually, the gems are "lucky stones," pearly white pebbles of quartz found in Sharon Conglomerate, a sandstone made during the Pennsylvanian geological period some 300 million years ago. Truth is the "diamonds" are either the leftovers of a lobe of overlaying conglomerate that has eroded away, or they have been carried here by the current of Swine Creek.

The steep slopes swelling above Swine Creek and its tributaries are primarily composed of thick strata of clay deposited by the Wisconsinan glacier about 12,000 years ago. Notice the "slumps," or huge blocks, of clay that have broken from the slope.

The nameless creeks carving the ravines alongside the Valley and Siltstone trails expose Sharpsville sandstone atop Orangeville shale. Both bedrocks, once the sediments at the floors of ancient seas, date back to the Mississippian period (330 million years ago). Downstream, Swine Creek reveals Bundysburg sandstone.

WILDLIFE

Fret not, wild swine (boars) do not roam in these woods. You are more likely to see deer, fox, mink, and birds, notably eastern meadowlark, bobolink, horned lark, ruffed grouse, snow bunting, screech owl, Savannah sparrow, and killdeer.

Cottonwood, walnut, sycamore, and willow shade Swine Creek where the long-legged great blue heron and plunging kingfisher hunt for fish. Beech, maple, wild black cherry, white and red oak, and wild azalea occupy the slopes and ridges.

Spring brings the colorful eruption of wildflowers led by large-flowered trillium, various violets, columbine, bee balm (or Oswego tea), and lobelia.

HISTORY

The reservation used to be part of a 1,200-acre hunting preserve owned by Windsor Ford, a well-to-do man from Mesopotamia (the Trumbull County community not the ancient civilization). He supposedly descends from Seabury Ford, who voters elected governor of Ohio by a thin margin in 1848.

Ford sold (268 acres) to the park district in 1977. (Some of the land on the east side of Hayes Road remains a hunting preserve.) The park district later bought 63 acres along Swine Creek, raising the total acreage to 331.

JOURNAL

Sometime in October: Whatever the season, the approach of dusk is always the best time of day here.

Though the sun has sunk beneath the ridge, the autumn leaves decorating the valley remain luminescent, the embers of departed daylight. The tiny rill is a phosphorescent brushstroke of gold and crimson sprinkled with chips from a bluish-white icicle.

Nature sounds fill the valley—the brook, a chipmunk rustling leaves, a plaintive birdsong, a barred owl concluding an overture with a long vibrating "awwwww." No echo of interstate traffic rising from the horizon, no distant drone of industry, no jets screeching overhead. Just afterglow and coral blue soaking into the ridge.

◆ ◆ ◆　　JEFFERSON COUNTY　　◆ ◆ ◆

Information can be found by contacting Friendship Park, P.O. Box 530, Smithfield, OH 43948, (740) 733-7941.

Friendship Park, county fairground, CR 23 (Chandler Road). Car racing, fishing, horse arena, camping picnic shelters, pavilion, ice rink, lake, boating, off-road vehicles.

◆ ◆ ◆　　LAKE COUNTY　　◆ ◆ ◆

Information can be found by contacting Lake Metroparks, 11211 Spear Road, Concord Township, OH 44077, (440) 639-7275 or 1-800-227-7275.

Chapin Forest Reservation

You must climb to the top of this flat-topped sandstone summit for the expansive, smiling panorama—the best in northeastern Ohio. When you finish your blinking at the overlook, explore the pebbly, sandstone ledges and a grand forest of oaks, maples, beech, tuliptree, and hemlock. These, too, should not be overlooked.

LOCATION

Southwestern Lake County, near Kirtland.

SIZE

390 acres.

ACCESS

From I-90 (or SR 2) travel south on SR 306 across the East Branch of the Chagrin River (a state scenic river), pass the Kirtland Temple of the Church of the Latter-Day Saints, to Eagle Road. Here you have a choice. Continue straight on SR 306 and enter the reservation at the Chapin Parkway entrance, or turn right (west) on Eagle Road, then left (south) on Hobart Road, and visit the park starting from the Pine Lodge and Twin Ponds Picnic Shelter.

Trails: At the Twin Ponds - Pine Lodge entrance on Hobart Road. Look for a driveway-sized gravel path heading east from the parking lot and the blue blazes of the Buckeye Trail, the main trail through the reservation. Printed guides are available at the trailhead.

The Buckeye Trail and Arbor Lane Trail share the path into the woods. This wide, smooth, moderately challenging trail slowly winds up the hill, generally heading easterly. Several smaller paths branch to the right as you walk—first the Ash Grove Link, then the Parcourse Trail (twice), Ruffed Grouse Trail, Lucky Stone Loop, Mourning Cloak Link, and the Wintergreen Link.

Special Places & Events: Back at the Twin Ponds Picnic Area you will find drinking water, rest rooms, picnic tables, and a ball field. Fishing is permitted in the Twin Ponds (license required). Pine Lodge is the site of education programs, meetings, and cross-country ski rentals.

The reservation's Pine Lodge Ski Center at the Hobart Road entrance has become a cross-country skiing headquarters with lessons, ski rentals, trails (5.5 miles), races, and snowshoeing. Open December through March, depending on snow conditions. Call (440) 256-3810 before skiing.

Geology

The rounded, milky pebbles that you see in the ledges and scattered on the ground are called "lucky stones." Supposedly, the pebble acts as an amulet if tucked into a pocket.

Sharon Conglomerate, a sandstone, is one of the oldest deposits in the Pennsylvanian geologic period, roughly 320 million years ago. It formed after mountain streams, originating from the north and east, dumped truckloads of gravel along the coast of the ocean then covering Ohio. This deposit stretched out in a wide fan, or delta, larger than the present Mississippi River delta. Over time the sea retreated and the sediment compacted into the coarse sandstone conglomerate.

The quartz pebbles became rounded from the constant tossing and tumbling in the quick, ancient streams. Water seeping through joints and seams in the formation created the deep and narrow crevices characteristic of the "ledges." Trees roots sinking into the cracks have contributed to the erosion.

Sharon Conglomerate once was mined from the abandoned quarry. The rock was pulverized then sifted to separate the pebbles and sand. These products were used in local construction. The foundation of the nearby Kirtland Temple of the Church of the Latter-day Saints, completed in 1836, supposedly is made of this sandstone.

Wildlife

Chapin Forest is a mature (full-grown) woodland packed with beech, oak, maple and tuliptrees. As trail names (Ash Grove and Whispering Pine) imply, ash

and pine cover some of the ground, though the latter species was planted years ago for reforestation.

The forest sponsors the growth of wildflowers typical in Ohio—trillium, hepatica, bloodroot, etc. Fragrant wintergreen blossoms along the short trail that carries its name.

Look for deer, flying squirrels, red fox and barred owls in the woods. Though I failed to flush a ruffed grouse (called a partridge in New York) along the Ruffed Grouse Trail, I did spy a pileated woodpecker clinging to a hickory before it flew away. Fox tracks, faint in the dust beside the trail, pointed to a northerly flight. Chipmunks seem to enjoy running through the cracks, crevices, roots, and pockets of the ledges. Please do not feed them, however.

The fern growing in the cracks of the sandstone is appropriately called rock cap fern, a common plant living in a fragile habitat.

The driveway from the entrance on SR 306 to the Ledges Picnic Area goes through four types of forest. Red maples dominate first, then beech and sugar maples, followed by red maples again, and oaks at the ledges. See if you see these different communities of life.

History

The stony knob, also known as Gildersleeve Mountain, has paid a steep price to present a vista. Miners long ago gave the cobble the equivalent of a frontal lobotomy, gouging from its north face an enormous block of rock and the forest that covered it. The cliff offering the view is the scar of this quarry.

To save this forest from further logging and mining Frederic H. Chapin, a Cleveland area industrialist, purchased Gildersleeve Mountain in 1949 and donated it to the state. The property became Chapin State Forest. The Ohio Division of Forestry used this woodland for some selective cutting and to study the growth of trees. Some trees still bear the faint white-painted numbers of the study trees. The last quarry closed sometime in the 1960s.

Later, Lake Metroparks began leasing the forest from the Ohio Department of Natural Resources. The park district now manages the site as a park and natural area.

Journal

July 17: It is a clear day, low humidity. I yearn to camp on this quarry ledge tonight and simply watch the stars of the northern sky open after the melon-colored glow of the sunset fades. The blinking lights of barges on Lake Erie would drift in the distance. Perhaps a shooting star will streak across the horizon and fall into the lake.

The ancient people observed celestial luminaries much more than we, especially the shiny bodies that rose and fell on the horizon. They studied the heavens purposefully and reverently. That was how they connected with the cosmos, set their calendars, got their bearings, and followed the rythmns of nature. To them stardom meant the realm and vitality of the eternal nighttime sparks, not some attraction to human celebrities who momentarily glow in the white-hot electronic world. Ask yourself which kind of star—heavenly or earthly—from where you tend to get your bearings.

On the open and bare quarry floor 100 feet below some humans have positioned rocks in a circle. The diameter of the circle is about 10 feet. The darkest stone points north, toward Lake Erie. Is the circle the site of a nightly ritual, an extraterrestial landing site, a target for tossing "lucky stones," or did children playing pretend put them in this order? Ah, if only I could camp on this ledge tonight and learn the answer

Penitentiary Glen Reservation

The only penitentiary here is a rock-bottomed, steep-walled gorge which, like a prison, is easy to get into, but hard to get out of. Penitentiary Glen offers freedom from the humdrum of daily rigors, and the beguiling charm of the place may get locked up in your heart.

LOCATION
Southwestern Lake County, in Kirtland.

SIZE
383 acres.

ACCESS
Exit I-90 and travel south on SR 306. After crossing the East Branch of the Chagrin River, a state scenic river, bear left on Kirtland-Chardon Road (follow the signs). The entrance will be on the right, after a long climb.

Trails: This natural area has four miles of trails through a variety of habitats. Pick up a trail guide at the nature center.

Special Places & Events: Its nature center has exhibits for youngsters, an auditorium, gift shop, rest rooms (outside access, too), and classrooms. Nature programs are held here regularly.

A wildlife center is part wildlife hospital, part zoo for injured critters, part educational facility for humans. The rehab center is open to the public.

Another oddity is the Penitentiary Glen Railroad, a pint-sized steam railroad, operated by full-sized members of the Lake Shore Live Steamers (toy railroads not cooked clams) Club. The railroad cars are big enough to pull people on free rides to the gorge during the warm months. The schedule, like this attraction, may be irregular, so call the park beforehand.

More, *metroparks*

Other Lake County Parks

Hidden Valley, 109 acres, Klasen Road, Madison Township. Grand River, rare flora and fauna, canoe landing, picnic tables, playground, sledding hill, birdwatching.

Girdled Road, 643 acres, Girdled Road between SR 86 and SR 608. Forested, Big Creek, picnic tables, playground, fishing, Buckeye Trail, rare plants.

Hogback Ridge Park, 413 acres, Emerson Road, Madison Township. Grand River, forests, wildflowers, steep ravines.

Hell Hollow Wilderness Area, 643 acres, Leroy Center Road, Leroy Township. Trails, picnic area, playground, ball fields, creek.

Arcola Creek, Dock Road, Madison Township. Mecca for steelhead trout angler, picnic area.

Also, Chagrin River Park, Indian Point Park, Children's Schoolhouse Nature Park, Concord Wood Nature Park, Fairport Harbor Lakefront Park, Helen Hazen Wyman Park, Lake Farmpark, Lakefront Lodge, Lakeshore Reservation, Mason's Landing Park, Paine Falls Park, Painesville Township Park, Parsons Gardens, Riverview Park, Veterans Park, Erie Shores Golf Course, Pine Ridge Country Club.

Bathing Beach Lake Glacier Mill Creek Park, Youngstown

GEOLOGY

Like a freedom-hungry prisoner who has been sawing the iron bars of his cell with dental floss, tiny Stoney Brook has been scratching at the bedrock that has confined it in Penitentiary Gorge for millenia. So far, it has removed layers of Berea sandstone and Bedford formation (shale and siltstone), both products of the Mississippian geologic period 345 to 320 million years ago.

You will best see sandstone overhangs and other odd shapes from the overlook near the wildflower garden (Glen Meadow Loop). Halfway through its high-walled dungeon Stoney Brook tumbles about 20 feet over Bedford rock (Stoney Brook Falls via the Gorge Rim Loop). Downstream, it cuts into older, Devonian-aged rocks—Cleveland and Chagrin shales—once the sediment of a shallow, murky sea. You cannot see these latter strata from a trail. Take one of the scheduled naturalist-led hikes for a closer look of these formations, and other curiosities in the gorge.

Stoney Brook does not appear to be a current created by glacial outwash, the water melting from an ancient glacier. It may have started as rain or snowmelt running off higher ground south of the reservation. As it flowed north it found a depression or crack in bedrock and began its scouring action.

A mile outside the reservation Stoney Brook joins the East Branch of the Chagrin River, which soon merges with the Aurora Branch from the south. The river drains north to Lake Erie where the water once confined by Penitentiary Gorge can freely spread out.

In the forest encircled by the Gorge Rim Loop you will see many boulders looking out of place. They did not roll off a hill because there is no hill, nor did they drop from the sky as some medieval charlatan might imagine. These huge stones, called "erratics," are part of the rubble left behind by the melting Wisconsinan ice mass that passed over this surface some 10,000 to 12,000 years ago. The erratics are the tombstones of that mile-high body of ice.

WILDLIFE

The tall hemlocks that carpet the rim and gorge walls are remnants, or refugees, of the Ice Age. This species of the cold northwoods arrived in the vanguard of the glaciers. When the climate warmed and the ice mass retreated to the polar caps, the surviving hemlocks found refuge in the cool, shady ravines in Ohio. Another tree of the northern clime, mountain maple, grows in a patch on the south side of the gorge. Look for its white foamy flowers in the spring.

The realm of the hardwoods lies beyond the rim. Some rather stout red oaks thrive in the forest alongside buxom maples, chestnut oak, tupelos, some beech and hickory. (Study them at the trailside bench on the Gorge Rim Loop).

A recovering forest of young trees, berry patches, vines is characteristic along the edges of fields and mature forests. The Rabbit Run, Bobolink and Glen Meadow trails visit these habitats on the road to becoming full-bloom forests again.

Wildflowers brighten the forest floor in the spring. One of them is the small whorled pogonia, a state and national endangered plant. Stemless lady slipper, round-leaved violet (stemless yellow blossom), and trailing arbutus are some of the members of this colorful ensemble. In summer, Indian pipe and squawroot were abundant beneath the shady canopy. Bulblet and long-beech are some of the ferns living here.

The forest attracts warblers of several varieties, as well as scarlet tanager, rose-breasted grosbeak, and pileated woodpecker. As you could have guessed, bobolinks have nested in the meadow encircled by the Bobolink Loop. Their ecstatic, raspy song is a favorite of many birders. In summer, the male appears to be dressed in a tuxedo, black-bellied with white plumage on top, with an orange brushstroke on the back of the neck. Also look for bluebirds and tree swallows in this habitat.

Waterfowl—Canada geese and ducks mostly—can be seen in the marsh and pond behind the nature center. Occasionally great blue and green herons appear. Naturalists expect more birds will call these newly-created wetlands home in the future.

HISTORY

Sam and Blanche Halle, owners of the Cleveland department store chain, bought this old farm (180 acres) in 1912 and built a weekend and summer cottage above the gorge for the family. Farming continued until after World War II. Lake Metroparks obtained the Halle property in the mid-1970s.

◆ ◆ ◆   LORAIN   COUNTY   ◆ ◆ ◆
Information: Lorain County Metroparks, 12882 Diagonal Road, LaGrange, OH 44050, (440) 458-5121 or 1-800-LCM-PARK

Black River Reservation

The Black River cuts a curling, picturesque path across a floodplain, swamp forest, and upland meadow. Spectacular shale cliffs poke through the forest and prairie plants rise head high in July.

LOCATION

Northern Lorain County, Sheffield and Elyria townships.

SIZE

833 acres.

ACCESS

Entrances are on Ford Road and 31st Street. SR 254, off I-90/SR 2, bisects the site.

Trails: The centerpiece of the reservation is the Bridgeway Trail, 3.5-mile hike and bike path along the Black River. The 12-foot wide paved route favors hikers, bicyclists, in-line skaters, wheelchair users, and strollers (no skateboards). Highlight of the trail is a 1,000-foot bridge span which crosses the Black River twice and raises visitors into the tree canopy.

More, *metroparks*

Other Lorain and Mahoning County Parks

LORAIN COUNTY PARKS

Mill Hollow-Bacon Woods Memorial Park, Vermilion Road, Brownhelm Township. Vermilion River, sledding hill, hiking, Benjamin Bacon Museum, nature center.

French Creek Reservation, 428 acres, SR 611 and 4530 Colorado Avenue, Sheffield. Hiking trails, French Creek, nature center, birding.

Caley National Wildlife Woods, 500-acres, West Road, Pittsfield Township. Nature trails, small lake, observation area.

Indian Hollow Reservation, west of Grafton between Parsons and Indian Hollow roads.

Charlemont Reservation, New London-Eastern Road, Rochester-Huntington township line. Hunting.

North Ridgeville Reservation, between US 20 and Otten Road.

Shoepfle Garden, 20 acres, in Birmingham, Erie County.

MAHONING COUNTY PARKS

Yellow Creek Park, Bridge Street, SR 616, Wetmore Ave., Lowellville Road, in Struthers. Hiking, lodge, pavilion.

Vickers Nature Preserve, 275 acres, US 224, Ellsworth Township. Trails, education farm.

A dozen interpretive signs explain the river valley's natural history.

Special Places & Events: An electric tram, departing from Day's Dam Picnic Area, takes passengers into the valley during the warm months. The park has three picnic areas with shelters and rest rooms. Park is open 8 a.m. to 9:30 p.m. daily.

WILDLIFE

Check out the large prairie remnant and extensive oxbow swamp. Depending on the season, birders are likely to see the belted kingfisher, northern oriole, rough-winged swallow, wood duck, eastern woodcock, gray catbird, and common yellow-throat warbler.

Carlisle Reservation

The West Branch of the Black River meanders across the reservation, which offers mature forests, flood plain meadows, and abandoned river channels that have evolved into wetlands.

LOCATION
Carlisle Township.

SIZE
Nearly 1,700 acres.

ACCESS
The entrance to the visitor center is on Nickel Plate-Diagonal Road, near its junction with SR 301. US 20 forms the northwestern border of the park.

Trails: Seven interconnecting trails totaling 5.5 miles start here; ten miles total. Duck Pond Picnic area, off Nickel Plate-Diagonal Road, offers two shelters, two ponds, fishing pier, drinking water, and rest rooms.

Special Places & Events: Carlisle Visitor Center serves as a nature education center, wildlife observation area, trailhead for hiking trails, conference room, gift shop, and park district headquarters. The Equestrian Center is a staging area for horseback riders who can enjoy two loop trails totaling nearly three miles. The area also has picnic areas, ice skating area, rest rooms, amphitheater, water, sledding hill, and horse ring for exhibitions and events. The park has a Bluegrass Festival in July, horse-drawn wagon rides in autumn, and horse-related activities (barrel races) sponsored by local 4-H clubs on Sunday afternoons in summer.

WILDLIFE
Discovery of a stand of pumpkin ash, an imperiled tree in Ohio, enhanced the status of the reservation.

The reservation's bottomlands are ruled by sycamores, cottonwoods, boxelders, willows and walnuts. Higher ground supports ash, elm, sugar maple, beech, red oak, basswood, tulip and hickory. A seven-acre wetland created in 1993 complements a natural wetland arising from an abanoned river channel.

Waterfowl linger at the duck ponds, and shorebirds, heron, and egrets now visit the new wetland. Summer birdwatchers can seek bluebirds, bobolinks, willow flycatchers, swamp sparrows, American kestrels, and ever-present turkey vultures.

✦ ✦ ✦ *MAHONING COUNTY* ✦ ✦ ✦

For information contact Mill Creek Metropolitan Park District, 7574 Columbiana-Canfield Road, Box 596, Canfield, OH 44406-0596, (330) 702-3000, www.neont.com/millcreek.

Mill Creek Metropolitan Park District

Mill Creek Gorge is the Wisconsinan glacier's scenic signature in Youngstown and nature's centerpiece in a mammoth metropark that has something for everybody.

LOCATION
This linear, north-south park flanks Mill Creek in the heart of Youngstown.

SIZE
2,530 acres.

ACCESS
The park spreads from US 224 (Canfield-Boardman Road, off SR 11) to its confluence with the Mahoning River, near Mahoning Avenue (off I-680). US 62 and Shields Road cross the park's midsection.

Trails: Seventeen miles of foot trails travel along both banks of Mill Creek. Trailheads and parking are available at East Newport Drive and Shields Road, Stitt Pavilion off West Golf Drive, Newport Boathouse, Chestnut Hill and Valley drives, West Glacier Drive and Glacier Boathouse. The featured section is the East Gorge Trail and Boardwalk between historic Lanterman's Mill and Lake Cohasset. Admire the natural waterfall and the lateral ravines along the way. Evergreens, notably hemlock, and hardwoods cloak the precipitous ravines.

Motoring through the park, which boasts 21 miles, has been a long-time pastime. Three "pleasure" (artificial) lakes were created with dams made of local sandstone. Lake Newport is the largest, 100 acres, followed by Lake Glacier, 44 acres, and Lake Cohasset, 28 acres.

Special Places & Events: Fellows Riverside Gardens is an arboretum and botanical garden at the north end of the park, off Price Road. Named after Elizabeth A. Fellows, who bequeathed the land and money for the public garden in 1958, the cultivated setting includes rose gardens, rock garden, pavilions, fountains, Victorian gazebo, statues, rhododendrons, conifers, seasonal plantings, scenic views and terraces. Hundreds of thousands of humans visit this jewel box yearly. The site includes the Fred W. Green Memorial Garden Center, a place for meetings, flower shows, horticultural displays, and gifts. Wedding sites and tours are offered (330) 740-7116.

Lanterman's Mill is a restored, historic gristmill on Canfield Road (US 62). The park district restored the 1846 mill in the mid-1980s. In 1976 the mill was entered in the National Register of Historic Places by the U.S. Department of the Interior. For information about the mill (and gift shop) call (330) 740-7115.

Ford Nature Education Center features natural history exhibits, nature programs, and trail walks. Located at Robinson Hill Drive (east bank) at Old Furnace Road. Phone (330) 740-7107. James L. Wick Jr. Recreation Area, off McCollum Road, has an ice rink, and par-3 golf course. Other facilities are boathouses at Lake Glacier (Price Road) and Lake Newport (West Newport Drive); 36-hole golf course along West Golf Drive, pavilions and day-use cabins for group activities, a 1.5-mile hike and bike trail beginning at Shields Road and East Newport Drive, picnic table, fishing ponds, covered bridge, sledding hill, tennis and basketball courts, garden center, and athletic fields.

GEOLOGY

Torrents of glacial meltwater are responsible for the carving of Mill Creek. The northerly part of the park includes Mill Creek gorge and parts of the lateral ravines that enter it. This narrow valley extends from the confluence of Mill Creek with the Mahoning River at the extreme north end of the park to the Lake Newport Dam at its southerly end. Through this section of the park, the hillsides are steep and beautifully covered with deciduous and evergreen trees. There are bold outcroppings of sandstone rock and numerous grass covered meadows. A fine variety of shrubs, vines, ferns and wildflowers are native to the gorge section of the park.

Above the gorge the land is rolling and partly wooded but much of it was formerly good farmland. Lake Newport covers the bottom land in this part of the park. The extreme south end is quite flat and includes both dense woods and extensive swamps. The finest stands of wildflowers in the county are found here.

WILDLIFE

Small furry creatures and deer are plentiful (perhaps too abundant in the case of whitetails).

Beaver have reappeared in quiet wetlands after a century's absence. Birdwatching can be productive. Look for great blue and green-backed herons, screech owls, eastern kingbirds, swallows (barn and rough-winged), hummingbirds, scarlet tanager and indigo bunting.

HISTORY

Community mover and shaker Volney Rogers was instrumental in establishing Mill Creek Park in 1891, then known as the Youngstown Township Park District. A statue of Rogers stands near the north entrance. The inscription reads, "Conceived in his heart and realized through his devotion," a reminder that hard work is required for dreams to become realities.

Lanterman's Mill reminds visitors of the area's early pioneer history. John Young, the founder of Youngstown, originally owned the mill site. In August 1797, Phineas Hill and Isaac Powers bought the spot (300 acres and a waterfall) from Young, and built a saw and grist mill fashioned from logs within 18 months. This mill ran from 1799 to 1822, then was replaced by a frame structure. A flood wiped out the second mill in 1843. Enter German Lanterman, who erected the present gristmill in 1845-46.

Lanterman used three sets of grinding stones at his mill, which prospered until its closing in 1888. The nascent park district purchased the mill in 1892 and over the next eight decades used it as a dance hall, concession stand, bath house, boat storage, and nature and historical museums. The mill became a mill again after a major renovation in the mid-1980s. Other fixtures nearby included a covered bridge and boardwalk trail. You can buy corn meal for Johnnycakes in the mill's gift shop.

◆ ◆ ◆   M E D I N A   C O U N T Y   ◆ ◆ ◆
For information, contact the Medina County Park District, 6364 Deerview Lane, Medina, OH 44256, (330) 722-9364.

◆ ◆ ◆   P O R T A G E   C O U N T Y   ◆ ◆ ◆
For information, contact the Portage County Park District, 449 S. Meridian St., Ravenna, OH 44266, (330) 673-9404.

Towner's Woods

George Towner was a curious man. In 1932 he sifted through gravel atop a dome that had aroused his curiosity. He found some curious beads and some bones. Towner notified archeologists at Kent State University and the Ohio Historical

Society. The hillock turned out to be a burial mound of 11 Hopewell people who lived there 1,500 years ago.

LOCATION
Between Ravenna and Kent, on the Franklin-Ravenna township line.

SIZE
175 acres.

ACCESS
From Kent, take SR 43 north, then go right on Ravenna Road. Ahead, bear right at a fork with Lake Rockwell Road. After a sharp right turn look for a gravel driveway and parking lot to Towner's Woods beside an old railroad blockhouse.

Trails: A 2.5-mile perimeter route combining the Lakeside, Eagle, Meadow Circuit, and Fencepost Path trails visits the celebrated Hopewell mound, the shore of Lake Pippen, one of Akron's water supplies, and Barnacle Bog, a thick sphagnum moss wetland that shelters imperiled plants like leather-leaf and wild calla. The hillocks you climb here are kames, formed when sediments in meltwater slid through cracks in a glacier and were deposited hourglass fashion at bottom of the ice slab.

Interior trails called Mosquito, King's, Ginseng, Swann's Way, and Warm-up can lengthen (or shorten) your adventure. A loop for cross-country skiing is provided on the eastern side of the park. The half dozen shelters scattered along trails are meant for wildlife observation, and breathers, though some folks use them for picnics. (Carry out your trash!) There are picnic tables and primitive rest rooms near the parking lot.

HISTORY
George Towner sold his place to Portage County in 1972, and park development began in 1975 with federal grant money. However, in 1983, Portage County Probate Judge Robert Kent dissolved the park board with the blessing of county commissioners who feared a park board could seek tax levies without their consent. Protesters, who included The Friends of Towner's Woods, somehow maintained the park with meager funding. A park board was re-established in 1991. The Friend of Towner's Woods now support a rail-to-trail route from Kent to Warren.

✦✦✦   RICHLAND   COUNTY   ✦✦✦
For more information about Richland County Park District, 2295 Lexington Avenue, Mansfield, OH 44907, (419) 884-3764.

✦✦✦   STARK   COUNTY   ✦✦✦
For more information about Stark County park areas, contact   Stark County Park District, 5300 Tyner Avenue NW, Canton, OH 44708, (330) 477-3552.

Sippo Lake Park

Sippo Lake is one of those something-for-everybody parks. And there's something for critters, too—a wildlife rehabilitation clinic for injured animals at the Sanders Center of Outdoor Education.

LOCATION
A few miles west of Canton, Perry Township.

SIZE
278 acres.

ACCESS
Entrances are on Tyner Ave. (off Perry Drive NW), 12th St. NW., Genoa Road NW.

Special Places and Events: Try out the 97-acre lake, marina, food, boat rentals, boat shelter, club-house, picnic areas and shelter, playground, Perception Park for people with special needs, bird blinds, observation tower, trails, parking, rest rooms, and fishing pier.

If you enjoy irony, go to the Sanders Center for Outdoor Education. Part of it houses the Sanders Collection (hence its name) consisting of 65 mounted animals, many of them big game mammals exotic and native to North America. Another part patches up injured critters, and cares for animals "positively orphaned." There are, of course, other exhibits explaining the area's natural history.

HISTORY
Sippo Lake was a private hunting and fishing club from 1910-1977. The lake is stocked with catfish, walleye, bass, perch.

✦✦✦   SUMMIT   COUNTY   ✦✦✦
For information, contact Metroparks of Summit County, 975 Treaty Line Road, Akron, OH 44313, (330) 867-5511.

Furnace Run Metropark

Though it has been disturbed by the construction of two major highways and a row of steel towers toting power lines,

Furnace Run Metropark is bouncing back, attracting beavers, deer and herons once again.

LOCATION
Northwestern Summit County, Richfield Township.

SIZE
890 acres.

ACCESS
Northbound travelers on I-77 can take the SR 21/Ohio Turnpike (Brecksville Road) exit. (There is no exit here for southbound cars.) The exit lane travels north, so you will have to turn around in nearby parking lots and head south on Brecksville Road (SR 21). Go under I-77, ignore the southbound ramp for I-77, and take the next right, Townsend Road. The park entrance will be on the right in a mile.

From the Ohio Turnpike, exit at SR 21 (Gate 11) and go south 1 mile to Townsend Road, then turn right to the park entrance.

Trails: The trailhead for nature paths totaling 3.2 miles is located at the end of a short trail that begins to the left of the Brushwood Shelter. Brushwood Lake, beside the shelter, grew behind an old mill dam blocking Rock Creek. You have choices at the trailhead, where you will find maps in a wooden box.

The trails are wide and easy to follow. There are a few brief steep climbs up and down creek banks, nothing too strenuous. You'll be crossing streams on stepping stones, but after a heavy rain the current is likely to wash over these steps. Be prepared for muddy trails and wet feet.

Special Places and Events: More than two-thirds of the park is off limits to the public. Here, wildlife gets a breather from the intrusions of humans. Much of that land is roughly bordered by I-77 on the west, Boston Mills Road, Black Road, and SR 303. These oak-hickory tracts can be explored during the annual "Stream Stomp." You can peek into this forbidden zone while tiptoeing on the half-mile H.S. Wagner Daffodil Trail, located off Brush Road. This trail is especially beautiful when the daffodils bloom in early spring.

Recently modernized Brushwood Shelter accommodates 100 people. It has a food service area, nearby picnic area, and rest rooms. Call the park office for reservations and fees.

GEOLOGY
Geologically speaking, you won't find narrow gorges, cliffs, or ledges along the hiking trails. Instead, study the smaller scenes—stream bank erosion that exposes roots and topples trees; sand and gravel beaches on the bends; and pools deep enough for tiny fish.

In the protected (non-public) area of the park the terrain is steeper and more rugged. Tributaries pouring into Furnace Run have carved several ravines.

WILDLIFE
Canada geese, almost as common as pigeons, and ducks of several varieties float on Brushwood Lake. Occasionally, a great blue heron will wade in the creek, hunting for tasty morsels. The park attracts a fair number of warblers in the warm months, and protects permanent residents such as owls, bluejays, sparrows, and cardinals.

Trees associated with an oak-hickory forest dominate the higher ground above Furnace Run in the protected area of the park. The hiking trails, however, traipse through the land of beeches and maples, with sycamore, willow, and walnut clinging to stream banks. You will find groves of pines and spruces scattered throughout the park. Many were planted in the 1930s and have grown to maturity.

From time to time, beavers will establish a colony along the creek. I found deer and raccoon tracks on the trail, and I hear that fox run wild in the hollows.

HISTORY
Furnace Run Metropark took shape in 1929 when the family of Charles Francis Brush Jr. donated 272 acres to the newly-formed Akron Metropolitan Park District. It was opened that year, one of the first in the park district.

Park development hastened during the Depression years (1930s) when work crews from the Civilian Conservation Corps built trails, roads, bridges, and other structures.

Brushwood Lake was a favorite swimming hole until construction of the Ohio Turnpike and other human developments upstream sped up erosion. The park district recently scooped out the muck so that waterfowl and ice skaters could return.

Gorge Metropark

Gorge Metropark lets visitors peek into a gorge that exposes pages of geological and human history. The site's scenic appeal would triple if the useless power company dam could be removed to reveal "copacaw," the majestic waterfalls hidden by the dam lake.

LOCATION
At the border of Akron and Cuyahoga Falls in Summit County.

SIZE
205 acres.

Exit SR 8 at Howe Road then go south to Front Street. The park entrance is off Front Street near the bridge over the river.

Trails: Two trails, each covering 1.8 miles, emerge from the parking lot. The Gorge Trail, a loop path, heads west, beyond the dam, and visits the Mary Campbell Cave, a channel cut through sandstone called Chuckery Race, and the narrow gorge itself. It returns to the parking lot. The Glens Trail travels east on the north bank of the river, and finishes at Front Street. Retrace your steps to the parking lot.

Special Places & Events: The park has a picnic shelter, picnic area, rest rooms, fishing access, and ice skating pond.

GEOLOGY

For 12,000 years, the Cuyahoga River has been slicing through this chasm. It has already washed away the glacial topsoil and a thick layer of pebbly,

More, *metroparks*

Other Medina, Richland, Stark, and Summit County Parks

MEDINA COUNTY PARKS

River Styx Park, 83 acres, Blake & River Styx roads, Guilford Township. River Styx Valley, ravines, fishing pond, hiking, picnic areas.

Buckeye Woods Park, mile east of Lafayette on SR 162. Chippewa Creek, trails, Schleman Nature Preserve, fishing, picnicking, ball fields.

Hidden Hollow Park, Richman Road off SR 421, Harrisville Township. Clear Creek Fork, group camping, nature study, hiking.

Also, Green Leaf Park, Hubbard Valley Park, Letha House Park, Plum Creek Park, Alderfer-Oenslagr, Princess Ledges, Chippewa Lake and Allardale.

RICHLAND COUNTY PARKS

Gorman Nature Center, 130 acre, Hanley Road. Nature study, trails, ponds, spring, forests, prairie, covered bridge, streams, and meadows.

STARK COUNTY PARKS

Petros Lake Park, 94 acres, Perry Township. Fishing lake, picnic area, volleyball, ball fields, trail, wildflower/butterfly trail.

Ohio & Erie Towpath Trail, a 25-mile multipurpose trail along Tuscarawas River from north of Canal Fulton to county line. Canal rides at Lock 4 Park.

SUMMIT COUNTY PARKS

Silver Creek Metropark, 610 acres, Medina Line Road. Silver Creek Lake, swimming beach, boat launch, fishing, picnic area, trails for hikers and horse riders.

Deep Lock Quarry Metropark, 77 acres, Riverview Road south of Peninsula. Old sandstone quarries, hiking, Towpath Trail, part of Cuyahoga Valley National Recreation Area.

Hampton Hills Metropark, 278 acres, Bath Road and Akron-Peninsula Road. Tough hiking trails, part of Cuyahoga Valley National Recreation Area, historic farm.

F.A. Seiberling Naturealm & Sand Run Metropark, 100 acres, Sand Run Parkway off Ghent Road. Naturealm nature center, arboretum, overlooks, paths, bridle and hiking trails, canoe access, ice skating, picnic areas, playground, sledding hill.

Munroe Falls Metropark, South River Road. Swimming lake, athletic fields, tennis, horseshoe, and basketball and volleyball courts, playground, sledding hill, picnic areas, trail, beaver pond.

300 million-year-old Sharon Conglomerate. Now it is working on sheets of shale. Several springs spill from the ledges, but don't drink the water.

WILDLIFE

You will see oak, blackgum, tulip trees, yellow birch, and bunches of spring wildflowers nourishing themselves on the valley walls. Don't expect to see a wide variety of flying and four-legged creatures here, except for the mainstays who endure urban environments. However, spring and fall migratory birds can be spotted in this protected corridor.

HISTORY

In 1759, little Mary Campbell was abducted in Pennsylvania by Lenni Lenape (Delaware) Indians and brought to the cave here to live with Chief Netawatwees. Mary went home, five years later, at the end of the French-Indian War.

In 1844, workers began cutting a channel through the sandstone, a project called the Chuckery Race. Water flowing in the race was supposed to bring prosperity to a new boomtown called Summit City. The city went bust, but the race got listed on the National Register of Historic Places.

From 1882 to the 1920s, folks flew on the roller coaster and kicked up their heels at the "commuter park" High Bridge Glens, located here. The Northern Ohio Traction and Light Company, the forerunner of Ohio Edison, gave 144 acres of land to the park district in 1930.

O'Neil Woods Metropark

This hilly park offers scenic views of Summit County, and its trail explores forest, meadow, floodplain, and creek.

LOCATION

Bath Township, Summit County.

SIZE

274 acres.

ACCESS

The entrance is on Martin Road. Park in the Lone Pine Picnic Area.

Trails: Deer Run Trail, a 1.8-mile loop path, begins and ends at the Lone Pine Picnic Area (where toilets also are located). This path heads south along a narrow ridgetop before crossing Bath Road and swooping into the Yellow Creek Valley. It follows the creek then bends north to the trailhead. Picnic tables with grills, and rest rooms, are provided at the parking lot.

GEOLOGY

Hilly terrain sets off the park. Yellow Creek flows over a shale bed and drains into the Cuyahoga

River to the east.

WILDLIFE

Oaks prevail on the ridges but along Yellow Creek the black walnut, sycamore, eastern cottonwood, and black willow spread their branches. Ferns and wildflowers are especially abundant in the forest. The hiking trail visits one of the few alder swamps in the county.

The park is known for its deer, which quiet hikers are apt to see in the leafless months. The many habitats provide shelter for a thriving collection of birds, notably ruffed grouse and barred owls (oaks and ridges), woodcocks and bluebirds (meadows), kingfishers (creek), as well as song sparrows.

HISTORY

The family of William and Grace O'Neil donated their family farm to the park district in 1972. The O'Neils founded the General Tire & Rubber Company. For two decades, beginning in the 1930s, the farm served as a family and weekend retreat for horseback riding and gentleman farming.

Firestone Metropark

Boasting the Tuscarawas River, two ponds, a marsh, and a race, Firestone Metropark is a wetland paradise.

LOCATION

Summit County, just south of Akron.

SIZE

255 acres.

ACCESS

Entrances are located on Axline Avenue, Warner Road, and two on Harrington Road.

Trails: The 1.6-mile Willow Trail is accessible from each entrance. Start at the Little Turtle Pond and Spring Pond entrance off Harrington Road. Little Turtle Pond is a popular fishing hole for anglers 15 years and younger.

The Willow Trail starts its loop in the parking lot, passes the ponds, follows the Tuscarawas River, visits the Axline Avenue Picnic Area, traces Tuscarawas Race and the river, crosses the Tuscarawas Picnic Area, then runs along the shore of the swamp back to the starting point. Other amenities are a playground, toilets, fitness trail, shelter, sledding hill, and drinking water. The park provides access to canoers who want to paddle the Tuscarawas River.

WILDLIFE

More than 175 species of birds have been counted in this park of many habitats. The creek and

Union Park Akron, Ohio

Trumbull County

For information, contact
Trumbull County
Metropolitan Park District,
(330) 898-6635
Canoe Trail Park, *Newton*
Township, on Newton Falls-
County Line Road. Canoe
launch on tributary of
Mahoning River, picnic area,
hiking.
Canoe City Park, *Warren*
Township, in Leavittsburg,
North Leavitt Road. Canoe
launch into Mahoning River,
dock, bait, snacks, picnic area,
handicapped accessible, trail,
parking.
Clarence Darrow Park,
Champion Township. Frisbee
golf course, hiking trail, picnic
area.

ponds sponsor fish, crayfish, turtles, frogs, salamanders and other aquatic creatures. Look for fox, raccoons, muskrats, skunks, mice, voles in the swamp and wet meadows.

HISTORY

Some 189 acres of land was given to the park district in 1949 by the Firestone Tire and Rubber Company. The place had been a dairy farm.

The Tuscarawas Race, a channel built in the 19th century to fill the Ohio-Erie Canal, runs through the south section of the park.

Goodyear Heights Metropark

Oaks and other hardwoods are slowly pushing out the Scotch pines that were planted 60 years ago. Anglers and birdwatchers will satisfy their natural desires around Alder Pond.

LOCATION
Summit County, Akron.

SIZE
410 acres.

ACCESS

From I-76, head north on SR 91 (Darrow Road), turn left on Newton Street, then right on Frazier Avenue.

Trails: Midway to the pond, the Alder Trail (1.8 miles) goes off to the right. This trail soon splits again. The Alder Trail goes left (north) and shares the path with the Piney Woods Trail. Go right at the next intersection, eastbound on Piney Woods Trail.

Piney Woods Trail (two miles) journeys through a growing hardwood forest, a pine plantation on the east side of the park, and back to the Alder Trail. Turn left (south) when you reach this last junction, and return to the trailhead. Don't let the fitness trail confuse you.

Fishing: Anglers will make a beeline to Alder Pond via the half-mile Lake Trail (toilets nearby).

Facilities: The park permits horseback riding, and has picnic areas, fitness trail, ball field, bus stop, playground, picnic shelter, toilets, and sledding hill.

WILDLIFE

Trees more typical of the woods of northeastern Ohio are replacing the pines that relief workers planted in the 1930s. In one area on the north side of the park, acidic soil allows sassafras trees to flourish above a mat of sarsaparilla.

Some areas of Alder Pond are becoming bog-like, sponsoring colonies of yellow birch and cattail. Muskrats, who live in cattail lodges, Canada geese, and mallard ducks call the pond home.

SOUTHEAST

◆ ◆ ◆   G A L L I A   C O U N T Y   ◆ ◆ ◆

For information, contact O.O. McIntyre Park District, Gallia County Courthouse, 18 Locust Street, Gallipolis, OH 45631-1262, (740) 446-4612, ext. 256.

Raccoon Creek County Park

Nestled in the foothills of Southeastern Ohio, the park is bounded by Raccoon Creek, a stream the Shawandase called

Etha-Petha. The place could rightfully be called Cyperus refractus after the reflexed umbrella sedge, an endangered plant that earned the park designation as an Ohio Natural Landmark.

LOCATION
Perry Township.

SIZE
About 700 acres.

ACCESS
From Gallipolis, go west on SR 141, south four miles on SR 775, right on Dan Jones Road (CR 28) (after crossing the creek). Recreation facilities are a half-mile ahead, the natural areas .75 miles.

Trails: The natural areas upstream from the recreation area have separate trails branching from the west side of Dan Jones Road (CR 28). As its name implies, Natural Gorge Trail (half mile) visits a gorge carved by a tiny tributary to Raccoon Creek. Deer Hollow Trail comprises three loops of 1.25 miles.

Facilities: Facilities at the recreation area include six shelterhouses (reservable), picnic areas with grills, two-mile fitness trail, canoe access, "ad-

More, *metroparks*

Other Monroe and Gallia County Parks

OTHER MONROE COUNTY PARKS
Clarington Park, 254 acres, end of Fish Port Road, Salem Township.
Keidaish Point Park, 230 acres, off Short Ridge Road, Ohio Township. Overlooks Ohio River.
Veterans Memorial Community Park, 66 acres, SR 145, near Beallsville.
Monroe Park & Marina, 11.2 acres, off SR 7, Lee Township. Former Lock 15, boat access to Ohio River,

fishing, picnic area.
Also, Parry Museum, Hannibal Pool & Tennis Complex, Lee Lads & Lassie 4-H Park, Fly Park, Stafford Park.

OTHER GALLIA COUNTY PARKS
Elizabeth L. Evans Waterfowl & Bird Sanctuary, 60 acres, along Chickamauga Creek, Gallipolis. Hiking trails, observations decks for wildlife viewing.

Life is summer, sunshine, watermelon, and the pits.

venture" playgrounds, rest rooms, drinking water, parking, park office, ball fields, tennis and basketball courts, horseshoe pits, badminton and volleyball, and open areas for frisbees and cloud watching.

WILDLIFE

The park's diverse habitats—woodlands, wetlands, shady gorges, meadows, and lawns—support ruffed grouse, wild turkey, fox, raccoon, deer, waterfowl, songbirds, and favorites like the eastern bluebird and killdeer. Raccoon Creek is an enjoyable and easy canoeing stream. The stretch from Bob Evans' Farm to the park is about seven miles. The creek could easily be called *Castor canadensis* because beavers have returned big time and put deadfalls into the current.

HISTORY

Beavers recall frontiersman Daniel Boone who trapped and hunted in this valley in the 1790s.

◆ ◆ ◆   GUERNSEY COUNTY   ◆ ◆ ◆

For information, contact Guernsey County Park District, (740) 432-9200.

Jackson Park, 16.7 acres, SR 821, south of Byesville. Fishing pond, playground, hiking trail, volleyball, picnic tables.

◆ ◆ ◆   MONROE COUNTY   ◆ ◆ ◆

For information, contact Monroe County Park Board, 101 W. Main St., Courthouse, Woodsfield, OH 43793, (740) 472-1328.

Piatt Park

The star of this park district features a scenic gorge, cave, and campgrounds in the heart of the county.

LOCATION

On TR 2308 four miles east of Woodsfield.

SIZE

199 acres.

ACCESS

The park has a campground with 10 sites equipped with water and electric hookups, rest rooms, and picnic pavilion.

Trails: An interpretive nature trail departs from the camp, as well as a trail to the park's attractive gorge and shelter cave. The trail to the cave traverses a few steep hills and stairways.

WILDLIFE

Piatt Park's quiet woodlands provides a sanctuary for mountain laurel, ground pine, New York and interrupted ferns, mayapples, fairy wand, alum root, Virginia creeper, wild ginger, mountain cress, and other plants.

HISTORY

Founded in 1972, the park district today manages 10 parks totaling 700 acres.

CENTRAL

◆◆◆ CLARK COUNTY ◆◆◆

For information, contact Clark County Park District, 930 S. Tecumseh Road, Springfield, OH 45506, (937) 882-6000.

The district has 5 parks, nearly 500 acres—George Rogers Clark Park, Estel Wenrick Wetland, Little Miami Bikeway, Aberfelda Nature Preserve, Peckuwe Village Battlesite.

◆◆◆ DELAWARE COUNTY ◆◆◆

Preservation Parks of Delaware County, 40 N. Sandusky St., Suite 201, Delaware, OH 43015, (740) 368-1805.

Blues Creek Preserve, 97.5 acres, Scioto Township. Trails, picnic area, playground, stream.

◆◆◆ FAIRFIELD COUNTY ◆◆◆

For information contact Fairfield County Historical Park District, 407 E. Main St., Lancaster, OH 43130, (740) 681-7249.

Cross Mound Park

This park features a cross-shaped mound, likely the work of the Hopewell people.

LOCATION

Southwestern Lancaster County, Clear Creek Township.

SIZE

More than 20 acres.

ACCESS

From SR 159 in Tarlton (midway between Chillicothe and Lancaster), take Sixteenth Road north a half mile to the park.

Trails: A half-mile nature trail, called a land lab by the local Boy Scouts who built it, features interpretive signs that challenge your powers of observation and intuition. It gets the gray cells warmed up for the bigger questions rising from the cross. The answers to the land lab queries are written on the back of a signpost at the trailhead bridge. A few picnic tables and rest rooms are available.

The park was formerly a state historical site called Tarlton Mound. Cross Mound may be located alongside an ancient road connecting the large mound complexes in Chillicothe and Newark.

JOURNAL

I reached Cross Mound, compass steady in my open palm. Sure enough, the earthen cross points north, with just a bit of error. My heart pumps questions into my head, so I open the floodgate. Is the orientation of the cross coincidental, or had the Hopewell people discovered the cardinal directions (north, south, west and east)? Did they take their bearings from a star? If so, which one? Dead north in Hopewell times (100 B.C. to 400 A.D.) was between Polaris, the current North Star, and Thuban, the North Star about 3,500 years ago when slaves built monuments for Egyptians. Why does each linear mound in the cross measure 90 feet, a number equal to the angle between each leg? Coincidence, again?

◆◆◆ FRANKLIN COUNTY ◆◆◆

In the 1930s, the members of the Wheaton Club, avid birdwatchers and naturalists, surveyed Franklin County and compiled a list of precious sites worth preserving. On August 14, 1945, the Columbus and Franklin County Metropolitan Park District was formed. The sites researched by the Wheaton Club served as the park district's acquisitions list.

More information about the parks can be obtained by contacting the Metropolitan Park District of Columbus and Franklin County, P.O. Box 29169, Columbus, OH 43229, (614) 891-0700.

Battelle-Darby Creek Metropark

The trails in this wooded metropark take you to a stream considered to be the most vital and diverse aquatic ecosystem of its dimension in the Midwest—bar none. If that is not impressive enough, then consider the thick oak-hickory woods and the tallgrass prairie meadows that cover the creek banks, the half dozen ancient Indian burial mounds hidden in the forest, and the thousands of migratory birds who either bed down here, or, like their ancestors, get their north-south bearings from the creek.

LOCATION
Southwestern Franklin County, Pleasant Township.

SIZE
3,500 acres.

ACCESS
From I-70 (west of Columbus and I-270), travel south on Rome-Hilliard Road, then west (right) on US 40 (National Road). Turn south (left) on Darby Creek Drive. The Cedar Ridge entrance to the park will appear on the right in about three miles. The Indian Ridge entrance, also on the right, occurs in four miles.

Trails: A two-mile path called the Ancient Trail goes to an Adena Indian mound. A 3.2-mile trail for cross-country skiers and hikers exists at the Little Darby Picnic Area. Two mile Terrace Trail stems from the Indian Ridge area.

Facilities: Park brochures (with trail maps) can be found at the ranger station (Cedar Ridge). Rest rooms and drinking water are located at Cedar Ridge, Indian Ridge and the canoe access. Vault toilets are found at the fishing site on Gardner Road. Cedar Ridge and Indian Ridge have plenty of picnic areas, playgrounds, and open space.

Special Places & Events: Park naturalists conduct programs here all the time. The program schedule is posted on bulletin boards in the parking lots.

GEOLOGY
Adding to its natural gifts, the metropark possesses any geological splendors, notably a steep 50–70-foot bluff on which the Cedar Bluff Overlook sits, and several steep cuts.

The creeks are outwashes of the Wisconsinan glacier, which scoured this terrain about 12,000–15,000 years ago and spread a layer of till, a mixture of gravel, sand, and cobble. This till stratum varies in thickness and composition in the Darby Creek watershed. For most of their journey, the creeks flow over and carry away this till. In the park, tributaries have carved steep slopes into the east bank.

In spring, the Darbies cannot hold their water. This frequent flooding has been a blessing because it has discouraged human development. The high water often overwhelms the creekside trails, and inundates portions of the floodplain in the park.

WILDLIFE
The Darby Creek watershed is a paradise for small fish and mollusks. Eighty-nine varieties of fish have been recorded in the watershed, including imperiled darters, minnows, and shiners that spawn in the shallow, cobbly riffles of the stream.

Thirty-eight species of mollusks, more than in Europe and Australia combined, thrive here. A half dozen are rarities. Oddly, the streamline chub and verigoot darter, uncommon residents elsewhere, are familiar faces in the Darby.

These critters, of course, attract herons—great blue and green—and kingfishers and osprey, occasionally. Ducks also ply the waters. All totaled, 176 species of birds have been observed in the region. Some of these are the pileated woodpecker, yellow-throated warbler, rose-breasted grosbeak, barred owl, and several brands of hawk. Look for the eastern meadowlark, bobolink, and Henslow's sparrow in the meadows. The last bird carries "special interest" status by the Ohio Division of Wildlife, meaning it is potentially threatened.

The usual assemblage of quadrupeds are present—deer, raccoons, squirrels, and fox. Recently, beaver and coyote have moved in. Visitors and park neighbors have seen the feisty badger.

In July and August the park's tallgrass prairies brighten the landscape. The park district began cultivating prairie species here in the late 1970s. The seeds came from other pockets of prairie lands in the Darby Plains. (See the Darby Plains prairies.)

The entrance to the Indian Ridge section of the park is lined with prairie dock, prairie coneflower, bergamot, purple coneflower, and others. Elsewhere, royal catchfly (a potentially threatened species), tall larkspur, and blazing stars compete with grasses called little and big bluestem.

Forest wildflowers are abundant, especially in the Cedar Ridge section. Keen observers may find yellow lady slipper, showy orchis, and pale jewel-weed (touch-me-not).

Nine kinds of oak (among them white, pin, chinkapin, burr) and five types of hickory dwell here. Some mammoth white oaks preside over the main trail in the Cedar Ridge area. You will also discover red, sugar, and silver maple, pawpaw, aspen, blue ash, sycamore, and osage orange, whose wood made the stoutest bows and arrows on the Great Plains. This tree from Texas may have been planted here as a fencerow thicket. Altogether, some 50 species of trees and shrubs grow in the park.

HISTORY
The ancient Indians favored the banks of Darby Creek. Six of their burial mounds have been discovered in the park (though they are off limits to the public). Stories are told of local farmers filling barrels with arrowheads, pottery, pipes, and other artifacts that they collected after plowing the fields. The bones of wolves, bears, and sandhill cranes, animals now extirpated or rare in Ohio, also have been unearthed found.

The Shawnee nation used this land before white settlers pushed them out in the late 18th century. Because Columbus has expanded fastest north and east, the Darby watershed (west of Columbus) has avoided the natural degradation associated with unchecked urban development. When farmers began to employ intensive farming techniques in the 1970s water quality in the currents began to decline due to greater amounts of chemicals and silt. Still, it is an area of small towns, small farms, and clean water—relatively speaking.

In the 1960s, the U.S. Army Corps of Engineers planned to dam Darby Creek near SR 665. The reservoir was to quench the thirst of burgeoning Columbus. The Corps bought the land marked for flooding, and evacuated people. Fortunately, that is as far as the project progressed.

The dam stalled following the discovery of numerous endangered species in the water and the ancient Indian earthworks in the floodplain. Seizing the chance, the park district bought the Cedar Ridge section from the Corps for $2 million. The Corps of Engineers still holds title to several hundred acres north of SR 665 (the public hunting area).

Blacklick Woods Metropark

(Walter A. Tucker State Nature Preserve)

Though encircled and threatened by the vagaries of development, this quiet forest preserve of huge beeches and maples, a National Natural Landmark, remains a peaceful place amidst urban sprawl.

LOCATION
Northwestern Fairfield County, Violet Township, near the Franklin County border.

SIZE
632 acres.

ACCESS
From I-70 (east of Columbus) head north on Brice Road, then east on Livingston Avenue to the entrance of Blacklick Woods Metropark (not the golf course). The state nature preserve has four entrances. Park at the Beech-Maple Lodge, Ash Grove or The Meadows picnic areas, or the metropark nature center.

Trails: Two trails, both starting in the metropark, visit Blacklick Woods. A half mile, self-guided boardwalk, the Buttonbush Trail, begins and ends at the park's nature center. This wheelchair and baby stroller trail loops through the swampy southeast corner of the site, but does not connect to other trails. A longer and better loop path venturing into the

Tucker preserve has entrances near the Meadows Picnic Area and Beech-Maple Lodge, a day use facility. Look for maps at the lodge, nature center, or the ranger station at the Ash Grove Picnic Area. Check out the bike path, too.

Special Places & Events: The nature center has exhibits, books, and a wildlife viewing window that overlooks Ashton Pond and a meadow. Nature education programs are held at the lodge and nature center. The lodge is available for group activities. Rest rooms and drinking water are located throughout the park, but none are located within the preserve. Playgrounds and a bicycle-jogging trail are found in the park.

GEOLOGY
Two factors saved Blacklick Woods from the axe and plow—flat terrain, and clay. The area is covered by a thin loamy topsoil atop a subsoil of firm clay that stops water from seeping deeper into the ground. Because of the level topography and clay, the topsoil becomes waterlogged. Excess water collects in shallow pools in the forest. Consequently, the location was unsuitable for farming, barring extensive draining.

Bedford shale of the Mississippian geologic period (330 million years ago) is exposed in Blacklick Creek, which serves as the southeast border of the metropark. (The creek does not pass through the preserve). The formation, however, is visible only if one wanders from the bike trail.

WILDLIFE
Blacklick Woods has some of biggest beech trees in Central Ohio. In fact, many giants in this forest are believed to be more than 200 years old. Their age is remarkable considering they are thin-skinned, susceptible to fire, frost, and fungi. They have spread their roots in the shallow soil on the ground above the swamp, often sharing it with sugar maple. Beech are identified by their smooth, gray bark, which, unfortunately, is easy to scar with a pocketknife. Beech trees growing beside trails carry the initials of humans far too often.

The extinct passenger pigeon favored beechnuts. Storytellers claim that roosting pigeons once were so numerous at Blacklick Woods that their weight bent beech branches to the ground. Turkeys and grazing hogs also like to fatten themselves on beechnuts.

Look closely around a big beech. Notice the many young sprouts that have climbed above the surface from roots. Sprouts also will rise from stumps and the depressions created by uprooted trees. Black bears, once prevalent in these woods, often chose the hollows and root cavities of toppled beech trees for dens.

Sugar maples and beeches seem to be inseparable, mostly because they enjoy the same habitat. They nurture each other. Beech seedlings grow best under the shade of the sugar maple, and vice versa.

Trees that do not mind "wet feet"—white ash,

swamp white oak, red maple, silver maple, pin oak—thrive in the swamp forest. You will also find elms (slippery and American), American hornbeam, wild black cherry, shagbark and pignut hickory, ironwood (also called musclewood), honey locust, other oaks (burr, northern red), tulip tree, Ohio buckeye, dogwood, sassafras, black walnut, black gum (black tupelo), sweet gum, black willow, box elder, and redbud. Along the creek the sycamore and eastern cottonwood preside. Pawpaw, whose buds deer refuse to eat, is increasing in number.

Due to overbrowsing by deer, a problem in other Columbus metroparks (see Sharon Woods Metropark), the varieties of wildflowers has decreased in recent years. Still, about 100 kinds can be observed in the preserve and park, such as cardinal flower, corn salad, spring beauties, Miami-mist, wild sweet William, Star of Bethlehem, hooked crowfoot (buttercup), lizard's tail, and pasture rose. Ferns are represented by Christmas, sensitive, rattlesnake, and oblique grape.

The woodland ponds and swamps (scarce habitats in Ohio) attract a large assemblage of life, much of it tiny and inconspicuous. The waters in the park contain catfish, smallmouth bass, bullhead, bluegill, fairy shrimp, fingernail clams, snails, crustaceans, frogs, salamanders, and crayfish.

Snakes like the black rat, blue racer, garter, DeKay's, and the water snake are free to slither. Both terrestrial (eastern box) and aquatic (midland painted) turtles dwell here.

Ducks (mallard and wood ducks are common), great blue herons, swallows, and Canada geese visit the ponds. Try spotting the common flicker (listen for "klee-yer" call in the hardwoods), cedar waxwing, cuckoo (occasional), flycatchers (several types), rufous-sided towhee, pine siskin (winter), and these warblers—American redstart, yellow-rumped, cerulean, black-and-white, and prothonotary. The black-crowned night heron, indigo bunting, and oriole have been seen near Blacklick Creek. Cooper's hawk, barred owl, great horned owl and the screech owl find homes here.

Mammals include the usual collection for this type of woodland: deer (too many actually), bats, opossum, squirrels (gray, red, flying, fox), muskrat, jumping mouse, weasel, mink, red fox, mole, vole, and shrew.

HISTORY

White settlers arrived after an 1801 congressional act set aside more than 100,000 acres in this area, the so-called Refugee Tract, for Canadians dispossessed of their land during the American Revolutionary War. In 1823, pioneers organized a wolf hunt (a massacre, really) to exterminate predators from the woods. They shot one black bear, three wolves, 49 deer, 60–70 turkeys, and 1 owl.

William Ashton bought 160 acres from a "refugee" settler and took up farming. He operated a steam-powered sawmill near the pond behind the nature center, and allowed his livestock to graze except in the forbidding swamp forest that is Blacklick Woods. The property was handed down to family members until 1948 when much of it was sold to the park district. Some of Ashton's descendants still live nearby.

The state nature preserve in the metropark honors a former park district director, Walter A. Tucker.

Blendon Woods Metropark

This bucolic setting at the edge of sprawling Columbus offers a variety of natural attractions for humans and wildlife—a waterfowl refuge, hardwood forest, brooks, and ravines.

LOCATION
Northeast Franklin County, Blendon Township.

SIZE
646 acres.

ACCESS
Leave I-270 (the beltway surrounding Columbus) at SR 161 (Dublin-Granville Road) east. Exit at the Little Turtle exit and follow signs west to the park entrance. Stay on the main road through the park, following signs to the nature center. You will find parking beside the new nature interpretation center, the best place to begin your visit.

Trails: Walk all the trails for a 2–2.5-mile hike. The paths are wide and smooth. Interpretive nature signs add to your understanding of the woods. Look for trail maps at the nature center and ranger station.

Facilities: Take your first right after entering the park to reach the open picnic areas, ranger station, and disc golf course. The nature trails also can be reached from the picnic areas. Groups can reserve picnic areas in other parts of the park.

Special Places & Events: The new, modern nature center is the departure point for the many scheduled nature programs. Drinking water and toilets are found here, too. The center is usually staffed by a naturalist who is ready to answer questions. The center has a small bookshop, and natural artifacts (deer antlers, turtle shells, skulls, etc.) for children.

GEOLOGY
The forest grows above what once was a relatively flat and thick layer of till, that wonderful mixture of gravel, sand and clay deposited by the last glacier (the Wisconsinan) some 15,000 years ago. It has taken centuries for the many small seasonal streams that meander in the park to wear away the till and form hollows.

Other Columbus Metroparks

Three Creeks Metropark,

1,000 acres, off Bixby Road, Madison Township. Confluence of Alum, Big Walnut, Blacklick creeks, trails, picnic areas, fishing, nature study.

Prairie Oaks Metropark,

1,000 acres, Western Franklin County along Big Darby Creek. Due to open in 2000.

In some places (Ripple Rock Trail), the streams have reached the bedrock of shale (composed of compressed mud or clay). The "ripples" in the rock were shaped by water currents (or waves) that once flowed over this deposit.

All of the brooks flow southwesterly into Big Walnut Creek, creating ridges with slopes facing north and south. Consequently, you will see more beech and maple trees on the north slopes because these plants prefer shadier, cooler and moister sites. On the other hand, oaks and hickory, which prefer sunnier and drier soil, will dominate the southern slopes.

The Hickory Ridge Trail passes through a small and unique swamp forest. (It is located about 100 yards in a straight line from the nature center.) Water that has been unable to penetrate a stratum of impervious shale close to the surface has created a woodland swamp in this flat location. Many trees have toppled here from their own weight because the wet soil and shale prevented them from sinking deep roots.

Thoreau Lake is a manmade pond, freshened somewhat by tiny rills. Yes, it honors philosopher Henry David Thoreau.

WILDLIFE

Thousands of waterfowl and other birds may gather in the waters of Thoreau Lake during the spring and autumn migrations. Bring your bird guides and binoculars. Ask a naturalist for a bird checklist at the nature center.

In the spring of 1993 some owls hatched their young in baskets placed by naturalists in a hollow tree beside the lake. Hawks often circle overhead, and perch in trees overlooking the pond.

During my visit that spring I twice spotted a wood duck flying in the woods along the Ripple Rock Trail. I suspect the bird was darting back and forth between its hidden tree nest and Thoreau Lake. Farther along this trail, a trio of pileated woodpeckers flushed in a crisscross pattern from the ground to the safe heights of nearby shagbark hickories. They clung to the bark long enough for me to fix them in my field glasses.

More than 160 kinds of wildflowers carpet the grounds. Pick up a checklist and blooming schedule for 50 cents at the nature center. Monkey flower, beardtongue, small skullcap, mouse-ear chickweed, heal-all, clammy ground cherry, naked-flowered tick-trefoil (say that one fast three times) are some of the little miracles you can see at Blendon Woods.

JOURNAL

Memorial Day. The volunteer naturalist at the observation blind said the lithesome, long-necked, white bird swimming in Thoreau Lake was a mute swan. The bird is rarely seen in these parts—an accidental tourist. Sure enough, the mute swan was not listed on the bird checklist given to me at the nature center.

This Eurasian import resides along the northeast-ern coast of the U.S., roughly from Cape Cod to Chesapeake Bay. However, my trusty Peterson's field guide reports that the bird has established colonies in the Great Lakes region.

This is the swan I remember in fairy tales. The graceful S-curved neck, the distinctive black lobe at the base of an orange bill that pointed down, an effortless, buoyant swimmer.

Chestnut Ridge Metropark

"Chestnut Ridge is a place that doesn't fit easily into human plans and categories," wrote David Rains Wallace, who lived in a cabin below the ridge in the late 1970s. His observations that year led to his nationally-acclaimed book Idle Weeds: The Life of an Ohio Sandstone Ridge, which briefly placed Chestnut Ridge in a pantheon of special places alongside Walden Pond and Sand County.

LOCATION

Northwestern Fairfield County, Bloom Township.

SIZE

486 acres.

ACCESS

Drive northwest from Lancaster about eight miles on US 33 (or southeast 15 miles on US 33 from Columbus) and turn right onto Winchester Road at the traffic light in Carroll. In three miles, bear right at the "Y" intersection to stay on Winchester Road (Old Route 33). Go another half mile to the entrance on the left.

Trails: A two-mile loop trail takes visitors through mature woodlots, a large meadow, a tiny bog, and along a creek. From the trailhead in the parking lot bear right, paralleling the road. The trail becomes steep as it ascends the ridge but it levels off when you reach a boardwalk. At the end of the boardwalk the trail hooks southward along the top of the ridge through an old orchard, woods, and some open areas. The terrain is hilly, and the trail can be steep in places.

Facilities: The parking area offers picnic tables, drinking water, a small playground, and toilets. The manmade fishing pond is a new addition to the park.

GEOLOGY

Chestnut Ridge lies at the edge or the boundary between the region of Ohio influenced by the

Wisconsinan glacier and the region that missed the ice pack.

Blackhand sandstone above beds of shale forms the shell of the ridge. These strata were made during a span of time called the Mississippian Period, 350–325 million years ago. Here's what happened.

Ohio, at that time, was covered by an ocean. However, to the east, the continental plates of Europe and North America collided head on. This tremendous clash caused the bedrock layers in North America to fold up like an accordion. You can simulate this action by spreading a tablecloth across the dining room table. Put books on one edge of the table to secure the cloth, then slide the cloth across the table from the other side. The long wrinkles represent the Appalachian Mountains (though they were more like the Alps 350 million years ago).

Rain water eroded these new mountains. Streams transported the sediment westward and dumped them in a delta (or beach) that stretched across Eastern Ohio. These sediments later dried and compressed to form the shale and sandstone of the Appalachian Plateau, also known as the Allegheny Escarpment.

The shales beneath the Blackhand sandstone are made from the finer, lighter sediments, such as mud and silt, which the mountain streams carried farthest offshore. The coarser, pebbly, and heavier sediments landed on the beach and became the Blackhand sandstone. (See Blackhand Gorge State Nature Preserve)

Over tens of millions of years, weathering and erosion sculpted the sandstone into the knobs, gorges, bony ridges, and shelter caves characteristic of eastern and southeastern Ohio.

Now comes the Ice Age (Pleistocene Epoch), which began about two million years ago. At least three and maybe four different glaciers swept across Ohio. The last and most recent one, the Wisconsinan, covered about two-thirds of the state from 18,000–12,000 years ago.

The Wisconsinan glacier stopped near Lancaster. Scientists think the ice mass surrounded Chestnut Ridge to its neck, but did not swallow it. The ridge's height—1,110 feet—may have been too much for the thin vanguard of the glacier. In similar fashion, the glacier may have wrapped around the bases of the knobs at Shallenberger State Nature Preserve, just south of Lancaster. From a satellite these knobs would have looked like stepping stones in a stream.

The glacier heaped soil, gravel and pebbles—collectively called glacial till—on the west slope of the ridge. The east slope is steeper because less till was left behind when ice released Chestnut Ridge from its grip. A pair of moraines—long rolls of till—running across Bloom Township mark the advance of the glacier.

WILDLIFE

Chestnut Ridge owes its name to the American chestnut trees that attracted nut gatherers at harvest time from as far away as Columbus. The trees are gone now, victims of the blight in the 1930s. Occasionally,

though, a sprout emerges from the roots of a stump, a slim reminder of its giant ancestors.

The chestnuts probably attracted thousands of passenger pigeons to the ridge. Like the tree, this bird, is gone. Passenger pigeon flocks once were dense enough to blacken the sky. Bears and bobcats also lived here before 1900.

The chestnuts and their oak kin grew best on the steep, acidic, east side of the ridge, while beech and maple dominated where the glacial till covered the sandstone. These boundaries continue today, though there has been mixing. You will find black cherry, hickory and other trees and shrubs typical of the forests in this region. Mature pines, surrounding a home in the center of the park, were planted by previous landowners.

An especially luxuriant forest (look for the grove of sugar maples) lies to the east of the nature trail, just before it comes into a big meadow. Willows, sycamores and some poplars and walnuts thrive along two intermittent rills that feed Little Walnut Creek. Multiflora rose and berry patches have invaded the open spaces in the forest.

White-tailed deer, once scarce in the area, browse the ridge, and wild turkey recently were spotted here for the first time in this century. A pair of red salamanders, typical in the Appalachians but uncommon in Central Ohio, were sighted in 1989. The flowers and birds typical of the area's forests and meadows can be counted. The park district manages the growth of the open areas to protect the species who thrive in this varied habitat.

HISTORY

Did the ancient people come here for chestnuts, too? Early woodlands Indians (Adena culture, 1500–100 B.C.) did settle here and built five mounds, but they look like all the other little forested knolls and without a map or guide you won't find them. One of them, Old Maid's Orchard Mound, is conical, with a diameter of 60 feet. It is listed on the National Registry of Historic Places.

Early pioneers built cabins and barns near the springs that trickle from the base of the ridge. Sandstone quarried from the ridge became the foundations of local structures and perhaps canals in the 19th century, but nature has covered these scars too with hardwoods.

After decades of dormancy, the ridge was bought in 1918 by an Army veteran who cleared it, and planted apple trees. People drove many miles to buy fruit at the family's farm market (known as the Smith Sisters' Market). Homes rose along the dirt roads that bordered the ridge.

A developer had a different view from the ridge—a subdivision of country estates. Little by little neighbors who worried about the encroaching city began selling tracts to the metropark district. By 1970 the park district had bought all the land.

In the late 1970s, nature writer David Rains Wallace lived in a cabin at the base of Chestnut Ridge and wrote *Idle Weeds*. He saw more skyscrapers on the horizon and wrote, "Even if the ridge becomes the only green spot in a hundred square miles of skyscrapers its fundamental value will not be in rarity, in diversion from the human world, but in commonness, in union with the biosphere on which the human world depends."

Clear Creek Metropark

Clear Creek has become the crown jewel among the Columbus metroparks, and the largest state-designated nature preserve. The park district wants to keep the valley the way it found it—semi-wild, crowded with critters, a place reserved for nature, and a simple and relaxing spot for humans.

LOCATION
Hocking County, Good Hope Township; Fairfield County, Madison Township.

SIZE & DESIGNATION
4,400 acres. It became a preserve in 1998.

Nature
Notable

Columnist's Appreciation of the Outdoors Was Clear

Ed Thomas was Central Ohio's nature-writing laureate for six decades. In more than 3,000 weekly columns for the Columbus Dispatch, he either brought strange, uncelebrated critters to our attention—freshwater jellyfish, massasauga rattlers, wall-rue spleenwort, black-horned tree crickets and the Allegheny woodrat come to mind—or served as guide on field trips to Cedar Bog, Goll Woods, Fort Hill, Mentor Marsh, Kelley's Island, or Old Man's Cave. He could identify 60 species of grasshoppers and crickets, and scores of birds just by listening to their songs. Of all the scenic spots he visited, Thomas unashamedly proclaimed his stomping ground, Clear Creek Gorge in Hocking County, "the garden spot of the State of Ohio."

The Woodsfield native started his professional life as a Columbus lawyer, but he yearned for the outdoors. The nature columns began in March 1922, then he somehow managed a doctorate of science degree from Capital University. At age 40, Thomas abandoned law to become the curator of the Ohio Archeological and Historical Society, a position he held from 1931 until 1962.

He was a founding member of the Wheaton Club, a nature club of Ohio State scientists and prominent alumni that identified nature spots now protected as Columbus metroparks. He presided over the Columbus Audubon Society and Ohio Academy of Science. Thomas also served as a commissioner for Columbus metroparks for twenty years. The E.S. Thomas State Nature Preserve in Sharon Woods Metropark commemorates his work. Thomas' beloved farm in Neotoma Valley is now part of Clear Creek Metropark.

ACCESS

From US 33, at a filling station half mile south of the Hocking-Fairfield county line, turn west on CR 116 (Clear Creek Road). Follow the road to the Creekside Meadows Picnic Area, on the left at the junction with Starner Road (TR 117); to Fern Picnic Area, and to the Hamilton Day Use Area.

Trails: The metropark's "primitive" eight-mile trail system explores ravines and ridges on the north side of Clear Creek Road. Trailhead for the Ridgetop Trail is the Creekside Meadows Picnic Area, while the Fern Picnic Area serves as the terminus for the Fern Trail. Hemlock Trail starts between the parking lots and intersects the Ridgetop and Fern Trails. The easy mile-long Creekside Meadows Trail joins the picnic areas, and as its name suggests goes through meadows along Clear Creek. Rest rooms are available at the picnic/parking areas.

To its credit, Columbus metroparks plans to leave these trails steep, natural, somewhat narrow—what it calls primitive. These trails aren't the typical golf cart paths found in other parks for city slickers, baby strollers, and joggers. Additional trails at the Hambleton Day Use Area were in the works or recently completed at presstime.

Fishing: Seven small parking areas are spaced along Clear Creek Road for anglers who can cast for bass, catfish, and trout, the latter being introduced by the Ohio Division of Wildlife. (Trout anglers must use a barbless hook, and catch only one fish per day.)

Special Places & Events: Plans are to designate some natural areas with limited access to humans. These are the Beck Nature Preserve, a state-designated natural area bounded by Clear Creek and Opossum Hollow roads and US 33; Benua Nature Preserve, the former estate of William E. Benua; and Neotoma Valley, the fabled homeland of Edward Sinclair Thomas, the park district's first director. Clear Creek contains a ravine called Rhododendron Hollow, but this place should not be mistaken for nearby Rhododendron Cove State Nature Preserve (permit required).

GEOLOGY

Clear Creek has been a two-way stream, according to a venerable valley resident named Ed Thomas. Besides being the curator of natural history at the Ohio Archaelogical and Historical Society (1931-1962) and first director of the Columbus Metroparks, Thomas wrote a weekly column for the Columbus Dispatch for 40 years. Here's how he described the valley's origins in an article dated May 5, 1968.

"It is easy for the practiced eye to recognize Clear Creek and its gorge as a 'young' or recently formed valley, geologically speaking. The 'col' or neck of the gorge is extremely narrow, with precipitous hills rising steeply on either side of the stream. This is the gorge proper. The valley widens gradually both to the east and the west, evidence of the fact that two streams once found their source at the col, heading in opposite directions."

Clear Creek straddles glaciated and unglaciated Ohio. Its western edge claims deposits left behind by the Illinoian glacier, and its eastern side barely escaped the grip of the Wisconsinan glacier, which touched the knob at Wahkeena Nature Preserve just three miles north.

The gorge walls that Thomas mentioned are Blackhand sandstone, dating back 325 million years to the Mississippian Period. Although better exposures of this bulky rock stand out in nearby Hocking Hills State Park and Rockbridge State Nature Preserve, you cannot miss two striking examples of it along Clear Creek Road.

Leaning Lena serves as the valley's eastern portal. Lena is barn-sized chunk of Blackhand sandstone that liberated itself from the canyon wall. The slump rock tilts toward its descendant formation, and the road barely squeezes between Lena and the cliff. Another pile of boulders arranged in a maze called Penitentiary Rocks makes scientists suspect that an earthquake (aided by water erosion) is chiefly responsible for the abundance of "slumps" in the park.

A sandstone outcrop called Written Rock stands as the park's west portal, about five miles from US 33. Its name stems from the human names, some dating back 150 years, that appear on it. Unfortunately, recent scribblers have used spray paint.

WILDLIFE

Thomas called his place "Neotoma" after an endangered woodland creature he discovered there in the summer of 1923. The resident was Neotoma floridana, a.k.a the Allegheny or Eastern woodrat, or packrat. While observing and photographing a roosting black vulture, an imperiled bird still colonizing Clear Creek Valley, Thomas and his party noticed a pair of woodrats beneath a rock ledge. The next weekend, Thomas live-trapped one; two others evaded capture. It was only the second sighting of this Neotoma in Ohio, and the first in the 20th century.

The curious naturalist inventoried the items in Neotoma's cave dwelling: mushrooms (more kinds than Thomas had seen in the valley), leaves and twigs from trees, vines, ferns, and berry bushes, tufts of rabbit fur, a black vulture feather, a mink skull, and a handful of empty shotgun shells. Park district administrator and naturalist Jim Stahl was the last human to see the reclusive rat, his sighting being in 1984.

Neotoma may be the most obscure endangered critter in the valley, but it's not the only one. Here, too, flourish rarities such as great rhododendron (state-threatened), mountain laurel, and creeping phlox. The northernmost colony of a fern called little gray polypody, or resurrection fern, thrives on Leaning Lena, which explains why climbing the landmark is forbidden. All totaled, flocks of scientists have recorded 850 vascular plants, and 40 kinds of ferns (maidenhair and ostrich being noteworthy) in this slim valley.

Wildflower lovers can look for foam flower, miterwort, pink ladies' slipper, showy orchis, firepink, jack-in-the-pulpit, Indian pipe, pine sap, bee balm, yellow passionflower, swamp milkweed, oxeye, Joe-pye-weed, and turtlehead, the host for a butterfly called Baltimore checkerspot. Some 4,300 acres of the park is forested, most of it the mixed Appalachian deciduous forest characteristic of Southeastern Ohio. These hardwood ridges are streaked by hemlock-lined ravines that offer cool shade in summer, and green refreshment in winter. Dogwood and redbuds trim creekside meadows; their vernal colors contrasting brilliantly against hemlocks. See if you can find wild plum, Kentucky coffeetree, black birch, witch hazel, and sour gum in the thatch.

Thomas made Clear Creek Valley a birder's mecca as early as the 1920s. Audubon members have held annual warbler walks for decades, and Tom Thomsom, author of *Birding in Ohio* and one of Ohio's leading birders, has taken a yearly breeding census here for a quarter century. The various habitats support 110 nesting species, though the number fluctuates yearly. These include 19 warblers, such as the cerulean, magnolia, Canada, hooded, worm-eating, Kentucky, northern parula, black-and-white, American redstart, and yellow. Bring binoculars for closeup views of the scarlet tanager, indigo bunting, hermit thrush, rufous-sided towhee, cedar waxwing, yellow-breasted chat, and Louisiana waterthrush. At dusk listen for whippoorwills, and great horned and screech owls. The reverberating gobbles of tom turkeys echo down the valley in April. Overhead, hawks red-shouldered, broad-winged, and red-tailed circle with turkey vultures. A small colony of black vultures nests here at its northernmost range in the state. Common ravens (uncommon in the Ohio Valley) nested here in the late 1980s. Occasional visitors—peregrine falcon, eagles, osprey, evening grosbeak, and Bewick's wren—rarely miss being seen by astute observers.

The ledges and ravines above Clear Creek once harbored endangered timber rattlesnakes, the last one seen in 1971. Amphibians and reptiles are still diverse. Thirty to 40 species are found in yearly surveys, including salamanders slimy, red-backed, and dusky and snakes called hognose, garter, and black racer.

A growing list of butterflies, now at 45 species, is led by the monarch, wood satyr, and mourning cloak. Park naturalists have counted 400 varieties of moths—polyphemous and buck moths being notables—but they figure the list will reach 2,000. Rare dragonflies called tiger spiketail and Eastern spangled skimmer reside here.

Hikers may encounter deer, raccoons, skunks, beavers, coyote, and possibly the harmless and endangered bobcat. In spite of its clarity and health, Clear Creek lacks mussels and large populations of invertebrates. Naturalists suspect that earlier pollution wiped out these species, which have been unable to recolonize due to their absence in the Hocking River, the parent stream.

HISTORY

Clear Creek's protection preceded its formal preservation. Ed Thomas' neighbors kept their for-ested tracts as pristine as possible. In 1973, the family of Allen F. Beck gave the park district 2,234 acres of land the wealthy Columbus businessman bought for preservation in the 1920s. The donation became the largest state-designated nature preserve and the nucleus of the metropark. A few years later the park district bought Neotoma Valley from Thomas, then an active octogenarian.

More than 660 acres was acquired in the 1990s from the descendants of William Ellsbury and Emily Platt Benua. This gift included an elegant French-styled stone chalet, a 4,700-square foot dwelling featuring a sandstone floor. It is referred to as the Benua Castle. The park district will rent the home, built in the early 1960s, until it gets a new purpose—nature center, corporate retreat, etc. Mrs. Benua was the sister of Ohio-born nature writer, lecturer, and film narrator Rutherford Platt.

Later in the decade the park district purchased the Barneby Environmental Studies Center from Ohio State University, and other properties. The site includes Lake Ramona. Money for that purchase partially came from the sale of land given to the park district by Wallace Hambleton, the namesake of the day-use area.

Visitors will find old cabins on the property, the most obvious one being the Mathias Homestead, a log home (minus its mortar) alongside Clear Creek Road before Leaning Lena. The cabin (mistaken for Thomas' place) marks the entrance to the park. Ed Thomas' beloved Neotoma Valley, up the first northside driveway after turning off US 33, is considered an ecologically-sensitive area, a euphemism for a shrine.

Clear Creek officially became a metropark in July 1996, and Ohio's largest state nature preserve in early 1998.

JOURNAL

Summer: I reach Clear Creek Road after hiking the Ridgetop and Fern Trail. A clipboard carrying park ranger approaches me. I wondered if I had somehow trespassed, parked in the wrong place, broken a rule, spat where I shouldn't have. None of the above. He asked me for an opinion of the trails. "Don't change a thing," I said. His smile indicated I gave him the correct answer. We agreed that Clear Creek was a special place that should retain its ruggedness, wildness, and aloofness. Keep this park simple and chaotic, I told him, and make sure park developments go on already "disturbed" land and never intrude on critters. I made sure he wrote that remark on his clipboard. Two year later, however, the trail has been widened and improved, enought for a mountain biker to illegally use it for free.

Highbanks Metropark

(Highbanks State Nature Preserve)

It has taken the Olentangy River eons to

slice through the bedrock shale that formed the "high banks" in this preserve. From these strategic bluffs Adena Indian warriors guarded a slumbering village, smoked "kinnikinnick," stargazed, and watched for the silhouettes of canoes moving like dark shadows against the silver moonlight that glistened on the Olentangy below. Today, their spirit soars on the wings of the red-tailed hawks. The echo of their chants and prayers still swirls in the hollows and cliffs.

LOCATION

Northern Franklin County, Sharon Township, and Delaware County, Orange Township.

SIZE & DESIGNATION

The preserve comprises 206.5 acres; the metropark is 1,050 acres. The Olentangy River, a state designated scenic river, flows on the western border of the sanctuary.

ACCESS

The nature preserve comprises the southwest section of Highbanks Metropark. Exit I-270 at US 23 (north of Columbus), and travels north about four miles. The entrance will be on the left. Park in the Oak Coves Picnic Area.

Trails: The wooded preserve can be reached by a trail that begins in Highbanks Metropark. Pick up a map at the new nature center, then park in the westernmost lot in the Oak Grove Picnic Area. (It's okay to see the exhibits in the nature center first.) A 2.5-mile foot trail begins here. Head southerly (or left as you face the woods) and bear right at each fork, following the Overlook Trail. Just after the first fork, the wooded path passes through a meadow favored by bird-watchers. Most trail intersections display a "You Are Here" map. At the southernmost spot on the trail (near the Indian earthworks) an arrow points to a path to the observation deck.

Please don't wander off the viewing deck. Exploring the bluffs tramples the fragile plants growing there, and climbing is prohibited. Loose turf on the edge of the 100-foot tall cliffs makes them dangerous.

Special Places & Events: The observation deck offers a decent view of the valley, but photographers may be disappointed if they are expecting a panorama free of obstructions and human intrusions. Unfortunately, development on the west bank of the Olentangy River is spoiling the view.

Nature programs and special events are held in the park all the time. One is the "Hike to the Giants," a journey to a secret place where a pair of sycamore trees believed to be more than 500 years old hide from humans. Each of the giants is 23–24 feet in circumference!

Check out the exhibits in the nature center, and trails on the northside of the park. One goes to an Adena Indian mound. You will find restrooms, picnic areas, playgrounds, open areas for ball playing and kite flying, reservable barn for group activities, pioneer cemetery, and canoe access in the park.

GEOLOGY

The "high banks" are actually cliffs of Devonian era shale formed about 350 million years ago when a shallow, murky ocean covered most of Ohio. Later, the land swelled and this former mud-clay sea floor hardened into bedrock. The shale that you see in the bluffs, known as Ohio black shale (so-called because of its charcoal gray color) sits above lighter-colored Olentangy shale, and a bed of limestone. Rotting plants that washed and settled into the Devonian sea account for the dark hue of Ohio shale.

The glaciers that scrubbed the land many millennia ago piled till (a mixture of gravel, sand, silt, and rocks) on top of the shale. The Powell end moraine, a roll of till that stretches east-west into Indiana, goes through the park. The moraine is hard to detect in the park, but travelers driving north from Columbus on US 23 might notice the gentle undulation of this feature before reaching the park.

Water running off the last ice mass, the Wisconsinan glacier some 15,000 years ago, created the Olentangy River, which has washed away the till and cut through the Ohio shale.

At Highbanks, the river now scours Olentangy shale and in places limestone (Columbus limestone), the compressed remains of an even older sea floor. In midsummer, when the water level is low, the limestone layer is exposed.

Southwesterly moving tributaries, fed by rain and snow, have roughed up the terrain by gouging ravines into the bluffs. These hollows run perpendicular to the river, and give a "whaleback" (or hogback) look to the relief.

Though it is hard see them from the overlook, the "high bank" is chock-full of round rocks, some the size of wrecking balls, oddly stuck among the horizontal layers of shale. These are concretions. From the river it looks like some giant creature long ago threw mud balls into the cliff, or that some army from the Middle Ages catapulted them randomly into a mud dome.

Scientists believe concretions began as pieces of organic matter (a tree branch perhaps) that secreted minerals, such as iron, and attracted sediment. The concretions grew in concentric layers, like pearls or onions. You might see smashed ones at the bottom of deep ravines, or in the river during low water.

WILDLIFE

It has been said life at the top is tough. That is true

at the top of the "high banks" where it is thin-soiled and dry due to constant pounding by westerly winds and long sun exposure. Nevertheless, this environment is good enough for lichens and mosses, and shrubs such as viburnum and blackhaw. This fragile spot harbors some plants uncommon in Central Ohio, such as star toadflax, butterfly weed, smooth aster, and nodding wild onion.

Not far from the edge a forest takes over with hickories, oaks, maples, and beeches stretching skyward. Walnuts, Ohio buckeyes, and hackberries like the moist soils near the ravine mouths. Cottonwoods and sycamores prefer the river's edge. Dogwoods, redbuds, pawpaws, and hornbeams spread out in the understory soaking up whatever sunlight penetrates the canopy.

Winter's dreariness ends when the wildflowers blossom. Overbrowsing by deer has trimmed the wildflower patches, but you will still find large-flowered trillium, ragworts, phlox, violets, Dutchman's breeches, and bloodroot.

A reclusive reptile called the Jefferson salamander resides at the Indian earthworks. The creature is named after President Thomas Jefferson, an amateur naturalist. When the early spring rains fall these tiny lizards emerge from their tunnels and begin a 2–3 week breeding spree. Then they return to their burrows and pray for rain next spring.

The surrounding metropark offers wooded and open natural areas worth exploring. These former farm fields and orchards, which are in various stages of succession, yield milkweed (the host plant of monarch butterflies), grasses, goldenrod, briar patches, and pioneer trees like sumac, hawthorn, crabapple and ash. If left undisturbed, these fields will eventually give way to the woodland.

Birds are abundant. As many as 150 species have been tallied. Bald eagles and osprey have loitered here, though none have been seen recently. More promising for birders are red-tailed hawks or owls (barred, great horned, and screech) who perch in trees at the edge of meadows hunting prey. Sometimes Cooper's, broad-winged, and kestrel hawks are observed. At night, swarms of swallows dart in the fields. Look for bluebirds at one of the 71 nesting boxes standing in the meadows.

A specially built garden attracts butterflies and hummingbirds when deer don't devour the flowers. Quiet walkers may see these deer (abundant), and perhaps a red fox.

The Olentangy sponsors aquatic creatures such as the eastern softshell turtle, water and queen snakes, crayfish (a favorite prey of queen snakes), many insect larvae, and small fish called darters, notably the blue-breasted darter, considered a rarity. The park also supports black, ring-necked, and milk snakes.

HISTORY

Humans have been fond of the "high banks" and the Olentangy for hundreds of years.

Archeologists continue to wonder about a horse-shoe-shaped, 1,500-foot earthen mound and moat built by the so-called "late woodlands" Indians of the Cole Culture about 1,000 years ago. It is hard to detect it near the overlook because erosion has worn it down and vegetation conceals it.

Most believe it was a U-shaped fortification protecting a settlement. The open end of the horse-shoe ends at the "high bank," and deep ravines border the sides. The moat bolstered the defensive position at the bottom of the "U." The site also may have served as a ceremonial plaza. Two burial mounds of the Adena culture, located elsewhere in the park, indicate that the area also was sacred to our forebears. The earthworks are listed on the National Registry of Historic Landmarks.

Inniswood Metro Gardens

Although the main attractions of this metropark are its cultivated gardens, a half-mile boardwalk trail loops through two distinct forests and offers a glimpse into nature's wilder side. Gardeners, landscapers, and nature lovers should make Inniswood Gardens a destination.

LOCATION
Northeast Franklin County, City of Westerville.

SIZE
92.3 acres.

ACCESS
Leave I-270 at the SR3 North Westerville exit; travel north a half mile on SR 3 (State Street), then turn right (east) on to Schrock Road. Follow Schrock Road to its end (about 1.4 miles), then turn right (south) on Hempstead Road. The entrance is on the left in .3 mile.

Trails: The half-mile nature trail begins at the edge of the woods to your right as you walk from the parking lot to the gardens and Innis House. The boardwalk trail is flat and accessible to visitors in wheelchairs, but don't try to jog there unless you enjoy being chased by park administrators. Benches along the trail provide rest and views of the wet woods. The trail concludes at the north lawn. Just follow the sidewalk to the gardens.

Special Places & Events: Visitors can tour the gardens and natural area daily from 7 a.m. until dark. Innis House, a former estate, is open from 8 a.m.–4:30 p.m. Tuesday–Friday, and on weekends for scheduled gardening, nature and art programs. Maps of the grounds can be found at a small reception area by the parking lot or at Innis House.

The grounds feature a herb garden, rock garden, rose garden, and a memorial garden. Beds of irises and peonies are located west of the rock garden (bottom of the hill). The park brochure has a blooming schedule for the many flowers that add color to the park. Obviously, the best time to visit are the warm months.

A multipurpose room in Innis House seats up to 100 people for lectures and meetings. Art exhibits and horticultural programs are also held in this air-conditioned building. Dining facilities are available, too. Tours led by staff naturalists or volunteers begin at Innis House.

Facilities: Rest rooms and drinking water are located at the east end of the parking lot and at Innis House (handicapped accessible). Unlike other metroparks, Inniswood does not have picnicking or recreational facilities. Activities such as jogging, kite flying, ball playing are not allowed—and leave your radio at home.

GEOLOGY

The Wisconsinan ice mass that swept across the state 15,000 years ago left the terrain here relatively flat. Nevertheless, there are subtle and important changes in elevation. For instance, the divide separating the watersheds of Big Walnut and Alum creeks runs through the gardens. The water on the eastside of park ends up in Big Walnut Creek, but water on the westside slowly flows into Alum Creek.

Divide aside, water hardly drains quickly to either stream, so the wooded natural area remains swampy year-round (another reason for the boardwalk). You will notice several intermittent (seasonal) rills in the woods, but the main brook winds through the west side of the park. Innis House lies above the floodplain of this picturesque brook.

WILDLIFE

Notice, as you negotiate the boardwalk, that buxom beech and maples dominate the southside of the natural area, but that oaks, hickory, and their kin rule on the northside. An almost imperceptible change in topography allowed the oak-hickory community to claim the higher ground, leaving the beech-maple group on the lower ground.

You also will see a smattering of wild black cherry, American hornbeam, dogwood, and ash in this wet forest.

People come to Inniswood mostly to see the gardens. Here the planted flowers and herbs are identified by small plaques. In the woods, however, the blossoms emerge without the advantage of brass plates. Look for bloodroot, blue phlox, cut-leaf toothwort, jack-in-the-pulpit, trillium, purple bittercress, rue anemone, violets, Virginia bluebell, wild geranium, wild ginger, and white baneberry. A small cattail pond on your left at the end of the nature trail teems with colorful dragonflies in the spring and summer. Walk to the shore and watch them dip and climb for mosquitoes. Dragonflies, also known as darning needles and stingers, are not at all

harmful to humans. Their elongated bodies are designed for flight, not for piercing skin.

The pond grew out of a mistake during park development. An errantly excavated hole filled with water and was neglected. It developed into a pond that attracted frogs, snakes, and other wildlife. People liked it, so the pool stayed.

These woods are thick with squirrels and chipmunks, perhaps too many for the habitat. I suspect the surrounding residential developments have forced these critters into the park. They appear smaller and much more tame than their brethren in oak forests of southeast Ohio. These animals, and the rabbits, are chased by the foxes who reside in the woods, perhaps in the hollows of fallen beech trees.

Inniswood lures the usual collection of birds in Central Ohio. The challenge for birders will be spotting the owls (barred and great horned), Cooper's hawk, red-tailed hawk, eastern bluebird, and pileated woodpecker, whose shrill song does not match its beauty.

Hungry deer fleeing suburban development raid the gardens. In 1993, they wiped out the day lilies (400 varieties) and all of the hostas.

HISTORY

Inniswood reflects the lifelong interests of Grace and Mary Innis, whose 37-acre garden estate forms the nucleus of this metropark. Grace Innis was an avid horticulturist, Mary an ornithologist.

Grace Innis, the surviving sister, donated the estate to the park district in 1972 and during the next decade worked with officials to develop a master plan for the grounds. She died in 1982.

The remaining 54 acres, the wooded natural area, was purchased with grant money from the Innis sisters, metropark funds, and matching grants from the U.S. Land and Water Conservation Fund of the U.S. Department of the Interior. The herb garden was completed in 1987 with funds from the Columbus Foundation, Lancaster Colony, individual benefactors, and the Inniswood Society, a support and fund-raising group created to improve the grounds and boost interest in gardening and horticulture. The group holds a flower sale in the spring to raise money for the gardens.

The park district will be adding gardens and other facilities to fulfill the master plan of the Innis sisters.

JOURNAL

June 13: Dozens of people in their Sunday best are milling around Innis House. Unknown to me, it is the Inniswood Society's annual meeting and garden party. Inside the Innis House, a horticulturist is talking about Japanese gardens. Outside, a string quartet seated in the shade of an oak tunes up; golf carts arrive laden with punch bowls.

As usual I am dressed for the woods—khaki pants, boots, T-shirt, wrinkled Aussy hat, camera gear vest, and tripod. Add a quart of sweat to my apparel, and my seven-year-old son who dressed himself that day and— you get the picture. Not the day to pick the brain of staffers and volunteers. They are up to their necks in fruit punch, napkins, and pressed clothes.

Indeed, a certain natty decorum reigns at Inniswood. Shoes and shirts must be worn at all times. Keep that in mind, all of you bare-chested, bare-footed, halter-topped, cutoff jeans, radio-blasting and Frisbee throwers, when visiting Inniswood.

Pickering Ponds Metropark

(Pickerington Ponds State Nature Preserve)

The calamitous and chaotic honking of thousands of waterfowl can be downright rapturous when they converge at the glacier-formed ponds. The cacophony climaxes in the spring and again in the fall during the height their cross-country migration. Here you have a front row seat for aerial performances. Observe the tight flying formations and graceful landings of incoming Canada geese. Over there, ducks bob and dive for food.

LOCATION
Southeastern Franklin County, Madison Township, and northwestern Fairfield County, Violet Township.

SIZE
406 acres.

ACCESS
From Columbus take US 33 southeast to Gender Road. Head north (left) on Gender Road for two miles, then east on Wright Road. Bowen Road, which connects with Wright Road, also passes through the preserve.

Special Places & Events: Visitors can observe wildlife from observation areas on Bowen or Wright roads. The Bowen Road area has a shelter, rest room, and drinking water. Feel free to walk along the roadside, but do not climb fences for a better look. Don't enter private property. The refuge is open everyday during daylight hours. Call (614) 895-6222 for a recorded message of weekly waterfowl sightings.

GEOLOGY
Most lakes in Ohio are manmade, but not the Pickerington Ponds. These are ancient kettle lakes created when enormous blocks of ice split from the withdrawing Wisconsinan glacier some 15,000 years ago. The weight of these chunks caused depressions which filled with water when the ice melted. The marsh in the preserve also is a kettle that has filled in with vegetation.

Long ago, there were hundreds of kettle ponds in glaciated Ohio, providing habitat for migratory waterfowl and other animals. The birds still follow this ancient trail of teardrops left behind by the glacier. All but a few kettles have vanished, the victims of draining.

The knolls surrounding the ponds are kames formed when gravel, sand, and clay washing across the top of the glacier fell through a hole in the ice. The kames serve as a watershed for the ponds.

WILDLIFE
Birdwatching is the big (and only) attraction here. Some 212 different species have been sighted, including rarities like the sandhill crane (just stopping for a visit) and the marsh wren, an endangered species. At the height of the spring and fall migrations 2,000–4,000 birds stop for rests and refills.

On any day, birders are apt to observe any of the waterfowl known to Ohio waters, such as teals, mergansers, pintail and ring-necked ducks. Shore-birds (sandpipers, woodcock, killdeer), rails, and gulls visit the ponds. Hawks might be seen perched on trees at the edge of the ponds and marsh.

The marsh sponsors muskrats, those painted turtles and other shelled species, frogs (just listen to the croakers on a summer evening), northern water snakes (hunting frogs), and even fox and deer on its edges. You might see herons and bitterns hanging out here.

HISTORY
In the early 1970s, developers eyed these ponds. That prompted William W. Ellis, Jr., a Columbus attorney, to organize the Pickerington Ponds Committee under the leadership of the Ohio Chapter of The Nature Conservancy. The groups raised money and bought the ponds, marsh, and surrounding higher ground. Major contributors were The Columbus Foundation, the Jeffrey family, the Schumacher Foundation, Wolfe Associates, and the Columbus Audubon Society.

The park district has bankrolled about half the project, relying on tax dollars and matching funds from the Federal Land and Conservation Fund which were obtained by the Ohio Department of Natural Resources. The conservancy has deeded the land to the metroparks as a wildlife refuge. Improvements like observation shelters will be built when money becomes available. In 1998, park supporters successfully defeated a housing developers' scheme to surround the preserve with hundreds of homes.

JOURNAL
October: Every preserve has its challenge. Here, it's goose feces the size of small Tootsie Rolls. It litters Bowen Road and produces a mild, but persistent stench. Hard not to step in it. Hard not to gag. How fast can you roll up the car windows? Hundreds, maybe thousands, of geese collected here

recently. Hard to criticize that. The stink and manure they left behind is what you expect when any large number of animals gathers in any location.

At another collecting point just 15 miles away—downtown Columbus—hundreds of thousands of humans sweat, rev their smelly engines, and add to the waste stream everyday.

The nauseous odor at Pickerington Ponds makes geese feel right at home. It is their place, and we humans will just have to live with their litter.

Sharon Woods Metropark

(Edward S. Thomas State Nature Preserve)

Curious whitetailed deer may tiptoe within an arm's length of you in this sanctuary of meadows and hardwood trees in suburban Columbus. You can hike or bike to the state-dedicated nature preserve in this metropark.

LOCATION

Northern Franklin County, Sharon Township. The Edward S. Thomas State Nature Preserve occupies the western third of Sharon Woods Metropak, which is wedged into the northeast corner of the junction of interstates 71 and 270.

SIZE

762 acres.

ACCESS

From I-71 drive east on I-270 about a mile and take the Cleveland Avenue (Westerville) northbound exit. Go north on Cleveland Avenue about a mile to the park entrance (traffic signal) on the left. Park at the Maple Grove Picnic Area for the bicycle path (also a foot trail); or at the Schrock Lake Picnic Area for the mile-long nature trail.

Trails: The Edward S. Thomas Nature Trail, a flat, wooded, one-mile loop, starts and ends at the Schrock Lake Picnic Area. About half of the trail meanders through the preserve. A wildlife observation deck at the boundary of the preserve and metropark offers a magnificent view of a long meadow, the evening gathering point for the park's deer herd.

The paved bicycle trail, measuring 3.8 miles, wanders deeper into the preserve from the Maple Grove Picnic Area. Folks in wheelchairs or pushing strollers can use this trail, but expect several steep slopes when the trail crosses ravines. Bikers must follow the arrow and stay in their designated lane. All other visitors should travel in the pedestrian lane.

Benches are conveniently spaced along the trail, and there is a water fountain midway. Trail maps are located at the ranger station and information boards.

Facilities: The park offers three picnic areas (with toilets), playgrounds, shelters, sledding hill, ice skating, and open spaces.

Fishing: Youngsters 15 years and under can fish for bass, bluegill, and catfish at 11-acre Schrock Lake.

Special Places & Events: Metropark naturalists and local conservation groups hold meetings, workshops, and programs at the Spring Hollow Outdoor Education Center, reached from the entrance to the park district headquarters on West Main Street, Westerville. Natural history programs are held in various locations within the park throughout the year.

GEOLOGY

The general terrain is flat, though some gentle knolls and ravines exist. Till, a mixture of sand, gravel, rocks, clay, and silt, deposited here by the Wisconsinan glacier some 15,000 years ago, rests upon shale of the Devonian geological period (roughly 375 million years ago). Intermittent streams and forest wetlands can be viewed from trails. Many of the boulders in the preserve are refugees from Canada, some of the debris left behind by the receding glacier. Geologists call these rocks erratics, though none of them show much erratic behavior.

WILDLIFE

Sharon Woods Metropark is famous for its abundance of whitetailed deer. It is easy to spot them roaming through the woods and across the meadows. Come July, stately bucks browse in the fields, their formidable racks still sheathed by velvet. Cautious does, at the edge of the woods, guard curious, spotted fawns. In the autumn bucks who wandered from the park return to mate (a season called rut). Lucky visitors may see the bucks fighting for supremacy by clashing their antlers. Enjoy the scenes. What you don't see, however, is a small ecological disaster.

Study the vegetation carefully. Notice the "browse line" among the trees and shrubs, marking the reach of the deer. The whitetails, in fact, have been overbrowsing, eating everything in their reach. Several hundred varieties of wildflowers once grew in the park, but overbrowsing by an ever-growing herd of deer has drastically reduced the number of species.

The deer, of course, cannot be blamed for the decline in wildflowers. Rapid residential and commercial growth that destroyed their habitat has packed them into Sharon Woods. The metropark is just not big enough to sustain the wildflowers and all those deer. Overbrowsing also is blamed for the drop in the rabbit and groundhog populations, and for diminishing the habitat of ground nesting birds, such as the woodcock. The herd also did not look healthy. Many deer, especially young ones, looked malnourished, undersized, and deformed. After years of study, park administrators decided that the deer herd had to be trimmed to reinvigorate the wildflowers and the deer.

Licking County Metroparks

Licking Park District

4309 Lancaster Road,

Granville, OH 43023,

(740) 587-2535

Infirmary Mound Park,

326-acres, SR 37, three miles

south of Granville. Fishing

lake, wetland, hiking and bridle

trails, senior building, shelter

houses, playground, nature

programs.

Riverview Preserve,

300 acres, along the Licking

River, Newark. Hiking trails

visit woods, wetlands,

wildflowers.

Taft Reserve,

276 acres, Franklin Township

on Flint Ridge Road. Hiking

and horseback riding trails,

hilly terrain, wildflowers

Metropark in Central Ohio

Park officials opted to relocate some deer in 1993 rather than shoot them.

In spite of the overbrowsing, some bloomers persist, notably trillium, violets, daisy, thistle, flea-bane, chicory, and Queen Anne's lace. Swampy hollows showoff skunk cabbage, marsh marigold, and turtlehead. Higher on the ridge live showy orchis and twin leaf.

In the bottom of ravines look for sycamore and black walnut growing alongside Ohio buckeye, pawpaw, and red elm trees. The pawpaw is abundant here because the deer find its sprouts and buds distasteful. Higher ground supports beech, white oak, swamp white oak, red oak, chinkapin oak, burr oak, and white ash. Several huge oaks (bur and chinkapin), believed to be 250 years old, preside along the Thomas Trail in the nature preserve. Other trees include hickories (shagbark and pignut), elm, ash, silver maple, locust (black and honey), dogwood, hawthorn, and crabapple, a remnant of the orchard that once flourished here.

Schrock Lake attracts Canada geese and other waterfowl. At dusk, watch bats and swallows gobble insects. The usual cast of birds resides here. Keep your eyes open for bluebirds, killdeer, woodcocks (dusk), and barred owl.

HISTORY

The preserve is named after Edward S. Thomas, a park board commissioner until the late 1960s and former curator of natural history at the Ohio Archeological and Historical Society. Land purchases in the 1960s culminated in the opening of the park in 1968.

More than a third of the land was set aside for nature preservation. In September 1975 the Ohio Department of Natural Resources, Division of Natural Areas and Preserve, designated the undisturbed parcel a scenic nature preserve.

JOURNAL

July: Some folks snicker at slogans like "Think Planet First," thinking them banal or self-righteous. But the "deer problem" at Sharon Woods (and other Columbus metroparks) illustrates the conflict underlying the slogan. Metropark officials wrestled with the "deer problem" for several years. The debate focused on the fate of the animals. The "real" problem—controlling human development—was not publicly addressed. Land developers still see wildlife as an obstacle; and few elected officials are willing to stop suburban spread to protect critters.

Slate Run Metropark

Easterners settling here mistook the black shale beside the creek for slate, hence the name. Nevertheless, the beauty of the oak-covered ravines and the "slate" run are still unmistakable.

LOCATION
Northeast Pickaway County, Madison Township.

SIZE
1,707.8 acres.

ACCESS
From US 23, running south from Columbus, turn left (east) on Duvall Road (two miles south of the Franklin County line) and go about eight miles to SR 674. Turn right (south) to the main park entrance a half mile away on the right. Continue south on SR 674, then right (west) on Marcy Road to reach the historical farm. Go north on SR 674, and west on Neiswanger Road to the youth camp entrance. From US 33 exit at Canal Winchester and head south on SR 674, about 7.5 miles, to the park.

Trails: The double-loop nature trail starts at the west end of the parking lot and journeys through various habitats—an oak-hickory forest, meadows, successional growth, and creeks. The inner loop, the Five Oaks Trail, measures 1.6 miles, while the outer loop, or Sugar Maple Trail, takes 2.3 miles. Study the map at the trailhead before departing.

The path begins by following the crest of an oak-hickory ridge which overlooks the scenic ravine of Slate Run to the right. Notice the young trees to the left and mature trees to the right, indicating that farming and grazing once took place up to the edge of the ravine and stream. This demarcation between new, successional growth and mature trees is evident throughout the trail.

The trails are wide, smooth and well-marked. A couple of climbs up and down the ravine are a little steep, but brief. Interpretive signs explain some of the natural history of the woods.

Special Places & Events: A visit to the Slate Run complex, combining a tour of the living, 1880s-era historical farm and the natural area, is an ideal family outing. The natural area has picnic areas, toilets, drinking water, and outdoor classroom for nature programs.

Naturalist-led programs on natural history topics are held almost weekly. Program schedules can be found at the information board near the drinking fountain.

The youth camp (reservations only) has a two-mile trail, rest rooms, drinking water, and a picnic shelter. Two picnic areas are available at the main park entrance.

GEOLOGY
The shale wrongly identified as slate is actually Ohio shale which formed at the bottom of shallow, murky ocean about 350 million years ago during the Devonian geologic period. Unfortunately, very little of this formation, whatever you call it, can be seen on the nature trail. The best examples lie upstream from the trailhead. (Winter offers a better view from ridgetops.)

It is easy for amateurs to confuse these rocks. Both are dark gray in color and composed of clay and tiny quartz crystals. Shale is a sedimentary rock created from bits (or sediments) of ancient rock that broke off due to erosion or weathering. Slate, a metamorphic rock, is shale whose mineral composition or texture has been changed, or metamorphosed, because of higher temperature or pressure in the earth.

During the mountain-building period many millions of years ago, extreme pressure transformed particles in shale into mica and drew foliations (waves or cleavages) in the layer, sometimes perpendicular to the direction of the rock bed. Slate slabs sliced from these cleavages have been used for roof tiles.

So, Slate Run has really been washing away shale, sandstone and glacial till all these years. Younger Bedford shale, also dark gray, and Berea sandstone of the Mississippian geologic era (a mere 325 million years old), are above the Ohio shale. Above all of this sedimentary bedrock is till (sand, gravel, clay) left behind by the Wisconsinan glacier 15,000 years ago.

The Slate Run you see is a meandering brook which empties into Little Walnut Creek, then Walnut Creek, and the Scioto River.

WILDLIFE
The woods here are the typical Central Ohio blend of oaks, hickories, maples, and beech, called a mixed mesophytic forest. You will also find slippery elm, whose inner bark was used by Indians and early settlers as a fever and cold remedy. The extinct passenger pigeon once favored the tree's wafer-shaped fruit.

An interpretive sign on the trail pointing to a pignut hickory explains that white settlers give the tree its derisive name because its bitter nuts were fit only for pigs. The nuts of the shagbark hickory are edible.

Several mighty specimens of northern red oak grow on the ridgetop near the trailhead. This hardwood was prized for its sturdiness and was used to prop up coal mines and for railroad ties. Many years ago, 300 acres of northern reds would be cut annually to make the charcoal needed to feed an iron furnace.

A board at the trailhead listed the warblers nesting in the woods. I spotted several species in the valley but they moved too fast to identify. A scarlet tanager greeted me near the entrance. We studied each other for 2–3 minutes until the next group of hikers disturbed him. A solitary killdeer stood in grass near the entrance when I arrived.

Listen for the hooting of the barred owls, and the shrill cries of the flicker and pileated woodpecker.

HISTORY
The land here has been settled and farmed since the early 1800s. The living historical farm recreates farm life in Central Ohio in the 1880s when Samuel Oman owned this acreage.

A former metroparks commissioner, Walter A. Tucker, foresaw the ecological value of the farm and woods.

SOUTHWEST

◆◆◆　　*BUTLER COUNTY*　◆◆◆
For information, contact Metroparks of Butler County, 2200 Hancock Avenue, Hamilton, OH 45011, (513) 867-5835.

◆◆◆　　*CLERMONT COUNTY*　◆◆◆
Clermont County Park District, 2228 U.S. 50, Batavia, OH 45103, (513) 732-9733. Sites - 7; acres - 208.

Crooked Run State Nature Preserve

(Robert J. Paul Memorial Wildlife Sanctuary)

The calm backwaters behind "Paul's Island" provide perfect hatcheries for Ohio River's fish, and feeding areas for long-legged herons, thousands of waterbirds, and migrating bald eagles. Humans come here for the calming water too.

LOCATION
Southeastern Clermont County, Franklin Township.

SIZE
The freshwater estuary is a state nature pre-serve totaling 77.5 acres.

ACCESS
In the Village of Chilo (US 52) follow Green Street to County Park Road. Enter Chilo Lock 34 Park, which is the gateway to the sanctuary. The preserve includes an easy and scenic one mile nature trail highlighted by observation blinds and a tower, views of the Ohio River, and the estuary of Crooked Run.

GEOLOGY
The preserve protects a unique freshwater estuary receiving water from Crooked Run and the Ohio River.

WILDLIFE
Scientists are trying to figure out how a water mysid found in the Gulf of Mexico got into this Ohio River backwater. Maybe *Taphronmysis lousianae* is extending its natural range, or is it an anomaly who stowed away on a tanker and jumped off here. Brook pimpernel, a potentially endangered fish when it was discovered here in 1984, swims in the estuary.

Visitors are more likely to see deer, beaver, great blue heron, green heron, waterfowl, wild turkey, mink, fox, and an occasional bald eagle. Sycamore, silver maple, pawpaw, hickory, black walnut, black locust, boxelder and others represent the tree kingdom.

HISTORY
Mimi Ford Paul, the former publisher and editor of the Bethel Journal, donated this site, known as Paul's Island and Damsite Farm, to the State of Ohio in 1978 with the stipulation that she could live there the rest of her days. In June 1980, the Ohio Department of Natural Resources dedicated the place a state nature preserve, co-named the Robert J. Paul Memorial Wildlife Sanctuary in honor of Mrs. Paul's husband. After many days on Earth, she died in November 1991. The Division of Natural Areas and Preserves leased the location to the Clermont County Park District in 1993.

◆◆◆　　*DARKE COUNTY*　◆◆◆
Darke County Park District, 603 S. Broadway, Greenville, OH 43512-2628, (937) 548-0165. Sites - 5; acres - 230.

◆◆◆　　*GREENE COUNTY*　◆◆◆
For information contact Greene County Park District, 651 Dayton-Xenia Road, Xenia, OH 45385, (937) 376-7445.

Indian Mound Reserve

You pay tribute to early Ohioans in this compact natural setting which features Adena earthworks, a pioneer's log cabin, a picturesque gorge, a waterfall, marsh, and a wooded floodplain.

LOCATION
Northeast Greene County, Cedarville Township.

SIZE
165 acres. The Williamson Mound and Pollock Works are national historic sites.

ACCESS
From Cedarville travel west (or south) toward Xenia on US 42. Just beyond the outskirts of town the first of three parking areas for the reserve appears on the right. Stop here to view Cedar Cliff Falls (manmade) and the small gorge carved by Massie Creek. To visit the Indian sites continue on US 42 to the next parking lot, about a half mile down the road on the right. From Xenia go northeast on US 42 past Wilberforce. The reserve will be on the left just

More,
metroparks

Other Clermont and Butler County Parks

BUTLER COUNTY PARKS

Indian Creek Preserve, 135 acres, Springfield Road, Reilly. Hiking trails, Indian Creek, Adena mound, American Discovery Trail, creeking, fossil finding, picnicking, fishing.

Governor Bebb Preserve, 174 acres, off SR 126, Morgan Township. Log cabin birthplace of Ohio governor William Bebb, covered bridge, camping, picnic area, nature trails, playground, youth group lodge, amphitheater.

Sebald Park, 267 acres, Elk Creek Road, Wayne Township. Hiking trails, picnic area and shelter, fishing, wildlife watching.

Rentschler Forest Preserve, 258 acres, Reigert Road, Fairfield Township. Great Miami River, Miami-Erie Canal, towpath trail, canoe access, fishing, nature and fitness trails, amphitheater, playground, picnic area, bike rentals.

Gilmore Ponds Interpretive Preserve, 195 acres, Symmes and Gilmore roads. Wetlands sanctuary with trails, wildlife, historic home.

Also Indian Creek Pioneer Church and Burial Ground, Bunker Hill Universalist Pioneer Cemetery, Monument Cabin, Crawford House, Chrisholm Historic Farmstead, Excello Locks, Pater Park State Wildlife Area, William F. and Cora Dudley Woods, Miami River Preserve.

CLERMONT COUNTY PARKS

Kelley Nature Preserve, 42 acres, Miami Township near Miamiville. Little Miami River, nature trails, prairie wildflowers, near Little Miami bike trail.

Pattison Park, 40 acres, US 50 near Owensville. Lodge, park district office, trails, fishing, playground, picnic area, ropes course, property of former Ohio governor.

Sycamore Park, 23 acres, SR 32 near Batavia. Picnic area, athletic fields and courts, hiking.

Chilo Lock 34 Park, 14 acres, County Park Road, Chilo. Historic dam, lock, picnic area, camping, playground, near Crooked Run Nature Preserve.

Route 222 Roadside Park, SR 222, Batavia. Canoe launch into East Fork of Little Miami River, picnic area.

Hartman Log Cabin, five acres, US 50 & Aber Road, Jackson Township. 1800s log cabin, gardens, nature trail, pioneer cemetery.

Conservatory in Eden Park, Cincinnati, Ohio

before you reach Cedarville.

Cedar Cliff Falls has several observation points where you can gaze upon a cascade that once powered a flour mill. The bridge arching over Massie Creek presents a clear view of the falls and the dolomite gorge. You can hike to the Adena Indian ruins from here by following Cedar Cliff Trail downstream (west) after crossing the bridge.

Facilities: Scaling the falls and gorge walls is prohibited. Rest rooms and picnic tables are located in the parking area.

The middle section of the reserve contains the ruins of earlier Ohioans, but the first large artifact you see is a restored log cabin in the parking lot.

The trail to the ancient Indian site begins at the right on the far side of a grassy area. Bear left at the first fork, following the Marsh Trail and arrows to the earthworks. After passing a small cattail marsh, stay left and enter the inside of a circular Indian earthwork known as the Pollock Enclosure. A short trail loops within the earthwork.

If you follow the left leg of this loop, you will find another trail going left through a gap in the mound—the Wall View Trail. This path descends into Massie Creek where steping stones help you across a ford. On the north bank, turn left on the Dolomite Trail and go downstream. (The Cedar Cliff Trail merges from the right.)

Notice the dolomite wall, 20-40 feet tall, on the right. Soon you will walk on a ridge (a dike really) separating two sunken areas which used to be reservoirs. After crossing a wooden bridge over a tributary of Massie Creek, turn right at the next intersection. This trail, the Mound Trail, leads to a field and the Williamson Indian Mound.

Sixty-two steps (count them) lead to the top of this memorial. Retrace your steps to the bridge, only turn right before the footbridge and follow the wide Mound Trail back to an access road and the parking lot. Go left when you reach the gravel road.

Figure on walking about two miles. The trails are well-marked and easy to follow, and the terrain is relatively flat with some low riverbanks to climb. The trail becomes thin and rocky around the earthworks. Your feet may get wet crossing Massie Creek at the ford.

Rest rooms, drinking water, and picnic tables are located in the parking lot. The reserve opens at 7 a.m. and closes at dark.

GEOLOGY

During its withdraw from Ohio some 12,000 years ago, the Wisconsinan continental glacier bore rivers of melting ice. One of these currents was Massie Creek, a tributary of the Little Miami River.

Since its birth Massie Creek has removed the bed of loose glacial till (gravel, stones, sand, and clay) that laid in its path. It also has cut a gorge into the hard dolomite rock formed 425 million during the Silurian geological period. Sometimes confused for limestone, dolomite contains high concentrations of calcium-magnesium carbonate derived from the remains of small marine creatures. Unlike limestone, however, dolomite contains few fossils because the remnants dissolved in the rock. The dissolution of the fossils accounts for the porosity of this sedimentary rock.

You can see outcroppings of dolomite (once known as olostone) at the Falls Overlook (though the Cedar Cliff Falls is manmade) and along the Cedar Cliff and Dolomite Ridge trails.

Massie Creek flows through the gorge in a relatively straight channel contained by the dolomite. However, downstream, near the circular earthwork, the dolomite disappears enabling Massie Creek to follow a freer, casual snaking course.

WILDLIFE

The reserve protects two rare trees. One is arbor vitae, or northern white cedar, a potentially threatened species in Ohio. The other is mountain maple. Both trees are much more common in the boreal forests in Canada. They probably followed the vanguard of the Wisconsinan glacier (15,000 years ago) when the climate in Ohio was much cooler. After the glacier retreated, these survivors found a congenial, but tiny, habitat in the reserve.

Common flowers are large-flowered trillium, nodding trillium, wild columbine, Dutchman's breeches, and squirrel corn, similar to the breeches only its flower is heart-shaped. The "corn" name derives from its root tubers which resemble corn kernels.

Warblers arrive en masse in the spring and stay until early autumn. Look for the prothonotary, common yellowthroat, and black-throated green warblers. Great blue and green herons favor the creek, while great horned, barred, and screech owls prefer the forest.

The reserve supports the common furry critters. One special resident is the coyote.

HISTORY

Indian Mound Reserve is rich in human history, as well as natural history. Ancient people called the Palaeo Indians probably migrated to this area as the Wisconsinan glacier withdrew, about 10,000-12,000 years ago. They hunted mastodons, mammoths, giant beavers, muskox, and caribou.

Descendents of the Palaeo people, known as Archaic Indians, lived in this vicinity around 9,000 years ago. They too were hunters, though their quarry, instead, may have been deer, bear, wild turkey, and fish. Plants became a greater part of their diet.

The Williamson Mound is a relict of the Adena Culture, 1,000 B.C. to 800 A.D. Though the mound has never been excavated (and I hope it stays that way), experts believe it is the grave of tribal leaders.

The Pollock earthworks were built by ancient people called the Hopewell Indians, who established villages in Central and Southern Ohio between 100 B.C. to 600 A.D. The Hopewell people raised corn to supplement their diet. They are known for their well-crafted decorative art on tools, weapons, household items, and personal possessions; and for their numerous earthen structures—circles, squares, octagons, and crescents.

The Pollock Works are small compared to other sites, where 100 acres may be enclosed. The purpose of the earthworks remains a mystery. At first they resemble military forts, but most students today think they might be gathering places for religious ceremonies or commercial activities (trading, markets).

The people of the Miami and Shawnee nations later settled in the region, but as the losers in frontier wars they had to give up their holdings to the victorious white settlers.

Mills grew up on the banks of Massie Creek after the Civil War. In 1868, Harbison Mill, a flour mill, was built on the south bank, just west of the waterfall. A 40-foot dam was erected in 1887 for turbine power and to divert water to a mill race. Notice that the dam arches upstream so that the force of water presses the stones together.

The Harbison mill stayed in business until 1917. Later, several rows of stone were removed from the top of the dam so that Massie Creek would cascade over it. The Williamson family donated the land containing the Adena mound to the public in the 1920s.

The Hager Straw Board and Paper Company occupied the site in the 1930s. Pipes, sluiceways, and ditches carried toxic effluent to settling ponds located west of the waterfall. The pools are the sunken areas beside a levee now serving as part of the Dolomite Ridge Trail. Specifically, the pits are located between the Pollock Works and Williamson Mound. Some of the contraptions of this sewage system are evident on the trail.

The park district began acquiring land the for the park in 1968. The parcels are now returning to their normal, natural state, and the Indian earthworks are protected from industrial waste.

The Narrows Reserve

The reserve's name suggests that the Little Miami River must fit through a tight squeeze of rock walls and boulders. It doesn't. The "narrows" refers to the slender shape of the property comprising the park, not the shape of the land. Still, the river flows by placidly, sometimes languidly, in a U-shaped ravine that few could deny is scenic, except the narrow-minded.

Putting aside the "narrows" issue, the preserve's riverside trail offers some of the best views of this national and state scenic river and the riparian woodland that comforts it.

LOCATION
Western Greene County, Beavercreek Township.

SIZE
162 acres.

ACCESS
Take Bellbrook Road (not Lower Bellbrook Road) southwest from downtown Xenia. In a little more than four miles, turn right (northwest) on Indian Ripple Road for about 1.5 miles. Just after crossing the Little Miami River, turn left into the reserve parking lot (for canoe launch and hiking trails). The entrance to the nature interpretation center is the next left. There are numerous trails in the preserve. I recommend heading for the river (the canoe launching area) and turning right (downstream) on the River Trail. This trail parallels the river and has several side paths to the water, good spots for nature viewing, wading, or napping.

Big Wood Trail branches from River Trail at the reserve boundary, and climbs a moderately steep riverbank to the "big woods."

Folks who want to visit the interpretive center should turn left on the Vista Trail, mount the steep bluff, and go left on the Old Road Trail to the center. Follow the Old Road Trail back to the parking lot.

Back at the parking lot you will find picnic tables, and a rest room. Fishing, canoeing, and primitive camping (by permit) are allowed in the reserve. The interpretive center has nature exhibits. The grounds are open daily from dawn to dusk.

GEOLOGY
Like neighboring Clifton Gorge (which does have narrow canyons) the Little Miami River flows through The Narrows. And, like Indian Mound Reserve, the bedrock exposed in places is dolomite, dating back 425 million years to the Silurian geological period.

The Wisconsinan glacier covered the bedrock with a thick layer of till, an unsorted mixture of gravel, sand, silt, and boulders. As the glacier retreated northward, around 12,000-15,000 years ago, its meltwater created the Little Miami River. Since then the Little Miami has worn a path through the till and into the ancient bedrock.

WILDLIFE
The Narrows boasts a collection of wildlife similar to the Indian Mound Reserve, only it lacks the northern white cedar and mountain maple trees.

The Little Miami has a large variety of fish: largemouth and smallmouth bass, bluegill, suckers, shiners, and Johnny and greensided darters being common.

HISTORY
An "open space" master plan developed by the regional planning commission in the 1960s targeted this location for a nature park. After the Little Miami River's national and state scenic river designation, the Ohio Department of Natural Resources acquired "the narrows," and in the mid-1970s leased it to the park district.

Sara Lee Arnovitz Preserve

Methotasa could go no farther, not even another mile to Chalagawtha where other women could help deliver the baby kicking in her womb. Pucksinwah, the father and a leader among the Shawandase, found a comfortable camp beside a spring on the banks of a creek the whites now call Oldtown. His attendance at a council in the village would have to wait a day.

That night, Pucksinwah and his son, Chiksika, watched a star streak across the sky, a portentous celestial event which a Shawandase legend said was a panther looking for its den in the south. It was a powerful sign, perfect "unsoma"—an event involving an animal during a human birth—for the boy born a minute later on March 13, 1768. Pucksinwah named his son, Tecumseh, meaning Panther Across the Sky.

The story of Tecumseh's birth has strong parallels to Christianity's story of the birth of Jesus Christ. After birth, both led charmed and haunted lives, both became "saviors" and died as young martyrs.

The spring where Tecumseh sprang to life is 100 yards away from the Arnovitz preserve, on the grounds of the Division of Wildlife's district office. Some of the large trees along the creek may have been Tecumseh's companions when he splashed in the creek after frogs.

LOCATION

Xenia Township. From Downtown Xenia, go north on US 68. Just north of town, turn right on Kinsey Road. The reserve will be on the left where Oldtown Creek crosses the road.

ACCESS

A half mile trail explores a wet meadow and forested bank above Oldtown Creek, which flows into Massie Creek just before its meeting with the Little Miami River. A boardwalk, bridge and stairway goes for a third of the distance, and a platform provides opportunities for wildlife watching.

GEOLOGY

The wetland beside the creek is partly the work of rainwater that has seeped through the porous glacial moraine beside the creek and spread laterally upon striking bedrock.

WILDLIFE

Consider the preserve a jewelbox for flora and birds. Check out blossoms called spotted jewelweed, boneset, ox-eye, guara, thistle, mountain mint, gray-headed coneflower, dodder, tall lobelia, and cattails. Red-winged blackbirds are common. Red-tailed hawks perch atop snags, and songbirds are lively in spring. Trees include black walnut, black locust, hackberry, and young oaks.

HISTORY

The descendents of Sara Lee Arnovitz and area residents donated the parcel to the park district in 1984.

◆ ◆ ◆   *HAMILTON COUNTY*   ◆ ◆ ◆

Nature lovers near Cincinnati can satisfy their open-air vigor at one of the 16 sites (12,000 acres) owned by the Hamilton County Park District. Since 80 percent of the parkland is reserved for wildlife, Hamilton County does not boast a maze of footpaths. Not that this is bad. Much of the parkland remains trackless and consequently, undisturbed by humans.

Seven favorite sites are reviewed. Hamilton County Park District also owns four state-designated nature preserves, which can only be visited on appointment and therefore not featured here. The same limited visitation policy exists for Richardson Forest Preserve and Kroger Hills, both designated conservation and wildlife areas owned by the park district.

Please note that these metroparks are not free. Visitors must pay a fee, called a motor vehicle permit, upon entering a park. The annual charge is $3 (the best option if you plan to visit often); the daily fee, $1. Buy the permits at any park facility (visitor or nature centers, golf courses, marinas, ranger stations, gift shops, etc.) or from rangers and technicians. You can purchase an annual $3 motor vehicle permit through the mail by writing the Hamilton County Park District, 10245 Winton Road, Cincinnati, Ohio 45231; phone (513) 521-7275. You can hike with your dog provided he's on a leash no longer than six feet. (You're responsible for scoop-ups.) The parks are open everyday from dawn to dusk.

Miami Whitewater Forest

Ohio's own badlands offer a rugged, deep woods experience close to the city.

LOCATION

Northwestern Hamilton County, Crosby and Whitewater townships.

ACCESS

From Exit 3 on I-74, travel north on Dry Fork Road for a mile, then turn right on West Road. At the park's tollgate turn left and follow the driveway (Timberlakes Road) to the parking lot (on the left) for the Badlands and Oakleaf hiking trails. A nature center is located beside the parking lot.

Trails: Nature hikers can choose among three foot-paths, totaling about 3.6 miles. The Oakleaf and Badlands trails depart from the same location. To reach the tallgrass Prairie Trail turn right at the park entrance on West Road, or enter from Harrison Avenue.

Facilities: The park also has horseback riding trails, a boathouse, fishing (boat only), picnic areas, fitness trail, campground, frisbee golf course (the first in Ohio), golf course, and playgrounds.

GEOLOGY

The "badlands" in Miami Whitewater Forest hardly resemble the Badlands in North Dakota. Still, they do fit the common definition of badlands—an odd-shaped terrain with soil unsuitable for farming.

Sinkholes give this spot its "badlands" look. These are the numerous cup-shaped depressions, or sinks, surrounded by hillocks. Sinkholes form when acidic water dissolves the underlying limestone bedrock. A cave-in occurs when the limestone (a rock containing the alkaline mineral calcite) weakens and can no longer support the soil above.

The limestone is 450 million years old (Ordovician geological period) and composed of the sediment that spread across the floor of an ancient ocean. The alkalinity of the rock derives from the remains of the marine animals that fell to the bottom of the sea. The fossils of these ancient creatures, much older than the dinosaurs, appear in the limestone.

About 20,000 years ago the vanguard of the Wisconsinan glacier stopped just north of the park. When the climate warmed huge volumes of water poured from the melting glacier and created streams like Dry Fork Creek and Whitewater River. The two currents, stems of the Great Miami River watershed, have been eroding the land ever since.

Dry Fork Creek meanders through the park before emptying into the Whitewater River. One of the creek's tributaries was dammed in 1971 to create the Miami Whitewater Forest Lake.

WILDLIFE

Exhibits inside the nature center at the trailheads of the Oakleaf and Bandlands trails explain the animals and plants you might see in the park's various habitats.

In the mature forest, for example, look for beech and sugar maple, oaks (white, red, burr), ash, shagbark and pignut hickory, tulip tree, and wild black cherry, among others. Here live birds like the barred owl, pileated woodpecker, scarlet tanager, tufted titmouse, red-eyed vireo, wood pewee, ovenbird; mammals—gray squirrel, short-tailed shrew, white-footed mouse; mourning cloak (butterfly) and luna moth; reptiles and amphibians, such as black rat snake, two-lined salamander, and fence lizard.

Areas of successional growth (usually a young woodlot or thicket meadow en route to becoming a mature forest) include trees like elm, black cherry, box elder, dogwood, yellow buckeye, honey locust, black gum; birds—blue-winged warbler, woodcock, goldfinch, indigo bunting, catbird; mammals—deer, woodchuck, skunk, pine vole; bugs—cicada, bald-faced hornet, walking stick; rough green snake and box turtle.

Plants such as bluegrass, broom sedge, goldenrod, and milkweed prevail in open meadows and grasslands. Here lives the red fox, rabbit, meadow vole, weasel, least shrew; birds—eastern meadowlark, dickcissel, grasshopper sparrow, bluebird; insects—monarch butterfly, bumblebees, praying mantis; reptiles and amphibians—black racer snake and toad.

In wetland habitats (ponds, streams, swamps) observe cattail, willow, water lily, skunk cabbage,

More, *metroparks*

Other Darke and Hamilton County Parks

DARKE COUNTY PARKS

Coppess Nature Sanctuary, 32 acres, Young Road, Jackson Township. Nature trail, woods, bird blind, prairie wildflowers.

Routzong Preserve, 55 acres, Van Buren Township. Trails, boardwalk, great wildflowers, butterfly meadow.

Shawnee Prairie Preserve, Greenville (SR 502). Site of Tenskwatawa's Shawnee village, nature center, trails, wetlands, observation tower.

Tecumseh Point, Greenville, at the confluence of Mud and Greenville creeks. Place where Shawnee chief Tecumseh lit bonfires to protest the Treaty of Greene Ville.

HAMILTON COUNTY PARKS

Embshoff Woods & Nature Preserve, 226 acres, Delhi Township, Paul Road. Nature preserve, fitness trail, Frisbee golf, picnic area, ice skating, amphitheater, athletic fields.

Lake Isabella, 77 acres, Symmes Township, Loveland-Madeira Roads. Lake, Little Miami River, fishing, boathouse, picnic area, playground, lodge, canoe access, wildlife observation area.

Farbach-Werner Nature Preserve, 23 acres, Colerain Township on Poole Road. Ellenwood Nature Barn, nature programs, gift shop, trails.

Triple Creek Park, 136 acres, Colerain Township, Buell Road.

Kroger Hills, 214 acres, near Terrace Park. Old-growth forest, Little Miami River.

Newberry Wildlife Sanctuary, 100 acres, Colerain Township.

Richardson Forest Preserve, 256 acres, Colerain Township. Freshwater wetland with rare plants and animals.

swamp white oak (swamp forest), or critters like raccoon, mink, muskrat; birds—kingfisher, marsh wren, red-winged blackbird, least bittern, great blue heron; bugs—dragonfly, mayfly, mosquito; reptiles and amphibians—leopard frog, bullfrog, snapping turtle, and banded watersnake.

The Badlands Trail wanders through groves of eastern red cedar that can survive on rocky and impoverished soil. The tree provides excellent cover for many birds and usually indicates the presence of limestone in the soil, which is certainly the case in this forest. Cedars prefer open areas, but here encroaching hardwoods may someday "shade" them to death.

The Tallgrass Prairie Trail journeys to a five-acre planted prairie where beauties such as blazing star, rattlesnake master, prairie dock, purple cone-flower, mountain mint, gray coneflower rise along-side grasses called switchgrass, little bluestem, big bluestem and Indian grass.

Elsewhere, feast your eyes on wildflowers such as mayapple, rockcress, Joe-pye weed, jack-in-the-pulpit, whitetop, wild quinine, field pussytoes, Venus' looking-glass, stickseed, and monkey flower, among others.

Miami Whitewater Forest is noted for its fungi, both the nonpoisonous and the poisonous kinds. Eating wild mushrooms is risky, and picking them is prohibited. Here are some of the ones you could see on the Oakleaf Trail: earthstars, scarlet cup, stinkhorns, mycena, birds nest, emetic russula, and morels.

The park boasts 33 species of reptiles and sala-manders, the greatest variety among the county's metroparks. One member of this community is the rare and endangered cave salamander, a colorful creature that lives near the entrance of limestone caves only in Hamilton and Adams counties.

Birdwatchers spotted 77 sandhill cranes (visiting migrants), and 32 dark-eyed (or northern) juncos in the park during an annual winter bird count in 1993. Both birds are endangered species in Ohio.

History

Miami Whitewater Forest encircles an old Shaker village, founded at New Haven in 1824. It was one of three Shaker villages in southwestern Ohio. The sect formed in Manchester, England in 1747 after splitting from the English Quaker church. They called themselves the United Society of Believers in Christ's Second Appearing. Outsiders knew them as Shakers because of their "shakings" (gyrations and spins) during worship services.

Many Shakers moved to New York and New England after 1774 to escape religious persecution in England. Later, some moved to Ohio and established Union Village near Lebanon and Watervliet Village near Kettering, both in 1806. Next came North Union Village near Cleveland (1822) and Whitewater Village (1824), near New Haven, an offshoot of Union Village.

The Shakers lived a celibate, communal, and agriculture life. The Whitewater Village grew from 18 members on 40 acres in 1824 to 200 members on 1,700 acres in Hamilton and Butler counties in 1857. The colonies began to decline after 1870 and by 1916 Whitewater Village had ended.

The park district has acquired several Shaker buildings for restoration and public visitation. One of them is the only brick meeting house (1827) in the country. Shaker meeting houses elsewhere were made of wood. Other local Shaker buildings are privately owned.

The park opened in 1949 following the pur-chase of 709 acres for $141.18 per acre. It has grown to 3,906 acres, making it the largest in the district. In 1978, Ohio's first frisbee golf course was con-structed here.

Journal

The heads of four deer, all does, raised in unison to face me on an oak-covered ridge. They took turns watching me while they browsed for acorns, which rained from the trees. Through the binoculars I could see that their breath, like mine, steamed in the frosty autumn morning.

Suddenly, the most skittish in the bunch sprang to another ridge, adding 70 yards to her distance from me. The others, following their leader, bounded away in a wedge formation. They disap-peared the way fog melts into clouds. Saplings, twigs, bark, leaves, and a ridge hid them except for an occasional flick of a whitetail. Soft footfalls revealed their presence. Later, I would surprise them in the "badlands," a woods of mounds, sinkholes, and gullies where these clever brows-ers can frustrate any hunter.

Mitchell Memorial Forest

A quotation from William Shakespeare is posted at the trailhead. "This, our life away from public haunt, finds tongues in the trees, books in the running brooks, sermons in stones, and good in everything."

The din of urban progress vanishes in this hill preserve. The pervading susurrus is sung by a chorus of rustling leaves, scurrying creatures, croaking old trees, rapturous birdsong, and the drumming of a woodpecker. Alert deer, fleeing at my footfall, seem to be the only animals frightened by my presence. The rest take

no notice of me.

LOCATION
   Western Hamilton County, Miami Township.

SIZE
   1,340 acres.

ACCESS
   Leave I-74 at Exit 7 and head north on SR 128 into the Village of Miamitown. At the traffic light, turn right (eastbound) on Harrison Road. About 1.5 miles, turn right (south) on Wesselman Road, then right on Buffalo Ridge Road (CR 177), and left on Zion Road (CR 186). The entrance is a few hundred feet ahead on the right. Park at the lot for the Wood Duck Trail on your left.

   Facilities: Most of Mitchell Memorial Forest is a heavily wooded nature preserve and off limits to the public. Don't come expecting to play golf, Frisbee golf, softball, or to pursue other recreational activities. However, you will find picnic areas, a playground, rest rooms and drinking water, and a fishing pond.

GEOLOGY
   As Shakespeare foresaw, there is a book in this running brook, and sermons in its stones: fossil-rich limestone slabs lay scattered in the creek bed. From the fragments we assemble a picture of life on earth during the Ordovician Period, some 450 million years ago, but we are far from knowing the whole story.

   The fossils embedded in the rock are the remains of extinct creatures who flourished near the bottom of an ancient tropical ocean. When they died, their bodies settled to the sea floor and mixed with other sediments. Most dissolved, but many became encased, entombed in the soup. Later, the sea floor solidified into limestone and was lifted to the surface.

   Much later, the rock was buried beneath the rubble and debris left behind by the continental glaciers that swept across Ohio during the Ice Age (within the last million years). Streams born from the glaciers have cut through the debris to reveal the template of the Ordovician Period.

   I lifted one fragment from the water and saw a congealed colony of fossilized snails (gastropods) piled atop one another as if they had been the victims of a mass execution. A larger plate beside it revealed a community of brachiopods, their fan-shaped, symmetrical shells widely and evenly spaced like cemetery gravestones. Lying side-by-side, the pieces did not seem to come from the same jigsaw puzzle. This discovery provokes a sermon, a possible rule of geological exploration; that overturning every stone can still leave mysteries unsolved.

WILDLIFE
   Though heavily wooded, much of Mitchell Memorial Forest is a young second growth forest, meaning that it was previous logged (perhaps several times), cleared for cultivation, grazed, or all three.

Now this old farmland is being allowed to grow back.
   Notice the numerous small sugar maples, the wild grape vines and berry patches, multiflora rose, redbud and dogwood trees, and wildflowers such as white snakeroot, bedstraw, and hog peanut (weeds to some people). These are some of the "indicators" of a young woods.

   You will see a number of large sugar maples, sycamores, some oaks and hickories on higher, drier ground, pines (planted), and beeches, too. Box elder thrives in moist spots. Eastern red cedar, which prefers open areas and limestone soils, reminds us of the land's agricultural and Ordovician past.

   Birders can test their skill here searching for the wood duck (namesake of the trail), green heron, brown thrasher, wood thrush, Acadian flycatcher, rufous-sided towhee, Cooper's hawk, and warblers (blue-winged, Kentucky, pine, myrtle), brown creeper, red-breasted nuthatch, golden-crowned kinglet, and red-eyed vireo.

   Several rare and protected birds have been spotted in the park, including the dark-eyed junco, yellow-bellied sapsucker, barn owl, and sandhill crane (11 sighted in December 1993)—all endangered species in Ohio. Other beauties seen here are the sharp-shinned and red-shouldered hawks, and long-eared owl, all designated "special interest," or potentially threatened.

HISTORY
   Mitchell Memorial Forest became the 12th local metropark in 1977, thanks to a 617-acre gift by the late William Morris Mitchell. The donation honors his parents, William Henry and Lucille Morris Mitchell. Acquisitions have brought the total to 1,340 acres. Roughly 80 percent of the land will be retained in its natural state.

Sharon Woods Park

The fossils of extinct animals who lived in

an ocean 450 million years ago rise like

ghosts from the rocks in this spooky gorge.

Every so often the current of Sharon

Creek washes these "signatures in rock" off

the steep banks.

The creek, however, is no longer unruly.
The current, now just a trickle, lacks the
power, and perhaps the will, to remove
the rubble that hides other ghosts on the
stream bank. Few striking fossils turn up

anymore. Some say it is best to keep the ancient creatures locked in their tombs. Though hidden from eyes, their haunting presence can be felt by sensitive wanderers who stop for a moment at the waterfall overlook.

LOCATION

Northeastern Hamilton County, Sycamore Township.

SIZE

755 acres.

ACCESS

From I-275 drive south .8 mile on US 42 (Lebanon Road), then turn left at the entrance. The driveway crosses Sharon Creek, bends left past the visitor/nature center and historical village, crosses the creek again and curves to the right. Ignore the left turn to Sharon Harbor. Just after you travel over the bridge that spans the gorge, turn into the parking lot on the right. The lake appears across the street.

Trails: First, pick up a free park brochure and a guide for the gorge trail at the nature center. The park also features a hiking trail around a lake, a transplanted early 19th century small town called Sharon Woods Village, a boathouse and snack bar at Sharon Harbor, a fitness trail, ball fields, and numerous picnic areas. Rest rooms are located at these attractions.

Special Places & Events: The historical village opens to the public with an admission charge. Phone: (513) 563-9484.

GEOLOGY

Sharon Creek tumbles over limestone and shale beds, the oldest exposed bedrock in Ohio. The fossils frozen in the stone show the abundant life forms that swam in an ocean 450 million years ago, during the Ordovician geologic period. The names of these alien creatures sound otherworldly: Brachiopods, bryozoans, crinoids, trilobites (the official state fossil).

These were the earthly beings who lived in the ancient tropical sea, long before mammals and dinosaurs. Their remains sank to the depths and mixed with all the other sediment on the ocean floor. When the water disappeared the deposits dried, compacted, and solidified into limestone or shale. The ecoskeletons of many creatures became embedded, or fossilized, in the rock layers.

Illustrations of these fossils appear in the trail guide. The park's small nature center has some examples, but better specimens can be viewed at the Cincinnati Museum of Natural History and similar facilities in Ohio.

Long ago Sharon Creek excavated a channel nearly 100 feet deep through layers of limestone and shale. Now, the channel is a thin brook. Several large boulders in the creek suggest that the tip of a glacier reached this spot during the last million years or so. The boulders are called "erratics," chunks of igneous rocks brought here from Canada by the glaciers.

WILDLIFE

There is more to Sharon Woods gorge than fossils—a forest of tall timbers, a kaleidoscope of wildflowers, and a bustling community of birds.

Mature maples (sugar and silver mostly), oaks (white, red, bur), beech, sycamore, ash, tulip tree, walnut, hickories, and basswood form the canopy in this deep valley. (The flower of the basswood, or linden, supposedly produces tasty honey.) Beneath the canopy, in the understory, pawpaw, dogwoods, and ironwood (blue beech) flourish.

Closer to the ground look for these blossoms in the spring and early summer—jack-in-the-pulpit, green dragon, lady's thumb, wild comfrey, salt and pepper, white baneberry, and wild ginger, or heart's ease, used as a medicine by Indians and as a seasoning by white pioneers.

Late summer and autumn flowers include false foxglove, clammy ground cherry, Indian plantain, yellow wood sorrel, and touch-me-not (jewelweed), said to stop the itch of poison ivy, athlete's feet, and nettle. See if you can identify the Christmas, spinulose wood, and rattlesnake ferns.

Sixteen species of reptiles and amphibians, such as the red-backed salamander and ring-necked snake, were counted in the park in 1992.

During a winter count in 1992, birdwatchers recorded 32 species of birds. Around Sharon Lake, 103 mallards and 90 Canada geese floated on the water while 142 Carolina chickadees, 34 tufted titmice, and 18 nuthatches climbed trees in the woodlands searching for meals. Eighty-two robins scattered leaves on the forest floor to expose bugs and other eatables. Twenty downy and 10 red-bellied woodpeckers tapped into trees for burrowing insects. The cardinal, Ohio's state bird and a permanent resident, numbered 43. All totaled, 1,012 birds were counted.

Spring, of course, is a different story. Other birds arrive in waves, like the warblers who build nests in the canopy and raise their voices in song. The ominous-looking turkey vulture also returns, as well as some hawks, waterfowl, the scarlet tanager, hummingbird, and others. The bird population in late spring swells to many thousands.

HISTORY

Sharon Woods, originally called the Reading Tract, opened to hikers and picnickers in 1932, the first in the Hamilton County Park District. By 1938, most of the remaining parkland had been acquired.

During the years of the Great Depression, park developments were funded by the federal government, and built by workers employed by the Civilian Conservation Corps, Works Progress Administration, and Hamilton County Welfare Department.

Kreis Dam, the impoundment you see on the

Gorge Trail, was finished in 1937. It remembers L. Alvin Kreis, one of the first park commissioners. The dam created 35-acre Sharon Lake, but flooded a section of Sharon Gorge.

Recreational facilities have been added over the years, starting in 1937 with an 18-hole golf course christened by the legendary golfer Bobby Jones. A two-year lake restoration project, completed in 1987, returned 50-year-old Sharon Lake to its original state. A modern Sharon Harbor opened in 1990.

The Ohio Department of Natural Resources, Division of Natural Areas and Preserves, designated Sharon Woods Gorge a state scenic nature preserve on January 31, 1977.

Shawnee Lookout Park

Two centuries ago the Shawnees stood on this sacred hilltop and admired the majestic view above the confluence of the Great Miami and Ohio rivers. Back then, the wind just before sunset would be susurrous, and light with birdsong. Today, this natural fortress and important historical site is clouded by fumes, and crowded by steel bridges, railroads, smokestacks, and interstate highways. Birds still sing loudly and earnestly, but their cheer is drowned by the steady, monotonous whine coming from a looming electric power plant.

LOCATION
Southwestern Hamilton County, Miami Township.

SIZE
1,026 acres. Miami Fort has been listed on the National Registry of Historic Places.

ACCESS
From US 50, at a traffic light in the Village of Cleves, turn westerly on Mt. Nebo Road. After crossing railroad tracks, turn right on River Road. This road follows the Great Miami River and becomes Lawrenceburg Road. The park entrance (about four miles from the turnoff on River Road) will be on your left just past Dugan Gap Road (which appears on your left).

Trails: Go to the parking lot at end of the driveway to hike the Miami Fort Trail. The Miami Fort, Blue Jacket and Little Turtle trails take you on a time voyage through thousands of years of Indian history. As you enter, pick up a park brochure, as well as guides for each trail.

Facilities: The park, open daily from dawn to dusk, has a golf course, picnic areas, a playground, and a boat ramp on the Great Miami River, near the entrance. The Uhlmansiek Wildlife Sanctuary, bordering the Great Miami River, lies within the metropark but remains off limits to the public.

GEOLOGY
The ancient people could not have picked a better place to stage ceremonies, build villages, or simply to enjoy the scenery. The earthworks encircle the summit of a four-sided ridge that rises 300 feet above the Ohio and Great Miami rivers. A narrower ridge extends toward to the west from the main hilltop.

The tip of the skinny ridge presents a commanding lookout over the merger of two major rivers, the hillsides and bluffs to the south (Kentucky), and the gentler landscape west and north (Indiana). A dip, or trough, separates the ridges.

Notice the steep upper slopes of the ridges. If you peeled back the vegetation you would see that these slopes are composed of limestone layers, specifically Fairview (Maysville) limestone. The gentler slopes have alternating layers of shale and limestone. Geologically speaking, they are members of the Lower Kope or Eden formation. All of the bedrocks began as sea floors back in the Ordovician Period, some 450 million years ago.

A cross-section of the ridge would reveal a dividing line between the upper and lower formations at the 650-foot elevation. The earthworks are 80–100 feet above the dividing line.

A five-foot layer of windblown silt (loess) spreads across the ridgetop and may have been an important reason for putting the mounds on this particular hill. This soil, which originated from the meltwater outwash of Ice Age glaciers, is much easier to dig, haul, and dump than the heavy, sticky clay soil found at other sites.

The ancient builders also used slabs of the local rock in the earthworks and burial mound. A quarry below the fort may have been established by the Indians—nobody knows with certainty.

On a clear day, from the lookout, you can see in the distance the abandoned valley of a tributary that flowed into the ancient Teays River, the major river system in Ohio before the Ice Age. Look downstream along the Ohio River. Opposite Lawrenceburg, Indiana, on the Kentucky side, find the shelf-like terrace about 100 feet above the river, and 150 feet from the top of the bluff. That is the floodplain of the ancient tributary called the Kentucky River.

The Teays River roughly flowed from West Virginia and across the southern third of Ohio and into Indiana. The former Kentucky River flowed north into the Teays River. The Great Miami and Whitewater rivers flow in the opposite direction—south into the Ohio River.

The Great Miami River makes a couple of sweeping, and scenic S-shaped curves called ox-bows before spilling into the Ohio River. You can see the oxbows from an overlook on the north leg of the Miami Fort Trail.

These river brushstrokes beg us to look far ahead. Someday, perhaps, the river will wash over the base of the curves and straighten the current. The event, if it happens at all, could be thousands of years away. The relics of the abandoned channels would form crescent-shaped ponds, which over more time become marshes. What will humans see from this vantage a millennium from today?

WILDLIFE

Artifacts found here suggest humans have occupied the ridge at various times during the last 14,000 years. The ancestors of some of the plants and animals that you will see have lived on the ridge a good deal longer.

The abundance and diversity of life in the forest would have been an important factor to the Woodland Indians who were scouting sites for villages and "forts." The lush primeval forest that greeted their arrival is gone.

Most of the trees that are retaking this hill are newcomers. These include a new crop of oaks (white, red, burr), maple, tulip tree, hickory, wild black cherry, slippery elm, ash, black locust, beech, basswood, and a few sycamore that occupy the canopy. Beneath them grow box elder, hackberry, dogwood, sassafras, pawpaw, staghorn sumac, ironwood (blue beech), and Ohio buckeye, among others.

Hawthorn is especially prevalent along the Blue Jacket and Little Turtle trails. Deer and other animals enjoy its fruit, which resembles tiny apples. Apple and pear trees appear along the Little Turtle Trail, the remnants of the land's agricultural past.

The wildflower collection includes jack-in-the-pulpit (Indian turnip), wild delphinium, bindweed, jewelweed (touch-me-not), pokeberry, mouse-eared chickweed, asters (several kinds), squirrel corn, larkspur, fire pink, Joe-pye weed, and Miami mist, a waterleaf thickly populated in the park. According to the park district, this little blossom finds its beauty only in the Great Miami and Little Miami valleys, hence its name.

During the spring and fall migrations, the overlooks above the oxbows become hunting lodges for observing hawks, ospreys, bald eagles (endangered), comorants (designated special interest), and an occasional peregrine falcon (endangered). In 1971, a pair of black vultures, rare in Ohio, nested at Shawnee Lookout. When the bottomland floods, look for great blue herons, egrets, and wood ducks.

Warblers also flock to the area, including the prothonotary warbler and American redstart, as well as the rose-breasted grosbeak, considered a rarity in southwestern Ohio. Quiet walkers might catch a glimpse of a wild turkey on the Little Turtle Trail.

Winter can be rewarding for the birdwatcher. Participants in the park district's annual December bird survey counted 2,283 individual birds from 40 species. Sixty-eight bluebirds, 151 killdeers, 57 red-bellied woodpeckers, and 40 downy woodpeckers were seen, the most sightings of each of these birds in all the metroparks. Birders spotted several endangered birds—the dark-eyed junco (four), winter wren (three), and yellow-bellied sapsucker (four).

Shawnee Lookout may have the largest deer herd among the local metroparks, largely because it offers the animal a prime habitat. Twenty-six kinds of reptiles and amphibians also flourish here, such as the hognosed snake (a rarity), eastern spiny softshell turtle, Fowler's toad, Blanchard's cricket frog, and the Jefferson salamander.

HISTORY

Two years before he was elected the ninth president of the U.S., William Henry Harrison visited and studied many of the ancient Indian earthworks in Ohio, including the "fort" situated within a cannon's blast of his homestead on the north bank of the Ohio River. This famous frontier general, then 65 years old, imagined that the brave mound-builders chose this spot to make their last stand against invading tribes.

It was a natural conclusion. Harrison knew about military fortifications. Earlier in his career he fought in the Indian Wars with General Anthony Wayne, and commanded the American troops against the Indians and British in the War of 1812. His homestead was just a short walk from the ruins of Fort Finney, a stockade built by the British in the mid-1780s. It was this general-politician who would make his homestead near such an important military and political position—Miami Fort and Fort Finney being, in his mind, the outposts of two former empires that dominated North America.

Harrison's physical description of the site in 1838 still fits. "It occupies the summit of a steep insulated hill and consists of a wall carried along its brow, composed of earth, thrown from the interior; the wall conforms strictly to the outline of the hill, except at the west where there is a considerable promontory which is left unenclosed." The knoll on this promontory served as a lookout, according to Harrison. It is really a prehistoric Indian burial mound.

Relying on research unavailable to Harrison, scholars now believe Miami Fort, a 12-acre enclosure, primarily served as a ceremonial site.

Archeological digs in and around Shawnee Lookout in this century have uncovered artifacts indicating that the so-called Paleo Indians who lived in Ohio from 14,000–8,000 B.C. utilized this area. Their successors, categorized as the Archaic (8,000–1,500 B.C.), Woodland (1,000 B.C.–800 A.D.), and Ft. Ancient Indians (800–1650) also left their marks.

The Adena people (early Woodland period) established villages on the ridgetop, around 900–400 B.C., but they did not build the impressive earthworks. Those were built by the Hopewell people a century

Typical Camp in Hills and Dales Park Dayton, Ohio

or two later. After the Hopewell people, the Fort Ancient people came here, followed by the Miamis, Shawnees, and Europeans.

Michikiniqua, or Little Turtle (1752–1812), a chief among the Miamis, was a fearless warrior and able tactician in battle. He ruined the military campaigns of Generals Josiah Harmar and Arthur St. Clair. He often fought alongside the Shawnee chief known as Blue Jacket. After signing the Treaty of Greene Ville in 1794, supposedly ending the Indian wars, he met President George Washington. He died in Indiana in 1812.

As a white child, Blue Jacket was named Marmaduke van Swearingen. The Shawnees who adopted him in 1771 called him Wehyehpihehrsehnwah. His white enemies and admirers called him Blue Jacket. As a Shawnee warrior he captured the legendary frontiersmen Daniel Boone and Simon Kenton. He became a Maykyjay Shawnee chief in 1784, fought with the British during the Revolutionary War, signed the Treaty of Green Ville in 1794, and died of a fever in 1810.

The first white military expedition to this spot was led by French explorer Pierre Joseph Celoron, who buried a lead tablet at the confluence in 1749 and proclaimed Louis XV ruler of the land. The claim did not stick, of course, and the tablet has never been found.

During the last two centuries the forest has been cleared for farms, cities, industries, and housing developments. Many local Indian ruins—and they were numerous—have been bulldozed or looted. It is a wonder Miami Fort survived at all.

Though the park district discussed creating a park at this location in the early 1930s, action did not begin until University of Cincinnati scientists started poking through the ruins in the mid-1960s. In 1966, a citizens' committee raised $91,000 to buy 177 acres on Shawnee Lookout. The following year the park district received as gifts 684 acres from the Cincinnati Gas & Electric company, owner of the adjacent power plant, and 114 acres from the Cincinnati Park Board.

The Miami Purchase Association funded a major archeological survey of the site in 1968. In 1971 Shawnee Lookout was listed on the National Registry of Historical Places. The restored cabin arrived at the park in 1973, and the golf course opened in 1979. Miami Fort Trail was built in 1979–80.

JOURNAL

October: At Shawnee Lookout we remember lost civilizations, and the struggles of our ancestors, Indian and white. Those days have vanished, but the forest seen by our ancestors, if left undisturbed, will return.

Winton Woods Park

Hamilton County's busiest and most crowded metropark for humans has plenty of amenities for wildlife, too.

LOCATION
North-central Hamilton County, Village of Greenhills.

SIZE
2,628 acres.

ACCESS
Leave I-275 at Exit 39 and travel south on Winton Road to the entrance on the right. From I-75 take Sharon Road west, then Winton Road south (left turn). Park in the lot at the Kingfisher Picnic Area, also serving the hiking trail.

Trails: The park only has two footpaths for hikers—the Kingfisher and Great Oaks trails. Each traces a ridge overlooking a cattail pond called Kingfisher Lake. Park district rules urge hikers to stay on trails. Those who want to walk the Great Oaks Trail separately will find the trailhead near the Walnut Ridge Picnic Area. Do not cross the creek during periods of high, or swift water and flooding.

The metropark also has a three-mile paved hike-bike trail, a bridle trail and riding center on the south side of Winton Lake.

Fishing: Fishing is permitted in the lake, but check the restrictions published in the park brochure.

Facilities: You will also find a public campground, a visitor center (Winton Centre) with nature exhibits, more than a dozen picnic areas and nine reservable shelters, an 18-hole golf course, an 18-hole frisbee golf course, a mile-long parcourse fitness trail, ballfields, and a boathouse (rentals, scenic rides available). The park district's administration building also is located in Winton Woods.

GEOLOGY
On old trail maps, Kingfisher Lake looks bigger and deeper than its present size. Indeed, this pond and Lake Winton have shrunk due to the settling of excessive amounts of silt, tiny bits of clay or mud.

Since its construction in 1952, Lake Winton has lost half its volume to siltation, and about a third of the lake is no longer navigable by small boats. Black-crowned night herons, and the red-shouldered and sharp-shinned hawks (the latter two designated special interest birds by the Ohio Division of Wildlife) may have abandoned the lake because of pollution and silting.

WILDLIFE
In spite of silting, Kingfisher Lake remains a vital habitat for carp, catfish, and bass when the water level is suitable. Gizzard shad, bluegill, and bullhead also swim in Lake Winton, as well as stocked crappie, trout, and perch.

The Kingfisher Trail derives its name from the belted kingfisher, which feasts on the small fish in streams and ponds. Sometimes it hovers before diving on its victim. Greater yellowlegs, great blue heron, various flycatchers and woodpeckers, killdeer, and ducks have been observed here.

Kingfisher Lake, really more a marsh, occasion-ally attracts a muskrat or a mink. Footprints on a sand bank revealed the presence of raccoon and skunk.

The red-eared and snapping turtles, queen snake, and bullfrog may reside in this wetland, too. The park, in fact, protects 19 species of reptiles and amphibians, especially the endangered cave salamander, known to exist in Ohio only in Hamilton and Adams counties.

The long-beaked arrowhead (a potentially threatened plant in Ohio) and the rare water speedwell survive on the banks of the pond. Wildflowers like trout lily, wild delphinium, salt and pepper, Japanese honeysuckle, tall bellflower, jewelweed (touch-me-not), and lobelia will brighten your hike on Kingfisher Trail from spring to autumn.

As its name implies, the Great Oak Trail protects giant oaks. One stand of red oaks rises 75–100 feet, and probably have grasped the ridge for two centuries. An interpretive sign next to a set of twin oaks points out that each tree drinks 100 tons of water a year.

Besides the oaks, sugar maple, shagbark hickory, black walnut, sycamore, and tulip tree occupy the canopy while blackgum (tupelo), pawpaw, sassafras, and honey locust thrive in the understory. The honey locust, by the way, is the tree that bristles with spikes that Indians used for fish hooks.

The park as a whole provided a refuge to 2,747 birds representing 47 species, according to a December 11, 1993 winter bird count. That compares to 601 individuals from 37 species tallied in a 1984 winter survey. Either Winton Woods is attracting more birds, or bird watchers are becoming better counters.

Birders recorded a group of 44 dark-eyed juncos (an endangered bird in Ohio) in the December 1993 count, plus 31 golden-crowned kinglets, 542 robins, 257 chickadees and 191 mallards (the most in any local metropark), and two yellow-bellied sapsuckers, another endangered bird.

HISTORY
Winton Woods opened in 1939 when the U.S. Department of Agriculture agreed to lease 902 acres to the park district. Known at the time of its purchase as Greenhills Park, the park district considered calling its new site Simon Kenton Forest, Springfield Forest, and West Branch Forest. It settled on Winton Woods, derived from a pioneer named Mathew Winton who settled along the road that later carried his name. Winton Woods is the second oldest and second largest park in the district. Recreational facilities have been added as the park grew. Golfers started swinging on the park's 18-hole golf course in April 1951.

To control flooding in the industrialized Mill Creek Valley, the U.S. Army Corps of Engineers constructed West Fork Dam, completed in 1952. A year earlier the park district signed an agreement to lease 529 acres in Winton Woods from the corps.

The dam also created Winton Lake, whose surface size can increase from 188 acres to 557 acres when Mill Creek is fully restrained. Besides encouraging boating and fishing, the lake provides a habitat for aquatic wildlife.

Two sections of the metropark became state nature preserves on November 15, 1976. The Ohio Department of Natural Resources, Division of Natural Areas and Preserves made the designations. The Kingfisher Trail goes near Greenbelt State Nature Preserve, a 97-acre tract known for its mature beech-maple forest and expanding sinkholes. Spring Beauty Dell State Nature Preserve (41 acres), another beech-maple forest, is an excellent birding woods. Permission is required to visit these preserves.

Withrow Nature Preserve

This secluded spot, once the estate of Adelaide and Andrew Withrow, lays on a bluff some 300 feet above the Ohio River. In spring, the rugged woodland slopes are softened with wildflowers and the song of newly-arrived warblers.

LOCATION
Southeastern Hamilton County, Anderson Township.

SIZE
270 acres.

ACCESS
Exit I-275 at Five Mile Road. Head west on Five Mile Road to the preserve entrance on the left. From Kellogg Avenue on the bank on Ohio River, turn north on Five Mile Road to the entrance on the right. The parking lot is at the end of the driveway.

Trails: Two footpaths wander through this rugged terrain, but none is especially strenuous. You will have to climb several sets of stairs on the trail as you traverse ridges. As you face Highwood Lodge at the end of the parking lot, both trails begin to the left, at the edge of the woods. Consult the trail map near the parking lot before departing.

Folks looking for solitude and quiet should find it here (though the distant echo of traffic on I-275 sometimes intrudes upon the silence). The preserve lacks picnic areas, rest rooms and drinking water (except when Highwood Lodge is open), and the recreation facilities familiar in other county metroparks.

GEOLOGY
The small brook that has carved the deep ravine in this preserve empties into Five Mile Creek and the Ohio River. It has washed away soil dumped here by the Illinoian glacier, roughly 125 million years ago.

WILDLIFE
The mature forest that you see is a beech-maple climax forest, meaning that the land has reached the last stage of successional growth (from field to forest) and has become self-perpetuating with beech and sugar maples being the dominate trees in the woods. Mixing with the beech-maple giants are healthy examples of red and white oak, shagbark hickory, black cherry, and ash.

Aside from the mature wooded areas in the ravine and river slope, much of the preserve shows various stages of successional habitats from open fields packed with grasses, wildflowers, and fencerow plants like bittersweet, to young forests of rising maples, cherry, and beech. Thickets of shrubs, sumac, briars, and wild grape vines are also present.

The trails honor two spring wildflowers abundant in the preserve. The hepatica (meaning liver) has small, dainty white to lavender flowers. Its leaves were used by Indians and early white settlers to treat liver ailments.

The nodding yellow blossom of the trout lily appears from late March through early June. It is sometimes called the dogtooth violet because of the toothlike shape of its subsurface bulb. This delicate lily (not a violet) got its name from its mottled leaves, which resemble the markings of a brook or brown trout.

Also search for flowers called sessile trillium, salt and pepper, twinleaf, shooting star, and ferns named Christmas and maidenhead.

In the field, find the round, brown, tumorous balls growing on goldenrod stems. If it looks like the plant tried to swallow a large marble, they are goldenrod galls. In the summer, gall flies lay eggs on the stem. A chemical secreted by the flies swells the galls. The balls become cozy winter homes for larvae (maggots), which hatch in the spring and eat their way through the gall to the surface. They complete their development inside the gall and later emerge as adult gall flies.

Elliptical shaped goldenrod galls house moth larvae, instead of maggots. Sometimes an ichneumon wasp emerges from these elliptical galls. This predator injects its eggs into the gall next to the moth larvae. The wasp larva eats the moth larva, then beds down in a cocoon and comes out in late summer.

The preserve also attracts birds of many varieties. Woodpeckers are abundant judging from the constant rapping on trees. During the park district's December 1993 winter bird count, 10 red-bellied, eight downy, and three hairy woodpeckers, plus three yellow-bellied sapsuckers, endangered in Ohio, were counted. Birders also sighted 10 golden-crowned kinglets.

HISTORY
Adelaide and Andrew Withrow bought this piece of paradise in the 1930s. The hilltop offered a remarkable view of the Ohio River, Kentucky hillside, and Five Mile Creek valley. Though the couple landscaped around the home, and planted some exotic trees, like ginko, they largely left the land alone.

In the 1970s the Withrows approached the park district about buying the land for a nature preserve. The first purchase, 145 acres, was completed in 1977 with the help of the Ohio Chapter of The Nature Conservancy. In 1979, Adelaide Withrow Farny and Eugene Farny donated an adjoining 126 acres to the park district.

The nature preserve opened to the public in 1983. It is a favorite site for outdoor weddings and nature programs.

Woodland Mound Park

Humans have been surveying the Ohio River valley from this hilltop for 14,000 years. For centuries, perhaps for millennia, hawks and vultures have floated on the thermals rushing up the steep slope. Early morning visitors might catch the fog floating above the river. Soon sunlight bakes the fog and it dissolves into the air.

LOCATION
Southeastern Hamilton County, Anderson Township.

SIZE
949 acres.

ACCESS
Going eastbound on US 52, turn left (north) on Eight Mile Road, then an immediate right on Old Kellogg Avenue. The entrance is ahead on the left. Park at the Seasongood Nature Center.

Trails: Two footpaths leave the hilltop. First, though, enjoy the best view of the Ohio River valley. The half-mile Seasongood Trail goes from the rear of the nature center into the woods. The mile-long Hedgeapple Trail is quieter and a little more strenuous. It departs from the parking lot for the Weston Amphitheater to the right of the fitness trail. Pick up a map for this trail at the nature center. The numbered stops will give you insights on the natural habitats you will observe.

Facilities: The park also has a top-rated golf course, The Vineyard, and the Weston Amphitheater, a 10,000-seat outdoor concert hall. Picnic areas, Frisbee golf course, ballfields, snack bar, and playground are found in the park.

Special Places and Events: The modern Seasongood Nature Center features interactive nature exhibits, interior overlooks, outdoor decks, wildlife viewing windows, an auditorium, restrooms and drinking water, and Nature's Niche Gift and Bookshop. A gift from the estate of Murray and Agnes Seasongood paid for the construction of the attractive building; Murray Seasongood advocated for the creation of a metropark district when he was mayor of Cincinnati, 1926–30.

GEOLOGY
Limestone and shale created back in the Ordovician geological period, some 450 million years ago, provide the foundation for steep hills overlooking the Ohio River. These bedrocks started as soupy sea floors enriched with the remains of the era's marine life. The fossils of the ancient sea creatures are found in the exposed Ordovician rocks.

Recently, say within the last 500,000 years, continental glaciers, notably the Illinoian, laid blankets of sand, silt, gravel, rocks, and boulders—a deposit called till—atop these bedrock formations. The soil on the ridgetop of this park is made of glacial till.

Some streams running off the steep hills have washed away the till and brought the old rocks and sea creatures back into the sunlight. None of the hiking trails mentioned above visits one of these streams.

WILDLIFE
The wrinkled yellowish-green "brains" found along the Hedgeapple Trail in autumn are the softball-sized fruits of the osage orange, or hedgeapple, tree. Though common in Ohio, it is not a native. It was imported and planted by farmers, usually in rows, as a hedge or fencerow. Its thorny, rot-resistant, intertwining branches kept livestock from fleeing a field. Barbed wire replaced osage orange as a fence, but the tree survives as a relic. Pioneers put the fruit in their cabins as an insect repellent. Today, squirrels and quails munch on the seeds.

You also will see honey locust and black locust trees, distinguished by their thorns and rows of small leaves. Don't lean on a honey locust. In spite of its sweet-sounding name, its thorns, or spikes, can pierce your flesh. The thorns have been used as pins and fish hooks.

Numerous vines creep alongside the Hedgeapple Trail. Poison ivy (whose oil makes your skin itch) and Virginia creeper often grow side by side up the trunk of a tree. Five leaves spring from the stem of the Virginia creeper, three from the poison ivy vine.

Wild grape vines, the thick, woody, "Tarzan" vines we swung on as youngsters, produce dark blue or purple grapes that are enjoyed by wildlife, especially raccoons. Sweet-scented white or yellow blossoms appear from the tendrils of Japanese honeysuckle, a non-native vine imported to control soil erosion. The plant has become overabundant in some areas and suffocates native plants.

Elsewhere in the park, oaks called black, shumard, pin, and yellow thrive, along with beech, hackberry, red cedar, cottonwood, ailanthus (tree of heaven), redbud, ash, black willow, box elder, silver and black maple, black walnut, shagbark and bitternut hickory, and others.

The park's diverse wildflower assemblage includes beauties found in woodlands and meadows. Look for these—Virgin's bower, thimbleweed, black nightshade, black snakeroot, moth mullein, spring beauty, St. John's wort, wild bergamot, sessile trillium, jack-in-the-pulpit, white and purple dwarf larkspur, jewelweed (touch-me-not), catnip, giant hyssop, and many others.

The ponds on the Hedgeapple Trail differ slightly. As noted above the vernal pond teems with life—insect larvae and tadpoles—when water fills it in the spring. By mid-summer the pond is empty, but dragonflies feast on swarming mosquitoes, and the great crested flycatcher preys on dragonflies.

The woodland pond is shaded and usually keeps its water year-round. It is a watering hole for animals, a place for turtles to bask, and for salamanders, frogs and toads to hibernate. Bullfrogs croak in raspy-basso notes at the cattail pond, more open than the neighboring woodland pond. Red-winged blackbirds nest in the cattail stands. Freshwater snails in the ponds provide meals for nocturnal visitors.

At the last count 20 species of amphibians and reptiles have been recorded in the park, such as the hognosed (becoming rare), black rat, and rough green snakes, and the slimy and ravine salamanders.

The ridgetops are proven viewing spots for hawks, vultures, waterfowl, and other migratory birds. The park attracts the usual crowd of warblers, and sparrows, plus regulars like cardinals, robins, bluejays, and crows. The meadows fill with butterflies in summer, notably the tiger swallowtail and monarch.

HISTORY

It is possible that ancient people called the Palaeo Indians roamed atop these hills 14,000 years ago. Later groups (so-called Archaic, Woodland, and Fort Ancient Indians) occupied the slopes, according to the park district. Ten sites discovered in the park—small villages, campsites, two mounds, and the Eight Mile Earthworks—remind us of their presence. (See Shawnee Lookout.)

The Miami and Shawnee people moved into Ohio in the early 1700s, a few decades before the first whites began to explore the region. Though no major Indian paths passed through the park, the nearby Ohio River, of course, was a major transportation route for Native Americans and white pioneers.

According to early pioneer diaries and letters, the parkland in 1750 was 95 percent forested, with some trees boasting girths of six feet and heights of 100 feet. That, of course, changed. By the 20th century the forest had been cleared. Elk, bison, black bear, wolf, mountain lion, and bobcat had been killed off.

The park district "penciled in" a park for this area on a 1934 master plan, but scant resources and other park developments delayed the project until 1974. By 1976 some 700 acres had been acquired. The park opened on July 20, 1980, marking the park district's 50th anniversary.

The Weston Amphitheater is named after Mrs. Sara K. Weston whose donation of 40 acres in 1976 helped the district obtain a matching federal land grant. The nature center opened on May 19, 1990.

◆◆◆   MIAMI   COUNTY   ◆◆◆
For more information, contact 2535 E. Ross Rd., Tipp City, OH 45371, (937) 667-1086. Sites - 4; acres - 663.

Charleston Falls Reserve

The petite Charleston Creek emerges from a subterranean source and flows several miles west before dropping 37 feet over a precipice made of the same ancient bedrock that trips the Niagara River 350 miles northeast of here. Except for this quirky geological link, the so-called "Miniature Niagara" of Miami County hardly compares with the thunderous Niagara. No matter. It has a charm of its own, though showering under it is no longer allowed.

LOCATION
Southeast Miami County.

SIZE
169 acres.

ACCESS
Leave I-70 at the exit for SR 202 and drive north on SR 202 about 3 miles. Turn left (west) on Ross Road for about a mile to the entrance on the right. Follow the driveway to the parking lot.

Trails: Charleston Falls Preserve has 2.5 miles of foot trails that travel along rock escarpments, and brooks, and visit hardwood forests, meadows, and prairies. Pick up a preserve brochure/trail map at the bulletin board in the parking lot.

The waterfall, of course, is the big attraction. The .3-mile trail from the parking lot heads east for a few paces then joins the main trail. A right turn at this junction goes to a picnic area. Turn left for the trail to the falls, and bear right at the first fork.

At the falls I recommend the trail at the left, marked "lower viewing platform," which descends a moss-covered limestone escarpment into the gorge and amphitheater at the base of the waterfall. Here you can best observe the size and depth of the cascade, the forces of erosion, as well as the geological storybook expressed in the rocks. On a hot summer day the fine, powdery mist of the falls, combined with the canopy of the forest, provide cool relief.

Unfortunately, showering under the cascade is no longer allowed. Climbing the cliffs is unlawful and foolhardy. Thousands of humans before you bathed and climbed, and in doing so trampled the plants and mosses living around the falls. Such frolicking aided erosion, and caused numerous injuries.

Facilities: Picnickers can head for the picnic area (no fires). You will find drinking water and toilets in the 32-car parking lot. Motorcyclists should park in a designated lot.

GEOLOGY

Charleston Falls performs daily, and continually, in a natural amphitheater of its own creation, built upon some of the oldest uncovered rock in Ohio.

The story began 440–500 million years ago (Ordovician geologic period) when Ohio was covered by a shallow, muddy sea. Eventually the ocean receded, allowing the mud to dry into a flaky sedimentary rock called shale, specifically the Elkhorn variety of Cincinnatian shale.

Another ocean washed over the bedrock of shale. This one teemed with sea creatures—crustaceans, jellyfish, sponges, trilobites, brachiopods. Their skeletal remains fell to the sea floor in calcium-rich beds. Many skeletons became embedded in the sediment, and became fossils.

When this ocean withdrew, the limey soup hardened into limestone. The brand of limestone at both Charleston and Niagara Falls is called Brassfield limestone. It is chunky (scientists call it blockular), resistant to erosion, and rich in fossils.

More oceans came and went, and each dumped a layer of sediment atop the limestone. When the last sea retreated, the erosive power of rain, wind, and sun slowly eat away the strata until it reaches the limestone.

Water is predictable. It always goes to the lowest place, and takes the path of least resistance. Here, it seeped into the fissures (cracks) of the limestone blocks. Over millennia, erosion widened the cracks and formed caves. Rain water ran to low spots on the surface, then carved troughs that became streams and gorges.

Then, mile-high glaciers pushing south from the polar cap arrived. The ice mass slid across Earth on melted water produced by the friction of its own enormous weight. When the planet's temperature rose, the shrinking glacier sent roaring torrents of meltwater down channels like Charleston Creek and the Great Miami River. The currents carved deeper gorges and wider paths. Underground caverns literally burst and collapsed. Where limestone had been removed, the mad torrents attacked the softer shale "as easily as we tear pages out of a loose-leaf notebook," said one writer. That left limestone outcrops hanging over the valley.

The last glacier (Wisconsinan ice mass) scoured this part of Ohio about 12,000–15,000 years ago. It deposited mounds of glacial till (sand, gravel, rocks, etc.) in its wake. The demise of the glacier forced the Great Miami River to feed itself with tributaries like Charleston Creek.

At the falls, stream water has eroded the shale layers beneath the limestone, forming a recess cave. Limestone overhangs that lose their shale foundation eventually fall into the creek.

Diversions in the current can change the location of the spout on the precipice. The drape of the falls may be in a different location each year. Notice, too, that Charleston Creek has fashioned a charming little gorge before it enters the floodplain and the Great Miami River a mile downstream.

WILDLIFE

Charleston Falls is the centerpiece of the preserve. The limestone walls surrounding the cool, shady glen support some uncommon plants, notably wild columbine, walking fern, purple cliffbreak, and rock honeysuckle. The boardwalk and platform at the falls protects these plants from human trampling.

The preserve is largely wooded, containing trees common in Ohio—oaks, beech, maples, hickory, tulip tree, etc. In an abandoned farmlot, redbud, black-haw, and cedar have moved in. Redbud Valley Trail gets its name from the tree that blossoms there every spring.

Black and honey locust grow here in healthy groves. Locust Grove Trail passes through a community of this hardwood. Park staff used black locust found in the preserve for the split-rail fences you see.

A special place is Cedar Pond and the adjacent planted tallgrass prairie. The spot looks still and passive enough, but it actually overflows with life. In summer, dragonflies diving for mosquitoes may be swallowed by a rough-winged swallow. Butterflies intoxicate themselves on the nectar of the prairie blossoms. On a hot summer day, I watched a group of regal fritillaries feast on a single milkweed plant for 20 minutes. One of them landed briefly on my shoulder.

The preserve's brochure says the pond, built in 1977, will be a marsh in 100 years, and a forest two centuries hence. Until then, it will be a collecting point for frogs, turtles, crustaceans, raccoons, as well as humans. If you sit on a bench at dusk, silent and still, a deer might tiptoe to the shore for a drink.

Elsewhere, mink and fox hunt for mice and rabbits in the bushes. Purple finches and pine warblers hide in the pines. Listen for the sonorous hoot of the barred owl: "who cooks for you, who cooks for you all."

You are apt to look twice at the sign in the pond. The writing makes no sense until you study its reflection in the pool. Only in the reflection can you read, "Cedar Pond." On the ride home, parents can get the kids to write their name upside-down and reversed so that it reads correctly in a mirror.

Sinewy, young trees growing in dense groves tell us that the land had been cleared for human use not too long ago.

HISTORY

The Indians who gathered here for centuries undoubtedly skinny-dipped under the falls without fear of provoking a ranger, and without harming the wildlife. They left behind fire pits, artifacts, and burial mounds to prove that they visited the site.

White landowners enjoyed the falls for its peace and beauty, too. Though much of the land surrounding the cascade was cleared for agriculture, park officials say they left the falls itself "relatively undisturbed."

The Ohio Chapter of The Nature Conservancy, aided by the George Gund Foundation, purchased the site in 1975. The next year the park district acquired the preserve from the conservation group with tax levy money and a matching federal grant. Charleston Falls was the county park district's first acquisition.

JOURNAL

June 15: I have arrived in time to see the last wild columbine blossom on the cliff, and to feel the soft spray of spring water that has fallen two-score feet over the lip of this limestone bowl. The mist offsets the mid-June heat and recharges body and soul.

Goode Prairie State Nature Preserve

The crest and slope of a south-facing bluff that overlooks the Stillwater River brightens with tallgrass prairie blossoms in midsummer.

LOCATION

Northwest Miami County, Newberry Township.

SIZE

28 acres.

ACCESS

Start in Piqua and drive west on SR 185 about eight miles. Go north (right) on Fink Road, then left on Union Church Road. Where Union Church Road turns sharply right, look for the preserve entrance on the left (west) side of the road.

Trail: A short loop trail goes from the parking lot to the preserve's hillside prairie and returns—a half mile.

GEOLOGY

The prairie grows and the Stillwater River flows atop thin, well-drained limey soil formed on a gravelly base. The bedrock beneath it all is dolomite dating to the Silurian Period.

WILDLIFE

The floral community includes wild bergamot, prairie dock, butterflyweed, big bluestem, rough goldenrod, gray-headed coneflower, nodding ladies' tresses, partridge pea, nodding wild onion, gaura (morning honeysuckle), and hoary puccoon, a yellow-orange tubular blossom with hairy, or "hoary," leaves and stems. Puccoon comes from an Indian word for several plants that yield colored dyes. Flattened wild oat grass, a potentially endangered plant, also grows here. Frequent slumping, or soil sliding, has actually benefitted this prairie pocket.

Trees are represented by the sycamore, red cedar, several oaks, Ohio buckeye, and ashes blue, white, and prickly.

HISTORY

The preserve derives from a gift from Leona Goode, wife of the late Walter Goode, former Miami County Commissioner. Goode was also a co-founder of the Stillwater River Association, a conservation group advocating preservation of the Stillwater River and its designation as a scenic river. The preserve is owned by the Ohio Department of Natural Resources, Division of Natural Areas and Preserves, but managed by the Miami County Park District.

✦✦✦ MONTGOMERY COUNTY ✦✦✦

Information about these Dayton-area parks can be obtained from Five Rivers Metroparks, 1375 East Siebenthaler Avenue, Dayton, OH 45414, (937) 275-PARK (7275).

The Five Rivers (Dayton) Metroparks owes its existence to a terrible flood on Easter Sunday, 1913, that swallowed Dayton and other communities along the Great Miami River and its tributaries. By the end of the decade the Miami Conservancy District, the first watershed management program of its kind in the U.S., had constructed five flood-control dams in the area. The land surrounding the impounded lakes became parkland managed by the conservancy district. The park district, established in 1963, has more than tripled its holdings since it began leasing reserves from the Miami Conservancy District. The district now manages 20 sites and more than 20,000 acres.

Carriage Hill Metropark

The park district transformed 900 acres of played out farmland into a historical farmpark, and recovering natural area with woodlands, ponds, marsh, and meadows. The restored farmstead of Daniel Arnold reenacts farm life in the 1880s, including chores like hog butchering.

Northeastern Montgomery County, Wayne Township; Southeastern Miami County, Bethel Township.

SIZE

898 acres.

ACCESS

From I-70 (southern border of the park), go north on SR 201 (Brandt Pike) about a half mile, then turn right (east) on Shull Road to sites within the park. Shull Road continues east to Bellefontaine Road, the eastern border of the park.

Eastbound on Shull Road you pass the staging area for horseback riding (left), parking for the Red Wing Picnic Shelter and Marsh-Boardwalk Trail (left), entrance and parking to the historical farm (right), parking for the Cedar Lake Picnic Shelter (left), and driveway to the Activity Center (right). Start at the Activity Center, which has park brochures, trail map (you might need one), exhibits and rest rooms.

Accommodations: Free overnight camping (primitive) is available to organized groups at the Redbud and Day Camp sites, at the end of a gated service road off Bellefontaine Road. For camping and other information call the park office at (937) 879-0461.

Trails: Nature hikers will enjoy the Marsh Boardwalk Trail and branching walks to North Woods Pond, South Woods, and along the shore of Cedar Lake. Choose from several routes shown on the park brochure. The Marsh Boardwalk Trail goes across the shallow northwestern tip of Cedar Lake. Stop at the interpretive signs and observation points

Silt
Siding

Sediments from Development Threaten Aquatic Life

Silt is a common particle suspended in Ohio streams. The sediment travels like wind-borne pollen or dust and gives many streams their muddy appearance. Swift streams can carry silt great distances and distribute it all along its banks. Obstacles that slow down the current, such as logs or dams, can become silt collecting points.

The currents of the Mill Creek watershed carry silt to the lakes. Water running off from surrounding hills also contains silt. When the silt reaches the peaceful lake water behind West Fork Dam it settles and accumulates. The bottom of the lake rises with sediment and water inches up the shoreline.

The silting of a lake is a natural process. Barring a catastrophic event, it usually takes hundreds or thousands of years for sediment to fill a lake bed. Humans, however, can make Nature's clock tick faster. Intense development around the park over the last four decades is responsible for the high silt content in Lake Winton and Kingfisher Lake in Hamilton County. Precipitation run-off transports silt from construction sites into the Mill Creek watershed, and into the lakes.

Excessive silt affects the aquatic life of a lake or pond. Though some life forms benefit, others may suffer, especially critters higher up the food chain such as fish, frogs, crayfish, snakes, and some birds. Silt from development sites also may be charged with contaminants that can harm wildlife.

along the way. Distance is 4-4.5 miles, depending on your route, and you will tramp over fields, woods, and wetlands.

Hikers and cross-country skiers also can venture on the perimeter bridle trail covering five miles. Two small loops within the perimeter increase the distance to six miles. The bridle path is largely through fields, and shrub land. Start at the staging area for horse riders.

Fishing: Visitors can also fish in the ponds (no license, no charge, check limits).

Special Places & Events: Don't leave without visiting the historical farm for several hours. The site includes barns, live animals, smokehouse, icehouse, blacksmith shop, old farming machines, the Daniel Arnold House (1836), sawmill, croplands, rest rooms, and Country Store. Farm Hours 10 a.m. to 5 p.m. weekdays, 1-5 p.m. weekends. Activities are posted at the Country Store and Activity Center.

GEOLOGY

The park lies in the till plains physiographic region, a level to gentle rolling landscape massaged by the Wisconsinan glacier 12,000 years ago. Glacial erratics, granite or gneiss boulders, are sprinkled throughout the park. These rocks got a free ride from Canada via the glacier.

WILDLIFE

Carriage Hills has diverse habitats—meadows, fields, woods, and wetlands. Birders should look for the great blue heron and puddle ducks by the lake, and woodcocks, orchard and northern orioles, rufous-sided towhees, screech owls, and common yellowthroats. Warblers are few and far between. Feeders attract the usual cast of sparrows, finches, cardi-

More, *metroparks*

Other Miami and Montgomery County Parks

OTHER MIAMI COUNTY PARKS

Garby's Big Woods Sanctuary, 272 acres, Statler Road, Spring Creek Township. Mature woods, boardwalk trail, wildflowers, picnic tables, fishing pond.

Stillwater Prairie Reserve, 217 acres, SR 185, Newberry Township. Stillwater River, tallgrass prairie, boardwalk, hiking, picnic area, fishing ponds.

OTHER FIVE RIVERS METROPARKS

Aullwood Garden, 32 acres, next to Englewood Metropark and Aullwood Audubon Center on Aullwood Road, Gardens, strolling paths, displays.

Cox Arboretum Metropark, 159 acres, Springboro Pike. Theme gardens, visitors center, ponds, pavilion, trails, gift shop, greenhouse, gazebo.

Crains Run Metropark, Crains Run Road, Miami Township. Merger of Crains Run and Great Miami River, River Corridor Bikeway, fishing, picnic areas.

Eastwood Metropark, 437 acres, SR 4, Harshman Road and Springfield Pike. Eastwood Lake, Mad River, boating, picnic areas, water skiing, fishing, playground, Buckeye Trail, paths.

Huffman Metropark, 368 acres, Lower Valley Pike, Greene County, Bath Township. Huffman Lake, fishing, sailing, boating, picnic areas, Buckeye Trail.

Island Metropark, Downtown Dayton (Helena Street). Merger of the Stillwater and Great Miami rivers, River Corridor Bikeway, Buckeye Trail, picnicking, canoe access, fishing, playground.

Stillwater Gardens/Wegerzyn Center, 46 acres, Siebenthaler Avenue. Horticultural education center, vignette gardens, metroparks headquarters, bike path, River Corridor Bikeway.

Twin Creek Metropark, 688 acres, German Township, SR 123 and Eby Road. Hopewell Indian mounds, fishing, hiking, picnicking.

Wesleyan Metropark, 41 acres, Wesleyan Road in Dayton. Picnic pavilion, playground, trails, nature center.

nals, titmice, chickadees, and nuthatches. Long-eared and saw-whet owls, American pipit, Henslow's sparrow, and the sedge wren have been visitors.

Meadows stir with butterflies, the monarch being the most noticeable. Willow and cottonwoods crowd the marsh. Red cedar invaded when farming stopped but many of these are being replaced (a gentle way of saying killed off) by overtopping hardwoods. Purple coneflower, black-eyed Susan, common milkweed (the host plant for monarchs), and asters lead the wildflower bouquet.

Frogs, turtles and muskrats hang out in the park. Deer browse in the field and rabbits are nibbling shrubs and leaving evidence of their presence.

HISTORY

Back in the mid-1960s, Eugene Kettering fueled his private plane and took Richard Lawwill, park superintendent, and William P. Patterson for a ride. Kettering had just donated $250,000 to the park district for park land and he wanted to show his passengers a piece of property "up north." That aerial reconnaissance mission led to the purchase of Dry Lick Run Reserve from the Grusenmeyer brothers. Dry Lick Run Reserve became the core parcel of Carriage Hill Metropark.

JOURNAL

During my visit to the Arnold Farm, I was treated to a hog butchering, and so were two busloads of school kids of various ages. The demonstration curdled the lunch of some kids, but it recalled fond memories of my father, who earned extra money by butchering cattle and hogs on weekends.

Carriage Hill is one of those "the best is yet to come" parks. In a half century the trees will be taller and the land will be more fertile.

Englewood Metropark

The trails through the natural area in this metropolitan park visit waterfalls, natural springs, a state natural landmark, and a state scenic river. The floral scent in the air reminds visitors of gardens that surround the Aull estate in the southeast section of this park.

LOCATION

Northern Montgomery County, Randolph Township, near Englewood.

SIZE

1,925 acres. Aullwood Garden is 32 acres.

ACCESS

From Dayton travel north (about six miles) on I-75, west a few miles on I-70, and exit northbound US 48. Less than a mile on US 48 turn right (east) on US 40, and turn left into the reserve just after crossing the Englewood Dam. To reach the trails described below, drive beyond the lake at your left to the end of the road, turn right (Patty's Road) and pull into the parking lot on the right. The trail begins across the street. To reach Aullwood Garden, bear right after crossing the dam, and turn right on to Aullwood Road. Just beyond the Aullwood Audubon Center, pull into the drive on the right, which goes to a parking lot beside Stillwater River.

Trails: Twelve miles of trails wander through the reserve. Maps are usually available at the trailheads. The trail to Martindale Falls, round trip 1.5 miles, begins across the street from the parking lot designated for the picnic area and shelter house on the left side of Patty's Road (not the riding center). You will find rest rooms at this location. The path goes north, on the side of a ridge. Halfway to the falls, the River Trail joins from the left. Several paths loop through the Big Spring section of the reserve bordered by Meeker and Aullwood roads. Trailheads are at the Aullwood Audubon Center.

Facilities: You also will find rest rooms, picnic areas, bicycle paths, fishing areas, and horse riding trails in the preserve.

Special Places & Events: Aullwood Garden is open Tuesday–Saturday, 8 a.m.–7 p.m. It remains closed on Sunday and Monday, and January–February.

GEOLOGY

At Martindale Falls and Patty's Falls, notice the alternating layers of limestone and shale. These strata date back more than 450 million years ago to the Ordovician geologic period when Ohio was covered by a shallow, warm inland sea.

When the creatures living in this ancient ocean died their shells and skeletons floated to the bottom and mixed with other sediment. Eventually, this limey soup hardened into limestone. The waterfalls show a process called undercutting at work. The Stillwater River and its tributaries have been eroding, or undercutting, these limestone and shale walls for centuries.

The creeks that tumble over Patty Falls and snake through Aullwood Garden emerge from underground water sources. The Patty family, once owners of the land, tapped this spring for its water.

WILDLIFE

A rare pumpkin ash community, population 80 and growing, thrives in a swamp forest just off the trail connecting Martindale and Patty Falls. This tree was believed to be extinct in Ohio. The spot is now a state natural landmark.

Just a few hundred yards away is a pine plantation planted nearly 60 years ago by the Civilian Conservation Corps. Three whitetailed deer tiptoed within 50 feet of me. The May breeze, brisk in my face, never carried my odor to them. Either that, or they, like me, lingered to inhale the pine vapors.

The land here has been farmed and grazed, and much of the vegetation is in various stages of succession growth. Birds and other critters common in Ohio reside here. Look for waterfowl in Englewood Lake.

Though not a wild, natural area, take a peek at luxuriant Aullwood Garden, especially if you are a devoted gardener and landscaper. A plaque on the trail from the parking lot to the garden reminds you that some of the trees along the river have been there for 300 years. Swarms of butterflies as well as bees float like confetti above the blossoms in the summer.

HISTORY

After a devastating flood in 1913 dams and other flood control projects were constructed under the management of the Miami Conservancy District (MCD). In spite of pressure from developers, the agency wisely left most of the land surrounding the impoundments for park and recreation land. One of these dams blocked the Stillwater River at Englewood.

The Dayton-Montgomery Park District was founded in 1963 and began leasing land around the MCD for parks and natural areas. One of these projects became the Englewood Preserve. Quite by accident the preserve's size grew in the early 1970s when 100 acres along Meeker Road were acquired through eminent domain to block construction of a housing development and waste treatment plant.

In 1907 John Aull, a businessman, bought 150 acres along the Stillwater River as a refuge. He built a modest home on the site and reconfigured Wiles Creek after the 1913 flood. In the ensuing years, he and his wife, Marie, developed a garden that maintains a natural look.

To revive the woodland floor cover that had been beaten down by grazing, the Aulls planted native wildflowers, such as the thousands of Virginia bluebells that cover the hillsides and the blue-eyed Marys rescued from a nearby farm. Each week of each season has a different look in the garden.

In 1977, Marie Aull donated her home and garden to the park district.

Germantown Metropark

Twin Creek has lacerated this land right down to the bone, in this case the bone being 450 million-year-old limestone packed with fossils of creatures that lived on Earth long before the dinosaurs. Nature bandaged the wound with a forest.

LOCATION

Southwestern Montgomery County, German Township.

SIZE

1,412 acres.

ACCESS

From Germantown, travel west on SR 725 roughly four miles, then turn right (north) on Boomershine Road. The entrance is a mile up the road on the right. Park at the nature center, located on the west bank of Twin Creek. The east side of the reserve is accessible from Conservancy Road running between SR 725 and Manning Road.

Trails: Hikers can take pleasure in 10 miles of trails that visit forests, steep ravines, meadows, streams, and ponds. The well-marked, color-coded trails are open daily from 8 a.m. to dusk (closed Christmas and New Year's Day) but during spring floods the paths along Twin Creek may be impassable.

Get a trail map at the modern nature center and study the color-coded trail sign before departing. I recommend the route that follows the yellow blazes.

Hiking trails on the north side of Twin Creek, accessible from the Conservancy Road entrance, lead to the Broad-Winged Prairie, a colony of red cedars, Sunfish Pond, and the Valley Overlook, which presents a scenic view of the Twin Creek valley.

Facilities: The reserve also has picnic areas (some reservable), and two group campgrounds. Fishing is allowed in Twin Creek (south of the Germantown Dam, Creek Road entrance) and at Sunfish Pond (off the Conservancy Road entrance). Canoeing is permitted below the dam (use the Creek Road entrance). Fossils are reportedly abundant in the vicinity of the dam.

Special Places & Events: The underground, energy-efficient nature center features one of the best wildlife windows in the state. Speakers amplify the songs of the birds that flock to the outdoors feeders. There are plenty of exhibits in the nature center, even some live critters. Rest rooms and drinking water are available here.

GEOLOGY

The fossils embedded in rock are the remains of extinct creatures that clung to the floor of an ocean around 450 million years ago. A wall at the entrance of the nature center describes the ancient sea critters. The most common fossil is the bryozoan, which grew in colonies like moss. They look like small bones or twigs. Brachiopods, or lamp shades, had tiny, symmetrical fan-shaped shells. Snail-like gastropods preyed upon brachiopods. Horn corals have radiating lines inside their cups and striations around their horn-shaped bodies. Cephalopods, identified by coiled shells, are related to modern squid.

An uncommon discovery here was a predatory trilobite, now the official state fossil. Finding a whole specimen is a prize, fragments are common. All types had two grooves running from head to toe, and a body split into three sections. One variety reached a length of two feet.

The flood control impoundment known as Germantown Dam (built in the late 1910s) has slowed the pace and increased the depth of the creek.

WILDLIFE

Germantown Reserve protects land on the mend, and southwestern Montgomery County's largest mature forest. Evidence of the land's agricultural past—patches of grass in the forest, ground hogs, fencerows, and barbed wire scars on tree trunks—still faintly exist, but these reminders eventually will disappear.

Though white settlers deforested the upland and gentle slopes for farms in the first half of the 19th century, many trees avoided the axe. These lucky ones live in rugged nooks and crannies, or steep slopes, or soggy bottomland, places loggers simply ignored.

Some mammoth beeches are thought to be more than 200 years old, and there are maples and oaks just as old, and just as big. And some of the grandfather cottonwoods near the creek must be older. The reserve also boasts buxom tulip trees, shagbark hickories, and wild black cherries.

Red cedar groves dot the landscape. This pioneer tree (one of the first to populate a played-out field) likes open areas with alkaline soil. Some 50 species of birds consume the tree's berries, including bobwhite quail, pheasant, grouse. The tree also appeals to two rare birds—the saw-whet and long-eared owls. The Ohio Division of Wildlife has declared both of them "special interest" birds, a designation roughly equal to potentially threatened. Quiet walkers hiking through the cedars in the winter might catch a glimpse of the diminutive saw-whet, the smallest owl in Ohio. Great-horned, screech, and barred owls are also present.

Broad-winged hawks supposedly nest near a prairie patch discovered in 1982, hence the name Broad-winged Prairie. The Cooper's, red-tailed, red-shouldered (special interest), and kestrel hawks often glide above the valley.

Look for these colorful birds—indigo bunting, scarlet tanager, cerulean warbler, ruby-throated hummingbird, and slate-colored junco. The northern waterthrush, an endangered species, has been spotted here, along with the cedar waxwing, eastern meadowlark, pileated woodpecker, redstart, and evening grosbeak. Waterfowl residents include mallard and wood ducks. Great blue herons and kingfishers occupy the creek habitat.

Wildflowers, hundreds of varieties, brighten the landscape from the dawning of the skunk cabbage in late February to the waning of the New England aster in late October. For kicks, try to find the spring larkspur, yellow goatsbeard, dewberry, wild columbine, Greek valerian, toadshade (one of the trillium family), deptford pink, jack-in-the-pulpit, white beard-tongue, and firepink.

The prairie, a relict of the sweeping grassland that thrived here just 4,000 years ago, sponsors little bluestem (a grass), wild bergamot, purple coneflower, oxeye daisy, sunflower, and prairie coneflower.

Insects named great-spangled fritillary, pink-edged sulfur, and clear wing sphinx moth represent the butterfly kingdom.

Bass (smallmouth, largemouth, and rock), bluegill, and crappie swim in Twin Creek, a good spot to look for the two-lined, red-backed, smallmouth, and long-tailed salamanders.

Germantown Metropark is the only known habitat in Montgomery County for the eastern hognose snake, a reptile becoming rare in Ohio. More common are the black racer, water, and queen snakes. Five kinds of turtle get old here—the box, painted, softshell, map, and snapping.

HISTORY

People of the Miami and Shawnee nations moved into the region during the first half of the 18th century but by the time white settlers arrived only a small band of Shawnees survived south of Germantown.

Most of the land comprising the reserve was cleared by farmers in the first half of the 19th century. One cash crop, tobacco, rapidly depleted the soil.

The terrible flood that swamped Dayton on Easter Sunday, 1913, inspired the creation of the Miami Conservancy District two years later. The MCD was the first major watershed district established in the U.S., according to historian George W. Knepper. The Germantown dam was one of a six earthen impoundments built by the MCD in the late 1910s.

Arthur Morgan, the MCD's hired engineer, recommended that the land surrounding the dams be used for recreation. The suggestion was adopted, enabling Twin Creek valley above the dam to return to its natural state. The newly-formed Park District of Dayton-Montgomery County began leasing four MCD park sites, including Germantown, in the early 1960s. The park district has been improving it since then.

Possum Creek Metropark

Local old soldiers remember the Argonne Forest—the one they fought in during the First World War, and the one they played in before the Second World War. The former amusement park now amuses prairie flora, human nature lovers, and a grove of old beeches above the banks of Possum Creek.

LOCATION
Central Montgomery County, Jefferson Township.

SIZE

550 acres.

ACCESS

From Dayton follow SR 4 (Germantown Pike) southwesterly. Just outside the city limits turn left (east) on Frytown Road, and right at the north park entrance. This driveway leads to parking lots for Argonne Lake, hiking trails, and fishing ponds. To reach the Possum Creek Metropark Farm (south entrance) continue south on SR 4, then left on Infirmary Road and left on Shank Road to the entrance.

Accommodations: The Sycamore Campsite for organized groups is located here, too. A walk-in group camp is located near Argonne Forest. Permits are needed for overnight camping.

Trails: About five miles of trails await foot travelers. Most paths start at the parking area for Argonne Lake, smack in the middle of the park. Picnic tables, shelters, rest rooms, and brochures showing trail routes are available here. Youngsters head for the trail that encircles the kidney-shaped lake. Slow them down by putting a fishing pole in their hands and letting them catch dinner. Take the trail at the northwest shore of the lake and head for Argonne Forest. Consult your park guide carefully, for there are some tricky turns.

Short loop trails near the restored farm (one with a bird blind) are intended for time-pressed people, and nature education for young visitors. Horse riders have a 1.5-mile trail that traces Possum Creek. The trail begins at a small staging area on Shank Road, west of the south entrance.

Fishing: A foot trail running along the fishing ponds connects the campsite with the parking area for anglers. Another runs from the farm to a park service road near the fishing ponds. Fishing is free and no license is needed. There is a 10-inch minimum size for bass, and six-fish limit per day. The northernmost pond is "catch-and-release." Good places to start kids off with the right tackle and bait.

Facilities: The North Entrance Road leads to a parking area for anglers (rest rooms, phone) and ends at a parking lot south of Argonne Lake. Picnic tables, shelter, and rest rooms are present there. Two reservable picnic shelters are available on a park road east of the north entrance.

Special Places & Events: Possum Creek Farm features an 1830s farmhouse, an 1880s barn, plus pastures, rabbit hutch, orchard, corral and chicken house. Polly Possum's Math Farm consists of 15 math stations offering a variety of ways to solve math problems while learning about the farm. Some 200 public gardens are available to conventional and organic cultivators. Each plot measures 25 X 40 feet. Registration is held on the first Monday in April. Livestock appears in the barn on Saturday and Sunday, 1-4 p.m. For information on farm tours and events call (937) 268-1312.

GEOLOGY

Possum Creek is a small tributary of the Great Miami River. It flows over glacial till deposited by the Wisconsinan continental glacier at least 12,000 years ago.

WILDLIFE

The Argonne Forest here is a mature beech-maple woodlot in the northwest corner of the park. The spot is also choked with shrubs, briar patches and honeysuckle. Oaks, cottonwoods, sycamores, and black cherry trees are also represented.

The park district has planted four tall grass prairies in the park. The three areas between the fishing ponds and Argonne Lake (vintage 1980) may represent the largest planted prairie in Ohio. In July and August these meadows become a "sea of grass" mixed with wildflowers reaching heights of eight feet. The prairie southwest of Argonne Lake was planted in 1990.

HISTORY

In September 1917, Null Hodapp, age 23, and his best friend, Ralph Clements, went to Camp Sherman in Chillicothe with 600 other draftees from Montgomery and Preble counties. Four years earlier, Hodapp and Clements had faced danger together when they were marooned by the Great Flood of 1913. They encountered worse danger in 1918. The two joined the 322nd Field Artillery Unit and were shipped to France. Their unit attacked strong German lines in the Argonne Forest, in the last and decisive Allied offensive of the war. Near the end of the battle, Clements was killed by shrapnel and died an hour before the Armistice was signed.

Back home in Dayton, Hodapp became a judge in the municipal and common pleas courts. He also became the owner and operator of an amusement park called Argonne Forest Park, in memory of Clements and the 322nd Field Artillery Unit. On his 400-acre property Hodapp built a small Coney Island-type amusement park with midway games, several shooting ranges, swimming area, concession stands, figure-eight auto track, dance hall, horseback riding, streetcars for overnight camping, battle reenactments, and fireworks on July 4 before crowds of 8,000-10,000 people. Attendance dropped during World War II. Hodapp failed in his attempt to move the Montgomery County Fairground to his location. He died in late 1945. Though some parcels were sold, the park district acquired 300 acres through arrangements with Hodapp's estate.

A hike through Argonne Forest today is something of an archeological journey. Keen observers will see the cement slab of the dance floor, remnants of three streetcars, and the old swimming pool. Argonne Lake covers the old race track.

JOURNAL

The forest, lakes, prairie and shrubs have hidden the former amusement park. In a decade or two only memories of its past glory will be visible.

Sugar Creek Metropark

The Three Sisters, a hoary and revered triumvirate of white oaks, have presided over their redoubtable slope for more than 550 years. They have seen the forest reduced to cornfields, and the cropland reverting back to forest. In spite of their many years, they look fit enough to carry on for another five centuries. It is said that the secrets of eternity rise from the sweet water of Sugar Creek to their roots, then spread, like gossip, into their brittle, intertwining branches.

LOCATION
Southwestern Greene County, Sugarcreek Township.

SIZE
596 acres.

ACCESS
From Xenia, go southwest on US 42 to Spring Valley, then turn right (west) on SR 725 to Bellbrook. Go left (south) on Waynesville Road in downtown Bellbrook. Just south of the village turn right on Ferry Road, and right on Conference Road, which takes you to the entrance on the right.

Accommodations: A primitive campground for groups is located next to the picnic area.

Trails: Five miles of trails are open daily (except Christmas and New Year's Day) from 8 a.m. to dusk. Trails are color-coded with lettered signposts at intersections. Study the trail map, available at the trailhead, before departing. A separate brochure on the Three Sisters Trail is available, too.

The reserve also boasts 6.5 miles of bridle trails, accessible from the Riding Center at the Wilmington Pike entrance, although horseback riding is not allowed on the footpaths described above. Rental horses are available.

Facilities: Archers can test their aim at the free, 50-target archery range located off Ferry Road. The Sugarcreek Archers maintain the site. Archers must bring their own equipment. Rest rooms are found at the picnic area, riding center, and archery range.

GEOLOGY
The last of three or four continental glaciers affecting the area, the Wisconsinan glacier, left behind a dense layer of sand, gravel, boulders, and clay (called till) about 12,000 years ago. A cigar-shaped deposit of the glacier called an esker, formed by sediments carried in a stream beneath the ice mass, rises near the Three Sisters at Point H on the map.

Though nobody knows for certain, this land may lie above a buried tributary of the ancient Teays River, which coursed northwest toward Indiana about a million years ago. The Wisconsinan glacier and its predecessors covered this vast river system under tons of sediment.

The swift streams of water rushing off the melting Wisconsinan glacier carved valleys in the till. Sugar Creek is one of these post-glacial streams. In the reserve, Sugar Creek has gnawed down to bedrock Ordovician-aged limestone dating back 450 million years. The rock is filled with the fossils of sea creatures that lived on the sea floor. The remains of these ancient animals mixed with other sediments to form the limestone (see Germantown Reserve).

White settlers found the water sweet tasting, hence the name Sugar Creek. Later, when sewage flowed into the stream, the water was everything but sweet. Waste treatment facilities have cleansed the water considerably, but noone is advised to drink it.

WILDLIFE
Somehow the Three Sisters missed the axe, lightning bolts, forest fires, and diseases. Test bores suggest they were already 50 years old when Christopher Columbus landed on Hispanola in 1492.

Indeed, these ancient ones inspire veneration and curiosity. White oaks that rise in a mature forest sport tall, straight trunks and narrow crowns; and their branches appear 40–50 feet above the ground. But the Three Sisters have stocky, squat trunks and wide-spreading crowns, suggesting that they grew in a clearing rather than a forest. Seeing the burly scars on the trunk (the former location of lower branches) loggers may have concluded the trunks were too knotty for timber. Later, farmers saw the advantage of letting them flourish because their sprawling limbs shaded livestock in summer.

At Sugarcreek Reserve, the best is yet to come. In the two decades or so that it has been a nature park, this former farmland has begun to change back to forest land. Look closely; notice how hundreds of small trees, many the same size and age, have migrated into the fields. Just before you reach Point O on the Three Sisters Trail map, look for the stand of wild black cherry trees (on the right). In 1968, corn grew on that spot. These youngsters are probably the offspring of the mammoth grandfather cherry that presides a few paces north (near Point N on the map).

American beech dominates the southeast corner of the reserve. Elsewhere, the forest supports a mix of oak, maple, hickory, walnut, and other hardwoods. Even tulip trees are returning in numbers. White settlers favored these straight trees for log homes and barns.

Sycamore trees love moist soil, which explains

their presence in floodplains and along stream banks. Sugar Creek Reserve protects a stand of sycamores that strangely thrives on the top of a ridge west of the picnic area. Park officials suspect the trees are fed by water that percolates beneath the ridge.

Wildflowers have rebounded, especially hepatica, bloodroot, large-flowered trillium, phlox, twinleaf, spring (purple) larkspur, and firepink. White snakeroot (white fuzzy flower heads) grows here. Consuming milk from cows that eat snakeroot can be fatal. Abraham Lincoln's mother supposedly died after drinking "snakeroot" milk.

The prairie planted in an old cornfield blooms from mid-July–Labor Day. Grasses called big bluestem, Indian switchgrass, and nodding rye live here, alongside flowers named royal catchfly (potentially threatened in Ohio), purple coneflower, compass plant, prairie dock, and tall coreopsis, to recall a few.

Birders will find the forest canopy teeming with warblers in the spring, including the yellow-rumped (myrtle), and yellow-throated varieties. Trained eyes will find these tiny triumphs—the golden-crowned kinglet, red-eyed vireo, fox sparrow, Louisiana waterthrush, and yellow-breasted chat. You also might see an indigo bunting, kingfisher, pileated woodpecker, red-tailed hawk, bobolink, great horned owl, and yellow-crowned night heron, an endangered critter in Ohio.

Coyotes have been seen in the preserve, but they will not disturb you. The biggest four-legged animal found in these woods is the whitetailed deer.

Bass, sunfish, daces, and minnows swim in Sugar Creek. Common snakes are the black rat, black racer, and water snakes.

HISTORY

Sugarcreek Reserve was the second property purchased (late 1960s) by the newly-created park district.

Local archers manage a 50-target range in one section of the reserve, an uncommon but creative recreational activity in a metropark. Recent neighborhood developments, Spring Lakes Park, and a new 18-hole golf course have increased the traffic and could intrude on the solitude of Sugarcreek Reserve.

Taylorsville Metropark

As it passes through this reserve, the Great Miami River, born 15,000 years ago from a shrinking glacier, is refreshed by spring-fed rivulets that emerge from ruptured layers of 450-million-year-old bedrock. The rock is limestone, composed of the shells and skeletons of extinct sea creatures all churned with other sediments. Now water oozes from the depths of the Earth. Is it the nectar of that venerable sea or a liquid remnant of the glacier?

LOCATION

Northeastern Montgomery County, Wayne Township.

SIZE

865 acres.

ACCESS

Leave I-70 at the exit for SR 202. Drive south on SR 202 for a half mile and turn right (west) on Taylorsville Road. Drive north (right turn) on Bridgewater Road (crossing over I-70) to its end at US 40. Turn right on US 40, then left .5 mile to the reserve entrance, marked by a wooden park sign. A sign says you have arrived at Location TR-5 in the reserve. Park here.

Trails: Some of the trails are moderately rugged by Ohio standards (piece of cake for Adirondackers), but easy to follow. They often become rocky, narrow, and steep in ravines, but benches appear every so often to rest weary legs. A half dozen connecting trails shorten the walk. Pick up a guide to the reserve (found in the parking area or shelter house) before setting out.

The famous Buckeye Trail passes through the reserve. From I-70 the "blue-blazed" foot trail traces the east bank of the river, crosses the dam, then splits. One trail heads straight north beside the old Miami & Erie Canal; the other goes east to the river then north along the west bank of the river. The trails converge again near the powerline on the west bank of the river.

Folks seeking a quick walk can hike the Forest Ridge Trail, a one-third-mile loop trail which starts at the shelterhouse, travels to the Rock Outcrop, to the overlook, and back to the start. Look for the trail guide at the shelterhouse.

Fishing & Boating: Fishing (license required) is permitted south of the dam. The Taylorsville Dam is a favorite canoeing destination, and a canoe pick-up road west of the dam (Cassel Road) is open April through October. Canoes are not allowed through the dam. Swimming is not allowed either.

Facilities: Picnic areas are located throughout the reserve. The departure site has drinking water (Baker pump) and rest rooms near the shelter-house.

Special Places & Events: Reserve naturalists hold a variety of nature programs in the park throughout the year. A schedule of events usually hangs in the bulletin board near the shelterhouse. Sledding hills are found at the TR-1 site off Brown School Road.

GEOLOGY

The landmark called "rock outcrop" near the shelterhouse reveals the geological history of the reserve. Some 450 million years ago (Ordovician geological period) this limestone was an ocean floor, a calcareous stew of dead sea creatures, mud, and other soggy sediments. When the ocean disappeared this limey soup, now on the surface, hardened into rock. The layer is jam-packed with fossils, but removing them is illegal.

The Great Miami River started as a storm sewer of the Wisconsinan glacier, the last ice mass to bulldoze over Ohio (18,000–12,000 years ago). The outwash of the glacier eventually formed a river, which knifed through the limestone and underlying layers. The rim of the limestone escarpment once served as the river bank.

Notice that a spring gushes from the base of the outcrop. It is one of many tiny springs in the reserve that recharge the river. Look for these fountains on the hiking trail. (Although the water looks pure, drinking it is not advised because many springs are refilled by surface water which may be contaminated.) Their streams have sculpted the ravines that you must trudge across on the trail.

At this spot in 1984, when nobody was watching, 375 tons of overhanging limestone slid off the cliff and piled up at the base of the wall. The boulders crushed a trail bridge. Park officials blamed the rock slide on a combination of factors such as seeping water erosion, freezing and thawing of water in cracks, tree roots wedging into cracks, and the vibrations of traffic on US 40. If left undisturbed, these factors will someday, perhaps thousands of years from now, swallow the highway.

WILDLIFE

Trees that typically grow in an Ohio hardwood forest can be appreciated here—oaks, beech, maples, hickory, tulip tree, black walnut, ash, and the like. "Wet feet" trees like sycamore, cottonwood, and willow grace the river banks. Clusters of planted pine and spruce struggle to hold their ground against encroaching hardwoods.

From mid-March to mid-May wildflowers such as skunk cabbage, bloodroot, trillium, hepatica, spring beauty, Virginia bluebell, and mayapple brighten the forest floor. By June, most of these little miracles have vanished because "leafed out" trees have stolen the sunlight and darkened the ground. Animals like deer become invisible in all that summer green camouflage. Color returns in autumn, and falling leaves open the canopy.

The Great Miami River is a corridor for migrating birds—waterfowl and warblers. Adept observers may count as many as 60 different species moving through the preserve during the spring and autumn migrations. The river, in fact, may be an ancient skyway, a path these nomadic birds have followed for millennia.

During the summer, woodland birds are hard to find amidst all the greenery. On very hot days, as is the case with all wise animals, they stay hidden in shade and motionless as much as possible. Birders will have better luck along the river where they might spot a great blue heron quietly fishing, or flush a noisy kingfisher.

The reserve has the usual year-round residents—chickadees, nuthatches, blue jays, and cardinals. You might hear the barred owl's emphatic eight-hoot toot more often in winter. Deer are easier to see in the colder months.

HISTORY

For centuries, the Great Miami River was an important waterway for the Native American tribes who lived here. Early white settlers also plied the waters in canoes, but as commerce increased the canoe was replaced by the canal boat.

A remnant of the Miami & Erie Canal, completed in 1845, runs through the west side of the preserve. It took 20 years to hand-dig the channel that linked Cincinnati, Dayton, and Toledo. The Buckeye Trail follows the old canal route. The foundations of a canal aqueduct still stand a couple hundred yards north of the dam.

The canal brought prosperity to the village of Tadmor, located at the intersection of the canal, National Road (US 40), the Great Miami River, and the Dayton-Michigan Railroad. Tadmor vanished after the canal and railroad died, and the National Road lost its traffic to the interstate highway.

The Taylorsville Dam was one of five flood control projects built in the early 1920s by the Miami Conservancy District. (The Easter Sunday flooding of Dayton in 1913 inspired the dam projects.) The land around the dam was managed as a recreational area by the Civilian Conservation Corps. When the CCC disbanded, the conservancy resumed management.

The park district, formed in 1964, began leasing the Taylorsville Dam acreage from the conservancy in the mid-1960s. The district has developed portions of the land for recreation but most of it has been set aside as a natural area. The conservancy still manages much of the land on the west bank of the river.

JOURNAL

July 5: Except for some matted grass seen in the early morning of the 90-degree day, I have seen no evidence of whitetailed deer, and few squirrels and chipmunks. That is not surprising; animals reduce their activity in extreme heat, plus the overwhelming greenery of the woods lets them hide easily, and escape unseen. Deer will simply freeze in their tracks and let hikers pass them undetected. In summer they survive by hiding; in leafless months they flee for their lives.

❖ ❖ ❖   *W A R R E N   C O U N T Y*   ❖ ❖ ❖
For information, contact Warren County Parks, 300 E. Silver St., Lebanon, OH, 45036, (513) 933-1109.

Landen Deerfield Park, 95 acres, Maineville. Hiking, bicycling, picnic area, athletic fields. Kesling Park, 17 acres, Red Lion-Five Point Road, Springboro. Picnic area, athletic fields. Also, Hatton Luken Park, Bowman Park, Ivins Memorial Park.

NORTHWEST

◆ ◆ ◆   A L L E N   C O U N T Y   ◆ ◆ ◆

Information contact the Johnny Appleseed Metropolitan Park District, 235 Ada Road, Lima, OH 45801, (419) 221-1232

Kendrick Woods Metropark

The former owners of this place almost turned Allen County's largest woodlot into a trailer court. Fortunately, at the last minute, they were persuaded to sell to the park district. The action saved a grove of venerable, regal oaks who have lived here for three centuries. These trees watched the militia of General "Mad" Anthony Wayne march on the Defiance Trail to the Battle of Fallen Timbers. The army that defeated the Indians, also brought white settlers who, in turn, defeated the forest.

LOCATION

Southwestern Allen County, Amanda Township. From Downtown Lima go west on SR 81 about 12 miles. Immediately after crossing the Auglaize River turn right (north) on Defiance Trail. The park entrance is a half mile ahead on the left. Park to the right of the rest rooms, near the trailhead.

SIZE

218 acres.

ACCESS

The park, open daily during daylight hours, offers five miles of trails, picnic area, playground, fishing and ice skating pond, rest rooms and drinking water. Folks in wheelchairs or pushing strollers can take the boardwalk, or All People's Trail.

Pick up an interpretive guide for the South Trail at the trailhead. Get to the South Trail via the Hickory Trail. The route goes through a grove of ancient hardwoods and along Six Mile Creek. The park district schedules nature walks and programs at Kendrick Woods during the year.

GEOLOGY

An issue of the park district's newsletter, Cider Press, acknowledges that the region lacks "the scenic hills and gorges of southern Ohio. Our rivers do not measure up to the mighty Ohio. We don't even have rocky hillsides or scenic overlooks."

Still, visitors can find beauty in this flat land from a different perspective. Here you have the feeling of being at the bottom of the sky, rather than at the top of the Earth.

Frozen tidal waves called continental glaciers shaped the surface into elongated undulations and spread a thick blanket of till (gravel, sand, clay, and other sediments) which became the fertile ground for the forests and farms of the region.

Certainly, there are slight changes in elevation, and nature has taken advantage of these thin distinctions. Your job is to detect the subtleties in this wild realm.

The water currents crawling through this level of the preserve, Six Mile Creek and the Auglaize River (forming the eastern border), appear vapid and cloudy most of the year. Auglaize means muddy, in French, the language of the first Europeans on the scene. The sleepy streams, of course, become devilish torrents after thaws and heavy rains.

As you traipse along the South Trail you cannot miss the whiff of sulfur. The odor comes from an artesian spring gurgling at the surface. According to the trail guide "the spring was formed when the water-bearing rock layer underground, called the aquifer, was either drilled into or naturally met the surface of the ground. A bubbling, flowing spring like this one indicates that the aquifer is under pressure from the layers of soil and rock above, thus causing the water to constantly flow out."

The swamp around the spring results from water seeping to the surface and spreading over the ground year-round. Grazing cattle drank from this water hole.

Another sulfur spring emerges near the Auglaize River. Local folks filling jugs at the spot called it the "Fountain of Youth" and claimed the water was good for health.

WILDLIFE

Somehow a small community of aged white

oaks, about 12–15 trees, avoided the axe. Others were not as lucky and their rotting stumps stand as tombstones. They are all that remains of the thick, mature forest that once covered Allen County.

They are joined by 55 other kinds of trees and shrubs in this predominantly oak-hickory woodland. Six other oaks (red, swamp white, pin, burr, black, and chinkapin) and three types of hickory (shagbark, pignut, and bitternut) grow in the deep woods. Sycamores, their branches reminiscent of crossed swords, arch over Six Mile Creek. Their partners in the floodplain include cottonwood, box elder, Ohio buckeye, black walnut, silver maple, among others.

You will find basswood, honeylocust, beech, bigtooth aspen, white and green ash, American and slippery elm, and pawpaw. Some of the shrubs represented are nannyberry, trumpet honeysuckle, and running strawberry bush.

Naturalists have counted more than 65 types of wildflowers on the forest floor. For a challenge, look for false mermaid, Greek valerian, lopseed, enchanter's nightshade, heart-leaved skullcap, and horsebalm. Wild columbine is supposedly abundant here. A three-acre prairie, planted in 1987, returns these blossoms to Allen County.

Birds are plentiful—85 species have been spotted, even a bald eagle, hermit thrush, yellow-crowned night heron, and yellow-bellied sapsucker. These creatures are endangered in Ohio.

Birders can fix their field glasses on these warblers: black-throated green, yellow-throated, myrtle, blackburnian, black and white, baybreasted, chestnut-sided, and American redstart. Try to find the redheaded woodpecker, ruby-crowned kinglet, rose-breasted grosbeak, eastern meadowlark, and many others. Hawks include the American kestrel, Cooper's and red-tailed.

The streams harbor reptiles such as the five-lined skink and northern water snake. The small-mouth salamander, an amphibian, inhabits these woods. The common woodland mammals thrive here—deer, squirrels, fox, mink, muskrat, raccoon, opossum and the rest.

HISTORY

The preserve is located along the historic Defiance Trail, the path taken by General Anthony Wayne to the Battle of Fallen Timbers on the Maumee River in August 1794. Avenging an American loss three years earlier, Wayne defeated a combined Indian force commanded by Tecumseh and Blue Jacket. Wayne's victory opened this area for white settlers. The new human inhabitants cut down the forest for farms, cities, roads, railroads, and industries—the march of uncontrolled progress.

By the 1960s, this woodlot, known as Strayer's Woods, became an anomaly, an isolated copse of tall timbers surrounded by a flat, open, checkerboard region of farms and small towns. When word got around that the landowners wanted to build a mobile home village here, conservationists persuaded the owners to sell the woods to the park district.

Using money from the estate of Florence Kendrick (in memory of her husband Ray) the park district purchased the property in 1976. More land was acquired in 1985 and 1991 to bring the total acreage to 218. The metropark opened in 1987. The Ohio Department of Natural Resources designated the woods, now called Kendrick Woods, a state nature preserve in May 1992.

◆ ◆ ◆   CRAWFORD COUNTY   ◆ ◆ ◆

For information, contact Crawford County Park District, 117 E. Mansfield St., Bucyrus, OH 44820-2302, (419) 562-8394.

Unger Park, 36 acres, Nevada Road, Bucyrus Township. Sandusky River, hiking, birdwatching, nature study, fishing, cross-country skiing, prairie garden.

◆ ◆ ◆   ERIE COUNTY   ◆ ◆ ◆

For information contact Erie Metroparks, 3910 E. Perkins Avenue, Huron, OH 44839, (419) 625-7783.

Castalia Quarry Reserve

The walls of the former limestone quarry show the signature of the last glacier, and provide a habitat for a dozen imperiled plants. An observation deck offers views into the old excavation and distant Sandusky Bay.

LOCATION
Margaretta Township.

SIZE
152 acres.

ACCESS
Take SR 101/412 from Sandusky, or SR 269 to Castalia. Continue southwesterly on SR 101. Just outside Castalia parking for the preserve will appear on the right; trails on the left.

Trails: The 1.8-mile perimeter trail, and shorter paths to the quarry floor, can be used by hikers and mountain bikers. Ecologically sensitive areas are off-limits to visitors. A wheelchair-accessible observation deck built by the Ohio Civilian Conservation Corps presents vistas of the quarry, Sandusky Bay, and Perry's Monument on South Bass Island on a clear day. Two picnic areas and rest rooms are available.

Glacial grooves in the rock can be seen along the trail. Though not as impressive as the grooves on Kelleys Island, these represent more opportunities to view the unique geological formation.

WILDLIFE

Birding is productive year-round. Turkey vultures nest in the cliffs and cuckoos in the woods. Hawks are commonly seen from trail vistas.

HISTORY

Stone from the quarry was used in the construction of the nearby Ohio Turnpike and the Edison and Bay bridges across Sandusky Bay. Wagner Quarries Company donated 110 acres to the park district in 1987. The rest, 42 acres north of SR 101, was purchased later.

Dupont Marsh State Nature Preserve

A corporate gift saved this riverine marsh for imperiled wetlands plants and fish. For humans the preserve is a gateway to marsh creatures, and to a rail-to-trail path across the county. Erie (County) Metroparks leases the site from the Ohio Department of Natural Resources, Division of Natural Areas and Preserves.

LOCATION

Central Erie County, Huron Township.

SIZE

114 acres.

ACCESS

From Huron, go south on River Road on the east side of the Huron River. In three miles the preserve entrance will be on the right (sharp turn) near a water tower. Leave your car in the parking lot.

Trails: Two trails depart from the preserve's parking area. To see the marsh, take a mile-long loop trail that features an observation platform. The Huron River Greenway, an abandoned railroad bed converted to a recreation trail, goes to Huron (north) and Milan (south). The preserve is open daily during daylight hours.

GEOLOGY

The two forks of the Huron River start near the Huron-Richland county line and flow northerly to a junction in Milan State Wildlife Area. Flat terrain along the river encouraged creation of riverine marshes as the river neared Lake Erie.

WILDLIFE

Roughly half the preserve is marshland along the east bank of the Huron River. The location of plant life depends on the depth of water. Cattail, burreed, and spatterdock grow in the shallows along the edge, while pondweeds and water-milfoil survive in deeper water. Rarities here include leafy blue flag, an endangered iris, and hairy-fruited sedge. Other specimens are water dock and pickerel weed.

In the 1970s, endangered fish called spotted gar, pugnose minnow, banded killifish, and blacknose shiner swam in these waters.

The marsh is a vital fish hatchery and refuge for waterbirds. Birders are apt to see great egrets, various herons, and armadas of waterfowl from the observation area.

HISTORY

The E.I. duPont deNemours Corporation, better known as DuPont Chemical Company, donated the wetland to the Ohio Chapter of The Nature Conservancy in 1977. The Ohio Division of Natural Areas and Preserves took possession in 1980, but did not open it to the public until 1996. DNAP leased the preserve to Erie Metroparks in early 1997, which will manage it for 30 years.

◆ ◆ ◆   HANCOCK COUNTY   ◆ ◆ ◆
For information contact Hancock Park District, 1833 Historical Courthouse, 819 Park Street, Findlay, OH 45840, (419) 425-7275

Oakwoods Nature Preserve

It is hard to tell that this place once was a limestone quarry and railroad yard. Shank Lake and Miller Quarry Pond remind us of this land's past and its future as a natural attraction. A nature center and prairie meadow enhance this rehab effort.

LOCATION

From Downtown Findlay head west on Sandusky Street.

SIZE

76 acres.

ACCESS

Just past I-75, turn left on CR 144. The entrance will be on the right before railroad tracks and I-75.

Trails: Loop trails named Prairie, Aurand Run, and Shank Lake total 1.4 miles. Eighteen-foot deep Shank Lake has an observation deck off Shank Lake Trail and fishing spots for bass, crappie and catfish.

Ah, stovepipe cuisine, canvas canopy. Who could ask for anything more?

Horseback riding is available with a permit.

Special Places & Events: A 1,260-foot boardwalk takes visitors from the parking lot to the Richard S. "Doc" Phillips Discovery Center, which features a "window on wildlife," meeting rooms, rest rooms, water, and natural history exhibits. A 1,000-foot boardwalk goes from the Discovery Center to Shank Lake. The center is named after a devoted nature lover, teacher and local preservationist.

Sections south of Aurand Run and around Miller Quarry Pond are nature sanctuaries.

GEOLOGY

The preserve's second-growth woods grows over a thin layer of glacial till atop Silurian limestone. Shank Lake drains into Aurand Run, a tributary of the Blanchard River. The hills, or rather mounds, in the preserve are made of the dirt removed above bedrock before excavation.

Oakwoods is hemmed in by farmland still in cultivation, active railroad tracks, and suburbia. The north stretches of the Aurand Run and Shank Lake trails follow an old railroad bed.

WILDLIFE

Wildflowers explode beneath the canopy in spring and later in the successional meadows. Prairie blossoms called tall coreopsis, gray-headed coneflower, and prairie dock open in July and August, and some last until asters arrive in September. These beauties were planted here in 1986 from stock in nearby Big Spring Prairie. Meadows are managed for food and nesting cover for small critters like rabbits, foxes, bluebirds, owls, and red squirrels.

Riverbend-Findlay Reservoir Area

Once an old Indian hunting camp above a bend in the Blanchard River, the forest and meadow at the "riverbend" now provides outdoor recreation opportunities and natural experiences for the current human occupiers.

LOCATION
Marion Township.

SIZE
Approximately 1,200 acres.

ACCESS
From Findlay drive east on Sandusky Street (SR 568). The north entrance to the park will be on the right (TR 241) just past the Marion Township Building. The south entrance, by Findlay Reservoir 1, is on CR 205, off SR 37. TR 207 traces the northern shore of Findlay Reservoir 2 from River Road (TR

208) to the east entrance on TR 234.

The Riverbend area north of the Findlay reservoirs offers two "activity" areas, four hiking trails, and fishing in the Blanchard River.

Big Oaks, so named for its large oaks, is the first activity area after entering the park from Sandusky Street. The location on River Road has picnic shelters and tables, amphitheater, drinking water, rest rooms, primitive camping (permit required), Payne Arboretum, and a playground. Oxbow Bend Activity Area has a picnicking area, water, rest rooms, playground, plus a pavilion for 200 people, and a mini-airport for model airplanes. Park naturalists stage activities at both locations.

Trails: A scenic section of the county's 20-mile Heritage Trail and 37-mile Old Mill Stream Bikeway follows the wooded corridor of the Blanchard River from where they enter the park at junction of TR 234 and Sandusky Street (west of the Riverbend entrance) and CR 205 by Findlay Reservoir 1. Anglers take this route to their favorite spots along the Blanchard River. Hikers must register at the park office on River Road to venture on these trails beyond park boundaries.

In Riverbend, 4.5 miles of trails called Old Oxbow, Meadow, and Woodland Loop depart from the activity areas and join the Heritage and Old Mill Stream routes. Old Oxbow (orange blazes) cuts across abandoned, dried out river channels from the Big Oaks area. Other trails are meadow Trail (blue

More, *metroparks*

Other Allen, Erie, Hancock County Parks

ALLEN COUNTY PARKS

Heritage Park, 81 acres, Reed Road, Shawnee Township. Hiking, picnicking, fishing, volleyball, ice skating, horseshoes, Rotary Riverwalk.

McLean-Teddy Bear Park, 55.5 acres, North Dixie Highway, Bath Township. Braille Discovery Trail for visually-impaired humans, pond fishing, nature trail, picnicking, playground, horseshoes.

Ottawa Metropark, 214 acres, on SR 81, east of Lima. Lima Lake offers fishing, swimming at a separate pond, amphitheater, picnic area, camping, boating.

Allen County Farm Park, Bath Township, features a large farm barn, playing fields, volleyball, and horsehoes. Reservations only.

ERIE COUNTY PARKS

Coupling Reserve, 20 acres, SR 13 (Mud Brook Road). Railroad cars are bunkhouses, hiking, picnic area, sledding, cross-country skiing, canoe rental.

Edison Woods Reserve, 1,400 acres, SR 61 (Ceylon Road), Berlin Township. Features fields, oak forest, sandstone cliffs, trails (seven miles) for hikers, cross-country skiers, horse riders.

James H. McBride Arboretum, 57 acres, campus of Bowling Green University, Firelands Campus near Huron. Parker Lake, meadows, trails, wood lot.

Hoffman Forest Reserve, 40 acres, Berlin Township. Outdoor education programs.

Osborn Recreation Area, park headquarters, ball fields, picnic shelters, swimming pool, trails, fishing ponds, garden plots, Frost Center.

Pelton Park, 20 acres. Woods, picnicking, hiking, cross country skiing, wildflowers.

Birmingham School Park, three acres. Former school yard.

HANCOCK PARK DISTRICT SITES

Blue Rock Nature Preserve, 11 acres, Bank Street in Findlay. Reclaimed dump has trail, meadow, woods, observation deck, pond, picnic area.

Litzenberg Memorial Woods, 227 acres, US224/SR 15. Woods, historic farm, ravines, trails, Blanchard River, observing deck.

Old Mill Stream Parkway, a 23-mile canoe route along the Blanchard River.

blazes) and Woodland Loop (red). The latter path loops through a young forest (40 years old) of hawthorn, elm, box elder, locust, and hackberry.

The dikes around the reservoir offer more hiking (and jogging) opportunities of various lengths, though their appeal is limited. The outside perimeter (both reservoirs) covers 4.2 miles. Distance around Reservoir 2 is 4.1 miles, while the perimeter of Reservoir 1 is 1.9 miles.

Horsemen can ride their mounts in open areas below the dikes. The same area is generally available for snowmobiling and cross-country skiing. The slopes off the dikes are good for sledding. Horses, bicycles, and snowmobiles cannot ride on the dikes.

Fishing & Boating: Fishers and boaters enjoy their sports at the reservoirs. Boat ramps and parking are located near the south and east entrances. Boat length limits are 10-26 feet. Motors up to 9.9 horsepower are allowed on Reservoir 2, while Reservoir 1 accepts electric motors up to six horsepower. Canoers face portages at lowhead dams before and after the 90 degree bend. Swimming is not allowed in the reservoirs nor river.

Bluegills, bass (smallmouth, largemouth, and white), channel catfish, yellow perch, bullhead, crappie, carp, and walleye await the angler's offering. Some 7.5 miles of shorelines is open for bank fishermen but they will have to contend with riprap in places. The lakes are periodically stocked, and given "structure" in the form of submerged Christmas trees. Ice fishing for panfishing is popular when the park district says the ice is thick enough.

HISTORY

Findlay Reservoir 2, completed in 1971, holds five billion gallons and is Ohio's largest upground reservoir. The reservoirs have a combined total of 815 surface acres. Water for the reservoirs comes from the Blanchard River and wells at Limestone Ridge near Vanlue.

◆ ◆ ◆   LUCAS   COUNTY   ◆ ◆ ◆

The Metropolitan Park District of the Toledo Area was created in 1928. It manages nine parks covering some 6,700 acres. Oak Openings Preserve is one of the largest metroparks in the state and a rare wildlife paradise. Folks longing for a walk along the Maumee River, a state scenic river, can go to Bend View, Farnsworth, Providence and Side Cut metroparks.

To learn more, contact, Metroparks of the Toledo Area, 5100 West Central Avenue, Toledo, OH 43615, (419) 535-3050

Oak Openings Preserve

This preserve protects one of the rarest and most unique habitats in the state, if not the world—an oak opening. More than 1,000 different plants flourish in this bounteous place. The cornucopia of life includes the largest assemblage of rare and threatened plants and animals in Ohio. With so much life at risk, it is no surprise that conservationists have declared the oak openings and nearby savannas a globally threatened habitat.

LOCATION
Western Lucas County, Swanton Township.

SIZE
3,668 acres.

ACCESS
From I-475 on the west side of Toledo, travel west on SR 2 for 8 miles. SR 295 joins SR 2 at the Toledo airport and both roads continue west. In a mile, the roads split. Take SR 295 south (left) for a half mile then bear right on Wilkins Road. Follow Wilkins Road for 2.5 miles to its end, then go right (west) on Oak Openings Parkway. Turn at the next right and park at the lot for Mallard Lake and the Buehner Walking Center.

Trails: Oak Openings Preserve teases the hiker with seven marked trails totaling 28.1 miles, including its famous 17-mile loop around the perimeter of the park land. Beyond this, hikers can ramble down 50 miles of unmarked fire lanes, and a 5.5-mile stone-surfaced all-purpose trail. That's nearly 85 miles of foot trails! Generally trails are well-marked and easy to follow. The trail map on the park brochure is detailed. Merging fire lanes may cause a moment of indecision, however. Frequent visitors seeking new trails might try those unblazed paths.

In addition, 23 miles of trails beckon horseback riders. The riding center is located on Jeffers Road.

If you can only choose one path, take the Sand Dunes Trail. Before leaving, grab a park brochure (which includes a trail map) and study the big trail map at the Buehner Walking Center.

Folks in wheelchairs or pushing strollers can enjoy the .6-mile Lake Circuit Trail (aqua blazes) that circles Mallard Lake. Small kids might prefer this short hike, which features an observation deck on the west shore.

A special four-mile trail for cross-country skiers begins at Evergreen Lake. You will find rest rooms and a warm fire at a shelter halfway on the trail. Call (419) 382-7669 for skiing conditions. Skating is permitted on Mallard Lake when the ice is thick enough. (Call first.)

Fishing: Fishing is permitted at Evergreen, Springbrook, and Mallard Lakes (the latter only for children 14 years and under).

Special Places & Events: The Buehner Walking Center has rest rooms and drinking water. Please deposit your trash in the receptacles if you picnic at Mallard Lake. Group camping sites are available to youth and educational organizations, but reservations are required. The center also is a good place to access the north and south legs of the Wabash Cannonball Bike Trail. Follow Wilkins Avenue north to the north leg, an abandoned rail bed going through the preserve, or south to the southern leg. Oak Openings Lodge can be reserved for meetings and social events. The dormitory and food service can handle 52 guests.

GEOLOGY

To understand how this land received the gift of so much plant life, we have to journey back 10,000 years or so when water, not vegetation, covered this land. Back then, a large freshwater lake, one of Lake Erie's predecessors, flooded much of northwestern Ohio. The lake level reached far inland because the Wisconsinan glacier blocked the Niagara/St. Lawrence outlet to the east. Rivers and glacial meltwater carried fresh water and sediments (sand, silt, etc.) into the series of lakes on the same site, known as Lake Warren, Lake Wayne, or Lake Lundy, depending on the location of its shoreline. The water level of Lake Warren, for example, was 93 feet higher than Lake Erie's.

Sand deposited off the western and northwestern shores of the ancient lake (off the shore of eastern Michigan) traveled to the flat beaches on the southwestern and southern shores (Ohio) by way of southbound longshore currents. When the ice jam finally broke, the lake drained and left the beaches high and dry.

At first, the landscape probably resembled a flat, sandy, barren plain. Quickly, though, wind dried the plain and began blowing sand into shifting dunes. The terrain now looked corrugated and wind swept.

In Ohio the sand belt stretched for 25 miles and varied in width from 3–7 miles. The dunes continued into Michigan. The sand ridges now rise from 15–50 feet above their clay base. Water drains slowly (if at all) in this sandy area, and may settle within three feet of the surface. Where the sand is thin between sand ridges, swamp forests or bogs commonly form.

The soil on the crest of sandy ridges tends to be acidic, due to decomposing vegetation. However, in depressions it is usually slightly alkaline because it lays just above glacial till (gravel, silt, rocks, etc.) that is alkaline. These slight variations in soil pH levels add to the diversity, and mystery of the oak openings.

Swan Creek, one of two currents naturally draining the sand belt, avoids disturbing the highest dunes as it snakes through the preserve. In places, you can see where the current has cut below the sand layer and into the clay. Dammed tributaries have created Mallard Lake, Springbrook Lake, and Ever-

green Lake (the biggest pond in park).

WILDLIFE

The geological forces that sculpted this terrain created six distinct habitats in the oak openings.

Two of the habitats are found on the dunes themselves. One setting has widely spaced black and white oak, and some red oak, growing on the top of the ridges. Black oak seedlings grow best in dry and open areas, which explains why they have found a home on the sandy ridges. This habitat also sponsors bracken and sweet ferns, huckleberry, dewberry, shrubby St. John's wort, New Jersey tea, everlasting, wintergreen, wild indigo, chokeberry, lupine, sweet pea, butterfly weed, and others.

Prairie-type plants, like little bluestem grass, Indian grass, coreopsis, and sunflowers thrive on the dunes and abandoned farm fields. Some of these plants are remnants of the prairie vegetation that moved into Ohio during a warm spell 4,000 years ago. These plants could grow beneath the scattered oaks. Butterflies (fritillaries and monarchs), honeybees, and sand (digger) wasps are abundant in this area.

At the dunes, study the small, delicate details—the footprints of beetles (gray tiger and brown beetles) and birds, the twisting path of a hognose snake, or the thin, crescent-shaped traces of windblown grass or a tree branch on the sand. Look for ripples on the dunes, and the different colors in the sand.

Small swamp forests rise in the hollows between dunes. In this living place, you are apt to find pin oak, red oak, black cherry, blackgum, pawpaw, spicebush, and bigtooth aspen trees. The ferns (cinnamon, interrupted and royal) grow to great heights, as do clumps of buttonbush, blackberry, spikenard, bedstraw, spicebush, white baneberry, stinging nettle, meadowsweet (spirea), and wild lily-of-the-valley.

In the scattered bogs, also found at the base of sand dunes, look for speckled alder, willows, meadowsweet, buttonbush, elderberry, berry patches, skunk cabbage, marsh marigold, jack-in-the-pulpit, spotted jewelweed (touch-me-not), yarrow, and marsh ferns.

The Swan Creek floodplain supports typical bottomland plants such as green ash, sycamore, walnut, silver maple, basswood, box elder, plus wood nettle, smartweed, giant ragweed, and lizard's tail. This type of habitat is not unique to the oak opening and can be found along other floodplains in northwestern Ohio.

The sixth habitat of the oak openings region—the wet prairie, or savanna—is best viewed at nearby Irwin Prairie State Nature Preserve or Kitty Todd Preserve (owned by The Nature Conservancy)—though some elements exist here. These moist areas look like typical wide-open grasslands with clusters of shrubs and small trees. Many plants associated with wet prairies are found in the Oak Openings Preserve.

The evergreen stands of red, white, and Scotch pines, spruce and fir were planted by relief workers nearly 60 years ago. Many have become diseased, or are dying of old age (Scotch pines). Since these are not native Ohio trees, the land will be allowed to return to its natural condition.

Edwin L. Moseley studied the vegetation of the sand belt back in the late 1920s. He recorded 715 plant species in his 1929 book. Sixty-one of these plants were found in only two other Ohio counties, and 168 species were more common here than the rest of Ohio. He counted 17 kinds of asters, and 20 varieties of goldenrods. Since his report, almost 300 more plants have been discovered and recorded on the inventory.

A recent park district survey of the flora and fauna revealed the existence of 157 protected species in the preserve. That is the largest gathering of endangered and threatened life in any preserve in Ohio.

In dry areas, look for these endangered plants—Junegrass, southern club moss, plains muhlenburgia, southern hairy panic grass, Canada hawkweed, limestone rockcress, Carolina whitlow-grass, narrow leaf pinweed, prairie tick-foil, sessile tick trefoil, dotted horsemint, hoary mountain mint, one-flowered wintergreen, green-flowered wintergreen, fern-leaf false foxglove, and old field toadflax. Eighteen threatened and 17 potentially threatened plants enlarge this grouping of rarities.

Wet areas provide a sanctuary for rare sedges (Bicknell's, hay, pale umbrella), grass-like beak rush, Atlantic blue-eyed grass, Greene's and inland rush, long-bracted orchid, yellow lady's slipper, purple fringed orchid, bushy aster, Missouri ironweed, spathulate-leaved sundew, prairie gentian, soapwort gentian, Bicknell's geranium, fire weed, cross-leaved milkwort, gay wings, Canada plum, and Skinner's foxglove. Add to this list northern blue-eyed grass, thought to be extinct in Ohio, and 20 threatened and 27 potentially threatened species.

Tachysphex pechumani, a small sand wasp, is the latest discovery at Oak Openings. The insect is so rare it lacks a common name. It is known to exist only in isolated spots in New Jersey's pine barrens and Michigan's Pinckney Recreation Area.

The mostly black bug burrows into sand to lay eggs. It stuffs the tiny tunnel with insects so that young, hatching wasps have food. Close up, the male measures only .5-.75 inches, while the larger female grows from .75–1 inch. Females have orange antennae, which distinguishes them from other wasps. Males have amber-colored wing bases.

Other endangered insects found here are the Persius dusky wing, frosted elfin, regal fritillary, and Karner blue butterflies, and the unexpected cycnia and brown satyr moths. The Karner blue butterfly has not been seen since 1989, however. If you see one, report it and mark its location.

The Karner blue, Persius dusky wing, and frosted elfin deposit their eggs solely on wild lupine. The plant is the larval host for these struggling butterflies. If the lupine declines, so do these beautiful aviators. To improve the chances for these butterflies, park managers must bolster the lupine population by controlling the spread of shrubs and trees by trimming and mowing.

Birders should keep their eyes peeled for a glimpse of these endangered birds—American bittern, northern harrier, bald eagle, peregrine falcon, king rail, sandhill crane, winter wren, magnolia and Canada warbler (these all being migratory, stopover birds), sedge wren, hermit thrush, golden-winged warbler, and lark sparrow, the latter being nesters in the preserve.

Some unusual birds, unusual because they are not commonly seen in northwestern Ohio, pay a visit—prairie, pine and yellow-throated warblers, summer tanager, and blue grosbeak. The preserve, of course, claims a long list of common and unprotected birds—rufous-sided towhee, bluebird, wood thrush, and common flicker being in this company.

Though it has not been observed recently, the endangered Indiana bat dwells in the preserve, along with the evening bat, considered a rarity. The oak opening region is one of the last Ohio habitats for the badger, a special interest (potentially threatened) mammal.

The blue-spotted salamander, an endangered amphibian, finds refuge here, along with four "special interest" reptiles, notably Blandings turtle and the poisonous eastern massasauga rattlesnake, though the latter has not been sighted for awhile.

The preserve has a large herd of whitetailed deer, and its streams attract muskrat, mink, and long-tailed weasel. The red fox, gone from the region in 1900, is common again, but the gray fox is infrequently seen.

Earlier studies identified 70 kinds of fungi living in the openings. Twenty to 30 years ago, naturalists talked about the lichen prairies in the preserve—good open spots to view the stars, they said. The Evergreen Trail boasts the preserve's most colorful colonies of lichens and mosses.

HISTORY

Humans arrived at the oak openings about 12,000 years ago, judging from their discarded artifacts. But they apparently never established a permanent settlement in the sands. The sand ridges became trails for early European explorers and trappers traveling from Detroit to the Maumee River. (The paths probably were first blazed by deer). Hiking and camping in the "opening" was easier than trudging through the surrounding swamp forest, known as the Great Black Swamp.

Settlers began "developing" the openings in the 1830s. They cleared the land of timber oaks, plowed the prairie, and drained the wetlands with a series of ditches. Because of the high degree of leaching in the sandy soil, farmers countered with great amounts of fertilizer that found its way into the soil and water.

Crushed limestone used in road building changed acidic soils to alkaline soil along roadsides. This allowed new vegetation to enter the area. Lime also blew into the preserve from adjacent farmland.

Local farmers robbed orchids from the forest and sold them for a pennies in Toledo along with their vegetables and fruits. The buyers tried to plant the orchids in their own gardens, but most discovered too late that few orchids survive transplantations. The forest and dunes also were ravaged by mushroom hunters, wildflower pickers, motorcyclists, and folks who simply liked to frolic in the sand (not realizing the damage they were doing).

The coming of the automobile brought more people into the region and put greater stress on the openings. By the mid-1920s much of the original oak savanna had vanished.

The park district was founded in 1928. One of its first projects was saving the oak openings. In 1932, 67-acre Springbrook Park, the preserve's predecessor, opened. More land was purchased as funds became available, and today the preserve protects 3,668 acres.

JOURNAL

December 27, 1993. I am reading old accounts of the vanished wildlife that once lived here and enriched this land. For instance, 15 pairs of sandhill cranes nested in the area until 1875. Today, a few cranes may stop briefly to rest and refuel before continuing their migration.

A metroparks naturalist named Paul Goff wrote about the preserve "having an abundance of hognosed snakes." That was back in 1968. Today, one kind of hognosed snake, the eastern hognose, is considered a rare find in the preserve.

We mourn the loss of the creatures who have disappeared.

Pearson Metropark

This verdant relict of the Great Black Swamp forest survives today thanks to a newspaper reporter's 20-year campaign to liberate these trees from the grip of local bankers. Long ago local folks called the place the Bank Lands because banks held it as a security on loans. Now it's public land and everybody's collateral for the future.

LOCATION
Eastern Lucas County, City of Oregon.

SIZE
320 acres.

ACCESS
Traveling on I-280 southbound motorists should exit at Starr Avenue (or SR 2, Navarre Road, see below) and head east, then right (south) on Lallendorf Road, and left into the park entrance (one-way road). Northbound travelers on I-280 should exit at Wheeling Road and go right (north) a short distance, then right (east) on Navarre Road/SR 2, left on Lallendorf Road, and an immediate right at the park entrance. Park in the lot on the right just past the Packer-Hammersmith Center. The one-way road through the park exits on Starr Avenue.

Trails: From the parking lot proceed to the modern Packer-Hammersmith Center, dedicated in 1988. Visit the "window on wildlife." open daily from 7 a.m.–dark (the same as the park hours) and grab a trail map before departing. Both footpaths begin at the nature center.

Heading east from the center the 1.3-mile Black Swamp Trail (orange trail markers) rambles through a remnant of the Great Black Swamp forest. Bear right at the first fork (start of the loop). Ahead, the trail splits near a gazebo, a good spot for watching wildlife. The Wood Thrush Trail, also 1.3 miles, heads west from the center, crosses the driveway and visits the Pearson Memorial. Follow the blue-blazed path into an open area, and bear right at the first junction. (The path to the left goes to a lake.) The loop begins ahead at the edge of the woods. You choose the way. Each leg wanders through field and forest.

The park also features a 3.3-mile bicycle trail and a 2.9-mile jogging trail around the perimeter. These trails are designed for faster-paced folks.

Special Places & Events: Children enjoy the pedal-boats that can be rented at the Lake Activities Center. In the winter, the pond is lighted for ice skating, and cross-country skiing is permitted on all trails.

Pearson Metropark also attracts many people to its numerous softball fields, tennis courts, soccer field, picnic areas, and playgrounds. Restrooms are located at the nature center, soccer field, lake activities area, and tennis courts.

GEOLOGY
Pearson Metropark is a fragment of the Great Black Swamp, a vast swamp forest that once covered much of northwestern Ohio. The forest arose on the lake floor (Lake Erie's predecessor), which stretched from western New York to Fort Wayne, Indiana some 13,000 years ago. Water running off the Wisconsinan glacier and surrounding countryside filled Lake Maumee.

When the glacier withdrew farther north into Canada, outlets opened and Lake Maumee drained through the St. Lawrence/Niagara gateway. It left behind a flat plain more than 100 miles long and 30–40 miles wide. The Great Black Swamp sprawled out on this plain.

The impermeable clay soil of this plain stopped water from percolating into the earth, and the level land retarded drainage. Consequently, this flatland remained soggy most of the year. Plants took root as the temperatures warmed.

WILDLIFE

The woodland canopy in this natural area boasts a variety of mature hardwoods, such as sugar and red maple, American beech, basswood (linden), swamp oak, shagbark hickory, sycamore and cottonwood. Dutch elm disease wiped out the impressive stands of elm. Their stumps and rotting trunks remind us of their former glory.

Pawpaw, ironwood, spicebush, redbud, and dogwood dominate the understory, the growth area between the forest floor and canopy represented by smaller trees and shrubs.

On the ground, a bouquet of wildflowers blooms according to Nature's staggered schedule. These miracles include snakeroot purple cress, stinging nettle, spring beauty, trillium, jack-in-the-pulpit, wild ginger, wild geranium, and garlic mustard.

In spring, the woods brighten with warblers. Sharp eyes may spot an endangered hermit thrush, or a northern oriole, red-eyed vireo, ovenbird, scarlet tanager, American redstart, wood thrush, downy and hairy woodpeckers, and Acadian flycatcher. The sharp-shinned hawk, designated a special interest (potentially threatened) bird in Ohio, and the great horned and screech owls are less frequent guests.

HISTORY

The metropark honors George W. Pearson, an East Toledo resident and a reporter for The Blade, Toledo's daily newspaper. Pearson's many articles about the swamp forest inspired hundreds of citizens to join his effort to save it as a park.

For many years the property was known as the Bank Lands because banks held it as a security on loans. The park district bought the first parcel, a 280-acre tract, right off the auction block, using money from an anonymous donor. A fundraising scheme called "Living Memorials," where donors get their names "plaqued" and tacked to trees secured cash to buy the remaining 40 acres. The park was dedicated on August 30, 1934.

One benefit of establishing the park in the early 1930s was that it created jobs. Beautifying the Great Black Swamp cured a few woes of the Great Depression. Laborers working for the Works Progress Administration and Civilian Conservation Corps built many of the park's facilities, notably the distinctive stonework. Workers dug the manmade ponds (renovated in 1986–87) with picks and shovels.

The Packer-Hammersmith Center pays tribute to a trio of school teachers whose hefty bequests built the nature education facility. The teachers were Dorothy Packer-Hammersmith, Edward Packer, and George Hammersmith. The center was dedicated in 1988.

Secor Metropark

It is hard to believe that the long, rolling mound yonder, the one topped by oaks and wildflowers, once was a naked sand dune on the beach of an ancient lake. Towering tulip trees also spread their roots wide in the sandy and soggy forest.

LOCATION

Northwestern Lucas County.

SIZE

600 acres.

ACCESS

From I-475 travel west on US 20 (Central Avenue) about 4.5 miles to the entrance on the left side of the highway. Follow Tupelo Way, the entrance drive, a mile to the Nature Discovery Center.

Trails: Obtain a park brochure at the Nature Discovery Center (more on this facility later) and go to the trailhead for the Woodland Pond, Forested Dune, and Trillium trails, located behind and to the right of the center. Follow the blue markers of the Woodland Pond Trail. The All-Purpose Trail (3.4 or 2.7 miles) is designed for joggers, bicyclists, and for visitors traveling in wheelchairs and strollers.

Special Places and Events: The nature center, rededicated in 1990 after a facelift, brings people, especially children, closer to nature. Toddlers can crawl through a chipmunk tunnel, a treehouse teaches children about life in the forest canopy. Birds and other critters can be observed at the "Window on Wildlife", a picture window looking out on birdfeeders and other critter attractions. Hands-on exhibits, drinking water and rest rooms also are located in the center.

The park also has three picnic areas, featuring open spaces for outdoor games, a playground (Walnut Grove only), toilets, and drinking water.

GEOLOGY

This park lies at the edge of the oak openings region of Northwestern Ohio, a land characterized by forested sand dunes and shallow, swampy areas. You will walk beside some of these dunes on the Forested Dune Trail.

For about 10,000 years, the lakeshore of Lake Erie's predecessor, Lake Warren, extended farther inland because the Wisconsinan glacier blocked the natural outlet (the Niagara-St. Lawrence valley) for accumulating water.

Glacial meltwater and rivers to the north (Michigan) dumped sand and heavier sediment into the lake. Southbound longshore currents carried the lightweight sand to the southwestern coast of the lake, then waves distributed it on flat beaches and offshore shallows.

When the ice jam broke the lake drained, leaving its former beach and shore high and dry. Wind then dried the sand and tossed it into shifting dunes. Eventually, vegetation sank roots and sta-bilized most of the dunes. (See Oak Openings Preserve.)

Prairie Creek courses through the northwestern third of the park before entering Tenmile Creek. One of its diminutive tributaries, Wiregrass Creek, has traced a shallow trough in the southwestern corner of the park. Both of these currents expose the layer of sandy topsoil on their banks. Beneath the sand is a bed of impermeable clay, which explains why water collects in the hollows between sand ridges and gives rise to the trees of the wet woods.

WILDLIFE

The wet forest in Secor Metropark sponsors the growth of buxom tulip trees, black cherry, beech, basswood (linden), black walnut, sprinkled with some oaks on the ridgetops. Note that many of these trees have buttressing trunks, meaning their roots have spread farther than normal for extra support in the unstable sandy topsoil.

Various oaks rim Woodland Pond. Their de-composing leaves emit tannic acid and give the pond its dark color. A pair of white oaks, the oldest trees in the park, stand sentry in front of Wolfinger Cemetery.

The understory, the trees growing below the forest canopy, consists of black gum, spicebush, pawpaw, sassafras, and flowering dogwood. Secor, in fact, boasts the largest concentration of native dogwoods in northwestern Ohio.

At ground level, ferns (cinnamon, interrupted, royal) and wildflowers called bloodroot, cut-leaf toothwort, garlic mustard, jack-in-the-pulpit, jewel-weed (touch-me-not), white baneberry (doll's eyes), mayapple, wild geranium, and stinging nettle display their colors and shapes.

Common woodland animals dwell here—rac-coon, downy woodpecker, flicker, tufted titmouse, and fox squirrel, among others. Tracks in the sandy soil gave away the presence of deer.

In the meadow are dogwoods, milkweed, Queen Anne's lace, yarrow, sensitive fern, berry patches, asters, thistles, common vetch, and others. Black oak (which likes open areas), blazing star, tall coreopsis, bergamot, prairie dock, lupine, puccoon, and big and little bluestem grasses flourish in the planted prairie.

The prairie blossoms arrived en masse during a warm spell 4,000 years ago. Though temperatures later cooled, sparking the comeback of the decidu-ous forest, the prairie persisted in isolated pockets. Settlers wiped out most of the native prairie remnants in Lucas County.

In these open areas, you might see birds like the woodcock (spring), red-winged blackbird, goldfinch, bobwhite quail, ring-necked pheasant, brown thrasher, bluebirds, and sparrows. Hawks may fly overhead hunting for field mice.

Other aviators include swallowtail, monarch, crescent, cabbage white, and sulfur butterflies. Grasshoppers, honeybees, ladybugs, and garter snakes reside in the fields, too. Furry critters such as the red fox, ground hog, and cottontail rabbit prefer this habitat.

HISTORY

Oddly, the metropark owned a parking lot at the corner of Jefferson and Erie in downtown Toledo. That busy corner was given to the park district in 1941 by Arthur J. Secor in memory of his parents Joseph K. and Elizabeth T. Secor.

The profit from the parking lot paid for the park land in 1949. The park opened in September 1953, followed in 1959 by the Nature Discovery Center. The proceeds from the 1985 sale of the parking lot funded most improvements at the Nature Discovery Center, rededicated in 1990.

The Wolfinger family used to live on this land. Their family cemetery is preserved on the park grounds.

The Shepherst Memorial pays tribute to J. Max Shepherst, the park district's first director-secretary. Shepherst was one of the leading advocates for the preservation of the oak openings region.

Swan Creek Preserve

Don't be fooled by the placid pace of meandering Swan Creek. Like a restless snake, this current has shed its skin, scattering fragments of flesh in the form of oxbow-shaped wetlands in its floodplain. Examining these oxbows—sometimes ponds, sometimes morasses, sometimes dry—is one of the treats in this suburban metropark.

LOCATION
Lucas County, South Toledo.

SIZE
417 acres.

ACCESS
Leave I-475 at the exit for SR 2 (Airport High-way) and travel east a little more than a couple of miles to the entrance on the right. Park at the lot for the Yager Center. Another entrance is located on Glendale Avenue.

Trails: After parking, pick up a park brochure and trail map at the Yager Center, which features outdoor nature exhibits, the indoor "Window on Wildlife", drinking water, and rest rooms with out-door entrances. The park has five nature paths, none measuring more than 1.5 miles, and a 3.3-mile All Purpose Trail for bicyclists, joggers, and recreational walkers.

The longest footpath, the North Trail, begins to the east of the Yager Center, and swings northeast (follow blue blazes) to pavement and a wooden observation deck that overlooks Swan Creek. Folks in wheelchairs and pushing strollers can reach this spot, too. Birdwatching is a favorite pastime at this view. Departing from the Yager Center, the All-Purpose Trail wanders into the northwest section of the park. Another connecting spur travels to the Glendale Avenue entrance. Cross-country skiers can use all the trails.

GEOLOGY

Swan Creek makes curling brushstrokes as it wanders through this preserve. The scenic S-shaped curves are called meanders, which occur only when a stream passes over flat terrain.

Though Swan Creek looks peaceful it continues an earth-moving process that it has carried out for centuries. Look carefully at the creek bank. The current quickly washes away loose bits or chunks of dirt, largely clay. This soil is composed of fine clay particles and silt that washed into a large lake (Lake Erie's predecessor) that grew in front of the stalled Wisconsinan glacier around 10,000 years ago. Tree roots, relieved of soil by the creek, dangle over the water.

The sediment lifted by the current upstream may be dumped downstream at places where the water slows, such as the inside of bends or behind logs and other obstacles that fall into stream. Sand bars, tiny islands, new banks, or small beaches may form in these slack areas.

During the spring flood period and after heavy rains Swan Creek becomes a wild current. It will overflow its banks and inundate the floodplain. It might even form a new channel, as it has done many times already, by cutting through the neck of a curve. The abandoned, horseshoe-shaped channel, like a snake's discarded skin, becomes a stagnant oxbow pond.

Floods may occasionally freshen some of these ponds; some become intermittent pools. Those farthest from the everchanging current may dry up entirely and host lush vegetation.

Water takes a long time to drain from and percolate through the clay-based floodplain soil. This creates swampy conditions.

WILDLIFE

The soggy swamp forest at Swan Creek sustains plants that can stand being flooded from time to time. These include trees like sycamore, willow, black walnut, and cottonwood on the creek banks, and elm, ash, and red maple. Aspen, beech, dogwood, black cherry, mulberry, Ohio buckeye, bladdernut, tulip tree, and butternut (a potentially threatened species) reside in the preserve. Combined, 44 types of trees have been counted.

Arrowhead, purple cress, and stinging nettle might be some of the first wildflowers to settle in the swamp area. More than 180 species of blossoms have been recorded, notably jack-in-the-pulpit and beauties such as poor man's pepper (peppergrass), deadly (climbing) nightshade, Virginia creeper, lizard's tail (look for an arching flower-head), gall-of-the-earth, beggartick, twisted stalk (a tiny lily with a twisting stalk), black snakeroot (supposedly a healer) and white snakeroot (supposedly a killer if cow's milk containing its toxin is consumed by humans).

Nine ferns thrive here. Look for the interrupted, ostrich and rattlesnake ferns.

Sometimes a badger (a protected mammal in Ohio) lives in the preserve. Otherwise, expect the regulars to appear—red and gray foxes, deer, woodchuck, rabbit, mink, striped skunk, and others.

Along the creek you are apt to see a belted kingfisher swooping for food, or a great blue heron stabbing the current with its beak. Seventy-four other birds join the preserve's checklist. Try to find the Swainson's thrush, the nighthawk, scarlet tanager, evening grosbeak, indigo bunting, wood duck, northern oriole, golden-crowned kinglet, and bobwhite quail.

Thirteen reptiles (turtles and snakes) and 11 brands of amphibians might be identified by the observer.

HISTORY

Back in 1928, wishful park planners, zeroed in on this acreage, but money for its purchase did not become available until the 1960s. This once rural setting now had become suburban.

Some of the funds for the park land came from the federal government—compensation for the loss of Toledo park land during the construction of interstates 75 and 475. After additional purchases, the park opened on October 27, 1973.

The Yager Center is named for the late Joseph A. Yager, a park district board member from 1943–1962, and his son, John W. Yager, a park board member from 1970–1985 and a board president for 12 years.

The Mary Jane Gill Picnic Shelter honors a 12-year board member who retired in 1987.

Wildwood Preserve

Wildwood Preserve once was the estate of a millionaire who made his fortune selling spark plugs. But the "spark" to protect this natural land was ignited in the early 1970s when a developer revealed a plan to carve up the place into luxury housing lots. Citizens and conservation groups persuaded voters to buy it. The effort restored a stately manor house, saved the upland and floodplain forests, kept the meadows alive for birds, and gave people a striking view of the Ottawa River— something to cherish for a long time.

LOCATION
North Central Lucas County.

SIZE
460 acres.

ACCESS
Leave I-475 from either the US 20/Central Avenue or Talmadge Road exits. If you exit I-475 at Central Avenue, travel east about a mile to the entrance on the left. From the latter exit, head south on Talmadge Road, then west (right) on Central Avenue to the park drive on the right. Park in the main lot serving the visitor center and estate.

Trails: Wildwood's five nature trails visit different habitats. All of them can be reached from the trailhead behind the Visitor Center. The All-Purpose Trail (1.6 miles) for bicyclists, joggers, and visitors in wheelchairs and strollers starts in the parking lot. Cross-country skiers can use all the trails in the winter.

Special Places & Events: After traipsing through the wild, dust off your hat, wipe your feet, and tour the Manor House, the former estate of Robert A. Stranahan Sr. The mansion is open Wednesday through Sunday from noon–5 p.m.

The Visitor Center, the former stables of the estate, has a wildlife viewing window, outdoor nature education panels, rest rooms, and drinking water. The Window on Wildlife is open daily from 8 a.m. to dusk. Park offices are located here. Picnic tables and a play area are nearby.

Metroparks Hall boasts nature art exhibits, a gift shop, and offices for the Citizens for Metroparks. The building used to house Stranahan's limousines.

GEOLOGY
The sand beneath your feet in the forest was once either part of an ancient beach, sand dune, or sand bar.

The Ottawa River, a post-glacial stream, curls through the park. In places it has eroded through the sand and exposed the layer of clay beneath it. Spring floods reshape the banks, lick new channels, and deposit new sediments—actions that redistribute and replenish the plant life in the floodplain.

WILDLIFE
Some 32 types of trees grow in Wildwood Preserve. Red and white oak rule in the upland woods. Here you also find sugar maple in abundance, and healthy specimens of wild black cherry, bitternut hickory, sassafras, viburnum, and pin oak. Sycamore and cottonwood preside over the floodplain. Ohio buckeye, black walnut, box elder, silver maple, willow, and river birch also occupy this moist habitat.

Fifty-nine varieties of wildflowers have been counted. After spring floods look for wild phlox, bittercress, and buttercups along the river. In summer, these are replaced by nettles, coneflowers, cup plant (a member of the sunflower family), and others. The upland forest yields many blossoms including sweet cicely, trout lily, spring beauty, and white baneberry (also known as doll's eyes), whose white berries are poisonous. The prairie hosts grasses, like big bluestem and Indian grass, which can grow to 10 feet, and blossoms named bergamot, black-eyed Susan, and blazing star. In the meadows, look for the swaying doily of Queen Anne's lace and vetches on the higher terrain. Joe-pye weed and ironweed will occupy the lower ground.

The resplendent, feathery wings of ferns appear everywhere. Representatives include the sensitive, interrupted, bracken, and maidenhair ferns.

Foxes, owls, and hawks will hunt for mice, voles, and small birds in these clearings. Deer browse throughout the park. You are likely to see the tracks of raccoons on the banks of the Ottawa River. This furry critter, and the great horned owl, find homes in the hollows of tall trees.

An old "walker's companion" published by the park district listed the 68 different birds that had been seen in Wildwood Preserve. The checklist included two endangered species—the dark-eyed junco and magnolia warbler.

The platforms along the Upland Woods Trail are excellent places to observe birds of the forest, such as the pileated woodpecker, chickadee, and nuthatch. The floodplain attracts the belted kingfisher, eastern phoebe, and great blue heron. The fields hide the eastern meadowlark, woodcock, and eastern bluebird.

HISTORY
Only a few sand dunes, if any, remained uncovered by the time French explorers reached northwestern Ohio. Since then, human development has altered the land substantially.

Wildwood Preserve encompasses the former estate of Robert A. Stranahan, Sr., co-founder of the Champion Spark Plug Company. The Stranahan Mansion (now called Manor House), styled after the Georgian Colonial homes of the 18th century, was completed in 1938. An Italianate formal garden with brick walkways and gazebos lies east of the home.

A local developing company caused a stir in

1973 when it unveiled plans to build a residential community on the Stranahan property. Concerned local conservationists organized the Citizens Campaign to Save the Stranahan Estate.

The Ohio Chapter of The Nature Conservancy bought the property in 1973 and served as an interim owner. Voters approved a levy in 1974 to buy back the land from the conservancy. The estate reopened on Memorial Day 1975 as Wildwood.

◆◆◆ SANDUSKY COUNTY ◆◆◆

For information about all the Sandusky parks, contact Sandusky County Park District, 1970 Countryside Place, Fremont, OH 43420, (419) 334-4495.

White Star Park

The flagship of the park district is a reclaimed limestone quarry transformed into a park with outdoor opportunities for everybody.

LOCATION
Madison Township.

SIZE
572 acres.

More, *metroparks*

Other Toledo, Shelby and Sandusky County Parks

SANDUSKY COUNTY PARKS

Blue Heron Reserve, 160 acres, CR 260 off US 6. Great Black Swamp, fen, boardwalks, Pickerel Creek, wetland restoration project.

Wolf Creek Park, 93 acres, south of Fremont on SR 53. Sandusky River, Wolf Creek, camping, canoe access, fishing, Buckeye Trail, playground, picnic area, covered bridge nearby.

SHELBY COUNTY PARKS

Bornhorst Woods, 12 acres, Staley Road. Hiking, picnic area, wildlife observation blind.

Hardin Park, SR 47 and Hardin-Wapakoneta Road, Hardin. Historical marker.

Lockington Reserve, 200 acres, Kaser Road, Washington Township. Lockington Dam, hiking, picnic area, camping, rental camps, fishing, canal locks, wildlife blinds, Loramie Creek, Buckeye Trail, canoeing.

LUCAS METROPARKS

Bendview/Canal Lands & Farnsworth Metroparks, 195 acres, along US 24, Waterville Township. Maumee River, Miami & Erie Canal Towpath Trail, boat launch, Buckeye Trail, fishing.

Providence Metropark, 407 acres, US 24, Lucas-Henry county line. Maumee River, canal boat and sternwheeler rides, historic mill, canal locks, Miami & Erie Canal Towpath.

Side Cut Metropark, 562 acres, River Road or Wayne Street, Monclova Township. Battle of Fallen Timbers Monument, picnic areas, Maumee River, Lamb Heritage Center, Siegert Wildlife Observation Area, canal locks, trails, ponds, tennis courts, ballfields, playground, fishing.

ACCESS

From Fremont, travel west on US 6, then go north (right) on SR 300. The park entrance is on the right south of Gibsonburg. CR 65 bisects the park, and CR 60 forms the eastern border.

Accommodations: White Star Campground across the main entrance has 24 primitive camping sites April 1-December 31. Fees are charged for swimming, camping, day use barn, shelters, and scuba diving.

Trails: The park also has nature trails (south of CR 65).

Swimming, Boating & Fishing: The centerpiece of the park is 15-acre White Star Quarry Pond for swimming, fishing, non-motorized boating, and scuba diving. Except at a well-maintained swimming beach, average depth of the quarry is 40 feet, but scuba divers can explore a tunnel descending to 80 feet. Diving season is April 1 to December 31. Common fish catches from boat or shore are bluegill, bullhead, catfish, bass, trout, yellow perch, and pike. Night fishing (to midnight) permitted on Fridays from Memorial Day to end of September.

Facilities: The park hosts ball fields, a playground, reservable picnic shelters, picnic tables with grills, fishing platform, scuba platform, water, rest rooms, volleyball, horseshoes, day camp and barn (permit required), and boat ramp.

HISTORY

Part of the money to develop this park was derived from the sale of scrap metal salvaged from the quarry machinery.

❖❖❖   SHELBY   COUNTY   ❖❖❖
Shelby County Park District, 9871 Fessler-Buxton Road, Piqua, OH 45356, (937) 773-4818

❖❖❖   WOOD   COUNTY   ❖❖❖
Wood County Park District, 18729 Mercer Road, Bowling Green, OH 43402, (419) 353-1897.

Buttonwood-Betty C. Black Recreation Area, 26 acres, Hull Prairie Road, off SR 65. Maumee River, walleye fishing, hiking, playfields, camping, boat access. Also, Otsego Park, Cedar Creek Preserve, Fuller Preserve, William Henry Harrison Park, Zimmerman School, and Wood County Historical Center.

Metropark
web sites

Metropark Websites

Cleveland Metroparks
www.clemetparks.com/
reservations.html

Columbus Metroparks
http://metroparks.co.franklin.oh.us/

Crawford County Park District
www.cybrtown.com/~crawford
parkdistrict

Darke County Park District
www.darkecountyohio.com/

Five Rivers Metroparks
www.dayton.net/Metroparks

Greene County Park District
www.erinet.com/data/parks.htm

Hamilton County Metroparks
www.hamiltoncountyparks.org/

Hancock (County) Park District
www.hancockparks.com/
facilities.htm

Lake (County) Metroparks
www.lakemetroparks.com/

Licking County Park District
www.msmisp.com/lpd/

Miami County Parks District
http:/tdn-net.com/miami/content/
miami_co_nature.html

Mill Creek Park District
www.neont.com/millcreek

Stark County Park District
www.starksparks.com

Summit County Metroparks
www.neo.rr.com/metroparks/
maimenu.htm

Toledo Metroparks
www.metroparkstoledo.com/
indes_map.html

Wood County Park District
http://wcnet.org/~wcpd

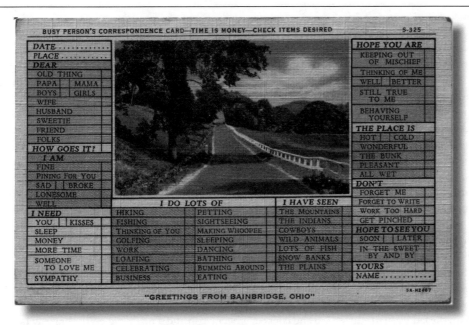

Wishing you were outdoors.

Ohioans "get back to nature" in a variety of ways, for a variety of reasons. They drive to metroparks for a picnic, paddle upstream for the view, bike across state for the exercise. Some head to the hills as escape, an attempt to find a smaller set of rules to live by.

We told everybody that we bought land in the country for the usual reasons—open space, weekend escapes, fresh air, simplicity, camping with friends, private hunting, sanity, peace and quiet, nature study. Looking back, we bought it impulsively, before guilt or remorse could set in. The whole deal went down capriciously, like our wedding and our first child.

But there was another reason for buying that 30 acres in Morgan County, I just couldn't put a finger on it for years. That reason kept escaping into the bushes of my subconscious. It nagged me the way a pebble does when it squeezes into my hiking boot and presses into my heel. Only this time when I remove the shoe, no pebble appears. I knew it would take a while to trap the reason; then I would shake the everlasting truth out of it.

Building a cabin on the property was my wife's idea. I favor a warm, cozy hovel on a fierce winter day, but I'm also content in a tent or a shed made of scrap lumber. Bury me in a sleeping bag, a la Edward Abbey, and throw me to the coyotes, I always say.

After several false starts and five years of dreaming, planning, designing, belt-tightening, bickering and arm-twisting, we assembled a work crew one Labor Day weekend. The congregation consisted of weekend bikers with beards to their bellies, a fellow who learned accounting as a resident in a penal system, several college professors, a few college students, a couple of blokes my father would have called "operators," a computer programmer, a salesman, a lawyer (just in case), drop outs (put me there), drop ins and lost souls (all the rest). Several among them actually knew what they were doing, or so they said, so I paid them believing they did.

Several human languages tangoed with birdsong and buzzsaws. One tongue—the grunts,

Wild Ohioans

Two out of three Ohioans surveyed by the Ohio Divison of Natural Resources in 1995 reported that they make a special effort to watch photograph, feed or listen to wildlife.

stutters, curses and jargon of carpenters—was new to me. Women of French descent muttered as they served up such haute cuisine as burgers, brats and beer, a great leveling experience for these fussy gourmands. Around the campfire we wondered where else this odd assortment would ever gather. "A Grateful Dead concert," someone offered. We toasted the band's leader Jerry Garcia, who had recently fallen off the twig.

Mishaps nearly doomed the project on Saturday. First, the crew "Boss" shot a 16-penny nail through his left index finger with a nail gun. The dart passed cleanly through flesh, just missing a bone, and etched the chest of a goateed business major before stabbing the forest floor. After cursing the inventor of the nail gun, Boss dunked the wounded digit in iodine, wrapped it in gauze and climbed back on the ladder, nail gun loaded and cocked. "Happens all the time," he shrugged as if talking about hard work or taxes. Me? I would have fainted and required a hospital, an attorney, possibly a surgeon, and maybe a priest.

Next, a pony-tailed, bearded chap with a Teddy Roosevelt grin popped the rib he had cracked the week before breaking up a brawl at a rock concert. He grimaced when his wife poked the stick back into place. "Happens all the time," he said nonchalantly.

The compressor that powered the nail guns died at noon. The college boys panicked, threatened to strike, so Boss showed them how a hammer drove a nail into wood. "Part of your edgy-cation," he explained. "Remember to hit the nail, not your hand." While the college boys practiced their new trick, a mechanically minded biker bonded with a French electrical engineering professor and revived the sputtering compressor.

Later, a wood chip dove into the eye of the mechanically minded biker. He fished out the chip, iced and patched the swollen socket and tried to work. But it was no use. He wheeled around like a half-blind, drunken pirate. When he poured a Pepsi down his chin instead of in his mouth, Boss fed him some bourbon and sleeping pills and pushed him into a tent. By supper—an encore of beer, brats and burgers—the swelling had vanished and sight had been restored.

"Happens all the time," he mumbled. The beer had found its mark.

At dusk, under the glow of halogen lights, the whole crew lined up to wiggle the center beam into place across the roof peaks. In hindsight, we should have postponed this tricky task until morning. Halfway up the roof ridge the beam shifted and fell flush on a friend. Miraculously, he survived without a scratch. Boss and I inspected the victim. Other than being shaken, his senses and functions were normal. "A complete miss," Boss announced, "Happens all the time."

"A 24-foot beam body slams a guy and you say it happens all the time?"

"No, man. Accidents that don't cause injuries are complete misses. *They* happen all the time," Boss explained.

I rose before dawn and sneaked to the swimming hole to bathe. Two days of sweat, sawdust, and swill swirled on the glassy surface. A raccoon had eaten a crayfish and a turtle egg on the gravelly beach. Wild turkeys had watered here several days earlier.

As is my habit, I melted into the woods for a while to become invisible. Long ago, humans walked across the land without leaving a trail, but now that skill must be learned. Nature rewards invisibility. It gives its heartbeat, its bosom, its energy—its true nature, in other words—to those who live in its obscure, shadowy world. Take the eastern box turtle, clad in a masterfully camouflaged carapace. It moves carefully and precisely within a few acres of forest. Longevity is the payoff. The reptile may live 80 years, far longer than its roving predators and many humans.

The soprano scream of a band saw cutting yellow pine fetched me back to the human world. At the campground, I greeted new arrivals, fresh troops in clean, creased overalls. These buddies owned rental properties and understood building codes, floor plans, builders' lingo. They inspected the premises, blueprints in hand.

"Excellent foundation. Contractor must have used a laser beam," one observed. "How many bids did you get?"

"I got one estimate over the phone. We shook on it, and the guy did the work with a level and a string. No contract, no down payment, no cost overruns. Same deal with the excavator and electrician," I summarized.

"So the building inspector has signed off on all this already?" another inquired circumspectly.

"Building inspector?" I confronted stunned comrades. "I don't need a building inspector here."

Circa 1920: A beach baptism. Circa 2000: "Beach fun" is top-ranked by outdoor faithful.

Then came an avalanche of polite queries. Did the window openings meet code? Legal-sized ingress and egress? House wrap the correct thickness? Was I adequately drained, minimally ventilated, properly plumbed? Did I account for this and that? Consider such and such? And so on.

I halted the inquest with a raised palm and began one of my speeches.

"Friends, this is the country, not the city. You have crossed into a different world, where English common law and the Old Order prevail. A man's home is his castle. (Women grumbled.) There is no zoning down here, no building permits, no building codes, no building inspector. Nobody's looking over our shoulders and second-guessing. If I want, I can build a house of cards or a skyscraper of Styrofoam. I can build one without windows or one with a hundred, and glass is optional. I can paint it pink with purple polka dots or never paint it. I can build it any size, any shape and anywhere in my realm, with siding or sans siding. The roof can be pointed like a spruce, or flat as a beaver's tail. Down here, people live happily with a smaller set of rules."

Boss finally broke the spell. "Time to go to work, boys. The big bad wolf isn't gonna blow this house down. Now somebody hand me that plywood so we can finish the roof by sunset."

A week later, the city service department mailed to my permanent suburban address its new regulations governing autumn yard waste and street parking. Tree limbs and "like matter" now had to be bundled into lengths no longer than a yardstick and no heavier than 20 pounds (a maximum of three bundles per week). The bundles had to be stacked besides trash cans in the alley and clearly marked "yard waste"—to avoid confusing them with auto parts, I suppose.

On page two, I learned that I now needed a permit and sticker to legally park in front of my house; penalties for violations were noted. The service director thanked me in advance for my cooperation.

The following day the regulations kindled the campfire in Morgan County. I'll be a law-abiding citizen and properly affix that parking sticker in a week or so. But right now, as flames lick a foot high, I'm savoring my moment of defiance. Down here, I live by a smaller set of rules—my rules, mostly. ✒

—SO

est Ohio Has to Offer

by Stephen Ostrander

Top Nature Preserves for Wildflowers

You may photograph, admire, and sniff, but please don't pick.
- Brown's Lake Bog Nature Preserve (*Wayne*)
- Cedar Bog State Memorial (*Champaign*)
- Clifton Gorge State Natural Area (*Greene*)
- Darby Plains Prairies (*Madison, Union*)
- Edge of Appalachia Preserves, Lynx Prairie (*Adams*)
- Flint Ridge State Memorial (*Licking*)
- Fort Hill State Memorial (*Highland*)
- Fowler Woods State Nature Preserve (*Richland*)
- Glen Helen Nature Preserve (*Greene*)
- Lake Katharine State Nature Preserve (*Jackson*)
- Rockbridge State Nature Preserve (*Hocking*)
- Cincinnati Nature Center (*Clermont*)

Fifty Steps to Better Geology: Hocking Hills

Best Scenic Over-look and Views

Look, but don't leap
- Shawnee Fire Tower, Wayne National Forest (*Hocking*)
- Fire towers in Ohio state forests
- Tinker's Creek Gorge, Bedford Reservation (*Cuyahoga*)
- Chapin Forest Reservation (*Lake*)
- Clear Fork Gorge, Mohican State Park (*Ashland*)
- Conkles Hollow State Nature Preserve (*Hocking*)
- Edge of Appalachia Preserves, Buzzardsroost Rock (*Adams*)
- Hach-Otis State Nature Preserve (*Lake*)
- Shawnee State Forest (*Scioto*)
- Rocky River Reservation (*Cuyahoga*)

🐾Shallenberger State Nature Preserve (*Fairfield*)
🐾Shawnee Lookout Park (*Hamilton*)
🐾Woodland Mound Park (*Hamilton*)
🐾Great Seal State Park (*Ross*)
🐾 Fort Ancient State Memorial (*Warren*)

Best Birding Places

Take binoculars, and gawk.

🐾 Ottawa National Wildlife Refuge (*Ottawa*)
🐾 Clear Creek Gorge Metropark (*Hocking, Fairfield*)
🐾 Old Woman Creek State Nature Preserve (*Huron*)
🐾 Magee Marsh State Wildlife Area (*Ottawa*)
🐾 Maumee Bay State Park (*Lucas*)
🐾 Aullwood Audubon Center (*Montgomery*)
🐾 Cincinnati Nature Center (*Clermont*)
🐾 Glen Helen Nature Preserve (*Greene*)
🐾 Pickerington Ponds Metropark (*Fairfield*)
🐾 Sheldon Marsh State Nature Preserve (*Huron*)
🐾 Springville Marsh State Nature Preserve (*Seneca*)
🐾 Mentor Marsh State Nature Preserve (*Lake*)
🐾 Stage's Pond State Nature Preserve (*Pickaway*)
🐾 Hocking Hills State Park, Hocking State Forest (*Hocking*)
🐾 The Dawes Arboretum (*Licking*)

Special Outings for Children

You can't go wrong at any of the metropark nature centers, arboretums, or private nature centers because they cater to children and young adults. Here are some kid-tested selections.

🐾 **Aullwood Audubon Center** (*Montgomery*) —
Combined with a tour of the historical farm, fossil collection spot, and Aullwood Gardens, this site may be everybody's top choice.

🐾 **Glen Helen Nature Preserve** (*Greene*) —
It has everything—nature center, exhibits, foot trails, bike trails, cable bridge, raptor rehab center, summer nature camp, quirky geological structures, and Little Miami River.

🐾 **Rocky River Reservation** (*Cuyahoga*) —
A replica of an ancient, armored shark named Dunk hangs from the ceiling. The nature center

has a deck over the river. Hiking trails lead to Indian earthworks.

🐾 **Fort Ancient State Memorial** (*Warren*) —
Youngsters get big doses of early Ohio human history and current natural history, plus views of the Little Miami River gorge.

🐾 **Blackhand Gorge State Nature Preserve** (*Licking*) — A perfect outing for the beginning biking family. The flat, paved trail along the lush Licking River always satisfies.

🐾 **Maumee Bay State Park** (*Lucas*)—
Ditch the lodge frills and hike the boardwalk trail at dusk. Every kid should see and hear the geese and ducks landing for the night.

Geological Gems

Looking for some rocky cliffs, ledges, outcrops? Some odd formations? Some waterfalls? Try these.

🐾 Hocking Hills State Park (*Hocking*)
🐾 Chapin Forest Reservation (*Lake*)
🐾 Charleston Falls Reserve (*Miami*)
🐾 Clifton Gorge State Nature Preserve (*Greene*)
🐾 John Bryan State Park (*Greene*)
🐾 Flint Ridge State Memorial (*Licking*)
🐾 Fort Hill State Memorial (*Highland*)
🐾 Hinckley Reservation (*Medina*)
🐾 Lake Katharine State Nature Preserve (*Jackson*)
🐾 The Holden Arboretum, Little Mountain & Stebbins Gulch (*Lake*)
🐾 Rockbridge State Nature Preserve (*Hocking*)
🐾 Nelson-Kennedy Ledges State Park (*Portage*)
🐾 Conkles Hollow State Nature Preserve (*Hocking*)

Solitude, Silence, and Slow Pace

These off-the-beaten-track, hard-to-reach places offer solitude, timelessness, and few distractions. This is where you go to escape from civilization, forget responsibilities, and dodge the maddening crowd.

🐾 Wayne National Forest (take a deep woods backpack trail)
🐾 Shawnee State Forest (*Scioto*)
🐾 Zaleski State Forest (*Vinton*)

Recreation Resources

From time to time Ohioans are asked what they do in the great outdoors. The poll is called SCORP, short for Statewide Comprehensive Outdoor Recreation Plan. The information helps outdoor recreation planners prepare for the future. The last SCORP was released in 1993. Some of the findings follow.

Ohio ranks unfavorably compared to other states in terms of per capita acreage for outdoor recreation (48th in one survey). Only five percent of Ohio land is available for outdoor recreation, or 131 acres per 1,000 residents. Ohio's growing number of outdoor enthusiasts, therefore, often find themselves competing over public land use.

The top five counties in total outdoor recreation acres (land and water) were Scioto, Lawrence, Hocking, Pike, and Jackson. The bottom five were Hardin, Paulding, Madison, Putnam, and Union. Vinton County ranked first in acres per 1,000 residents, 3,401 acres; while Hardin County finished last with 16 acres per 1,000.

Acreage (land and water) for outdoor recreation in Ohio totaled 1,417,557 acres.

Outdoor Participation

According to the 1993 SCORP, Ohioans spend an estimated $5.7 billion on outdoor recreation in their state.

Almost two-thirds of the households polled indicated they "walked for pleasure," and more than half picnicked, worked in a garden, fished from shore, and went to the beach. (Respondents could list more than one outdoor activity in the poll.) Here's how the activities stacked up (at right), with a comparison to 1989. The figures reflect the percentage of polled households that participated in the activity (na = no data).

Participants of an outdoor activity were asked if they were "satisfied" with the experience. The most satisfying experiences were boating, trail activities, bicycling, and swimming. The least satisfying were field sports, horseback riding, wildlife observation, golf, and winter sports.

The top five "barriers" to participating in outdoors activities were lack of time, lack of information about sites, overcrowded sites, other family commit-

ments, and distance to site.

Some outdoor enthusiasts say they go to great lengths for an optimum experience. The typical Ohio camper travels an average of 44.5 miles to a favorite campground, a fisher 33.3 miles, hunters and boaters, 32.7 miles. Bicyclers only go 8.6 miles to their site, and golfers 11.5 miles to tee off.

Percentage of respondents who said they participated in outdoor activities are as follows:

Activity	1993	1989
Walking	64.9	na
Picnicking	59.2	67.1
Gardening	55.7	na
Fishing (shore, wading)	54	na
Beach fun	52.1	48.1
Wildlife, observation	48.9	na
Fishing from boat	41.8	na
Gathering	40.1	na
Outdoor pool	39.5	41.9
Power boating	35.7	28.2
Day hiking	31.8	na
Bicycling	30.9	28.7
Small game hunting	29.2	20.5
Backpack/tent camping	25.1	23.1
Deer/turkey hunting	25	na
Golf	23.4	26.5
Softball	22.3	na
Motorized camping	22.5	20.5
Other boats (pontoon, tubes)	22.1	16.7
Canoeing	20.9	23.7
Jogging/running	20.6	na
Shooting sports	19.8	na
Volleyball	18.1	na
Basketball (outdoors)	18.1	na
Waterskiing	18	17.6
Baseball	15.9	na
State park lodge/cabin	15.5	17.1
Other hunting	14.1	9.7
Horseback riding	12.7	12.2
Off-road vehicles	11.7	7.9
Tennis	10.1	na
Ice Skating	9.5	na
ORV (vehicles 50" wider)	8.7	na
Snow skiing	7.3	na
Snowmobiling	6.8	na
Soccer	6.6	na
Waterfowl hunting	6.5	4.4
Sailing	4.4	7.9

Greetings from Lynchburg, Ohio.

*P*retend to draw a complete, unabridged and unabashed map of every trail by every creature in Ohio, from interstate to insect trace.

Make sure you add the shadows brushed by birds of feather and steel, the silver threads of rivers and rills, the zigs and zags of swallowtails and shiners, and the routes of rodents, reptiles, roots, and rails. Capture all cart paths, conveyances, canoe currents, and canals, every path for pedestrian and pedaler, every ditch, driveway, and detour. Remember the highways for hooves, heels, and wheels. Pencil in the prevailing ways of the wind, the random course of pollen, the predictable trip of ants and bees. Include the veins of commerce, the avenues of escape, the boulevards for browsers, the roll of rockslides, the slow slide of slugs, the angle of snowflakes, the stations for migrations.

When finished, with all trails drawn, heart-shaped Ohio would appear somnolent in a cocoon, or compressed in tightening coils of copper wire. Just thinking about all the simultaneous squirming on those trails makes me itch. All that gyrating, buzzing, and humming; all those claustrophobic collisions, and rush-hour contentions; and all that electricity pulsing and tickling the turf. It is enough to produce malarial shakes.

So let's instead simplify the map. Unravel a few strands, purify the picture, and scratch several itches. Just focus on the trails for hikers, horse riders, bicyclers, cross-country skiers, and ATVers, and only the routes that go through forests and meadows, over hills and streams, around lakes and towns: paths that challeng the legs, heal the heart, and explore the soul. Now Ohio looks at ease, recovered, and roomy enough for deep breaths.

The trail you choose to follow, the course you set, and the way you move belongs to you.

Here's a guide to set you in motion. Remember, whoever gets off the trail last wins. ✑

—SO

Walk This Way

Thoreau once postulated that we walk in the wilderness because an *"unknown force moves us."* Had the philosopher been hiking with couch-loving teenagers, that compelling force would have been easily identifiable: griping from the ranks.

Halfway up a steep slope I let the slow-pokes catch their breath—the slow pokes being a rag-tag band of teenagers of assorted shapes, sizes, and genders. We were northbound on the Shawnee State Forest backpack trail, destined for Copperhead Fire Tower and a picnic lunch to be delivered by a motor vehicle. At my feet a husky man-child dropped like a dead tree and sprawled spread-eagle on the trail. Another draped himself limply over a fallen chestnut oak, and muttered monosyllables between oceanic breaths. The rest staggered, gasped, reeled, then collapsed with the paroxysms of marathoners at the finish line.

"It gets easier when you catch your second wind," I assured them.

"What about third and fourth winds?" an athlete wheezed.

"Are we there yet?" another asked weakly.

"Just a couple more miles," I lied cheerfully. Groans, growls, gags and guffaws.

"Why didn't we just drive there?" scowled son David, acetylene-torch eyes cutting quick to my aorta.

Two hours later the mob reached the tower to find it deserted. No food, as I had promised, no beverages, no extended Dodge minivan for the ride back to base camp. "Looks like we beat them here," I responded like a winning coach. "Looks more like we beat the odds," shouted a smart aleck.

An hour passed; no deliverance. The animals were becoming restless. I resorted to sanguine proclamations from a miniature chapbook. "Thoreau wrote, 'The swiftest traveler is he that goes afoot.'" The innocent quote kindled panic. Starvation and denial of a sugar fix could be endured, but not a forced march back to camp. The lynch-mob voted unanimously for calling a cab on a cellular phone that one of them disguised as a sandwich and slipped into her haversack. My abstention drew predatory stares. Two brutes with crooked smiles circled behind me. I looked for a tree.

Just then the chuck wagon arrived. The wolves pounced on the larder.

"Sorry we're late. Got a flat outside Portsmouth," explained our rescuers. "Couldn't find the lug wrench, so we had to call AAA. Took us two hours to fix it." Flat tire, blistered heel, wrong turn—all the same.

Late that night, when the campfire coals shrank to the size of distant city lights, I thought about the protest concluding the day's long hike. Why so much resistance from fit teenagers, 30 years my junior, to walking? Had I become an old fogy hopelessly besotted to an activity which in their eyes is a museum artifact, like handwritten letters, LP record jackets, and black and white TVs with rabbit ears. Maybe they had a point.

Why, indeed, trudge overland to an anachronistic landmark when a car and a road gets there easier and faster? Why do anything slowly, let alone on foot, in this hyperactive, supersonic, instantaneous, pushbutton, at-your-fingertips, in-your-face, high-tech age? Life is short, so see, do, be as much as you can. What then, is so special about walking?

Using a flashlight, I jotted down reasons for walking—walking, that is, in forests and fields, and along shores and streams, where walking is best.

Walking is good exercise, healthy. Though I prefer my walking to be a craving, an addiction that requires abstinence after overindulgence, then a backsliding to paradise.

It is subversive. A way of snubbing the human rat race, mass transit, and driving between the lines; a way of disappearing, of crawling into a hole, of getting away. Anybody who walks to work nowadays, especially a soul rich enough to own a car, gets dubbed a weirdo, eccentric, fool, and misanthrope. Perhaps, then, this is the best reason to walk.

Walking is elemental, the only mode of movement shared by every capable human, and many creatures on the planet. My legs are an axle for the engine in my body.

It is purgative. A panacea. The cure for minor aches and pains, frustration, anger, wounded egos, boredom, not unlike drugs, booze, and sex.

It is the best way to examine, experience and admire the natural world, and to quench an inherent curiosity about life. But one could argue that this can be accomplished with videos, PBS shows, microscopes, zoos, encyclopedias, computers, drugs, booze, and sex.

Walking can be like time tripping, traveling back to a comfortable place and simpler time.

It is certainly cheaper than psycho-analysis. It can be self-reconnaissance or a journey into the soul, until you trip over a root and bump your head.

To walk is to find freedom, un-encumbered, stripped down, a spore for a breeze.

I can daydream as I walk, something I dare not do while driving a car. I sample the moveable feast, snapshots of trail vistas, fords, flowers, trees, lakes, waterfalls, skinny dips, and creatures that appear in my diurnal and nocturnal dreams.

Sometimes walking is an unscratchable itch driven largely by curiosity, and somewhat by boredom, immobility, collapsing walls, despair, and fetid indoor air.

But ultimately, walking is an activity beyond analysis. If mountain climbers can scale a peak "because it is there," then hikers can slink along a trail "because it is the only way to get *there*," *there* being no place in particular.

British poets Samuel Taylor Coleridge and William Wordsworth, and Scottish essayist Thomas Carlyle were obsessive, long-distance walkers. They chalked up counties on daily hikes, and adhered to the British tradition of walking for fitness, vigor, and keeping the limbs and lungs limber. Wordsworth figured his lifetime peregrinations totaled 175,000 miles. Carlyle logged 54 miles one day, and Coleridge averaged 40 miles per hike. They largely stuck to tame lanes and ancient, trodden trails over land subdued and measured. Their base camps were village inns and gin mills. Along the way they scribbled stirring stanzas, and compressed vast thoughts into sentences. Mileage mattered as much to these literary energies as the magic and memories harvested by their motion.

America's sojourning literati, by contrast, strode across an overripe wilderness for spiritual workouts. Each excursion, wrote Henry David Thoreau with characteristic elevation, became a "saunter toward the Holy Land," or in modern parlance, a rebirth.

Although Thoreau was a fastidious counter, observer, and measurer of things on walks, he never kept track of his miles and rarely seemed concerned with destination.

Some thinkers consider Thoreau's last essay, entitled "Walking," to be the quintessential explanation, though lately it has produced a bounty of T-shirt and greeting card sentiments, such as "In Wilderness is the preservation of the World." In the essay, HDT suggests we walk because some "unknown force moves us," or for the "subtle magnetism of Nature." Perhaps, he suggests, the activity was "the reminiscence of a previous state of existence" which provided "absolute freedom and wildness, as contrasted with a freedom and culture merely civil."

But Thoreau's transcendental observations don't satisfy the nuts-and-bolts, what's-in-it-for-me fanatics, however. For that I turned to Colin Fletcher, author of *The Man Who Walked Through Time*, recounting his solo hike through the Grand Canyon. Fletcher talks about crossing boundaries of time, culture, and space—moving across worlds. Walking just for joy is high on his list. Like a runner, Fletcher gets adrenaline rushes while walking, "At some stage of every day's walking....there comes a moment when your cerebral synapses seem to click into gear....you fire on all cylinders. You soar, embrace the universe, see everything, solve the insoluble at a glance—you operate, that is, the way you wish you always did." To Fletcher, it is better to discover the "feel-how" of walking, than the "how-to" of it.

The why of walking still nagged me, though. Thoreau and Fletcher could not explain why I was periodically compelled to leave the recliner and hike across a wild place. The feeling comes over me like rut to a buck, and goes away as a howl freed by a wolf. So for explanation I went to Ohio's own John Glenn of hikers, Steven Newman. The Clermont County native circumambulated the globe alone in the mid-1980s and shared his adventures in *Worldwalk*. When I caught up with Newman on a trail at Fort Hill State Memorial, I asked him the big "why" question.

"Because it's natural," he explained easily, without a hesitation in his stride. "We can't get it out of our system. It's in our genes." His response was concise, polished to a nugget, practiced to perfection. ◐

The Buckeye Trail

The idea of a trans-Ohio hiking trail evolved for years. Merrill Gilfillan, a nature writer, finally bottled it in a story for the *Columbus Dispatch* in 1958. What Ohio needed more than another highway, he said, was a footpath connecting the Ohio River and Lake Erie, a mini-Appalachian Trail. A corps of hikers herded together and formed the Buckeye Trail Association (BTA) in 1959. Co-founder Emma "Granny" Gatewood, one of Ohio's legendary long-distance hikers, bought the first bucket of blue blaze paint.

The Mentor (Lake Erie) to Cincinnati leg opened in 1975. By 1981, the Buckeye Trail had grown to 1,200 miles, and linked the "Four Corners of Ohio." The "Long Blue Line," referring to the distinctive blue blazes that mark the trail, is now among the nation's longest single-state loop trails. It winds through 40 of the state's 88 counties, and is never more than 75 miles from a major city.

Members of the BTA, now 1,000 strong, have carefully and lovingly designed and maintained the route for 40 years. It passes through state parks, metroparks, state and national forests, historical landmarks, state wildlife areas, nature preserves, museums, wineries, and private land. It utilizes canal towpaths, abandoned railroad beds and logging roads, covered bridges, primitive footpaths, country roads, and a few miles of asphalt. Roughly half of the BT is "off-road."

Today the Buckeye Trail lets a traveler tour Ohio at a pilgrim's pace. It wanders across farmland, through forests and fens. It tracks along dry ridgetops and soggy streams, dives into gorges carved by glaciers, and climbs to hilltops once part of a plateau. Hikers also tramp through a spectrum of human history, from the puzzling earthen mounds of ancient inhabitants and canals of pre-industrial America, to the skyscrapers and highways of modern times. The trail is easy and smooth in places, and downright difficult elsewhere. It cures life's bumpy road, and toughens those who have grown soft and stale.

The trail is blazed by vertical light blue paint strokes, roughly two-by-six inches, every hundred feet, give or take. Look for the blazes on trees and utility poles. Additional blue blazes, left or right of the main mark, indicate changes in direction. White blazes show side trails.

BTA sells waterproof section maps, each covering 50 miles, showing the route, public roads, campsites, water sources, parking, emergency phone numbers, and places of interest. Section maps (not topographical) are valuable guides for hikers venturing into new areas. The Buckeye Trail is free and open year-round. Portions of the path allow horseback riding, bicycles, and roller blades. Backpackers must camp in approved campgrounds noted on section trail maps. Camping on trails, roadsides, and private land is forbidden. Hunting, fishing, and trapping occur along the trail where permitted.

Volunteer work crews toting shovels, pickaxes, and other gear keep the trail cleared, blazed, and litter-free. If you don't like hiking alone, the BTA schedules group hikes and trail maintenance outings. BTA also cooperates with many trail partners, such as the Ohio Department of Natural Resources, Ohio Historical Society, U.S. Department of Agriculture, Forest Service, Muskingum and Miami conservancy districts, American Electric Power, local park districts and trail councils, and private landowners.

Two longer "through" trails—North Country and American Discovery trails—use portions of the Buckeye Trail for their routes through Ohio. BTA members serve on the local councils for these national trails.

For information about the Buckeye Trail, membership information, and trail maps contact the BTA at the address below. For a circuit hiker's checklist of the trail, see the Appendix.

BUCKEYE TRAIL ASSOCIATION
P.O. Box 254
Worthington, OH 43085
www.ne-ohio.net/bta/

American Discovery Trail

At Cape Henlopen State Park, on Delaware's Atlantic coast, triangular badges of the American Discovery Trail (ADT) point the hale and hearty westward—on foot to California's Pacific Coast. At the historic Roebling Suspension Bridge in Cincinnati, a sign says the Atlantic Ocean is 960 miles behind, and that 3,875 miles stands between there and the Pacific Ocean—just 20 percent of the journey completed. Hikers can sneer at the sign and truck to the lighthouse at Point Reyes National Seashore in California; or sigh with satisfaction and save the rest for another lifetime.

The American Discovery Trail is not a joke. It is America's first coast-to-coast, multiple-use hiking trail. Hatched in 1989 by the American Hiking Society and *Backpacker* magazine, the ADT serves as a transcontinental backbone for radiating national and local trails, such as the Buckeye, Appalachian, and North Country trails. ADT comprises 6,356 miles, including miles for twin paths between Cincinnati and Denver. Along the way, it connects people to large cities, small towns, mountains, rivers, wilderness, forests and deserts.

Scouts charted the route through Ohio in 1990. Most of the trail's 400-plus miles in the state tracks the southern leg of the Buckeye Trail (also the route of the North Country Trail). The ADT enters Ohio at Belpre, then zigzags across Washington County to join the Buckeye Trail at Chesterhill, Morgan County. At Cincinnati, ADT breaks from the Buckeye Trail and dips into Kentucky, only to reenter Ohio downstream at Anderson Ferry. Just passed North Bend, ADT divides into the Northern Midwest and Southern Midwest routes. The southern route goes directly to Lawrenceburg, Indiana. The northern pathway heads to Oxford, Hueston Woods State Park, Richmond, Indiana, and points west. The legs converge in Denver and continue to California. Like the Buckeye Trail, the ADT in Ohio is free and open year-round. Portions of the trail are used by horse riders, bicyclists, and other travelers.

The ADT publishes a map of the Ohio-Kentucky route with detail maps of portions through Belpre, Burr Oak State Park, Hocking Hills State Park, and Cincinnati and Kentucky. The map lacks clear directions for the segments from Belpre to Chesterhill, and from Anderson Ferry westward on both legs of the Midwest route. Contact the local trail coordinator for more details. Refer to maps for the Buckeye Trail for the ADT route between Chesterhill and Eden Park, Cincinnati. Also note that stretches of the trail remain unmarked.

AMERICAN DISCOVERY TRAIL SOCIETY
P.O. Box 729
Orinda, CA 94563
(510) 283-6800
E-mail: ADTSociety@aol.com

ADT OHIO COORDINATOR:
Paul M. Daniel
7 Peabody Drive
Oxford, OH 45056
(513) 523-4851

North County Trail

The North Country Trail (NCT) is one of eight national scenic trails in the making. When it is finished, it will stretch 3,200 miles from Lake Champlain in New York to Lake Sakakawea in North Dakota. Much of its 700-mile, U-shaped sweep through Ohio overlaps the existing Buckeye Trail.

Through part of the national trail network administered by the U.S. Department of the Interior, National Park Service, much of the organizational work for trail maintenance and promotion is done by the North Country Trail Association. This group, founded in 1981, develops partnerships with local trail councils, such as the Buckeye Trail Association, national forests, and state and local parks. The NCT's triangular trail emblem—a gold star beaming within an inner blue triangle—appears along segments officially "certified" by the National Park Service. "Certified" means the trail segment has been developed and managed in accordance with the National Trails System Act of 1968 and the trail's master plan. Roughly 1,300 miles have been certified. Long stretches of the trail are open, but not yet certified. Other portions are still being designed. Some 1,600 miles will be located on private land.

From Pennsylvania, the NCT enters Ohio north of East Liverpool. Planners call for it to head westward along the Sandy & Beaver Canal corridor, the Little Beaver Creek State Scenic River through Beaver Creek State Park, to the Buckeye Trail near Zoarville. It stays on the BT except for detours into Wayne National Forest, along the Little Miami River, and around Dayton. Roughly 70 miles of the NCT have been developed in Wayne National Forest, but connections to the Buckeye Trail have not yet been established. Trail blazers believe it will depart the BT at Seneca Lake and angle southeast to Woodsfield and the WNF. From Lane Farm, northeast of Marietta, the NCT will swing northwesterly and rejoin the BT at Burr Oak State Park (though some suggest Chesterhill, the confluence of the BT and American Discovery Trail). In Northwestern Ohio, just east of Independence Dam State Park, the NCT veers north into Michigan. It is likely to follow the Wabash Cannonball Bike Trail and pass through Oak Openings Preserve.

Like the Buckeye and American Discovery trails, the NCT in Ohio is free and open year-round. Portions of the trail are used by horse riders, bicyclists, and other travelers. Contact the Wayne National Forest for a

Hiking Trails

Michigan

Lake Erie

Pennsylvania

WILLIAMS | FULTON | LUCAS | OTTAWA | NCT
DEFIANCE | HENRY | WOOD | SANDUSKY | ERIE | LORAIN | CUYAHOGA | LAKE | GEAUGA | ASHTABULA
PAULDING | PUTNAM | HANCOCK | SENECA | HURON | **Buckeye Trail** | MEDINA | SUMMIT | PORTAGE | TRUMBULL | MAHONING
VAN WERT | ALLEN | WYANDOT | CRAWFORD | ASHLAND | WAYNE | STARK | COLUMBIANA
MERCER | AUGLAIZE | HARDIN | MARION | RICHLAND | HOLMES | **North Country National Scenic Trail** | CARROLL
SHELBY | LOGAN | UNION | MORROW | KNOX | COSHOCTON | TUSCARAWAS | HARRISON | JEFFERSON
DARKE | MIAMI | CHAMPAIGN | DELAWARE | LICKING | GUERNSEY | **BT/NCT** | BELMONT
BT/NCT | CLARK | MADISON | FRANKLIN | MUSKINGUM
PREBLE | MONTGOMERY | GREENE | FAIRFIELD | PERRY | MORGAN | NOBLE | MONROE
ADT | FAYETTE | PICKAWAY | HOCKING | WASHINGTON | **NCT**
BUTLER | WARREN | CLINTON | ROSS | VINTON | ATHENS | **American Discovery Trail**
HAMILTON | HIGHLAND | PIKE | JACKSON | MEIGS | **West Virginia**
CLERMONT | BROWN | ADAMS | SCIOTO | GALLIA
Kentucky | LAWRENCE

Indiana

Ohio River

N

.... **Buckeye Trail (BT)**
• • • • • • **American Discovery Trail (ADT)**
▪ ▪ ▪ ▪ **North Country National Scenic Trail (NCT)**

map of the NCT through the federal holdings, otherwise refer to maps printed by the BTA. A checklist for the North Country Trail will be included when the trail is fully mapped. In the meantime, see an Ohio trail checklist in the Appendix.

NORTH COUNTRY TRAIL ASSOCIATION
49 Monroe Center, Suite 200B
Grand Rapids, MI 49503
Phone: (616) 454-5506
Email: NCTAssoc@aol.com
http://people.delphi.com/wesboyd/ncnst.htm

NCTA OHIO COORDINATOR:
Jim Sprague
4406 Maplecrest
Parma, OH 44129
(216) 884-4757

NORTH COUNTRY NATIONAL SCENIC TRAIL
National Park Service
c/o Bill Menke
700 Rayovac Drive, Suite 200
Madison, Wisconsin 53711
(608) 264-5610

WAYNE NATIONAL FOREST
Athens District
219 Columbus Road
Athens, OH 45701
(740) 592-3223

➤(continued on page 494)

Their Feet Were Made for Walking

Queen of the Trail

After raising eleven kids and four grandchildren in Ohio hill country during the Depression and war years, Emma Rowena Gatewood wasn't content to occupy a rocker on the front porch of her Mercerville farm. Not after she read an article on the Appalachian Trail (AT) in *National Geographic* magazine. The author mentioned that no woman had hiked the length of the Appalachian Trail in one season. Gatewood decided to make history in 1955 by becoming the first woman to through-hike the 2,300 mile Georgia-to-Maine route. It took her 146 days; a pace of 15.75 miles a day. She was 67 years old, and had no prior long-distance hiking experience.

"Grandma" Gatewood through-hiked the AT again in 1957 and 1964. Her walk on the 2,000-mile Oregon Trail in 1959 gave her national fame and appearances on TV shows, such as Groucho Marx's "You Bet Your Life." She was a co-founder of the 1,200-mile Buckeye Trail in 1959, and trained Peace Corps volunteers at Ohio University in 1964.

Sporting her trademark red beret, "Grandma" led group hikes across Ohio for the Buckeye Trail Association and Ohio Department of Natural Resources. Her favorite route, the six-mile stretch in Hocking Hills State Park between Old Man's Cave and Ash Cave, was dedicated as the Grandma Gatewood National Recreation Trail in 1979. A devout Christian, she walked into the valley of the shadow of death in the spring of 1973.

The Worldwalker

In April 1983, Steven Newman, then age 28, strode from his hometown of Bethel with Clinger, the pet name of his backpack, and the notion of circumnavigating the globe on foot, alone. His mission: to find out if the world still had a peaceful core of kindness, compassion, and love. Privately, some people doubted his sanity. Ohioans followed his progress across five continents and 20 countries through correspondences published in the *Columbus Dispatch, Cincinnati Post, Sandusky Register* and *New York Times.* Four years and 15,000 miles later, Newman returned to a hero's welcome in Bethel. The *Guinness Book of World Records* noted in its 1988 edition that Newman was the first human to walk around the world solo.

Newman's book, *Worldwalk,* ranks among the best "walking" adventure stories of this century, right up there with Colin Fletcher's *The Man Who Walk Through Time.* And yes, Newman found the world a wondrous place for one man, on foot, relying on his wits and his backpack. Ohio paid tribute to Newman by naming the backpacker's trail at East Fork State Park the Steven M. Newman Worldwalk Trail. Today, Newman lives in Ripley, and continues to write and lecture about his travels. He still wears out a pair or two of hiking boots every year. ☜

RECOMMENDED LONG WALKS

PLACE & TRAIL NAME	COUNTY	TRAILHEADS	MILES	USES
Northwestern Ohio				
MAUMEE STATE PARK				
Bike Trail	Lucas	Lake beach	6 (LP)	B,H
LAKE LORAMIE STATE PARK				
Miami-Erie Towpath	Shelby	Beach	7 (LN)	B,H
OAK OPENINGS PRESERVE				
Seventeen Mile Loop	Lucas	Springbrook Lake	17 (LP)	H
Area, SR 64				
Northeastern Ohio				
BEAVER CREEK STATE PARK				
Bridle Trail	Columbiana	Horseman's Camp	25 (CT)	E,H
Vondergreen & Loop	Columbiana	Echo Dell Bridge	7 (CT)	H,B,C
CUYAHOGA VALLEY NATIONAL				
RECREATION AREA				
Ohio & Erie Canal	Summit	Canal Rd., Pine Hill	23 (LN)	H,B,C
Towpath	Cuyahoga	Rd., Highland Rd.,		
		Peninsula, Hunt		
		Farm, Indian Mound		
METROPARKS SERVING				
SUMMIT COUNTY				
Bike and Hike	Summit	Silver Springs Park,	23 (LN)	B,H
	Cuyahoga	Darrow Road,		
		Boston Mills Rd., Steel		
		Corners Road		
MILL CREEK PARK				
West/East Gorge Trail	Mahoning	Lanterman's Mill,	6.7 (LP)	H
(also Witchbroom Trail)		Lake Newport		
		Boat Center		
MOHICAN MEMORIAL				
STATE FOREST				
Horsetail Run (blue blaze)	Ashland	SR 97 bridle area	13 (LP)	E,H,C
MOHICAN STATE PARK				
Clear Fork Gorge &	Ashland	Park cabins,	5 (CT)	H
Lyons Falls Loop		Pleasant Hill Lake		
		dam		
MOSQUITO LAKE STATE PARK				
West Multi-Purpose	Trumbull	Bazetta Road	10 (LN)	H,E,B,C,S
SANDY & BEAVER CREEK CANAL				
The Sandy Beaver Trail	Columbiana	Elkton, Ohio River	21 (LN)	H
(See Beaver Creek SP)				
TAPPAN LAKE & PARK				
Fox Trail	Harrison	Campground	6 (LP)	H
Fox-Deer Trails	Harrison	Campground	8 (CT)	H
WEST BRANCH STATE PARK				
Bridle	Portage	Copeland/Esworthy	20 (CT)	E,H
		Road		
Buckeye Trail segment	Portage	Rock Spring Rd.,	8 (LN)	H
		Knapp	Road	

Key: H-Hiking; B-Bicycling; E-Equestrian (Bridle Trail); C-Cross Country; S-Snowmobile; LP-Loop; LN-Linear (one-way); CT-Combined Trail

Place & Trail Name	County	Trailheads	Miles	Uses
Southeastern Ohio				
BARKCAMP STATE PARK Bridle Trail	Belmont	Horseman's camp, Park Road 6	9 (LP)	E,H,S
BLUE ROCK STATE FOREST Bridle	Muskingum	Forest Rd. 8	5-8 (CT)	E,H
BURR OAK STATE PARK Backpack	Morgan	Ranger Station, boat docks 1-4, beach, dam, campground	19 (LP)	H
Bridle	Athens	CR 58, park office	8 (LP)	E,H,S
CLEAR CREEK METROPARK Ridgetop, Fern, Creek- side Meadow trails	Hocking	Clear Creek Rd. picnic areas	5-6 (LP)	H
GREAT SEAL STATE PARK Shawnee Ridge	Ross	Campground via Sugarloaf Mt. Trail	7.8 (LP)	H,E
Mount Ives Ridge Tr.	Ross	Lick Run Road	6.4 (LP)	H,E
HOCKING HILLS STATE PARK Grandma Gatewood Trail	Hocking	Old Man's Cave, Ash Cave, Cedar Falls	6 (LN)	H,E,C
HOCKING STATE FOREST Bridle (Main Trail)	Hocking	Keister Rd	12 (CT)	E,H
LAKE HOPE STATE PARK Little Sandy, Hope Furnace, Hebron Hollow	Vinton	SR 278, Grouse Pt. Picnic Area, Camp- ground	5 (CT)	H
AEP RECREATION LAND Footpath	Morgan	CR 11, SR 78, Bristol TR 952	9-10 (LN)	H,C
Buckeye Trail segment	Morgan	TR 944, SR 83, CR 27, SR 78	9 (LN)	H
PERRY STATE FOREST Bridle (outer loop)	Perry	CR 48	6 (LP)	E,H
PIKE STATE FOREST Bridle/Buckeye	Pike	Auerville Rd.	5-10 (CT)	E,H
SALT FORK STATE PARK Bridle Trail (orange loop) Bridle Trail (blue loop)	Guernsey Guernsey	Horse Camp Horse Camp	18+(LP) 10 (LP)	E,H E,H
SCIOTO TRAIL STATE FOREST Long Branch Trail & loops	Ross	North Ridge, Stoney Creek rds.	5-7 (CT)	E,H
SHAWNEE STATE FOREST Backpack	Scioto	SR 125	42.8- 57.9 (LP)	H
Cabbage Patch	Adams, Scioto	Lower Twin Creek Road	8-10 (LP)	E,H

PLACE & TRAIL NAME	COUNTY	TRAILHEADS	MILES	USES
Silver Arrow	Scioto	Camp Oyo, horse camp (Bear Lake)	14 (LP)	E,H
Mackletree Pond Lick	Scioto	Pond Lick Rd., SR 125	5-6 (LN)	E,H
STROUDS RUN STATE PARK				
Bridle	Athens	TR 21	8.5 (CT)	E,H
Lakeview	Athens	CR 20	5 (LP)	H
TAR HOLLOW STATE PARK & STATE FOREST				
Chief Logan	Ross, Hocking, Vinton	Pine Lake, Spillway, Fire Tower	22.6 (LP)	H
WAYNE NATIONAL FOREST **LAKE VESUVIUS RECREATION AREA**				
Backpack (yellow blaze)	Lawrence	Boat dock, Vesuvius Furnace	16 (LP)	H
Lakeshore (blue blaze)	Lawrence	Boat dock, Vesuvius Furnace	8 (LP)	H
Horse (Main Loop) (gray diamonds)	Lawrence	CR 29, TR 245, CR 4	31 (CT)	E,H
WAYNE NATIONAL FOREST **IRONTON DISTRICT**				
Symmes Creek	Gallia	Symmes Creek Rd.	6 (LP)	H
Morgan Sisters	Gallia	Symmes Creek Rd., Pumkintown Rd.	8 (LP)	H
WAYNE NATIONAL FOREST **ATHENS UNIT**				
Wildcat Hollow Backpack	Morgan	CR 58	15 (LP)	H
Stone Church	Perry	CR 38	21 (LP)	E,H
WAYNE NATIONAL FOREST **MARIETTA UNIT**				
Ohio View	Washington	SR 7&260	7 (LN)	B,H
Archers Fork	Washington	Grandview Twp.Rd. 14, Jackson Run Rd.	9.5 (LP)	B,H
Covered Bridge	Washington	Hune Bridge Rinard Bridge	5 (LN)	B,H
Lamping Homestead	Monroe	SR 537	5 (LP)	H,B
ZALESKI STATE FOREST				
Backpack (trail begins in Lake Hope State Park)	Vinton	SR 278	23.5 (LP)	H
Bridle (Light Blue)	Vinton	Horse Camp	10.8 (LP)	E,H
Bridle (Dark Blue)	Vinton	Horse Camp	16.4 (LP)	E,H
Bridle (Red)	Vinton	Horse Camp	6.9 (LP)	E,H
Bridle (Black)	Vinton	Horse Camp	6.5 (LP)	E,H
Bridle (Orange)	Vinton	Horse Camp	5.5 (LP)	E,H

Southwestern Ohio

PLACE & TRAIL NAME	COUNTY	TRAILHEADS	MILES	USES
BUCK CREEK STATE PARK				
Buckhorn Trail	Clark	Tailwater parking	6.5 (LN)	H
SnowmobileTrail	Clark	North Marina picnic area	9 (LP)	S,H
BRUSH CREEK STATE FOREST				
Bridle Trail	Scioto, Adams	Ranger Station, Coffee Hollow Road	10 (LN)	E,H

PLACE & TRAIL NAME	COUNTY	TRAILHEADS	MILES	USES
CAESAR CREEK STATE PARK Perimeter Trail (lakeshore)	Warren	Visitor Ctr., Furnas boat ramp, dam	10 (CT)	H
Solidago Downs Trail (bridle trail)	Warren	Furnas Rd. horse camp, boat ramp	20 (LN)	E,H
CLIFTON GORGE NATURAL AREA & JOHN BRYAN STATE PARK North Rim, South Gorge, North Gorge trails	Greene	Clifton (Jackson & Washington sts.), park campground	5.5 (CT)	H
EAST FORK STATE PARK Backpack	Clermont	Campground, park office, Bethel ramp	12 (LP)	H
Newman Worldwalker (Backcountry) Trail	Clermont	Park entrance road	37+ (LP)	H,E
FORT HILL STATE MEMORIAL Deer Trail	Highland	Parking lot	5 (LP)	H
GLEN HELEN NATURE PRESERVE Boy Scout	Greene	Museum	5-10 (LP)	H
LITTLE MIAMI STATE PARK Little Miami Scenic Trail	Greene Warren Hamilton Clermont	Corwin, Ft. Ancient State Memorial, Morrow, Loveland, Terrace Park	50 (LN)	All
PAINT CREEK STATE PARK & STATE WILDLIFE AREA Rattlesnake Bridle Trail	Highland	Rattlesnake boat ramp	12 (LN)	E,H,C
Log Cabin Bridle Trail	Highland	Snake Road	8 (LP)	E,H,C
Snowmobile Trail	Highland	Snake Road	13 (LP)	S,H,E
PAINT CREEK STATE PARK Main Loop (bridle)	Highland	Horse camp	18 (LP)	E,H
Middle Loop (bridle)	Highland	Horse camp	13 (LP)	E,H
Short Loop (bridle)	Highland	Horse camp	7 (LP)	E,H
SYCAMORE STATE PARK Bridle Trail	Montgomery	Wolf Creek Pike parking area	6.8 (CT)	E,H,C
Central Ohio **ALUM CREEK STATE PARK** Winterhawk, Maple Glen, Hunter's Hollow trails	Delaware	Howard Rd. horse camp, boat ramp	43 (LN, CT)	E,H
Multi-Purpose	Delaware	Boat Ramp	7 (LP)	H,C,E,S
KOKOSING GAP TRAIL	Knox	Phillips Park, Mt. Vernon; Howard; Danville	13.2 (LN)	H,B,C
A.W. MARION STATE PARK Hargus Lake Trail	Pickaway	Campground, west shore picnic area	5 (LP)	H

Pedal pushers in ponytails pumping across pavement.

WAYNE NATIONAL FOREST
Marietta Unit
Route 1, Box 132
Marietta, OH 45750
(614) 373-9055

Other Long Walks

In addition to designated hiking trails, Ohio walkers can also travel on so-called bike and hike paths (a.k.a multipurpose and all-purpose trails or rail-trails). These are rewarding and charming routes, but not as physically demanding as the backcountry walks. These smooth paths are perfect for families with small children and people with limited abilities.

Many hikers also follow bridle trails because the routes often venture into rugged territory, and tend to be less crowded. Novices should know that well-trodden riding trails become sloppy and slippery when wet; pocked and hard when summer-baked. But don't let these small obstacles stop you.

State wildlife areas also offer countless miles of paths for bushwacking, improved and otherwise, and thousands of acres. These areas are omitted in the preceding chart (some exceptions) because trails are unmarked and often leave novice walkers lost or confused. The greatest joy of walking in state wildlife areas, however, is going off the trail.

Cycling

Bike Trails

The dapper, freshly painted train depot in Trotwood looks ready for another half century of service. It is a busy place this Saturday. Cars fill the parking lot, and a cop keeps traffic flowing on Main Street. A flock of passengers, tourists mostly, mills around the platform. They finish snacks, shuffle gear, adjust clothing, prepare for departure.

But nobody gazes down the tracks, nor tilts an ear for the hollow hoot of an approaching train. There is no conductor in a baggy coat impatiently checking his pocket watch, no rumble and clatter of box cars; no squeal of brakes. Missing are the mad dash into the coach for a window seat, and the final call of "All aboard."

Instead the "passengers" board bicycles and head single-file along a ribbon of pavement called the Wolf Creek Bikeway. The cop halts traffic so the pack can safely pedal out of town. They leave leisurely and noiselessly, except for the incessant clicking and ticking of shifting Shimano gears. Their destination, Verona, is 13 miles due northwest. The landscape is flat, open farmland. The trail, crushed stone outside Trotwood, runs smooth and level. En route, they'll stop in Brookville and Sycamore State Park, and Verona. Meanwhile, small families, couples, and solo travelers on different schedules depart on foot and two-wheelers, destinations unknown. By four o'clock in the afternoon the bike pack will have departed from the depot, fully exercised and entertained.

Whatever you call them—bike and hike trails, rail-trails, multipurpose trails, bikeways, or all-purpose trails—these paths have irresistible advantages and charm for occasional, recreational bicyclers. They are safe, scenic, separate off-road trails that are easy to pedal, easy to find, and easy to navigate. And they are free, with no cars and trucks to dodge: perfect for families with kids. Depending on surfaces and local rules the trails also allow for other non-motorized activities such as hiking, backpacking, horseback riding, cross-country skiing, in-line skating, jogging, and wheelchair access.

It might be easy to confuse bike trails with established bike routes, bikeways, or bike lanes, which share the main road with autos, trucks, buses, RVs, and motorcycles; the terms are often used interchangeably, so check on the route before departing. Bike lanes are painted strips on streets or roads designated for bikes (no pedestrians please). Bikers get no special treatment on a bike route, which is simply the best "way to go" from place to place be it by road, street, bikeway, or bridge. Though bike trails invite riders of all skill levels, virtuosos seeking speed and thrills are better off on bike routes. The same applies to serious mountain and all-terrain bikers. Pump away on the bikeway, but don't expect an obstacle course.

Ohio's nascent bike-hike trails are driven by popular interest and a sudden, large inventory of abandoned transportation corridors. They are the latest trail system in Ohio.

Migratory animals made the first trails in Ohio's wilderness. Native Americans hunting these animals "improved" the paths and blazed others to connect their settlements. Euro-Americans (hunters, trappers, pioneers, soldiers) used these well-trodden trails to displace the indigenous population.

When its frontier economy grew beyond subsistence Ohio constructed an elaborate and expensive canal system to transport goods to the Atlantic seaboard. Engineers built the canals along rivers and streams. One side of the canal featured a parallel, level embankment called a towpath, along which mules, oxen, or horses towed overloaded, cumbersome canal boats. During the canal era, Ohio had a mule-driven economy.

Canals made Ohio prosperous. They were the engineering marvels in the early nineteenth century. But like the bison trace and Indian path, the canal was replaced by something bigger, faster, noisier, and dirtier—the train.

A century ago the railroad was every town's link to the outside world. It was as important to daily life as today's car, computer, and cable TV. The nation blasted through rock, bridged waterways and ravines, cleared forest, and constructed 300,000 miles of level earthen mounds for the railroads. At its peak in 1914, Ohio was knotted together by a ganglion of track totaling 9,150 miles. The Depression stung railroads, but cars, trucks, airplanes, and mass communications did them more harm. Trains seemed slow, remote, and inefficient compared to these more modern modes of conveyance.

From 1930 to 1975 railroads abandoned 38,000 miles of tracks nationwide. Deregulation of the industry in the 1980s accelerated the downsizing, and an additional 65,000 miles of rails was peeled off the landscape. Following the trend, Ohio lost a third of its track, down to less than 6,000 miles.

So, what can be done with 3,000 miles of orphaned railroad corridor and hundreds of miles of crumbling canal towpaths? One solution has been to turn them into multipurpose linear greenways, sometimes known as "skinny parks." The idea caught fire in the Ohio General Assembly, which in 1972 ordered the Department of Natural Resources to develop a network of recreational trails for non-motorized travel "to the maximum practical extent." Most of the energy for bike paths, though, has come from the local level. Grassroots bicycling and hiking clubs, rails-to-trail conservancies, county park districts, and transportation planners have forged partnerships to resuscitate dead railroad beds. Other advocates have picked up the torch for canals.

Ohio's new trailblazers are not predatory railroad busters. Fact is, they get railways to voluntarily "railbank," a preservation program that keeps inactive rail beds (and their easements) intact in case railroads make a comeback. Until then, the corridor can be used for recreation. Railbanking stops the fragmentation that occurs when a track is legally abandoned.

So far, 21 rails-to-trails projects have converted 221 miles of abandoned railroad grade into public trails. That mileage could double in a few years because 135 corridors have been railbanked. Four sections of canal towpaths, totaling nearly 60 miles, have become popular with novice and serious riders. Some 50-60 more miles of towpath are targeted for "green space." Parks around the state contain 244 additional bikeway miles. Mileage seems to keep growing steadily, but in low gear, complain enthusiasts. In spite of the 1973 mandate, bikeways never boil to the top in state budget battles.

Other efforts, though, provide new hope for two-wheelers. In the early 1990s, the Ohio Chapter of the Rails-to-Trails Conservancy proposed its ambitious Discover Ohio Trails System—a 1,255-mile network of interconnected paths, consisting of the 325-mile Ohio to Erie Trail linking Cleveland, Akron, Columbus, and Cincinnati, plus four regional trail systems. The conservancy figures it will take $76.3 million to finish the Discover Ohio Trails System, so it is expected to be a work-in-progress for many years to come. But highlights of the plan include:

• An *Ohio to Erie Trail*, comprising a string of regional trails, is targeted to be opened in time for state's bicentennial in 2003. Two of the Ohio's premier trails, the existing Little Miami Scenic and Ohio & Erie Canal Towpath trails, will serve as anchors for this pathway.

• The *North Coast Inland Trail* will stretch 61 miles across Sandusky, Lorain, Ottawa, Wood, Erie, and Huron counties.

• Ashtabula will be tied to East Liverpool by the 80-mile *Great Ohio Lake to River Greenway*. Another 35-mile bikeway will run between Akron and Warren.

• Athens will be a hub for trails branching to Belpre (34 miles, and across the Ohio River to West Virginia's North Bend Rail-Trail), Nelsonville (13 miles), and Chillicothe (50 miles).

• The *Tri-County Triangle Trail* (60 miles) will pass through Ross, Highland, and Fayette counties.

• Several bike and hike trails will radiate from Xenia. The spokes will go to Dayton, Springfield, and Washington Court House.

• Also in Southwestern Ohio, look for the 40-mile *Tri-County Greenway* running across Warren, Clinton, and Fayette counties; a 53-mile bikeway connecting Dayton and Cincinnati; and a 20-mile riverfront path in Cincinnati.

State-funded trails can take a decade to finish, but locally-driven projects, like the Wolf Creek Bikeway, can be up and running in two years with fewer bureaucratic hassles. At the local level, county park districts, local rail-to-trail groups, bicycle and hiking clubs, land trusts, foundations, and planning commissions spearhead trailblazing. Here's a sampler of what's in the works on this:

• *The Holmes County Trail* will go right through the heart of Holmes County and Ohio's Amish country. The 34-mile path passes through Millersburg, the county seat, and crosses Killbuck Creek, a canoeing destination.

• One of the marvels of the planned *Perry County Trail* is a 1,000-foot tunnel built in the nineteenth century. Thornport (at Buckeye Lake) and Shawnee are the trailheads on this 31-mile trail, which will connect the Ohio & Erie Trail and the Hocking Hills Trails System.

• The Geauga County Park District is constructing the *Maple Highlands Trail* (21 miles) from Middlefield to the Geauga-Lake county line. The trail will cross the Upper Cuyahoga River, a state scenic river, touch East Branch Reservoir, and cut through Chardon.

• The Ohio & Erie Canal Corridor Coalition pushes for a Cleveland-to-Zoar trail (87 miles) along the canal's towpath. The 20-mile section already developed in the Cuyahoga Valley National Recreation Area attracts more than a million humans annually, and the 24-mile portion in Stark County may soon achieve that level of use. Canal backers enthusiastically refer to the transportation legacy as the "region's Old Faithful."

• A seven-mile segment along the old Cincinnati and Whitewater Canal in Hamilton County is another potential trail.

• Park districts with foresight built multipurpose trails as they created or remodeled parks. Cleveland Metroparks' extensive all-purpose trail network is Ohio's best example. Separate bike and hike trails are appearing beside new interstate highways, such as I-480 in Cuyahoga County and I-670 in Columbus.

At all political levels bike trailblazing requires more brains than brawn, more patience than palaver, and more hutzpah than hype. It requires jumping through hoops, tying stray strands of trails together, keeping supporters on track and energized, obtaining easements, soothing opponents who worry about trash, intruders, maintenance, loss of local autonomy, negotiating with railroads, landowners, and government agencies. Some of the most scenic and promising proposed paths lack local support groups. Trail building also costs money—$60,000 for a mile of crushed limestone, $140,000 for a mile of pavement. If Ohio prospers and its citizens crave a recreational mode of transportation on pace with that of the founding pioneers, trail building will continue on.

The bike trails featured below come in various surfaces—asphalt, crushed gravel or limestone, grass, or the original rail bed. If the surface matters, call ahead for details. See page 508 for a map.

NORTHEAST

BIG CREEK RESERVATION

Location: Cuyahoga County

Trailheads: Brookpark Road, Valley Parkway

Big Creek Reservation is a linear strip of suburban green space (sort of) about 7.5 miles long. Big Creek Trail runs down the middle alongside Big Creek Parkway from Brookpark Road (north) to Valley Parkway in Mill Creek Run Reservation. At this junction (near US 42), bicyclists can travel on the Valley Parkway Trail. This commuter bikepath cuts through Brooklyn, Parma Heights, Middleburg Heights and Strongsville. Hop on at Eastland, Snow, Stumph, East Bagley, Fowles, and Whitney roads, and W. 130th Street. The best place to pull off is Lake Isaac, a glacial kettlehole pond serving as a waterfowl refuge. Don't feed the ducks. *Cleveland Metroparks, 4101 Fulton Parkway, Cleveland, OH 44144-1923, (216) 351-6300.*

BEDFORD RESERVATION

Location: Cuyahoga County

Trailheads: Union St., Alexander Rd.

Like a baby hugging its mother's leg, Gorge Parkway Trail (5.25 miles) sticks close to Gorge Parkway and Overlook Lane. At the Union Street trailhead in Bedford the route continues east along Hawthorn Parkway to South Chagrin Reservation. From here to the Alexander Road trailhead, bikers can enter via Egbert, Willis, and Dunham roads. Both trailheads offer parking, and picnic areas, foot trails, and dazzling views that encourage delays. A must stop is the overlook into Tinker's Creek Gorge, a National Natural Landmark. *Cleveland Metroparks, 4101 Fulton Parkway, Cleveland, OH 44144-1923, (216) 351-6300.*

BIKE & HIKE TRAIL (LORAIN)

Location: Lorain County

Trailheads: Train depot, SR 58

The memory of two railroads lives strong in Oberlin. Fugitive slaves knew the town as the northernmost station on the Underground Railroad; a network of clandestine routes and sanctuaries African-American slaves followed to escape southern slavery. The next stop, after crossing Lake Erie, was Canada. Oberlin remembers the Underground Railroad during an annual summer festival.

Conrail trains traveling east or west also deposited people in this progressive college town. The bike trail running across town recalls this link with the outside world. Oberlin stands midway in a 12-mile route that connects Elyria and Kipton. The North Inland Coast Trail may absorb the trail, too. A parking lot for trail use is located at the aboveground train depot in Oberlin. *Lorain County Park District, 85 South Main Street, Oberlin, OH 44074, (216) 775-1513.*

BIKE & HIKE TRAIL (SUMMIT)

Location: Summit County

Trailheads: Silver Springs Park, Kent, Highland Road

Ohio's second rail-to-trail goes diagonally across northern Summit County, stretching from Sagamore Hills to the western edge of Kent. It also connects with Cleveland's Emerald Necklace and the Cuyahoga Valley National Recreation Area's towpath trails.

The product of a partnership between Ohio Edison Company and the Metroparks Serving Summit County, the path opened in 1972. Metroparks leases the route from the utility and maintains the trail. It follows the course of the "Alphabet Railroad," short for the Akron, Bedford & Cleveland intercity electric trolley, and a former New York Central route. The trolley later merged with other electric lines to form the Northern Ohio Traction & Light Company, the precursor of Ohio Edison.

Most riders rate the section between the Ohio Turnpike and State Route 303 the most spectacular because it passes beneath tall ledges cut for the railroads. This segment also parallels the eastern border of the Cuyahoga Valley National Recreation Area. Another beauty rest is Brandywine

Falls, just west of I-271.

On a map the trail is shaped like a scoop. Just east of State Route 8 the path divides. From here the northern fork heads southeast to Silver Springs Park in Stow. The southern branch goes south to Cuyahoga Falls then east along the scenic Cuyahoga River to the Summit-Portage county line. Portions of the trail inside Cuyahoga Falls are paved, and so is the section from Cuyahoga Falls to the county line. Elsewhere the surface is crushed gravel. The trail follows city streets between Hudson Drive and Silver Lake.

Safety posts narrow the trail at road crossings. Riders must dismount and walk their bikes through the gates. This safety feature can be troublesome for bikers toting trailers and kid carts, and for wheelchair patrons. *Metroparks Serving Summit County, 975 Treaty Line Road, Akron, OH 44313; (330) 867-5511.*

BLACK RIVER RESERVATION BRIDGEWAY TRAIL
Location: Lorain County
Trailheads: Day's Dam Area, Burr Oak Area, in park

This 12-foot wide asphalt trail runs 3.5 miles along the wooded flood plain of the Black River. The reservation straddles the border of Elyria and Lorain. A 1,000-foot, elbow-shaped bridge crosses the river twice and winds around treetops. A tram, the only motorized vehicle allowed on the trail, runs through the valley from the Day's Dam Picnic Area. North end parking is at the Day's Dam Picnic Area, off 31st Street, while the Burr Oak Picnic Area (off Ford Road) serves as the south terminus parking lot. *Lorain County Park District, 85 South Main Street, Oberlin, OH 44074, (440) 775-1513.*

BRECKSVILLE RESERVATION VALLEY PARKWAY TRAIL
Location: Cuyahoga County
Trailheads: Valley Parkway at Brecksville Rd, Riverview Rd., Chippewa Road.

This 4-mile stretch links to the Towpath Trail. *Cleveland Metroparks, 4101 Fulton Parkway, Cleveland, OH 44144-1923, (216) 351-6300.*

COSHOCTON TOWPATH TRAIL
Location: Coshocton County
Trailheads: Lake Park, SR 83

Here's another way to experience historic Roscoe Village. The refurbished towpath of the Ohio & Erie Canal now serves as a bike and hike trail connecting Lake Park Recreation Area with Roscoe Village and the Monticello III canal boat. A bridge crosses the Walhonding River a mile above its merger with the Tuscarawas River in Coshocton. After pedaling, relax aboard the 1800s canal boat and let the mules do all the work. Camping, swimming, playground, golf available at Lake Park Recreation Area. *Coshocton County Park District, 23253 SR 83, Coshocton, OH 43812, (740) 622-7528.*

EUCLID RESERVATION
Location: Cuyahoga County
Trailheads: Euclid Parkway, Highland & Green roads

A 2.5-mile ride. *Cleveland Metroparks, 4101 Fulton Parkway, Cleveland, OH 44144-1923, (216) 351-6300.*

GARFIELD RESERVATION
Location: Cuyahoga County
Trailheads: Broadway Avenue, Turney Road

A 2.4 mile path. *Cleveland Metroparks, 4101 Fulton Parkway, Cleveland, OH 44144-1923, (216) 351-6300.*

GRAVEL BASED TRAIL
Location: Cuyahoga County
Trailheads: Alexander Road, Highland Road

Alexander Road serves as a starting point for the Gravel Based Trail, a five-mile crushed limestone route that rides atop an abandoned New York Central railroad bed. Some consider this path to Highland Road an extension of the 20-mile Bike & Hike Trail (see Metroparks Serving Summit County). Cleveland Metroparks maintains the trail between Alexander and Highland roads. Riders can reach Brecksville Reservation and the Cuyahoga Valley National Recreation Area via a path between the Bike & Hike and the Towpath trails. *Cleveland Metroparks, 4101 Fulton Parkway, Cleveland, OH 44144-1923, (216) 351-6300.*

HINCKLEY RESERVATION
Location: Medina County
Trailheads: Bellus Road, East Drive, West Drive

A 3-mile path. *Cleveland Metroparks, 4101 Fulton Parkway, Cleveland, OH 44144-1923, (216) 351-6300.*

HUNTINGTON RESERVATION

Location: Cuyahoga County

Trailheads: Lake and Wolf roads

A jaunt of one mile. *Cleveland Metroparks, 4101 Fulton Parkway, Cleveland, OH 44144-1923, (216) 351-6300.*

I-480 BIKEWAY

Location: Cuyahoga County

Trailheads: Great No. Blvd. & Country Club; Stearns Rd., North Olmstead

Don't worry, a fence separates bikers from motorists on the busy highway. Park at Great Northern Shopping Center, near the eastern terminus. *City of North Olmstead, 5200 Dover Center Road, North Olmstead, OH 44070, (216) 777-8000.*

HEADWATERS TRAIL

Location: Portage County

Trailheads: Village parks in Mantua; Garrettsville; SR 700, Hiram Station

Named for its proximity to the headwaters of the Cuyahoga and Mahoning rivers, Headwaters Trail runs east-west between Garrettsville and Mantua. The cinder-gravel (eventually rolled crushed stone) route passes Marsh Wetlands and Mantua Bog state natural areas outside Mantua. Headwaters Landtrust purchased the corridor and donated it to the *Portage County Park District, 449 South Meridian Street, Ravenna, OH 44266-2963, (330) 673-9404.*

LESTER RAIL TRAIL

Location: Medina County

Trailheads: Lester Road depot; Medina County Join Vocational School

The Village of Lester still has an active freight train station. Now bicyclists wheel into the depot from Medina. Park at the Medina County Joint Vocational School, 1101 West Liberty Street (SR 18), Medina. This is a section of a planned longer path across the county. Eventually, it will link with the Chippewa Rail Trail, bearing south of the county seat. Plans call for the crushed limestone surface to be paved at a later time. *Medina County Park District, 6364 Deerview Lane, Medina, OH 44256, (330) 722-9364 or 225-7100 ext. 9364.*

MOSQUITO LAKE STATE PARK

West & East Multipurpose Trails

Location: Trumbull County

Trailheads: Hoagland-Blackstub Road; West Main Street, Cortland

The park's West Multipurpose Trail, 5.5-mile earthen path fit for mountain bikes, runs straight along the western shore of Mosquito Lake between Everett Hull Road and SR 88 (11 miles roundtrip). The dirt trail, shared by hikers, equestrians, cross-country skiers and snowmobilers, becomes muddy and pocked, but there are plenty of lake views and chances to see waterfowl and other wildlife. The trail staging area is on Hoagland-Blackstub Road (Bazetta Road) north of Everett Hull Road. Some riders start at the fishing access at the end of Housel-Craft Road. The East Multipurpose Trail has loops branching from a 1.5-mile main stem, and if you ride them all figure on a five-mile journey. Look for the trailhead at the end of Main Street, west of SR 46. *Mosquito Lake State Park, 1439 SR 305, Cortland, OH 44410-9303, (330) 637-2856.*

NORTH CHAGRIN RESERVATION

Location: Cuyahoga County

Trailheads: SOM Center, Chardon Lake roads, Strawberry Lane

Pedal for four miles on the Buttermilk Falls Parkway Trail. *Cleveland Metroparks, 4101 Fulton Parkway, Cleveland, OH 44144-1923, (216) 351-6300.*

OHIO & ERIE CANAL TOWPATH TRAIL

Location: Cuyahoga, Summit counties

Trailheads: Rockside Road, Boston Mills, and points noted in text.

This path is simply irresistible, taking you on a nostalgic journey through time and place. The time is the early 19th century when dour mules dragged canal boats along the elevated towpath of the Ohio & Erie Canal. The place is the Cuyahoga Valley National Recreation Area, an enchanting and pastoral setting, somewhere between unshaven suburbia and upscale small town.

Since opening in 1993, the nearly 20-mile towpath has been the park's showcase, and a mecca for users. It attracts 1.5 to 2 million people annually. The towpath is the best way to enjoy the park's many historical sites, natural wonders, and abundant wildlife. Pick up a park brochure before pedaling.

Proceed at a mule's pace. Check out the locks, scope out the old stone farmhouses, see the exhibits in the visitors' centers, admire the towering highway bridges, stop for refreshments in Peninsula, and board the scenic railroad. Take branch foot trails to

Brandywine or Blue Hen Falls, or to Hale Farm and Blossom Music Center. Follow foot trails, count deer, find the heron rookery, smell wildflowers, sleep over at the hostel. Portions of the Towpath Trail serve as bridle routes, so watch out for horses.

The Ohio & Erie Canal Corridor hopes to extend the trail to Cleveland and Zoar Village.

The northern half of the route, 10.5 miles, runs between the Lock 39 Trailhead at Rockside Road to Lock 32 in Boston Mills. Staging areas (parking, rest rooms, and water) are located at the Station Road Bridge Trailhead, off Riverview Road at the entrance to Brecksville Reservation, Canal Visitor Center and Frazee House, both on Canal Road. Note that canal lock numbers decrease north to south (or as you go upstream), but mile markers (indicating distance from Lake Erie) increase. Just north of Mile 19, a connector trail (part of the Old Carriage Trail) leads to the Bike & Hike Trail. The American Youth Hostel organization operates a hostel in Boston Mills on Stanford Road.

Indian Mound Trailhead south of Bath Road marks the end of the southern section. Before you get there you will go beneath interstate highways, across beaver marshes on wood decks, through picturesque Peninsula (food, bike rental, scenic railroad), and by canal locks named Mudcatcher, Pancake, and Johnny Cake. Access points are located at Lock 29 in Peninsula, Hunt Farm Visitor Information Center, and Ira. *Cuyahoga Valley National Recreation Area, 15610 Vaughn Road, Brecksville, OH 44141, (800) 445-9667 or (216) 524-1497.*

OHIO & ERIE CANAL TOWPATH TRAIL (STARK COUNTY)

Location: Stark County

Trailheads: Canal Fulton Visitors Center, Lock 4 Park, Warmington Rd., Butterbridge Rd., Crystal Springs., Hudson Drive, Riverland Road

The Ohio & Erie Canal Towpath continues in Stark County along the Tuscarawas River. Five miles of improved trail—from Canal Fulton to Crystal Springs—is open for biking, hiking, and equestrian use. Mountain bikes, horses, and hikers can use the towpath in the following sections: Crystal Springs (Fulton Drive) to Lake Avenue, Massillon; Warmington Street (Perry Township) to north Navarre limits; south Navarre limits (Brinker Street) to Bolivar; and Canal Fulton north to Summit County line. That's 24 miles of towpath fun. The Buckeye Trail follows the towpath, too.

The segments in Massillon and Navarre, and a rail-trail spur to Dalton in Wayne County, may be open soon. Meanwhile, use city streets to bridge these gaps in the trail. Seven small parking areas are spaced along the path. *Stark County Park District, 5300 Tyner Avenue NW, Canton, OH 44708, (330) 477-3552.*

RICHLAND B & O TRAIL

Location: Richland County

Trailheads: North Lake Park, Mansfield; SR 95, Butler, SR 97.

The Clear Fork of the Mohican River and swelling hills of Richland County frames this new, sickle-shaped, 18-mile trail. It rides atop the old Baltimore & Ohio grade from Butler to Mansfield, and passes through Bellville, Lexington, and Alta. Between Butler and Lexington, riders span the river five times, and pedal beneath I-71.

Add the bikeway to the attractions and activities in Mohican Territory. Gorman Nature Center, headquarters of the Richland County Park District, is just 1.5 miles east of the trail on US 42 (off Hanley Road). At the Mansfield terminus, pedal a few blocks to see the Kingswood Center gardens and mansion.

Towns are conveniently spaced so the trail can be pedaled in segments. From the Butler terminus, Bellville is five miles; Bellville to Lexington, six miles; Lexington to Mansfield, seven miles. In Lexington, riders briefly use sidewalks so they can cross Main Street at a traffic light. Parking and rest rooms are located at Hitchman Park in Butler, Community Park in Lexington, and North Lake Park in Mansfield. You also find parking at Bellville, SR 97 (just east of I-71), and Deer Park, south of Alta. A detailed map and mileage chart are available at the *Gorman Nature Center, 2295 Lexington Avenue, Mansfield, OH 44907, (419) 884-3764.*

ROCKY RIVER AND MILL CREEK RUN RESERVATIONS

Location: Cuyahoga County

Trailheads: Detroit Road, W. 130th St.

Valley Parkway Trail is a 21.5-mile all-purpose path that braids with the Rocky River through both reservations, going from Detroit Road in Lakewood to West 130th Street (south of the Ohio Turnpike). There are tons of temptations along the route—picnic areas, fishing spots, nature center, wading pools, hiking trails, Indian earthworks, and scenic stops. In Rocky River Reservation you can enter the trail at Riverside Drive, Wooster and Mastick roads, Brookway Lane, and Cedar Point, Old Lorain, Spafford, Barrett and Bagley roads. Mill Creek entrances are at SR 82 and US 42, and Albion, Handle, Lee, Prospect, Eastland, Edgerton and Bagley roads, and South Rocky River Drive. *Cleveland Metroparks, 4101 Fulton Parkway, Cleveland, OH 44144-1923, (216) 351-6300.*

SOUTH CHAGRIN RESERVATION

Location: Cuyahoga County

Trailheads: Harper Ridge Picnic Area on Hawthorn Parkway, Squaw Rock Picnic Area

Pedal 3.5 miles on the Hawthorn Parkway Trail. *Cleveland Metroparks, 4101 Fulton Parkway, Cleveland, OH 44144-1923, (216) 351-6300.*

SOUTHEAST

ATHENS COUNTY BIKEWAY

Location: Athens County

Trailheads: Athens, Ohio University; W. State St. ballfields; Beaumont; Hocking Tech (Robins Crossing)

A recreation easement donated by American Electric Power permitted development of this pretty 13-mile rail trail along the Hocking River. Asphalt covers the rail bed from Ohio University in Athens to Hocking Technical College in Nelsonville. Beaumont, a crossroads hamlet on SR 682, is a convenient halfway stop. Plans for spokes branching from Athens to Zaleski and Belpre, and from Nelsonville to Shawnee in Perry County are still in the dream stage. *Athens County Commissioners, 15 South Court Street, Athens, OH 45701, (740) 592-4431.*

STAVICH BICYCLE TRAIL

Location: Mahoning County; Lawrence, Penn.

Trailheads: SR 289 at New Castle Road, Washington St., New Castle (Penn.)

The 12-mile paved route links Struthers and New Castle, Pennsylvania. The Stavich Foundation built the path in 1983 on an abandoned interurban grade that snaked along the Mahoning River. Active B&O tracks are alongside, but they are safely separated from the bikeway. Hills, farms, small towns, woods provide a pastoral setting. *Falcon Foundry, 6th & Water streets, Lowellville, OH 44436, (330) 536-6221.*

GALLIPOLIS BIKE PATH

Location: Gallia & Vinton counties

Trailheads: Pine St., Gallipolis; Kerr; Bidwell; Vinton; Minerton

Looking northwest from Gallipolis the terrain is generous with bumpy hills, and rocky slopes—all too steep for the feet of most humans and beasts. But that's the direction the bikeway takes, up through the hills. Fortunately, railroad builders used dynamite and bulldozer to flatten the grade, so the climb is gentle and postcard pretty.

The first paved section, about 2.5 miles, goes from Pine Street (SR 160) in Gallipolis to Old US 35. Asphalt appears again in Kerr (three miles north) and continues 4.5 miles to SR 554 in Bidwell. (To reach Kerr, go east on Old US 35, and north on SR 160). Unpaved portions of the cinder trail are open to mountain bikers and foot travelers. Eventually, the 25-mile route will be blacktopped from Minerton in Vinton County and to Kanauga, where US 35 crosses the Ohio River into West Virginia. Park on streets in Gallipolis, Kerr and Bidwell. *O.O. McIntyre Park District, Gallia County Courthouse, Gallipolis, OH 45631, (740) 446-4612.*

ZANESVILLE RIVERFRONT BIKEPATH

Location: Muskingum County

Trailheads: Riverview Park, Market Street in Zanesville

The three-mile bikeway tours the Muskingum

River as it passes through downtown Zanesville. It runs along the east bank from Riverview Park (north terminus) to Market Street. Trains still run on parallel tracks but riders are protected by a barrier. Sites include a restored train station (now a visitors bureau) near Market Street, the *Loreena* paddleboat, and the Y-shaped bridge (several blocks south of Market Street). Park at the train depot and in parks. *City of Zanesville, 401 Market Street, Zanesville, OH 43701, (740) 455-0609.*

CENTRAL

BLACKHAND GORGE TRAIL

Location: Licking County

Trailheads: Nature preserve in Toboso, Brushy Fork Road

Follow the 5.5-mile route through Blackhand Gorge used by Native Americans, canal travelers, and railroad passengers. Many rank this Ohio's most scenic bike trail. It travels through Blackhand Gorge State Natural Area, along the wooded south shore of the Licking River. Families can combine biking and hiking, as there are several footpaths branching from the paved path. Flint Ridge State Memorial is just a few miles away. Enthusiasts want to connect this route to the nearby Evans Bike Trail and Ohio Canal Greenway. *Ohio Department of Natural Resources, Fountain Square, Columbus, OH 43224, (614) 265-6395.*

BLACKLICK METROPARK BIKE TRAIL

Location: Franklin, Fairfield counties

Trailheads: Picnic areas, Livingston Ave.

Flat terrain makes this short course popular with families. The path traces the western and southern boundaries, and finishes in a loop in the southeastern corner of the park. Local residents start at the bike entrance on Livingston Avenue, but folks arriving in cars can enter the trail at the picnic areas or nature center. Visit (on foot) the huge beeches in Blacklick Woods (Walter A. Tucker State Natural Area), or linger at the observation window in the nature center. *Metropolitan Park Distirct of Columbus and Franklin County, 1069 W. Main St., Westerville, OH 43081, (614) 891-0700.*

HERITAGE TRAIL

Location: Franklin, Madison counties

Trailheads: Main St., Hilliard; Homestead Park; Plain City

From the center of Old Hilliard, where the train tracks cross Main Street, you can bike or hike straight northwest across farmland as flat and soft as a pancake. The path is paved to Hayden Run Road, 2 miles beyond Homestead Park. Planners hope to extend it to Plain City, where you'll cross Sugar Run via a turn-of-the-century stone arch tressle, and Big Darby Creek, a national and state scenic river. There are restaurants and parking at both ends of the journey. *Heritage Rails-to-Trails, Homestead Park, 4675 Cosgray Road, Amlin, OH 43002, (614) 876-9554.*

INTERSTATE 670 BIKEWAY

Location: Franklin County

Trailheads: Cleveland & Leonard avenues, Columbus.

Wise planners created a bike trail while drawing a new highway. The three-mile bikeway runs parallel to I-670, which cuts across Columbus. Somebody, however, forgot to add parking lots, so bikers will have to park on city streets. Master planners want to link this route to existing and planned paths. *City of Columbus, Division of Traffic Engineering, 109 North Front St., Columbus, OH 43215, (614) 645-7790.*

KOKOSING GAP TRAIL

Location: Knox County

Trailheads: Phillips Park, Mt. Vernon; US 36, Howard; Washington St., Danville

You can pedal along the Kokosing River a state scenic river, on the old Pennsylvania line from Mt. Vernon to Danville. The route, 13.2 miles long, goes through Gambier, home of Kenyon College, and Howard. Scenery includes woods, wetlands, and farms. Steel span bridges cross the river at two spots, and a stone arch lifts US 36 overhead in Howard. Projects are underway to continue the trail to Brinkhaven and diagonally across Holmes County. *Kokosing Gap Trail, P.O. Box 129, Gambier, OH 43022, (614) 427-4509 or (614) 587-6267.*

OHIO CANAL GREENWAY

Location: Licking County

Trailheads: Canal Park in Hebron, SR 79

Eventually this segment will join the Evans trail and become part of the grand Ohio & Erie Trail. For now this three-mile path goes from US 40 (National Road) in Hebron to SR 79, a mile west of Buckeye Lake on the Licking-Fairfield county line. It rides atop an abandoned rail line and the old towpath of the Ohio & Erie Canal. Just south of I-70, the trail spans a small stream via a covered wooden bridge. A good place to start is Canal Park in Hebron. Mountain bikes are recommended for this dirt track. *Licking County Park District, 4309 Lancaster Road, Granville, OH 43023, (740) 587-2535.*

OLENTANGY-SCIOTO BIKEWAY

Location: Franklin County

Trailheads: Frank Road, Berliner Park, Antrim Park, Wilson Bridge Road, OSU, Whetstone Park.

The bikeway offers pleasant pedaling along the riverfront of downtown Columbus, and through parks along the Olentangy River. The 1.5-mile section from Frank Road to Greenlawn Avenue became Ohio's first rail-to-trail in 1969. The trail continues along the east bank of the Scioto River in downtown Columbus to the confluence of the Scioto and Olentangy rivers. At Fifth Avenue, it goes through the campus of Ohio State University and Tuttle Park to Dodridge Street. It skips to Clinton Park on Weber Road, where the most scenic section begins. There are no interruptions for the next 6.5 miles. It concludes at Wilson Bridge Road.

Watch out for speed demons and joggers on this heavily used trail. The route is tricky north of Weber Road. *Columbus Recreation and Parks Department, 420 Whittier St., Columbus, OH 43215, (614) 645-3300.*

SHARON WOODS METROPARK

Location: Franklin County

Trailheads: Maple Grove Picnic Area

Watch out for deer. The park is loaded with them, but most have learned to stay off the paved bike path, a 4-mile loop. Expect some hills, too. Thoughtful engineers installed a trailside drinking fountain in the middle of the Edward S. Thomas State Natural Area (part of the park) and beverage machines at the staging area. Park at the end of the lot for the Maple Grove Picnic Area. *Metropolitan Park Distirct of Columbus and Franklin County, 1069 W. Main St., Westerville, OH 43081, (614) 891-0700.*

THOMAS J. EVANS BIKE TRAIL

Location: Licking County

Trailheads: Newark (W.&E. Main St., Cherry Valley Rd., White's Field), Johnstown (Douglas Ave.), Granville, Alexandria.

Some 13.5 miles of the route follows Raccoon Creek through woods, farms, meadows—a great outing for families or couples. Try this Chamber of Commerce itinerary: breakfast in Newark, lunch in Johnstown, dinner in historic Granville. Alexandria is a convenient midway stop on this 14-mile path. Riders slowly glide downhill from Johnstown to Alexandria, but the terrain becomes hilly near Newark.

Another leg journeys along SR 16 from East Main Street in Newark to SR 668, 5.5 miles east of the county seat. Go south on SR 668 a bit and hop on the Blackhand Gorge bikeway. A recently finished section (3.5 miles) starts at White's Athletic Field in downtown Newark and follows SR 16 westward to Cherry Valley Road. Go south on Cherry Valley Road and west on West Main Street to reach the main spur. *Thomas J. Evans Foundation, P.O. Box 4212, Newark, OH 43055, (740) 345-9711.*

SOUTHWEST

HAMILTON BIKEWAY

Location: Butler County

Trailheads: Soldiers and Sailors Monument, Joyce Park, in Hamilton

The Great Miami River is the backdrop for a 3.5-mile riverside bike trail through Hamilton. The path runs from the Soldiers and Sailors Monument in Downtown Hamilton to Joyce Park on Entrance Road. *City of Hamilton, Department of Parks and Recreation, Municipal Building, 20 High Street, Hamilton, OH 45011, (513) 868-5874.*

HUFFMAN PRAIRIE OVERLOOK TRAIL

Location: Greene County

Trailheads: Wright Bros. Memorial, Fairborn

The narrow corridor consists of working railroad tracks, a busy state highway, and a rough bike path down the middle. This route is supposed to improve with age, and be linked to other trails being developed by the Miami Valley Regional Bicycle Council. Mountain bikes can manage the original cinder trail, which serves as a segment of the Buckeye Trail.

The best place to start and finish is the west terminus (north side of tracks) by the Wright Brothers Memorial on Kauffman Road, near the SR 444 junction. Huffman Metropark lies just west of this starting point, and the path traces the northern edge of Wright State University. Central Avenue is the eastern trailhead; there you can cross the tracks and pedal on the Kauffman Avenue bikeway (two miles) and backtrack. *Miami Valley Regional Bicycle Council, 1304 Horizon Drive, Fairborn, OH 45324, (937) 879-2068 or (937) 255-4097.*

LITTLE MIAMI SCENIC TRAIL

Location: Hamilton, Greene, Clark, and Clermont counties

Trailheads: various, see below

If you had to ride just one trail, this is it. The route itself is a major attraction in one of the state's top travel destinations.

Ohio's premier bike trail goes flat out for 55 miles, most of it along the Little Miami River, a national and state scenic river. It traverses Hamilton, Clermont, Warren, and Greene counties. Right now, it is the state's longest bike trail, and when it is finished it will measure 72 miles. Asphalt makes for smooth riding.

More than 30 miles of the route go through Little Miami State Park. It also passes through or near (north to south) Glen Helen Nature Preserve, Antioch College, John Bryan State Park, Clifton Gorge State Natural Area, Old Town Reserve, Spring Valley State Wildlife Area, Caesar Creek State Park, Caesar Creek State Natural Area, Fort Ancient State Memorial, Halls Creek Natural Area and Kings Island amusement park. There are plenty of antique shops, restaurants, historic train stations, covered bridges, mills to explore along the way, not to mention bike rentals, canoeing, camping, fishing, wading and more.

Little Miami State Park has staging areas (parking, picnicking, rest rooms, and phones) in Loveland, Morrow, and Corwin. You can also park and hop on the trail at Spring Valley State Wildlife Area, Old Town Reserve, Glen Helen Nature Preserve (Yellow Springs), Fort Ancient State Memorial, Miamiville, Xenia, or in any of the towns on the route. Make sure you are legally parked.

A 31 mile stretch from Milford to Oregonia lies within the state park. The 11 miles between Corwin to southern edge of Xenia is co-managed by the Greene County Park District and the state park. The county park manages the 10 miles from Xenia to Yellow Springs. A separate three-mile segment crosses Springfield. Between Milford and Kroger Hill the road surface can be rough. All but the last two sections have parallel dirt trails for horseback riding. The Yellow Springs to Springfield path, and sections in Xenia and Springfield are completed.

Many abandoned railroad lines radiate from Xenia, once a train hub. Long-range plans call for bike paths branching from here to Columbus and Dayton.

Bikers can now find canoe liveries (some with

camping) in the valley, in case the urge is to paddle instead of pedal. Hikers, roller skaters, cross-country skiers, backpackers, and joggers also enjoy the trail, so be alert.

Don't hurry. Enjoy the valley's historic sites and rich natural history. See the Indian earthworks at Fort Ancient State, or stop at Old Town Reserve, birthplace of Tecumseh. Glen Helen Nature Preserve and Caesar Creek State Natural Area are must stops for nature lovers. Some 340 wildflower species reside in the river corridor, notably Virginia bluebells, wild ginger, bellworts, and wild columbine. The Little Miami River is an important flyway for birds, and you are apt see the great blue heron, kingfisher, and red-tailed hawk along the way. *Little Miami State Park, 8570 East State Route 73, Waynesville, OH 45068-9719, (937) 897-3055; Greene County Park District, 651 Dayton-Xenia Road, Xenia, OH 45385, (937) 376-7440; Springfield Parks & Recreation Department, City Hall, 76 E. High Street, Springfield, OH 45502, (937) 324-7348.*

LUNKEN AIRPORT HIKE AND BIKE TRAIL
Location: Hamilton County
Trailheads: Lunken Playfield, Wilmer St.
Watch buzzards and Beechcraft airplanes soar in holding patterns while you circle around Lunken Field on a six-mile loop trail. The municipally-owned airport is east of downtown Cincinnati, near the confluence of the Little Miami and Ohio rivers. From downtown Cincinnati, go east on US 50, right on SR 125, right on Wilmer Street. You can rent bikes (in season), and dine there. *Cincinnati Recreation Commission, 2 Centennial Plaza, 8th Floor, Cincinnati, OH 45202, (513) 352-4000.*

MIAMI-ERIE CANAL BIKEWAY
Location: Butler County
Trailheads: Rentschler Forest Preserve
Only a mile of the Miami-Erie Bikeway—the portion in Rentschler Forest Preserve—is "improved" for regular biking. Beyond this segment, mountain bikes are recommended and riders may encounter obstacles. The trail goes along the abandoned towpaths of the Miami-Erie and Hydraulic canals (2-3 miles) into Hamilton. The best place to start is Rentschler Forest Preserve, a Butler County metropark on Riegart Road (off SR 4). The park rents bikes during warm months. Long-range plans will connect the riverside and canal trails, and extend it to Middletown, via the towpath. *Metroparks of Butler County, 2200 Hancock Avenue, Hamilton, OH 45011, (513) 867-5835.*

MIAMI-WHITEWATER FOREST, SHAKER TRACE MULTI-PURPOSE TRAIL
Location: Hamilton County
Trailheads: Visitor Center & harbor
The trail takes its name from the members of the United Society of Believers in Christ's Second Appearing, or Shakers, who founded the communal settlement of Whitewater here in 1824. The villagers farmed and sold top-quality seeds, brooms, furniture and other crafts to support themselves. The community ended in 1916.

Today, Miami-Whitewater Forest, a Hamilton County Park District site, surrounds the Shaker settlement, now being restored. The 7.8-mile outer loop journeys through various wildlife habitats—forests, wetlands, prairies, and meadows—on the perimeter of the park. Bring binoculars for birding. Shelters are spaced along the course, and the route has mile markers. A bridle trail parallels the outer loop. A 1.2-mile inner loop features a fitness course. Beginners and toddlers should stick to this path. Both loops and bridle trail begin at the park's visitor center on Mt. Hope Road. *Hamilton County Park District, 10245 Winton Road, Cincinnati, OH 45231, (513) 521-7275.*

RIVER CORRIDOR BIKEWAY
Location: Montgomery County
Trailheads: Sinclair Park, Rice Field
This paved path goes along the Great Miami and Stillwater rivers from Sinclair Park in North Dayton, through downtown Dayton to Rice Field in Miami Township—a distance of 22 miles. The route also goes through Moraine, West Carrollton and Miamisburg, where the setting changes from urban to suburban. In downtown Dayton it runs on both levees of the Great Miami River. Bike commuters use the trail during rush hours.

The trail shares city streets in several places, but car traffic is light. Access in downtown Dayton (between Helena Street and Stewart Avenue) requires toting bikes down pedestrian stairs to the trails. Some stairways have grooved ramps so that bikes can be rolled on slopes. A detailed map from the Miami Valley Regional Bicycle Council shows the location of ramps, parking, rest rooms, and sites on a detailed map.

Points of interest include Carillon Historical Park, Dayton Museum of Natural History, DeWeese Park, Vietnam Veterans' Memorial Park, Riverbend Art Center, Dayton Playhouse, Wegerzyn Horticultural Center, Triangle and Island parks, Dayton Art

Institute, Kettering Field, and Sinclair College.

The east bank path briefly ascends the Mad River before crossing at Webster Street. A proposed trail along the Mad River will start here and go to Huffman Metropark. Use the west bank path to reach Wolf Creek Rail Trail. *Miami Valley Regional Bicycle Council, 400 Miami Valley Tower, 40 W. 4th St., Dayton, OH 45402, (937) 223-6323; Five Rivers Metroparks, 1375 E. Siebenthaler Avenue, Dayton, OH 45414, (937) 275-PARK.*

SHARON WOODS PARK BIKE TRAIL

Location: Hamilton County

Trailheads: Sharon Harbor

The park's 2.6-mile bike trail follows the shore of Sharon Woods Lake. Start and finish at the Sharon Harbor (boathouse and bike rental) off Kemper Road. At Kreis Dam, park the bike and hike into Sharon Woods Gorge, a state-designated natural area. *Hamilton County Park District, 10245 Winton Road, Cincinnati, OH 45231, (513) 521-7275.*

WINTON WOODS HIKE & BIKE TRAIL

Location: Hamilton County

Trailheads: Boathouse, picnic areas in park

Bring your own wheels or rent them at the boathouse. The paved ribbon sticks close to the curb of Lakeview Drive and Valleyview Drive, the main drag through the park, and to the north shore of Winton Lake. The designated terminus is the boathouse off Lakeview Drive, but riders can hop onto the path from any roadside picnic areas or at the visitor center. This metropark offers camping and trails for hikers and horseback riders. *Hamilton County Park District, 10245 Winton Road, Cincinnati, OH 45231, (513) 521-7275.*

WOLF CREEK RAIL TRAIL

Location: Montgomery County

Trailheads: Trotwood depot, Main St.; Golden Gate Park, Brookville; Verona

Bikers tired of the Dayton's urban River Corridor route should try this rural alternative. The path follows an old CSX rail bed (before that the Dayton & Union Railroad) from Trotwood to the Montgomery-Preble county line. Thank Trotwood, Brookville and Five Rivers MetroParks for cooperatively building the path. Woods, farms, meadows, and the Wolf Creek valley provide a backdrop for the route. Trotwood and Brookville have restored train depots that are worth a stop. The trail touches Sycamore State Park where bikers will find picnic tables, foot trails, and natural scenery.

The trail should soon hook up with the River Corridor and extend into Preble County. Eventually the route will be paved. Park at the trailheads (Verona and Trotwood), parks, nearby streets. *Five Rivers Metroparks, 1375 E. Siebenthaler Ave., Dayton, OH 45414, (937) 275-PARK.*

NORTHWEST

CELINA COLDWATER BIKEWAY

Location: Mercer County

Trailheads: Schunk Rd. and US 127 in Celina

When the Norfolk and Western train slows down in Celina, 12-year-old boys and girls on Huffy bikes get ready to race Casey Jones. Few go the distance on the 4.5-mile route to Coldwater.

For most riders, though, the pace is waltz-like on this popular family route. Huffy Corporation, once based in Celina, bought the right-of-way so employees could ride Huffy bikes to work. Local folks use the country path for socializing, and exercise. Some riders carry stringers of fish snagged in the lake at St. Marys. *Celina Engineers Department, 426 West Market Street, Celina, OH 45822, (419) 586-1144.*

LAKE LORAMIE STATE PARK, MIAMI-ERIE CANAL TOWPATH

Location: Shelby County

Trailheads: Park office, beach at SR 62

The state park serves as the departure point for a seven-mile trek on the Miami-Erie Canal towpath.

The Buckeye Trail and North Country Trail also follow this level route. Bikers can take the dirt trail from the park office (beach and campground area) north to Lock Two (Lock Two Road). En route, you can stop in Minster and New Bremen for refreshments, or a rest. *Lake Loramie State Park, 11221 SR 62, Minster, OH 45865-9311, (937) 295-2011.*

MIAMI & ERIE CANAL TOWPATH

Location: Lucas County

Trailheads: Providence, Bend View, Farnsworth metroparks

Mules once trudged canal barges along this elevated path. The route goes through three Toledo metroparks between Waterville and Grand Rapids on the north bank of the Maumee River, a state-designated scenic river. Most of the ride (between Providence and Farnsworth metroparks) is on a dirt surface, which gets bumpy in spots. Mountain bikes are recommended, but not essential. The route is closed from January to March and during wet periods. Visit restored locks, mills, canal boat reenactments, and other sites along the way. *Metropark District of the Toledo Area, 5100 West Central Avenue, Toledo, OH 43615, (419) 535-3050.*

MAUMEE BAY STATE PARK, BIKE & MOUSE TRAILS

Location: Lucas County

Trailheads: Campground, swimming beach

The six-mile, paved Bike Trail begins at the Inland Lake beach, loops around the lake, and connects with the Mouse Trail, a multipurpose dirt trail coming from the campground. Combined, these trails give an eight-mile ride. The Mouse Trail loops around a successional meadow of grasses, wildflowers, shrubs and young trees. Bikes are not allowed on the two-mile boardwalk through a wetland, but check it out on foot anyway. Maumee Bay State Park, 1400 Park Road 1, Oregon, OH 43618, (419) 836-7758.

OAK OPENINGS PRESERVE

Location: Lucas County

Trailheads: Buehner Walking Center

Peddle around one of Ohio's most unusual habitats—an oak savanna featuring shifting sand dunes and evergreen stands. The northern leg of the Wabash Cannonball Trail, and a connector to its southern leg, pass through the preserve. Begin the 5.5-mile All-Purpose Trail at the Buehner Walking Center on Oak Openings Parkway. *Oak Openings Preserve Metropark, 4139 Girdham Road, Swanton,*

OH 43558; (419) 535-3050. Toledo Metroparks, 5100 West Central Avenue, Toledo, OH 43615, (419) 535-3050.

PEARSON METROPARK

Location: Lucas County

Trailheads: Packer Hammersmith Center

The three-mile bike trail traces the wooded perimeter of the park for most of its course. *Pearson Metropark, (419) 691-3997. Toledo Metroparks, 5100 West Central Avenue, Toledo, OH 43615, (419) 535-3050.*

SECOR METROPARK ALL-PURPOSE TRAIL

Location: Lucas County

Trailheads: Nature Center, Lone Oak Area

The smooth stone path, perfect for beginners, travels across flat ground, through woods and fields. *Secor Metropark, 10000 W. Central Avenue, Berkey, OH 43504, (419) 829-2761. Toledo Metroparks, 5100 West Central Avenue, Toledo, OH 43615, (419) 535-3050.*

SLIPPERY ELM TRAIL

Location: Wood County

Trailheads: E. Broadway, N. Baltimore; Sand Ridge Rd., Bowling Green

Before Euro-Americans arrived this flatland was a vast wet forest known as the Great Black Swamp. Today it is mostly farmland, so pedaling the 13-mile route is easy. The rails on this short B&O line were made of slippery elm boards wrapped by a thin steel plate, hence the trail name. Construction of this rail section was completed in 1891, and linked Wood County's oil and natural gas fields to larger markets. Service stopped in 1978. There's parking at the trailheads in Bowling Green and North Baltimore. *Wood County Park District, 18729 Mercer Road, Bowling Green, OH 43402, (419) 353-1897.*

SWAN CREEK PRESERVE METROPARK

Location: Lucas County

Trailheads: Glendale Ave., Yager Center

This easy, lasso-shaped trail winds through the western half of the park. There is a trailhead at the State Route 2 and Glendale Avenue entrances. *Swan Creek Preserve Metropark, (419) 382-4664. Toledo Metroparks, 5100 West Central Avenue, Toledo, OH 43615, (419) 535-3050.*

UNIVERSITY-PARK HIKE & BIKE TRAIL

Location: Lucas County

Trailheads: King Road, Douglas Road

Major Bike Paths

Michigan

Lake Erie

Toledo

Wabash Cannonball Trail

Miami-Erie Canal Towpath

Bowling Green

Slippery Elm Trail

Kipton Oberlin

North Coast Inland Trail

Emerald Necklace Trail

Cleveland

Elyria

Towpath Trail

Bike & Hike Trail

Akron

Stavich Bicycle

Pennsylvania

Celina to Coldwater Bike Trail

Celina

Coldwater

Mansfield

Richland B & O Trail

Mt. Vernon

Kokosing Gap Trail

Thomas J. Evans Bike Trail

Newark

Wolf Creek River Bikeway

Springfield

Columbus

Olentangy-Scioto Bikeway

Dayton River Corridor Bikeway

Dayton

Creekside Trail

Cedarville

Xenia

Franklin

Athens County Bikeway

Athens

Indiana

Cincinnati

Little Miami Scenic Trail

West Virginia

Kentucky

Ohio River

Ohio River

N

━━━ Existing Trails

••••• Proposed Trails

The popular 6.3-mile trail runs from the University of Toledo nearly to Sylvania. Midway is Wildwood Preserve Metropark, which offers ample parking and 1.5-mile all-purpose loop. The setting is suburban, and the section between the college and metropark runs parallel to an active Conrail line, though a row of trees and shrubs grows between the tracks. *Toledo Metroparks, 5100 West Central Avenue, Toledo, OH 43615, (419) 535-3050.*

WABASH CANNONBALL TRAIL
Location: Lucas County
Trailheads: Oak Openings Metropark

Cute name. Makes me want to sing. When it is finished there will be plenty to sing about—65 miles! Right now only a 3.5-mile section is open, running from the Lucas-Fulton County Line to SR 295. The trail goes through Oak Openings Metro-park, which has a 5.5-mile All-Purpose Trail for two-wheelers. Someday the route (an abandoned Norfolk & Western rail) will reach Montpelier to the west and Maumee in the east, then southwest to Liberty Center. *Northwestern Ohio Rails-to-Trails Association, P.O. Box 234, Delta, OH 43515; phone 1-800-951-4788.*

WILDWOOD PRESERVE METROPARK
Location: Lucas County
Trailheads: Visitor Center

The 1.6-mile route through the park is a yawner, hardly worth the effort. Think of Wildwood as a station stop, or diversion, along the longer University-Park Hike & Bike Trail. *Toledo Metroparks, 5100 West Central Avenue, Toledo, OH 43615, (419) 535-3050.*

Mountain Bike Trails

Mountain bikers have learned to be creative about finding trails; they have few public, off-road trails exclusively their own. Nevertheless, the sport's popularity is growing, and public land owners are becoming more accommodating, though some conservation groups oppose these intrusive trails.

In Southeastern Ohio, bike trekkers can share 183 miles of trails in Wayne National Forest with hikers, horseback riders, and other users. These are the toughest and most demanding public bike trails in the state. Pedal on pavement if you have weak knees and a faint heart. Beginners go elsewhere. Reaching some of the trailheads demands a four-wheeled drive vehicle. Many go across reclaimed stripmined land. Trails are closed December 15 to April 15 except for hiking.

Five state forests and thirteen state parks allow mountain bikes on designated multiple use trails. So-called ORV (off-road vehicle) trails were primarily designed for motorcycles, snowmobiles, and small four-wheelers, but mountain bikers can ride on them too (note exceptions). Mountain bikes are not allowed on most hiking and bridle trails, nor on fire roads in these locations (except Scioto Trail State Forest). State park mountain bike trails are open year-round. Know the rules of the road at each site before departing.

Riders take note! Hunting is permitted beside bike trails in Wayne National Forest, state forests and state parks. Wear bright clothing in autumn, and make noise. Don't be mistaken for a fleeing deer.

NORTHEAST

BEAVER CREEK STATE PARK
Location: Columbiana County

Advanced cyclists should consider the 15-mile multi-use track at Beaver Creek State Park. The trail travels along the Little Beaver Creek between the campground and Hambleton's Mill. Steep hills and ravines make the passage tough for beginners. *Beaver Creek State Park, 12021 Echo Dell Road, East Liverpool, OH 43920-9719, (330) 385-3091.*

FINDLEY STATE PARK
Location: Lorain County

Two miles of bike trail are now available at Findley State Park. Head south from the beach and make a loop on the Larch and Black Locust trails. The Spillway Trail on the east bank of Findley Lake also can be wheeled. *Findley State Park, 25381 SR 58, Wellington, OH 44090-9208, (440) 647-4490.*

HOCKING TECHNICAL COLLEGE
Location: Athens County

A ganglion of unmarked and shared trails (eight miles) winds behind Hocking Technical College in Nelsonville. Entrances to the college stem from US 33 and SR 691. Trails start at the Horse Barn and behind dormitories. Park in areas designated for visitors. Stay on improved trails into the nature preserve. *Hocking Technical College, 3301 Hocking Parkway, Nelsonville, OH 45764, (740) 753-3591.*

JEFFERSON LAKE STATE PARK
Location: Jefferson County

This park has 12 miles of interlocking paths for bicyclists, hikers and equestrians. These trails will test intermediate and advanced peddlers. *Jefferson Lake State Park, Route 1, Richmond, OH 43944-9710, (740) 765-4459.*

KELLEYS ISLAND STATE PARK
Location: Erie County

The island offers the five-mile East Quarry Trail for novice and intermediate cyclists, and the 1.5-mile

North Shore Loop over hilly and rocky terrain for intermediates. Rental bikes available in town. *Kelleys Island State Park, 4049 E. Moore's Dock Road, Port Clinton, OH 43452-9708, (419) 746-2546.*

MICKEY'S MOUNTAIN

Location: Harrison County

Ohio's first pay-to-ride trail bears no relation to the Disney mouse. Trails for beginners and advanced riders total 15 miles. From US 22 in Hopedale, go north on CR 4. After crossing railroad tracks in Miller Station, head west (left) on CR 46, then turn right on Ford Road (TR 170). The road ends at the trailhead. Call in evening for rates and race schedule at *(614) 946-5631 or via Mickey's web site at http://www.cannet.com/~BillMick/*

SOUTHEAST

LAKE HOPE STATE PARK

Location: Vinton County

Little Sandy Trail, two miles, is now a mountain bike path in Lake Hope State Park. Trailhead is on Cabin Ridge Road (road to the beach) near the intersection with SR 278. *Lake Hope State Park, Rte. 2, Box 3000, McArthur, OH 45651, (740) 596-5253.*

PERRY STATE FOREST

Location: Perry County

These eight color-coded trails total 16 miles. The terrain of this reclamation area is hilly. Motorized vehicles are allowed. From New Lexington drive northward on SR 345. About 1.5 miles north of the hamlet of Rehoboth turn left on TR 154, and left on TR 153 to parking. Trails go on both sides of TR 154. *Blue*

RISING VALLEY PARK

Location: Summit County

This private area has 10 miles of cross-country trails in a developing area. From SR 303, just east of the Medina-Summit county line, go north on Oviatt Road (note signs for park and scout camp). Trail is maintained by Northeast Ohio Mountain Bike Association, 890 Iroquois Run, Macedonia, OH 44056.

VULTURE'S KNOB

Location: Wayne County

This privately-owned three-mile trail is north of Wooster. From Wooster, follow Mechanicsburg Road north. The entrance will be on the left between Flickinger and Smithville-Western roads. Fee possible. Call ahead at *(330) 345-5636 or (330) 264-7636.*

Rock State Forest, 6665 Cutler Lake Road, Blue Rock, OH 43720-9740, (740) 674-4035.

PIKE STATE FOREST

Location: Pike County

Pike State Forest has set aside a tract for all-terrain vehicles on SR 124 a few miles east of Sinking Springs. Fifteen miles of trails climb hills and wind through hollows. Snowmobiles, and other motorized ATVs allowed. The parking area on SR 124 has latrines. *Pike State Forest, 334 Lapparell Road, Latham, OH 45646-9722, (740) 493-2441.*

RICHLAND FURNACE STATE FOREST

Location: Jackson County

This forest features nine miles of two-way trails for mountain bikes and motorized all-terrain vehicles. Park on CR 32, off SR 327. *Zaleski State Forest, P.O. Box 330, Zaleski, OH 45698-0330, (740) 596-5781.*

SCIOTO TRAIL STATE FOREST

Location: Ross County

This forest welcomes mountain bikers with 26 miles of trails also open to hikers and horseback riders (no motorized vehicles). Some consider these wooded, hilly paths the best public trails in the state. Try the Long Branch Trail off Stoney Creek Road. The state forest hosts a mountain bike family campout each summer. From US 23, go east on SR 372, which becomes Stoney Creek Road at the fire tower. You will find parking spots along state forest roads (also good for biking) and in the state park. Scioto Trail State Forest, 124 North Ridge Road, Waverly, OH 45690-9513, (740) 663-2523.

WAYNE NATIONAL FOREST, IRONTON DISTRICT TRAILS

Location: Lawrence & Scioto counties
Trailheads: Telegraph Hill Rd. (CR 193); Howard Furnace Road; Forest Road 105, off SR 650

Two areas designed for "quad-tracs," snowmobiles, and motorbikes are open for mountain biking (and hikers). Motorized travelers have worn down these trails, portions of which are old logging or mining roads that go through reclaimed land. Though parking lots are plentiful, many riders "unofficially" park (at their own risk) at crossroads. Do not block public roads and trails.

Pine Creek Off-Road Vehicle (ORV) Trail (Lawrence County, Decatur and Washington townships, Scioto County, Vernon and Bloom townships) is a forked route measuring 20 miles. Riders can take a short loop starting from the Wolcott Trailhead, Clinton Furnace Road off SR 522. The main terminus is the Telegraph Trailhead, just .125-mile west of SR 93 on Telegraph Hill Road (CR 193). The Lyra Trailhead is located on Howard Furnace Road.

Land twice devastated—logged clean for iron furnaces, then strip mined for coal—now has off-road vehicles crawling over it. *Hanging Rock ORV Trail* (Lawrence County, Hamilton and Elizabeth townships) is a ganglion of nine trails with names that reflect the site's natural history (Copperhead, High Knob, Hanging Rock trails) and its industrial past (Sawmill, Gas Well, Powerline trails). The point of departure is a parking lot on Forest Road 105, off SR 650 (.75-mile north of the junction with US 52). Don't expect scenery.

A map and information is available from *Wayne National Forest, Ironton Ranger District, 6518 State Route 93, Pedro, OH 45659, (740) 532-3223.*

WAYNE NATIONAL FOREST, ATHENS DISTRICT TRAILS

Location: Hocking, Perry & Athens counties
Trailheads: Various, see below

Monday Creek Off-Road Vehicle Area is another elaborate "spaghetti bowl" of trails, 65 miles worth, bounded by Haydenville in Hocking County, New Straitsville in Perry County, and Buchtel in Athens County. Four entangled trails comprise this hilly, shaggy ORV ground.

Dorr Run Trail (Hocking County, Green Township), a ganglion of paths, has trailhead parking at two locations. From US 33, two miles southeast of the intersection with SR 595, follow signs (turning north on old Company Road) to the trailhead parking on gravel roads.

The trailhead for *Snake Hollow Trail* (Hocking County, Ward Township) is on CR 24 in a settlement known as Monday. CR 24 branches from SR 278 in Carbon Hill and runs to Buchtel. This spot also serves as the southern terminus of the Main Corridor Trail.

Getting to the parking lot for the *Long Ridge Trail* (Hocking County, Ward Township) used to require four-wheeled traction. Look for the trailhead sign along SR 78, a mile or so north of Buchtel. Forest Road 758 (or Smart Road on some maps) leads to parking.

Parking for the *Main Corridor Trail* (Perry Township, Coal Township) is off SR 595 south of New Straitsville. The southern trailhead is shared with the Snake Hollow Trail. Midway, a spur leads to a private campground.

Get a map from *Wayne National Forest, Athens Ranger District, 219 Columbus Road, Athens, OH 45701, (740) 592-6644.*

WAYNE NATIONAL FOREST, MARIETTA DISTRICT TRAILS

Location: Washington & Monroe counties
Trailheads: Various

Though blazed for hikers, mountain bikers with a death wish can ride these rugged trails if they dare. Expect to carry your bike most of the way. Expect to damage your body or bike. Expect the worst. For maps and information on these trails contact Wayne National Forest, Marietta Unit, Route 1, Box 132, Marietta, OH 45750; (614) 373-9055.

Archers Fork Trail (Washington County, Ludlow, Independence, and Grandview townships) traverses 9-1/2 miles of wooded land. Irish Run Natural Bridge, one of only seven in Ohio, is worth the effort. Parking is located off TR 407 (Ludlow Twp., closest to natural bridge), and Jackson Run Road.

Lamping Homestead Trail (Monroe County, Washington Township) offers loops of 1.8 miles and 3.2 miles. This former pioneer homestead has massive pines, and an old growth grove (though some dispute its "virginity"). From SR 26, head west on SR 537, then left (south) on TR 307, a thin dirt road, to parking.

Covered Bridge Trail (Washington County, Ludlow and Independence townships) goes five miles over hills, dales, and streams between two covered bridges that span the Little Muskingum River. Backtrack to your terminus via SR 26, or a combination of SR 26 and Smith and Becker roads. Or take TR 34 three miles to the North Country Trail. Park either at Rinard Covered Bridge (CR 406 at SR 26) or Hune Covered Bridge (SR 26 and Smith Road).

Ohio View Trail (Washington County, Grandview Township), a seven mile linear path, features sweeping views of the Ohio River Valley. A 3 1/2-mile connector path leads to the North Country Trail. Park at the trailheads—SR 7 north of Beavertown and SR 260 at Yellow House. Be ready for "cardiac" hills and a steep, ridgetop ride. Don't expect a rescue from Medivac copters.

Scenic River Trail (Washington County, Independence Township) begin its 3.4-mile journey at the Leith Run Recreation Area, off SR 7 upstream from Wade. It goes northerly to CR 9 on an estab-lished path. Leith Run Recreation Area allows camping and is a good staging area for nearby rides.

Mountain bikes (muscles permitting) can navigate on "The Wayne's" sections of the *North Country Trail*, a new interstate footpath under construction. More than 70 miles of the NCT crosses The Wayne, but only half of it is blazed with the trail's blue diamond.

ZANESVILLE VELO-Z TRAIL
Location: Muskingum County

Off northbound SR 60, south of Zanesville and Duncan Falls you *might* find the unmarked gravel lane leading to the trailhead (near confluence of Salt Creek and Muskingum River) of this private trail. Call ahead for schedule of races and open trails. *Velo-Z Bicycle Club, P.O. Box 4455, Zanesville, OH 43702, (740) 674-4297.*

CENTRAL OHIO

ALUM CREEK STATE PARK
Location: Delaware County

This series of trails caters to novice and experienced mountain bikers (no motors). Advanced riders take the North Bike Trail, a six-mile course over hills, ravines, creeks and other obstacles. Beginners start on the two-mile South Bike Trail. Trails begin at the parking lot on Lewis Center Road, located in the southeastern corner of the park. *Alum Creek State Park, 3615 S. Old State Road, Delaware, OH 43015, (740) 548-4631.*

DEER CREEK STATE PARK
Location: Pickaway County

This area offers a 1.2-mile track for beginner and intermediate bikers. From SR 207, take Crownover Mill Road to the beach entrance. Turn left at the beach, and follow the park road to its end at the trailhead. *Deer Creek State Park, 20635 Waterloo Road, Mt. Sterling, OH 43143, (740) 869-3124.*

FALLING ROCK BOY SCOUT CAMP
Location: Licking County

The bike trails at Falling Rock Boy Scout Camp are open only on race days. Beware of cliffs and tight squeezes on this route. From Newark, head north on SR 79 roughly 10 miles and go left on Rainrock Road, and left on Rocky Fork Road. Follow signs to the scout camp. Park in the Winter Parking Area. Call *(614) 890-4145 or (614) 745-5327.*

MOHICAN WILDERNESS CENTER
Location: Knox County

This private trail system has a three-mile loop with a tough hill and an easy glide downhill. From Loudonville, travel south on SR 3, then turn left on Wally Road (CR 3175). Trail begins south of camping. *Mohican Wilderness Center, (740) 599-6741.*

SOUTHWEST

CAESAR CREEK STATE PARK
Location: Warren County

The mountain bike trails at Caesar Creek State Park measure eight miles. Advanced and intermediate riders take the 6.5-mile path, novices the 1.5-mile path. Start at the campground (Center Road) or from parking lots at the end of Ward and Harveysburg roads. Motorized vehicles are prohibited on this trail. *Caesar Creek State Park, 8570 East SR 73, Waynesville, OH 45068-9719, (937) 897-3055.*

EAST FORK STATE PARK
Location: Clermont County

The park offers a pair of loop trails rated easy to moderate in difficulty. The trails (four miles total) start at the end of a gravel road branching from Park Road (just north of the park office). *East Fork State Park, P.O Box 119, Bethel OH 45106, (513) 734-4323; or Queen City Wheels, 185 Albright Drive, Loveland, OH 45140.*

HUESTON WOODS STATE PARK
Location: Preble County

Hueston Woods has seven trail miles with easy, moderate, and difficult sections. Trails branch from a staging area on Hedge Row Road in the campground. Rental bikes are available at the trailhead. *Hueston Woods State Park, Route 1, College Corner, OH 45003, (513) 523-6347.*

PAINT CREEK STATE PARK
Location: Highland County

Appaloosa Run is the name the double-loop mountain bike trail in Paint Creek State Park. The outer loop measures eight miles, the inner loop four miles. Appaloosa Run Trail, accessible from the campgrounds, is shared with hikers. *Paint Creek State Park, 14265 US Route 50, Bainbridge, OH 45612, (513) 365-1401.*

NORTHWEST

MARY JANE THURSTON STATE PARK
Location: Henry County

Cyclists now have six miles to peddle in the North Turkeyfoot Area of Mary Jane Thurston State Park. The trail, shared with horses and hikers, begins at the parking areas on SR 24 (upstream from the main park area). Novice riders can handle the flat terrain. *Mary Jane Thurston State Park, 1-466 State Route 65, McClure, OH 43534, (419) 832-7662.*

MAUMEE STATE FOREST
Location: Fulton County

This area has a five-mile, double-loop track on flat terrain. Motorized vehicles are allowed. Parking lots are located on CR C and CR 2. *Maumee State Forest, 3390 County Road D, Swanton, OH 43558-9731, (419) 822-3052.*

Cross State Routes

Ohio has hundreds of "designed" bike routes, ranging from neighborhood rides a mile long to cross-state adventures several hundred miles in length. Riders can acquire published maps, or design their own route. Remember, bike routes are trips bicyclists take on public roads (usually paved) shared with cars, trucks, motorcycles.

The best way to discover these routes, as well as tours, outings, and races, is to join a local bicycle club, or American Youth Hostel. Bicycle dealers sell route books and maps, too.

Cardinal Trail (314 miles) goes east-west and diagonally across Central Ohio, from New Paris in Preble County to Petersburg in Mahoning County. Look for route signs every five miles. The name honors the state bird.

Route A (239 miles) joins Cincinnati and Toledo along a gentle S-shaped route in Western Ohio. Runs near Hamilton, Middletown, Dayton and Lima.

Route B makes a 240-mile track from Cincinnati to Marietta, touching Hillsboro, Chillicothe, and Athens.

Route C takes a 294-mile journey from Cincinnati to Cleveland. Parts trace the Little Miami Scenic Bikeway, Ohio & Erie Towpath Trail, and Cardinal Trail. The route bypasses Columbus.

Route E is the longest route, 494 miles, connecting Portsmouth and Toledo. Connecting routes at each terminus continue into neighboring states.

Route F (281 miles) cuts across Central Ohio, from Bellaire in Belmont County to New Paris, also the western terminus of the Cardinal Trail. This is the most "backcountry" route in this group.

Hilly Eastern Ohio has *Route J*, connecting Marietta and Conneaut (244 miles).

The western terminus of *Routes K & N* is McGill in Paulding County. Route K splits from Route N in Putnam County and streaks across the flatlands to join the Cardinal Trail and Route C at Mifflin in Ashland County, covering 156 miles. Route N runs close to the Lake Erie shore for 300 miles and leaves Ohio near Pierpoint in Ashtabula County.

For route maps (for a fee) check at bike shops, outfitters, and local clubs. Or contact *Columbus Outdoor Pursuits, P.O. Box 14384, Columbus, OH 43214, (614) 447-1006.*

Bike Safety

An average of 3,000 bike-motor vehicle crashes are reported in Ohio. These statistics don't count bike collisions with immovable objects (parked cars, trees, etc.), other bikes, pedestrians, and unreported accidents. 75 percent of bike accidents are preventable by using defensive driving tactics, and 85 percent of fatalities can be avoided by wearing helmets. Nearly half of all bike deaths involve riders who ride at night without lights. So remember this tips:

- Wear a helmet—every time, everywhere.
- Know and obey traffic laws, as well as local regulations on bike trails. Children are especially lax in stopping at stop signs, looking both ways before entering traffic and intersections, and using hand signals. Walk bikes across roads.
- Night riders should equip bikes with lights and reflectors. Flags (orange) and "fanny bumpers" make you more visible.
- Ride with traffic and in single file. Stay in designated lanes on bikeways. Keep to the right side of road or trail.
- On bike trails, faster cyclists should pass slower riders, hikers, joggers, etc. on the left and shout loudly "Passing left!" well in advance. The slower biker should stay right and look forward. Too often, slower riders stray when they look back to see approaching bikes.
- Bikers on multi-use trails should yield to horses.
- Keep your bike in good repair. Check brakes, tires, chain, gears, steering, seat, frame before riding.
- Carry water. Keep maps handy.

75 percent of bike accidents are preventable by using defensive driving tactics, and 85 percent of fatalities can be avoided by wearing helmets.

The call of the equestrian trail; Heigh O Silver, Ohio!

Riding

Horse Trails

Two centuries ago Ohio's overland transportation system consisted of Zane's Trace, a few overgrown and hastily hacked military roads, and a vanishing web of thin Indian paths: not exactly easy routes for humans traveling atop a horse.

Calling those wilderness passages "roads" required sobriety and imagination. Ebenezer Zane's government-funded route arcing from Wheeling, West Virginia, to Zanesville, Lancaster, Chillicothe, West Union and Aberdeen was barely wider than a horse's rump. Yet, these primitive paths became the state's first bridle trails.

It didn't take pioneers long to widen the traces and trails into rough wagon roads. Horses and mules were abundant and ubiquitous in nineteenth century Ohio. Their backs and haunches powered Ohio's major industries, and carried goods to markets over mountains and rivers. For millions of humans they were conveyances and symbols of personal wealth, freedom and status until supplanted by the automobile in this century.

Today, the Old Grey Mare serves as a four-legged recreational vehicle for many Ohioans. These equestrians ride on nearly 1,000 miles of trails on public land (most of the journey off-the-road), plus hundreds of miles on private land. The trails travel through dark forests, across meadows and scenic streams, and to vistas with crimson and gold sunsets.

Though today's rider and horse usually end up where they start the day, each gambol recalls the carefree, wandering horseman, be it pioneer, warrior, or cowboy. The feeling goes beyond a longing for freedom, or for a trouble-free open road. Boats, planes, cars, bikes launch me wildly across landscape, but only on a horse do I get a rush of living wildness. Muscle, mane, breath, blood, hoof, heaving. Deep inside, the horse and I want to flee; at least that's what I tell myself.

Herein are places where you can saddle up and ride off into a sunset. More than 400 miles of bridle trails are available in 21 state parks. Add to that 367 miles in 13 state forests, and 78 1/2 miles in Wayne National Forest. County and metroparks account for the rest. The guide indicates the location of staging areas, parking lots, and primitive campgrounds used by horse riders. Horse camps are separated from family campsites. Riders must provide their own mount. Nearby riding stables sometimes lead groups along public trails. Know and follow local trail rules.

Local stables and horse clubs lead group rides and have access to trails on private land. See the chapter listing clubs and organizations. Other chapters in this book describe the sites in more detail. Refer to these for maps, addresses and phone numbers.

515

SELECTED PUBLIC HORSE TRAILS

Location	Miles	Trail Access	Horse Camp	Sites
OHIO STATE PARKS				
Alum Creek	50	Howard & Hogback rds.	Howard Road	25*
Barkcamp	15	Park Rd. 6	Park Rd. 9	25
Beaver Creek	23	CR 428	CR 428	100
Burr Oak	8	Park Office	none	--
Caesar Creek	33	Furnas-Oglesby Rd.	Furnas-Oglesby	25*
Deer Creek	14	Horseman's Camp	Road to lodge	3
East Fork	55	Park Road 4	Park Road 5	17
Great Seal	20	Campground, Lick Run	Campground	15
Hueston Woods	6	Four Mile Rd	Four Mile Rd.	1
Jefferson Lake	15	Park Office, CR 54	none	--
Little Miami	50	Loveland, Morrow, Corwin, Spring Valley Wildlife Area	none	--
Malabar Farm	12	Pleasant Valley Rd., off Bromfield Road	Off Bromfield Rd.	15
Mosquito Lake	10	Hoagland-Blackstub Rd.	none	--
Paint Creek	25	Pioneer Farm on Upp Rd.	Park campground	15
Quail Hollow	4-6	Shady Lane	none	--
Salt Fork	20	Park Road 1 (entrance)	Park Road 1	20
Strouds Run	8.5	TR 21 (Lake Hill Rd.)	none	--
Sycamore	6.5	Wolf Creek Pike, Providence Road	none	--
Van Buren	2-6	Park off TR 229, park road	none	--
West Branch	20	Copeland/Esworthy roads	Contact office	Permit
OHIO STATE FORESTS				
Blue Rock	26	Forest Rd. 8, Browning Rd., Ridgeview Road	**	--
Brush Creek	12	Ranger Station (SR 73), Coffee Hollow Road	none	--
Dean	20	SR 73	none	--
Harrison	24	TR 185, TR 182, TR 189	TR 185 (off SR 9)	20
Hocking	40	SR 374, SR 56, Fire Tower	Keister Rd.	23
Maumee	15	TR V (Henry County), Jeffers Rd. (Lucas County)	none	--
Mohican Memorial	22	SR 97	**	--
Perry	8	CR 3 (Hollow Road)	none	--
Pike	33	Auerville & Greenbriar roads	**	--
Scioto Trail	26	Stoney Creek Road (FR 1), North Ridge Road (FR 2)	**	--
Shawnee	75	Bear Creek Rd. (FR 4), Roosevelt Lake, Lwr. Twin Creek Road	Bear Creek Rd.	58
Tar Hollow	33	Poe Run Rd. off SR 327, Fire Tower	Poe Run Road	50
Zaleski	33	TR 20 (Crow Tract)	TR 20	16

* Permit needed
**Camping for humans available at adjacent state park

More Happy Trails

CLEVELAND METROPARKS

The "Emerald Necklace" boasts 82 miles of horseback riding trails in Bedford, Brecksville, Hinckley, Mill Stream Run, North Chagrin, South Chagrin and Rocky River reservations. Stables are found at Brecksville (216-526-6767) and Rocky River (216-267-2525) reservations.

For more information contact the nature centers at Brecksville (216-526-1012), Rocky River (216-734-6660), and North Chagrin (216-473-3370), Chagrin Valley Trails and Riding Club (216-351-6300), or Cleveland Metroparks, 4101 Fulton Parkway, Cleveland, OH 44144-1923; (216) 351-6300.

FIVE RIVERS PARK DISTRICT

Park	Miles	Access
Possum Creek	1.5	Shank Road (farm entrance)
Englewood	3.5	Patty's Road, Old National Trail Riding Center
Sugarcreek	6.5	Riding Center, Wilmington Road
Carriage Hill	5	Shull Road

HAMILTON COUNTY PARK DISTRICT

Park	Miles	Access
Winton Woods	>3	Daly Road, Riding Center (lessons, shows, day camps), call (513) 931-3057.
Miami Whitewater Forest (two trails)	7.8	Shaker Trace Multipurpose Trail. Park on Mt. Hope Road
	<5	Horse camp on West Road.

HANCOCK PARK DISTRICT

Horse riders can travel in designated areas in parks, such as the base of the Findlay Reservoirs. Contact: Hancock Park District, 819 Park St., Findlay, OH 45840; (419) 425-7275.

LAKE METROPARKS

This park district (Lake County) offers limited horseback riding in Girdled Road, Chapin Forest, and Penitentiary Glen reservations, and at Lake Farmpark. Call before saddling at 1-800-227-7275. Lake Metroparks, 11211 Spear Road, Concord Township, OH 44077.

TOLEDO METROPARKS

Twenty-three miles of horse trails track through Oak Openings Preserve, accessible via the Horse Rider Center, Jeffers Rd., north of SR 64. Riders will visit a globally-threatened oak savanna, oak opening habitat featuring shifting sand dunes deposited on the shores of Lake Erie's predecessor lakes. The flat terrain is largely forested. The horse center on Jeffers Road includes picnic areas, grills, water, and rest rooms. The southbound trail from here goes into Maumee State Forest.

Contact: Oak Openings Preserve Metropark, 4139 Girdham Road, Swanton, OH 43558; (419) 826-6463.

WAYNE NATIONAL FOREST

Camping is allowed along trails in the national forest, with these exceptions: Horse riders cannot camp in developed family campgrounds (Oak Hill, Burr Oak Cove, Iron Ridge, Leith Run, canoe access spots) nor along foot paths. Horse camping is prohibited in ecologically-sensitive places designated as Special Areas.

Trail Name	Miles	Trail Access
Lake Vesuvius	46	CR 29 (Sand Hill), TR 245 (Paddle Creek), CR 4
Stone Church	22.5	CR 38 (Old Town Rd), north of New Straitsville
Kinderhook	10	CR 244, north of Newport

Safety

When riding public horse trails, follow all the usual rules of smart horsemanship plus the following trail etiquette:

• Don't tailgate. Even the quietest horse will eventually kick another horse who has a nose in his tail.

• When going uphill, maintain two horse lengths between horses; when going downhill, leave three horse lengths.

• Pass on the left and only at a walk.

• Wait for a dismounted rider to remount before moving on.

• If your horse tends to kick, tie a red ribbon in his tail to warn other riders. ✎

Off-Road Vehicle Trails

Nothing unsettles "politically" correct hikers faster than the rev and rattle of ATVs on their footpath. The noisy intrusion of the motorized, helmeted heathens burns the collar of the gentle woodsy set who have climbed this ridge to get away from it all, not to hear the roar of the road.

ATV is short for all-terrain vehicle, also called ORVs, off-road vehicles. Better known as snowmobiles, trail bikes, four-wheelers, or quads. Detractors call them "always terrible vehicles" and "&^#*@! vehicles."

Originally designed as a "beast of burden" vehicle to work in remote, tough terrain, the ORV has evolved into a popular recreation vehicle. It has become, proclaim adherents, another way for time-pressured humans to explore the great outdoors, no different, say, than a motorboat churning across a lake. Just man and machine moseying over moraines and ravines, admiring nature above the sassy whine of a motor and through mud-splattered goggles.

For awhile, ORV operators were the outlaws on public trails, sneaking rides when it was safe, hiding from authorities when it wasn't. Like coyotes, they had to be selective, wily, and creative about where they roamed. Conflicts among trail users eventually prompted public land managers to establish separate ORV areas. Now off-road riders have their own personal recreation space, albeit a modest realm in their minds. There are no charges for use of public area trails, and some local clubs often have access to other areas.

Buckeye snowmobilers (and cross-country skiers) are a likewise patient lot, who look longingly toward the horizon for snow clouds. Most winters the northern third of the state gets enough white stuff to sustain these intrepid sledders, and that's where they congregate. South of Mansfield, snow is scarce some winters, and it is often altogether absent in Southern Ohio.

Snowmobile trails in state parks generally track across flat, or gently rolling terrain, and over fields and lightly forested areas (the exception being Punderson). Experienced riders who want hills and forests should go to Mohican Memorial State Forest. Several state park lakes also attract snowmobilers. Check ice conditions before departing; ice five inches thick is considered safe for the motorized sleds.

The ORV trails in state forests and Wayne National Forest travel over hilly, largely-forested areas, much of it reclamation land and old clear-cuts. Reaching a few of the staging areas in Wayne National Forest requires four-wheel drive vehicles. These worn trails are usually closed (except to foot travelers) in winter to curb erosion.

PUBLIC TRAILS FOR MOTORIZED VEHICLES

Site	Staging Area	Trail Miles	Vehicles
OHIO STATE PARKS			
Alum Creek	New Galena boat ramp, east shore	7	SM
Barkcamp	Park office	9	SM
Buck Creek	North picnic area, east side	8	SM
Buckeye Lake	Park office, boat ramps	Lake	SM
Caesar Creek	Clarksville & Middletown roads	5	SM
Deer Creek	Campground check-in station	12	SM
East Harbor	Causeway parking lot	3-4	SM
Geneva	Lake Rd., north end, by golf course	3.5	SM
Grand Lake	Park office, boat ramps	Lake	SM
Indian Lake	Lakeview Harbor parking lot	Lake	SM
Lake Loramie	Lakeside parking lots, boat ramps	Lake	SM
Maumee Bay	Park office	7	SM
Mosquito Lake			
West	Everett-Hull Rd., beach, marina	11	SM
East	CR 193 boat ramp	3	SM
Paint Creek	Northwest boat launch, Snake Rd.	15	SM
Portage Lakes	Boat ramps	Lake	SM
Punderson	Punderson marina	5	SM
Salt Fork	Lodge, boat ramp, camp check-in	16	SM
Sycamore	Providence Road	8	SM
West Branch	West boat ramp, off Rock Sprg. Rd.	20	SM

The Compleat Angler catches more colds than fish, but doesn't mind.

***t**he Mad River runs swiftly for 60 miles from glacial-bred springs near Bellfontaine to the Great Miami River in Dayton. For 30 miles of its life, the Mad is clear enough, and cold enough to make it Ohio's best trout stream. It is here, in the spring of 1996, that I tried, for the umpteenth time, to get hooked on fishing.*

Fishing has been a puzzle and fascination to me, as well as a fathomless source of frustration. I think of a fish as the proverbial needle secreted in a haystack. It is a finicky, invisible, and alien beast who succeeds in an environment hostile to humans—a habitat, by the way, far more common on this planet than our own. Catching a fish is a rarity. I have caught more colds than fish, and retrospectively I probably would have had more success tossing my hook into the air for sparrows. The way I see it, whenever a fish swallows the bait it gets torn from a happy realm to, not-so-happy one, similar to the way human literary characters enter strange dimensions by walking through mirrors or cornfields. Each cast of the line enters their dimension and becomes a drama.

I still carry the humiliation of a summer evening's angling with my father and uncle on the shore of my hometown reservoir in upstate New York. The three of us cast within a 50-foot zone, with me in the middle. Fish went to my elders' hooks like bees to clover. By dusk they had caught their limit and built a crackling bonfire that spewed sparks halfway across the lake--their victory ritual. My line stayed limp, as always.

Undaunted, I tried my luck, this time solo, during the next trout season, which ironically opened on April Fools Day. The venue changed to Claverack Creek, which flowed into the reservoir en route to the Hudson River. Oldtimers claim it was a boss trout stream before the Taconic Parkway brought hundreds of gear-laden, well-monied, city anglers to deplete the mountain-chilled waters. My outing was a disaster of line entanglements, property losses (transistor radio, a boot, bait, several lures, and assorted tackle), and unwanted bone-freezing immersions—all for an empty creel.

It took me three years to realize that cagey casters didn't throw a line until the city boys went home, usually by the fourth day, satisfied with a cooler filled with nursery-raised trout released two weeks earlier. On day five the monster browns who had been hiding and starving since day one would edge into the current again and strike anything remotely resembling food. If you knew their hideouts, you could have a couple of stiffs in the freezer and not be late for work. One Friday morning, just before I went to school, my father and uncle heaved four such brutes into our kitchen

A shiver runs through it: a boat,
a fish, a line in the water.

sink. Both of them stank of bonfire and fruity brandy, and they wheezed and giggled like coyotes holed up with blue ribbon hens. They knew things others would never know. I envied their devilish merriment, their natural gifts, and their discipline to remain mum.

Since then, dozens of times, I have wistfully waded through mall canyons of fishing gear wondering where to begin. Hundreds of poles bristle like saplings and cattails. Lures and lines, jigs and rigs, sinkers and swivels, rapalas and reels glittering on walleyed walls. Which bobber? Which bait? So many choices! Too many decisions make my head swim. A barracuda salesman named Gil

sees me for a sucker with a grand to drop on a boat load of tackle. I avoid his hook, and swim to fresh air. I'll stick with the unworthy spin caster I've repaired and cursed for twentysome years. I still yearn to fish, but is it fish I'm after?

Now I find myself immersed in clumsy waders in the swift Mad River learning the basics of fly fishing from Patrick Roblin, who shares the tricks taught to him by a St. Louis sculptor. Surprisingly, casting comes naturally to me, thanks to Patrick's tutelage. It helps to have a mentor and to think the stream is a canvas and your casts are brushstrokes. I grin when the tiny fly alights softly on the surface, and floats down a riffle, racing a locust leaf. But for what I know my tippet lands where a trout has never tread. Downstream, Patrick fishes where brown trout probably lurk, in calm backwaters, along shore, beside slowly stirring eddies.

Pretty soon casting becomes automatic, and my thoughts flood into abandoned channels, back to Hemingway's trout tales, Claverack Creek, and bonfires. I slosh upstream where the Mad's charged rush bounces, gyrates, wags, and splashes like an excited hound. Its wired current is a cat nudging and curling around my legs. Petting it gives me goose bumps, makes me feel alive. The next step, it playfully tries to trip me.

We went home healthier, wiser, and holier from the outing, and it mattered little that we did not land a single fish. What mattered was a pledge to fish again, so we can cast for rapture once more. ☜

—SO

Fishing

Walleye Fever

Some fishermen get a bad case of walleye fever. It's like gold fever, and they troll around Lake Erie panning and pining for a strike, a mother lode. They forget to send postcards, can't remember where they parked their car, don't come to shore until they run out of bait or beer. All this for a fish, feisty, wise, and tasty.

Come April, when Lake Erie water rises to 40-50 degrees half-crazed schools of walleyes start spawning on the shore, along reefs, and in tributaries called Maumee and Sandusky. When they finish, the adults spread out across the lake's shallow Western Basin to feast on shiners, shad, alewife, and other small fry. Newborn walleye chew on plankton and insects for a year, then switch to grown up food. Given this cuisine, and the wits to avoid a hit, a walleye can grow to ten inches in a year, and three feet and 16 pounds in a dozen seasons: tackle-busting, fry pan sizzling, freezer filling gold!

The walleye, a member of the perch family, has a "cloudy" eye enabling it to feed in murky water, in deep water, at dusk and dawn, and on cloudy days. Walleye anglers follow the seasonal habits of the fish. Pre-spawning times in March deep areas near off-shore reefs are best. Move toward shore and the spawning tributaries in April. Females scatter eggs on gravel bottoms or reefs, or at riffles in river. Move back to the Western Basin in May and June. The deeper and darker Central Basin fills with walleyes in August and September, but in fall the fishing becomes spotty, unpredictable. Come winter, the walleye is back in the Western Basin and ice fishing is choice around the Bass Islands.

Controlling walleye fever is the responsibility of the Lake Erie Committee of the Great Lakes Fishery Commission, comprised of representatives from Ohio, Pennsylvania, Michigan, New York, and the Province of Ontario. The committee determines the yearly "total allowable catch" for walleye, and other lake fish. The idea being to afflict future generations with walleye fever.

Taking Trout

In the 1880s somebody put Pacific Coast trout into Lake Erie. The steelheads survived in the warmer water and became a popular game fish in the Central Basin. Today, the Ohio Division of Wildlife annually dumps 200,000 nine-inch yearling steelheads into four Ohio rivers for the steelhead's and angler's success. They don't reproduce enough to sustain a "fishable" population.

The young smolts head downstream in May and into Lake Erie where their diet changes from zooplankton to shiners, shad, smelts, and alewives. In summer, they dive into the deeper and cooler water of the Central Basin, in depths 50-70 feet. Steelheads gather near the shore and mouths of tributaries in autumn. They migrate upstream from mid-October through winter. Most try to return to their original stocked stream, but all streams in Northeastern Ohio get wandering steelheads. Their migration depends on stream level—fast after rainfall and snowmelt, otherwise slow. Spawning starts in March when adults move from pools to gravelly riffles and shallows in gentle currents. Contrary to romantic myths and its close kinship with salmons, steelhead, a variety of rainbow trout, do not perish after spawning.

In its second summer a steelhead averages two feet and 6-7 pounds. Some live seven years, reaching a length of three feet and weight of 15-21 pounds.

Steelhead and lake brown trout, the other Lake Erie trout species, come from the London State Fish Hatchery. Rocky River, Grand River, Conneaut Creek, and Chagrin River receive the steelheads. Brown trout are released into Lake Erie at Geneva State Park.

Ohio's steelhead trout streams include the four stocking rivers, plus the Ashtabula River, Cowles Creek, Wheeler Creek, Arcola Creek, and Vermillion River. These currents also have coho and chinook salmon. Check fishing regulations before wetting your line.

Hooking a Muskie

Muskie means trophy to most Ohio anglers. Many good things can be said of the the state's largest game fish, but the greatest are that it makes the angler's adrenaline rush like no other freshwater creature can do, and he doesn't keep you long in doubt. He sees your lure wobbling along over his weed bed lair. You may drag it over him a dozen times, but if he's not in the mood or if the plug or spoon isn't presented just right, he lets it pass. He can catch his prey anytime he wants, and so can afford to be choosy. He will pick the occasion.

What's Our Line

🎣 The Ohio Division of Wildlife estimates that 1.5 million Ohioans go fishing each year.

🎣 Ohio ranks 11th among states in the number of anglers; 11 nationally with 17.8 million days spent fishing; and 12th with direct expenditures of $836 million. (1996)

🎣 The American Sport-fishing Association reports that fishing in Ohio generates $1.9 billion for the economy and supports 22,000 local jobs.

The time comes when he is hungry and ready for a choice forage fillet or in whatever mood it is that triggers a muskellunge into striking the approaching lure. That lunging strike gives the muskie away instantly. No other fish hits so savagely. If he strikes down deep, below the surface, it feels, as a veteran fisherman once described it, like hooking the arm of your own chair. If the muskie takes the lure at the surface he kicks up a commotion like no other fish. Either way, the power that surges through the line and rod says muskie loud and clear. You know what you have hooked almost before you rear back on the rod. If all goes well, the fish feels your hooks about the time you feel the strike. He greyhounds in a surging run, barrel-rolls, bucks at the top, and goes for the weeds, and he does it all with reckless fury and slashing strength that are almost impossible to believe.

As an old-time muskie fisherman once said, "There's no chance you're ever going to hook a muskie on the first cast, and there's no chance at all that you'll catch one every time you go out. But if you're looking for the fight of your life, plus a trophy to hang on the wall that'll make jaws drop, muskies can't be beat."

Most Ohio muskies are caught from April through October when the water temperature is 55 to 75 degrees. Some of the best lakes to fish for muskies are Piedmont, Leesville, Rocky Fork, Clear Fork, Buckeye, Cowan, Hargus, Berlin, Milton, Pymatuning, Knox, and Salt Fork. Good muskie streams are Paint Creek, Olive Green Creek, Grand River, Meigs Creek, Sunfish Creek, Wolf Creek, Little Muskingum

Fish
Stories

Fish Ohio

Anglers who catch a big fish may enter their fish in the Fish Ohio recognition program and receive a certificate and pin. The program is run by the Ohio Division of Wildlife, which manages 15,000 entries a year. A catch qualifies if it meets the minimum size requirements listed on the Fish Ohio application. Anglers who catch four or more different species of qualifying fish will receive a Master Angler certificate.

The qualifying fish and minimum lengths are (no fish stories allowed):

Brown Trout 25 in.

Rainbow trout 25 in.
Carp 26 in.
Saugeye 21 in.
Channel catfish 26 in.
Smallmouth bass 20 in.
Crappie 13 in.
Northern pike 32 in.
Flathead catfish 35 in.
Sunfish 9 in.
Freshwater drum 22 in.
Walleye 28 in.
Hybrid striped bass 21 in.
White bass 16 in.
Largemouth bass 21 in.
Yellow perch 13 in.
Muskellunge 36 in.

For more information on the Fish Ohio program, contact Fish Ohio, Division of Wildlife, 1840 Belcher Drive, Columbus, OH 43224-1329.

Source: Ohio Department of Natural Resources, Division of Wildlife

By bank and boat, Ohioans cast about on the state's waterways.

River, Rocky Fork Creek, Scioto Brush Creek, Salt Creek, Ohio Brush Creek, Wills Creek, and the Mahoning River. Lakes with good fishing for tiger muskies are West Branch, Salt Fork, Jackson, North Reservoir, and Acton.

Scientists reported Ohio's native muskellunge to be abundant as early as 1810 and it was still considered economically important as a commercial fish as late as 1930. After 1930, migration routes were blocked by dams and muskie populations were drastically reduced. (Siltation caused by deforestation, agriculture, mining also contributed to the decline.) The species was hardly known to latter-day fishermen until the Division of Wildlife began its artificial propagation program in 1952. The division first attempted to propagate the muskellunge in 1948. Native muskie breeders were trapped live from Ohio streams and placed in hatchery ponds at Kincaid Fish Farm, in hope that natural reproduction would occur. Because of poor success with this project, an artificial propagation program was started. Success was achieved in 1953 when 2,235 muskie fingerlings were stocked in selected lakes, inaugurating a new muskie era for Ohio. Since then the Division of Wildlife has greatly expanded its propagation and stocking program. As a result, opportunities for catching muskies are more widespread in Ohio today than ever before.

With the increased catch of muskellunge from Ohio waters, interest among fishermen grew and the Division of Wildlife needed to obtain information on the muskellunge harvest. So, in 1961 an organization was formed to officially record the large muskies caught each year. The name, Huskie Muskie Club, seemed a natural.

The objectives of the club are to foster and promote sport fishing for muskellunge and to provide the Division of Wildlife with statewide information on muskellunge harvest. The club has proven to be an excellent vehicle for obtaining such information, which is valuable in evaluating past fish management activities and planning for the future. Many states have copied Ohio's Huskie Muskie Club system to achieve the same results. Ohio ranks high among the states each year in total catch of muskellunge, and for the past several years has been among the leaders in size taken. Awards are given to anglers who catch trophy sized muskellunge. Membership applications are available at muskie lake marinas and Division of Wildlife offices.

Once abundant, muskies are rare in the Lake Erie drainage basin today. The Grand River, however, boasts a naturally reproducing population.

Muskies reproduce naturally in only one lake—Berlin Reservoir (and possibly Lake Milton).

The fish spawns in 10 southern Ohio streams, the best being the Little Muskingum River in Washington County.

Currently, muskies are stocked (one fingerling per acre) in eight lakes (reservoirs)—Leesville, Clear Fork, West Branch, Piedmont, Cowan, Salt Fork, Rocky Fork, and Alum Creek.

Leesville Lake is Ohio's top muskie lake with 4,933 trophies (30+ inches) over the last 24 years. Muskies Inc., a national organization, ranks it sixteenth among the top 20 muskie waters in North America.

A muskie measuring 30 inches or longer qualifies an angler for a Fish Ohio award and an honorable mention membership in the Ohio Huskie Muskie Club. Fishers catching a muskie 40 inches or longer and weighing 20 or more pounds qualify for regular memberships in the Ohio Huskie Muskie Club. Anglers who release muskies measuring 42 inches without being weighed earn regular release membership in the club. Since the founding of the Huskie Muskie Club in 1961, the state muskie record has been broken several times. The long-reigning record holder is Joe Lykins of Piedmont, who caught his trophy in 1972 in Piedmont Lake. The fish measured 50.5 inches, and weighed 55 pounds and two ounces.

Catch
and release

Something Fishy in the Creel

Grandpa called the fish on my plate "brain food." Back then, his advice was a no brainer. He caught clean fish from clean water. Today, however, eating too much of Grandpa's brain food can make a person sick or turn them into a "no brainer." Which leads me to a new meaning for "catch and release."

As a fisher's conservation ethic, "catch and release" teaches fair play and restraint. Catch a fish, then release it unharmed for another angler's line. Never catch more than you can eat, the moral says. Wizened old salts say released whoppers breed new whoppers, who will be next year's fun. Save the trophy, fish tomorrow. And so on.

Pollution, however, adds a perverse meaning to "catch and release." The ethic could save the angler's health, too. Fish store contaminants in their bodies, primarily in their fat. Eat fish from a dirty stream, the dirty stream gets in your veins. A constant diet of "dirty" fish, which may store contaminants like mercury and PCB, can be unhealthy, possibly lethal. Children and women of child-bearing age are especially susceptible to "fishy" substances.

What do you do? Use your brain cells. The Division of Wildlife's booklet "Ohio Fishing Regulations," available where fishing licenses are sold, has advice on cleaning and cooking fish, and consumption amounts. Note the "advisories" listed for certain fish caught in certain streams. For example, the division's 1997-98 booklet has "Do Not Eat" warnings for all fish caught in polluted sections of the Little Scioto, Ottawa, Black, Ashtabula, and Mahoning rivers, and Scippo and Little Beaver creeks; and for channel catfish landed from Maumee Bay, Ohio River, Scioto River (Columbus to mouth), and Great Miami River (Dayton to mouth).

The Ohio Department of Health is ultimately responsible for fish advisories. For the latest update contact the department at (614) 644-6447.

—SO

Fishing Holes

Ohio River

Last count, 159 fish species live in the Ohio River. Of these, 25 varieties are considered sportfish, notably sauger, basses (largemouth, smallmouth, spotted, white, and hybrid striped), walleye, bluegill, crappie, and catfishes (channel and flathead). Fishers from shore and boat cast in the tailwaters below dams, the pools, or the embayments (the backwaters, and tributary mouths). A 1992 survey of anglers along the Ohio segment of the river, revealed that two-thirds of all fish catches were landed in tailwaters, a spot representing just one percent of the river's surface area. Bass captured most of the anglers' attention. Catfishers ranked the middle section between Huntington and Louisville their most popular area.

Six states cooperatively manage the river's fisheries through the Ohio River Fisheries Management Team. For Ohio anglers, this team approach means their fishing license is valid in Ohio River waters within Kentucky and West Virginia. And vice versa. Ohio River water ends at the first riffle or dam in tributaries. Reciprocity extends to shore fishing. The game laws of the state you are fishing in apply.

MWCD

The ten lakes that make up the Muskingum Watershed Conservation District offer a variety of treasure for those who drop a line. For more information, see the chapter beginning on page 281, but below a brief menu follows:

Atwood — northern pike, channel catfish, bullhead, largemouth bass, crappie, bluegill, yellow perch, saugeye.

Beach City — muskellunge, channel catfish, bullhead, largemouth bass, crappie, bluegill, saugeye.

Charles Mill — muskellunge, northern pike, channel catfish, flathead catfish, bullhead, largemouth bass, smallmouth bass, crappie, bluegill, yellow perch, saugeye.

Clendening — muskellunge, channel catfish, flathead catfish, bullhead, white bass, largemouth bass, smallmouth bass, crappie, bluegill, saugeye.

Leesville — muskellunge, channel catfish, bullhead, largemouth bass, smallmouth bass, crappie, bluegill, yellow perch, walleye.

Piedmont — muskellunge, channel catfish, flathead catfish, bullhead, largemouth bass, smallmouth bass, crappie, bluegill, yellow perch, walleye, saugeye.

Pleasant Hill — muskellunge, channel catfish, flathead catfish, bullhead, white bass, largemouth bass, smallmouth bass, crappie, bluegill, yellow perch, walleye, saugeye.

Seneca — muskellunge, channel catfish, bullhead, white bass, striped bass, largemouth bass, crappie, bluegill, yellow perch, walleye.

Tappan — muskellunge, channel catfish, flathead catfish, bullhead, white bass, largemouth bass, smallmouth bass, crappie, bluegill, yellow perch, walleye, saugeye.

Wills Creek — muskellunge, channel catfish, flathead catfish, bullhead, white bass, largemouth bass, crappie, bluegill, saugeye.

Fish Facts

Division of Wildlife Offices

For more information about Ohio Fishing, consult these publications: Ohio Fishing Regulations (available where fishing licenses are sold); Ohio River Fishing, Publication 124, Ohio Division of Wildlife; and Ohio River Fishing Guide, published by the Ohio River Fisheries Management Team, available for the wildlife division. Also, contact your nearest Division of Wildlife office.

Ohio Division of Wildlife Headquarters
1840 Belcher Drive
Columbus, OH 43224-1329
(614) 265-6300
1-800-750-0750 (TDD)
1-800-WILDLIFE

Ohio Division of Wildlife
District Three
912 Portage Lakes Drive
Akron, OH 44319
(330) 644-2293

Ohio Division of Wildlife
District Four
360 E. State Street
Athens, OH 45701
(740) 594-2211

Ohio Division of Wildlife
District Five
1076 Old Springfield Pike
Xenia, OH 45385
(937) 372-9261

Ohio Division of Wildlife
District One
1500 Dublin Road
Columbus, OH 43215
(614) 644-3925

Ohio Division of Wildlife
District Two
952 Lima Avenue, Box A
Findlay, OH 45840
(419) 424-5000

Ohio Division of Wildlife
London Fish Hatchery
2470 Roberts Mill Road, SW
London, OH 43140
(614) 852-1412

Ohio Division of Wildlife
Hebron Fish Hatchery
10517 Canal Road
Hebron, OH 43025
(740) 928-8092

Ohio Division of Wildlife
Senecaville Fish Hatchery
57199 Seneca Dam Road
Senecaville, OH 43780-9697
(740) 685-5541

Ohio Division of Wildlife
Kincaid Fish Hatchery
7487 SR 124
Latham, OH 45646
(740) 493-2717

Ohio Division of Wildlife
Castalia Fish Hatchery
7018 Home Gardner Road
Castalia, OH 44824
(419) 684-7499

Ohio Division of Wildlife
St. Mary's Fish Hatchery
1735 Feeder Road

St. Mary's, OH 45885
(419) 394-5170

Ohio Division of Wildlife
Sandusky Fisheries & Enforcement Units
305 E. Shoreline Drive
Sandusky, OH 44870
(419) 625-8062

Ohio Division of Wildlife
Internet Address: http://www.dnr.state.oh.
us/odnr/wildlife/wildlife.html

Catch of the Day

The Outdoor Writers of Ohio, a group of journalists who scribble words about outdoors sports, keeps track of champion fish snagged in Ohio waters. If you think you have landed the big one, weigh it on certified scales (enclose printout if weighed on a digital scale) and freeze the specimen. A close-up photo of the fish must accompany the application (take picture before freezing), and two witnesses must verify the weigh-in. Since 1993 record fish have been determined by weight only, but you can submit the catch's length measured from the tip of the closed lip to the tip of the furthest tail. Mail the information within six months of the catch.

Sorry, the whoppers that got away, even after they posed for pictures, are ineligible. And so are fish pulled out of "pay" ponds, those caught illegally, and specimens caught in "foreign" waters.

For an application contact Jeffrey L. Frischkorn, Chairman, Record Fish Committee, Outdoors Writers of Ohio, 7821 Dehlia Drive, Mentor-on-the-Lake, OH 44060; phone 1 (800) 947-2737, extension 625.

Below is a list of the current record holders. No carping allowed.

Bass (Hybrid Striped/White)—16 lbs., 13 oz., 29 ½ inches. Little Three Mile Creek, Ralph E. Campbell, Milford, Jan. 23, 1985.

Bass (Largemouth)—13 lbs., 2 oz., 25 1/16 inches. Farm pond, Roy Landsberger, Kensington, May 26, 1978.

Bass (Rock)—1 lb., 15½ oz., 14 3/4 inches. Deer Creek, George A. Keller, Dayton, Sept. 3, 1932.

Bass (Spotted)—5 lbs., 4 oz., 21 inches. Lake White, Roger Trainer, Waverly, May 2, 1976.

Bass (Smallmouth)—9 lbs., 8 oz., length not recorded. Lake Erie, Randy Van Dern, Kalamazoo, MI, June 18, 1993.

Bass (Striped)—37.1 lbs., length unrecorded. West Branch Reservoir, Mark Chulfo, Ravenna, July 2, 1993.

Bluegill—3 lbs., 4 ¹/₂ oz., 12 ³/₄ inches. Salt Fork Lake, Willie D. Nicholes, Quaker City, April 28, 1990.

Bass (White)—4 lbs., 21 inches. Gravel pit. Ira Sizemore, Cincinnati, July 1, 1983.

Bowfin. 11 lbs., 7 oz., 33¹/₄ inches. Nettle Lake, Christopher A. Boling, Montpelier, May 9, 1987.

Bowfin (bowfishing)—8.79 lbs., 31 inches. East Harbor State Park, John Ehman, Brookpark, April 30, 1969.

Bullhead— 4 lbs., 4 oz., 18 ¹/₂ inches. Farm pond, Hugh Lawrence, Jr., Keene, May 20, 1986.

Burbot—11.85 lbs., Lake Erie. Bud Clute, Chardon, Dec. 20, 1999.

Burbot—17.33 lbs., 34 inches. Lake Erie. Walter G. Kaczoroski, Conneaut, April 21, 1998.

Carp—50 lbs., 40 inches. Paint Creek, Judson Helton, Chillicothe, May 24, 1967.

Carp (bowfishing)—39 lbs., 40 inches. Farm pond, Dennis Derheimer, Canton, May 3, 1961.

Catfish (Channel)—37 lbs., 10.4 oz., length not recorded. LaDue Reservoir, Gus J. Gronowski, Parma, August 15, 1992.

Catfish (Flathead)—76 lbs., 8 oz., 53 ³/₈ inches. Clendening Lake, Richard Affolter, New Philadelphia, July 28, 1979.

Crappie (Black)—4 lbs., 8 oz., 18 ¹/₈ inches. Private pond, Ronald Stone, Wooster, May 24, 1981.

Crappie (White)—3.9 lbs., 18.5 inches. Private pond, Kyle Rock, Zanesville, April 25, 1995.

Drum (Freshwater, or Sheephead)—22 lbs., 10.5 oz., West Branch of Little Hocking River, Joseph Allen, Little Hocking, May 31, 1997.

Gar—25 lbs., 49 inches. Ohio River, Flora Irvin, Cincinnati, August 31, 1966.

Gar (bowfishing)—11.57 lbs., Scioto River, Freddie G. Brown, Columbus, May 29, 1999.

Muskellunge—55 lbs., 2 oz., 50 ¹/₄ inches. Piedmont Lake, Joe D. Lykins, Piedmont, April 12, 1972.

Muskellunge (Tiger)—31 lbs., 8 oz., Turkeyfoot Lake, Ron P. Kotch, Canal Fulton, April 22, 1999.

Perch (White)—1.42 lbs., 14 ¹/₁₆ inches. Green Creek, John Nause, Fremont, May 3, 1988.

Perch (Yellow)—2 lbs., 12 oz., 14¹/₂ inches. Lake Erie, Charles Thomas, April 17, 1984.

Pickerel—6 lbs., 4 oz., 26¹/₄ inches. Long Lake, Ronald Kotch, Akron, March 25, 1961.

Pike— 22 lbs., 6 oz., 43 inches. Lyre Lake, Chris Campbell, Dayton, October 3, 1988.

Salmon (Chinook)—29 ¹/₂ lbs., 42 ⁷/₈ inches. Lake Erie, Walter Shumaker, Ashtabula, August 4, 1989.

Salmon (Coho)—13 lbs., 10 oz., 34 ³/₄ inches. Huron River, Barney Freeman, Kansas, Dec. 1, 1982.

Sauger—7 lbs., 5 oz., 24 ¹/₂ inches. Maumee River, Bryan Wicks, Maumee, March 10, 1981.

Saugeye—12.42 lbs., Lake Logan, Daniel D'Amore, Swanton, March 29, 1993.

Sucker (Buffalo)—45 lbs., 1 oz., 38 inches. Hoover Reservoir, Dave Heinselman, Gahanna, July 3, 1988.

Sucker (Buffalo by bowfishing)—37 lbs., 40 ¹/₄ inches. Hoover Reservoir, Don Paisley, Columbus, May 14, 1983.

Sucker (other species)—9 lbs., 4 oz, 27 ¹/₂ inches. Leesville Lake, Wayne Gleason, Wellsville, April 3, 1977.

Sucker (other species by bowfishing)—7.36 lbs., Hoover Reservoir, Michael Stumph, Westerville, May 18, 1997.

Sunfish (Green)—7.3 oz., 7.6 inches. Birchwood Pond, Lou Uecker, Mason, May2, 1998.

Sunfish (Hybrid)—1.43 lbs., Privat pond, Ken Herera, Garrettsville, May7, 1999.

Sunfish (Pumpkinseed)—.60 lbs. Private pond, Mark Schlater, Hillsboro, April 26, 1999. (.59 lbs. Private pond, Ramon Hinchliffe, anrora, April 27, 1999.

Sunfish (Redear)—3.58 lbs., Farm Pond, Bert Redman, Newark, Oct. 2, 1998.

Sunfish (Warmouth)—One pound. Private pond, Rich Campitelli, Athens, September 6, 1994.

Trout (Brook)—2 lbs., 11 oz., 18¹/₂ inches. East Branch of Chagrin River, S. Graboshek, Willoughby, June 30, 1955.

Trout (Brown)—14.65 lbs., 25 ¹/₄ inches. Lake Erie, Timothy L. Byrne, Brooklyn, MI, July 15, 1995.

Trout (Lake)—16 lbs., 11 oz., Lake Erie, Daniel Wilson, Hudson, June 6, 1993.

Trout (Rainbow)—20.97 lbs., 12 oz., 36 ¹/₂ inches. Lake Erie, Mike Shane, New Middleton, Oct. 2, 1996..

Walleye—15.95 lbs., 33 inches. Lake Erie, Mike Baidel, Fayetteville, PA, March 24, 1995.

Walleye—16.19 lbs., 33 inches. Lake Erie, Tom Haberman, Brunswick, OH, Nov. 23, 1999.

Landlocked but unbowed: Ohio ranks eighth nationally in number of registered watercraft.

Boating

By the Numbers

Boating is big fun and big business in the Buckeye State. Boating in this state is now a $400 million industry in Ohio, where the number of boat registrations continues to increase by three to four percent per year.

The popularity of boating has grown significantly since the 1960s. In 1961, there were only 129,091 registered watercraft in Ohio. By 1971, the figure increased to 224,800. In 1985, it was up to 357,000, an increase of 176 percent since 1961. Ohio currently ranks a remarkable eighth nationally in the number of recreational boats with an estimated 390,000 registered watercraft.

Although the 2,250,000 acres of Lake Erie is Ohio's most frequently used boating area, Ohio's 133,000 acres of inland lakes, 7,000 miles of rivers and streams, and 451 miles of the Ohio River all add to Ohio's playground for boaters. From power boats to sail boats, pontoons to canoes, boating activities are widespread. According to a report published by the Lake Erie Marine Trades Association, approximately 30 percent of Ohioans participate in recreational boating. This is a higher percentage than in California or Florida.

The recreational boating industry accounted for $486,500,000 in the sale of boats, motors, trailers, accessories and related-boating services in 1986. The overall sales tax contribution totaled $24,327,500. Boating added more than 8,400 full-time and seasonal employees to the work force with a total annual payroll of $67.5 million.

Yet another boost to the economy comes in the form of the many annual boat shows and boating events that bring people and dollars into Ohio cities. Each year, Cleveland hosts the nation's largest indoor boat show, the Mid-America Boat Show, in which about 385 U.S. and Canadian companies participate and which more than half a million people attend. In addition, the oldest and largest regatta in the country is held each year at Put-In-Bay on Lake Erie. Other events include sternwheel festivals, fishing tournaments, canoe races, and powerboat races.

Source: Reprinted with the permission of the Ohio Department of Natural Resources. See pp. xx-xx and xx-xx for a listing of Ohio lakes and rivers.

Registration

A watercraft registration is a state record that identifies a boat. It is similar to auto registration and provides two boat tags and a registration form containing the assigned Ohio boat number, owner information, and a description of the boat. The registration is valid for three years, expiring on March 1 of the year shown on the registration form and tags. Once a boat is registered, Ohio law requires the registration paper to be aboard the boat at all times when underway.

Most recreational boats, including U.S. Coast Guard documented vessels, must register in Ohio. Sailboards and nonmotorized inflatable craft without a Hull Identification Number are exempt. The boat owner must be able to prove ownership for the vessel before being registered. To prove ownership:

A. For boats 14 feet long or longer, present an Ohio title in your name issued from your county title office. Titles are required for boats 14 feet in length or longer, except for canoes and kayaks. Also, present the last registration paper, signed over on the back to you from the previous owner (if applicable).

B. For documented pleasure craft, present a current U.S. Coast Guard certificate of documentation.

C. For boats less than fourteen feet long, or not requiring titles, present:

1. Manufacturer's Statement of Origin, or
2. Previous registration form, or
3. Bill of sale, or
4. Cancelled check, or
5. Notarized affidavit of ownership (affidavits may be obtained from any watercraft registration agent).

Watercraft may be registered with any watercraft registration agent. Agents can be found by consulting the yellow pages under "license agents" or by contacting any State watercraft office. Registration can also take place at some state parks, any Division of Watercraft district office in Ohio, and the Ohio Department of Natural Resources, Publications Center 4383 Fountain Square Court, Building B, Columbus, Ohio.

In addition to normal registration fees, many Ohio boaters with craft longer than 16 feet in length are required to purchase a "recreational vessel fee" decal for their boat if operating in territorial seas, internal tidal waters, or internal non-tidal waters from which a 16-foot powered vessel with a displacement type hull can navigate to tidal waters during most of the boating season. In Ohio, these waterways include Lake Erie, the Ohio River, and connecting waterways which can be navigated downstream to these waters without obstructions preventing navigation (rapids, dams, etc.).

The annual fee ranges from $25 to $100 based on the length of the boat. Boats sixteen feet or less in length are exempt from the fee as are lifeboats, yacht tenders, sailboards, canoes, kayaks, rowboats, jonboats, rowing sculls, and foreign vessels temporarily operating in the United States. Also exempt are public vessels, certain Coast Guard Auxiliary vessels, boats used for public safety (fire department and rescue squad boats), and boats owned and used for training purposes by the Boy Scouts, Girl Scouts, Sea Explorers, and the YMCA.

Display

Numbers and decals must be displayed in block-type letters and numbers at least three inches high in a color contrasting with the hull. Boat letters and numbers should read from left to right and be spaced thus: OH-0000-AA or OH 0000 AA. Ohio validation decals must be placed six inches away from the OH numbers and toward the stern of the boat. Documented vessels do not display "OH" numbers. Documented vessels must display two Ohio validation decals on the forward half of the vessel to be visible on the port and starboard sides. They may be displayed in windows. ✎

Canal *Dipping*

All-Over Tans on the Towpath

*For some,
Ohio's longest
swimming hole was
early training
ground for
swimming with
the sharks
of politics.*

He displaced much less water in those days, but portly President William H. Taft admitted to stroking the summer away in au naturale as a boy along Ohio's canals. On hot summer days Taft and other youngsters sprinted on the canal towpath, stripped to the buff, and launched themselves into the channel. Brave lads unnerved lockmasters by diving into filling locks, swimming like dolphins beneath flatboats, or hitching rides behind a barge. When constables arrived, the skinny dippers signaled each other with a "V for victory" sign, the gesture later made famous by Winston Churchill. In those days the sign meant, "Cheese it, the cops!"

Charles Ludwig of Cincinnati recalled his dips into the Miami-Erie Canal in his book *Playmates of the Towpath*. In 1928 Ludwig started the Ohio Canal Swimmers Society. Members included Taft, then Chief Justice of the U.S. Supreme Court, House Speaker Nicholas Longworth, Governor Myers Cooper, Cincin-

nati Mayor Murray Seasongood, Congressman William Hess, and other Cincinnati high-muckity-mucks. As boys these celebs splashed in the canal, but there are no reports of them risking public exposure—of the physical kind—in later life.

Ludwig's nostalgic poem, *Playmates of the Towpath*, remembers the good old days.

*Oft to the canal we trooped as boys,
Shouting and laughing—what sweet noise!
"Follow the leader!" — blithe and gay—
The start of a perfect Towpath Day.
"Who'll jump in first?" Now there's a dash!
Clothes pulled off fast! Kerplunk! A splash!*

Source: Ohio Water Firsts by Sherman L. Frost and Wayne S. Nichols

Dog freezes; wings whirl; shotgun kicks.

these are, undeniably, the best of times, for Ohio's deer, wild turkey, and waterfowl hunters. The populations of deer and turkey (extirpated species at the start of the 20th century) were at record levels at the end of it. Their numbers are only expected to increase.

Habitat improvement (natural and managed), restocking, hunting regulations, and public land purchases contributed to the fast comebacks of Ohio's prized game animals. As populations of game animals increase, so do hunting opportunities offered by longer seasons and more counties open to hunting. Technological advancements in firearms accuracy and renewed interest in so-called primitive weapons has put more hunters into the field. The statistics in this chapter clearly show that hunters are having more success, and simultaneously improving the populations of these creatures.

Pheasant, quail and ruffed grouse hunters, however, sing the blues. Though rebounding, ring-necked pheasant numbers are nowhere close to the five million cocks that inhabited our Ohio's grasslands a half century ago, and bobwhite quails, at the northern edge of their natural range, seem to struggle with our cold winters. Ruffed grouse and squirrel numbers are down due to subtle changes in their prime habitat.

Overall, Ohioans hunt game on nearly 800,000 acres of public land (143,000 acres of it in state wildlife areas), a total that keeps growing. Private landowners allow hunting on as much land, provided hunters seek permission first. The sport is estimated to pump $400-500 million annually into local economies. About 390,000 nimrods paid $5.7 million for hunting licenses during the state fiscal year ending June 1996.

The prospects for Ohio's gun and bow touting outdoors enthusiasts will continue to improve if they share the philosophy of Dick Tschantz of Wyandot County: "For [the good hunter], life is continutous. If he manages like he should, there will always be more deer. That's why good hunters are always conservation minded."—SO

Top Counties For Trophy Bucks (1958-1995)

Typical Racks

Muskingum, 269

Licking, 206

Guernsey, 182

Hocking, 170

Washington, 153

Coshocton, 152

Athens, 149

Vinton, 142

Morgan, 135

Meigs, 134

Division of Wildlife

The Ohio Division of Wildlife (DOW) evolved from Ohio Fish Commission, which was created in 1873. In 1949, the DOW became a division of the newly formed Ohio Department of Natural Resources. It is the administrative steward of Ohio's animal life. Its duties include wildlife and fish management, law enforcement, licensing, research and education, wildlife habitat enhancement, wildlife propagation, and protection of endangered animal species.

Ohio sportsmen provide 95 percent of the funding for the division through fees for licenses and permits. Taxpayer contributions from the checkoff on the state income tax form (called Do Something Wild) has enabled the division to purchase 1,000 acres of wetlands. DOW has three research stations—Waterloo, Crane Creek, and Olentangy. Studies at Waterloo, located in Ohio's forest country, emphasize woodland animals, such as turkey, ruffed grouse, deer, squirrel, and black bear. Olentangy, situated in Central Ohio, concentrates wildlife associated with farmland—rabbits, quail, pheasant, and partridge (ruffed grouse). Research at Crane Creek focuses on wetlands wildlife, notably geese, ducks, swans, and shorebirds. Researchers also cooperate in studies done on other public land and on private holdings.

A DOW wildlife officer in each Ohio county enforces wildlife management laws. Many officers participate in Project WILD, the division's environmental conservation and education program aimed at school age youngsters, and assist in hunter education classes.

The DOW has a central office in Columbus and five district offices. The addresses are noted below.

Central Office
OHIO DEPARTMENT OF NATURAL RESOURCES
DIVISION OF WILDLIFE
1840 Belcher Drive
Columbus, OH 43224-1329
Phones: 1-800-WILDLIFE
(614) 265-6300
(614) 265-6994 (TDD)

District Offices
OHIO DIVISION OF WILDIFE

DISTRICT ONE
1500 Dublin Road
Columbus, OH 43215
(614) 644-3925
Covers Franklin, Pickaway, Fairfield, Licking, Morrow, Marion, Union, Logan, Champaign, Madison, Fayette counties.

OHIO DIVISION OF WILDLIFE
DISTRICT TWO
952 Lima Avenue, Box A
Findlay, OH 45840
(419) 424-5000
Covers Hancock, Hardin, Allen, Van Wert, Paulding, Defiance, Williams, Fulton, Henry, Putnam, Lucas, Wood, Ottawa, Sandusky, Seneca, Wyandot, Crawford, Richland, Huron, Erie counties.

OHIO DIVISION OF WILDLIFE
DISTRICT THREE
912 Portage Lakes Drive
Akron, OH 44319
(330) 644-2293
Covers Summit, Cuyahoga, Lorain, Medina, Ashland, Wayne, Holmes, Tuscarawas, Harrison, Jefferson, Carroll, Columbiana, Stark, Mahoning, Portage, Trumbull, Geauga, Lake, Ashtabula counties.

OHIO DIVISION OF WILDLIFE
DISTRICT FOUR
360 East State Street
Athens, OH 45701
(740) 594-2211
Covers Athens, Meigs, Gallia, Lawrence, Jackson, Scioto, Pike, Ross, Vinton, Hocking, Morgan, Washington, Perry, Muskingum, Coshocton, Guernsey, Belmont, Noble, Monroe counties.

OHIO DIVISION OF WILDLIFE
DISTRICT FIVE
1076 Old Springfield Pike
P.O. Box 576
Xenia, OH 45385
(937) 372-9261
Covers Greene, Clark, Miami, Shelby, Auglaize, Mercer, Darke, Preble, Montgomery, Butler, Warren, Clinton, Hamilton, Clermont, Brown, Adams, Highland counties.

Safety

Before going into the field, remember to
- Attached your license to your back;
- Wear orange blaze (see regulations for amount), preferably above waist;
- Carry water and snacks, and written permission slips of private landowners;
- Pack maps (tracking wounded game can put you in unfamiliar turf);
- Honor local hunting restrictions;
- Stay alert and sober (signal other hunters, don't use alcohol or drugs);
- Carry out all litter (even cigarette stubs);
- Report poaching, call 1-800-POACHING, and
- Be careful.

Regulations

Every hunter should obtain and read the latest booklet on hunting regulations published by the Ohio Division of Wildlife. Pick one up when you buy a license. The booklet explains weapons regulations, bag limits, licenses, checking stations, season dates, fees, wildlife offices, and huntable game. For example, new hunters (youngsters and adults) must attend hunter safety classes and pass a written exam before getting a license. Questions should be directed to the Division of Wildlife.

How Ohio Hunting Ranks

- 9th nationally in licensed hunters.
- 10th in the number of hunting days afield.
- 17th in hunting expenditures.

Nature Notables

The Hunter's Art

By age nine Arthur Robert Harding was trapping furbearers on the family farm near Kyger in Gallia County. Five years later, in 1885, the youngster was buying furs from other farmboys. He made his fur-buying rounds on horseback, twice a month for six years. Then he bought furs for a Zanesville firm, traveling now by train, in Ohio, West Virginia, Kentucky, and Pennsylvania.

Eventually Harding decided to cultivate two passions—journalism and the great outdoors. He started the *Gallia Times* in 1898, and used this experience to launch *Hunter-Trader-Trapper* in 1900. The latter linked the interests of hunters, trappers and fur traders, and was the first Ohio-based outdoors magazine with a national following. More importantly, Harding used the publication to pioneer trapping and hunting regulations—seasons, bag limits, trap sizes and the like—to conserve wildlife and perpetuate the industry. At the time, game and furbearing animals had disappeared or been decimated in Ohio and other states due to habitat loss, unchecked human enterprises, and overharvesting.

Poor health forced Harding to sell the magazine in 1914, but a decade later he returned with *Fur-Fish-Game*, adding articles for anglers, shooters, dog owners, campers, and even mushroom collectors. The magazine is still publishing practical advice and entertaining stories in Columbus.

—SO

Mystery Solved

Who (or What) Slayed Ohio's Biggest Whitetailed Buck?

It takes two strong men to lift and hang the palmated rack of the "Hole in the Horn" buck to a mounting frame beside other champions. It is the sacred centerpiece in a traveling show of trophies, and the guys hauling the hunk do it slowly and solemnly, as if they were moving the *Mona Lisa*.

Ohio's legendary "Hole in the Horn" buck was discovered dead by railroads tracks that ran alongside the Ravenna Arsenal, back in the early 1940s. Its outlandish, twisted, fused "non-typical" rack fooled finders into thinking they had stumbled on an elk or moose at first. But it was, indeed, a whitetail, weighing between 250-300 pounds, and sporting a crown that scored 328 $^2/_8$ points on the Boone & Crockett scale. It was largest whitetail rack in North America at the time. Most figured the giant was killed by a train, except for this hole in one antler tine. A hole the size of a .22-caliber bullet. The mysterious hole fed David-and-Goliath stories that the monster was downed or frightened into a train by a poacher firing the smallest lead in a hunter's arsenal, but an illegal size for hunting deer.

A railroad engineer donated the rack to the Kent Canadian Club, where it hung for 40 years and slowly accumulated stains and stories. By the time a collector acquired the trophy in 1983, its origins had become obscure. Old timers had died, and new members recalled vague accounts. The collector, noted hunter and writer Dick Idol, insisted on solving the mystery of the hole and the deer's demise. His break came in a ten-word letter written by a fellow from Florida who claimed he was present when the buck was found.

The eyewitness, George Winters, untangled the puzzler. A piece of the Ravenna Arsenal perimeter fence made the hole. In its death throes, the buck became entangled in the fence. Winters removed a fence spoke from the tine so the deer could be carried away. The deer had definitely collided with a train, said Winters. No reports on how the train looked after the fight.

The "Hole in the Horn" deer reigned as the North American champion until 1981, when a buck found in St. Louis scored 333 $^7/_8$ points.

The buck stopped here, but not the legendary "Hole-in-the-Horn"

PUBLIC SHOOTING RANGES

Site/County	Class	Phone
Deer Creek State Wildlife Area, Fayette	A	(614) 644-3925
Delaware State Wildlife Area, Delaware	A,C	(614) 644-3925
Fernwood State Forest, Jefferson	D	(740) 264-5671
Grand River State Wildlife Area, Trumbull	A	(330) 889-3280
Harrison State Forest, Harrison	D	(740) 264-5671
Indian Creek State Wildlife Area, Brown	C	(513) 875-2111
Monroe Lake State Wildlife Area, Monroe	B	(740) 594-2211
Spencer Lake State Wildlife Area, Medina	C	(216) 648-2621
Spring Valley State Wildlife Area, Greene	A,C	(937) 372-9261
Strouds Run State Park, Athens	D	(740) 592-2302
Tranquility State Wildlife Area, Adams	B	(937) 372-9261
Wolf Creek State Wildlife Area, Morgan	B	(740) 594-2211
Woodbury State Wildlife Area, Coshocton	A	(740) 824-3211
Zaleski State Forest, Vinton	D	(740) 596-5781

CLASS

A — Supervised (attendant on duty) rifle and pistol target ranges, permit (purchased off-site) required to shoot. Special dates and hours apply; rest rooms and benches available.

B — Unsupervised rifle and pistol ranges.

C — Unsupervised archery range (usually separated from gun ranges).

D — Unsupervised ranges, all weapons

Rack Envy

What's Typical of Trophies

The Buckeye Big Buck Club, a nonprofit conservation group, has settled Ohio's "my rack's bigger than your rack" debates since 1958. Each season the club's judges measure, inspect, and debate trophy antlered deer entries from hundreds of hunters.

So what makes a Big Buck? Judges consider only the "rack," the crown that grows from the mantle of noble rogues. They measure racks based on a cumulative scoring system devised by the Boone & Crockett and Pope & Young hunting clubs. The system considers the number of antlers (or points), length of each antler, spread and shape of the rack, circumference of the antlers, and other details. Racks are characterized "typical" or "non-typical." Typicals are classic, crescent-shaped, symmetric racks, almost manicured in appearance. Non-typical racks are asymmetric, lopsided, and show irregularities like oddly branched points, or fused antlers. To get into the record book, a typical must score 140 points, a non-typical 160 points.

While some hunters shoot only trophies, mistaking their prowess or heightened conservation awareness with rack size, the vast majority of hunters are not as choosy. Sure, they will shoot a centerfold that walks by, but they are content with less. Taking a doe actually improves the vitality of the herd, and their meat, frankly, is more tender and less gamey.   —SO

More, Deer

☞ The 1996-1997 result fell considerably below a state prediction of 190,000 kills.

☞ Ohio ranked fifth in North America in trophy deer killed per square mile, according to a Boone & Crockett Club survey. Illinois, Kentucky, Minnesota, and Wisconsin were ahead of Ohio.

☞ Antlerless deer comprised 56 percent of the total deer kill in 1998.

☞ The number of deer hunters (including those exempted from license) reached 425,000 in 1995. Statewide deer population has increased from 17,000 in 1965 to an estimated 425,000 today, or in other words, one deer per deer hunter.

DEER SEASON TALLY (1996-1998)

County	1998	1997	1996	County	1998	1997	1996
Adams	1,303	1,964	1,279	Licking	2,416	3,664	3,067
Allen	287	289	261	Logan	720	798	964
Ashland	887	1,510	1,642	Lorain	845	1,175	561
Ashtabula	1,387	2,460	2,197	Lucas	440	594	248
Athens	4,165	5,078	4,468	Madison	201	262	257
Auglaize	255	243	168	Mahoning	667	806	790
Belmont	2,334	3,313	2,304	Marion	256	292	184
Brown	1,022	1,492	1,192	Medina	636	940	682
Butler	596	1,027	863	Meigs	3,971	4,963	3,271
Carroll	1,337	2,125	1,719	Mercer	211	251	170
Champaign	566	621	765	Miami	294	324	230
Clark	426	446	627	Monroe	2,172	3,290	2,953
Clermont	2,154	2,441	1,621	Montgomery	303	481	316
Clinton	398	708	541	Morgan	3,700	3,931	2,331
Columbiana	1,224	2,067	1,558	Morrow	941	1,192	1,147
Coshocton	3,086	4,745	3,608	Muskingum	5,939	5,867	4,877
Crawford	378	424	555	Noble	3,738	3,626	2,633
Cuyahoga	300	327	228	Ottawa	237	254	145
Darke	343	387	302	Paulding	299	313	244
Defiance	532	551	497	Perry	2,231	3,469	2,950
Delaware	1,072	1,459	1,234	Pickaway	587	735	1,180
Erie	288	273	172	Pike	1,949	2,320	1,600
Fairfield	1,460	2,121	1,610	Portage	899	1,385	905
Fayette	213	267	398	Preble	310	423	289
Franklin	804	759	530	Putnam	239	211	205
Fulton	488	362	171	Richland	941	1,688	1,620
Gallia	4,155	5,391	3,313	Ross	3,583	4,109	3,443
Geauga	1,128	1,519	1,002	Sandusky	401	474	312
Greene	414	747	451	Scioto	1,640	1,979	1,748
Guernsey	2,679	4,749	3,973	Seneca	603	727	459
Hamilton	1,299	1,253	665	Shelby	325	361	604
Hancock	382	436	203	Stark	624	947	1,063
Hardin	405	407	388	Summit	903	1,002	449
Harrison	2,407	3,182	2,687	Trumbull	1,324	1,992	1,374
Henry	236	245	305	Tuscarawas	2,520	3,666	3,938
Highland	1,054	1,854	1,805	Union	400	413	605
Hocking	4,016	4,911	3,469	Van Wert	164	201	163
Holmes	1,663	2,314	2,015	Vinton	3,475	4,670	2,733
Huron	694	706	652	Warren	854	1,217	611
Jackson	3,433	4,753	3,763	Washington	3,864	4,304	3,645
Jefferson	2,367	3,534	3,625	Wayne	541	771	501
Knox	2,307	3,207	2,154	Williams	957	971	771
Lake	568	767	607	Wood	328	348	201
Lawrence	2,705	2,986	2,393	Wyandot	496	579	506

| TOTAL (all weapons) | | | | | 118,270 | 153,159 | 158,000 |

Source: Ohio Division of Wildlife. Based on the mandatory reporting of carcasses at check-in stations.

Hunting for History

🦌 Hunting licenses were first issued in Ohio in 1913. Non-resident licenses started in 1904.

🦌 Game wardens (today's wildlife officers) began their work in 1901.

🦌 The first wildlife laws were passed in 1799 when Ohio was part of the Northwest Territory. The laws established bounties on wolves and mountain lions (1800). Over the years bounties have encouraged the killing of crows, starlings, woodchucks, sparrows, squirrels.

WILD TURKEY SPRING HUNTING RESULTS (1966-1999)

Year	Counties	Permits*	Harvest	% Success**
1966	9	500	12	3.7
1967	9	898	18	2.5
1968	9	914	20	2.6
1969	9	945	37	4.5
1970(a)	14	909	30	3.9
		898	36	4.9
1971(a)	14	1,000	37	4.6
		1,000	17	2.2
1972(a)	14	917	32	3.9
		881	25	3.2
1973(a)	14	1,034	39	4.3
		1,034	32	3.6
1974(a)	14	999	61	6.8
		184	10	6.0
1975(a)	14	996	75	8.4
		267	19	7.9
1976	14	1,471	139	10.7
1977	14	1,751	137	9.1
1978	18	2,000	147	8.6
1979	18	2,000	265	15.5
1980	20	2,097	387	20.6
1981	20	3,458	577	19.5
1982	20	4,262	651	17.9
1983	21	5,141	764	17.4
1984	31	6,935	1,233	19.9
1985	31	10,084	1,583	17.3
1986	31	11,913	1,816	17.0
1987	32	13,396	2,268	18.9
1988	32	19,492	2,629	16.0
1989	36	24,740	3,171	15.6
1990	37	26,739	4,096	20.2
1991	38	32,431	5,009	19.9
1992	38	33,906	5,678	19.4
1993	42	29,538	7,470	15.4
		4,106(b)		(12.4)
1994	44	29,334	9,098	16.6
		5,187(b)		(10.6)
1995	44	30,837	10,892	17.0
		6,136(b)		(15.3)
1996	46	30,930	12,098	
		7,782(b)		
1997	46		12,301	14.9
1998	50		13,251	16.9
1999	57		14,419	

* Permits sold is the number of turkeys that can be legally killed by licensed hunters. Hunters exempted from having a license may take a turkey. Not all hunters with permits go hunting.

**Success means the percentage of permit holders who bagged turkeys.

(a) 1970-75 turkey season was split into two periods. A permit was issued for each session.
(b) Permits for an additional bird have been issued since 1993. Success rate in parentheses is for the second bird.

Source: Ohio Division of Wildlife Based on the mandatory reporting of carcasses at check-in stations. Length of season varies year to year. Results above do not include fall hunting which started in 1996.

Talking Turkey

- Loss of forest habitat and unregulated hunting resulted in the extirpation (local extinction) of turkeys in 1904. Transplanted birds and improved habitat restored the flock between 1956-1963.

- In 1998 the turkey population was estimated at 132,500 birds in 80 counties.

- Jakes, or juvenile males, comprised 33 percent of the spring 1998 harvest.

- Nearly 52,000 hunters pursued turkeys in 1998.

- Hunters bagged 1,226 birds in Ohio's first fall hunting season, October 21-26, 1996. Only 9,700 hunters applied for a fall turkey permit.

- During the 1999 spring season, of the 57 counties reporting, Ashtabula claimed the most birds bagged with 951.

DUCK HUNTING RESULTS (1985-1995)

YEAR	DUCK STAMPS SOLD	OHIO ACTIVE HUNTERS	OHIO SEASON HARVEST	MISSISSIPPI FLYWAY HARVEST	U.S. HARVEST
1985	29,419	23,500	90,000	3,965,800	9,145,800
1986	29,807	22,800	85,900	3,982,300	9,159,100
1987	27,347	21,400	69,400	3,605,100	8,839,700
1988	26,854	20,500	56,400	1,918,400	4,989,300
1989	27,007	21,500	74,900	2,597,200	6,217,800
1990	29,972	21,100	76,400	2,557,600	6,156,000
1991	25,887	21,400	70,700	2,835,400	6,206,000
1992	29,811	24,309	84,900	2,882,300	6,252,900
1993	31,785	26,059	88,200	2,957,500	6,800,900
1994	30,605	24,776	81,500	3,801,000	8,276,000
1995	32,749	25,887	107,600	6,191,700	459,300
1996	33,454	27,704	124,300	6,411,800	13,282,700
1997	35,748	30,481	134,200	7,439,900	15,349,900
1998	41,152	33,930	138,000	7,660,500	16,039,700

* Ohio birds migrate on the Mississippi Flyway

DUCK HARVEST BY SPECIES, PERCENTAGE OF STATE HARVEST (1996-1998)

SPECIES	1996	1997
Mallard	53.07	50.87
Black Duck	3.96	5.12
Gadwall	1.85	1.55
American Wigeon	1.80	.72
Green-winged Teal	3.02	7.03
Blue-winged Teal	4.64	4.49
Northern Shoveler	.61	1.18
Pintail	.88	2.98
Wood Duck	17.07	12.55
Canvasback	.42	.68
Redhead	.92	.69
Scaup	3.16	2.18
Ring-necked	2.12	2.09
Common Goldeneye	.58	.35
Bufflehead	2.47	2.96
Ruddy Duck	.86	.33
Scoters	0	.06
Hooded Merganser	1.37	.82
Others	.33	2.98
TOTAL HARVEST	129,208	140,414

Source: Ohio Division of Wildlife

GETTING GOOSE

In the 1998-99 season Ohio hunters got 81,600 Canada geese making the Canada goose the top waterfowl target in Ohio. Ohio ranks third in the Mississippi Flyway and eighth nationally in Canada goose kills.

MOURNING DOVES

In 1995, an estimated 40,000 dove hunters spent 225,000 days hunting to kill 415,000 birds. The year marked the first dove season since 1913. The autumn population of this common bird is four million.

RING-NECKED PHEASANTS

This native of northern China and Korea first came to Ohio's northwestern farmland in the 1890s. By the late 1930s the population soared to five million birds and hunters bagged 750,000 cocks annually. After World War II intensive farming practices and pesticides resulted in a fast decline. Harvest dropped to 100,000 to 300,000 cocks in the late 1960s. Conservation programs have stabilized the population at mid-1980s levels. Hunter success has roughly averaged three birds per 100 hours in the field since 1978. Like quail, pheasant populations fall after cold winters.

COTTONTAIL RABBITS

Rabbits are the favorite small game target of Ohio hunters, and like other farmland animals their numbers are affected by weather. Harsh winters, such as the 1995-96 winter, and cool spring temperatures increase mortality. Rabbit populations are rising slightly in southeastern Ohio.

BOBWHITE QUAIL.

Quail peaked when settlers cleared the forest for farms. However, urbanization and intensive farming in this century have culled the flock considerably. Quail live in every Ohio county, but they are concentrated in 18 counties in the southwestern and south-central parts of the state. Ohio is the northern limit of its natural range, so prolonged cold weather can be devastating to the flock. The fair weather bird still has not rebounded from the 1978 blizzard, which wiped out 90 percent of its population. Hunters should not expect much.

> *Rabbits are the favorite* **small game target of** *Ohio hunters, and like other* **farmland animals** *their numbers are affected by weather.*

RUFFED GROUSE

Ohio's quickest upland game bird has been around since the Ice Age. Historically, its population rises as the forest expands and falls when the woody plants disappear. However, since the 1970s grouse numbers have gradually declined, in spite of an increase in forested land in Ohio. Wildlife experts suspect loss of brushland is the culprit. As woods mature in the grouse's 46-county eastern Ohio range, brush and shrub acres shrink. Grouse need reverting land for food and cover. Theories that competition with resurgent turkeys and overhunting have harmed grouse have been ruled out.

GRAY AND FOX SQUIRRELS

Gray squirrels were so abundant at the time of European intrusion that white settlers had quotas of squirrel pelts to pay along with taxes. Since then the gray's range has shrunk to the unglaciated hill country. Meanwhile, reddish fox squirrels moved eastward from the Great Plains to thrive in the wood lots left standing by farmers, and along tree-lined streams. It now lives in every Ohio county. Although forested land has increased since World War II, the acreage of oak-hickory stands, the prime habitat of squirrels, has remained level, or decreased slightly. The trend, if it continues, could be unfortunate for squirrels. The animals thrive on acorns and nuts, whose production cycles can be influenced by the vagaries of weather. Hunting success, therefore, is dependent on abundance of the mast crop. 🦅

—SO

Just Ducky

🦆 *An estimated 89.5 million ducks migrated across North America in the autumn of 1996, according to surveys by the U.S. Fish & Wildlife Service, Canada Wildlife Service, and several states. That was the biggest fall flight since 1970.*

🦆 *Though fluctuations have occurred, duck populations (mid-winter surveys) have risen steadily since 1984, largely due to better nesting habitat.*